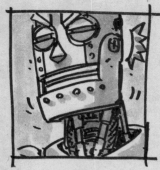

M...m...my jaw...hurts...*!!!*
What is this*?!* It's super-duper
painful... Even chewing tofu
hurts*!* Is this what they call
TMJD*?!*

—Masashi Kishimoto, 2013

岸本斉史

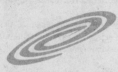

Author/artist Masashi Kishimoto was born in 1974 in rural Okayama Prefecture, Japan. After spending time in art college, he won the Hop Step Award for new manga artists with his manga **Karakuri** (Mechanism). Kishimoto decided to base his next story on traditional Japanese culture. His first version of **Naruto**, drawn in 1997, was a one-shot story about fox spirits; his final version, which debuted in **Weekly Shonen Jump** in 1999, quickly became the most popular ninja manga in Japan.

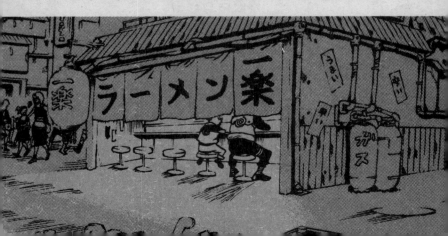

NARUTO

3-in-1 Edition
Volume 23
SHONEN JUMP Manga Omnibus Edition
A compilation of the graphic novel volumes 67–69

STORY AND ART BY MASASHI KISHIMOTO

Translation/Mari Morimoto
Touch-up Art & Lettering/ John Hunt
Design/Sam Elzway (Original Series), Alice Lewis (Omnibus Edition)
Editor/Alexis Kirsch (Manga Edition)
Editor/Erica Yee (Omnibus Edition)

Printed in the U.S.A.

Published by VIZ Media, LLC
P.O. Box 77010
San Francisco, CA 94107

10 9 8 7 6 5 4 3 2 1
Omnibus edition first printing, July 2018

PARENTAL ADVISORY
NARUTO is rated T for Teen and is recommended
for ages 13 and up. This volume contains fantasy
violence.
ratings.viz.com

THE WORLD'S
MOST POPULAR MANGA

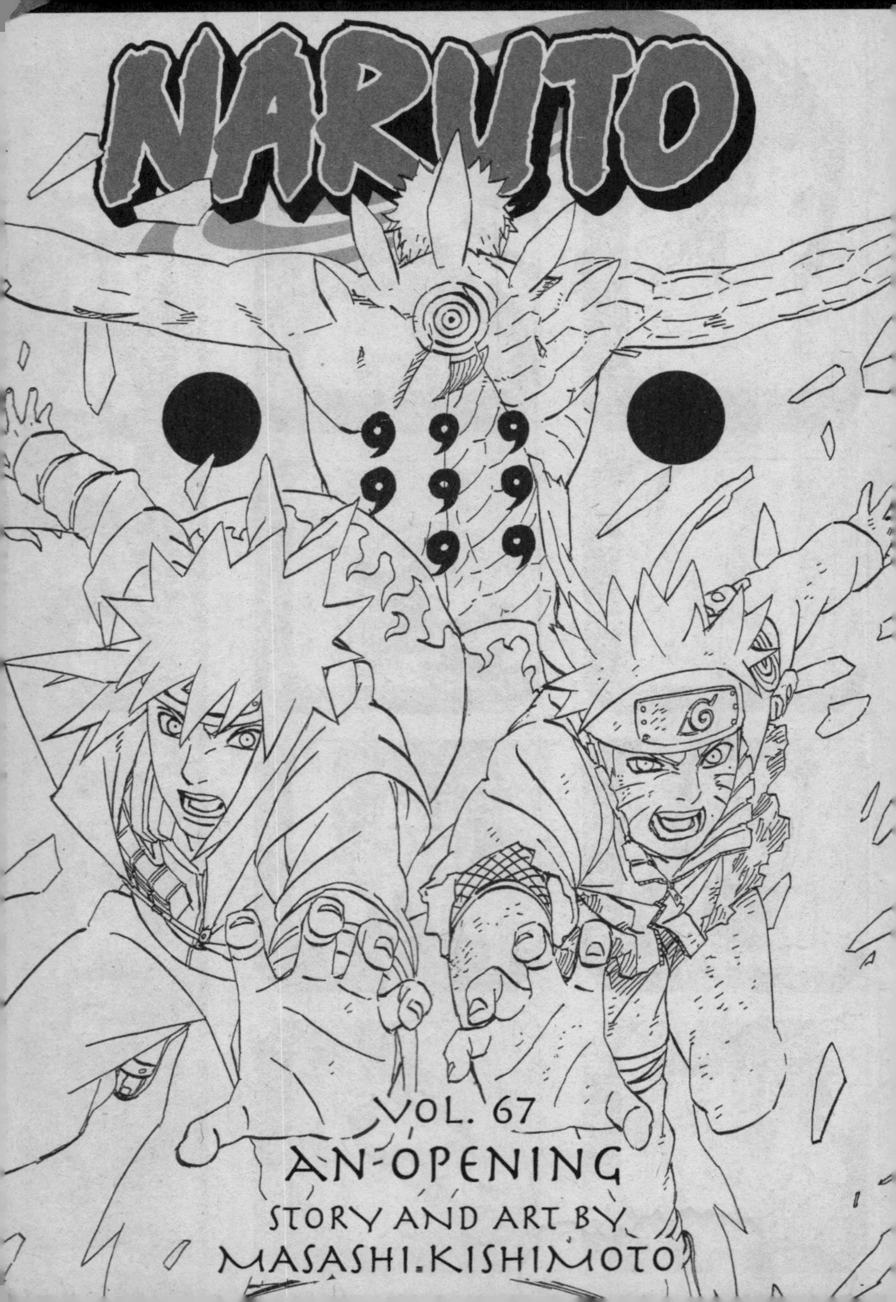
NARUTO
VOL. 67
AN OPENING
STORY AND ART BY
MASASHI KISHIMOTO

CHARACTERS

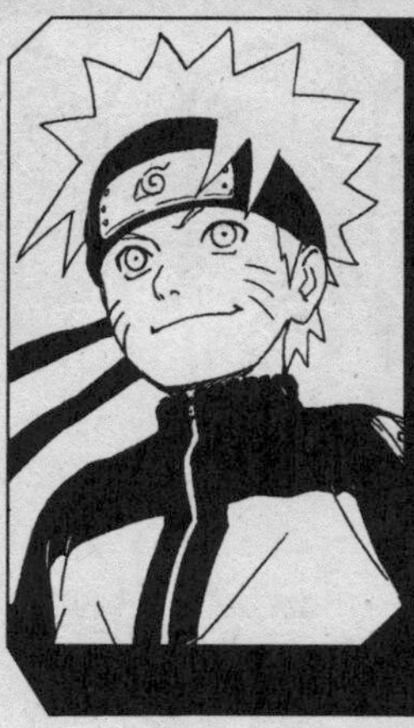

Naruto うずまきナルト

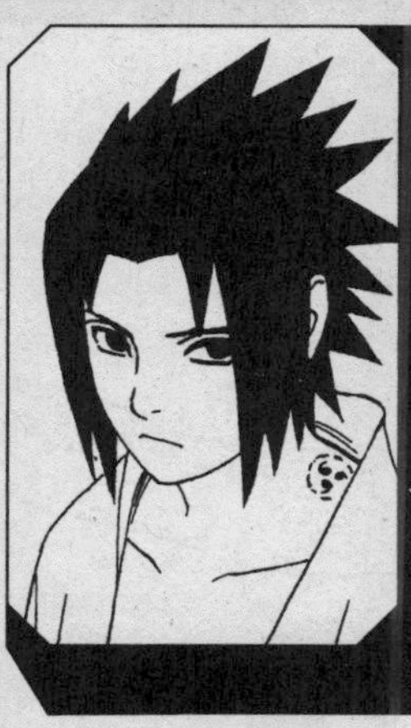

Sasuke うちはサスケ

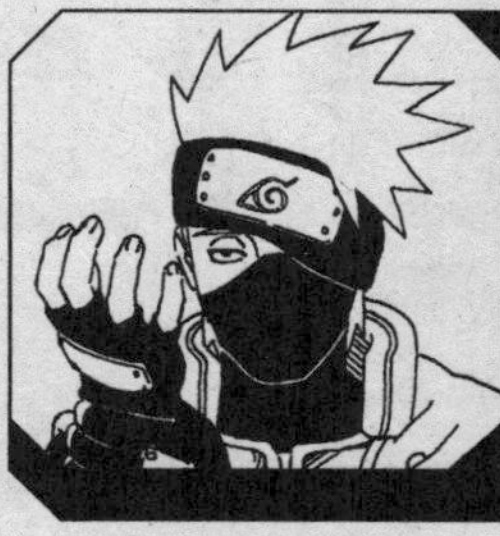

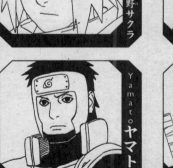

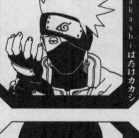

Kakashi はたけカカシ

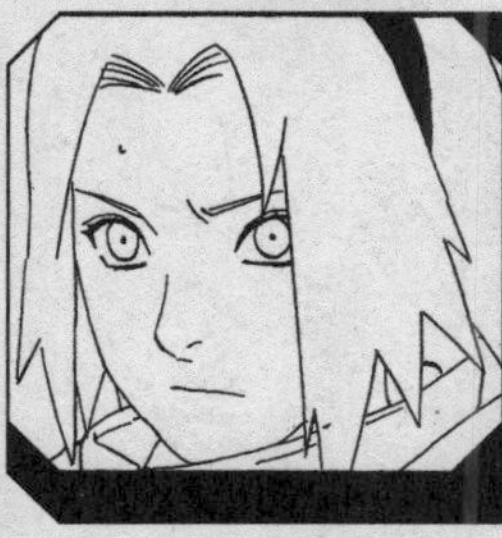

Sakura 春野サクラ

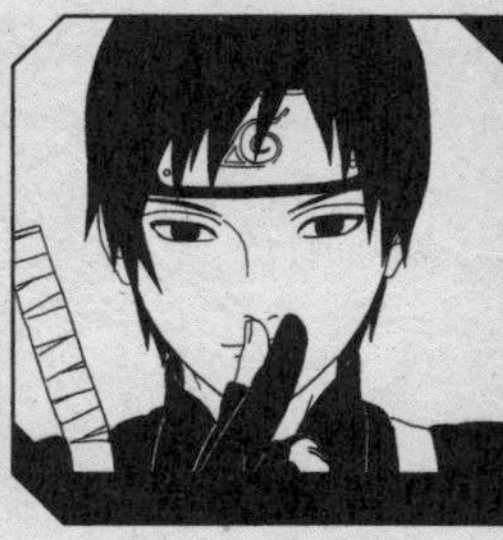

Sai サイ

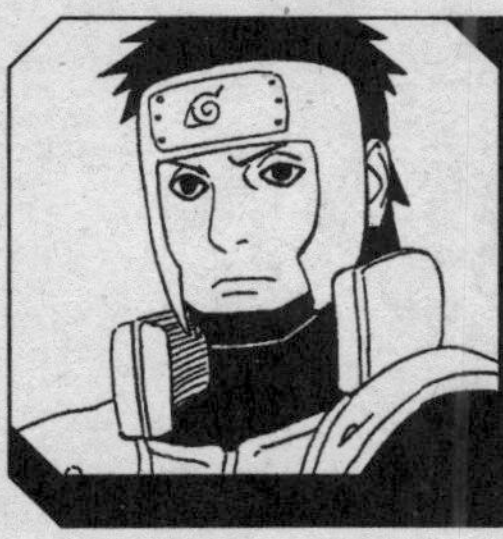

Yamato ヤマト

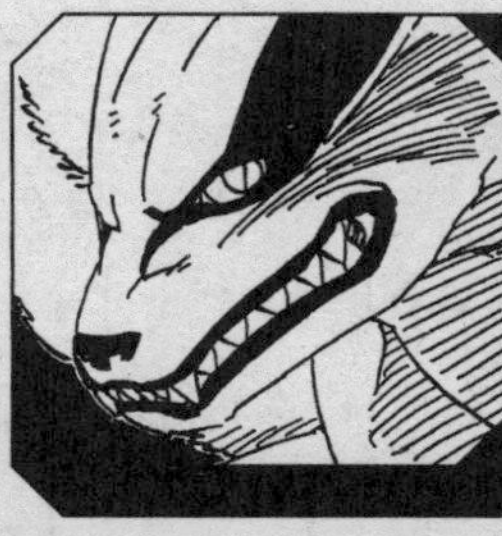

Kurama 九喇嘛

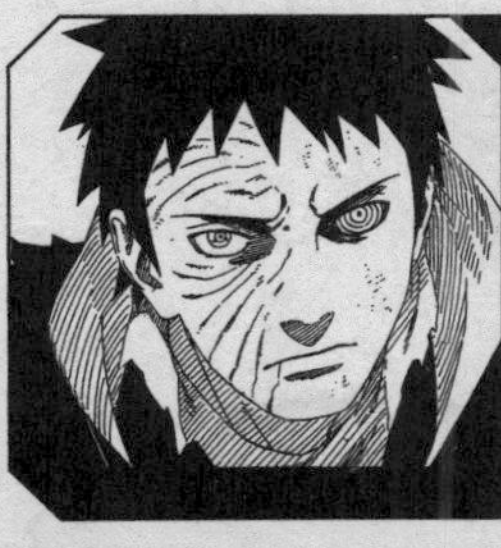

Obito うちはオビト

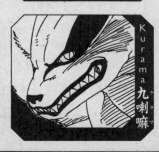

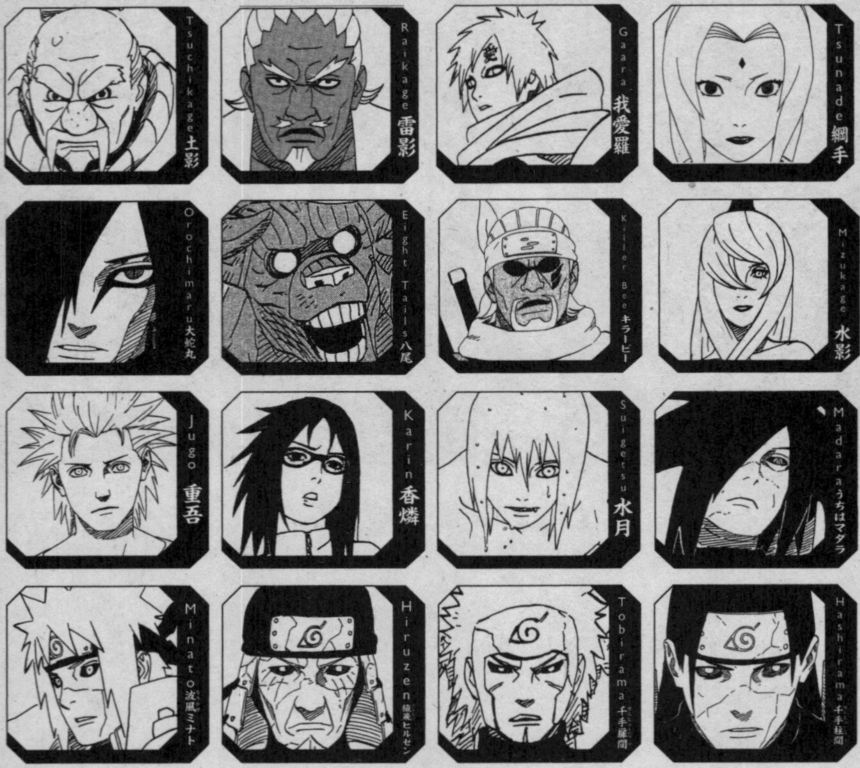

Tsunade 綱手
Gaara 我愛羅
Raikage 雷影
Tsuchikage 土影
Mizukage 水影
Killer Bee キラービー
Eight Tails 八尾
Orochimaru 大蛇丸
Madara うちはマダラ
Suigetsu 水月
Karin 香燐
Jugo 重吾
Hashirama 千手柱間
Tobirama 千手扉間
Hiruzen 猿飛ヒルゼン
Minato 波風ミナト

THE STORY SO FAR...

Naruto, the biggest troublemaker at the Ninja Academy in the Village of Konohagakure, finally becomes a ninja along with his classmates Sasuke and Sakura. They grow and mature through countless trials and battles. However, Sasuke, unable to give up his quest for vengeance, leaves Konohagakure to seek Orochimaru and his power...

Two years pass. Naruto grows up and engages in fierce battles against the Tailed Beast-targeting Akatsuki. And the Fourth Great Ninja War against the Akatsuki finally begins. Naruto and his companions face off against the reunited Obito and Madara in order to stop the resurrected Ten Tails! Ten Tails' power seems too great to handle, but Sasuke enters the battlefield along with the Edotensei-resurrected former Hokage. With Cell 7 reunited at last, the battle starts to turn in Naruto's favor. However, Obito the surprises everyone by becoming the Ten Tails' jinchuriki!

NARUTO

VOL. 67
AN OPENING

CONTENTS

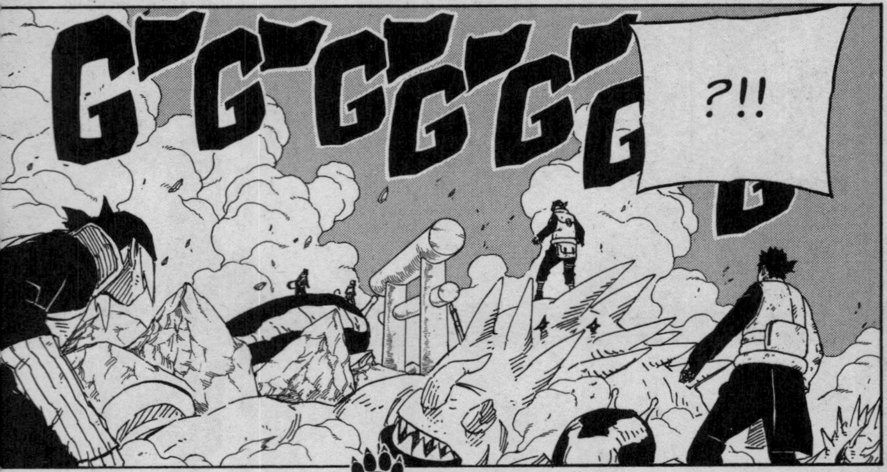
GGGGGGG
?!!

Number 638: Ten Tails' Jinchuriki, Obito

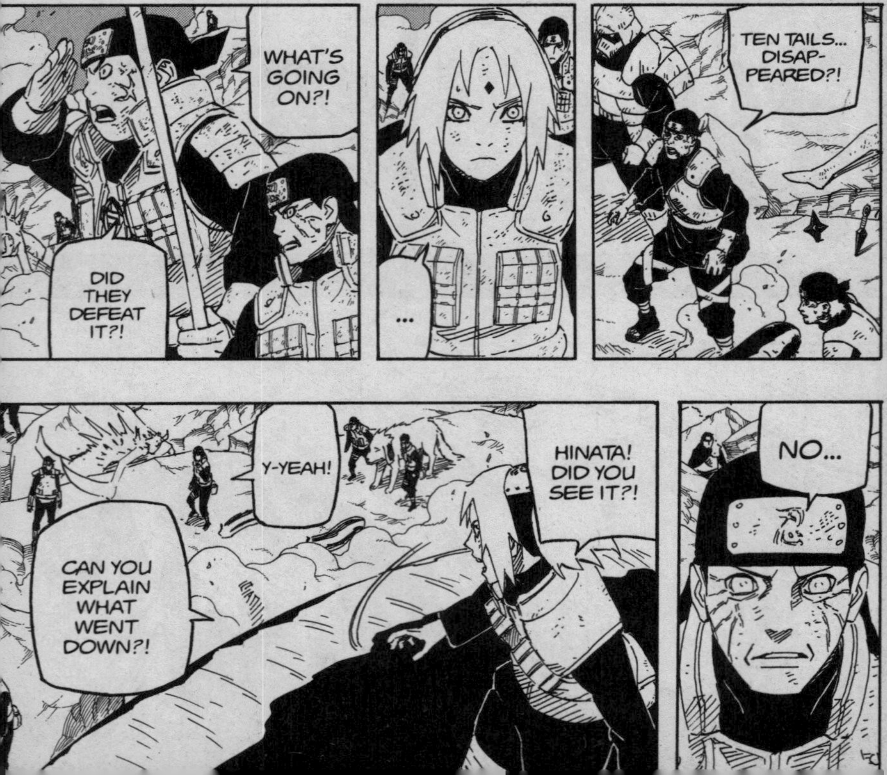
TEN TAILS... DISAP-PEARED?!
...
WHAT'S GOING ON?!
DID THEY DEFEAT IT?!
NO...
HINATA! DID YOU SEE IT?!
Y-YEAH!
CAN YOU EXPLAIN WHAT WENT DOWN?!

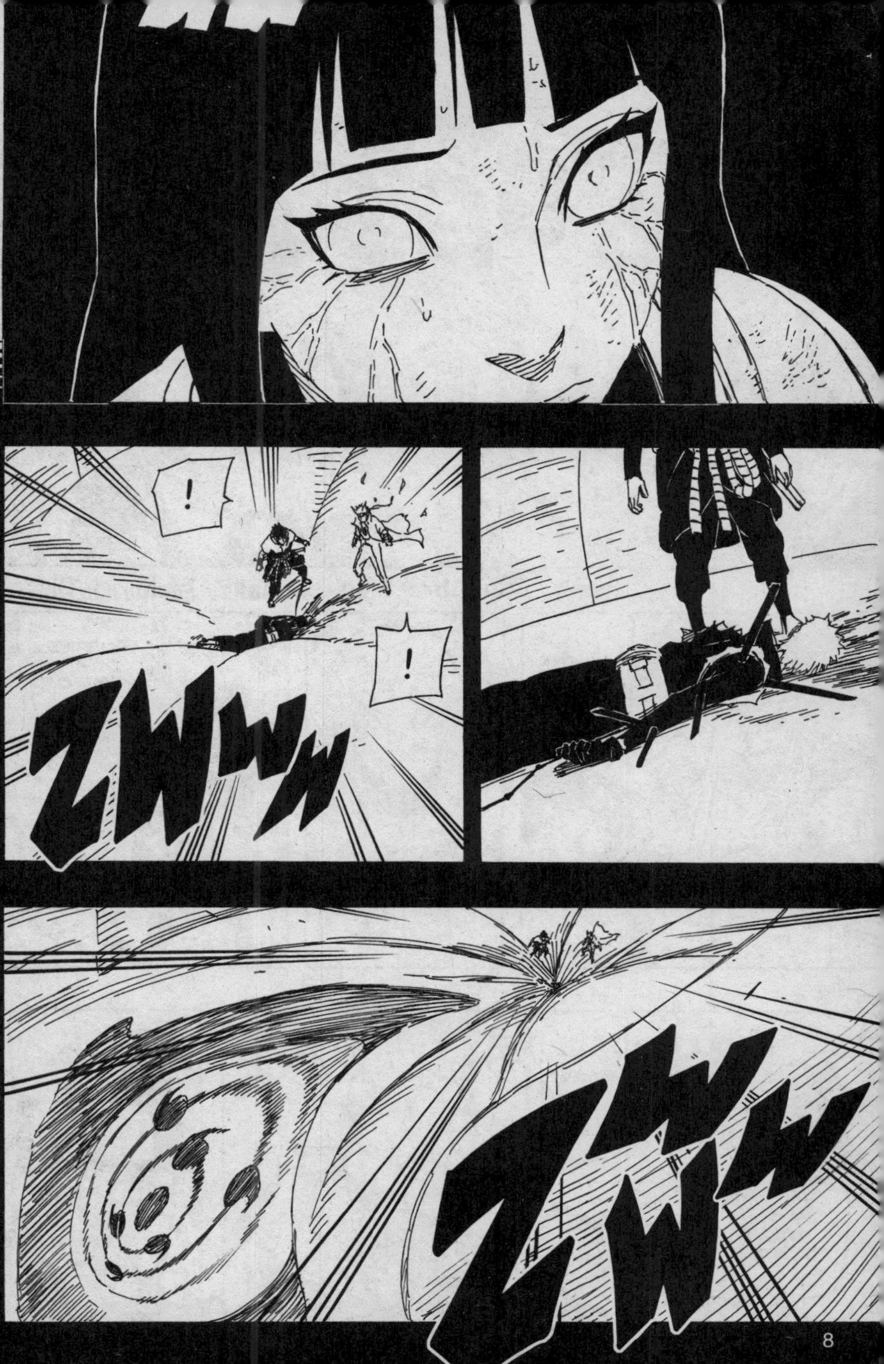
!
!

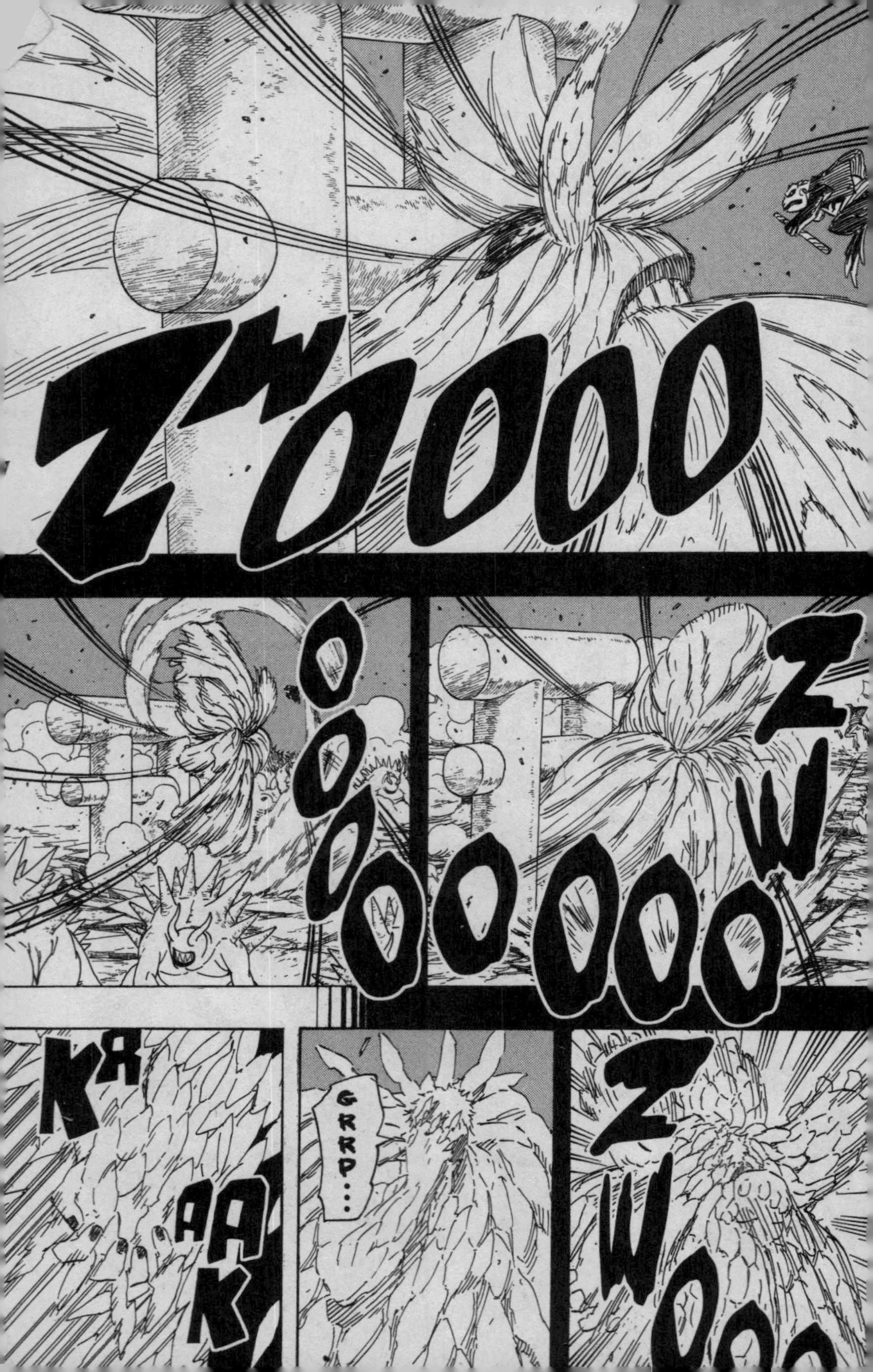

ZWOOOO
ZWOOOOOOOOOOO
GRRP...
KRAAK

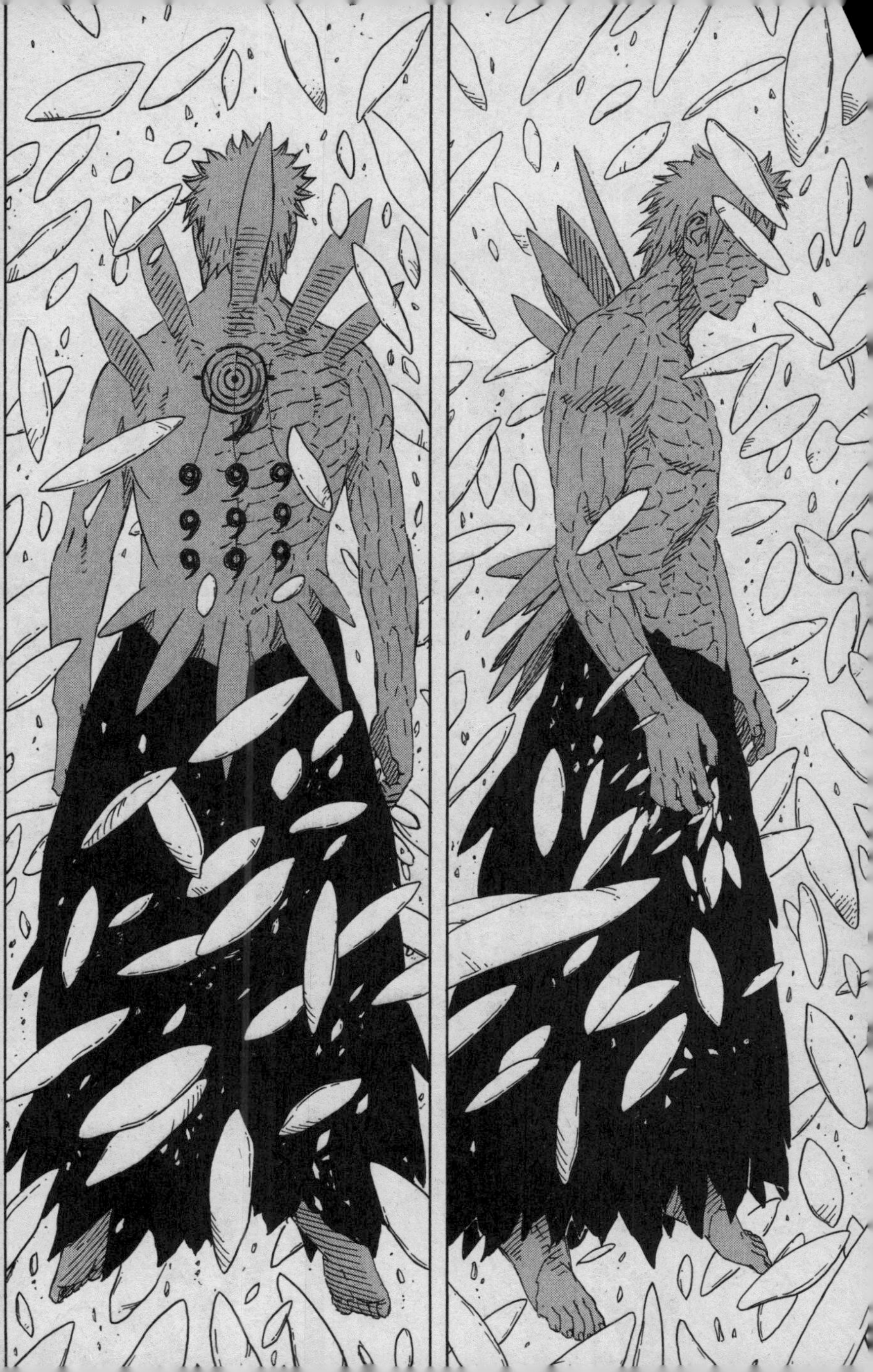

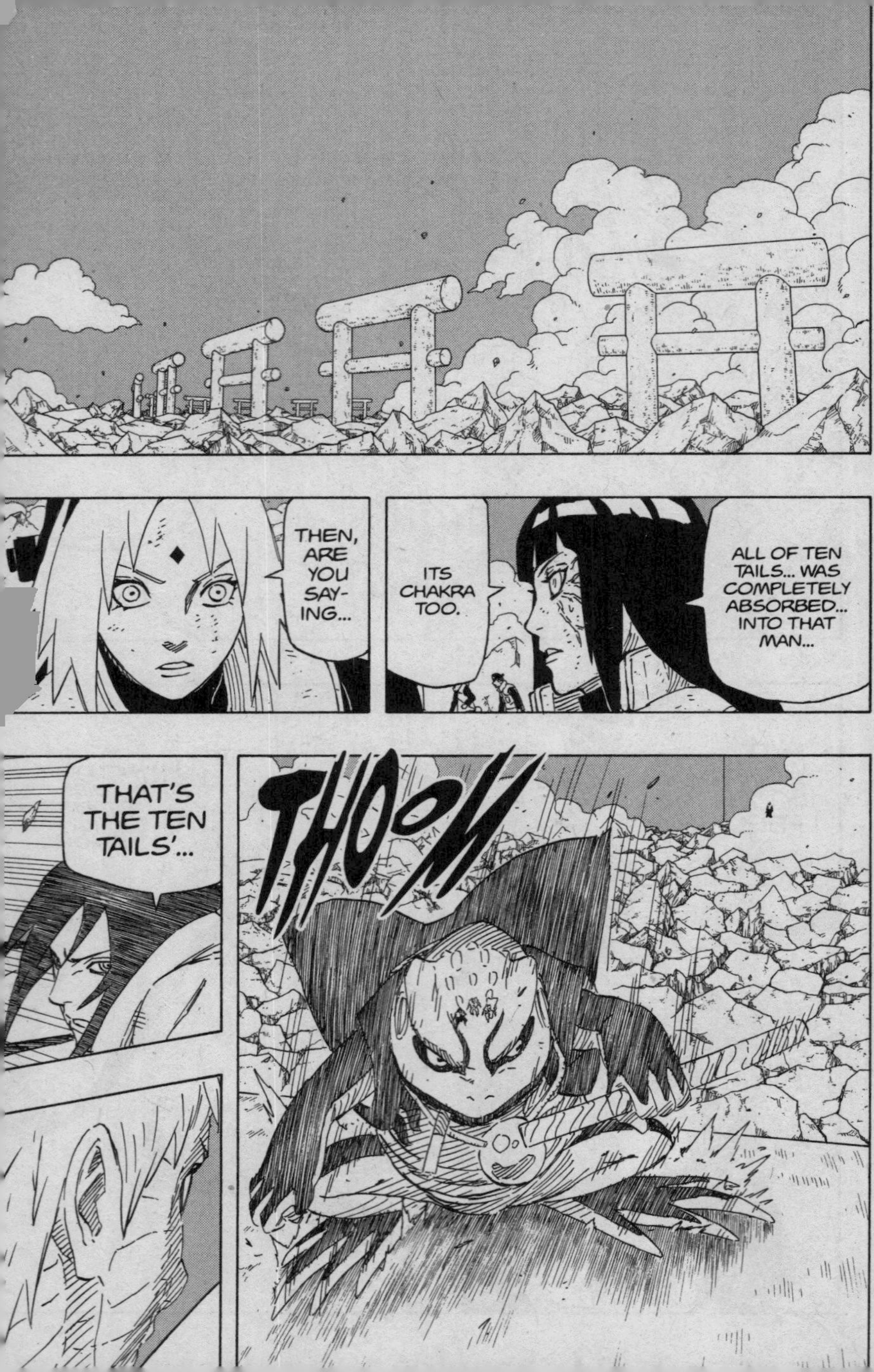
ALL OF TEN TAILS... WAS COMPLETELY ABSORBED... INTO THAT MAN...
ITS CHAKRA TOO.
THEN, ARE YOU SAYING...
THOOM
THAT'S THE TEN TAILS'...

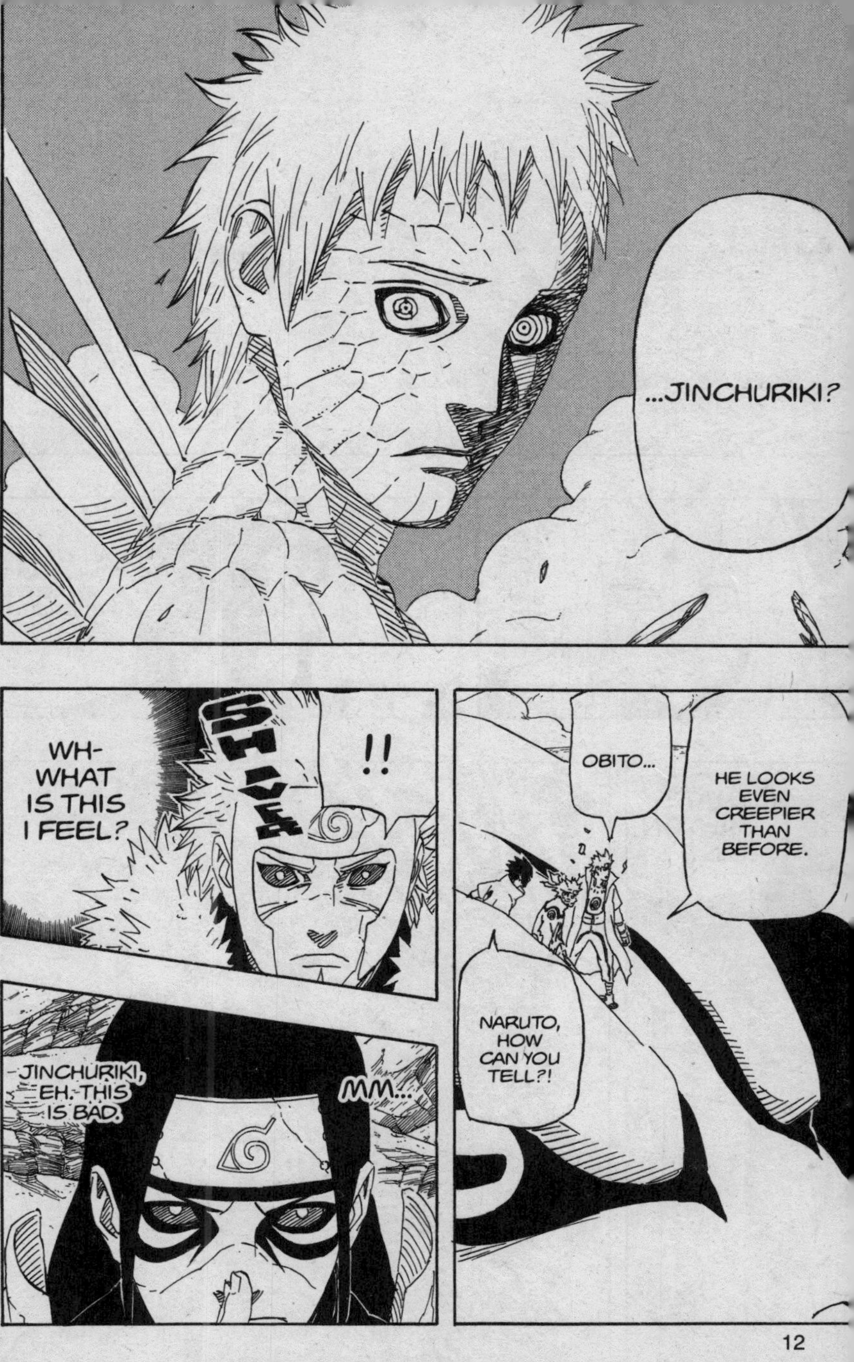
...JINCHURIKI?
HE LOOKS EVEN CREEPIER THAN BEFORE.
OBITO...
NARUTO, HOW CAN YOU TELL?!
!!
SHIVER
WH- WHAT IS THIS I FEEL?
MM...
JINCHURIKI, EH. THIS IS BAD.

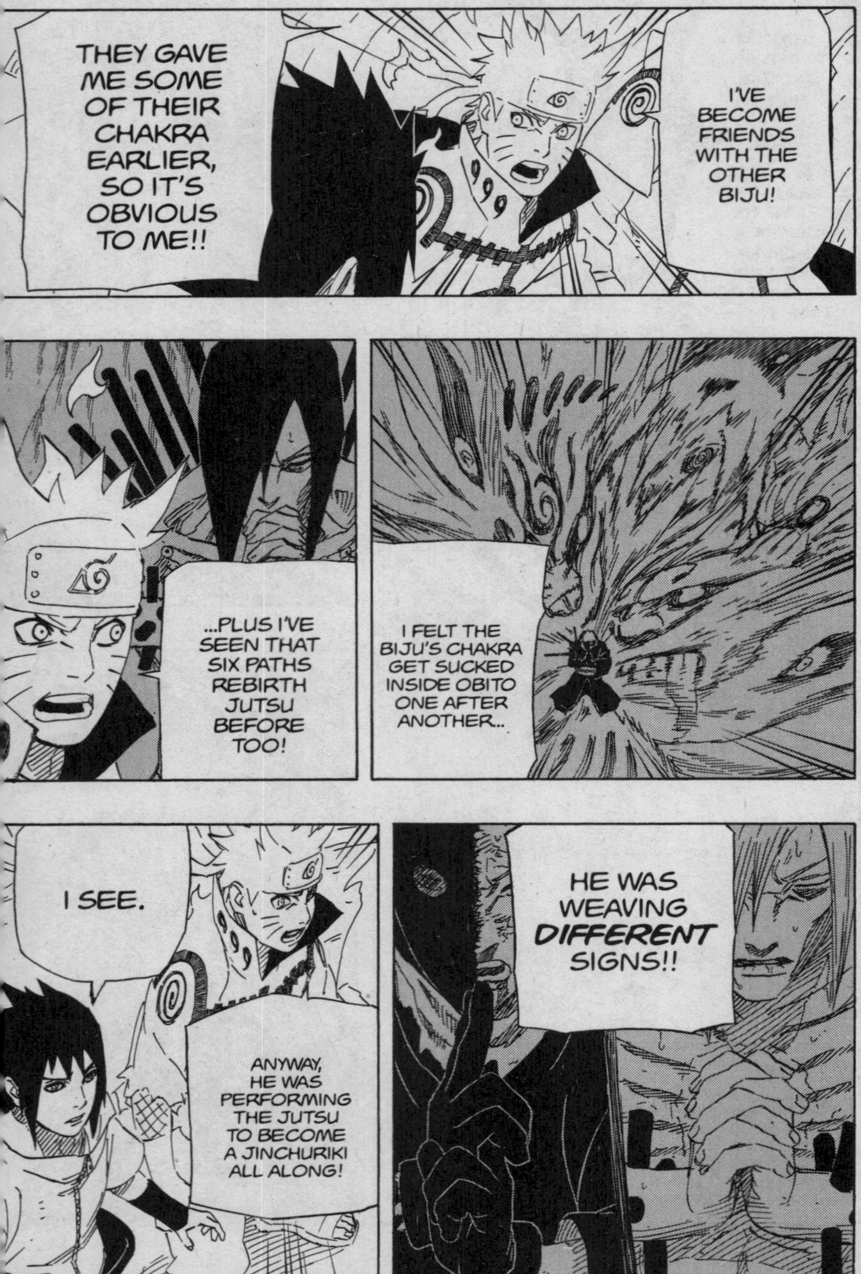
I'VE BECOME FRIENDS WITH THE OTHER BIJU!
THEY GAVE ME SOME OF THEIR CHAKRA EARLIER, SO IT'S OBVIOUS TO ME!!
I FELT THE BIJU'S CHAKRA GET SUCKED INSIDE OBITO ONE AFTER ANOTHER...
...PLUS I'VE SEEN THAT SIX PATHS REBIRTH JUTSU BEFORE TOO!
HE WAS WEAVING ***DIFFERENT*** SIGNS!!
I SEE.
ANYWAY, HE WAS PERFORMING THE JUTSU TO BECOME A JINCHURIKI ALL ALONG!

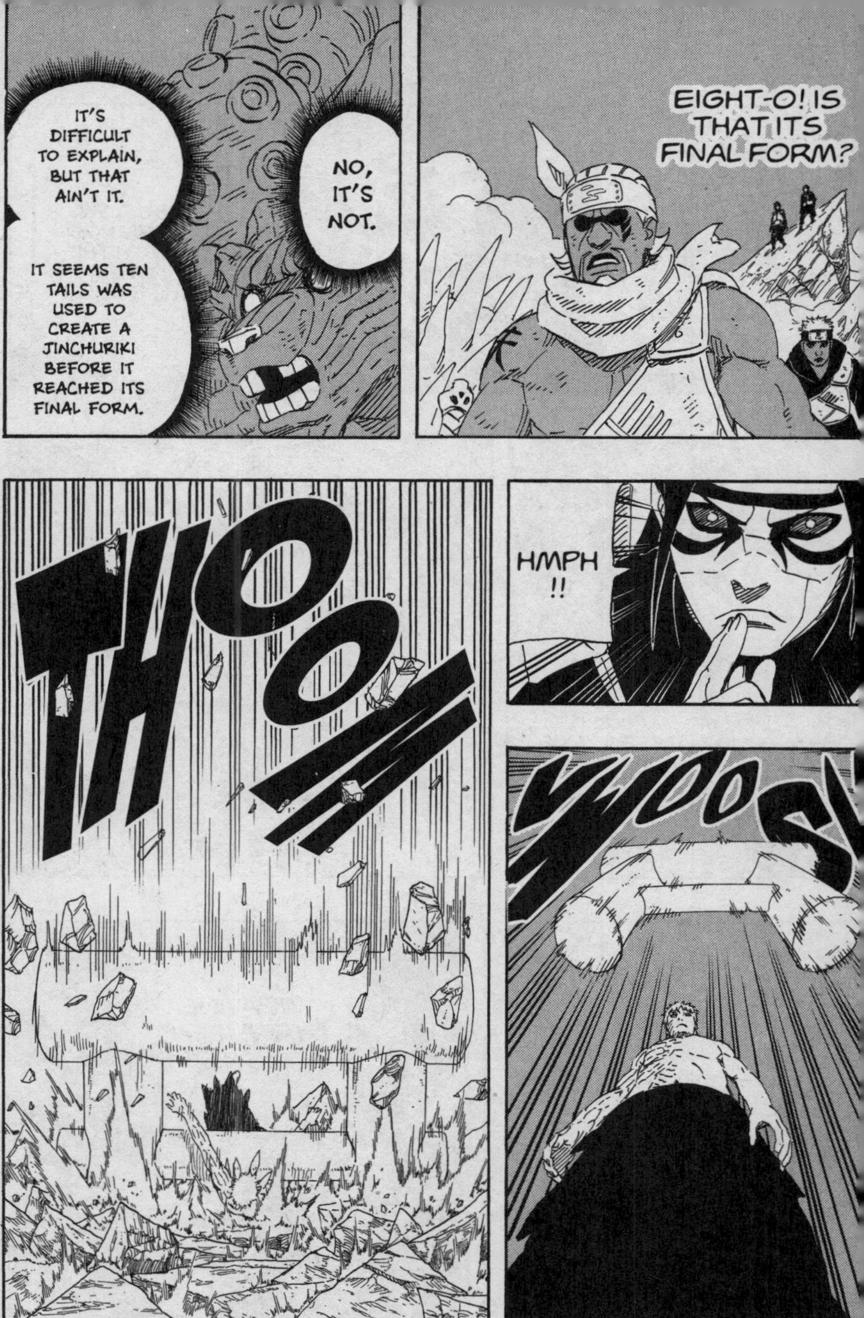
EIGHT-O! IS THAT ITS FINAL FORM?
NO, IT'S NOT.
IT'S DIFFICULT TO EXPLAIN, BUT THAT AIN'T IT.
IT SEEMS TEN TAILS WAS USED TO CREATE A JINCHURIKI BEFORE IT REACHED ITS FINAL FORM.
HMPH!!
THOOM

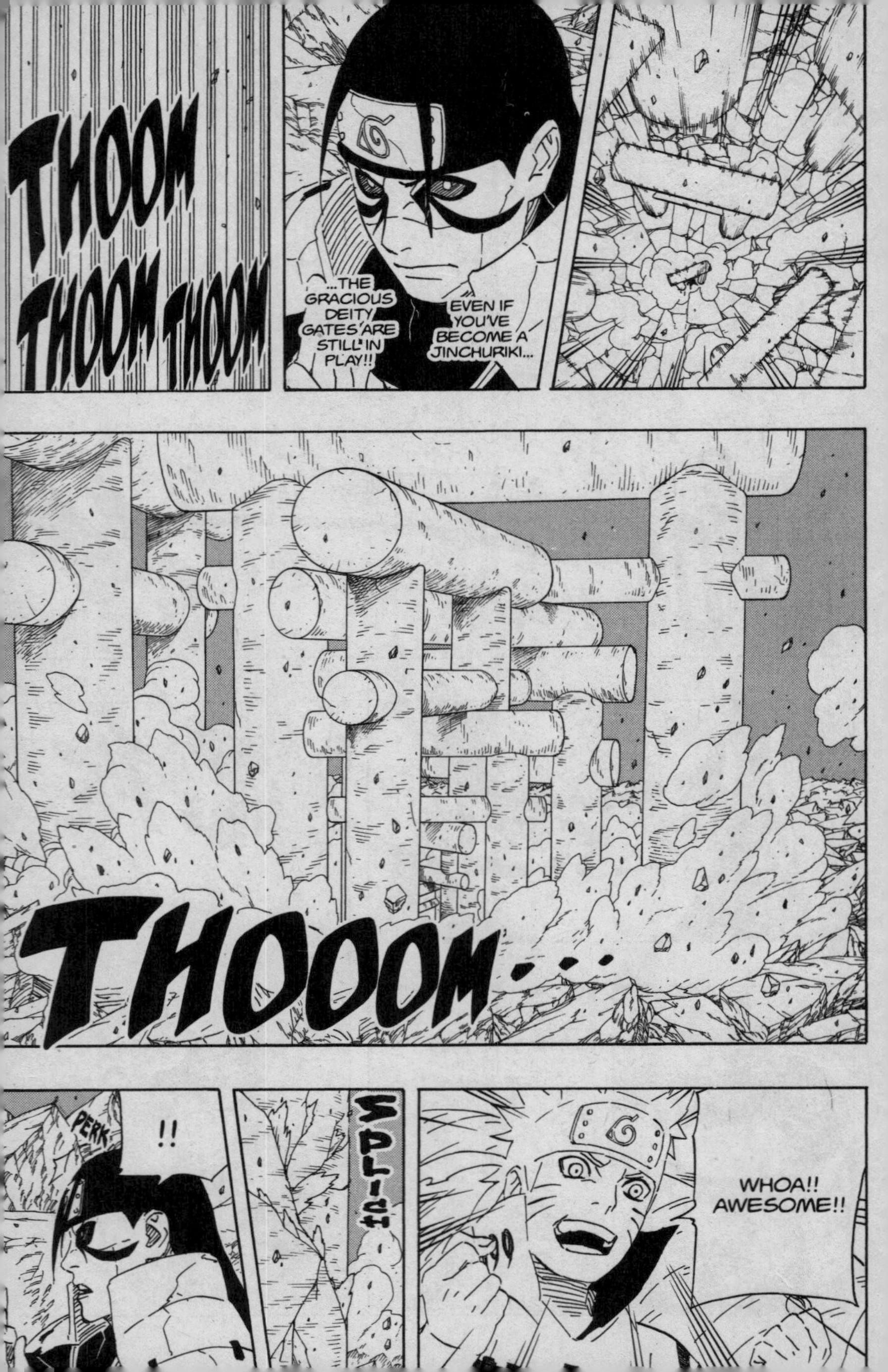
EVEN IF YOU'VE BECOME A JINCHURIKI...
...THE GRACIOUS DEITY GATES ARE STILL IN PLAY!!
THOOM
THOOM THOOM
THOOOM...
WHOA!! AWESOME!!
SPLICH
PERK
!!

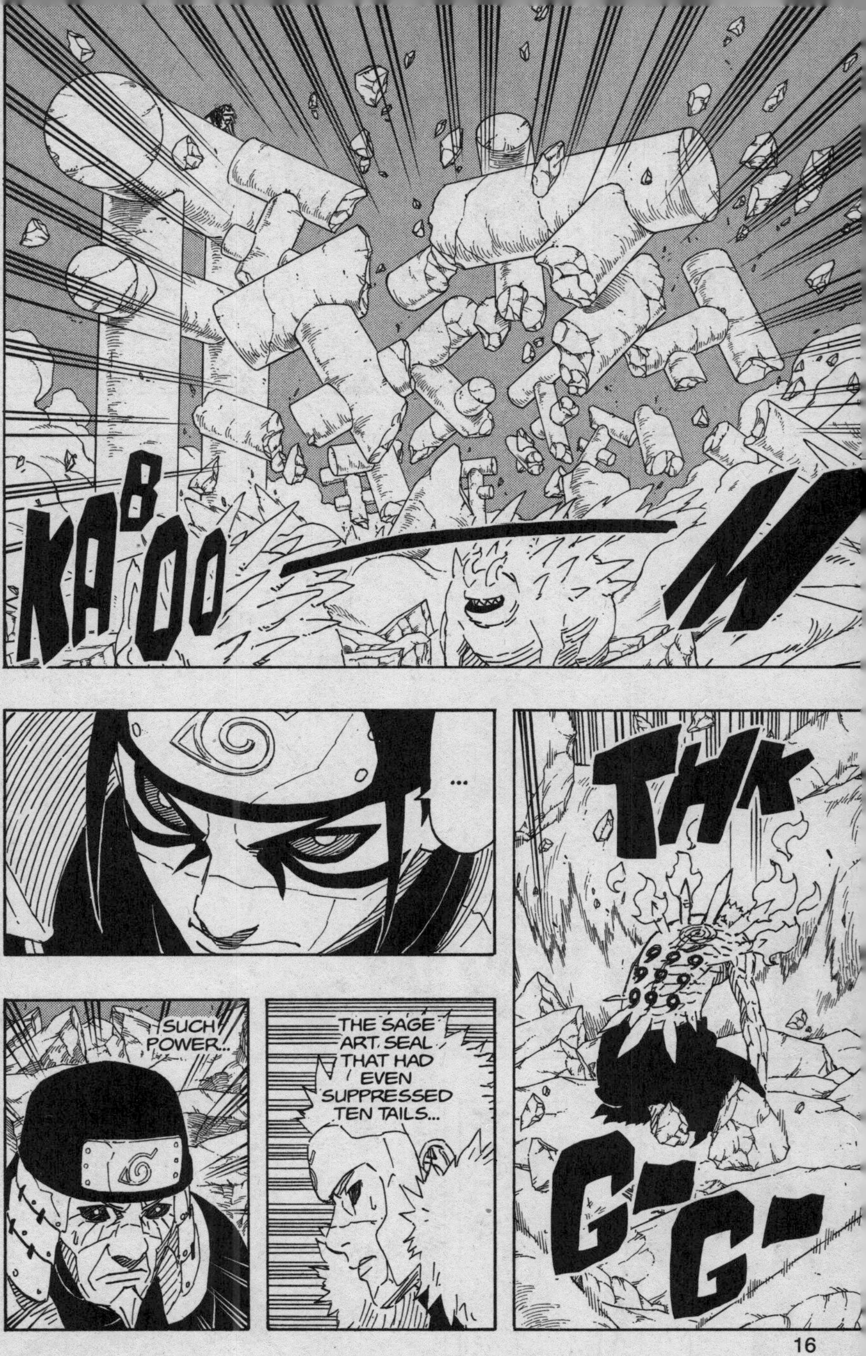
KABOOOM
THK
G-G-
...
THE SAGE ART SEAL THAT HAD EVEN SUPPRESSED TEN TAILS...
SUCH POWER...

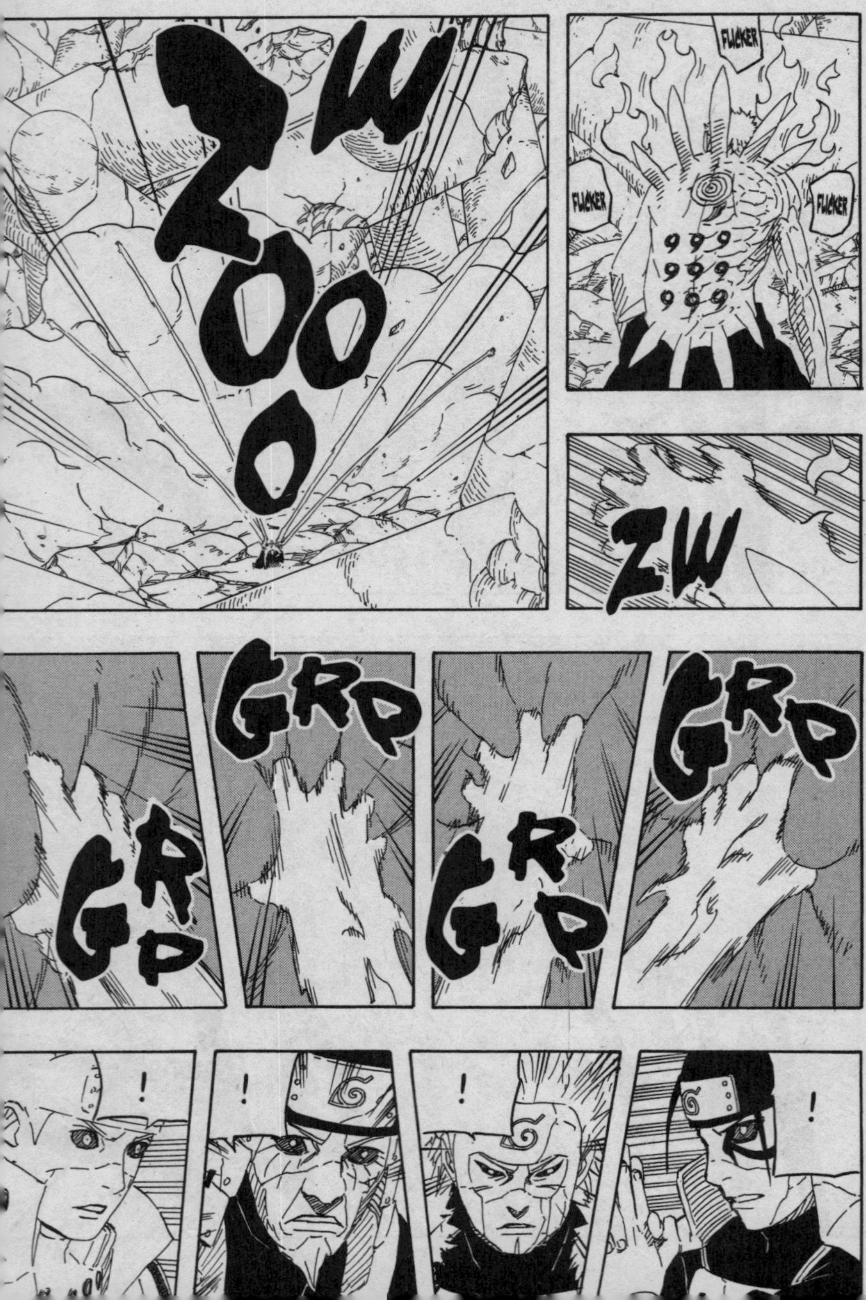
FLICKER
FLICKER
FLICKER
ZW
ZWOOO
GRP
GRP
GRP
GRP
!
!
!
!

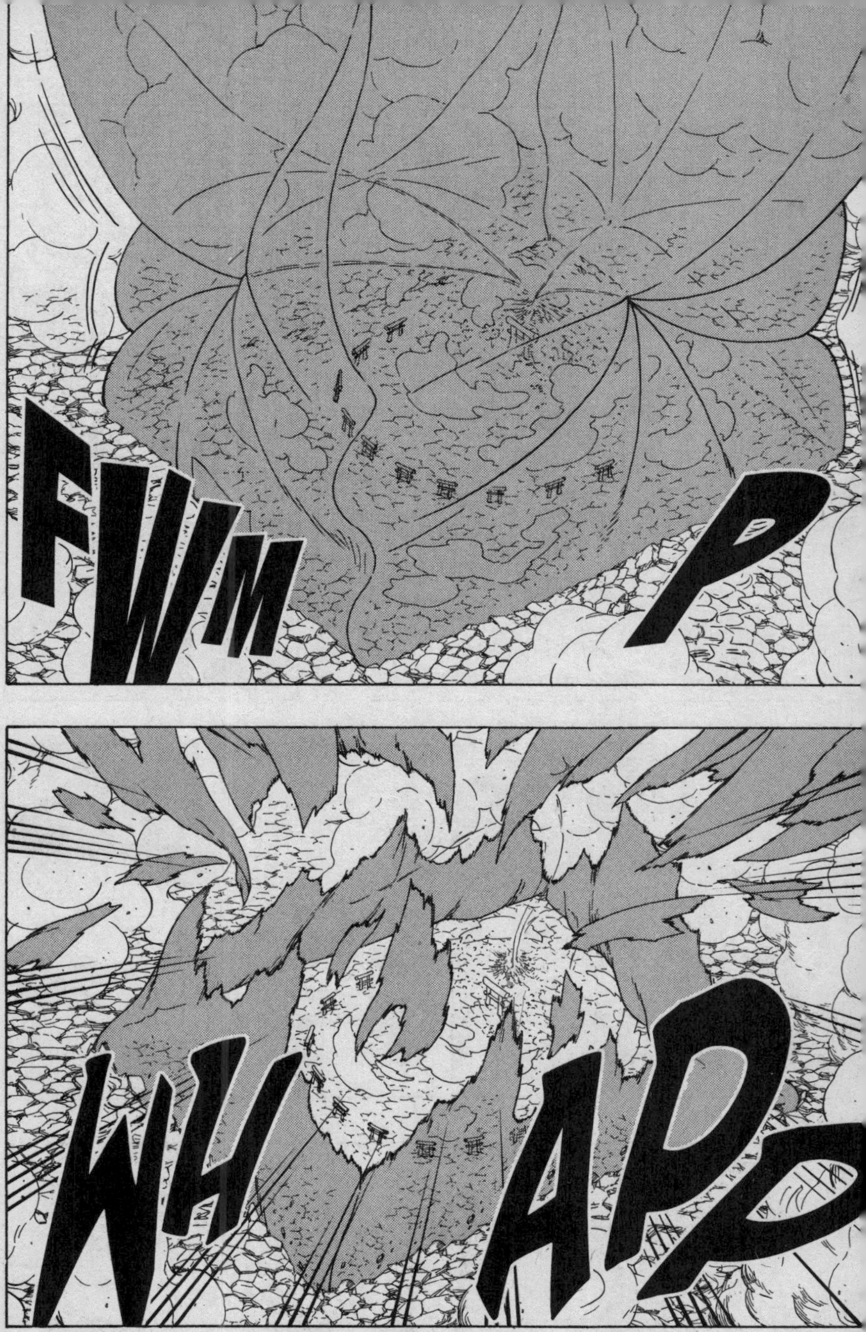
FWMP
WHAP

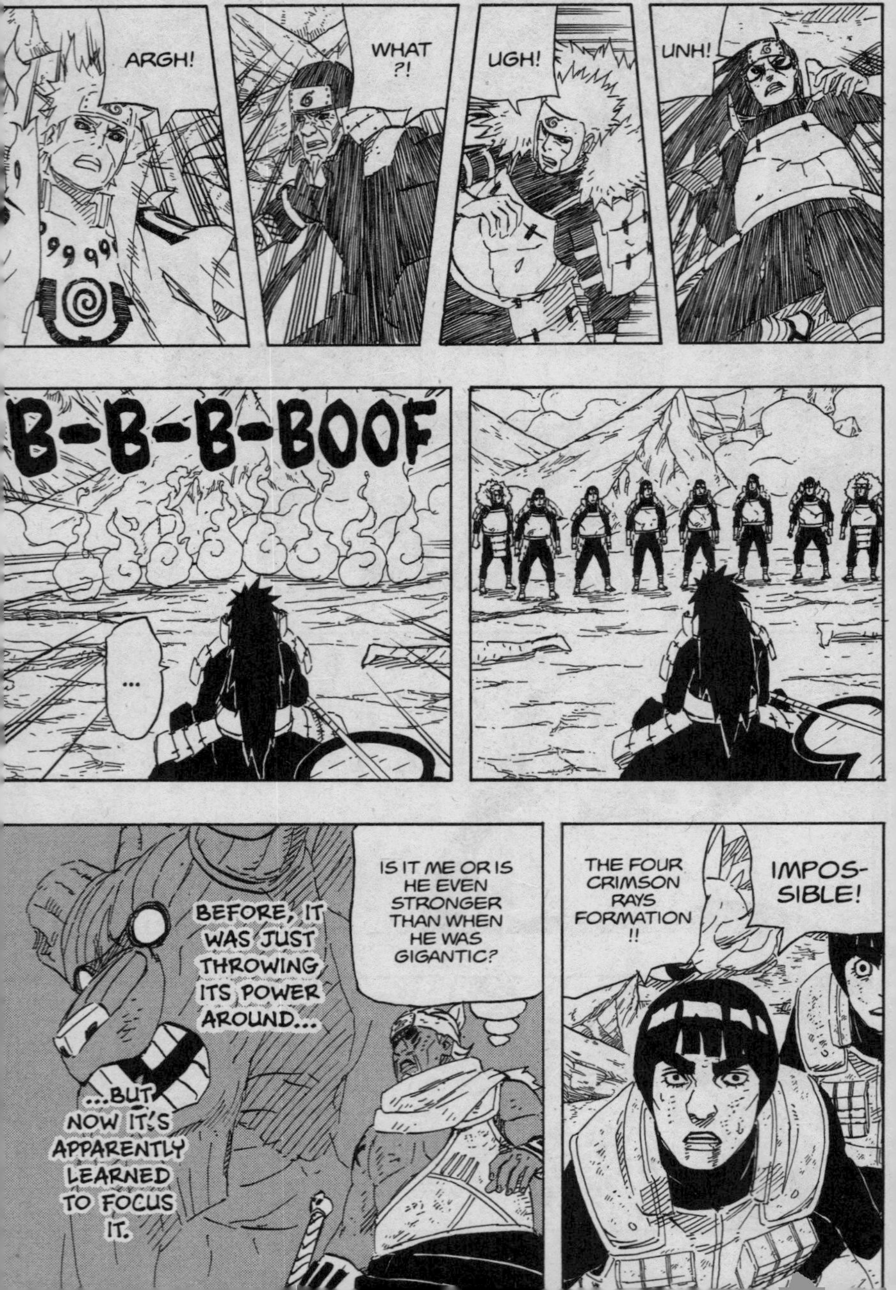
UNH!
UGH!
WHAT ?!
ARGH!
B-B-B-BOOF
...
IMPOS-SIBLE!
THE FOUR CRIMSON RAYS FORMATION !!
IS IT ME OR IS HE EVEN STRONGER THAN WHEN HE WAS GIGANTIC?
BEFORE, IT WAS JUST THROWING ITS POWER AROUND...
...BUT NOW IT'S APPARENTLY LEARNED TO FOCUS IT.

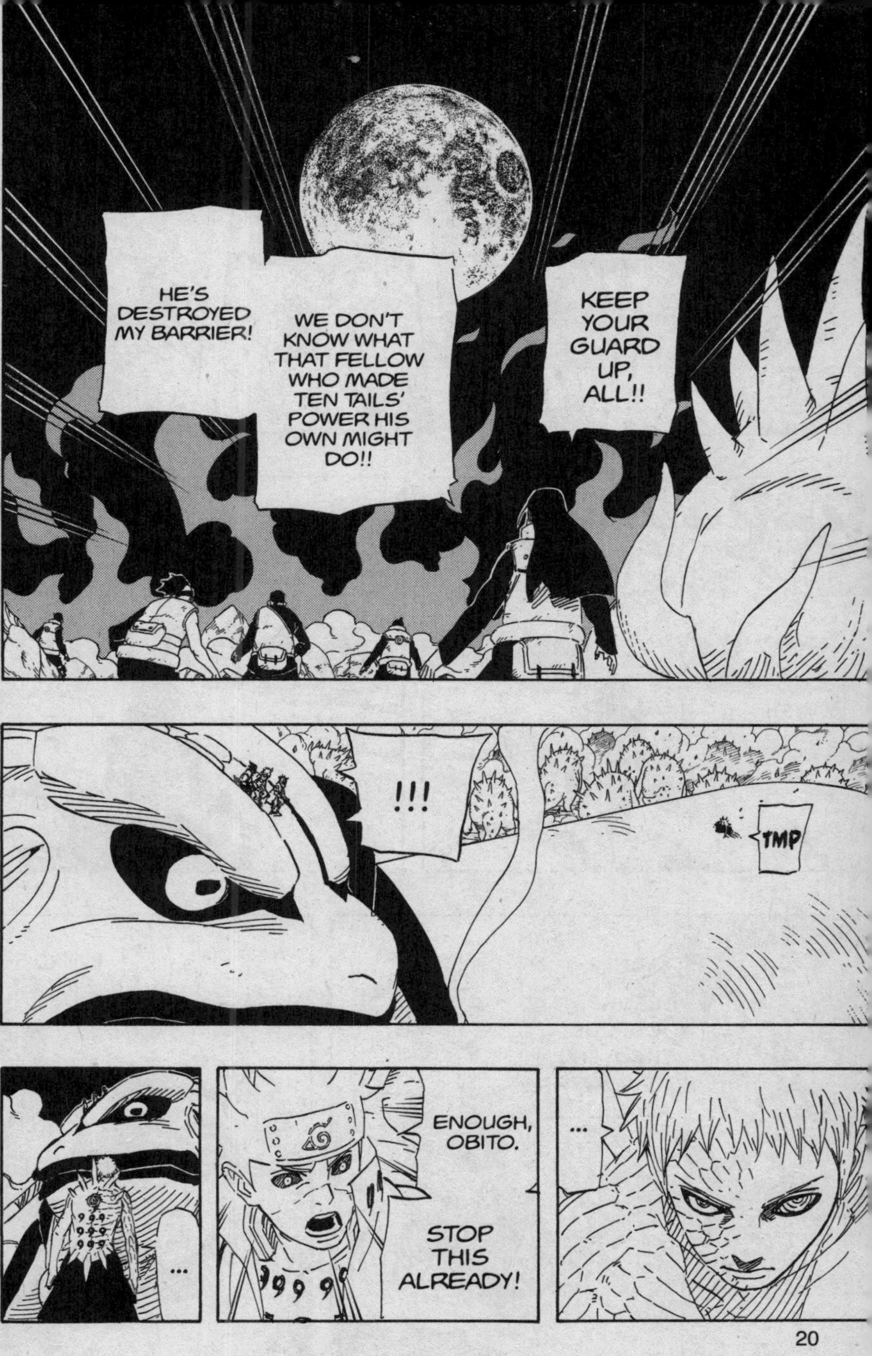
KEEP YOUR GUARD UP, ALL!!
WE DON'T KNOW WHAT THAT FELLOW WHO MADE TEN TAILS' POWER HIS OWN MIGHT DO!!
HE'S DESTROYED MY BARRIER!
TMP
!!!
...
ENOUGH, OBITO.
STOP THIS ALREADY!
...

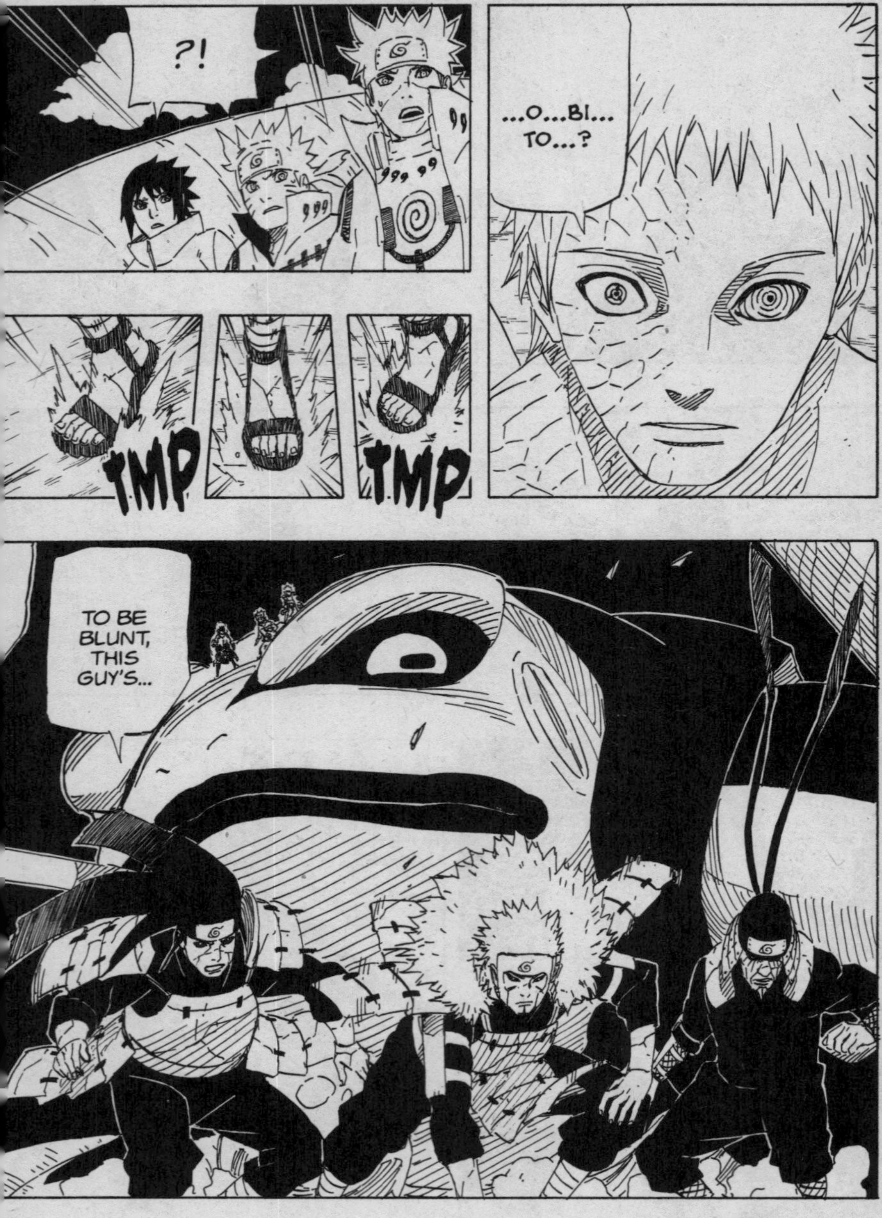
...O...BI... TO...?
?!
TMP
TMP
TO BE BLUNT, THIS GUY'S...

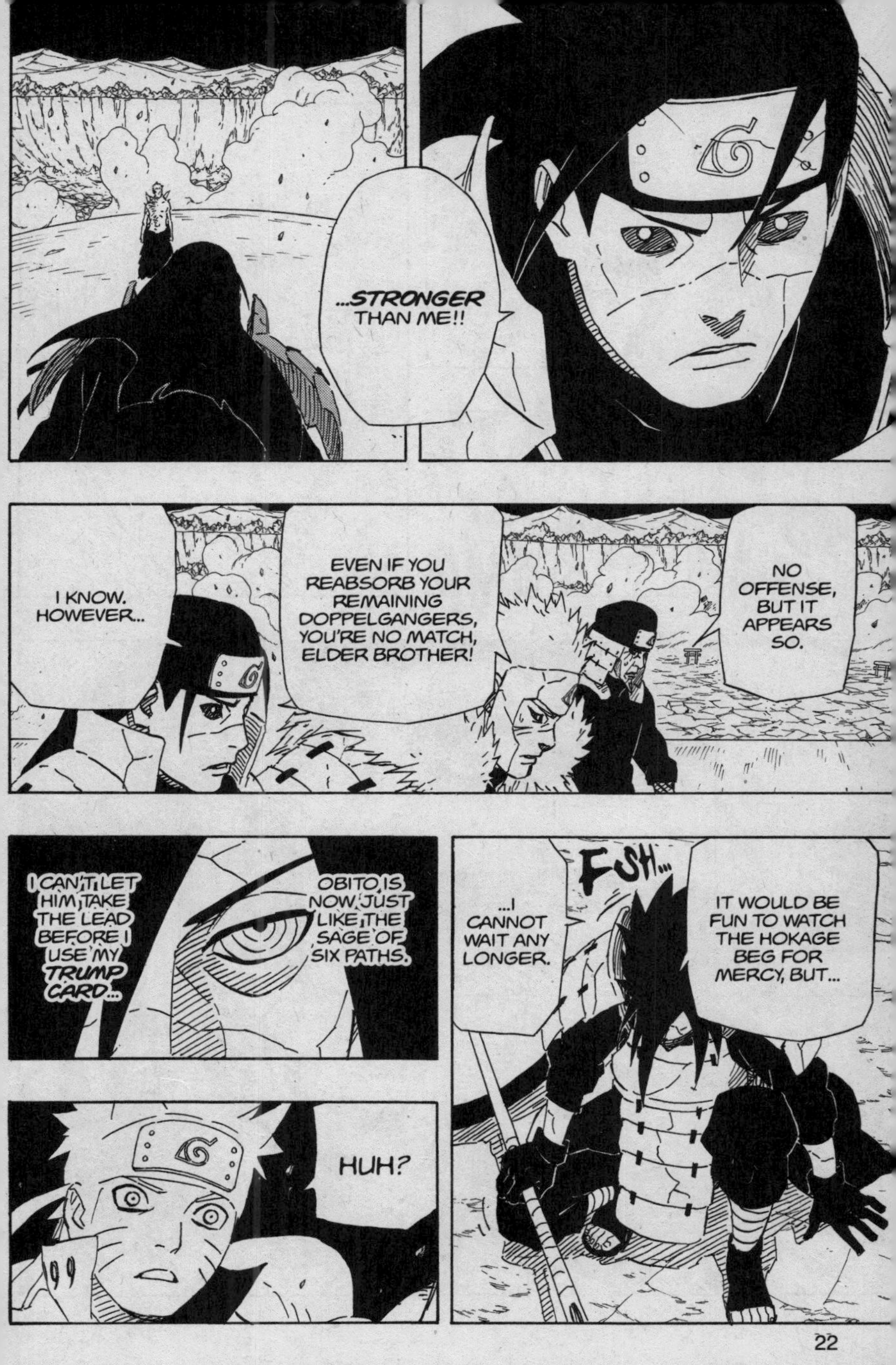
...STRONGER THAN ME!!
NO OFFENSE, BUT IT APPEARS SO.
EVEN IF YOU REABSORB YOUR REMAINING DOPPELGANGERS, YOU'RE NO MATCH, ELDER BROTHER!
I KNOW. HOWEVER...
IT WOULD BE FUN TO WATCH THE HOKAGE BEG FOR MERCY, BUT...
FSH...
...I CANNOT WAIT ANY LONGER.
OBITO IS NOW JUST LIKE THE SAGE OF SIX PATHS.
I CAN'T LET HIM TAKE THE LEAD BEFORE I USE MY *TRUMP CARD*...
HUH?

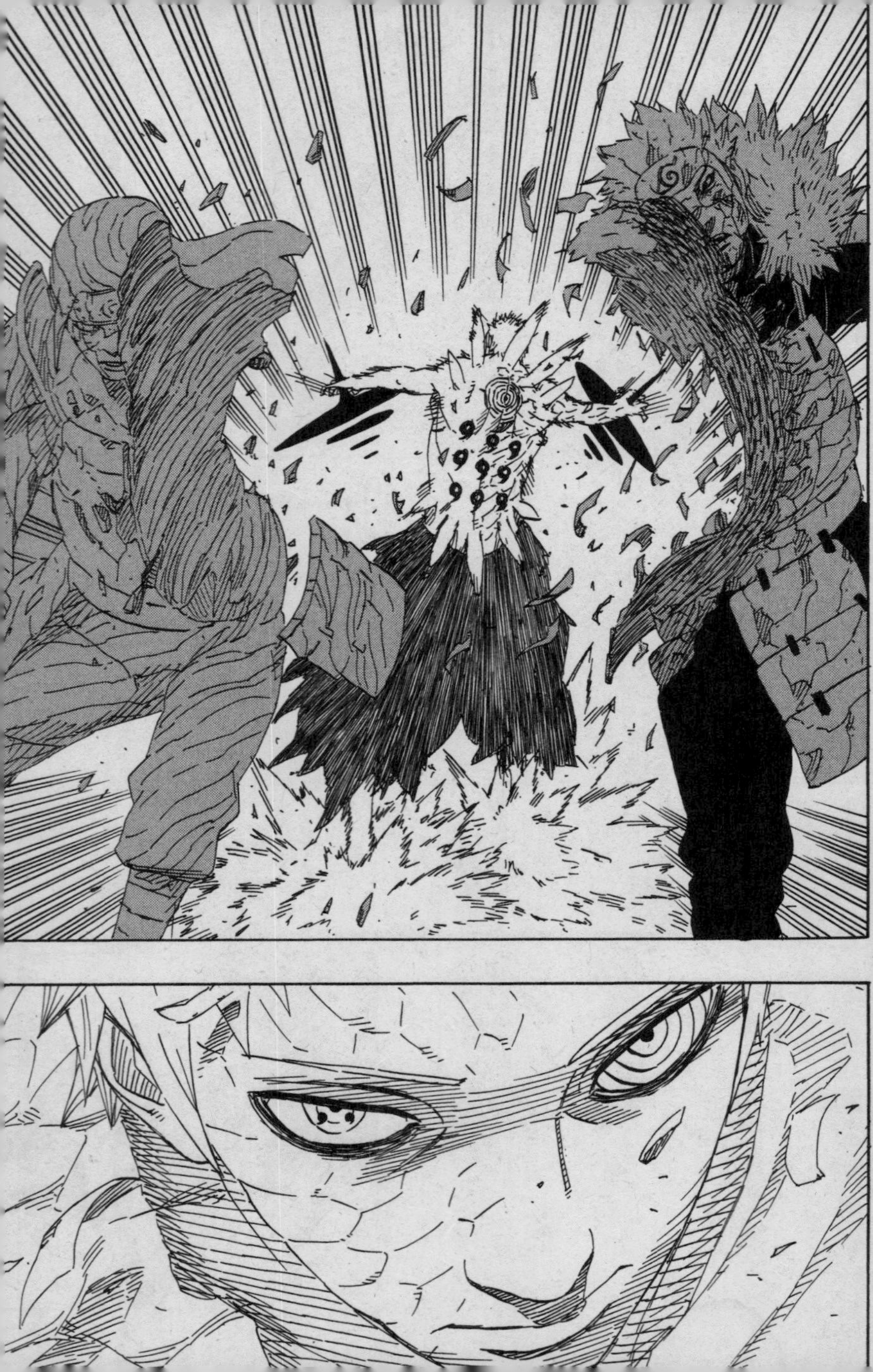

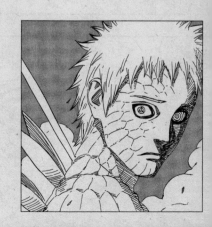

Number 639: Assault

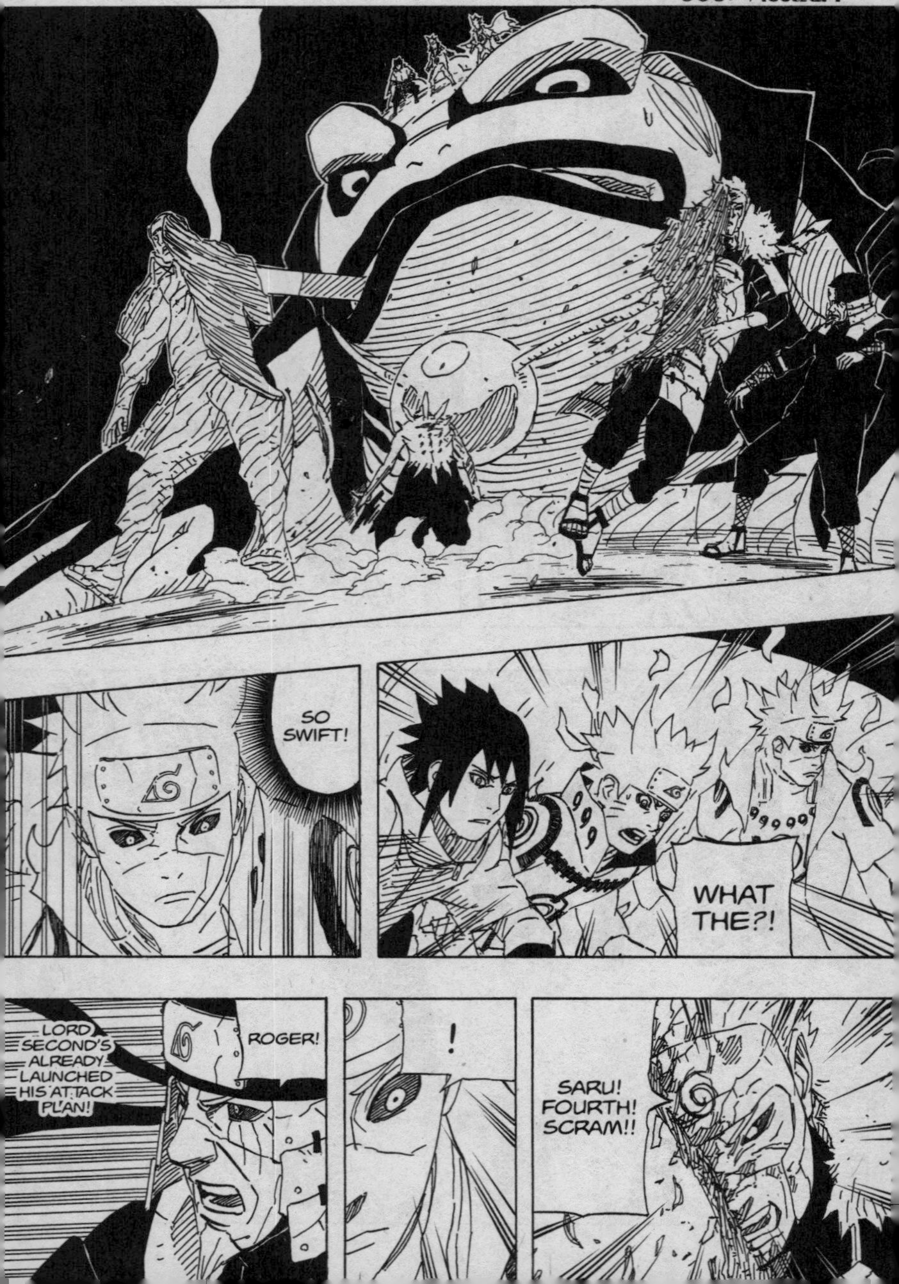
WHAT THE?!
SO SWIFT!
SARU! FOURTH! SCRAM!!
!
ROGER!
LORD SECOND'S ALREADY LAUNCHED HIS ATTACK PLAN!

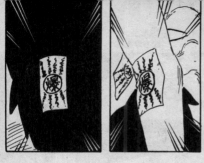

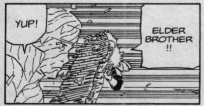

YUP!

ELDER BROTHER!!

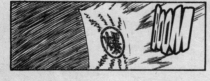

BOOM!

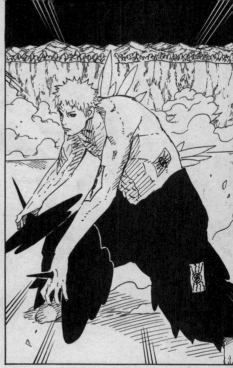

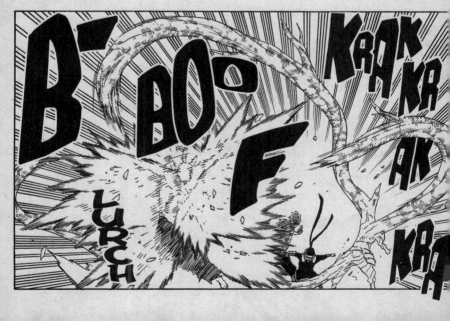

B-BOOF

KRAK KRAK KRA

LURCH

KRA

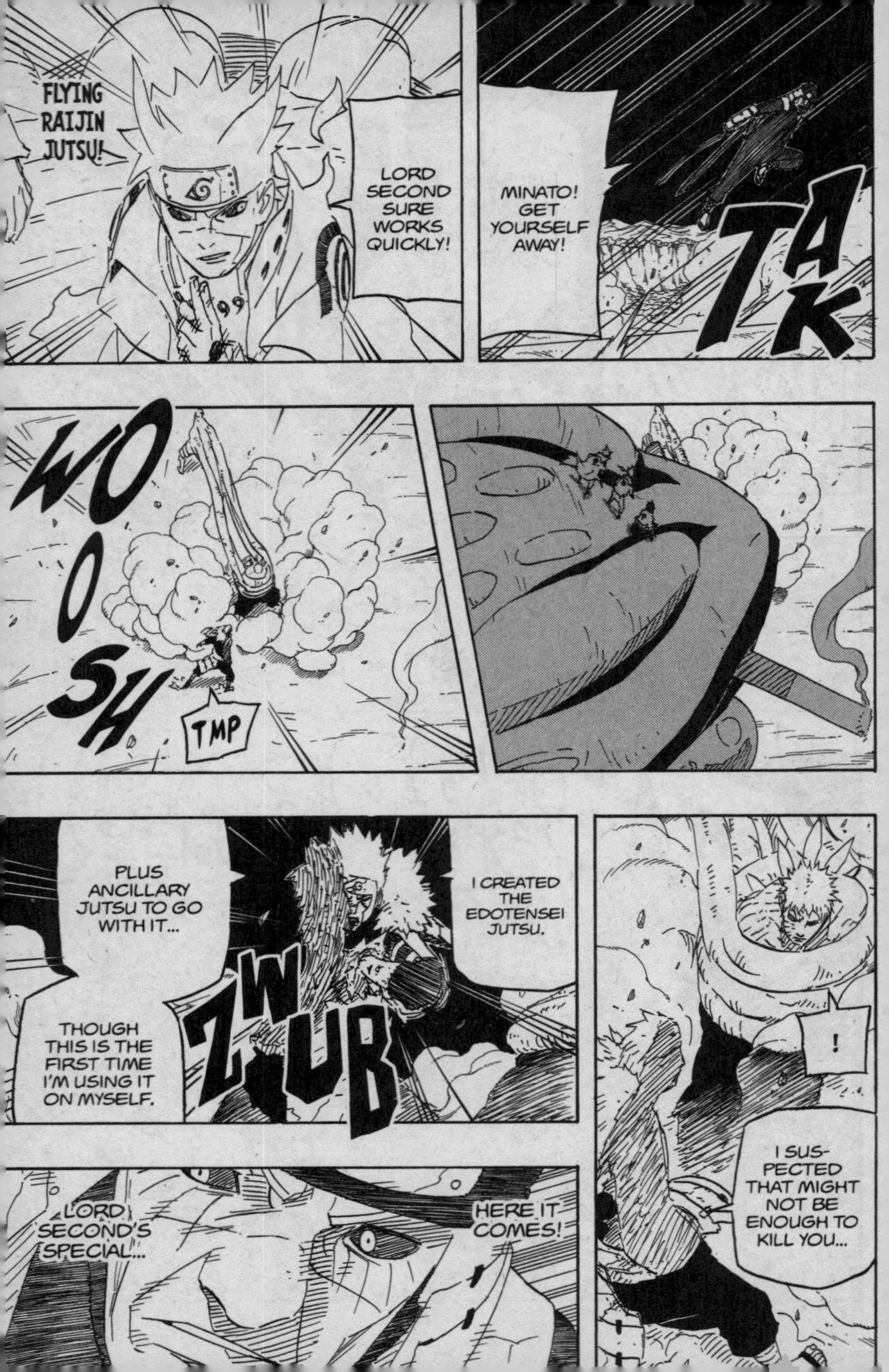
MINATO! GET YOURSELF AWAY!
TAK
LORD SECOND SURE WORKS QUICKLY!
FLYING RAIJIN JUTSU!
WOOSH
TMP
!
I SUS-PECTED THAT MIGHT NOT BE ENOUGH TO KILL YOU...
I CREATED THE EDOTENSEI JUTSU.
PLUS ANCILLARY JUTSU TO GO WITH IT...
THOUGH THIS IS THE FIRST TIME I'M USING IT ON MYSELF.
ZWUB
HERE IT COMES!
LORD SECOND'S SPECIAL...

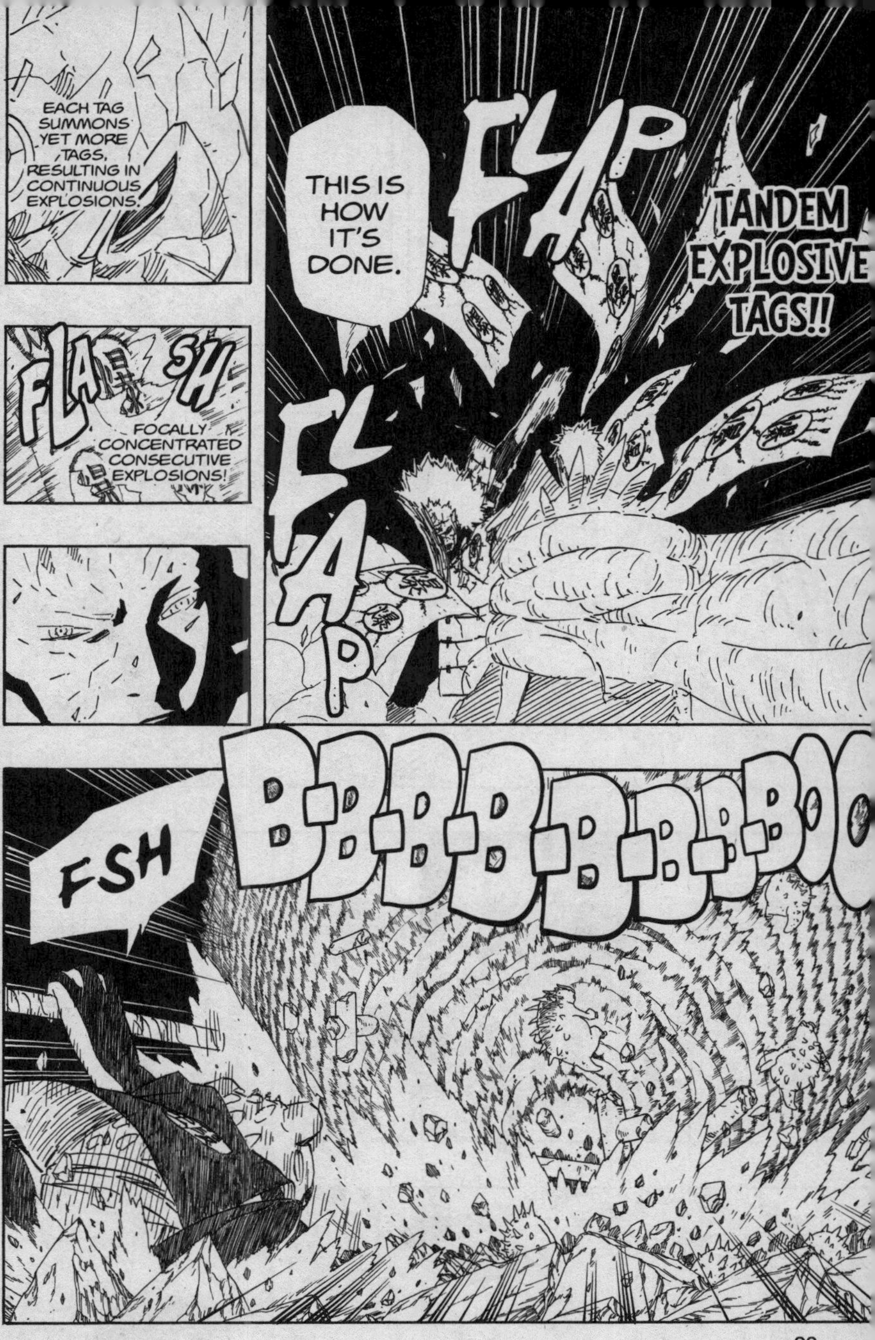

TANDEM EXPLOSIVE TAGS!!
FLAP
THIS IS HOW IT'S DONE.
FLAP
EACH TAG SUMMONS YET MORE TAGS, RESULTING IN CONTINUOUS EXPLOSIONS.
FLASH
FOCALLY CONCENTRATED CONSECUTIVE EXPLOSIONS!
B-B-B-B-B-B-B-B-BO
FSH

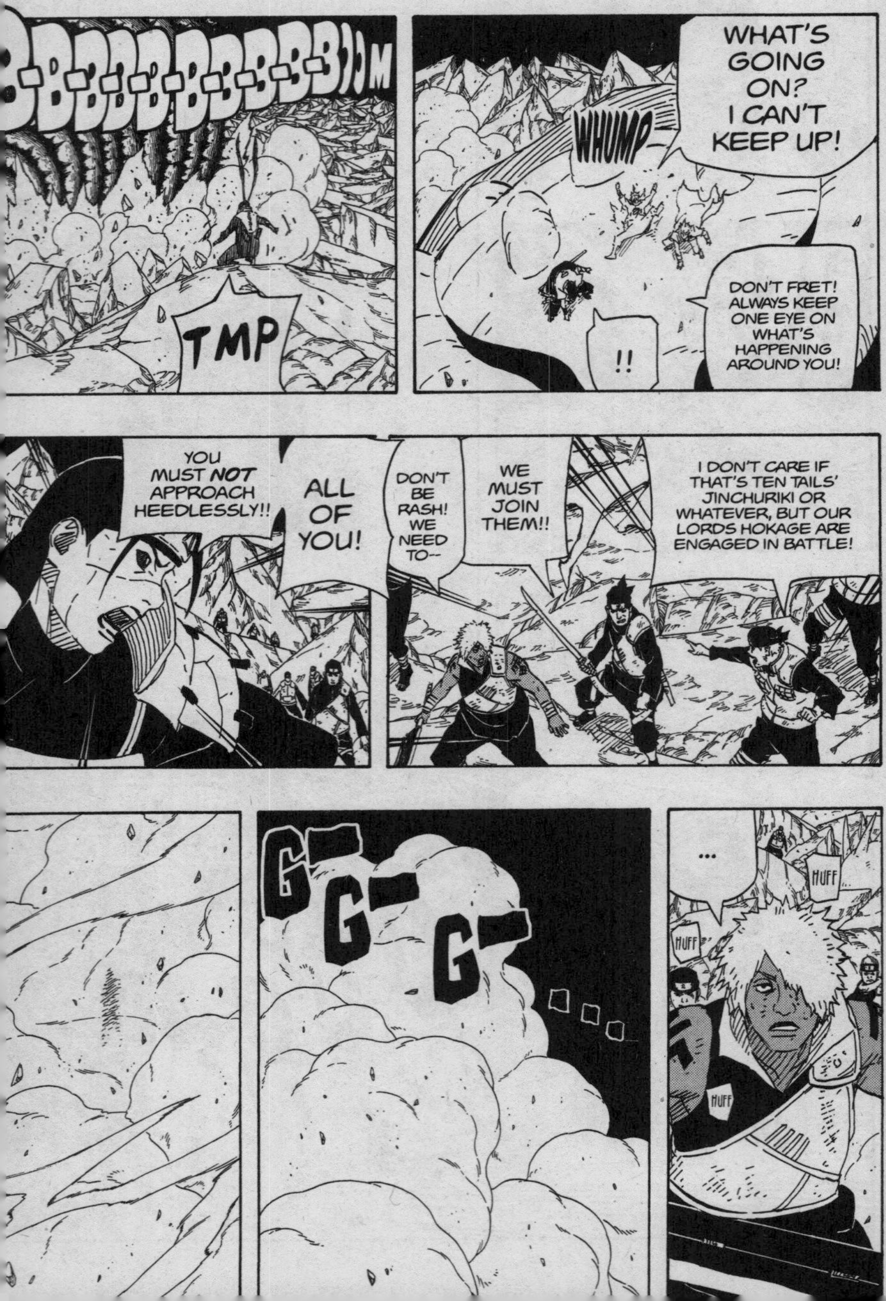
WHAT'S GOING ON? I CAN'T KEEP UP!
WHUMP
DON'T FRET! ALWAYS KEEP ONE EYE ON WHAT'S HAPPENING AROUND YOU!
!!
TMP
I DON'T CARE IF THAT'S TEN TAILS' JINCHURIKI OR WHATEVER, BUT OUR LORDS HOKAGE ARE ENGAGED IN BATTLE!
WE MUST JOIN THEM!!
DON'T BE RASH! WE NEED TO--
ALL OF YOU!
YOU MUST **NOT** APPROACH HEEDLESSLY!!
...
HUFF
HUFF
HUFF
G-G-G-

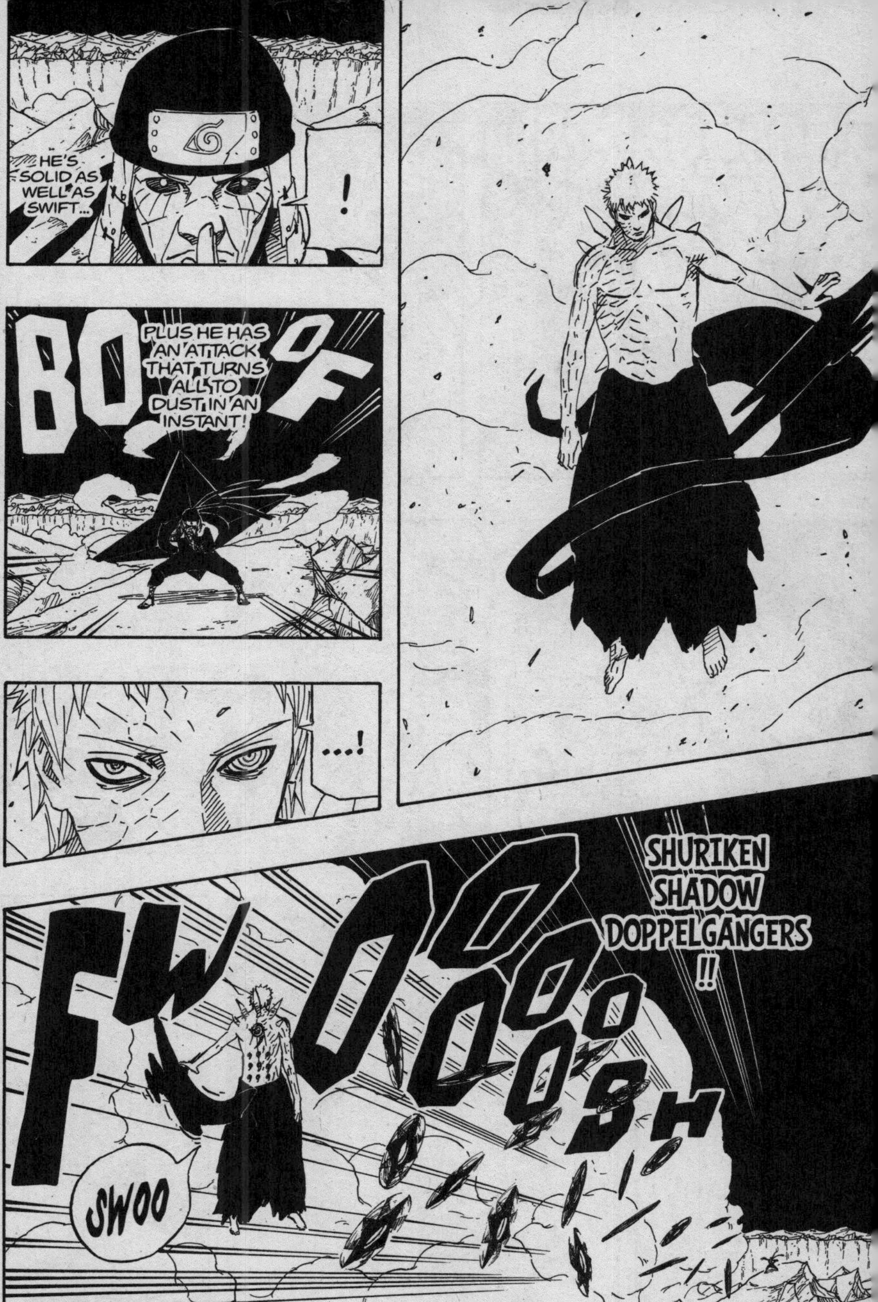
HE'S SOLID AS WELL AS SWIFT...
!
BOOF
PLUS HE HAS AN ATTACK THAT TURNS ALL TO DUST IN AN INSTANT!
...!
SHURIKEN SHADOW DOPPELGANGERS!!
FWOOOOOSH
SWOO

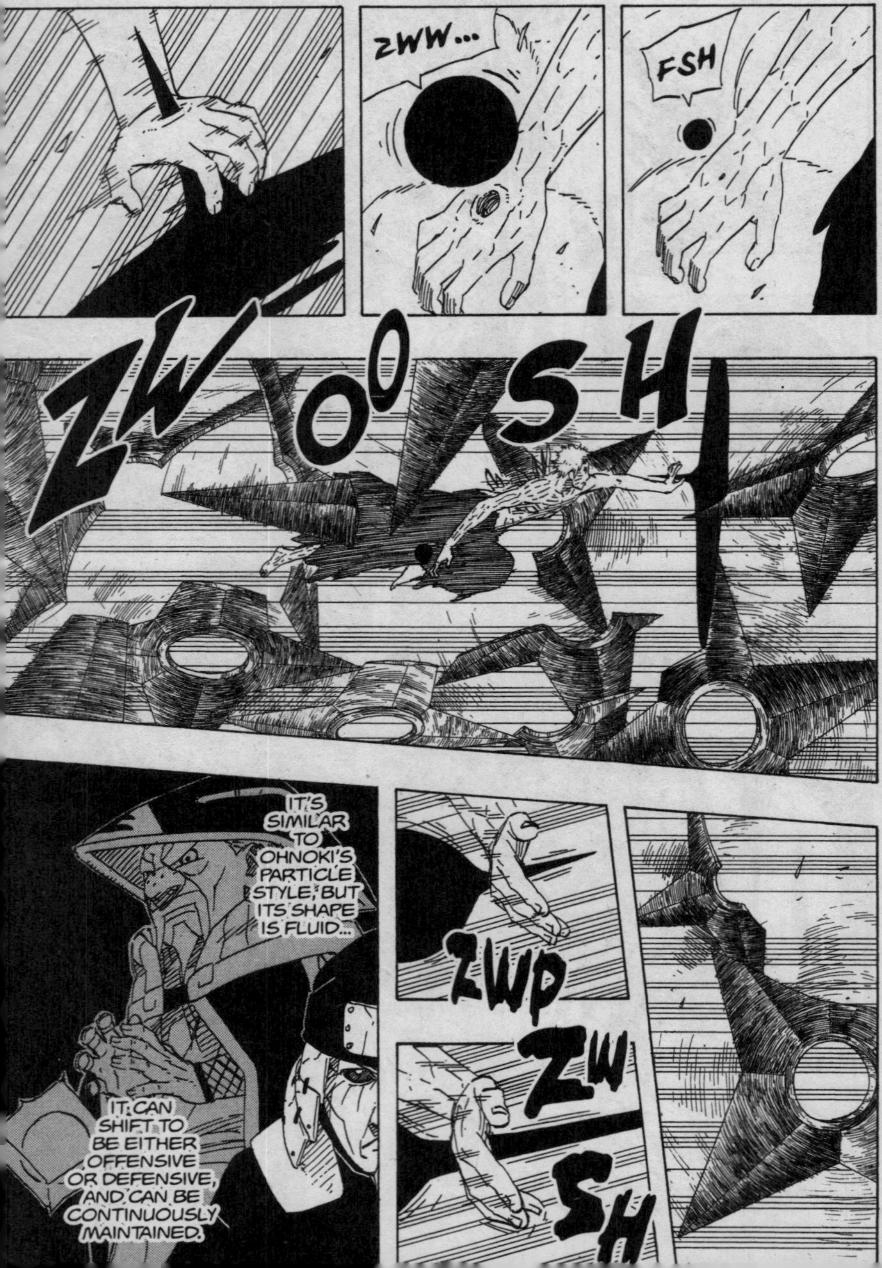
FSH
ZWW...
ZWOOSH
ZW
SH
ZWP
IT'S SIMILAR TO OHNOKI'S PARTICLE STYLE, BUT ITS SHAPE IS FLUID...
IT CAN SHIFT TO BE EITHER OFFENSIVE OR DEFENSIVE, AND CAN BE CONTINUOUSLY MAINTAINED.

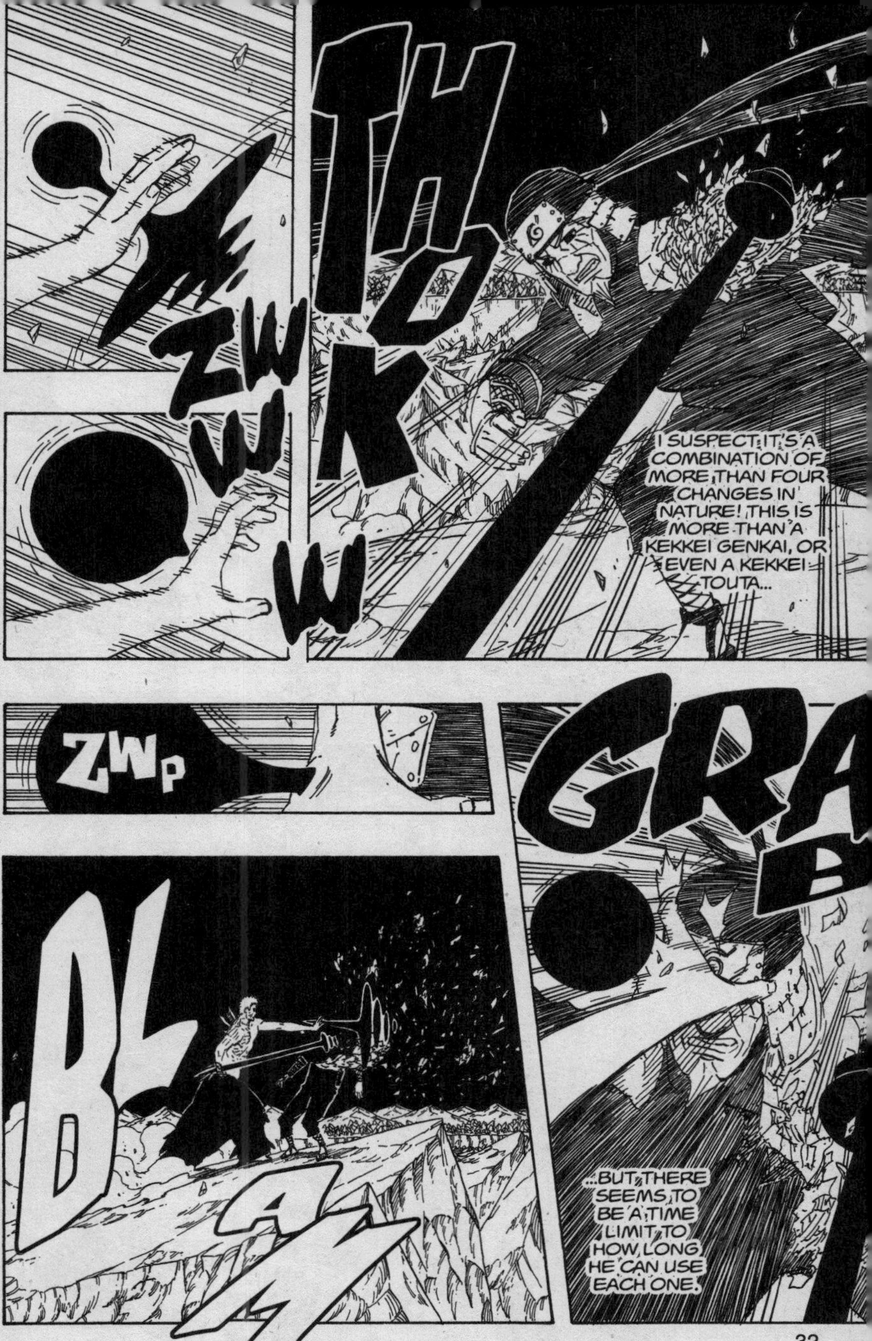
I SUSPECT IT'S A COMBINATION OF MORE THAN FOUR CHANGES IN NATURE! THIS IS MORE THAN A KEKKEI GENKAI, OR EVEN A KEKKEI TOUTA...
...BUT THERE SEEMS TO BE A TIME LIMIT TO HOW LONG HE CAN USE EACH ONE.
ZWP

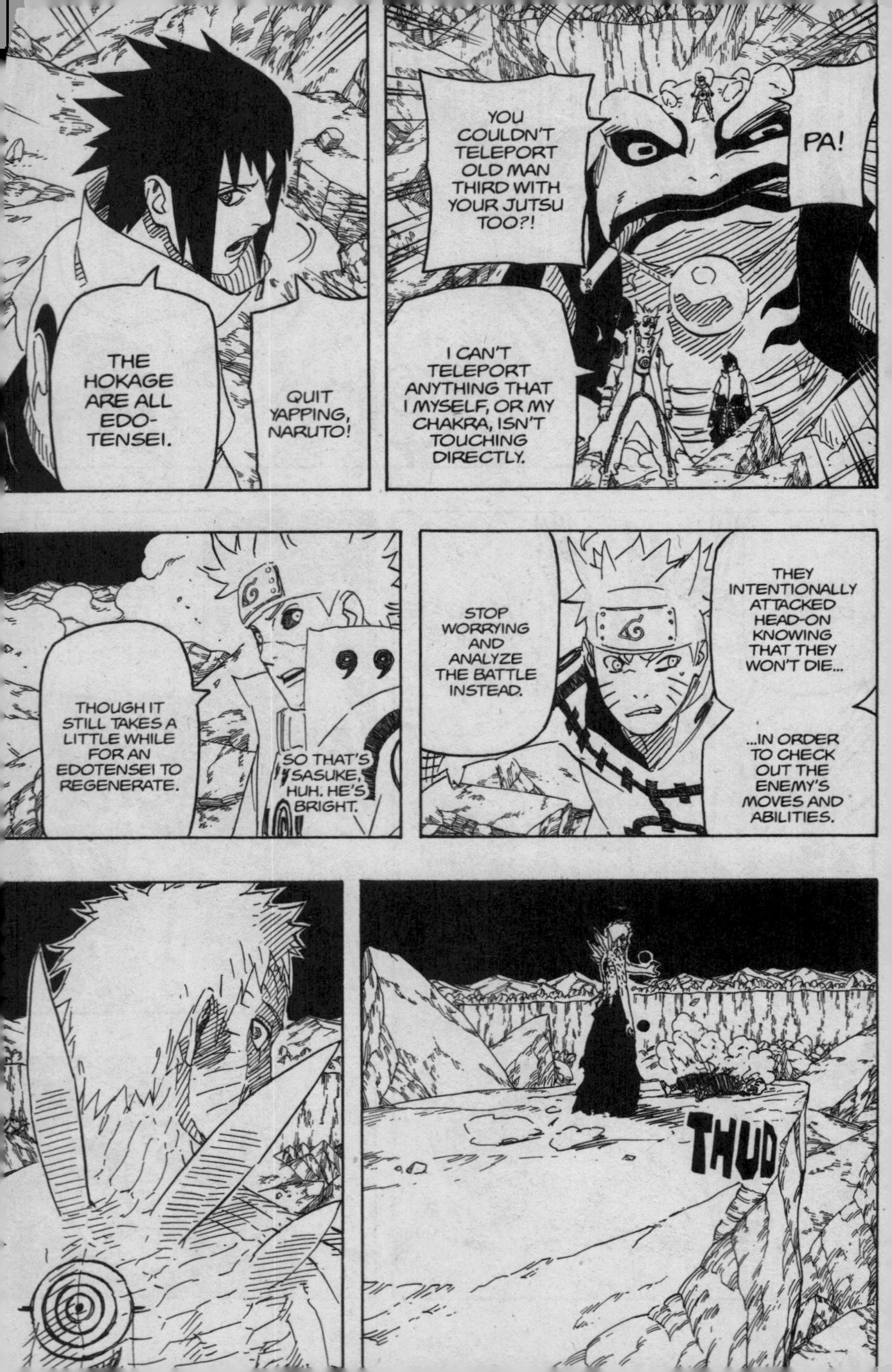
PA!
YOU COULDN'T TELEPORT OLD MAN THIRD WITH YOUR JUTSU TOO?!
I CAN'T TELEPORT ANYTHING THAT I MYSELF, OR MY CHAKRA, ISN'T TOUCHING DIRECTLY.
QUIT YAPPING, NARUTO!
THE HOKAGE ARE ALL EDO-TENSEI.
THEY INTENTIONALLY ATTACKED HEAD-ON KNOWING THAT THEY WON'T DIE...
...IN ORDER TO CHECK OUT THE ENEMY'S MOVES AND ABILITIES.
STOP WORRYING AND ANALYZE THE BATTLE INSTEAD.
SO THAT'S SASUKE, HUH. HE'S BRIGHT.
THOUGH IT STILL TAKES A LITTLE WHILE FOR AN EDOTENSEI TO REGENERATE.
THUD

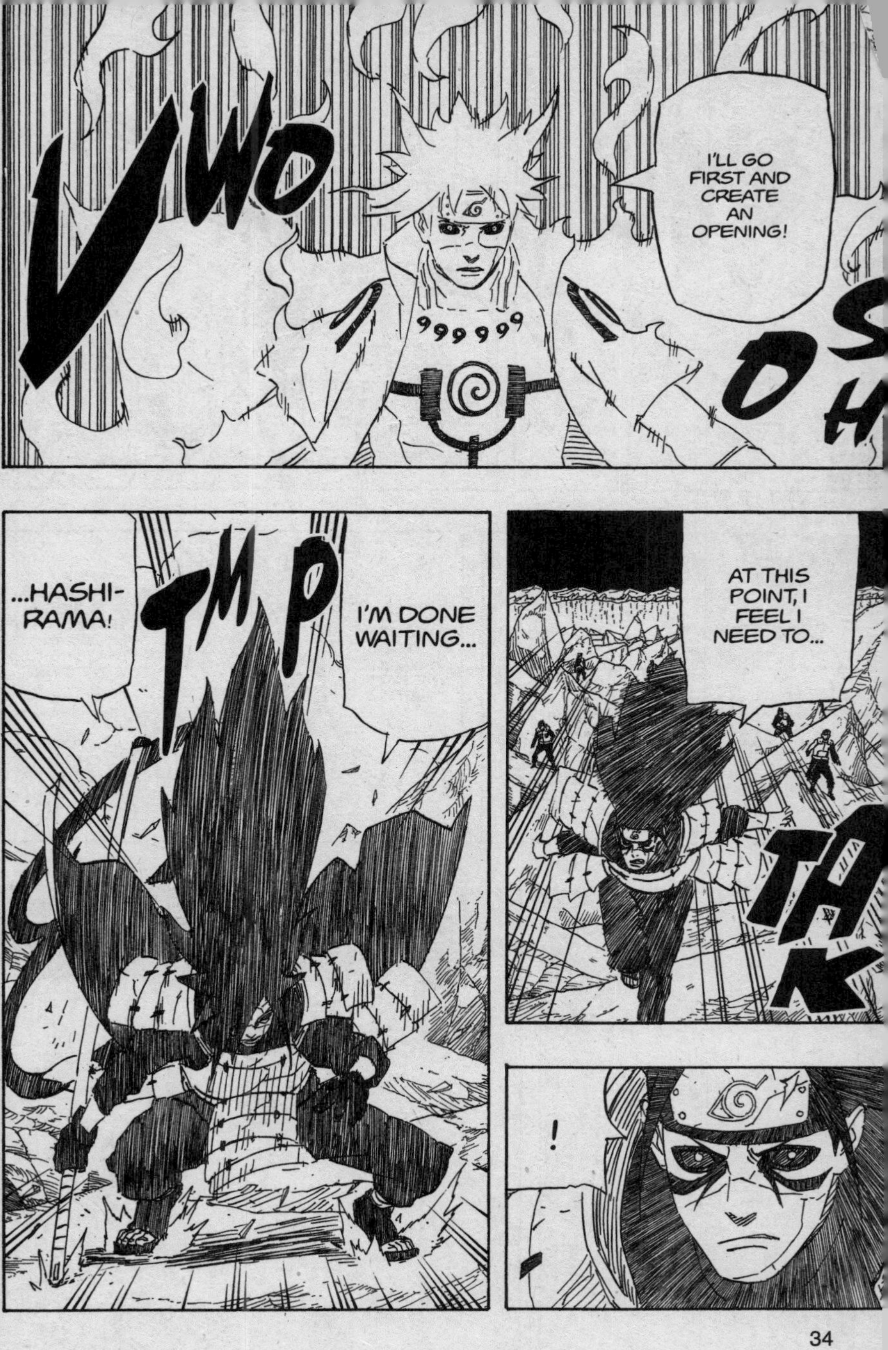
VWO
I'LL GO FIRST AND CREATE AN OPENING!
AT THIS POINT, I FEEL I NEED TO...
I'M DONE WAITING...
TMP
...HASHI-RAMA!
!

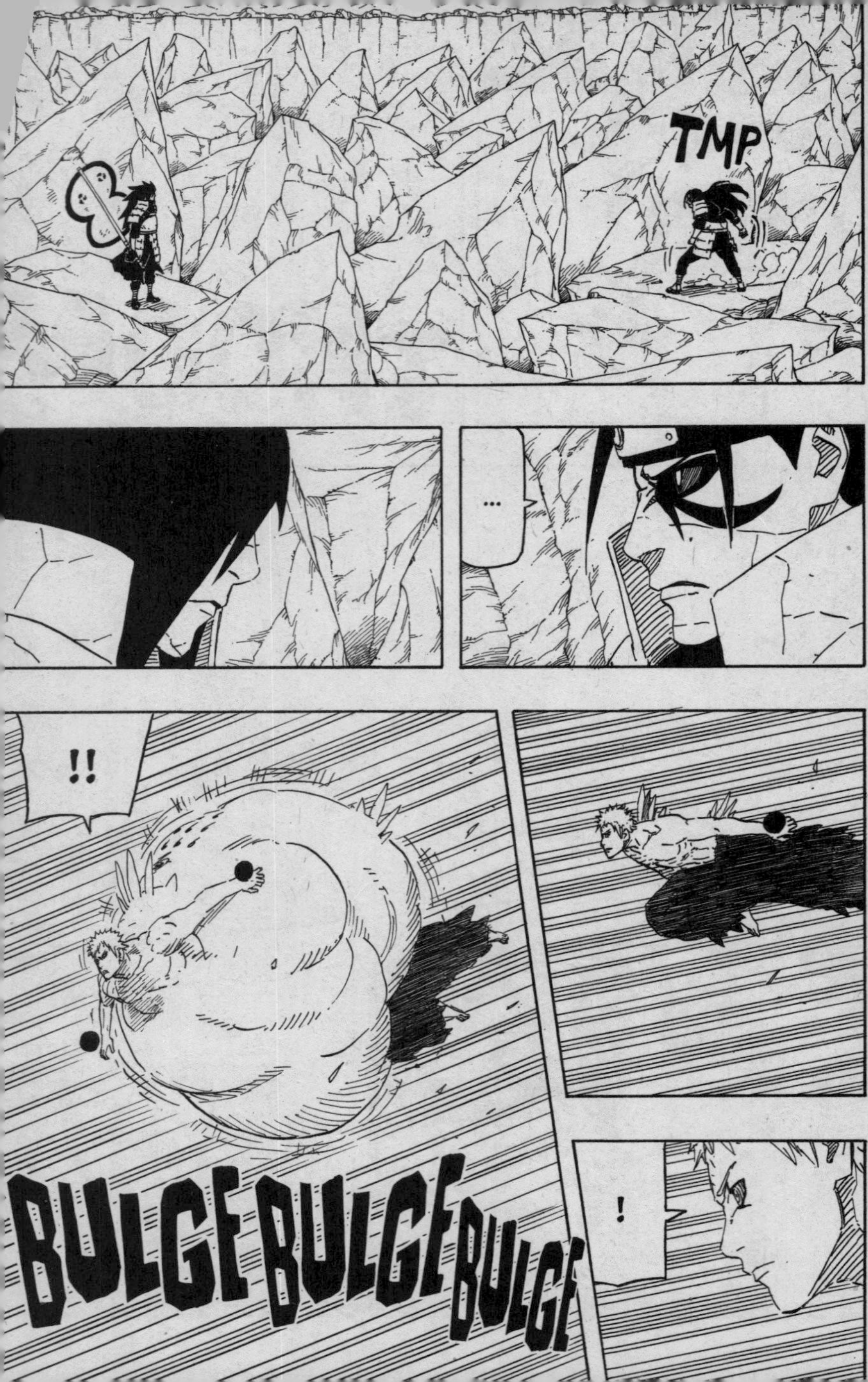
TMP
...
!
!!
BULGE BULGE BULGE

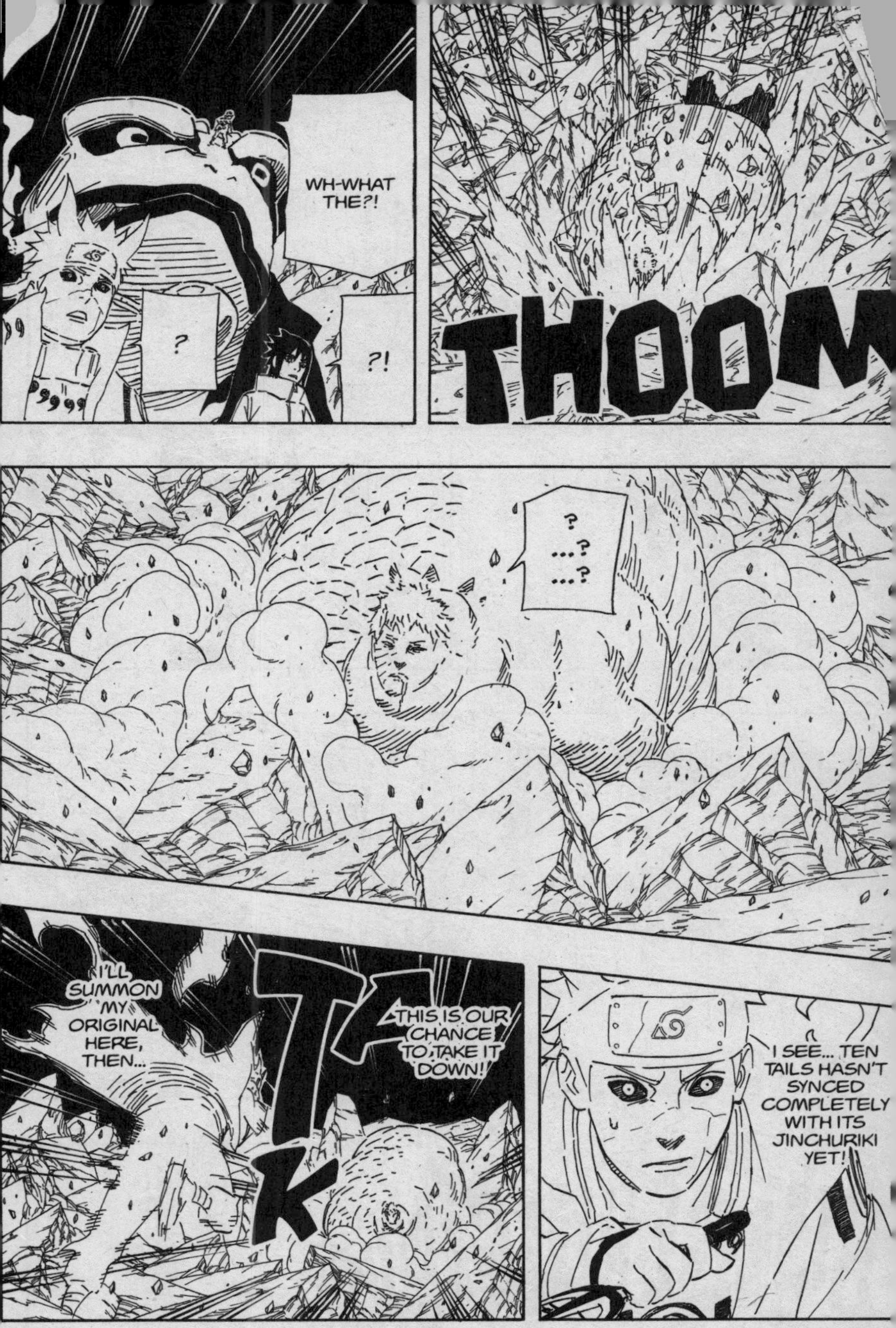
THOOM
WH-WHAT THE?!
?!
?
? ...? ...?
I SEE... TEN TAILS HASN'T SYNCED COMPLETELY WITH ITS JINCHURIKI YET!
THIS IS OUR CHANCE TO TAKE IT DOWN!
TAK
I'LL SUMMON MY ORIGINAL HERE, THEN...

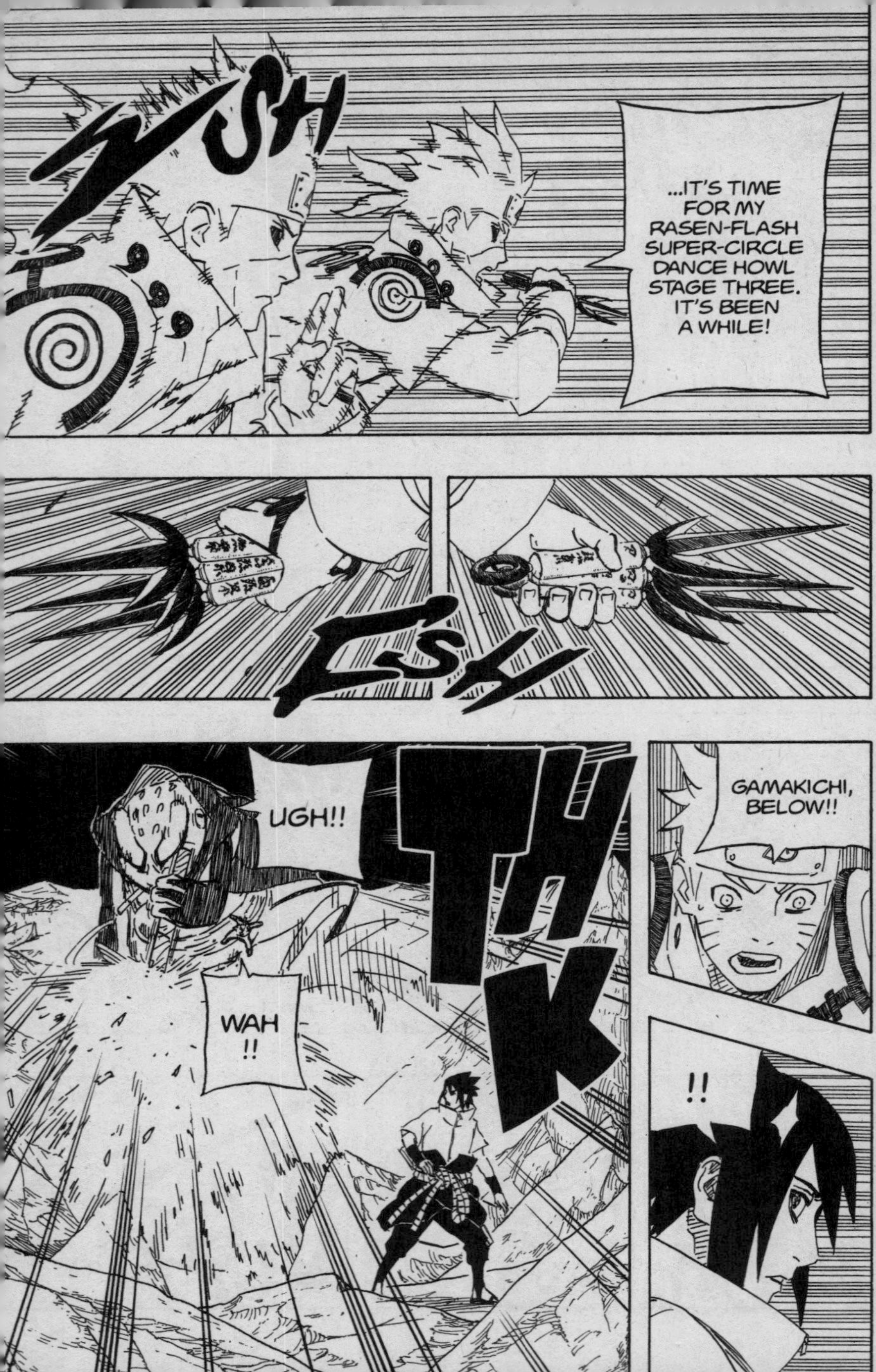
...IT'S TIME FOR MY RASEN-FLASH SUPER-CIRCLE DANCE HOWL STAGE THREE. IT'S BEEN A WHILE!
WHSH
FSH
GAMAKICHI, BELOW!!
!!
THK
UGH!!
WAH !!

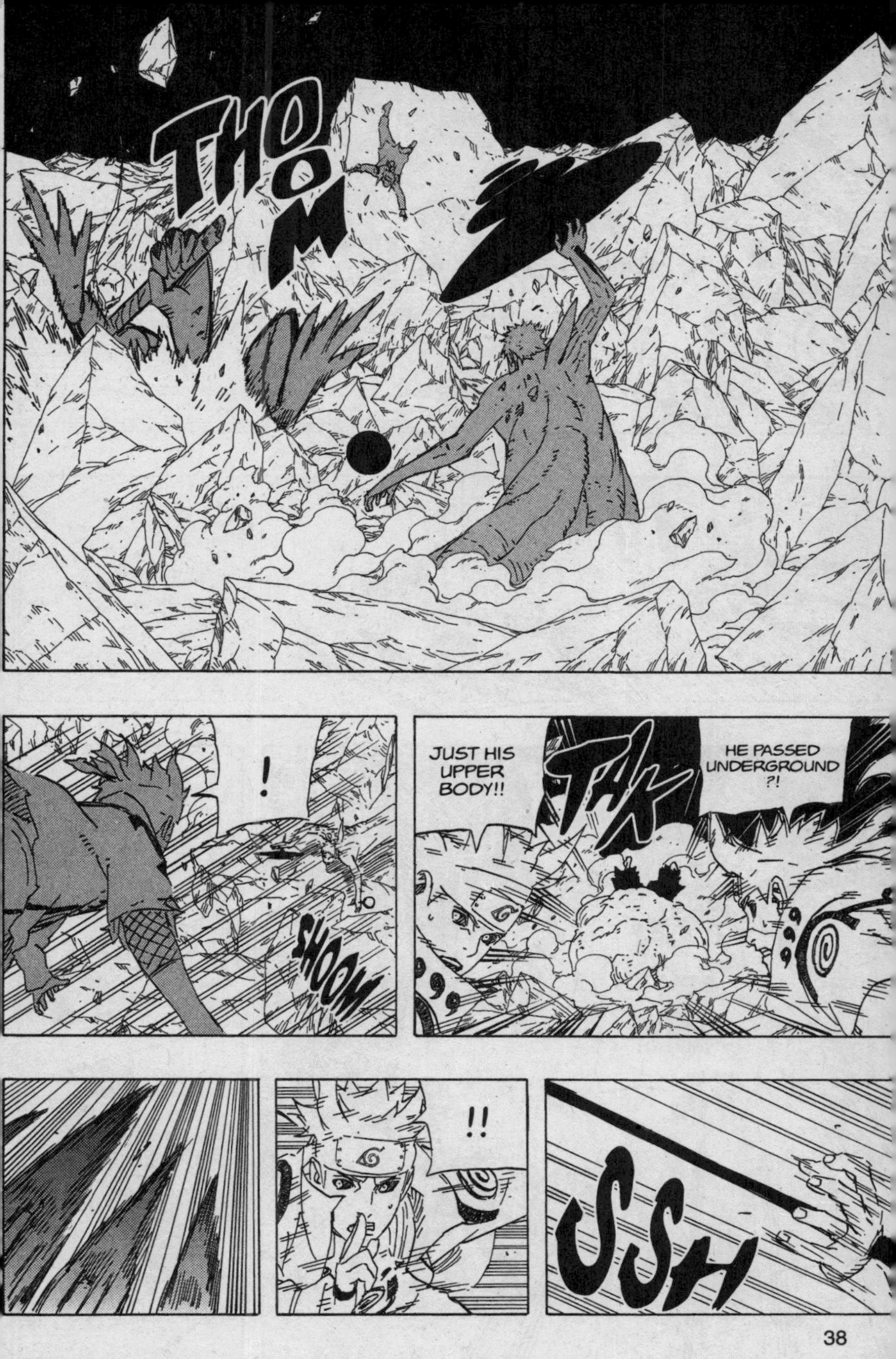
THOOM
HE PASSED UNDERGROUND ?!
TAK
JUST HIS UPPER BODY!!
!
SHOOM
SSH
!!

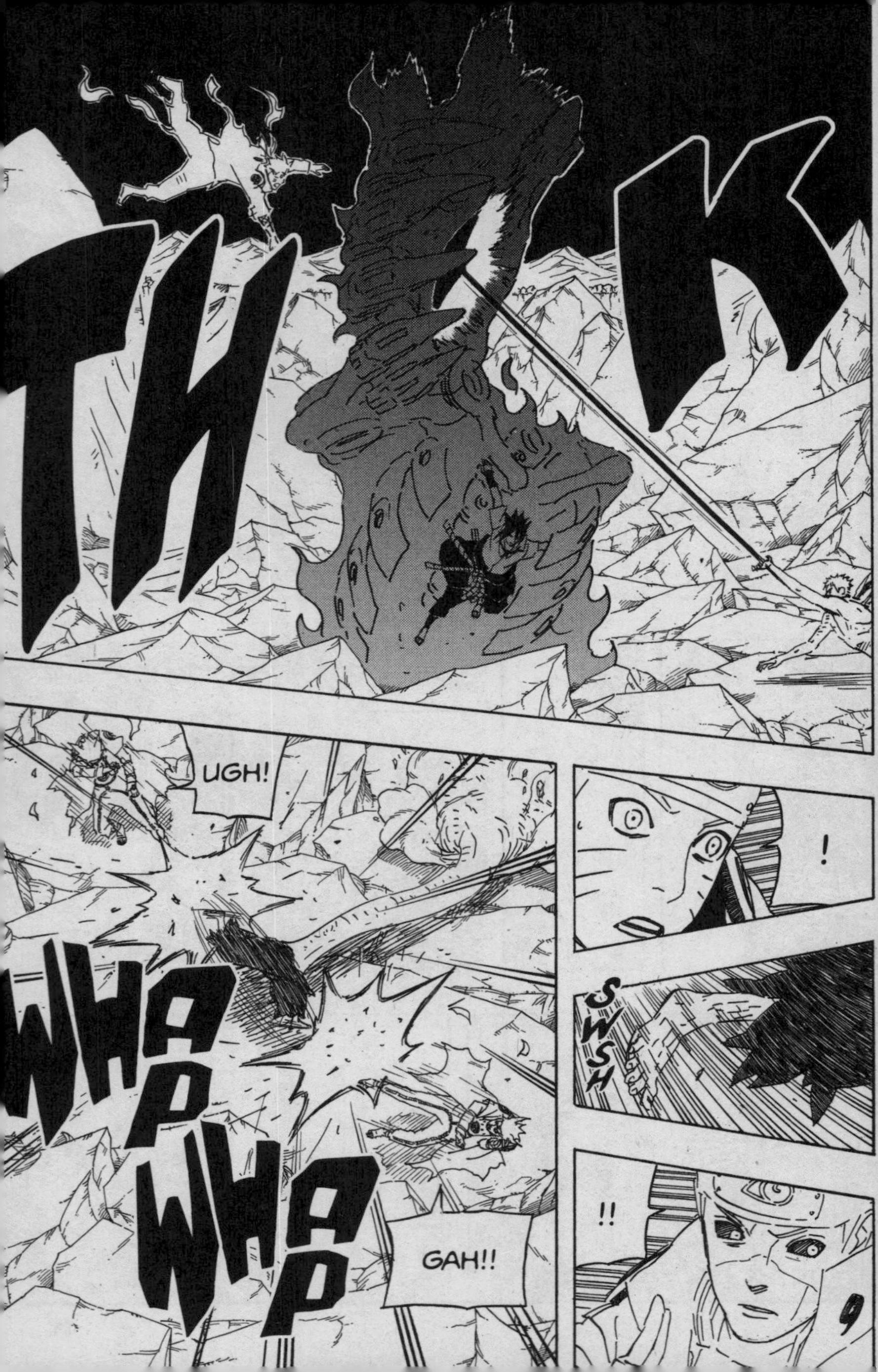
THWACK
!
SWSH
!!
UGH!
WHAP
WHAP
GAH!!

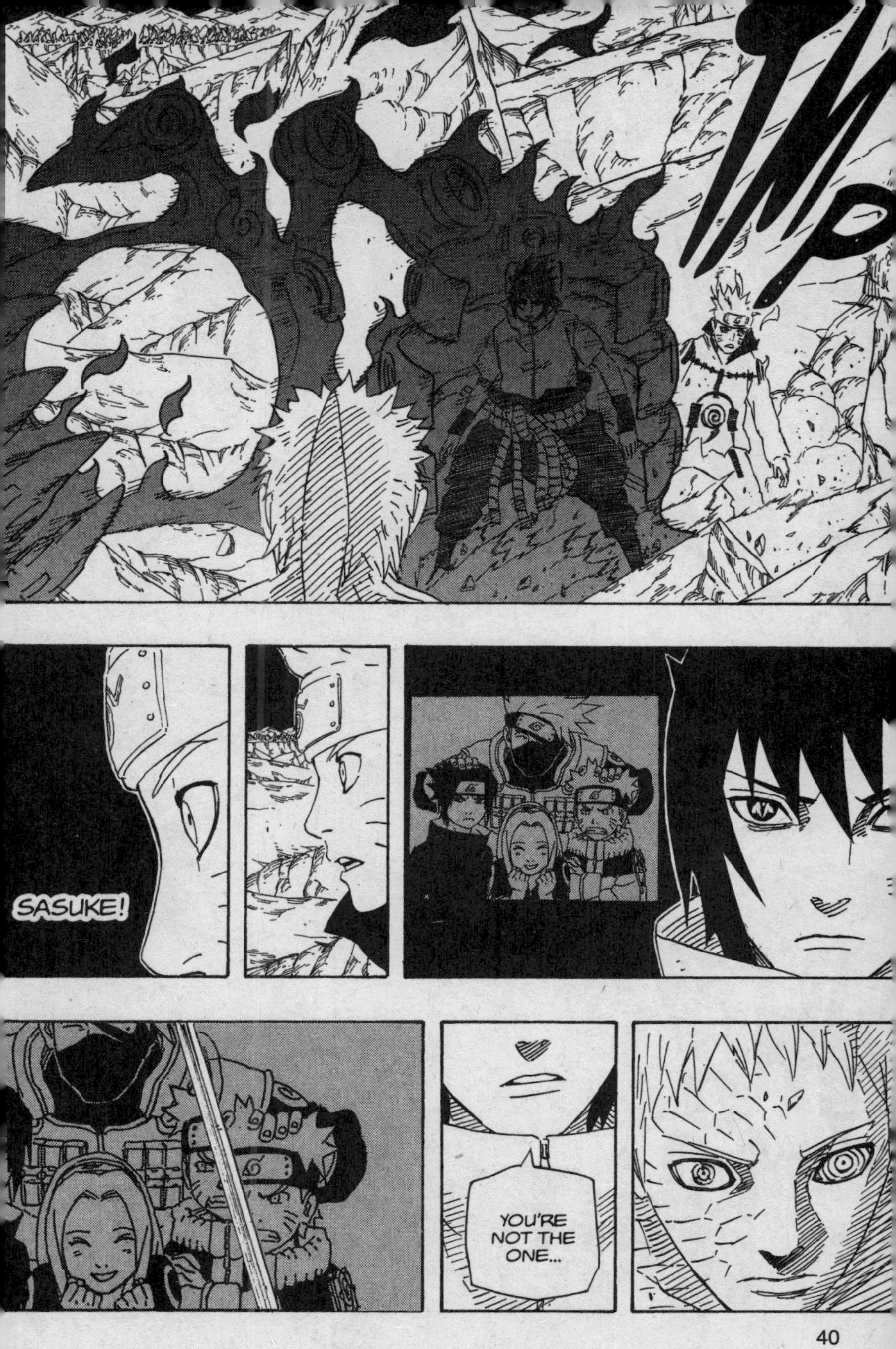
SASUKE!
YOU'RE NOT THE ONE...

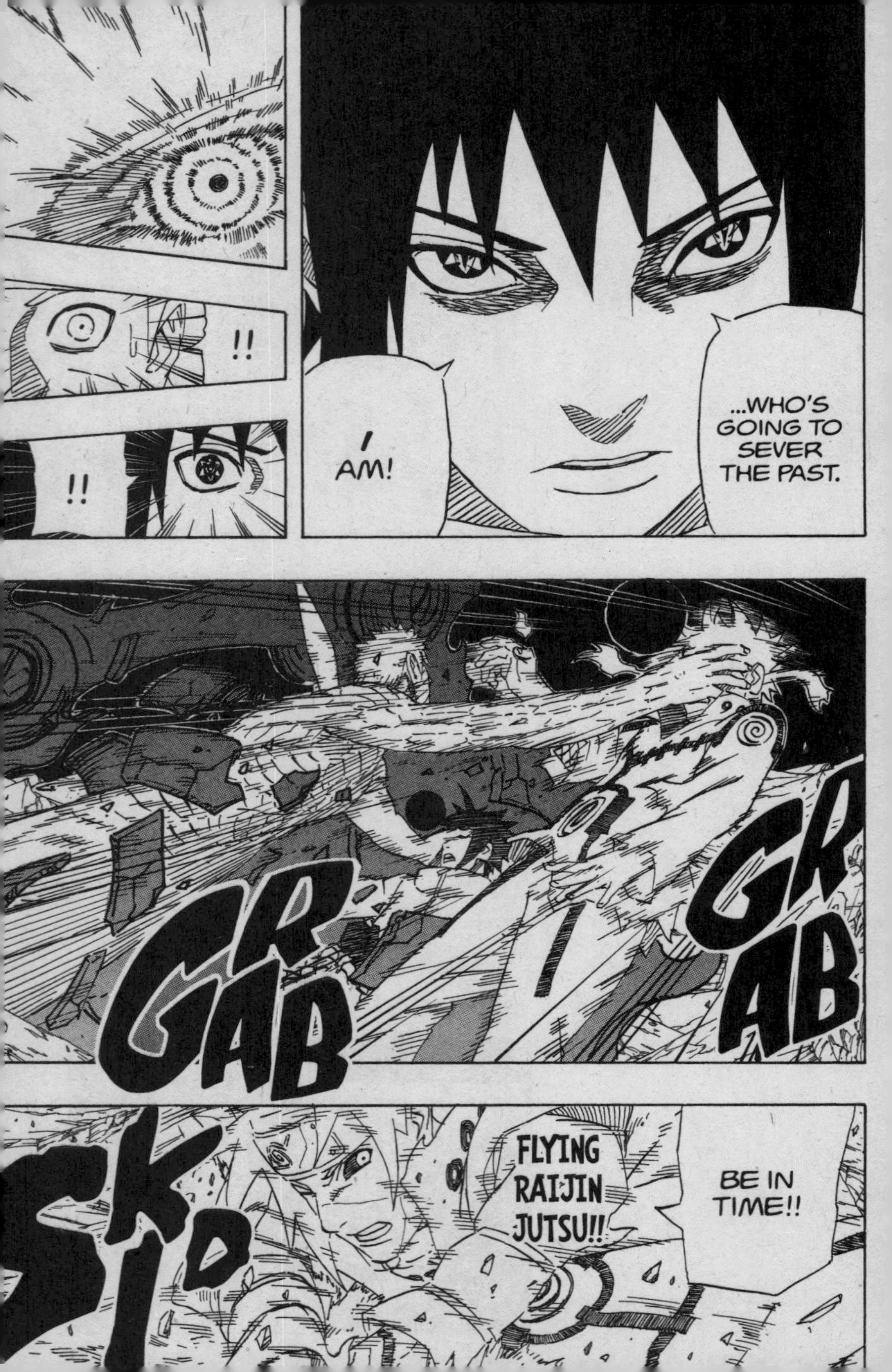
...WHO'S GOING TO SEVER THE PAST.
I AM!
!!
!!
GRAB
GRAB
BE IN TIME!!
FLYING RAIJIN JUTSU!!!

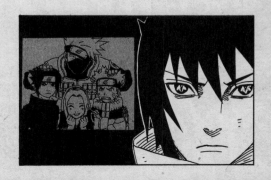

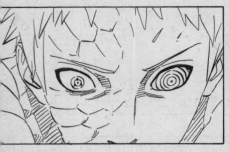

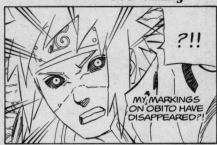

?!!

MY MARKINGS ON OBITO HAVE DISAPPEARED?!

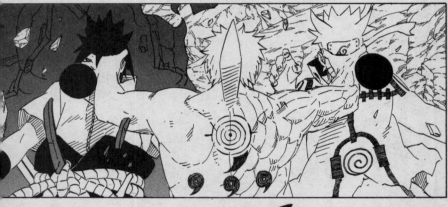

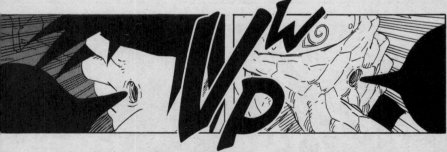

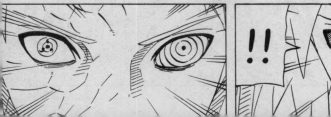

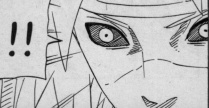

!!

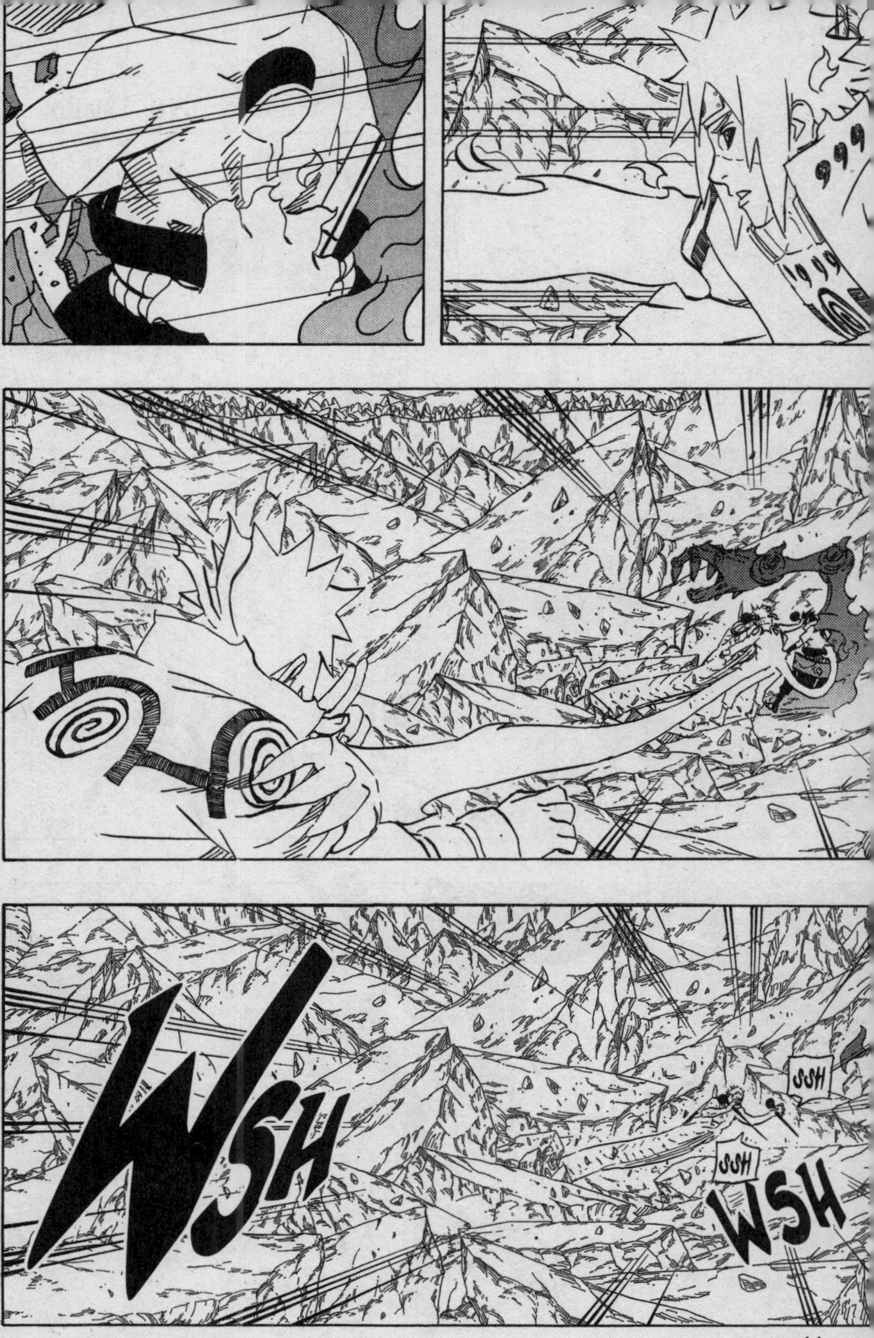
SSH
SSH
WSH
WSH

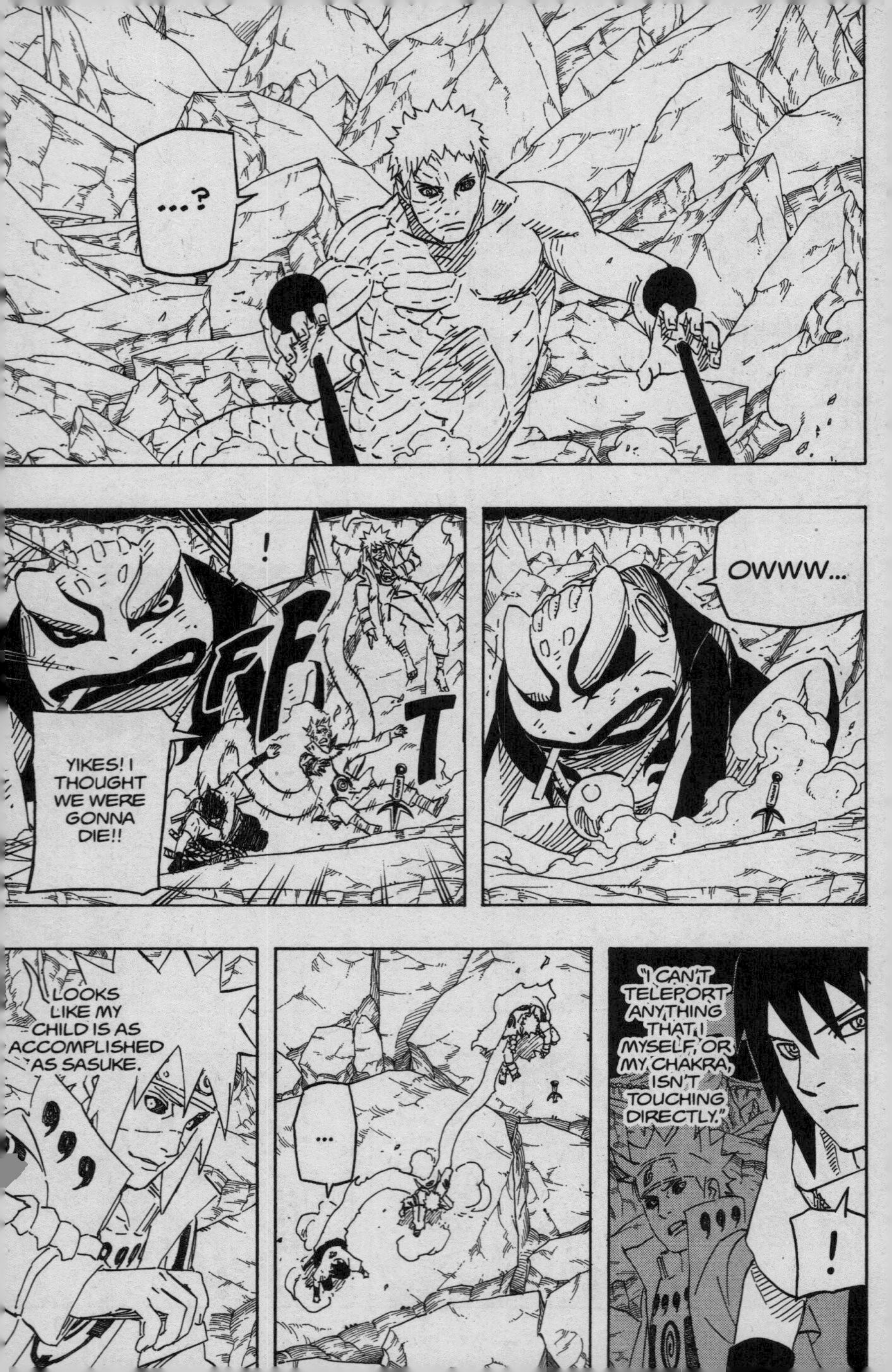
...?
OWWW...
!
FFT
YIKES! I THOUGHT WE WERE GONNA DIE!!
"I CAN'T TELEPORT ANYTHING THAT I MYSELF, OR MY CHAKRA, ISN'T TOUCHING DIRECTLY."
!
...
LOOKS LIKE MY CHILD IS AS ACCOMPLISHED AS SASUKE.

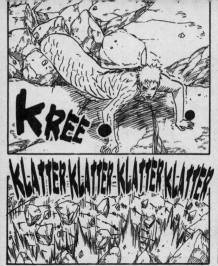

KREE

KLATTER KLATTER KLATTER KLATTER

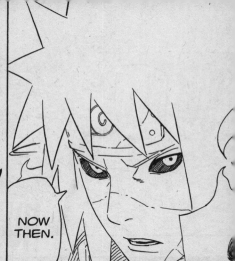

NOW THEN.

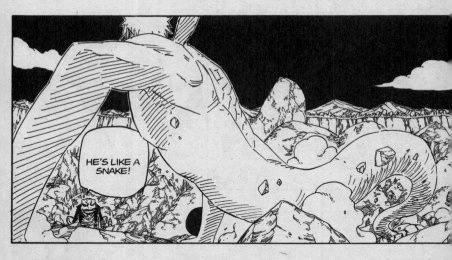

HE'S LIKE A SNAKE!

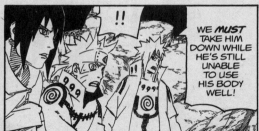

!!

WE *MUST* TAKE HIM DOWN WHILE HE'S STILL UNABLE TO USE HIS BODY WELL!

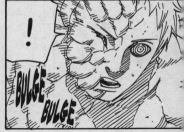

!

BULGE

BULGE

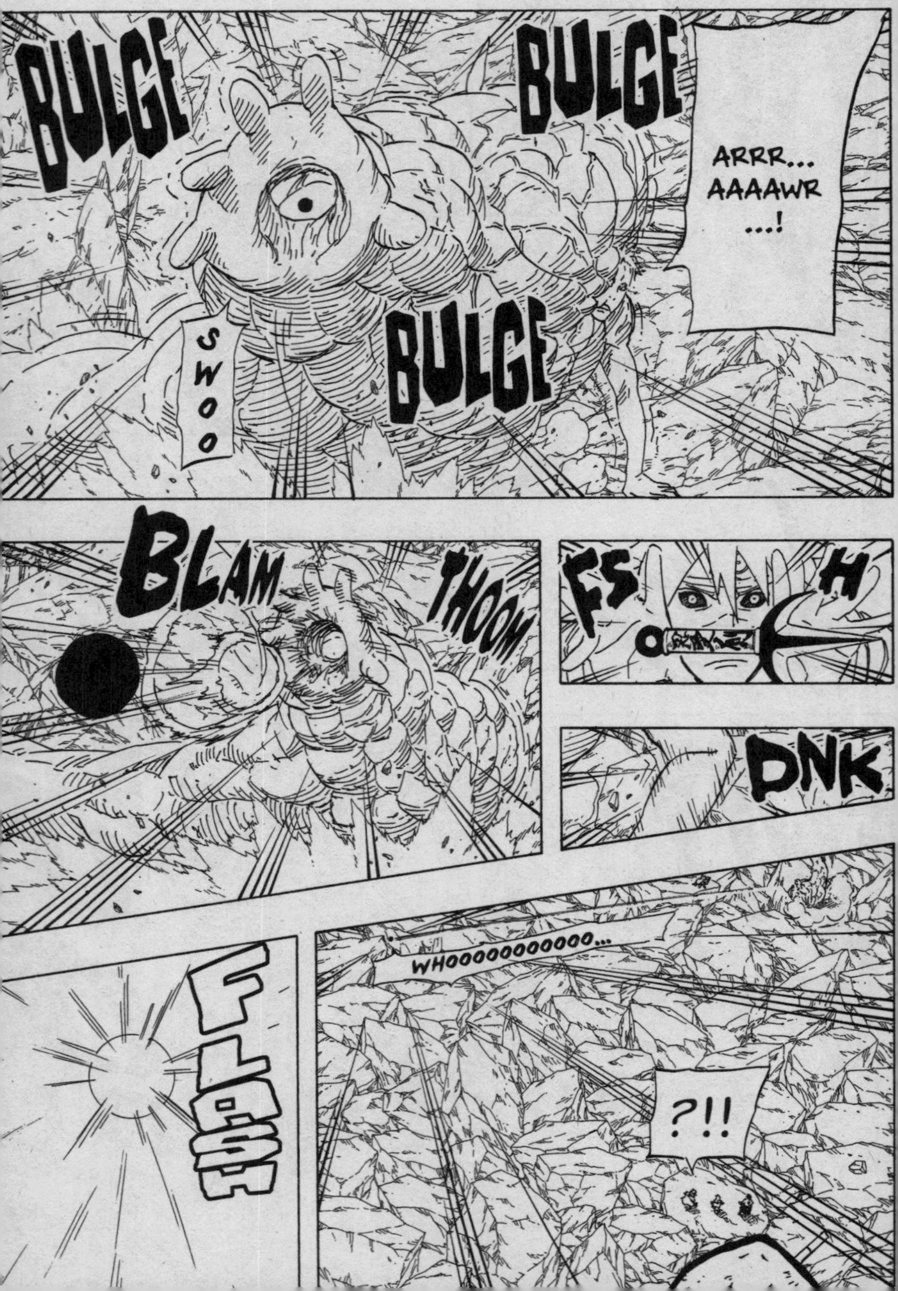
ARRR... AAAAWR ...!
BULGE
BULGE
BULGE
SWOO
FSH
DNK
THOOM
BLAM
WHOOOOOOOOOOO...
?!!
FLASH

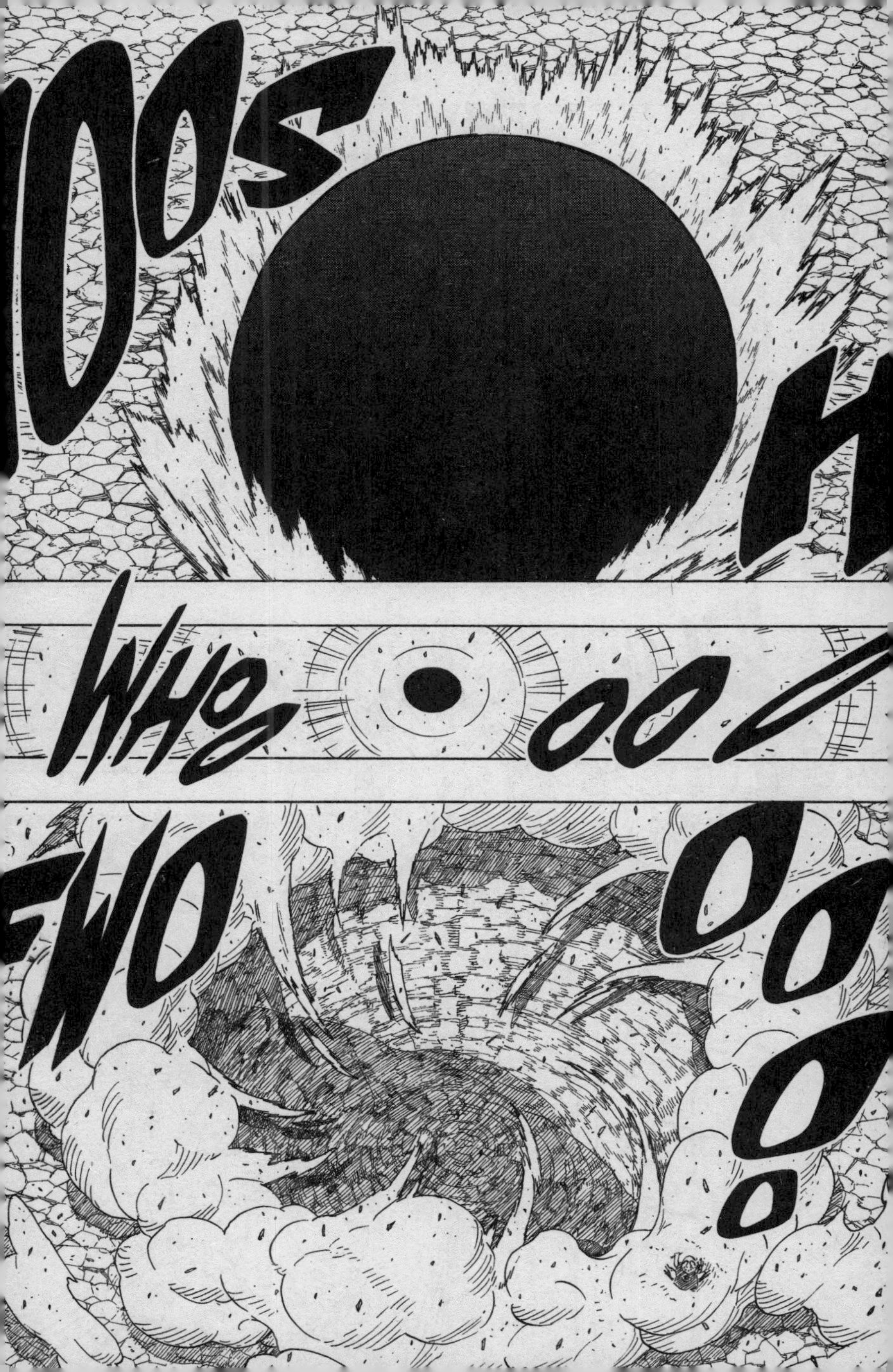
WHOOOO

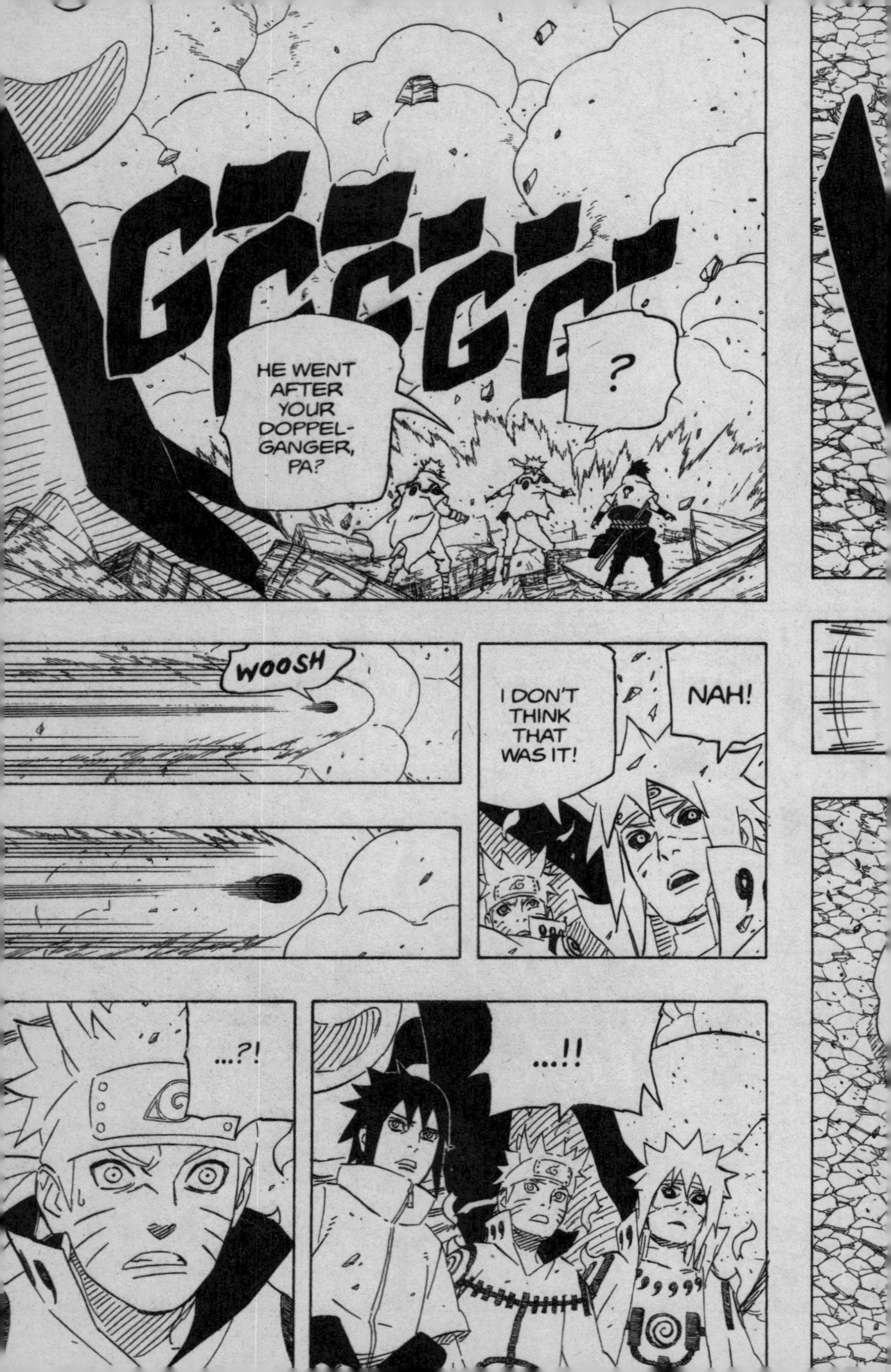
?
HE WENT AFTER YOUR DOPPEL-GANGER, PA?
NAH!
I DON'T THINK THAT WAS IT!
WOOSH
...!!
...?!

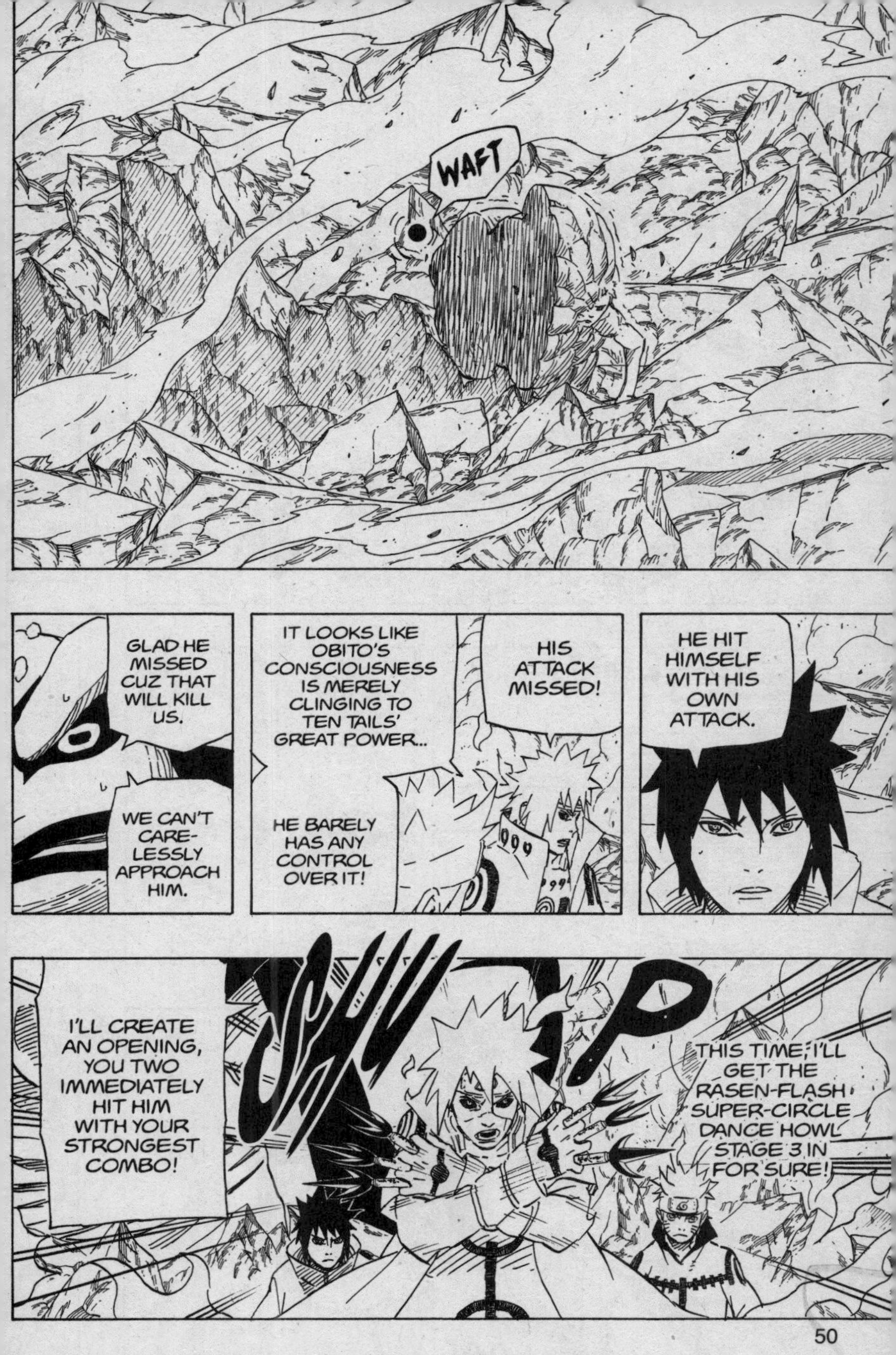
WAFT
HE HIT HIMSELF WITH HIS OWN ATTACK.
HIS ATTACK MISSED!
IT LOOKS LIKE OBITO'S CONSCIOUSNESS IS MERELY CLINGING TO TEN TAILS' GREAT POWER...
HE BARELY HAS ANY CONTROL OVER IT!
GLAD HE MISSED CUZ THAT WILL KILL US.
WE CAN'T CARE-LESSLY APPROACH HIM.
SHUP
I'LL CREATE AN OPENING, YOU TWO IMMEDIATELY HIT HIM WITH YOUR STRONGEST COMBO!
THIS TIME, I'LL GET THE RASEN-FLASH SUPER-CIRCLE DANCE HOWL STAGE 3 IN FOR SURE!

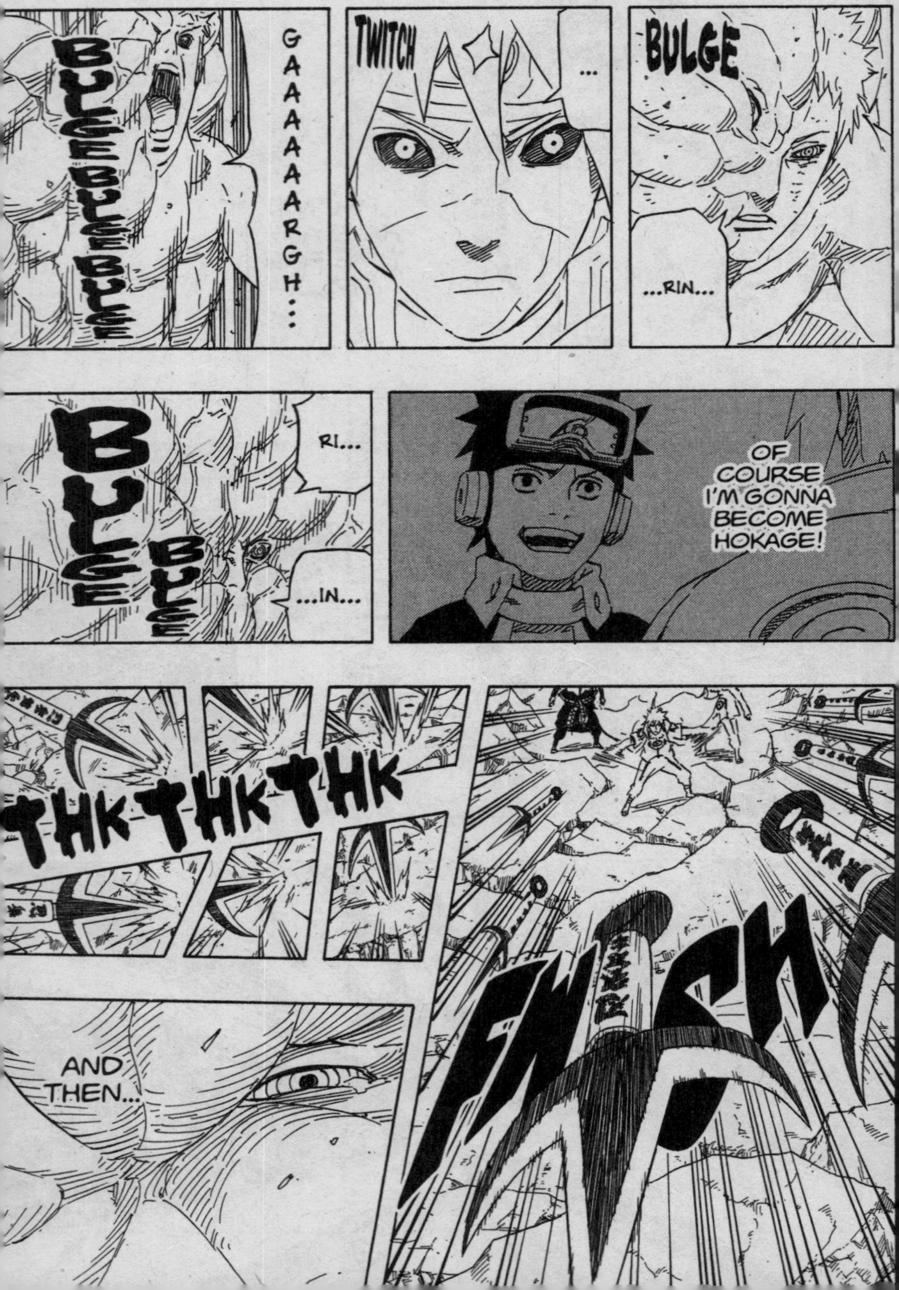
BULGE
...RIN...
TWITCH
...
BULGE BULGE BULGE BULGE
GAAAAAAARGH...
OF COURSE I'M GONNA BECOME HOKAGE!
RI...
...IN...
BULGE BULGE
THK THK THK
AND THEN...

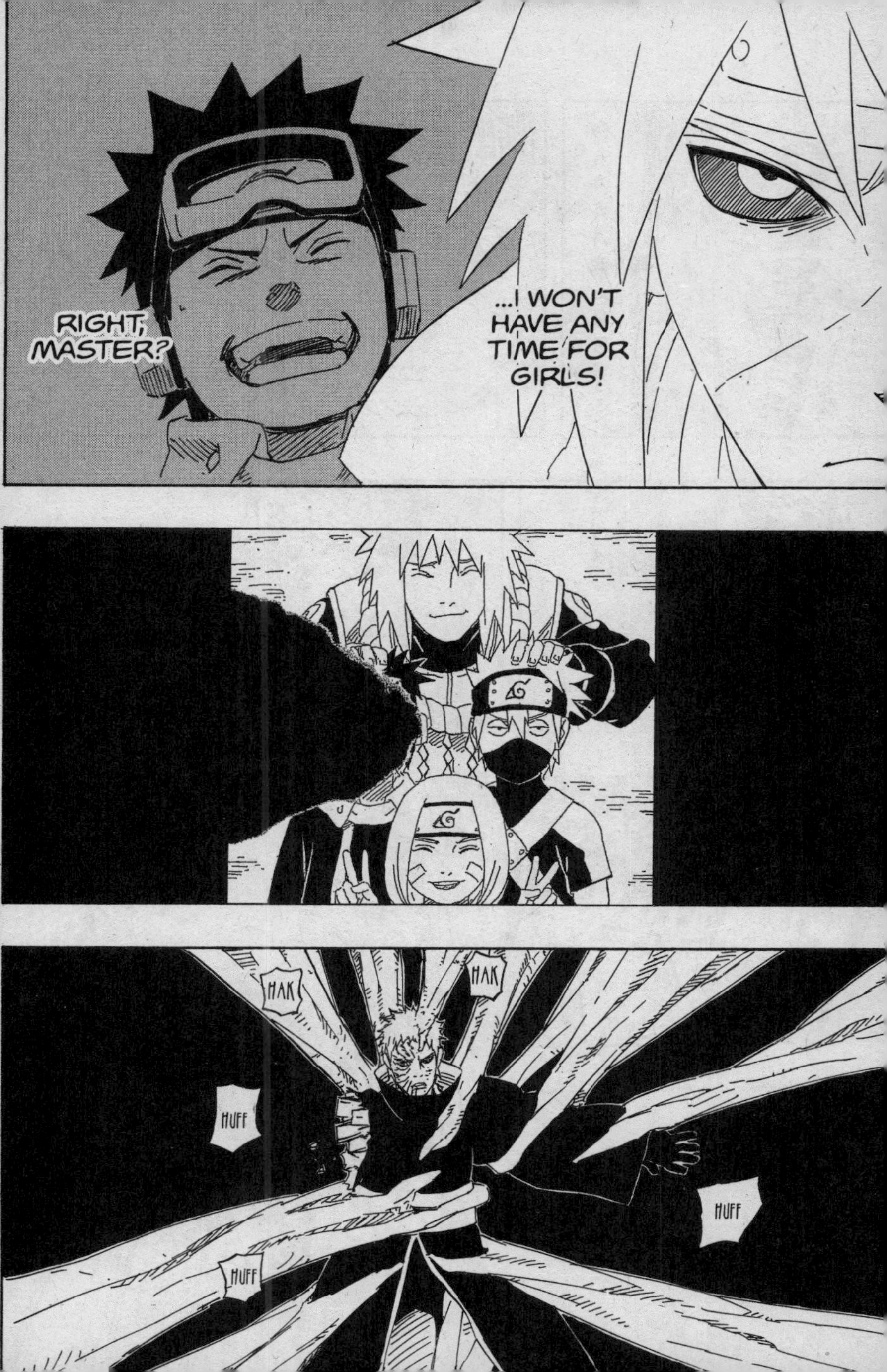
...I WON'T HAVE ANY TIME FOR GIRLS!
RIGHT, MASTER?
HAK
HAK
HUFF
HUFF
HUFF

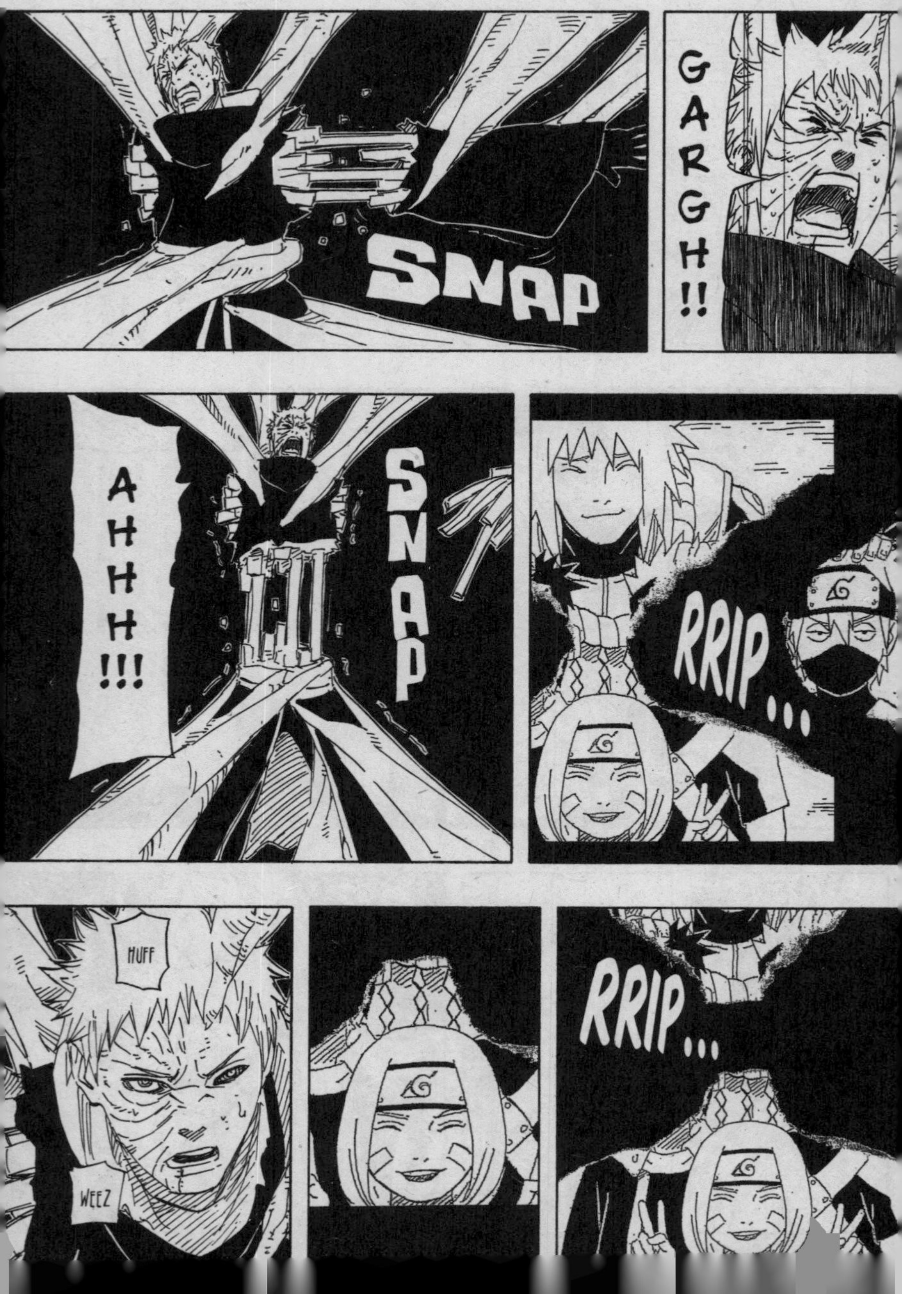
GARGH!!
SNAP
RRIP...
SNAP
AHHH!!!
RRIP...
HUFF
WEEZ

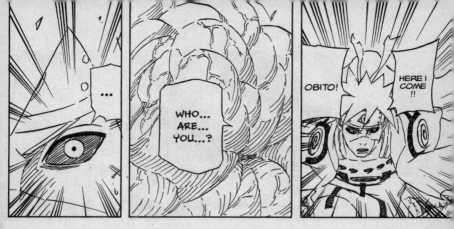

OBITO!

HERE I COME!!

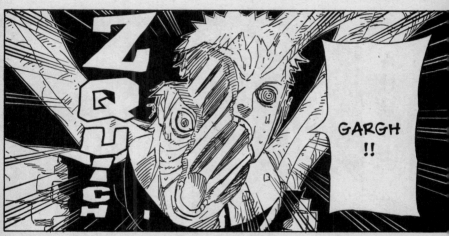

GARGH!!

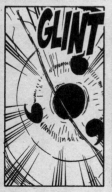

GLINT

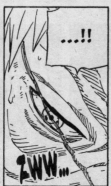

...!!

ZWW...

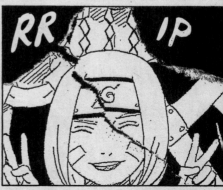

RR   IP

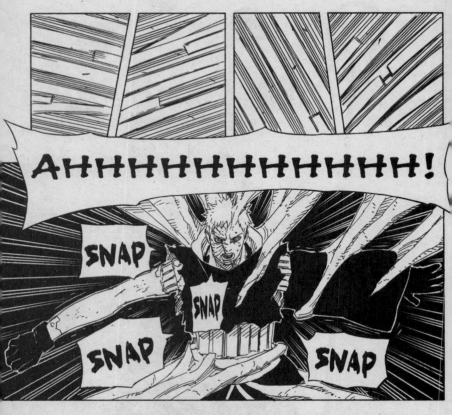

AHHHHHHHHHHHHH!

SNAP

SNAP

SNAP

SNAP

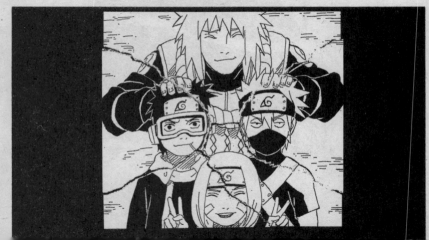

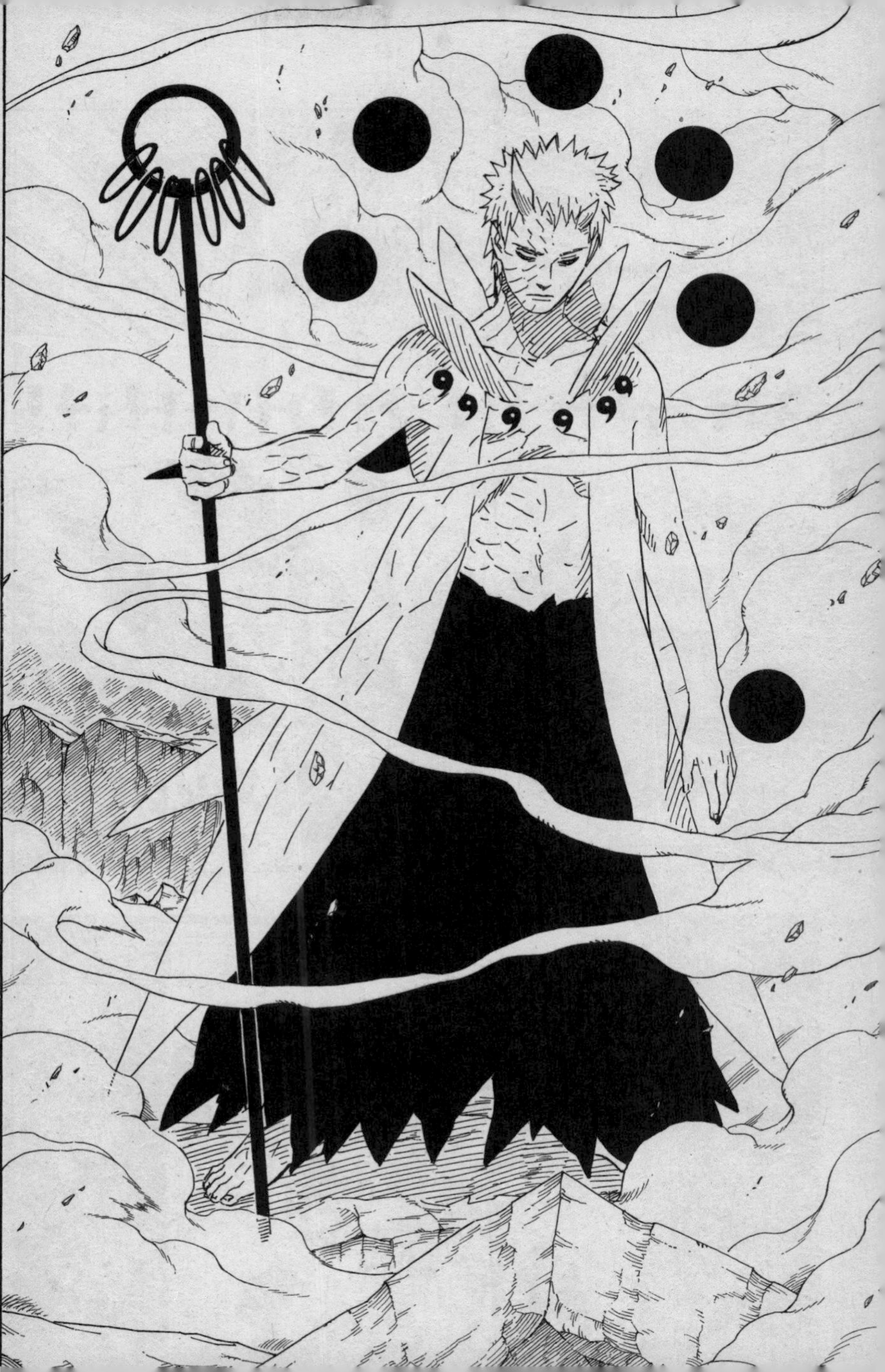

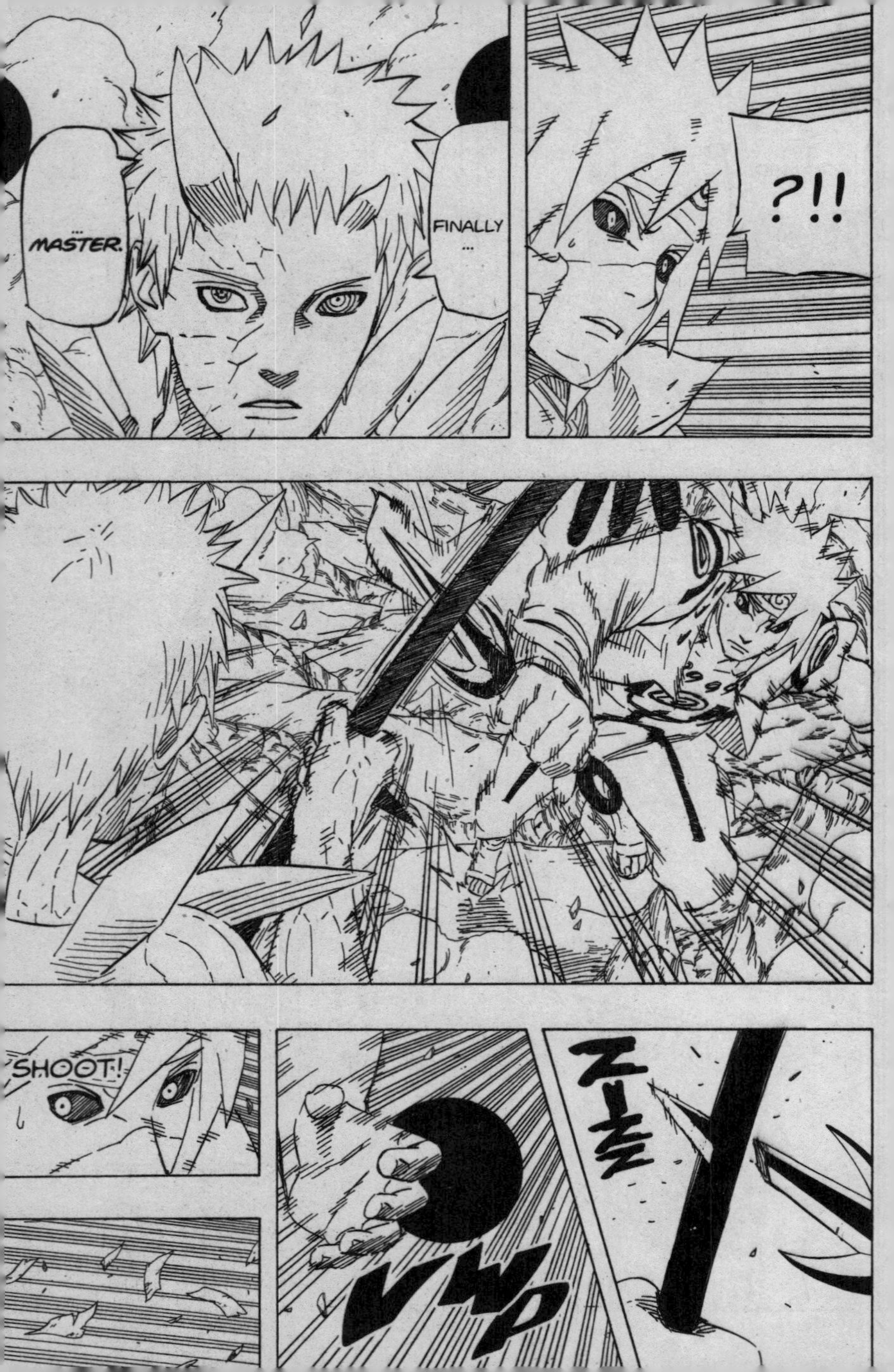
?!!
FINALLY ...
... MASTER.
ZIZZ
SHOOT!

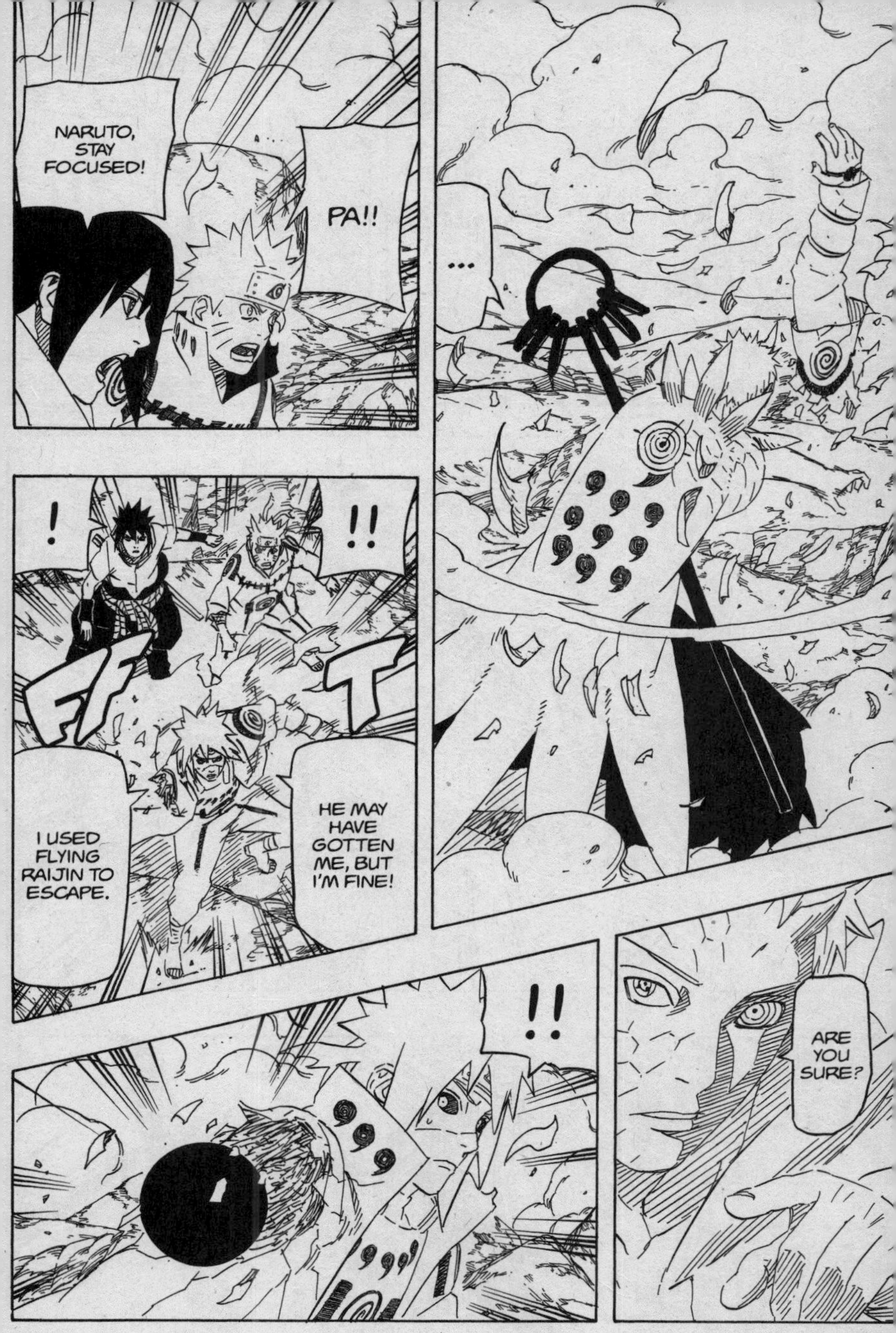
...
PA!!
A...
NARUTO, STAY FOCUSED!
!!
!
FFT
HE MAY HAVE GOTTEN ME, BUT I'M FINE!
I USED FLYING RAIJIN TO ESCAPE.
ARE YOU SURE?
!!

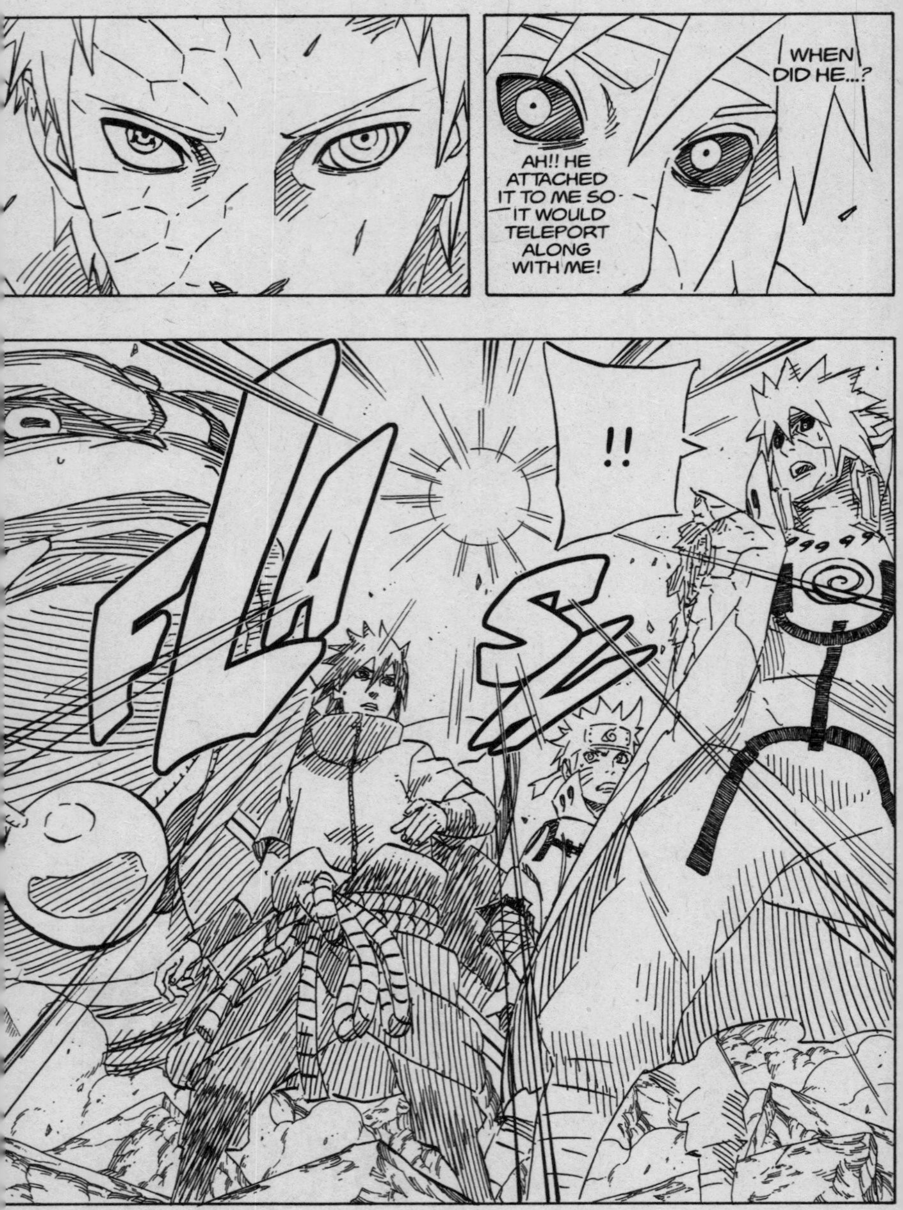
WHEN DID HE...?
AH!! HE ATTACHED IT TO ME SO IT WOULD TELEPORT ALONG WITH ME!
!!
FLASH

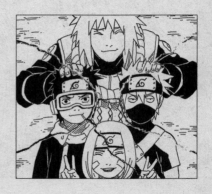

Number 641: You Two Are the Main Act!!

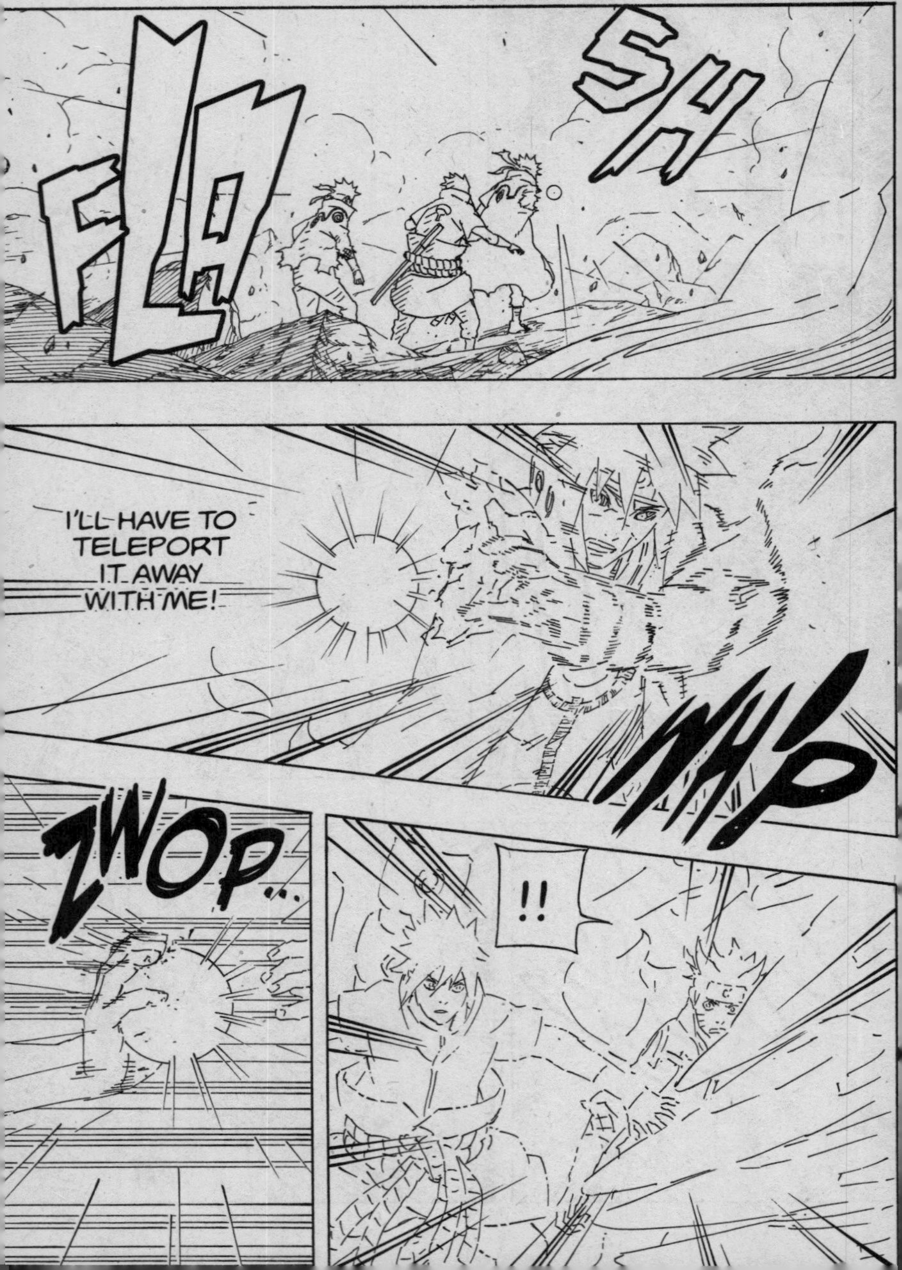
SH
FLA
I'LL HAVE TO TELEPORT IT AWAY WITH ME!
WHP
!!
ZWOP...

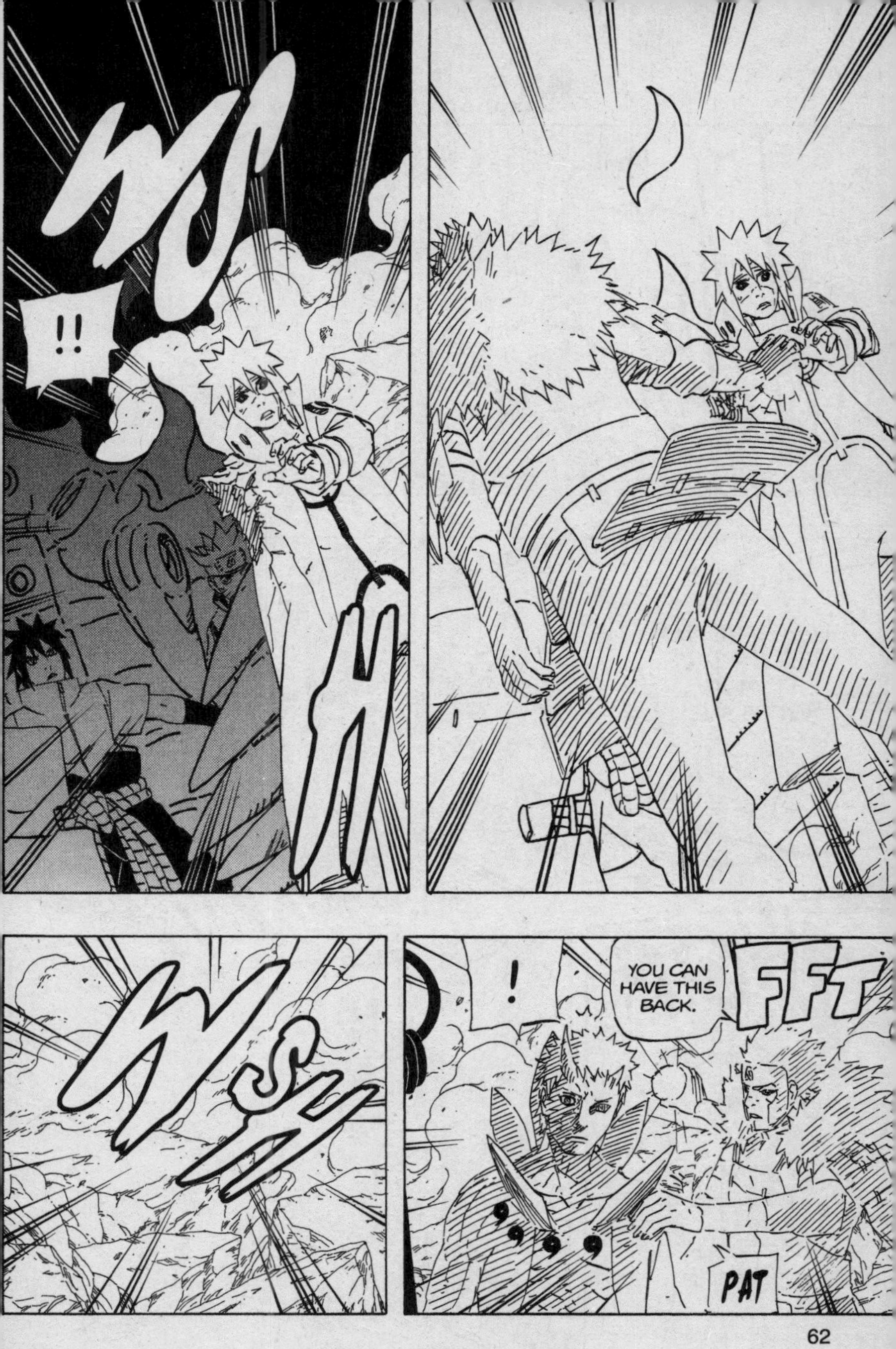
!!
!
YOU CAN HAVE THIS BACK.
FFT
PAT
WSH

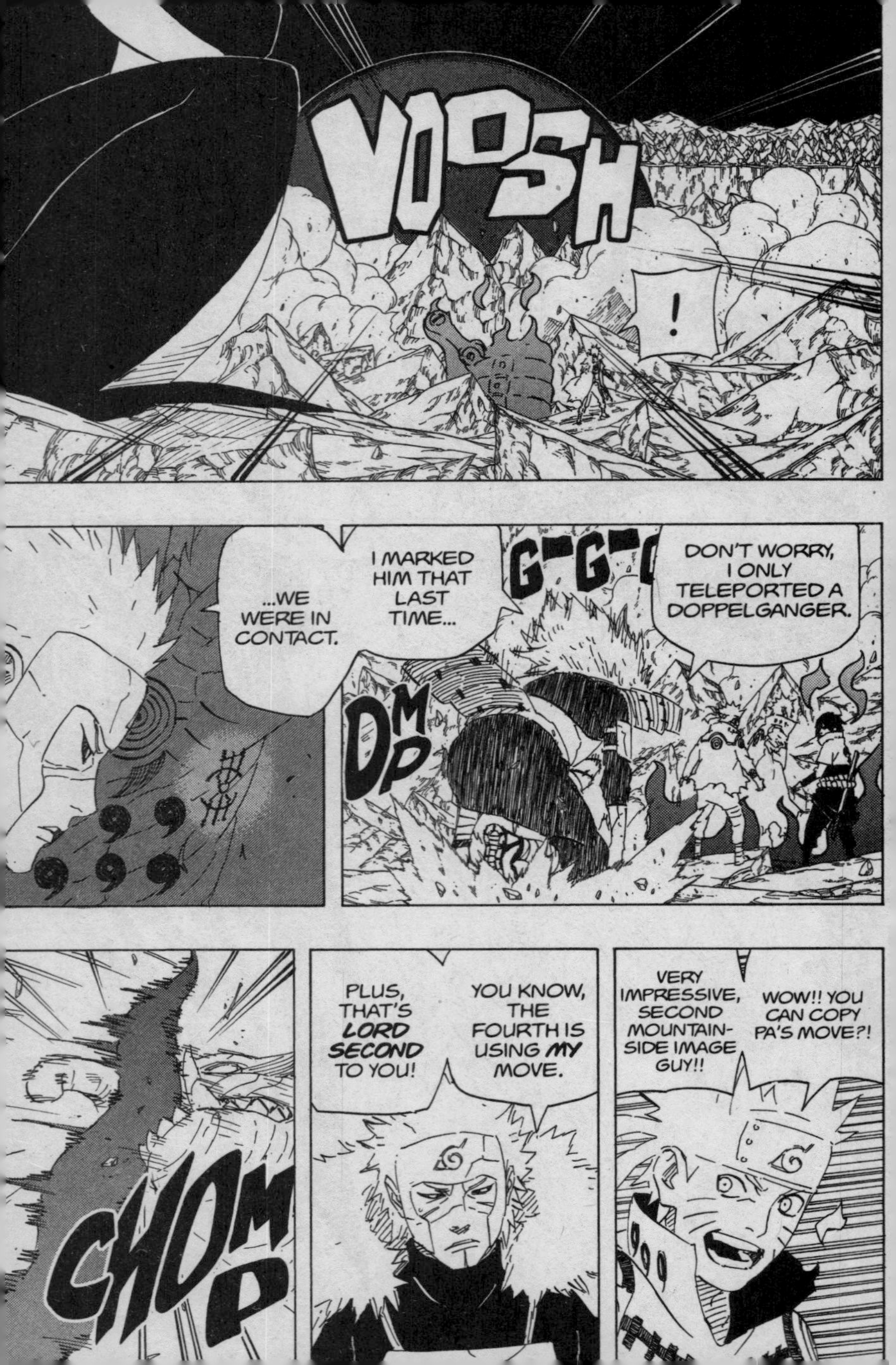

VOOSH
!
DON'T WORRY, I ONLY TELEPORTED A DOPPELGANGER.
G-G-G
I MARKED HIM THAT LAST TIME...
DMP
...WE WERE IN CONTACT.
WOW!! YOU CAN COPY PA'S MOVE?!
VERY IMPRESSIVE, SECOND MOUNTAIN-SIDE IMAGE GUY!!
YOU KNOW, THE FOURTH IS USING MY MOVE.
PLUS, THAT'S LORD SECOND TO YOU!
CHOMP

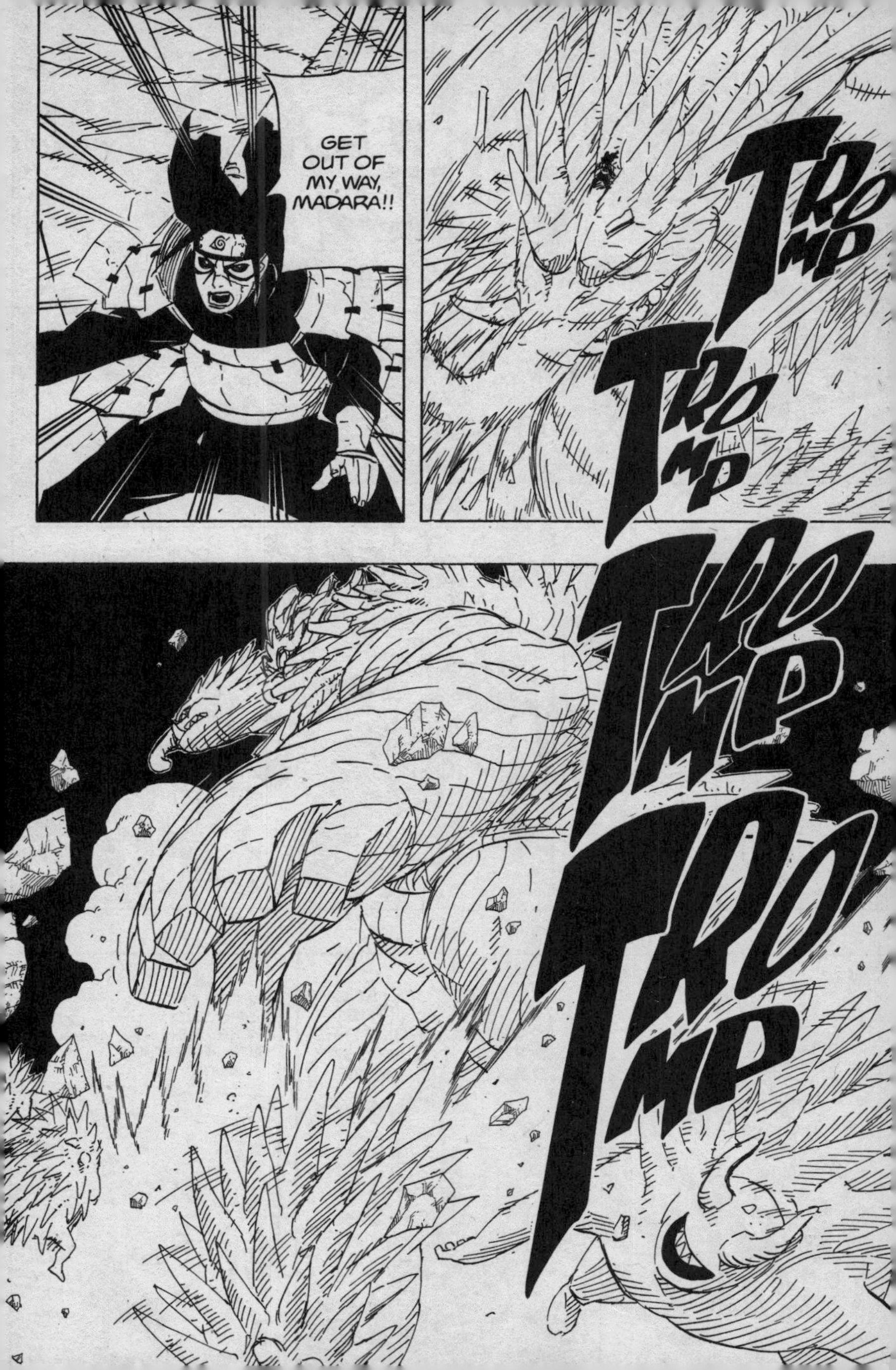
TROMP
TROMP
GET OUT OF MY WAY, MADARA!!
TROMP
TROMP

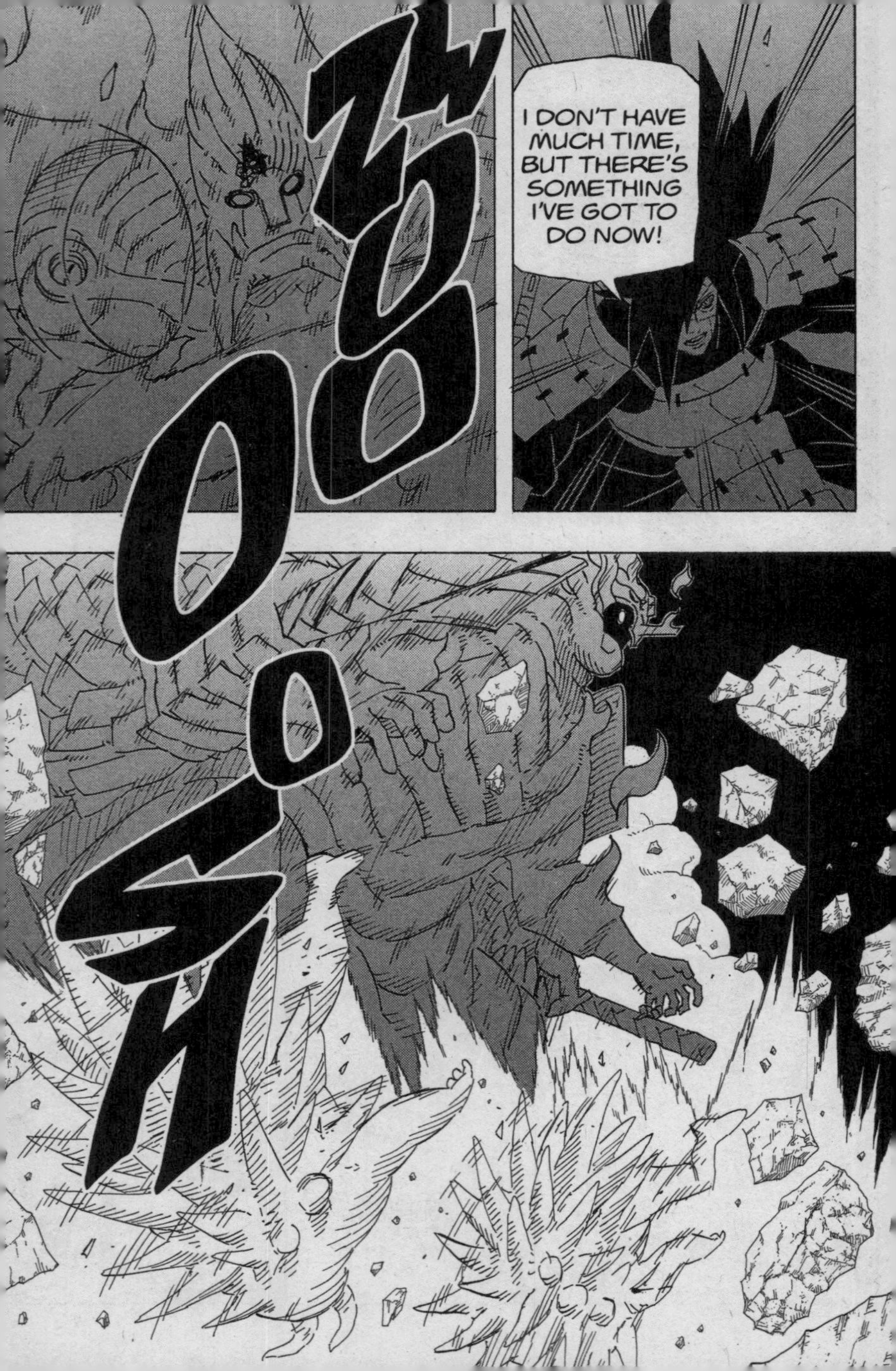
I DON'T HAVE MUCH TIME, BUT THERE'S SOMETHING I'VE GOT TO DO NOW!

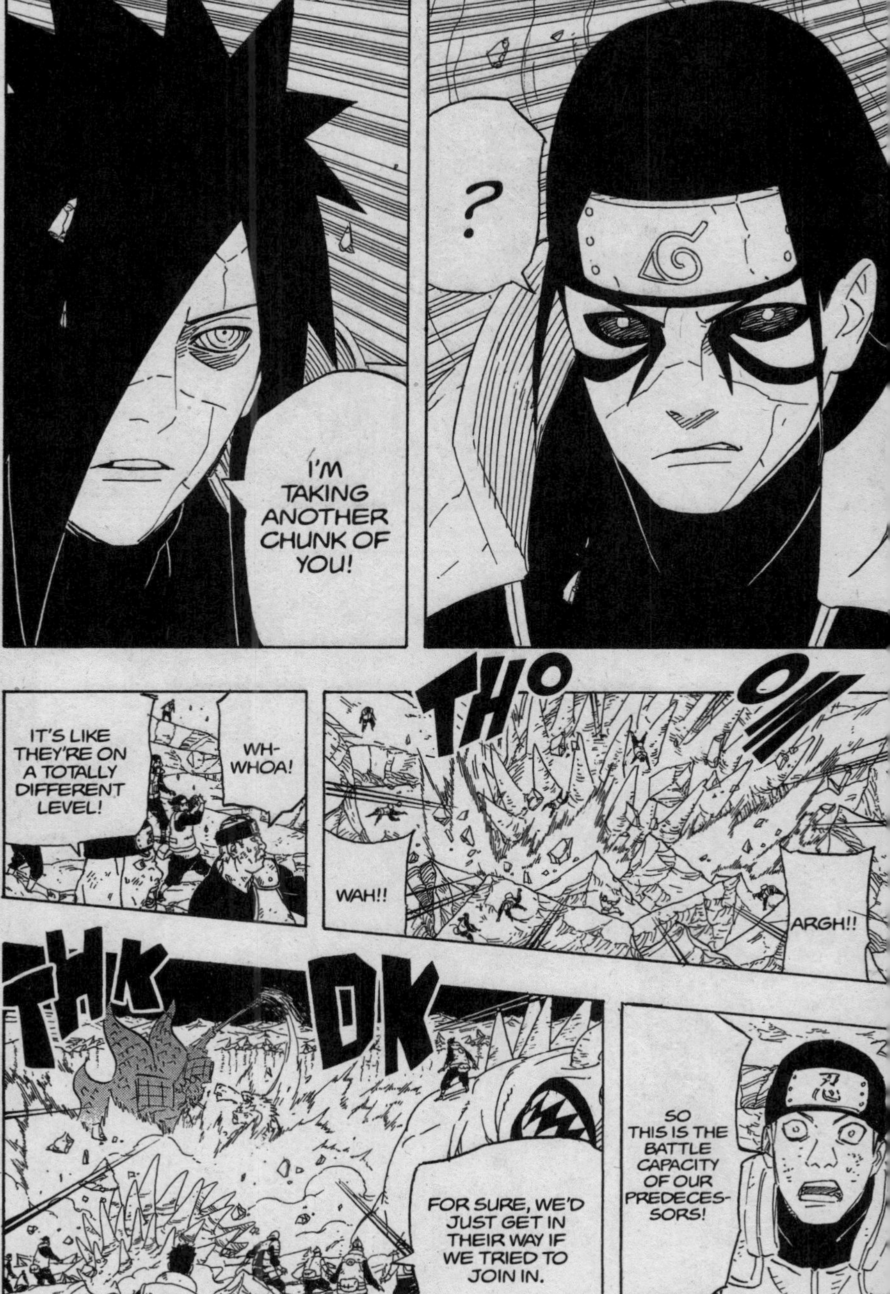
?
I'M TAKING ANOTHER CHUNK OF YOU!
THOOM
ARGH!!
WAH!!
WH-WHOA!
IT'S LIKE THEY'RE ON A TOTALLY DIFFERENT LEVEL!
SO THIS IS THE BATTLE CAPACITY OF OUR PREDECESSORS!
THK DK
FOR SURE, WE'D JUST GET IN THEIR WAY IF WE TRIED TO JOIN IN.

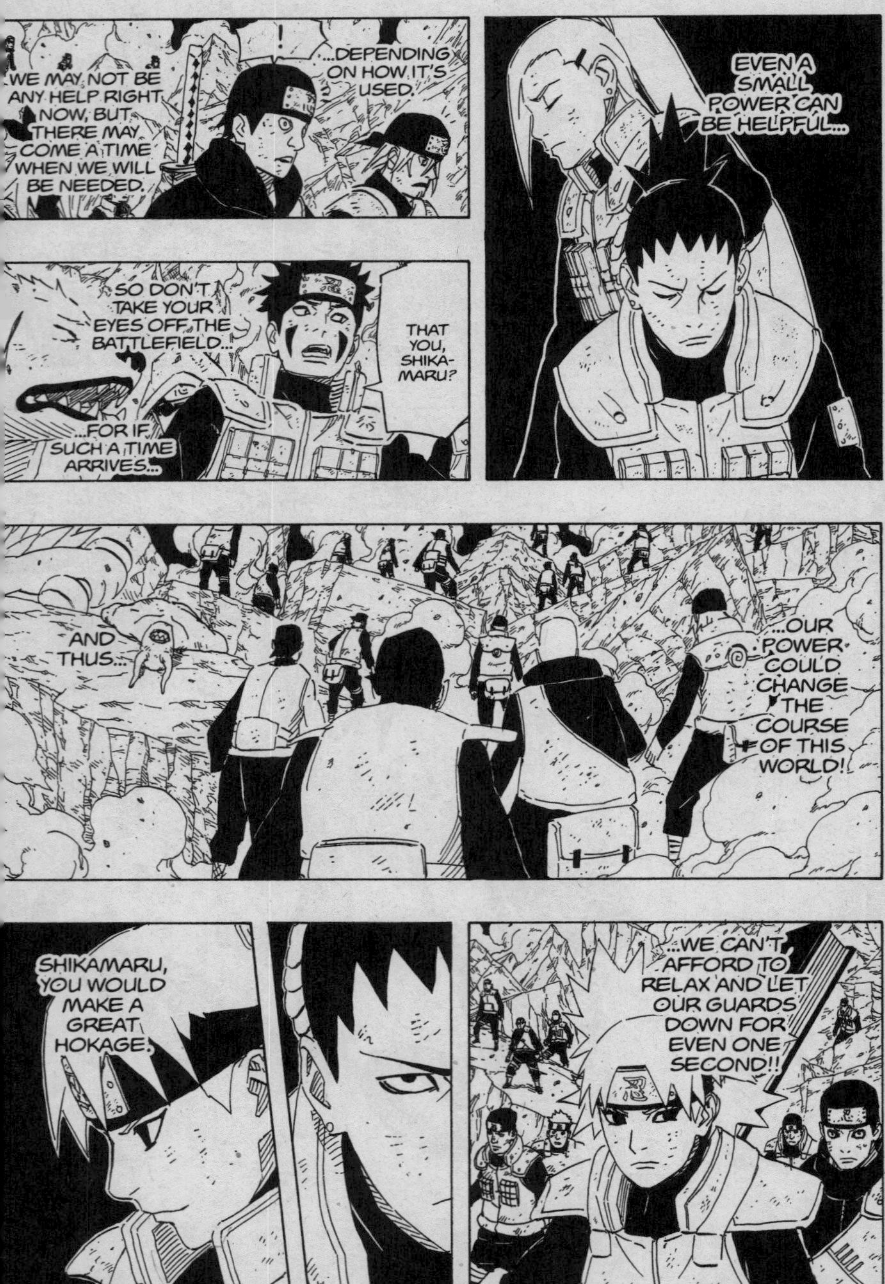
EVEN A SMALL POWER CAN BE HELPFUL...
!
...DEPENDING ON HOW IT'S USED.
WE MAY NOT BE ANY HELP RIGHT NOW, BUT THERE MAY COME A TIME WHEN WE WILL BE NEEDED.
THAT YOU, SHIKAMARU?
SO DON'T TAKE YOUR EYES OFF THE BATTLEFIELD...
...FOR IF SUCH A TIME ARRIVES...
...OUR POWER COULD CHANGE THE COURSE OF THIS WORLD!
AND THUS...
...WE CAN'T AFFORD TO RELAX AND LET OUR GUARDS DOWN FOR EVEN ONE SECOND!!
SHIKAMARU, YOU WOULD MAKE A GREAT HOKAGE.

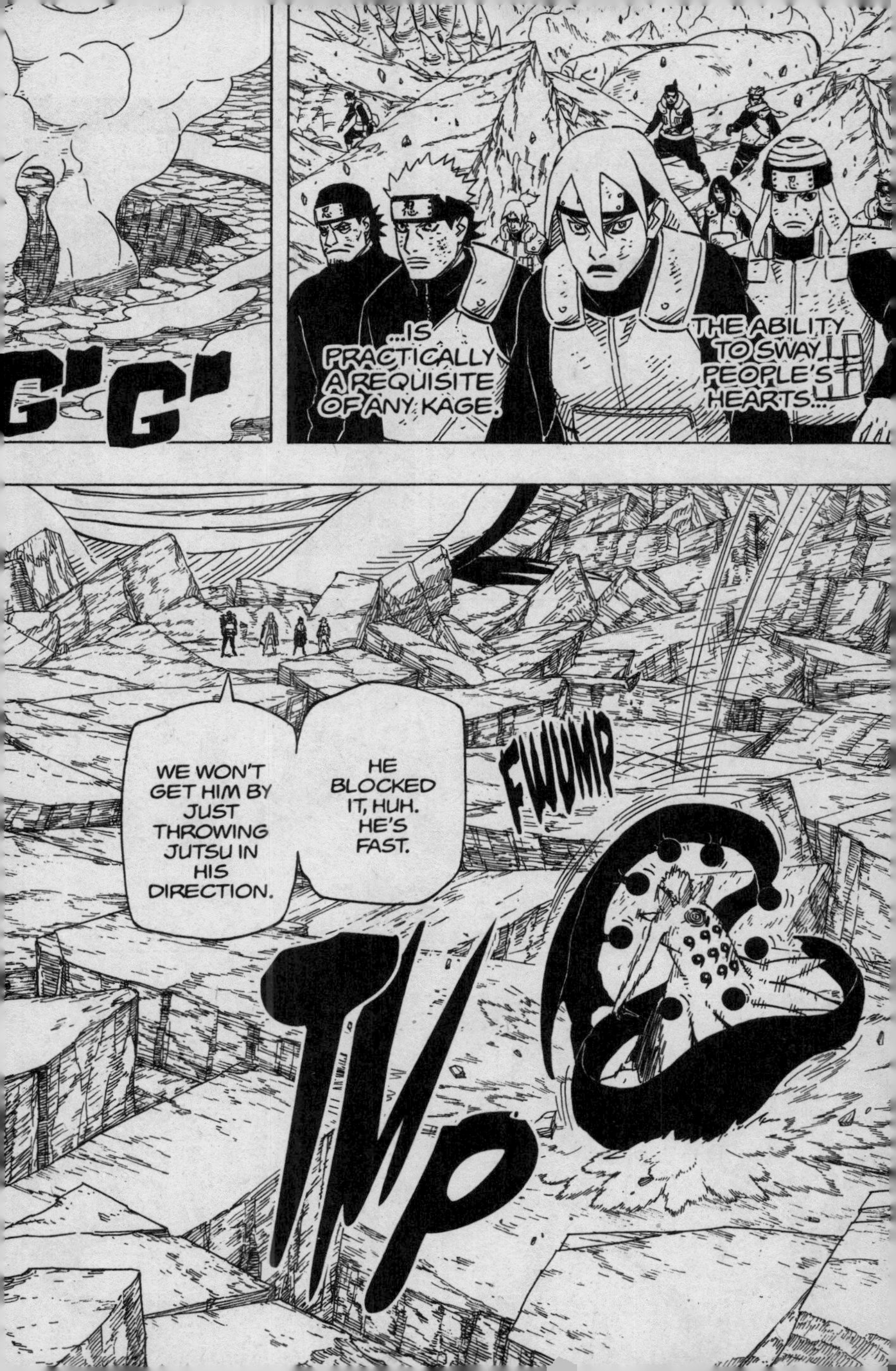
THE ABILITY TO SWAY PEOPLE'S HEARTS...
...IS PRACTICALLY A REQUISITE OF ANY KAGE.
G' G'
FWUMP
HE BLOCKED IT, HUH. HE'S FAST.
WE WON'T GET HIM BY JUST THROWING JUTSU IN HIS DIRECTION.
TMP

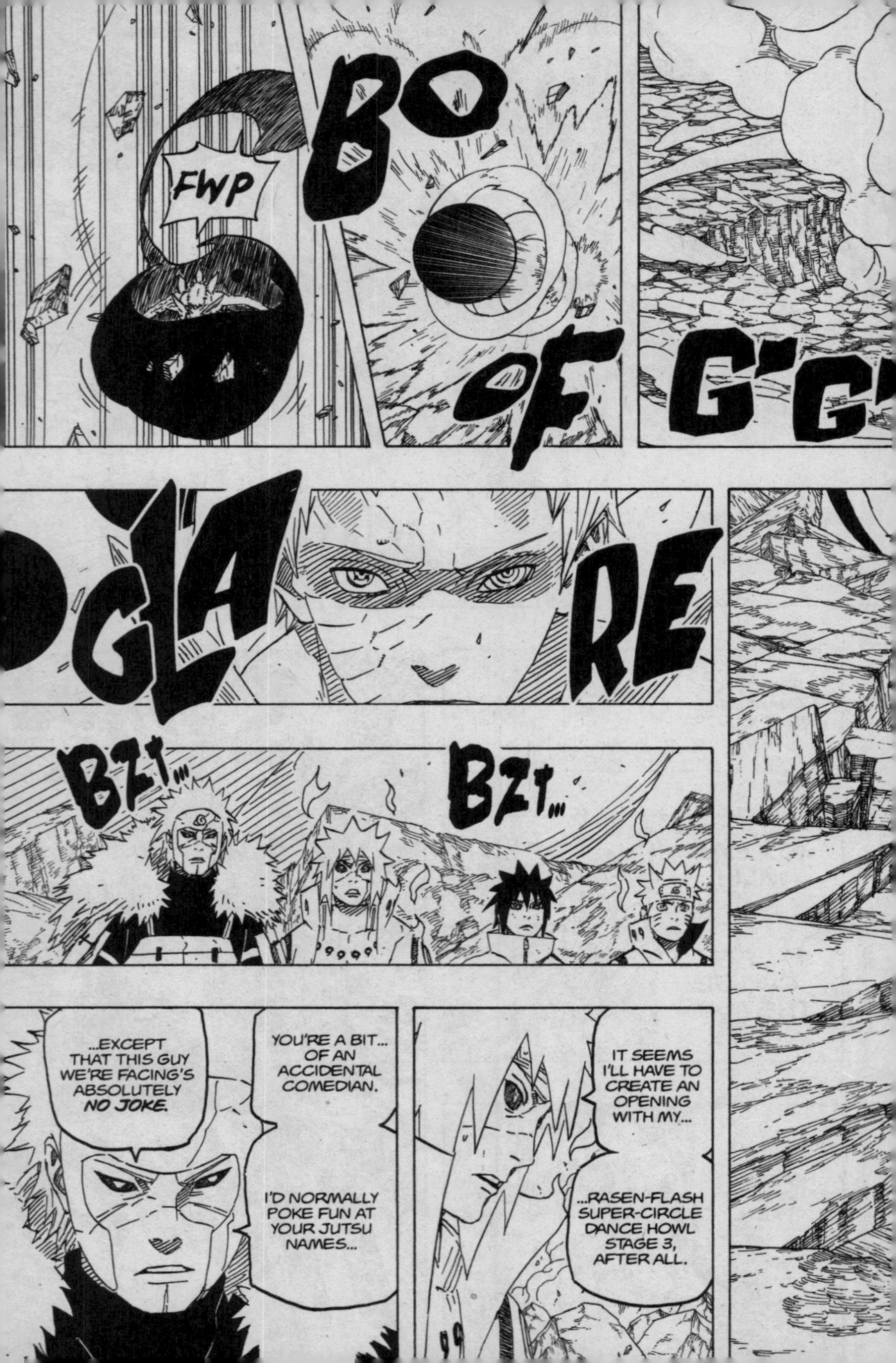
G'G'
BO
OF
FWP
GLARE
BZT...
BZT...
IT SEEMS I'LL HAVE TO CREATE AN OPENING WITH MY...
...RASEN-FLASH SUPER-CIRCLE DANCE HOWL STAGE 3, AFTER ALL.
YOU'RE A BIT... OF AN ACCIDENTAL COMEDIAN.
I'D NORMALLY POKE FUN AT YOUR JUTSU NAMES...
...EXCEPT THAT THIS GUY WE'RE FACING'S ABSOLUTELY NO JOKE.

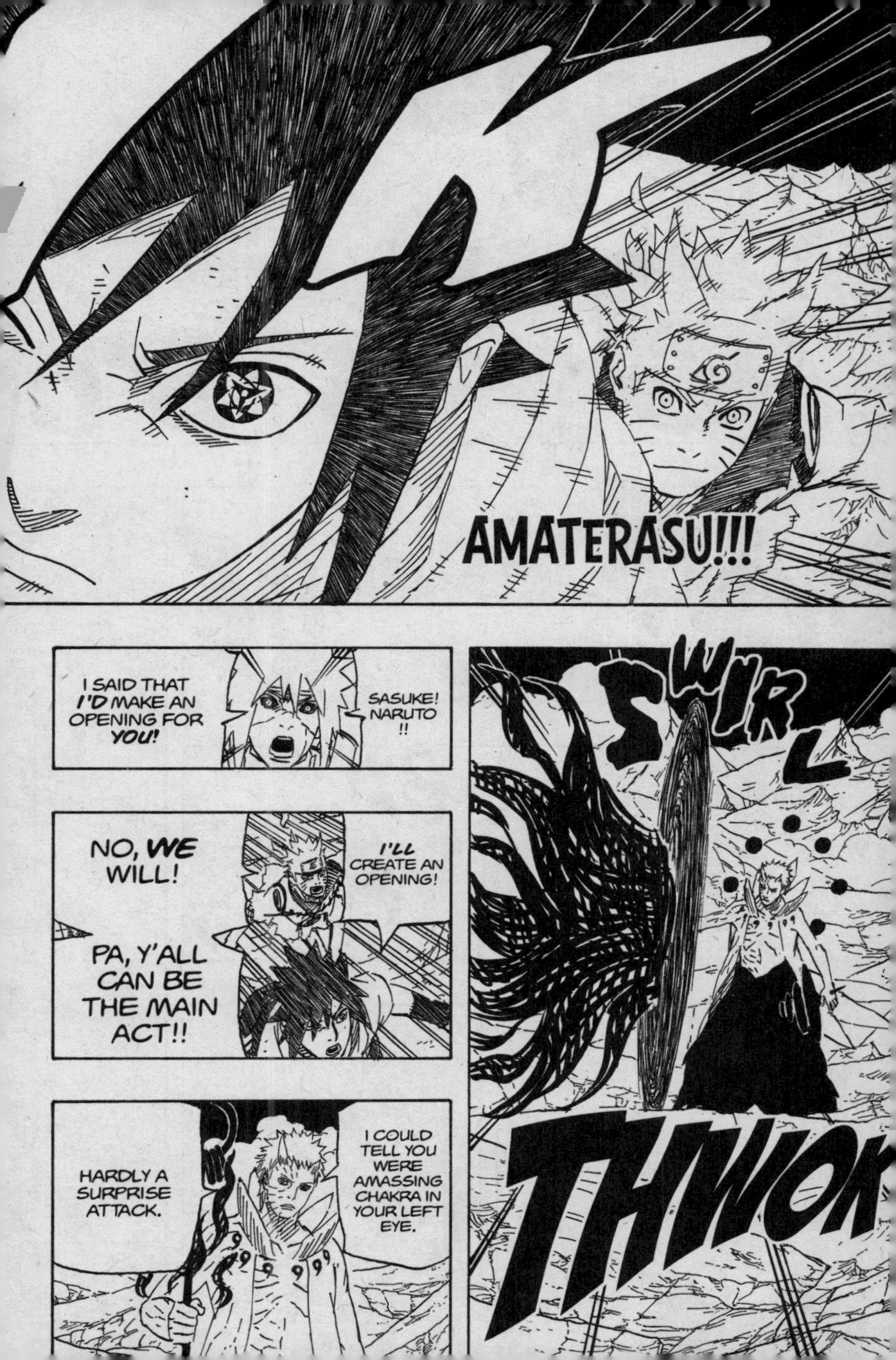
AMATERASU!!!
SWIRL
THWOM
SASUKE! NARUTO !!
I SAID THAT I'D MAKE AN OPENING FOR YOU!
I'LL CREATE AN OPENING!
NO, WE WILL!
PA, Y'ALL CAN BE THE MAIN ACT!!
I COULD TELL YOU WERE AMASSING CHAKRA IN YOUR LEFT EYE.
HARDLY A SURPRISE ATTACK.

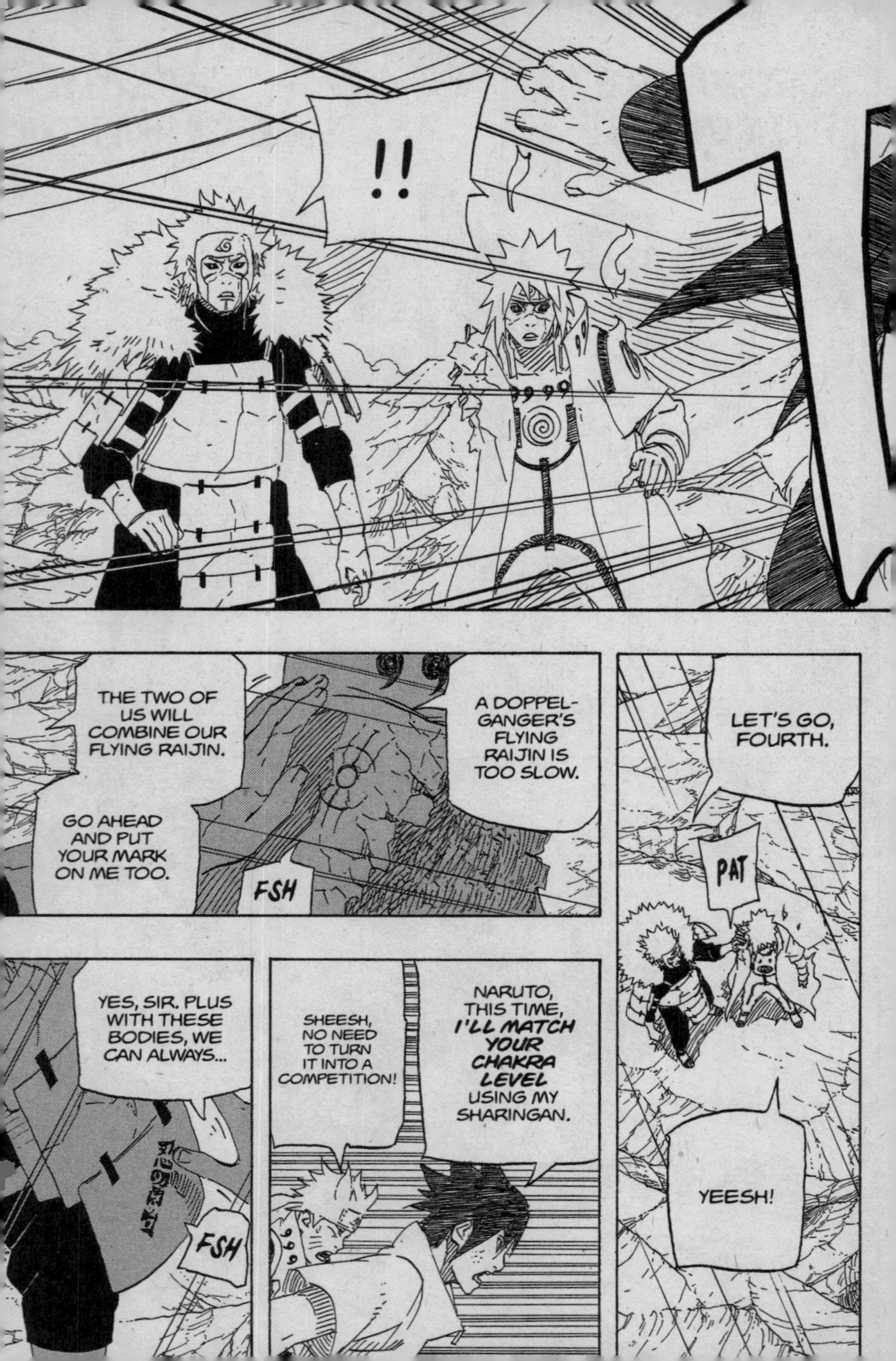
!!
LET'S GO, FOURTH.
PAT
YEESH!
A DOPPEL-GANGER'S FLYING RAIJIN IS TOO SLOW.
THE TWO OF US WILL COMBINE OUR FLYING RAIJIN.
GO AHEAD AND PUT YOUR MARK ON ME TOO.
FSH
NARUTO, THIS TIME, *I'LL MATCH YOUR CHAKRA LEVEL* USING MY SHARINGAN.
SHEESH, NO NEED TO TURN IT INTO A COMPETITION!
YES, SIR. PLUS WITH THESE BODIES, WE CAN ALWAYS...
FSH

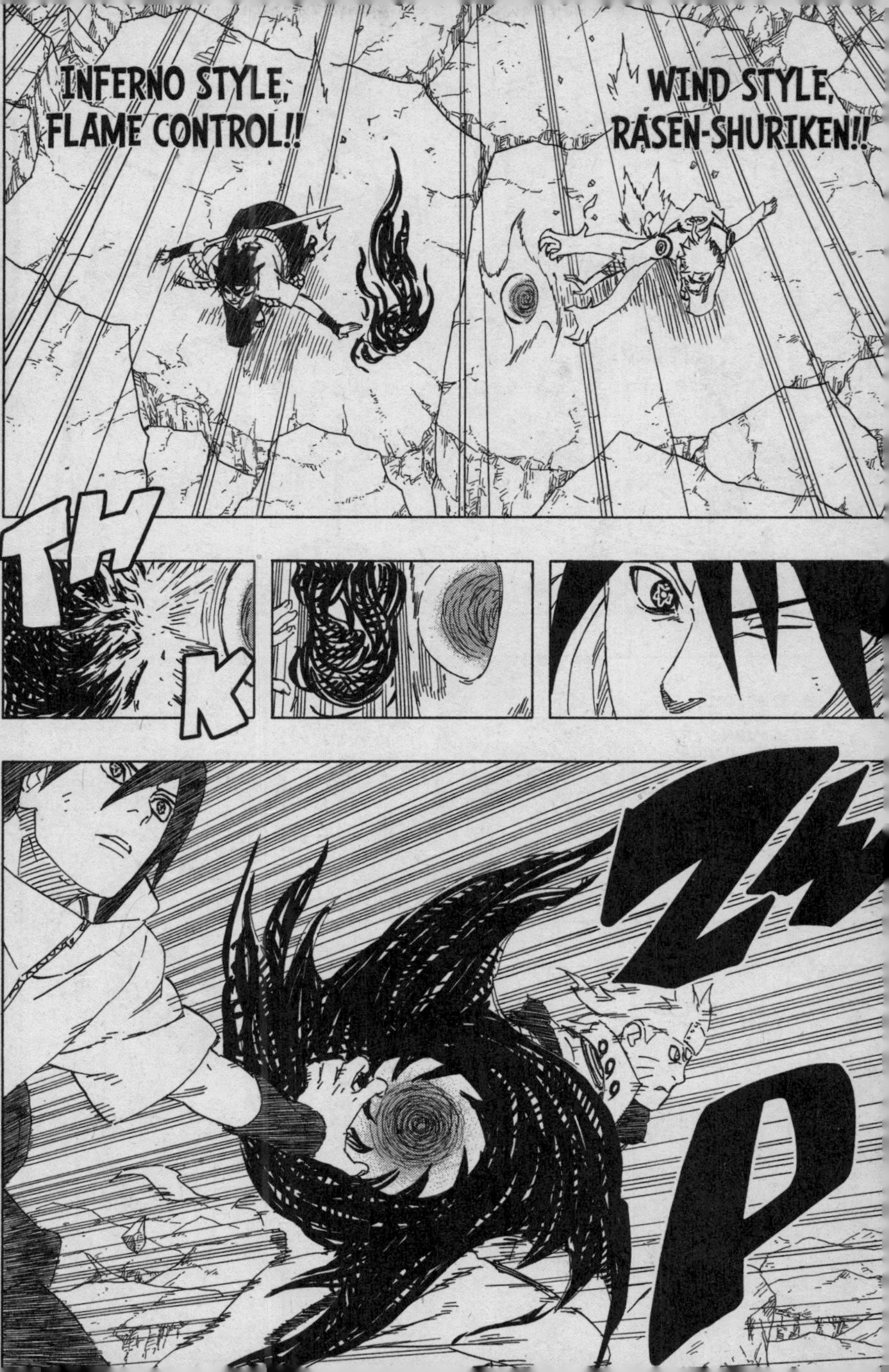
WIND STYLE, RĀSEN-SHURIKEN!!
INFERNO STYLE, FLAME CONTROL!!
THK
ZWP

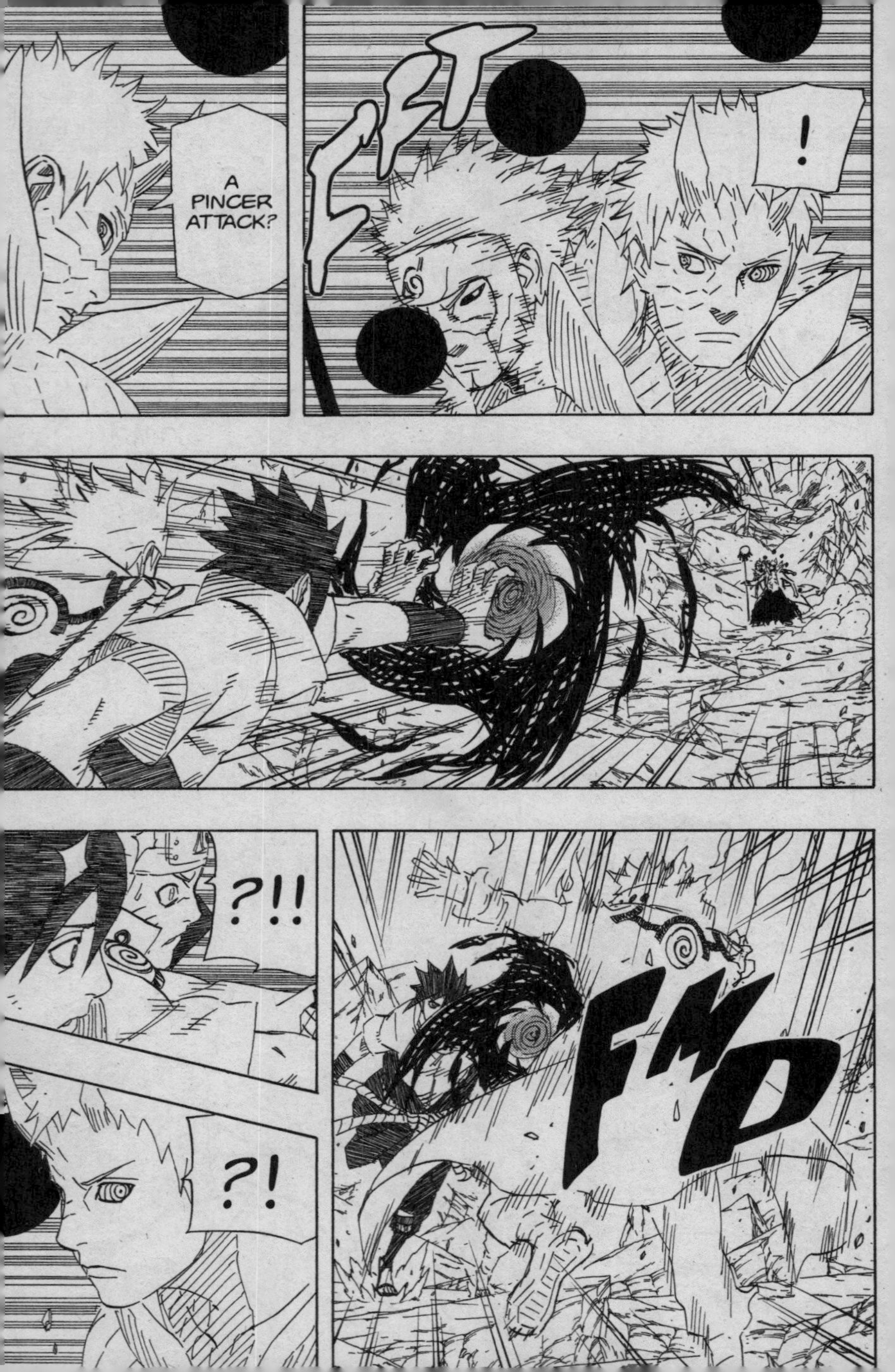
!
A PINCER ATTACK?
?!!
?!

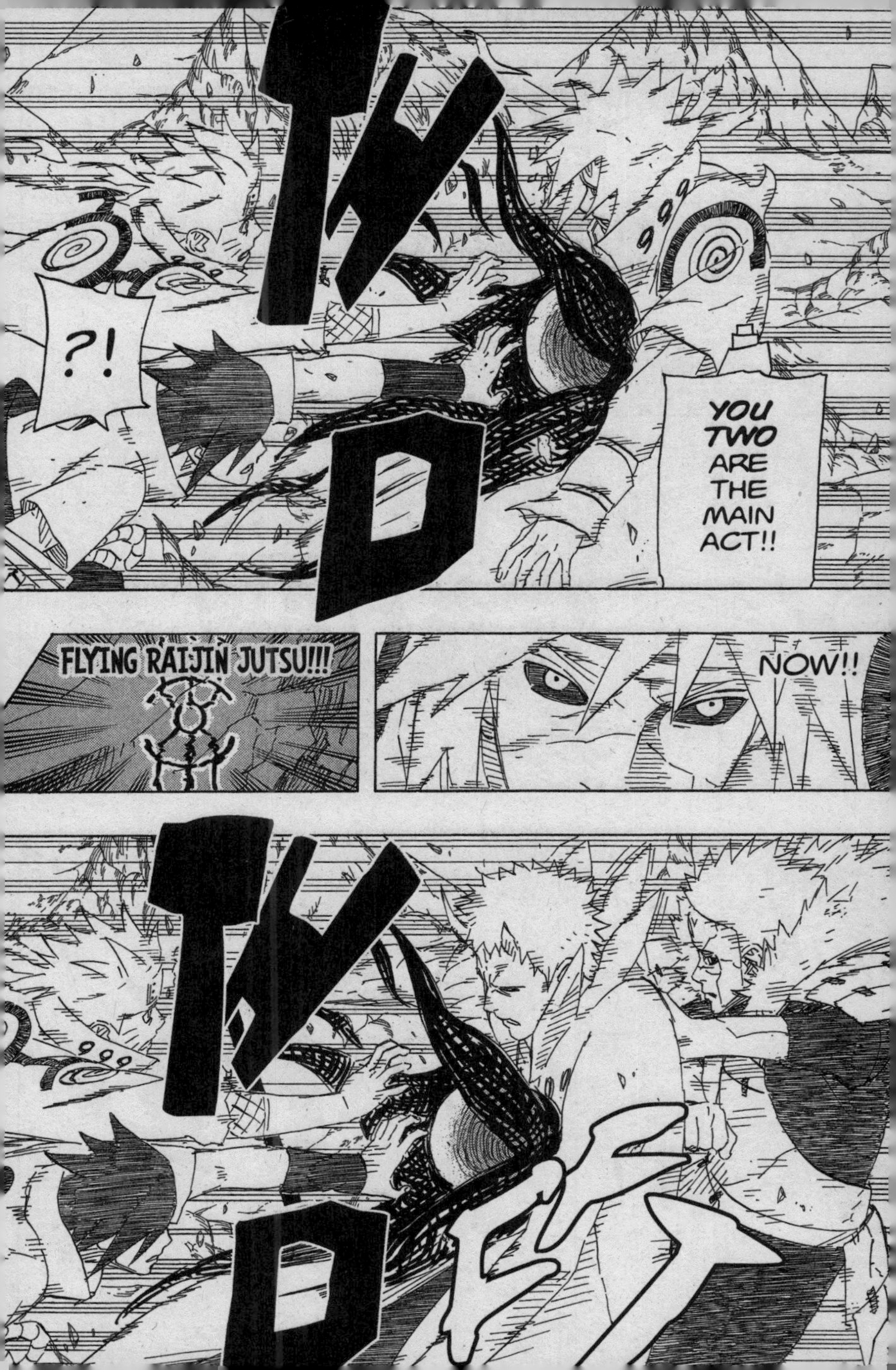
YOU TWO ARE THE MAIN ACT!!
?!
NOW!!
FLYING RAIJIN JUTSU!!!

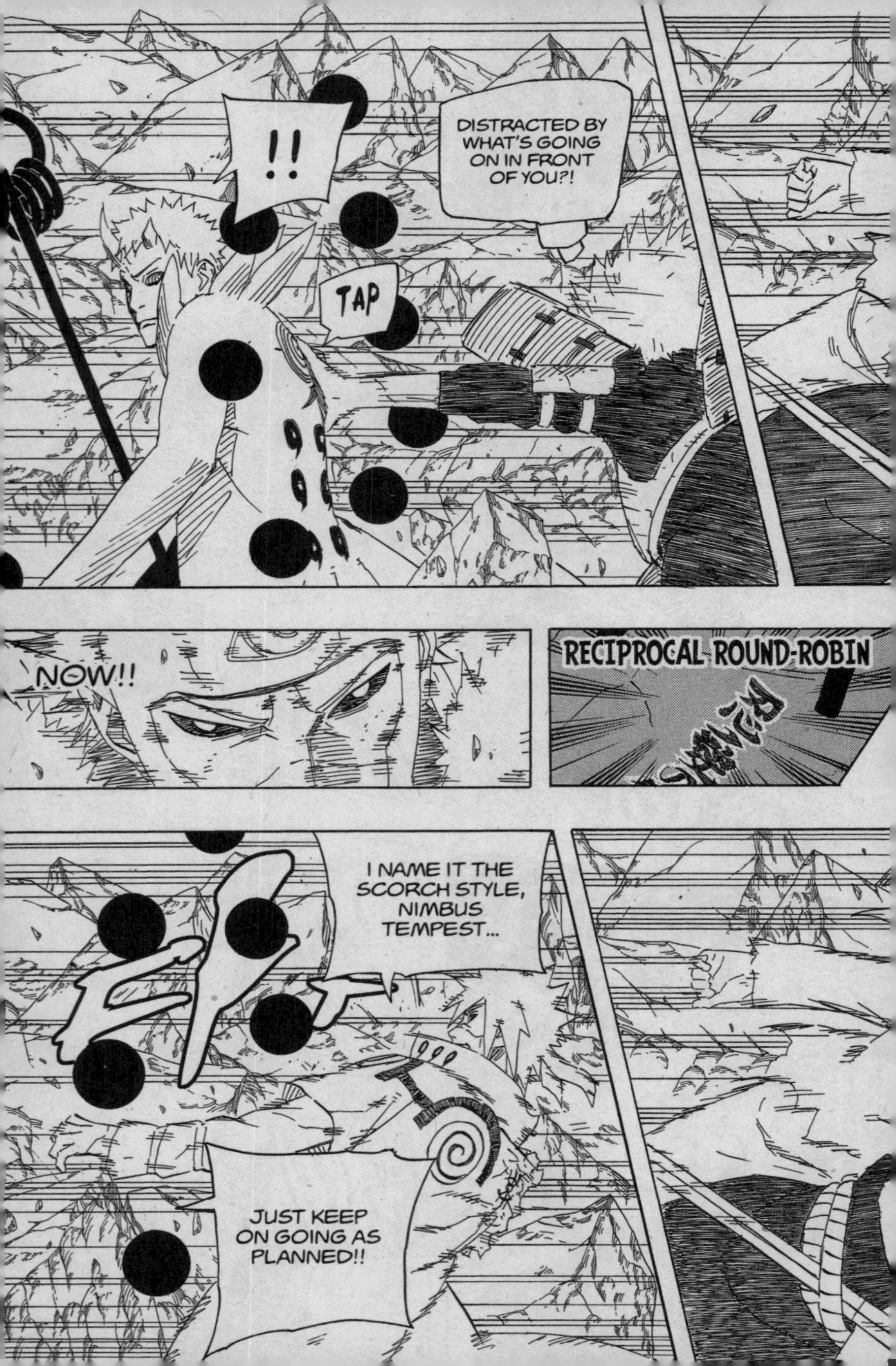
DISTRACTED BY WHAT'S GOING ON IN FRONT OF YOU?!
!!
TAP
RECIPROCAL ROUND-ROBIN
NOW!!
I NAME IT THE SCORCH STYLE, NIMBUS TEMPEST...
JUST KEEP ON GOING AS PLANNED!!

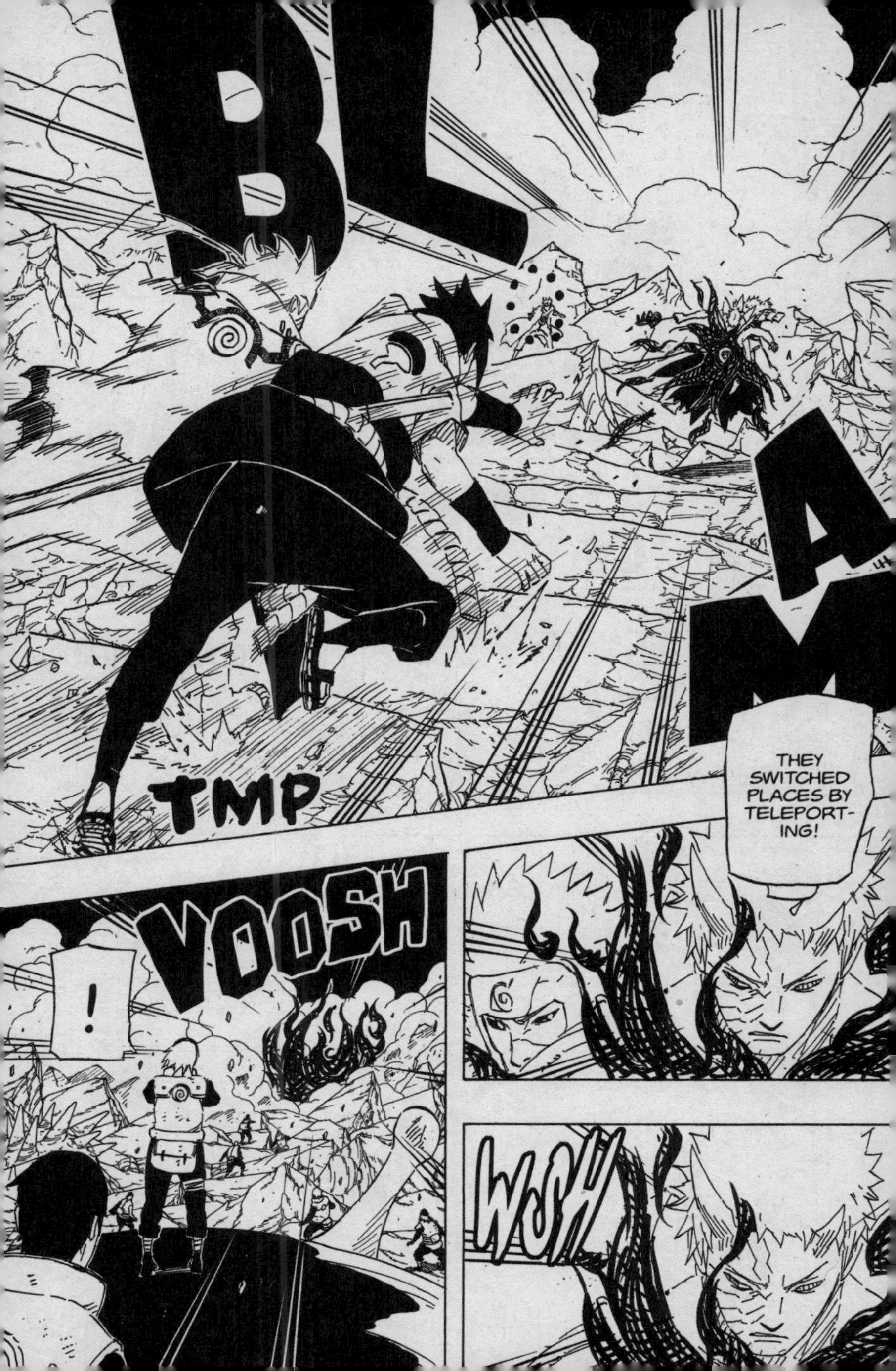
BLAM
TMP
THEY SWITCHED PLACES BY TELEPORTING!
WSH
VOOSH
!

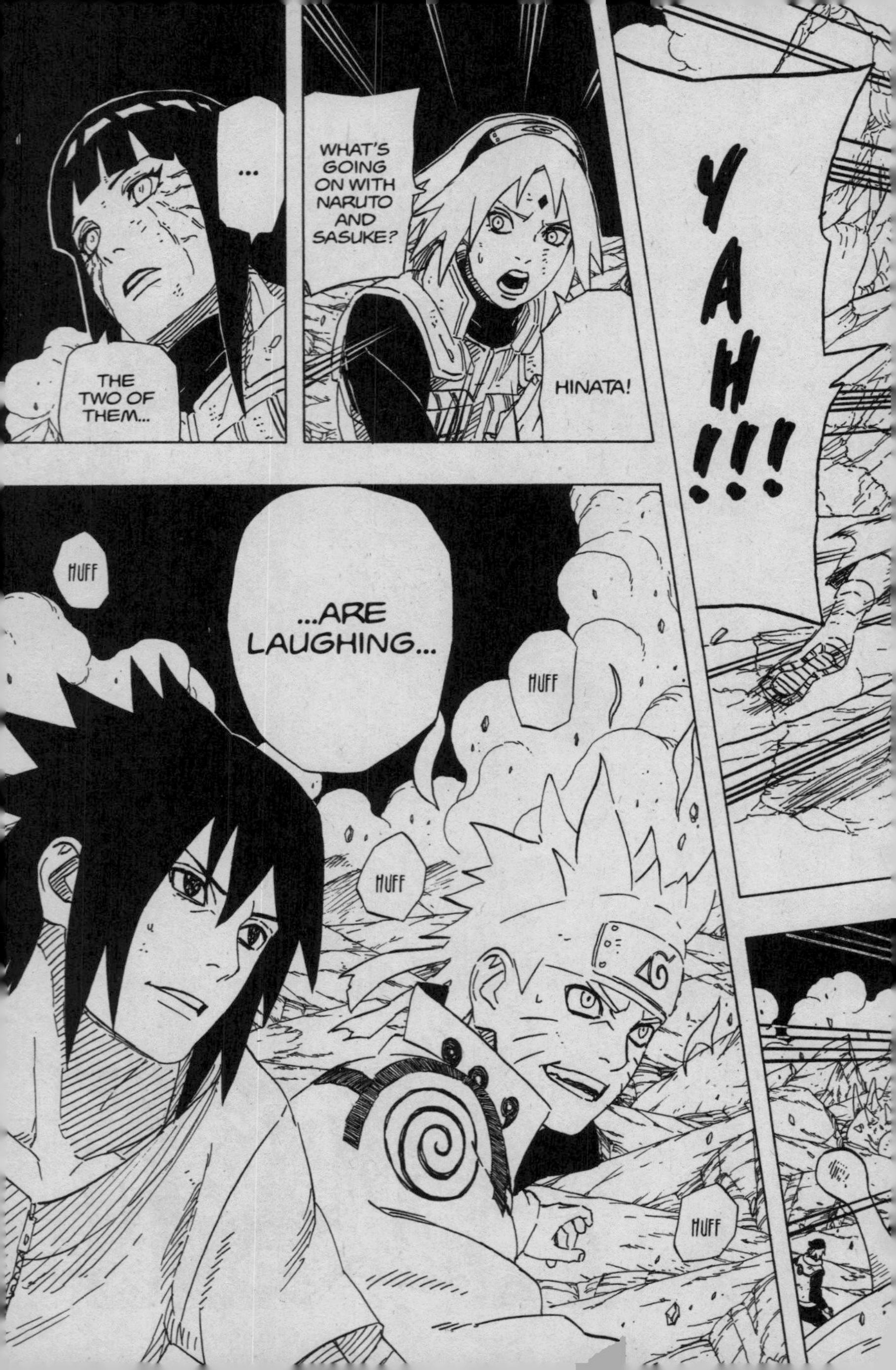
YAAH!!!
HINATA!
WHAT'S GOING ON WITH NARUTO AND SASUKE?
...
THE TWO OF THEM...
...ARE LAUGHING...
HUFF
HUFF
HUFF
HUFF

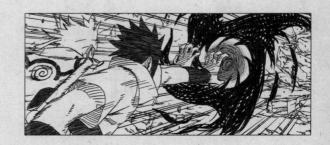

Number 642: An Opening

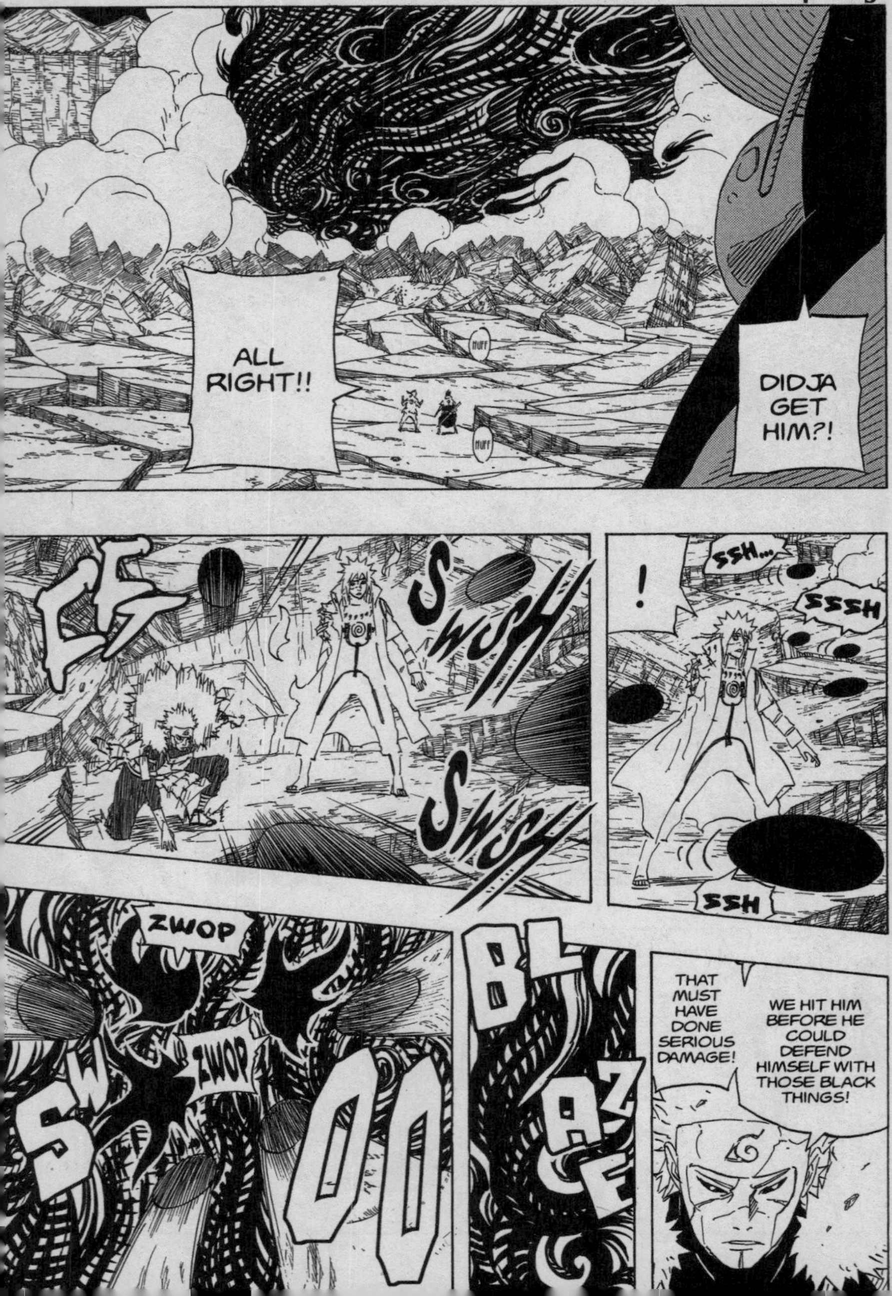
DIDJA GET HIM?!
HUFF
HUFF
ALL RIGHT!!
SSH...
SSSH
!
SSH
SWISH
SWISH
WE HIT HIM BEFORE HE COULD DEFEND HIMSELF WITH THOSE BLACK THINGS!
THAT MUST HAVE DONE SERIOUS DAMAGE!
ZWOP
ZWOP

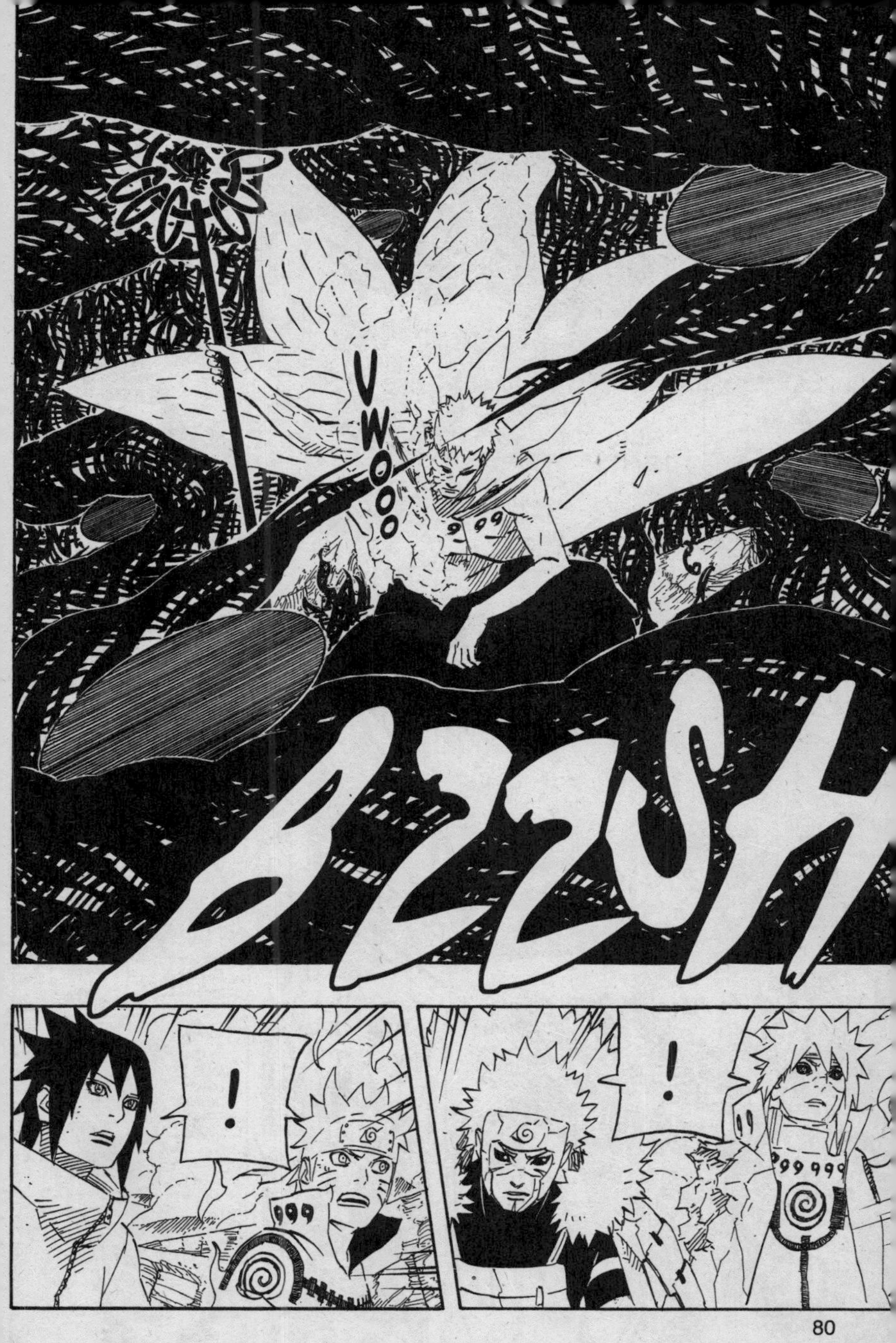

VWOOO
BZZSH
!
!

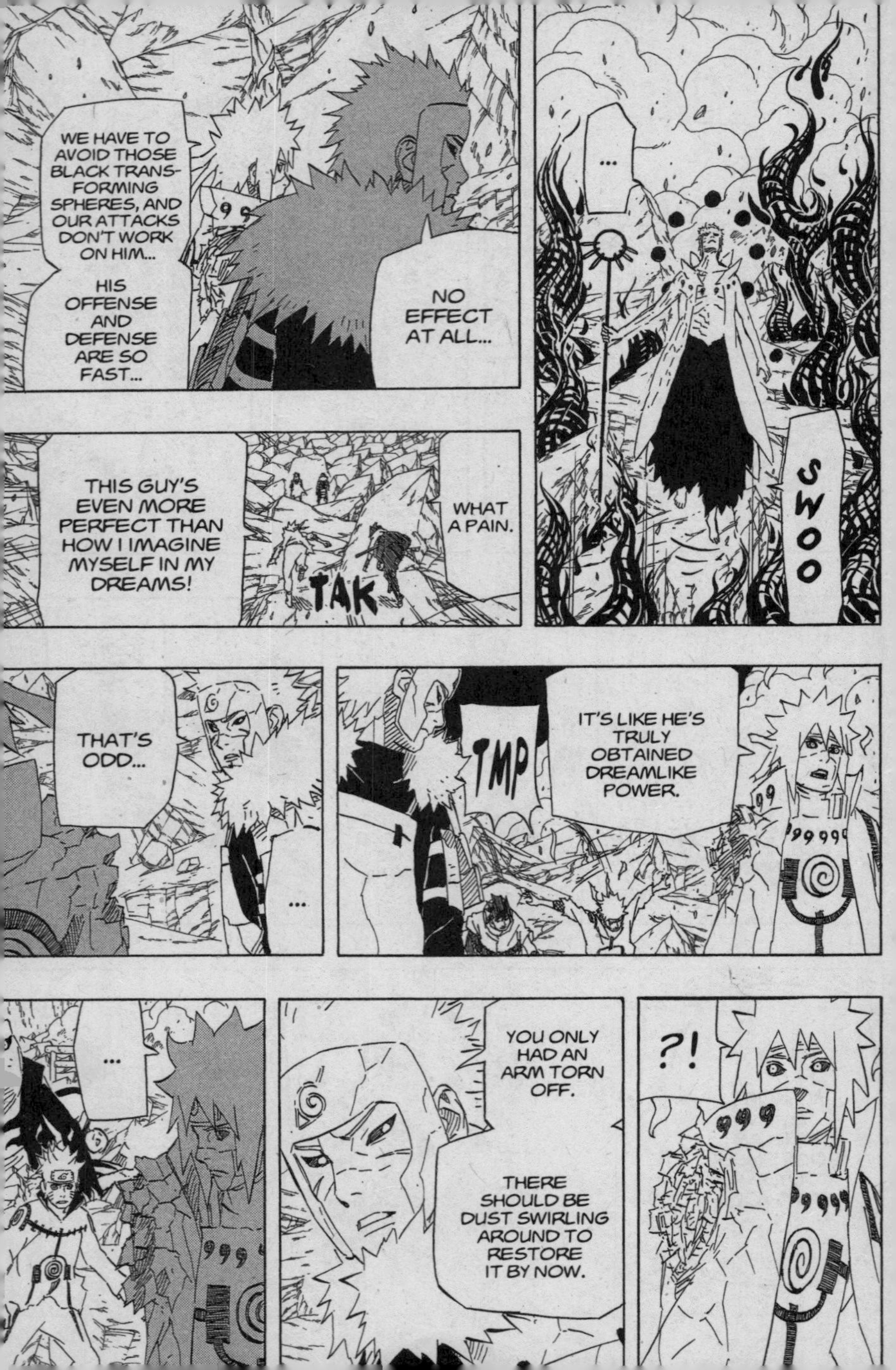
...
SWOO
WE HAVE TO AVOID THOSE BLACK TRANS-FORMING SPHERES, AND OUR ATTACKS DON'T WORK ON HIM...
HIS OFFENSE AND DEFENSE ARE SO FAST...
NO EFFECT AT ALL...
WHAT A PAIN.
TAK
THIS GUY'S EVEN MORE PERFECT THAN HOW I IMAGINE MYSELF IN MY DREAMS!
IT'S LIKE HE'S TRULY OBTAINED DREAMLIKE POWER.
TMP
THAT'S ODD...
...
?!
YOU ONLY HAD AN ARM TORN OFF.
THERE SHOULD BE DUST SWIRLING AROUND TO RESTORE IT BY NOW.
...

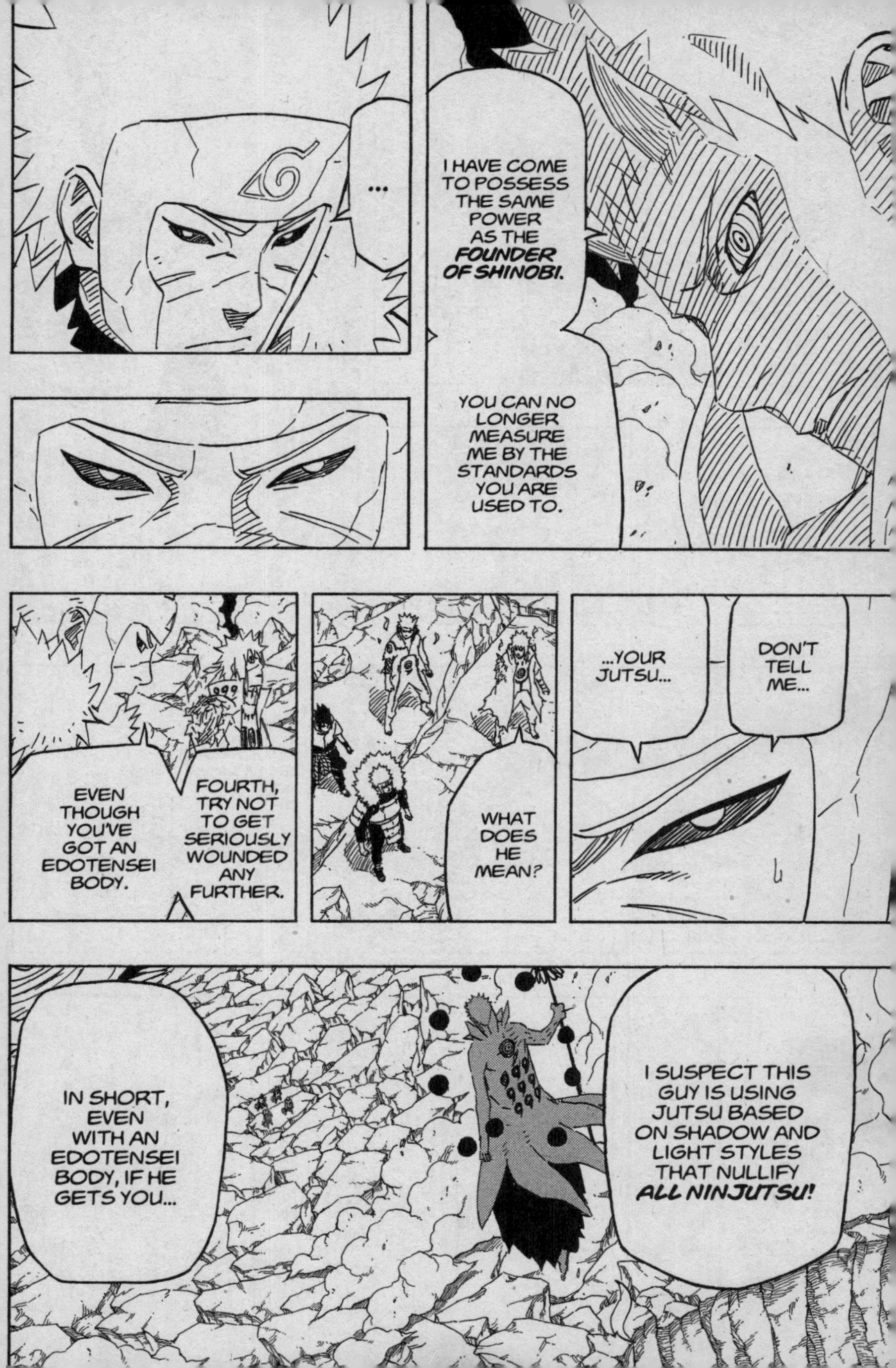
I HAVE COME TO POSSESS THE SAME POWER AS THE ***FOUNDER OF SHINOBI.***
YOU CAN NO LONGER MEASURE ME BY THE STANDARDS YOU ARE USED TO.
...
DON'T TELL ME...
...YOUR JUTSU...
WHAT DOES HE MEAN?
FOURTH, TRY NOT TO GET SERIOUSLY WOUNDED ANY FURTHER.
EVEN THOUGH YOU'VE GOT AN EDOTENSEI BODY.
I SUSPECT THIS GUY IS USING JUTSU BASED ON SHADOW AND LIGHT STYLES THAT NULLIFY ***ALL NINJUTSU!***
IN SHORT, EVEN WITH AN EDOTENSEI BODY, IF HE GETS YOU...

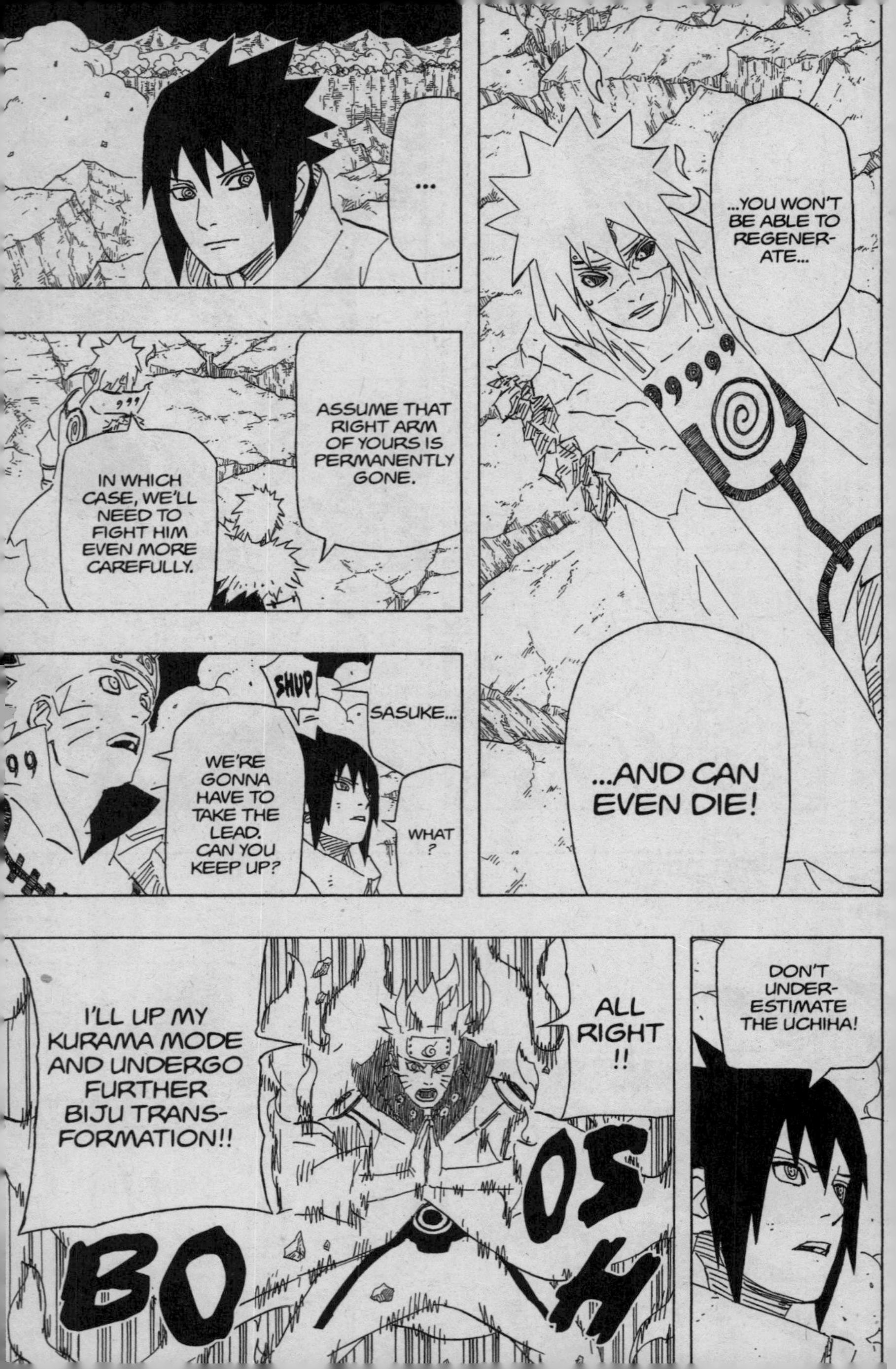
...YOU WON'T BE ABLE TO REGENER-ATE...
...AND CAN EVEN DIE!
...
ASSUME THAT RIGHT ARM OF YOURS IS PERMANENTLY GONE.
IN WHICH CASE, WE'LL NEED TO FIGHT HIM EVEN MORE CAREFULLY.
SHUP
SASUKE...
WE'RE GONNA HAVE TO TAKE THE LEAD. CAN YOU KEEP UP?
WHAT?
DON'T UNDER-ESTIMATE THE UCHIHA!
ALL RIGHT!!
I'LL UP MY KURAMA MODE AND UNDERGO FURTHER BIJU TRANS-FORMATION!!
BOOSH

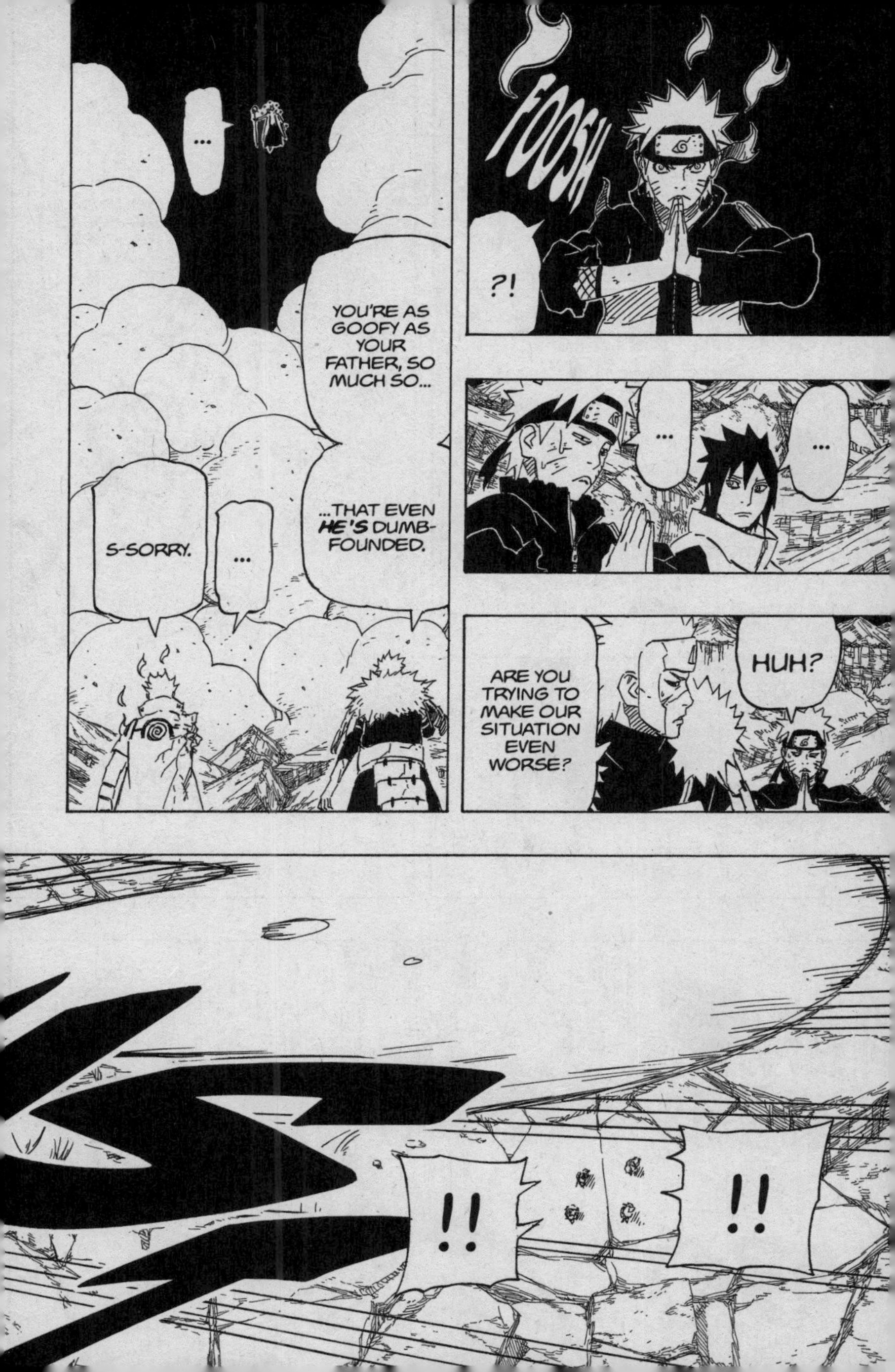
FOOSH
?!
...
...
HUH?
ARE YOU TRYING TO MAKE OUR SITUATION EVEN WORSE?
...
YOU'RE AS GOOFY AS YOUR FATHER, SO MUCH SO...
...THAT EVEN HE'S DUMBFOUNDED.
...
S-SORRY.
!!
!!

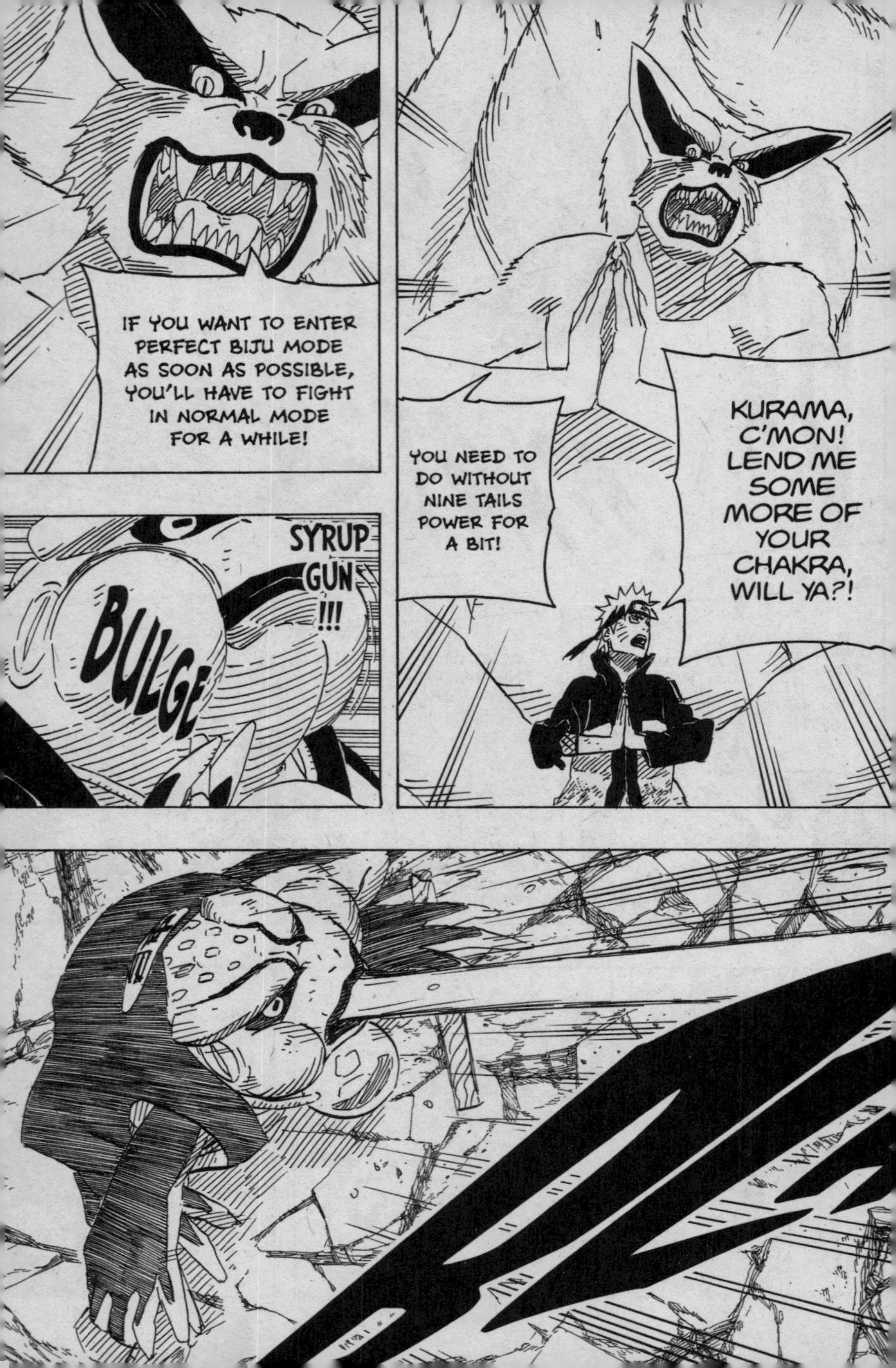
KURAMA, C'MON! LEND ME SOME MORE OF YOUR CHAKRA, WILL YA?!
YOU NEED TO DO WITHOUT NINE TAILS POWER FOR A BIT!
IF YOU WANT TO ENTER PERFECT BIJU MODE AS SOON AS POSSIBLE, YOU'LL HAVE TO FIGHT IN NORMAL MODE FOR A WHILE!
SYRUP GUN!!!
BULGE

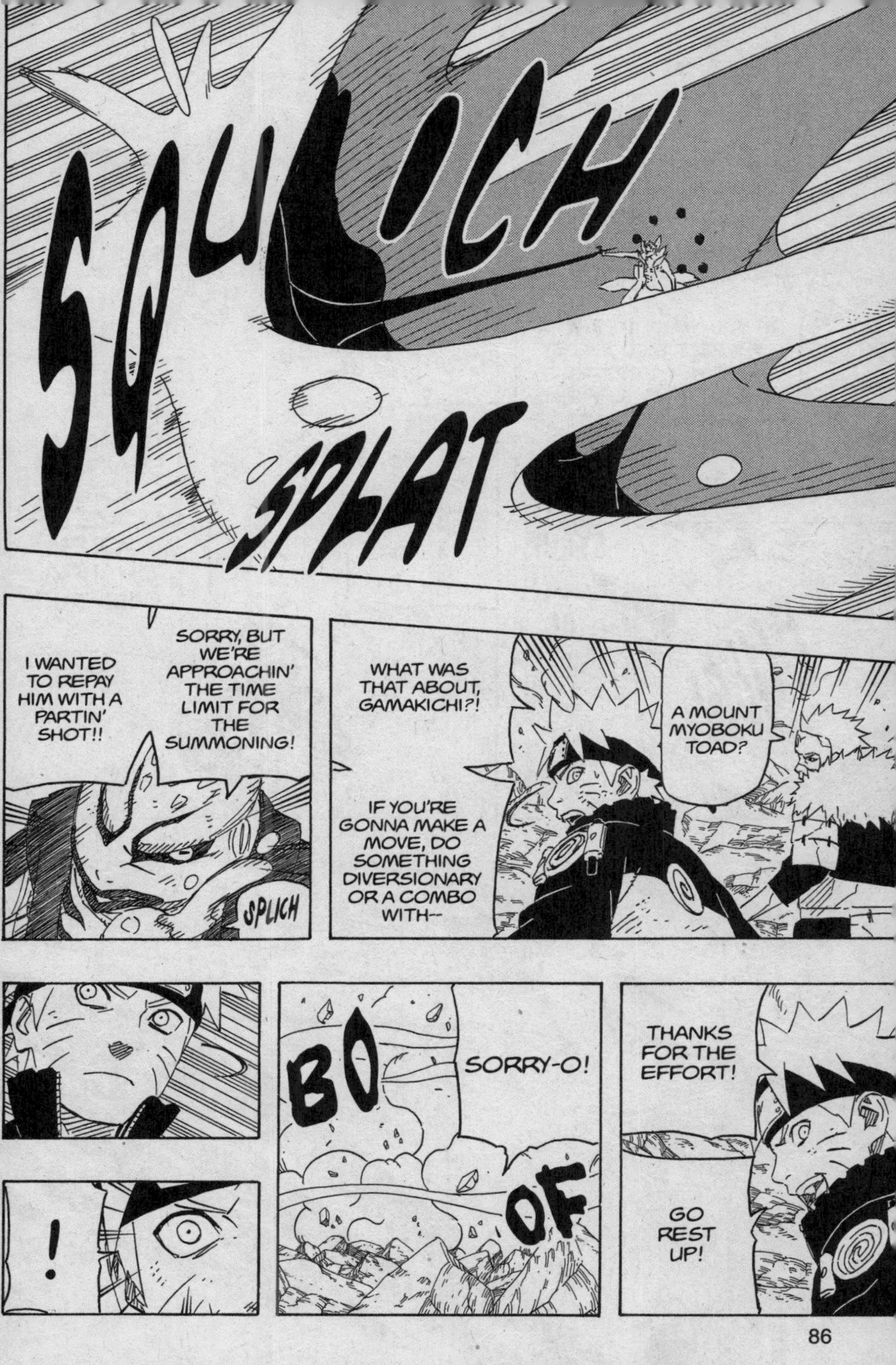
SQULCH
SPLAT
A MOUNT MYOBOKU TOAD?
WHAT WAS THAT ABOUT, GAMAKICHI?!
IF YOU'RE GONNA MAKE A MOVE, DO SOMETHING DIVERSIONARY OR A COMBO WITH--
SORRY, BUT WE'RE APPROACHIN' THE TIME LIMIT FOR THE SUMMONING!
I WANTED TO REPAY HIM WITH A PARTIN' SHOT!!
SPLICH
THANKS FOR THE EFFORT!
GO REST UP!
SORRY-O!
BO
OF
!

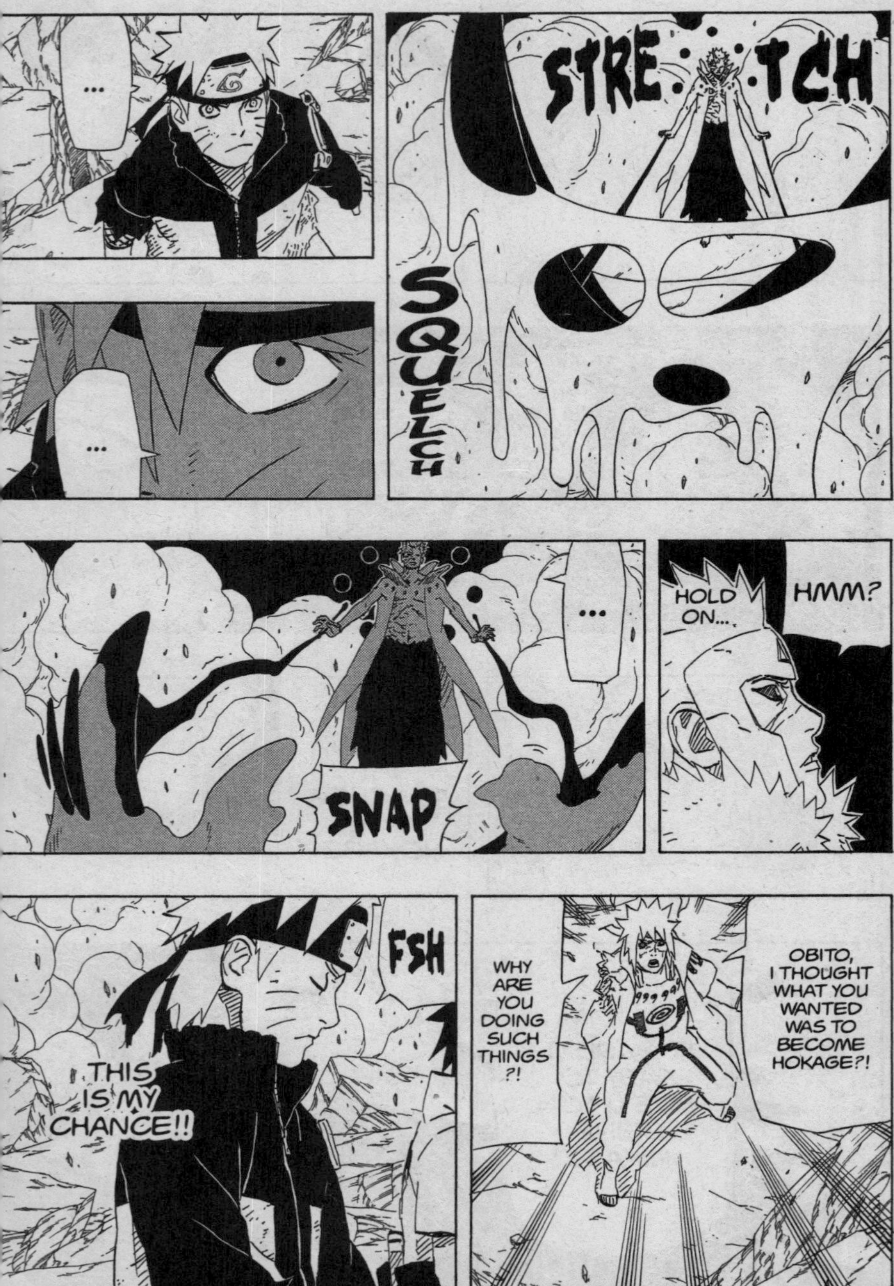
STRE...TCH
SQUELCH
...
...
HMM?
HOLD ON...
...
SNAP
OBITO, I THOUGHT WHAT YOU WANTED WAS TO BECOME HOKAGE?!
WHY ARE YOU DOING SUCH THINGS?!
FSH
THIS IS MY CHANCE!!

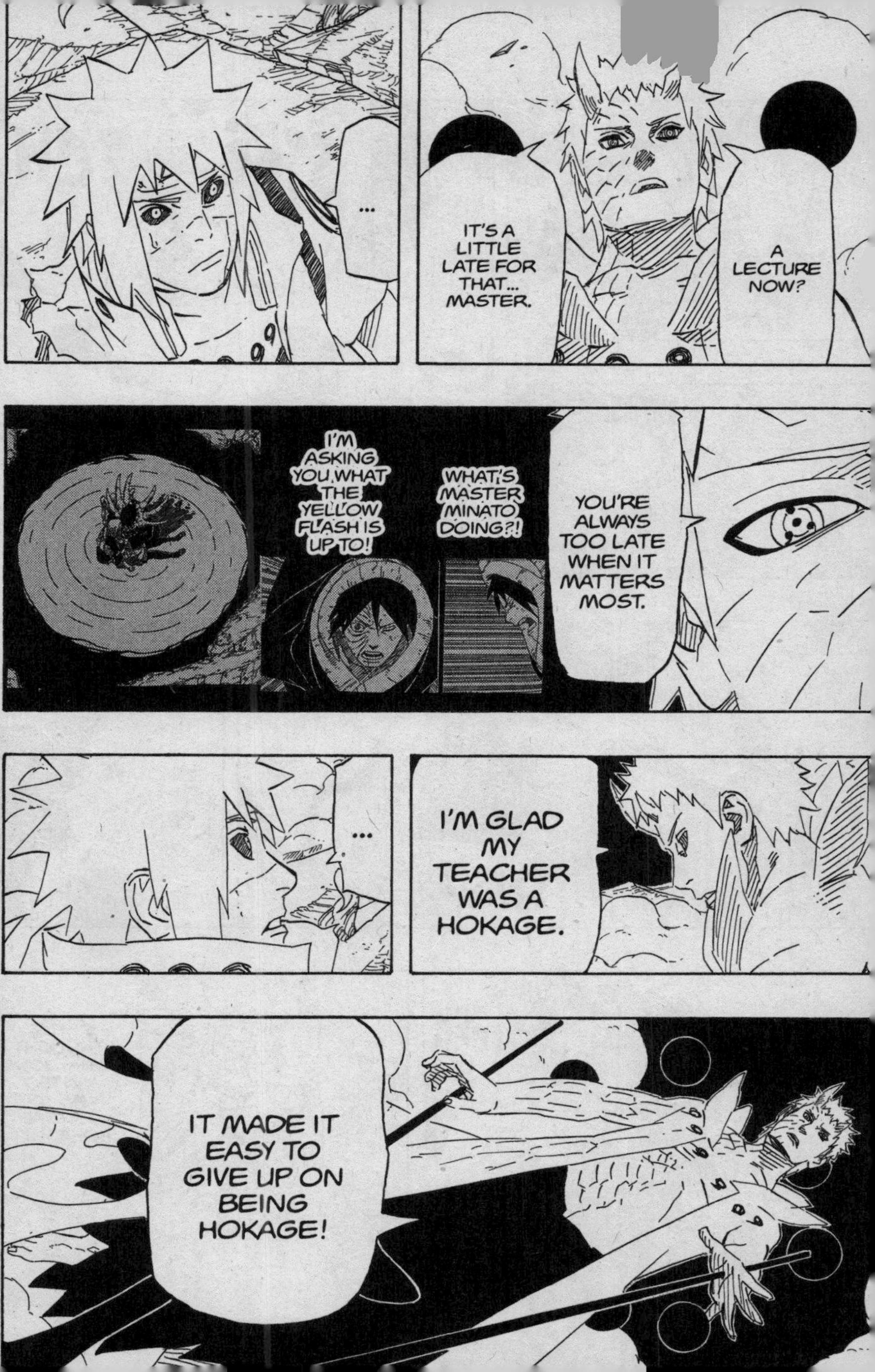
A LECTURE NOW?
IT'S A LITTLE LATE FOR THAT... MASTER.
...
YOU'RE ALWAYS TOO LATE WHEN IT MATTERS MOST.
WHAT'S MASTER MINATO DOING?!
I'M ASKING YOU WHAT THE YELLOW FLASH IS UP TO!
I'M GLAD MY TEACHER WAS A HOKAGE.
...
IT MADE IT EASY TO GIVE UP ON BEING HOKAGE!

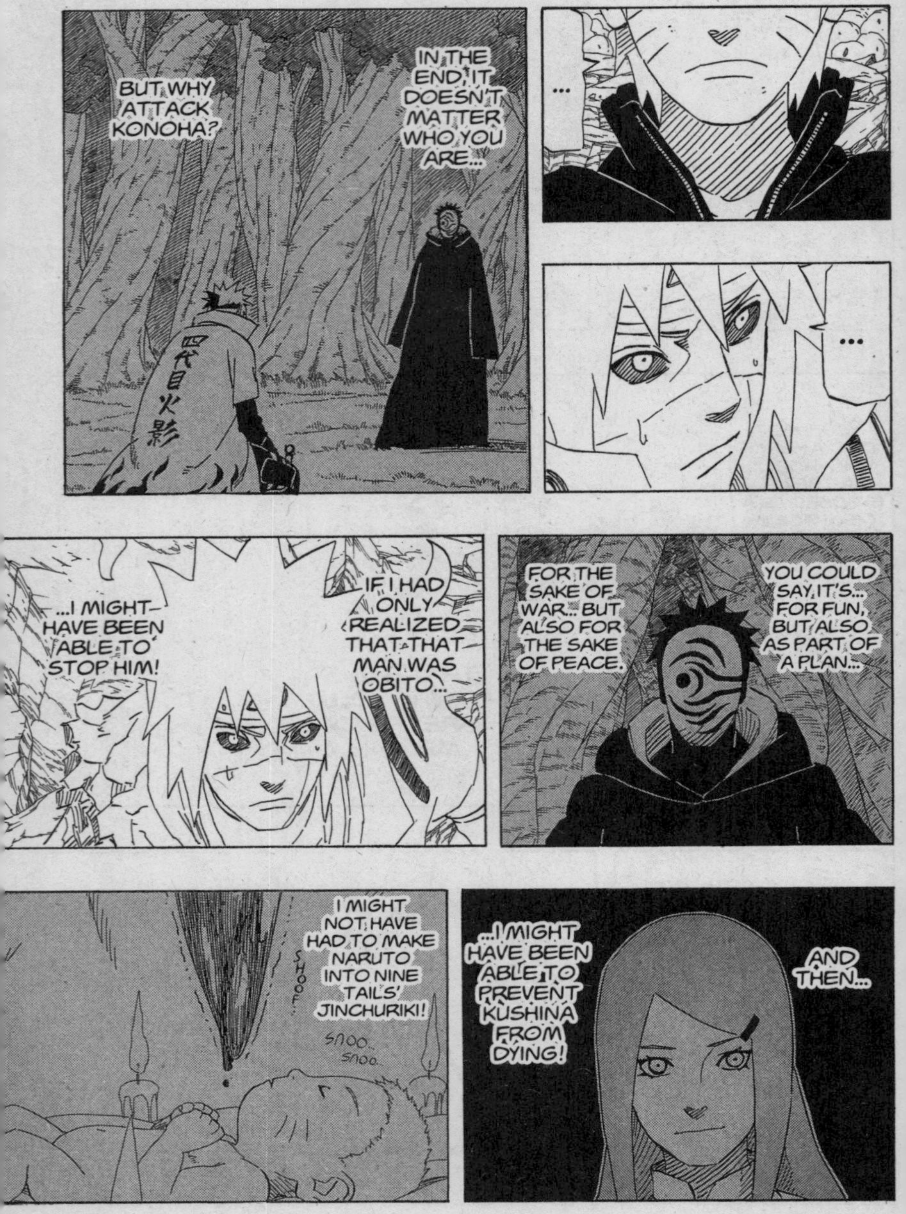
...
...
IN THE END, IT DOESN'T MATTER WHO YOU ARE...
BUT WHY ATTACK KONOHA?
YOU COULD SAY IT'S... FOR FUN, BUT ALSO AS PART OF A PLAN...
FOR THE SAKE OF WAR... BUT ALSO FOR THE SAKE OF PEACE.
IF I HAD ONLY REALIZED THAT THAT MAN WAS OBITO...
...I MIGHT HAVE BEEN ABLE TO STOP HIM!
AND THEN...
...I MIGHT HAVE BEEN ABLE TO PREVENT KUSHINA FROM DYING!
I MIGHT NOT HAVE HAD TO MAKE NARUTO INTO NINE TAILS' JINCHURIKI!
SHOOF...
SNOO... SNOO...

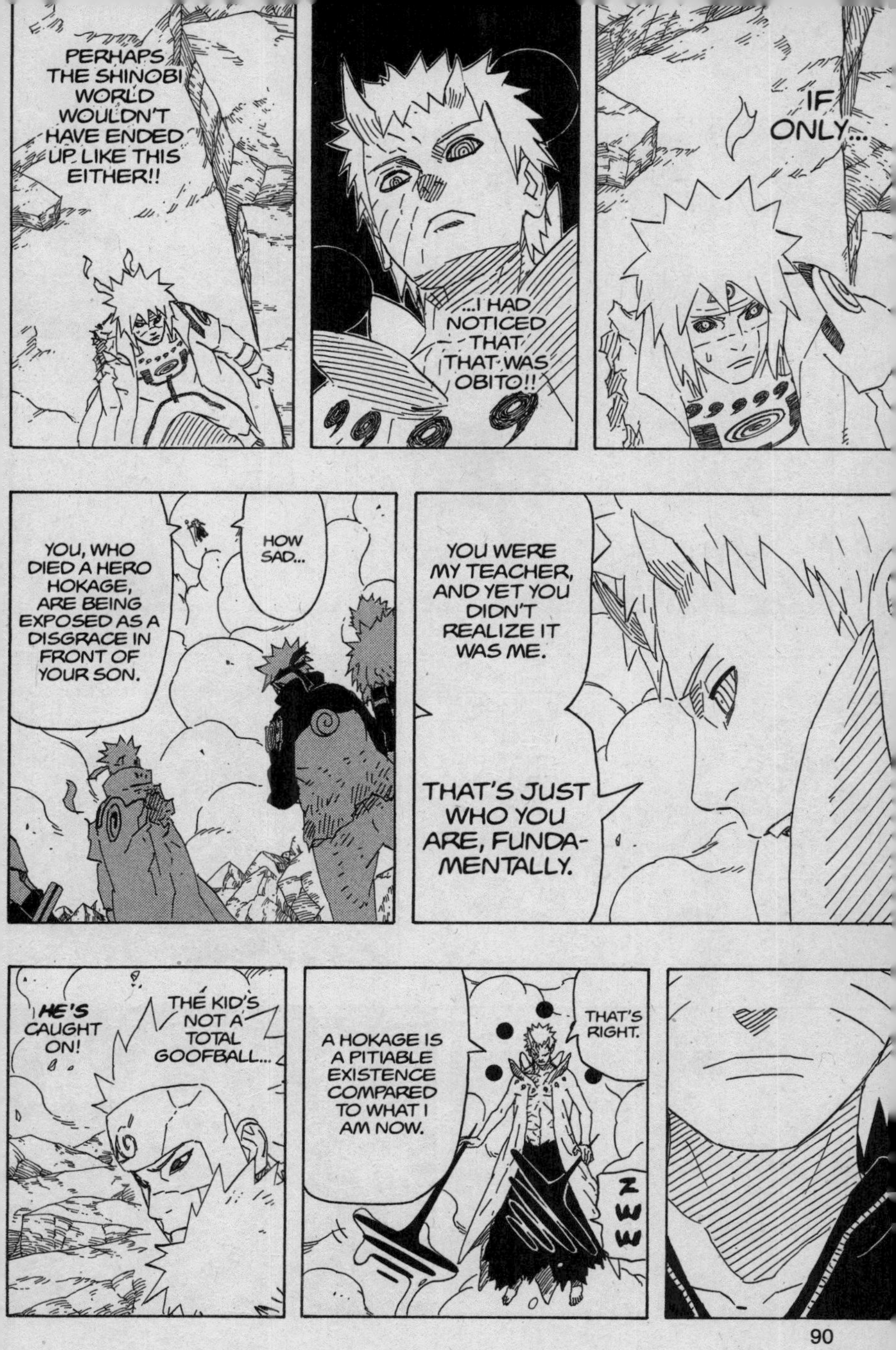
IF ONLY...
...I HAD NOTICED THAT THAT WAS OBITO!!
PERHAPS THE SHINOBI WORLD WOULDN'T HAVE ENDED UP LIKE THIS EITHER!!
YOU WERE MY TEACHER, AND YET YOU DIDN'T REALIZE IT WAS ME.
THAT'S JUST WHO YOU ARE, FUNDAMENTALLY.
HOW SAD...
YOU, WHO DIED A HERO HOKAGE, ARE BEING EXPOSED AS A DISGRACE IN FRONT OF YOUR SON.
THAT'S RIGHT.
A HOKAGE IS A PITIABLE EXISTENCE COMPARED TO WHAT I AM NOW.
ZWW
THE KID'S NOT A TOTAL GOOFBALL...
HE'S CAUGHT ON!

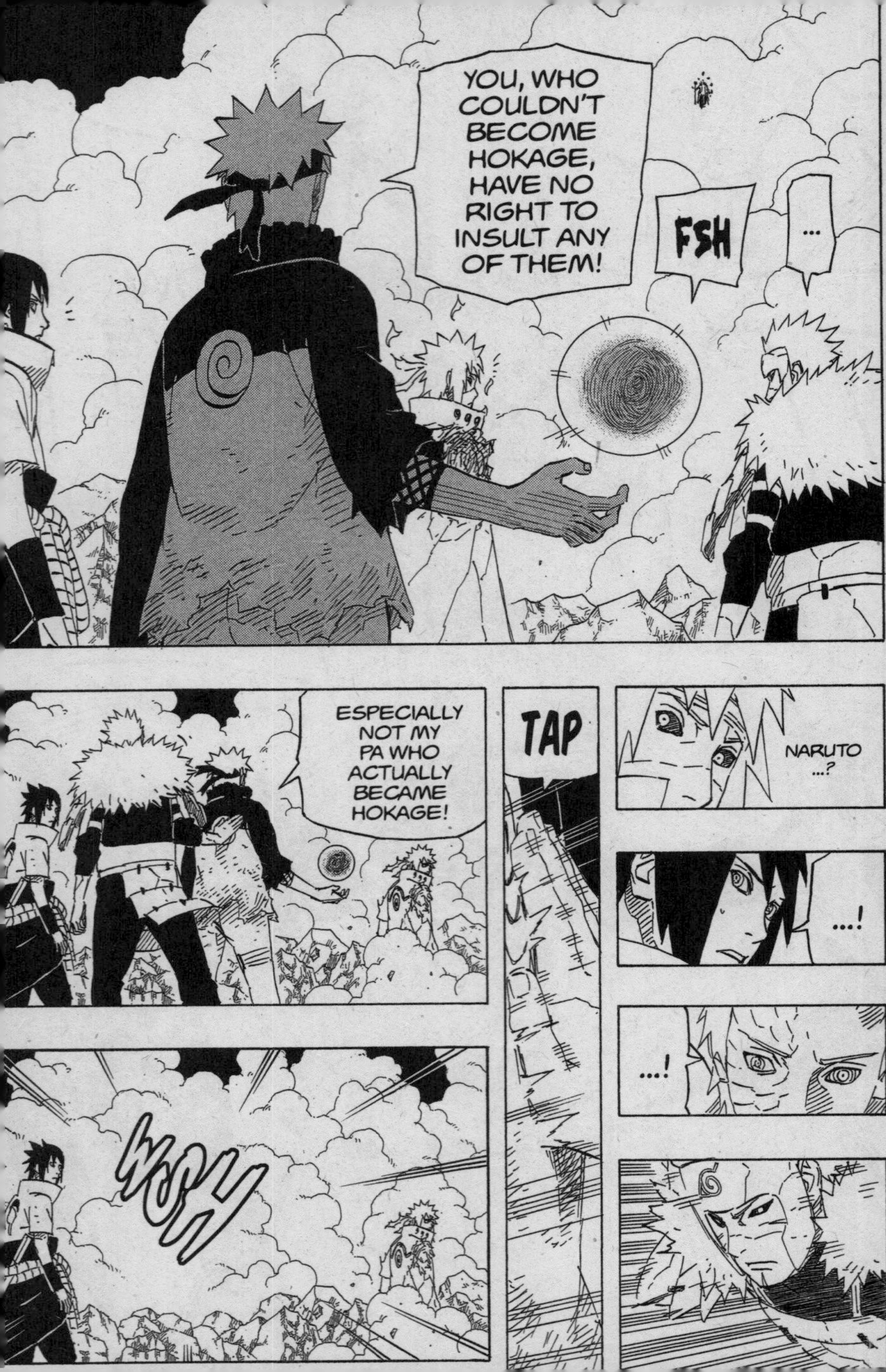
...
FSH
YOU, WHO COULDN'T BECOME HOKAGE, HAVE NO RIGHT TO INSULT ANY OF THEM!
NARUTO ...?
...!
...!
TAP
ESPECIALLY NOT MY PA WHO ACTUALLY BECAME HOKAGE!

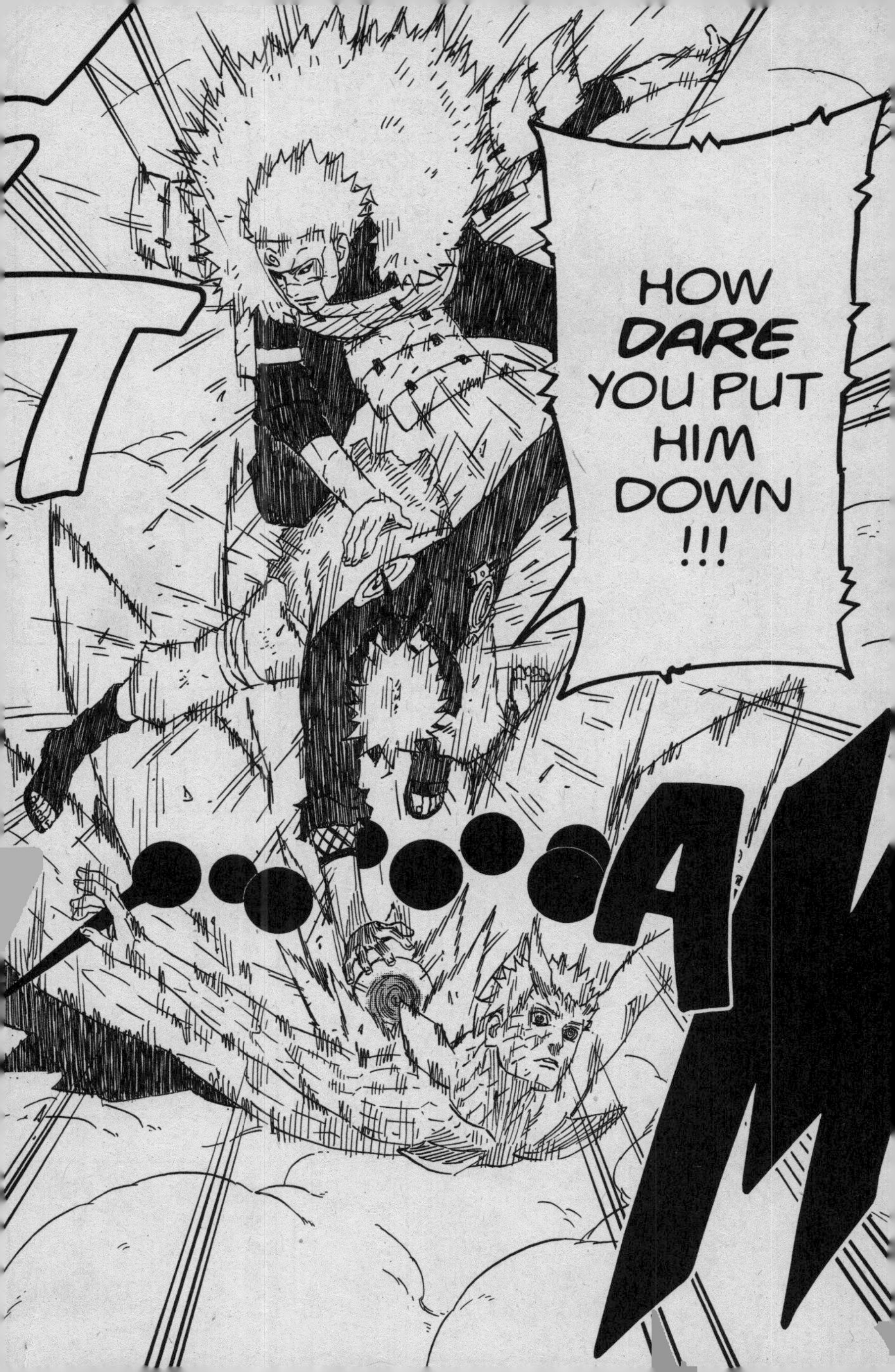
HOW DARE YOU PUT HIM DOWN !!!

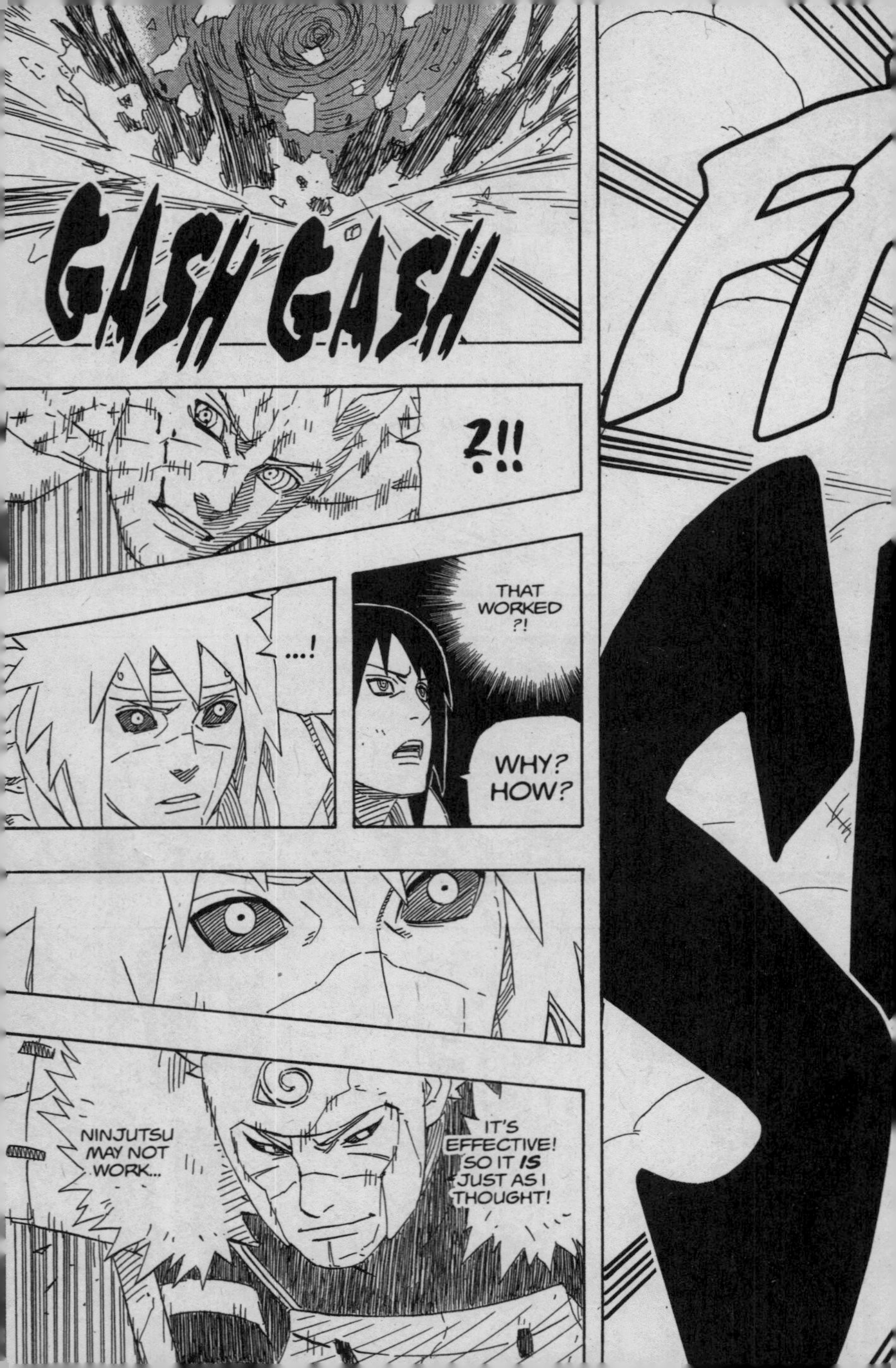

GASH GASH
?!!
THAT WORKED ?!
WHY? HOW?
...!
IT'S EFFECTIVE! SO IT **IS** JUST AS I THOUGHT!
NINJUTSU MAY NOT WORK...

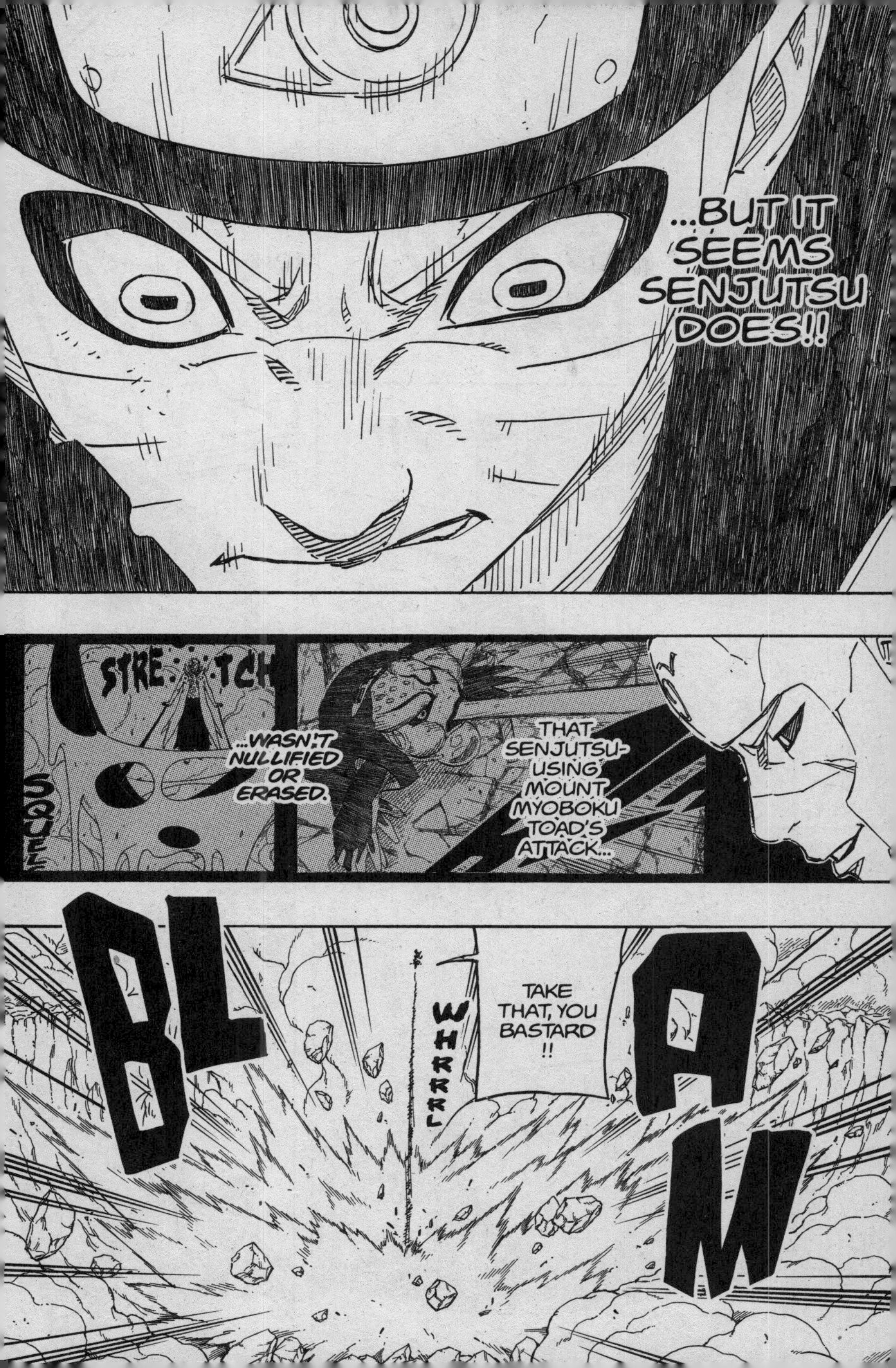
...BUT IT SEEMS SENJUTSU DOES!!
THAT SENJUTSU-USING MOUNT MYOBOKU TOAD'S ATTACK...
STRE TCH
...WASN'T NULLIFIED OR ERASED.
SQUEE
TAKE THAT, YOU BASTARD !!
WHRRRL
BLAM

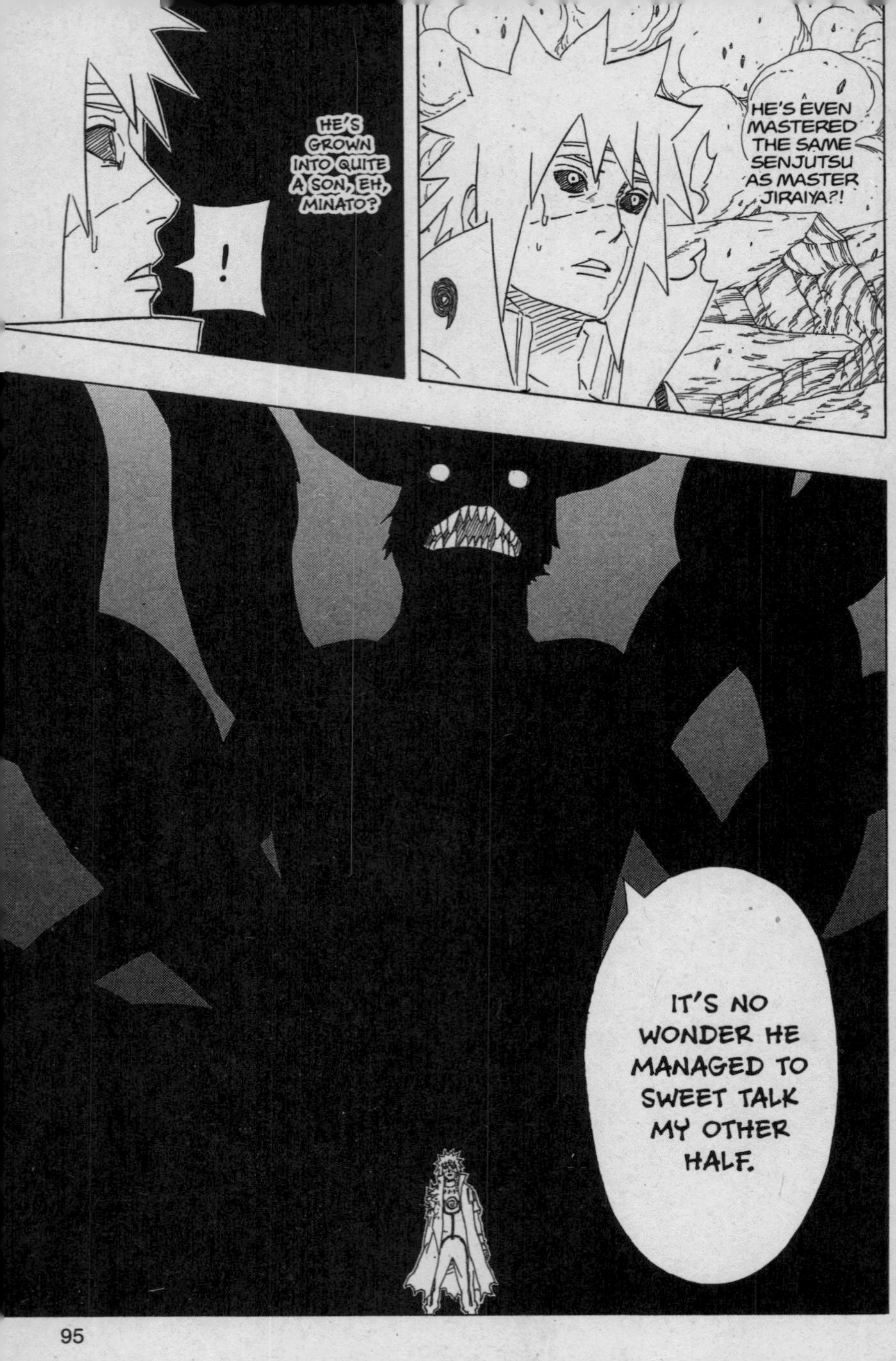
HE'S EVEN MASTERED THE SAME SENJUTSU AS MASTER JIRAIYA?!
HE'S GROWN INTO QUITE A SON, EH, MINATO?
!
IT'S NO WONDER HE MANAGED TO SWEET TALK MY OTHER HALF.

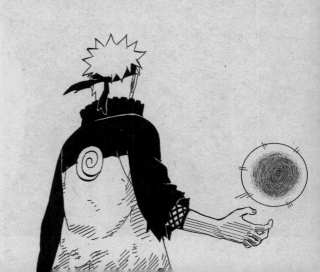

Number 643: Fist Bump

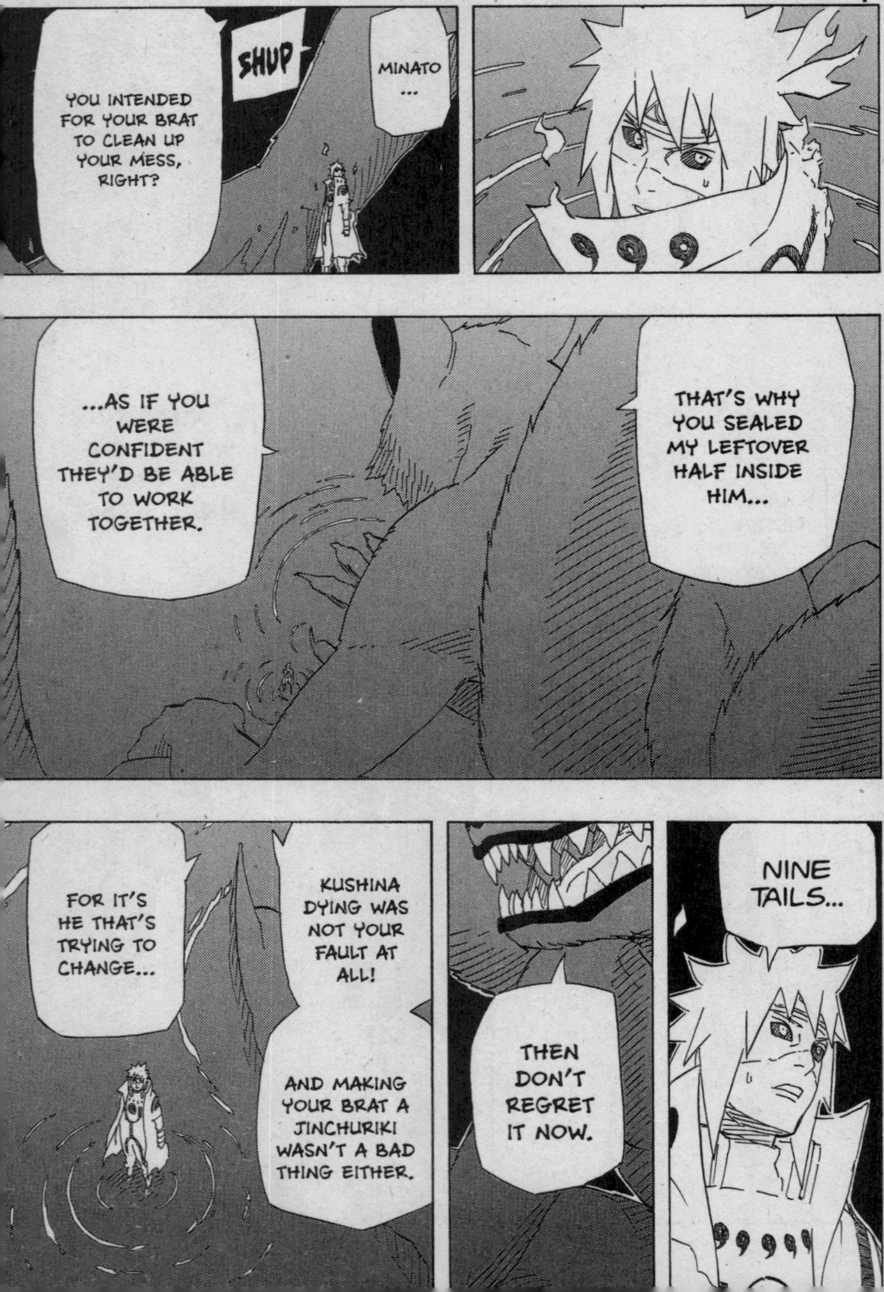
MINATO ...
SHUP
YOU INTENDED FOR YOUR BRAT TO CLEAN UP YOUR MESS, RIGHT?
THAT'S WHY YOU SEALED MY LEFTOVER HALF INSIDE HIM...
...AS IF YOU WERE CONFIDENT THEY'D BE ABLE TO WORK TOGETHER.
NINE TAILS...
THEN DON'T REGRET IT NOW.
KUSHINA DYING WAS NOT YOUR FAULT AT ALL!
AND MAKING YOUR BRAT A JINCHURIKI WASN'T A BAD THING EITHER.
FOR IT'S HE THAT'S TRYING TO CHANGE...

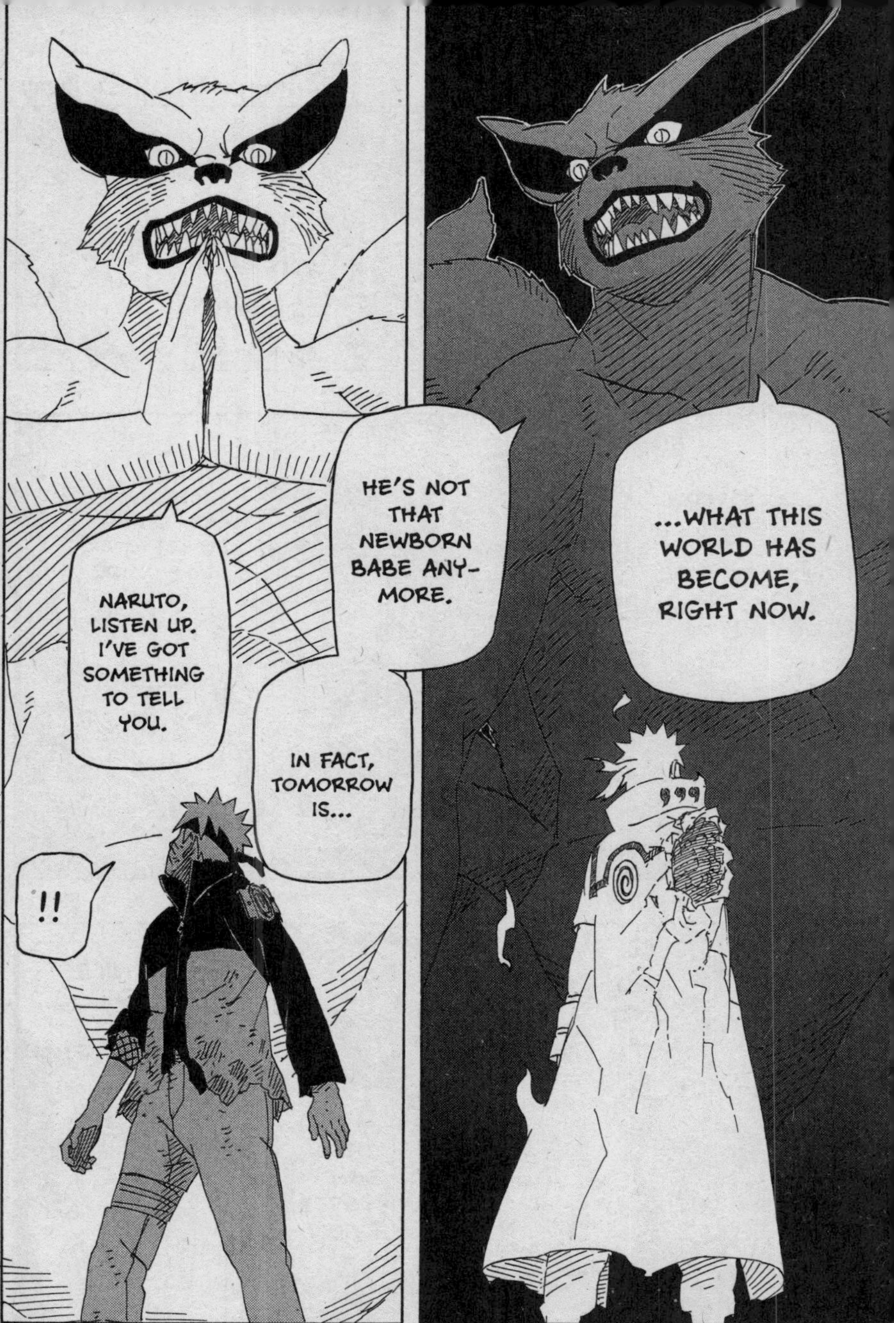
...WHAT THIS WORLD HAS BECOME, RIGHT NOW.
HE'S NOT THAT NEWBORN BABE ANY-MORE.
NARUTO, LISTEN UP. I'VE GOT SOMETHING TO TELL YOU.
IN FACT, TOMORROW IS...
!!

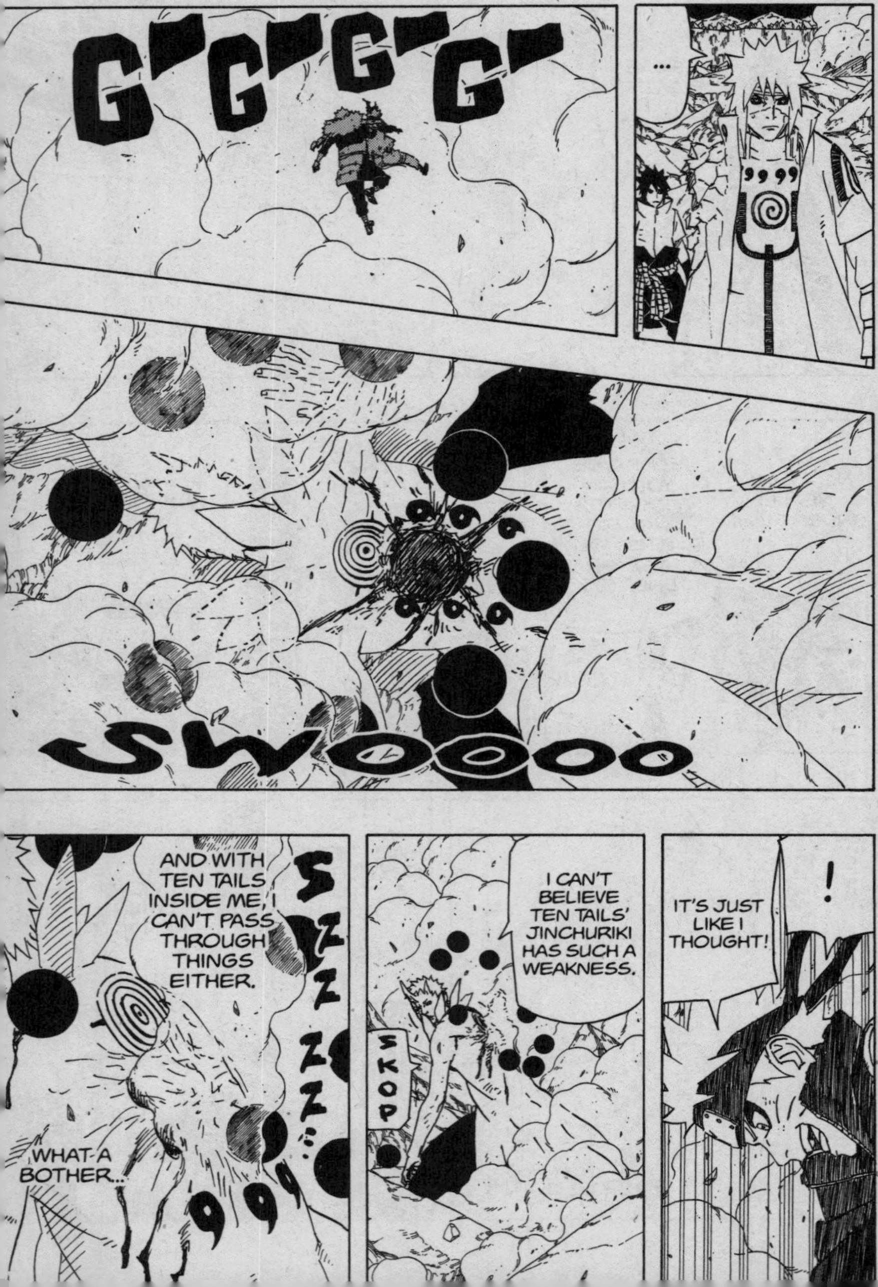
...
G-G-G-G-G
SWOOOO
!
IT'S JUST LIKE I THOUGHT!
I CAN'T BELIEVE TEN TAILS' JINCHURIKI HAS SUCH A WEAKNESS.
SKOP
AND WITH TEN TAILS INSIDE ME, I CAN'T PASS THROUGH THINGS EITHER.
SZZZZZ...
WHAT A BOTHER...

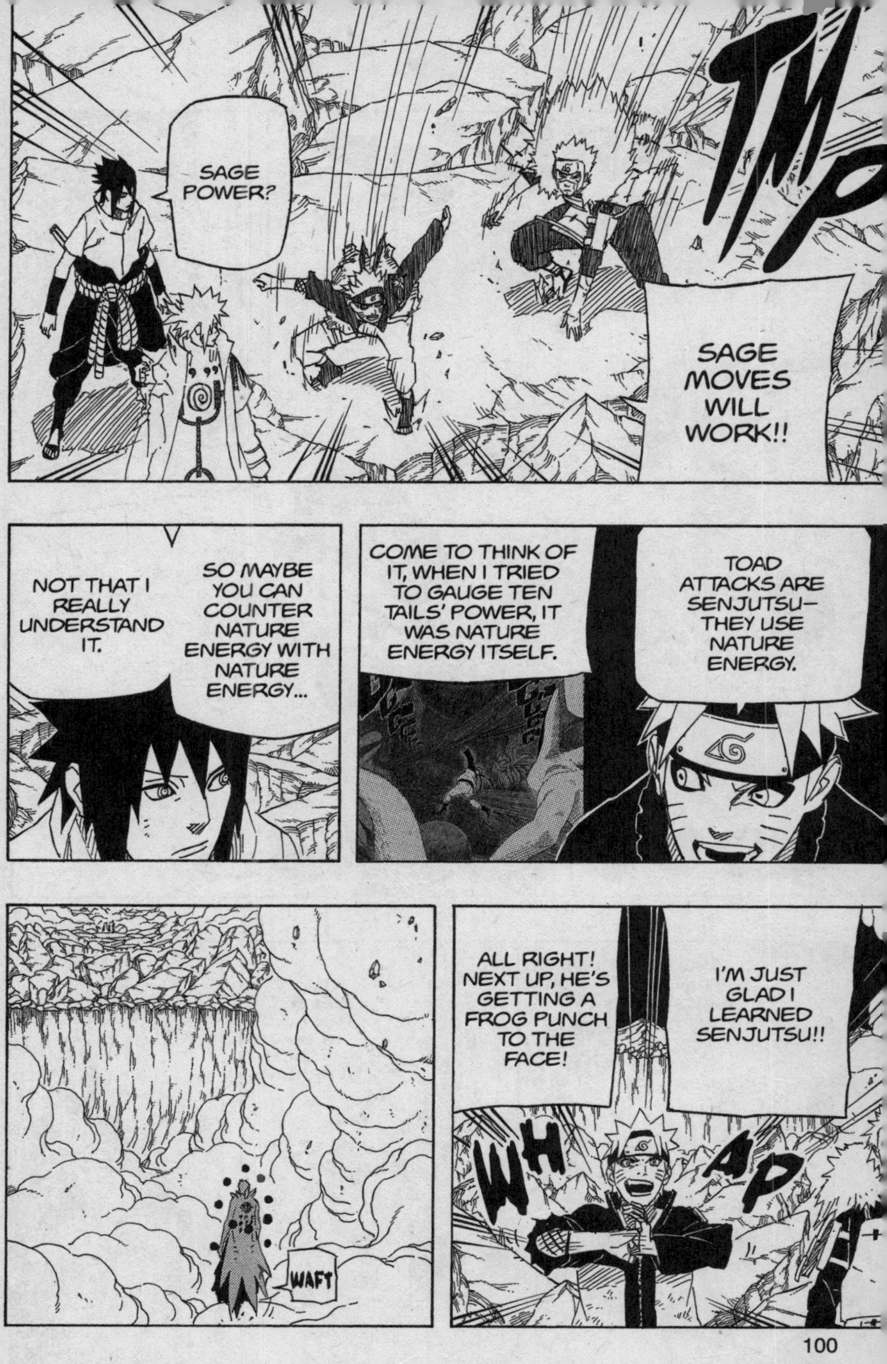
SAGE MOVES WILL WORK!!
SAGE POWER?
TOAD ATTACKS ARE SENJUTSU— THEY USE NATURE ENERGY.
COME TO THINK OF IT, WHEN I TRIED TO GAUGE TEN TAILS' POWER, IT WAS NATURE ENERGY ITSELF.
SO MAYBE YOU CAN COUNTER NATURE ENERGY WITH NATURE ENERGY...
NOT THAT I REALLY UNDERSTAND IT.
I'M JUST GLAD I LEARNED SENJUTSU!!
ALL RIGHT! NEXT UP, HE'S GETTING A FROG PUNCH TO THE FACE!
WHAP
WAFT

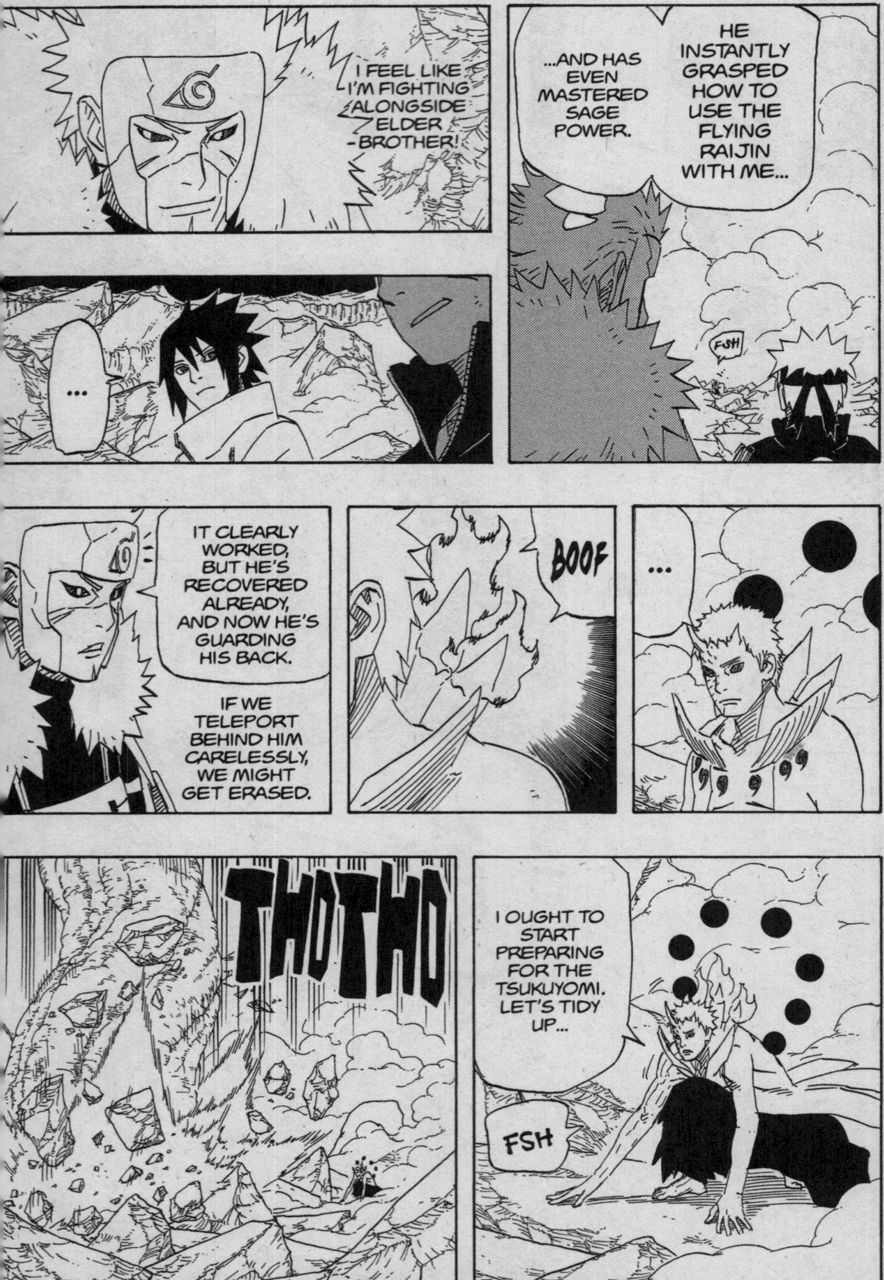
HE INSTANTLY GRASPED HOW TO USE THE FLYING RAIJIN WITH ME...
...AND HAS EVEN MASTERED SAGE POWER.
FSH
I FEEL LIKE I'M FIGHTING ALONGSIDE ELDER BROTHER!
...
...
BOOF
IT CLEARLY WORKED, BUT HE'S RECOVERED ALREADY, AND NOW HE'S GUARDING HIS BACK.
IF WE TELEPORT BEHIND HIM CARELESSLY, WE MIGHT GET ERASED.
I OUGHT TO START PREPARING FOR THE TSUKUYOMI. LET'S TIDY UP...
FSH
THOTHO

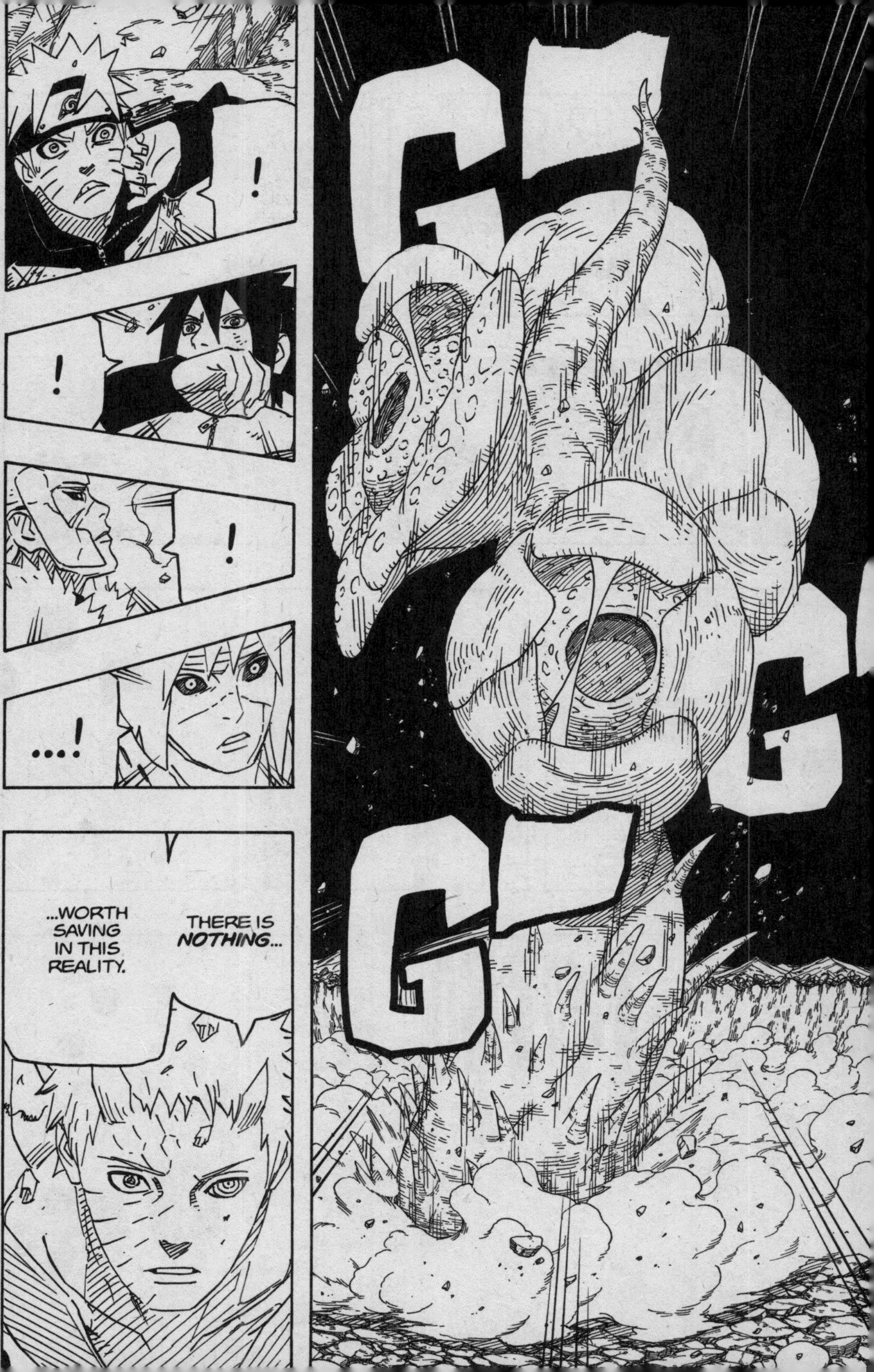
!
!
!
...!
THERE IS *NOTHING*...
...WORTH SAVING IN THIS REALITY.

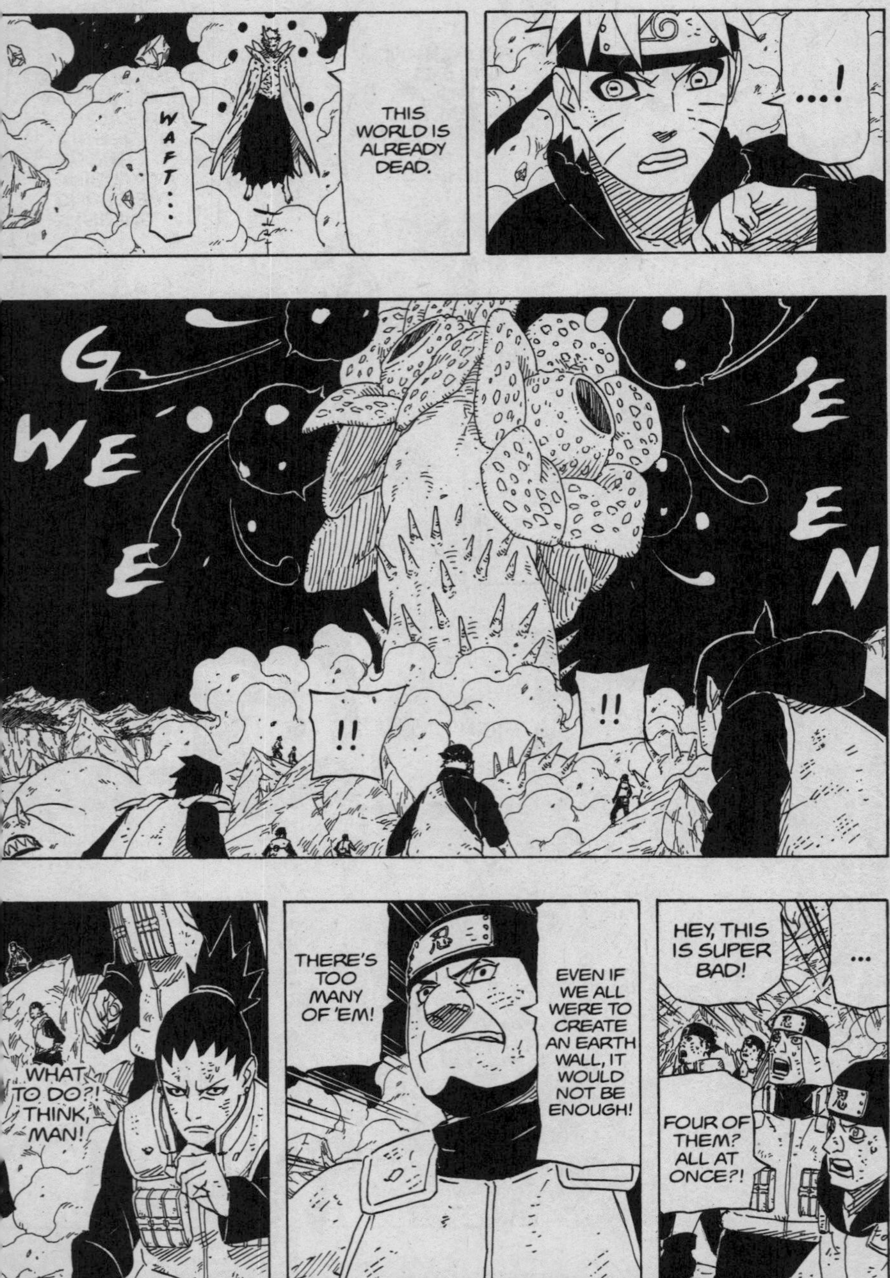

...!
THIS WORLD IS ALREADY DEAD.
WAFT...
GWEEEEN
!!
!!
...
HEY, THIS IS SUPER BAD!
FOUR OF THEM? ALL AT ONCE?!
EVEN IF WE ALL WERE TO CREATE AN EARTH WALL, IT WOULD NOT BE ENOUGH!
THERE'S TOO MANY OF 'EM!
WHAT TO DO?! THINK, MAN!

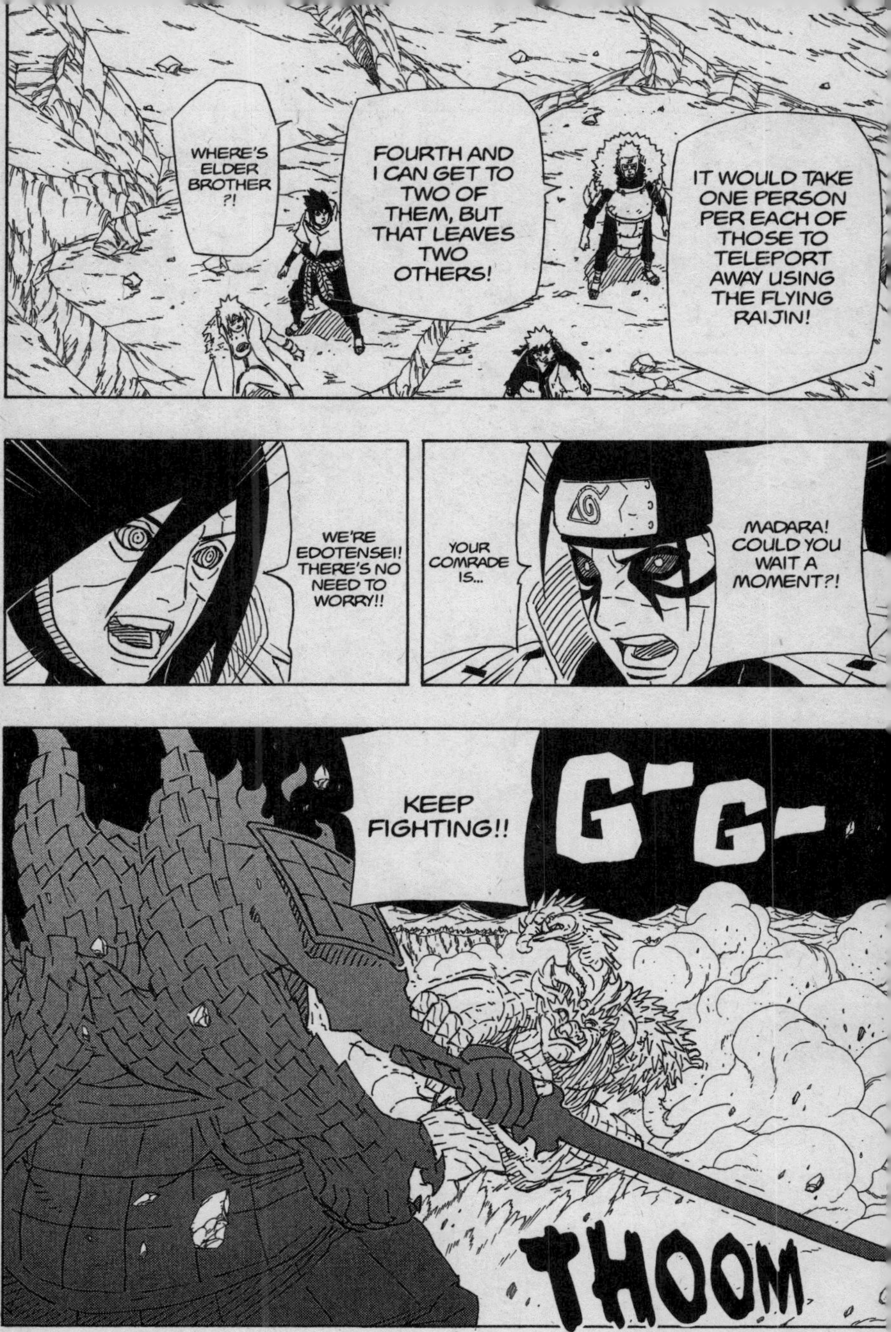
IT WOULD TAKE ONE PERSON PER EACH OF THOSE TO TELEPORT AWAY USING THE FLYING RAIJIN!
FOURTH AND I CAN GET TO TWO OF THEM, BUT THAT LEAVES TWO OTHERS!
WHERE'S ELDER BROTHER ?!
MADARA! COULD YOU WAIT A MOMENT?!
YOUR COMRADE IS...
WE'RE EDOTENSEI! THERE'S NO NEED TO WORRY!!
G-G-
KEEP FIGHTING!!
THOOM

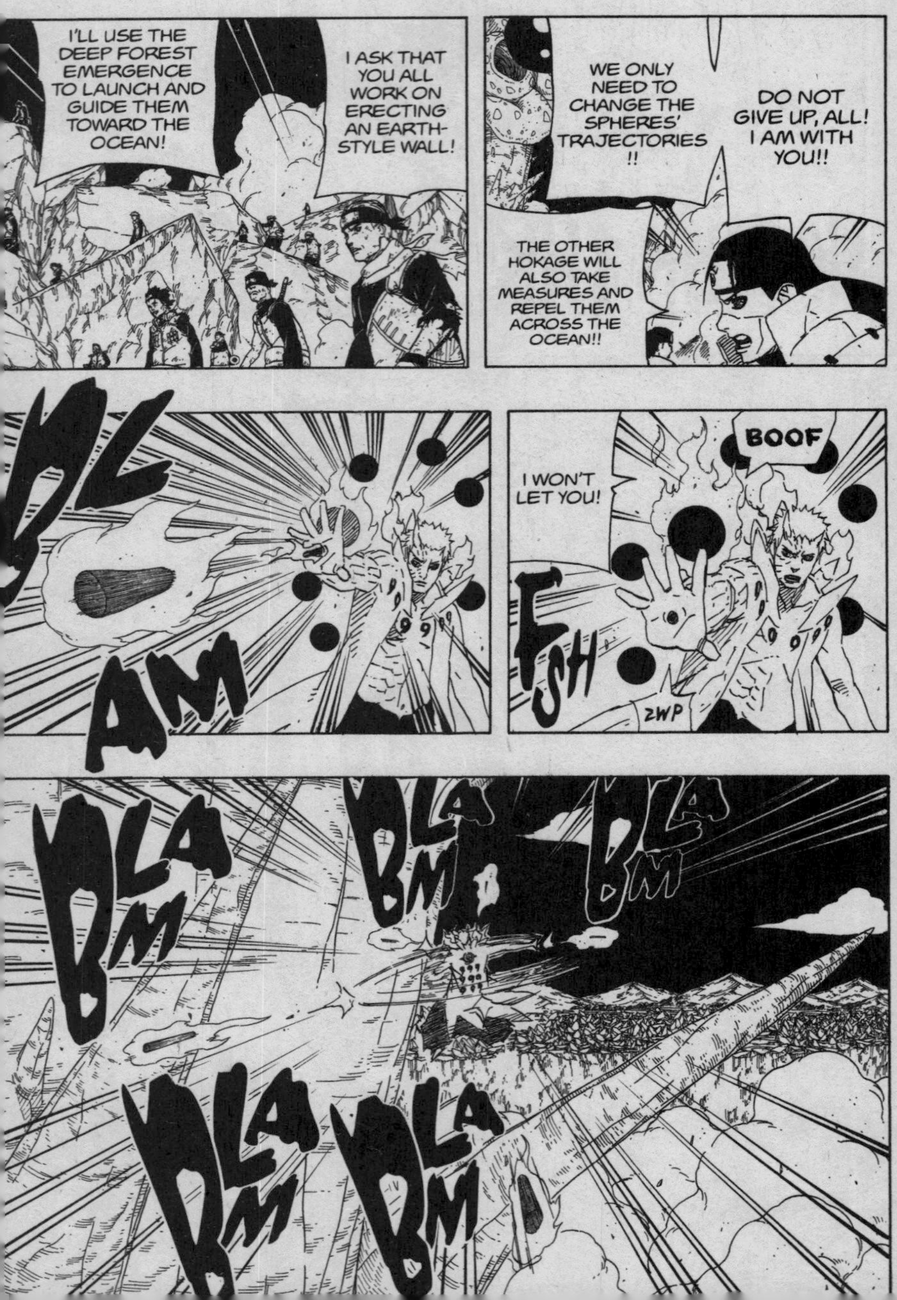
DO NOT GIVE UP, ALL! I AM WITH YOU!!
WE ONLY NEED TO CHANGE THE SPHERES' TRAJECTORIES !!
THE OTHER HOKAGE WILL ALSO TAKE MEASURES AND REPEL THEM ACROSS THE OCEAN!!
I ASK THAT YOU ALL WORK ON ERECTING AN EARTH-STYLE WALL!
I'LL USE THE DEEP FOREST EMERGENCE TO LAUNCH AND GUIDE THEM TOWARD THE OCEAN!
BOOF
I WON'T LET YOU!
FSH
ZWP

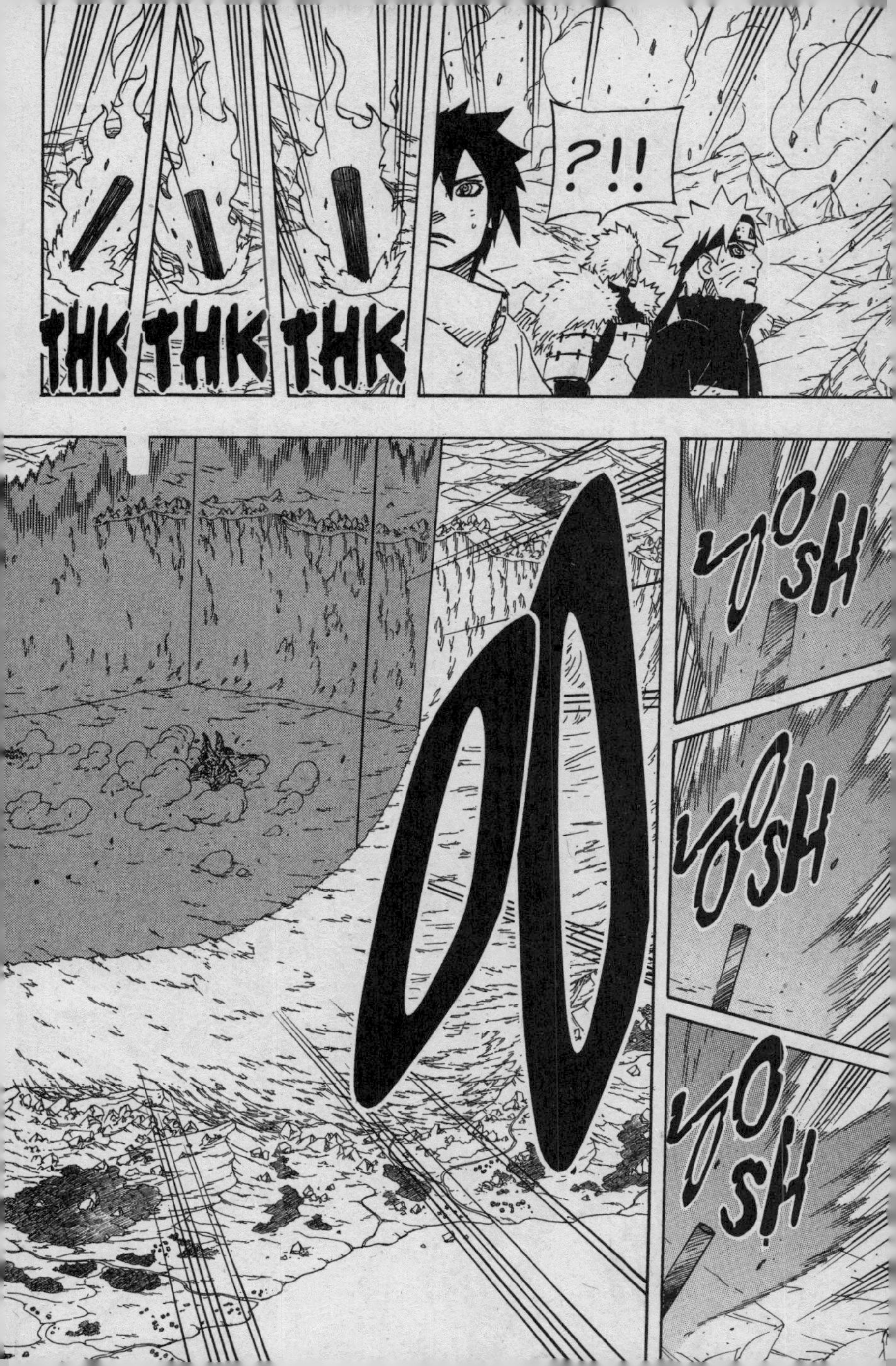
?!!
THK
THK
THK
VOOSH
VOOSH
VOOSH

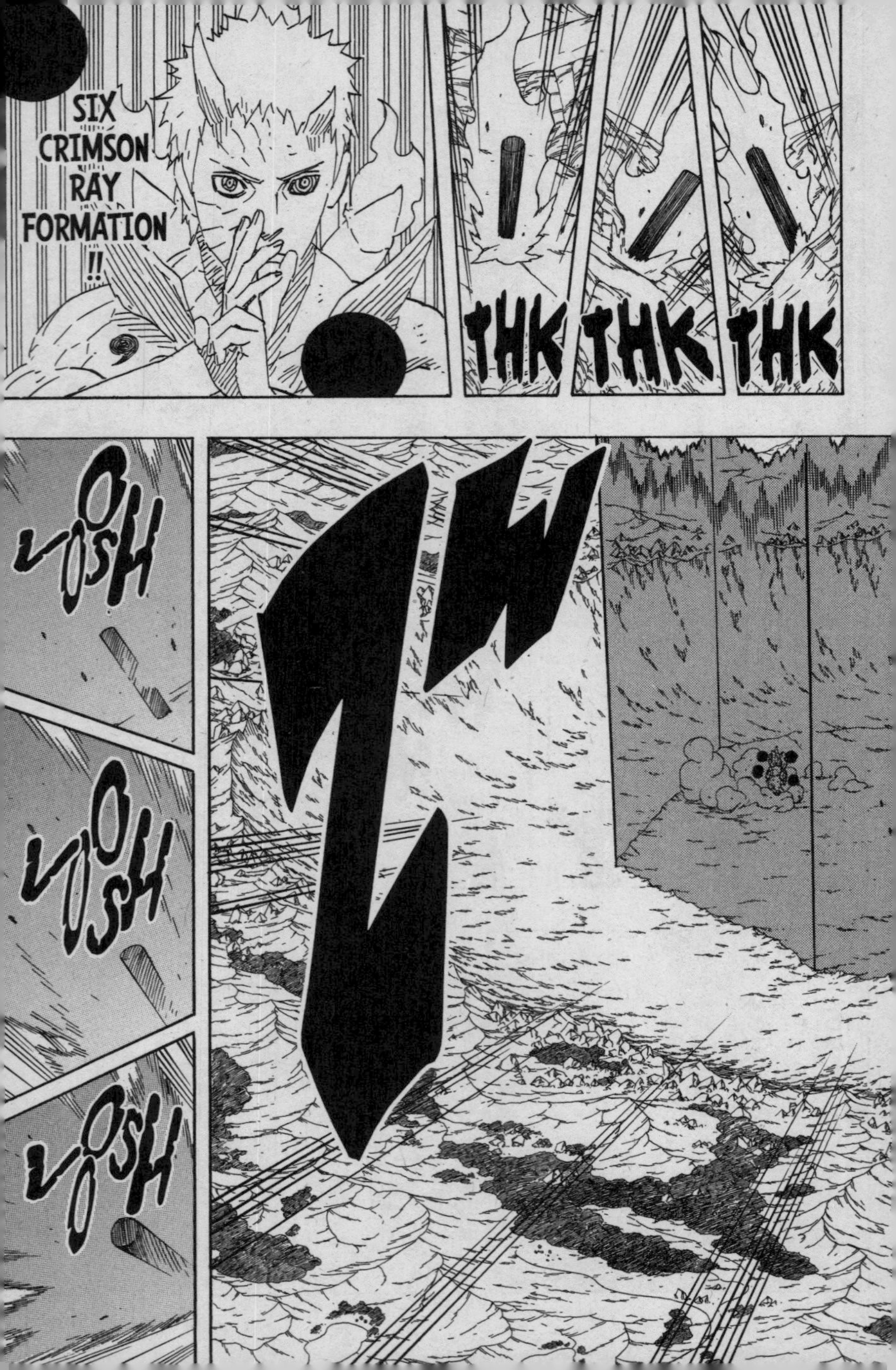
THK
THK
THK
SIX CRIMSON RAY FORMATION!!
VOOSH
VOOSH
VOOSH

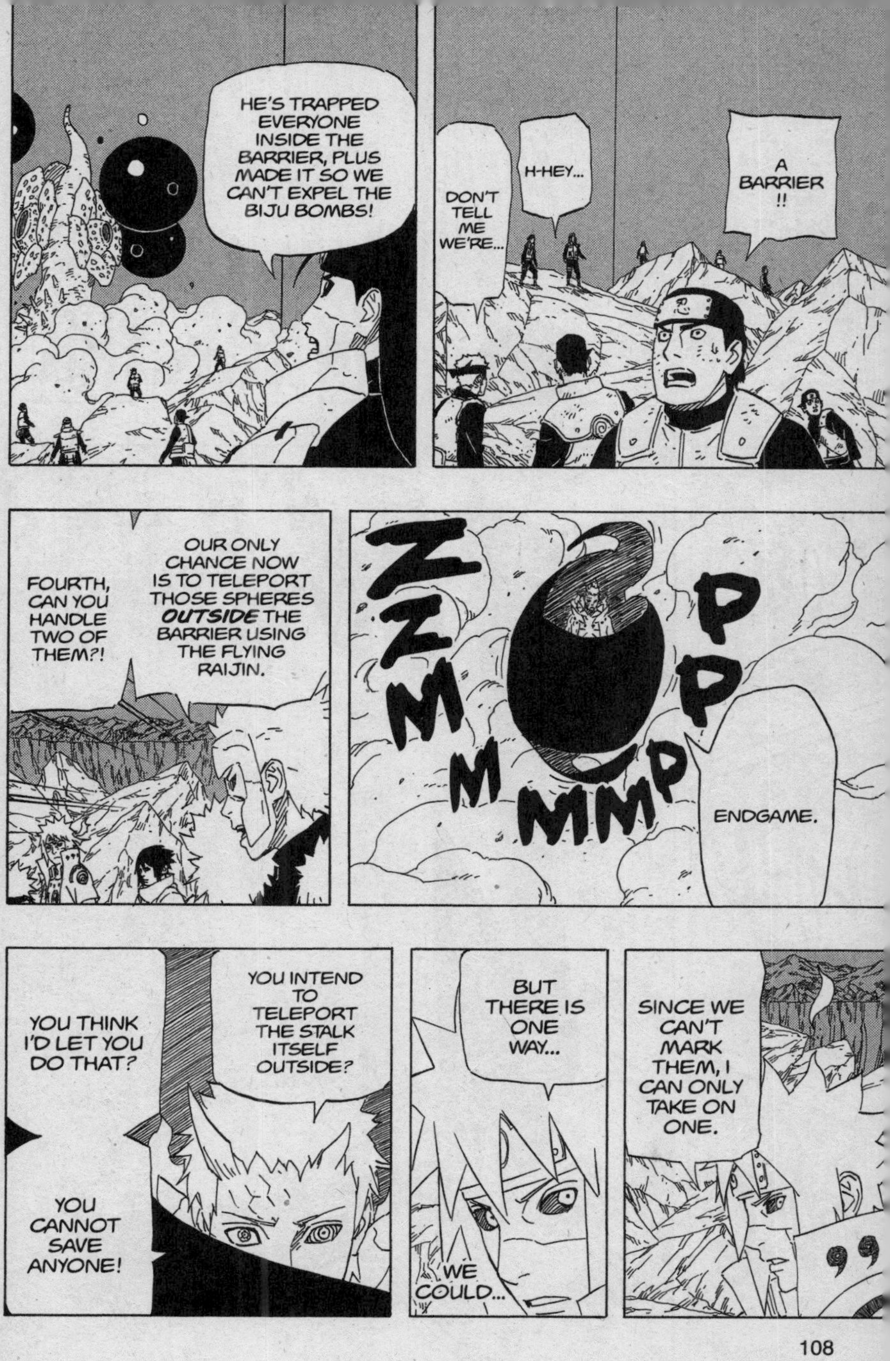
A BARRIER !!
H-HEY...
DON'T TELL ME WE'RE...
HE'S TRAPPED EVERYONE INSIDE THE BARRIER, PLUS MADE IT SO WE CAN'T EXPEL THE BIJU BOMBS!
ZZMMMMMPPP
ENDGAME.
OUR ONLY CHANCE NOW IS TO TELEPORT THOSE SPHERES *OUTSIDE* THE BARRIER USING THE FLYING RAIJIN.
FOURTH, CAN YOU HANDLE TWO OF THEM?!
SINCE WE CAN'T MARK THEM, I CAN ONLY TAKE ON ONE.
BUT THERE IS ONE WAY...
WE COULD...
YOU INTEND TO TELEPORT THE STALK ITSELF OUTSIDE?
YOU THINK I'D LET YOU DO THAT?
YOU CANNOT SAVE ANYONE!

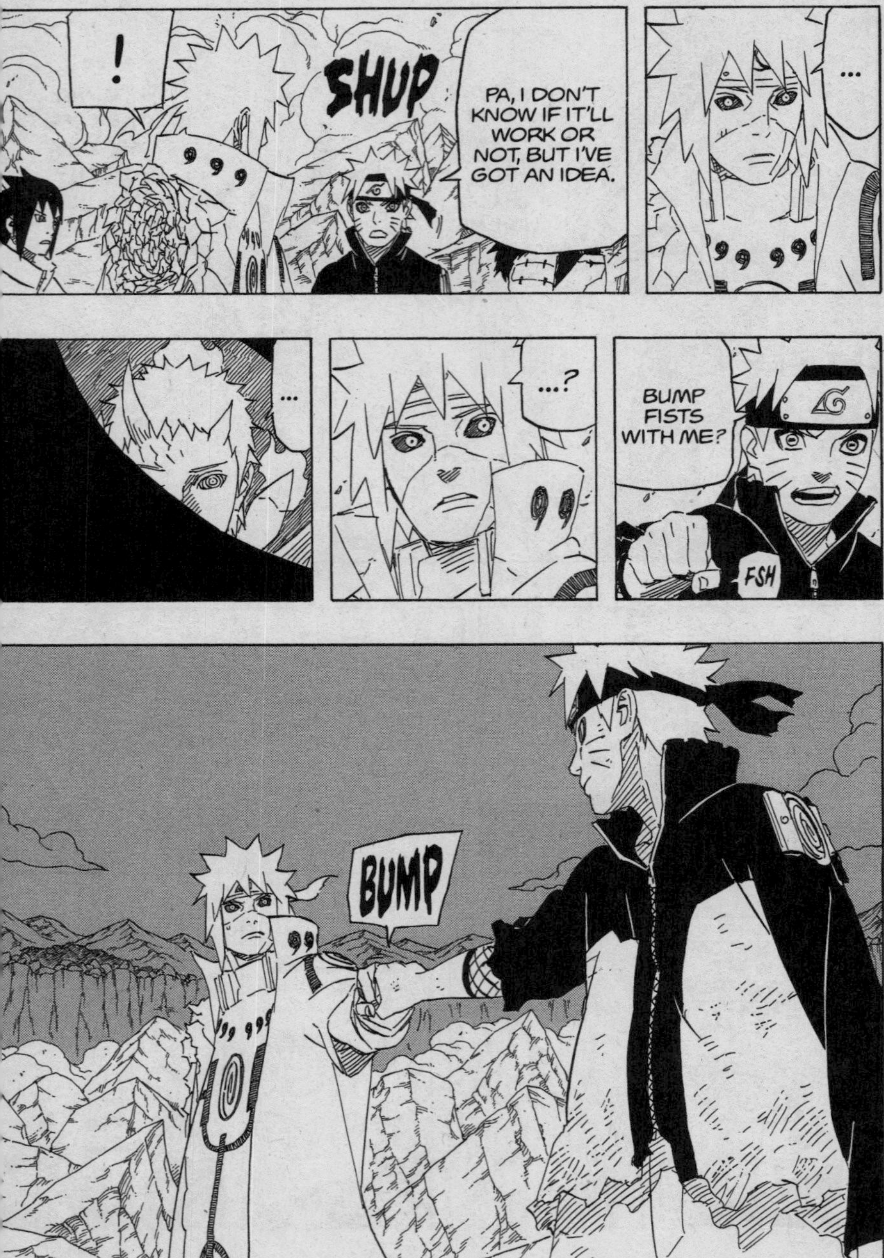
...
PA, I DON'T KNOW IF IT'LL WORK OR NOT, BUT I'VE GOT AN IDEA.
SHUP
!
BUMP FISTS WITH ME?
FSH
...?
...
BUMP

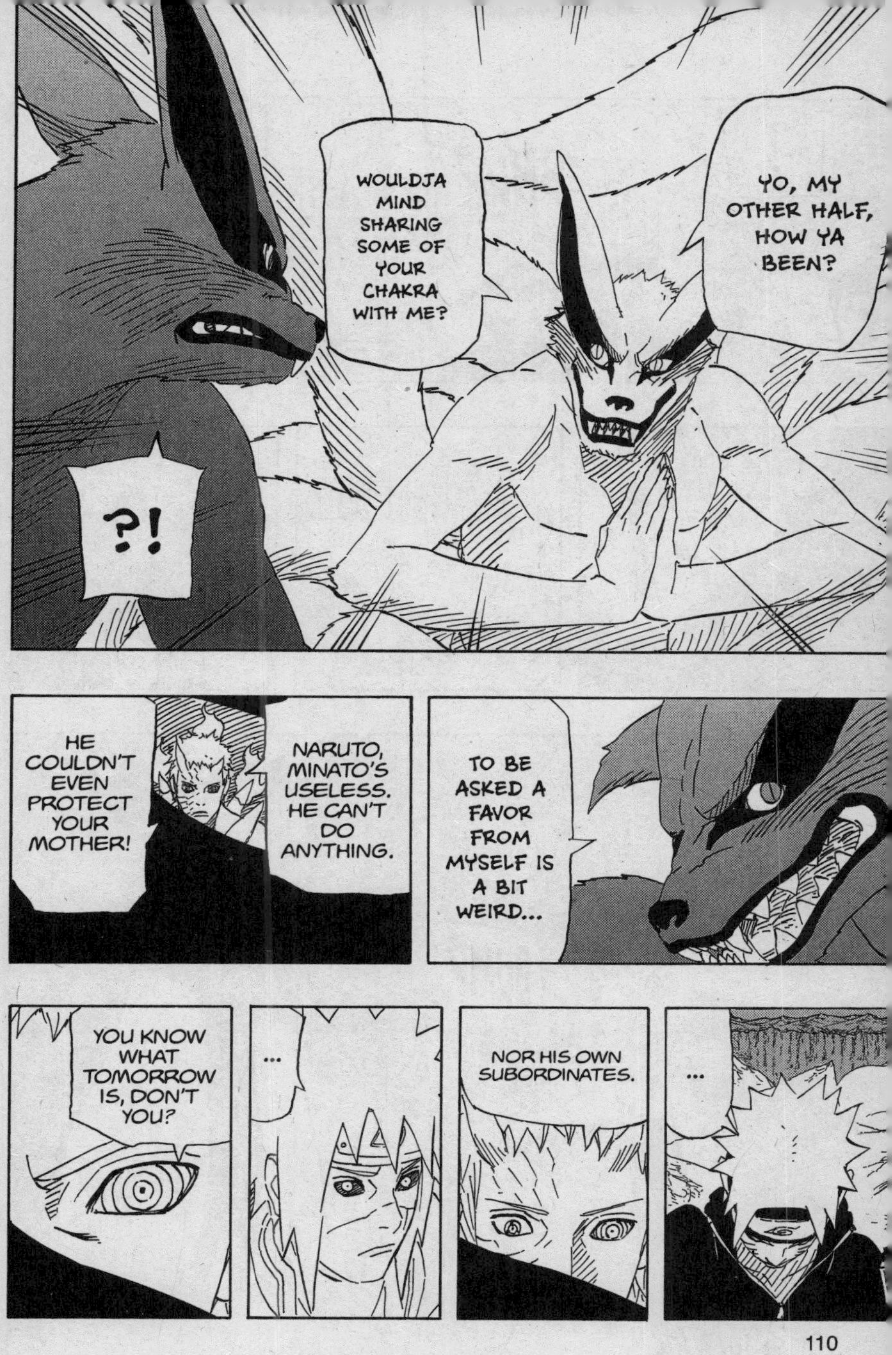

YO, MY OTHER HALF, HOW YA BEEN?
WOULDJA MIND SHARING SOME OF YOUR CHAKRA WITH ME?
?!
TO BE ASKED A FAVOR FROM MYSELF IS A BIT WEIRD...
NARUTO, MINATO'S USELESS. HE CAN'T DO ANYTHING.
HE COULDN'T EVEN PROTECT YOUR MOTHER!
...
NOR HIS OWN SUBORDINATES.
...
YOU KNOW WHAT TOMORROW IS, DON'T YOU?

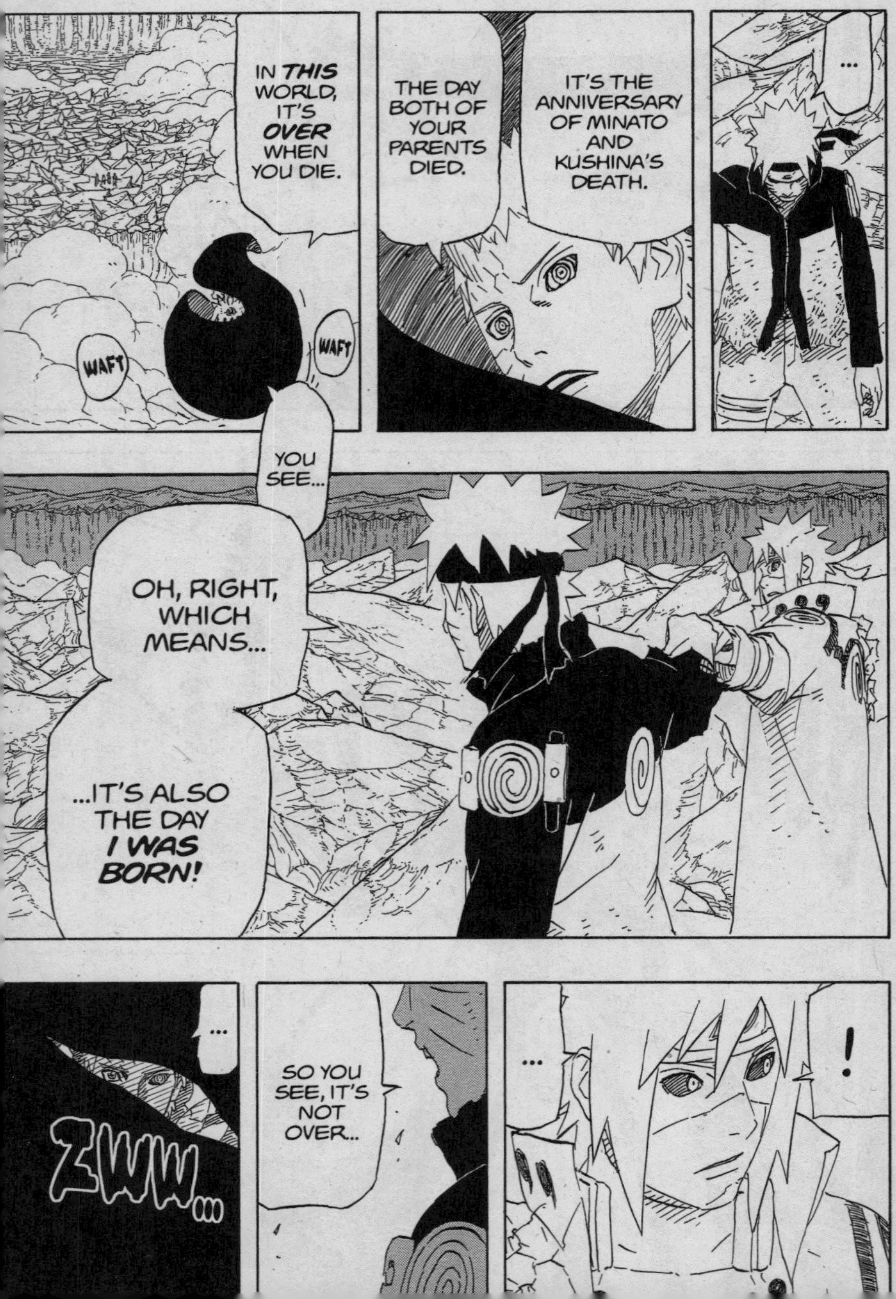
...
IT'S THE ANNIVERSARY OF MINATO AND KUSHINA'S DEATH.
THE DAY BOTH OF YOUR PARENTS DIED.
IN THIS WORLD, IT'S OVER WHEN YOU DIE.
WAFT
WAFT
YOU SEE...
OH, RIGHT, WHICH MEANS...
...IT'S ALSO THE DAY I WAS BORN!
!
...
SO YOU SEE, IT'S NOT OVER...
...
ZWW...

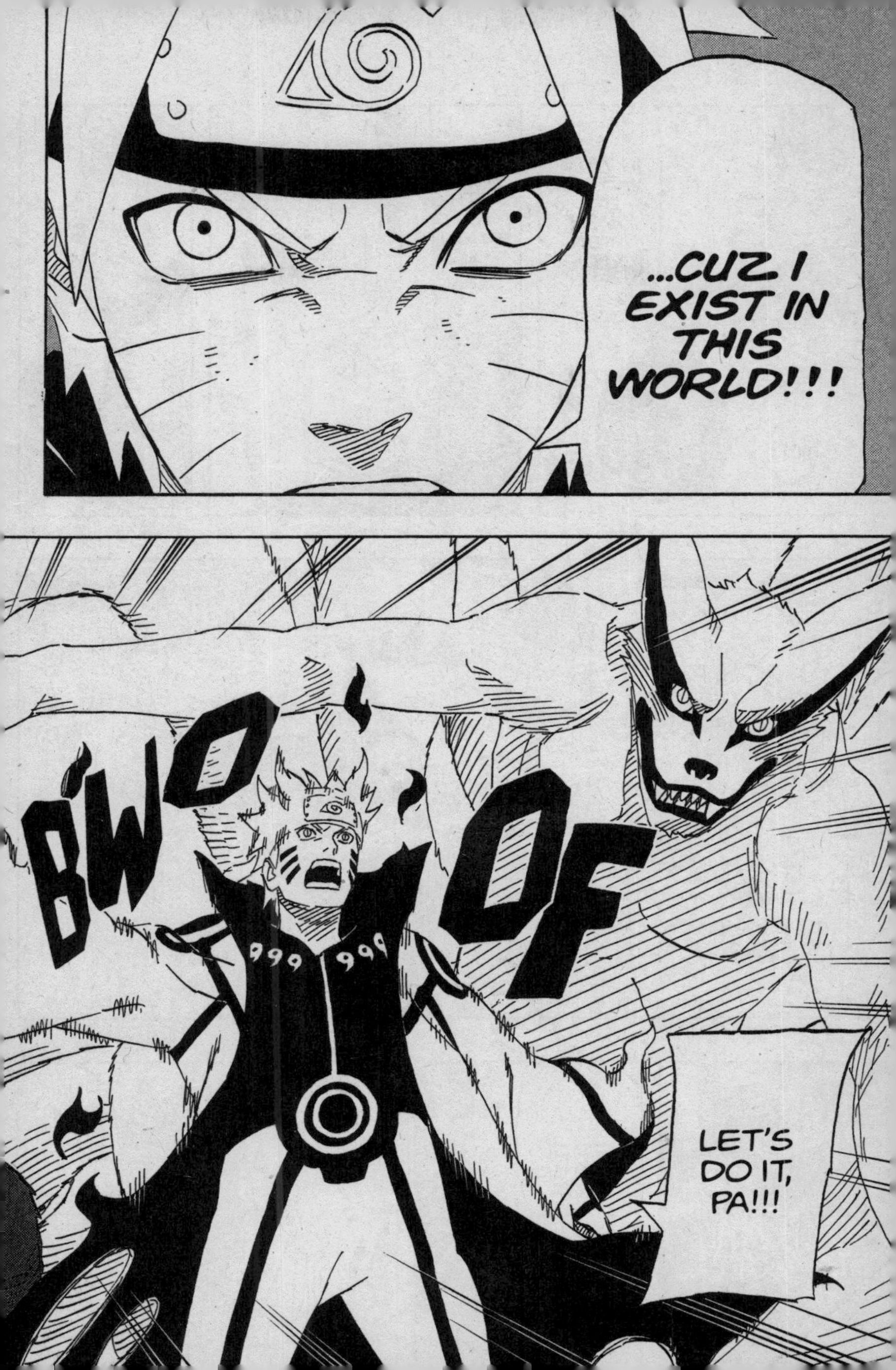
...CUZ I EXIST IN THIS WORLD!!!
BWOOF
LET'S DO IT, PA!!!

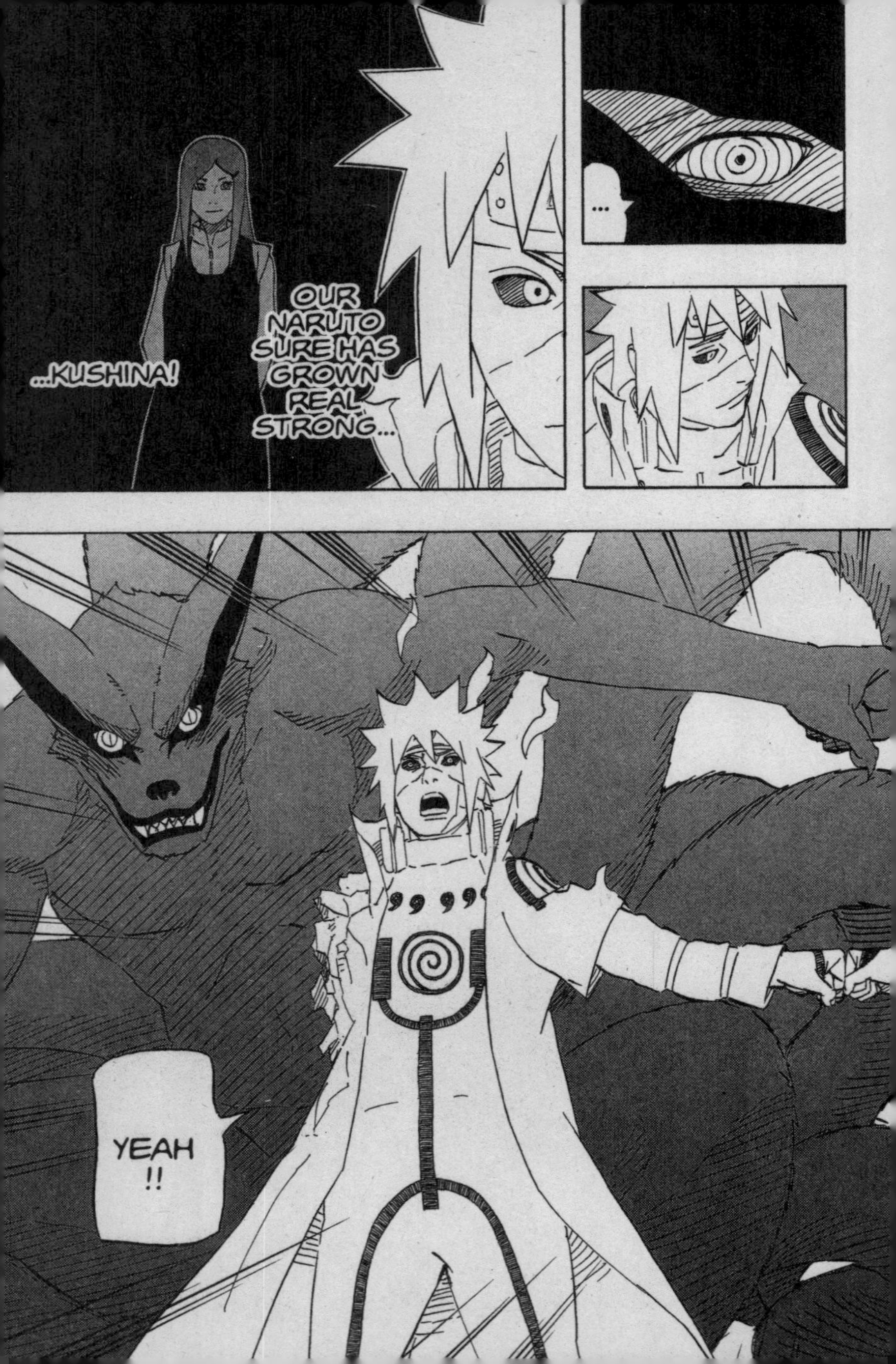
...
OUR NARUTO SURE HAS GROWN REAL STRONG...
...KUSHINA!
YEAH !!

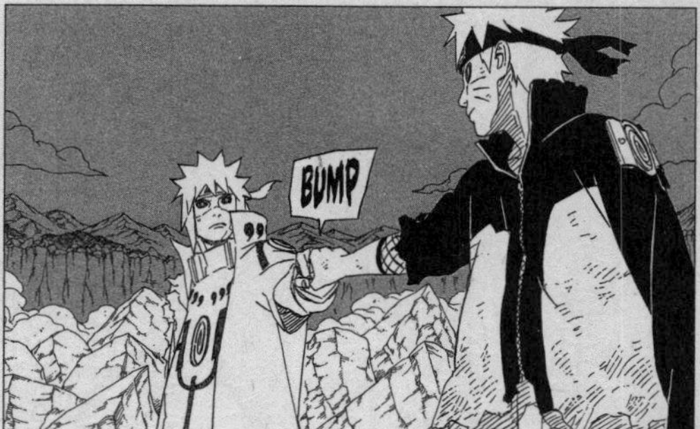
BUMP

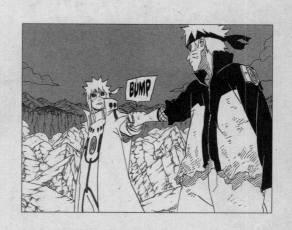

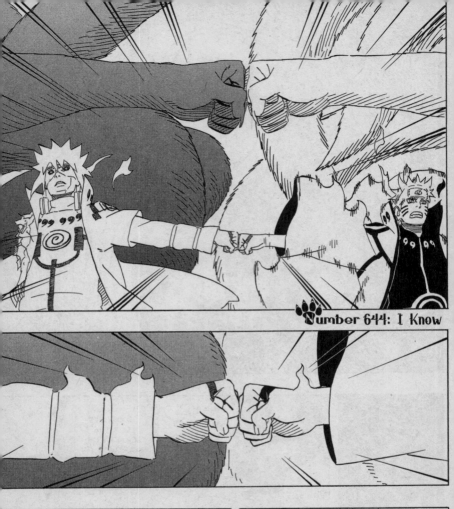

Number 644: I Know

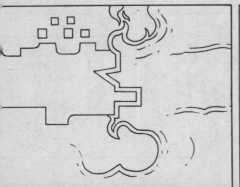

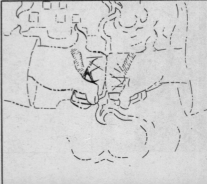

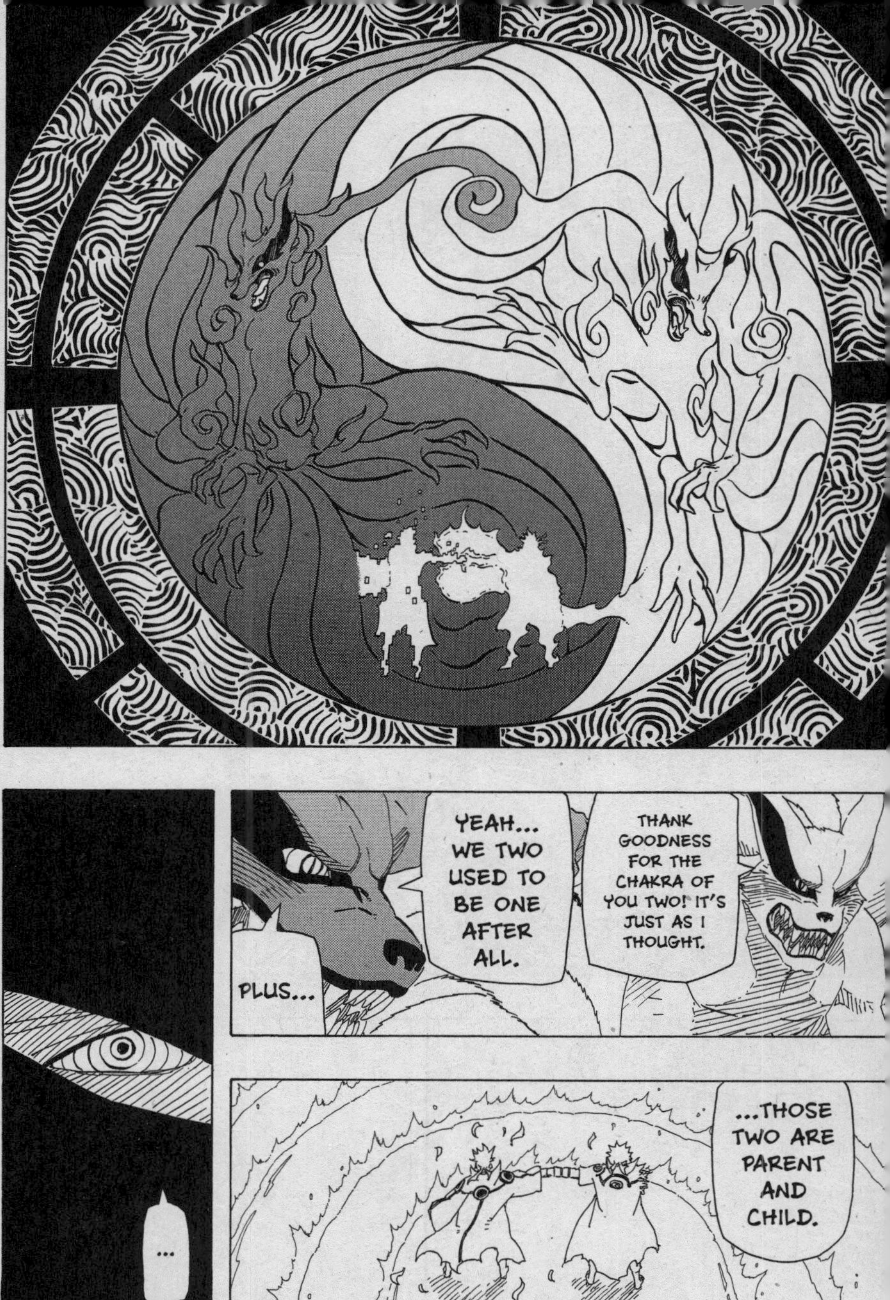
THANK GOODNESS FOR THE CHAKRA OF YOU TWO! IT'S JUST AS I THOUGHT.
YEAH... WE TWO USED TO BE ONE AFTER ALL.
PLUS...
...THOSE TWO ARE PARENT AND CHILD.
...

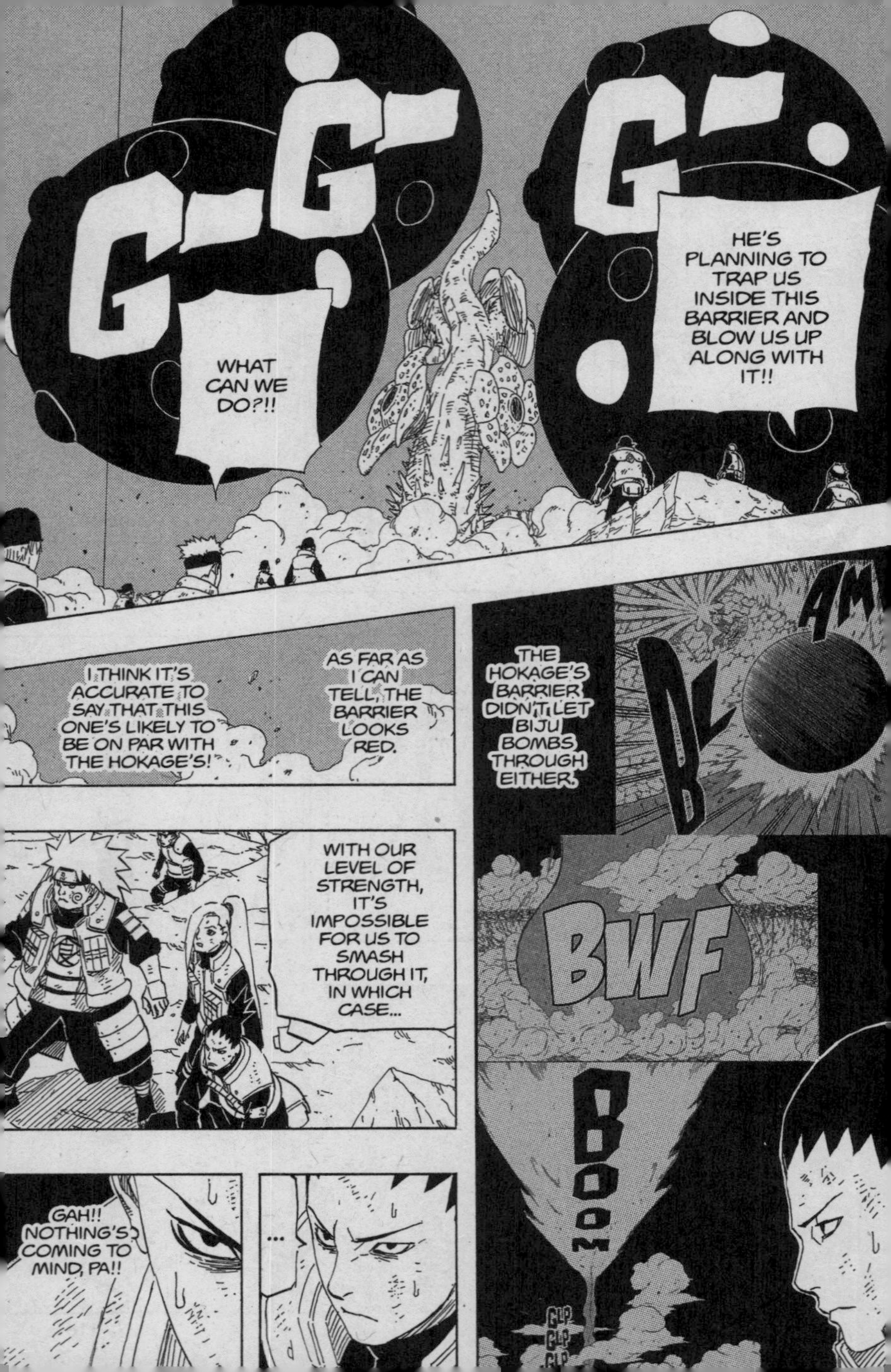

G-G-G-
HE'S PLANNING TO TRAP US INSIDE THIS BARRIER AND BLOW US UP ALONG WITH IT!!
WHAT CAN WE DO?!!
BLAM
THE HOKAGE'S BARRIER DIDN'T LET BIJU BOMBS THROUGH EITHER.
AS FAR AS I CAN TELL, THE BARRIER LOOKS RED.
I THINK IT'S ACCURATE TO SAY THAT THIS ONE'S LIKELY TO BE ON PAR WITH THE HOKAGE'S!
BWF
WITH OUR LEVEL OF STRENGTH, IT'S IMPOSSIBLE FOR US TO SMASH THROUGH IT, IN WHICH CASE...
BOOM
GLP GLP GLP
...
GAH!! NOTHING'S COMING TO MIND, PA!!

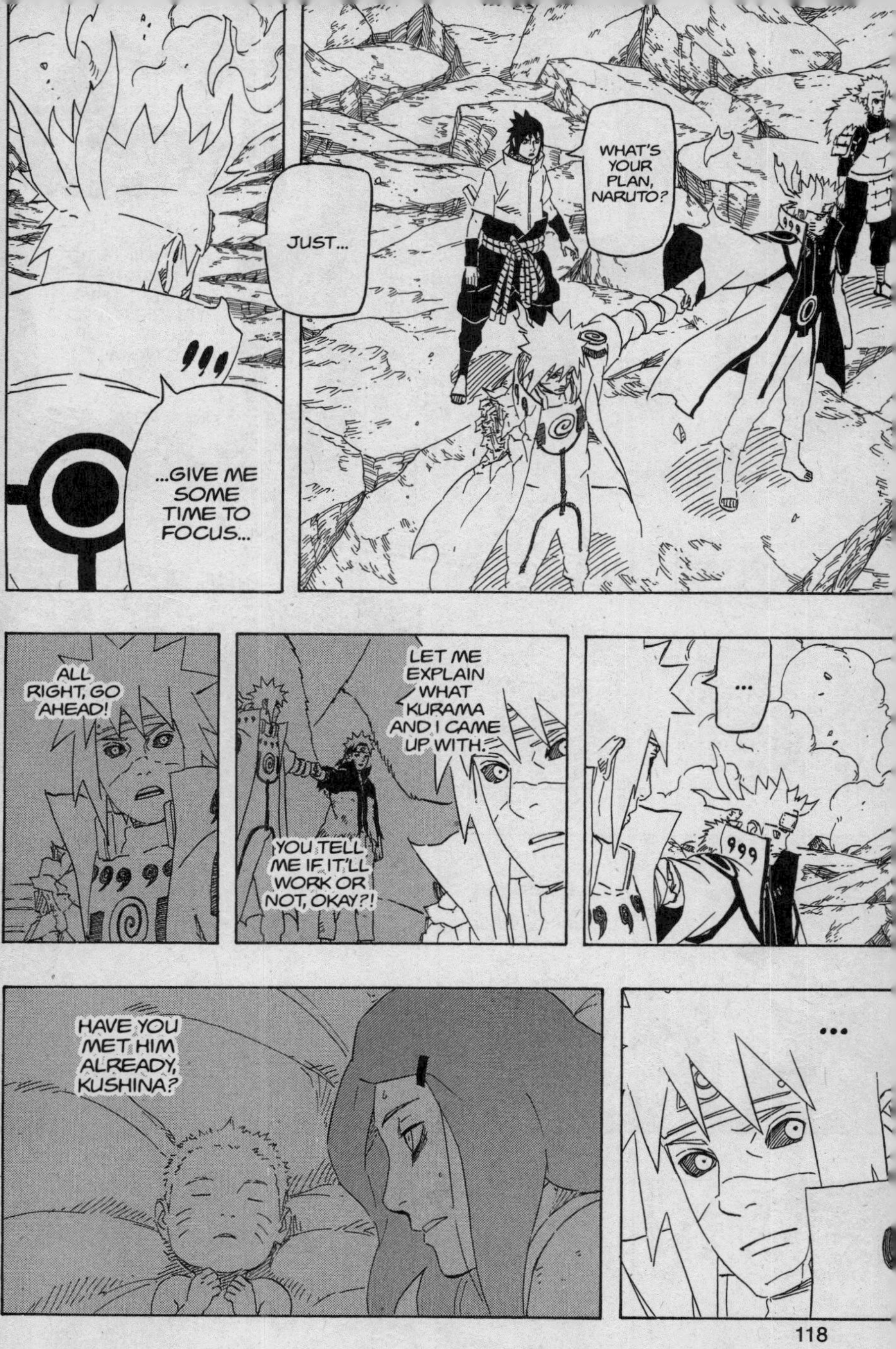
WHAT'S YOUR PLAN, NARUTO?
JUST...
...GIVE ME SOME TIME TO FOCUS...
...
LET ME EXPLAIN WHAT KURAMA AND I CAME UP WITH.
YOU TELL ME IF IT'LL WORK OR NOT, OKAY?!
ALL RIGHT, GO AHEAD!
...
HAVE YOU MET HIM ALREADY, KUSHINA?

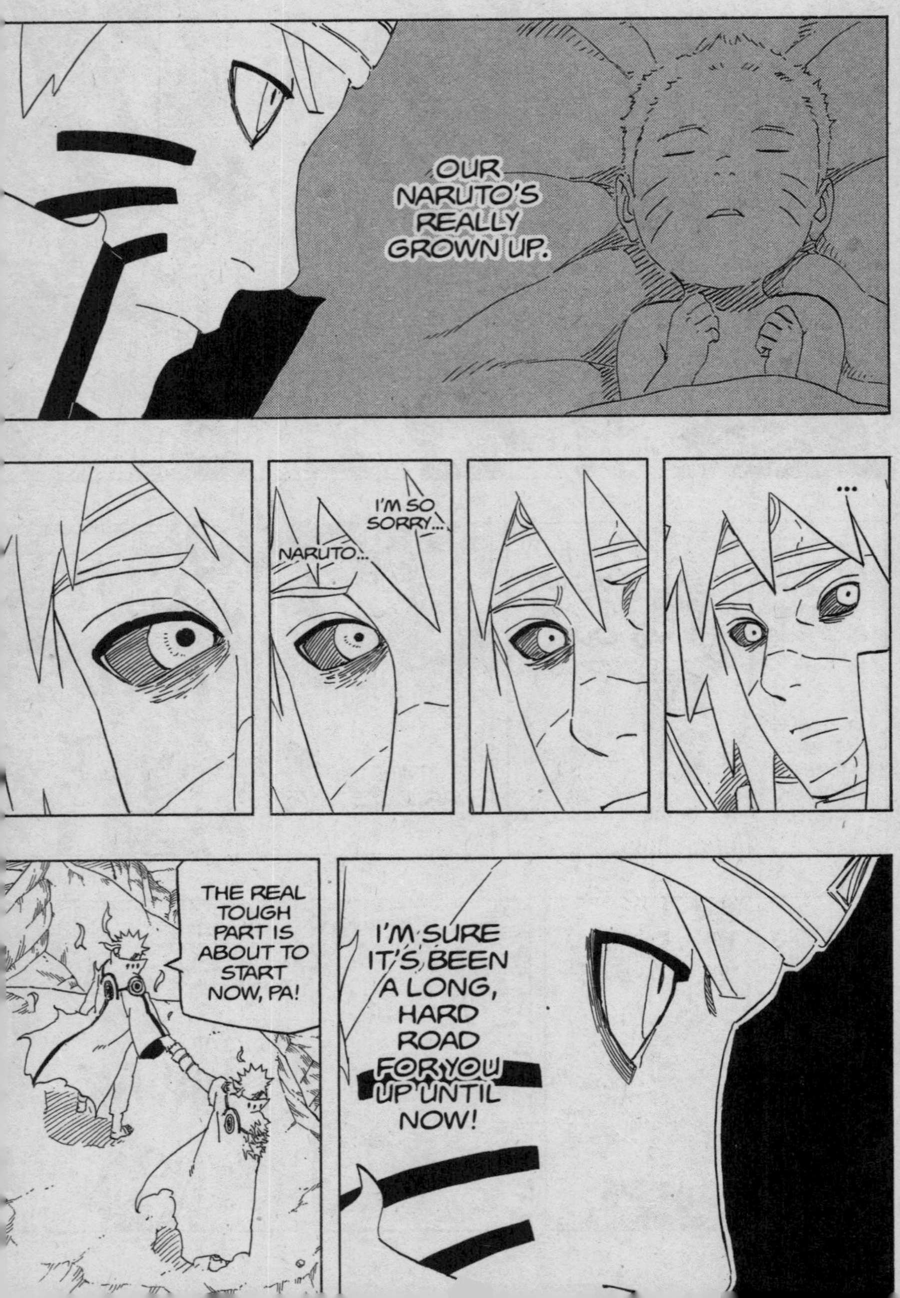
OUR NARUTO'S REALLY GROWN UP.
...
I'M SO SORRY...
NARUTO...
I'M SURE IT'S BEEN A LONG, HARD ROAD FOR YOU UP UNTIL NOW!
THE REAL TOUGH PART IS ABOUT TO START NOW, PA!

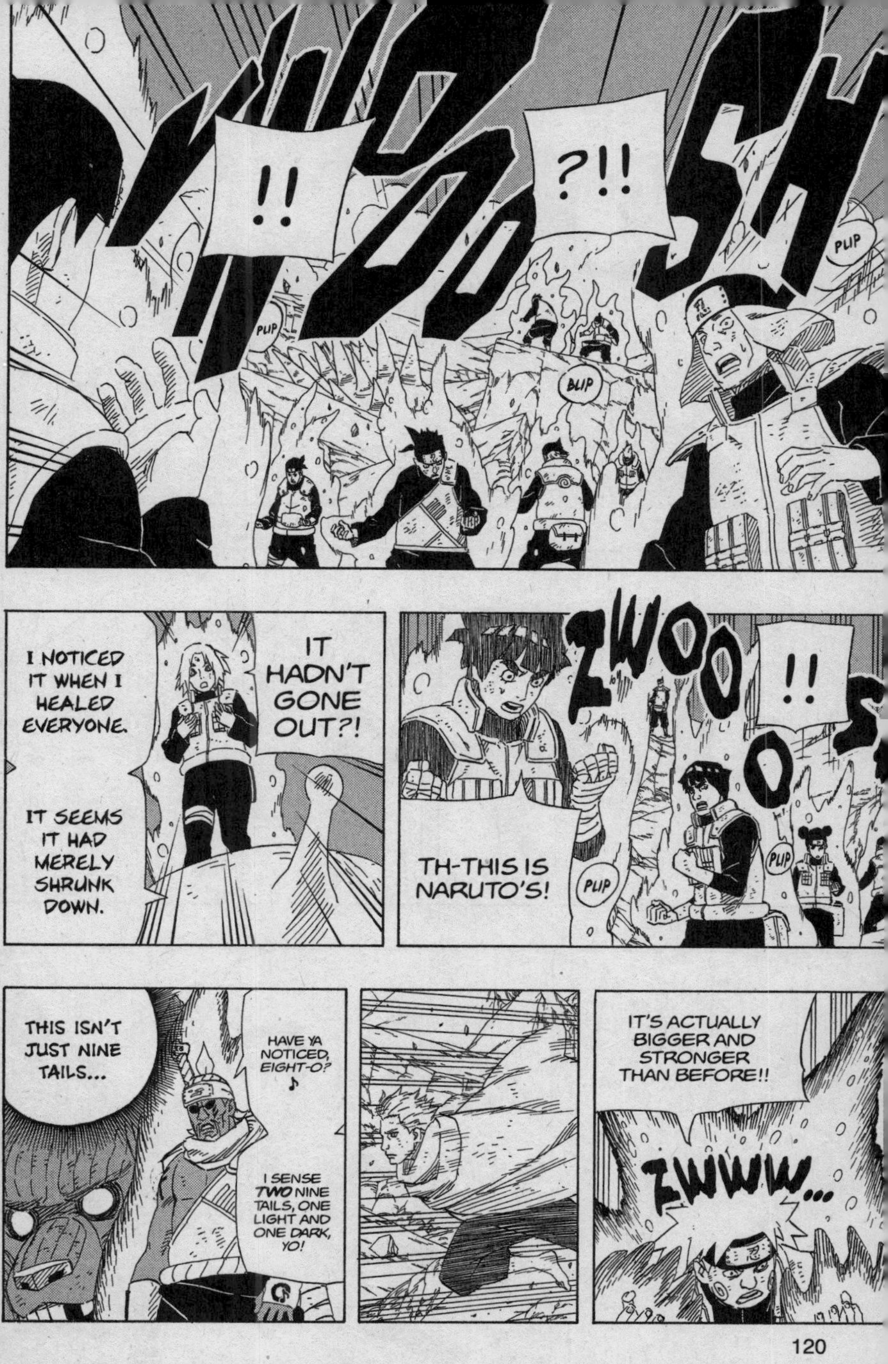
?!!
!!
PLIP
BLIP
PLIP
!!
TH-THIS IS NARUTO'S!
PLIP
PLIP
IT HADN'T GONE OUT?!
I NOTICED IT WHEN I HEALED EVERYONE.
IT SEEMS IT HAD MERELY SHRUNK DOWN.
IT'S ACTUALLY BIGGER AND STRONGER THAN BEFORE!!
ZWWW...
HAVE YA NOTICED, EIGHT-O? ♪
I SENSE *TWO* NINE TAILS, ONE LIGHT AND ONE *DARK*, YO!
THIS ISN'T JUST NINE TAILS...

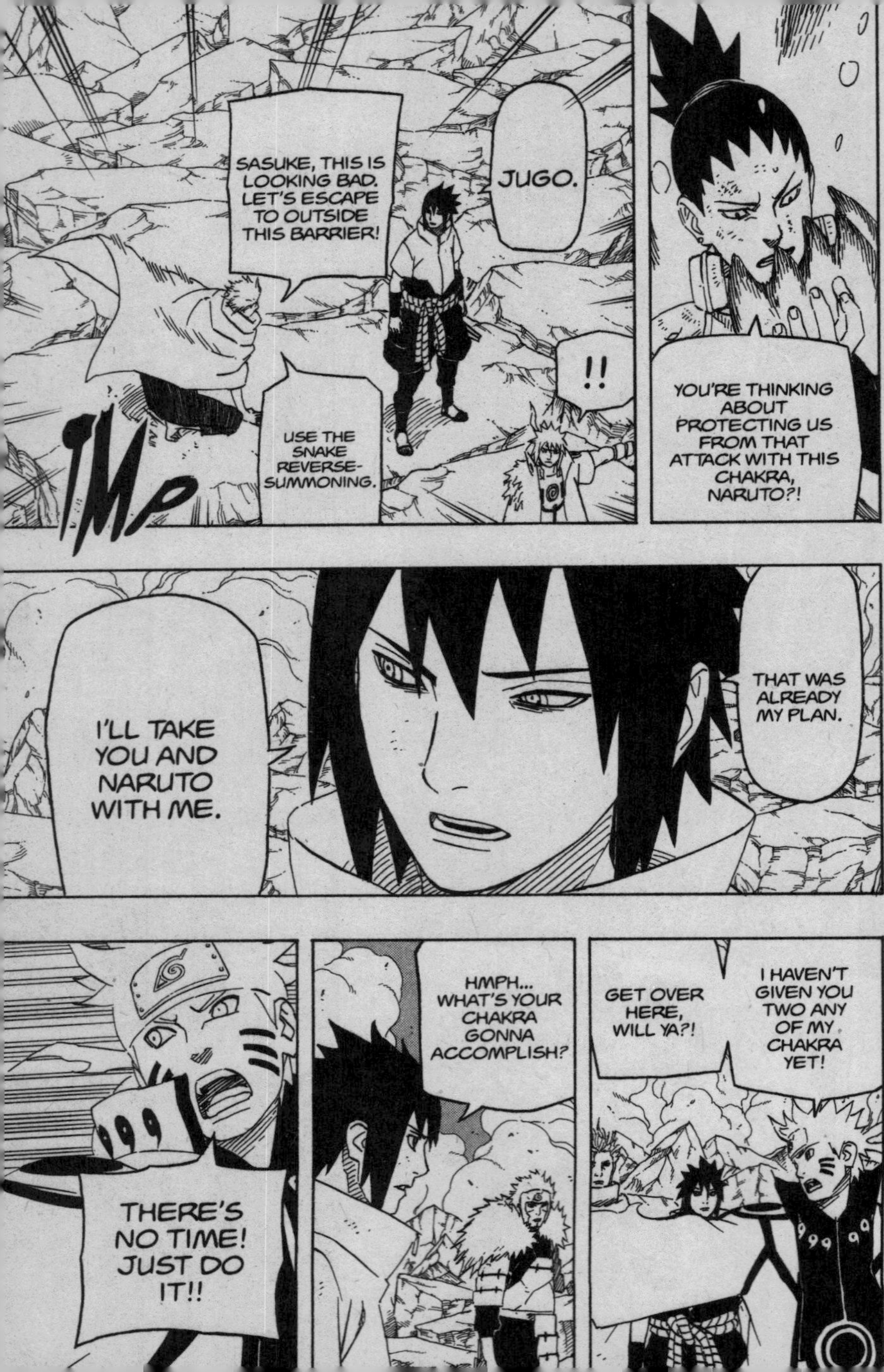
YOU'RE THINKING ABOUT PROTECTING US FROM THAT ATTACK WITH THIS CHAKRA, NARUTO?!
SASUKE, THIS IS LOOKING BAD. LET'S ESCAPE TO OUTSIDE THIS BARRIER!
JUGO.
USE THE SNAKE REVERSE-SUMMONING.
!!
TMP
THAT WAS ALREADY MY PLAN.
I'LL TAKE YOU AND NARUTO WITH ME.
I HAVEN'T GIVEN YOU TWO ANY OF MY CHAKRA YET!
GET OVER HERE, WILL YA?!
HMPH... WHAT'S YOUR CHAKRA GONNA ACCOMPLISH?
THERE'S NO TIME! JUST DO IT!!

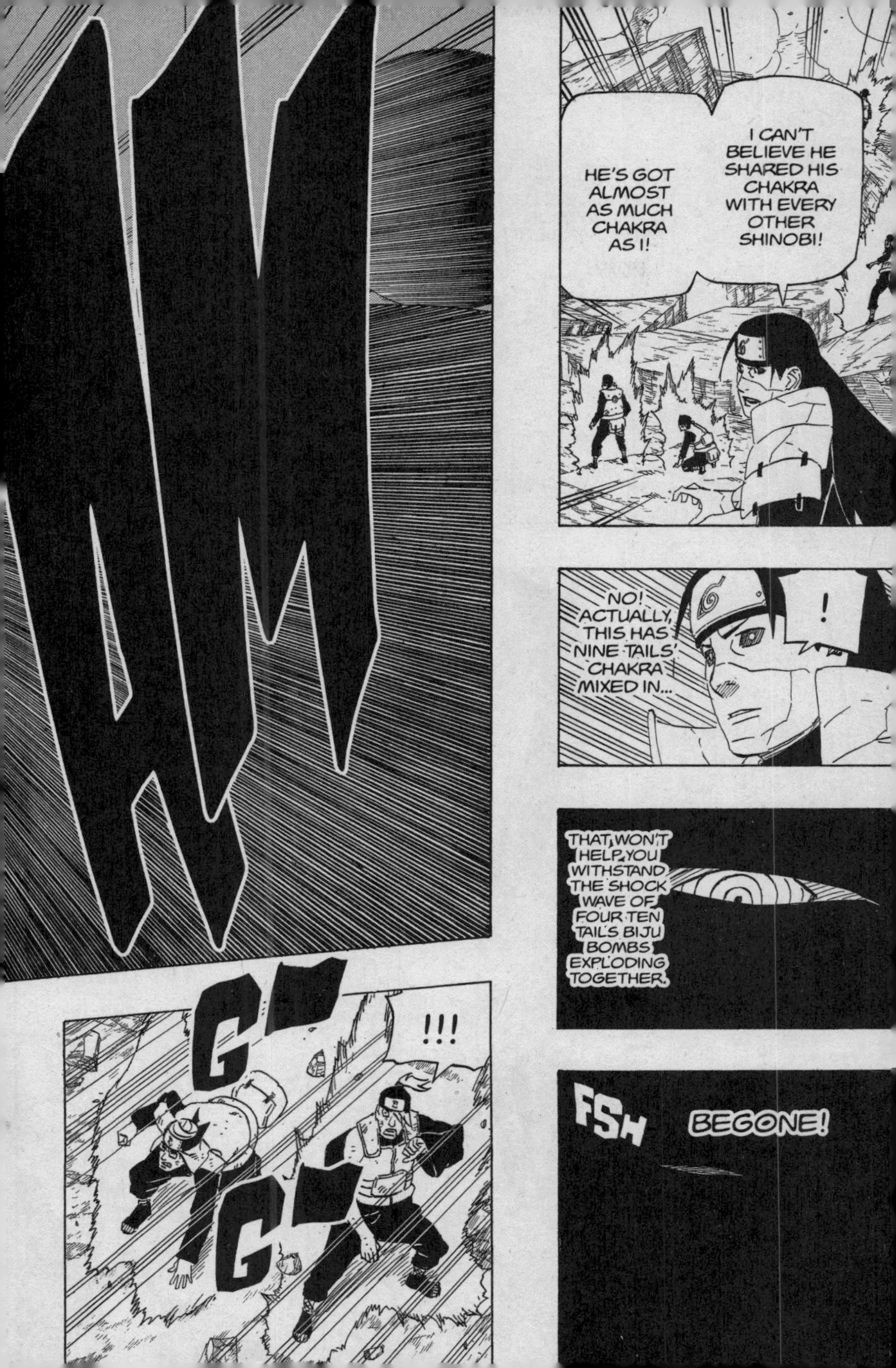
I CAN'T BELIEVE HE SHARED HIS CHAKRA WITH EVERY OTHER SHINOBI!
HE'S GOT ALMOST AS MUCH CHAKRA AS I!
!
NO! ACTUALLY, THIS HAS NINE TAILS' CHAKRA MIXED IN...
THAT WON'T HELP YOU WITHSTAND THE SHOCK WAVE OF FOUR TEN TAILS BIJU BOMBS EXPLODING TOGETHER.
FSH
BEGONE!
!!!

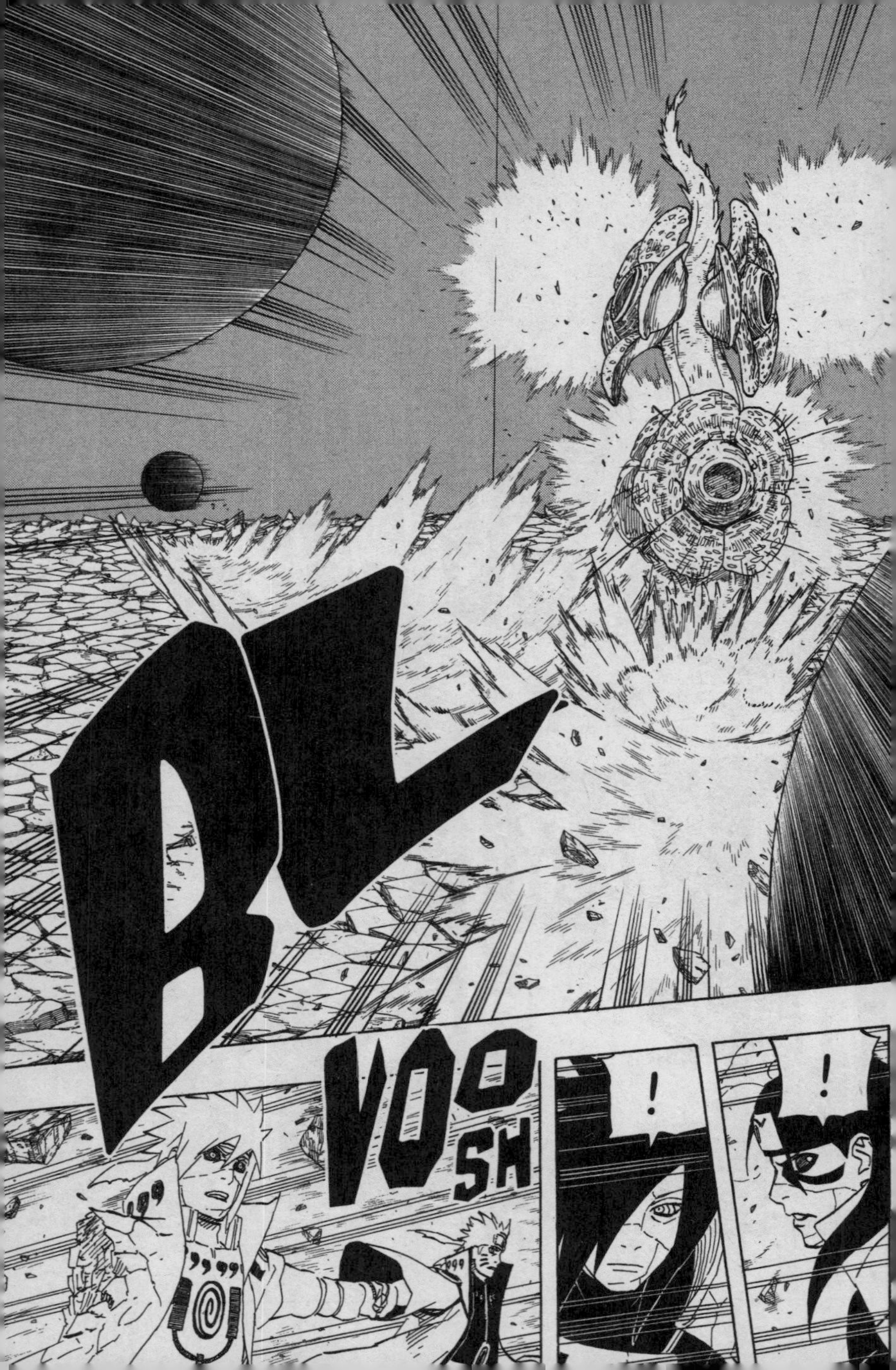
BL
!
!
VOOSH

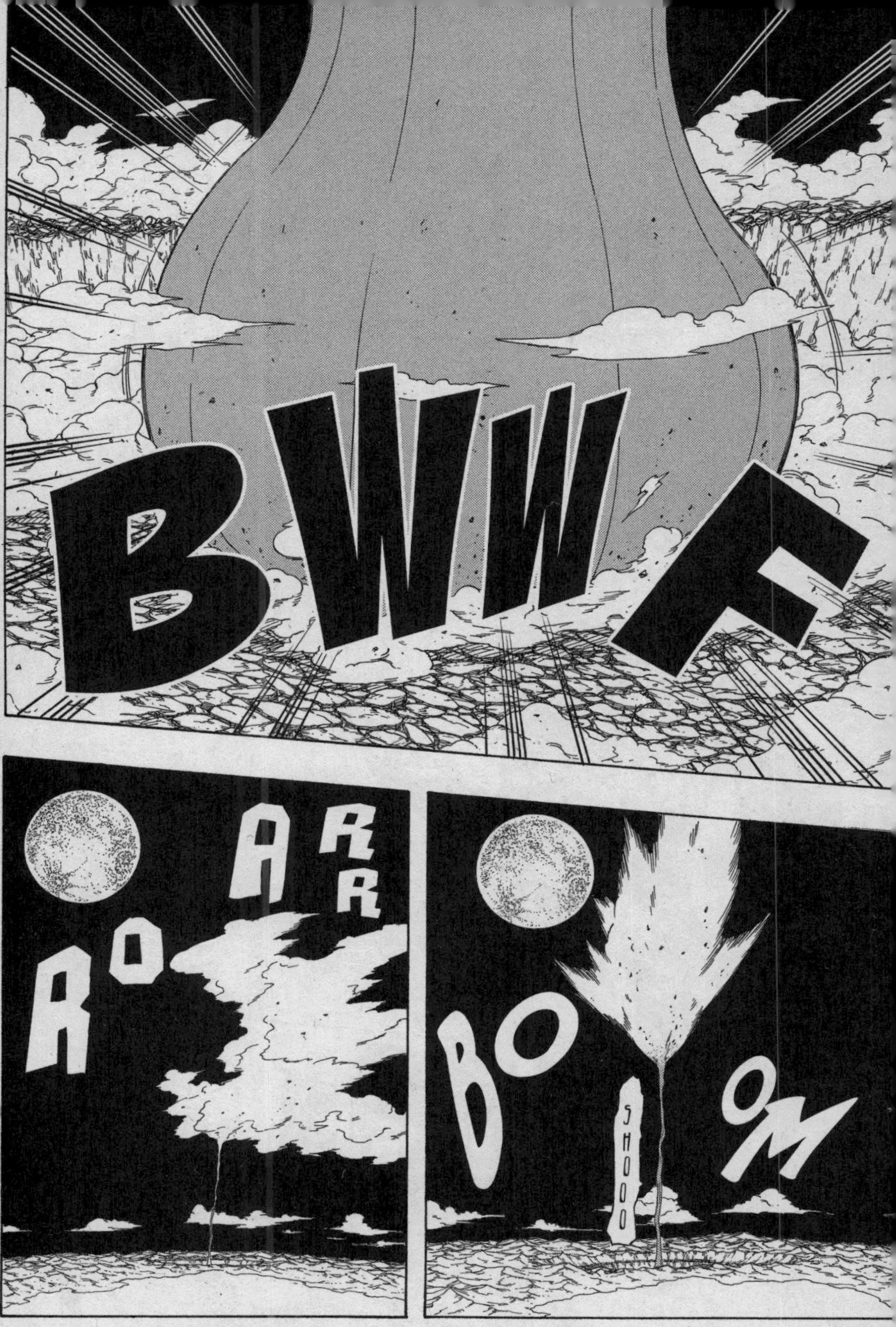
BWWF
BOOM
SHOOO
ROARR

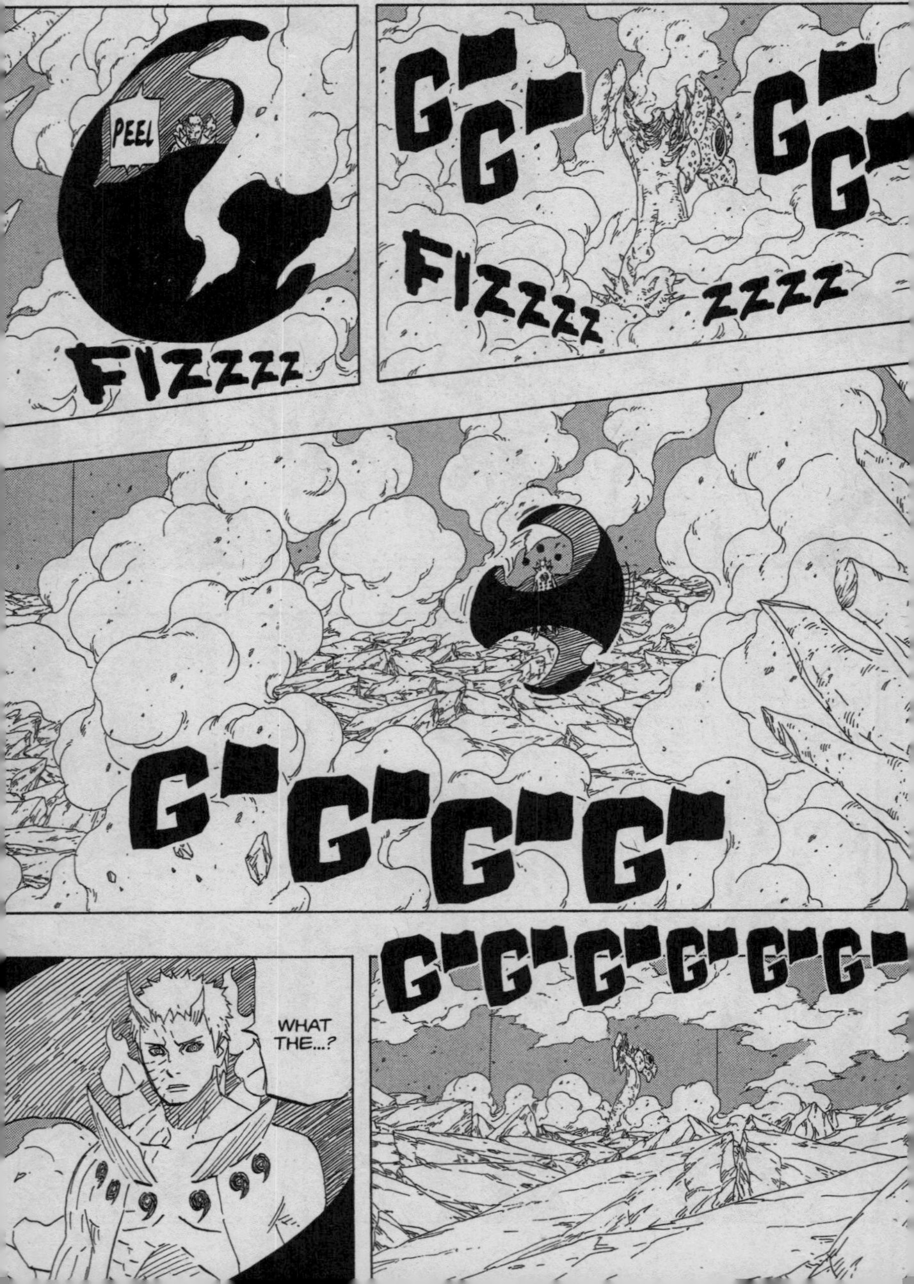
GG
GG
FIZZZZZ
ZZZZ
PEEL
FIZZZZ
GGGG
GGGGGGG
WHAT THE...?

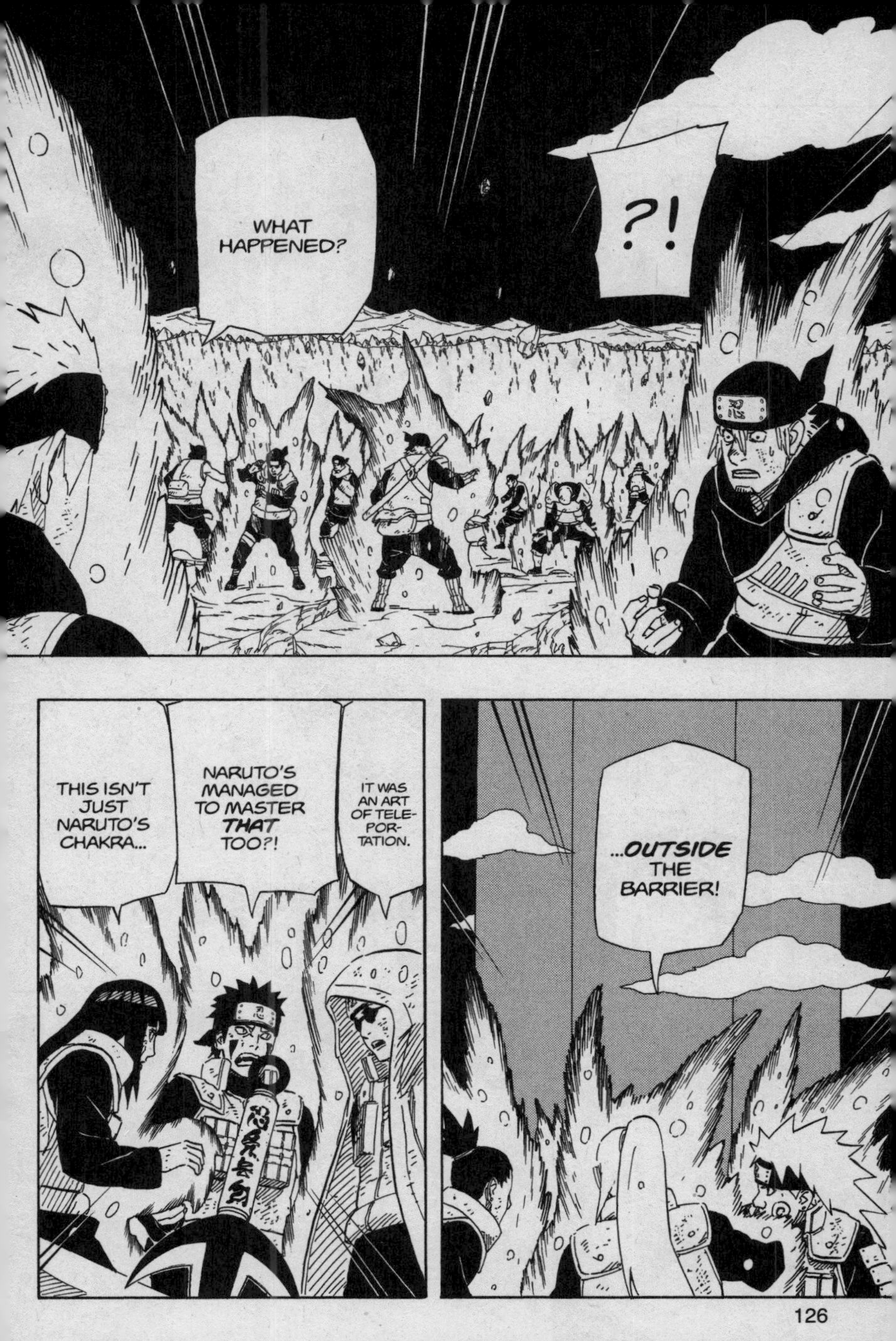
?!
WHAT HAPPENED?
...OUTSIDE THE BARRIER!
IT WAS AN ART OF TELE-PORTATION.
NARUTO'S MANAGED TO MASTER *THAT* TOO?!
THIS ISN'T JUST NARUTO'S CHAKRA...

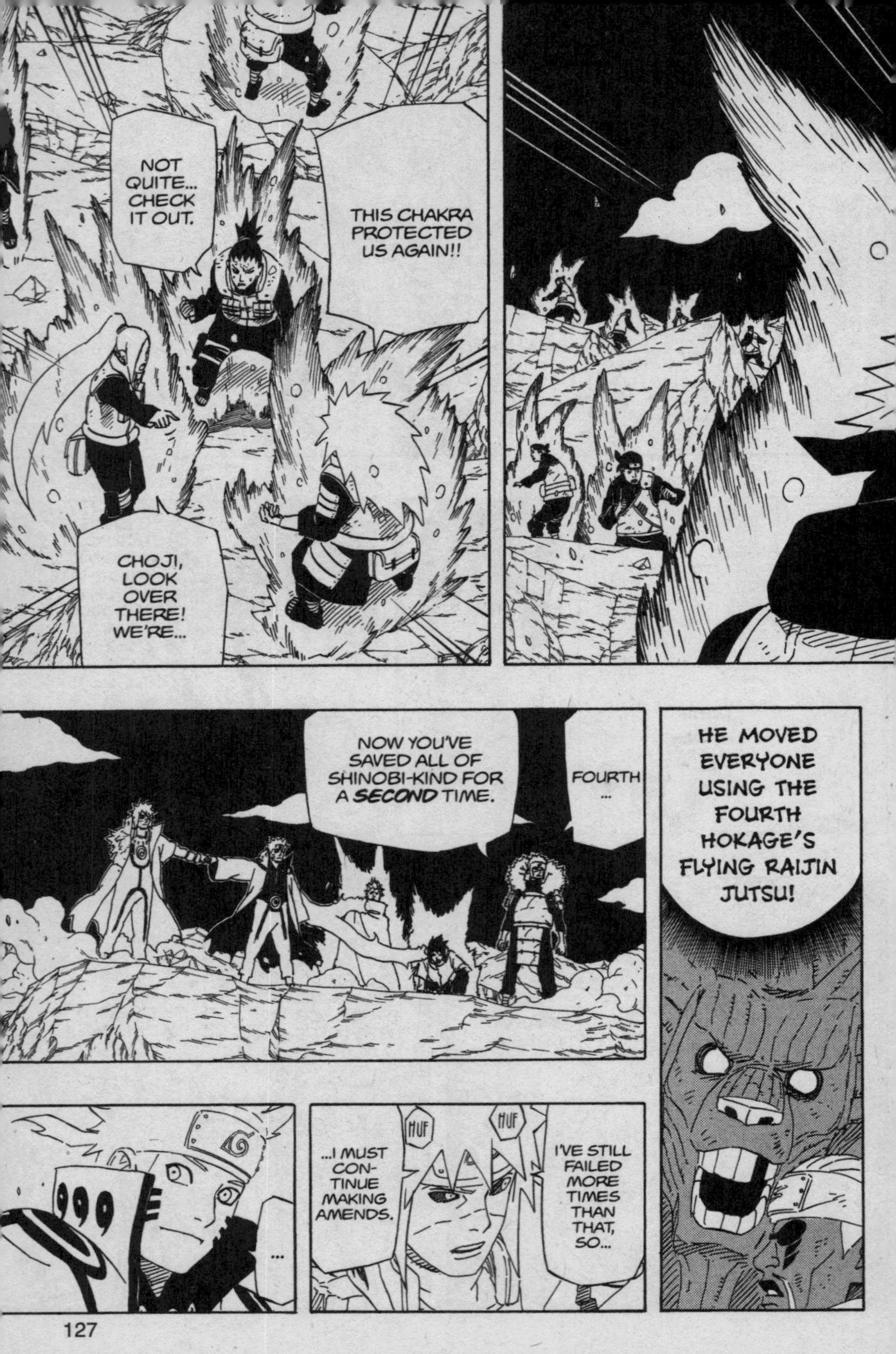
THIS CHAKRA PROTECTED US AGAIN!!
NOT QUITE... CHECK IT OUT.
CHOJI, LOOK OVER THERE! WE'RE...
HE MOVED EVERYONE USING THE FOURTH HOKAGE'S FLYING RAIJIN JUTSU!
FOURTH...
NOW YOU'VE SAVED ALL OF SHINOBI-KIND FOR A SECOND TIME.
HUF
HUF
I'VE STILL FAILED MORE TIMES THAN THAT, SO...
...I MUST CONTINUE MAKING AMENDS.
...

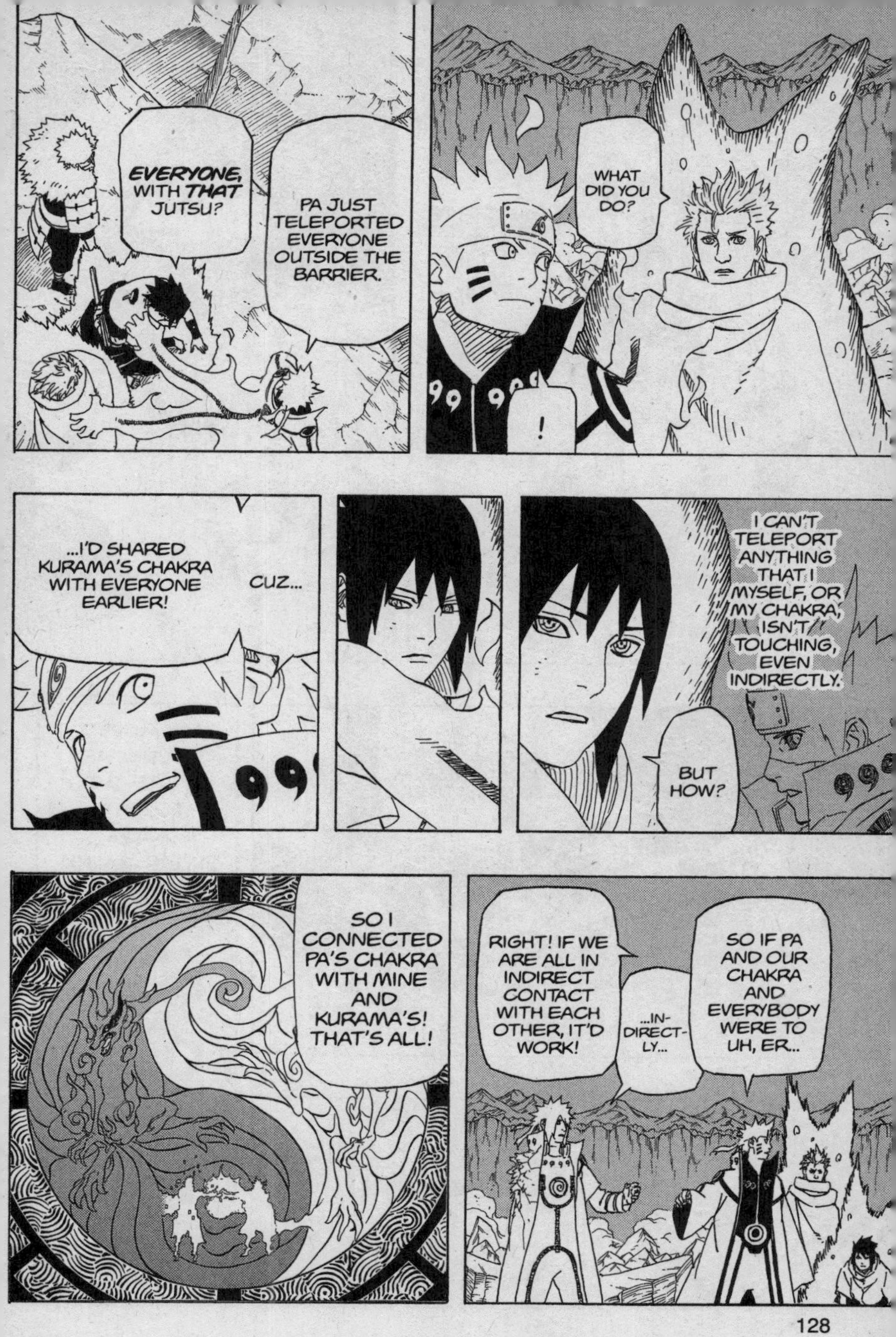
WHAT DID YOU DO?
!
PA JUST TELEPORTED EVERYONE OUTSIDE THE BARRIER.
EVERYONE, WITH *THAT* JUTSU?
I CAN'T TELEPORT ANYTHING THAT I MYSELF, OR MY CHAKRA, ISN'T TOUCHING, EVEN INDIRECTLY.
BUT HOW?
CUZ...
...I'D SHARED KURAMA'S CHAKRA WITH EVERYONE EARLIER!
SO IF PA AND OUR CHAKRA AND EVERYBODY WERE TO UH, ER...
...IN-DIRECT-LY...
RIGHT! IF WE ARE ALL IN INDIRECT CONTACT WITH EACH OTHER, IT'D WORK!
SO I CONNECTED PA'S CHAKRA WITH MINE AND KURAMA'S! THAT'S ALL!

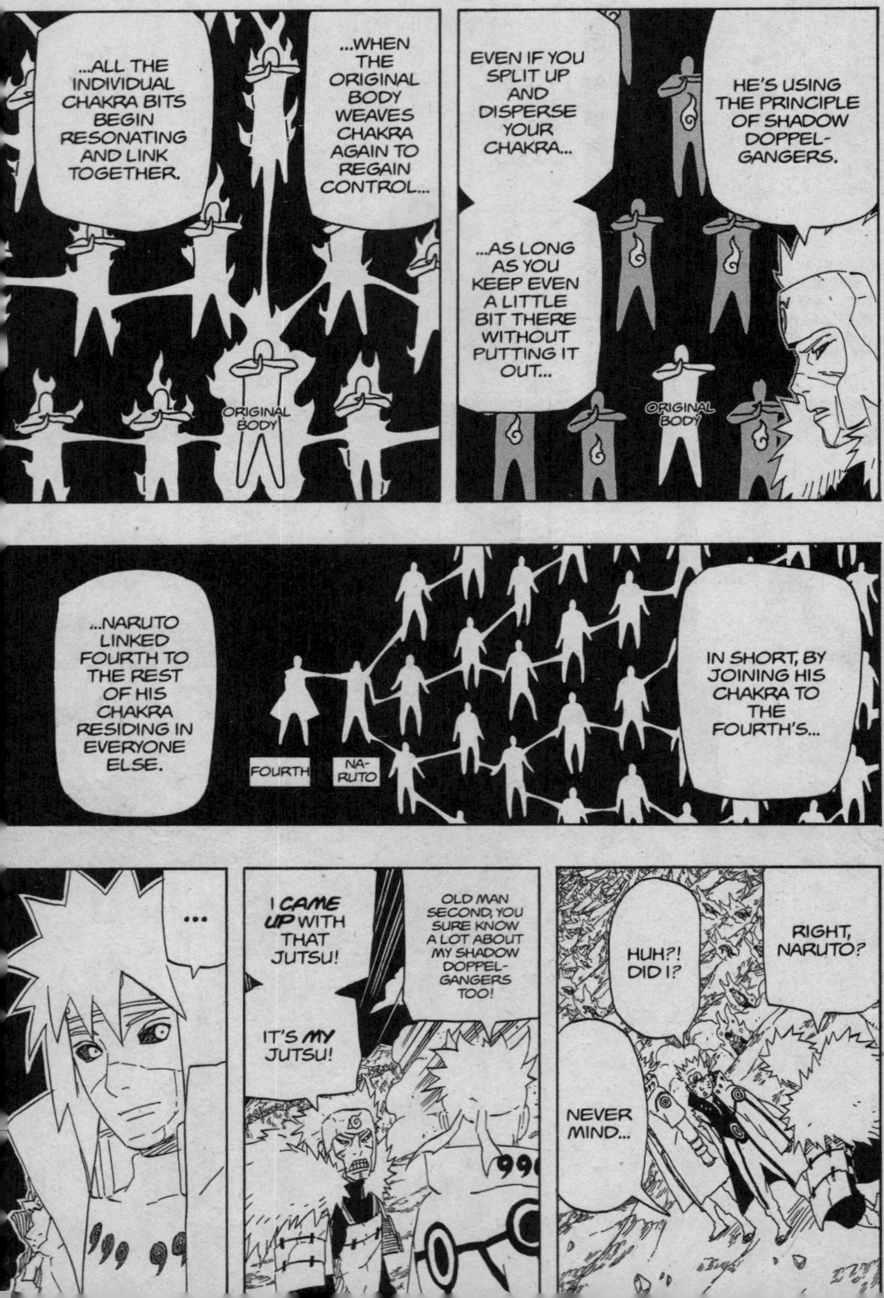
HE'S USING THE PRINCIPLE OF SHADOW DOPPEL-GANGERS.
EVEN IF YOU SPLIT UP AND DISPERSE YOUR CHAKRA...
...AS LONG AS YOU KEEP EVEN A LITTLE BIT THERE WITHOUT PUTTING IT OUT...
ORIGINAL BODY
...WHEN THE ORIGINAL BODY WEAVES CHAKRA AGAIN TO REGAIN CONTROL...
...ALL THE INDIVIDUAL CHAKRA BITS BEGIN RESONATING AND LINK TOGETHER.
ORIGINAL BODY
IN SHORT, BY JOINING HIS CHAKRA TO THE FOURTH'S...
NA-RUTO
FOURTH
...NARUTO LINKED FOURTH TO THE REST OF HIS CHAKRA RESIDING IN EVERYONE ELSE.
RIGHT, NARUTO?
HUH?! DID I?
NEVER MIND...
OLD MAN SECOND, YOU SURE KNOW A LOT ABOUT MY SHADOW DOPPEL-GANGERS TOO!
I *CAME UP* WITH THAT JUTSU!
IT'S *MY* JUTSU!
...

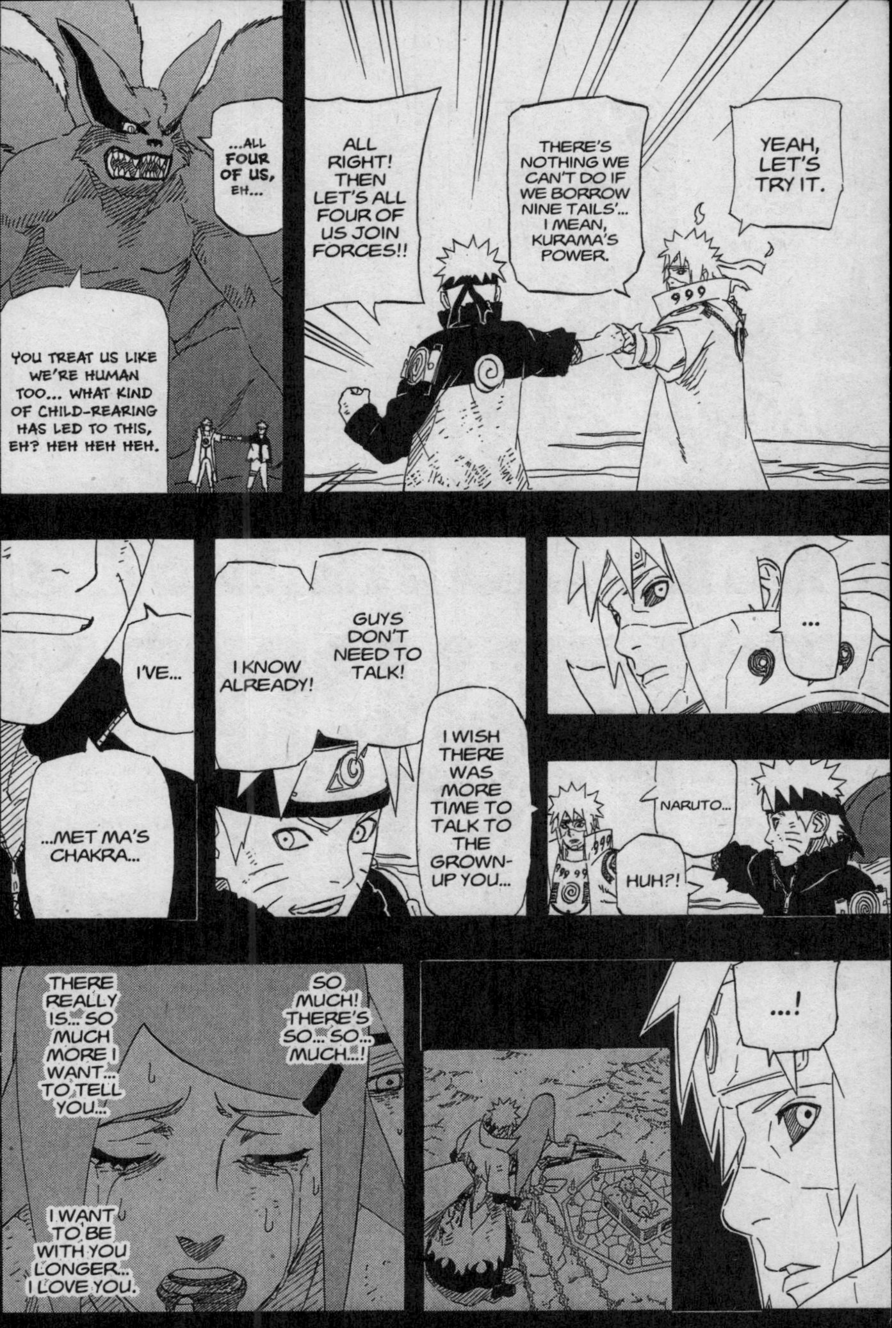
YEAH, LET'S TRY IT.
THERE'S NOTHING WE CAN'T DO IF WE BORROW NINE TAILS'... I MEAN, KURAMA'S POWER.
ALL RIGHT! THEN LET'S ALL FOUR OF US JOIN FORCES!!
...ALL FOUR OF US, EH...
YOU TREAT US LIKE WE'RE HUMAN TOO... WHAT KIND OF CHILD-REARING HAS LED TO THIS, EH? HEH HEH HEH.
...
NARUTO...
HUH?!
GUYS DON'T NEED TO TALK!
I KNOW ALREADY!
I WISH THERE WAS MORE TIME TO TALK TO THE GROWN-UP YOU...
I'VE...
...MET MA'S CHAKRA...
...!
SO MUCH! THERE'S SO... SO... MUCH...!
THERE REALLY IS... SO MUCH MORE I WANT... TO TELL YOU...
I WANT TO BE WITH YOU LONGER... I LOVE YOU.

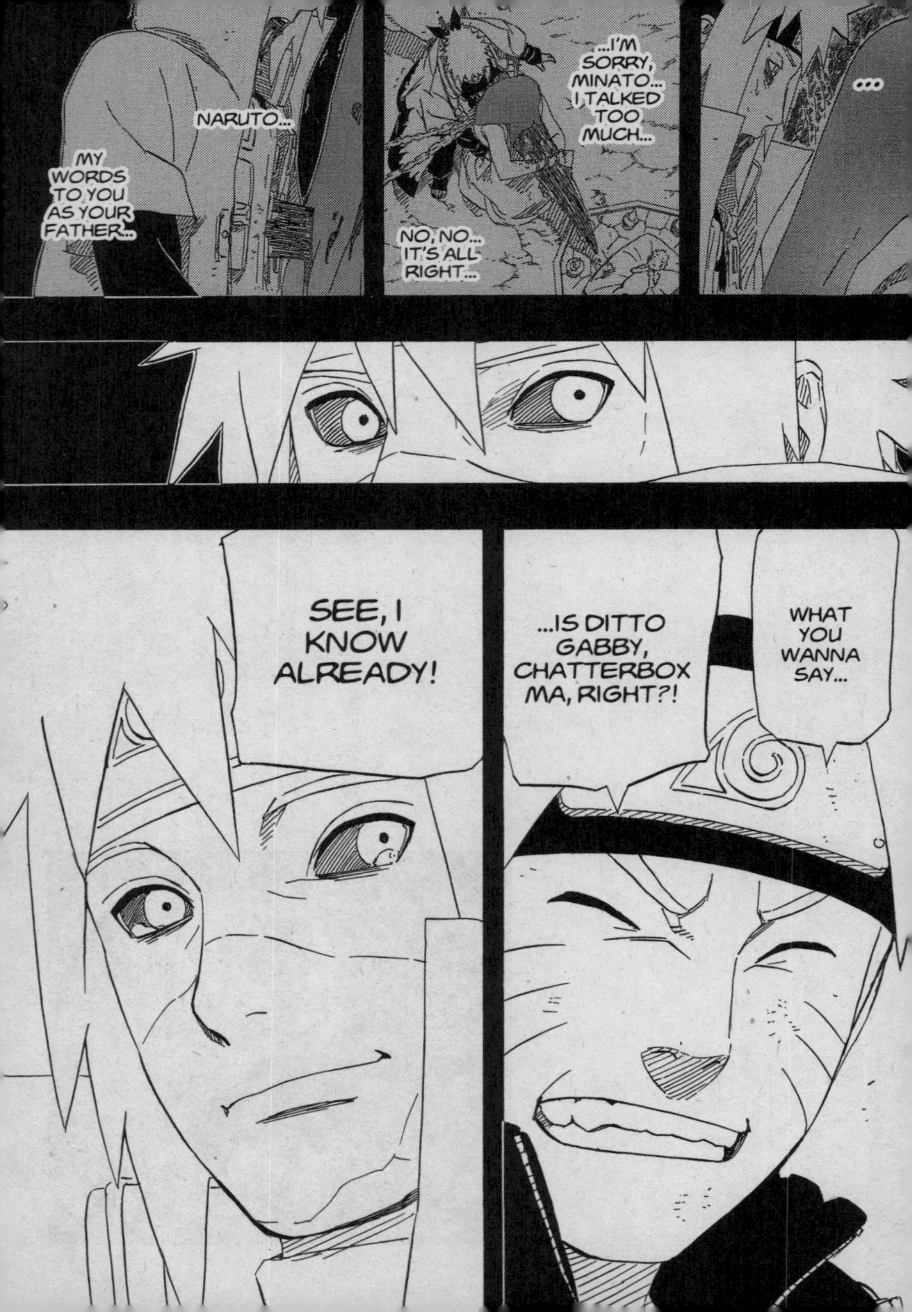
...
...I'M SORRY, MINATO... I TALKED TOO MUCH...
NO, NO... IT'S ALL RIGHT...
NARUTO...
MY WORDS TO YOU AS YOUR FATHER...
WHAT YOU WANNA SAY...
...IS DITTO GABBY, CHATTERBOX MA, RIGHT?!
SEE, I KNOW ALREADY!

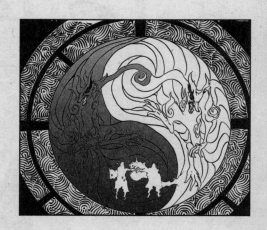

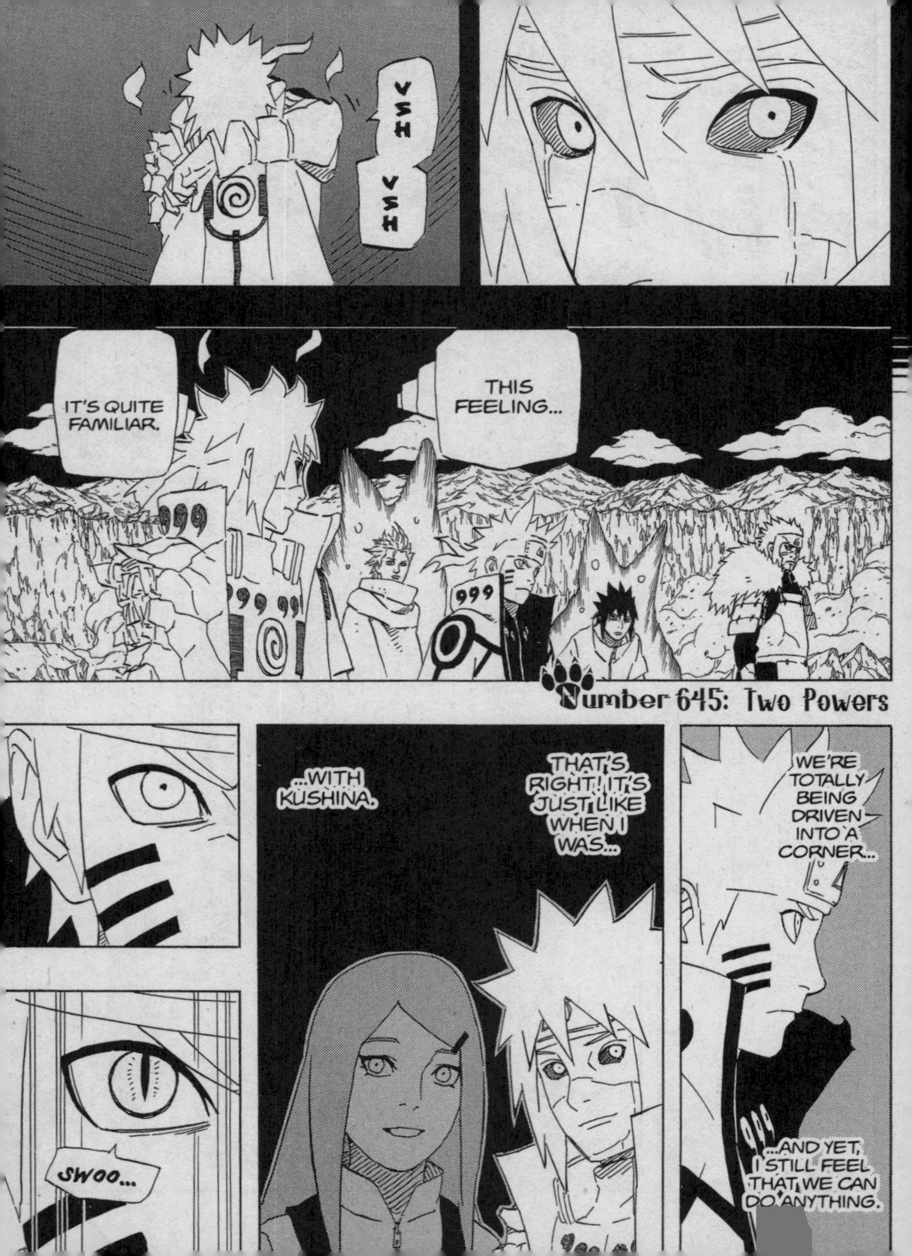
VSH
VSH
THIS FEELING...
IT'S QUITE FAMILIAR.
Number 645: Two Powers
WE'RE TOTALLY BEING DRIVEN INTO A CORNER...
...AND YET, I STILL FEEL THAT WE CAN DO ANYTHING.
THAT'S RIGHT! IT'S JUST LIKE WHEN I WAS...
...WITH KUSHINA.
SWOO...

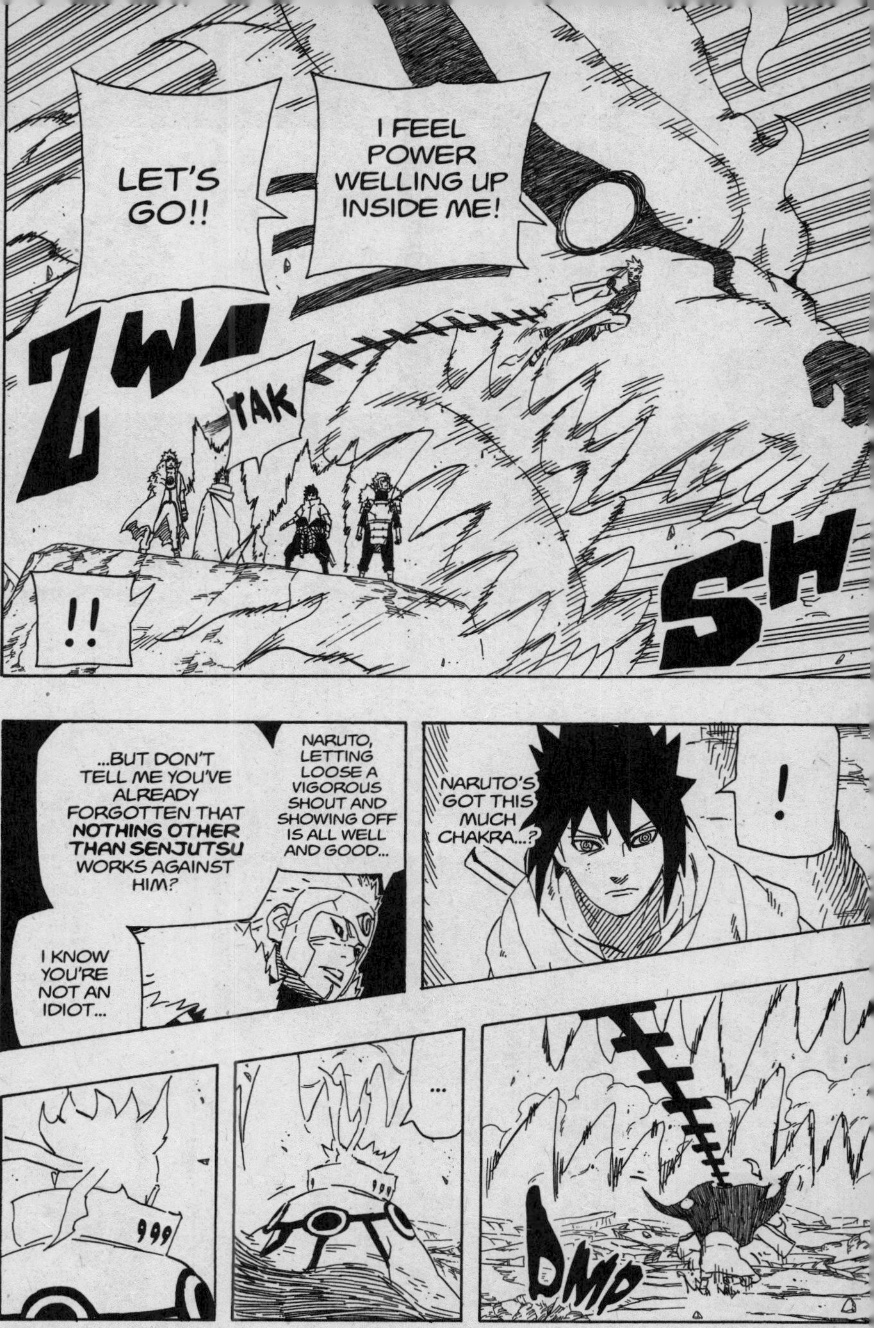
I FEEL POWER WELLING UP INSIDE ME!
LET'S GO!!
ZWI
TAK
SH
!!
!
NARUTO'S GOT THIS MUCH CHAKRA...?
NARUTO, LETTING LOOSE A VIGOROUS SHOUT AND SHOWING OFF IS ALL WELL AND GOOD...
...BUT DON'T TELL ME YOU'VE ALREADY FORGOTTEN THAT **NOTHING OTHER THAN SENJUTSU** WORKS AGAINST HIM?
I KNOW YOU'RE NOT AN IDIOT...
DMP
...

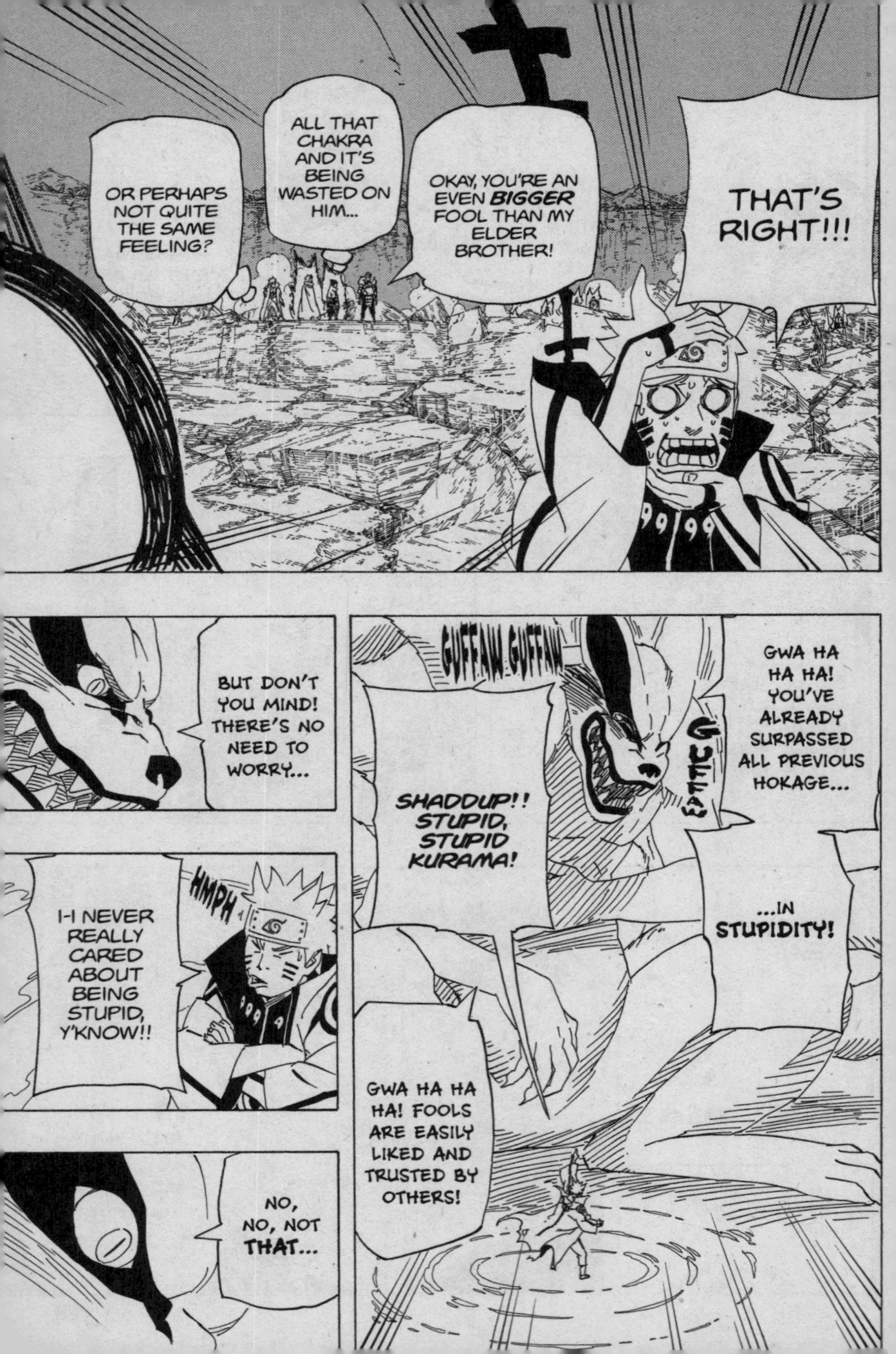
THAT'S RIGHT!!!
OKAY, YOU'RE AN EVEN **BIGGER** FOOL THAN MY ELDER BROTHER!
ALL THAT CHAKRA AND IT'S BEING WASTED ON HIM...
OR PERHAPS NOT QUITE THE SAME FEELING?
BUT DON'T YOU MIND! THERE'S NO NEED TO WORRY...
HMPH
I-I NEVER REALLY CARED ABOUT BEING STUPID, Y'KNOW!!
NO, NO, NOT **THAT**...
GUFFAW GUFFAW
GWA HA HA HA! YOU'VE ALREADY SURPASSED ALL PREVIOUS HOKAGE...
...IN **STUPIDITY!**
SHADDUP!! STUPID, STUPID KURAMA!
GWA HA HA HA! FOOLS ARE EASILY LIKED AND TRUSTED BY OTHERS!

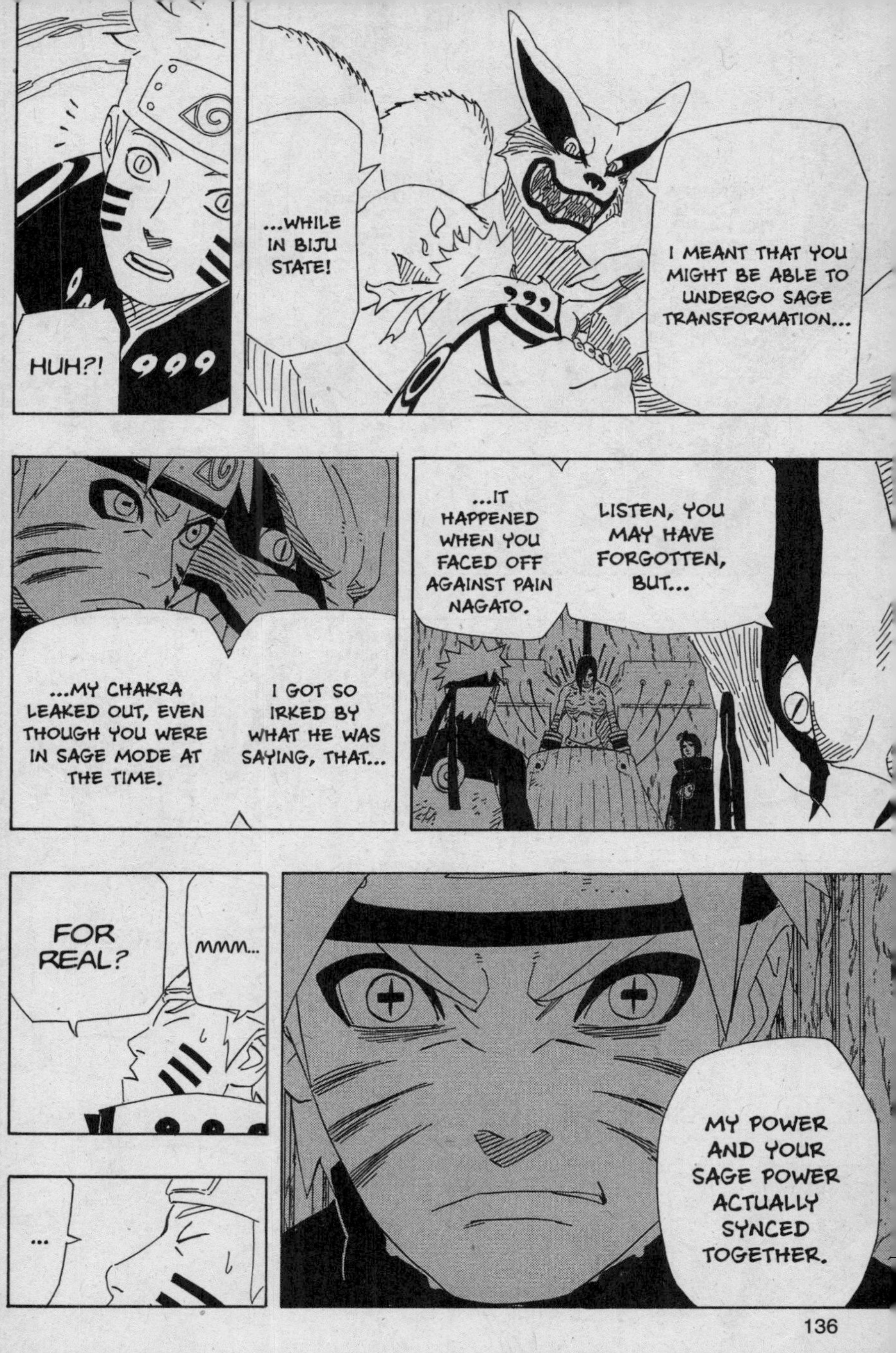
I MEANT THAT YOU MIGHT BE ABLE TO UNDERGO SAGE TRANSFORMATION...
...WHILE IN BIJU STATE!
HUH?!
LISTEN, YOU MAY HAVE FORGOTTEN, BUT...
...IT HAPPENED WHEN YOU FACED OFF AGAINST PAIN NAGATO.
I GOT SO IRKED BY WHAT HE WAS SAYING, THAT...
...MY CHAKRA LEAKED OUT, EVEN THOUGH YOU WERE IN SAGE MODE AT THE TIME.
MY POWER AND YOUR SAGE POWER ACTUALLY SYNCED TOGETHER.
MMM...
FOR REAL?
...

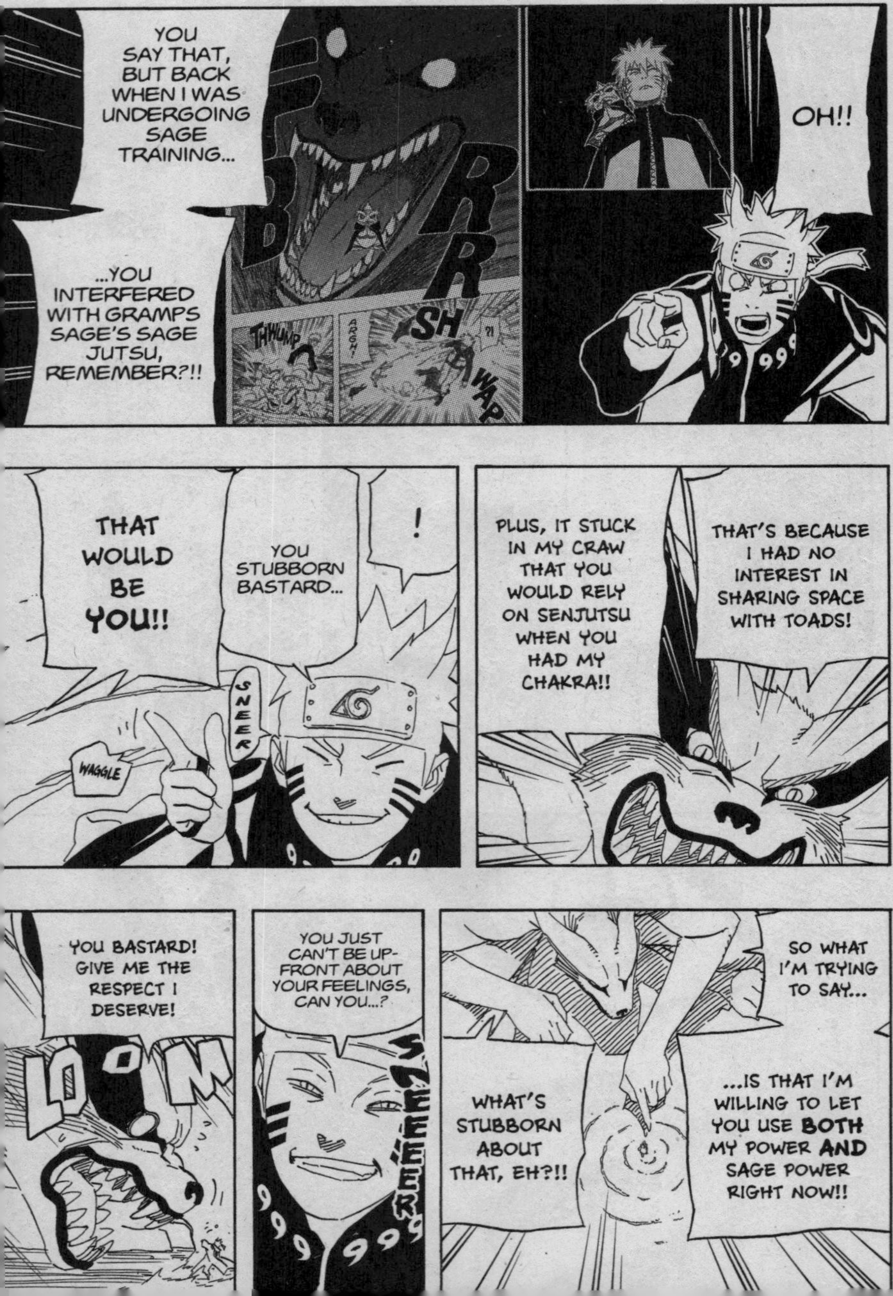
OH!!
YOU SAY THAT, BUT BACK WHEN I WAS UNDERGOING SAGE TRAINING...
BRR
...YOU INTERFERED WITH GRAMPS SAGE'S SAGE JUTSU, REMEMBER?!!
SH
ARGH!
WAP
THWUMP
THAT'S BECAUSE I HAD NO INTEREST IN SHARING SPACE WITH TOADS!
PLUS, IT STUCK IN MY CRAW THAT YOU WOULD RELY ON SENJUTSU WHEN YOU HAD MY CHAKRA!!
!
YOU STUBBORN BASTARD...
THAT WOULD BE YOU!!
SNEER
WAGGLE
SO WHAT I'M TRYING TO SAY...
...IS THAT I'M WILLING TO LET YOU USE BOTH MY POWER AND SAGE POWER RIGHT NOW!!
WHAT'S STUBBORN ABOUT THAT, EH?!!
YOU JUST CAN'T BE UP-FRONT ABOUT YOUR FEELINGS, CAN YOU...?
SNEER
YOU BASTARD! GIVE ME THE RESPECT I DESERVE!
LOOM

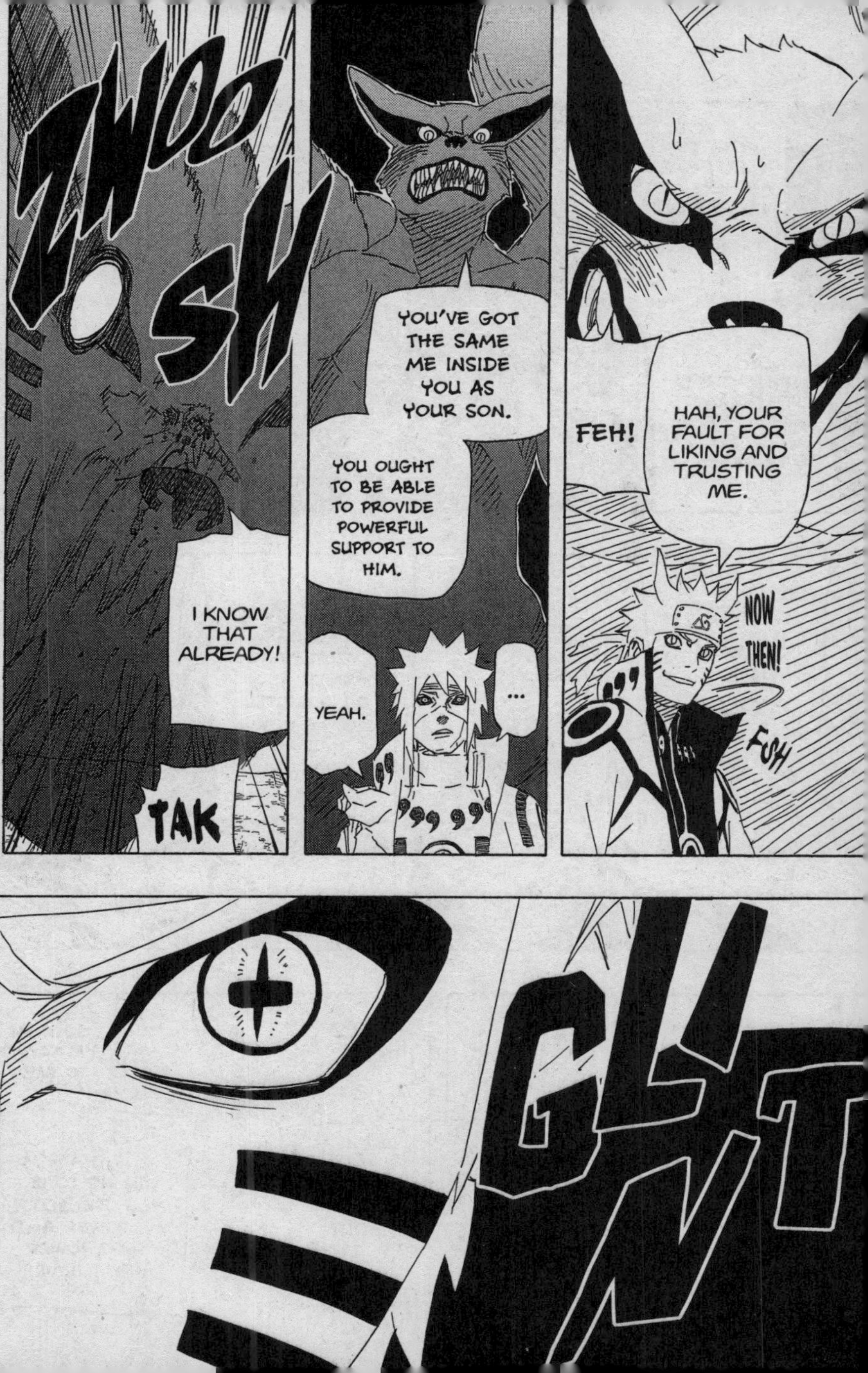
HAH, YOUR FAULT FOR LIKING AND TRUSTING ME.
FEH!
NOW THEN!
FSH
YOU'VE GOT THE SAME ME INSIDE YOU AS YOUR SON.
YOU OUGHT TO BE ABLE TO PROVIDE POWERFUL SUPPORT TO HIM.
...
YEAH.
ZWOOSH
I KNOW THAT ALREADY!
TAK
GLINT

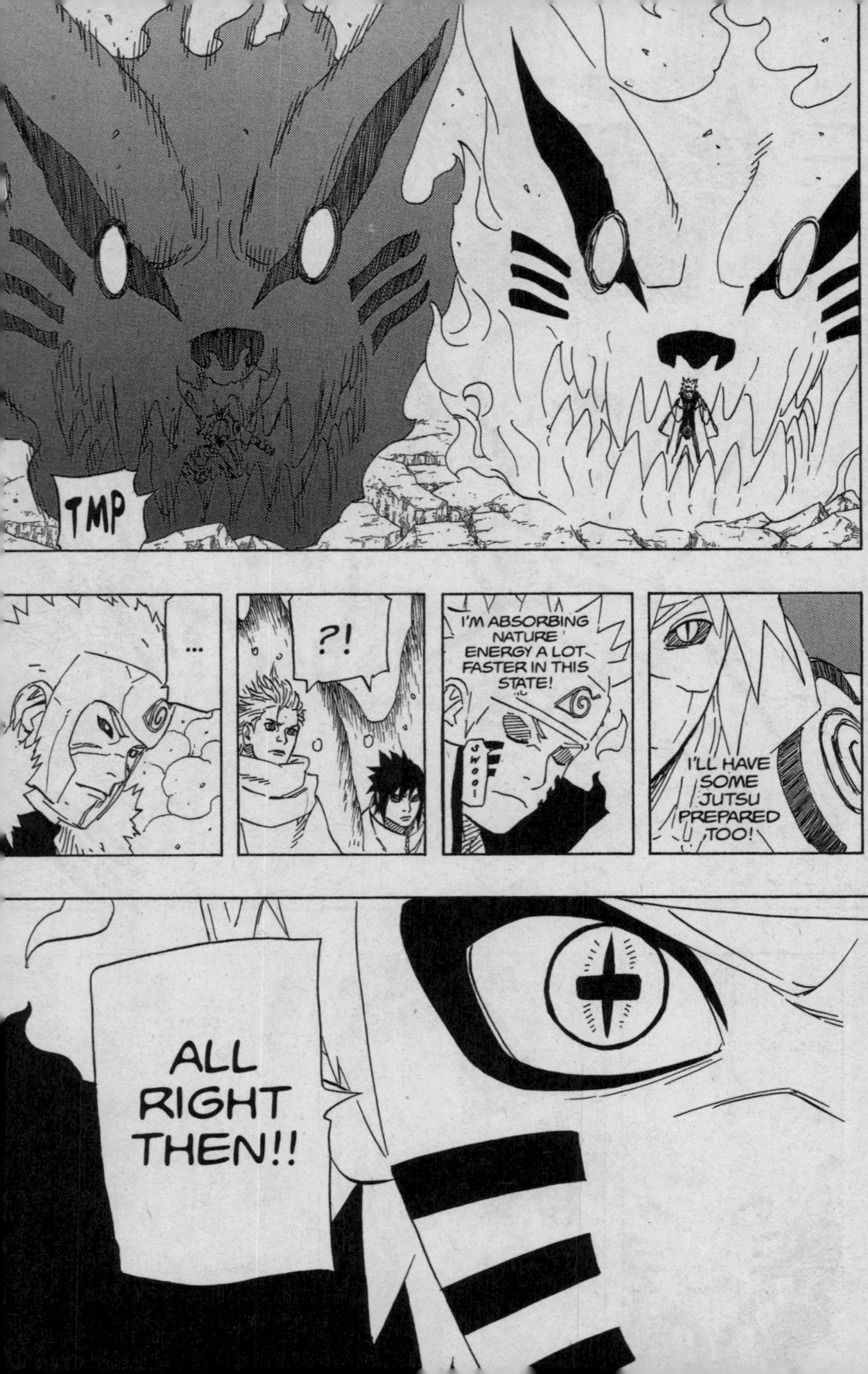
TMP
I'LL HAVE SOME JUTSU PREPARED TOO!
I'M ABSORBING NATURE ENERGY A LOT FASTER IN THIS STATE!
SHOO!!
?!
...
ALL RIGHT THEN!!

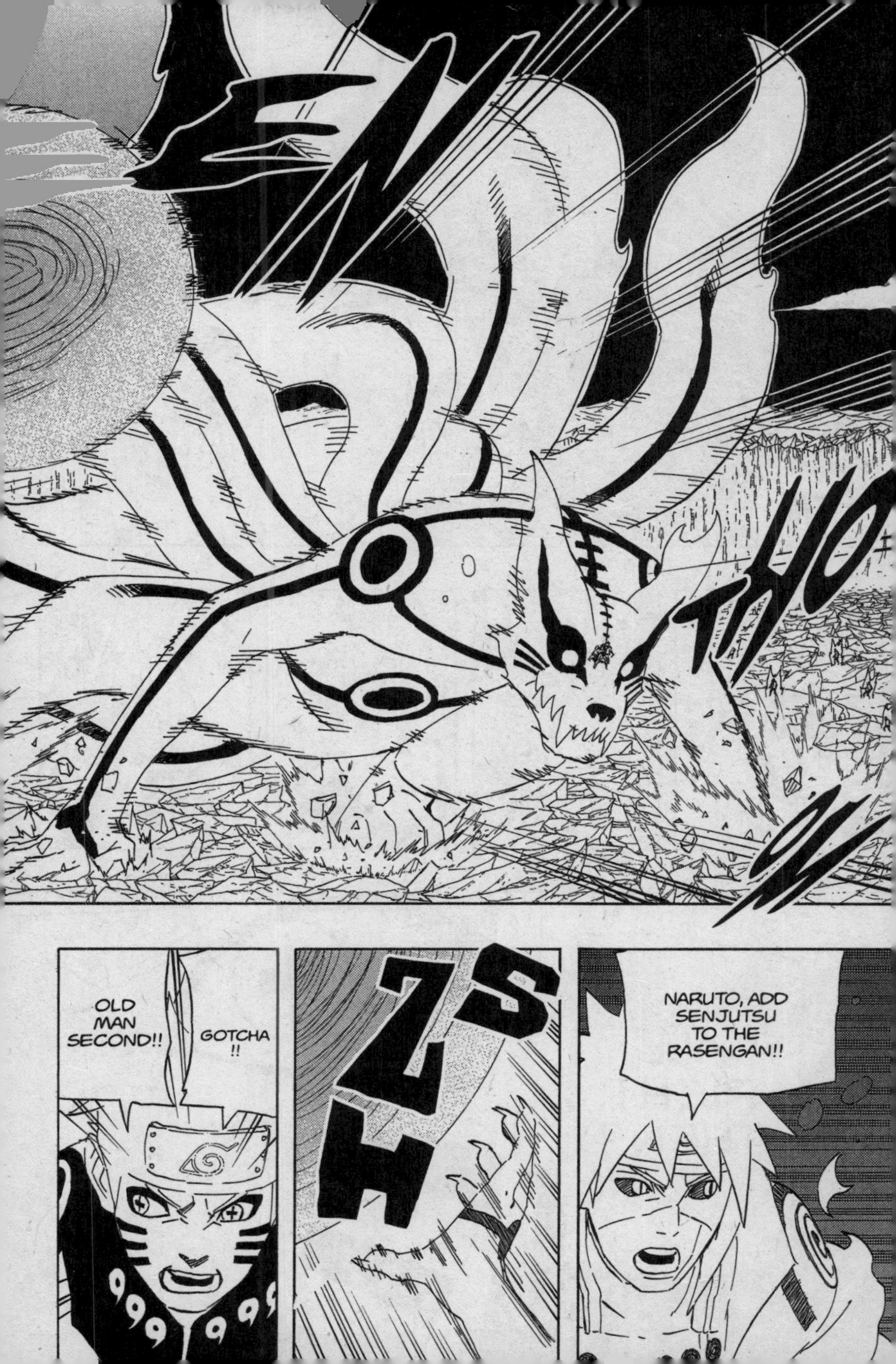
NARUTO, ADD SENJUTSU TO THE RASENGAN!!
GOTCHA !!
OLD MAN SECOND!!

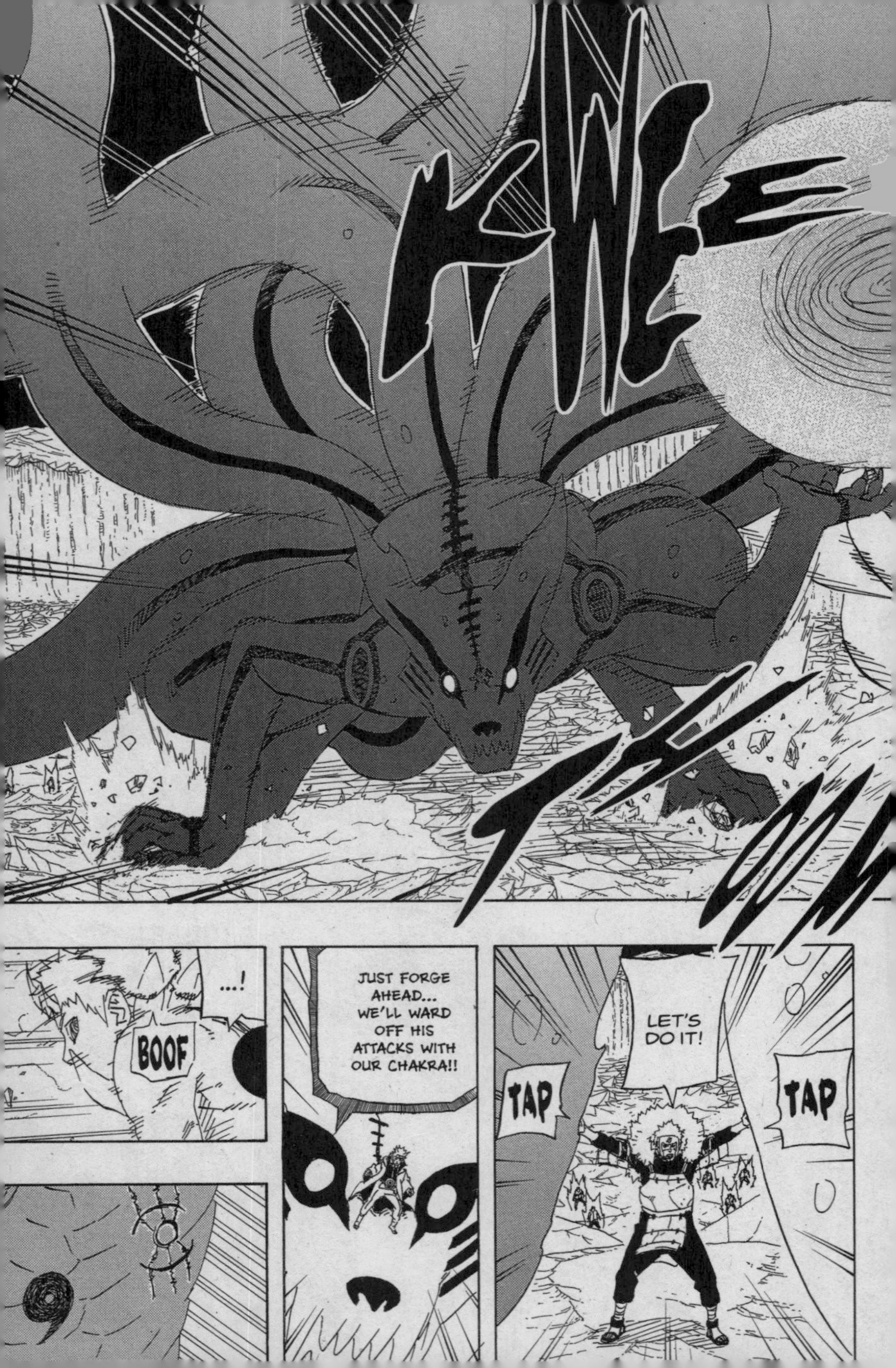
KWEE
TAP
LET'S DO IT!
TAP
JUST FORGE AHEAD... WE'LL WARD OFF HIS ATTACKS WITH OUR CHAKRA!!
...!
BOOF

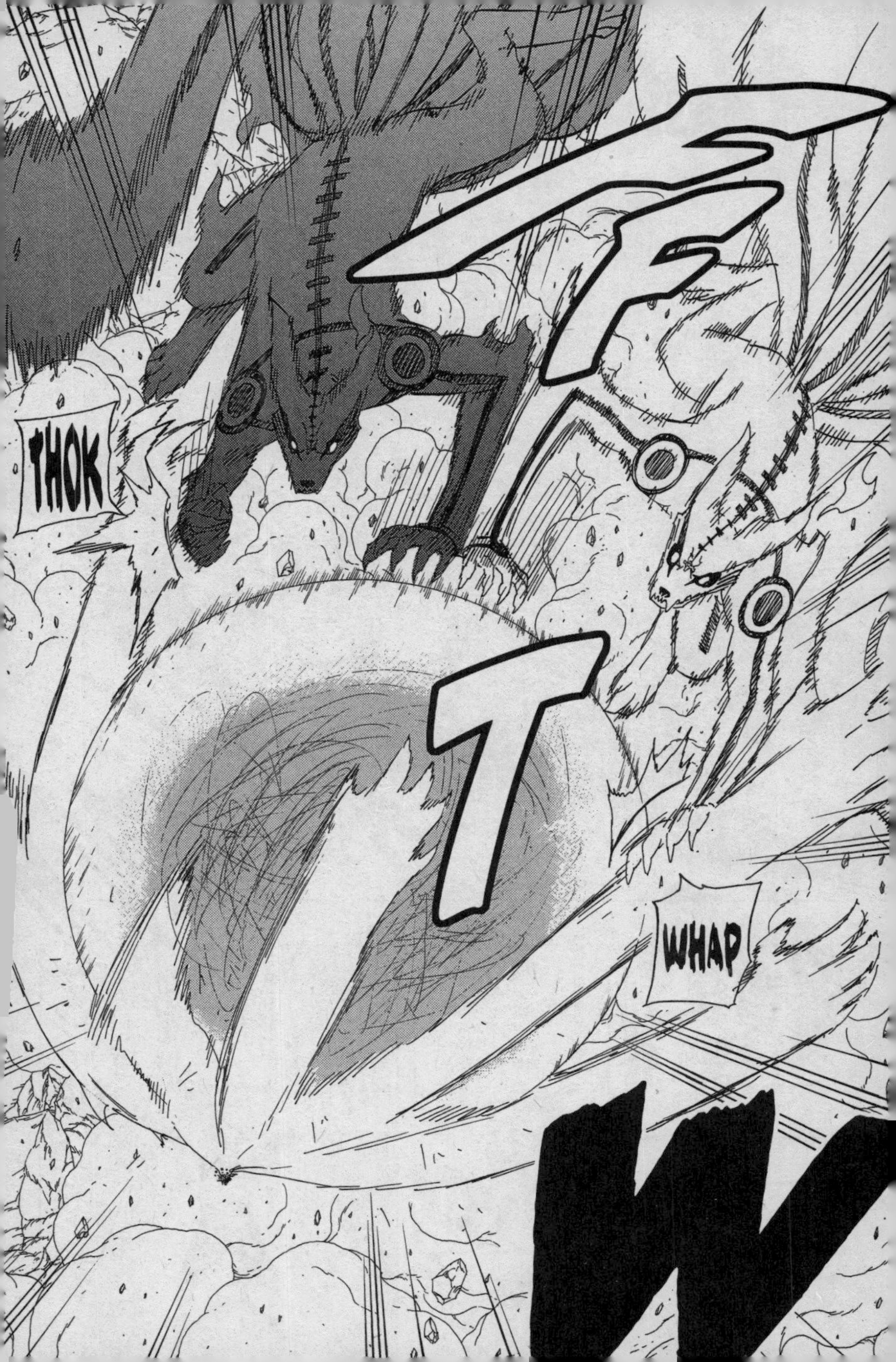
THOK
WHAP

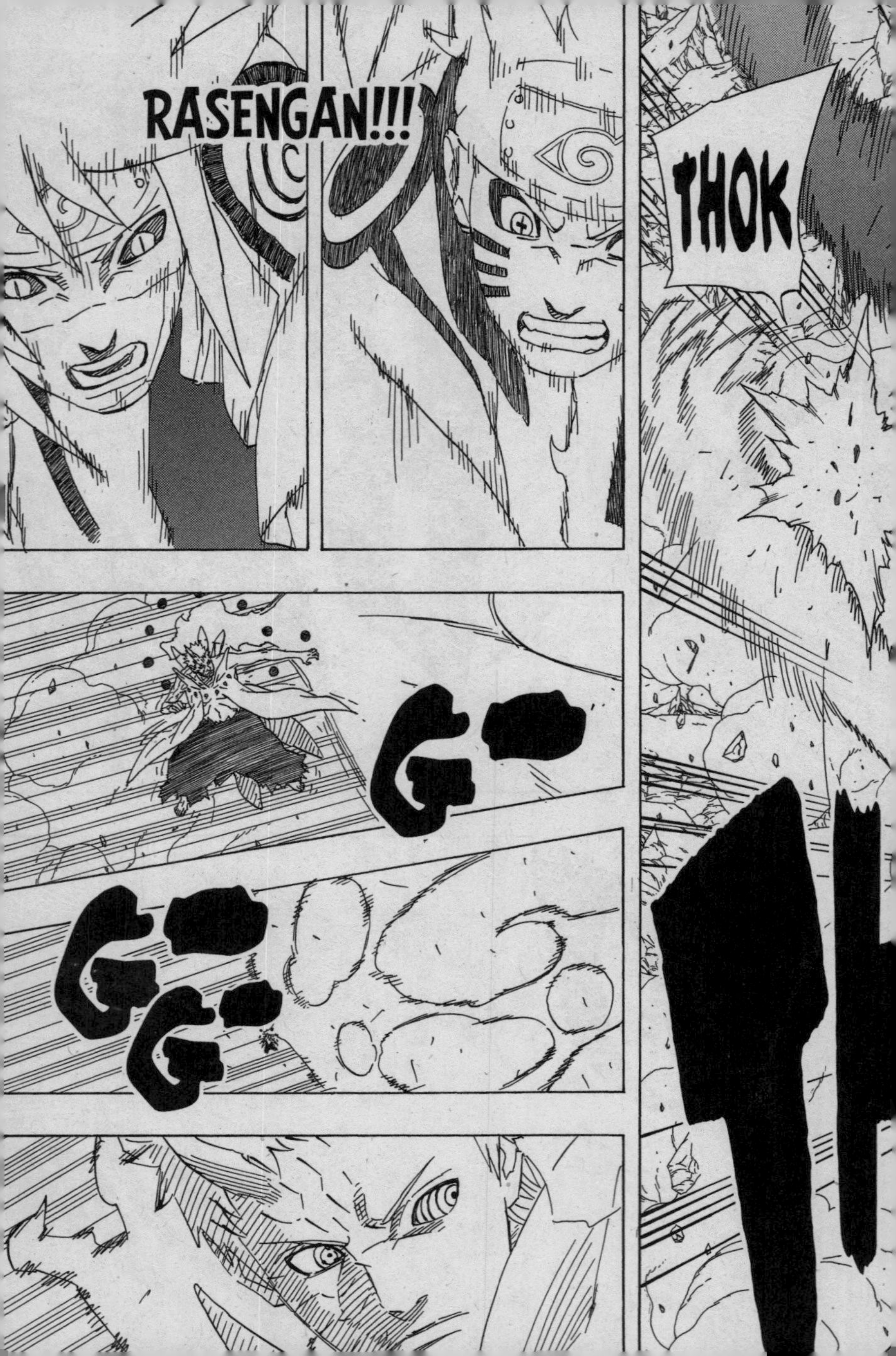
THOK
RASENGAN!!!

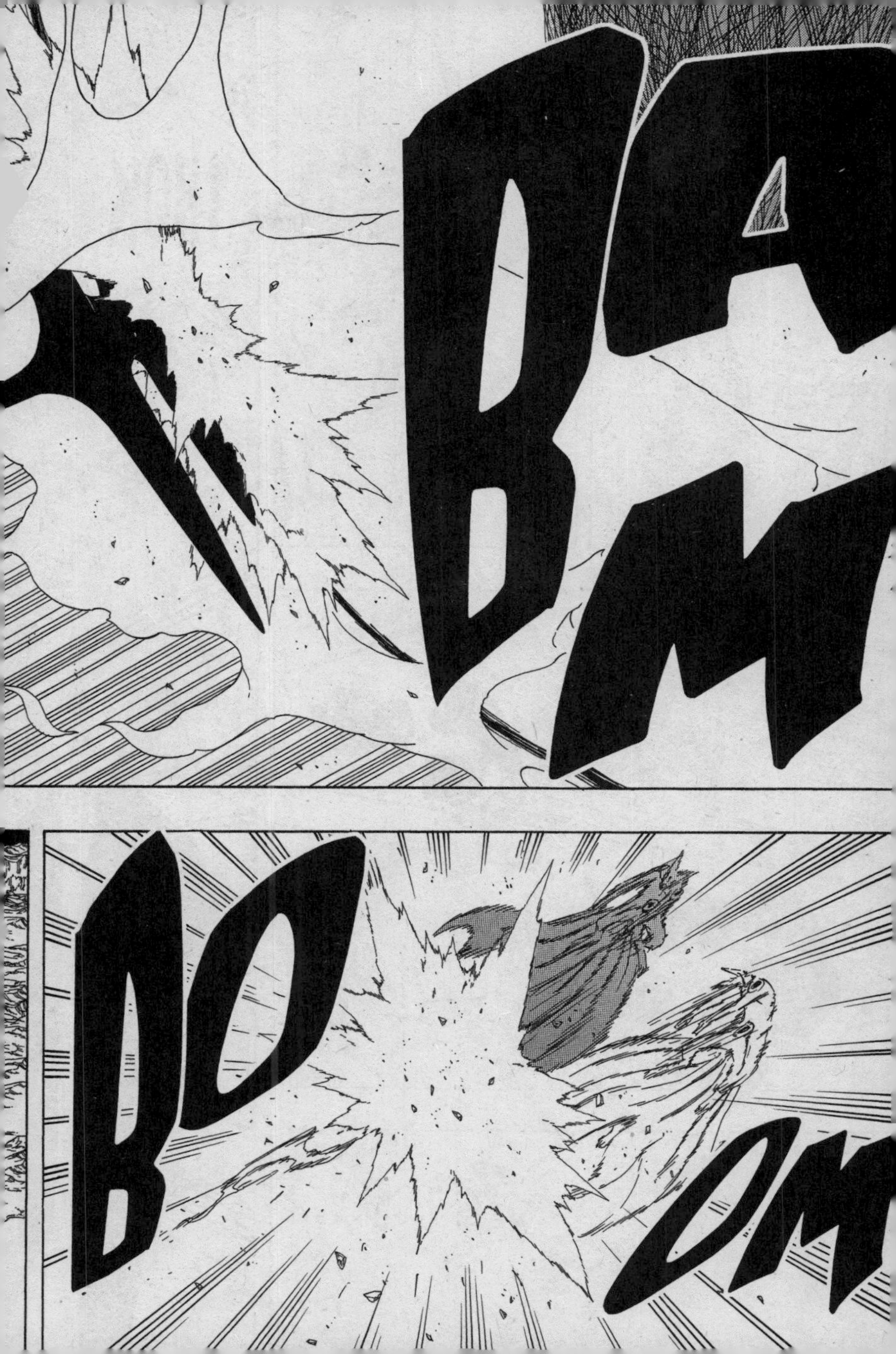
BAM
BOOM

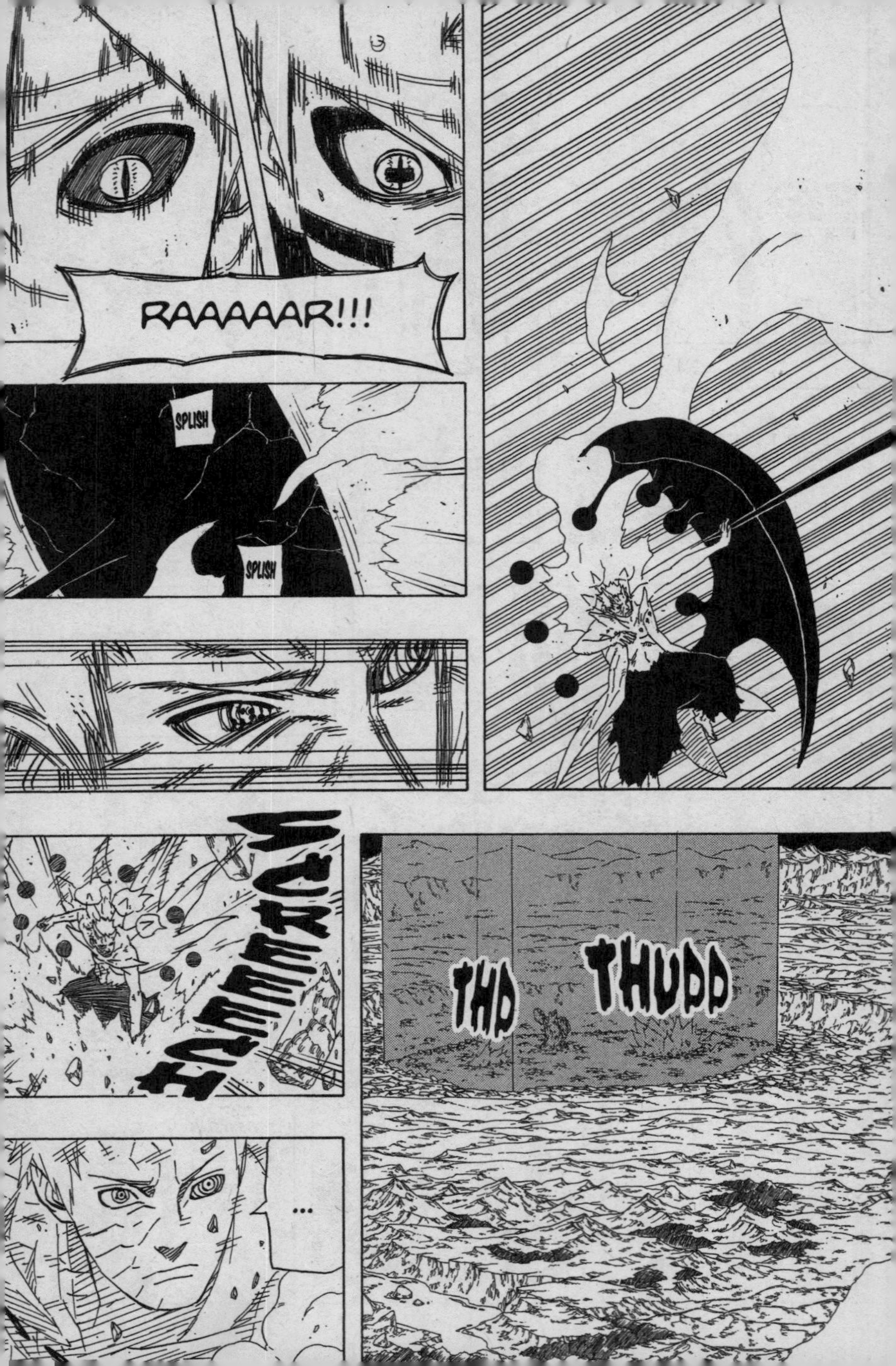
RAAAAAR!!!
SPLISH
SPLISH
THD
THUDD
SCREEECH
...

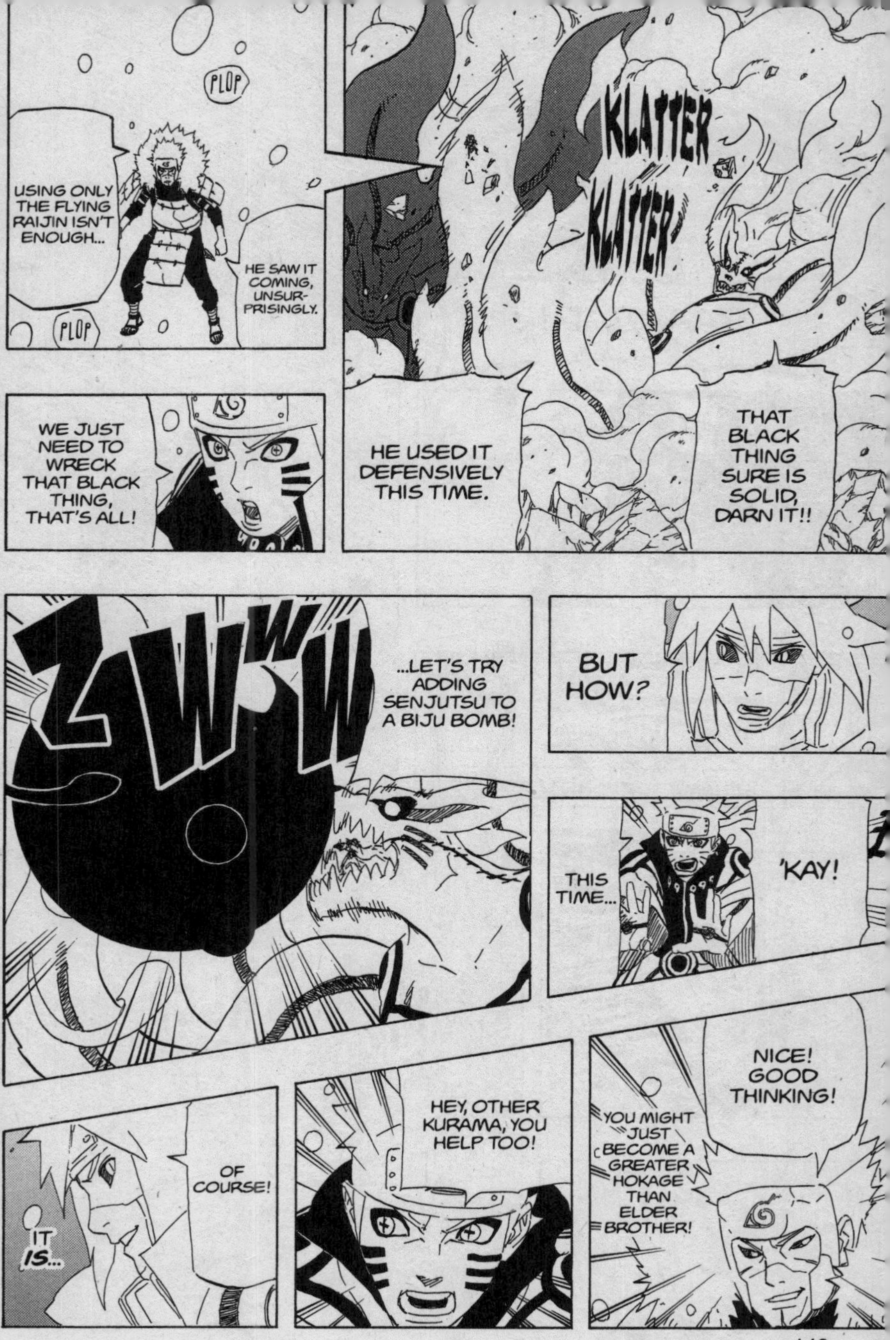
KLATTER
KLATTER
THAT BLACK THING SURE IS SOLID, DARN IT!!
HE USED IT DEFENSIVELY THIS TIME.
PLOP
HE SAW IT COMING, UNSURPRISINGLY.
USING ONLY THE FLYING RAIJIN ISN'T ENOUGH...
PLOP
WE JUST NEED TO WRECK THAT BLACK THING, THAT'S ALL!
BUT HOW?
'KAY!
THIS TIME...
...LET'S TRY ADDING SENJUTSU TO A BIJU BOMB!
ZWWW
NICE! GOOD THINKING!
YOU MIGHT JUST BECOME A GREATER HOKAGE THAN ELDER BROTHER!
HEY, OTHER KURAMA, YOU HELP TOO!
OF COURSE!
IT *IS*...

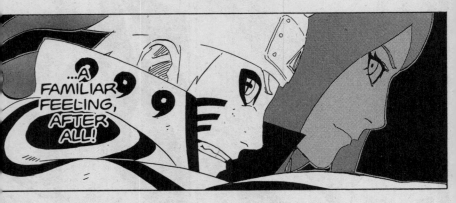

...A FAMILIAR FEELING, AFTER ALL!
ZWW
SWOO...
...
THIS IS NARUTO NOW?
WITH PERFECT CONTROL OVER THIS MUCH CHAKRA?
HOW FAR...
...WILL YOU...
CLENCH
NO HARM IN TAKING MEASURES EARLY.
KLAP

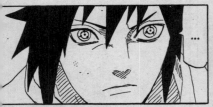

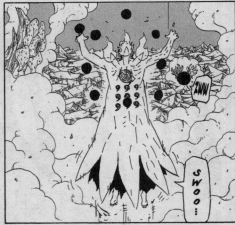

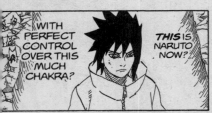

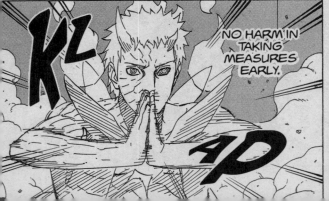

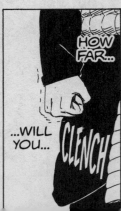

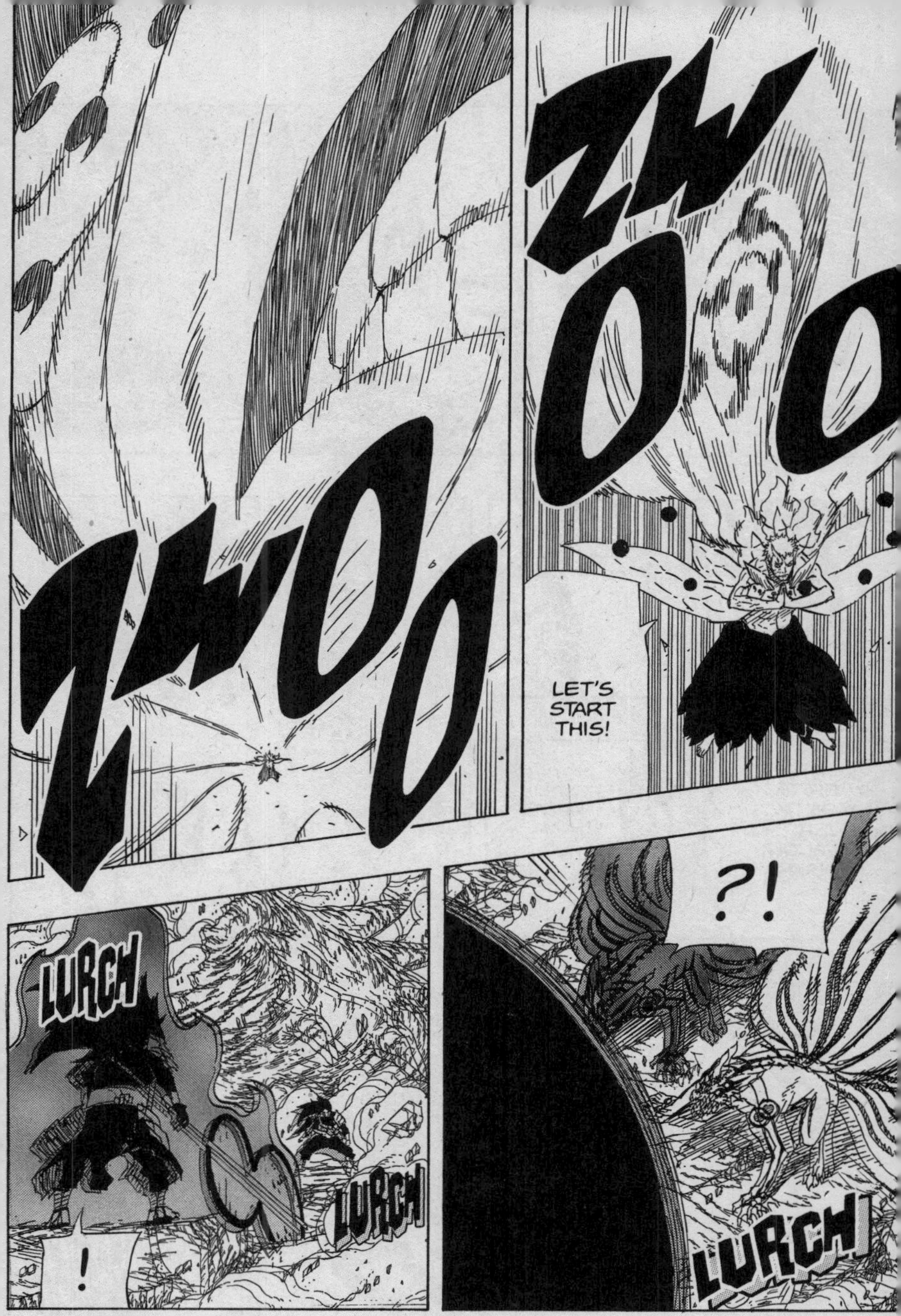
ZWOOO
LET'S START THIS!
ZWOOO
?!
LURCH
LURCH
LURCH
!

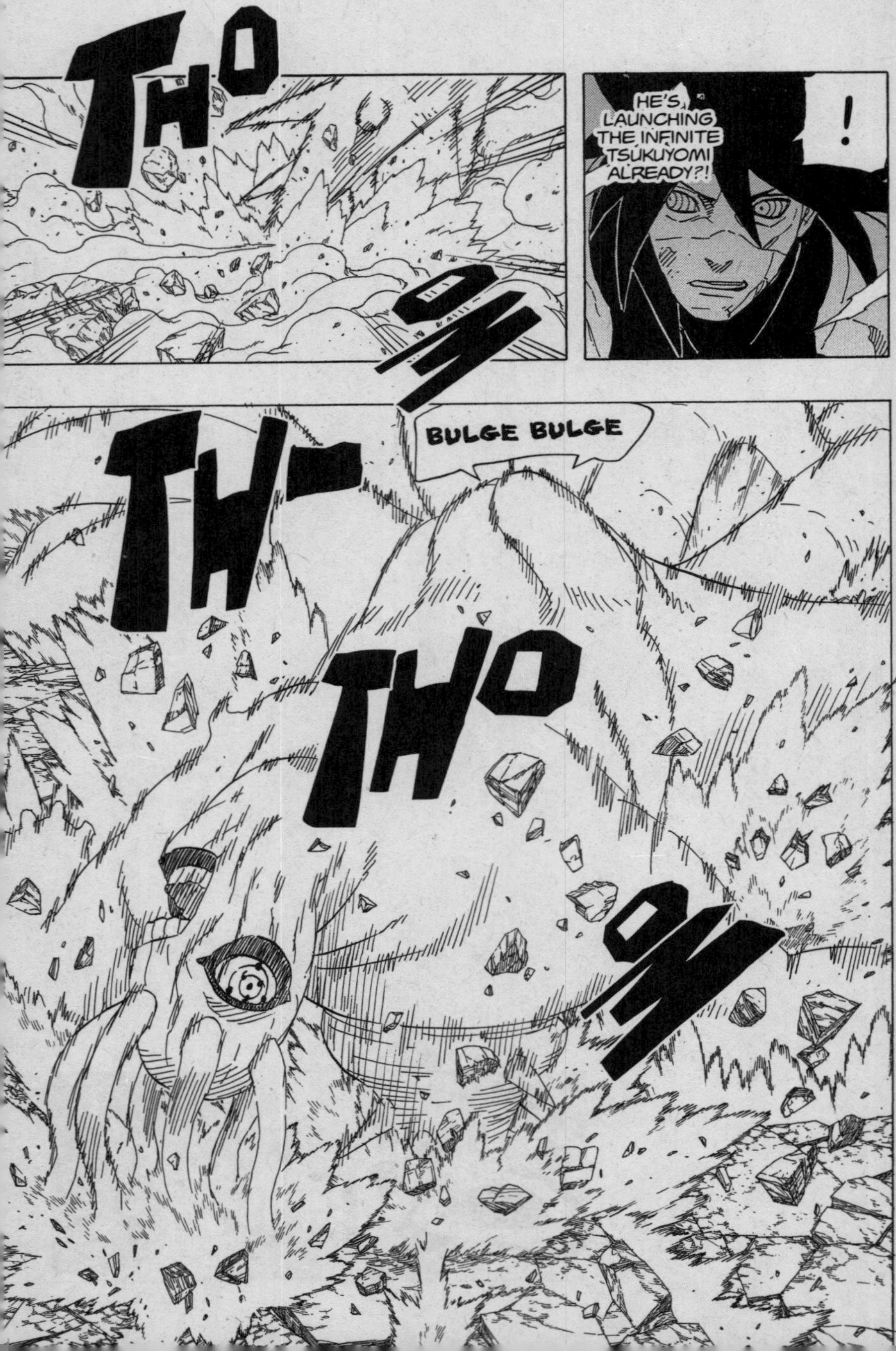
HE'S LAUNCHING THE INFINITE TSUKUYOMI ALREADY?!
!
THOOM
BULGE BULGE
TH-
THOOM

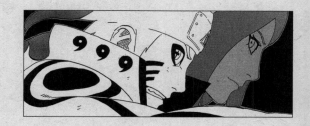

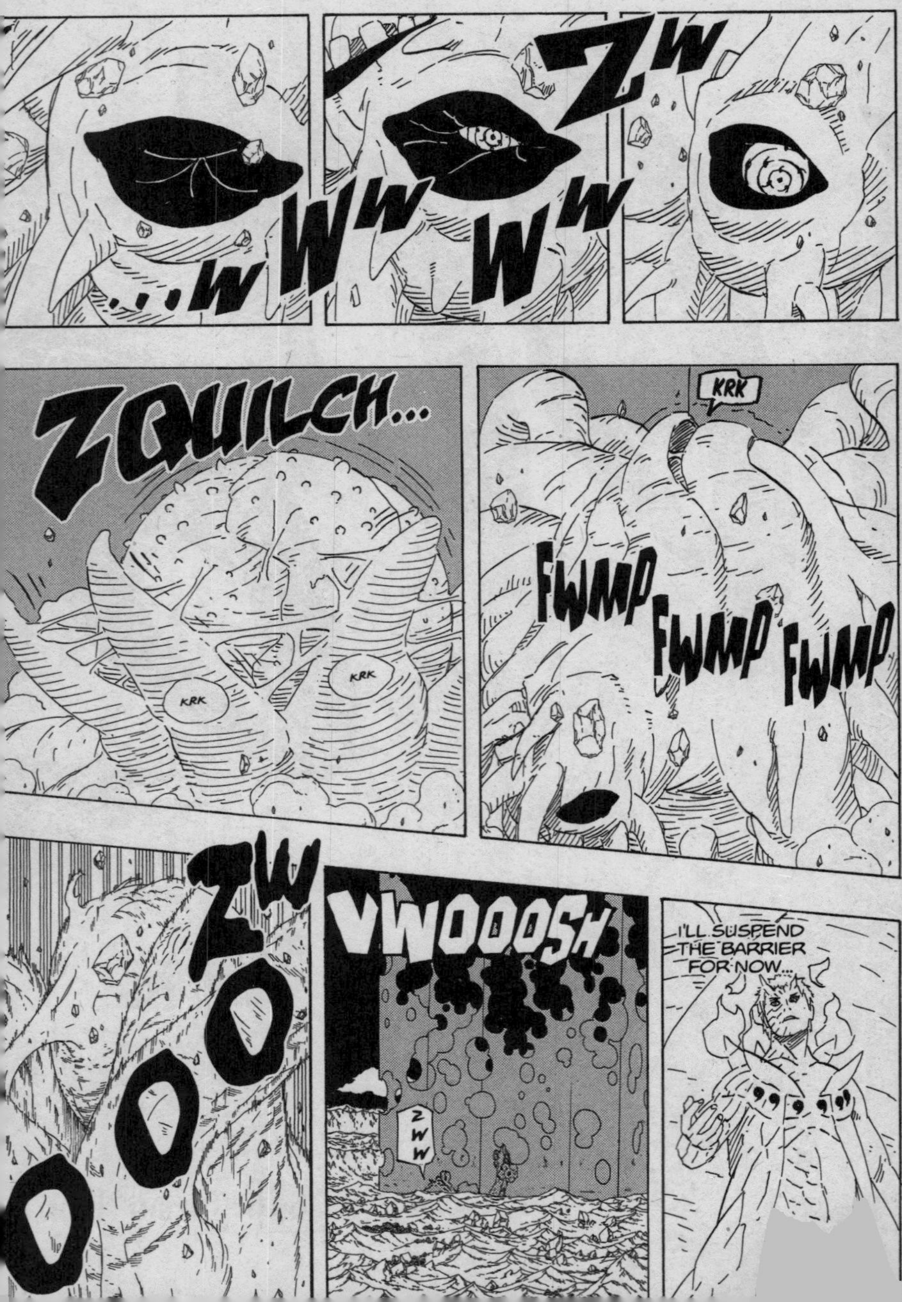

ZW
...WWWWW
KRK
FWMP
FWMP
FWMP
ZQUILCH...
KRK
KRK
I'LL SUSPEND THE BARRIER FOR NOW...
VWOOOSH
ZWW
ZWOOOO

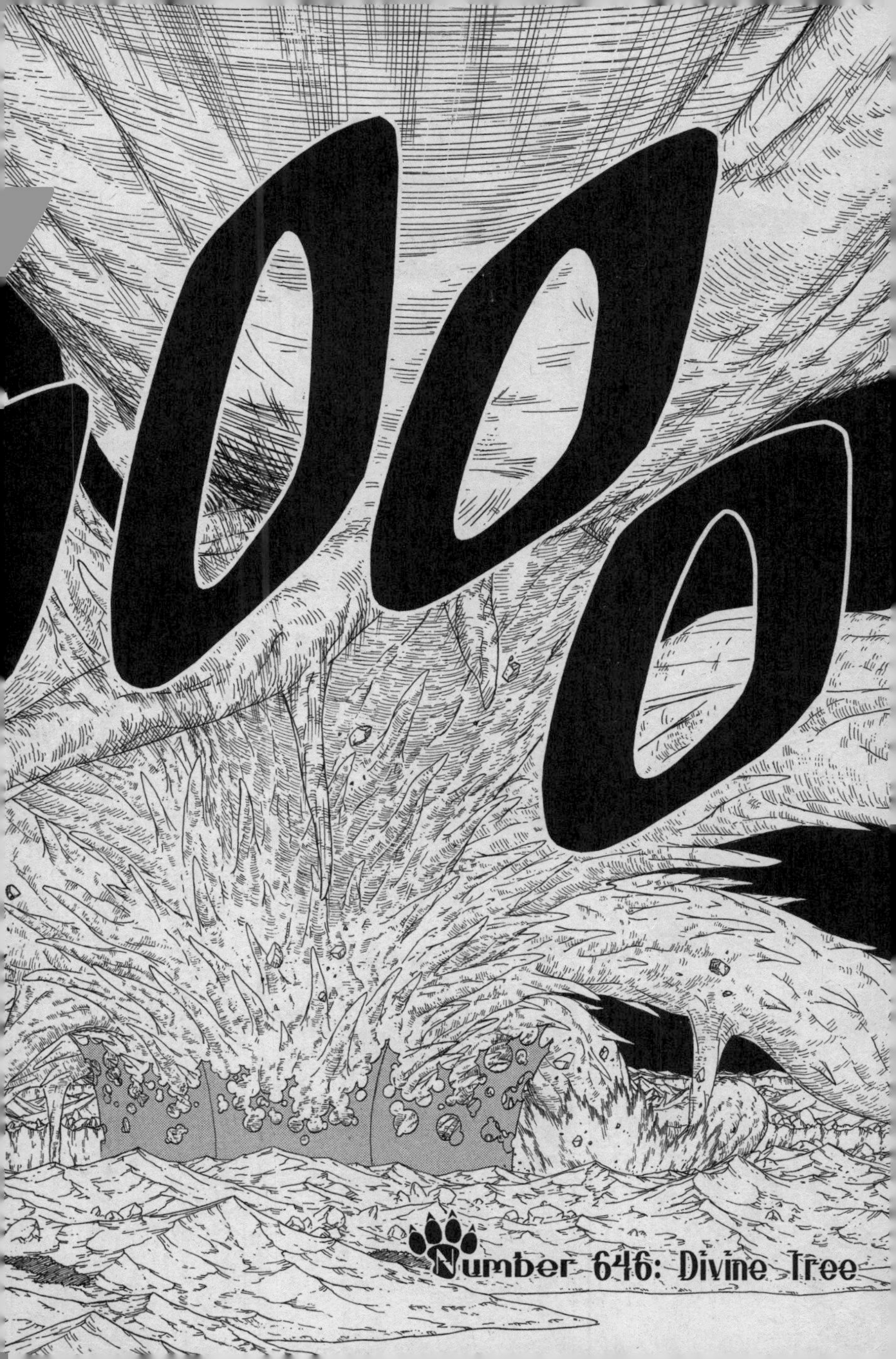
Number 646: Divine Tree

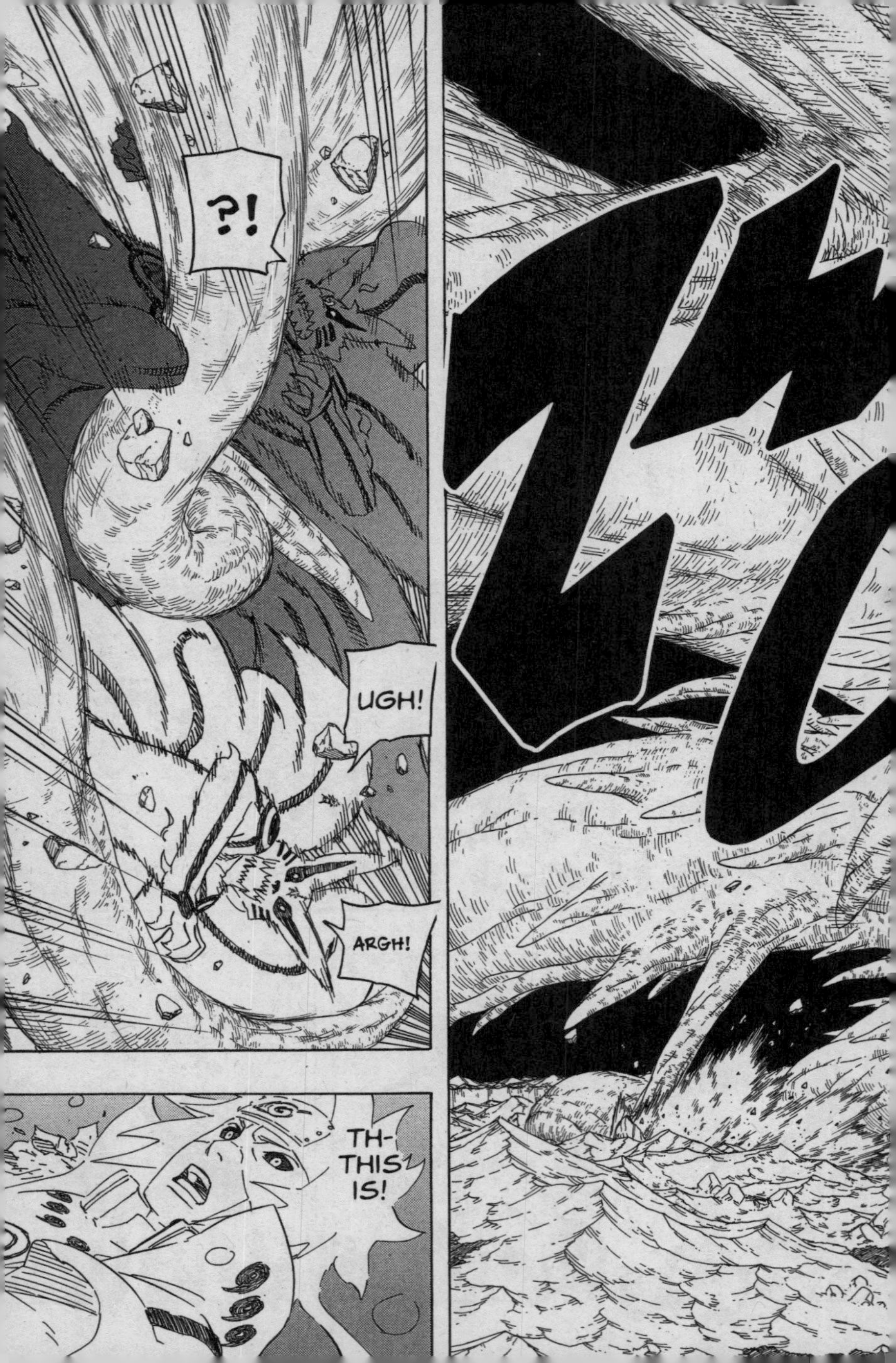
?!
UGH!
ARGH!
TH- THIS IS!

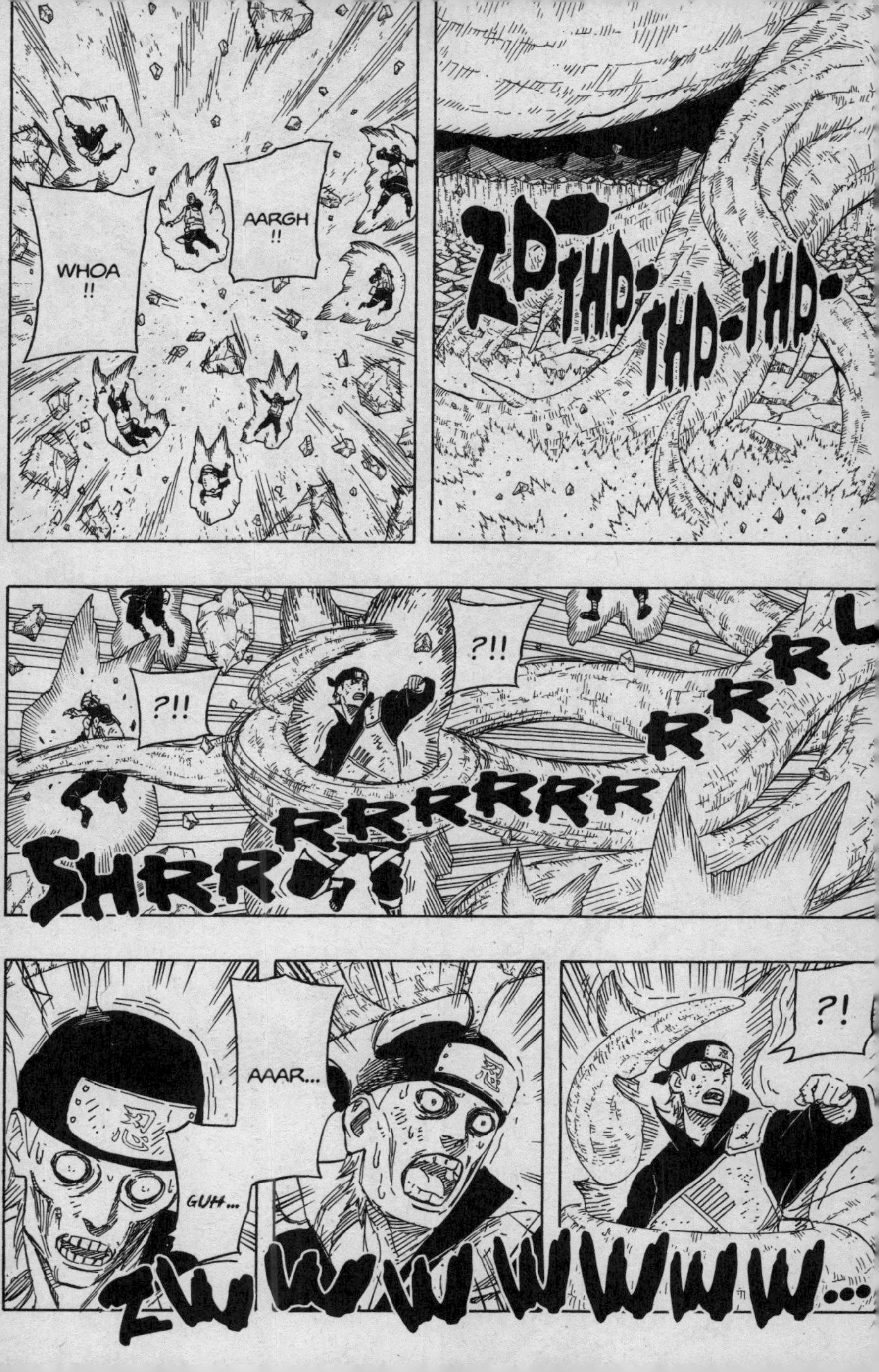

ZD
THD-THD-THD-THD-
AARGH!!
WHOA!!
?!!
?!!
SHRRRRRRRRRRRRL
?!
AAAR...
GUH...
ZWWWWWWWWWW...

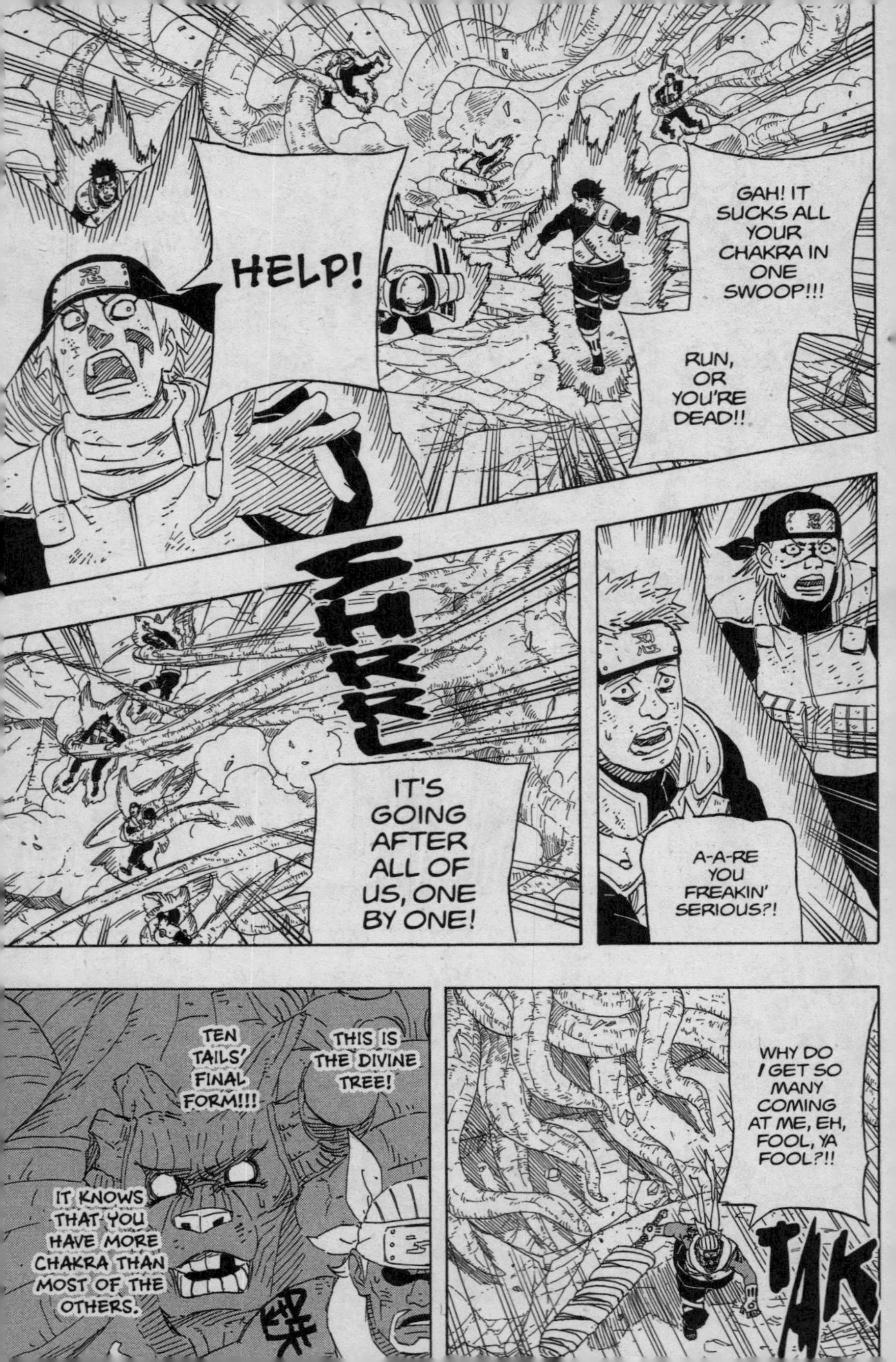
GAH! IT SUCKS ALL YOUR CHAKRA IN ONE SWOOP!!!
RUN, OR YOU'RE DEAD!!
HELP!
A-A-RE YOU FREAKIN' SERIOUS?!
SHRRL
IT'S GOING AFTER ALL OF US, ONE BY ONE!
WHY DO I GET SO MANY COMING AT ME, EH, FOOL, YA FOOL?!!
TAK
THIS IS THE DIVINE TREE!
TEN TAILS' FINAL FORM!!!
IT KNOWS THAT YOU HAVE MORE CHAKRA THAN MOST OF THE OTHERS.

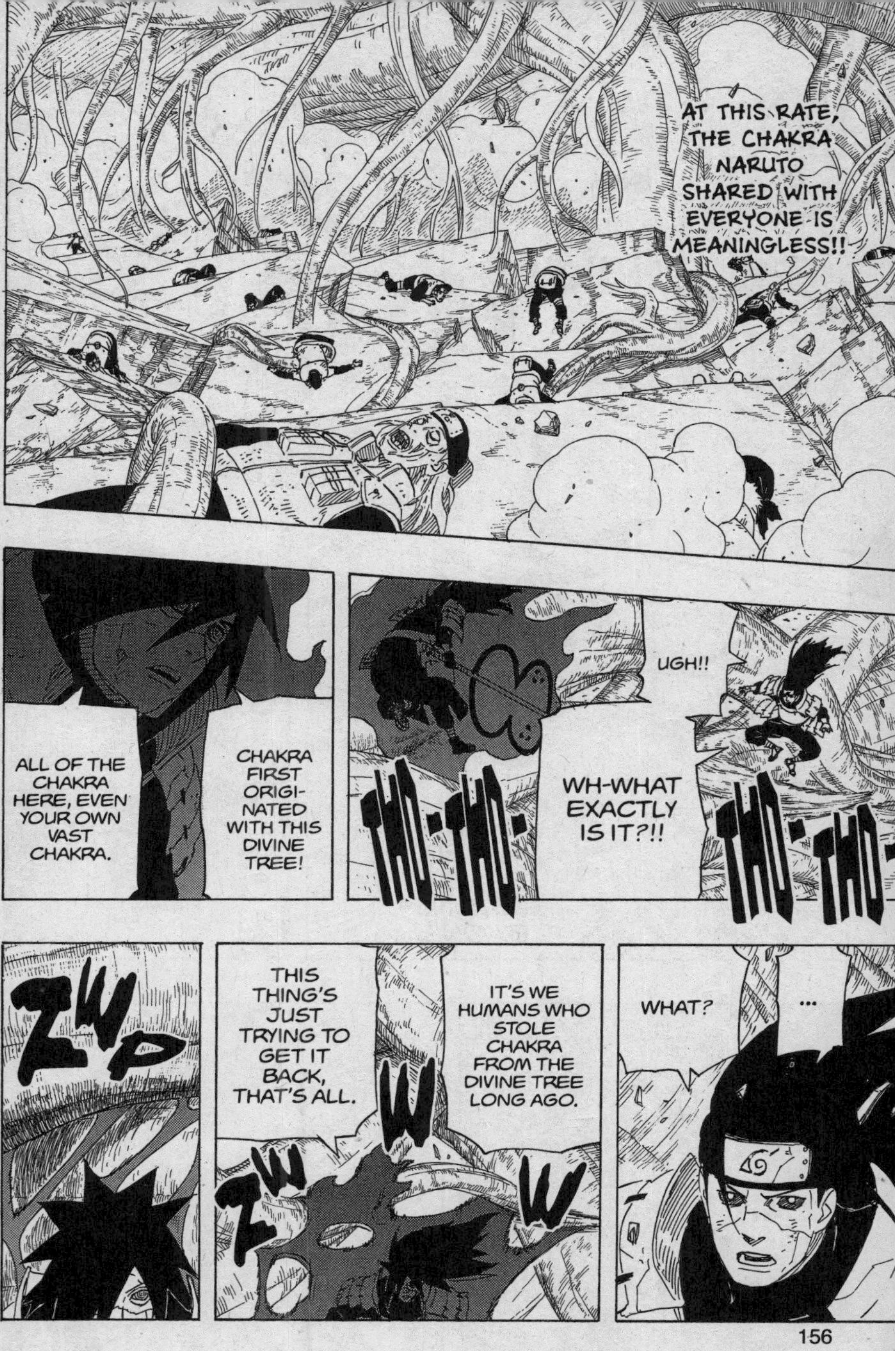
AT THIS RATE, THE CHAKRA NARUTO SHARED WITH EVERYONE IS MEANINGLESS!!
UGH!!
WH-WHAT EXACTLY IS IT?!!
THD-THD-
THD-THD-
CHAKRA FIRST ORIGINATED WITH THIS DIVINE TREE!
ALL OF THE CHAKRA HERE, EVEN YOUR OWN VAST CHAKRA.
...
WHAT?
IT'S WE HUMANS WHO STOLE CHAKRA FROM THE DIVINE TREE LONG AGO.
THIS THING'S JUST TRYING TO GET IT BACK, THAT'S ALL.
ZWP

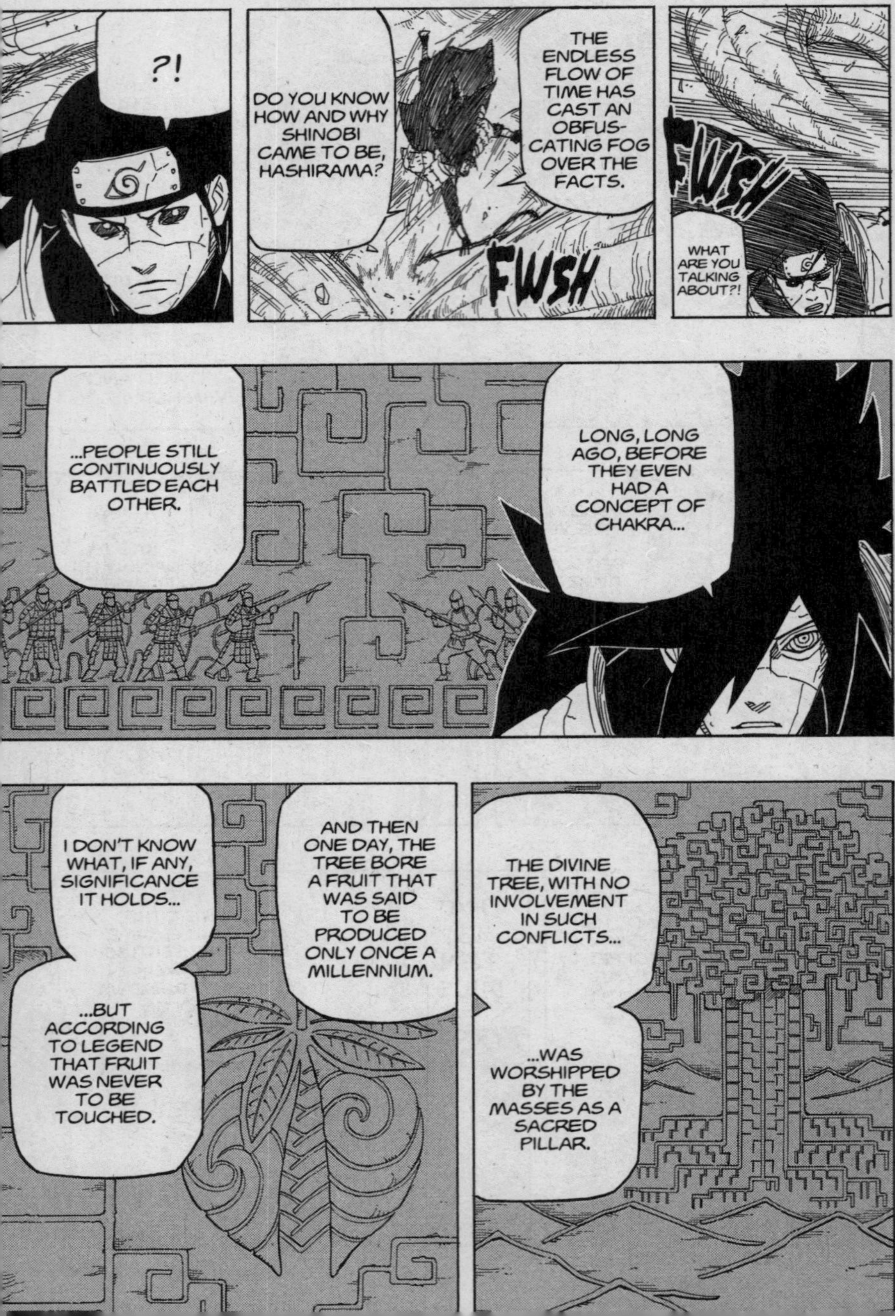
FWSH
WHAT ARE YOU TALKING ABOUT?!
THE ENDLESS FLOW OF TIME HAS CAST AN OBFUS-CATING FOG OVER THE FACTS.
DO YOU KNOW HOW AND WHY SHINOBI CAME TO BE, HASHIRAMA?
FWSH
?!
LONG, LONG AGO, BEFORE THEY EVEN HAD A CONCEPT OF CHAKRA...
...PEOPLE STILL CONTINUOUSLY BATTLED EACH OTHER.
THE DIVINE TREE, WITH NO INVOLVEMENT IN SUCH CONFLICTS...
...WAS WORSHIPPED BY THE MASSES AS A SACRED PILLAR.
AND THEN ONE DAY, THE TREE BORE A FRUIT THAT WAS SAID TO BE PRODUCED ONLY ONCE A MILLENNIUM.
I DON'T KNOW WHAT, IF ANY, SIGNIFICANCE IT HOLDS...
...BUT ACCORDING TO LEGEND THAT FRUIT WAS NEVER TO BE TOUCHED.

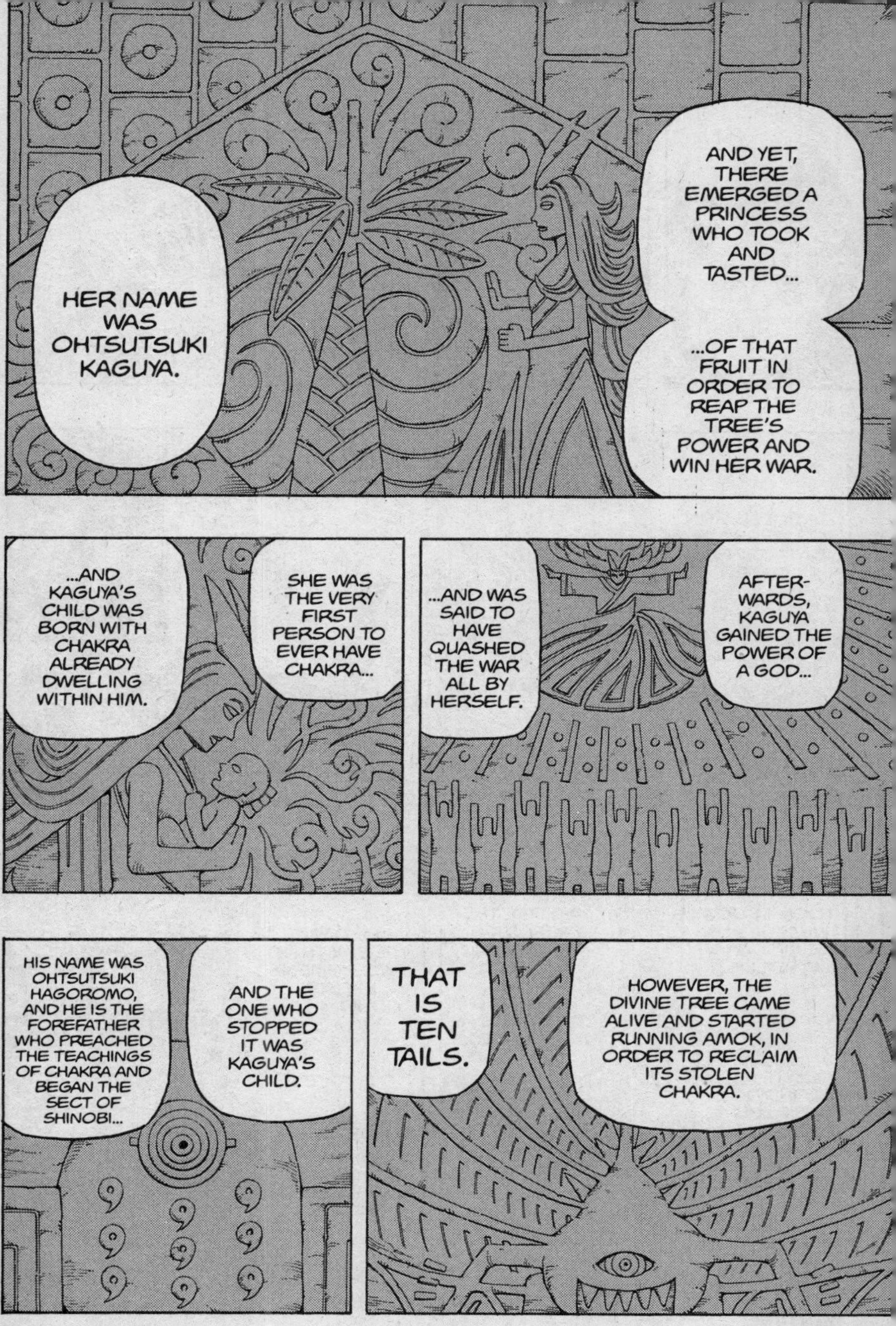
AND YET, THERE EMERGED A PRINCESS WHO TOOK AND TASTED...
...OF THAT FRUIT IN ORDER TO REAP THE TREE'S POWER AND WIN HER WAR.
HER NAME WAS OHTSUTSUKI KAGUYA.
AFTER-WARDS, KAGUYA GAINED THE POWER OF A GOD...
...AND WAS SAID TO HAVE QUASHED THE WAR ALL BY HERSELF.
SHE WAS THE VERY FIRST PERSON TO EVER HAVE CHAKRA...
...AND KAGUYA'S CHILD WAS BORN WITH CHAKRA ALREADY DWELLING WITHIN HIM.
HOWEVER, THE DIVINE TREE CAME ALIVE AND STARTED RUNNING AMOK, IN ORDER TO RECLAIM ITS STOLEN CHAKRA.
THAT IS TEN TAILS.
AND THE ONE WHO STOPPED IT WAS KAGUYA'S CHILD.
HIS NAME WAS OHTSUTSUKI HAGOROMO, AND HE IS THE FOREFATHER WHO PREACHED THE TEACHINGS OF CHAKRA AND BEGAN THE SECT OF SHINOBI...

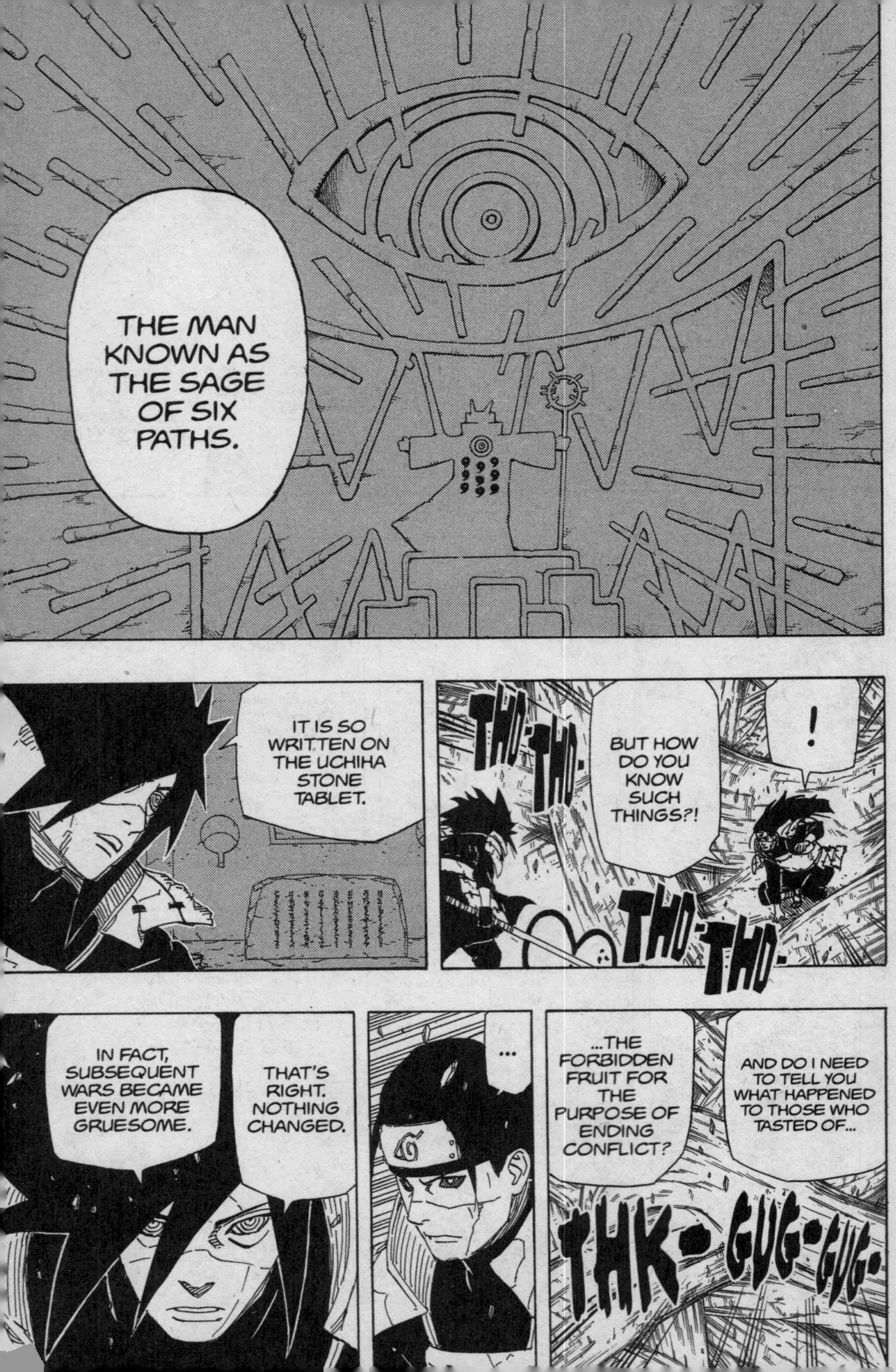
THE MAN KNOWN AS THE SAGE OF SIX PATHS.
!
BUT HOW DO YOU KNOW SUCH THINGS?!
THO-THO-
THO-THO-
IT IS SO WRITTEN ON THE UCHIHA STONE TABLET.
AND DO I NEED TO TELL YOU WHAT HAPPENED TO THOSE WHO TASTED OF...
...THE FORBIDDEN FRUIT FOR THE PURPOSE OF ENDING CONFLICT?
THK- GUG-GUG-
...
THAT'S RIGHT. NOTHING CHANGED.
IN FACT, SUBSEQUENT WARS BECAME EVEN MORE GRUESOME.

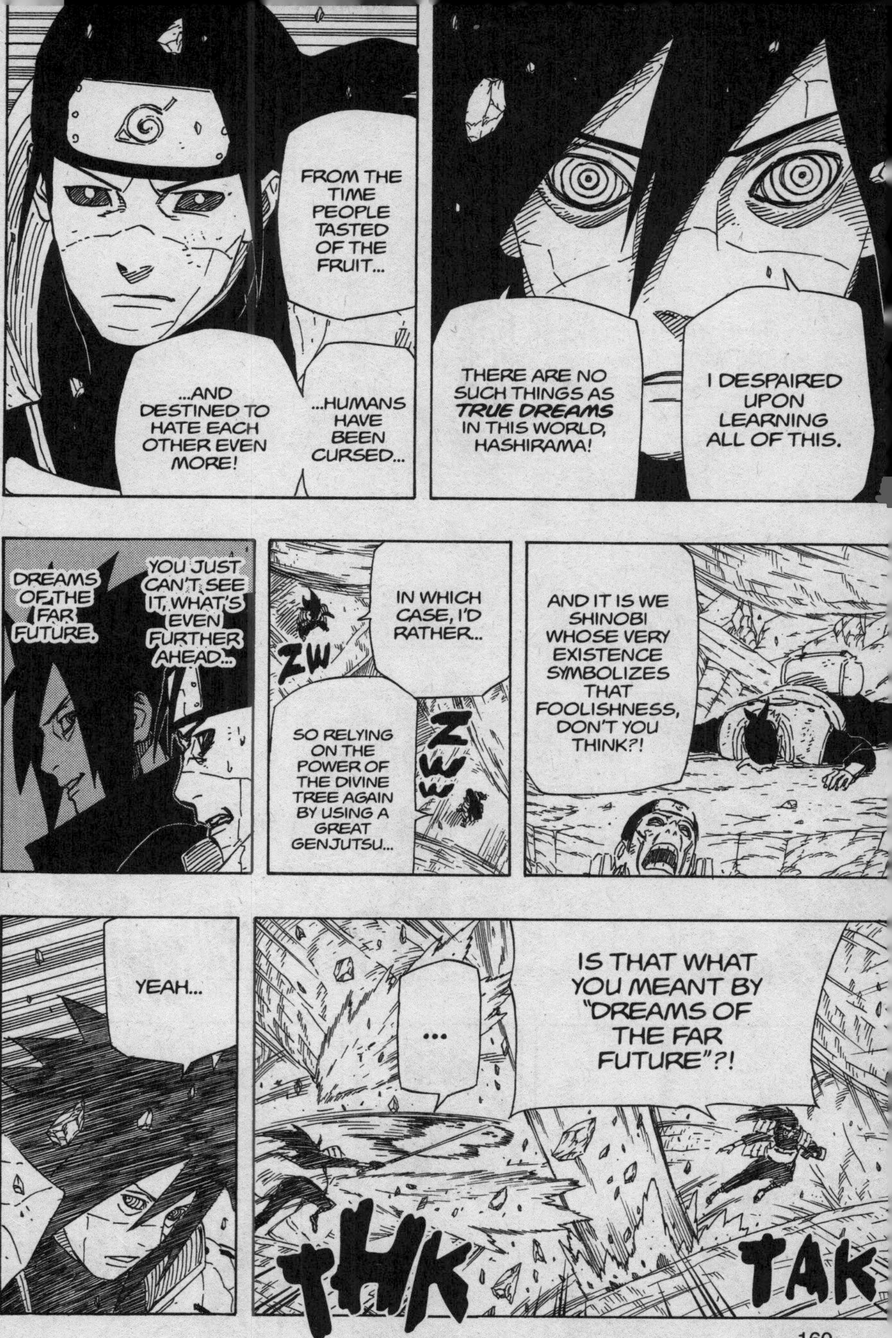
I DESPAIRED UPON LEARNING ALL OF THIS.
THERE ARE NO SUCH THINGS AS TRUE DREAMS IN THIS WORLD, HASHIRAMA!
FROM THE TIME PEOPLE TASTED OF THE FRUIT...
...HUMANS HAVE BEEN CURSED...
...AND DESTINED TO HATE EACH OTHER EVEN MORE!
AND IT IS WE SHINOBI WHOSE VERY EXISTENCE SYMBOLIZES THAT FOOLISHNESS, DON'T YOU THINK?!
IN WHICH CASE, I'D RATHER...
ZW
ZWW
SO RELYING ON THE POWER OF THE DIVINE TREE AGAIN BY USING A GREAT GENJUTSU...
YOU JUST CAN'T SEE IT, WHAT'S EVEN FURTHER AHEAD...
DREAMS OF THE FAR FUTURE.
IS THAT WHAT YOU MEANT BY "DREAMS OF THE FAR FUTURE"?!
...
TAK
THK
YEAH...

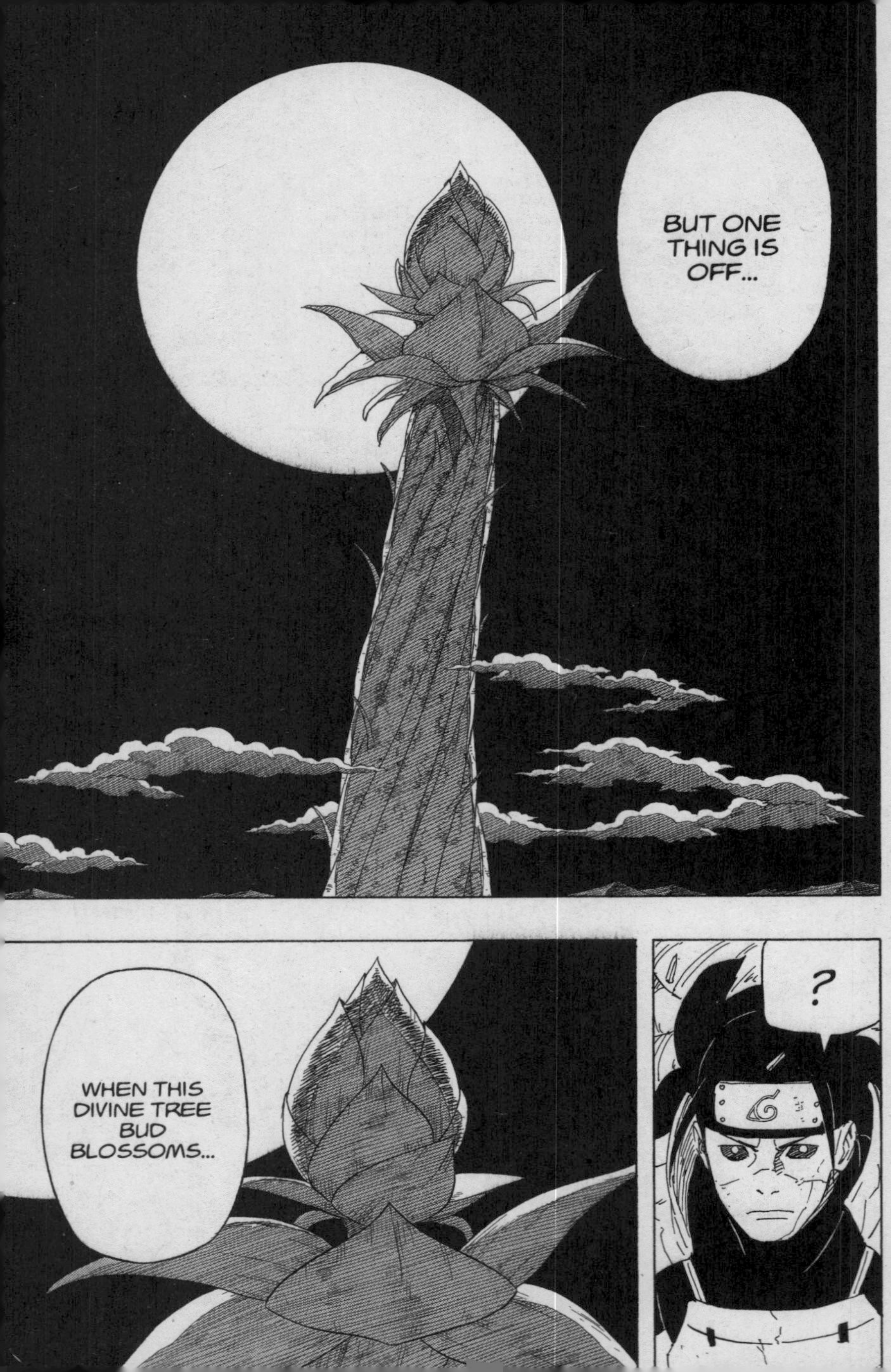
BUT ONE THING IS OFF...
?
WHEN THIS DIVINE TREE BUD BLOSSOMS...

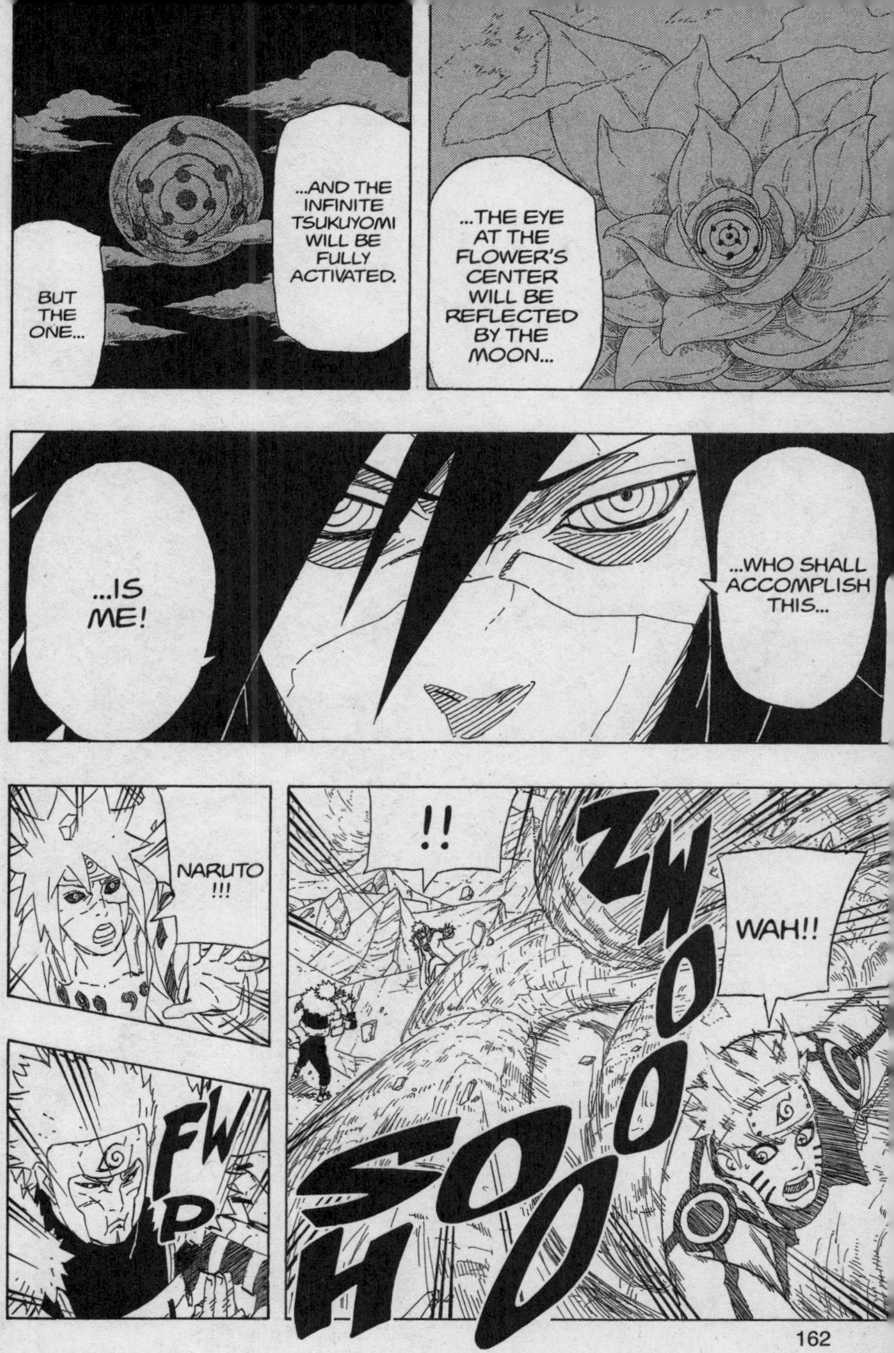
...THE EYE AT THE FLOWER'S CENTER WILL BE REFLECTED BY THE MOON...
...AND THE INFINITE TSUKUYOMI WILL BE FULLY ACTIVATED.
BUT THE ONE...
...WHO SHALL ACCOMPLISH THIS...
...IS ME!
WAH!!
ZWOOOOOOSH
!!
NARUTO!!!
FWP

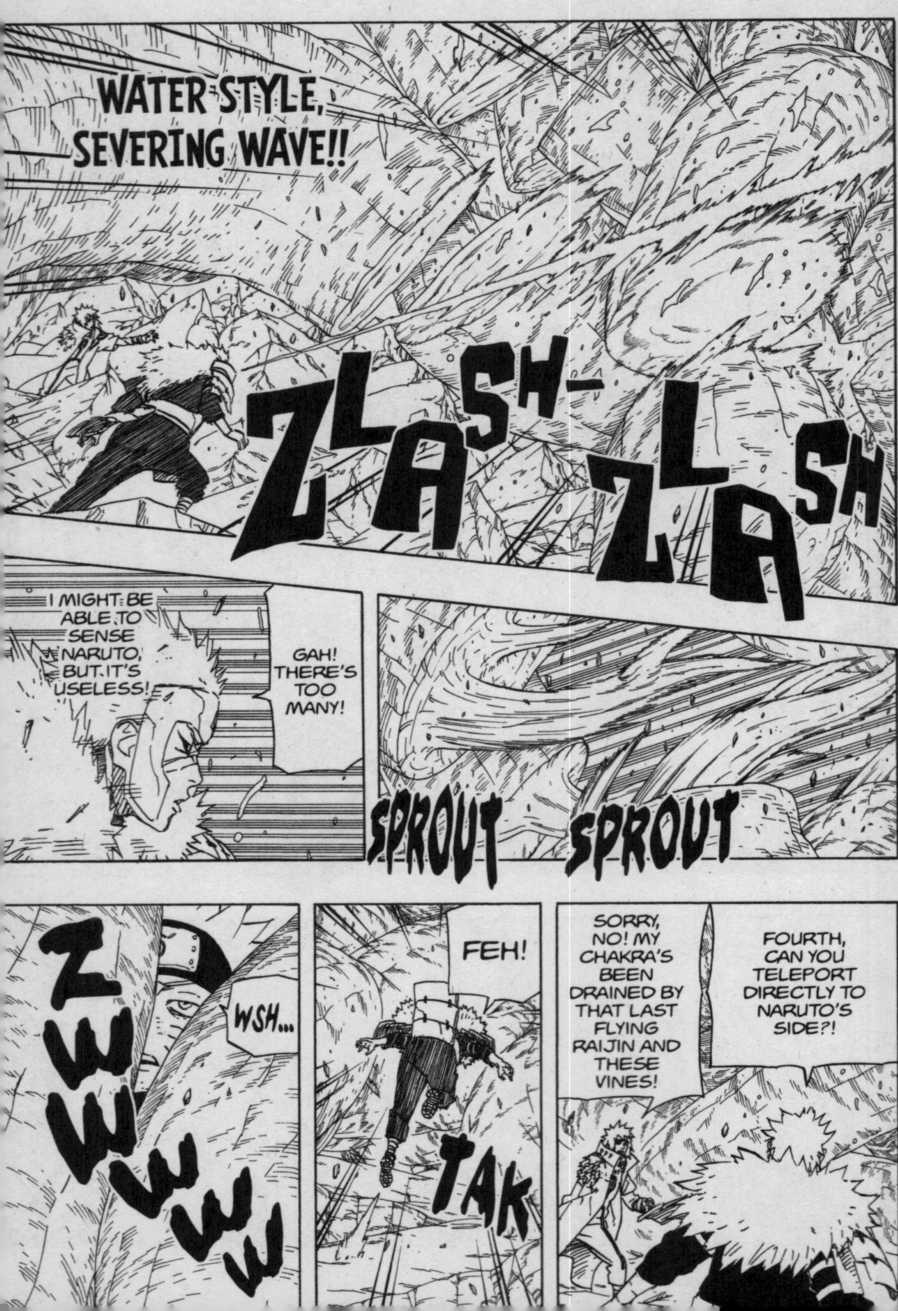
WATER STYLE, SEVERING WAVE!!
ZLASH-ZLASH
SPROUT SPROUT
GAH! THERE'S TOO MANY!
I MIGHT BE ABLE TO SENSE NARUTO, BUT IT'S USELESS!
FOURTH, CAN YOU TELEPORT DIRECTLY TO NARUTO'S SIDE?!
SORRY, NO! MY CHAKRA'S BEEN DRAINED BY THAT LAST FLYING RAIJIN AND THESE VINES!
FEH!
TAK
WSH...
ZWWWWW

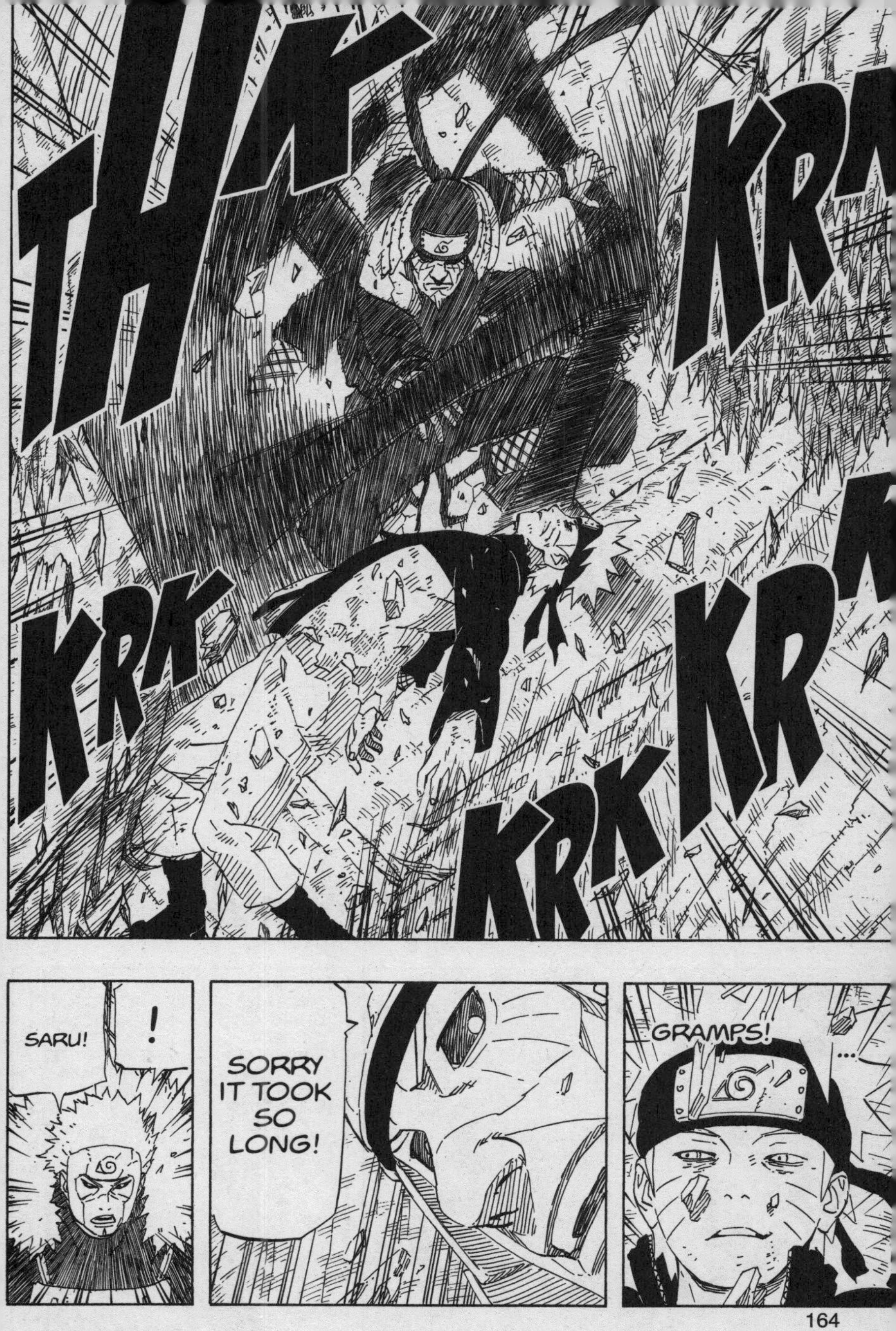
KRA
THK
KRK
KR
KRK
GRAMPS!
...
SORRY IT TOOK SO LONG!
!
SARU!

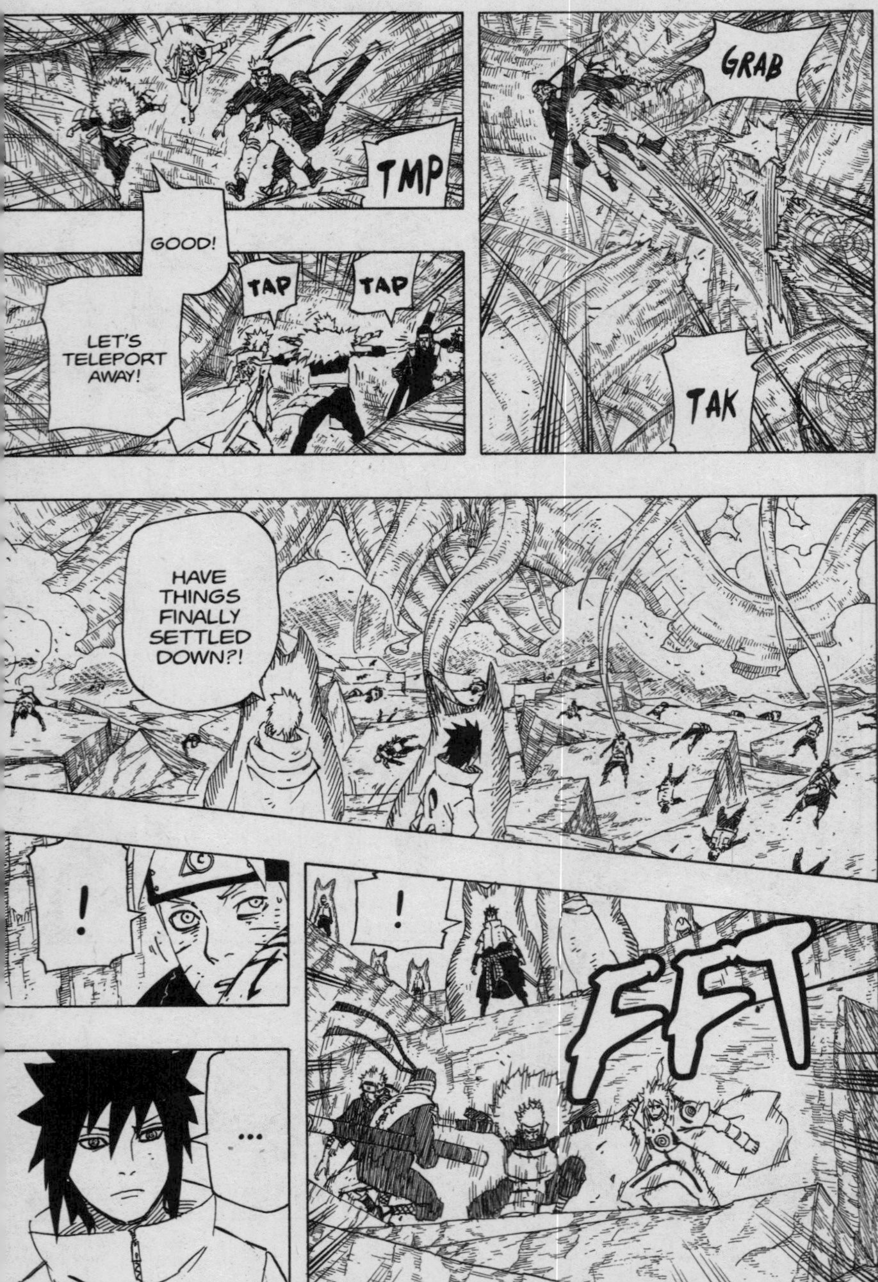
GRAB
TAK
TMP
TAP
TAP
GOOD!
LET'S TELEPORT AWAY!
HAVE THINGS FINALLY SETTLED DOWN?!
!
FFT
!
...

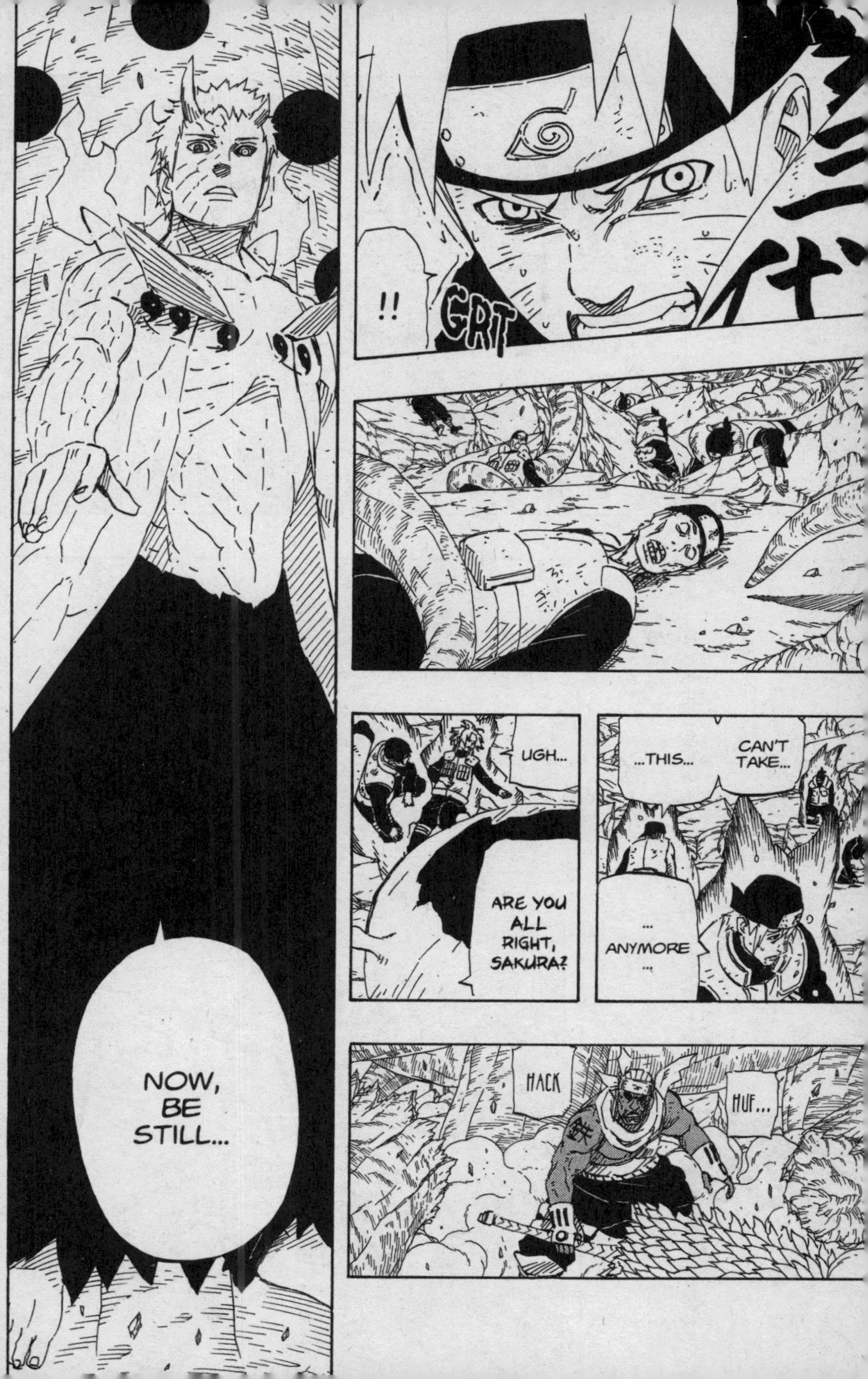

!!
GRT
CAN'T TAKE...
...THIS...
... ANYMORE ...
UGH...
ARE YOU ALL RIGHT, SAKURA?
HUF...
HACK
NOW, BE STILL...

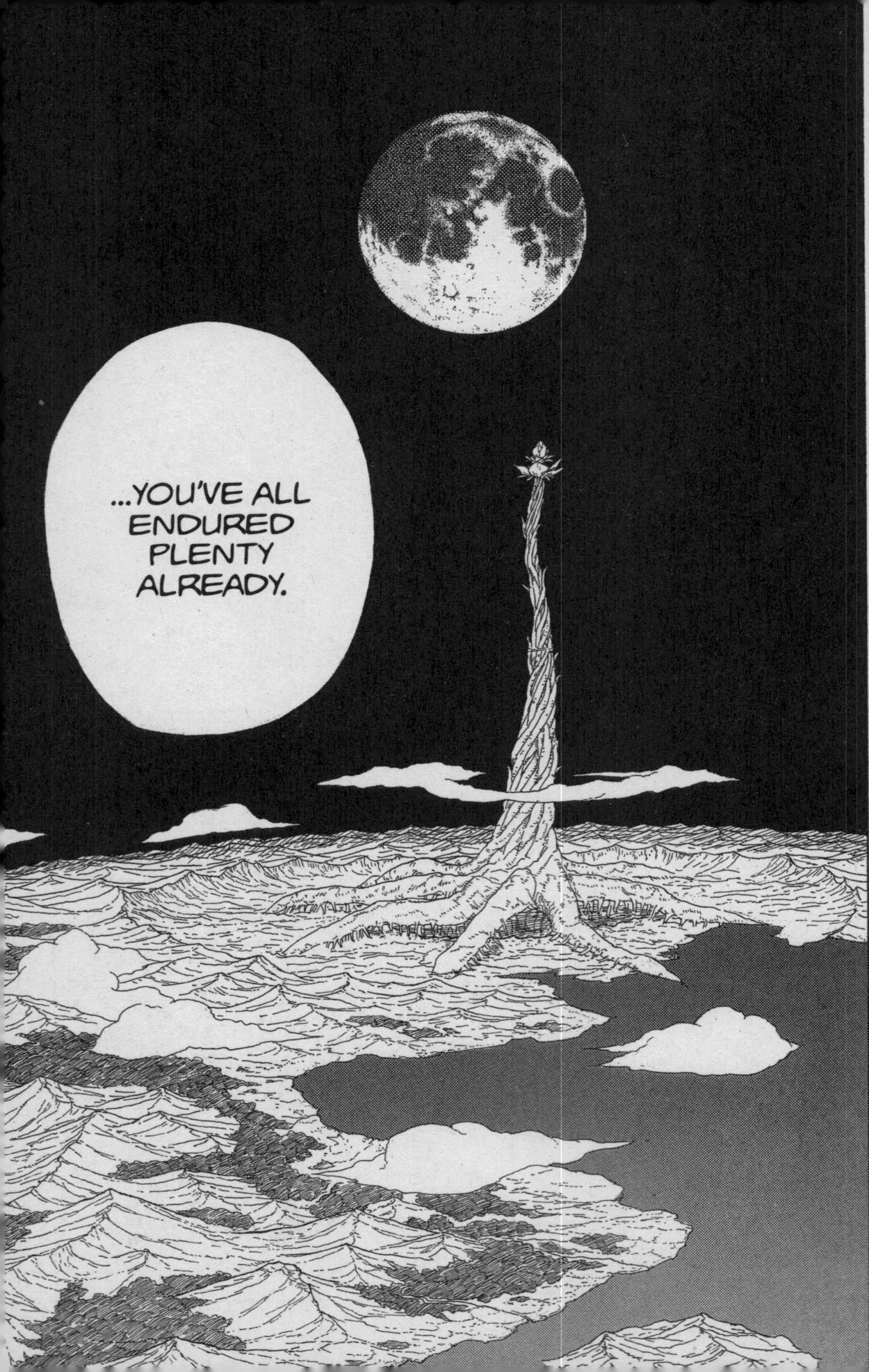
...YOU'VE ALL ENDURED PLENTY ALREADY.

ZWM
SWOO...

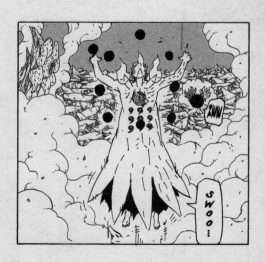

Number 647: Regret

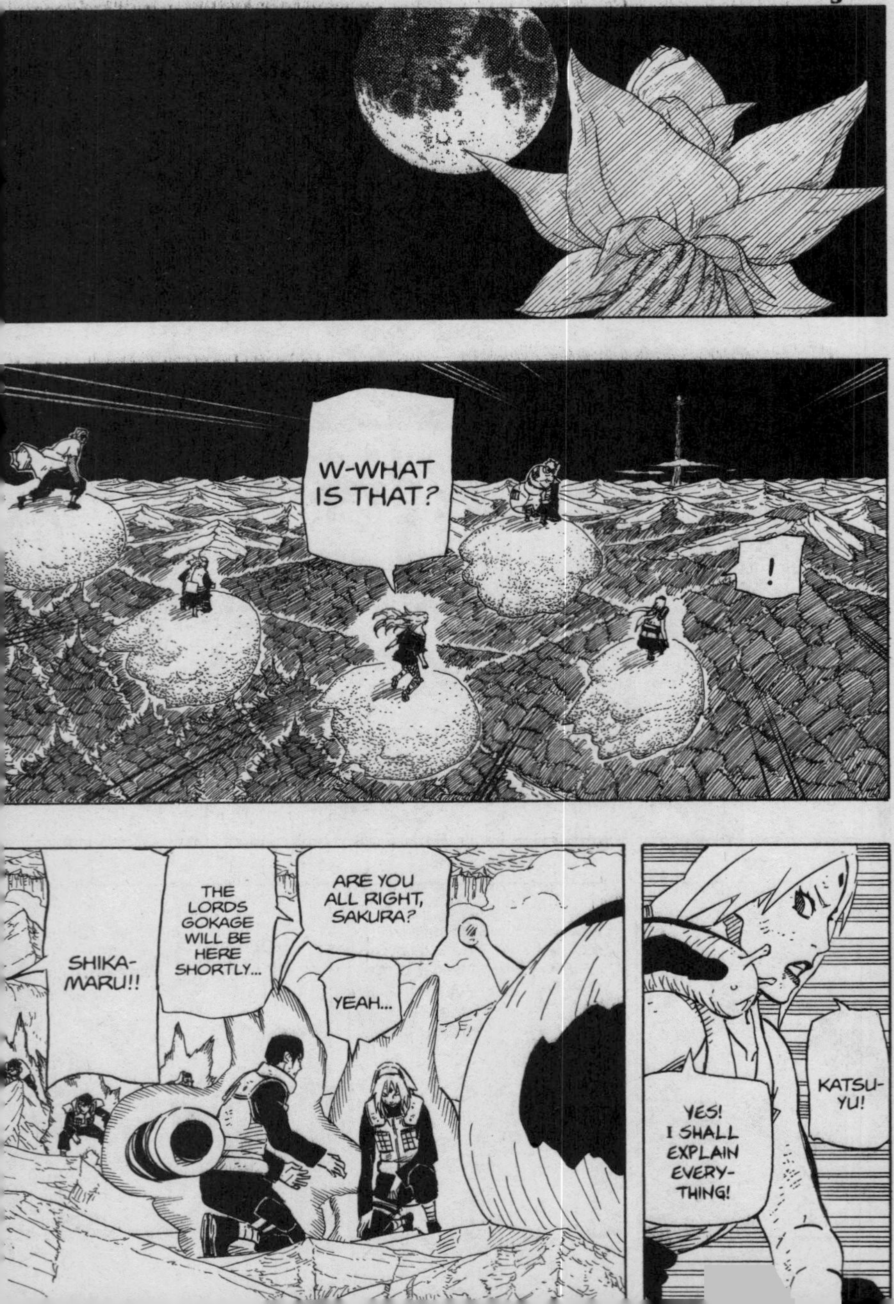
W-WHAT IS THAT?
!
KATSU-YU!
YES! I SHALL EXPLAIN EVERY-THING!
ARE YOU ALL RIGHT, SAKURA?
YEAH...
THE LORDS GOKAGE WILL BE HERE SHORTLY...
SHIKA-MARU!!

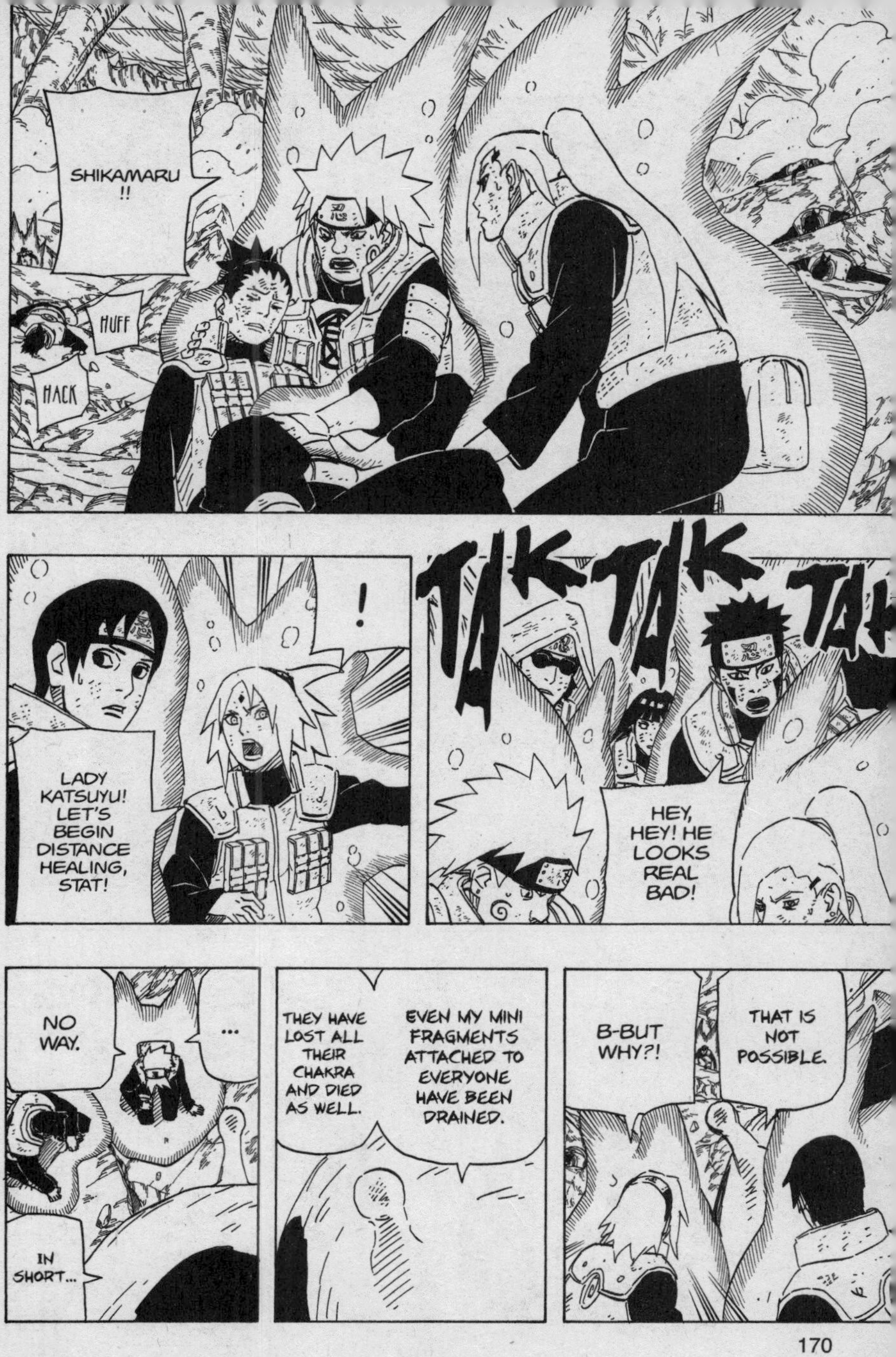
SHIKAMARU !!
HUFF
HACK
TAK
TAK
HEY, HEY! HE LOOKS REAL BAD!
!
LADY KATSUYU! LET'S BEGIN DISTANCE HEALING, STAT!
THAT IS NOT POSSIBLE.
B-BUT WHY?!
EVEN MY MINI FRAGMENTS ATTACHED TO EVERYONE HAVE BEEN DRAINED.
THEY HAVE LOST ALL THEIR CHAKRA AND DIED AS WELL.
...
NO WAY.
IN SHORT...

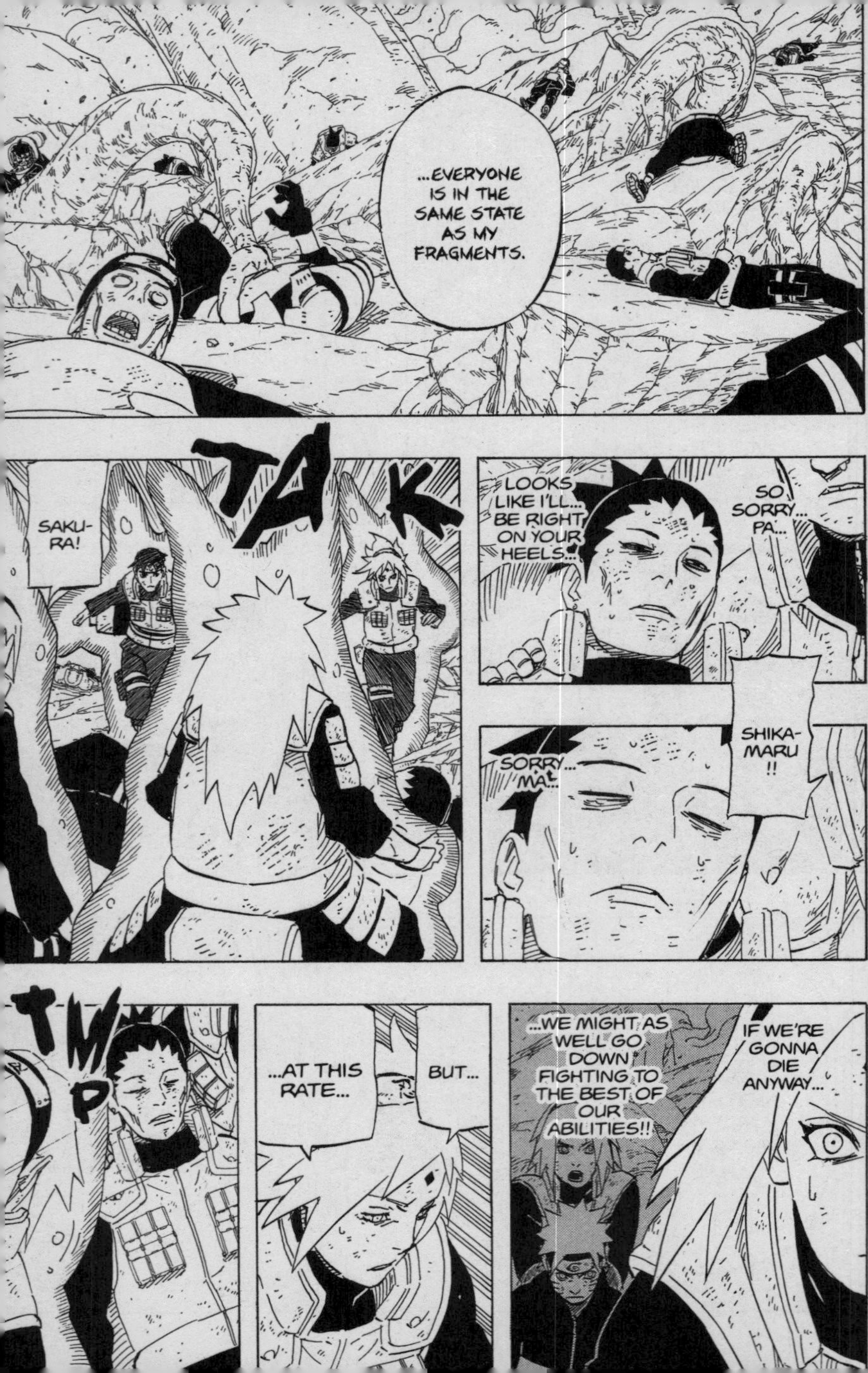
...EVERYONE IS IN THE SAME STATE AS MY FRAGMENTS.
SO SORRY... PA...
LOOKS LIKE I'LL... BE RIGHT ON YOUR HEELS...
SHIKA-MARU!!
SORRY... MA...
TAK
SAKU-RA!
IF WE'RE GONNA DIE ANYWAY...
...WE MIGHT AS WELL GO DOWN FIGHTING TO THE BEST OF OUR ABILITIES!!
BUT...
...AT THIS RATE...
THMP

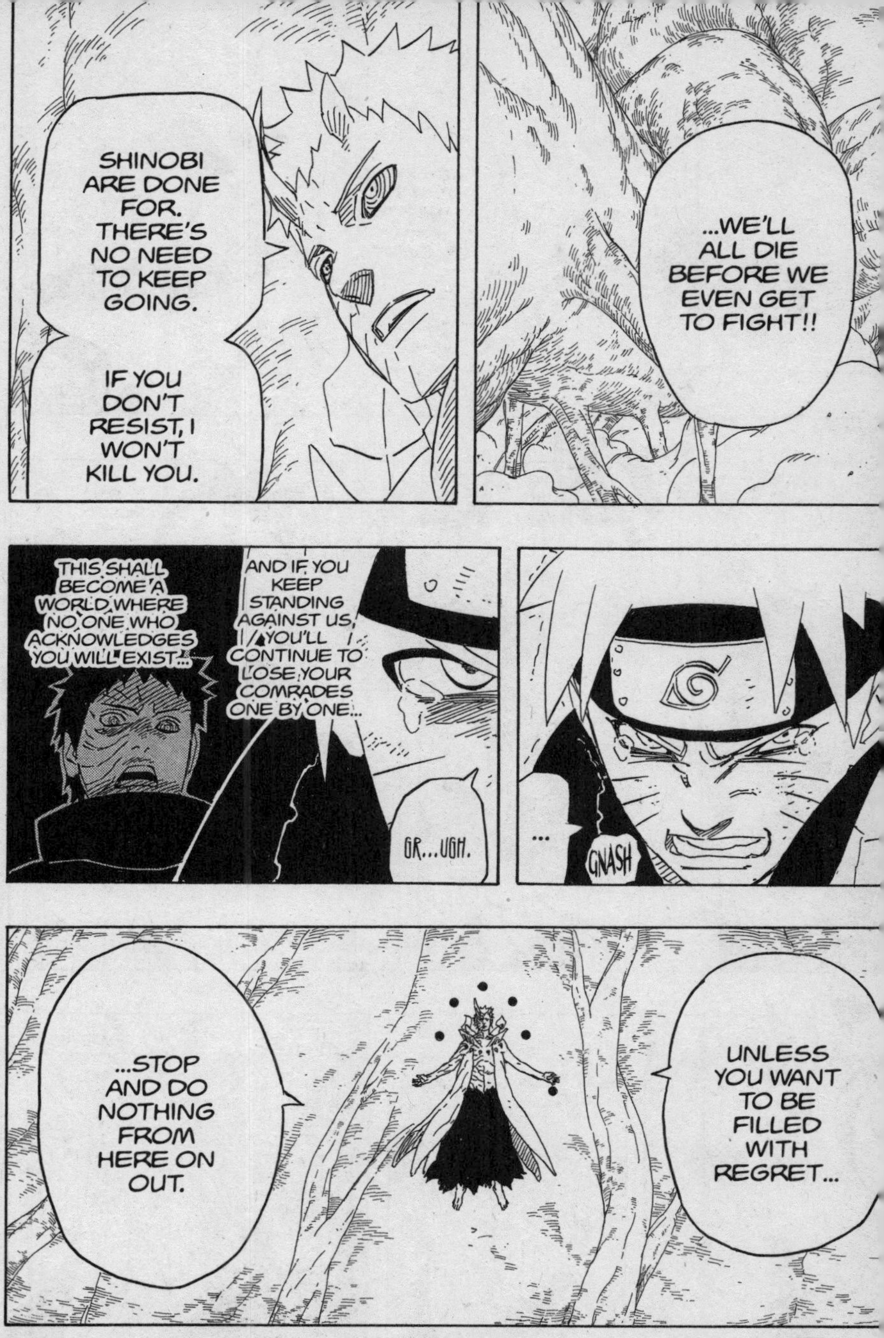
...WE'LL ALL DIE BEFORE WE EVEN GET TO FIGHT!!
SHINOBI ARE DONE FOR. THERE'S NO NEED TO KEEP GOING.
IF YOU DON'T RESIST, I WON'T KILL YOU.
...
GNASH
AND IF YOU KEEP STANDING AGAINST US, YOU'LL CONTINUE TO LOSE YOUR COMRADES ONE BY ONE...
THIS SHALL BECOME A WORLD WHERE NO ONE WHO ACKNOWLEDGES YOU WILL EXIST...
GR...UGH.
UNLESS YOU WANT TO BE FILLED WITH REGRET...
...STOP AND DO NOTHING FROM HERE ON OUT.

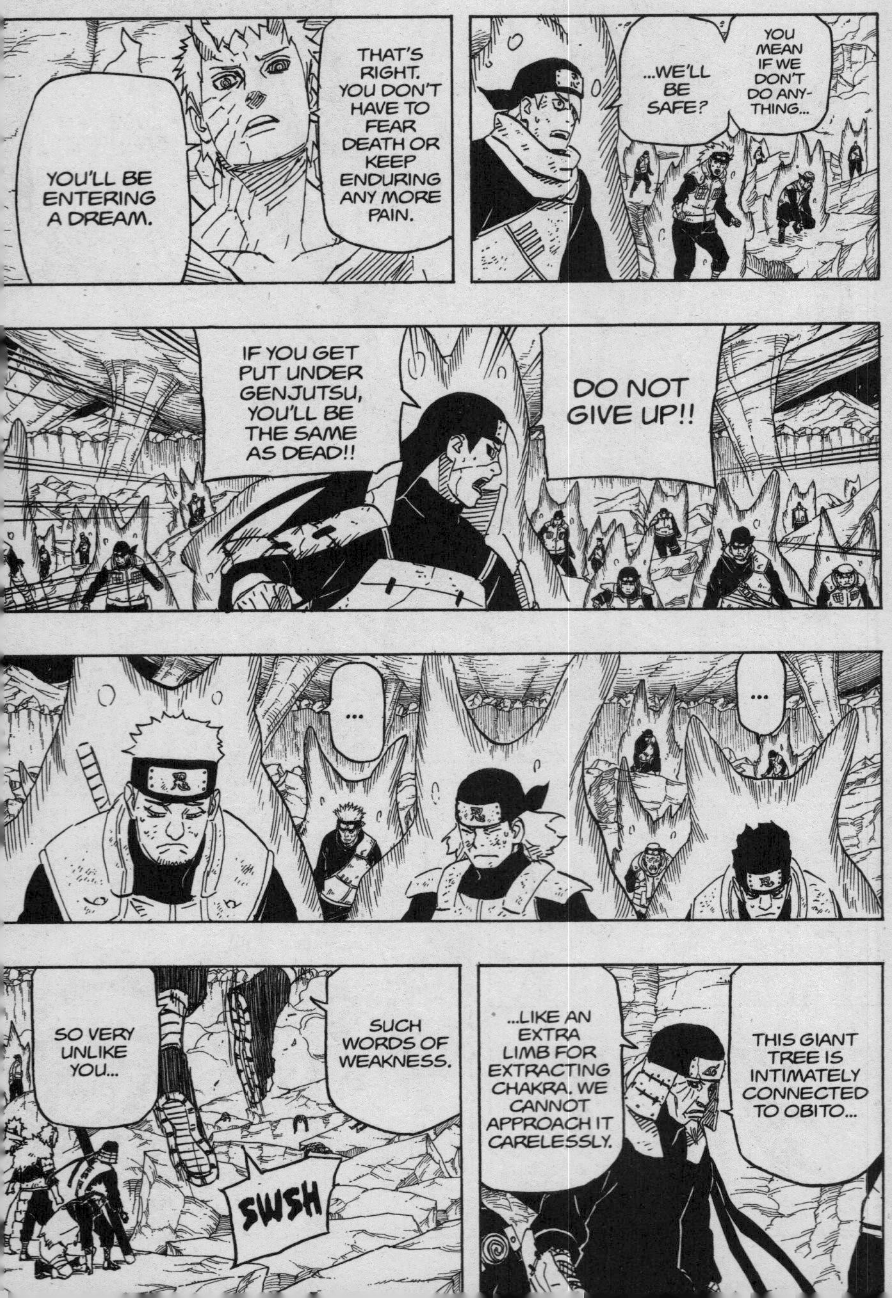
YOU MEAN IF WE DON'T DO ANY-THING...
...WE'LL BE SAFE?
THAT'S RIGHT. YOU DON'T HAVE TO FEAR DEATH OR KEEP ENDURING ANY MORE PAIN.
YOU'LL BE ENTERING A DREAM.
DO NOT GIVE UP!!
IF YOU GET PUT UNDER GENJUTSU, YOU'LL BE THE SAME AS DEAD!!
...
...
THIS GIANT TREE IS INTIMATELY CONNECTED TO OBITO...
...LIKE AN EXTRA LIMB FOR EXTRACTING CHAKRA. WE CANNOT APPROACH IT CARELESSLY.
SUCH WORDS OF WEAKNESS.
SO VERY UNLIKE YOU...
SWSH

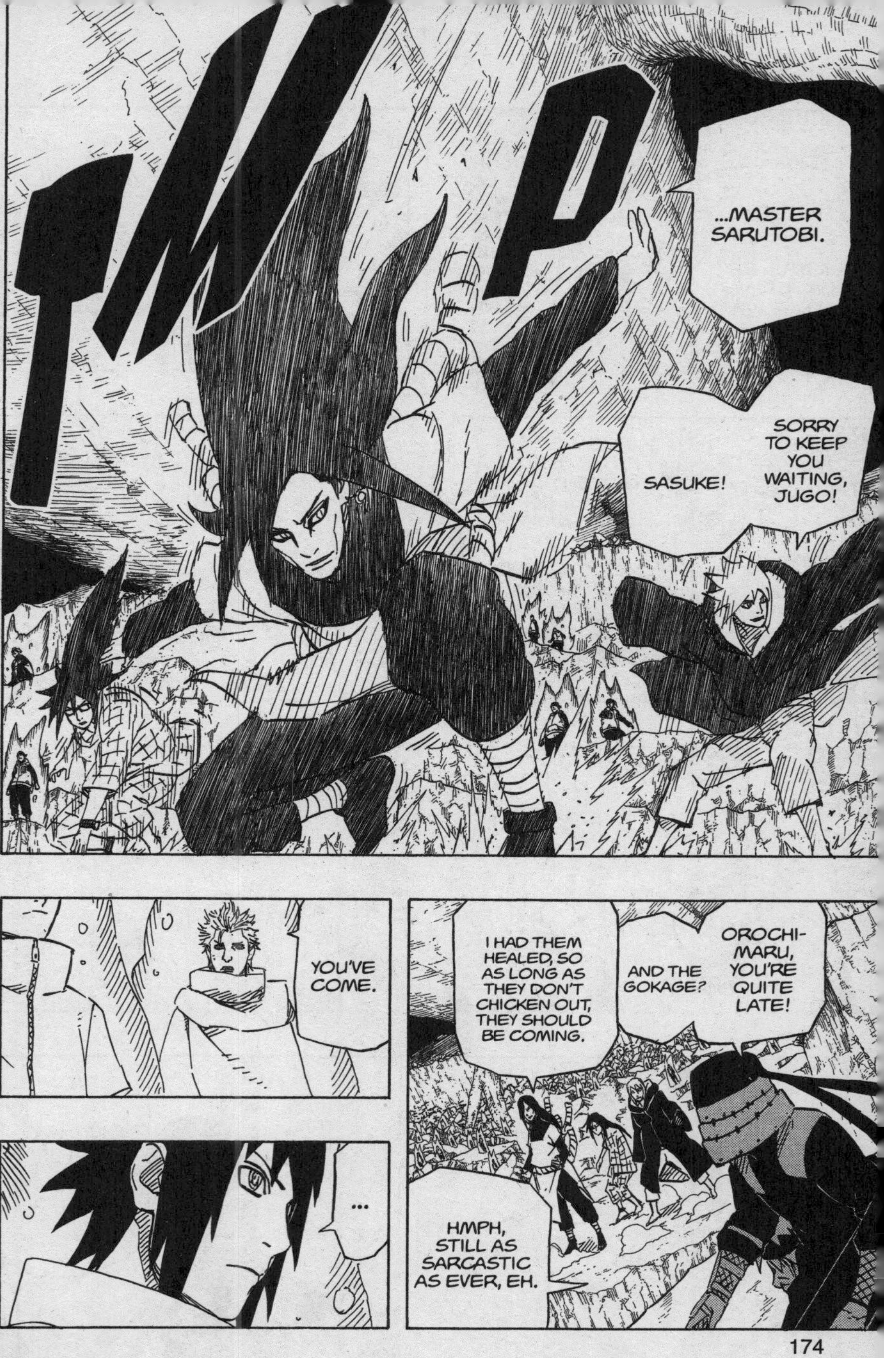
...MASTER SARUTOBI.
TWIP
SORRY TO KEEP YOU WAITING, JUGO!
SASUKE!
OROCHI-MARU, YOU'RE QUITE LATE!
AND THE GOKAGE?
I HAD THEM HEALED, SO AS LONG AS THEY DON'T CHICKEN OUT, THEY SHOULD BE COMING.
HMPH, STILL AS SARCASTIC AS EVER, EH.
YOU'VE COME.
...

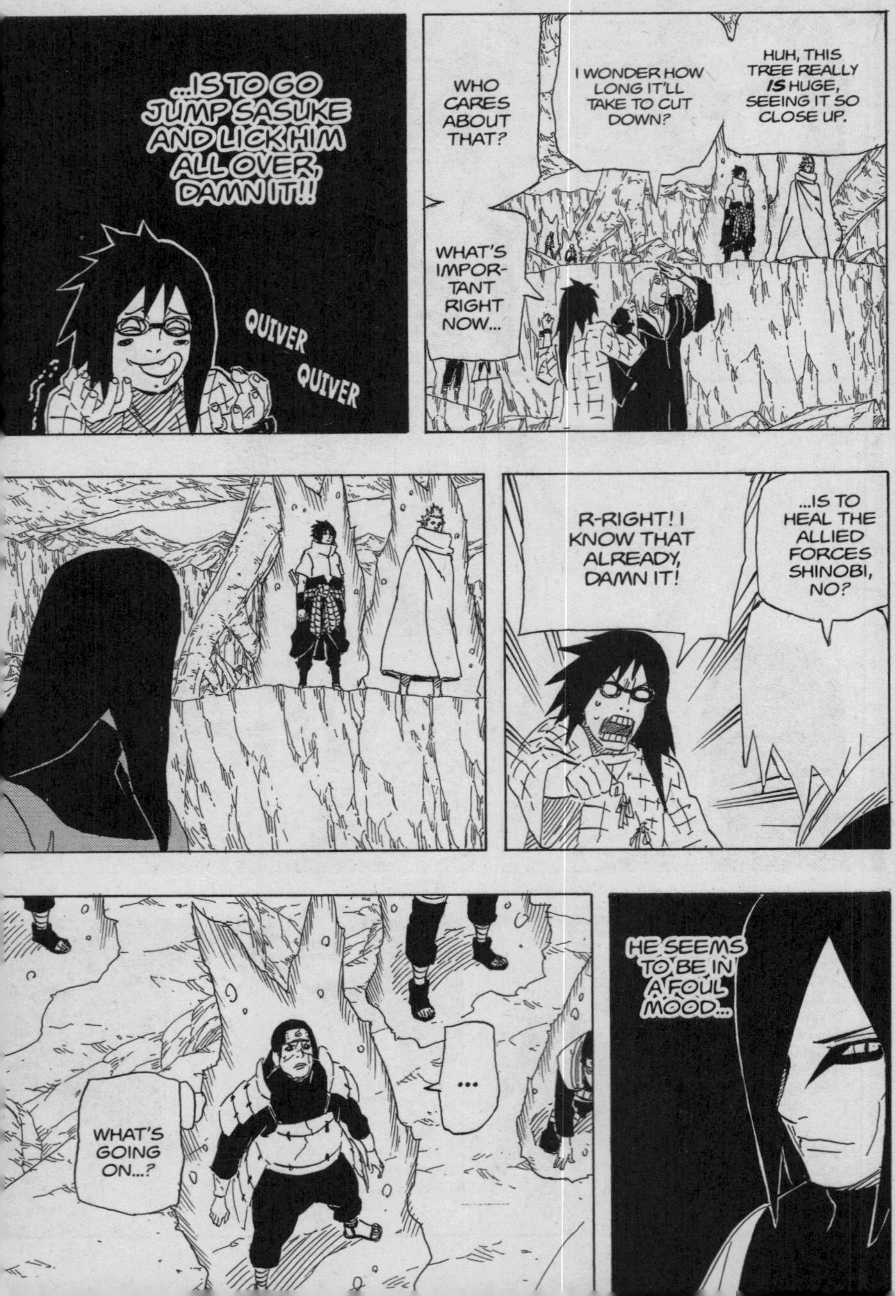
HUH, THIS TREE REALLY IS HUGE, SEEING IT SO CLOSE UP.
I WONDER HOW LONG IT'LL TAKE TO CUT DOWN?
WHO CARES ABOUT THAT?
WHAT'S IMPORTANT RIGHT NOW...
...IS TO GO JUMP SASUKE AND LICK HIM ALL OVER, DAMN IT!!
QUIVER
QUIVER
...IS TO HEAL THE ALLIED FORCES SHINOBI, NO?
R-RIGHT! I KNOW THAT ALREADY, DAMN IT!
HE SEEMS TO BE IN A FOUL MOOD...
...
WHAT'S GOING ON...?

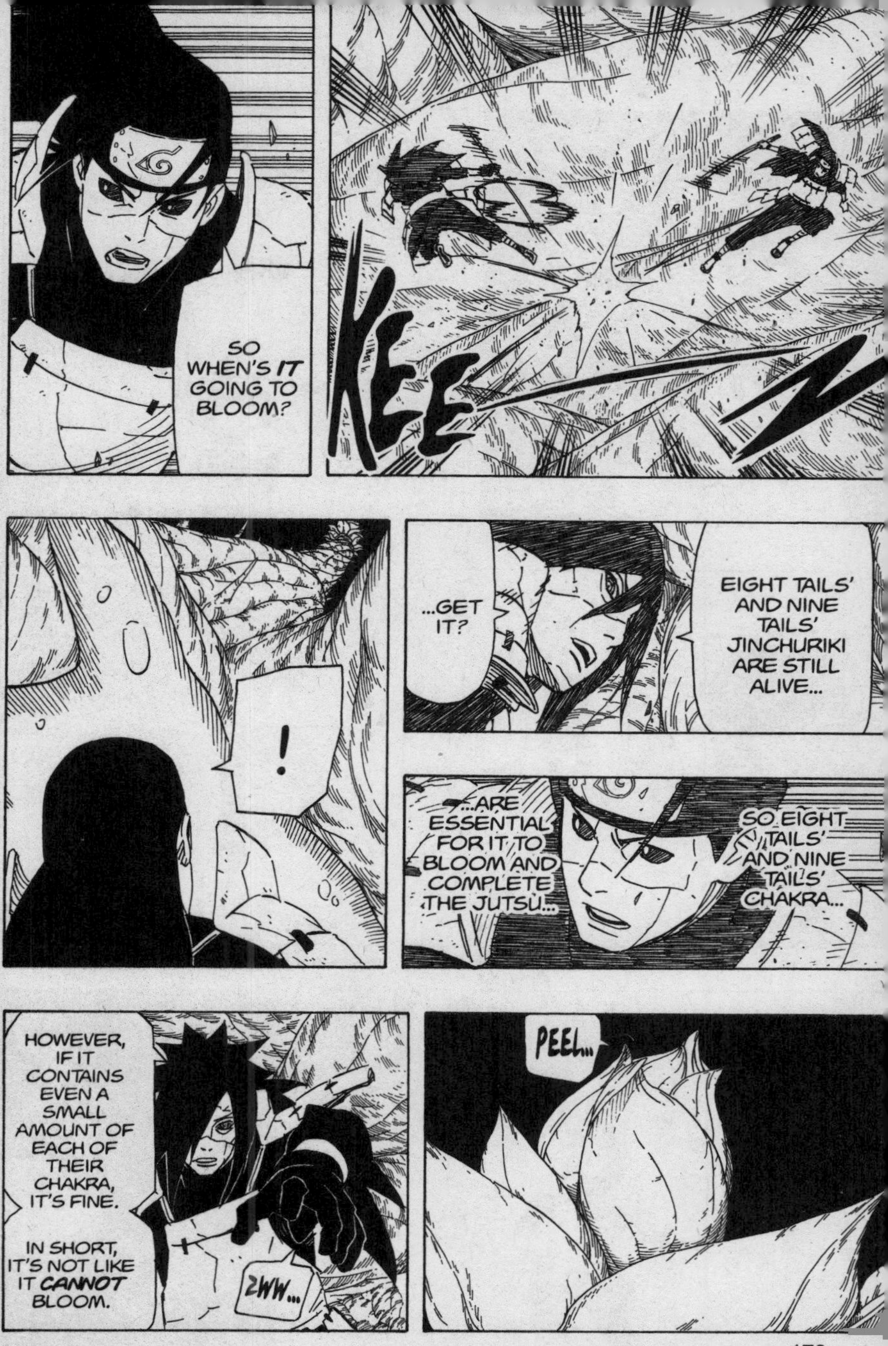
KEEN
SO WHEN'S *IT* GOING TO BLOOM?
EIGHT TAILS' AND NINE TAILS' JINCHURIKI ARE STILL ALIVE...
...GET IT?
SO EIGHT TAILS' AND NINE TAILS' CHAKRA...
...ARE ESSENTIAL FOR IT TO BLOOM AND COMPLETE THE JUTSU...
!
PEEL...
HOWEVER, IF IT CONTAINS EVEN A SMALL AMOUNT OF EACH OF THEIR CHAKRA, IT'S FINE.
IN SHORT, IT'S NOT LIKE IT ***CANNOT*** BLOOM.
ZWW...

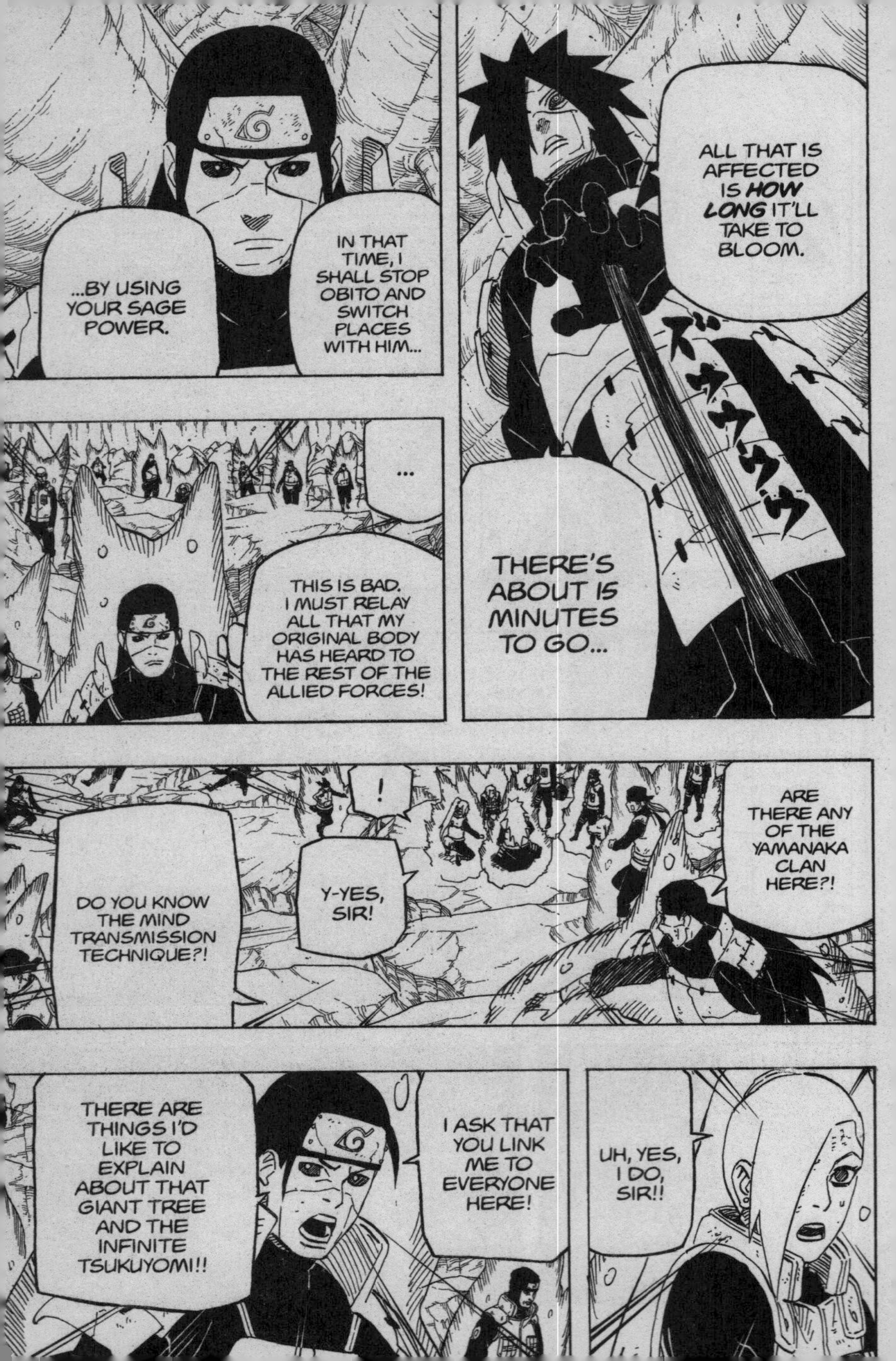
ALL THAT IS AFFECTED IS **HOW LONG** IT'LL TAKE TO BLOOM.
THERE'S ABOUT 15 MINUTES TO GO...
IN THAT TIME, I SHALL STOP OBITO AND SWITCH PLACES WITH HIM...
...BY USING YOUR SAGE POWER.
...
THIS IS BAD. I MUST RELAY ALL THAT MY ORIGINAL BODY HAS HEARD TO THE REST OF THE ALLIED FORCES!
ARE THERE ANY OF THE YAMANAKA CLAN HERE?!
!
Y-YES, SIR!
DO YOU KNOW THE MIND TRANSMISSION TECHNIQUE?!
UH, YES, I DO, SIR!!
I ASK THAT YOU LINK ME TO EVERYONE HERE!
THERE ARE THINGS I'D LIKE TO EXPLAIN ABOUT THAT GIANT TREE AND THE INFINITE TSUKUYOMI!!

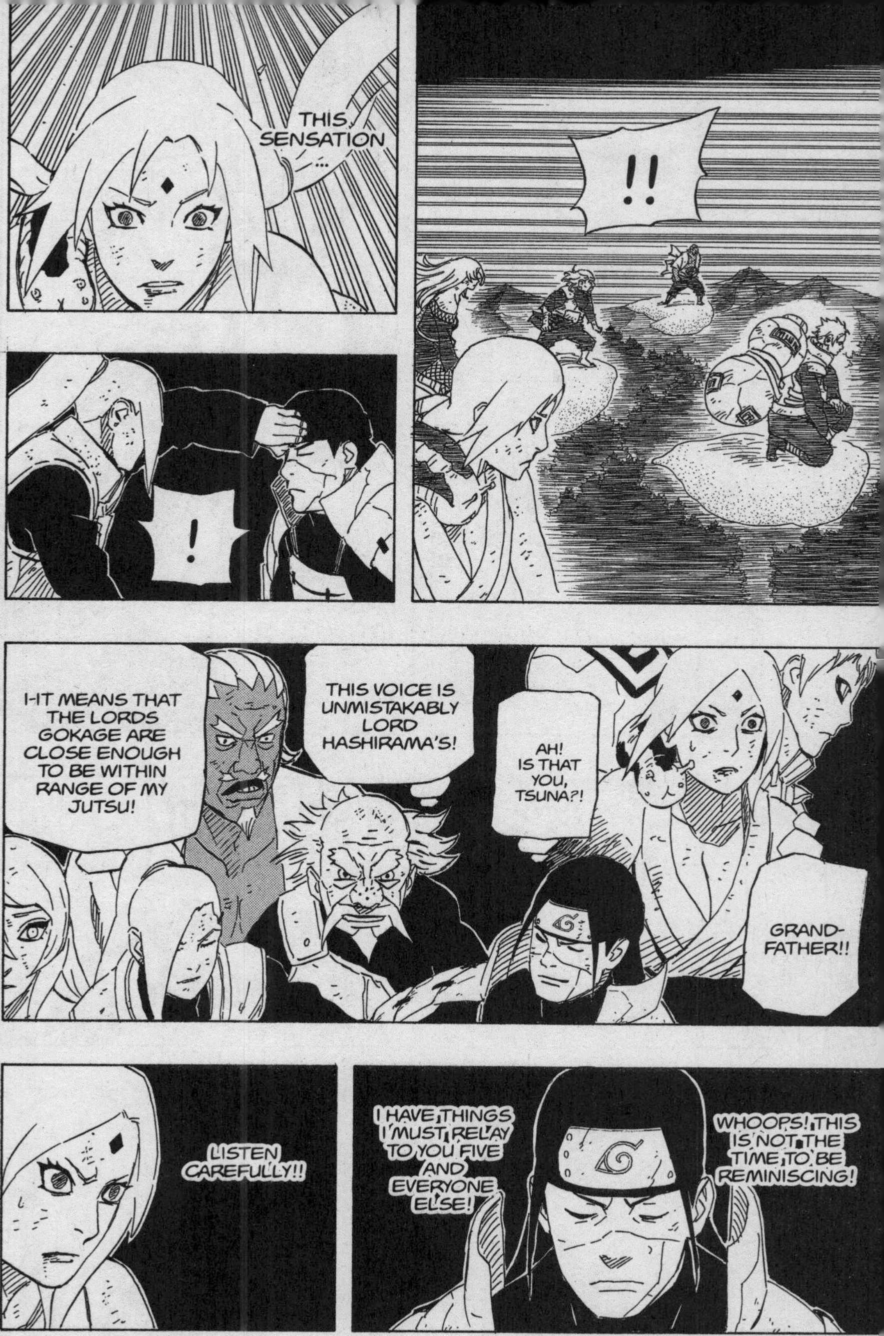
!!
THIS SENSATION...
!
AH! IS THAT YOU, TSUNA?!
GRAND-FATHER!!
THIS VOICE IS UNMISTAKABLY LORD HASHIRAMA'S!
I-IT MEANS THAT THE LORDS GOKAGE ARE CLOSE ENOUGH TO BE WITHIN RANGE OF MY JUTSU!
WHOOPS! THIS IS NOT THE TIME TO BE REMINISCING!
I HAVE THINGS I MUST RELAY TO YOU FIVE AND EVERYONE ELSE!
LISTEN CAREFULLY!!

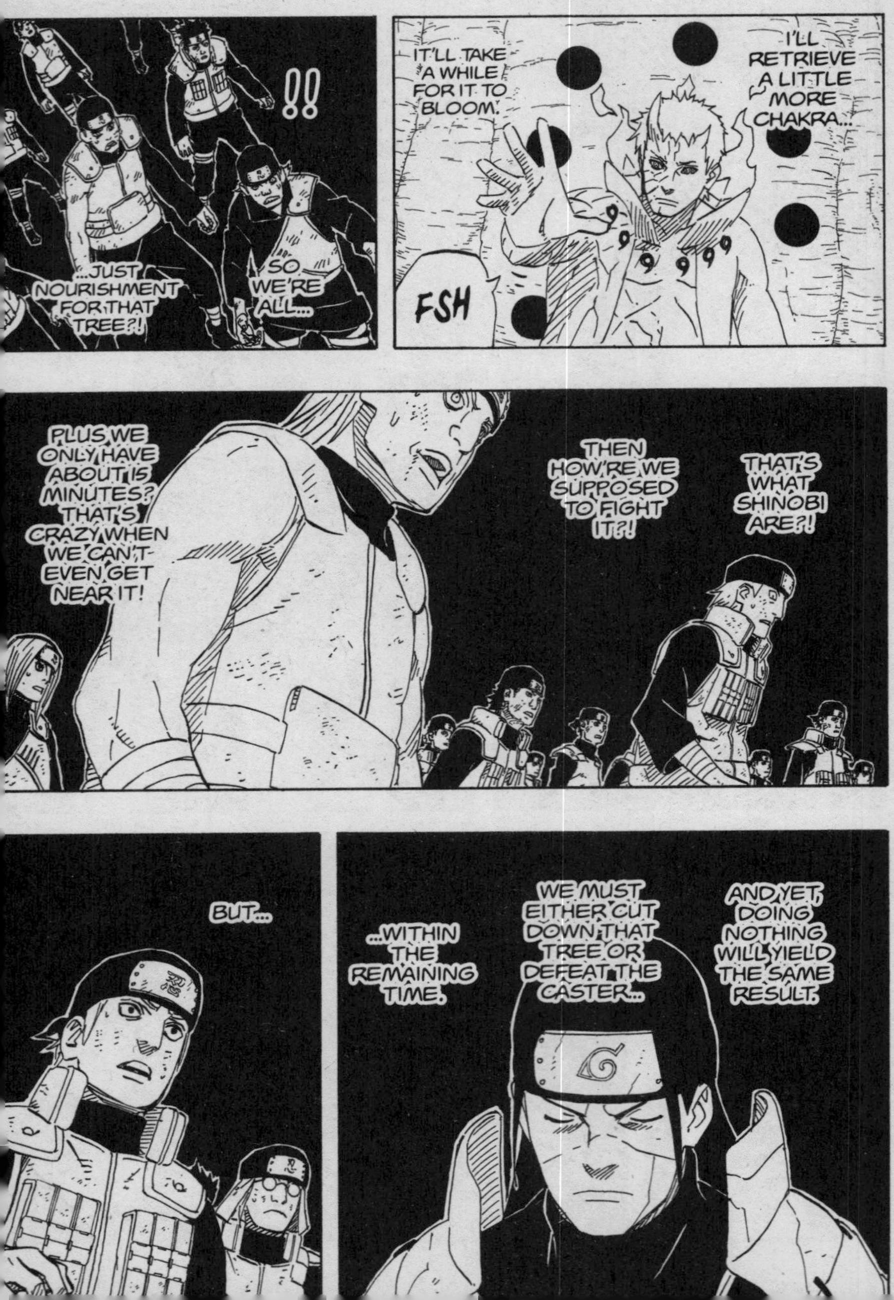
I'LL RETRIEVE A LITTLE MORE CHAKRA...
IT'LL TAKE A WHILE FOR IT TO BLOOM.
FSH
!!
SO WE'RE ALL...
...JUST NOURISHMENT FOR THAT TREE?!
THAT'S WHAT SHINOBI ARE?!
THEN HOW'RE WE SUPPOSED TO FIGHT IT?!
PLUS WE ONLY HAVE ABOUT 15 MINUTES? THAT'S CRAZY WHEN WE CAN'T EVEN GET NEAR IT!
AND YET, DOING NOTHING WILL YIELD THE SAME RESULT.
WE MUST EITHER CUT DOWN THAT TREE OR DEFEAT THE CASTER...
...WITHIN THE REMAINING TIME.
BUT...

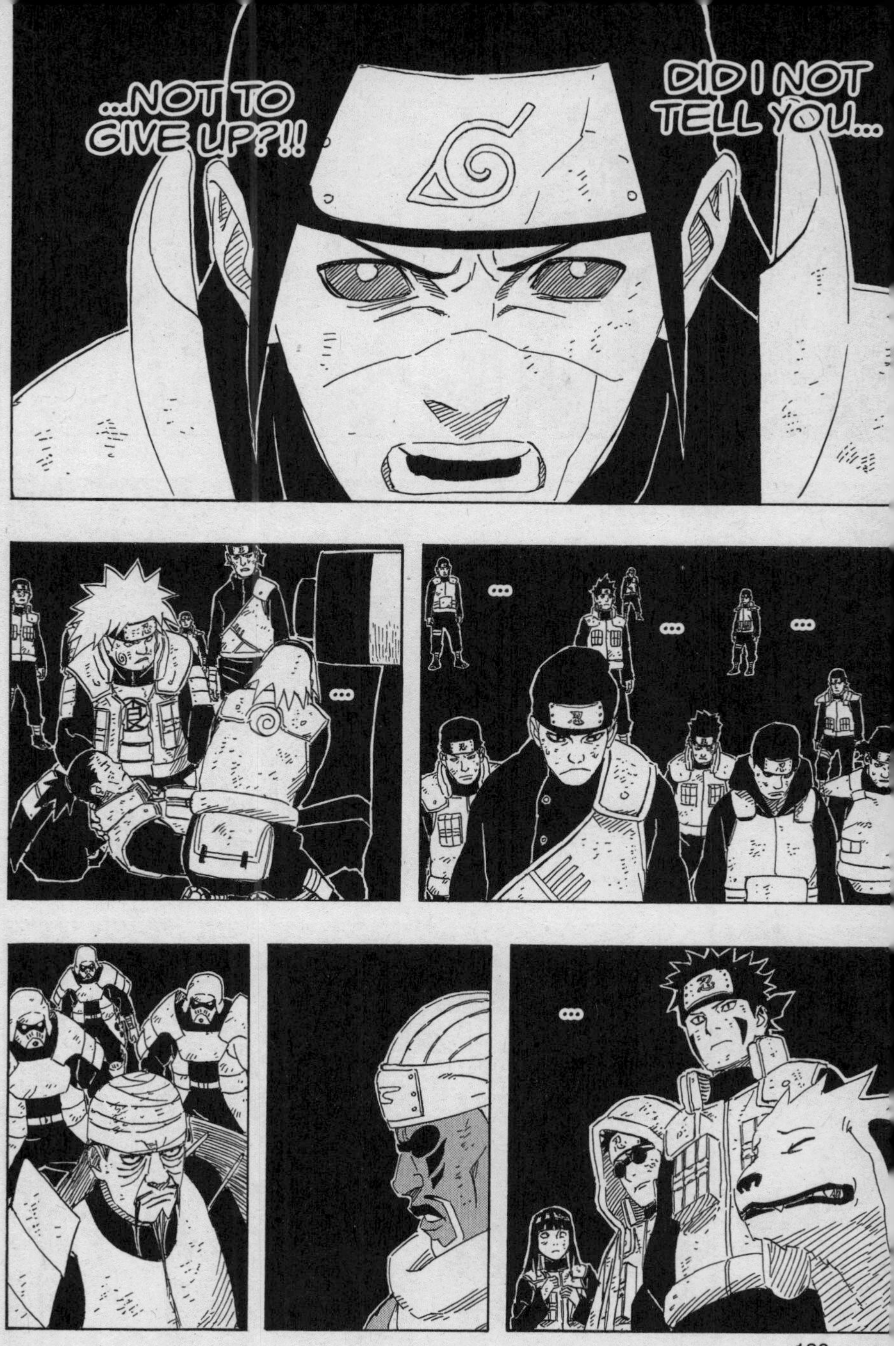
DID I NOT TELL YOU...
...NOT TO GIVE UP?!!
...
...
...
...
...

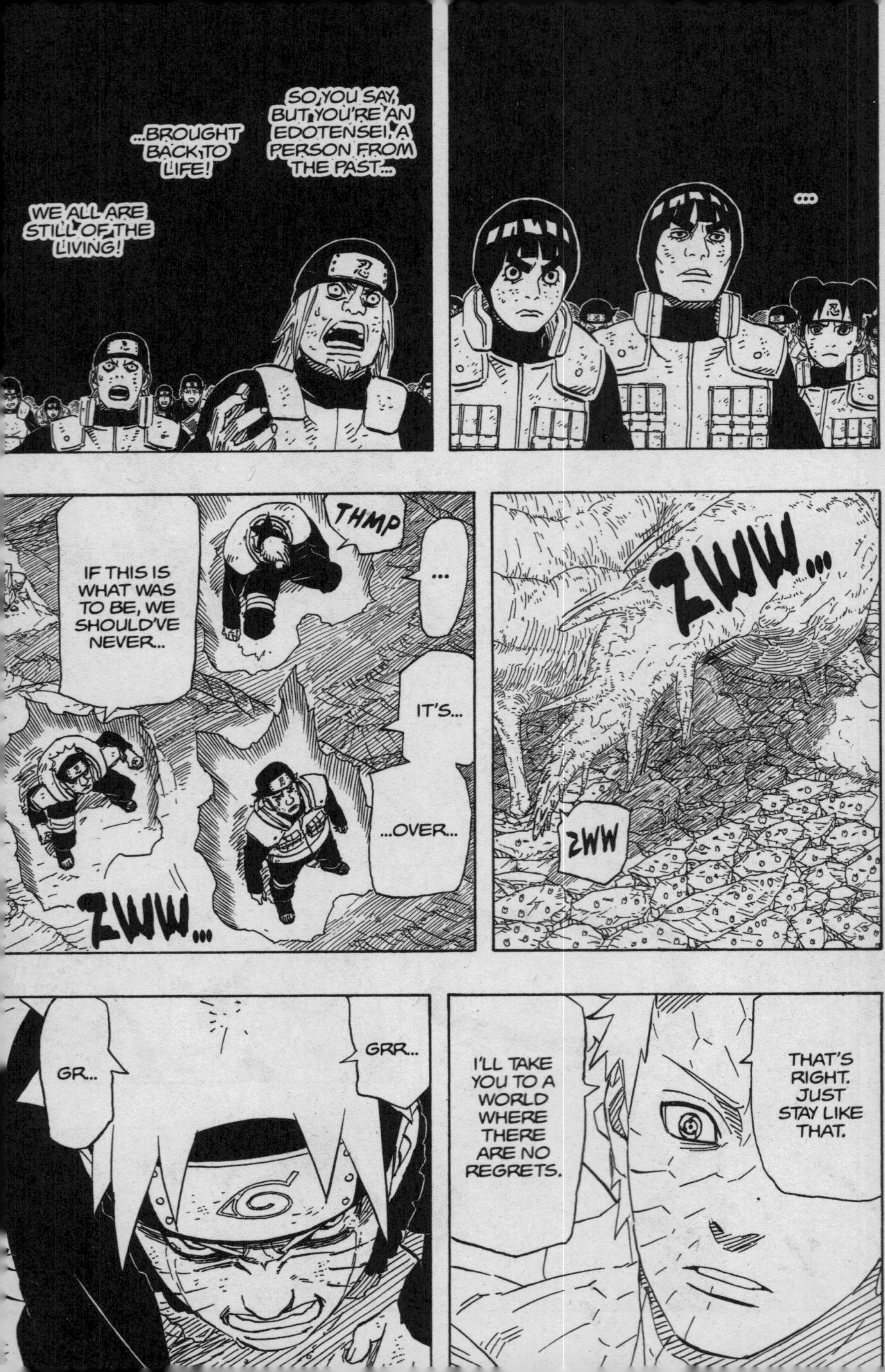
...
SO YOU SAY, BUT YOU'RE AN EDOTENSEI, A PERSON FROM THE PAST...
...BROUGHT BACK TO LIFE!
WE ALL ARE STILL OF THE LIVING!
ZWW...
ZWW
THMP
...
IT'S...
...OVER...
IF THIS IS WHAT WAS TO BE, WE SHOULD'VE NEVER...
ZWW...
THAT'S RIGHT. JUST STAY LIKE THAT.
I'LL TAKE YOU TO A WORLD WHERE THERE ARE NO REGRETS.
GRR...
GR...

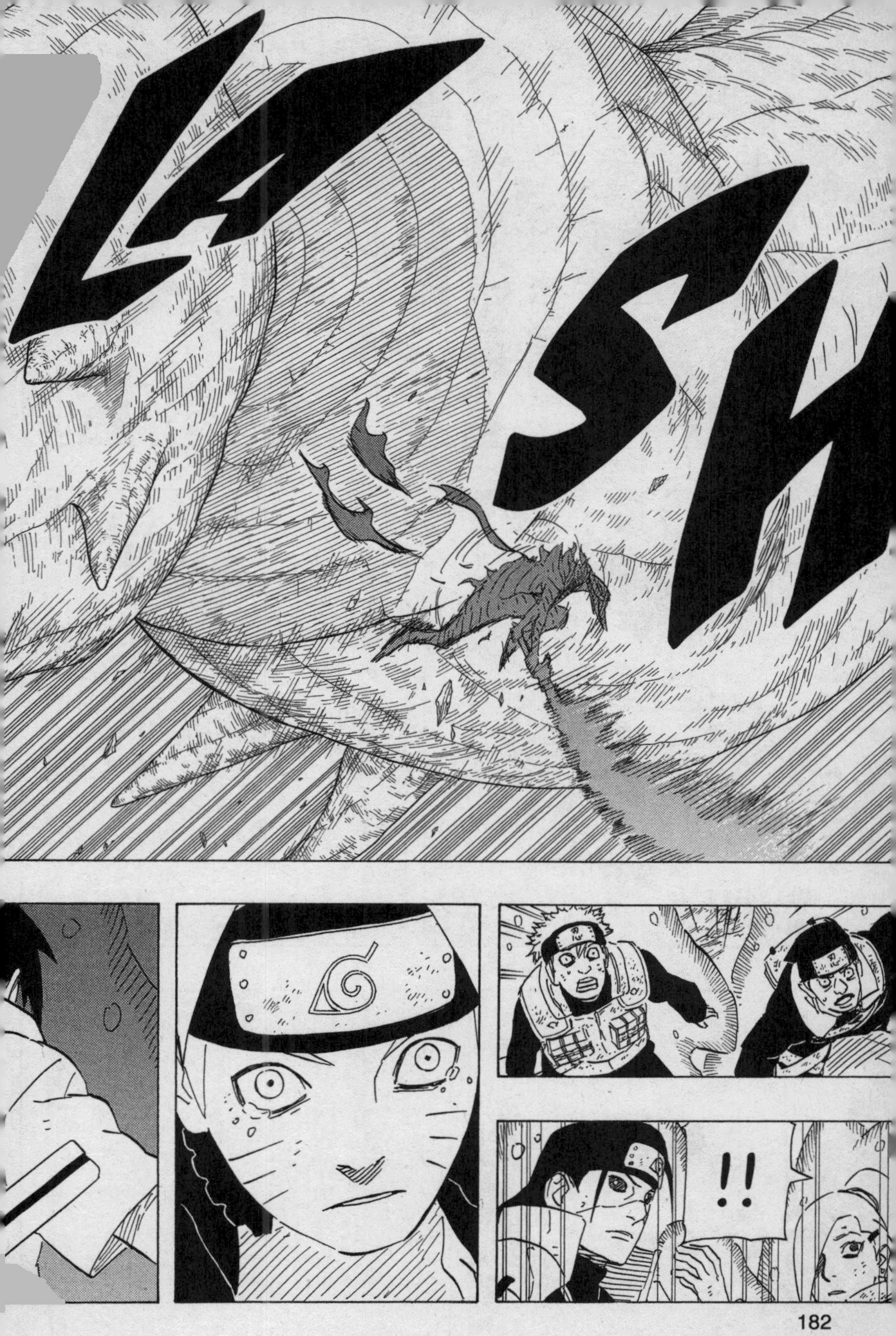
!!

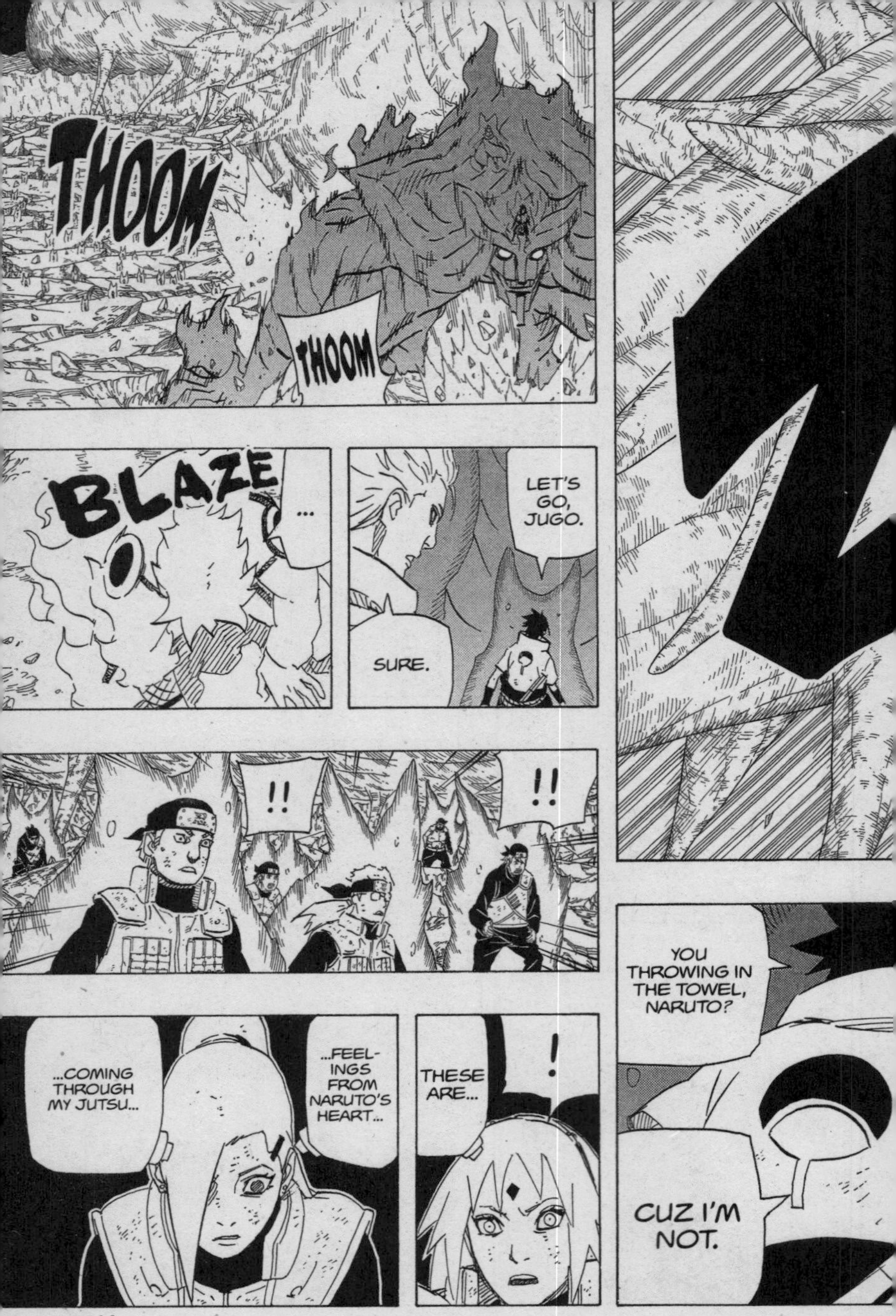
THOOM
THOOM
LET'S GO, JUGO.
SURE.
BLAZE
...
!!
!!
YOU THROWING IN THE TOWEL, NARUTO?
CUZ I'M NOT.
!
THESE ARE...
...FEEL-INGS FROM NARUTO'S HEART...
...COMING THROUGH MY JUTSU...

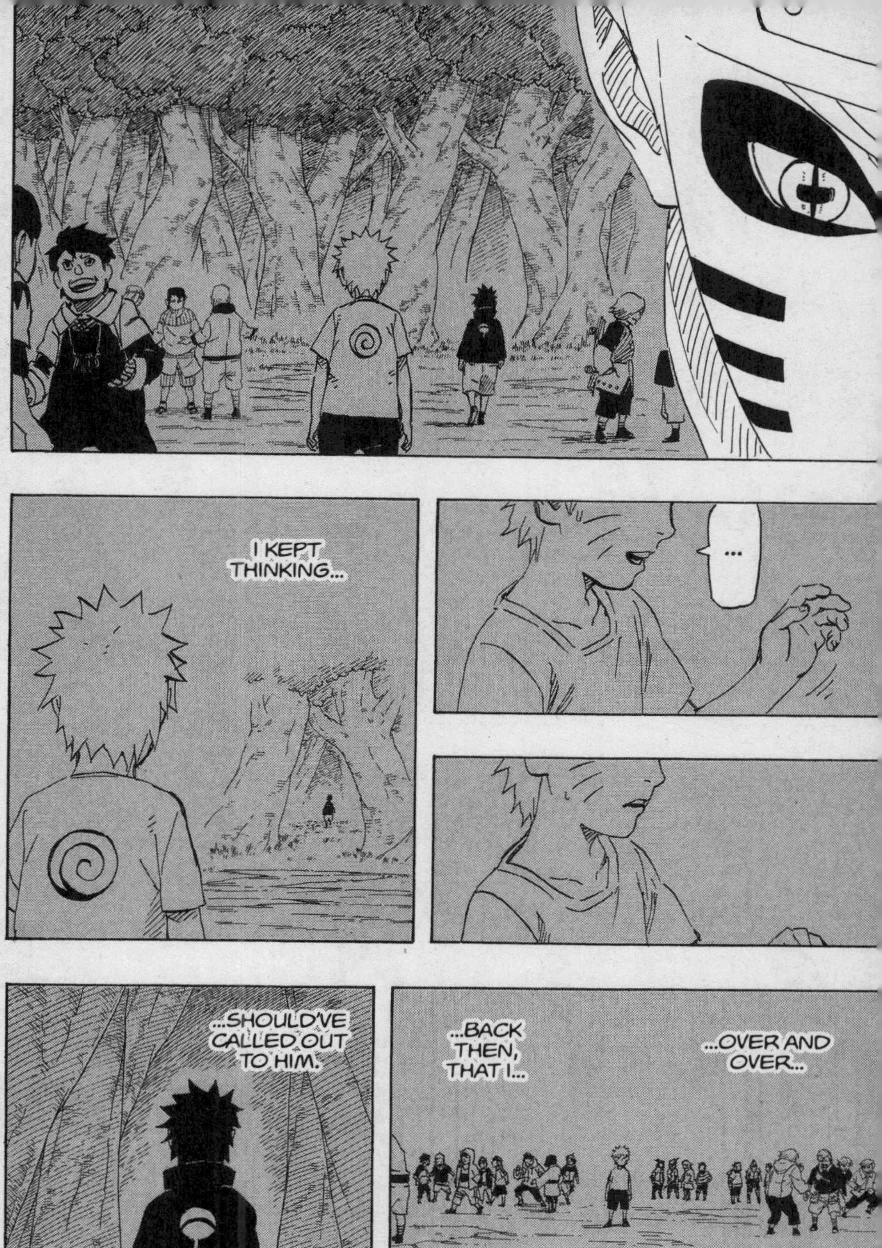
...
I KEPT THINKING...
...OVER AND OVER...
...BACK THEN, THAT I...
...SHOULD'VE CALLED OUT TO HIM.

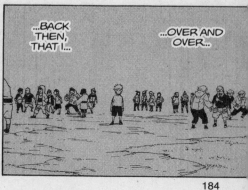

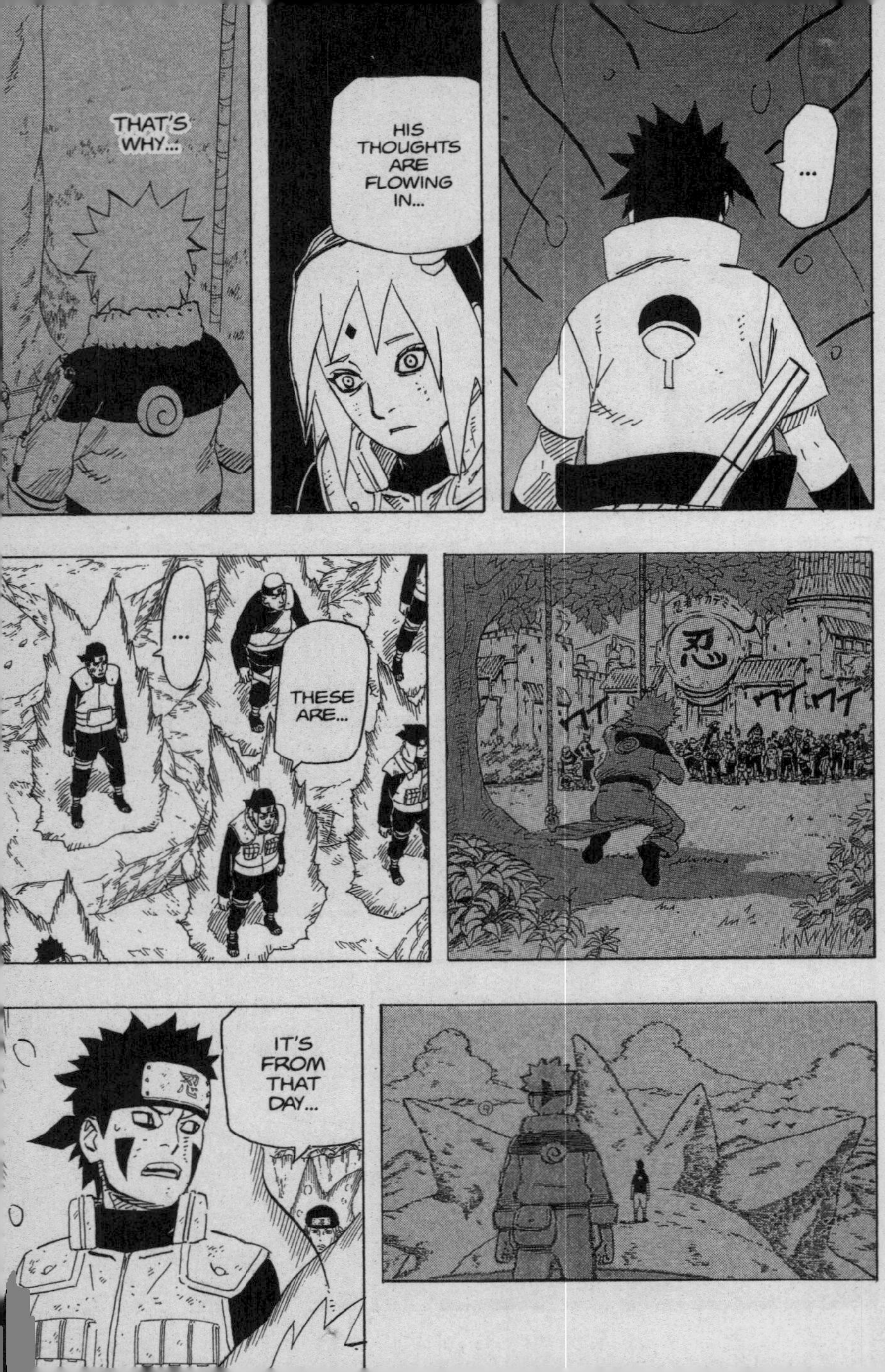
...
HIS THOUGHTS ARE FLOWING IN...
THAT'S WHY...
忍
ワイワイ
ワイ
...
THESE ARE...
IT'S FROM THAT DAY...

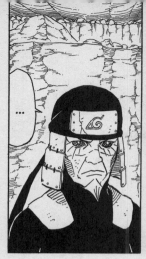

...

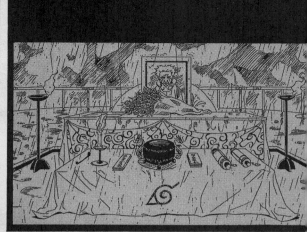

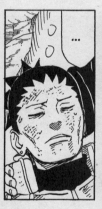

...

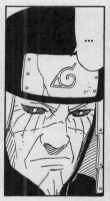

...

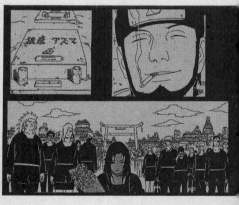

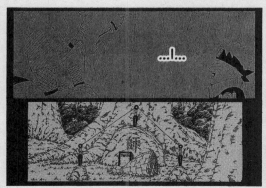

...l...

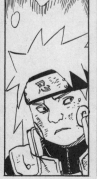

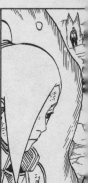

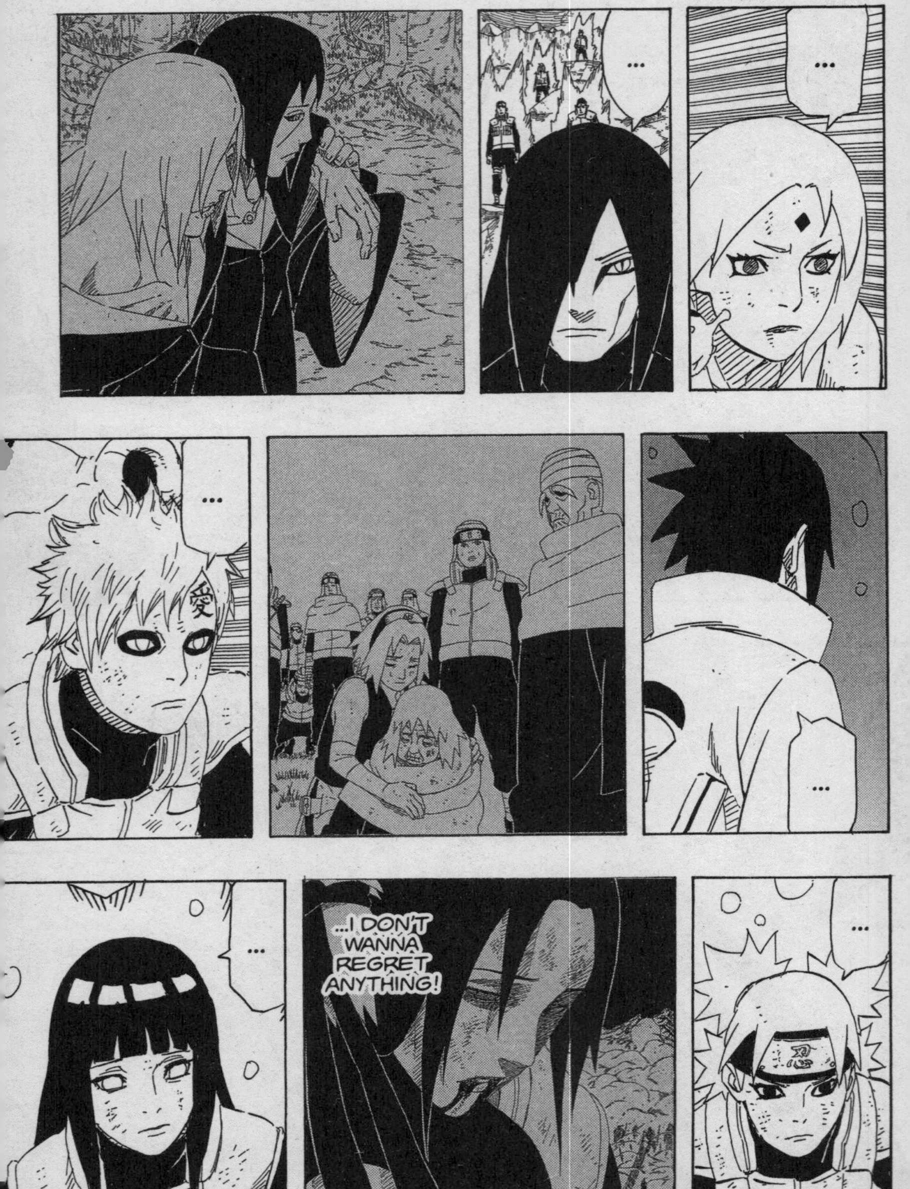
...
...
...
...
...
...I DON'T WANNA REGRET ANYTHING!
...

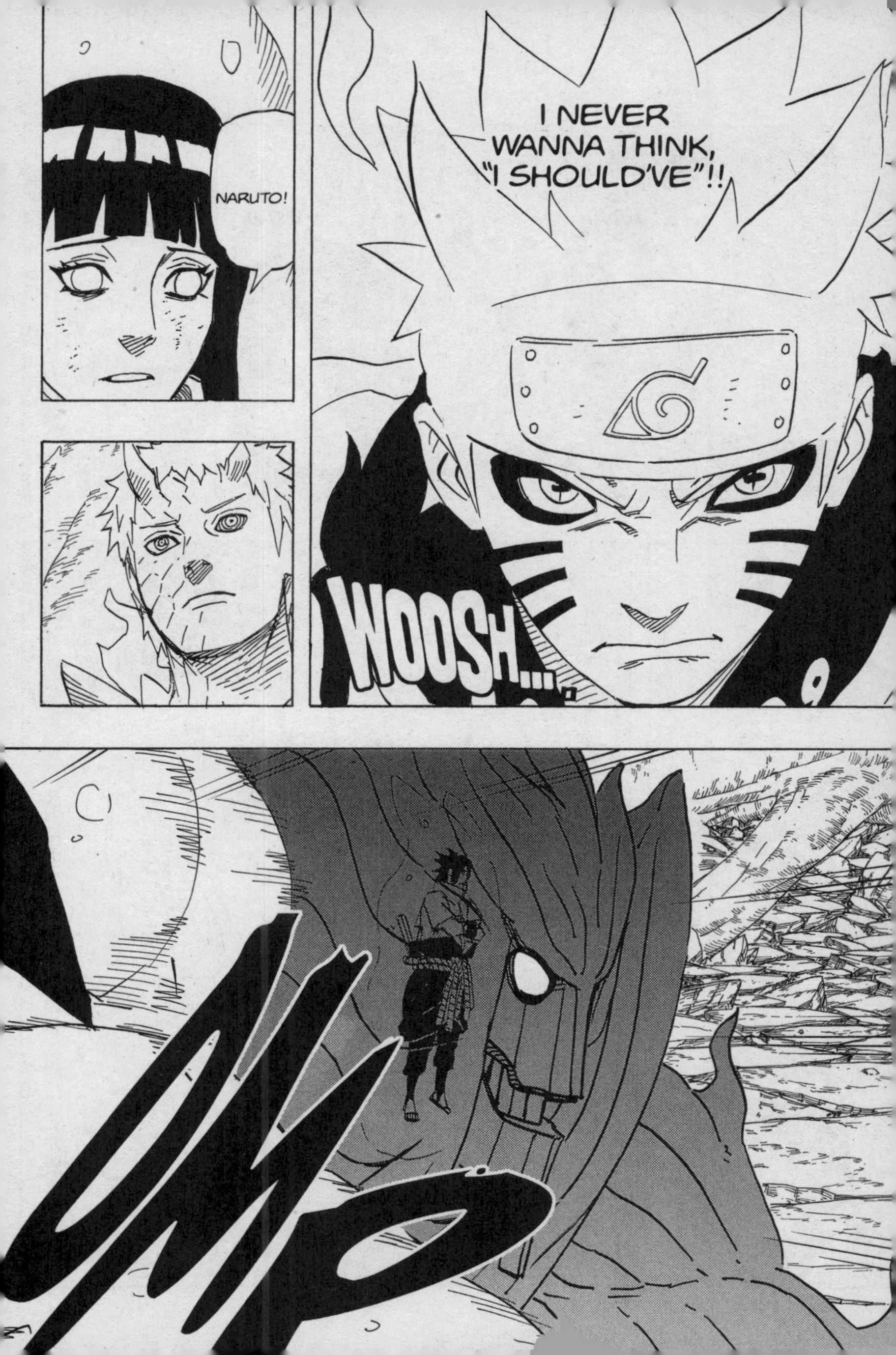
I NEVER WANNA THINK, "I SHOULD'VE"!!
WOOSH...
NARUTO!

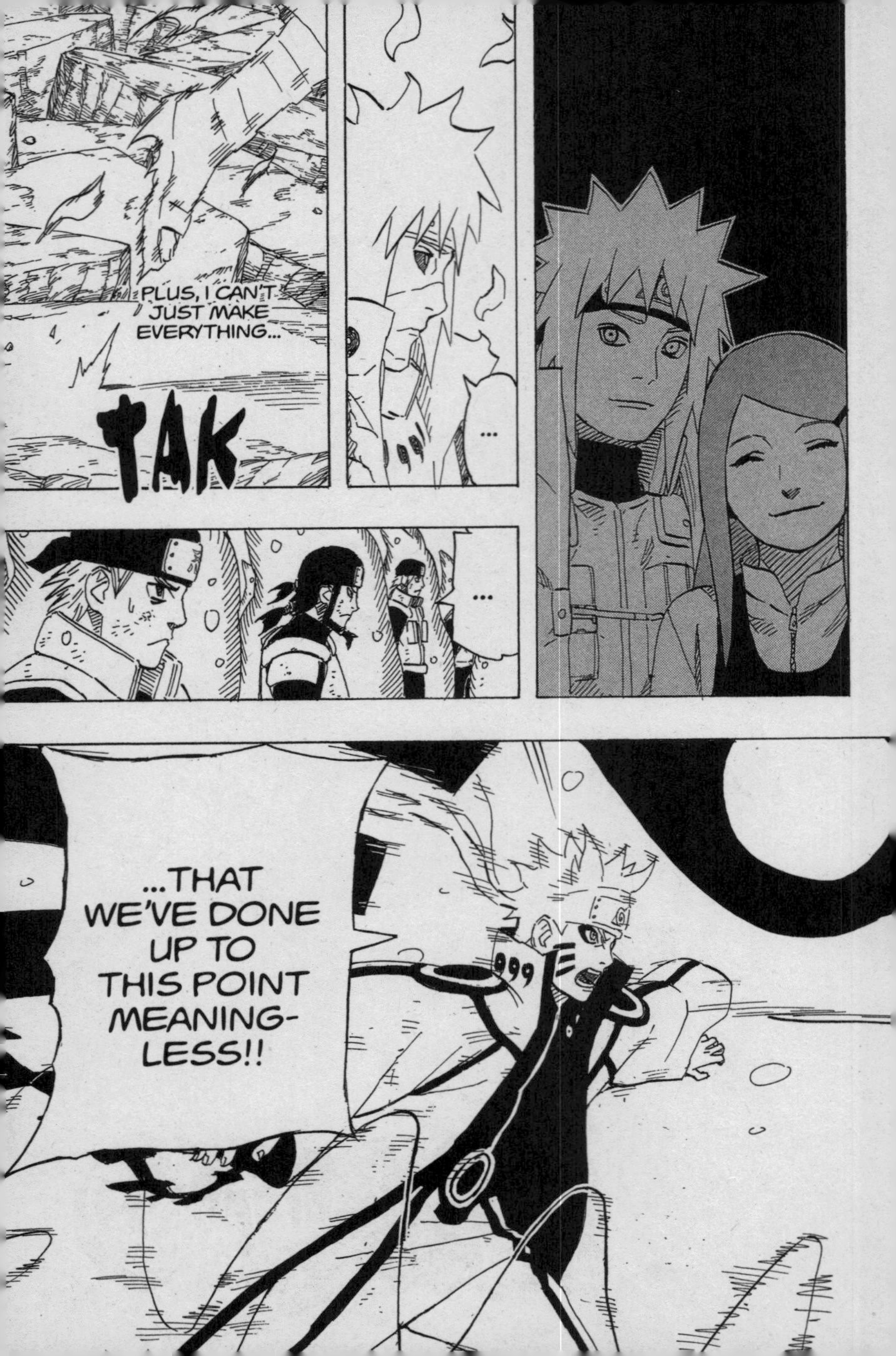
...
PLUS, I CAN'T JUST MAKE EVERYTHING...
TAK
...
...THAT WE'VE DONE UP TO THIS POINT MEANING-LESS!!

NARUTO

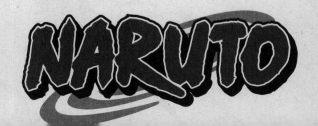

SHIVER
SHIVER
SHIVER

岸本斉史

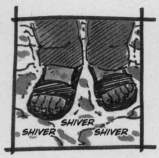

I visited my family home for the first time in a while and planned to take a really short stroll in the winter snow with my feet exposed. But everything was so nostalgic that I kept going and going. Though I was shivering from the cold, I'd walked over three miles before I realized it. I ended up having someone come give me a ride back.

—Masashi Kishimoto, 2014

一楽
ラーメン一楽
うまい

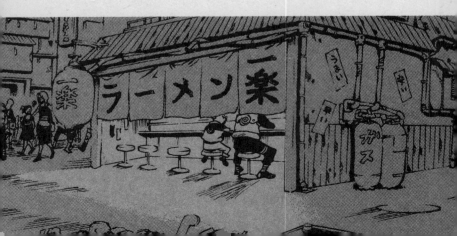

NARUTO

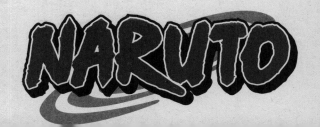

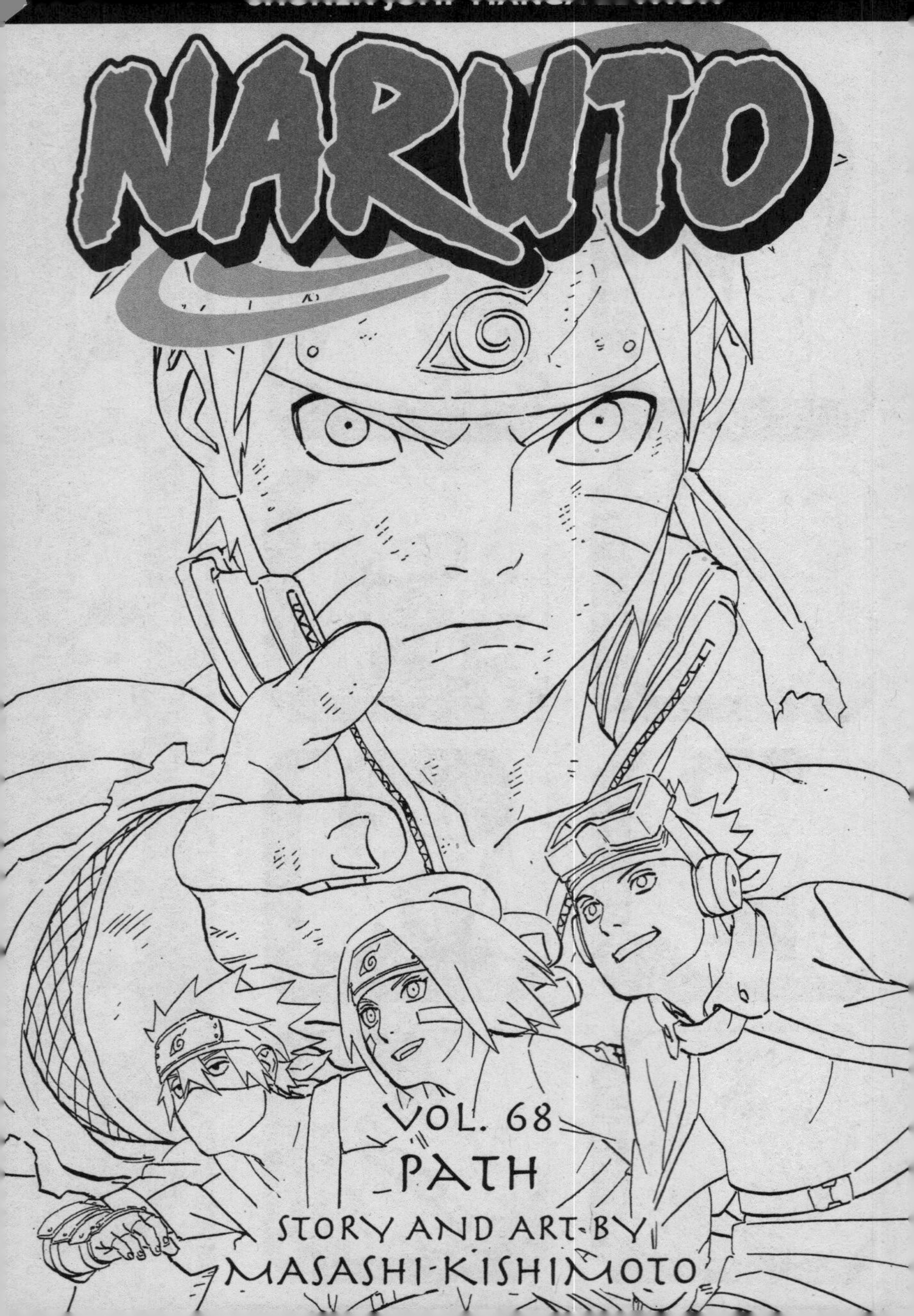
NARUTO
VOL. 68
PATH
STORY AND ART BY
MASASHI KISHIMOTO

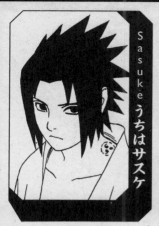

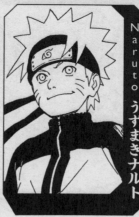

うちはサスケ
Sasuke

うずまきナルト
Naruto

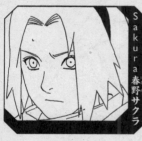

春野サクラ
Sakura

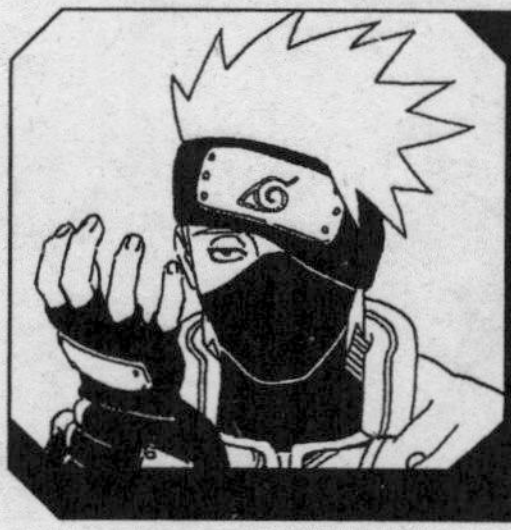

はたけカカシ
Kakashi

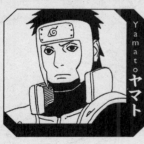

ヤマト
Yamato

サイ
Sai

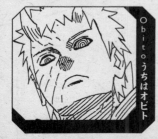

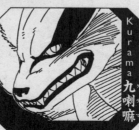

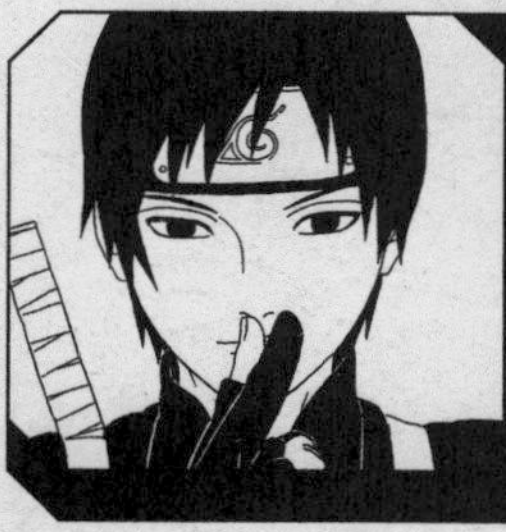

うちはオビト
Obito

九喇嘛
Kurama

CHARACTERS

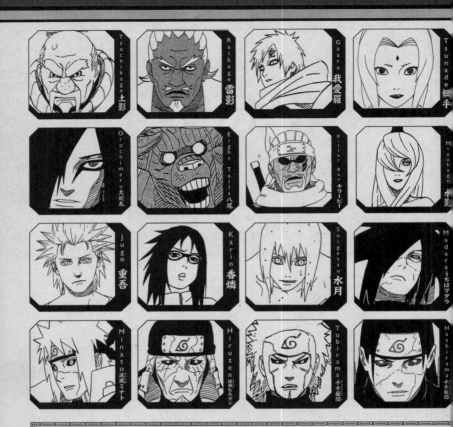

The character portraits are labeled (top to bottom, left to right): Tsuchikage 土影, Raikage 雷影, Gaara 我愛羅, Tsunade 綱手, Orochimaru 大蛇丸, Eight Tails 八尾, Killer Bee キラービー, Mizukage 水影, Jugo 重吾, Karin 香燐, Suigetsu 水月, Madara うちはマダラ, Minato 綱波ミナト, Hiruzen 綱波ヒルゼン, Tobirama 千手扉間, Hashirama 千手柱間

THE STORY SO FAR...

Naruto, the biggest troublemaker at the Ninja Academy in the Village of Konohagakure, finally becomes a ninja along with his classmates Sasuke and Sakura. They grow and mature through countless trials and battles. However, Sasuke, unable to give up his quest for vengeance, leaves Konohagakure to seek Orochimaru and his power...

Two years pass. Naruto grows up and engages in fierce battles against the Tailed Beast-targeting Akatsuki. And the Fourth Great Ninja War against the Akatsuki finally begins. Naruto and his companions face off against the reunited Obito and Madara in order to stop the resurrected Ten Tails! But soon, Obito absorbs the Ten Tails and becomes a Jinchuriki. Then, in order to complete the Infinite Tsukuyomi, he summons forth the Divine Tree. The alliance appears powerless against these forces but Naruto and Sasuke stand tall. Can they stop Obito?!

NARUTO

VOL. 68
PATH

CONTENTS

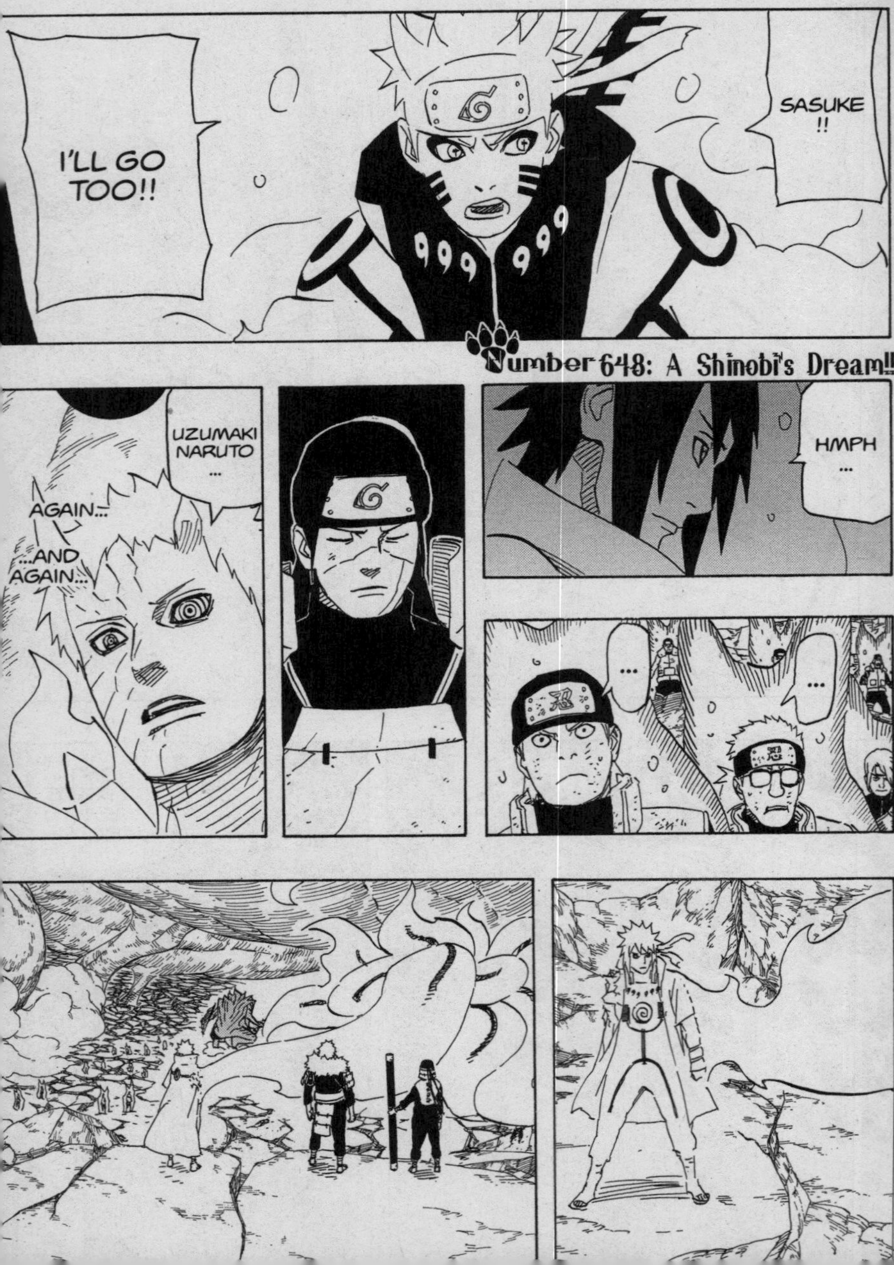
SASUKE!!
I'LL GO TOO!!
Number 648: A Shinobi's Dream!!
HMPH...
UZUMAKI NARUTO...
AGAIN...
...AND AGAIN...
...
...

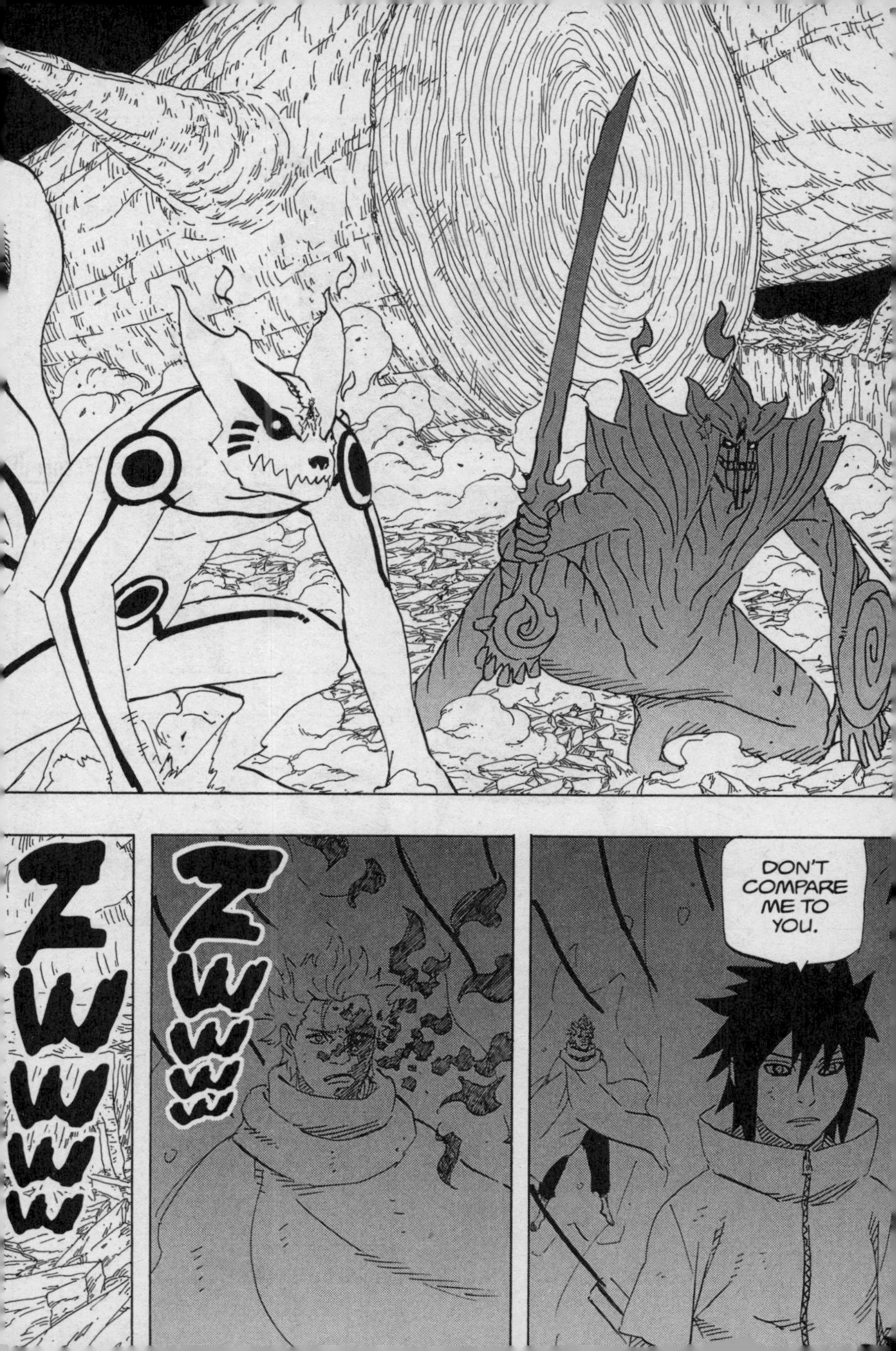
DON'T COMPARE ME TO YOU.
ZWWWW
ZWWWWW

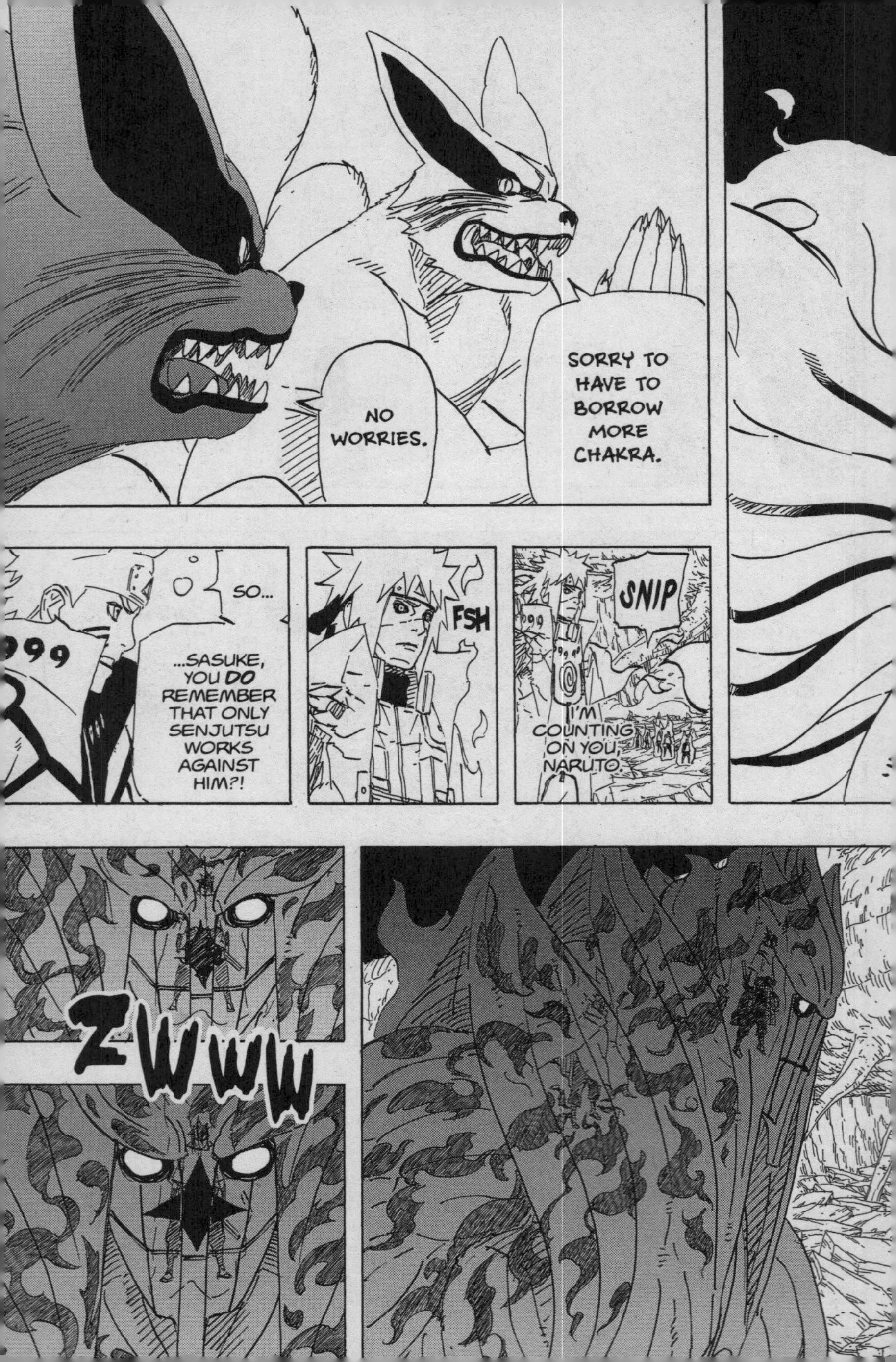
SORRY TO HAVE TO BORROW MORE CHAKRA.
NO WORRIES.
SNIP
I'M COUNTING ON YOU, NARUTO.
FSH
SO...
...SASUKE, YOU DO REMEMBER THAT ONLY SENJUTSU WORKS AGAINST HIM?!
ZWWW

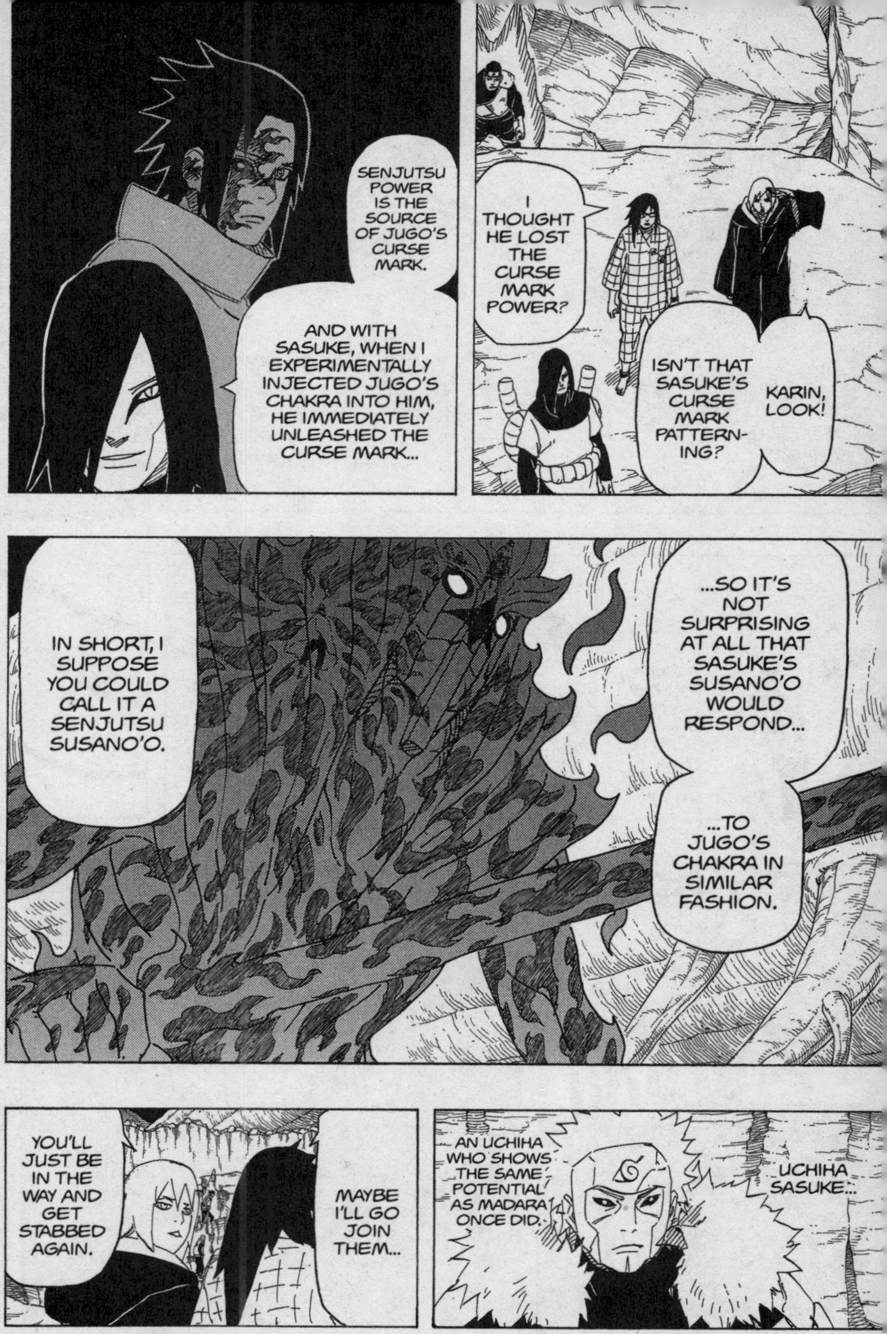
KARIN, LOOK!
ISN'T THAT SASUKE'S CURSE MARK PATTERNING?
I THOUGHT HE LOST THE CURSE MARK POWER?
SENJUTSU POWER IS THE SOURCE OF JUGO'S CURSE MARK.
AND WITH SASUKE, WHEN I EXPERIMENTALLY INJECTED JUGO'S CHAKRA INTO HIM, HE IMMEDIATELY UNLEASHED THE CURSE MARK...
...SO IT'S NOT SURPRISING AT ALL THAT SASUKE'S SUSANO'O WOULD RESPOND...
...TO JUGO'S CHAKRA IN SIMILAR FASHION.
IN SHORT, I SUPPOSE YOU COULD CALL IT A SENJUTSU SUSANO'O.
UCHIHA SASUKE...
AN UCHIHA WHO SHOWS THE SAME POTENTIAL AS MADARA ONCE DID.
MAYBE I'LL GO JOIN THEM...
YOU'LL JUST BE IN THE WAY AND GET STABBED AGAIN.

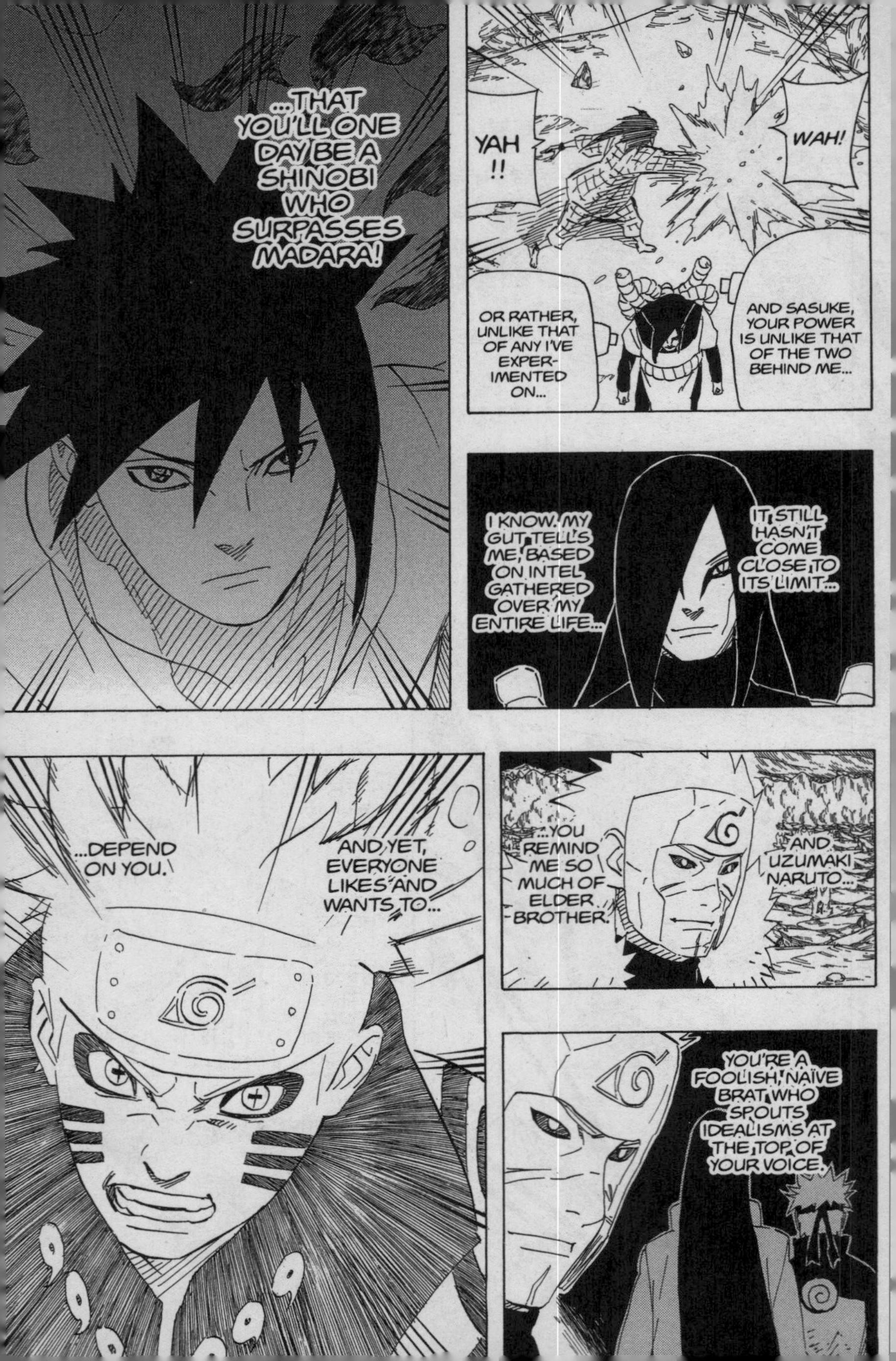
WAH!
YAH !!
AND SASUKE, YOUR POWER IS UNLIKE THAT OF THE TWO BEHIND ME...
OR RATHER, UNLIKE THAT OF ANY I'VE EXPER-IMENTED ON...
IT STILL HASN'T COME CLOSE TO ITS LIMIT...
I KNOW. MY GUT TELLS ME, BASED ON INTEL GATHERED OVER MY ENTIRE LIFE...
...THAT YOU'LL ONE DAY BE A SHINOBI WHO SURPASSES MADARA!
AND UZUMAKI NARUTO...
...YOU REMIND ME SO MUCH OF ELDER BROTHER.
YOU'RE A FOOLISH, NAÏVE BRAT WHO SPOUTS IDEALISMS AT THE TOP OF YOUR VOICE.
AND YET, EVERYONE LIKES AND WANTS TO...
...DEPEND ON YOU.

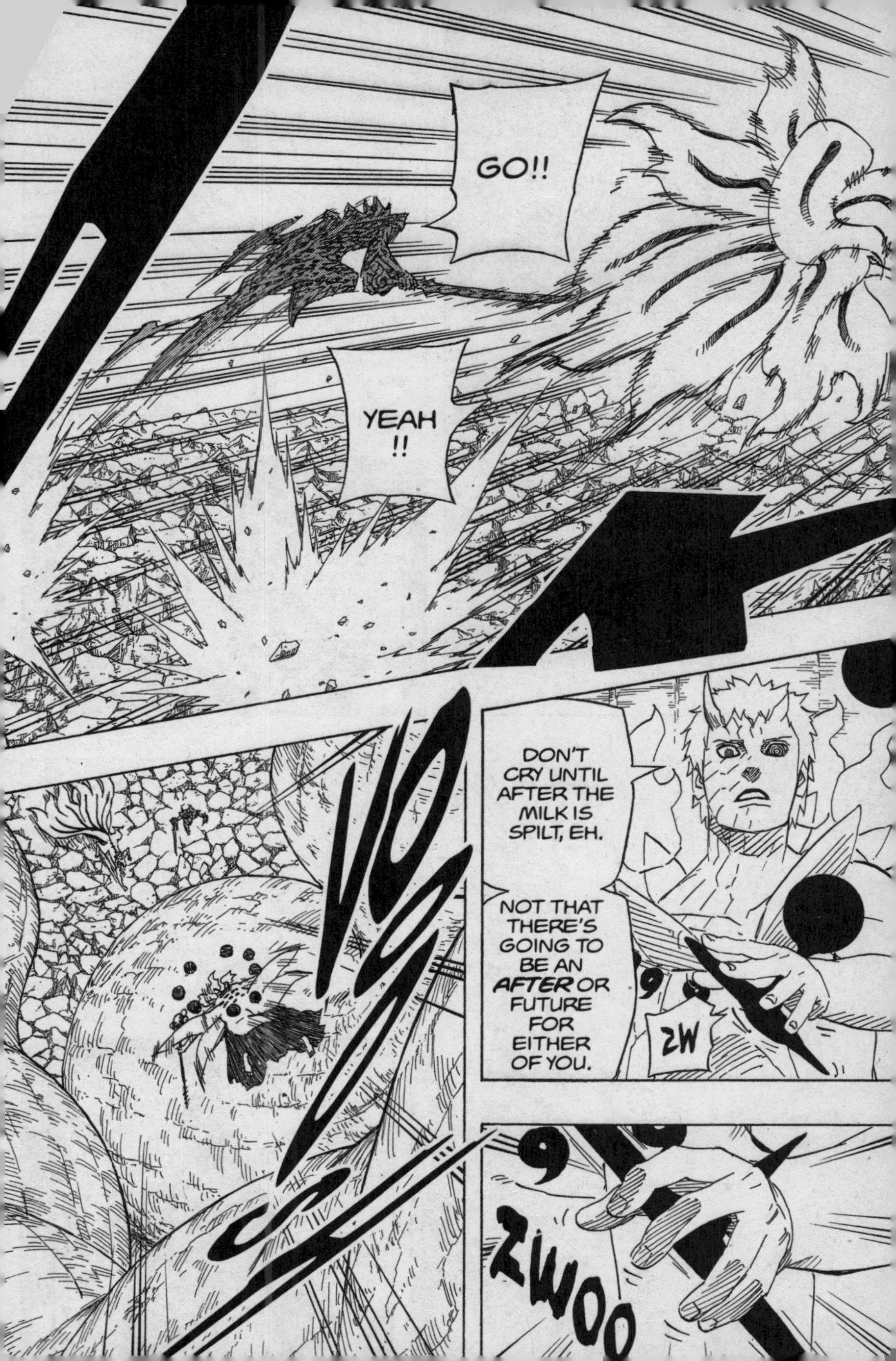
GO!!
YEAH!!
DON'T CRY UNTIL AFTER THE MILK IS SPILT, EH.
NOT THAT THERE'S GOING TO BE AN *AFTER* OR FUTURE FOR EITHER OF YOU.
ZW
ZWOO

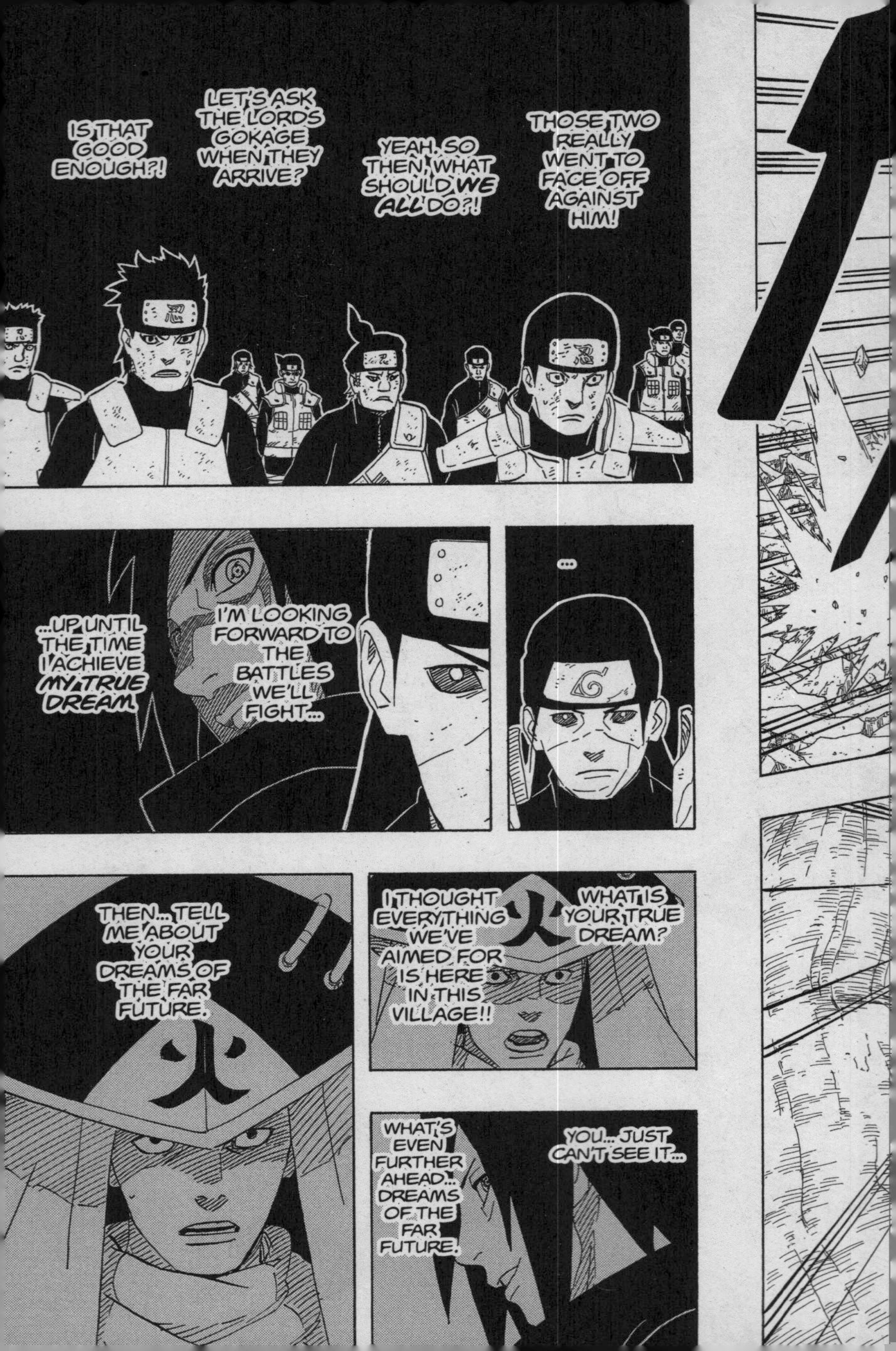
THOSE TWO REALLY WENT TO FACE OFF AGAINST HIM!
YEAH. SO THEN, WHAT SHOULD *WE ALL* DO?!
LET'S ASK THE LORDS GOKAGE WHEN THEY ARRIVE?
IS THAT GOOD ENOUGH?!
...
I'M LOOKING FORWARD TO THE BATTLES WE'LL FIGHT...
...UP UNTIL THE TIME I ACHIEVE *MY TRUE DREAM.*
WHAT IS YOUR TRUE DREAM?
I THOUGHT EVERYTHING WE'VE AIMED FOR IS HERE IN THIS VILLAGE!!
YOU... JUST CAN'T SEE IT...
WHAT'S EVEN FURTHER AHEAD... DREAMS OF THE FAR FUTURE.
THEN... TELL ME ABOUT YOUR DREAMS OF THE FAR FUTURE.

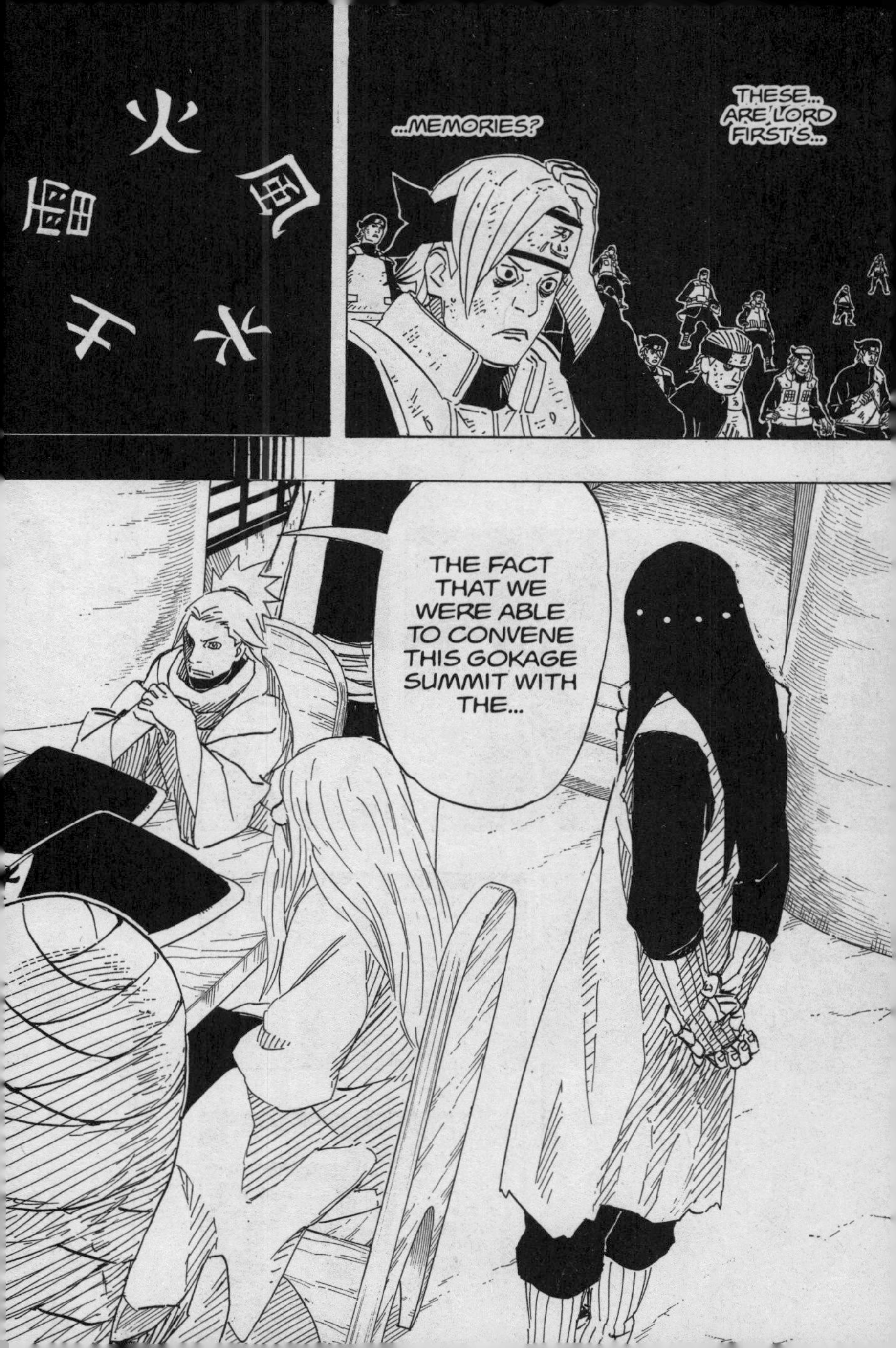
THESE... ARE LORD FIRST'S...
...MEMORIES?
火
風
水
土
雷
THE FACT THAT WE WERE ABLE TO CONVENE THIS GOKAGE SUMMIT WITH THE...

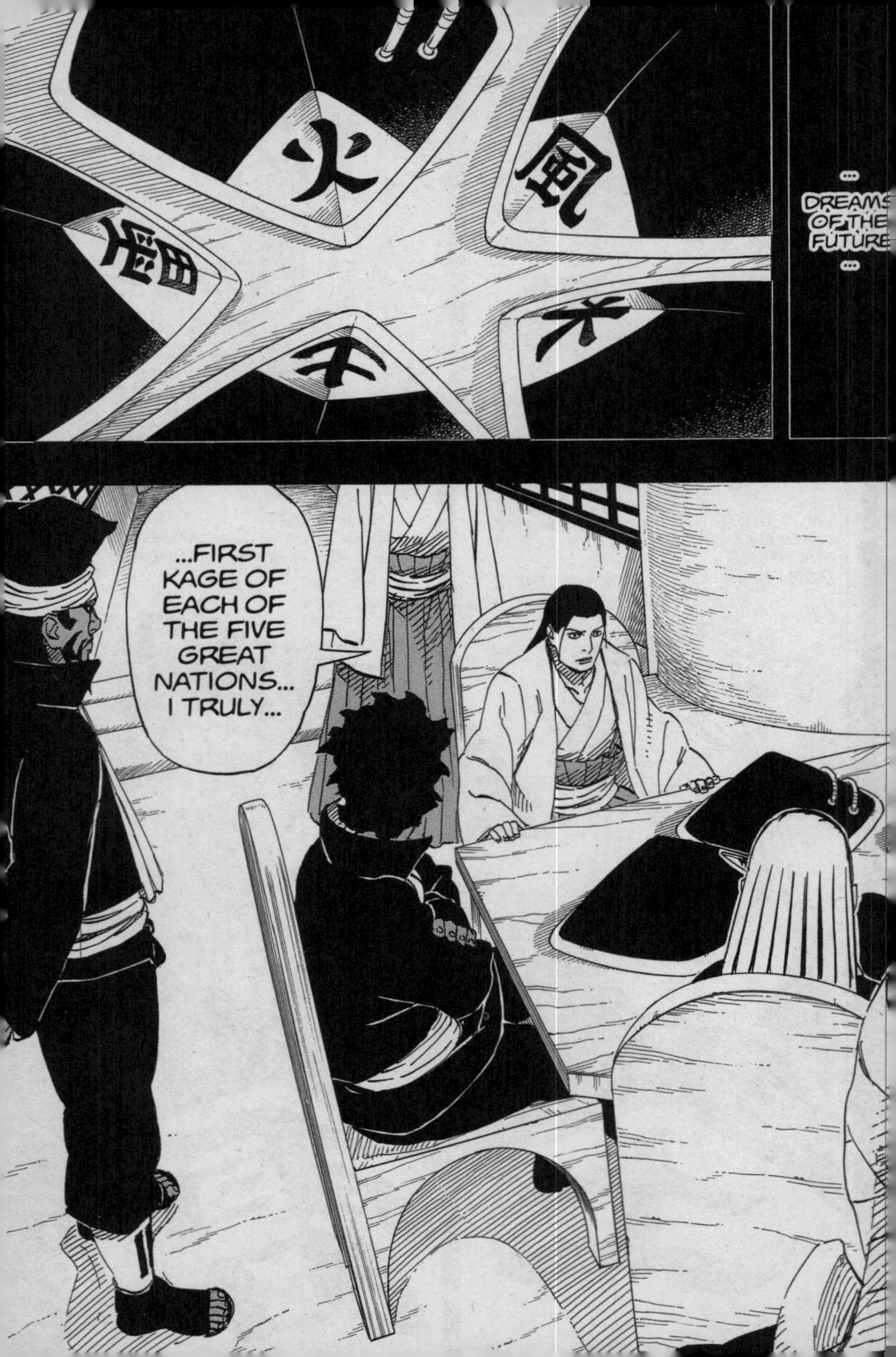
...DREAMS OF THE FUTURE...
...FIRST KAGE OF EACH OF THE FIVE GREAT NATIONS... I TRULY...

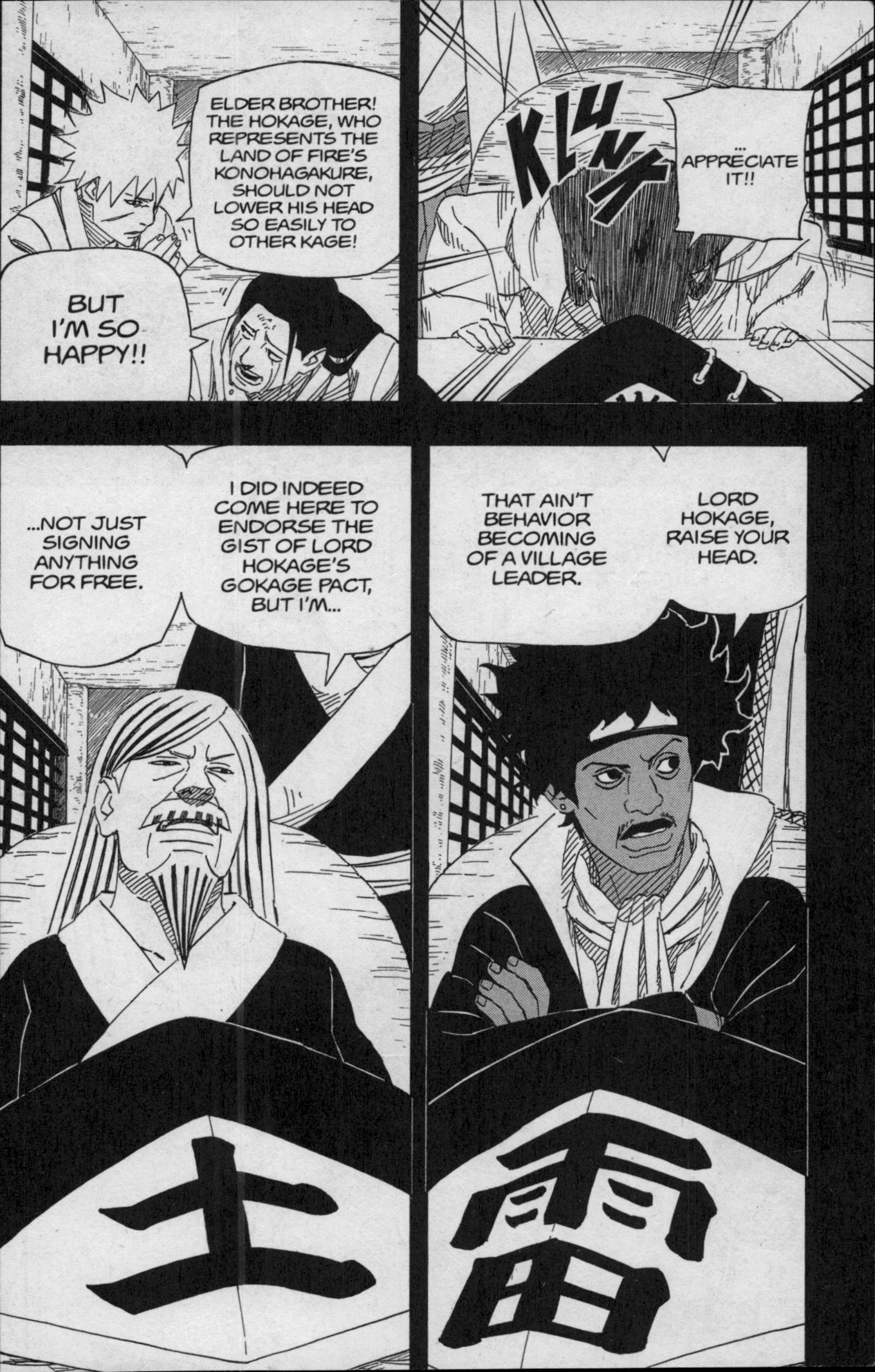

... APPRECIATE IT!!
KLUNK
ELDER BROTHER! THE HOKAGE, WHO REPRESENTS THE LAND OF FIRE'S KONOHAGAKURE, SHOULD NOT LOWER HIS HEAD SO EASILY TO OTHER KAGE!
BUT I'M SO HAPPY!!
LORD HOKAGE, RAISE YOUR HEAD.
THAT AIN'T BEHAVIOR BECOMING OF A VILLAGE LEADER.
雷
I DID INDEED COME HERE TO ENDORSE THE GIST OF LORD HOKAGE'S GOKAGE PACT, BUT I'M...
...NOT JUST SIGNING ANYTHING FOR FREE.
土

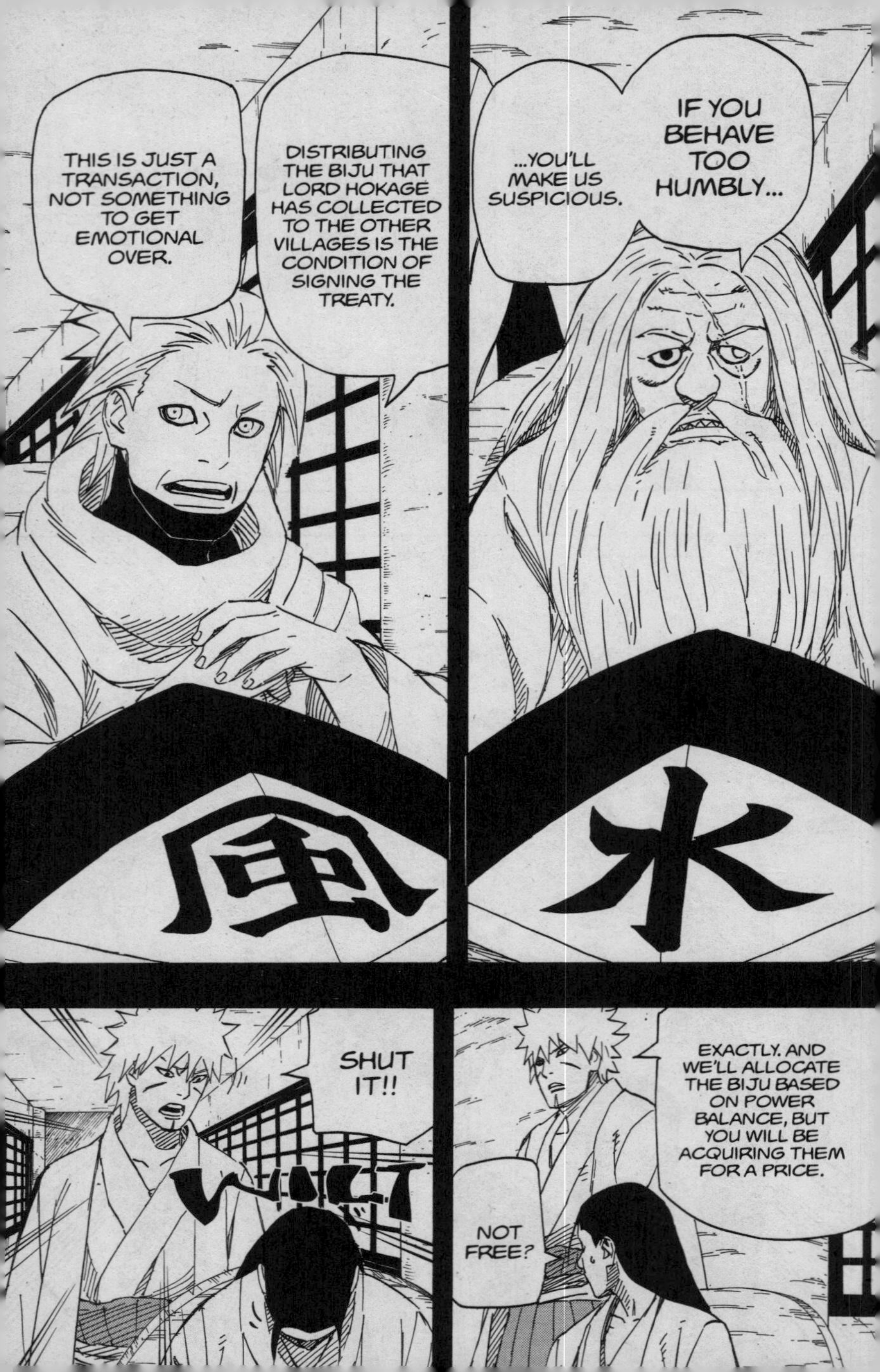
IF YOU BEHAVE TOO HUMBLY...
...YOU'LL MAKE US SUSPICIOUS.
DISTRIBUTING THE BIJU THAT LORD HOKAGE HAS COLLECTED TO THE OTHER VILLAGES IS THE CONDITION OF SIGNING THE TREATY.
THIS IS JUST A TRANSACTION, NOT SOMETHING TO GET EMOTIONAL OVER.
風
水
EXACTLY. AND WE'LL ALLOCATE THE BIJU BASED ON POWER BALANCE, BUT YOU WILL BE ACQUIRING THEM FOR A PRICE.
NOT FREE?
SHUT IT!!

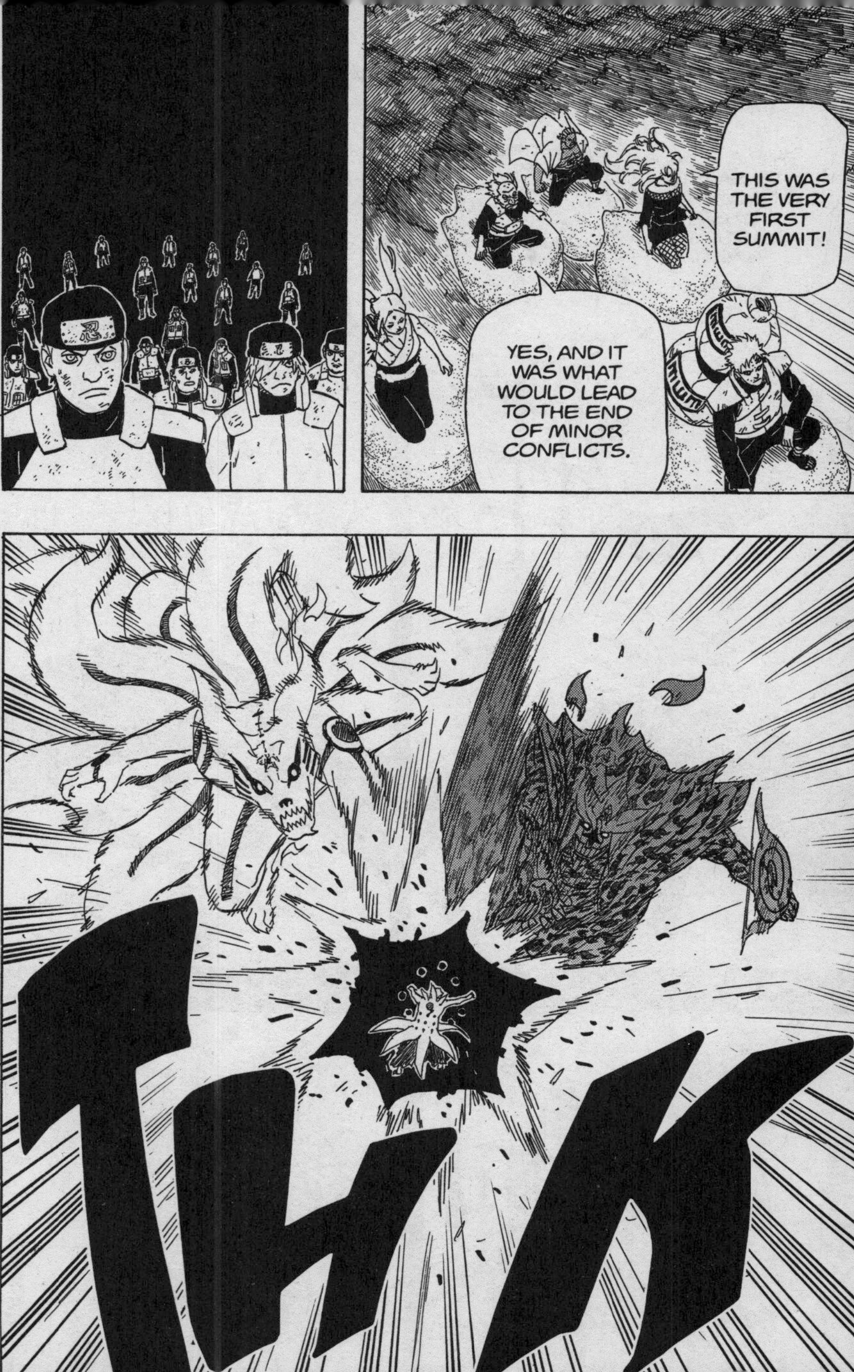
THIS WAS THE VERY FIRST SUMMIT!
YES, AND IT WAS WHAT WOULD LEAD TO THE END OF MINOR CONFLICTS.

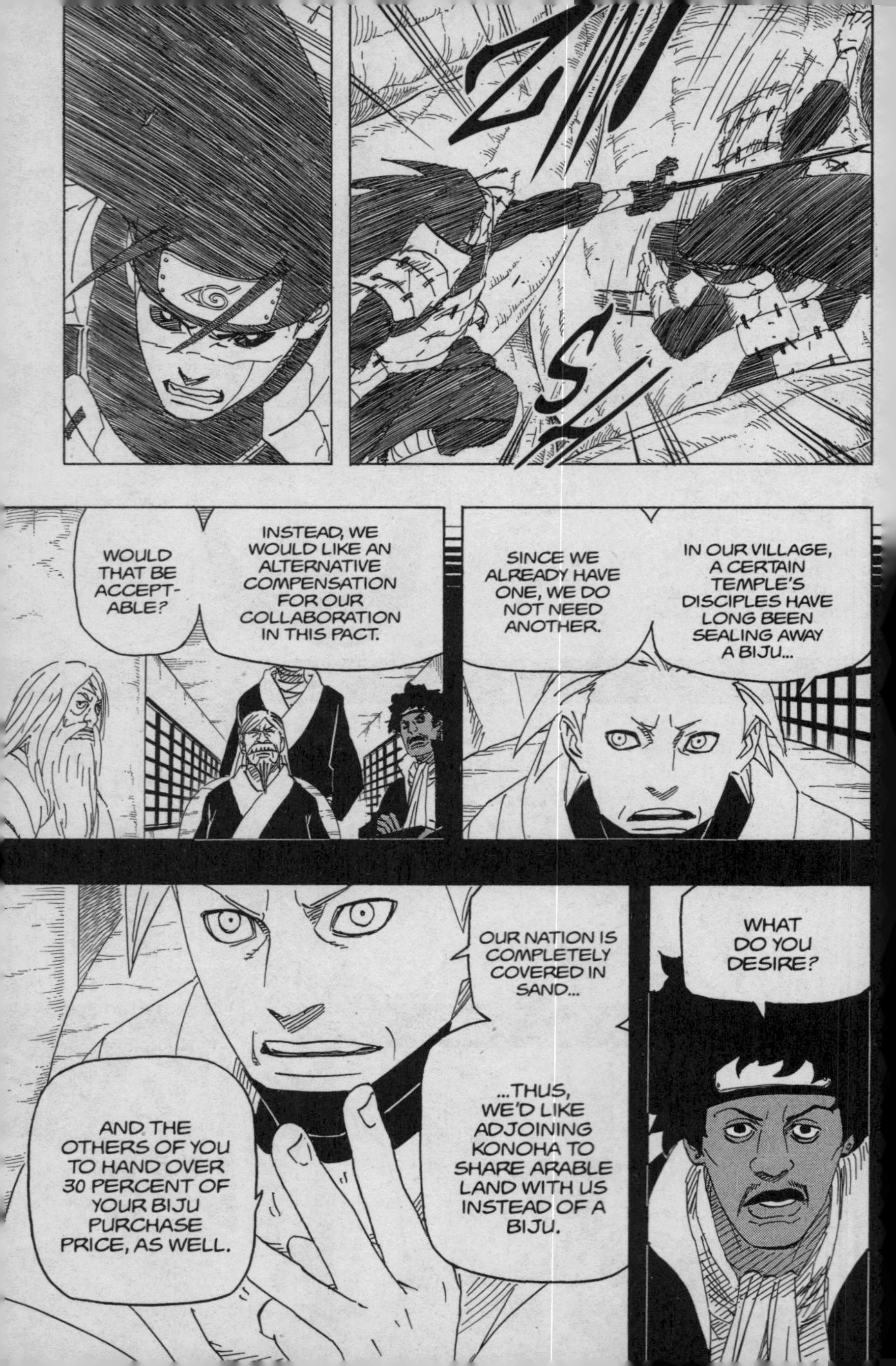
IN OUR VILLAGE, A CERTAIN TEMPLE'S DISCIPLES HAVE LONG BEEN SEALING AWAY A BIJU...
SINCE WE ALREADY HAVE ONE, WE DO NOT NEED ANOTHER.
INSTEAD, WE WOULD LIKE AN ALTERNATIVE COMPENSATION FOR OUR COLLABORATION IN THIS PACT.
WOULD THAT BE ACCEPT-ABLE?
WHAT DO YOU DESIRE?
OUR NATION IS COMPLETELY COVERED IN SAND...
...THUS, WE'D LIKE ADJOINING KONOHA TO SHARE ARABLE LAND WITH US INSTEAD OF A BIJU.
AND THE OTHERS OF YOU TO HAND OVER 30 PERCENT OF YOUR BIJU PURCHASE PRICE, AS WELL.

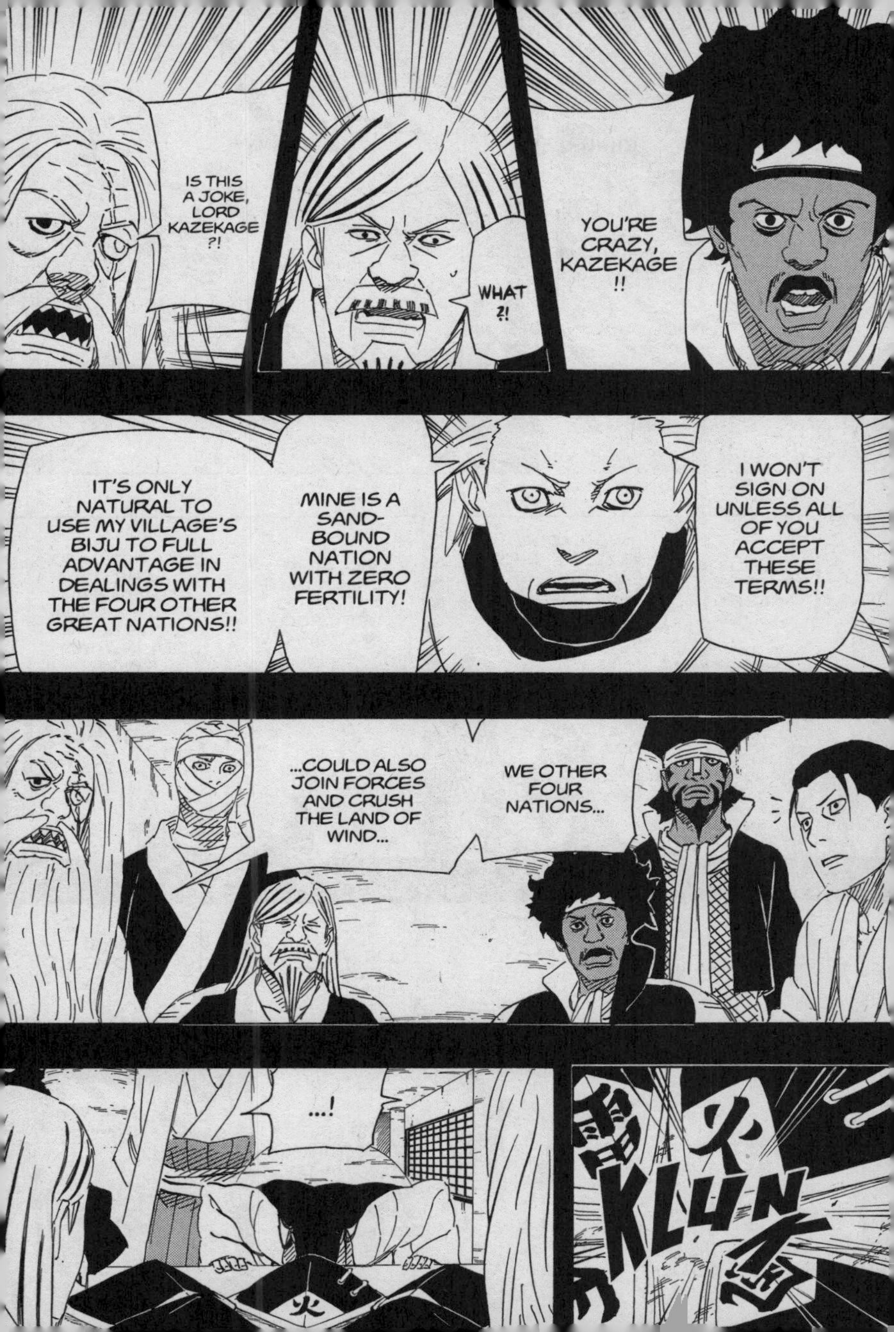
YOU'RE CRAZY, KAZEKAGE !!
WHAT ?!
IS THIS A JOKE, LORD KAZEKAGE ?!
I WON'T SIGN ON UNLESS ALL OF YOU ACCEPT THESE TERMS!!
MINE IS A SAND-BOUND NATION WITH ZERO FERTILITY!
IT'S ONLY NATURAL TO USE MY VILLAGE'S BIJU TO FULL ADVANTAGE IN DEALINGS WITH THE FOUR OTHER GREAT NATIONS!!
WE OTHER FOUR NATIONS...
...COULD ALSO JOIN FORCES AND CRUSH THE LAND OF WIND...
KLUN
...!

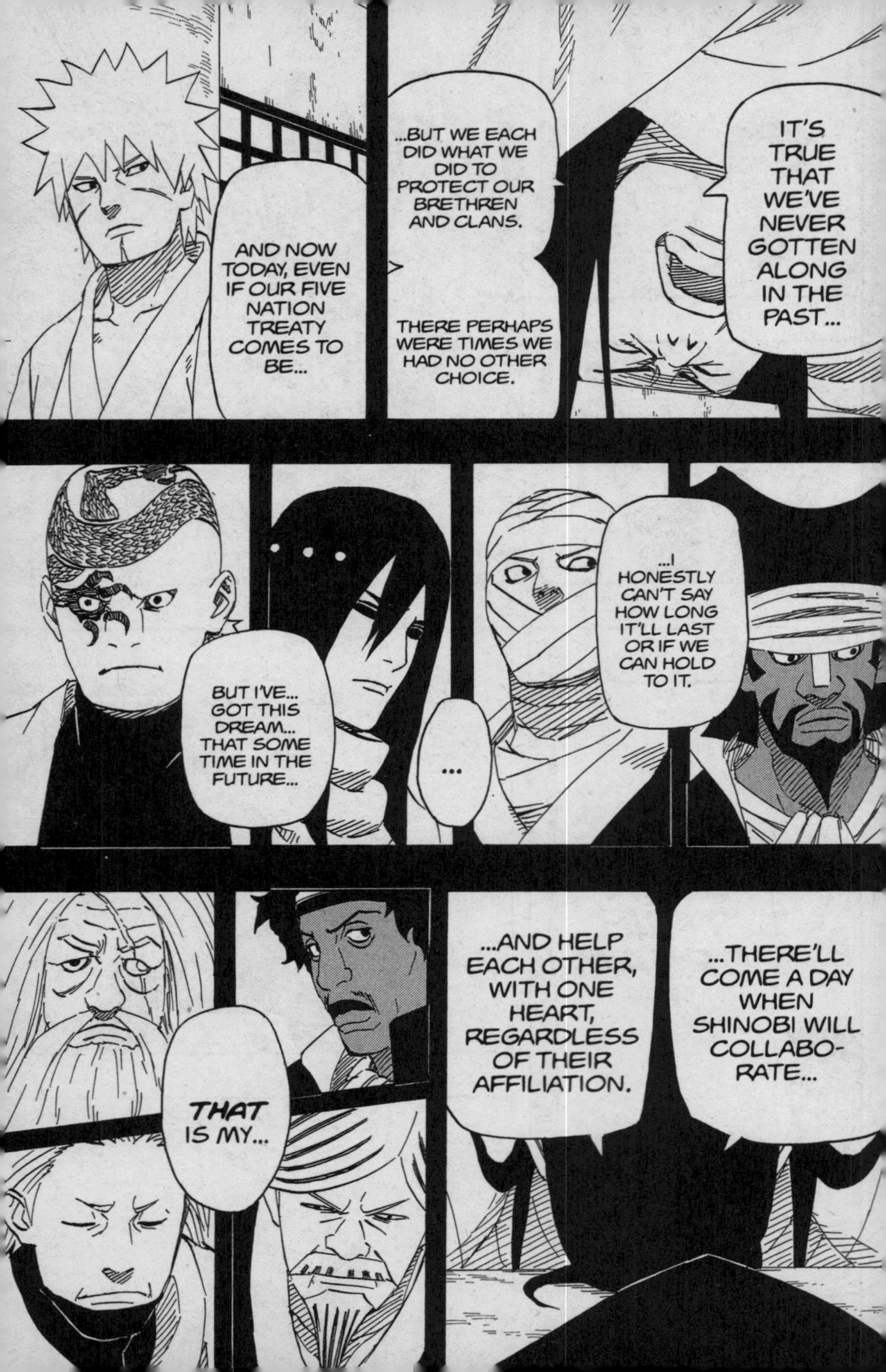
IT'S TRUE THAT WE'VE NEVER GOTTEN ALONG IN THE PAST...
...BUT WE EACH DID WHAT WE DID TO PROTECT OUR BRETHREN AND CLANS.
THERE PERHAPS WERE TIMES WE HAD NO OTHER CHOICE.
AND NOW TODAY, EVEN IF OUR FIVE NATION TREATY COMES TO BE...
...I HONESTLY CAN'T SAY HOW LONG IT'LL LAST OR IF WE CAN HOLD TO IT.
...
BUT I'VE... GOT THIS DREAM... THAT SOME TIME IN THE FUTURE...
...THERE'LL COME A DAY WHEN SHINOBI WILL COLLABO-RATE...
...AND HELP EACH OTHER, WITH ONE HEART, REGARDLESS OF THEIR AFFILIATION.
THAT IS MY...

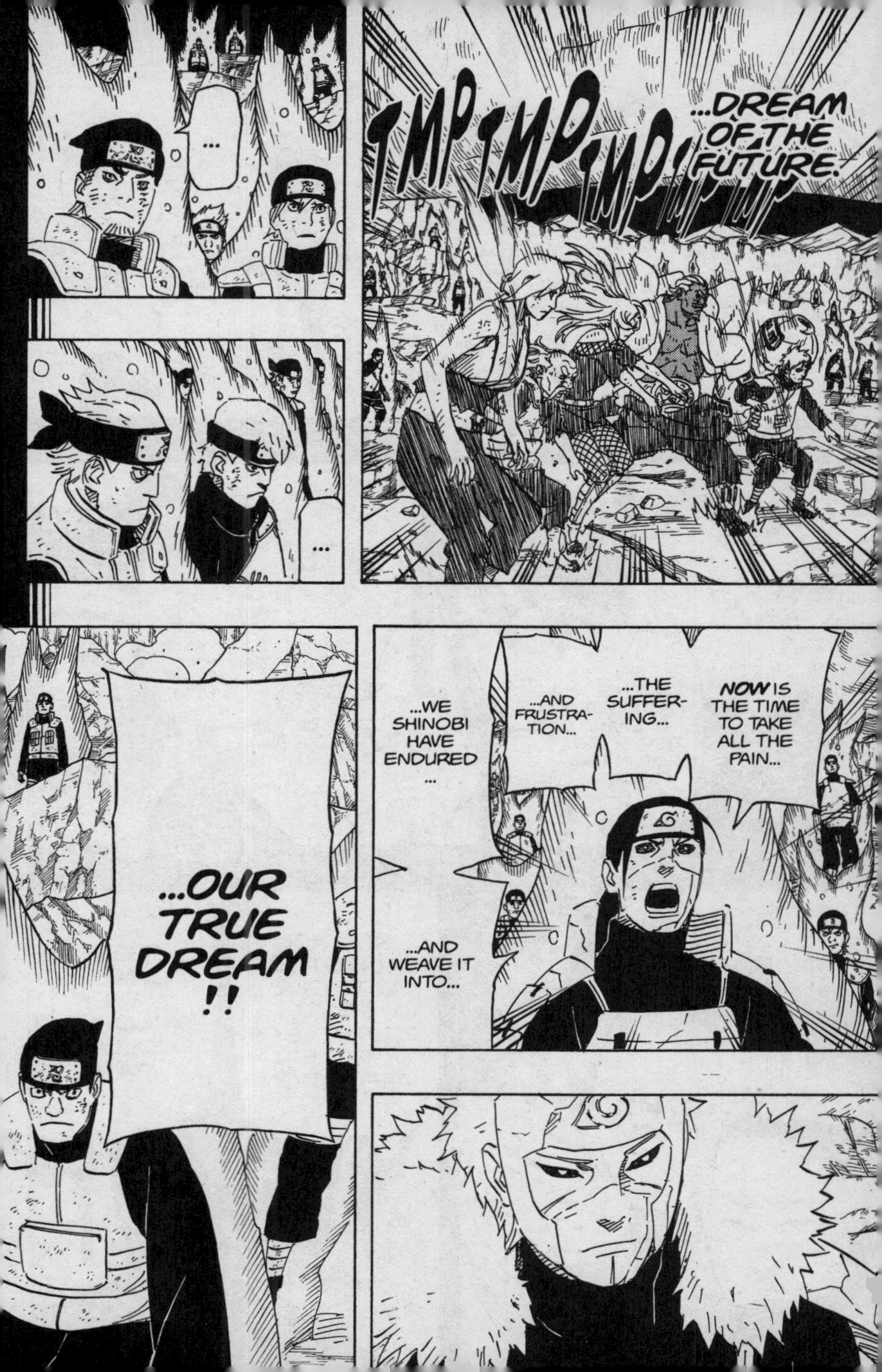
TMP TMP TMP
...DREAM OF THE FUTURE.
...
...
NOW IS THE TIME TO TAKE ALL THE PAIN...
...THE SUFFER-ING...
...AND FRUSTRA-TION...
...WE SHINOBI HAVE ENDURED ...
...AND WEAVE IT INTO...
...OUR TRUE DREAM !!

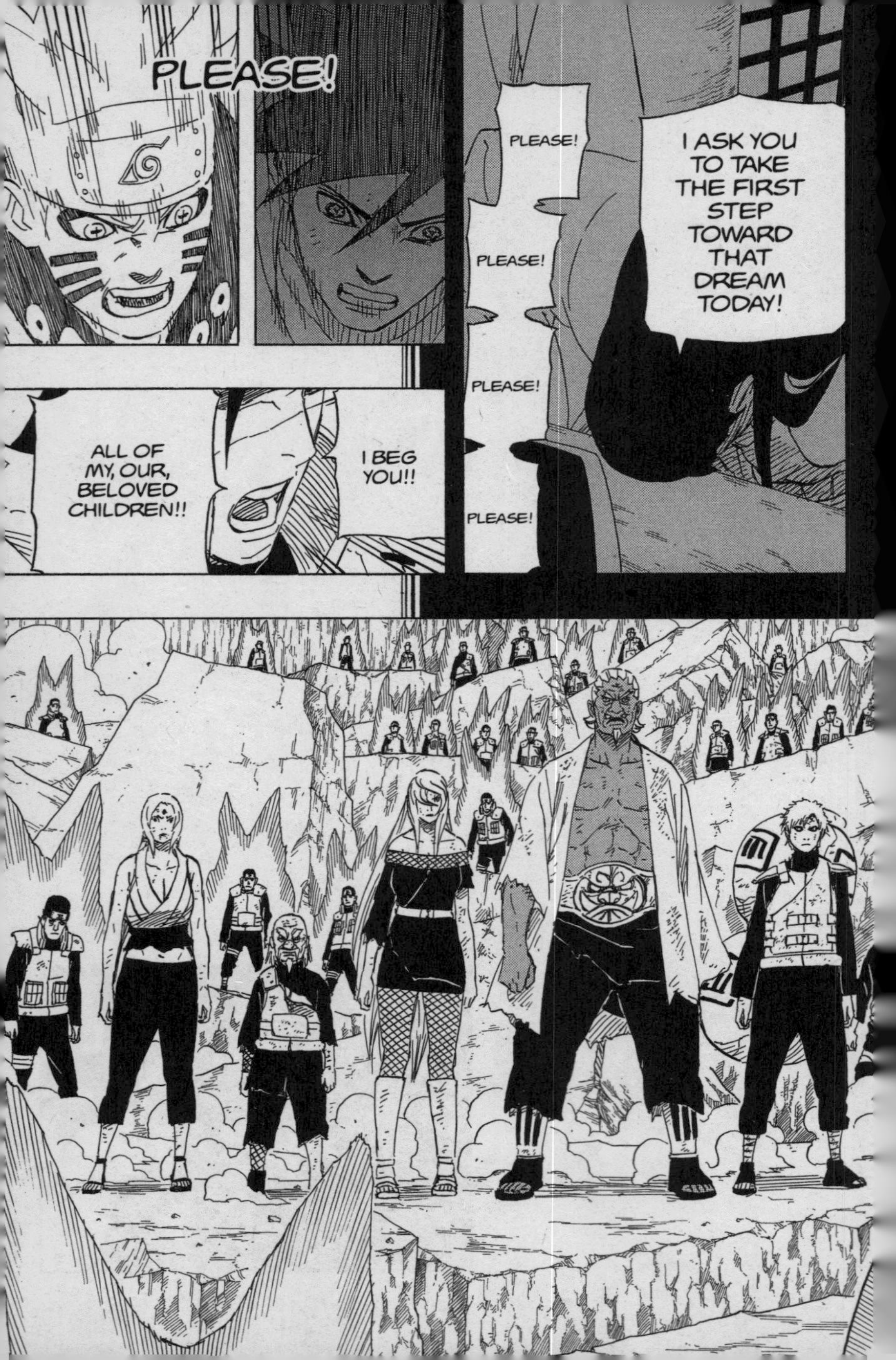
I ASK YOU TO TAKE THE FIRST STEP TOWARD THAT DREAM TODAY!
PLEASE!
PLEASE!
PLEASE!
PLEASE!
PLEASE!
I BEG YOU!!
ALL OF MY, OUR, BELOVED CHILDREN!!

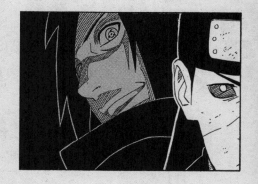

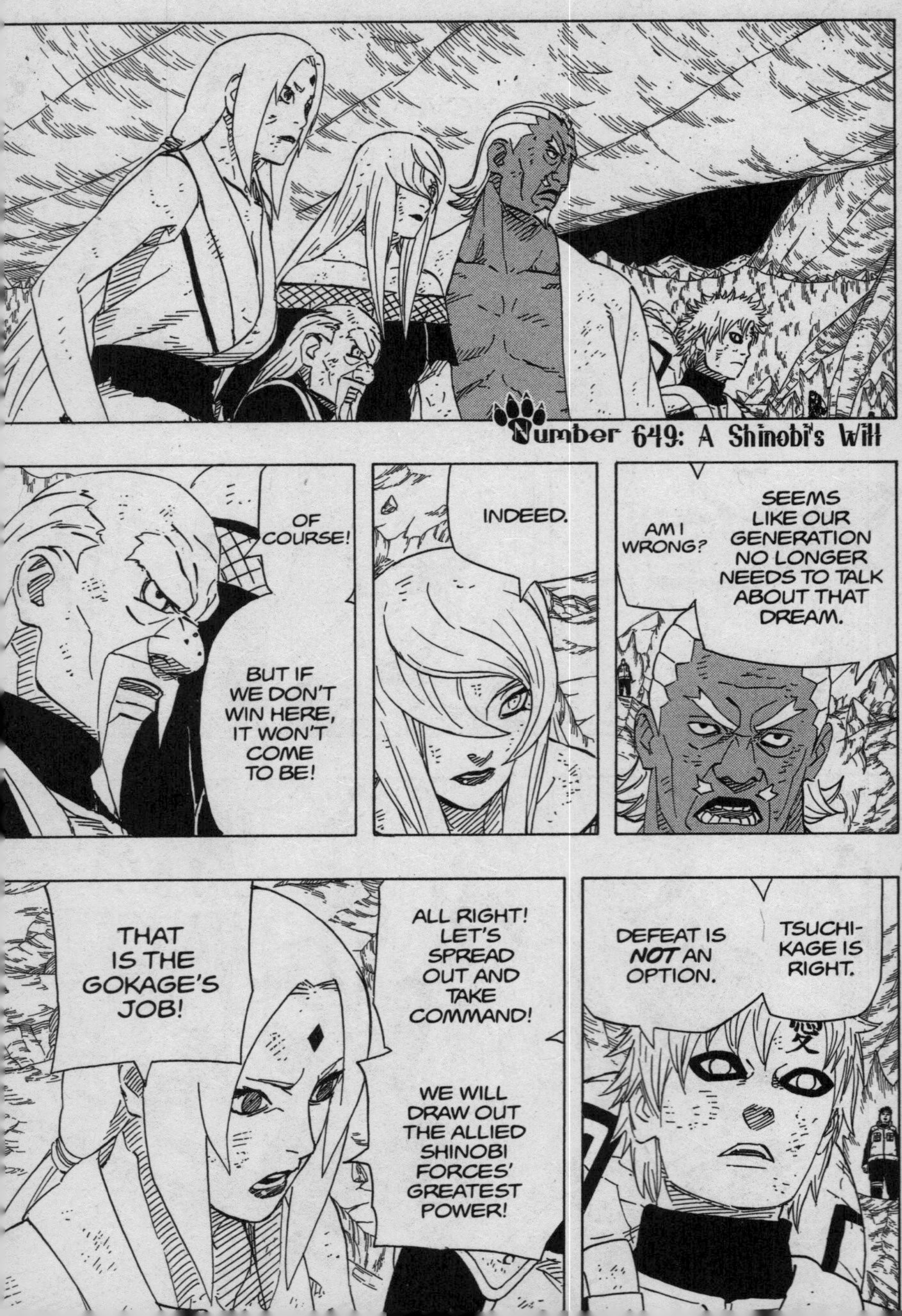
Number 649: A Shinobi's Will
SEEMS LIKE OUR GENERATION NO LONGER NEEDS TO TALK ABOUT THAT DREAM.
AM I WRONG?
INDEED.
OF COURSE!
BUT IF WE DON'T WIN HERE, IT WON'T COME TO BE!
TSUCHI-KAGE IS RIGHT.
DEFEAT IS ***NOT*** AN OPTION.
ALL RIGHT! LET'S SPREAD OUT AND TAKE COMMAND!
WE WILL DRAW OUT THE ALLIED SHINOBI FORCES' GREATEST POWER!
THAT IS THE GOKAGE'S JOB!

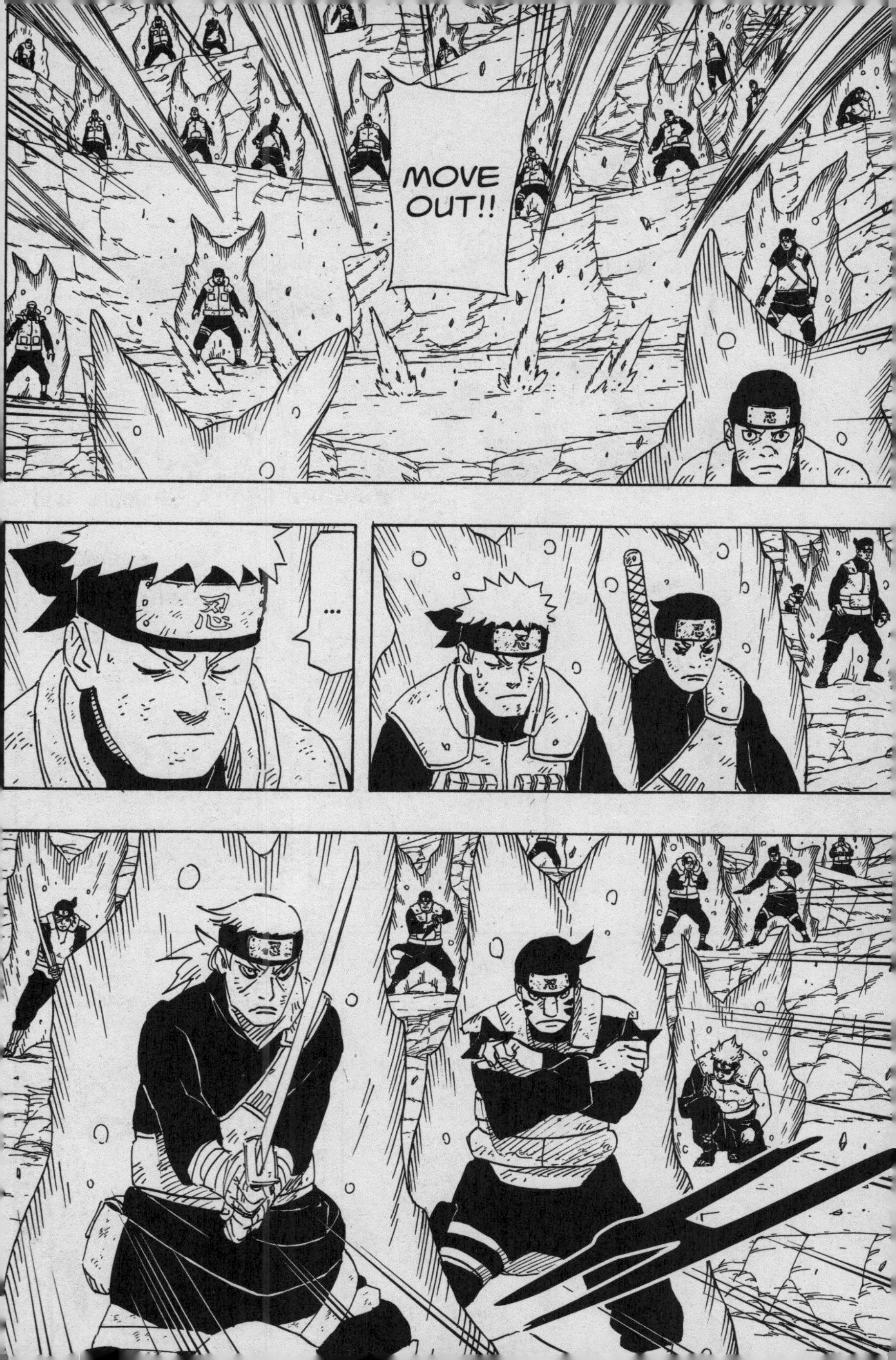
MOVE OUT!!
...

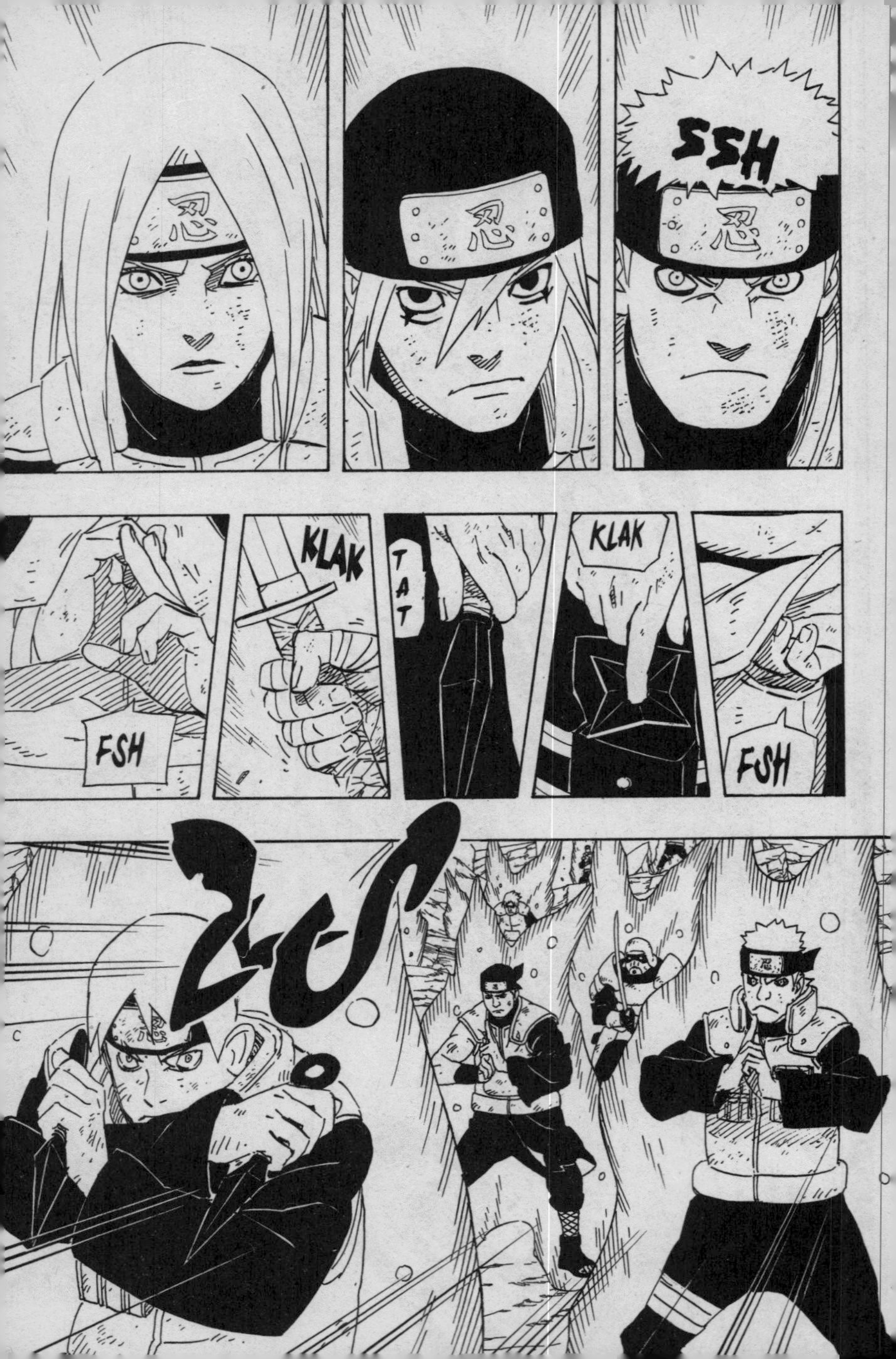
SSH
FSH
KLAK
TAT
KLAK
FSH

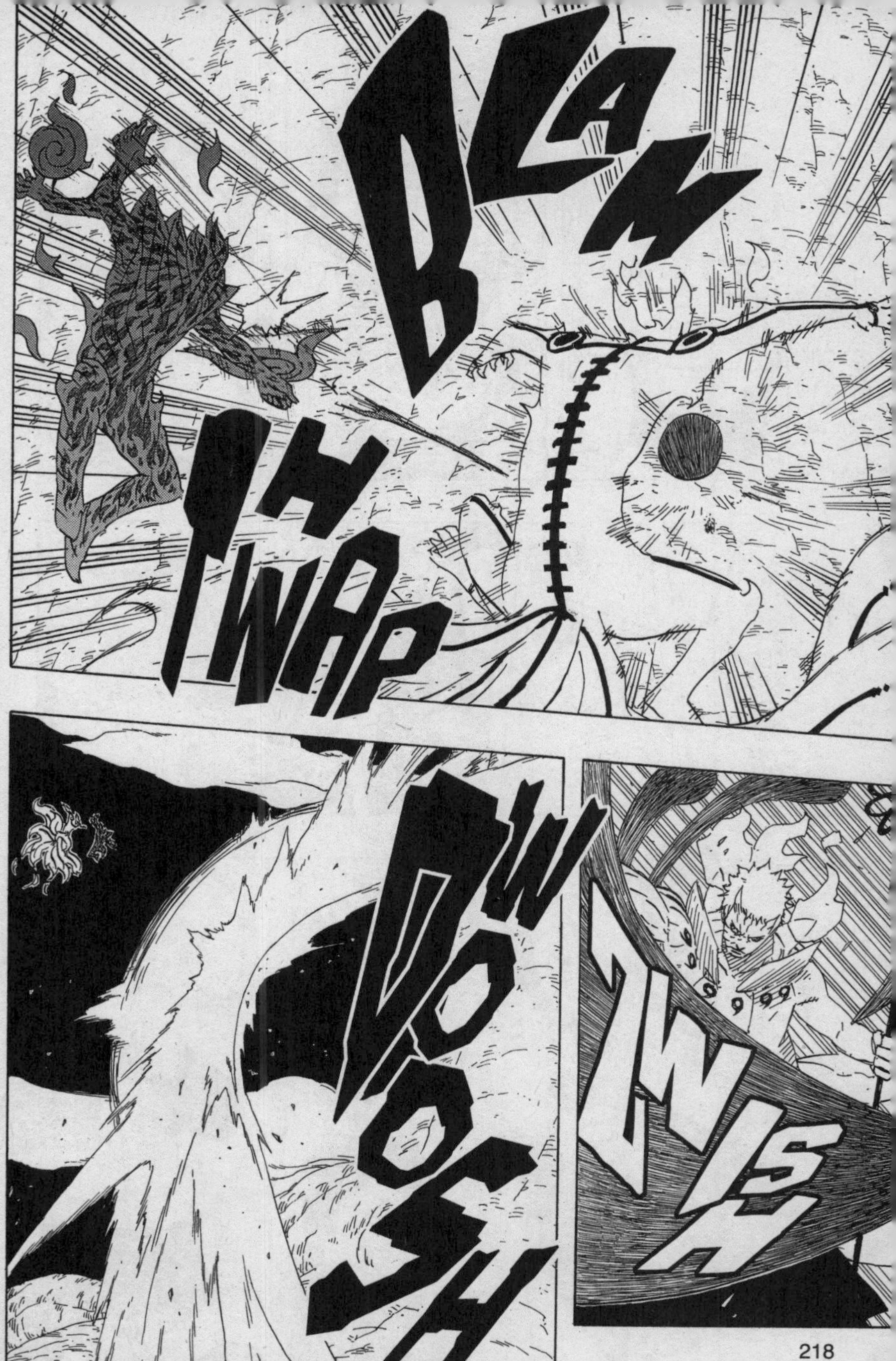
BLAM
THWAP
SWISH
DWOOSH

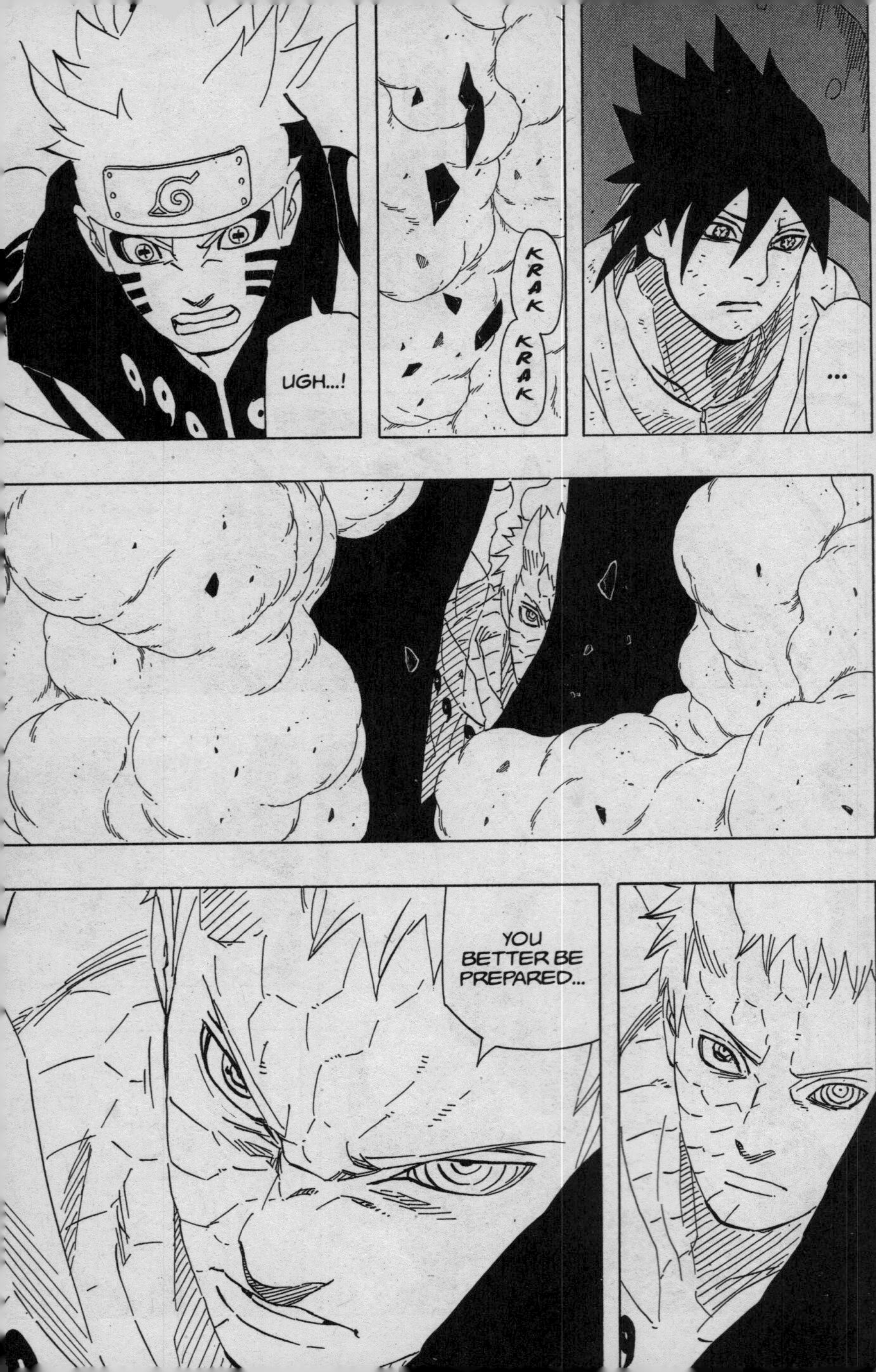
...
KRAK KRAK
UGH...!
YOU BETTER BE PREPARED...

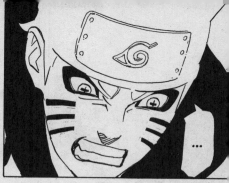

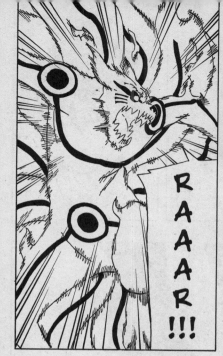

RAAAR!!!

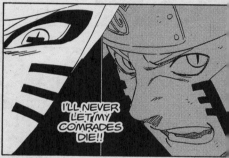

...

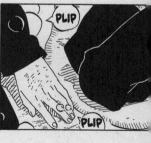

I'LL NEVER LET MY COMRADES DIE!!

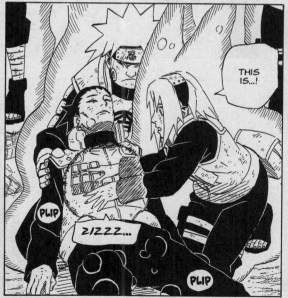

THIS IS...!

ZZZZZ...

PLIP

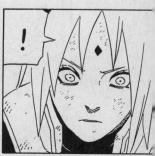

PLIP

PLIP

!

PLIP

220

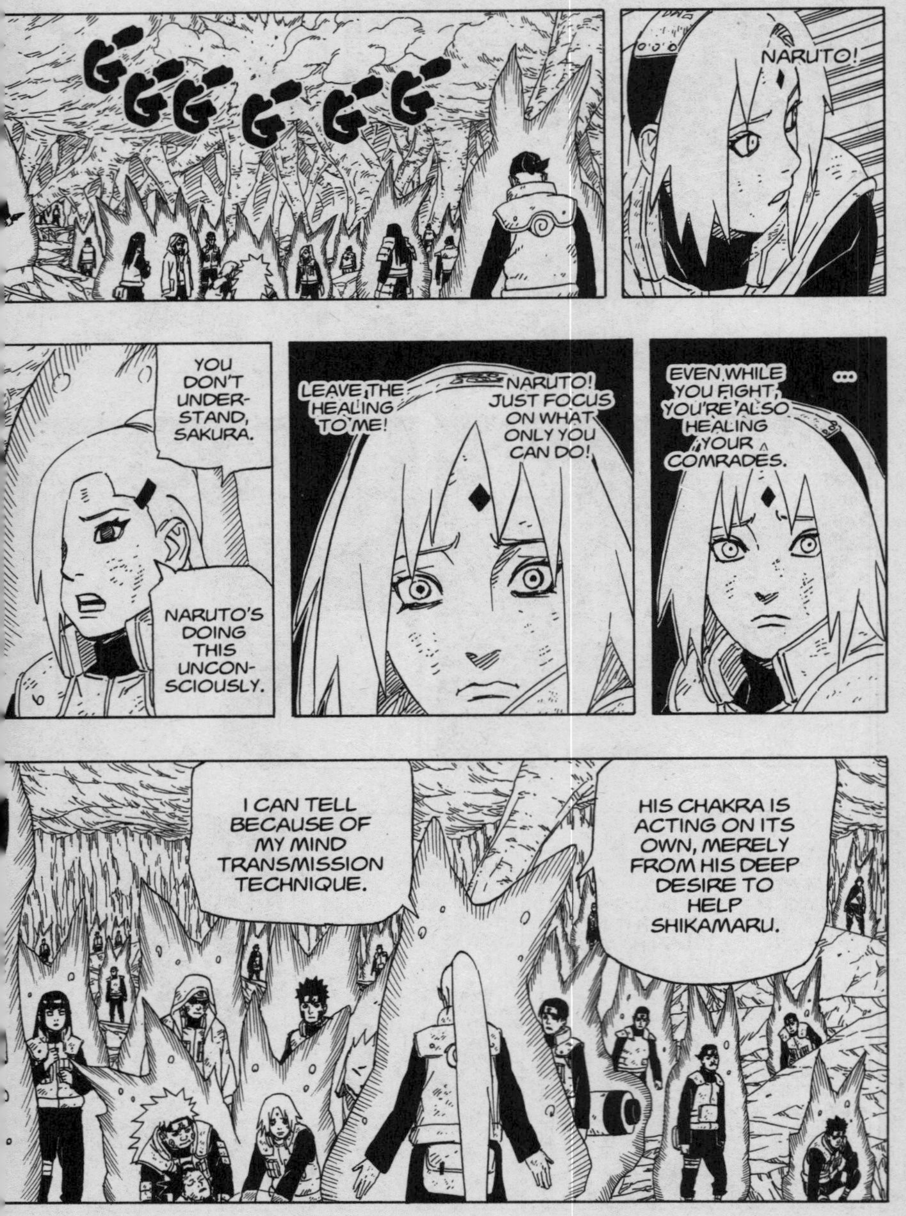
NARUTO!
GGGGGGG
...
EVEN WHILE YOU FIGHT, YOU'RE ALSO HEALING YOUR COMRADES.
NARUTO! JUST FOCUS ON WHAT ONLY YOU CAN DO!
LEAVE THE HEALING TO ME!
YOU DON'T UNDER-STAND, SAKURA.
NARUTO'S DOING THIS UNCON-SCIOUSLY.
HIS CHAKRA IS ACTING ON ITS OWN, MERELY FROM HIS DEEP DESIRE TO HELP SHIKAMARU.
I CAN TELL BECAUSE OF MY MIND TRANSMISSION TECHNIQUE.

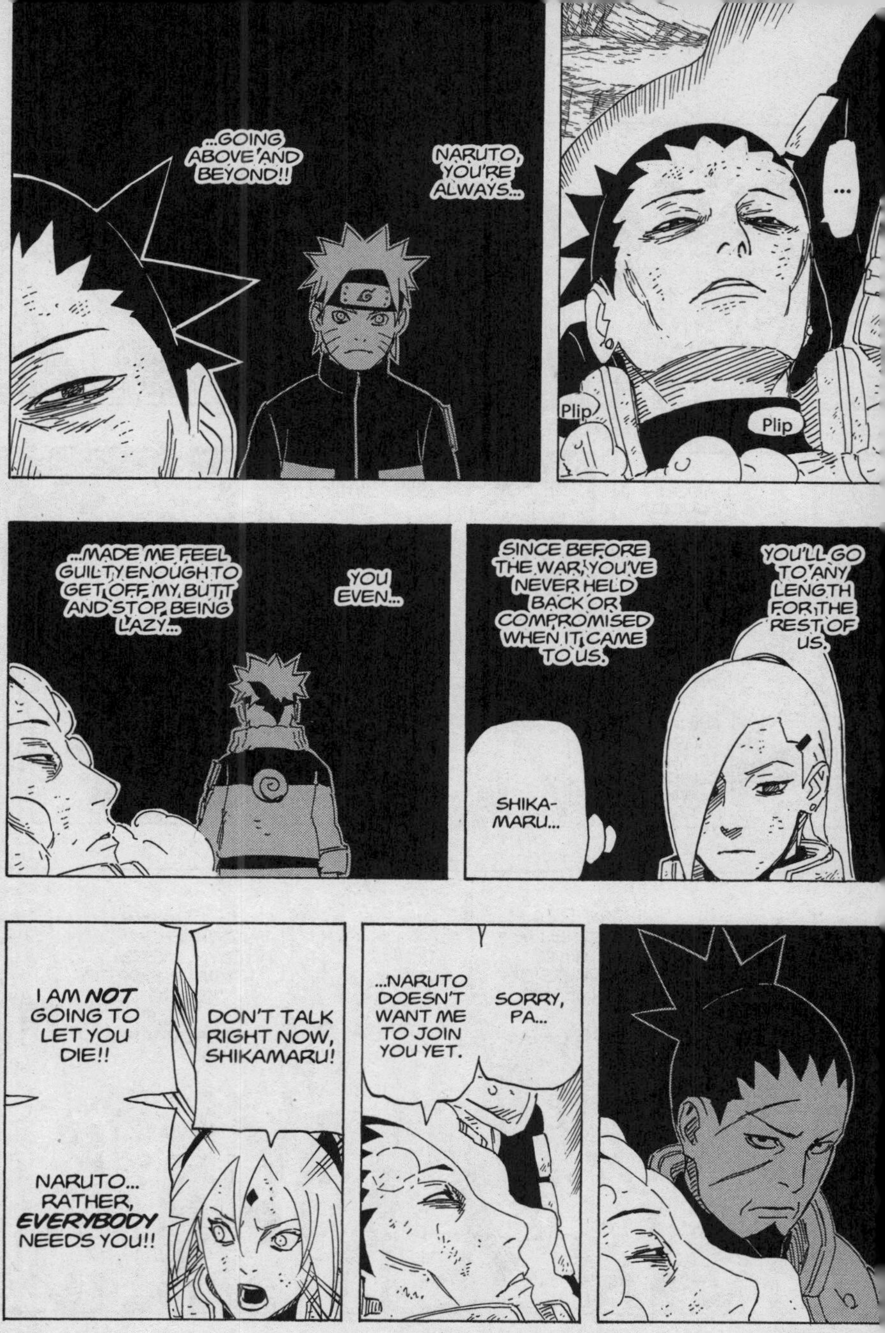
...
Plip
Plip
NARUTO, YOU'RE ALWAYS...
...GOING ABOVE AND BEYOND!!
YOU'LL GO TO ANY LENGTH FOR THE REST OF US.
SINCE BEFORE THE WAR, YOU'VE NEVER HELD BACK OR COMPROMISED WHEN IT CAME TO US.
SHIKA-MARU...
YOU EVEN...
...MADE ME FEEL GUILTY ENOUGH TO GET OFF MY BUTT AND STOP BEING LAZY...
SORRY, PA...
...NARUTO DOESN'T WANT ME TO JOIN YOU YET.
DON'T TALK RIGHT NOW, SHIKAMARU!
I AM **NOT** GOING TO LET YOU DIE!!
NARUTO... RATHER, ***EVERYBODY*** NEEDS YOU!!

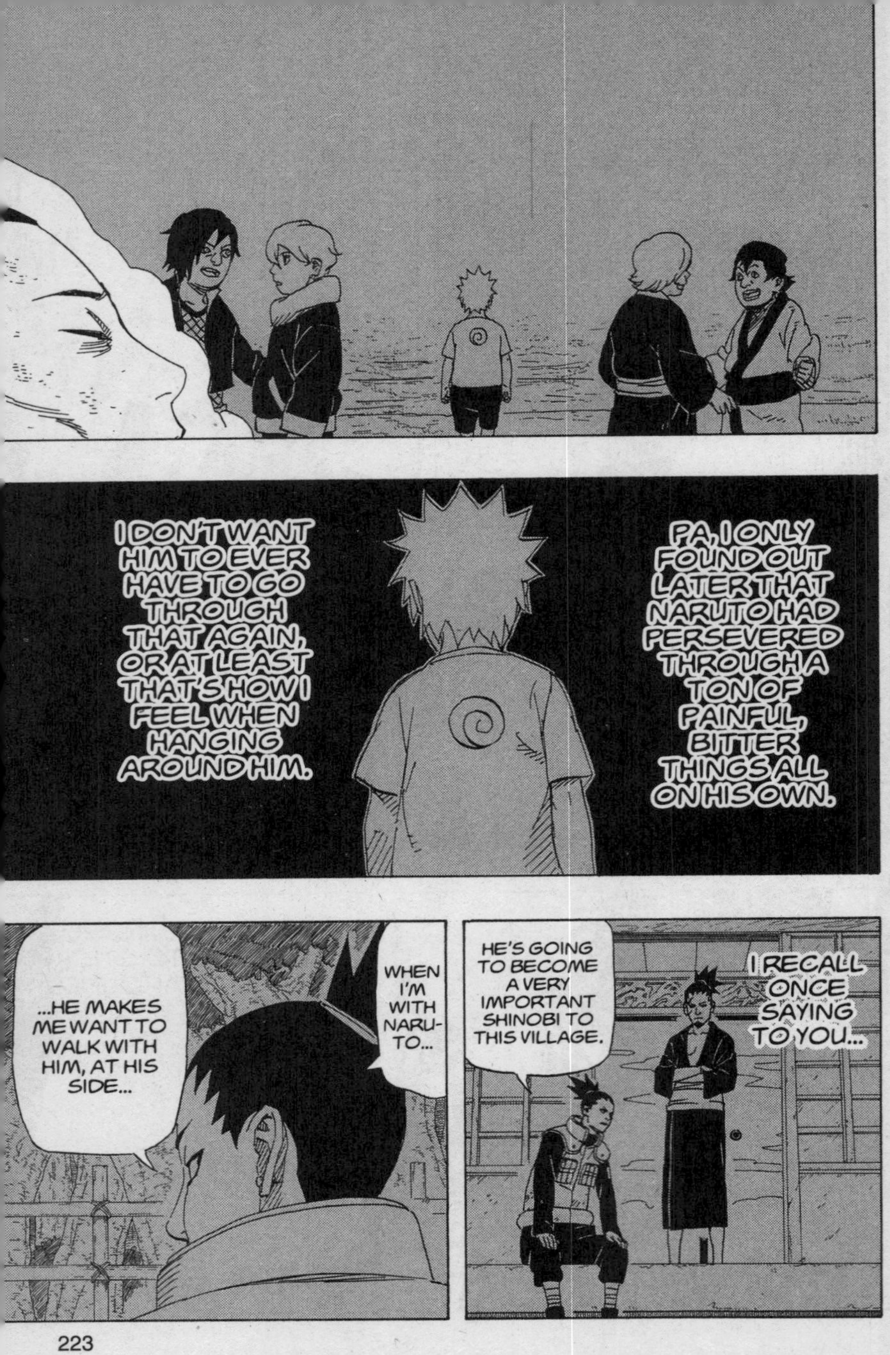
PA, I ONLY FOUND OUT LATER THAT NARUTO HAD PERSEVERED THROUGH A TON OF PAINFUL, BITTER THINGS ALL ON HIS OWN.
I DON'T WANT HIM TO EVER HAVE TO GO THROUGH THAT AGAIN, OR AT LEAST THAT'S HOW I FEEL WHEN HANGING AROUND HIM.
I RECALL ONCE SAYING TO YOU...
HE'S GOING TO BECOME A VERY IMPORTANT SHINOBI TO THIS VILLAGE.
WHEN I'M WITH NARU-TO...
...HE MAKES ME WANT TO WALK WITH HIM, AT HIS SIDE...

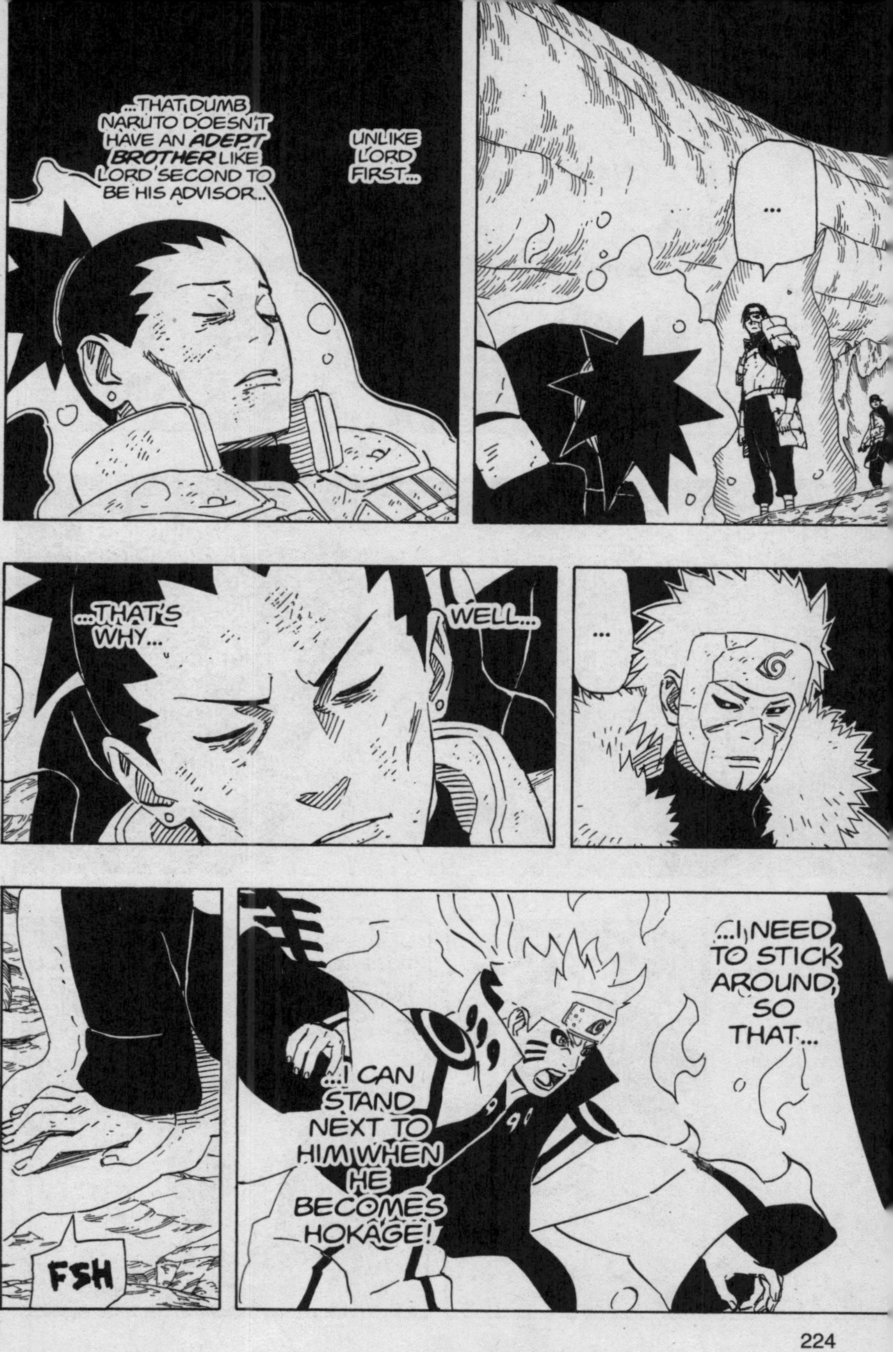
...
UNLIKE LORD FIRST...
...THAT DUMB NARUTO DOESN'T HAVE AN ADEPT BROTHER LIKE LORD SECOND TO BE HIS ADVISOR...
...
WELL...
...THAT'S WHY...
...I NEED TO STICK AROUND, SO THAT...
...I CAN STAND NEXT TO HIM WHEN HE BECOMES HOKAGE!
FSH

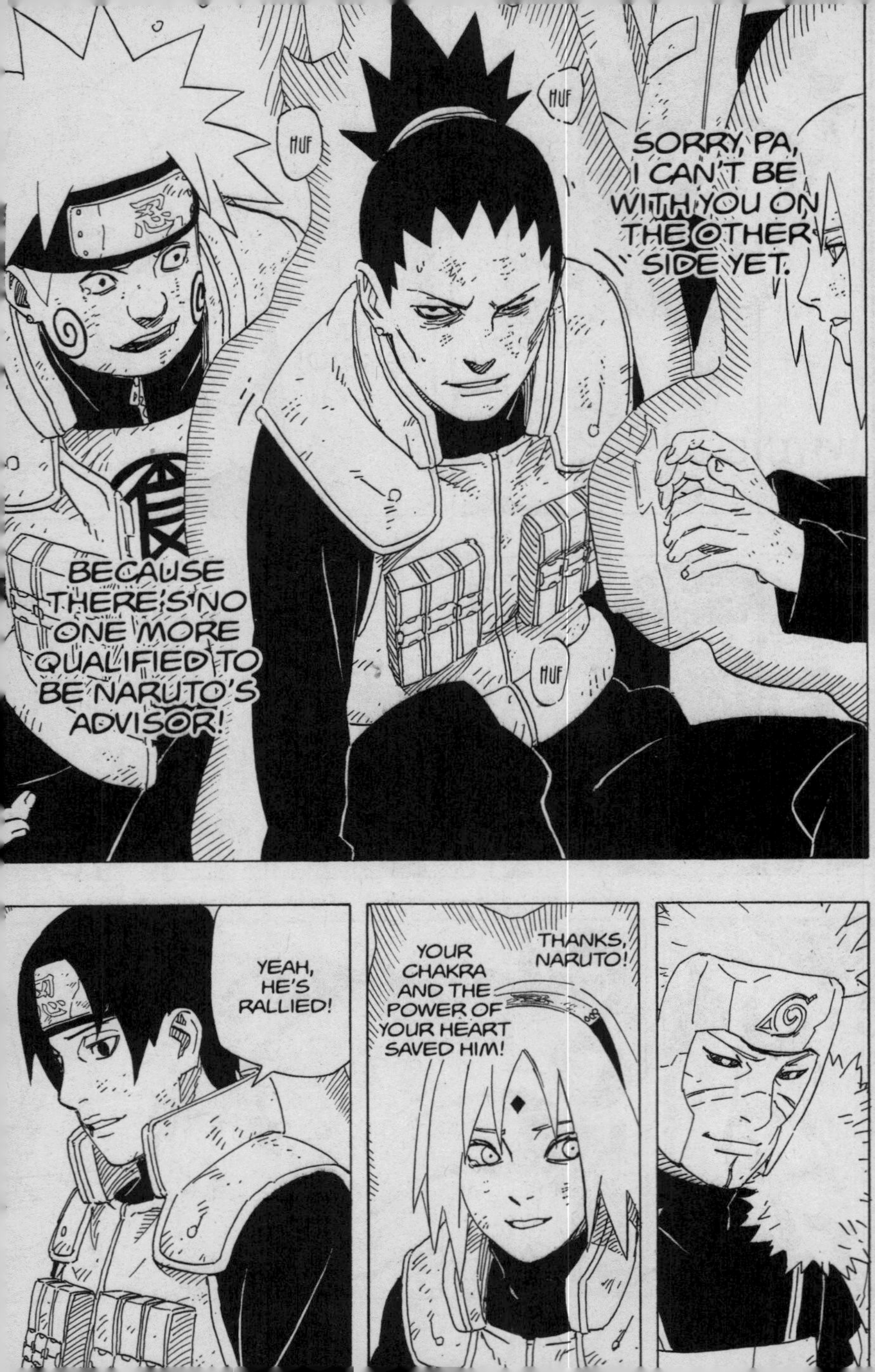
SORRY, PA, I CAN'T BE WITH YOU ON THE OTHER SIDE YET.
HUF
HUF
HUF
BECAUSE THERE'S NO ONE MORE QUALIFIED TO BE NARUTO'S ADVISOR!
THANKS, NARUTO!
YOUR CHAKRA AND THE POWER OF YOUR HEART SAVED HIM!
YEAH, HE'S RALLIED!

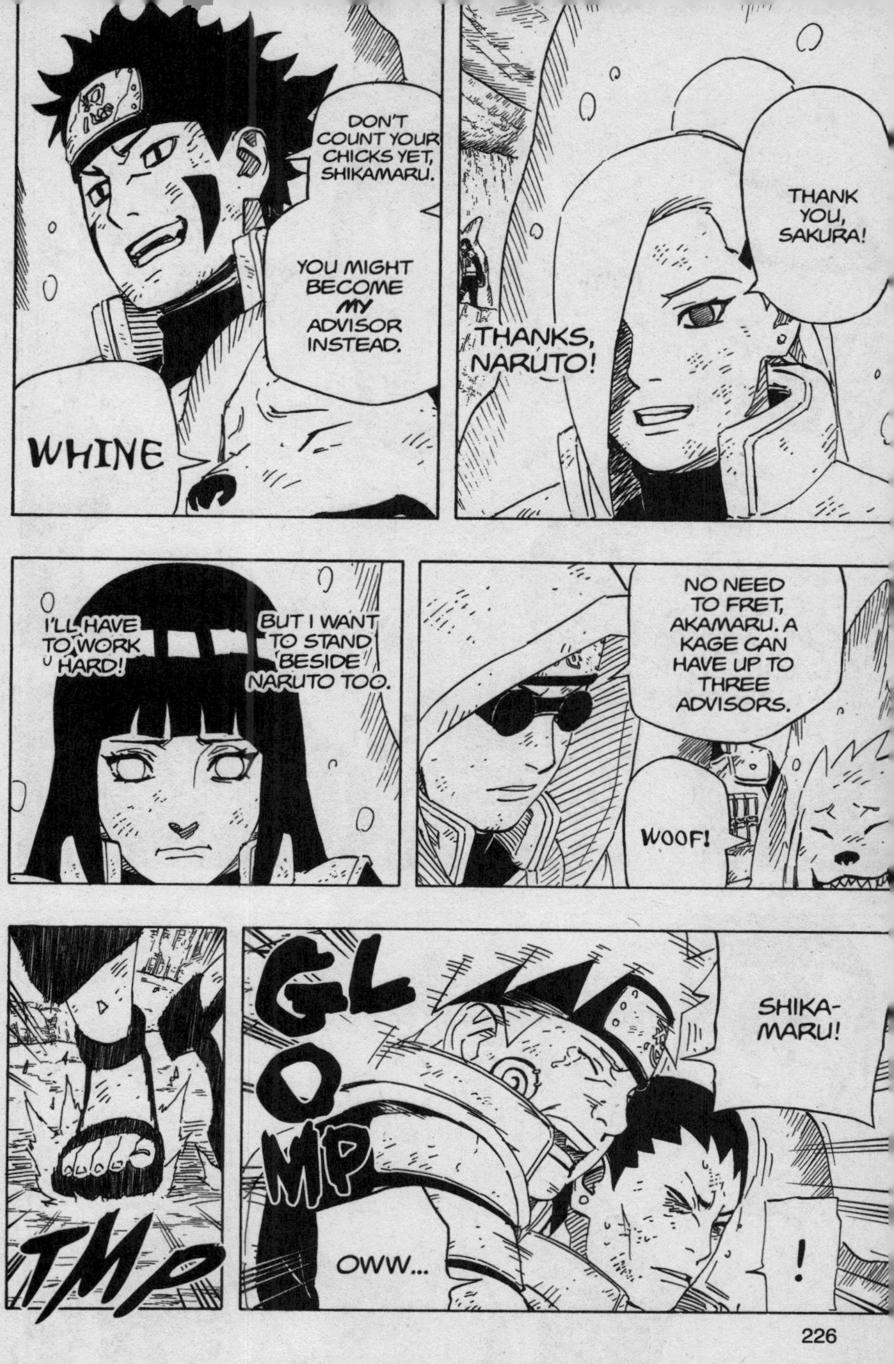
THANK YOU, SAKURA!
THANKS, NARUTO!
DON'T COUNT YOUR CHICKS YET, SHIKAMARU.
YOU MIGHT BECOME MY ADVISOR INSTEAD.
WHINE
NO NEED TO FRET, AKAMARU. A KAGE CAN HAVE UP TO THREE ADVISORS.
WOOF!
BUT I WANT TO STAND BESIDE NARUTO TOO.
I'LL HAVE TO WORK HARD!
SHIKA-MARU!
!
GLOMP
OWW...
TMP

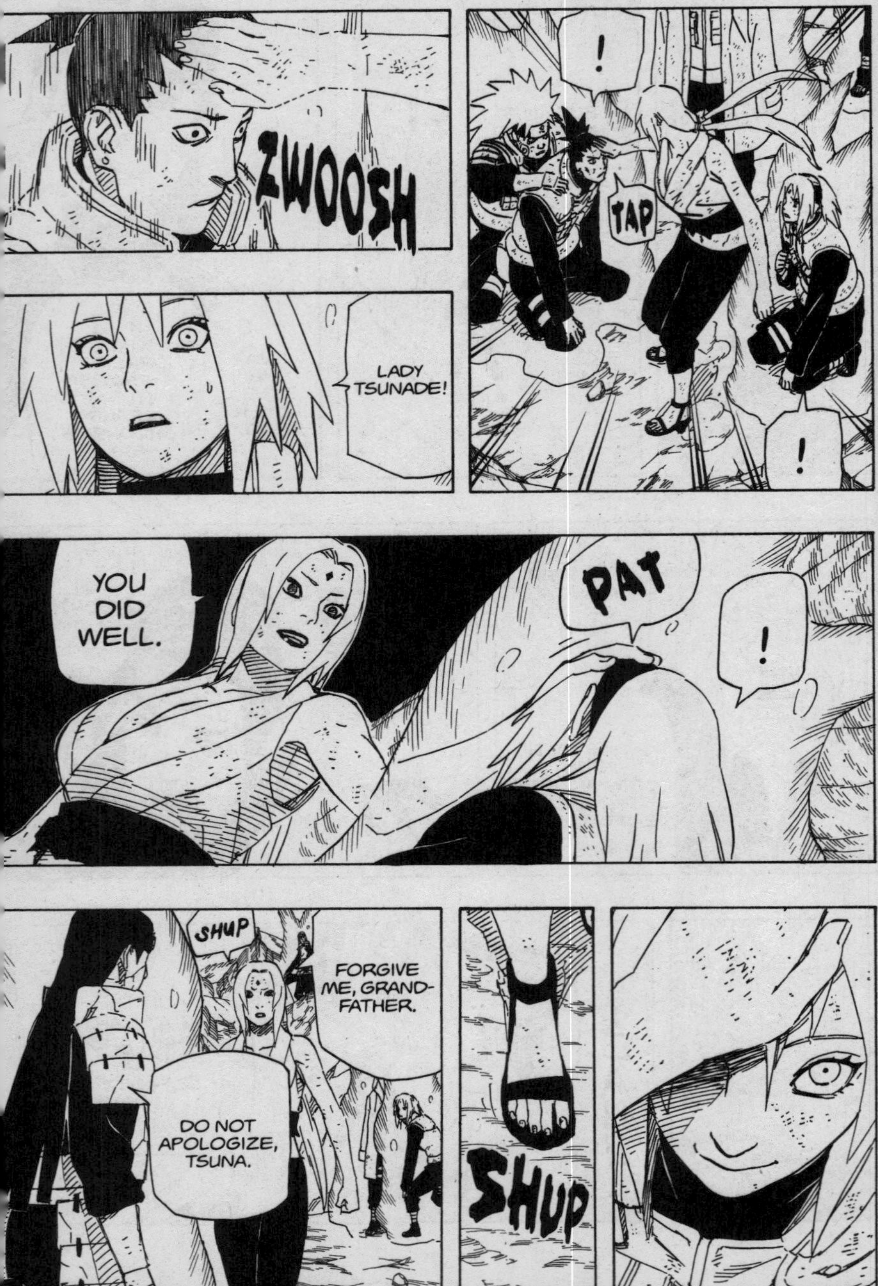

!
TAP
!
ZWOOSH
LADY TSUNADE!
!
PAT
YOU DID WELL.
SHUP
SHUP
FORGIVE ME, GRAND-FATHER.
DO NOT APOLOGIZE, TSUNA.

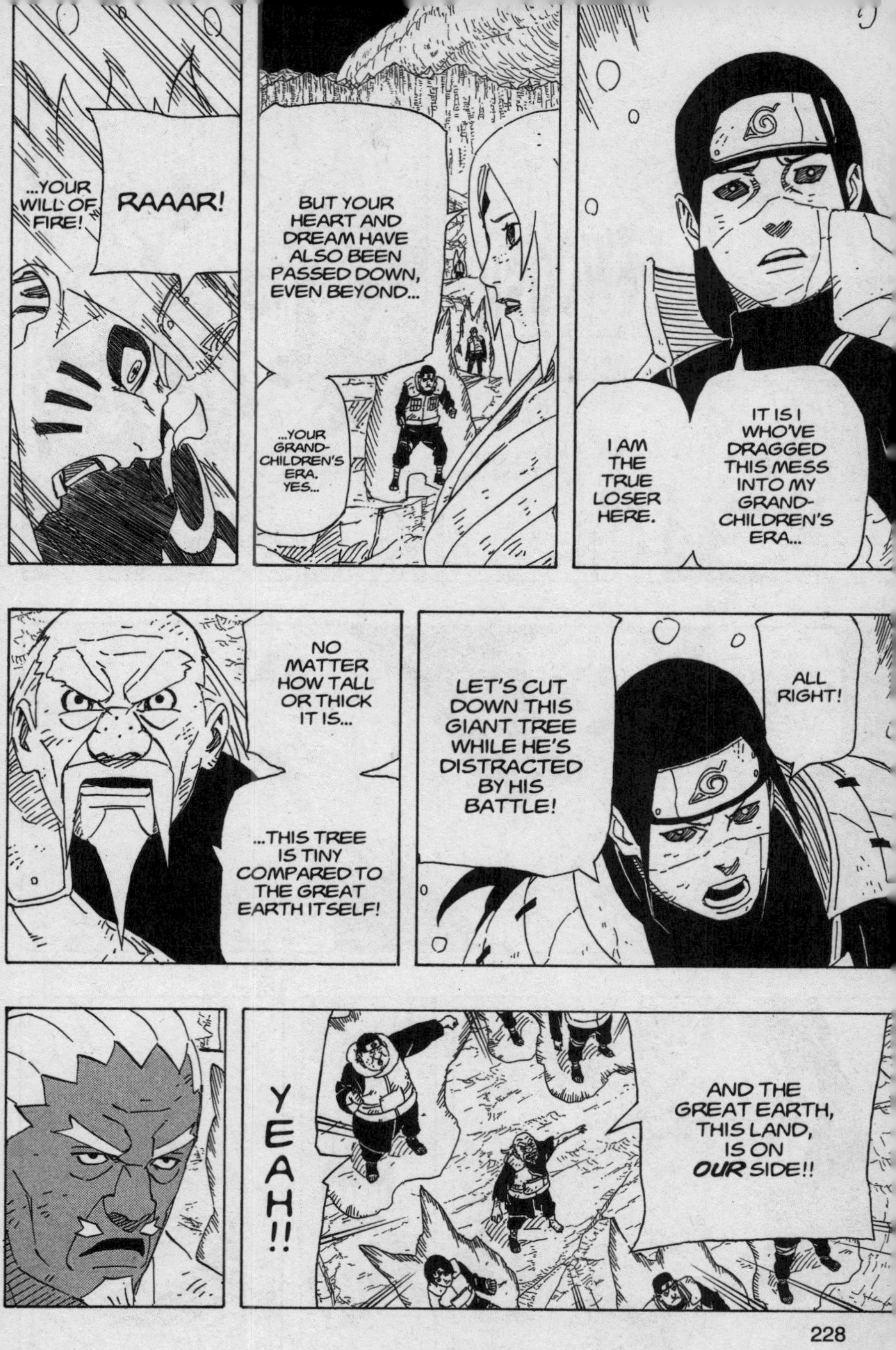
IT IS I WHO'VE DRAGGED THIS MESS INTO MY GRANDCHILDREN'S ERA...
I AM THE TRUE LOSER HERE.
BUT YOUR HEART AND DREAM HAVE ALSO BEEN PASSED DOWN, EVEN BEYOND...
...YOUR GRANDCHILDREN'S ERA. YES...
RAAAR!
...YOUR WILL OF FIRE!
ALL RIGHT!
LET'S CUT DOWN THIS GIANT TREE WHILE HE'S DISTRACTED BY HIS BATTLE!
NO MATTER HOW TALL OR THICK IT IS...
...THIS TREE IS TINY COMPARED TO THE GREAT EARTH ITSELF!
AND THE GREAT EARTH, THIS LAND, IS ON **OUR** SIDE!!
YEAH!!

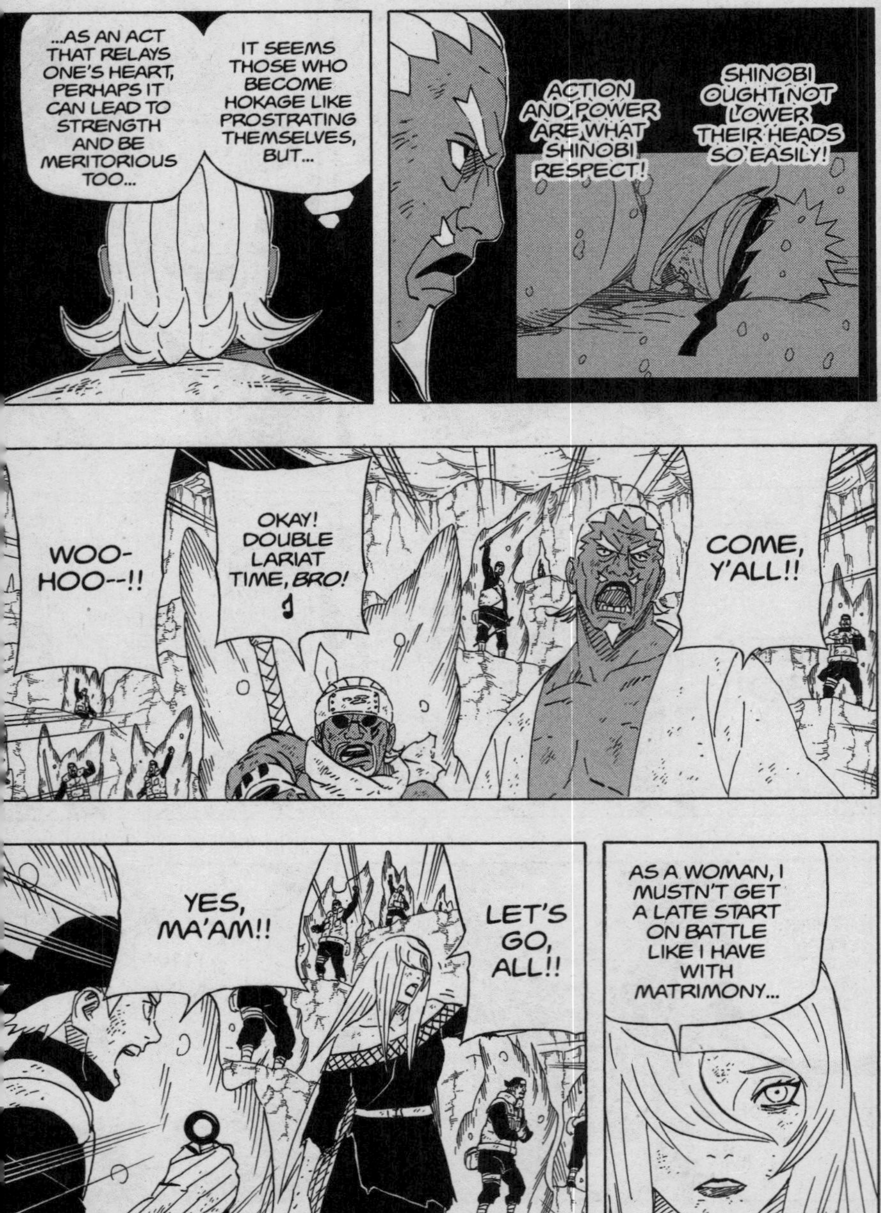
SHINOBI OUGHT NOT LOWER THEIR HEADS SO EASILY!
ACTION AND POWER ARE WHAT SHINOBI RESPECT!
IT SEEMS THOSE WHO BECOME HOKAGE LIKE PROSTRATING THEMSELVES, BUT...
...AS AN ACT THAT RELAYS ONE'S HEART, PERHAPS IT CAN LEAD TO STRENGTH AND BE MERITORIOUS TOO...
COME, Y'ALL!!
OKAY! DOUBLE LARIAT TIME, *BRO!* ♪
WOO-HOO--!!
AS A WOMAN, I MUSTN'T GET A LATE START ON BATTLE LIKE I HAVE WITH MATRIMONY...
LET'S GO, ALL!!
YES, MA'AM!!

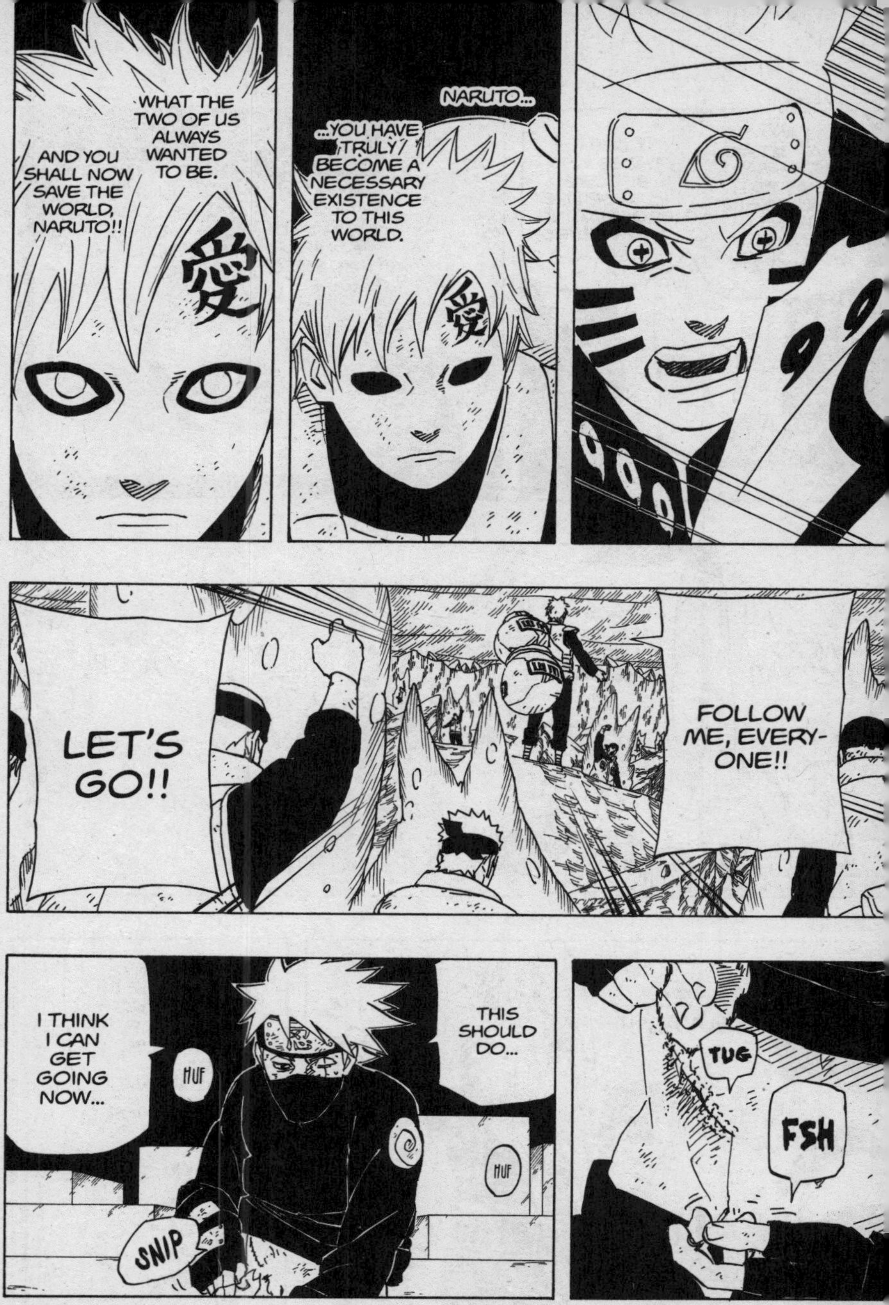
NARUTO...
...YOU HAVE TRULY BECOME A NECESSARY EXISTENCE TO THIS WORLD.
WHAT THE TWO OF US ALWAYS WANTED TO BE.
AND YOU SHALL NOW SAVE THE WORLD, NARUTO!!
FOLLOW ME, EVERY-ONE!!
LET'S GO!!
TUG
FSH
THIS SHOULD DO...
HUF
I THINK I CAN GET GOING NOW...
HUF
SNIP

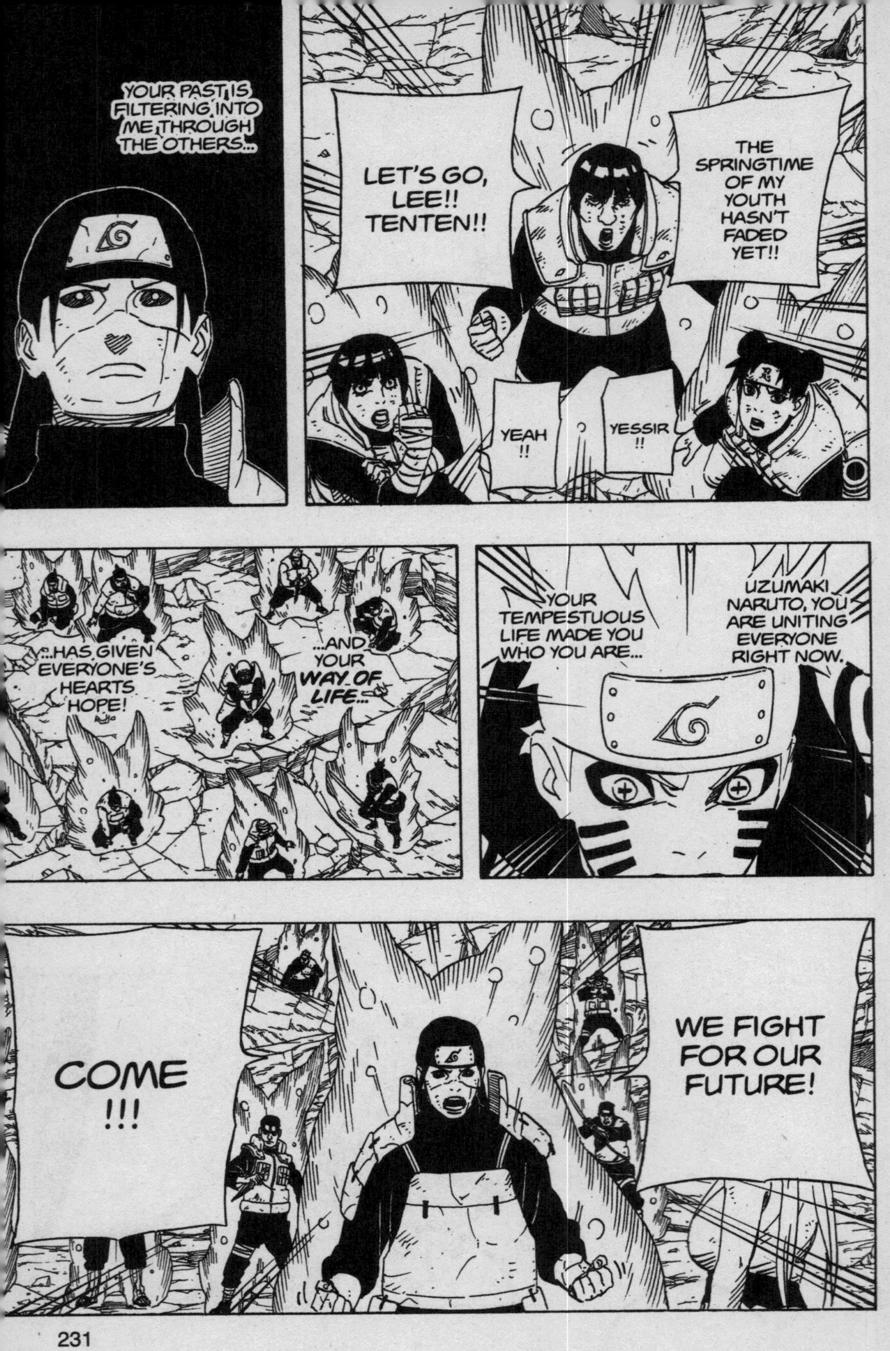
THE SPRINGTIME OF MY YOUTH HASN'T FADED YET!!
LET'S GO, LEE!! TENTEN!!
YESSIR!!
YEAH!!
YOUR PAST IS FILTERING INTO ME THROUGH THE OTHERS...
UZUMAKI NARUTO, YOU ARE UNITING EVERYONE RIGHT NOW.
YOUR TEMPESTUOUS LIFE MADE YOU WHO YOU ARE...
...AND YOUR WAY OF LIFE...
...HAS GIVEN EVERYONE'S HEARTS HOPE!
WE FIGHT FOR OUR FUTURE!
COME!!!

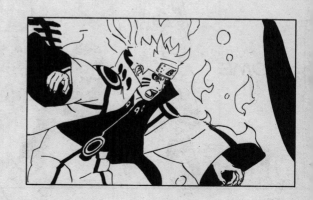

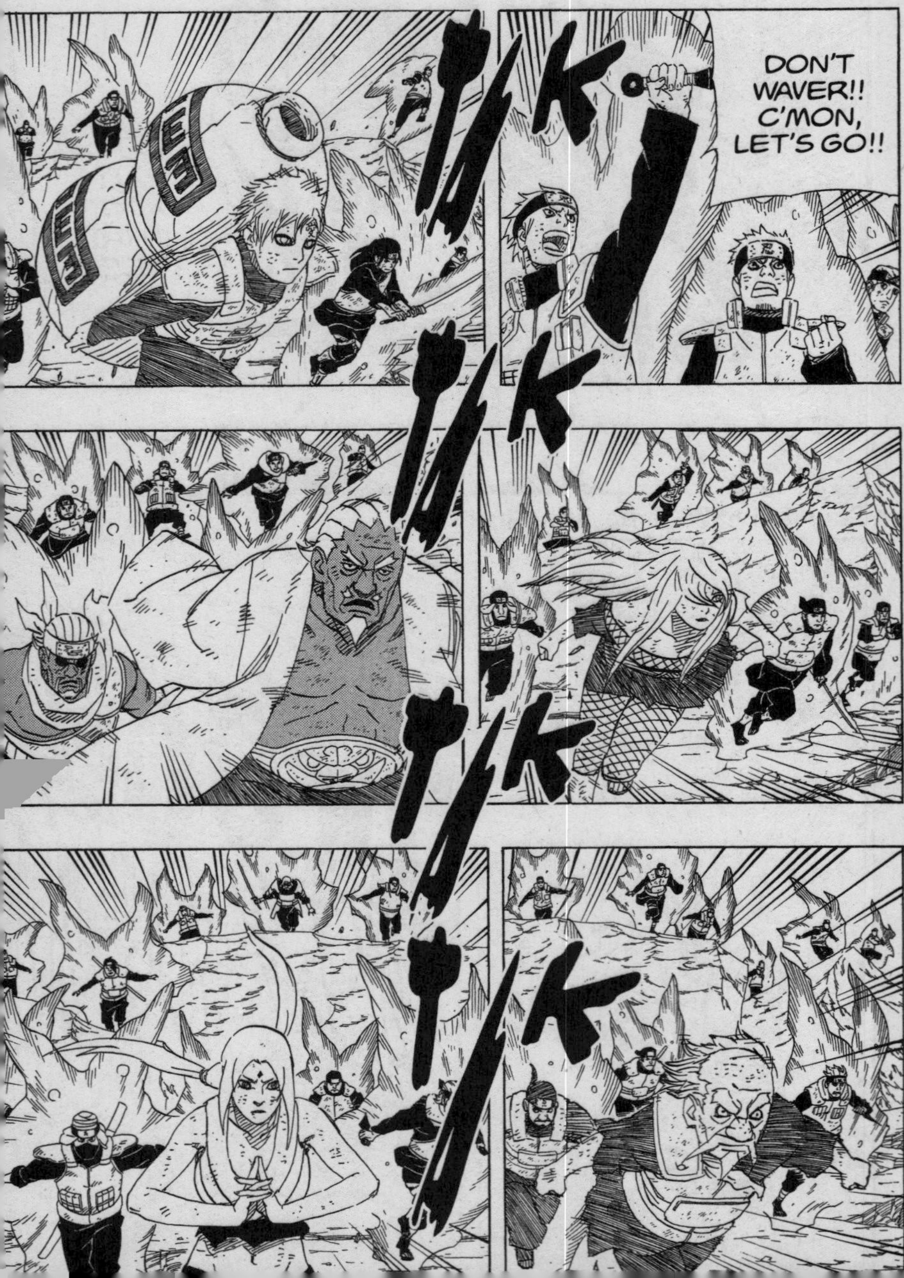
DON'T WAVER!! C'MON, LET'S GO!!

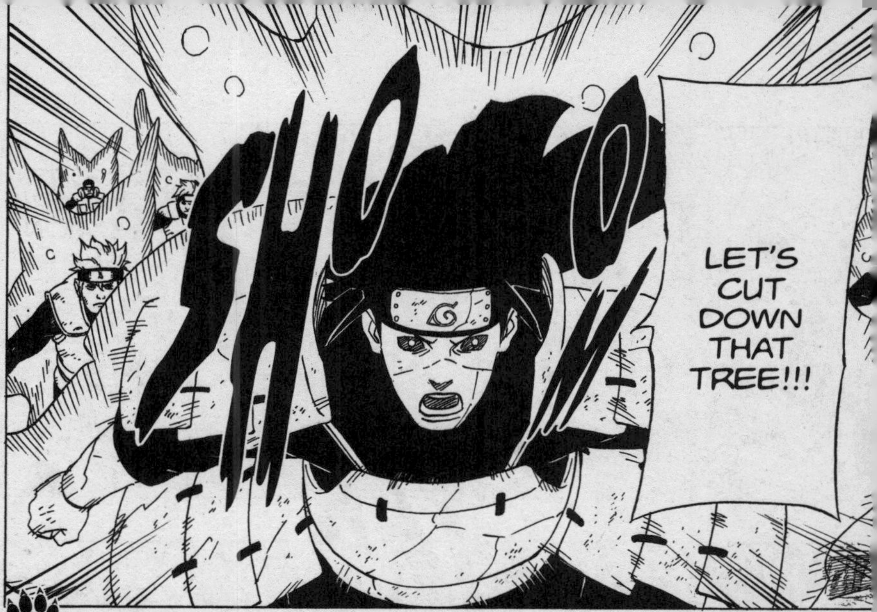
LET'S CUT DOWN THAT TREE!!!
SHOOM

Number650: Those Who Shall Sleep

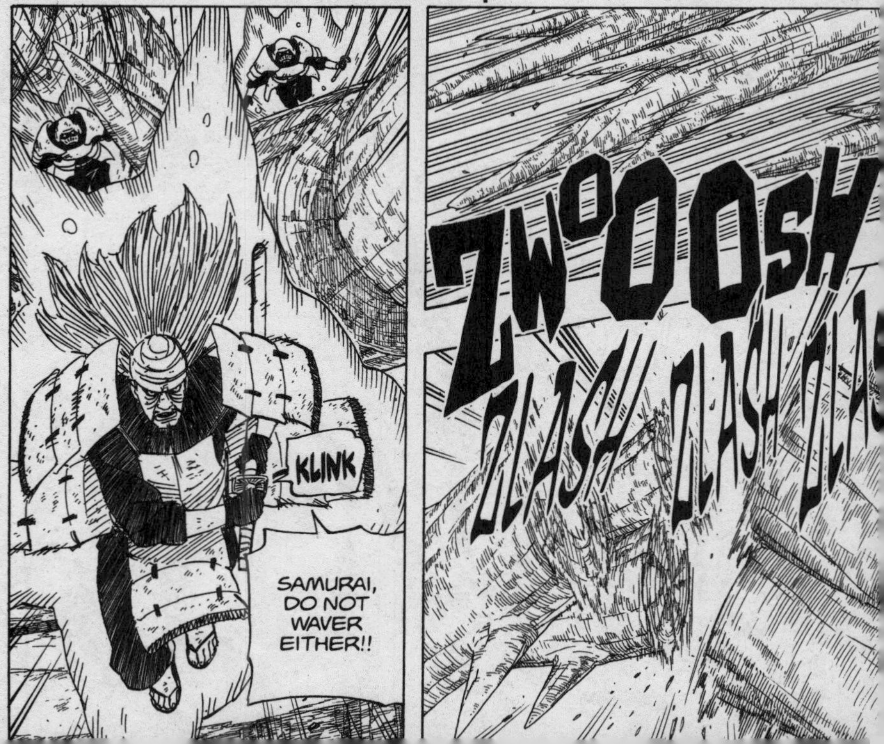
ZWOOOSH
ZLASH ZLASH ZLAS
KLINK
SAMURAI, DO NOT WAVER EITHER!!

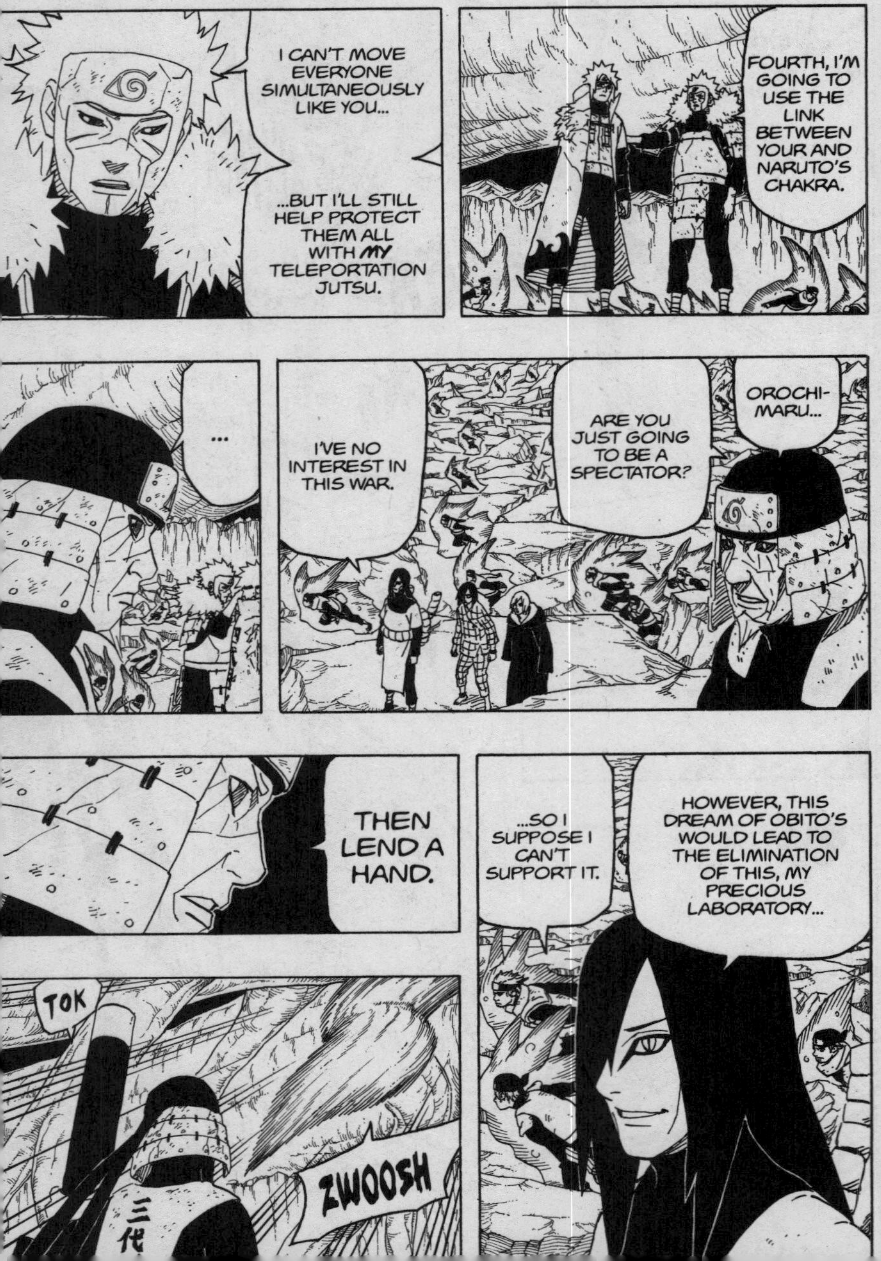
FOURTH, I'M GOING TO USE THE LINK BETWEEN YOUR AND NARUTO'S CHAKRA.
I CAN'T MOVE EVERYONE SIMULTANEOUSLY LIKE YOU...
...BUT I'LL STILL HELP PROTECT THEM ALL WITH *MY* TELEPORTATION JUTSU.
OROCHI-MARU...
ARE YOU JUST GOING TO BE A SPECTATOR?
I'VE NO INTEREST IN THIS WAR.
...
HOWEVER, THIS DREAM OF OBITO'S WOULD LEAD TO THE ELIMINATION OF THIS, MY PRECIOUS LABORATORY...
...SO I SUPPOSE I CAN'T SUPPORT IT.
THEN LEND A HAND.
TOK
三代
ZWOOSH

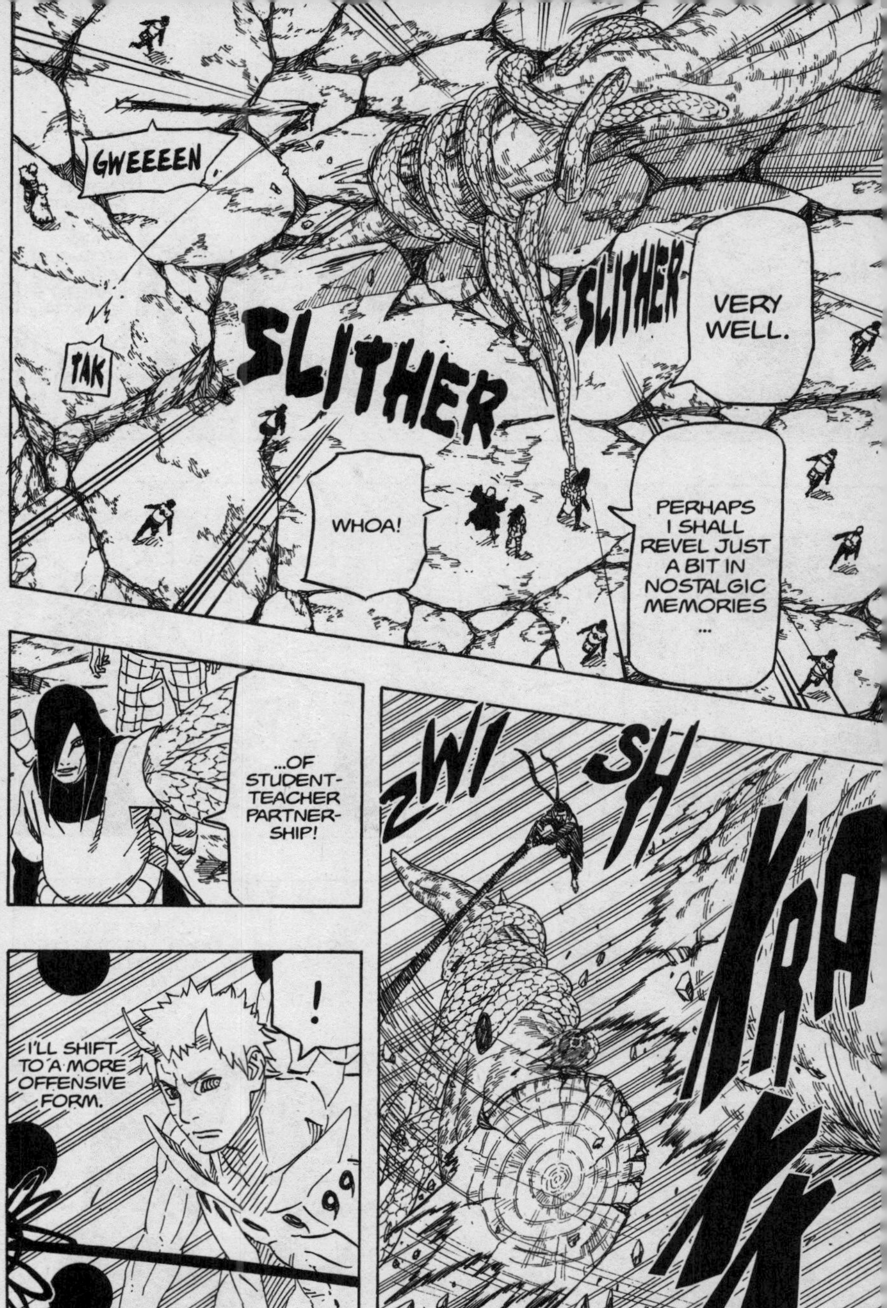
VERY WELL.
SLITHER
PERHAPS I SHALL REVEL JUST A BIT IN NOSTALGIC MEMORIES ...
GWEEEEN
SLITHER
WHOA!
TAK
ZWISH
KRAKK
...OF STUDENT-TEACHER PARTNERSHIP!
!
I'LL SHIFT TO A MORE OFFENSIVE FORM.

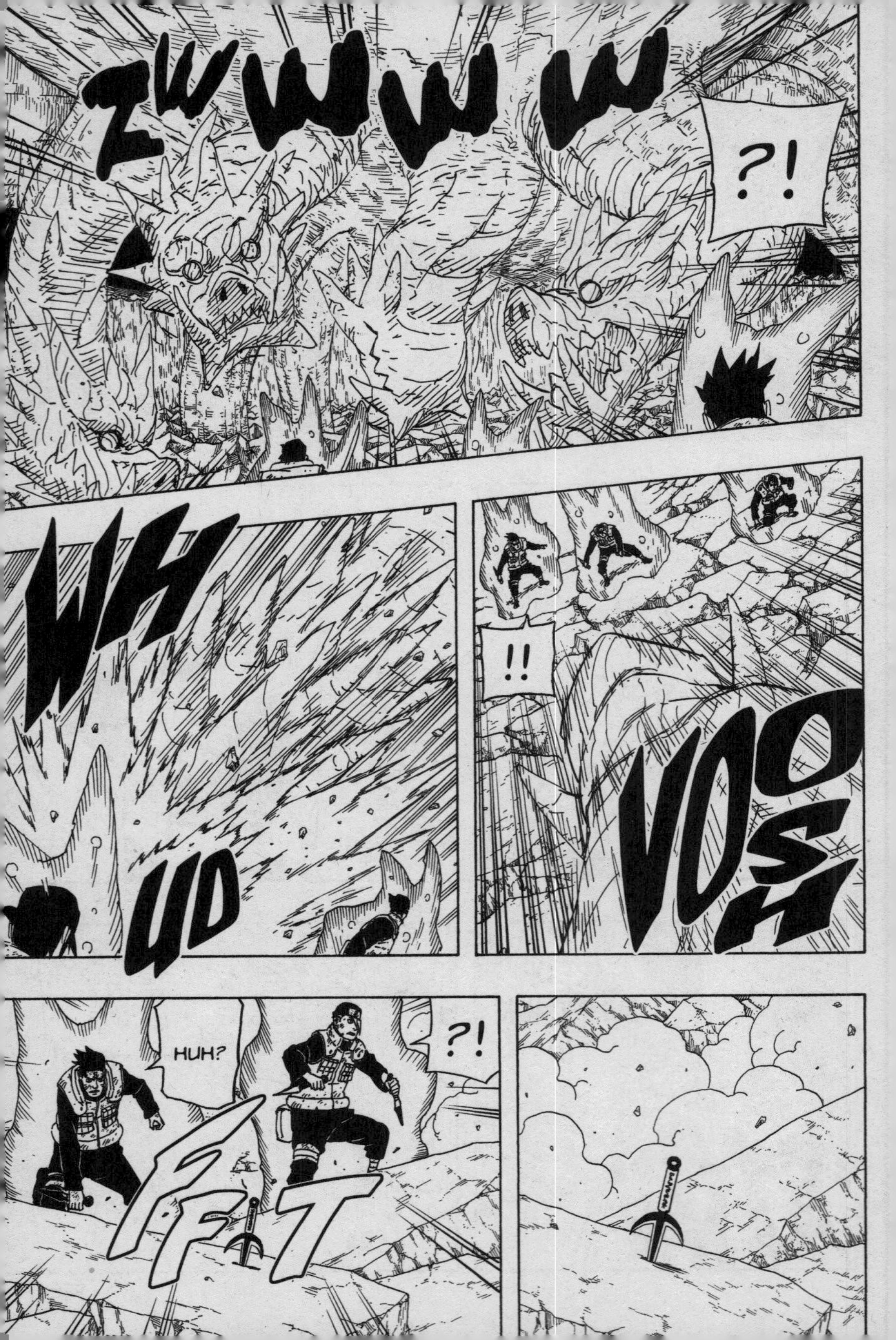
?!
ZWWWW
!!
VOOSH
WHUD
?!
HUH?
FFT

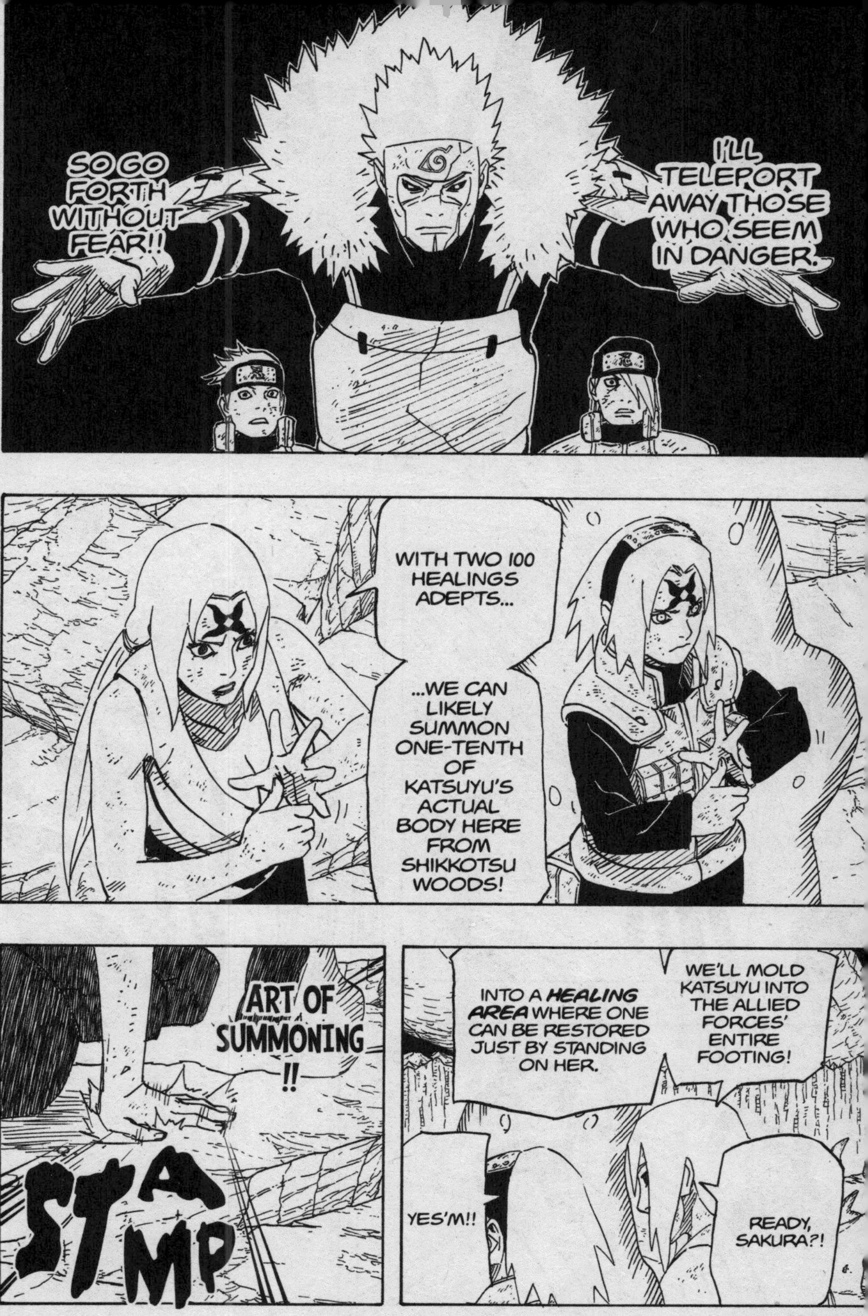
I'LL TELEPORT AWAY THOSE WHO SEEM IN DANGER.
SO GO FORTH WITHOUT FEAR!!
WITH TWO 100 HEALINGS ADEPTS...
...WE CAN LIKELY SUMMON ONE-TENTH OF KATSUYU'S ACTUAL BODY HERE FROM SHIKKOTSU WOODS!
WE'LL MOLD KATSUYU INTO THE ALLIED FORCES' ENTIRE FOOTING!
INTO A HEALING AREA WHERE ONE CAN BE RESTORED JUST BY STANDING ON HER.
READY, SAKURA?!
YES'M!!
ART OF SUMMONING!!
STAMP

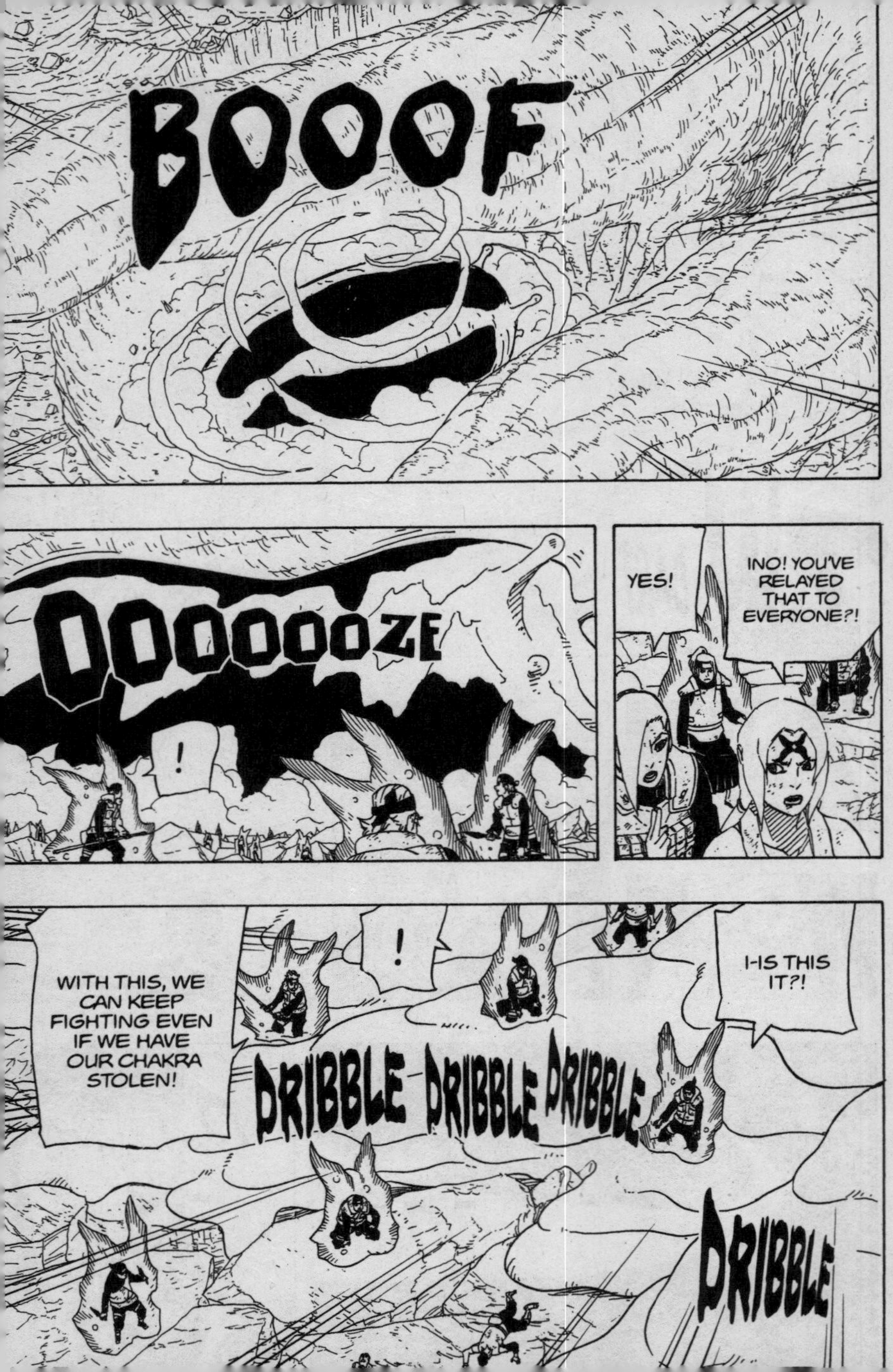
BOOOF
INO! YOU'VE RELAYED THAT TO EVERYONE?!
YES!
OOOOOOOZE
!
I-IS THIS IT?!
!
WITH THIS, WE CAN KEEP FIGHTING EVEN IF WE HAVE OUR CHAKRA STOLEN!
DRIBBLE DRIBBLE DRIBBLE
DRIBBLE

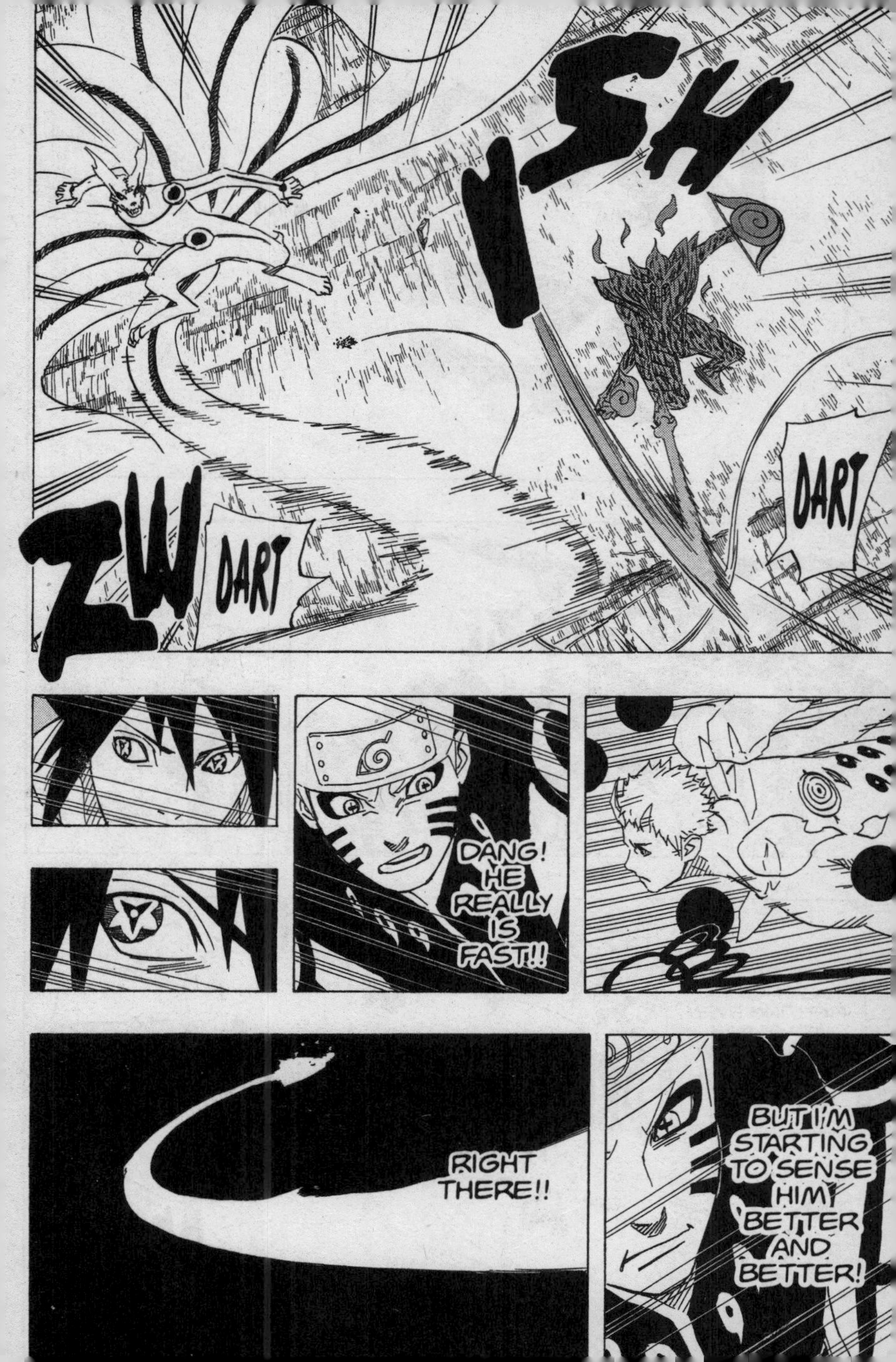
DART
ZWISH
DART
DANG! HE REALLY IS FAST!!
BUT I'M STARTING TO SENSE HIM BETTER AND BETTER!
RIGHT THERE!!

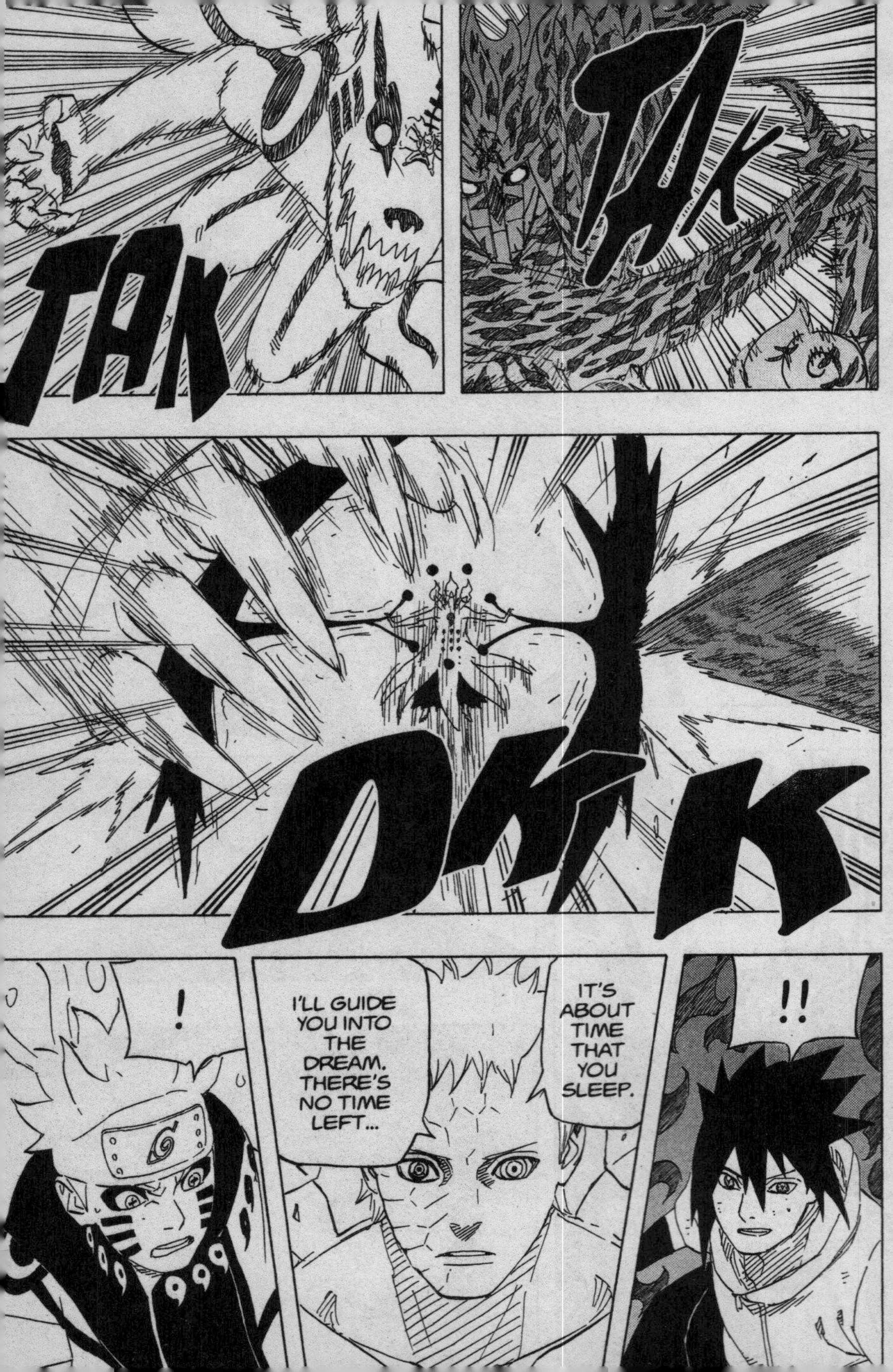
TAK
TAK
DAK
!!
IT'S ABOUT TIME THAT YOU SLEEP.
I'LL GUIDE YOU INTO THE DREAM. THERE'S NO TIME LEFT...
!

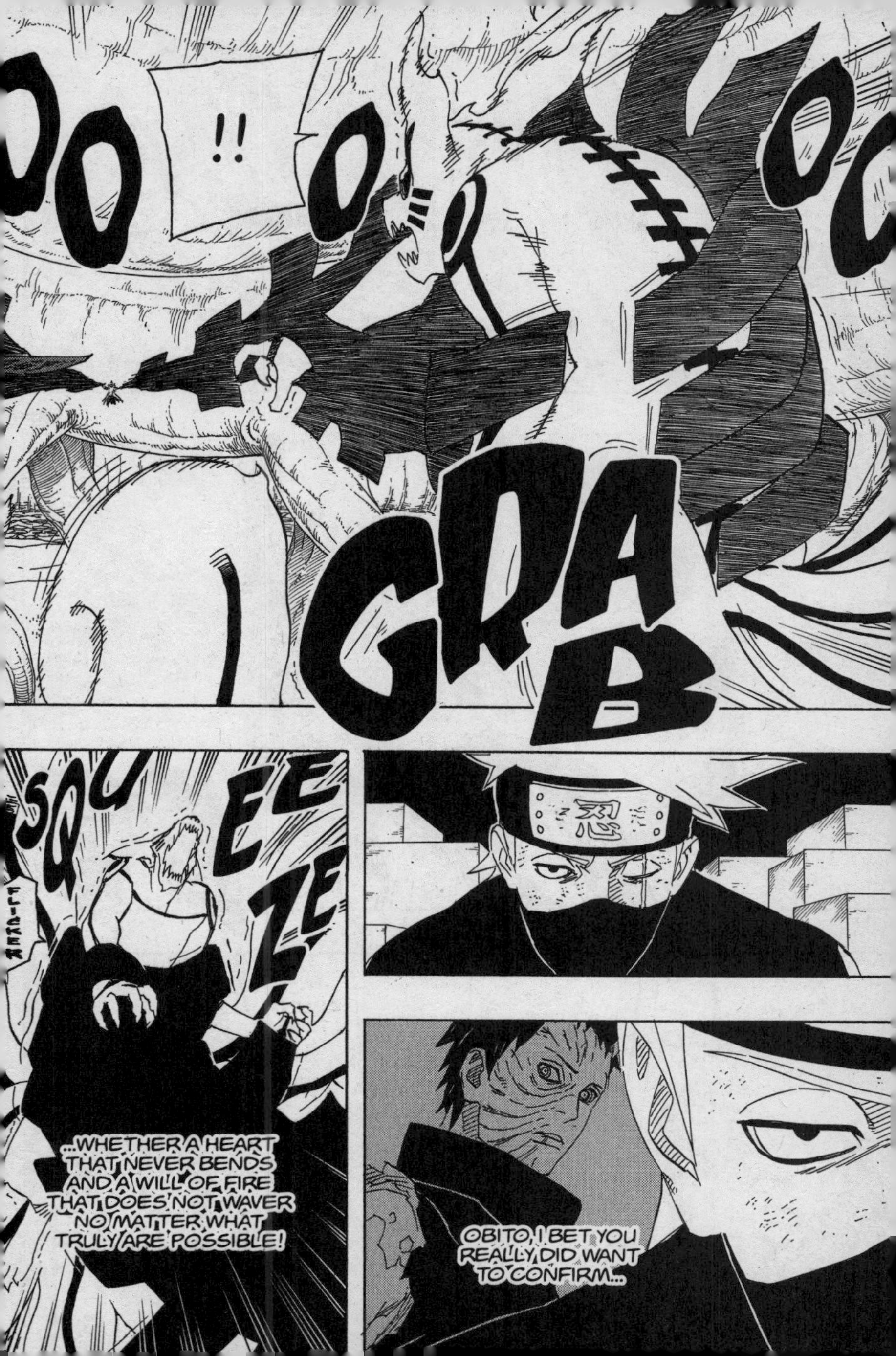
!!
GRAB
OBITO, I BET YOU REALLY DID WANT TO CONFIRM...
SQUEEZE
...WHETHER A HEART THAT NEVER BENDS AND A WILL OF FIRE THAT DOES NOT WAVER NO MATTER WHAT TRULY ARE POSSIBLE!

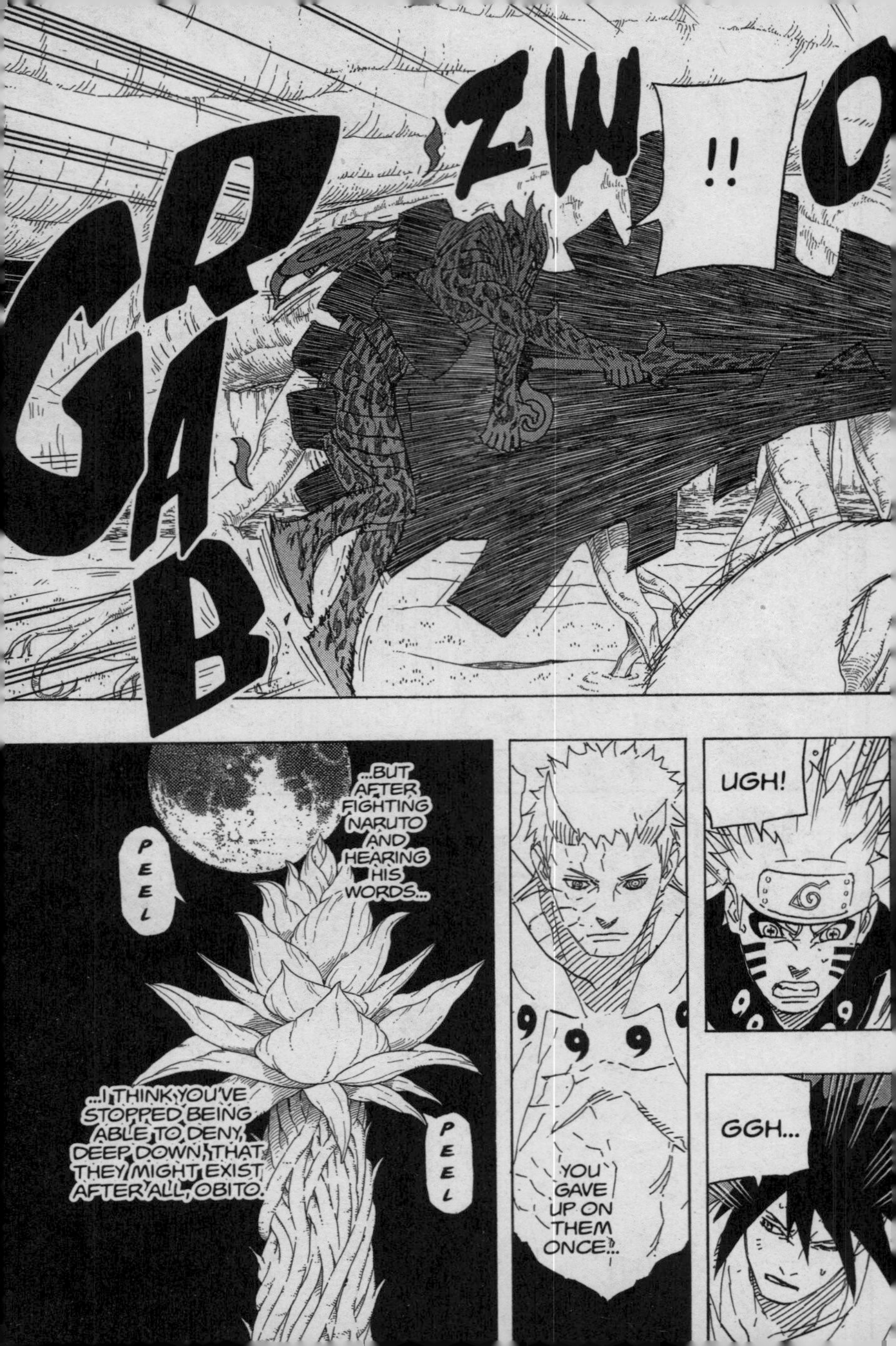

!!
ZWO
GRAB
UGH!
GGH...
YOU GAVE UP ON THEM ONCE...
...BUT AFTER FIGHTING NARUTO AND HEARING HIS WORDS...
PEEL
...I THINK YOU'VE STOPPED BEING ABLE TO DENY, DEEP DOWN, THAT THEY MIGHT EXIST AFTER ALL, OBITO.
PEEL

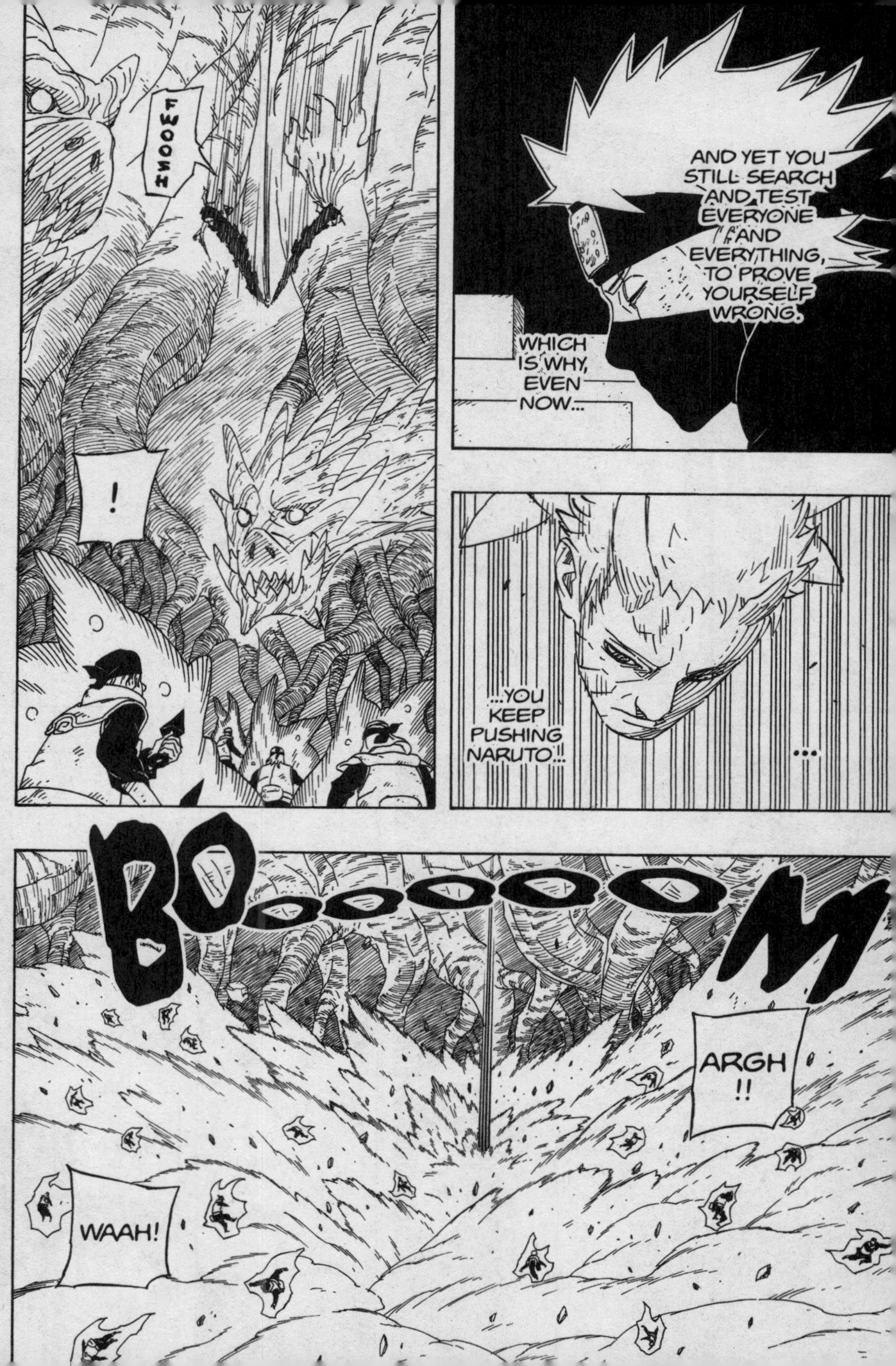
AND YET YOU STILL SEARCH AND TEST EVERYONE AND EVERYTHING, TO PROVE YOURSELF WRONG.
WHICH IS WHY, EVEN NOW...
...YOU KEEP PUSHING NARUTO!!
...
FWOOSH
!
BOOOOOM
ARGH!!
WAAH!

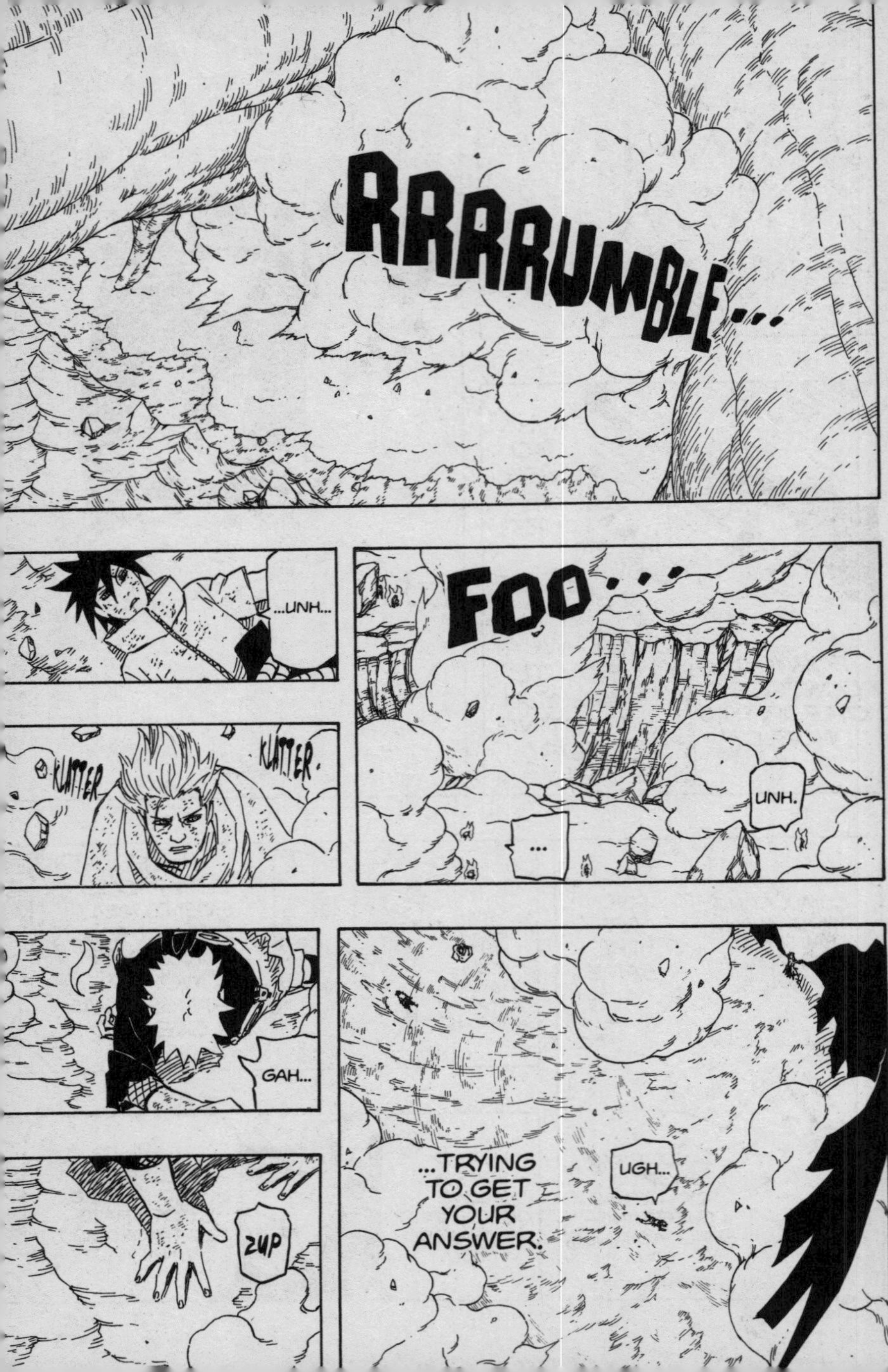
RRRRUMBLE...
FOO...
UNH.
...
...UNH...
KLATTER
KLATTER
UGH...
...TRYING TO GET YOUR ANSWER.
GAH...
ZUP

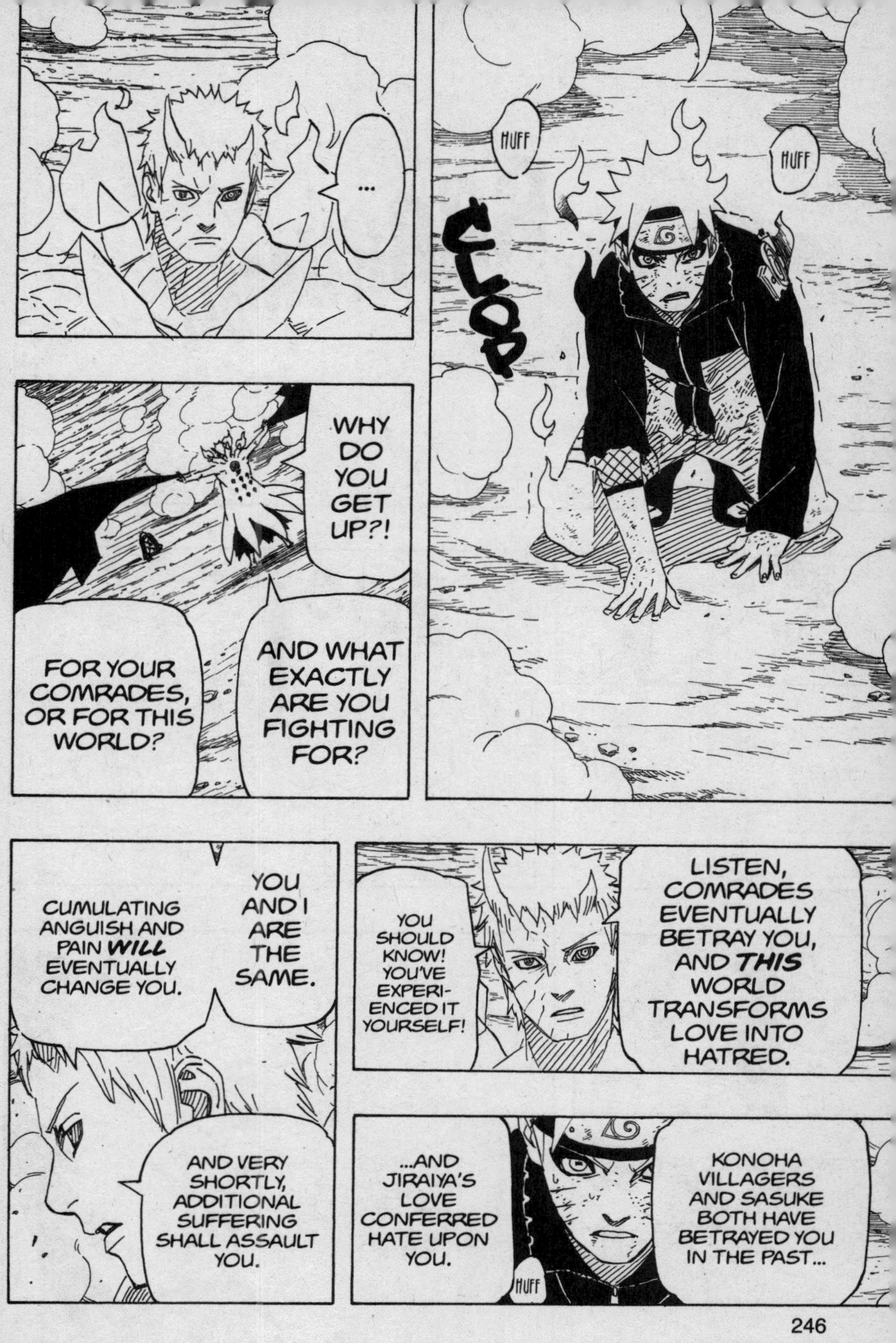
HUFF
HUFF
CLOP
...
WHY DO YOU GET UP?!
AND WHAT EXACTLY ARE YOU FIGHTING FOR?
FOR YOUR COMRADES, OR FOR THIS WORLD?
LISTEN, COMRADES EVENTUALLY BETRAY YOU, AND THIS WORLD TRANSFORMS LOVE INTO HATRED.
YOU SHOULD KNOW! YOU'VE EXPERI-ENCED IT YOURSELF!
KONOHA VILLAGERS AND SASUKE BOTH HAVE BETRAYED YOU IN THE PAST...
...AND JIRAIYA'S LOVE CONFERRED HATE UPON YOU.
HUFF
YOU AND I ARE THE SAME.
CUMULATING ANGUISH AND PAIN WILL EVENTUALLY CHANGE YOU.
AND VERY SHORTLY, ADDITIONAL SUFFERING SHALL ASSAULT YOU.

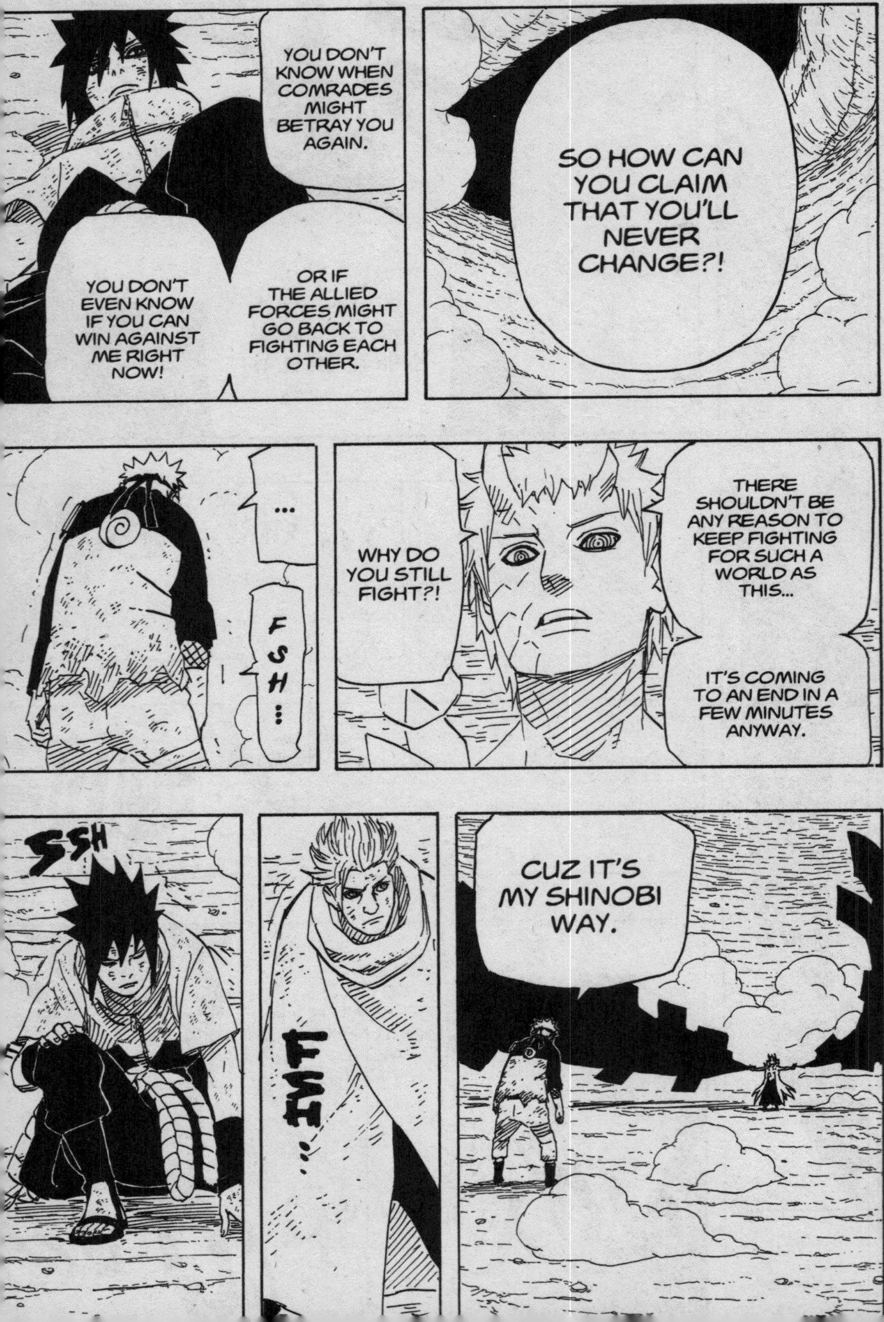
SO HOW CAN YOU CLAIM THAT YOU'LL NEVER CHANGE?!
YOU DON'T KNOW WHEN COMRADES MIGHT BETRAY YOU AGAIN.
OR IF THE ALLIED FORCES MIGHT GO BACK TO FIGHTING EACH OTHER.
YOU DON'T EVEN KNOW IF YOU CAN WIN AGAINST ME RIGHT NOW!
THERE SHOULDN'T BE ANY REASON TO KEEP FIGHTING FOR SUCH A WORLD AS THIS...
IT'S COMING TO AN END IN A FEW MINUTES ANYWAY.
WHY DO YOU STILL FIGHT?!
...
FSH...
CUZ IT'S MY SHINOBI WAY.
FSH..
SSH

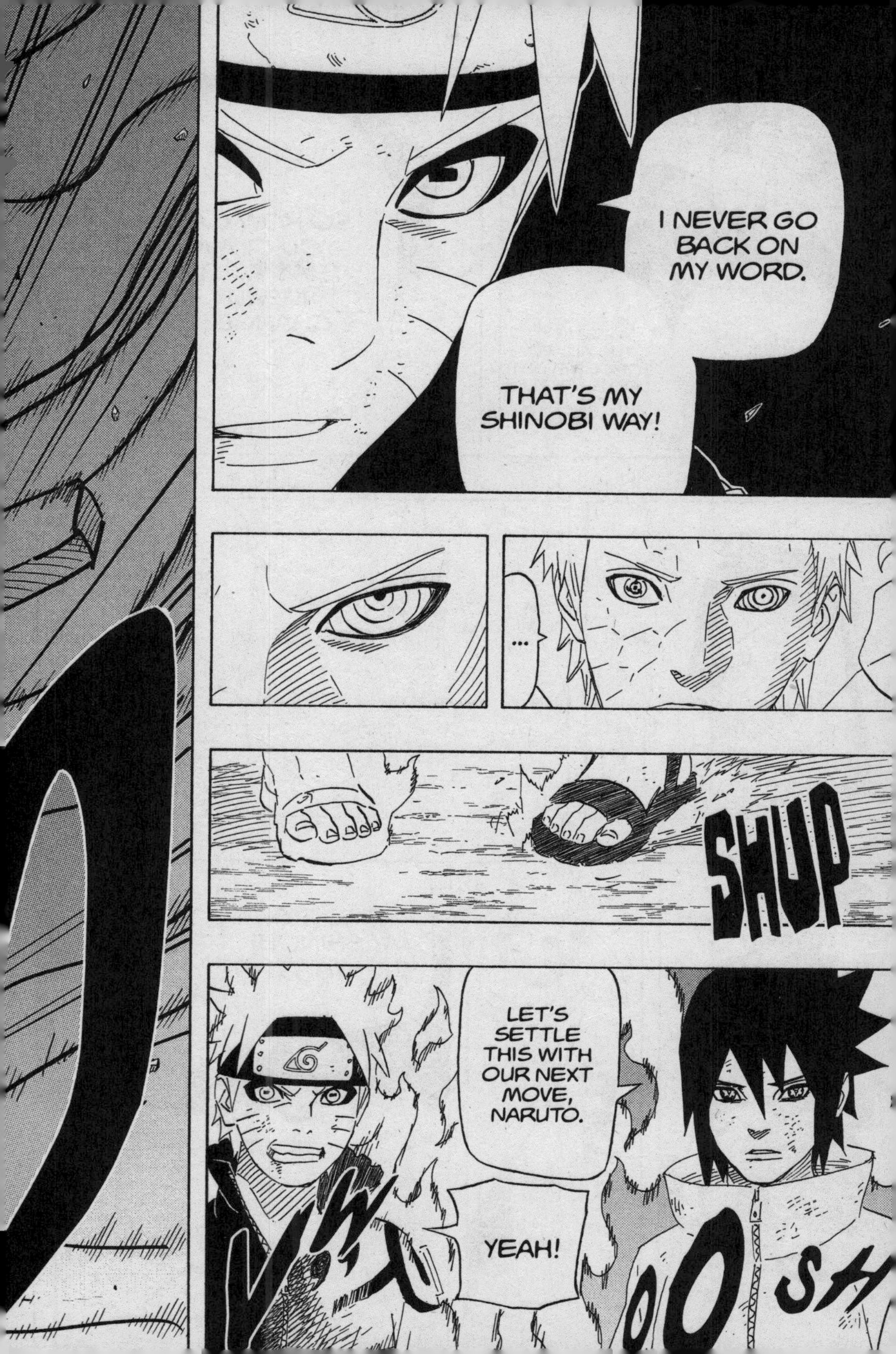

I NEVER GO BACK ON MY WORD.
THAT'S MY SHINOBI WAY!
...
SHUP
LET'S SETTLE THIS WITH OUR NEXT MOVE, NARUTO.
YEAH!

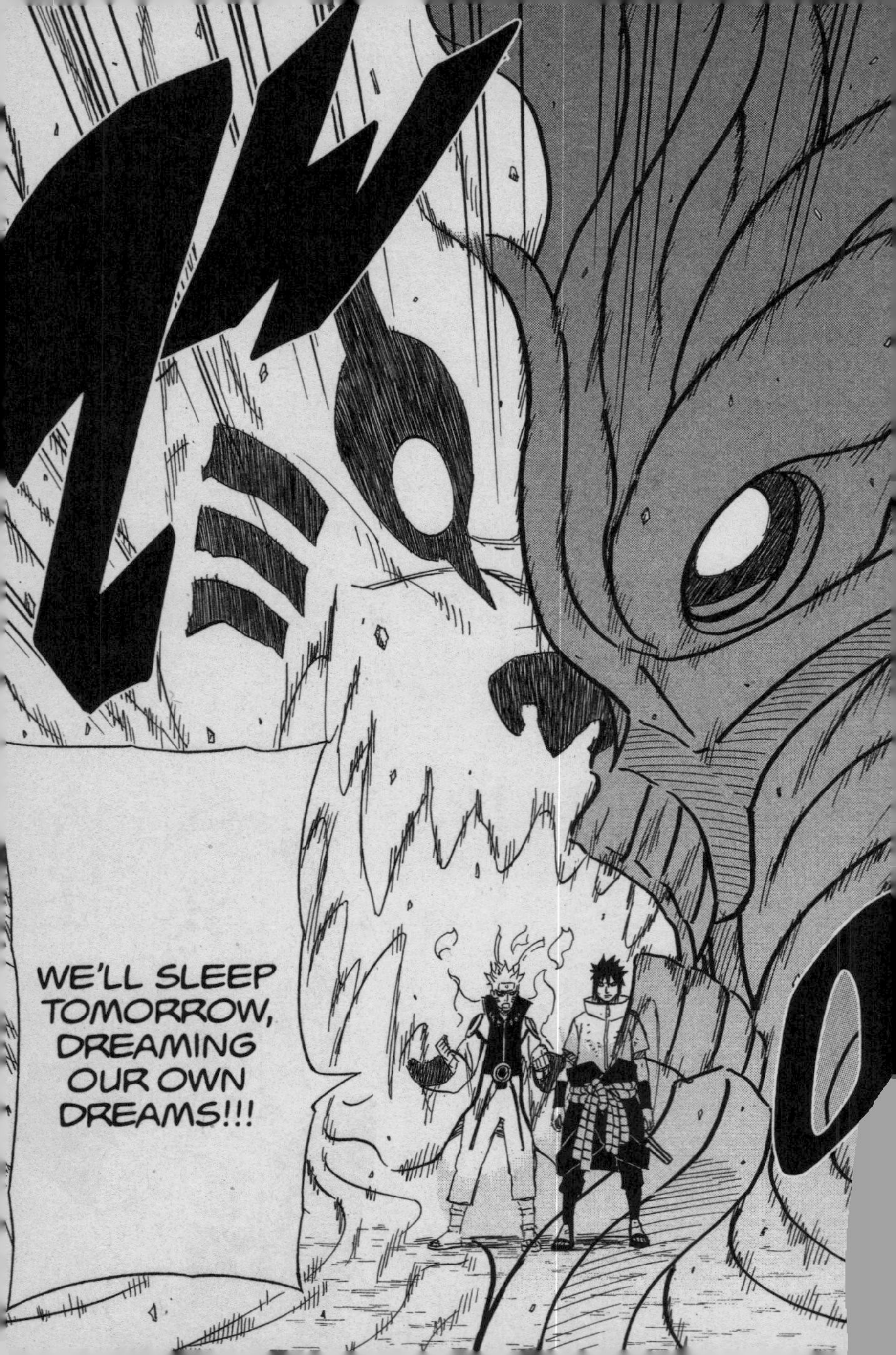
WE'LL SLEEP TOMORROW, DREAMING OUR OWN DREAMS!!!

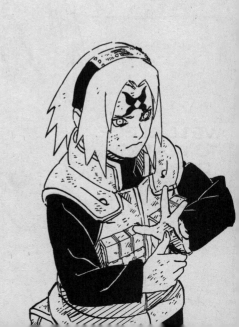

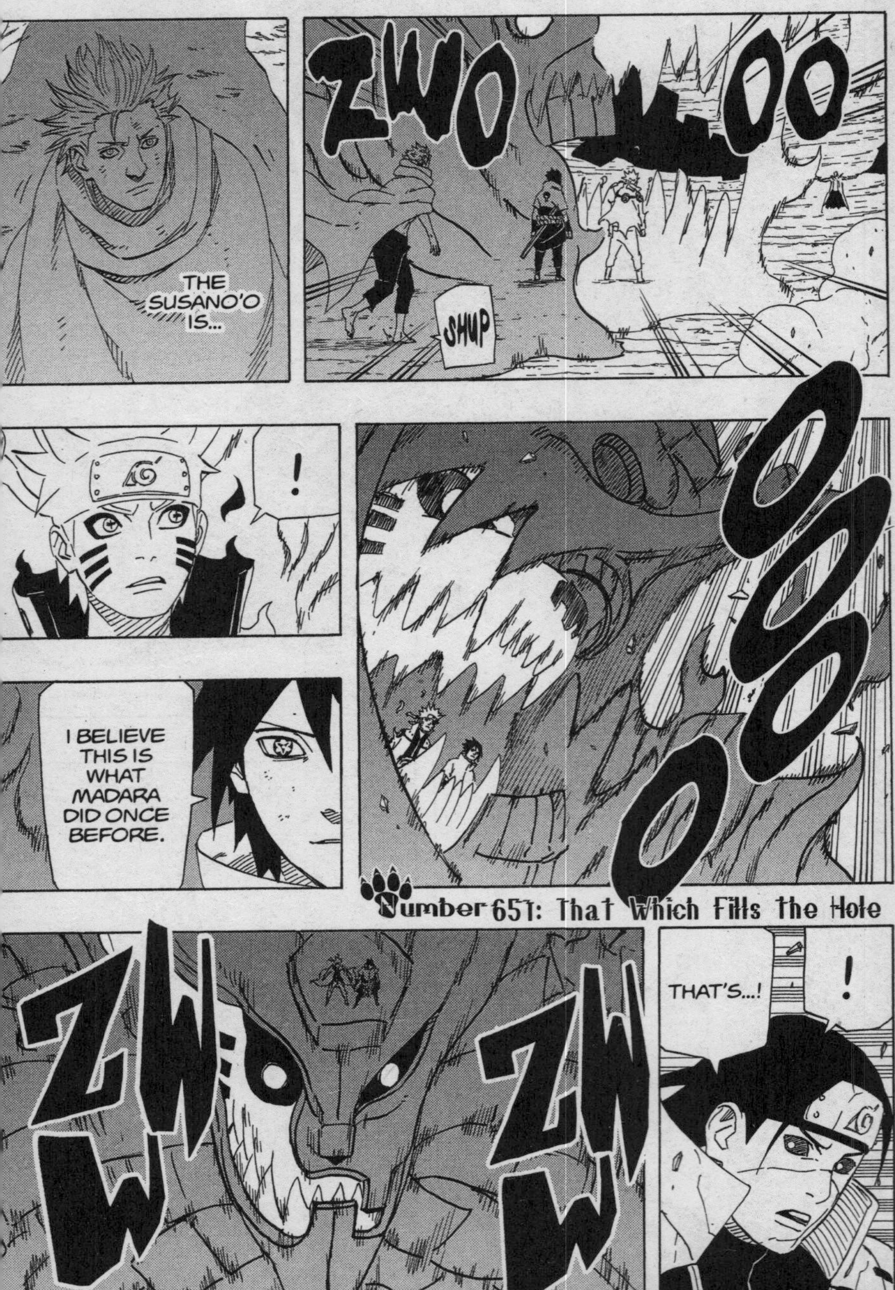
ZWOOO
SHUP
THE SUSANO'O IS...
OOOOOO
!
I BELIEVE THIS IS WHAT MADARA DID ONCE BEFORE.
Number 651: That Which Fills the Hole
!
THAT'S...!
ZWW
ZWW

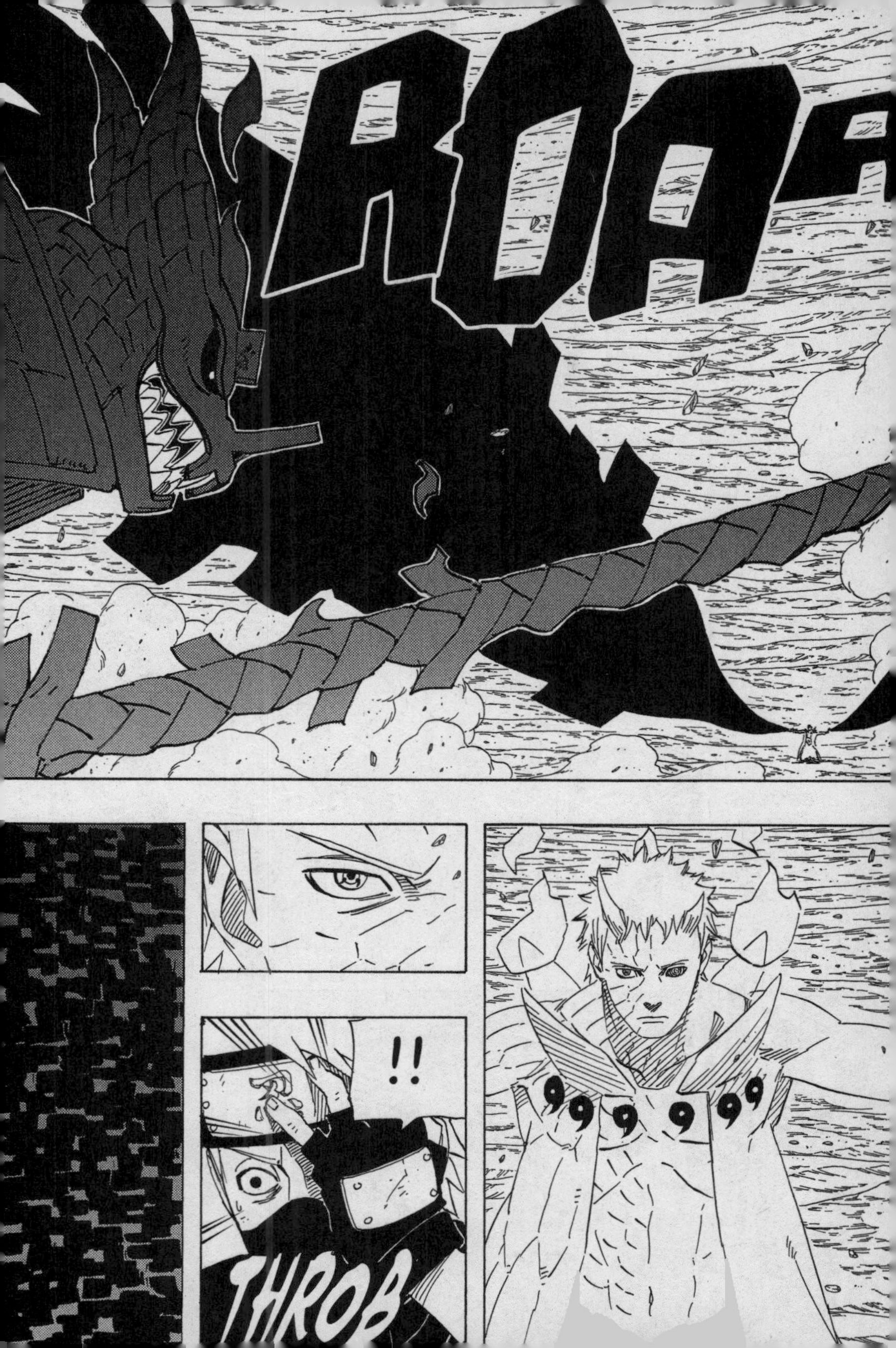
ROA
!!
THROB

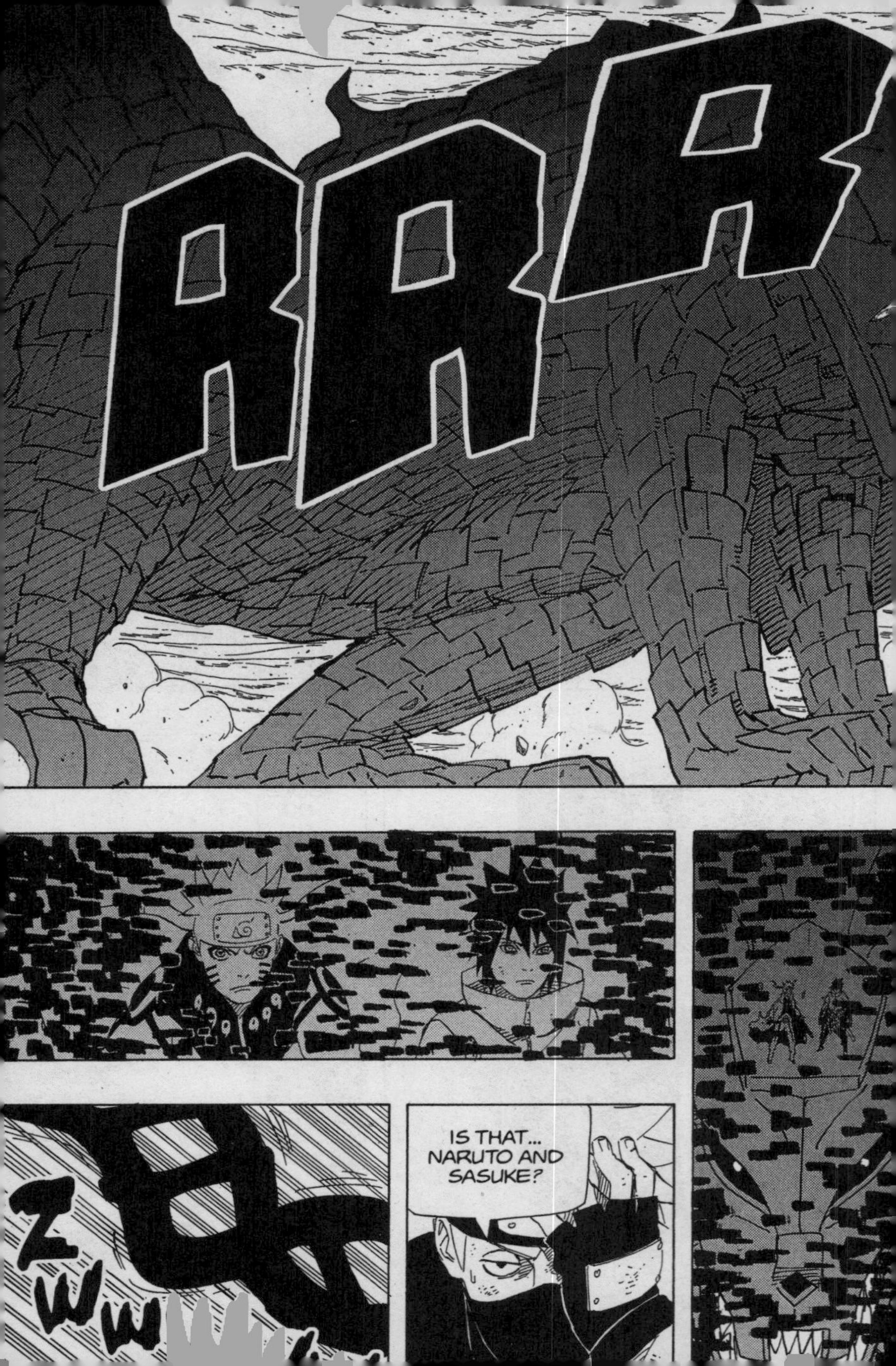
RRR
IS THAT... NARUTO AND SASUKE?
ZWWWB

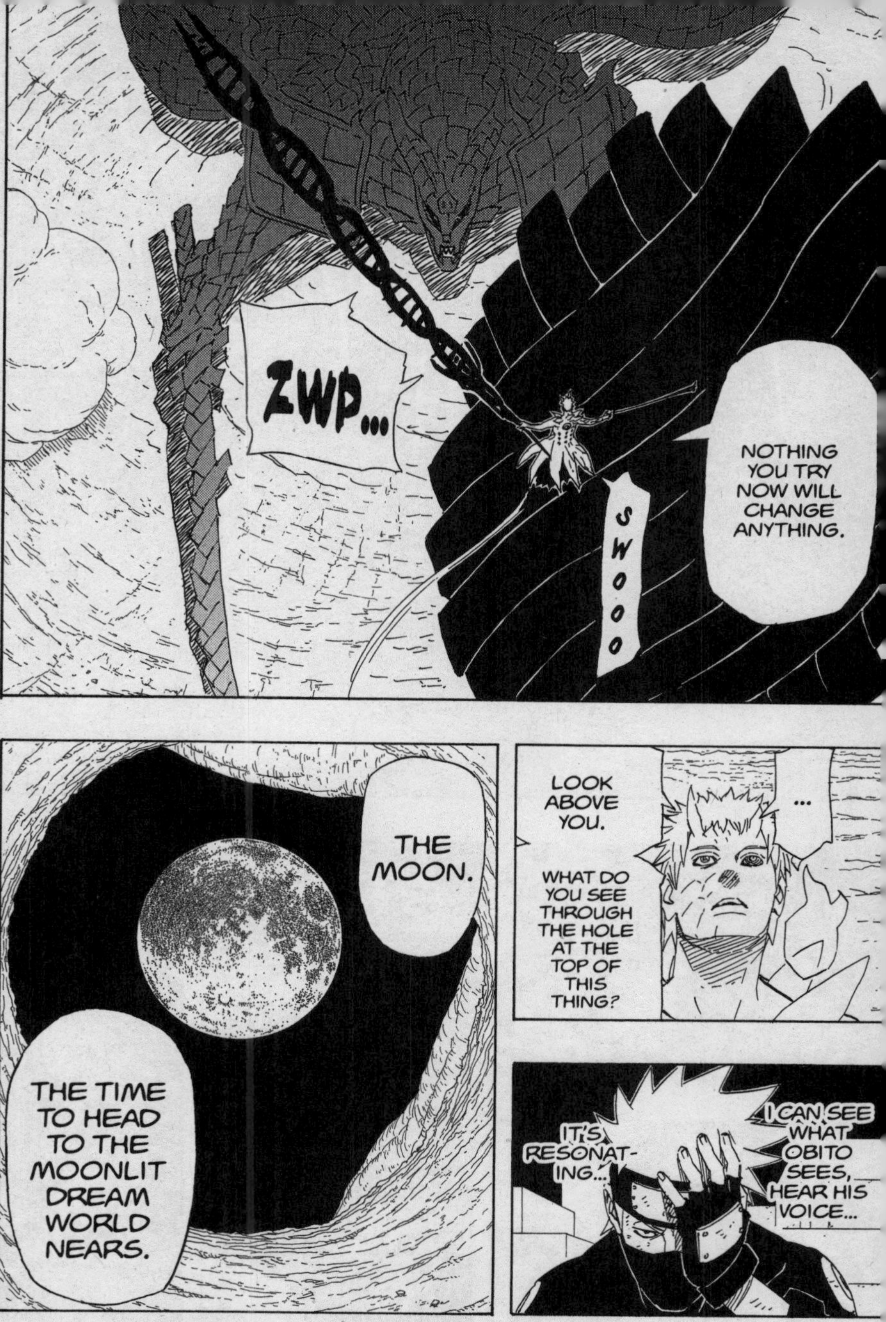
ZWP...
NOTHING YOU TRY NOW WILL CHANGE ANYTHING.
SWOOO
...
LOOK ABOVE YOU.
WHAT DO YOU SEE THROUGH THE HOLE AT THE TOP OF THIS THING?
I CAN SEE WHAT OBITO SEES, HEAR HIS VOICE...
IT'S RESONATING...
THE MOON.
THE TIME TO HEAD TO THE MOONLIT DREAM WORLD NEARS.

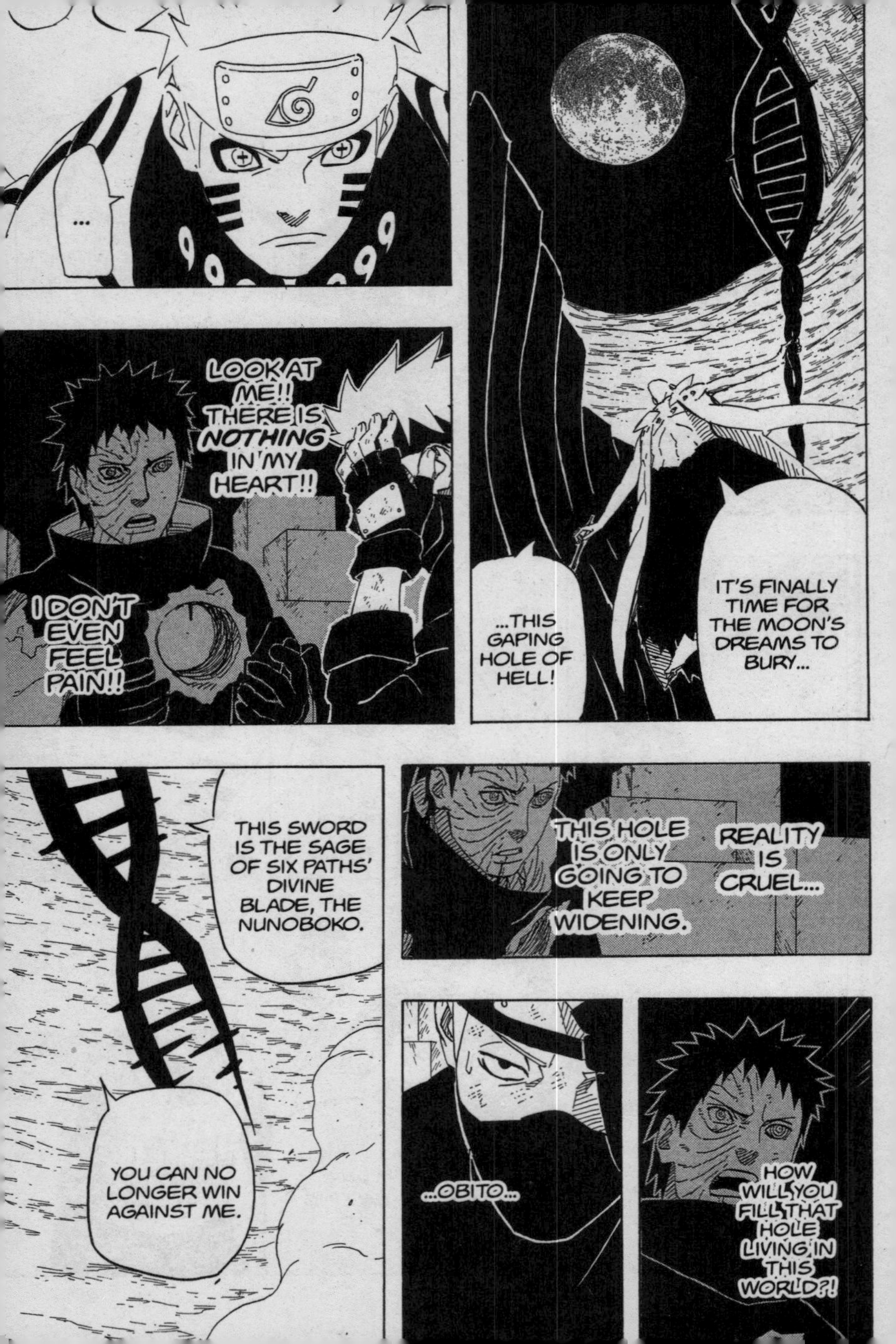
IT'S FINALLY TIME FOR THE MOON'S DREAMS TO BURY...
...THIS GAPING HOLE OF HELL!
...
LOOK AT ME!! THERE IS NOTHING IN MY HEART!!
I DON'T EVEN FEEL PAIN!!
REALITY IS CRUEL...
THIS HOLE IS ONLY GOING TO KEEP WIDENING.
HOW WILL YOU FILL THAT HOLE LIVING IN THIS WORLD?!
...OBITO...
THIS SWORD IS THE SAGE OF SIX PATHS' DIVINE BLADE, THE NUNOBOKO.
YOU CAN NO LONGER WIN AGAINST ME.

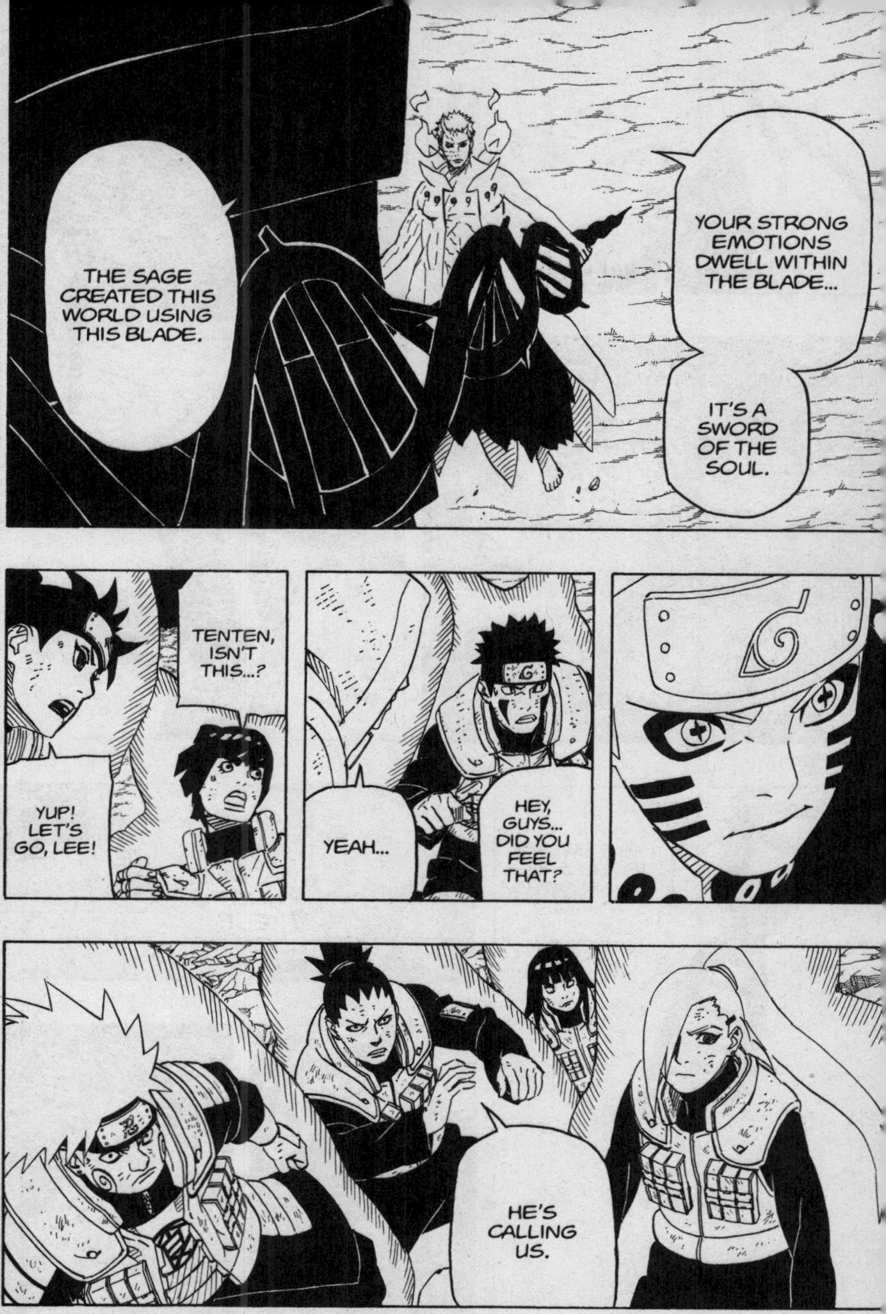
YOUR STRONG EMOTIONS DWELL WITHIN THE BLADE...
IT'S A SWORD OF THE SOUL.
THE SAGE CREATED THIS WORLD USING THIS BLADE.
HEY, GUYS... DID YOU FEEL THAT?
YEAH...
TENTEN, ISN'T THIS...?
YUP! LET'S GO, LEE!
HE'S CALLING US.

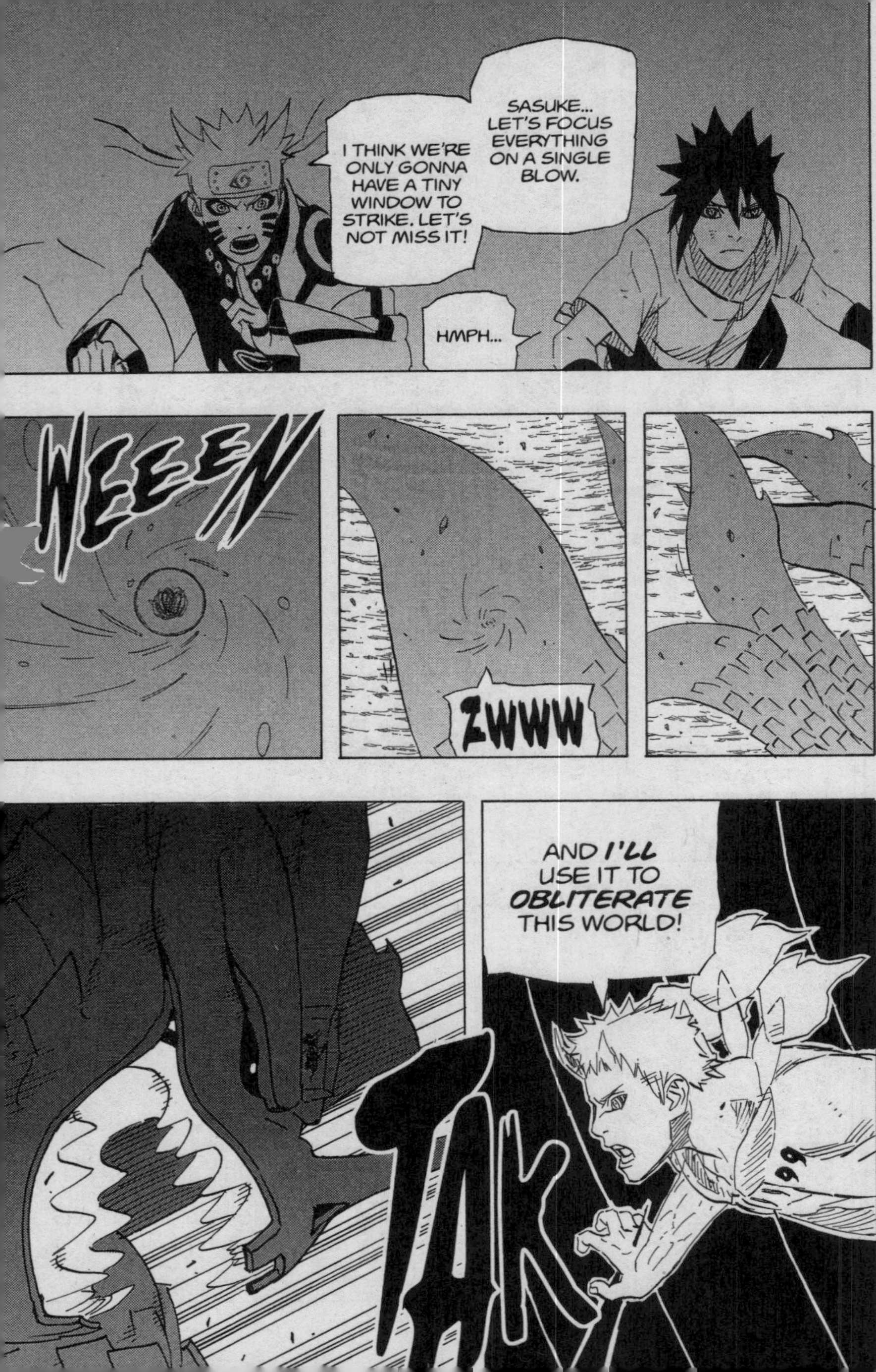
SASUKE... LET'S FOCUS EVERYTHING ON A SINGLE BLOW.
I THINK WE'RE ONLY GONNA HAVE A TINY WINDOW TO STRIKE. LET'S NOT MISS IT!
HMPH...
ZWWW
WEEEN
AND *I'LL* USE IT TO *OBLITERATE* THIS WORLD!
TAK

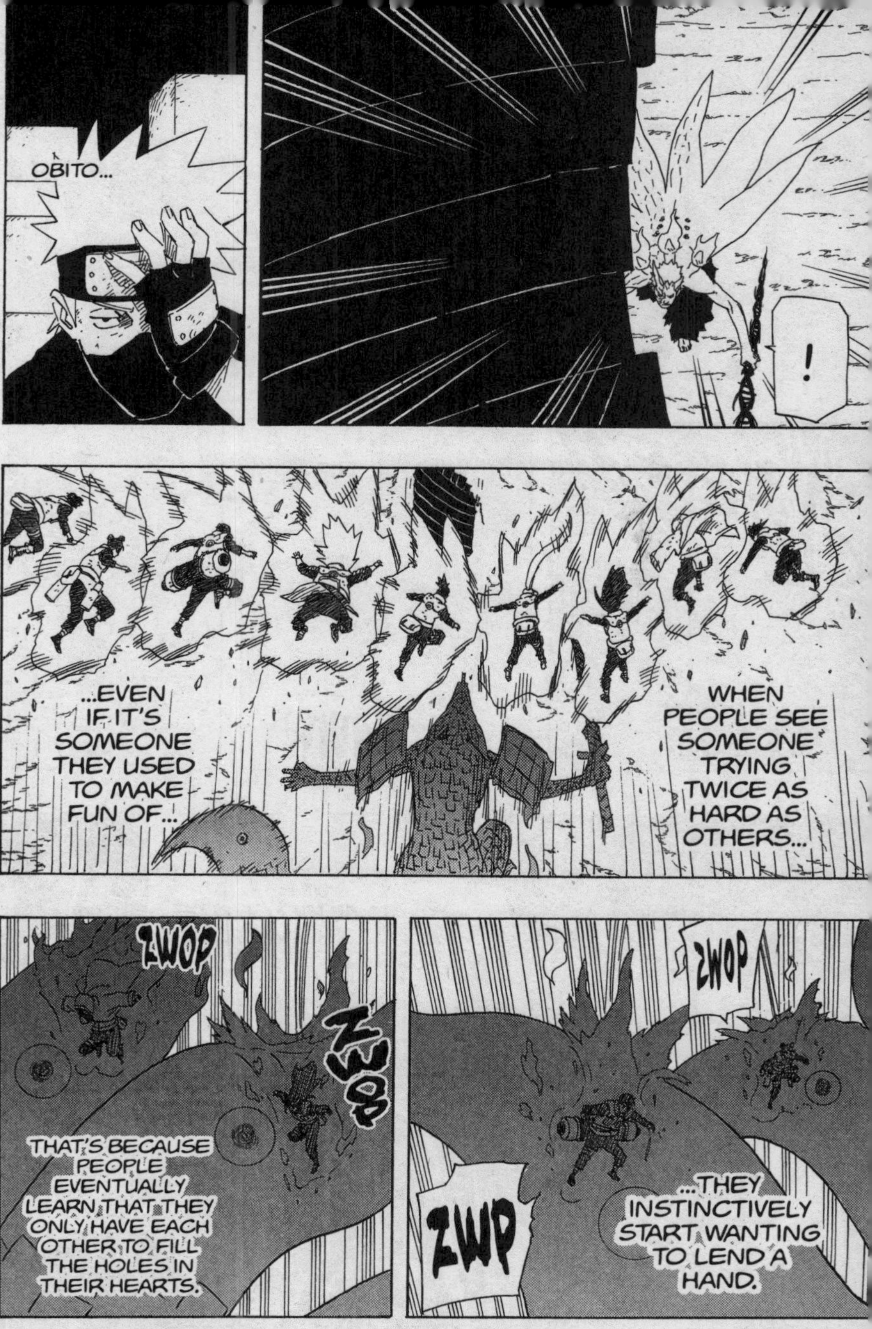
!
OBITO...
WHEN PEOPLE SEE SOMEONE TRYING TWICE AS HARD AS OTHERS...
...EVEN IF IT'S SOMEONE THEY USED TO MAKE FUN OF...
ZWOP
...THEY INSTINCTIVELY START WANTING TO LEND A HAND.
ZWP
ZWOP
ZWOP
THAT'S BECAUSE PEOPLE EVENTUALLY LEARN THAT THEY ONLY HAVE EACH OTHER TO FILL THE HOLES IN THEIR HEARTS.

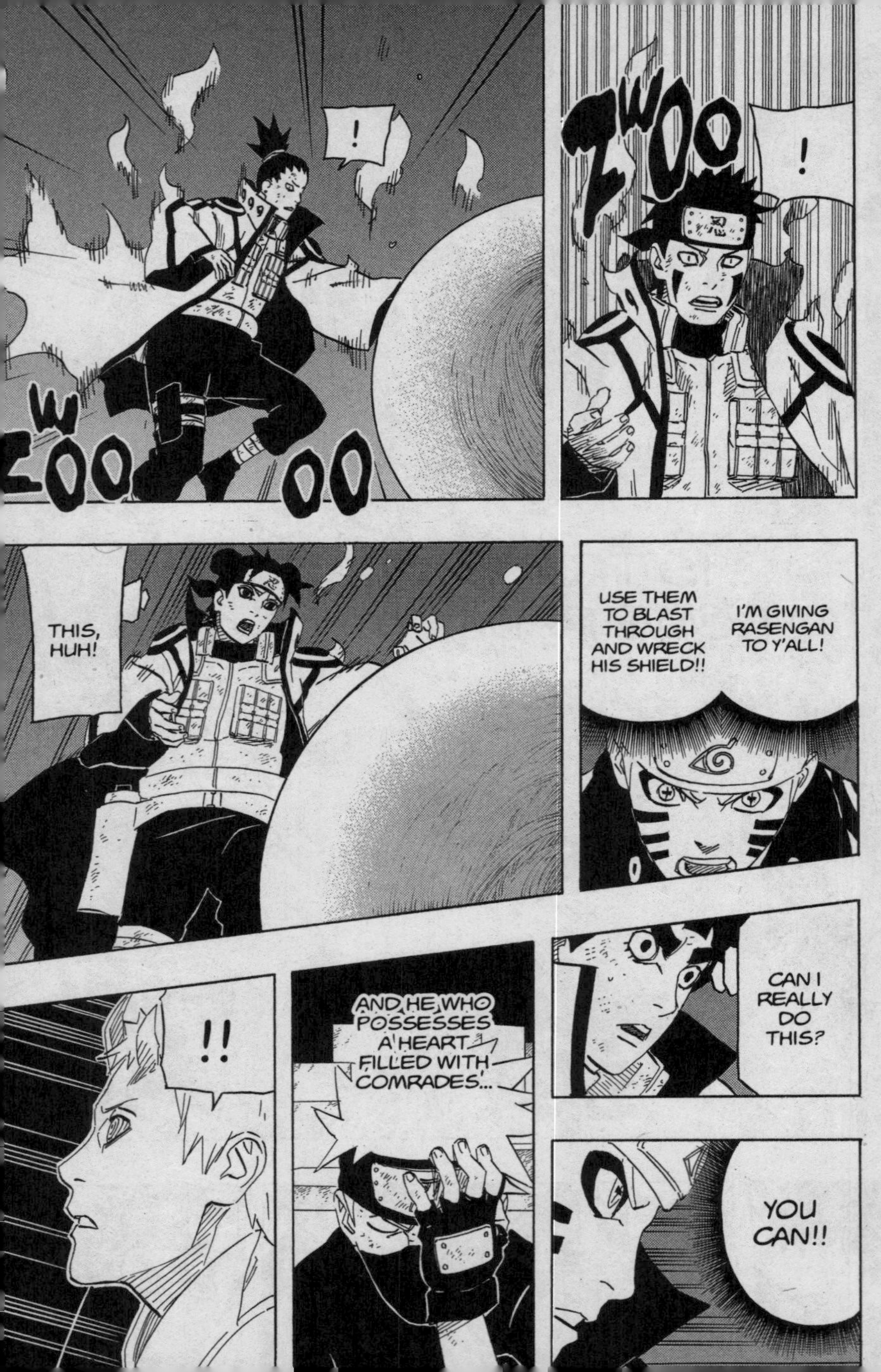
ZWOOO
!
!
ZWOOOO
I'M GIVING RASENGAN TO Y'ALL!
USE THEM TO BLAST THROUGH AND WRECK HIS SHIELD!!
THIS, HUH!
CAN I REALLY DO THIS?
YOU CAN!!
AND HE WHO POSSESSES A HEART FILLED WITH COMRADES...
!!

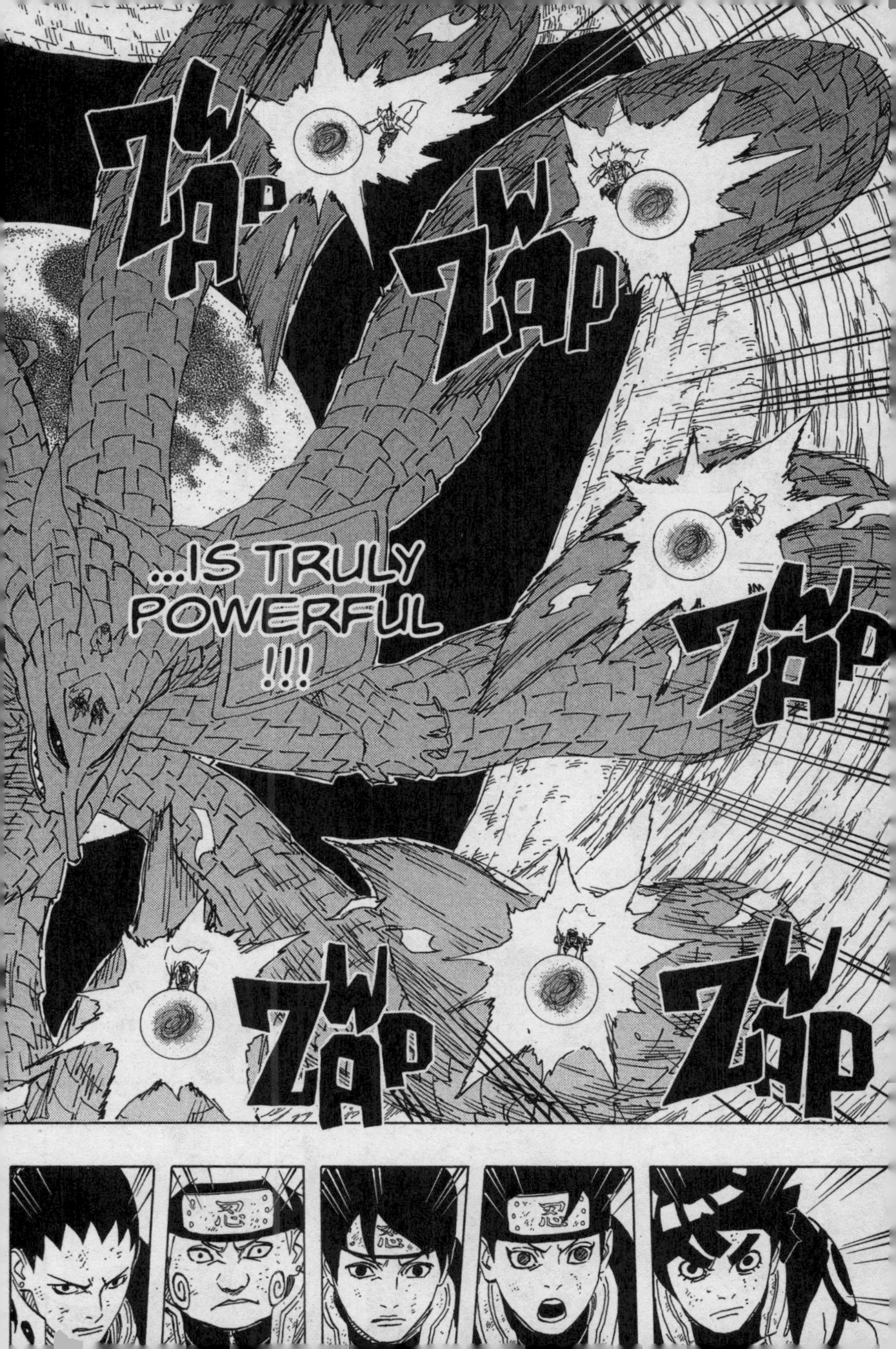
ZWAP
ZWAP
ZWAP
...IS TRULY POWERFUL!!!
ZWAP
ZWAP

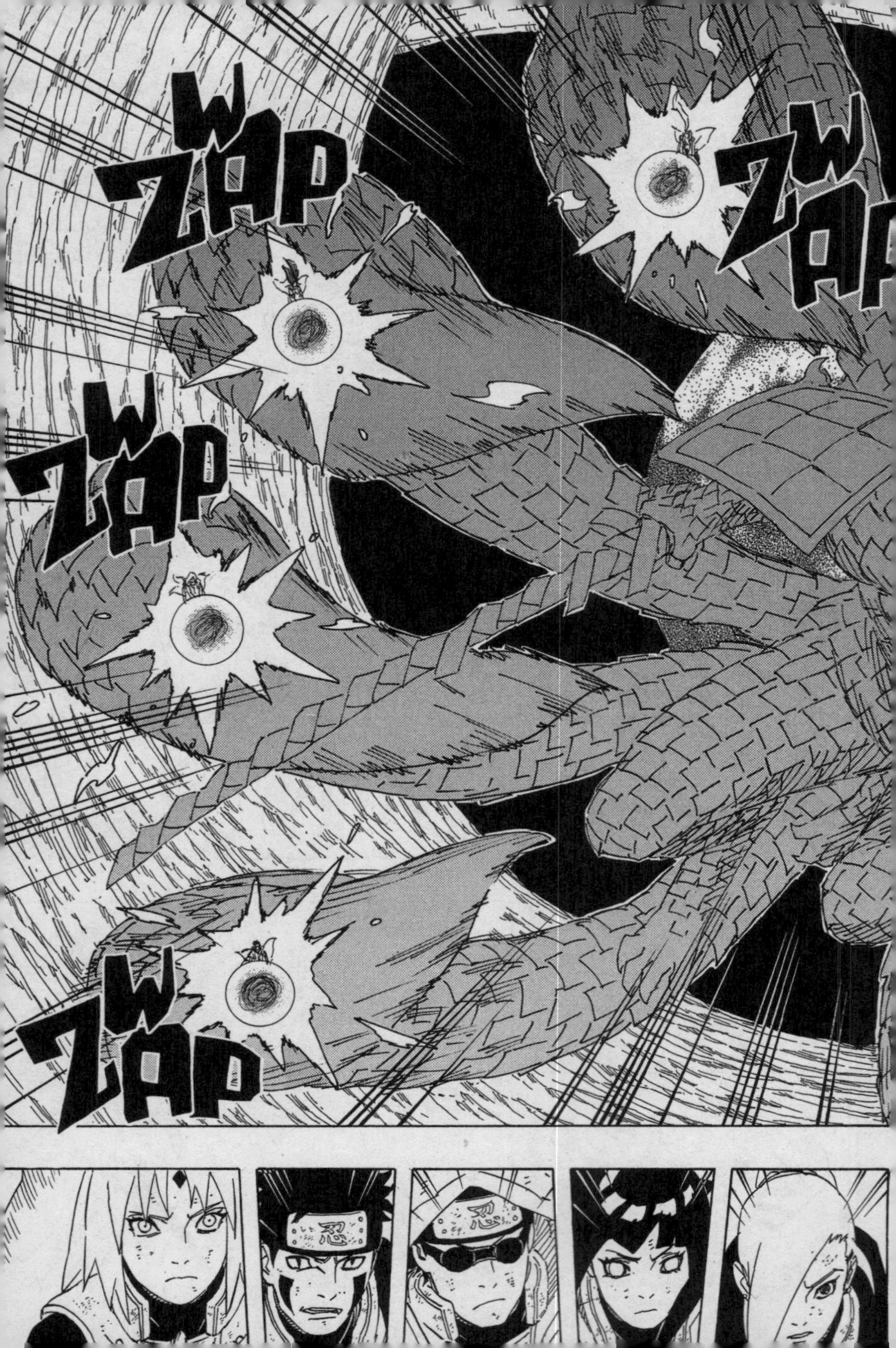
ZWAP
ZWAP
ZWAP
ZWAP

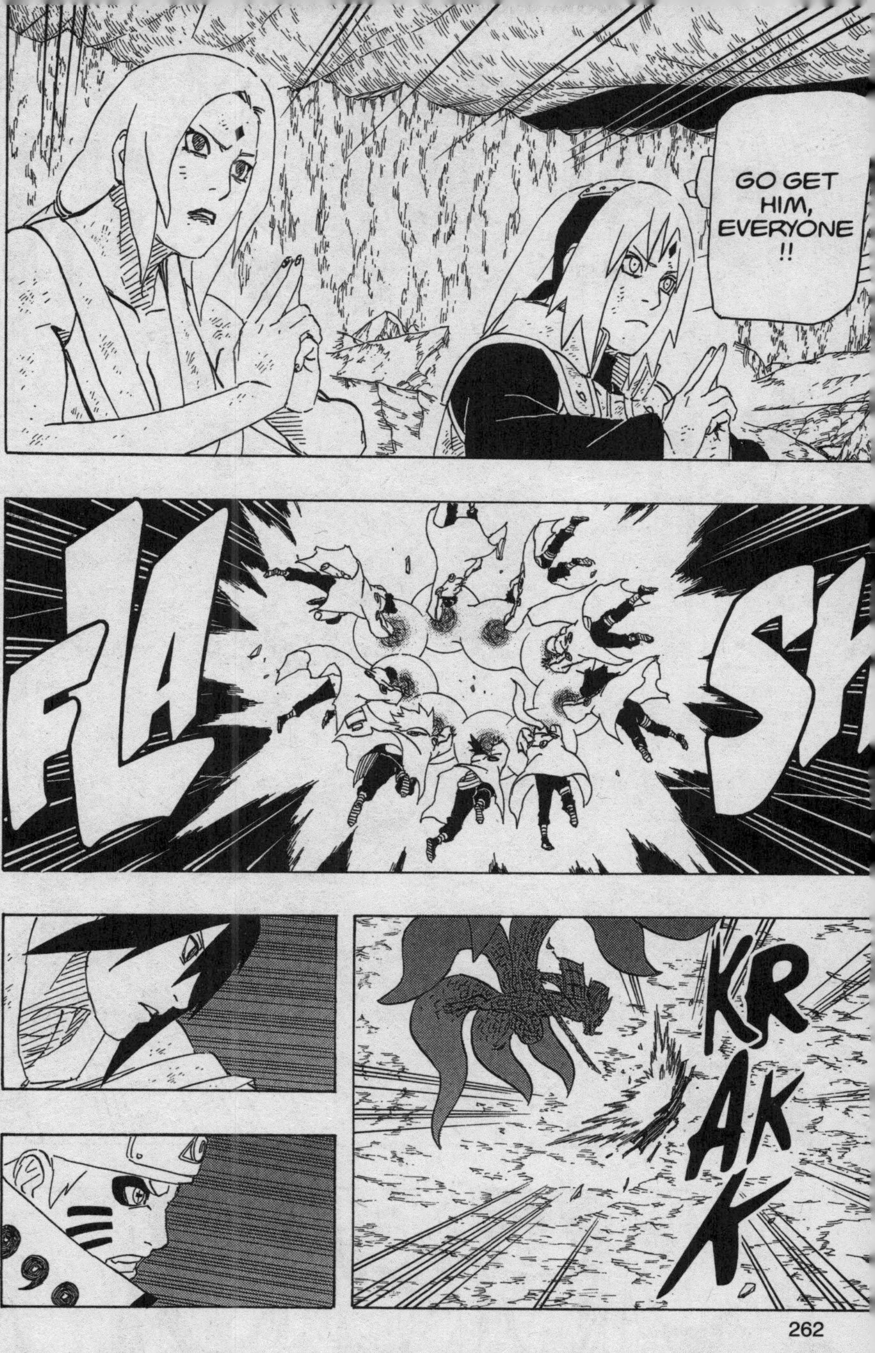
GO GET HIM, EVERYONE !!
FLA
SH
KRAKK

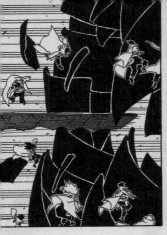

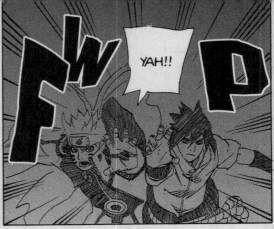

YAH!!

F'W P

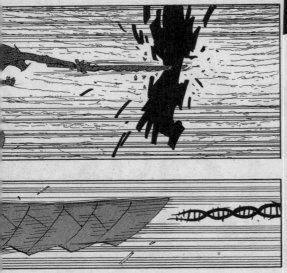

TA

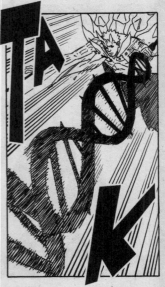

K

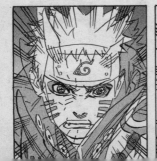

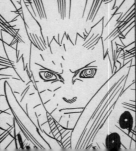

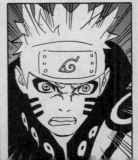

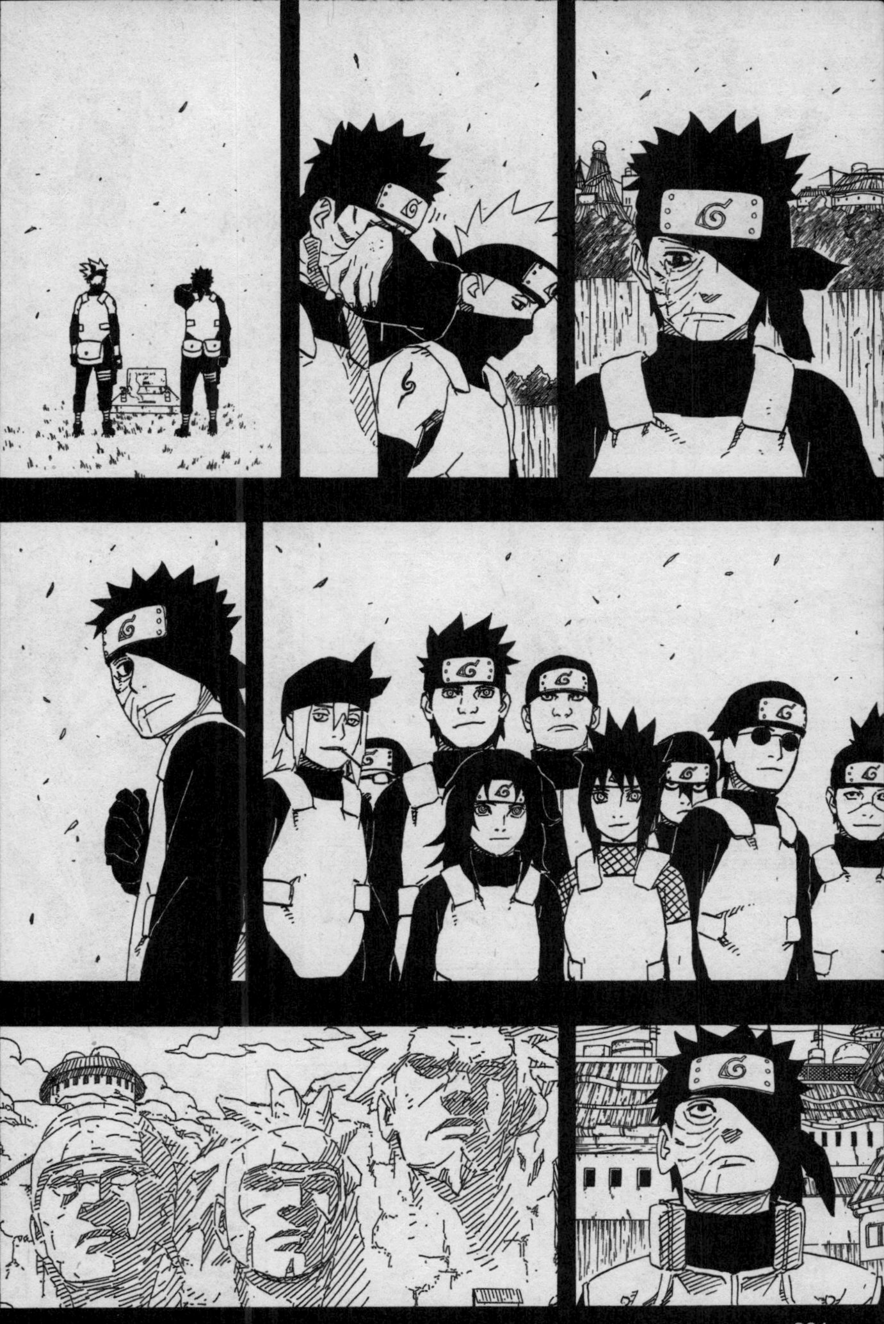

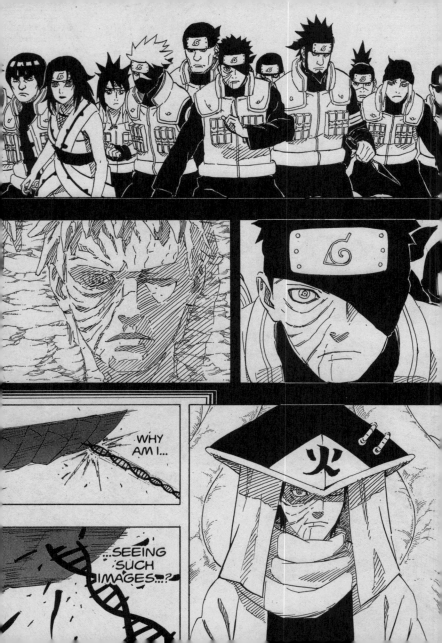

WHY AM I...

...SEEING SUCH IMAGES...?

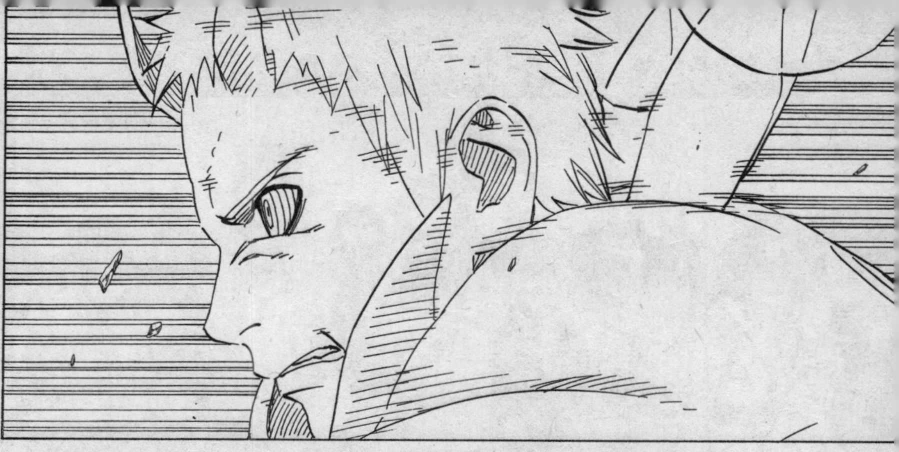
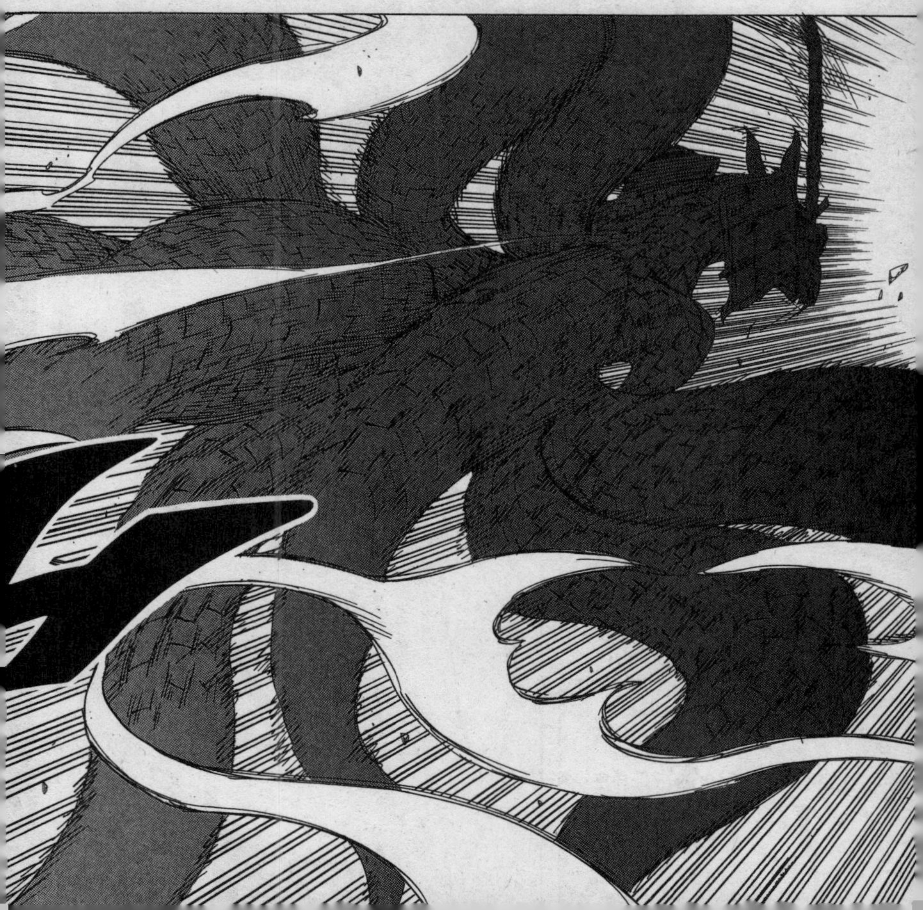

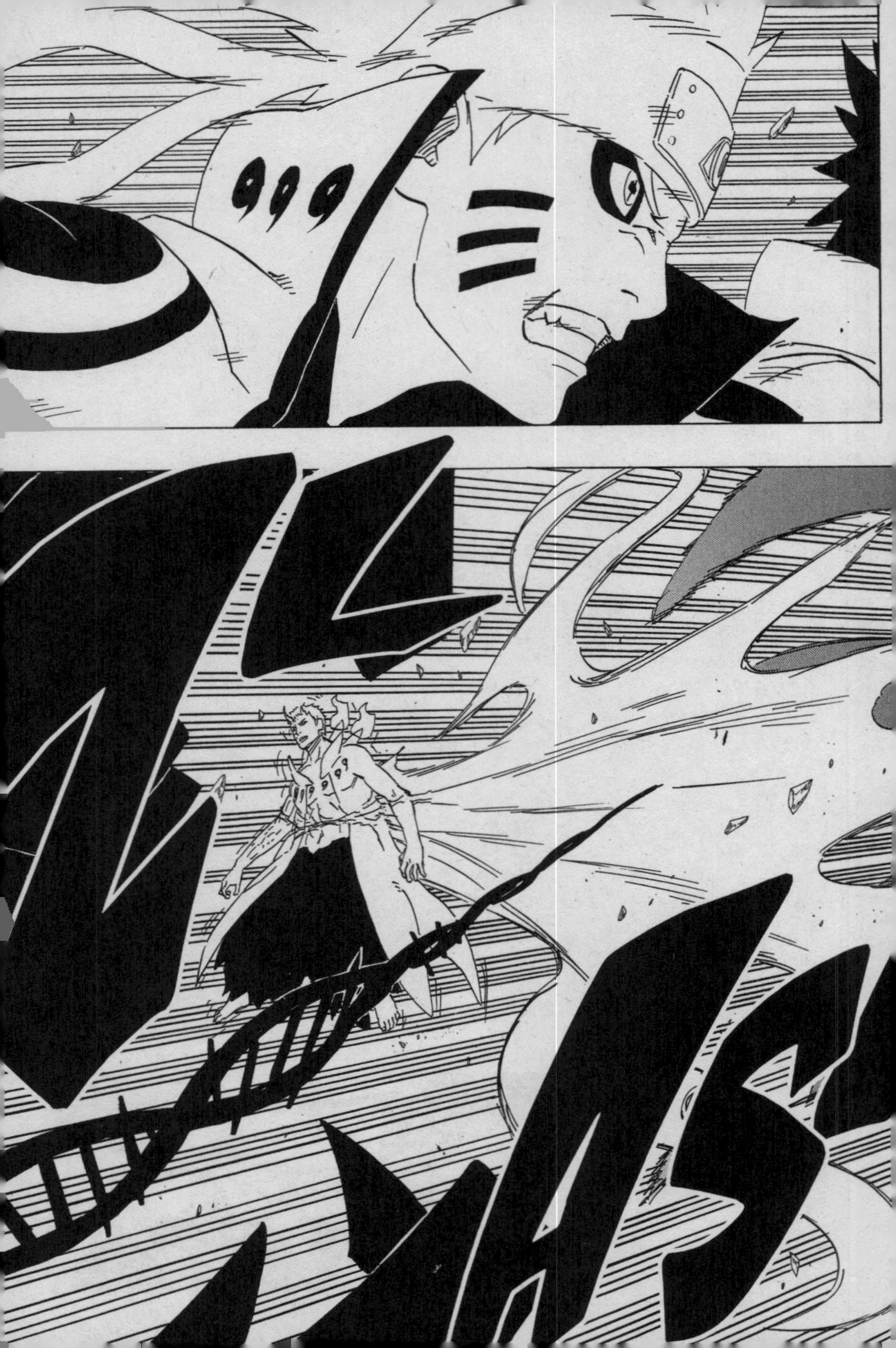

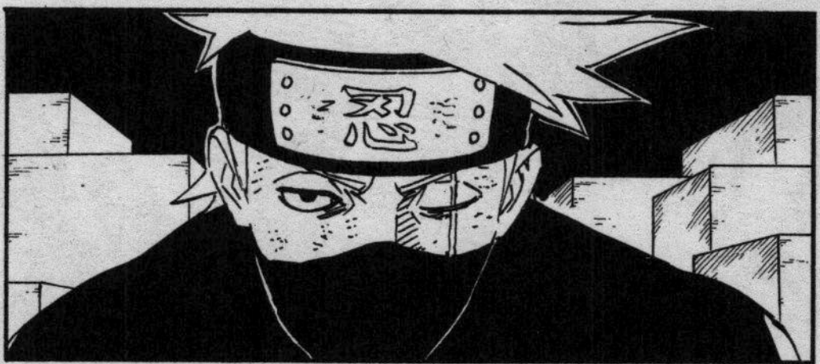
忍

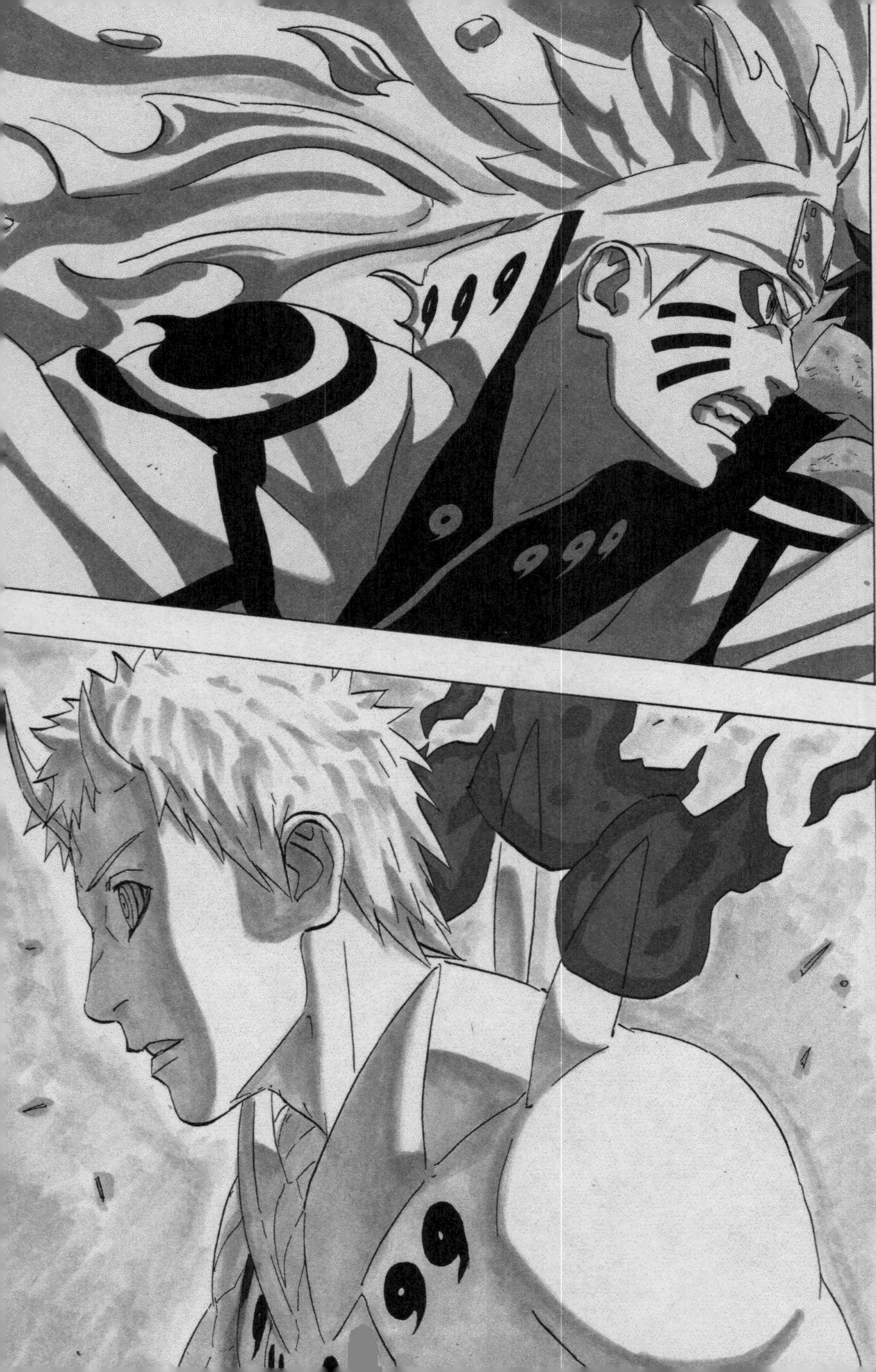

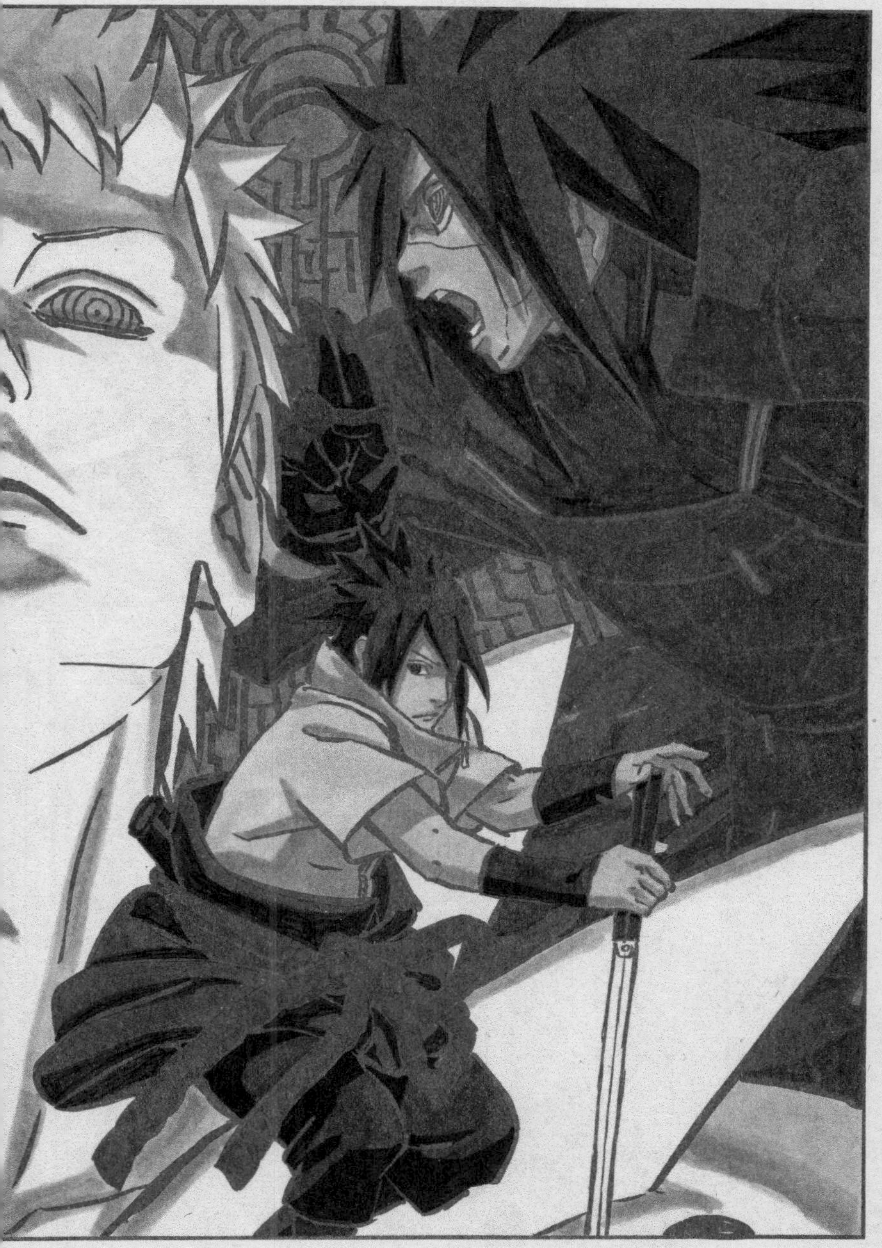

Number 652: Naruto's Path

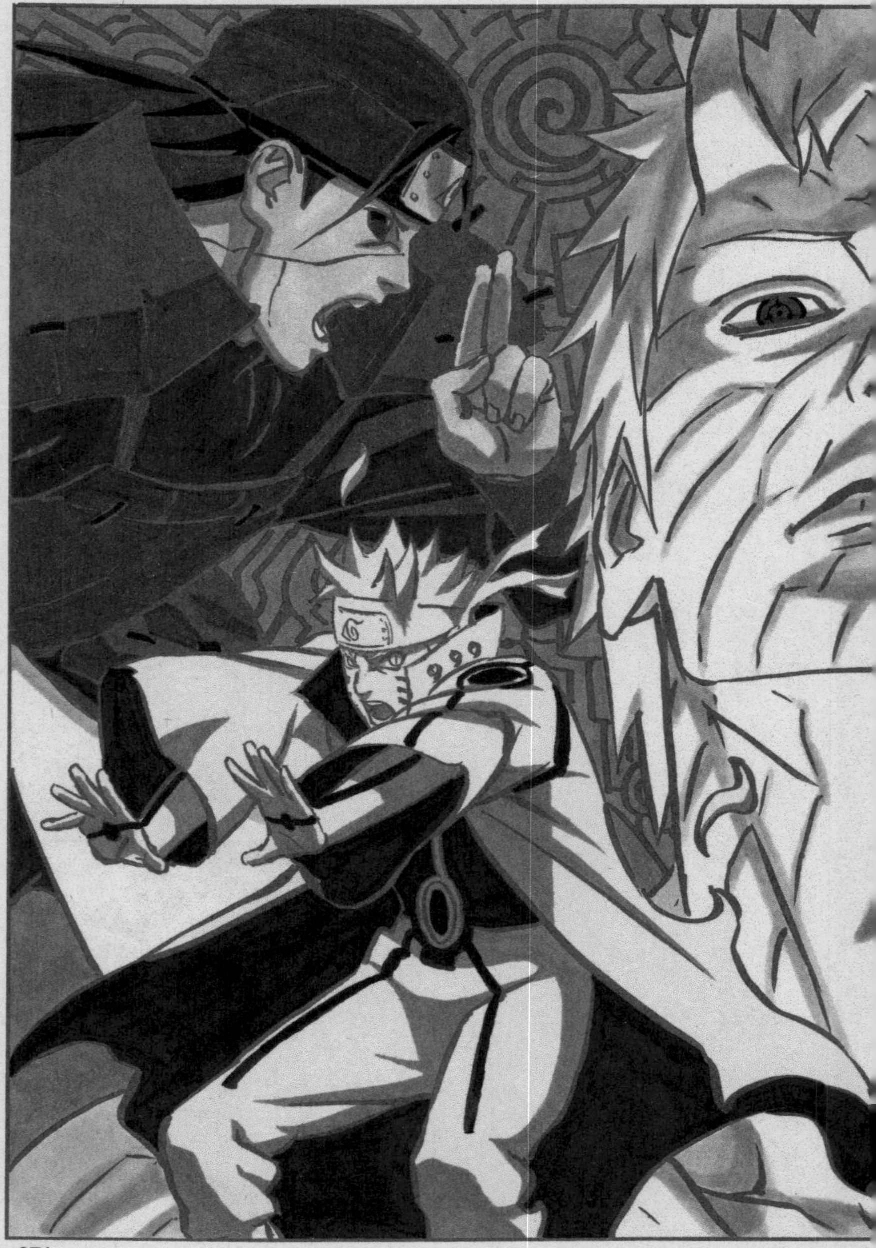

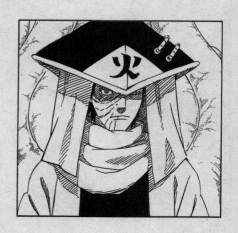

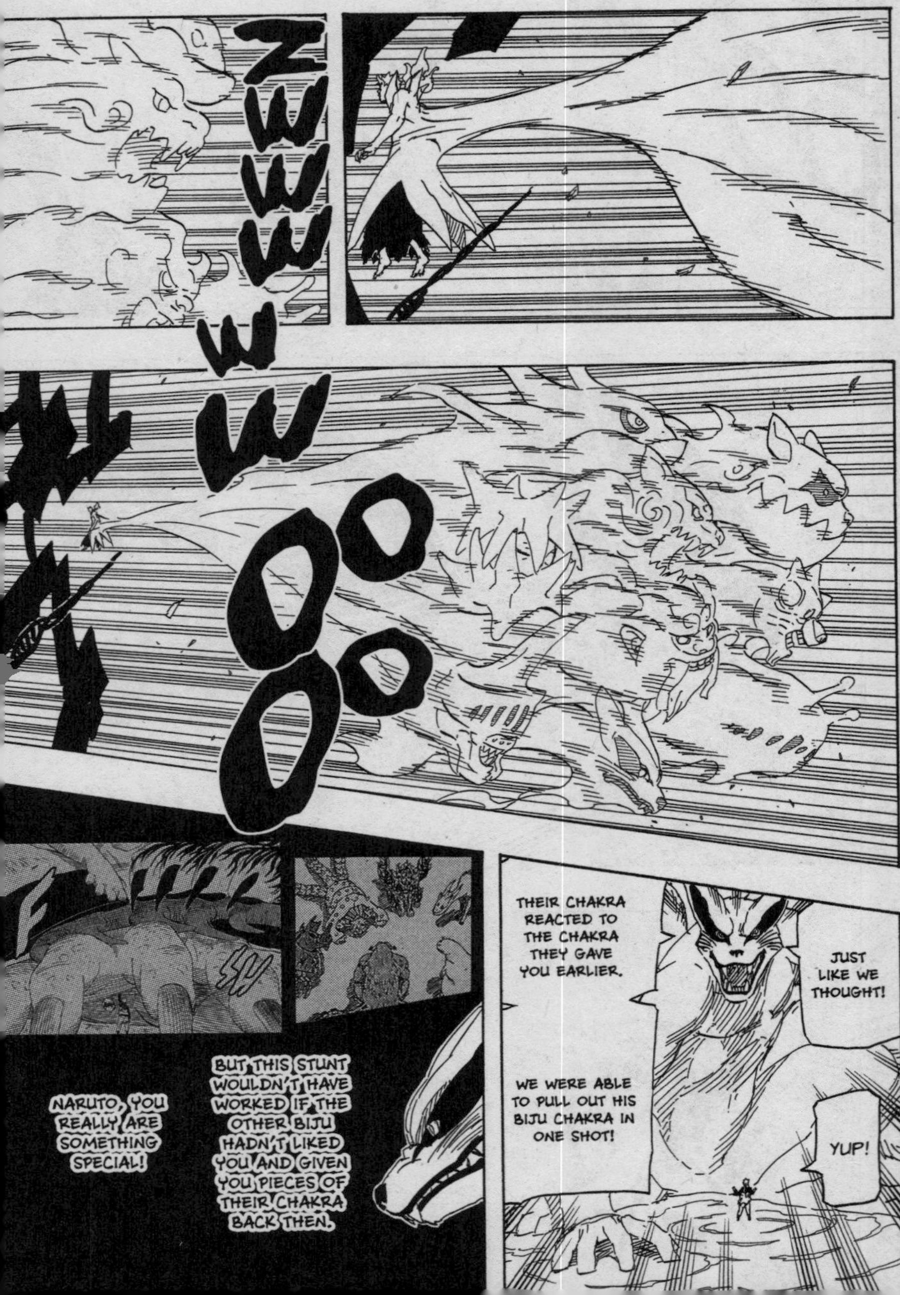
ZWWWWWOOOO
JUST LIKE WE THOUGHT!
THEIR CHAKRA REACTED TO THE CHAKRA THEY GAVE YOU EARLIER.
WE WERE ABLE TO PULL OUT HIS BIJU CHAKRA IN ONE SHOT!
YUP!
BUT THIS STUNT WOULDN'T HAVE WORKED IF THE OTHER BIJU HADN'T LIKED YOU AND GIVEN YOU PIECES OF THEIR CHAKRA BACK THEN.
NARUTO, YOU REALLY ARE SOMETHING SPECIAL!

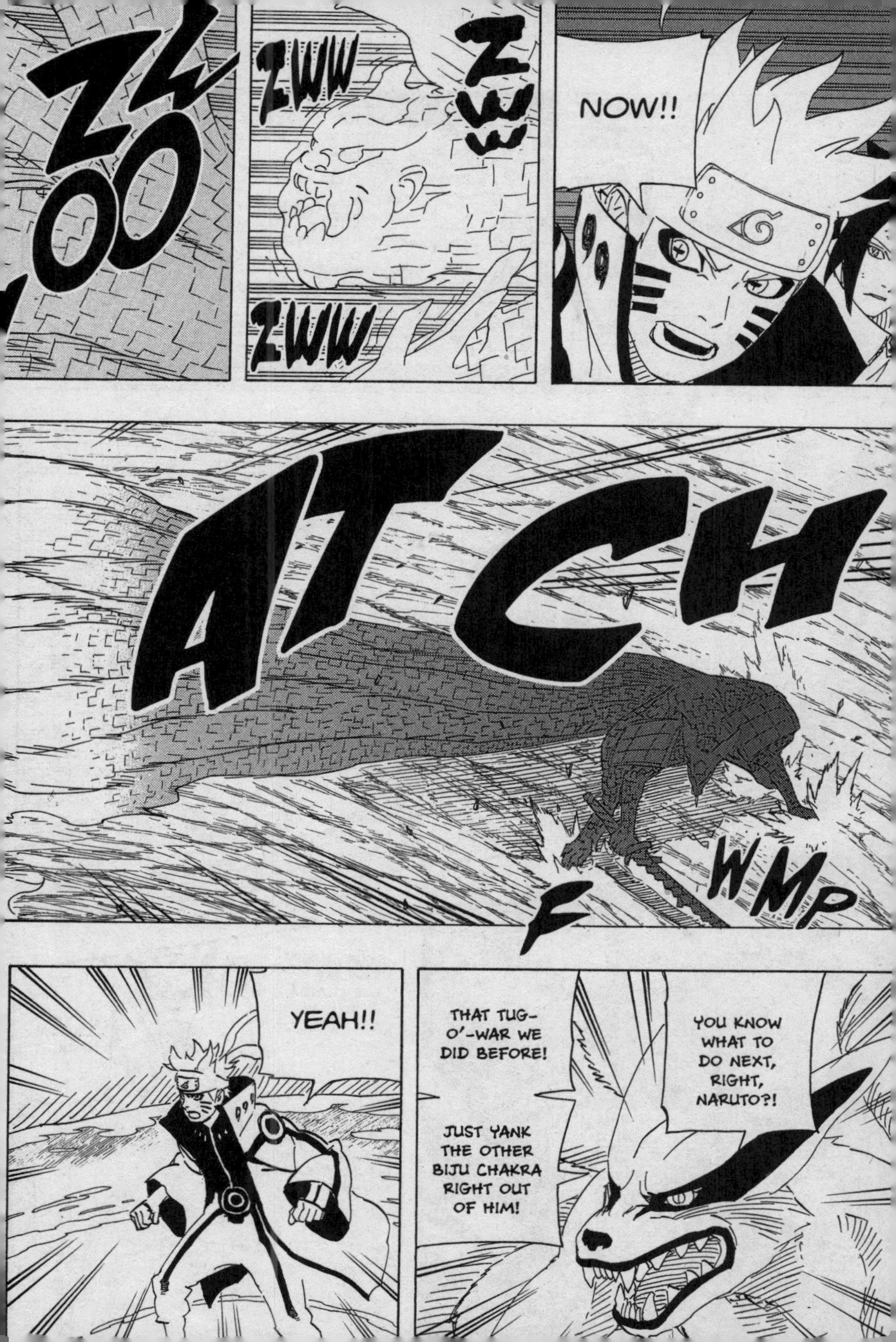
NOW!!
ATCH
FWMP
YOU KNOW WHAT TO DO NEXT, RIGHT, NARUTO?!
THAT TUG-O'-WAR WE DID BEFORE!
JUST YANK THE OTHER BIJU CHAKRA RIGHT OUT OF HIM!
YEAH!!

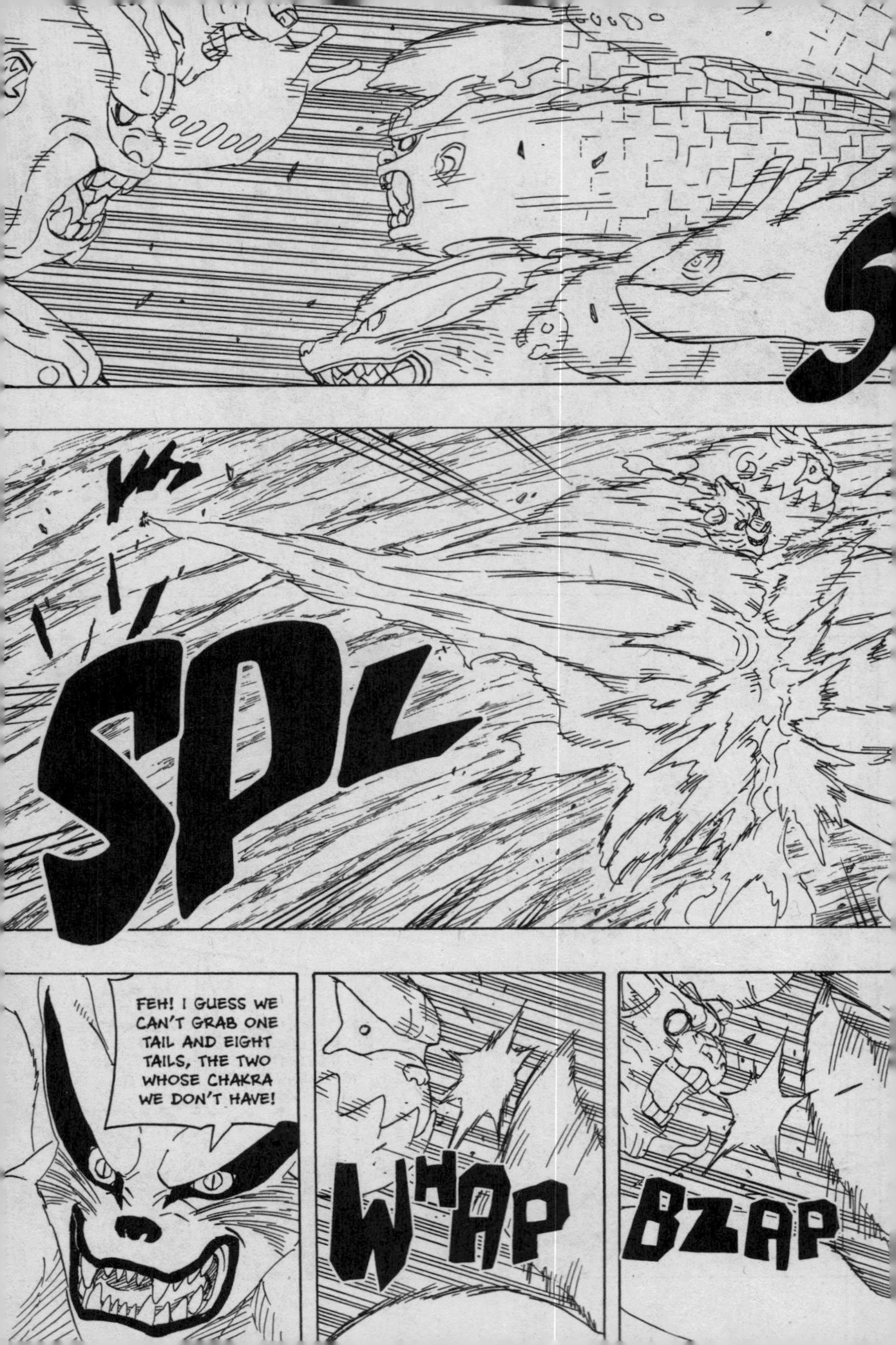
SPL
BZAP
WHAP
FEH! I GUESS WE CAN'T GRAB ONE TAIL AND EIGHT TAILS, THE TWO WHOSE CHAKRA WE DON'T HAVE!

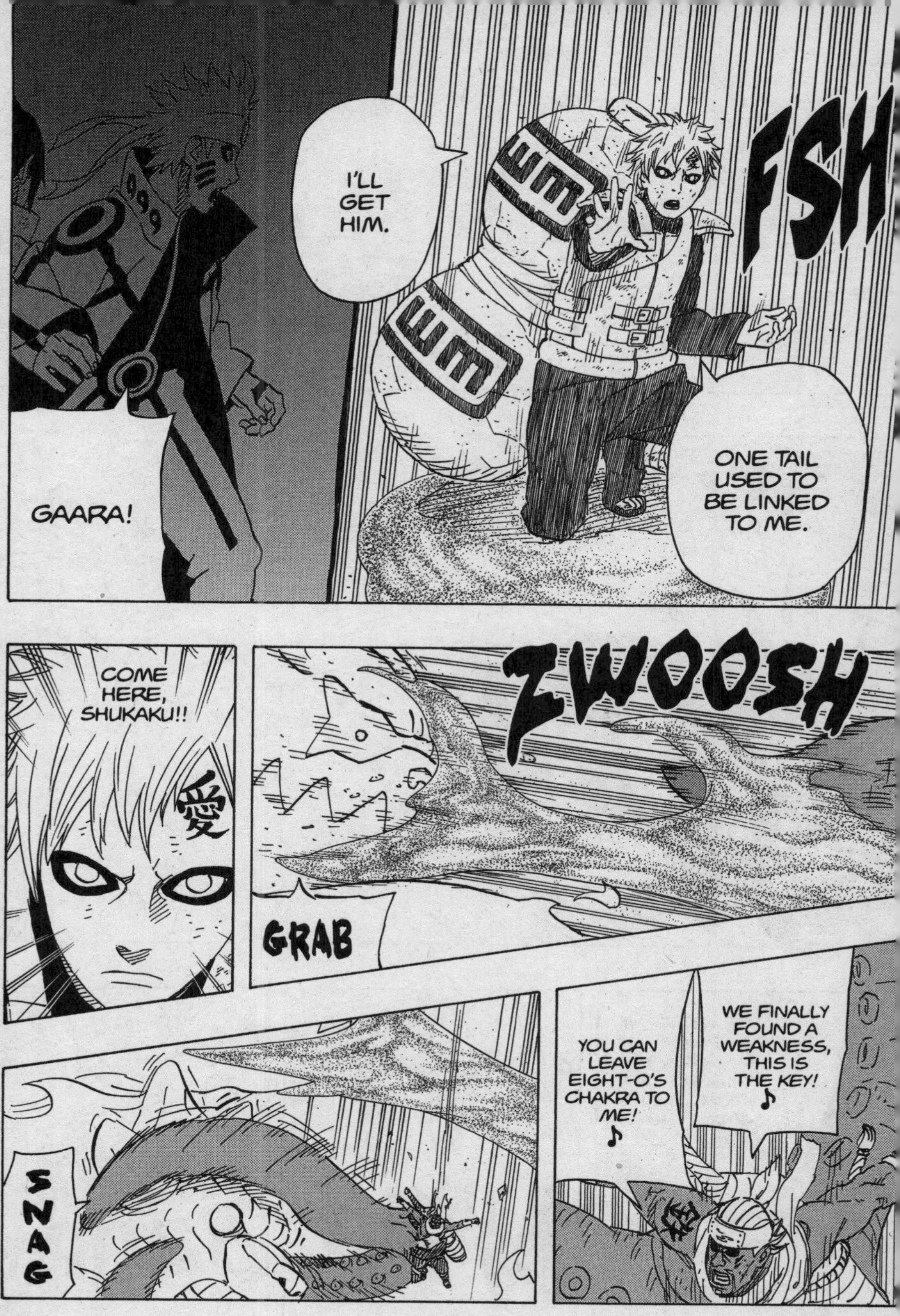
FSH
I'LL GET HIM.
ONE TAIL USED TO BE LINKED TO ME.
GAARA!
ZWOOSH
GRAB
COME HERE, SHUKAKU!!
WE FINALLY FOUND A WEAKNESS, THIS IS THE KEY! ♪
YOU CAN LEAVE EIGHT-O'S CHAKRA TO ME! ♪
SNAG

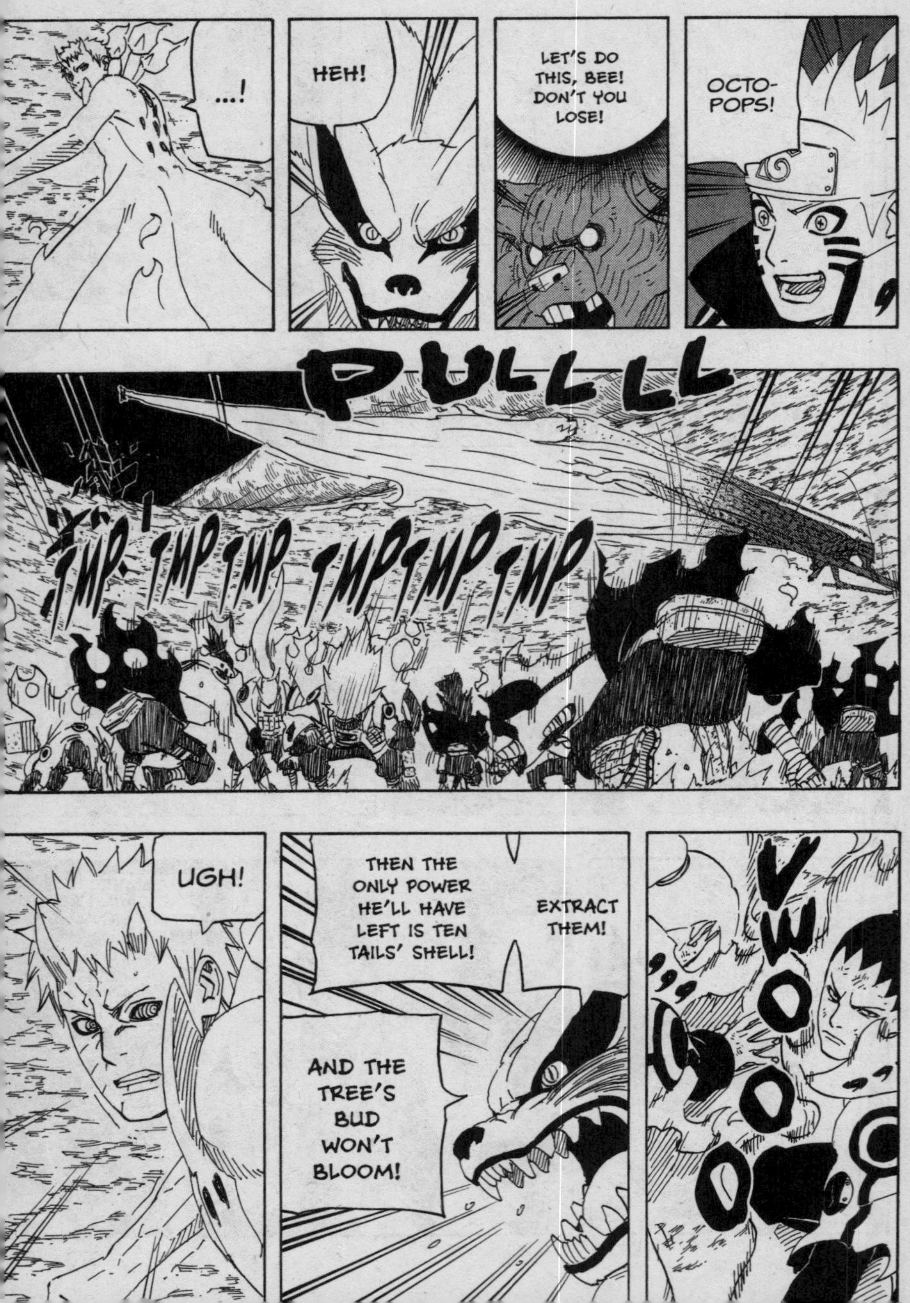
OCTO-POPS!
LET'S DO THIS, BEE! DON'T YOU LOSE!
HEH!
...!
PULLLL
TMP
TMP
TMP
TMP
TMP
TMP
TMP
VWOOOO
EXTRACT THEM!
THEN THE ONLY POWER HE'LL HAVE LEFT IS TEN TAILS' SHELL!
AND THE TREE'S BUD WON'T BLOOM!
UGH!

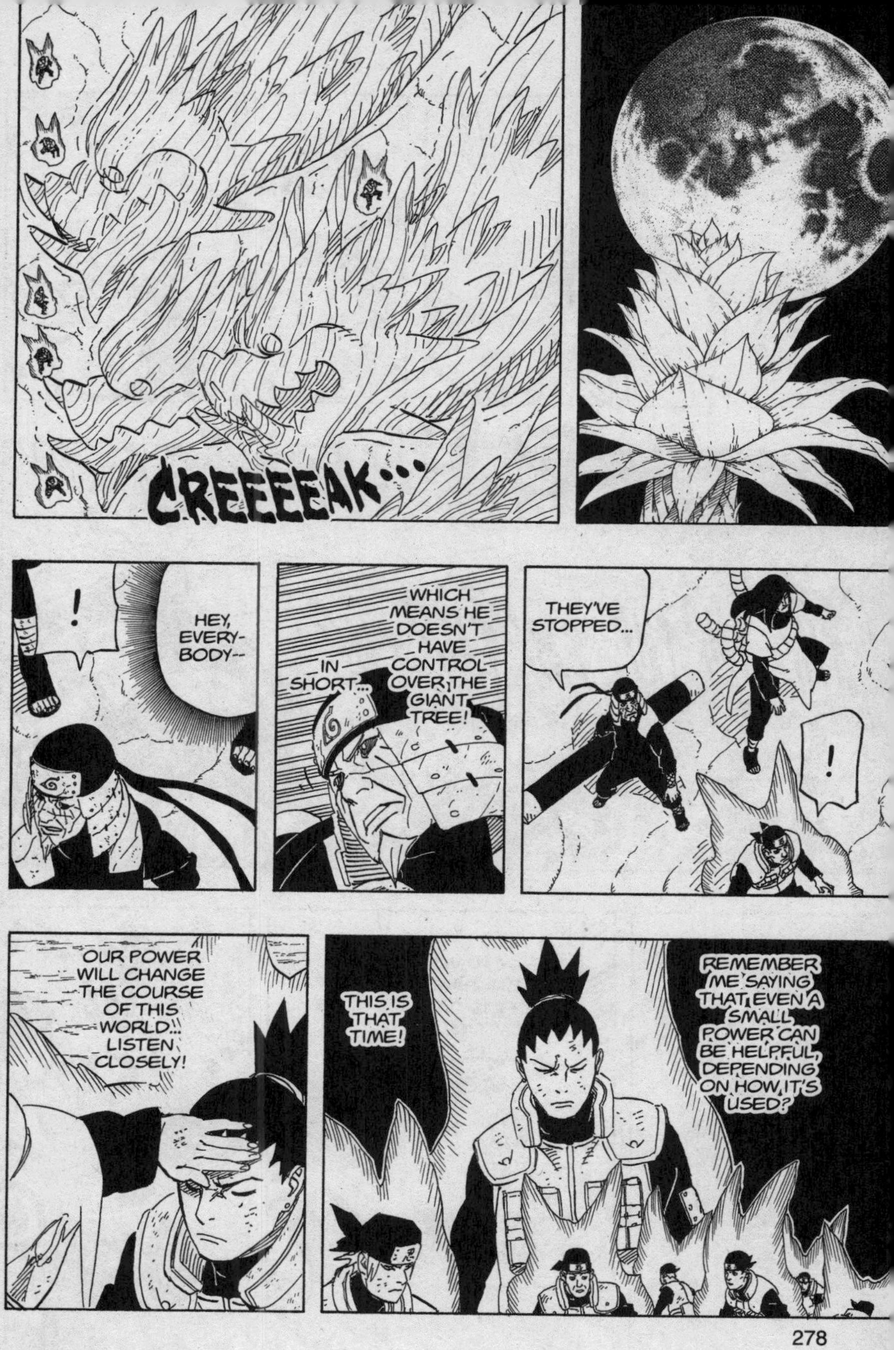
CREEEEAK...
THEY'VE STOPPED...
!
WHICH MEANS HE DOESN'T HAVE CONTROL OVER THE GIANT TREE!
IN SHORT...
HEY, EVERY-BODY--
!
REMEMBER ME SAYING THAT EVEN A SMALL POWER CAN BE HELPFUL, DEPENDING ON HOW IT'S USED?
THIS IS THAT TIME!
OUR POWER WILL CHANGE THE COURSE OF THIS WORLD!! LISTEN CLOSELY!

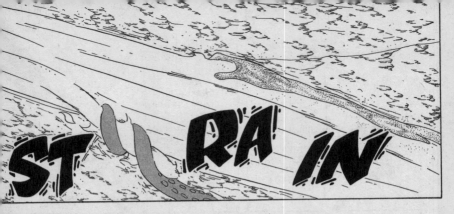

ST ‖ RA IN

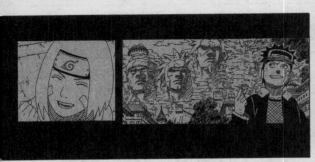

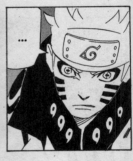

...

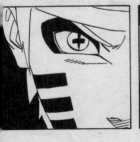

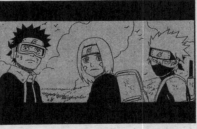

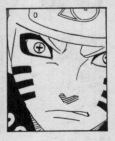

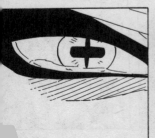

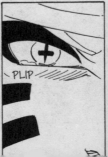

PLIP

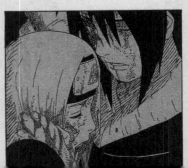

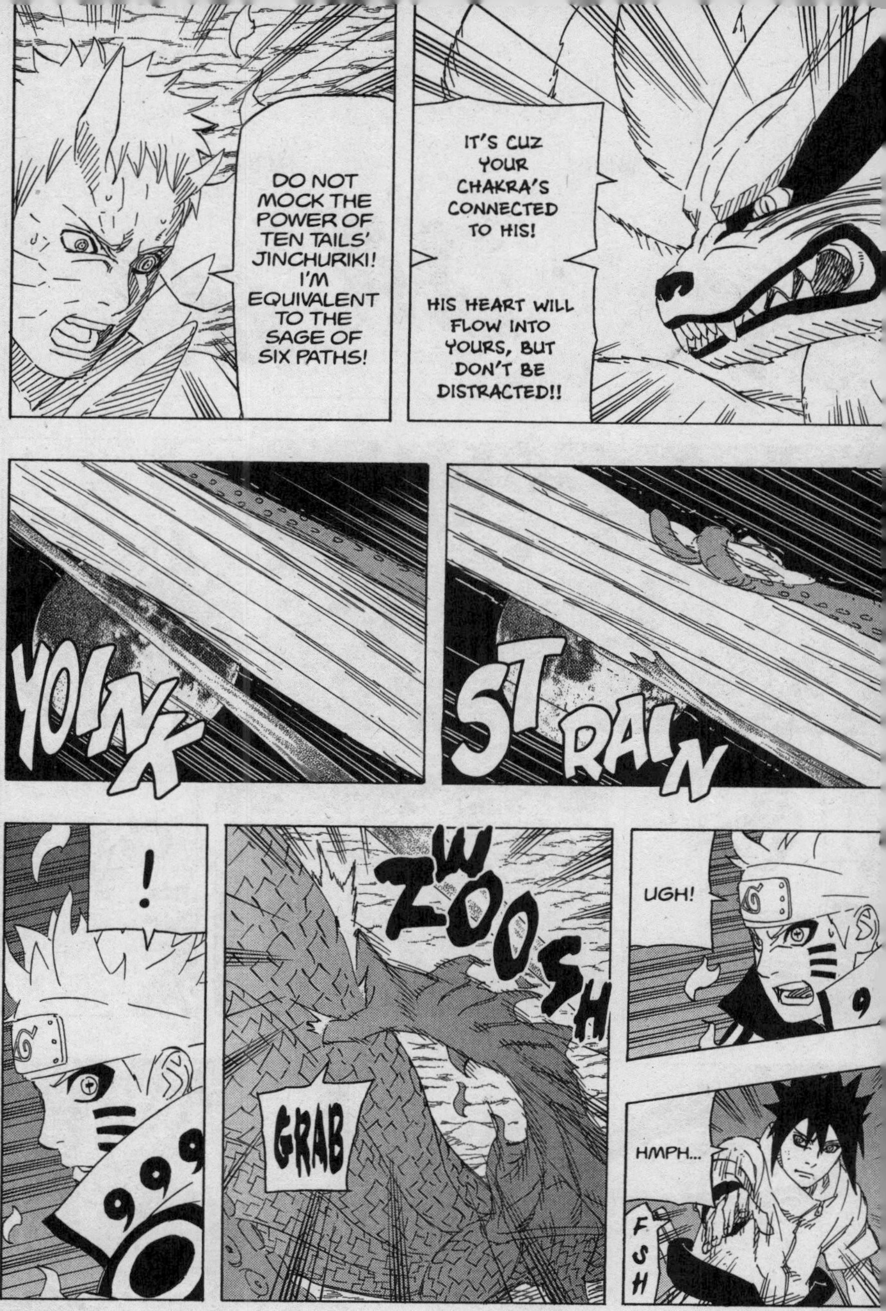
IT'S CUZ YOUR CHAKRA'S CONNECTED TO HIS!
HIS HEART WILL FLOW INTO YOURS, BUT DON'T BE DISTRACTED!!
DO NOT MOCK THE POWER OF TEN TAILS' JINCHURIKI! I'M EQUIVALENT TO THE SAGE OF SIX PATHS!
STRAIN
YOINK
UGH!
HMPH...
FSH
ZWOOSH
GRAB
!

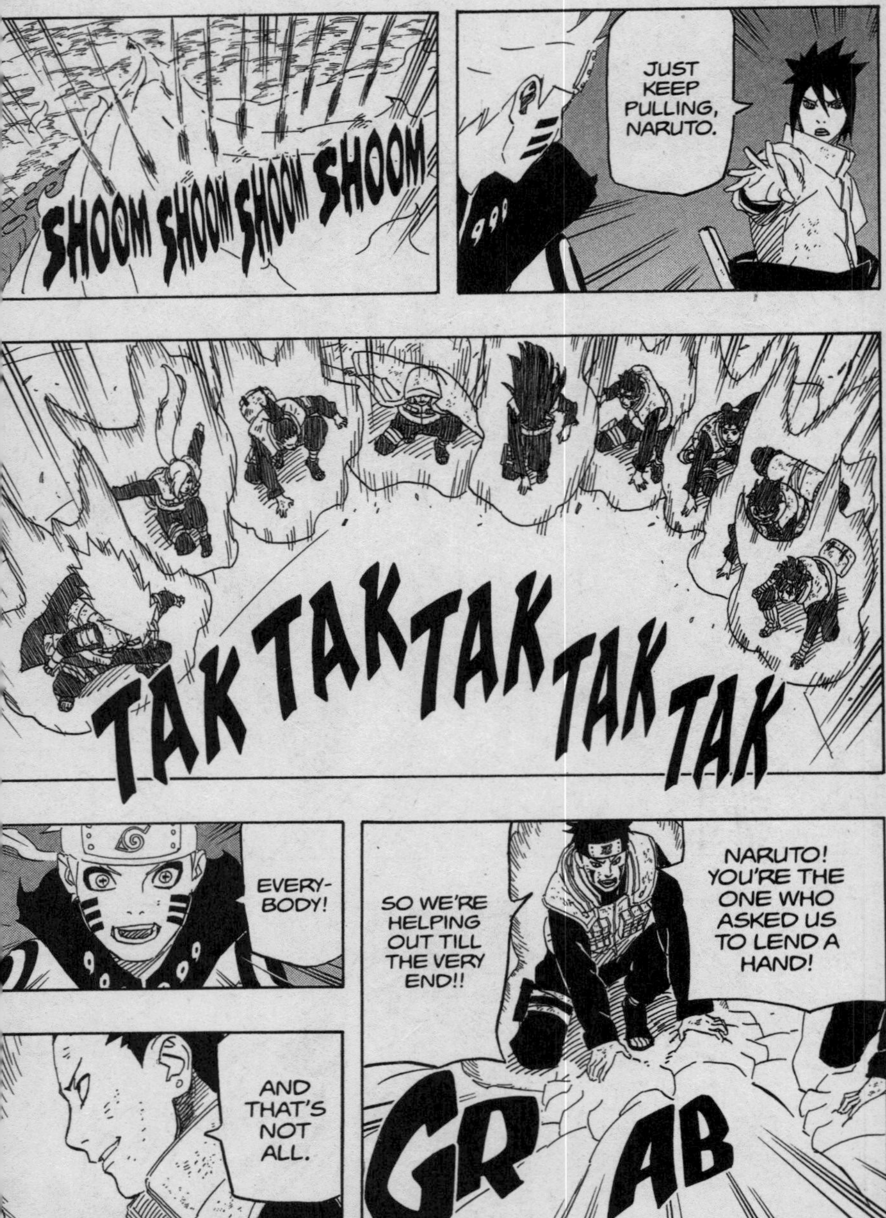
JUST KEEP PULLING, NARUTO.
SHOOM SHOOM SHOOM SHOOM
TAK TAK TAK TAK TAK
NARUTO! YOU'RE THE ONE WHO ASKED US TO LEND A HAND!
SO WE'RE HELPING OUT TILL THE VERY END!!
GRAB
EVERY-BODY!
AND THAT'S NOT ALL.

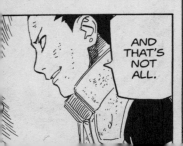

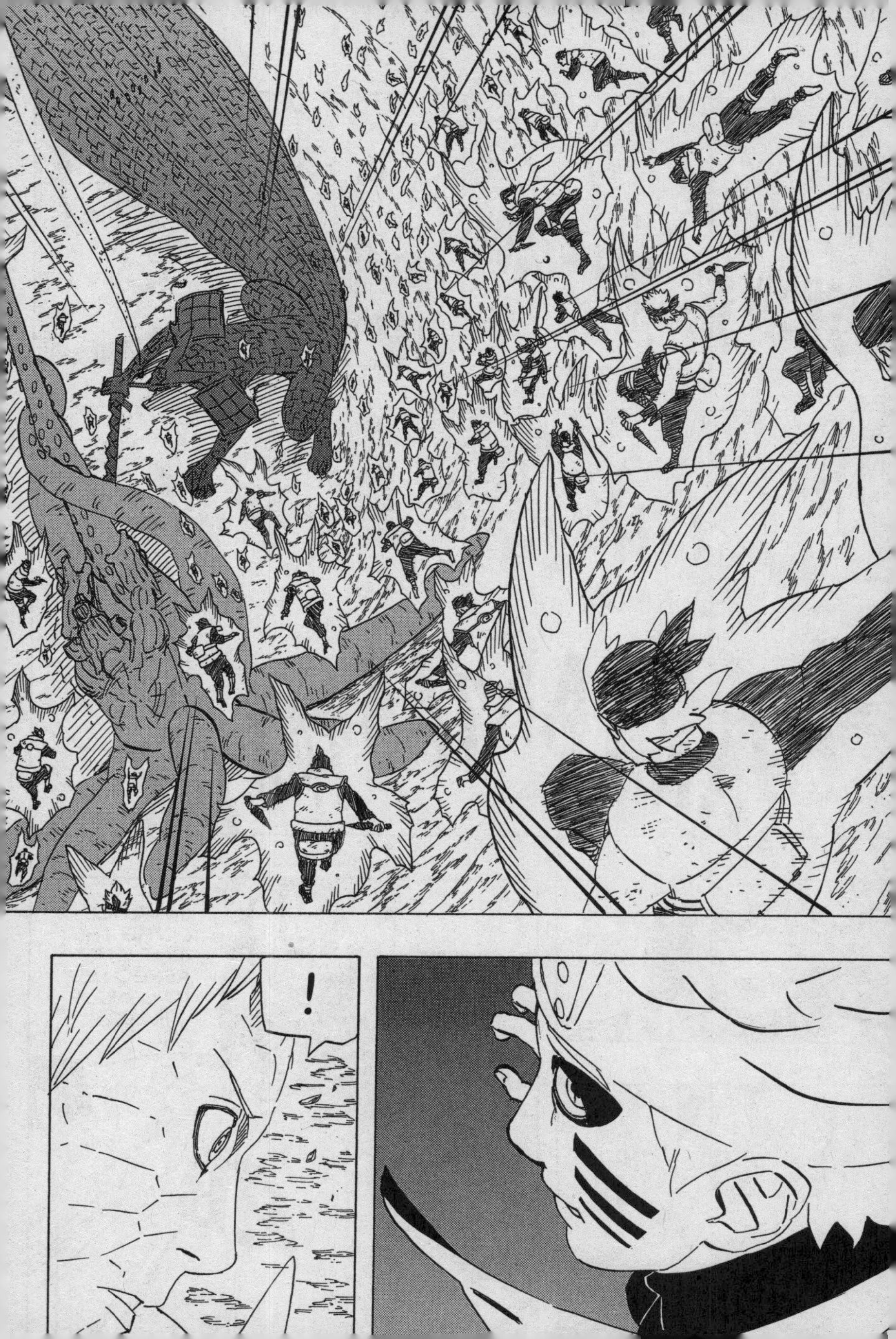
!

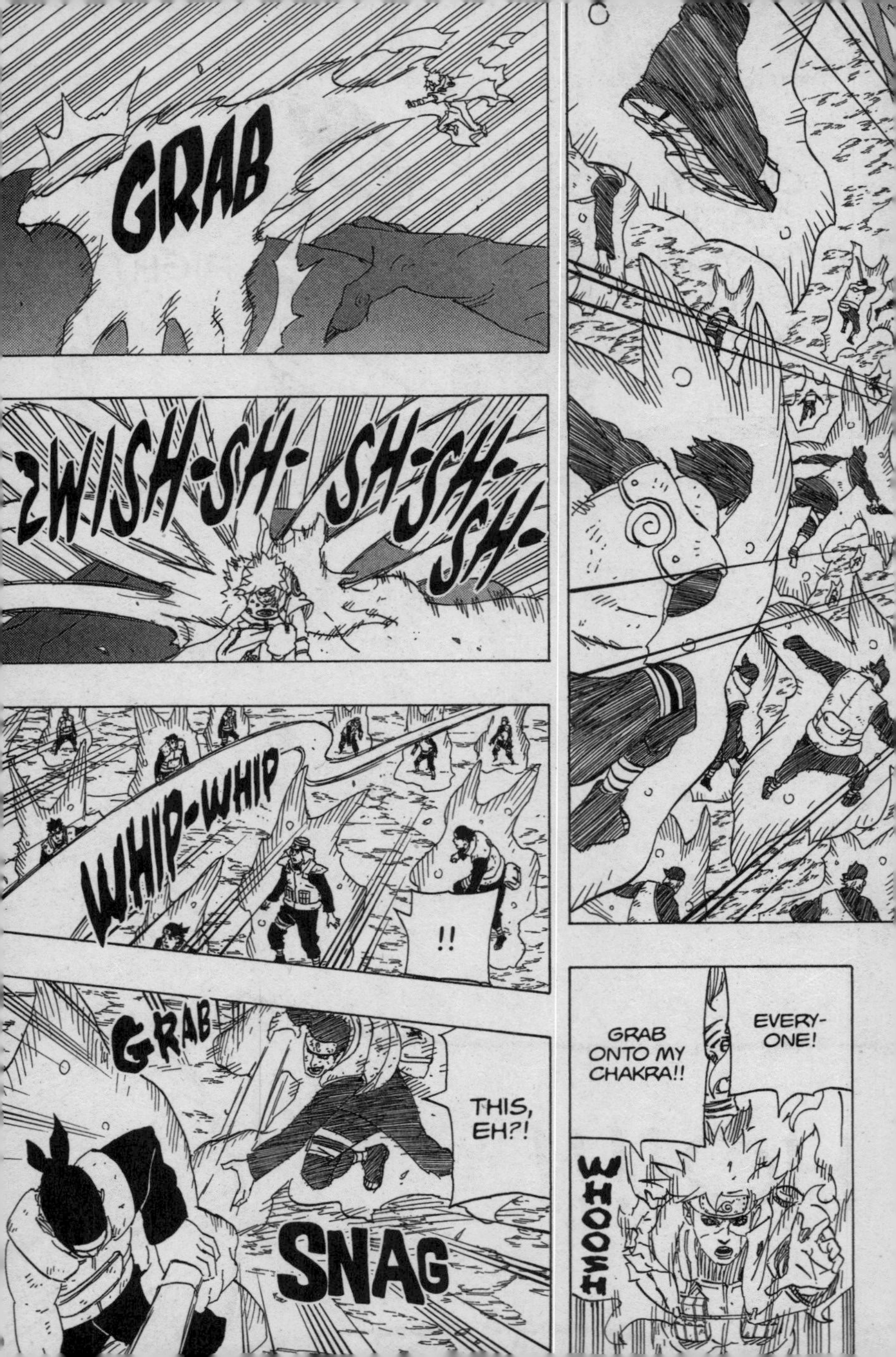
EVERY-ONE!
GRAB ONTO MY CHAKRA!!
WHOOSH
GRAB
ZWISH-SH-SH-SH-SH-SH-
WHIP-WHIP
!!
GRAB
THIS, EH?!
SNAG

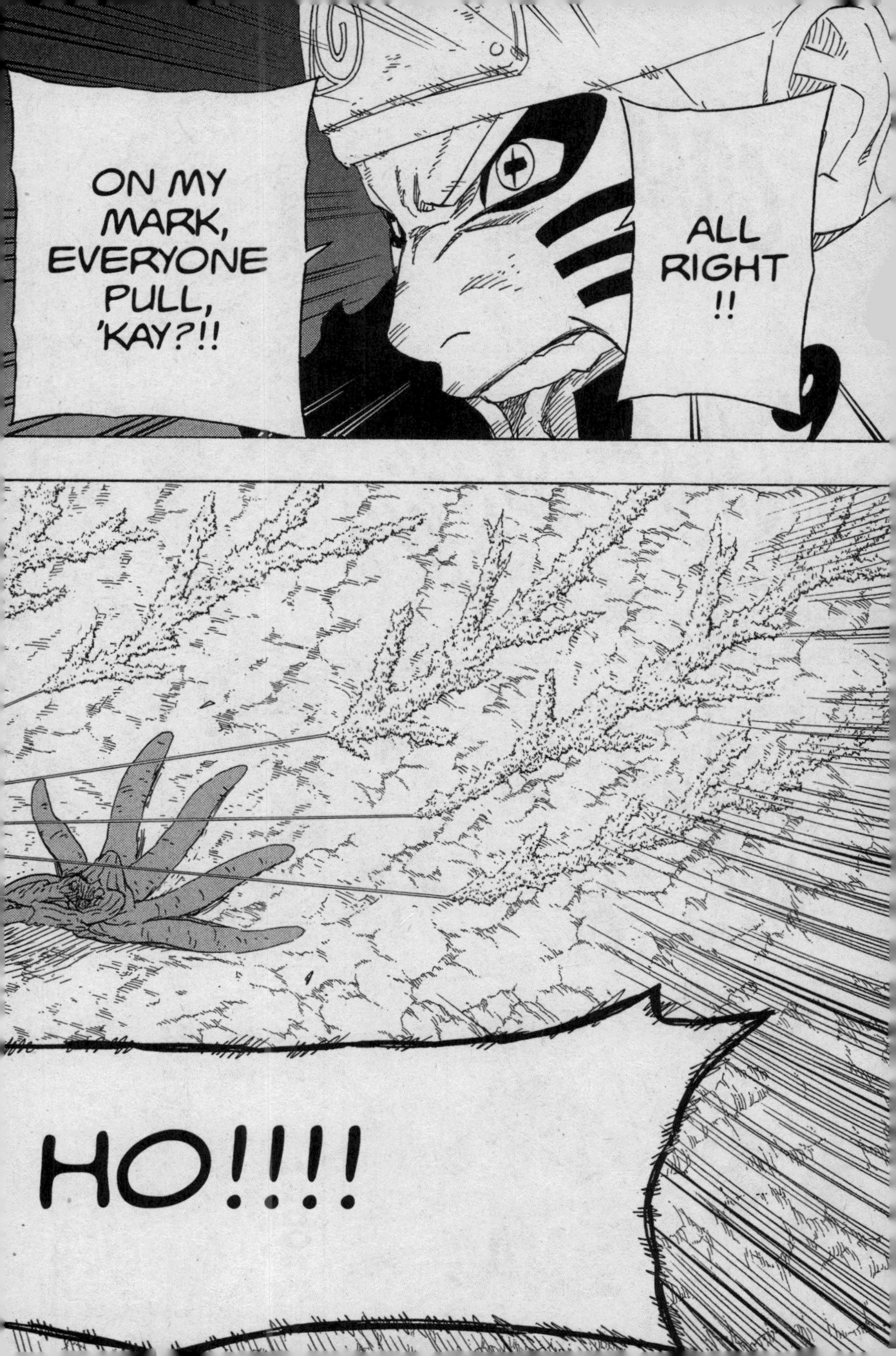
ALL RIGHT!!
ON MY MARK, EVERYONE PULL, 'KAY?!!
HO!!!!

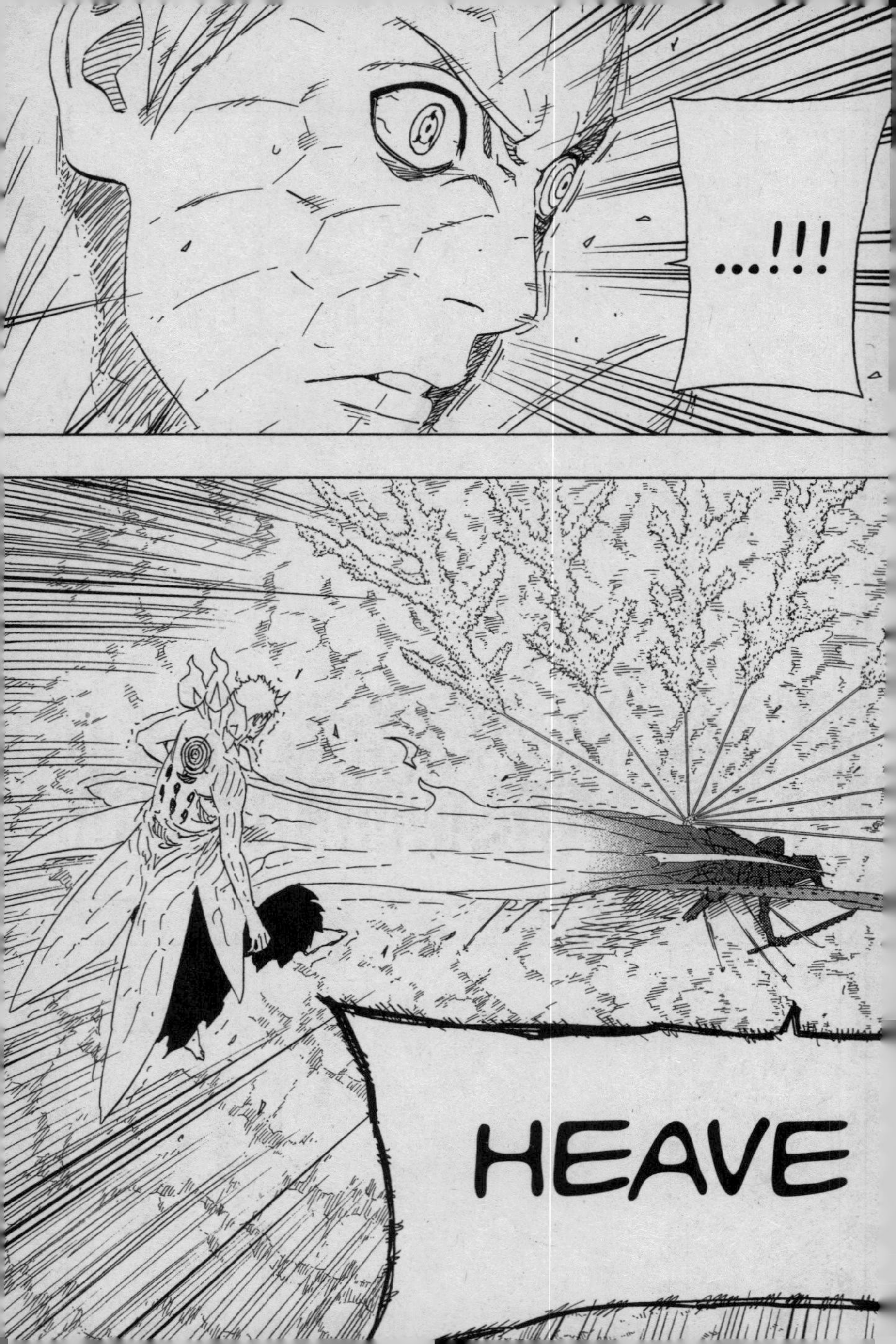
...!!!
HEAVE

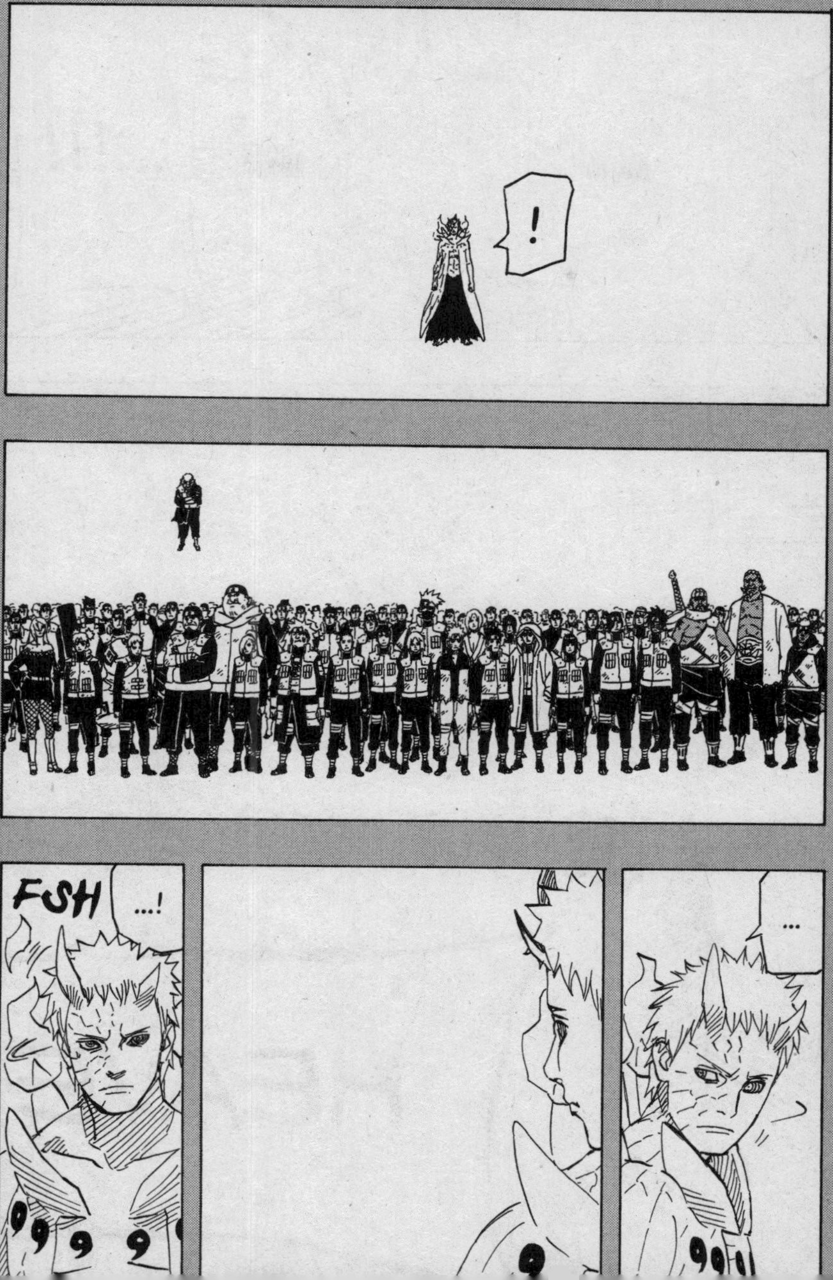
!
...
FSH
...!

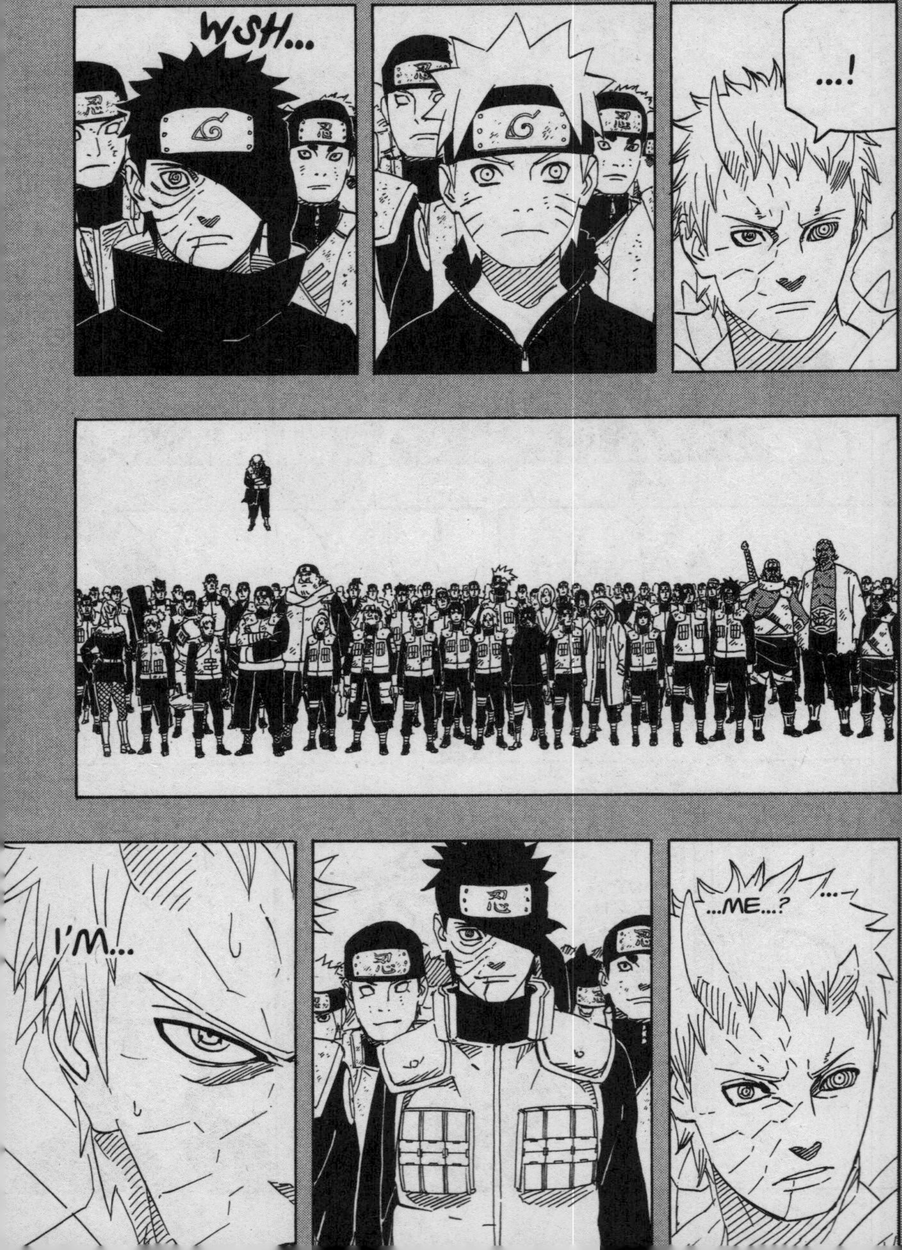
...!
WSH...
...
...ME...?
I'M...

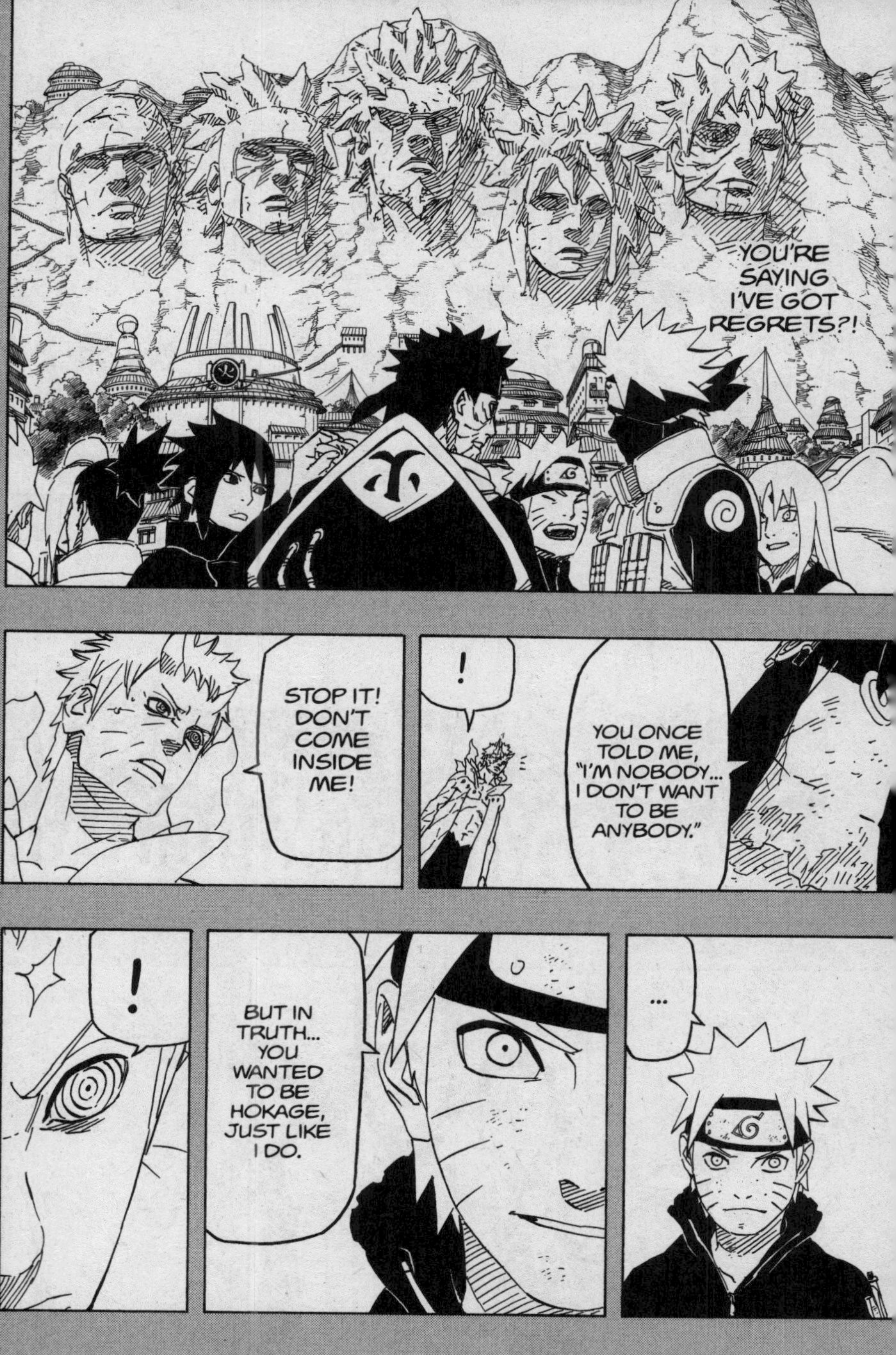
YOU'RE SAYING I'VE GOT REGRETS?!
YOU ONCE TOLD ME, "I'M NOBODY... I DON'T WANT TO BE ANYBODY."
!
STOP IT! DON'T COME INSIDE ME!
...
BUT IN TRUTH... YOU WANTED TO BE HOKAGE, JUST LIKE I DO.
!

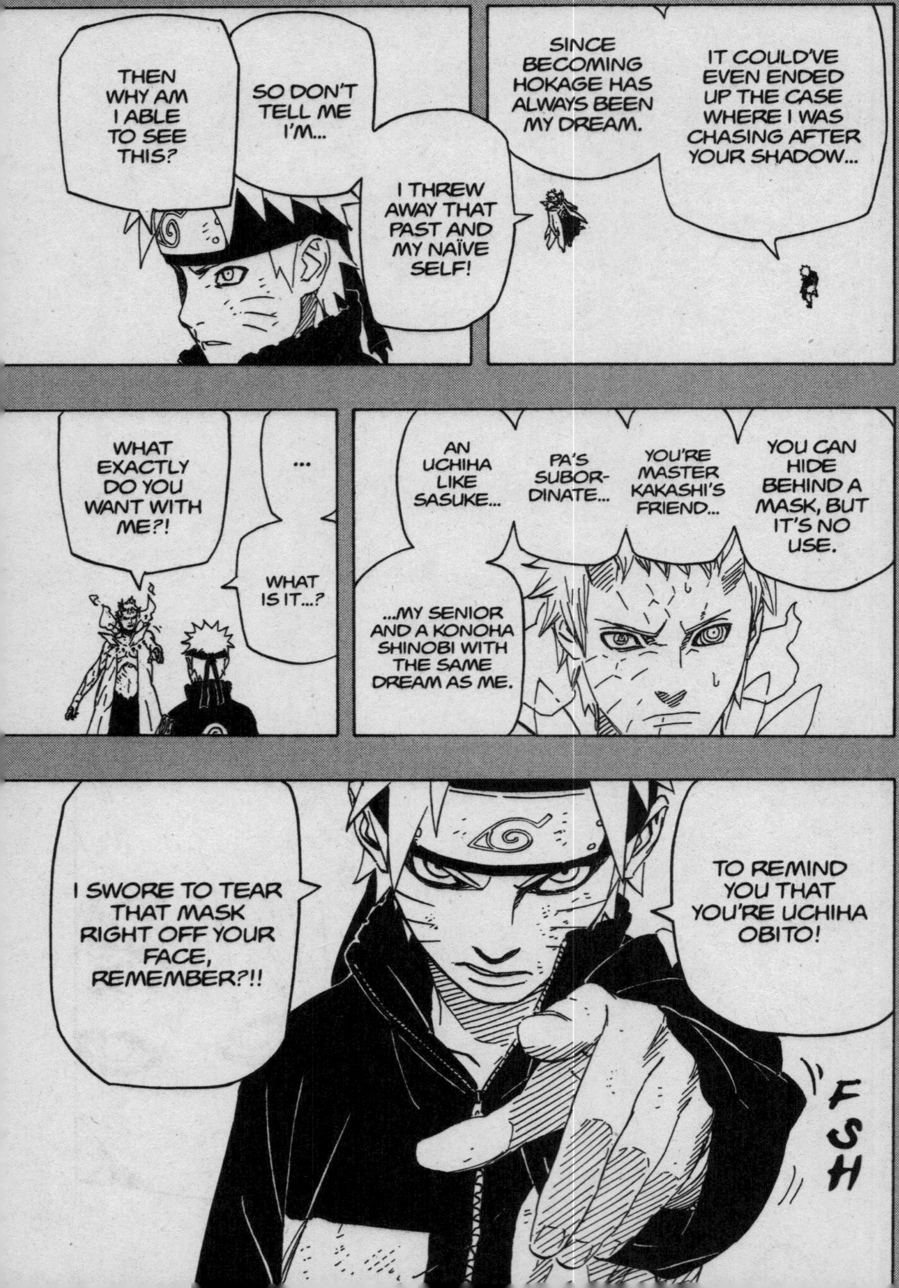
IT COULD'VE EVEN ENDED UP THE CASE WHERE I WAS CHASING AFTER YOUR SHADOW...
SINCE BECOMING HOKAGE HAS ALWAYS BEEN MY DREAM.
I THREW AWAY THAT PAST AND MY NAÏVE SELF!
SO DON'T TELL ME I'M...
THEN WHY AM I ABLE TO SEE THIS?
YOU CAN HIDE BEHIND A MASK, BUT IT'S NO USE.
YOU'RE MASTER KAKASHI'S FRIEND...
PA'S SUBOR-DINATE...
AN UCHIHA LIKE SASUKE...
...MY SENIOR AND A KONOHA SHINOBI WITH THE SAME DREAM AS ME.
...
WHAT IS IT...?
WHAT EXACTLY DO YOU WANT WITH ME?!
TO REMIND YOU THAT YOU'RE UCHIHA OBITO!
FSH
I SWORE TO TEAR THAT MASK RIGHT OFF YOUR FACE, REMEMBER?!!

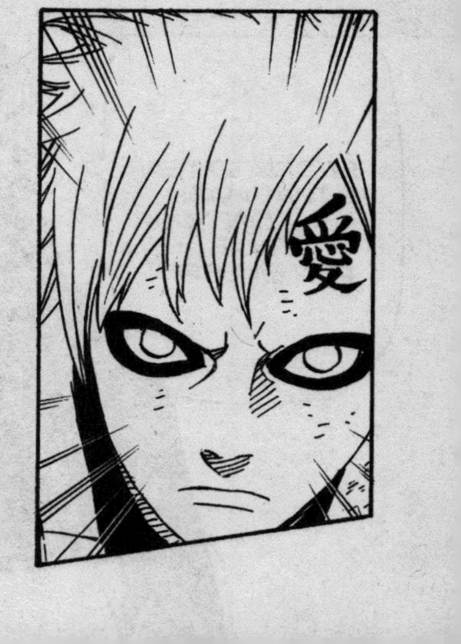
愛

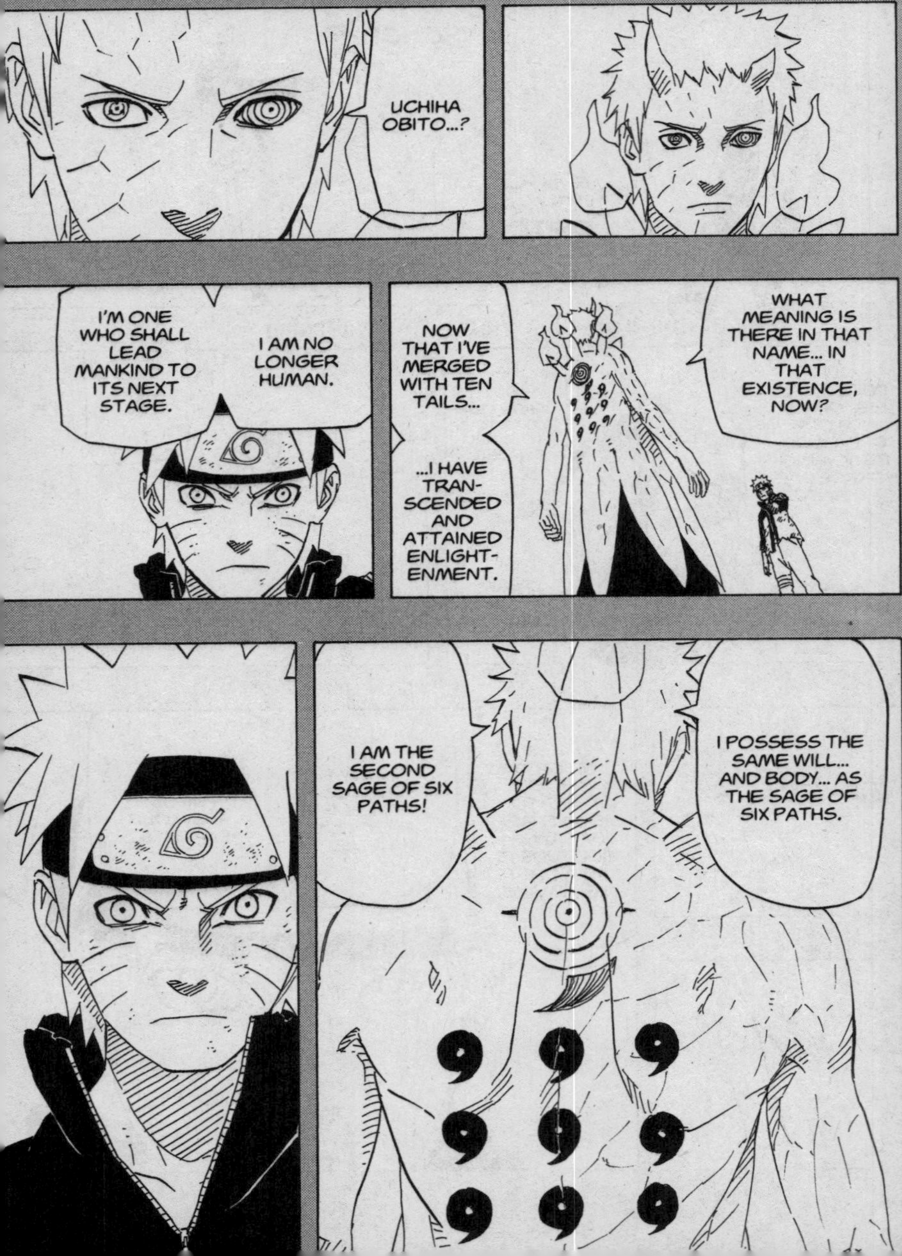
UCHIHA OBITO...?
WHAT MEANING IS THERE IN THAT NAME... IN THAT EXISTENCE, NOW?
NOW THAT I'VE MERGED WITH TEN TAILS...
...I HAVE TRANSCENDED AND ATTAINED ENLIGHTENMENT.
I AM NO LONGER HUMAN.
I'M ONE WHO SHALL LEAD MANKIND TO ITS NEXT STAGE.
I POSSESS THE SAME WILL... AND BODY... AS THE SAGE OF SIX PATHS.
I AM THE SECOND SAGE OF SIX PATHS!

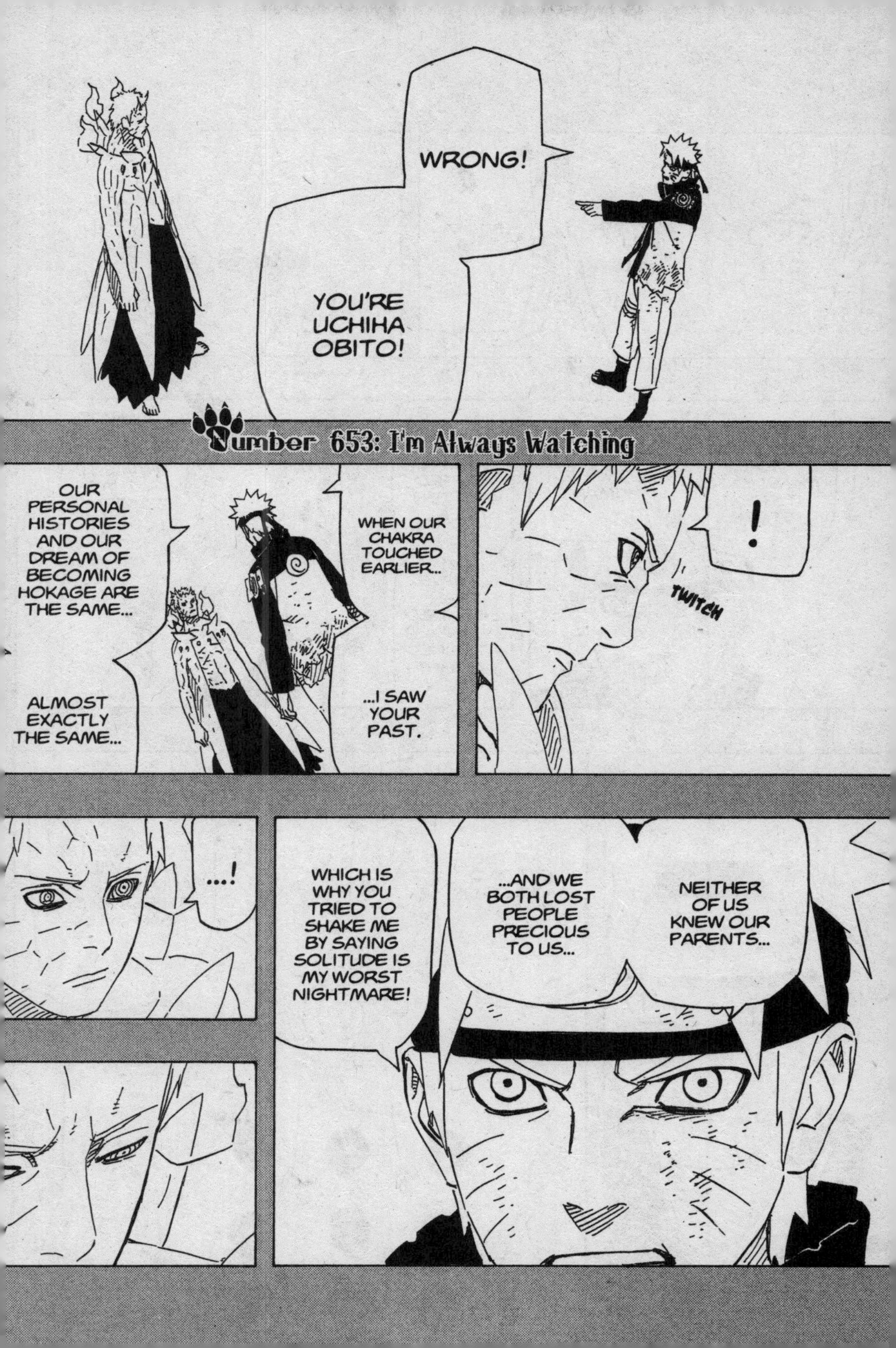
WRONG!
YOU'RE UCHIHA OBITO!
Number 653: I'm Always Watching
!
TWITCH
WHEN OUR CHAKRA TOUCHED EARLIER...
...I SAW YOUR PAST.
OUR PERSONAL HISTORIES AND OUR DREAM OF BECOMING HOKAGE ARE THE SAME...
ALMOST EXACTLY THE SAME...
NEITHER OF US KNEW OUR PARENTS...
...AND WE BOTH LOST PEOPLE PRECIOUS TO US...
WHICH IS WHY YOU TRIED TO SHAKE ME BY SAYING SOLITUDE IS MY WORST NIGHTMARE!
...!

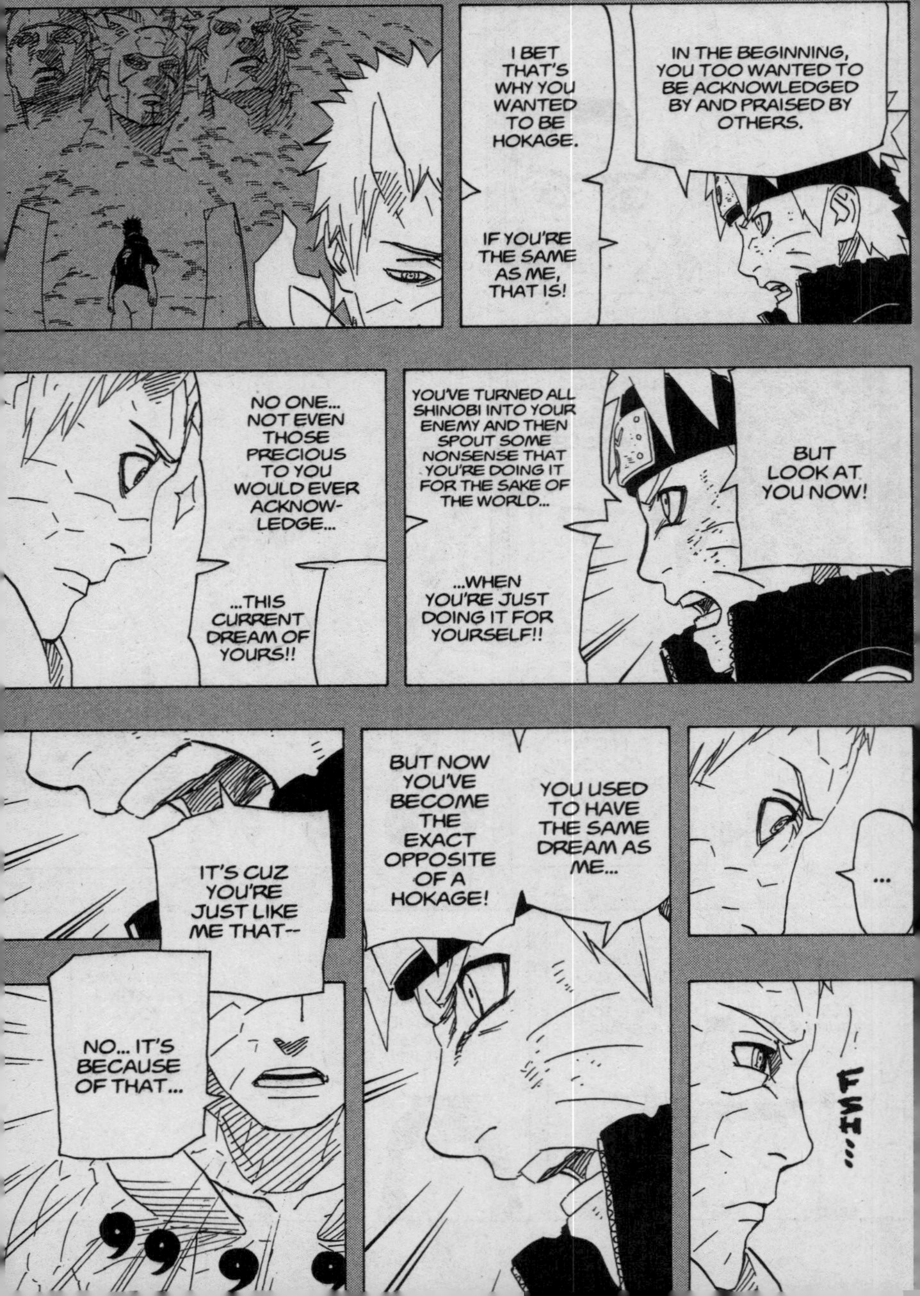
IN THE BEGINNING, YOU TOO WANTED TO BE ACKNOWLEDGED BY AND PRAISED BY OTHERS.
I BET THAT'S WHY YOU WANTED TO BE HOKAGE.
IF YOU'RE THE SAME AS ME, THAT IS!
BUT LOOK AT YOU NOW!
YOU'VE TURNED ALL SHINOBI INTO YOUR ENEMY AND THEN SPOUT SOME NONSENSE THAT YOU'RE DOING IT FOR THE SAKE OF THE WORLD...
...WHEN YOU'RE JUST DOING IT FOR YOURSELF!!
NO ONE... NOT EVEN THOSE PRECIOUS TO YOU WOULD EVER ACKNOW-LEDGE...
...THIS CURRENT DREAM OF YOURS!!
...
FSH...
YOU USED TO HAVE THE SAME DREAM AS ME...
BUT NOW YOU'VE BECOME THE EXACT OPPOSITE OF A HOKAGE!
IT'S CUZ YOU'RE JUST LIKE ME THAT--
NO... IT'S BECAUSE OF THAT...

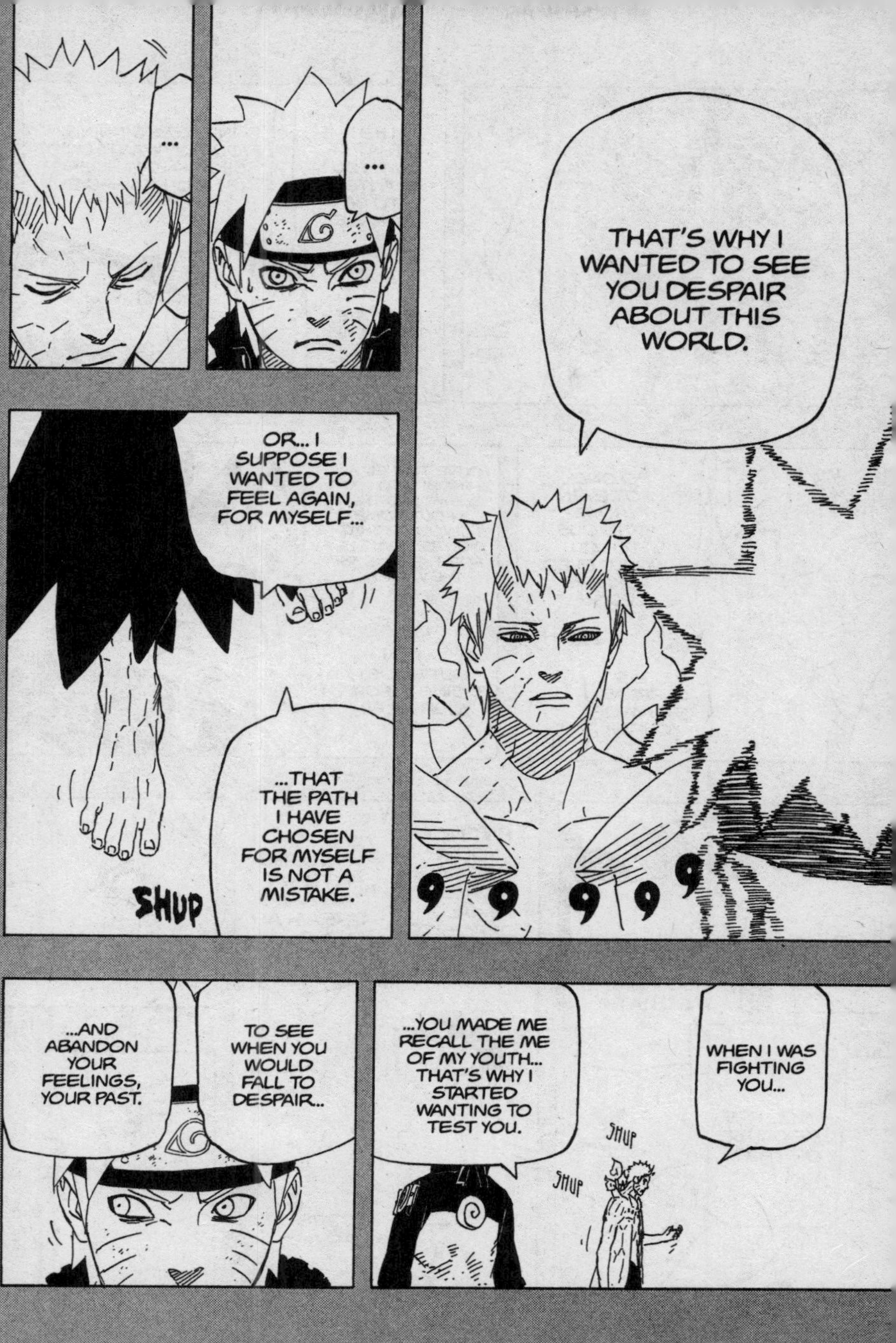
THAT'S WHY I WANTED TO SEE YOU DESPAIR ABOUT THIS WORLD.
...
...
OR... I SUPPOSE I WANTED TO FEEL AGAIN, FOR MYSELF...
...THAT THE PATH I HAVE CHOSEN FOR MYSELF IS NOT A MISTAKE.
SHUP
WHEN I WAS FIGHTING YOU...
...YOU MADE ME RECALL THE ME OF MY YOUTH... THAT'S WHY I STARTED WANTING TO TEST YOU.
SHUP
SHUP
TO SEE WHEN YOU WOULD FALL TO DESPAIR...
...AND ABANDON YOUR FEELINGS, YOUR PAST.

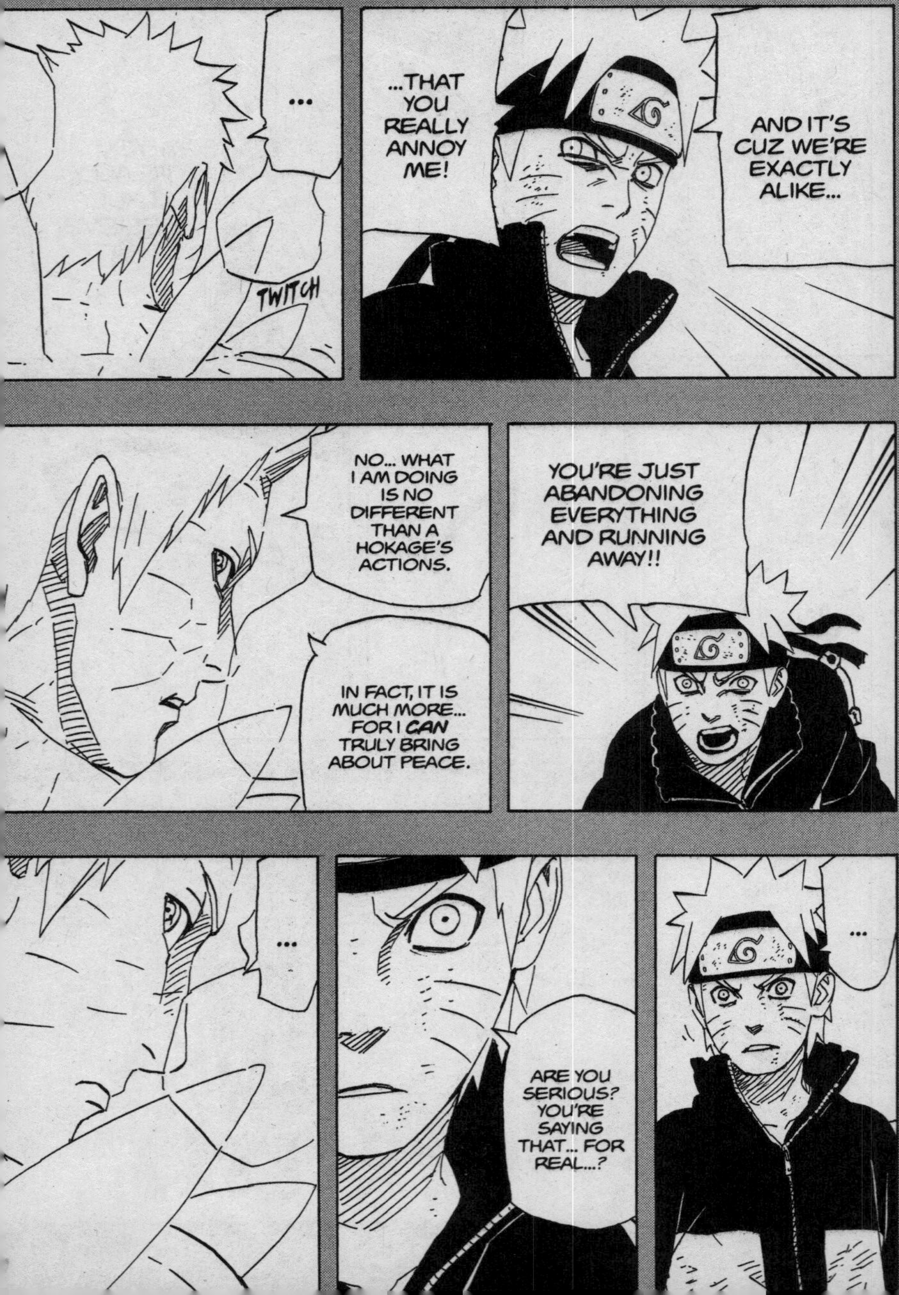
AND IT'S CUZ WE'RE EXACTLY ALIKE...
...THAT YOU REALLY ANNOY ME!
...
TWITCH
YOU'RE JUST ABANDONING EVERYTHING AND RUNNING AWAY!!
NO... WHAT I AM DOING IS NO DIFFERENT THAN A HOKAGE'S ACTIONS.
IN FACT, IT IS MUCH MORE... FOR I *CAN* TRULY BRING ABOUT PEACE.
...
ARE YOU SERIOUS? YOU'RE SAYING THAT... FOR REAL...?
...

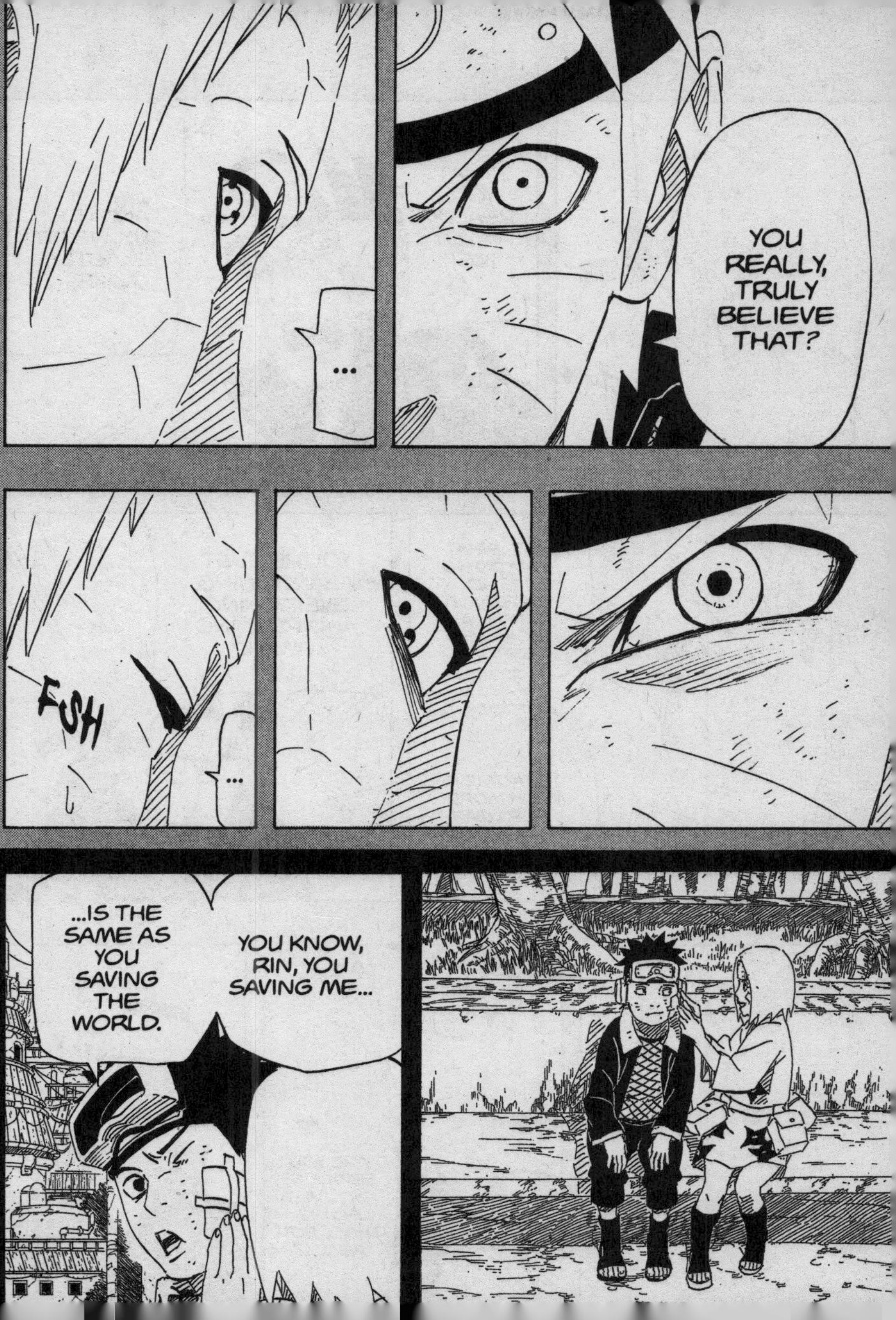
YOU REALLY, TRULY BELIEVE THAT?
...
FSH
...
YOU KNOW, RIN, YOU SAVING ME...
...IS THE SAME AS YOU SAVING THE WORLD.

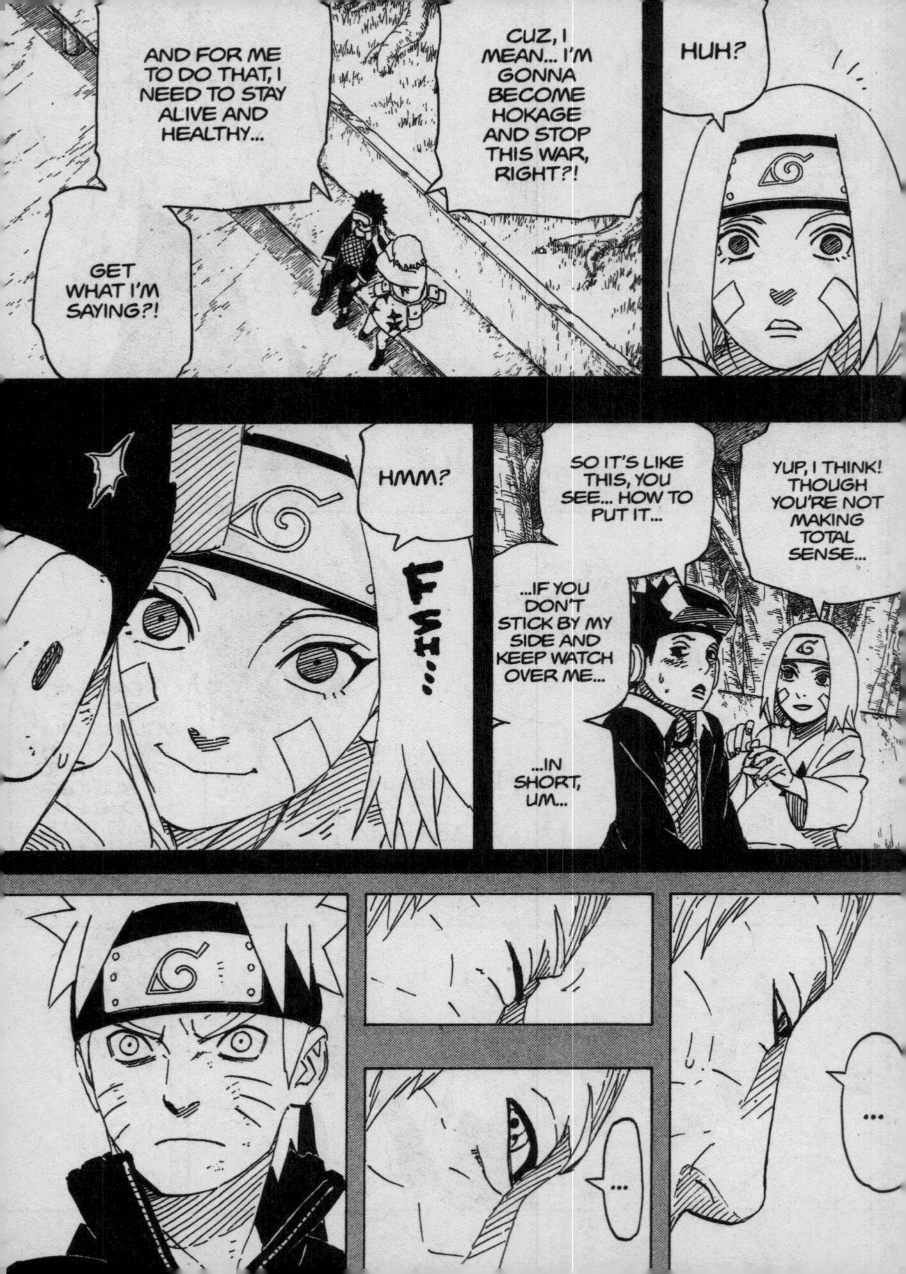
HUH?
CUZ, I MEAN... I'M GONNA BECOME HOKAGE AND STOP THIS WAR, RIGHT?!
AND FOR ME TO DO THAT, I NEED TO STAY ALIVE AND HEALTHY...
GET WHAT I'M SAYING?!
YUP, I THINK! THOUGH YOU'RE NOT MAKING TOTAL SENSE...
SO IT'S LIKE THIS, YOU SEE... HOW TO PUT IT...
...IF YOU DON'T STICK BY MY SIDE AND KEEP WATCH OVER ME...
...IN SHORT, UM...
HMM?
FSH..
...
...

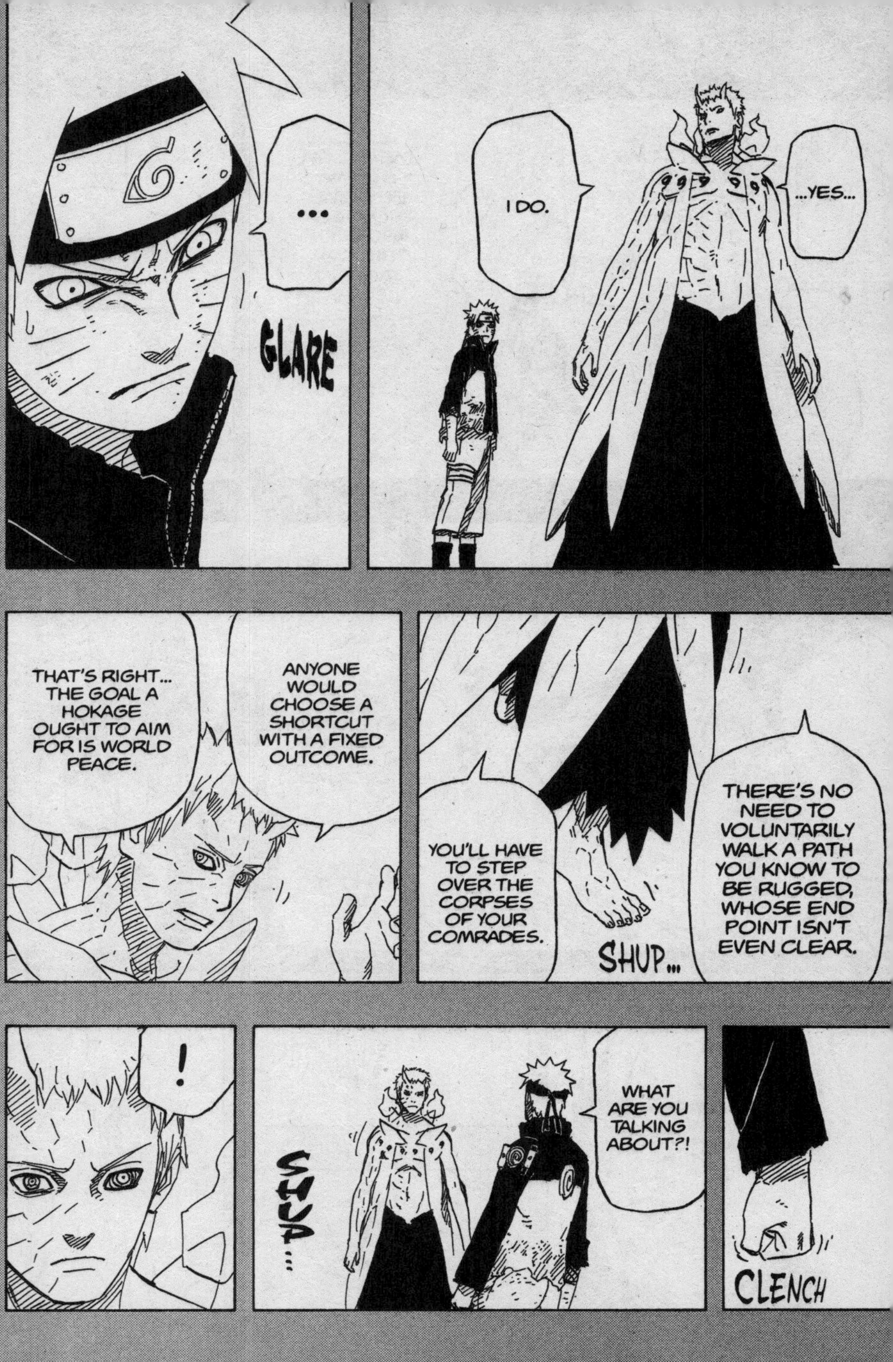
...YES...
I DO.
...
GLARE
THERE'S NO NEED TO VOLUNTARILY WALK A PATH YOU KNOW TO BE RUGGED, WHOSE END POINT ISN'T EVEN CLEAR.
YOU'LL HAVE TO STEP OVER THE CORPSES OF YOUR COMRADES.
SHUP...
ANYONE WOULD CHOOSE A SHORTCUT WITH A FIXED OUTCOME.
THAT'S RIGHT... THE GOAL A HOKAGE OUGHT TO AIM FOR IS WORLD PEACE.
CLENCH
WHAT ARE YOU TALKING ABOUT?!
SHUP...
!

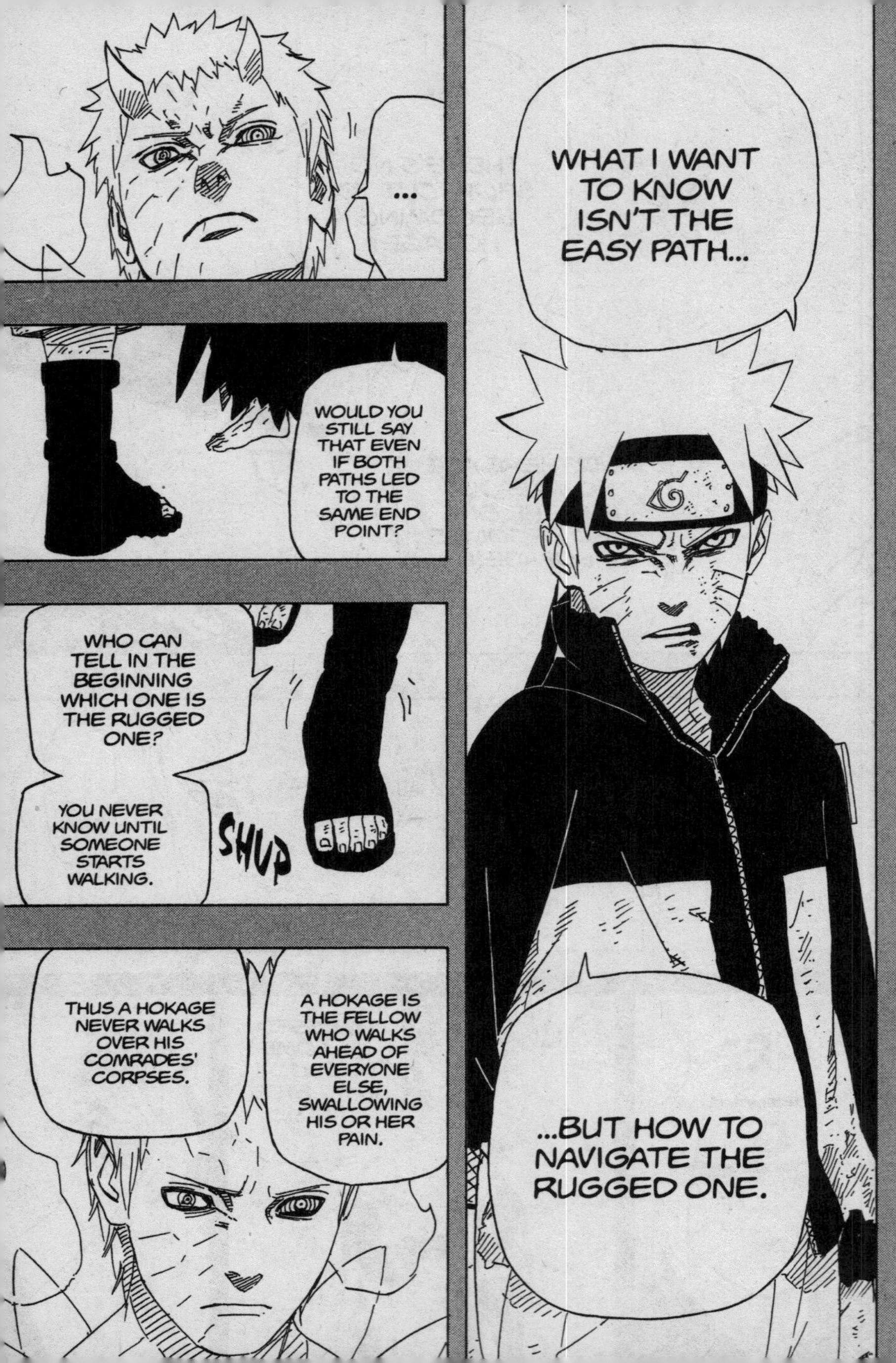
WHAT I WANT TO KNOW ISN'T THE EASY PATH...
...BUT HOW TO NAVIGATE THE RUGGED ONE.
...
WOULD YOU STILL SAY THAT EVEN IF BOTH PATHS LED TO THE SAME END POINT?
WHO CAN TELL IN THE BEGINNING WHICH ONE IS THE RUGGED ONE?
YOU NEVER KNOW UNTIL SOMEONE STARTS WALKING.
SHUP
A HOKAGE IS THE FELLOW WHO WALKS AHEAD OF EVERYONE ELSE, SWALLOWING HIS OR HER PAIN.
THUS A HOKAGE NEVER WALKS OVER HIS COMRADES' CORPSES.

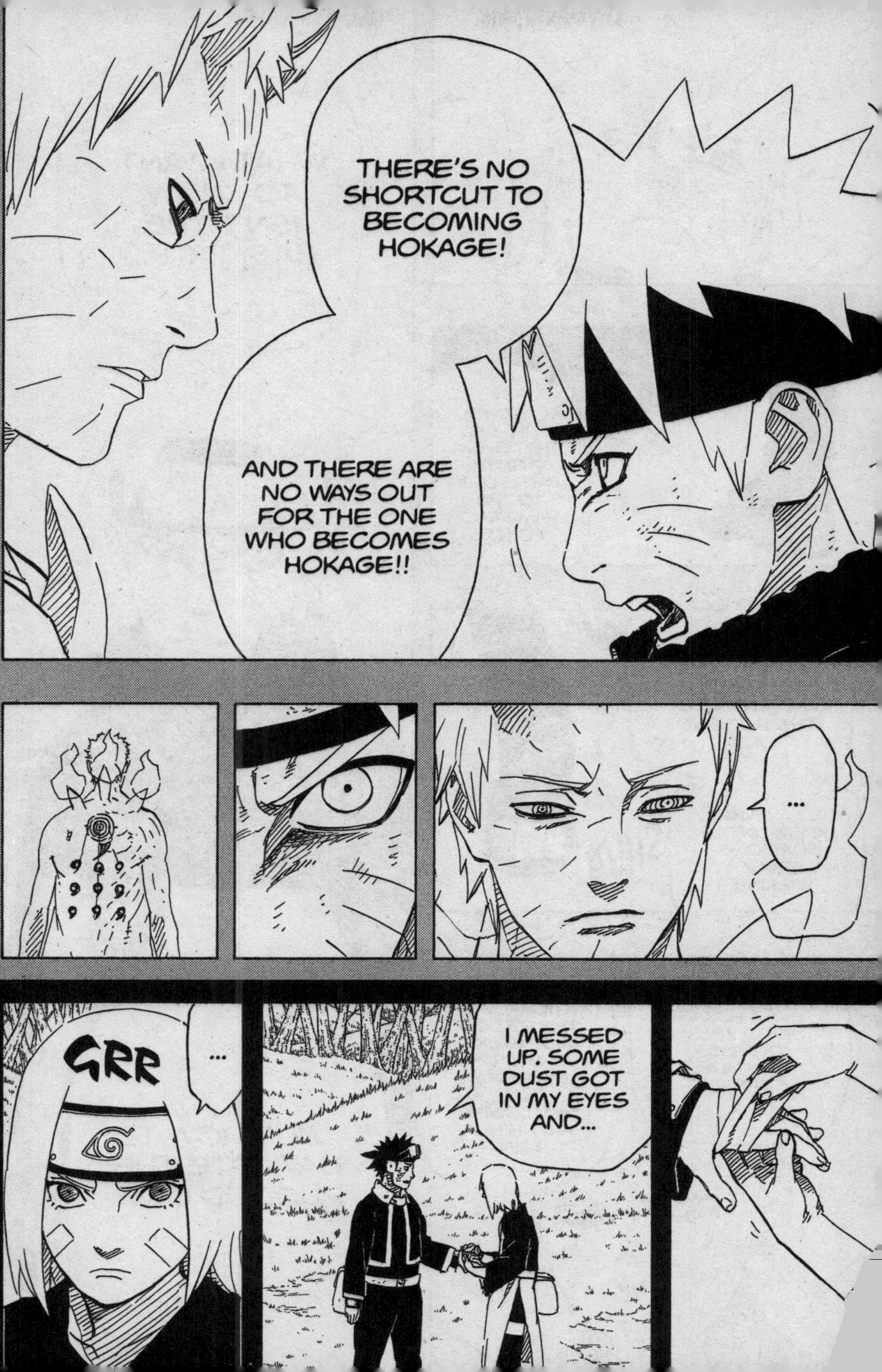
THERE'S NO SHORTCUT TO BECOMING HOKAGE!
AND THERE ARE NO WAYS OUT FOR THE ONE WHO BECOMES HOKAGE!!
...
I MESSED UP. SOME DUST GOT IN MY EYES AND...
...
GRR

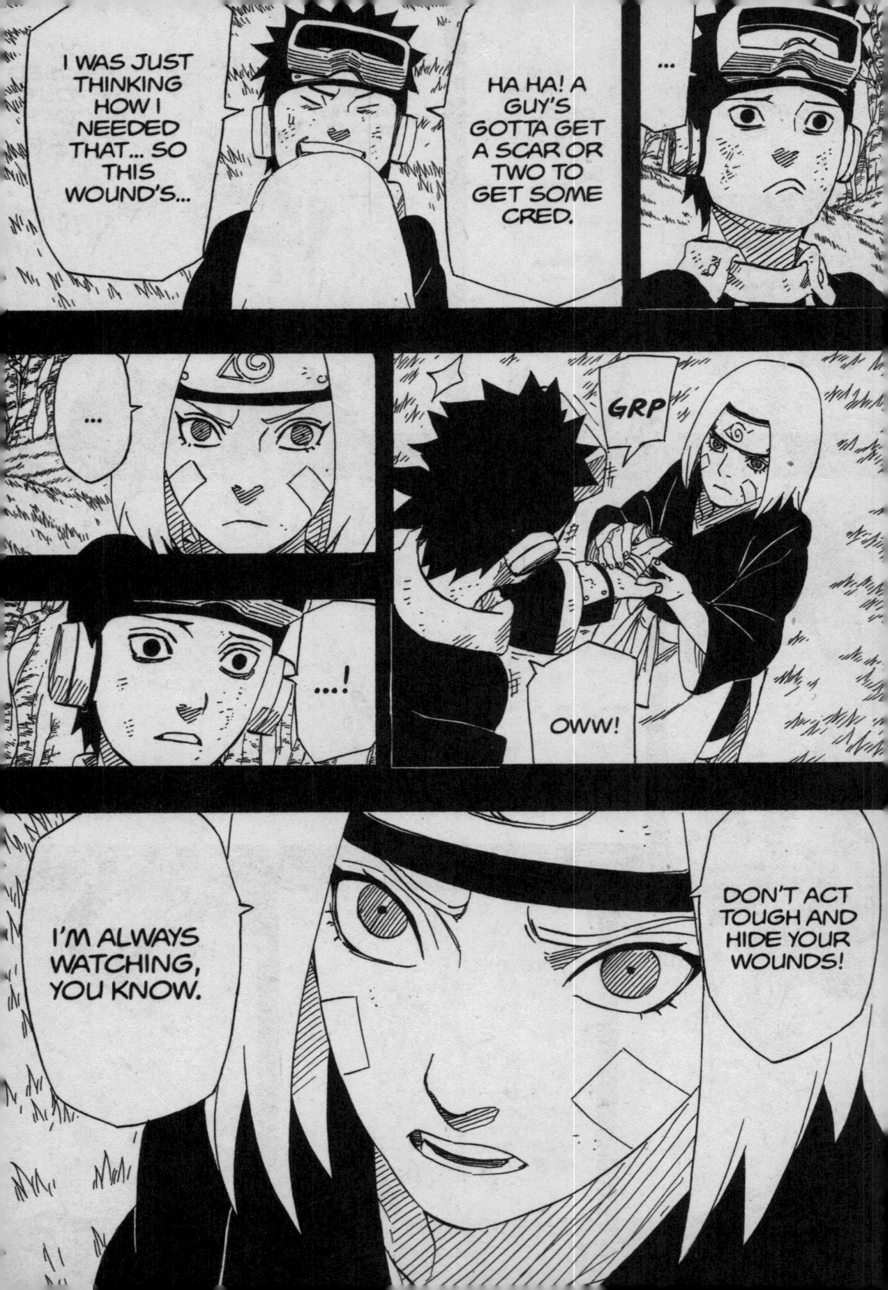
...
HA HA! A GUY'S GOTTA GET A SCAR OR TWO TO GET SOME CRED.
I WAS JUST THINKING HOW I NEEDED THAT... SO THIS WOUND'S...
GRP
OWW!
...
...!
DON'T ACT TOUGH AND HIDE YOUR WOUNDS!
I'M ALWAYS WATCHING, YOU KNOW.

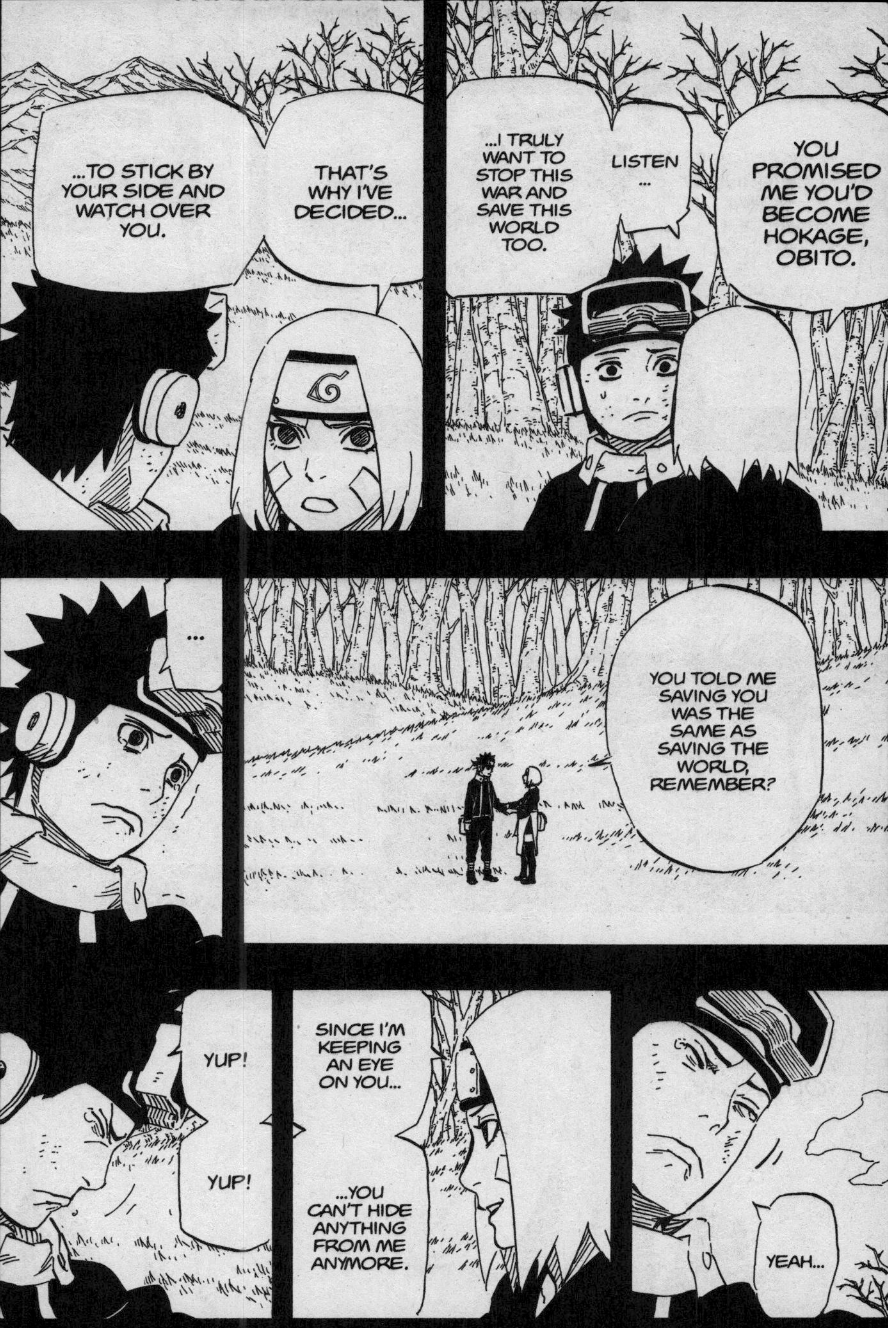
YOU PROMISED ME YOU'D BECOME HOKAGE, OBITO.
LISTEN...
...I TRULY WANT TO STOP THIS WAR AND SAVE THIS WORLD TOO.
THAT'S WHY I'VE DECIDED...
...TO STICK BY YOUR SIDE AND WATCH OVER YOU.
YOU TOLD ME SAVING YOU WAS THE SAME AS SAVING THE WORLD, REMEMBER?
...
YEAH...
SINCE I'M KEEPING AN EYE ON YOU...
...YOU CAN'T HIDE ANYTHING FROM ME ANYMORE.
YUP!
YUP!

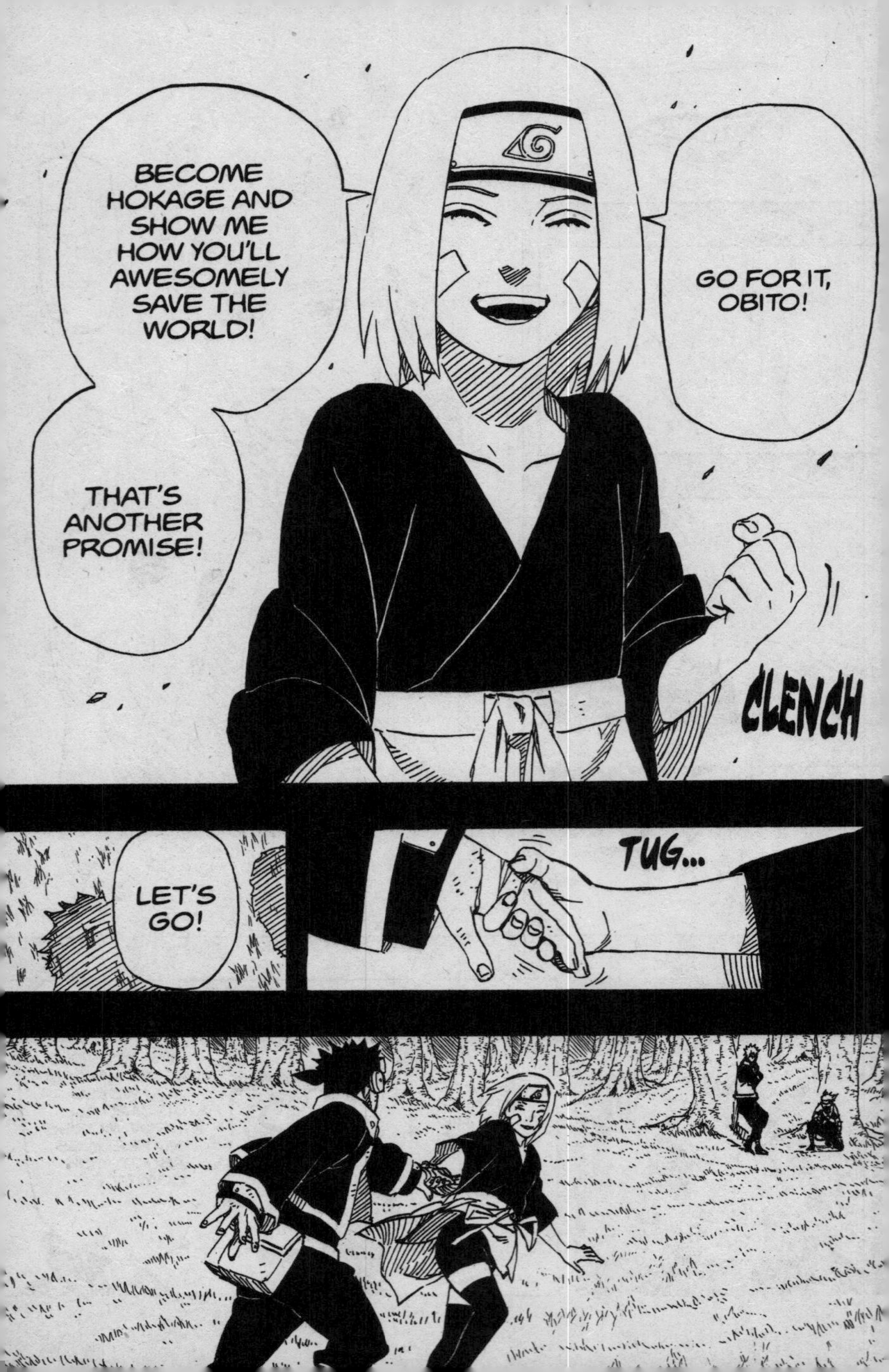
GO FOR IT, OBITO!
BECOME HOKAGE AND SHOW ME HOW YOU'LL AWESOMELY SAVE THE WORLD!
THAT'S ANOTHER PROMISE!
CLENCH
TUG...
LET'S GO!

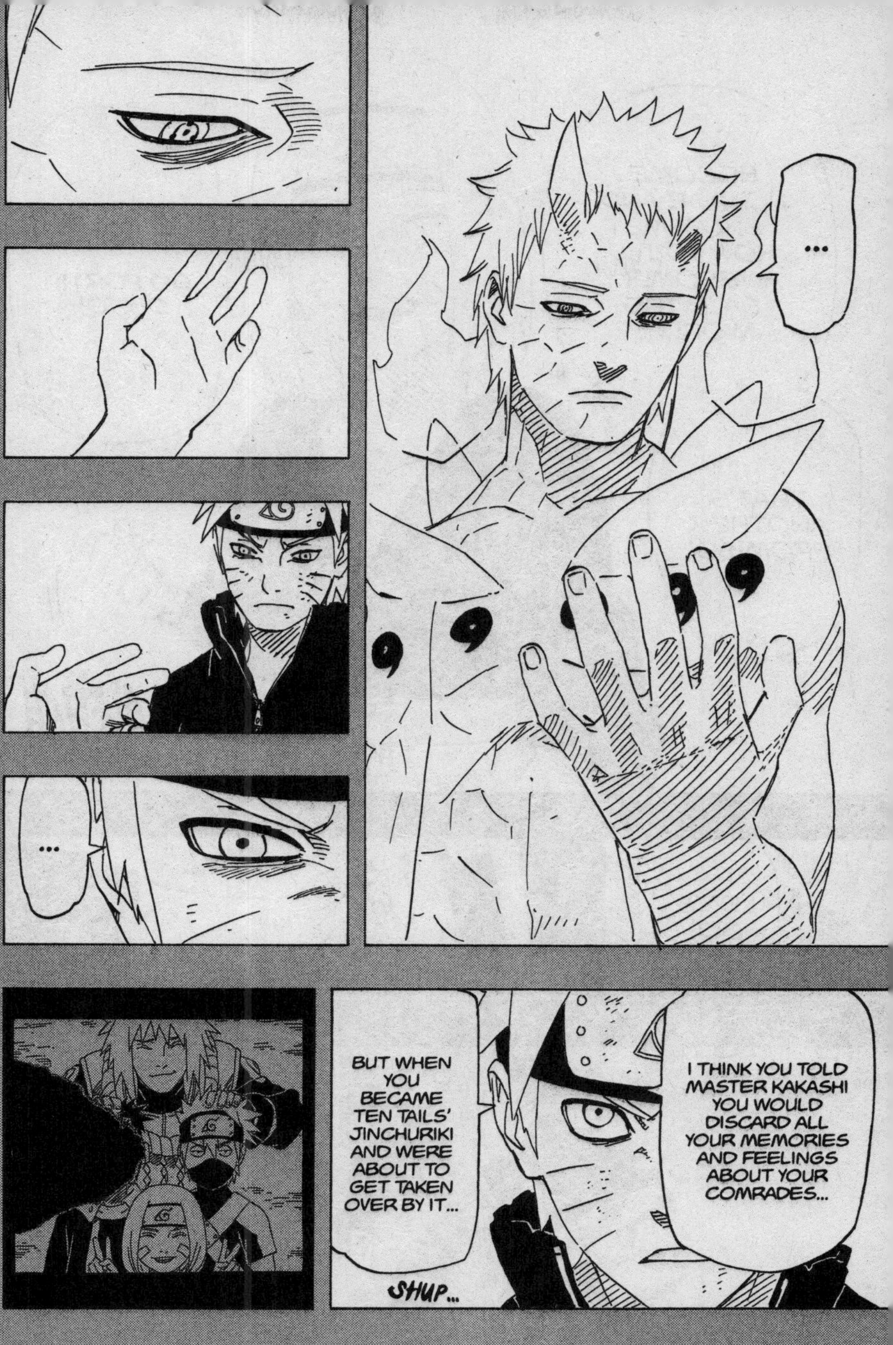
...
...
I THINK YOU TOLD MASTER KAKASHI YOU WOULD DISCARD ALL YOUR MEMORIES AND FEELINGS ABOUT YOUR COMRADES...
BUT WHEN YOU BECAME TEN TAILS' JINCHURIKI AND WERE ABOUT TO GET TAKEN OVER BY IT...
SHUP...

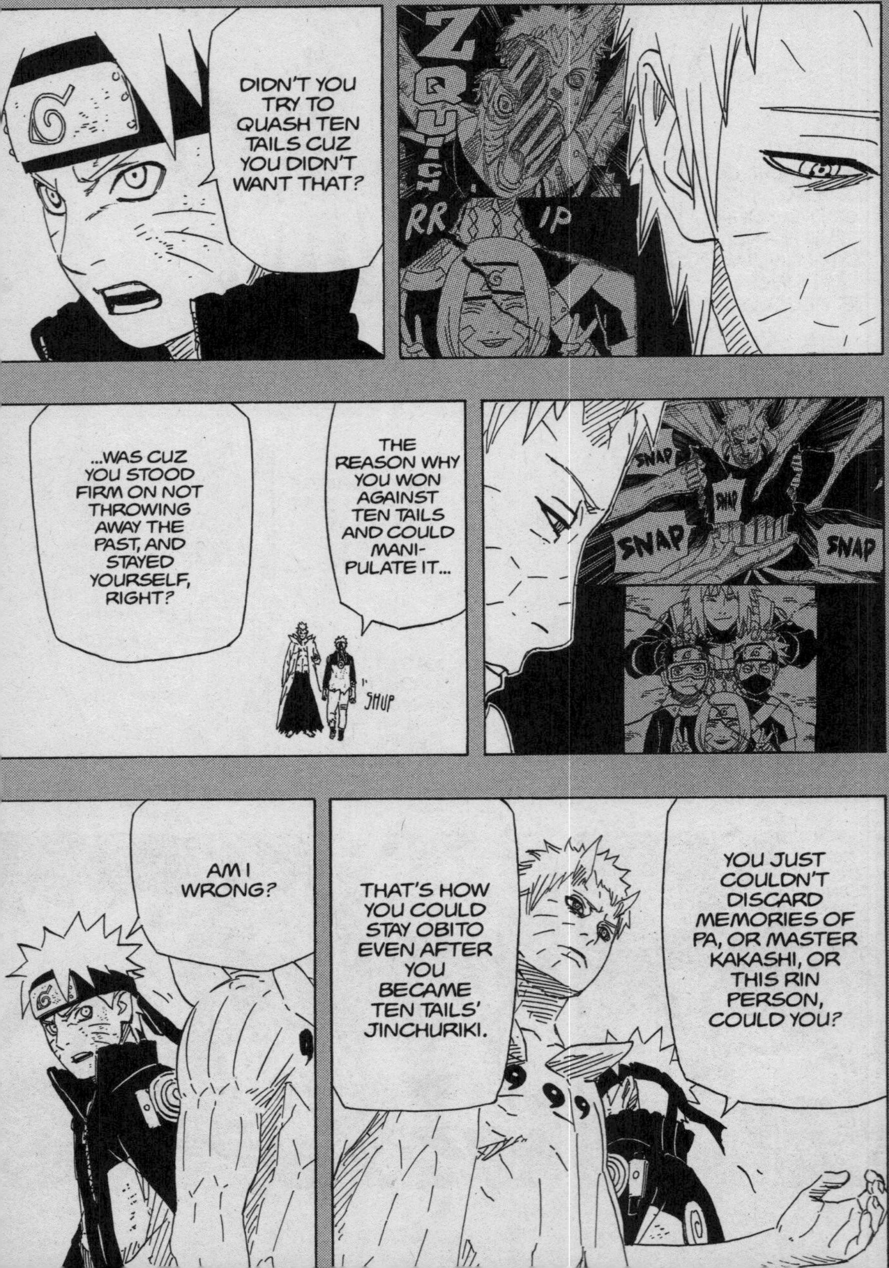
ZQUICH
RRIP
DIDN'T YOU TRY TO QUASH TEN TAILS CUZ YOU DIDN'T WANT THAT?
SNAP SNAP SNAP SNAP
THE REASON WHY YOU WON AGAINST TEN TAILS AND COULD MANI-PULATE IT...
...WAS CUZ YOU STOOD FIRM ON NOT THROWING AWAY THE PAST, AND STAYED YOURSELF, RIGHT?
SHUP
YOU JUST COULDN'T DISCARD MEMORIES OF PA, OR MASTER KAKASHI, OR THIS RIN PERSON, COULD YOU?
THAT'S HOW YOU COULD STAY OBITO EVEN AFTER YOU BECAME TEN TAILS' JINCHURIKI.
AM I WRONG?

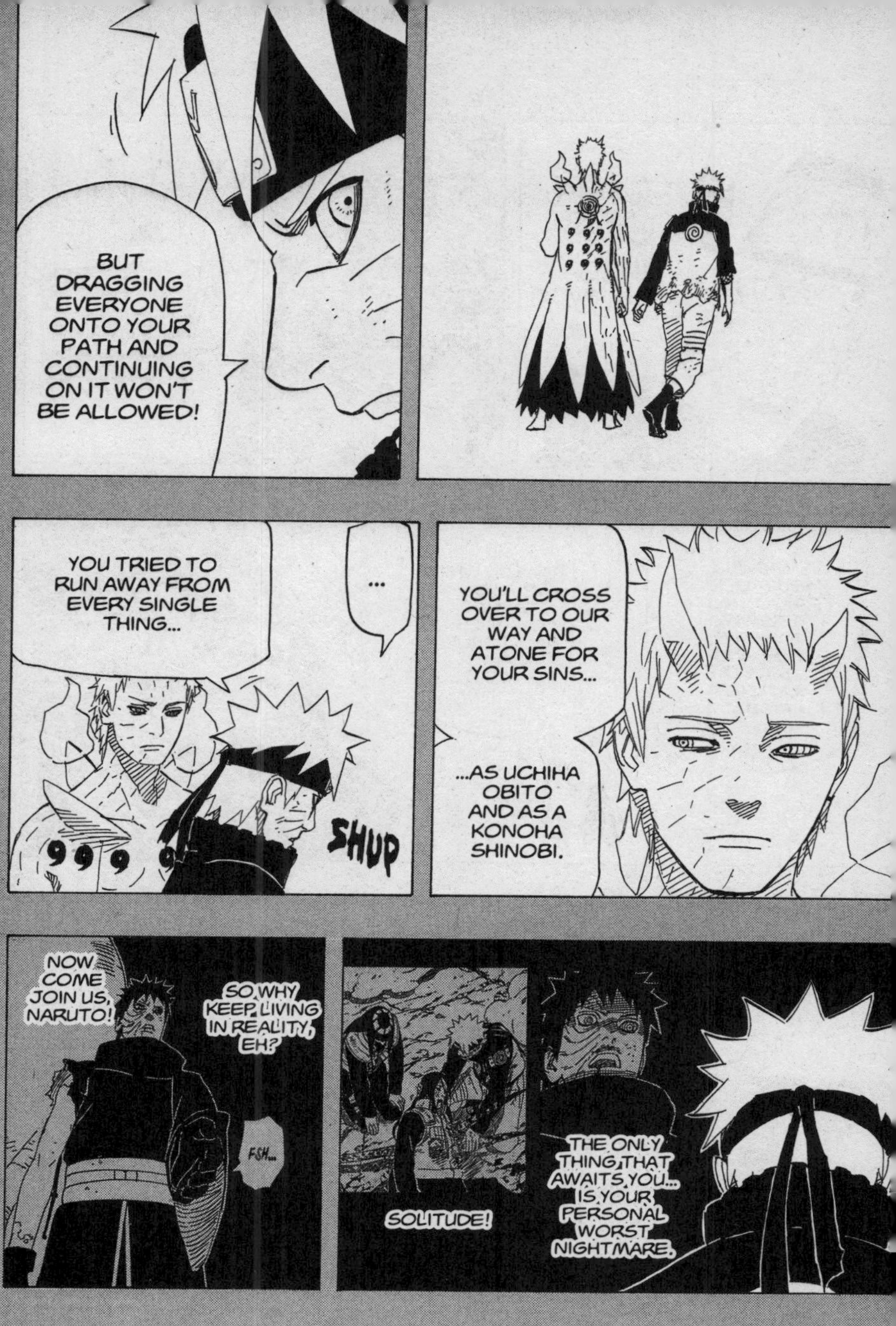
BUT DRAGGING EVERYONE ONTO YOUR PATH AND CONTINUING ON IT WON'T BE ALLOWED!
YOU'LL CROSS OVER TO OUR WAY AND ATONE FOR YOUR SINS...
...AS UCHIHA OBITO AND AS A KONOHA SHINOBI.
...
YOU TRIED TO RUN AWAY FROM EVERY SINGLE THING...
SHUP
THE ONLY THING THAT AWAITS YOU... IS YOUR PERSONAL WORST NIGHTMARE.
SOLITUDE!
SO WHY KEEP LIVING IN REALITY, EH?
NOW COME JOIN US, NARUTO!
FSH...

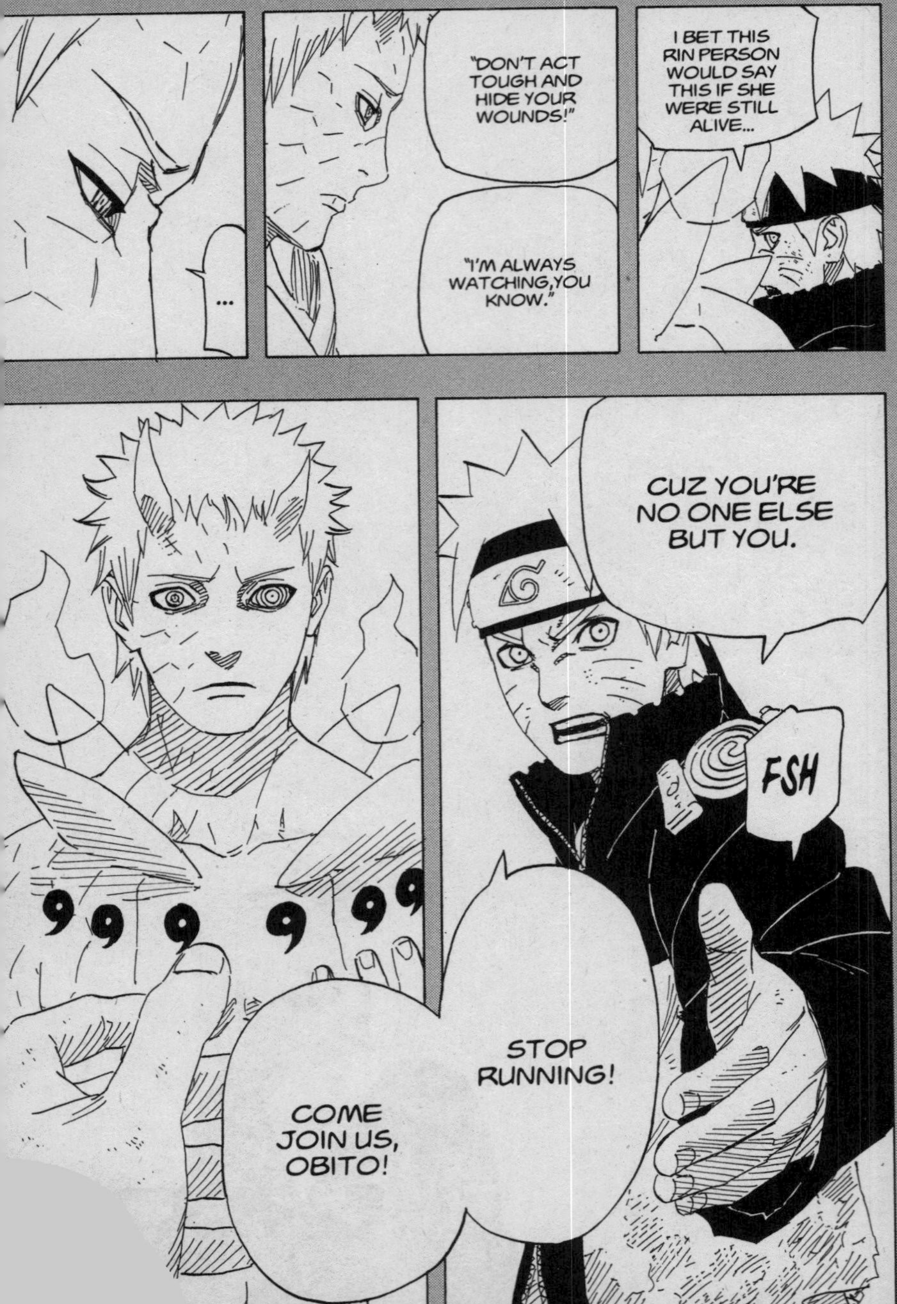
I BET THIS RIN PERSON WOULD SAY THIS IF SHE WERE STILL ALIVE...
"DON'T ACT TOUGH AND HIDE YOUR WOUNDS!"
"I'M ALWAYS WATCHING,YOU KNOW."
...
CUZ YOU'RE NO ONE ELSE BUT YOU.
FSH
STOP RUNNING!
COME JOIN US, OBITO!

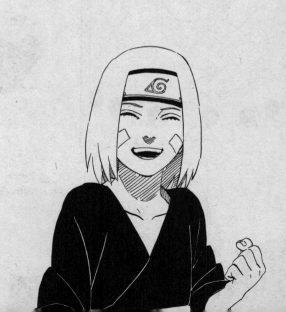

Number 654: I'm Uchiha Obito

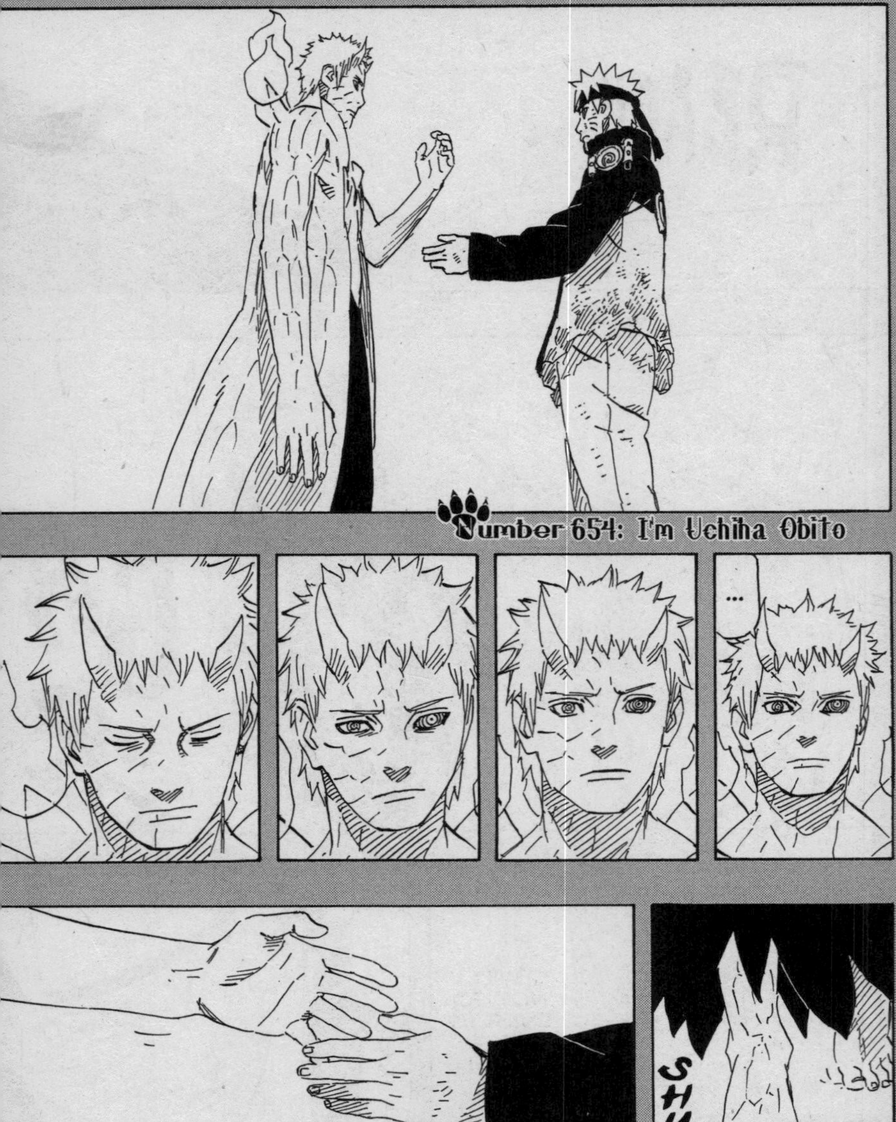
...
SHUP

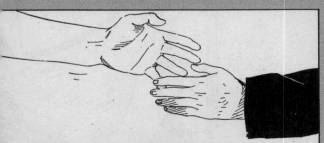

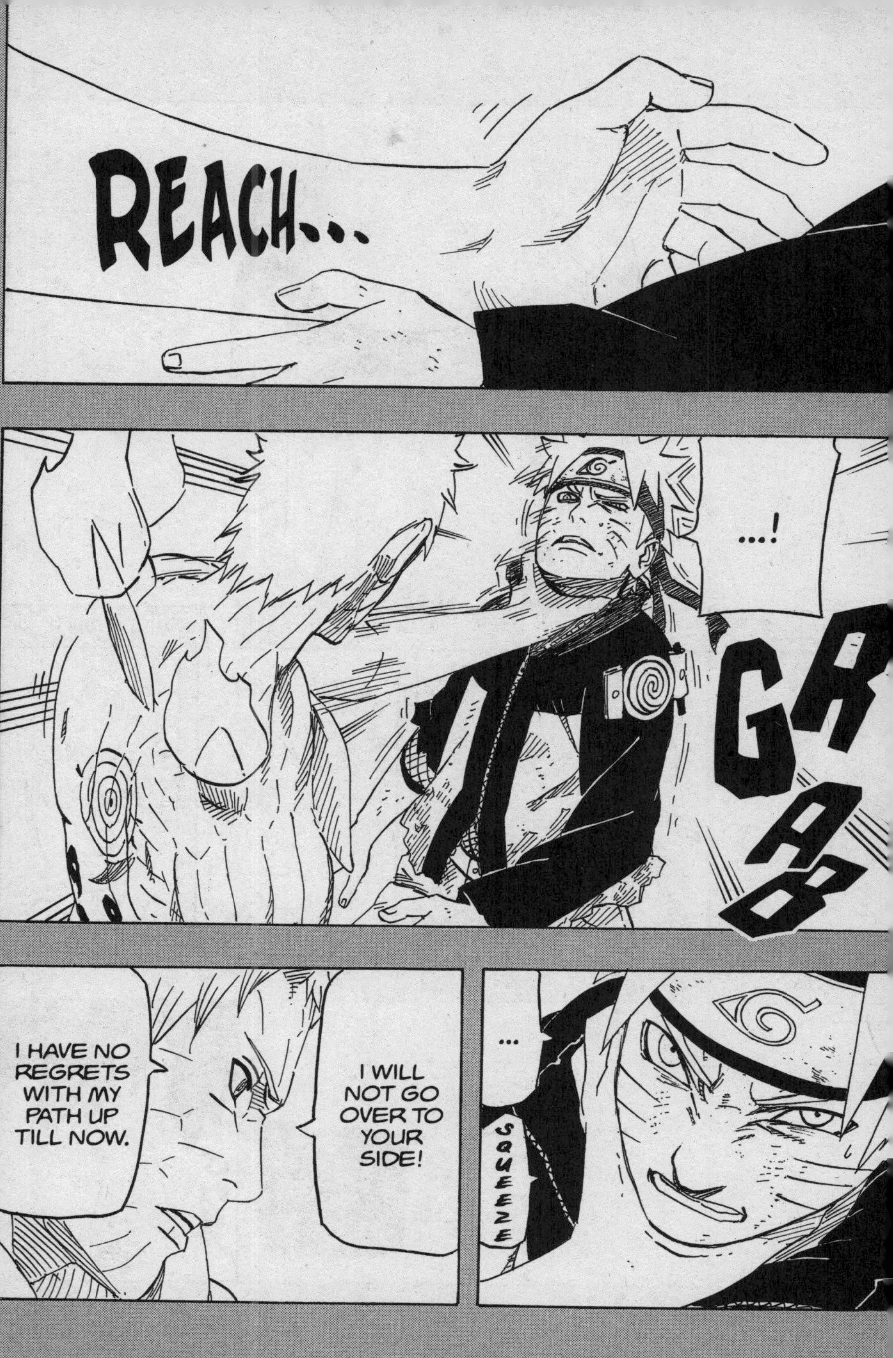
REACH...
...!
GRAB
...
SQUEEZE
I WILL NOT GO OVER TO YOUR SIDE!
I HAVE NO REGRETS WITH MY PATH UP TILL NOW.

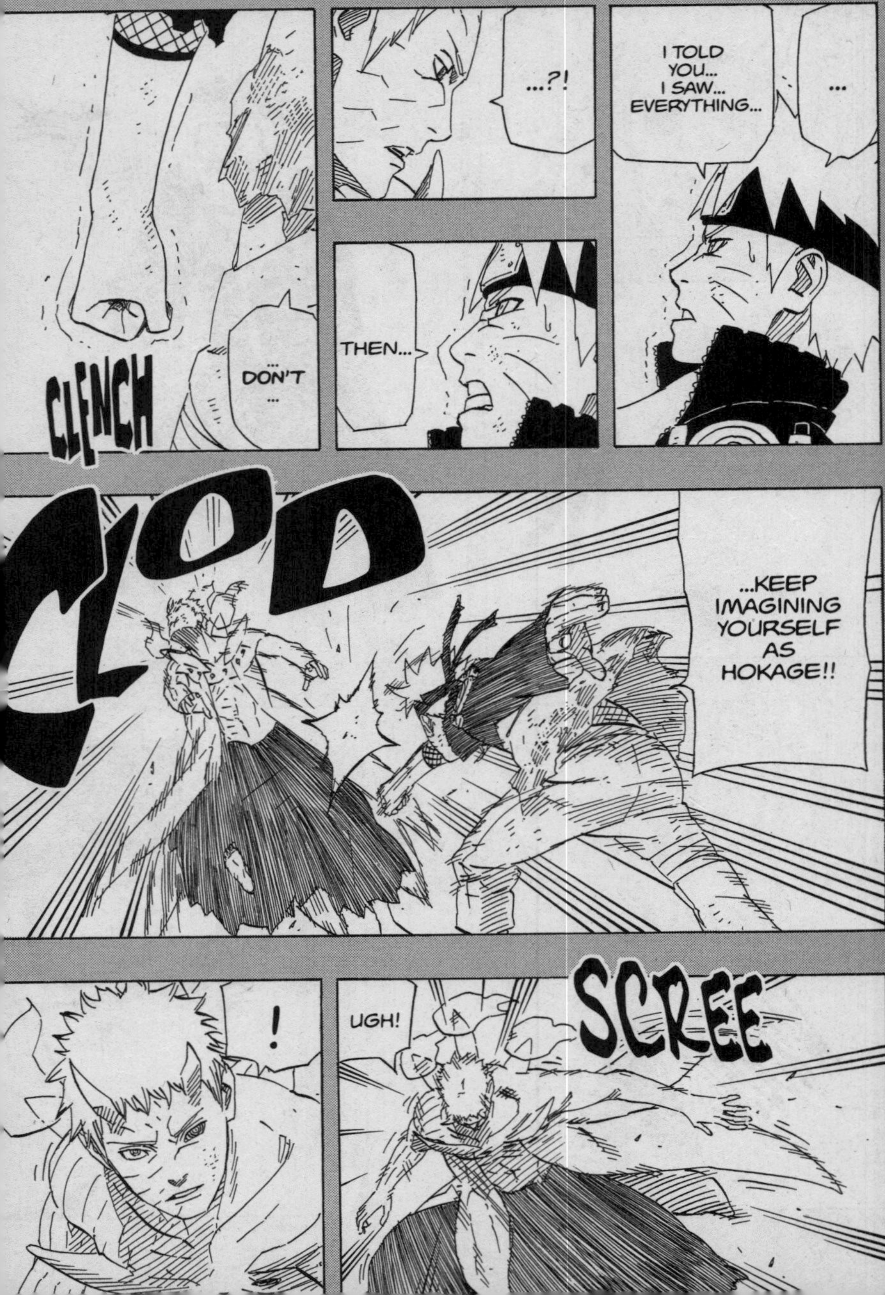
...
I TOLD YOU... I SAW... EVERYTHING...
...?!
THEN...
... DON'T ...
CLENCH
...KEEP IMAGINING YOURSELF AS HOKAGE!!
CLOD
SCREE
UGH!
!

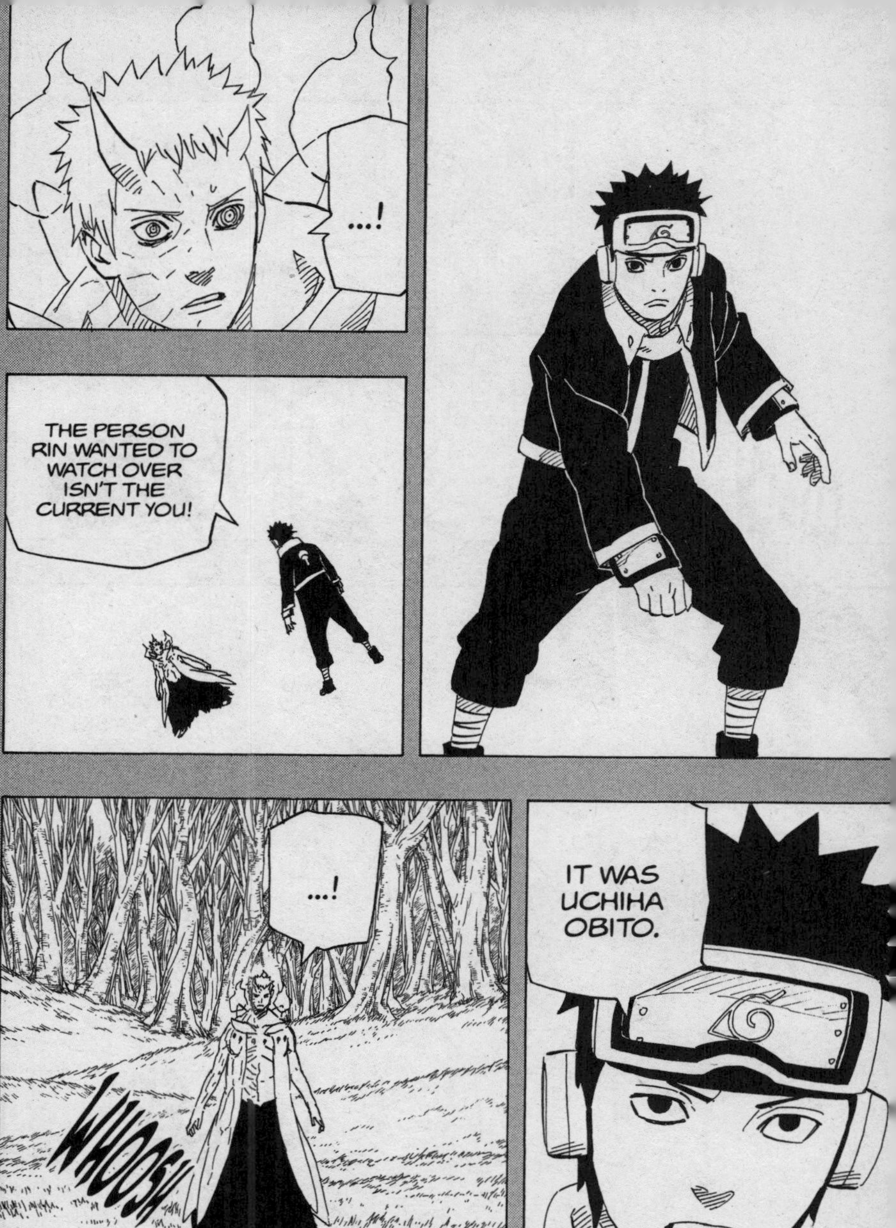
...!
THE PERSON RIN WANTED TO WATCH OVER ISN'T THE CURRENT YOU!
IT WAS UCHIHA OBITO.
...!
WHOOSH

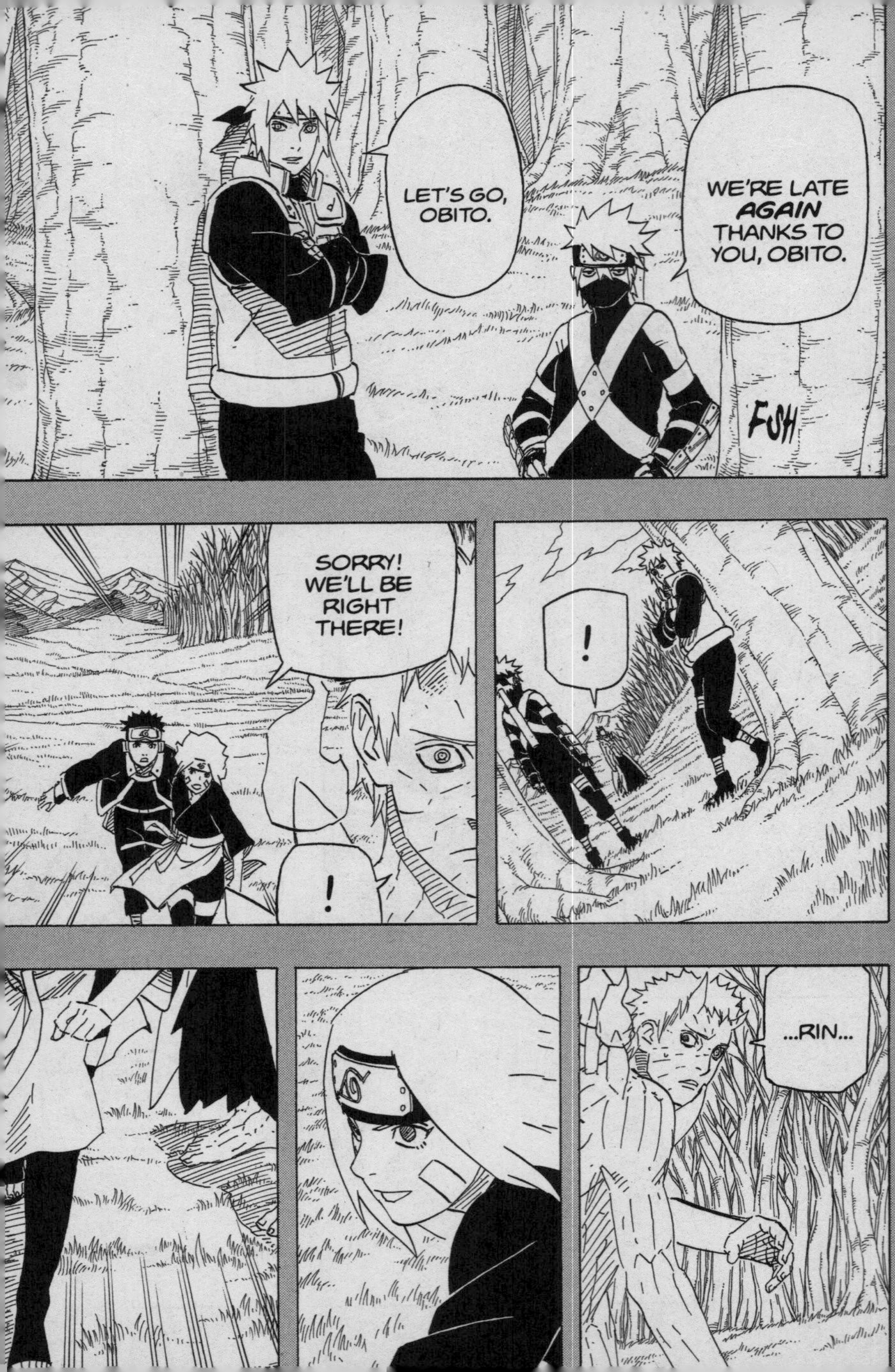
WE'RE LATE *AGAIN* THANKS TO YOU, OBITO.
LET'S GO, OBITO.
FSH
!
SORRY! WE'LL BE RIGHT THERE!
!
...RIN...

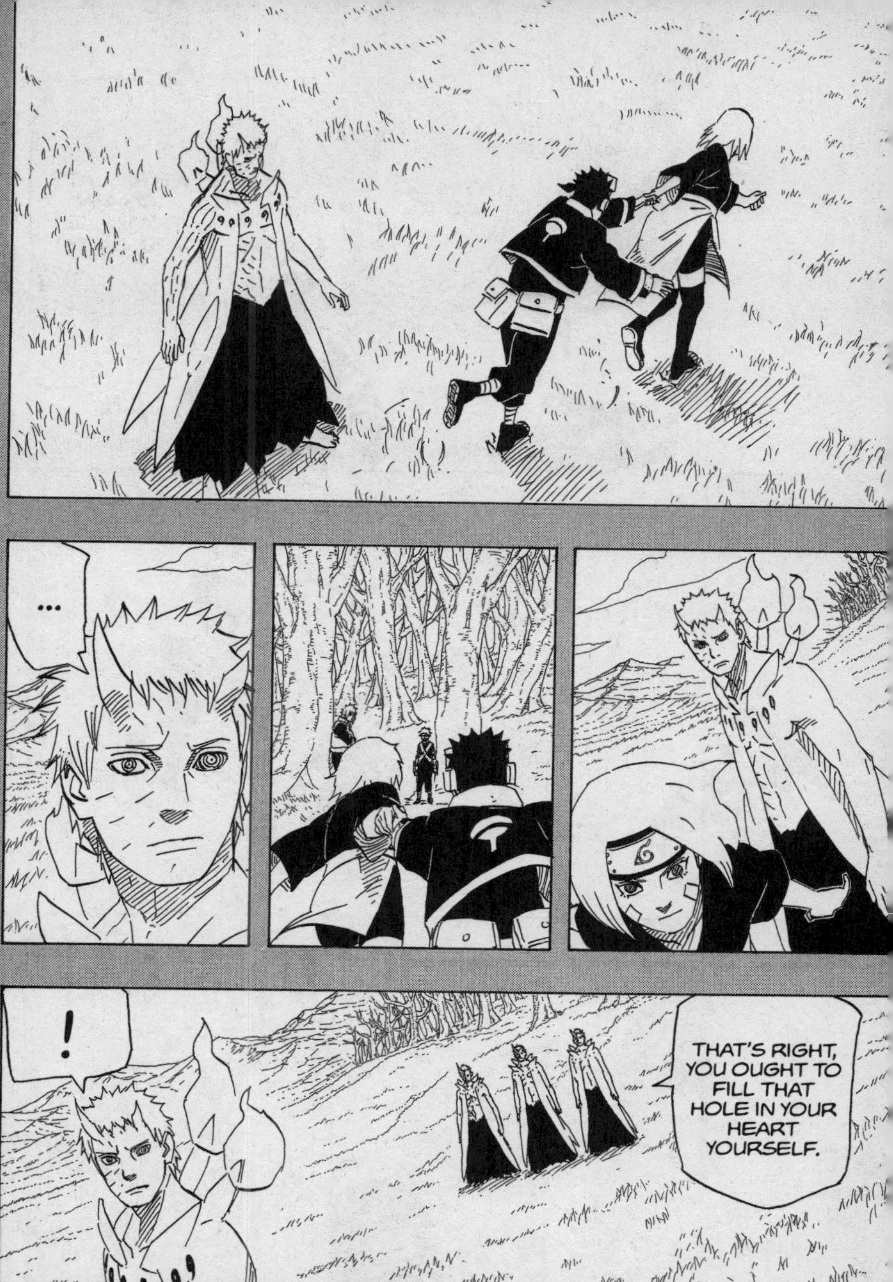
...
THAT'S RIGHT, YOU OUGHT TO FILL THAT HOLE IN YOUR HEART YOURSELF.
!

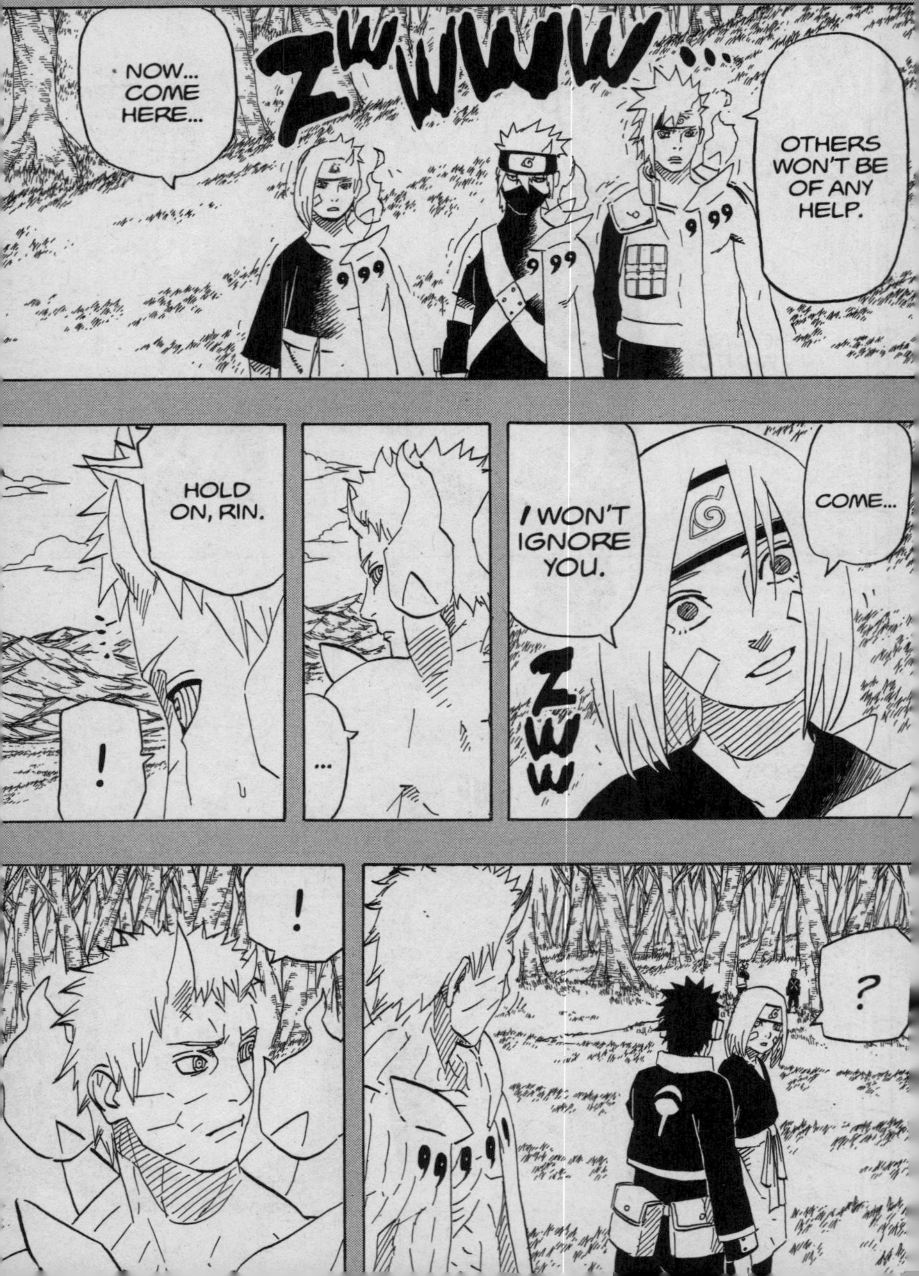
OTHERS WON'T BE OF ANY HELP.
ZWWWW...
NOW... COME HERE...
COME...
I WON'T IGNORE YOU.
ZWWW
...
HOLD ON, RIN.
!
?
!

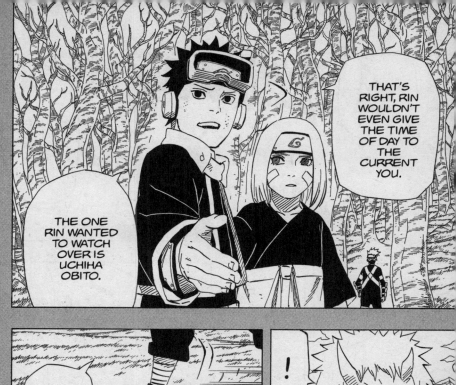

THAT'S RIGHT, RIN WOULDN'T EVEN GIVE THE TIME OF DAY TO THE CURRENT YOU.

THE ONE RIN WANTED TO WATCH OVER IS UCHIHA OBITO.

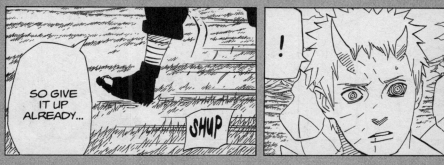

SO GIVE IT UP ALREADY...

SHUP

!

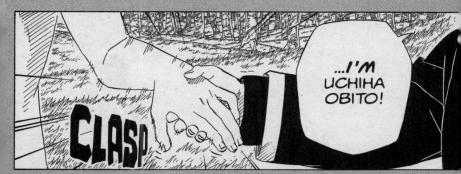

...I'M UCHIHA OBITO!

CLASP

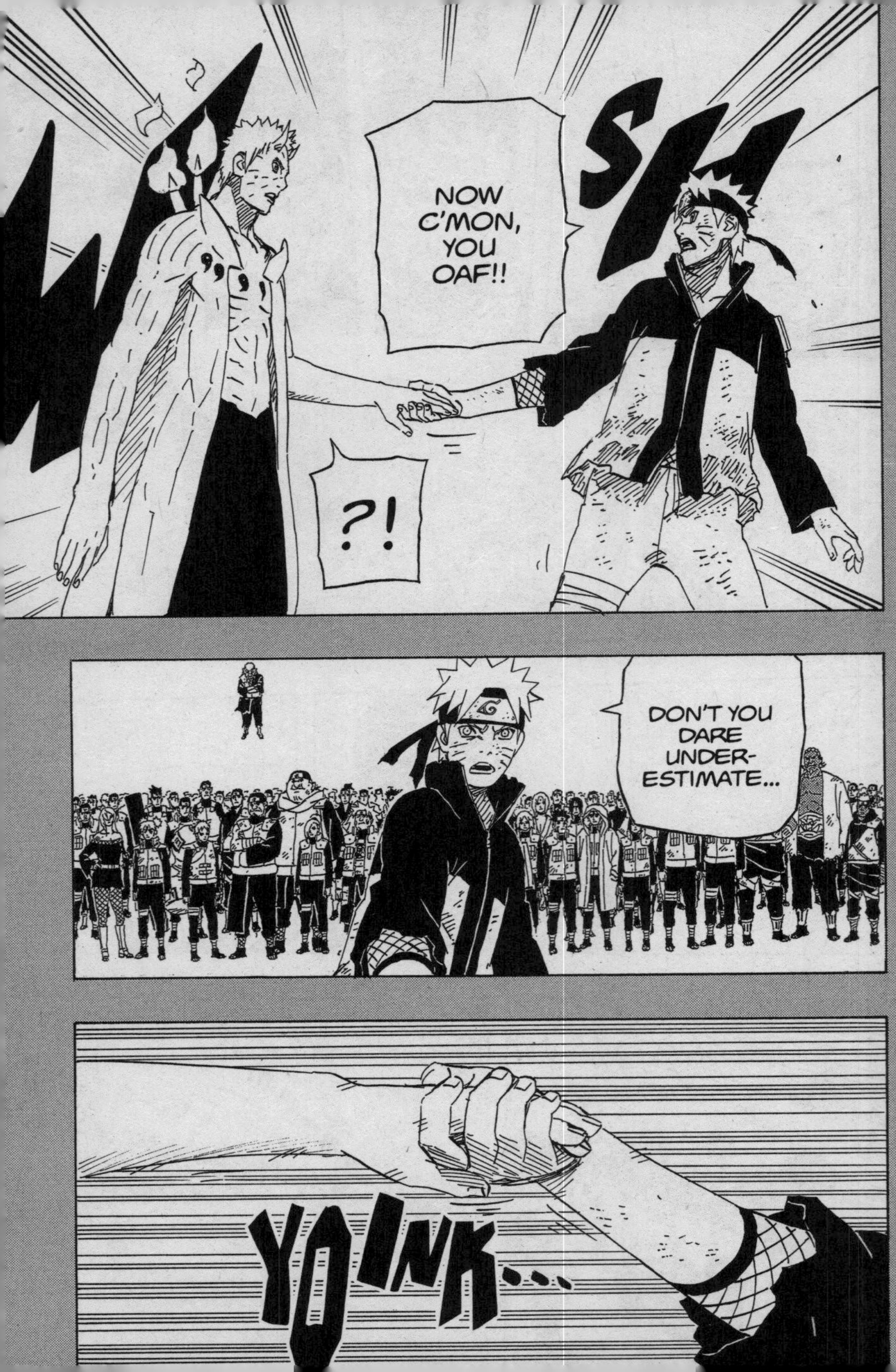
NOW C'MON, YOU OAF!!
?!
DON'T YOU DARE UNDER-ESTIMATE...
YOINK...

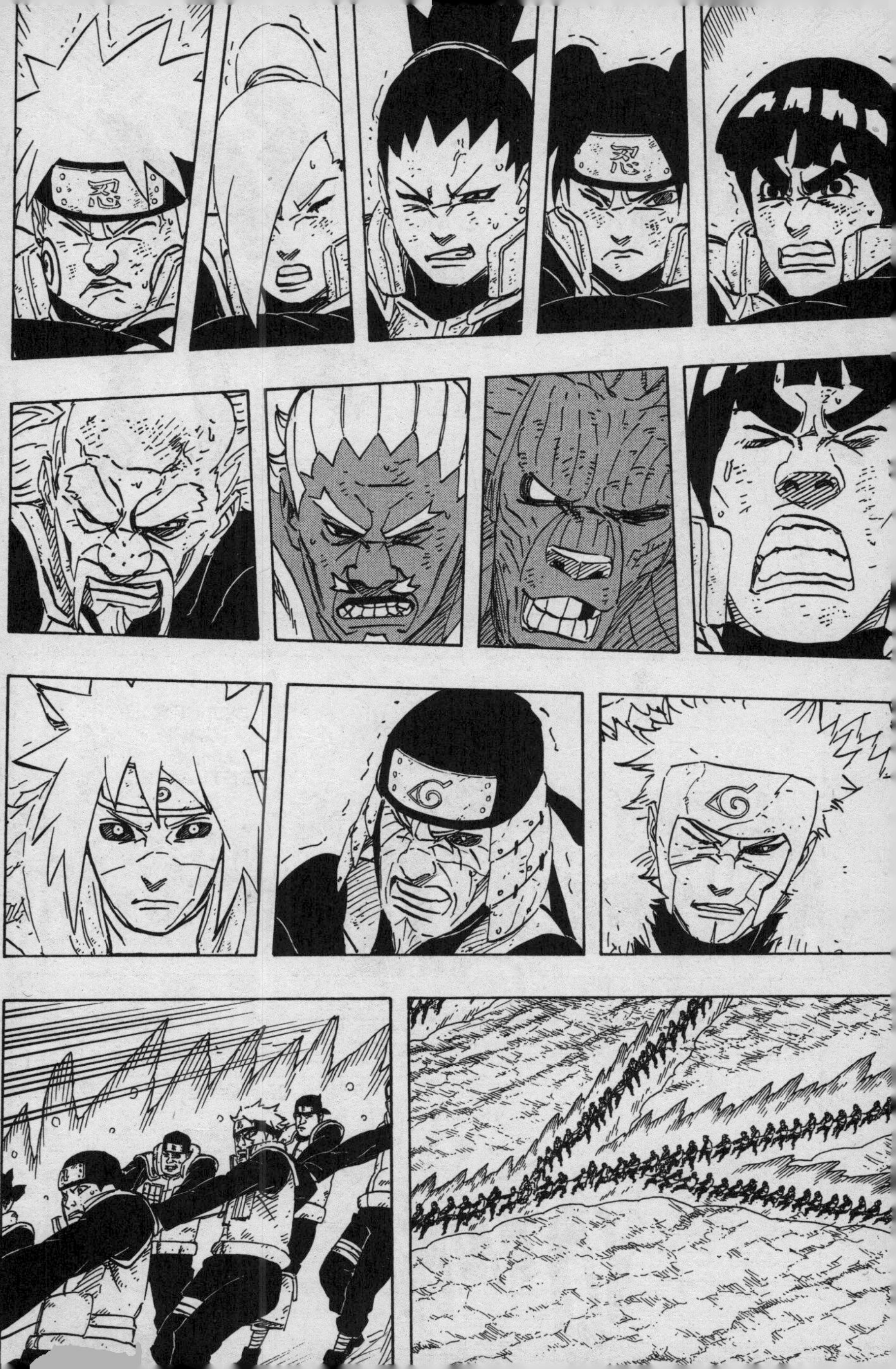

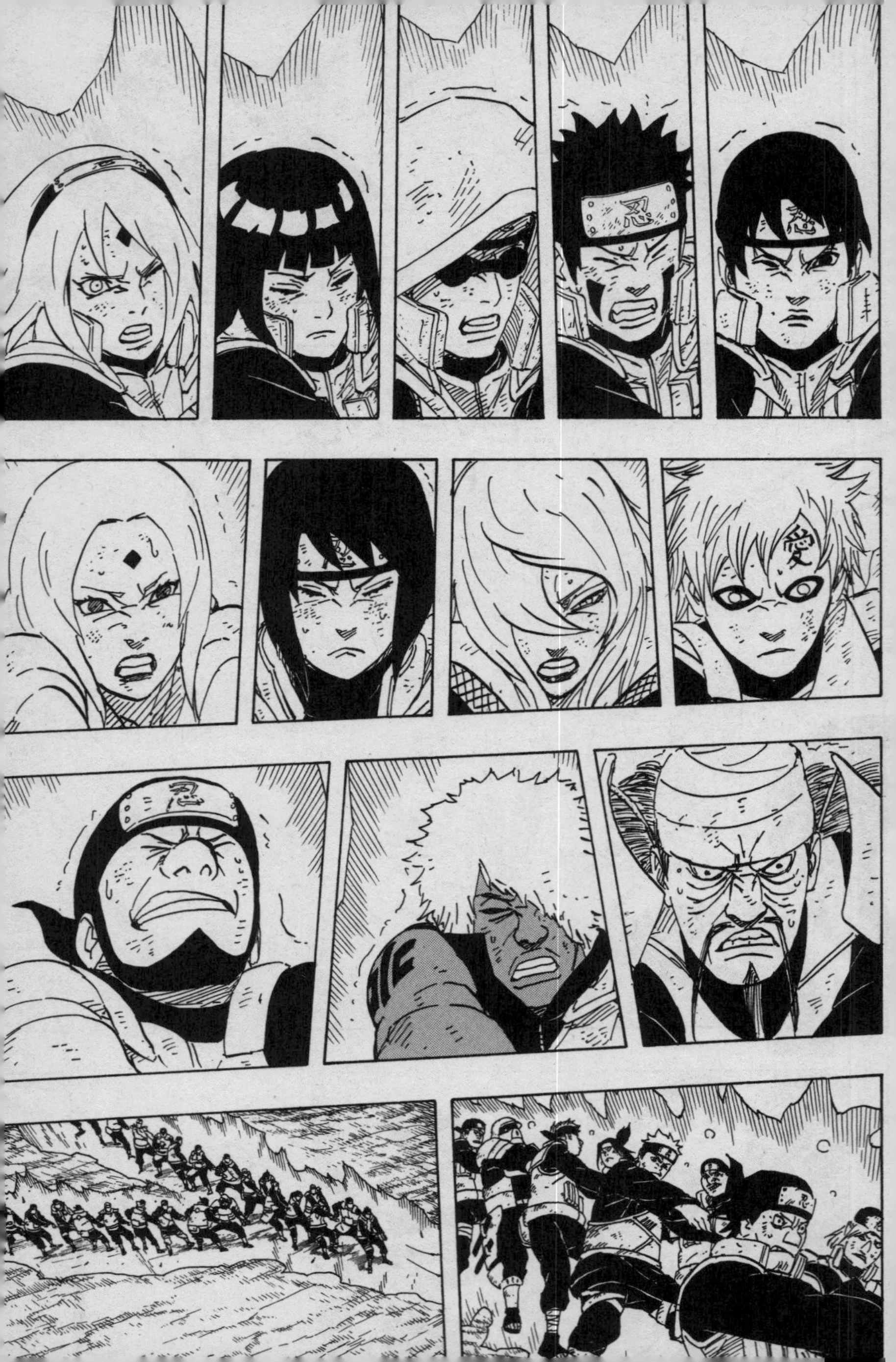

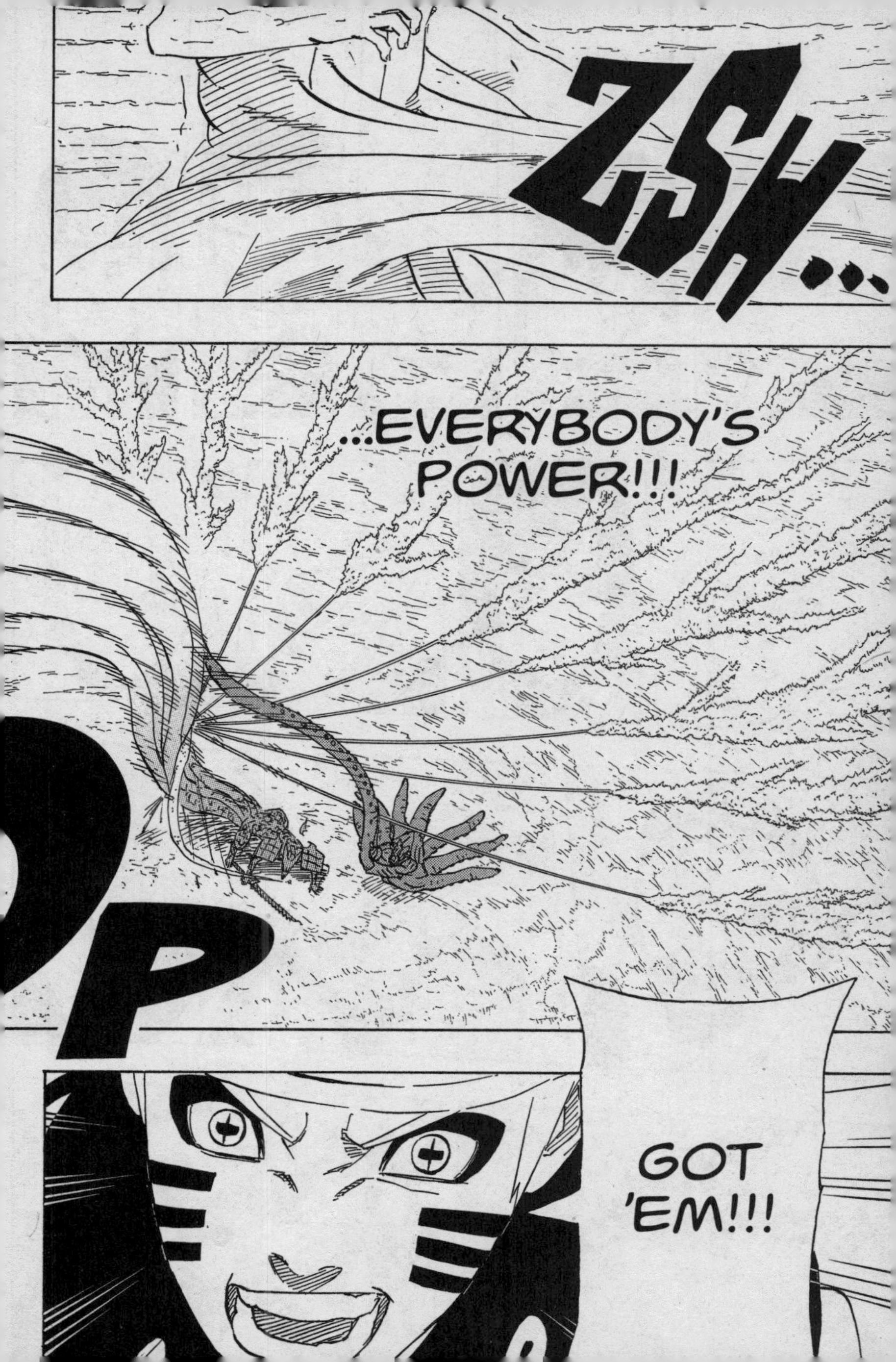
ZSH...
...EVERYBODY'S POWER!!!
GOT 'EM!!!

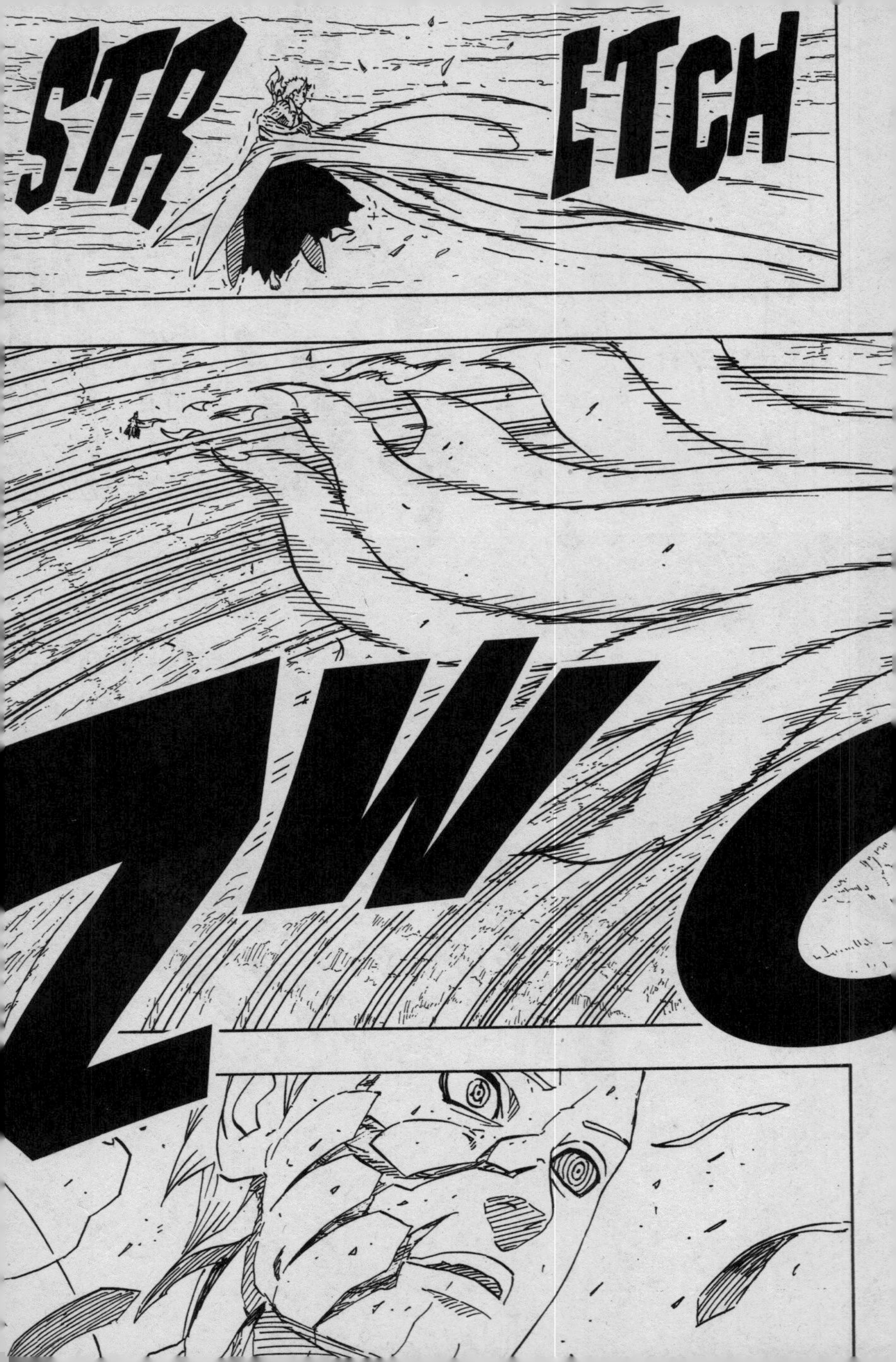
STRETCH
ZWO

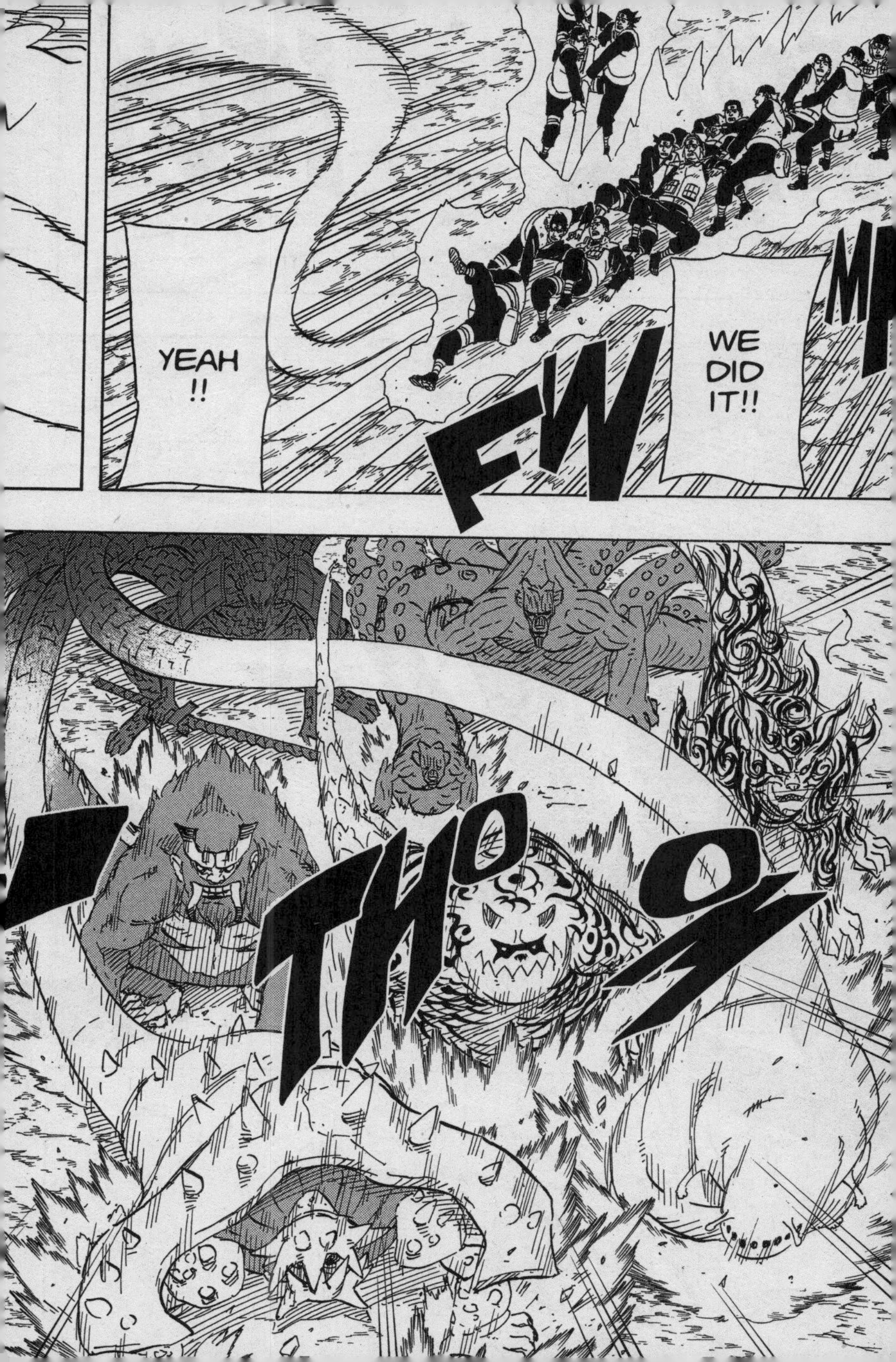
WE DID IT!!
FW
YEAH !!
THOOM

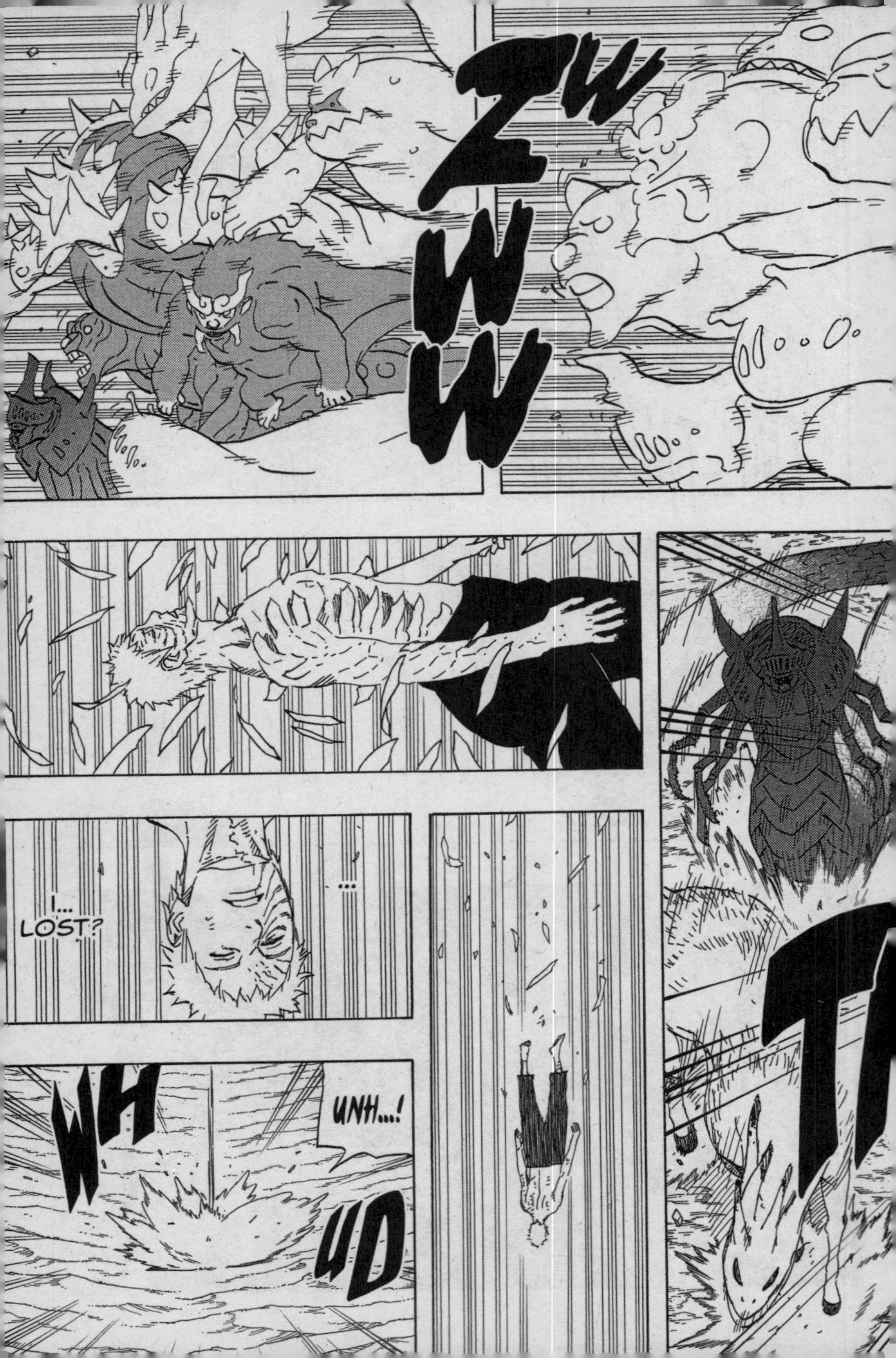
ZWWW
TT
...
I... LOST?
UNH...!
WHUD

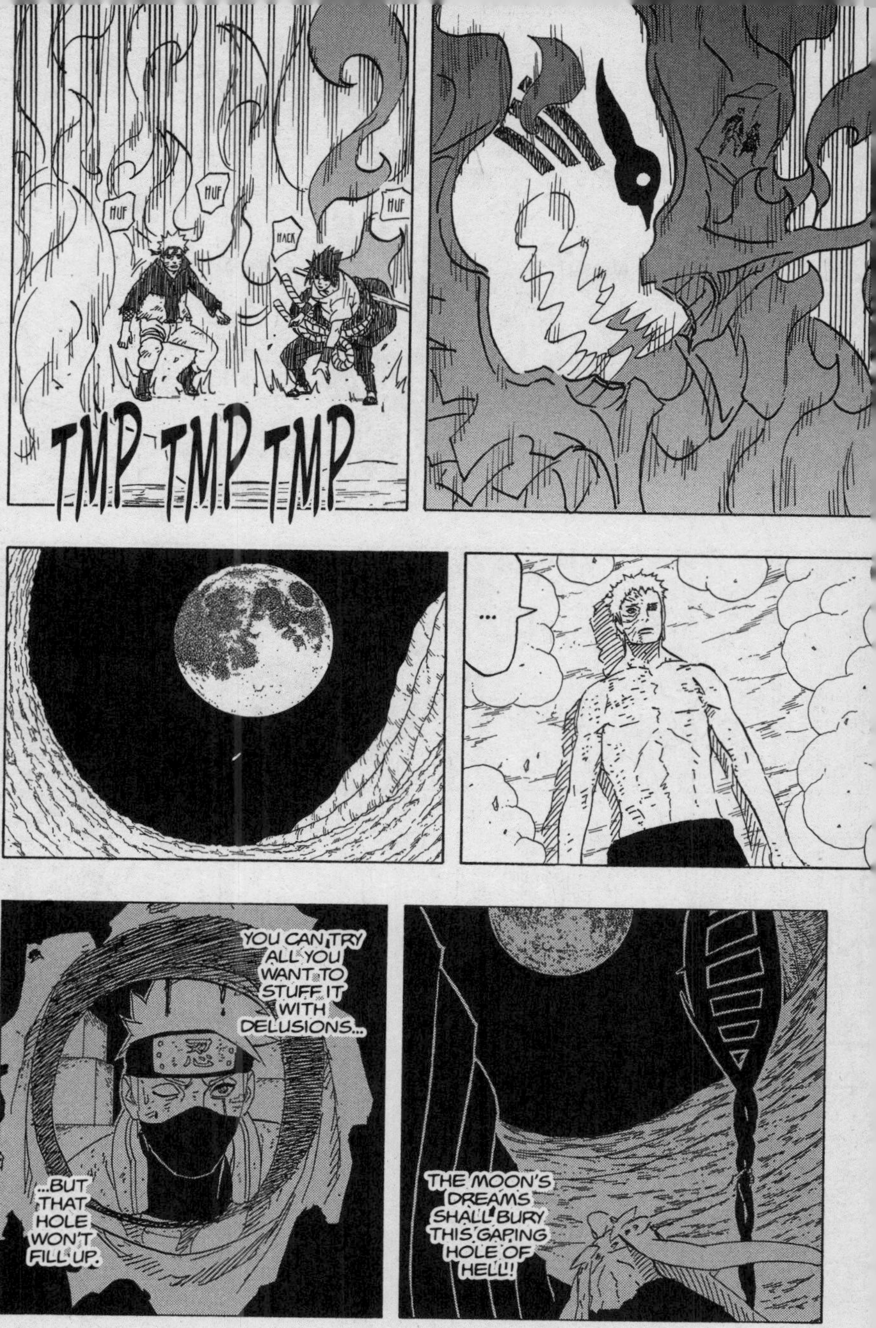
HUF
HUF
HACK
HUF
TMP TMP TMP
...
THE MOON'S DREAMS SHALL BURY THIS GAPING HOLE OF HELL!
YOU CAN TRY ALL YOU WANT TO STUFF IT WITH DELUSIONS...
...BUT THAT HOLE WON'T FILL UP.

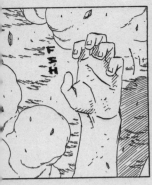

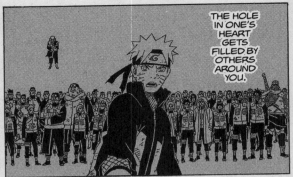

THE HOLE IN ONE'S HEART GETS FILLED BY OTHERS AROUND YOU.

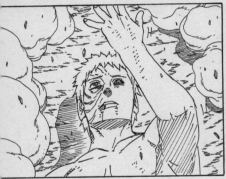

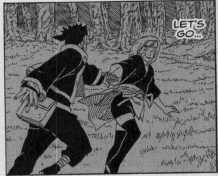

LET'S GO...

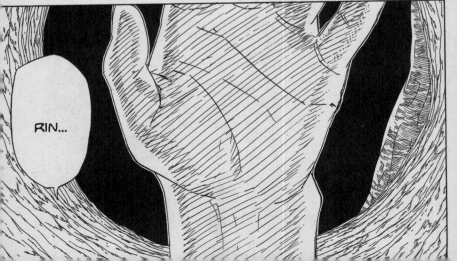

RIN...

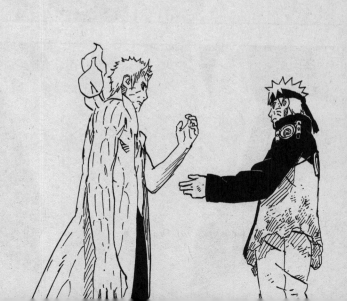

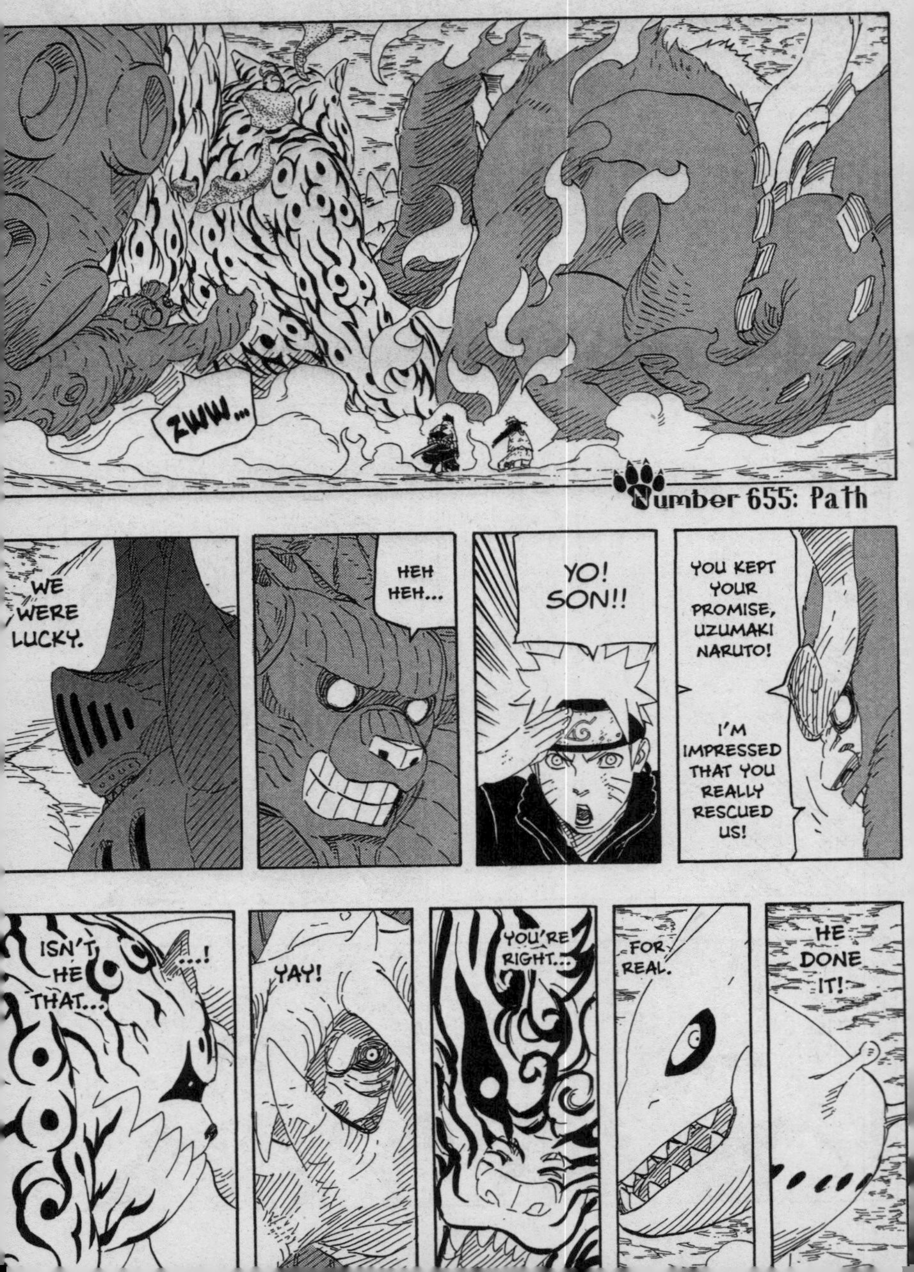
ZWW...
Number 655: Path
YOU KEPT YOUR PROMISE, UZUMAKI NARUTO!
I'M IMPRESSED THAT YOU REALLY RESCUED US!
YO! SON!!
HEH HEH...
WE WERE LUCKY.
HE DONE IT!
.....
FOR REAL.
YOU'RE RIGHT...
YAY!
...!
ISN'T HE THAT...

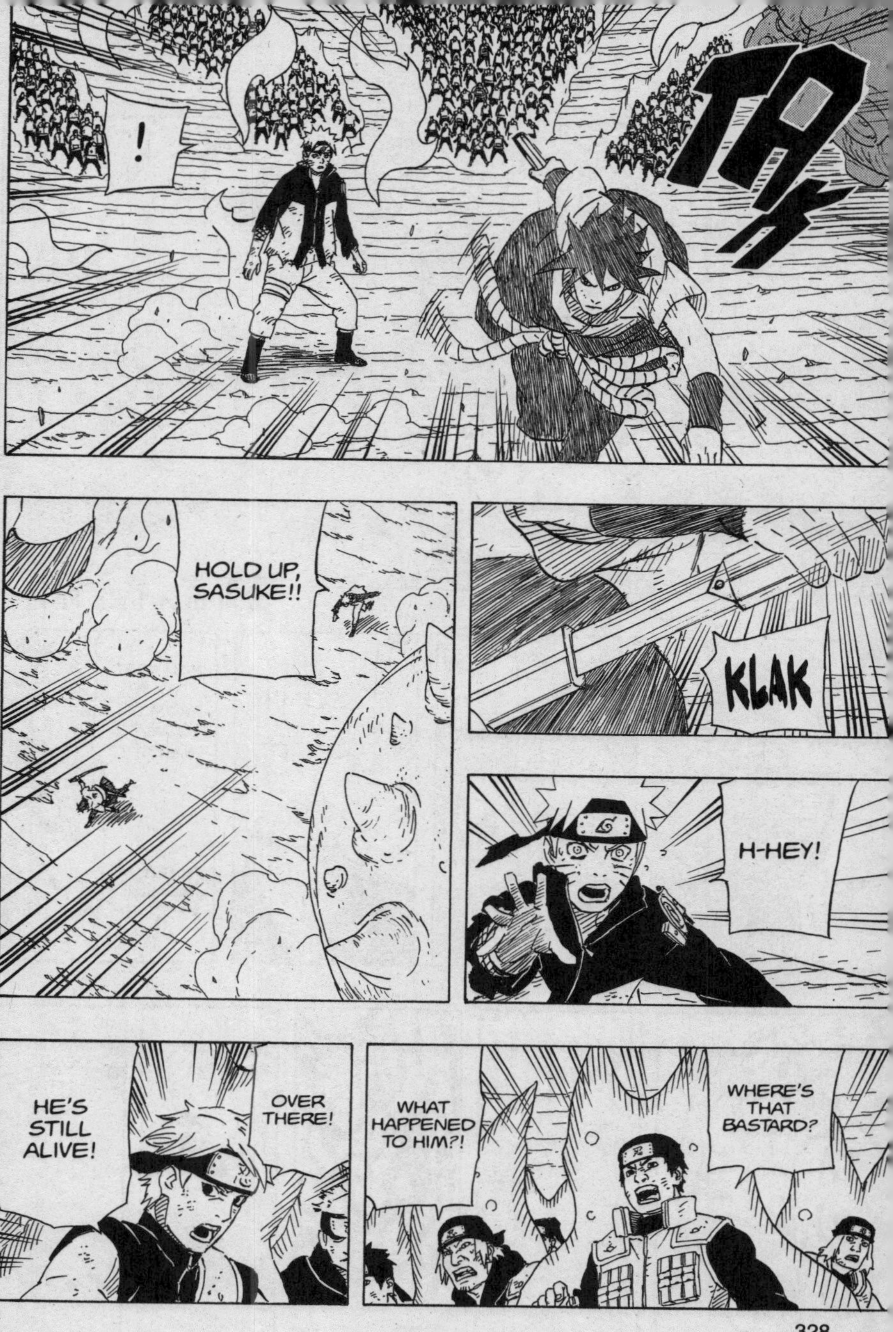
TA
!
KLAK
H-HEY!
HOLD UP, SASUKE!!
WHERE'S THAT BASTARD?
WHAT HAPPENED TO HIM?!
OVER THERE!
HE'S STILL ALIVE!

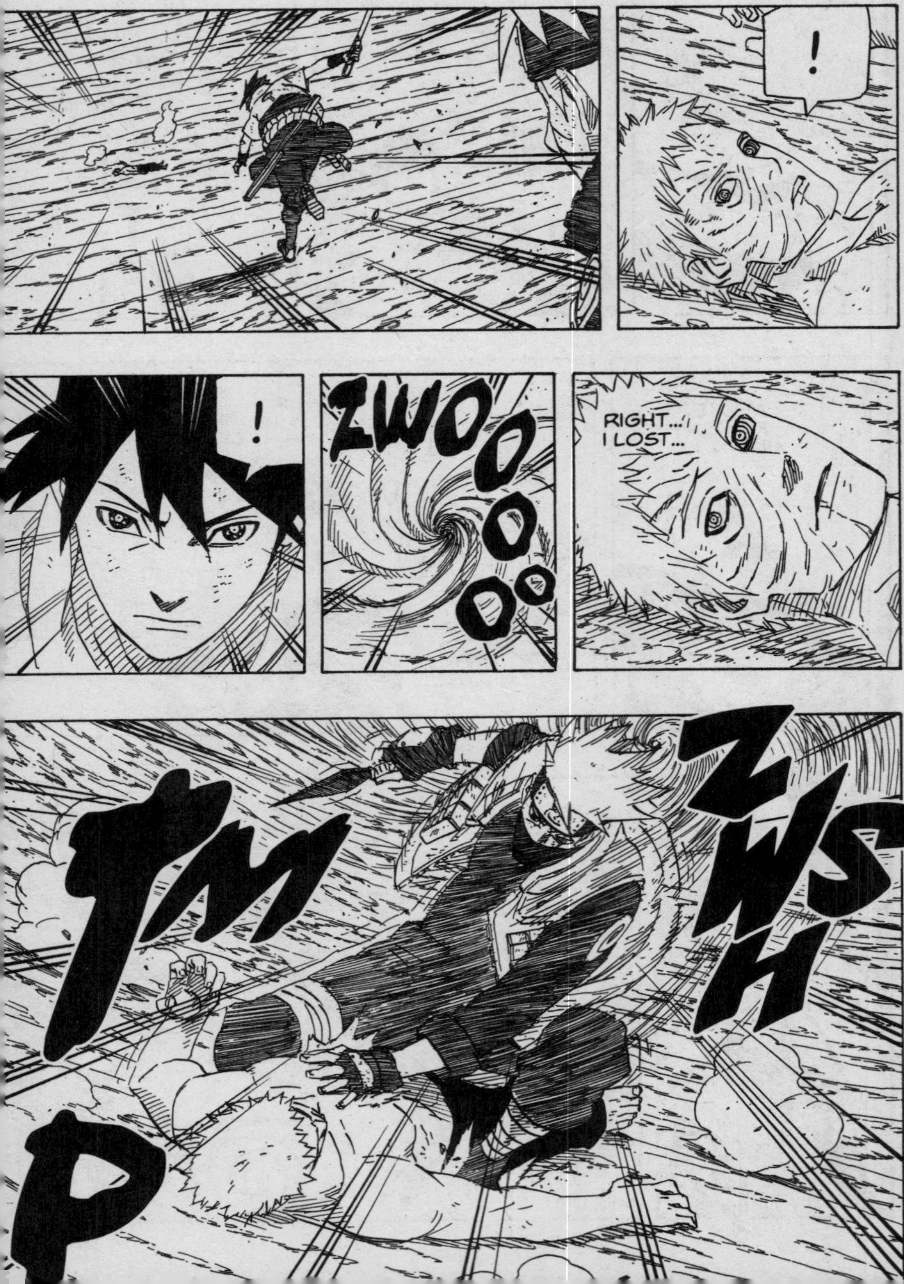
!
RIGHT... I LOST...
ZWOOOOOO
!
ZWSH

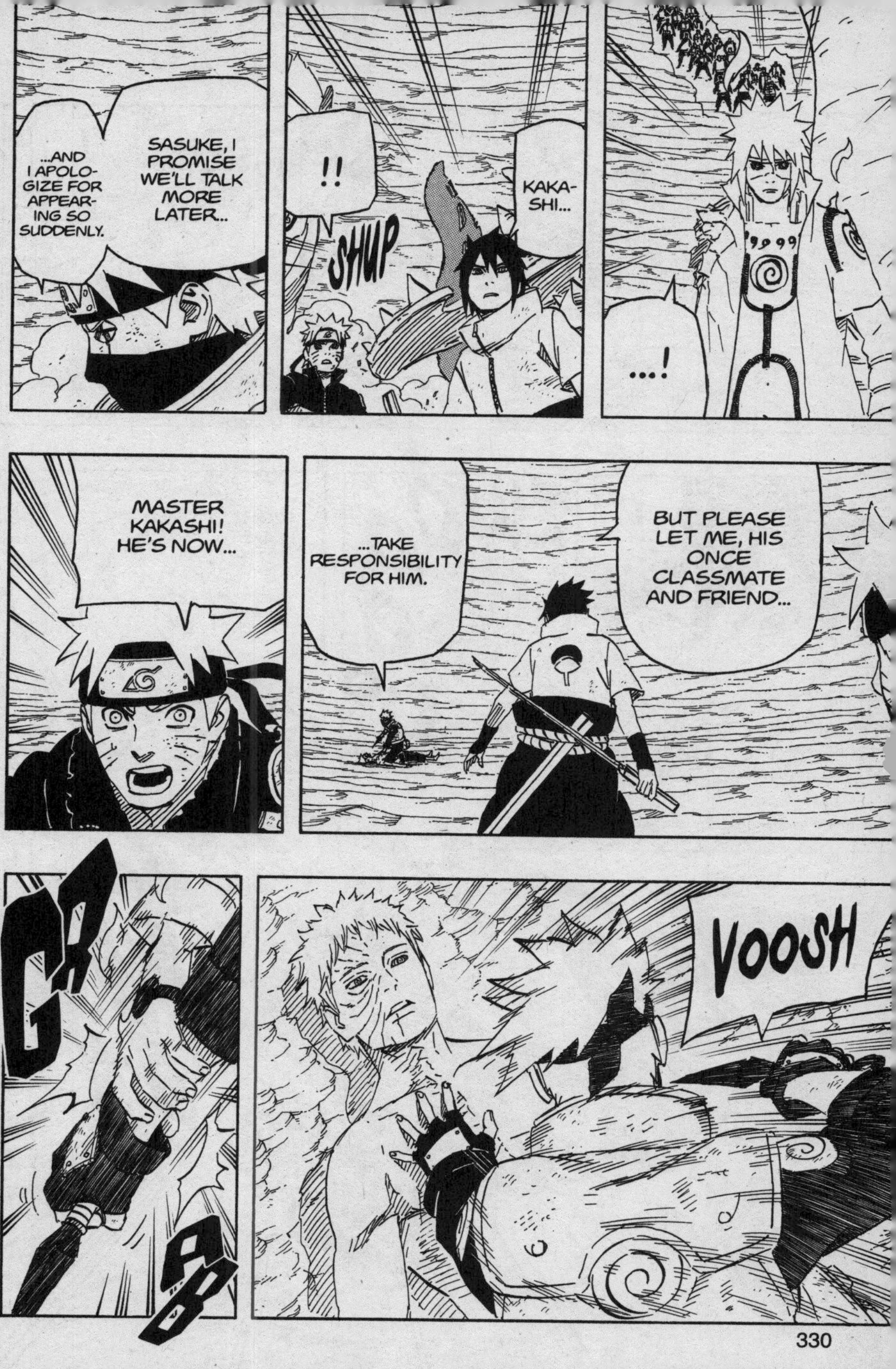
...!
KAKA-SHI...
!!
SHUP
SASUKE, I PROMISE WE'LL TALK MORE LATER...
...AND I APOLOGIZE FOR APPEARING SO SUDDENLY.
BUT PLEASE LET ME, HIS ONCE CLASSMATE AND FRIEND...
...TAKE RESPONSIBILITY FOR HIM.
MASTER KAKASHI! HE'S NOW...
VOOSH

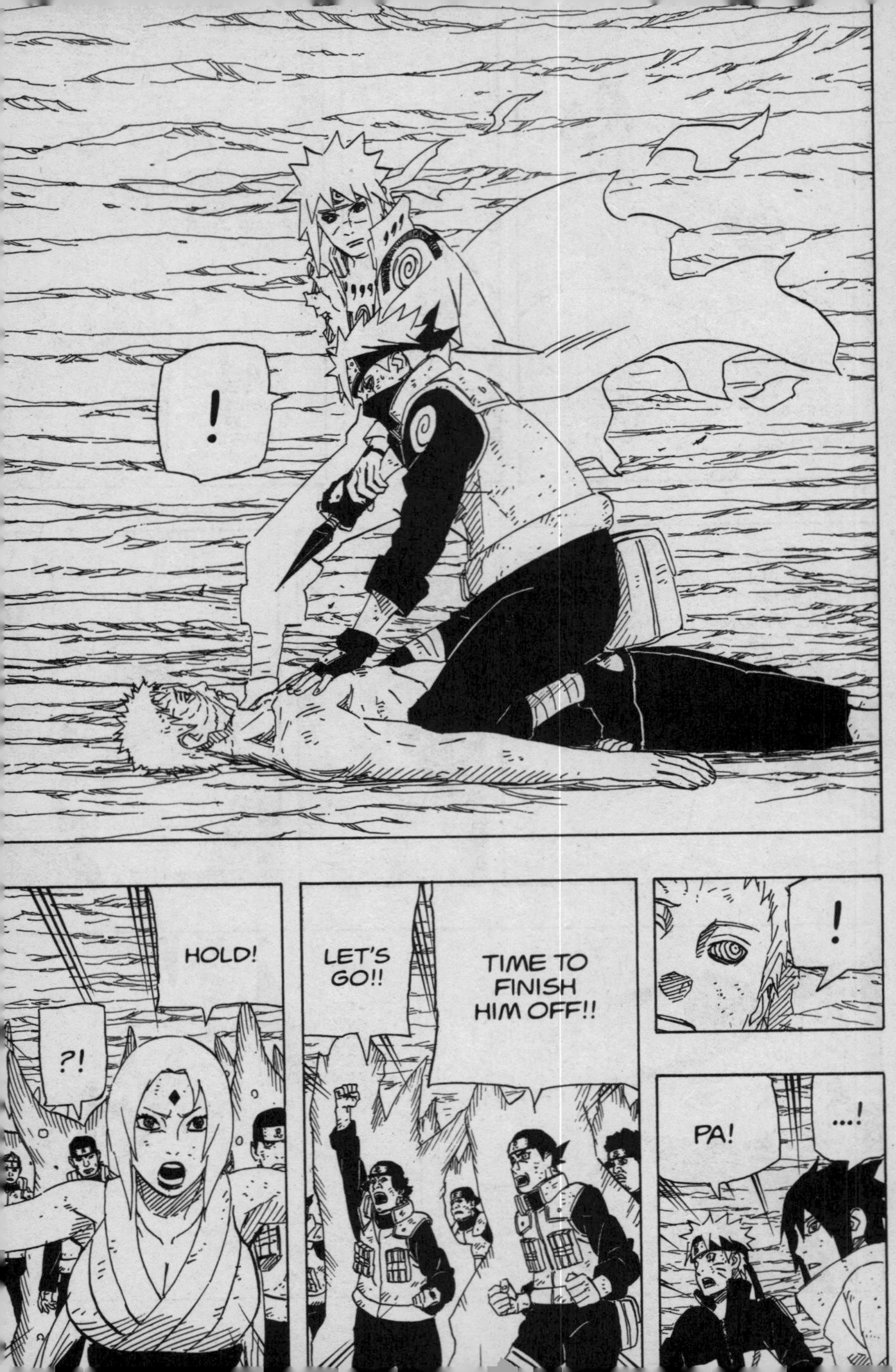
!
!
...!
PA!
TIME TO FINISH HIM OFF!!
LET'S GO!!
HOLD!
?!

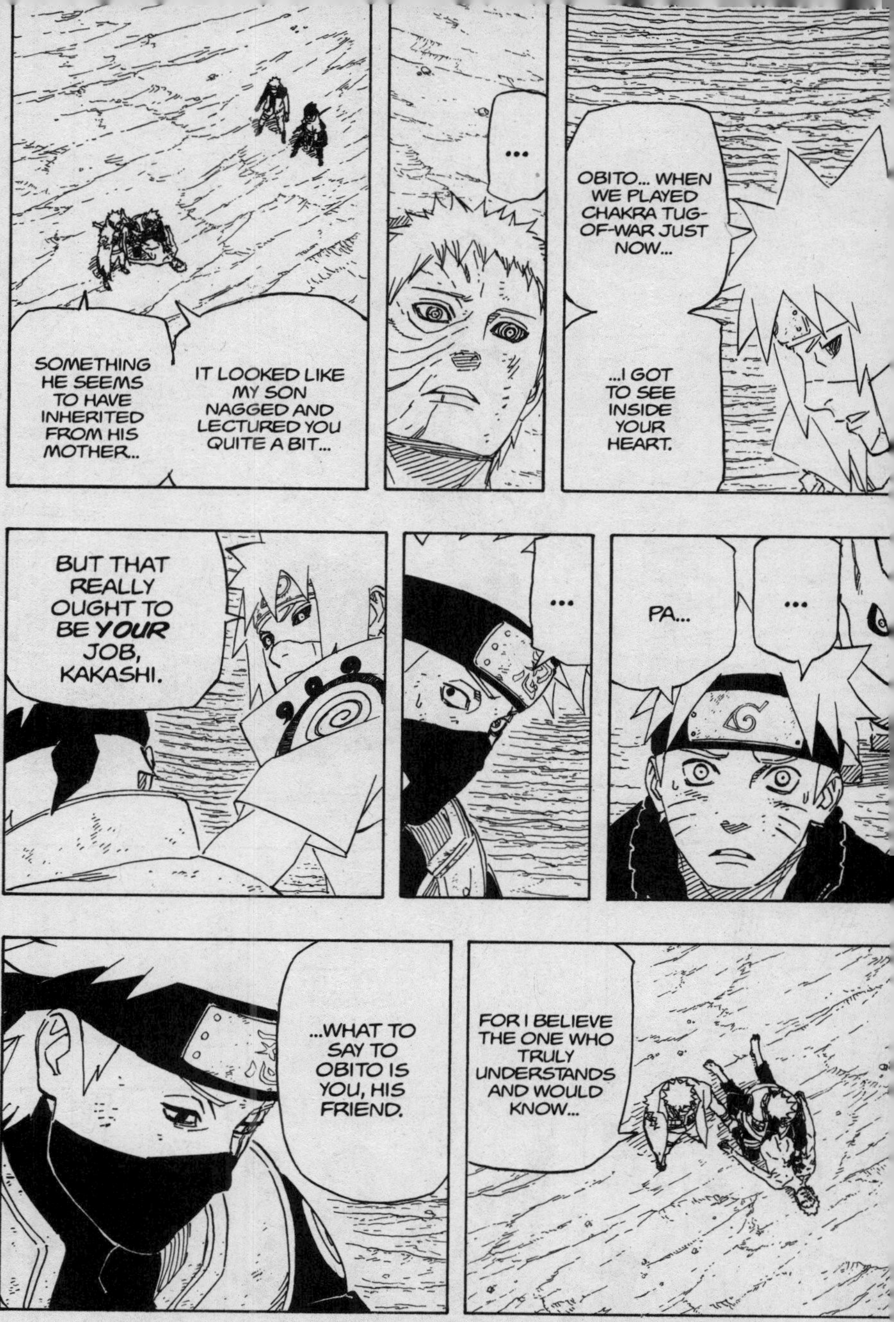
OBITO... WHEN WE PLAYED CHAKRA TUG-OF-WAR JUST NOW...
...I GOT TO SEE INSIDE YOUR HEART.
...
IT LOOKED LIKE MY SON NAGGED AND LECTURED YOU QUITE A BIT...
SOMETHING HE SEEMS TO HAVE INHERITED FROM HIS MOTHER...
...
PA...
...
BUT THAT REALLY OUGHT TO BE *YOUR* JOB, KAKASHI.
FOR I BELIEVE THE ONE WHO TRULY UNDERSTANDS AND WOULD KNOW...
...WHAT TO SAY TO OBITO IS YOU, HIS FRIEND.

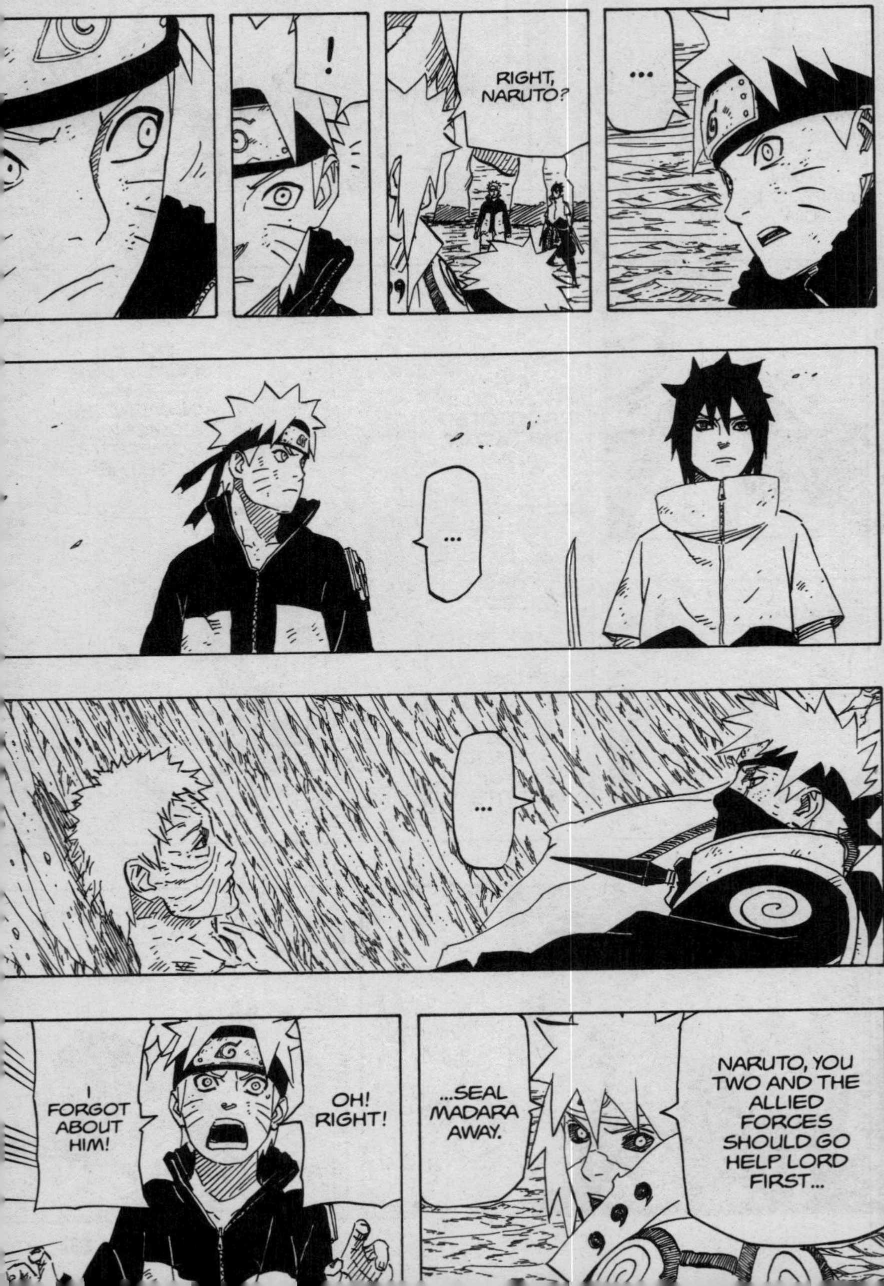
...
RIGHT, NARUTO?
!
...
...
NARUTO, YOU TWO AND THE ALLIED FORCES SHOULD GO HELP LORD FIRST...
...SEAL MADARA AWAY.
OH! RIGHT!
I FORGOT ABOUT HIM!

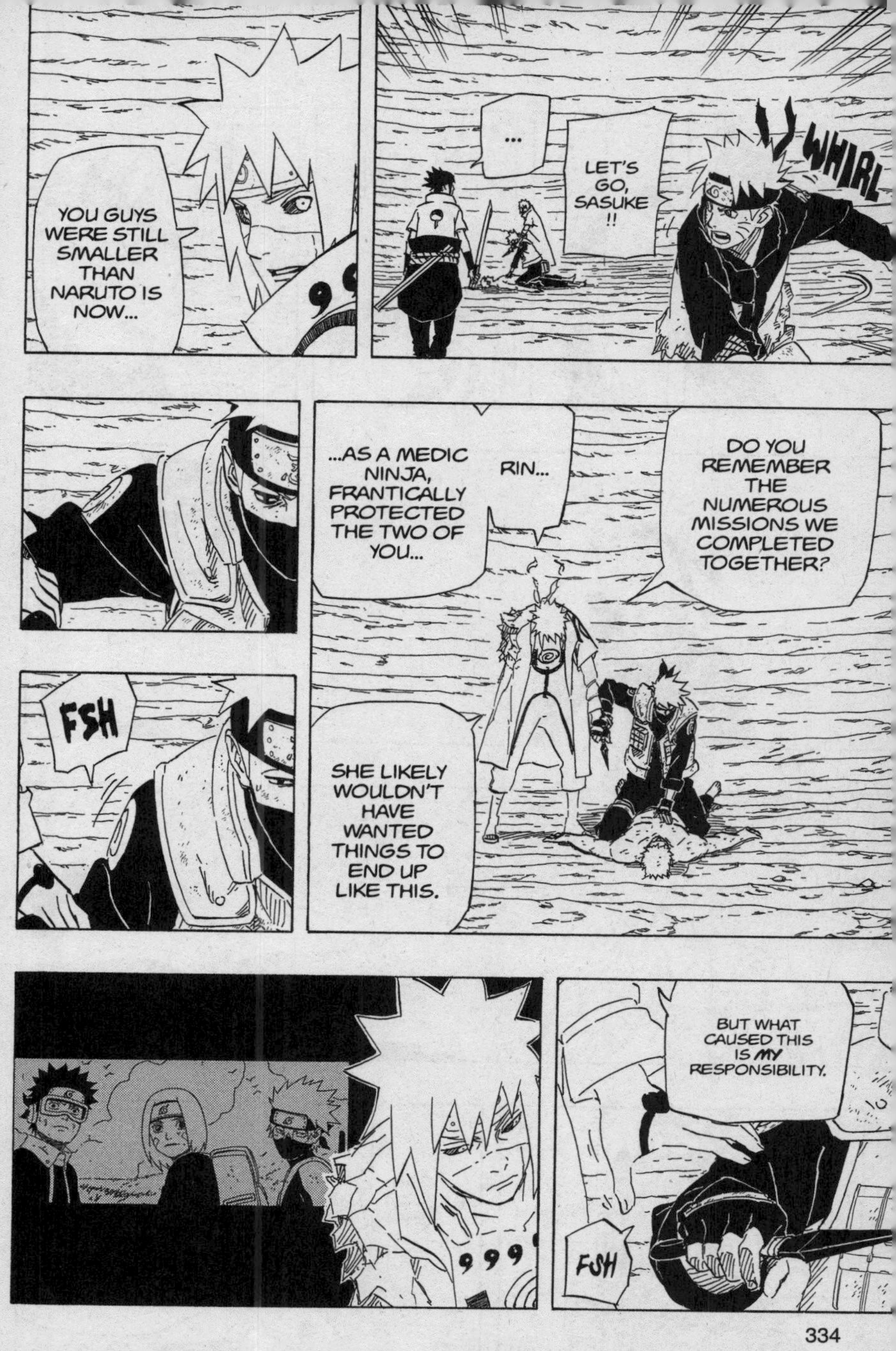
WHIRL
LET'S GO, SASUKE !!
...
YOU GUYS WERE STILL SMALLER THAN NARUTO IS NOW...
DO YOU REMEMBER THE NUMEROUS MISSIONS WE COMPLETED TOGETHER?
RIN...
...AS A MEDIC NINJA, FRANTICALLY PROTECTED THE TWO OF YOU...
SHE LIKELY WOULDN'T HAVE WANTED THINGS TO END UP LIKE THIS.
FSH
BUT WHAT CAUSED THIS IS *MY* RESPONSIBILITY.
FSH

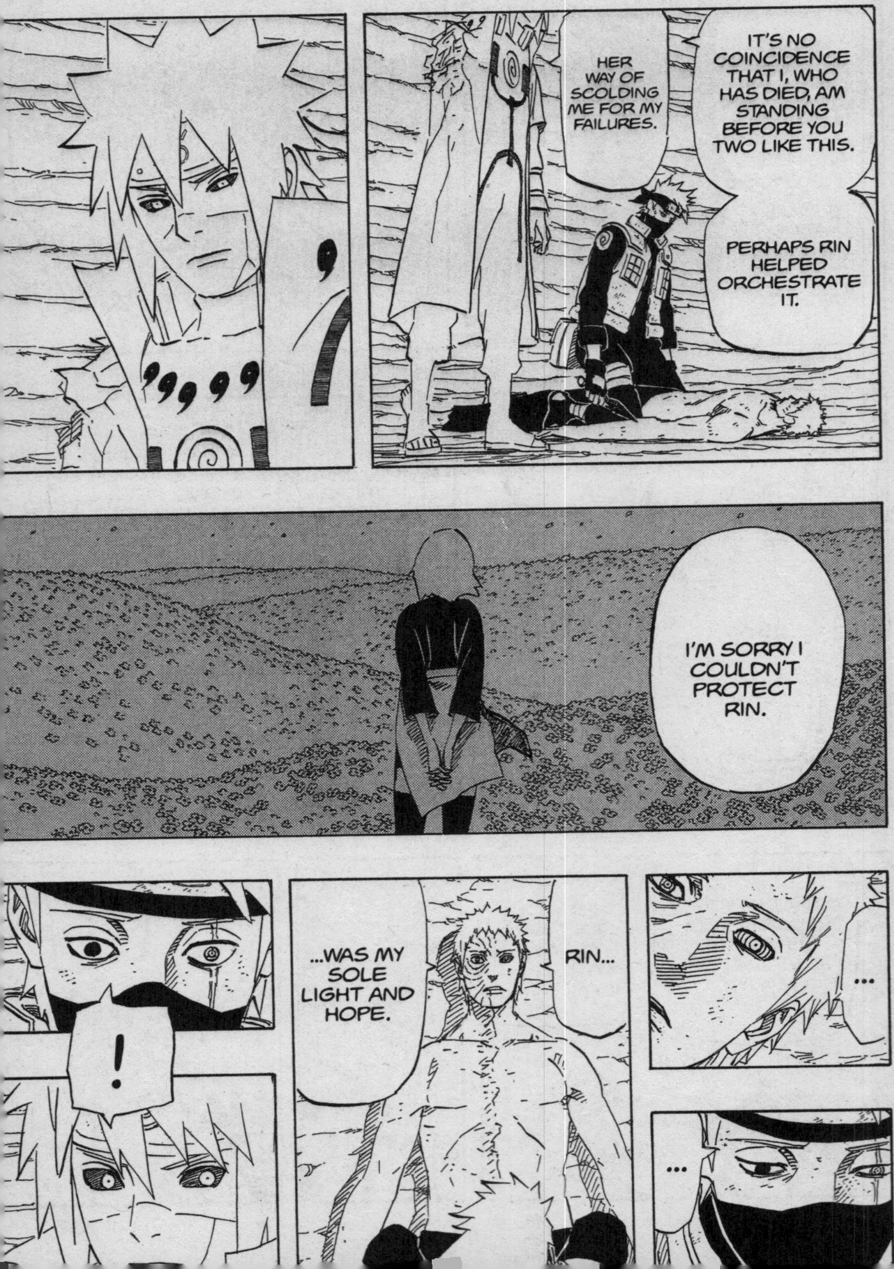
IT'S NO COINCIDENCE THAT I, WHO HAS DIED, AM STANDING BEFORE YOU TWO LIKE THIS.
PERHAPS RIN HELPED ORCHESTRATE IT.
HER WAY OF SCOLDING ME FOR MY FAILURES.
I'M SORRY I COULDN'T PROTECT RIN.
...
...
RIN...
...WAS MY SOLE LIGHT AND HOPE.
!

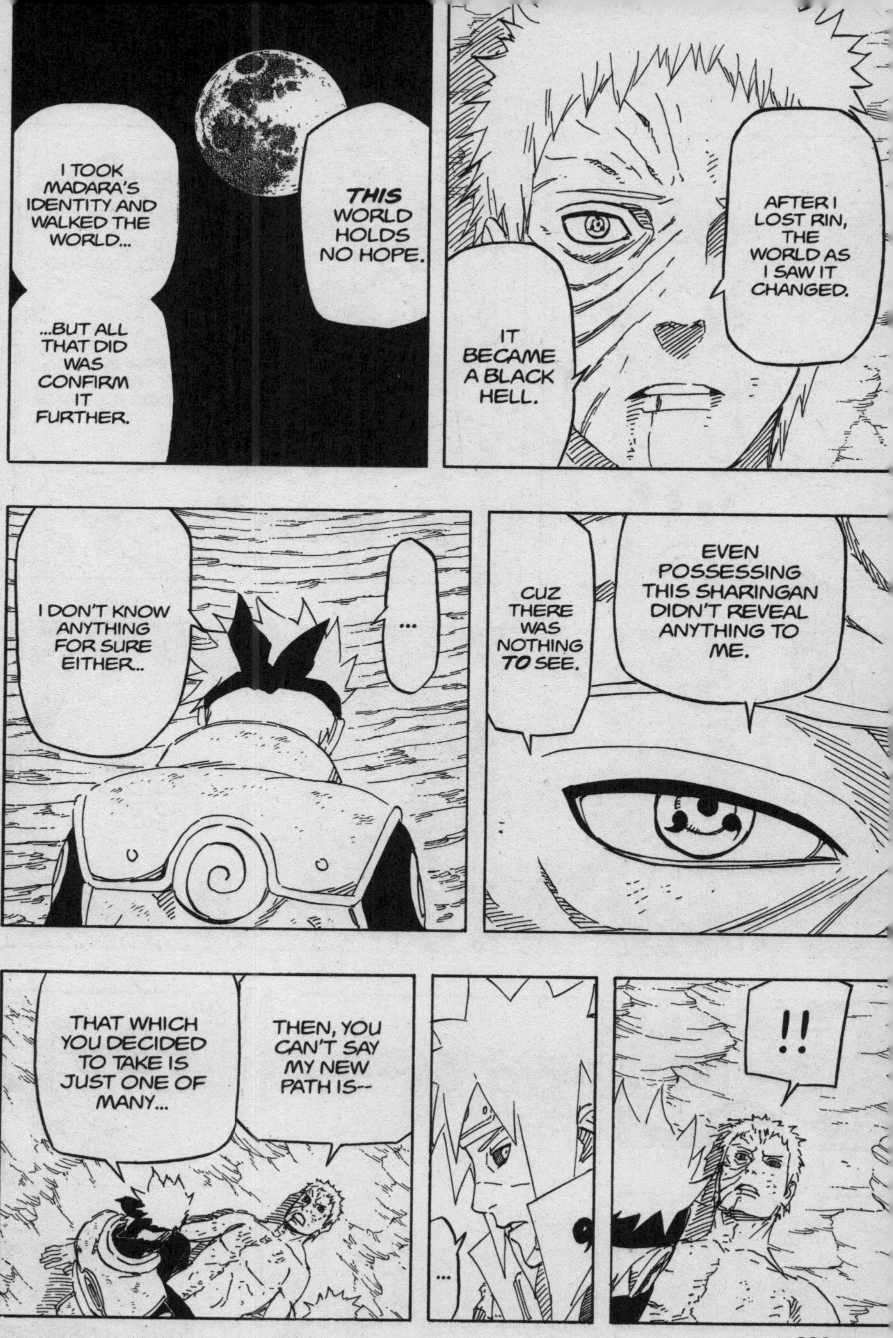

AFTER I LOST RIN, THE WORLD AS I SAW IT CHANGED.
IT BECAME A BLACK HELL.
THIS WORLD HOLDS NO HOPE.
I TOOK MADARA'S IDENTITY AND WALKED THE WORLD...
...BUT ALL THAT DID WAS CONFIRM IT FURTHER.
EVEN POSSESSING THIS SHARINGAN DIDN'T REVEAL ANYTHING TO ME.
CUZ THERE WAS NOTHING TO SEE.
...
I DON'T KNOW ANYTHING FOR SURE EITHER...
!!
...
THEN, YOU CAN'T SAY MY NEW PATH IS--
THAT WHICH YOU DECIDED TO TAKE IS JUST ONE OF MANY...

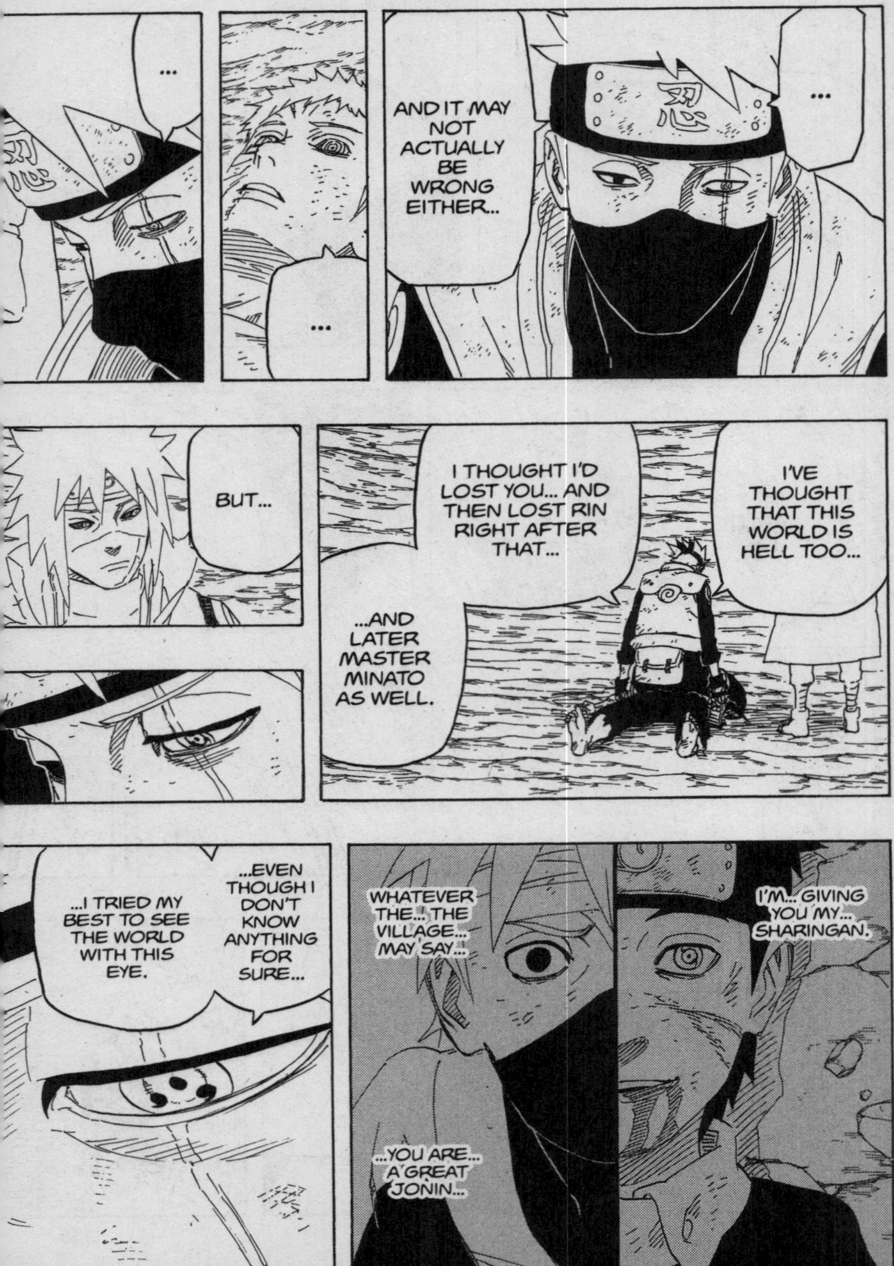
...
AND IT MAY NOT ACTUALLY BE WRONG EITHER...
...
...
I'VE THOUGHT THAT THIS WORLD IS HELL TOO...
I THOUGHT I'D LOST YOU... AND THEN LOST RIN RIGHT AFTER THAT...
...AND LATER MASTER MINATO AS WELL.
BUT...
I'M... GIVING YOU MY... SHARINGAN.
WHATEVER THE... THE VILLAGE... MAY SAY...
...YOU ARE... A GREAT JONIN...
...EVEN THOUGH I DON'T KNOW ANYTHING FOR SURE...
...I TRIED MY BEST TO SEE THE WORLD WITH THIS EYE.

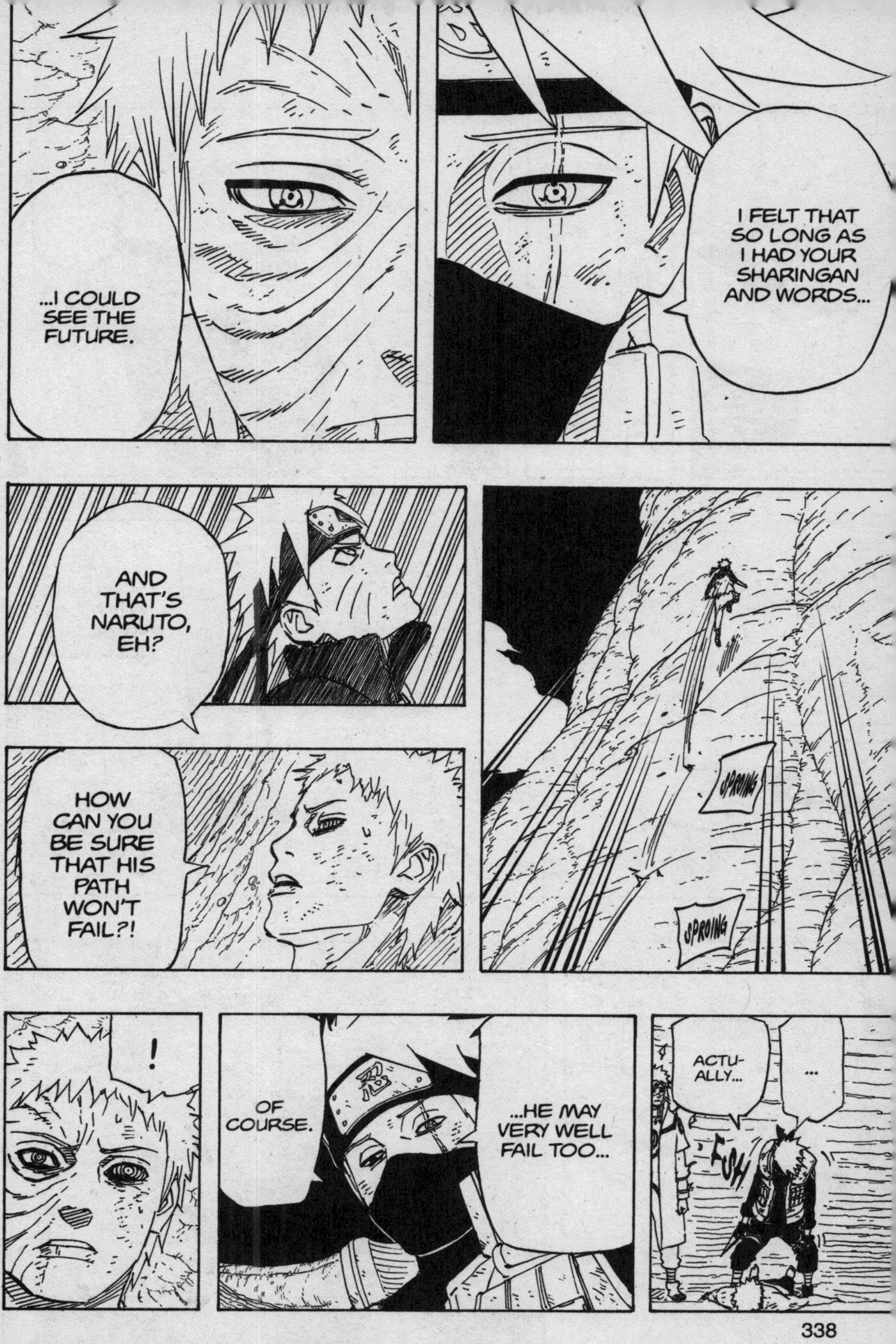
I FELT THAT SO LONG AS I HAD YOUR SHARINGAN AND WORDS...
...I COULD SEE THE FUTURE.
SPROING
SPROING
AND THAT'S NARUTO, EH?
HOW CAN YOU BE SURE THAT HIS PATH WON'T FAIL?!
...
ACTU-ALLY...
FSH
...HE MAY VERY WELL FAIL TOO...
OF COURSE.
!

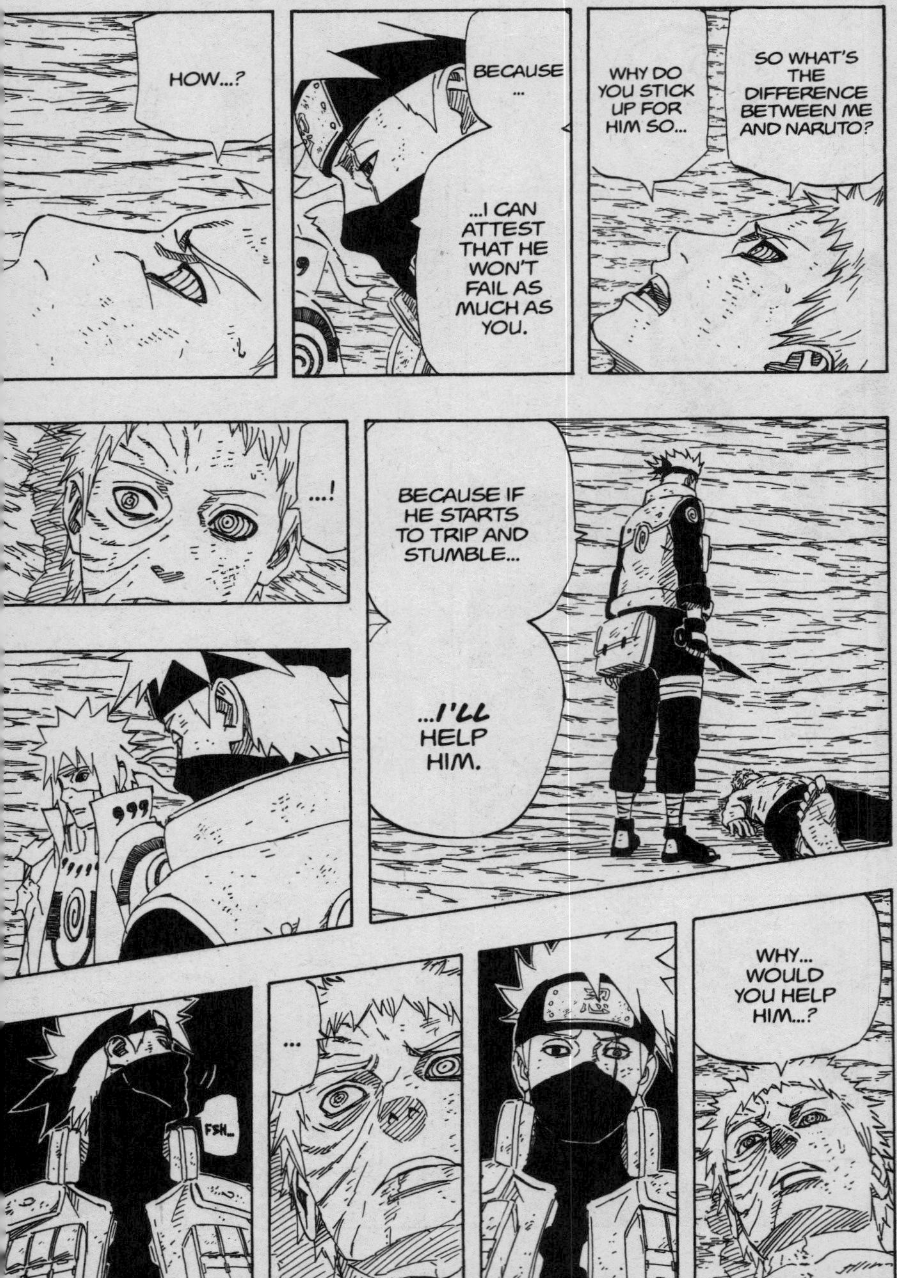
SO WHAT'S THE DIFFERENCE BETWEEN ME AND NARUTO?
WHY DO YOU STICK UP FOR HIM SO...
BECAUSE ...
...I CAN ATTEST THAT HE WON'T FAIL AS MUCH AS YOU.
HOW...?
BECAUSE IF HE STARTS TO TRIP AND STUMBLE...
...I'LL HELP HIM.
...!
WHY... WOULD YOU HELP HIM...?
...
FSH...

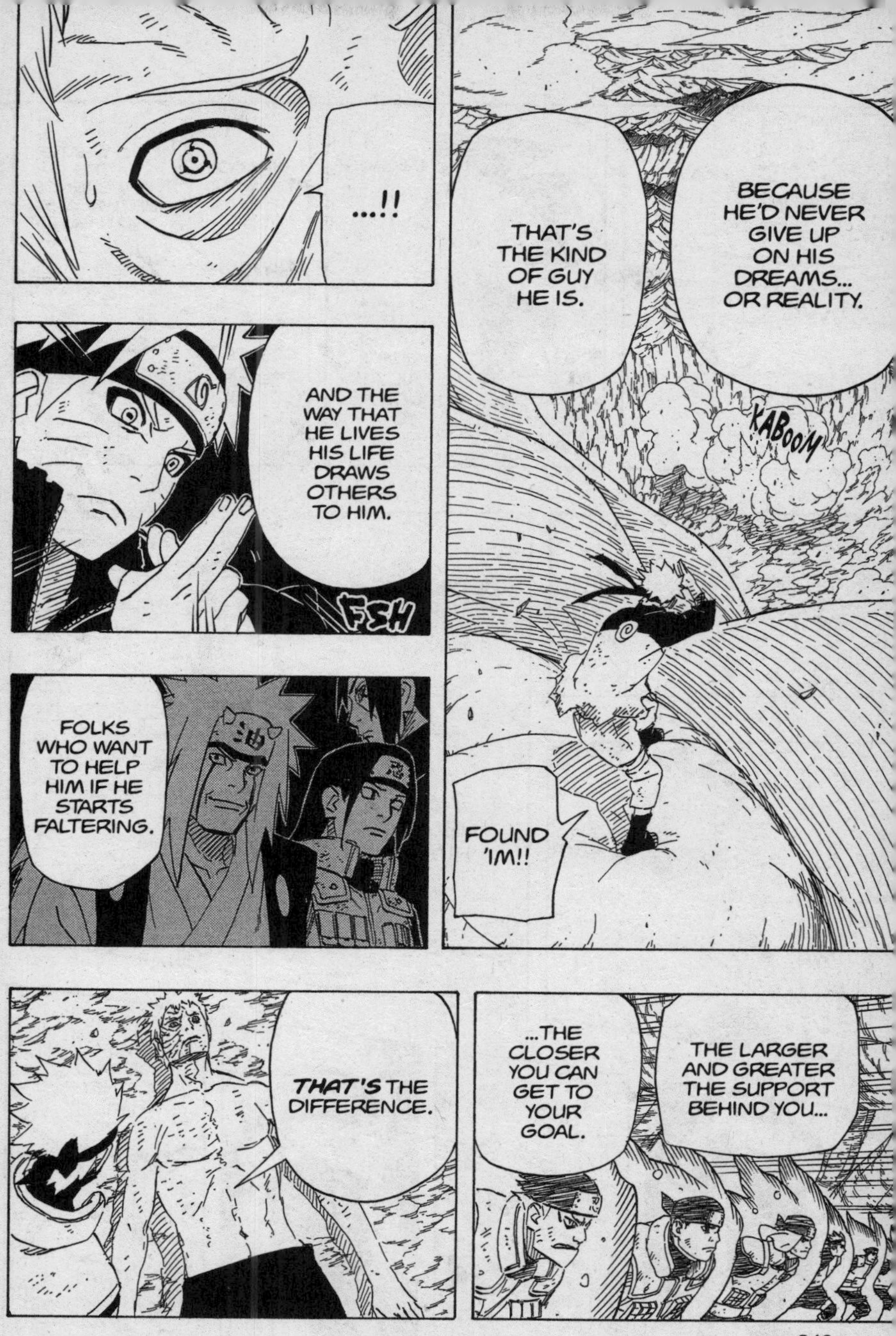
BECAUSE HE'D NEVER GIVE UP ON HIS DREAMS... OR REALITY.
THAT'S THE KIND OF GUY HE IS.
KABOOM
FOUND 'IM!!
...!!
AND THE WAY THAT HE LIVES HIS LIFE DRAWS OTHERS TO HIM.
FSH
FOLKS WHO WANT TO HELP HIM IF HE STARTS FALTERING.
THE LARGER AND GREATER THE SUPPORT BEHIND YOU...
...THE CLOSER YOU CAN GET TO YOUR GOAL.
THAT'S THE DIFFERENCE.

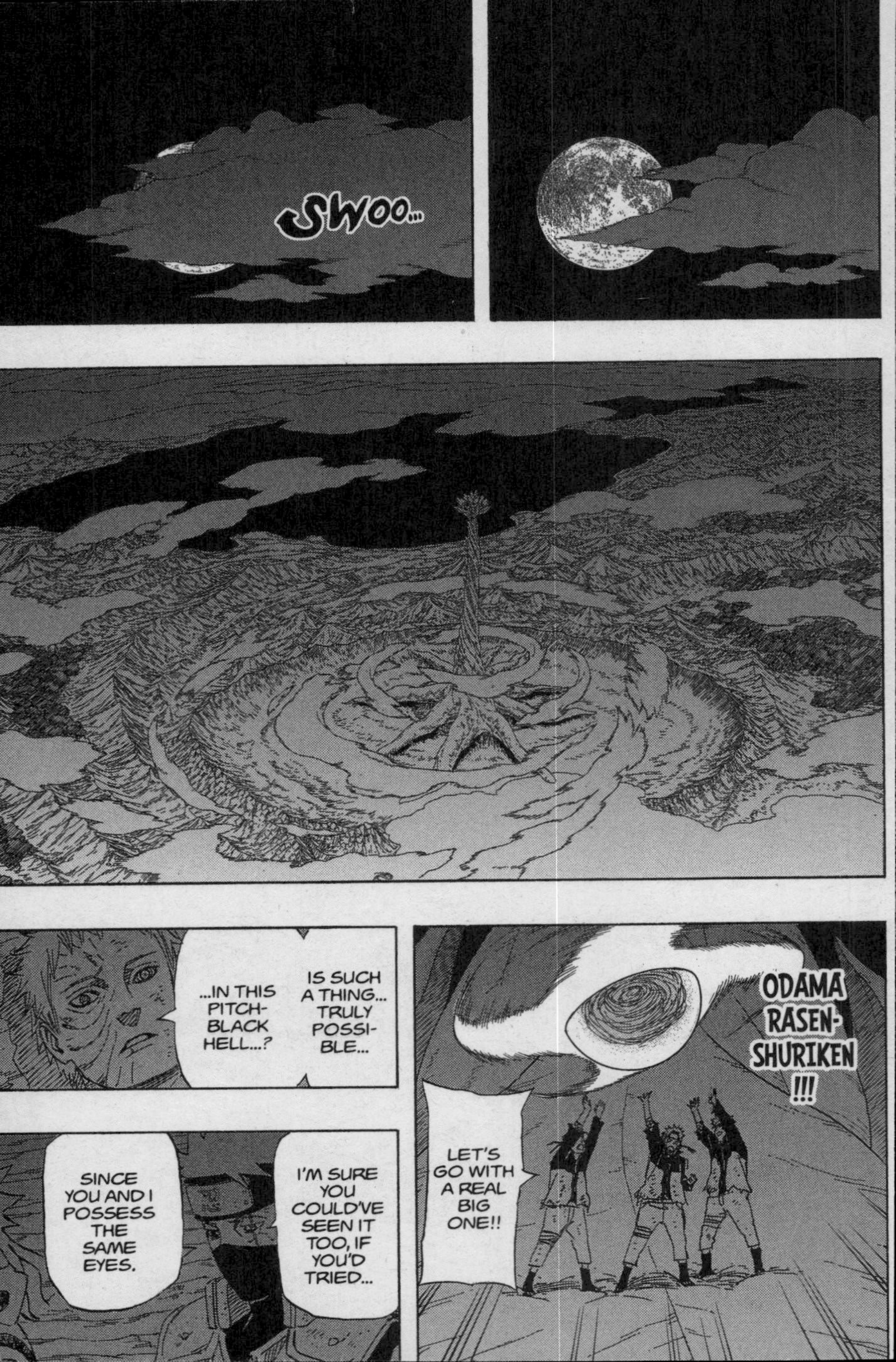
SWOO...
ODAMA RASEN-SHURIKEN!!!
LET'S GO WITH A REAL BIG ONE!!
IS SUCH A THING... TRULY POSSI-BLE...
...IN THIS PITCH-BLACK HELL...?
I'M SURE YOU COULD'VE SEEN IT TOO, IF YOU'D TRIED...
SINCE YOU AND I POSSESS THE SAME EYES.

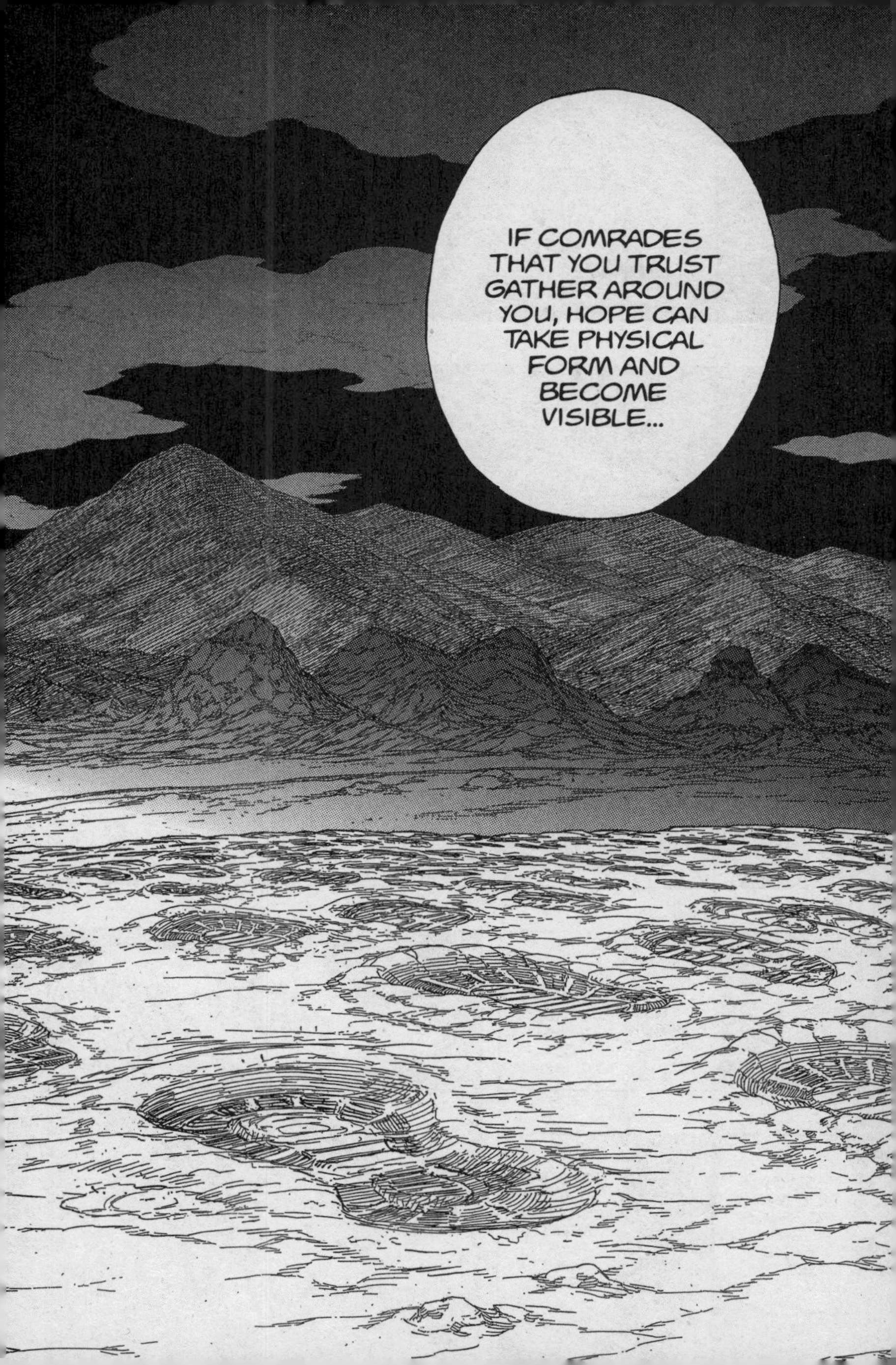
IF COMRADES THAT YOU TRUST GATHER AROUND YOU, HOPE CAN TAKE PHYSICAL FORM AND BECOME VISIBLE...

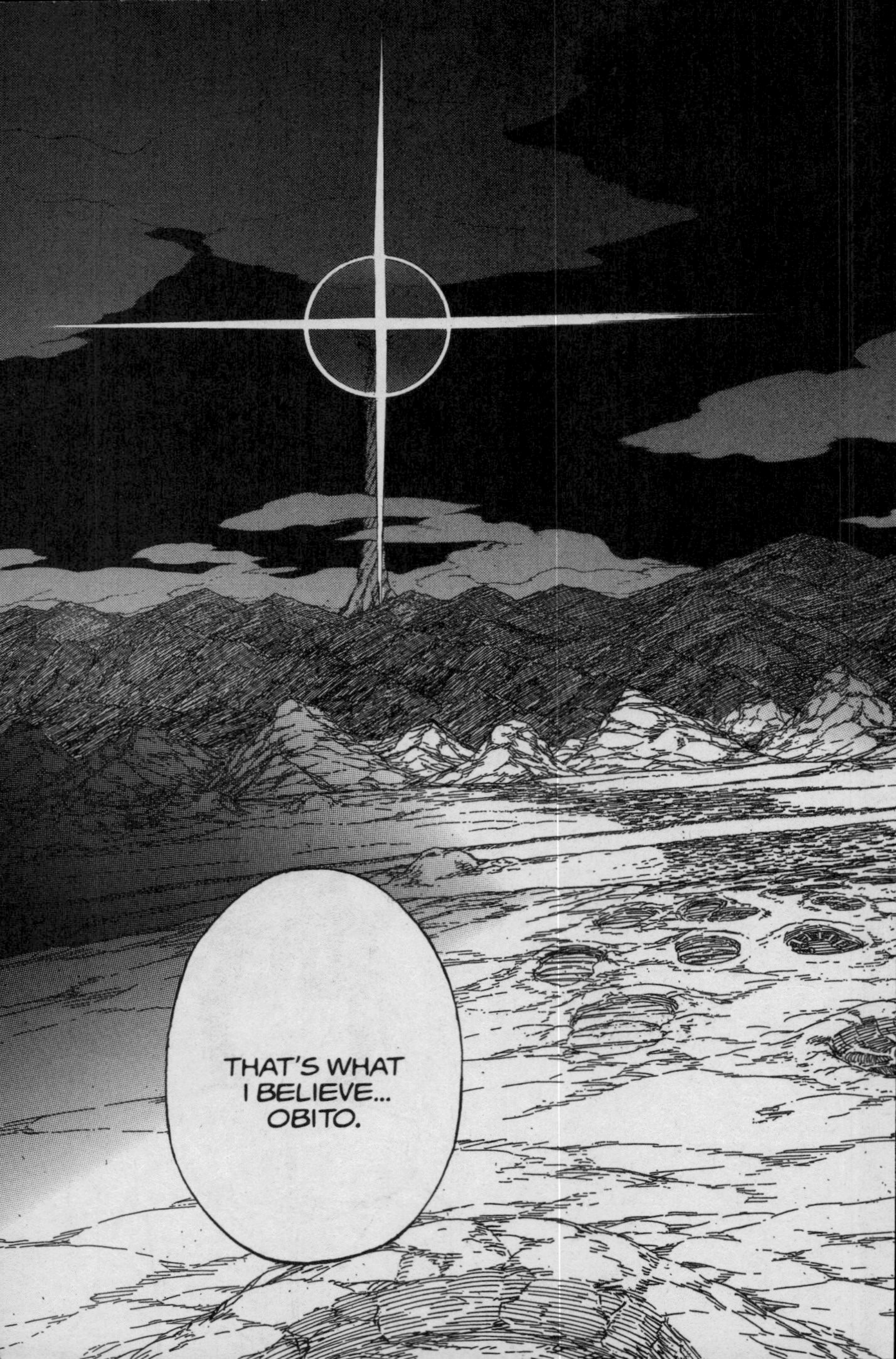
THAT'S WHAT I BELIEVE... OBITO.

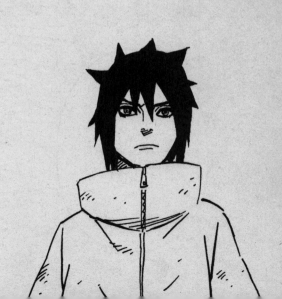

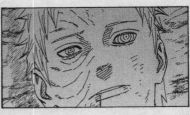

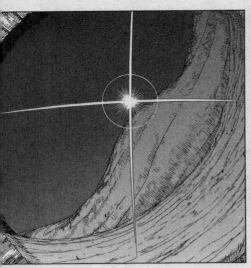

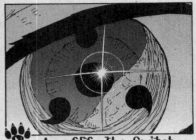

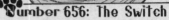

Number 656: The Switch

NARUTO'S PATH, HUH...

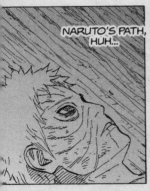

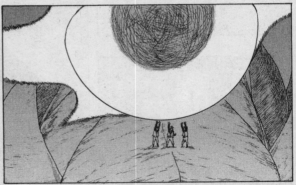

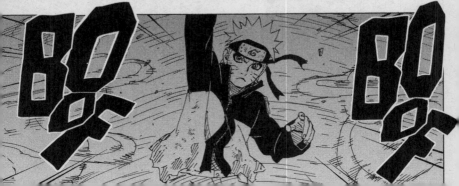

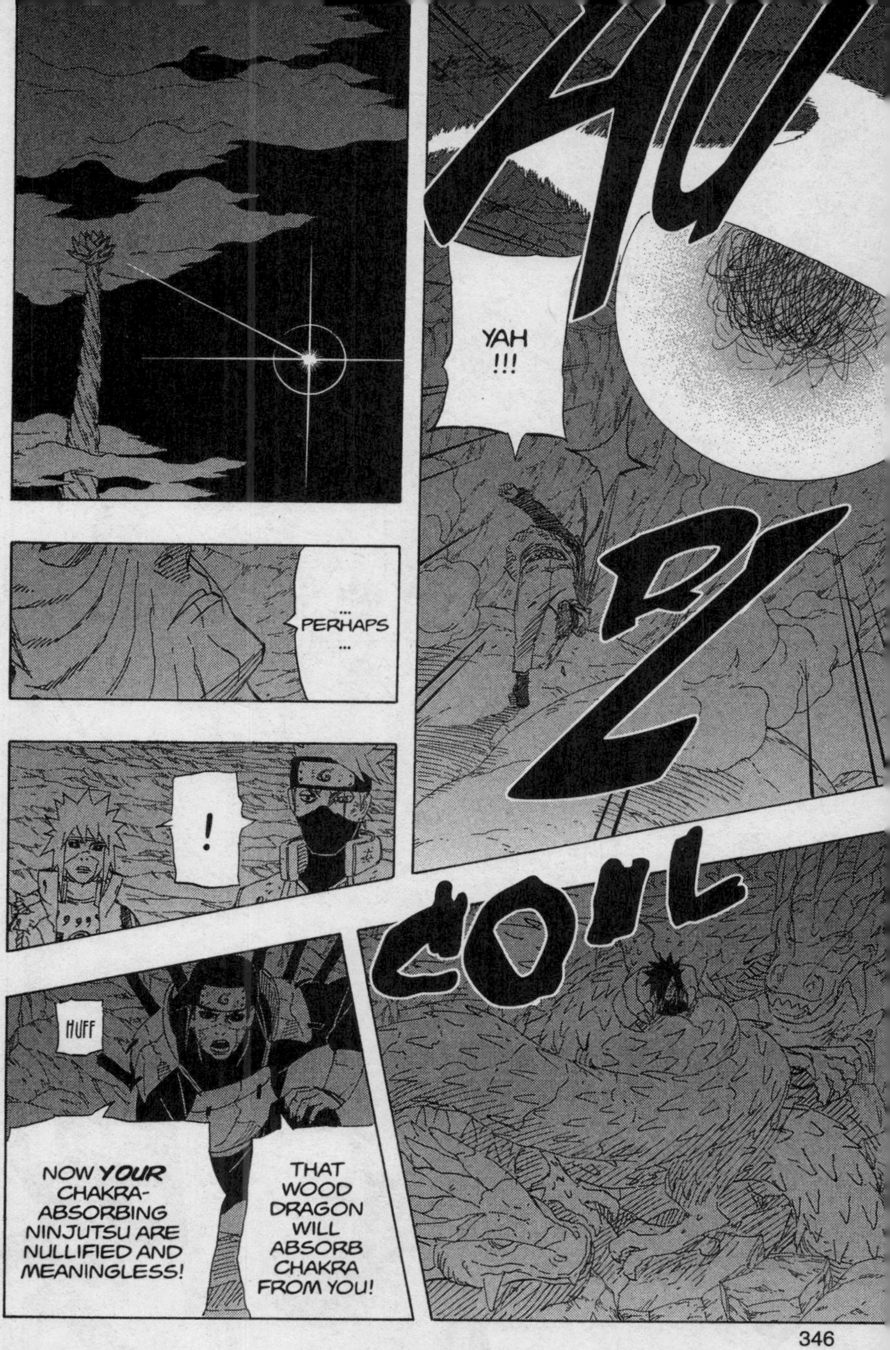
HYU
YAH !!!
DZ
... PERHAPS ...
!
COIL
HUFF
THAT WOOD DRAGON WILL ABSORB CHAKRA FROM YOU!
NOW **YOUR** CHAKRA-ABSORBING NINJUTSU ARE NULLIFIED AND MEANINGLESS!

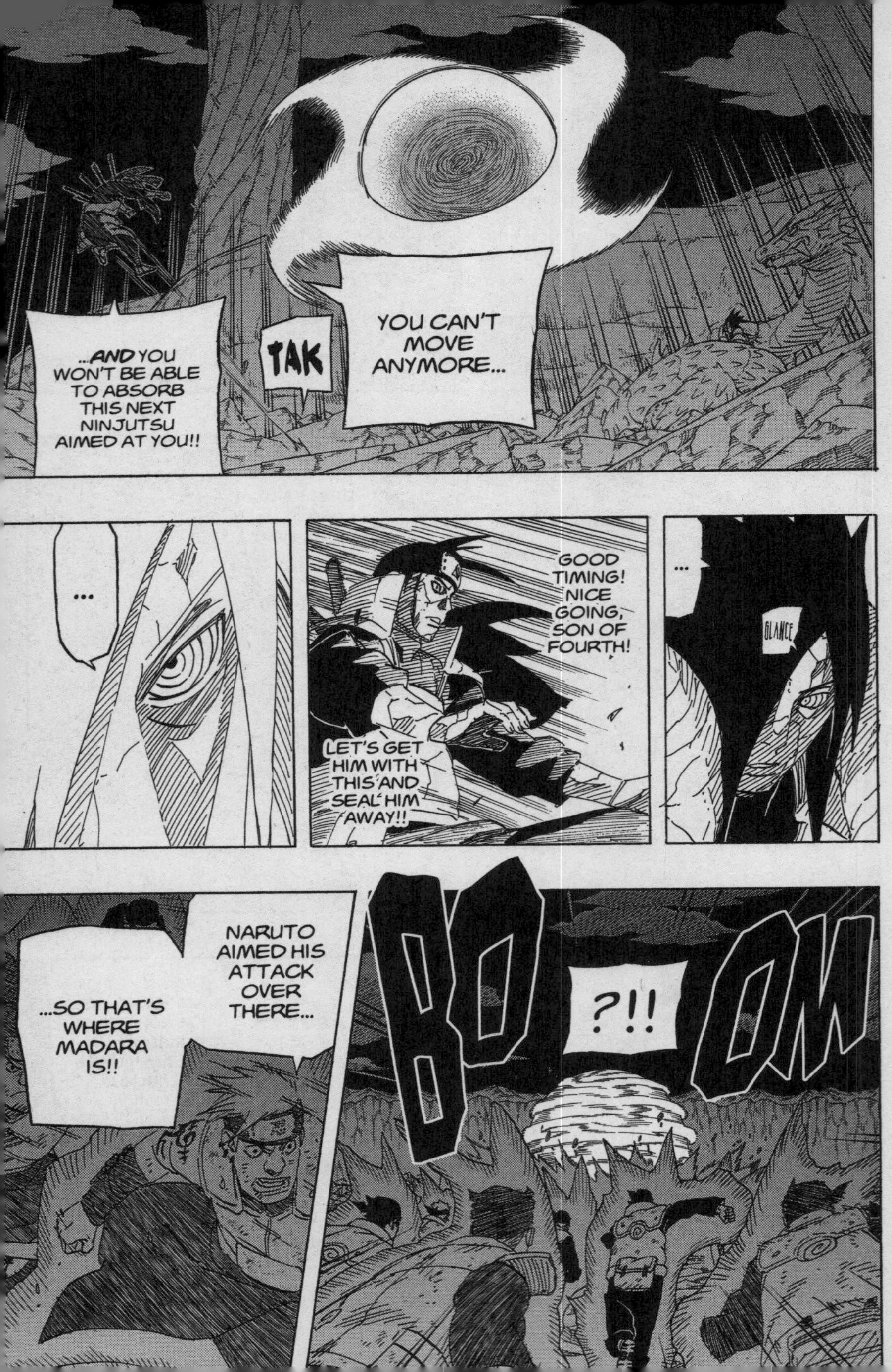
YOU CAN'T MOVE ANYMORE...
TAK
...AND YOU WON'T BE ABLE TO ABSORB THIS NEXT NINJUTSU AIMED AT YOU!!
...
GLANCE
GOOD TIMING! NICE GOING, SON OF FOURTH!
LET'S GET HIM WITH THIS AND SEAL HIM AWAY!!
...
BOOM
?!!
NARUTO AIMED HIS ATTACK OVER THERE...
...SO THAT'S WHERE MADARA IS!!

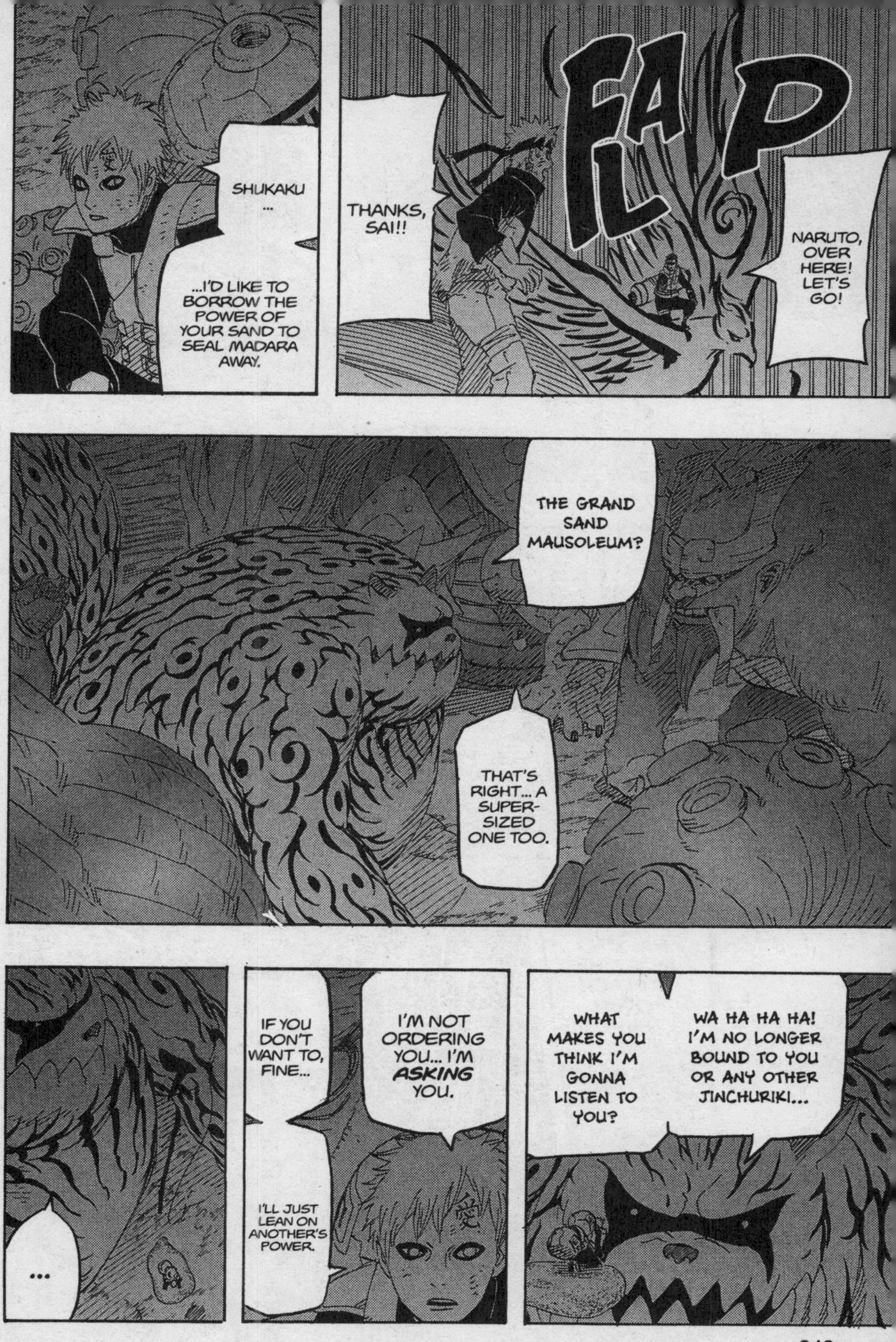
FLAP
NARUTO, OVER HERE! LET'S GO!
THANKS, SAI!!
SHUKAKU ...
...I'D LIKE TO BORROW THE POWER OF YOUR SAND TO SEAL MADARA AWAY.
THE GRAND SAND MAUSOLEUM?
THAT'S RIGHT... A SUPER-SIZED ONE TOO.
WA HA HA HA! I'M NO LONGER BOUND TO YOU OR ANY OTHER JINCHURIKI...
WHAT MAKES YOU THINK I'M GONNA LISTEN TO YOU?
I'M NOT ORDERING YOU... I'M **ASKING** YOU.
IF YOU DON'T WANT TO, FINE...
I'LL JUST LEAN ON ANOTHER'S POWER.
...

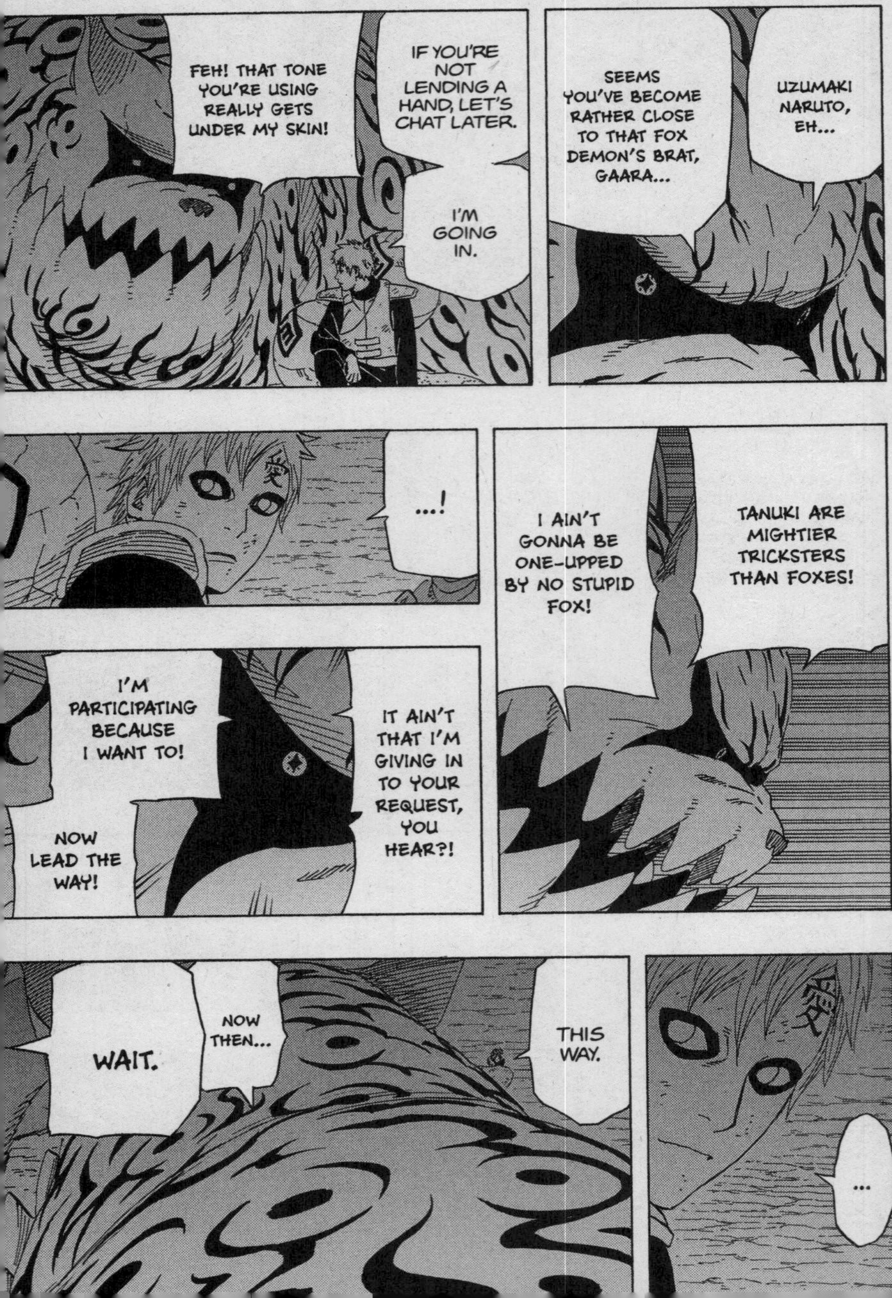
UZUMAKI NARUTO, EH...
SEEMS YOU'VE BECOME RATHER CLOSE TO THAT FOX DEMON'S BRAT, GAARA...
IF YOU'RE NOT LENDING A HAND, LET'S CHAT LATER.
I'M GOING IN.
FEH! THAT TONE YOU'RE USING REALLY GETS UNDER MY SKIN!
TANUKI ARE MIGHTIER TRICKSTERS THAN FOXES!
I AIN'T GONNA BE ONE-UPPED BY NO STUPID FOX!
...!
IT AIN'T THAT I'M GIVING IN TO YOUR REQUEST, YOU HEAR?!
I'M PARTICIPATING BECAUSE I WANT TO!
NOW LEAD THE WAY!
...
THIS WAY.
NOW THEN...
WAIT.

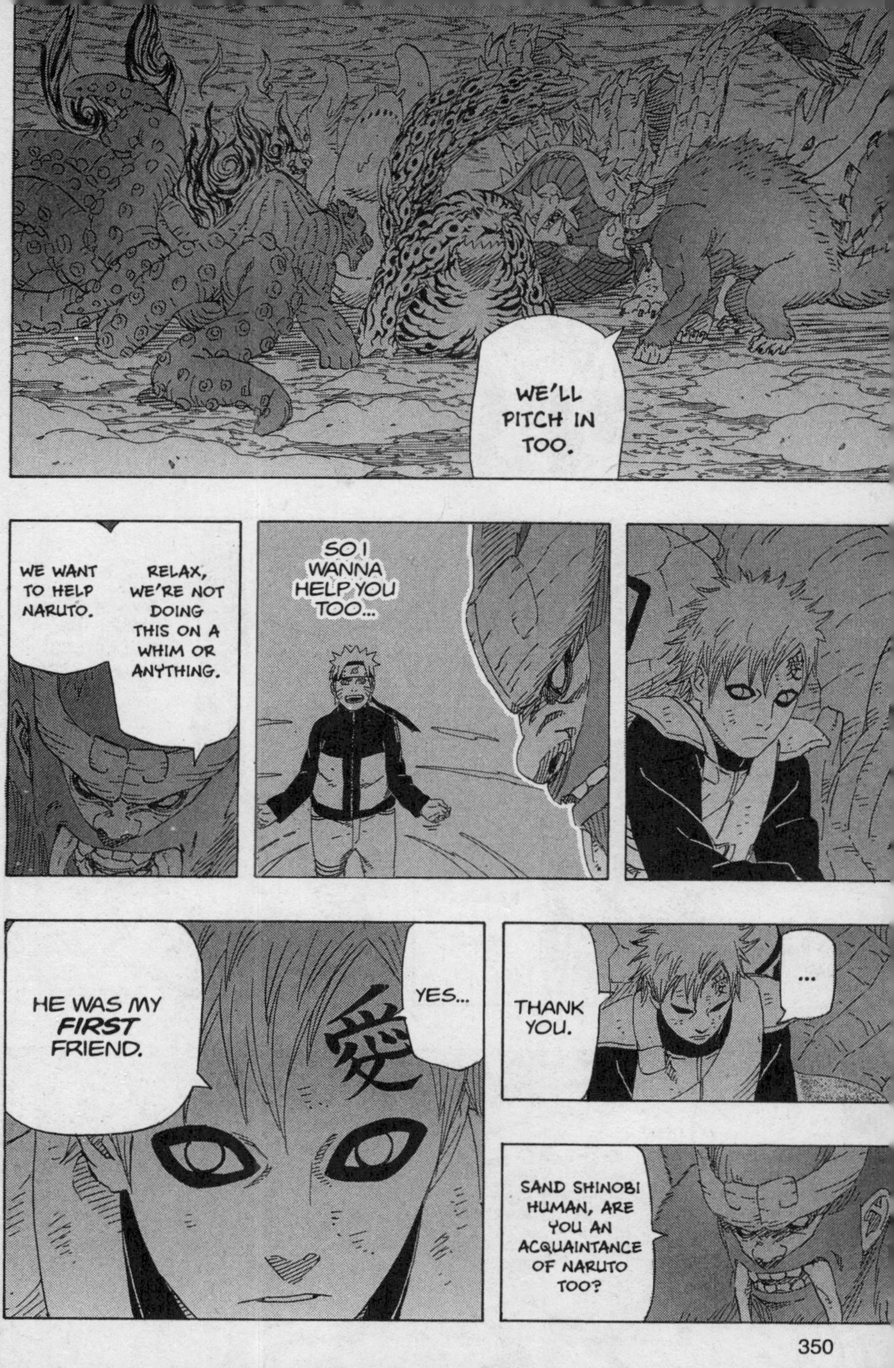
WE'LL PITCH IN TOO.
SO I WANNA HELP YOU TOO...
RELAX, WE'RE NOT DOING THIS ON A WHIM OR ANYTHING.
WE WANT TO HELP NARUTO.
...
THANK YOU.
SAND SHINOBI HUMAN, ARE YOU AN ACQUAINTANCE OF NARUTO TOO?
YES...
HE WAS MY FIRST FRIEND.

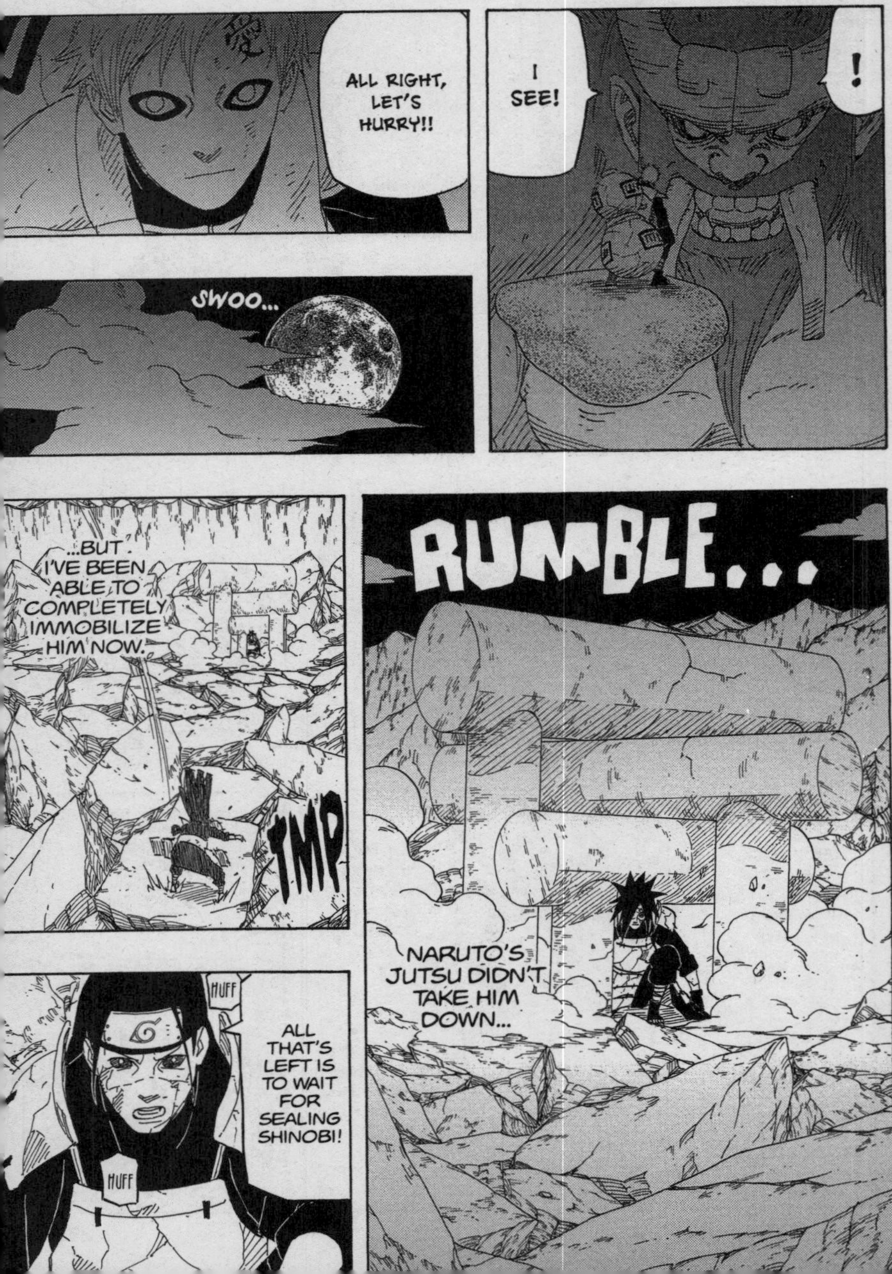
!
I SEE!
ALL RIGHT, LET'S HURRY!!
SWOO...
RUMBLE...
NARUTO'S JUTSU DIDN'T TAKE HIM DOWN...
...BUT I'VE BEEN ABLE TO COMPLETELY IMMOBILIZE HIM NOW.
TMP
HUFF
ALL THAT'S LEFT IS TO WAIT FOR SEALING SHINOBI!
HUFF

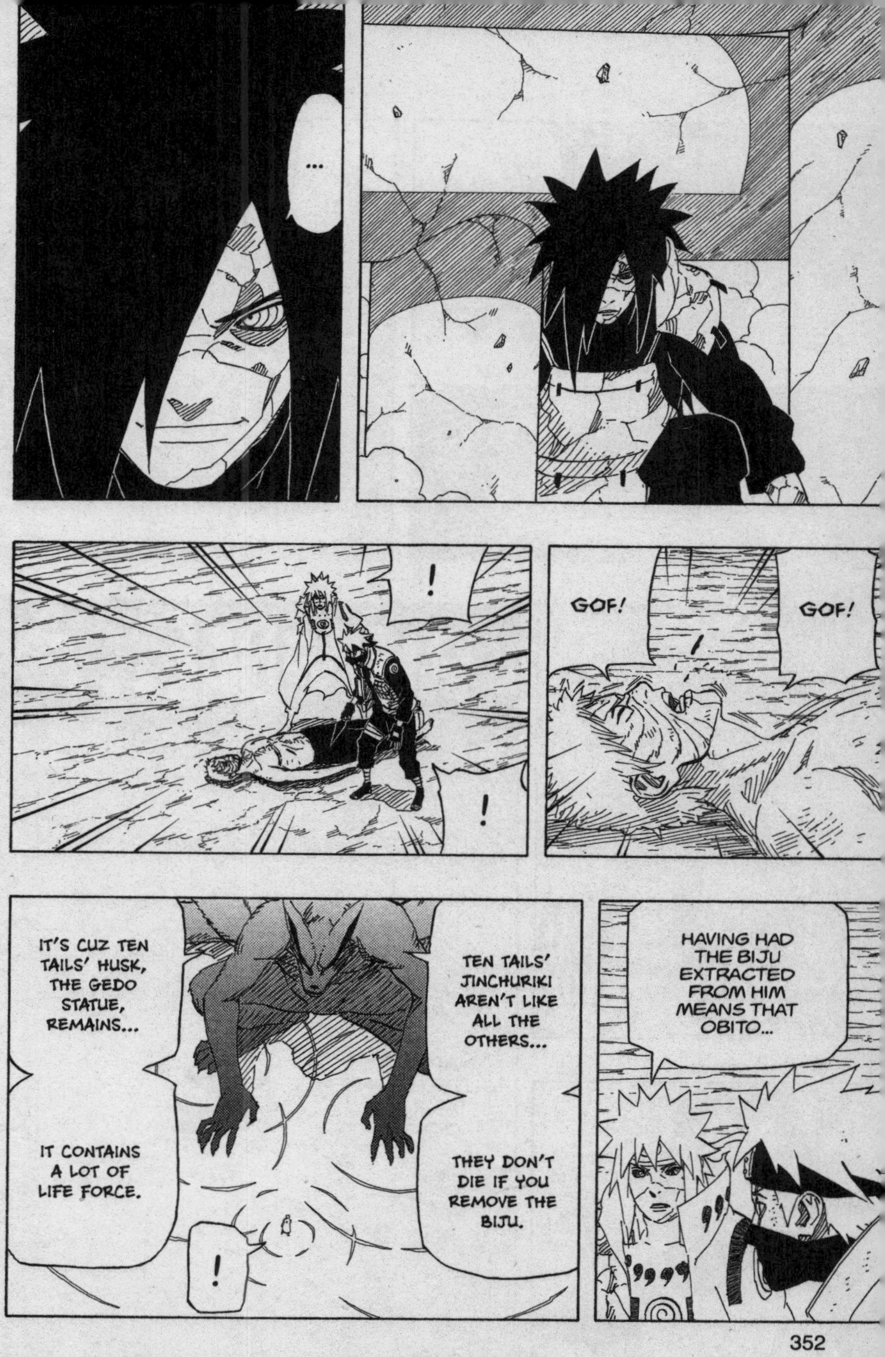
...
GOF!
GOF!
!
!
HAVING HAD THE BIJU EXTRACTED FROM HIM MEANS THAT OBITO...
TEN TAILS' JINCHURIKI AREN'T LIKE ALL THE OTHERS...
THEY DON'T DIE IF YOU REMOVE THE BIJU.
IT'S CUZ TEN TAILS' HUSK, THE GEDO STATUE, REMAINS...
IT CONTAINS A LOT OF LIFE FORCE.
!

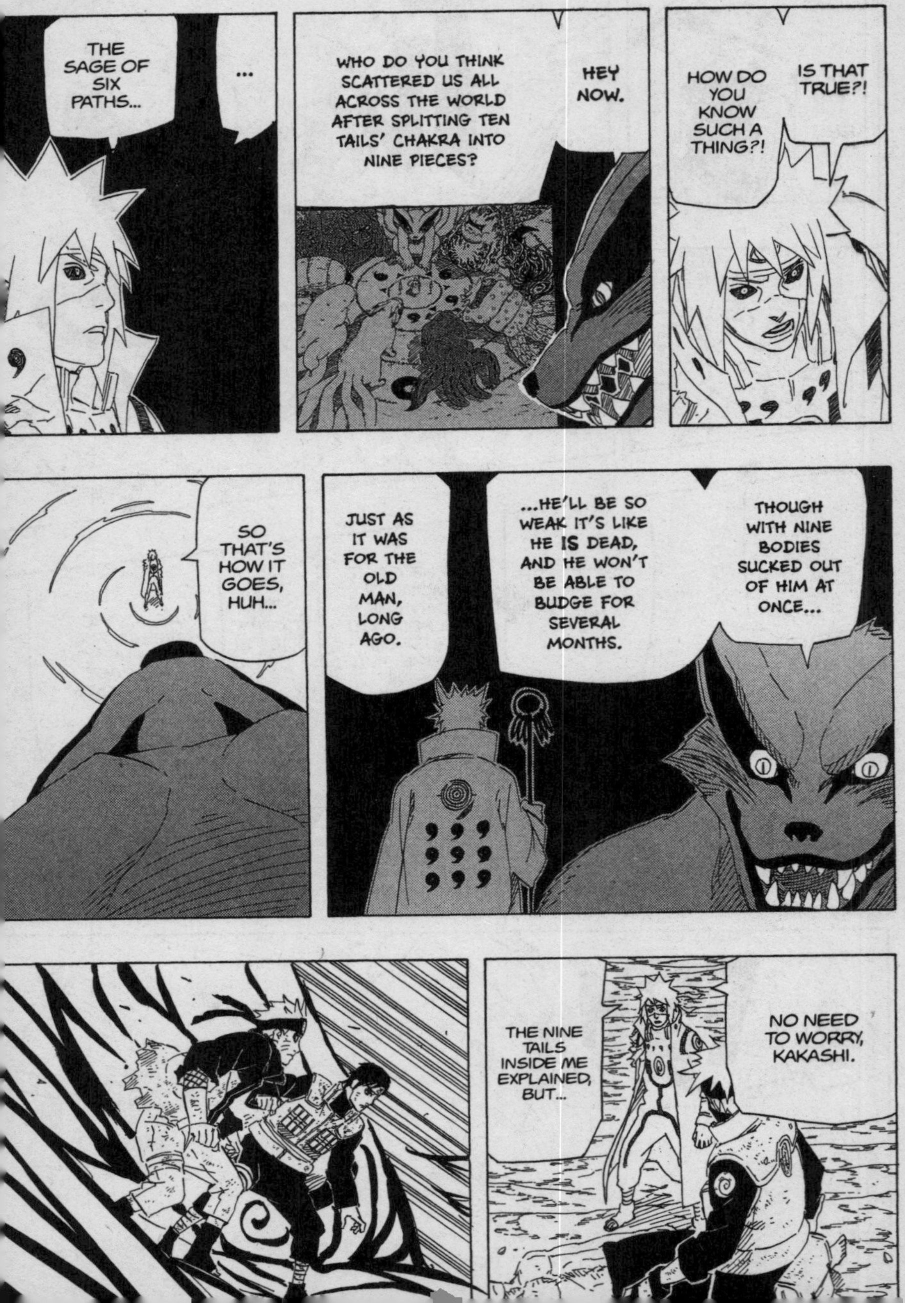
IS THAT TRUE?!
HOW DO YOU KNOW SUCH A THING?!
HEY NOW.
WHO DO YOU THINK SCATTERED US ALL ACROSS THE WORLD AFTER SPLITTING TEN TAILS' CHAKRA INTO NINE PIECES?
...
THE SAGE OF SIX PATHS...
THOUGH WITH NINE BODIES SUCKED OUT OF HIM AT ONCE...
...HE'LL BE SO WEAK IT'S LIKE HE IS DEAD, AND HE WON'T BE ABLE TO BUDGE FOR SEVERAL MONTHS.
JUST AS IT WAS FOR THE OLD MAN, LONG AGO.
SO THAT'S HOW IT GOES, HUH...
NO NEED TO WORRY, KAKASHI.
THE NINE TAILS INSIDE ME EXPLAINED, BUT...

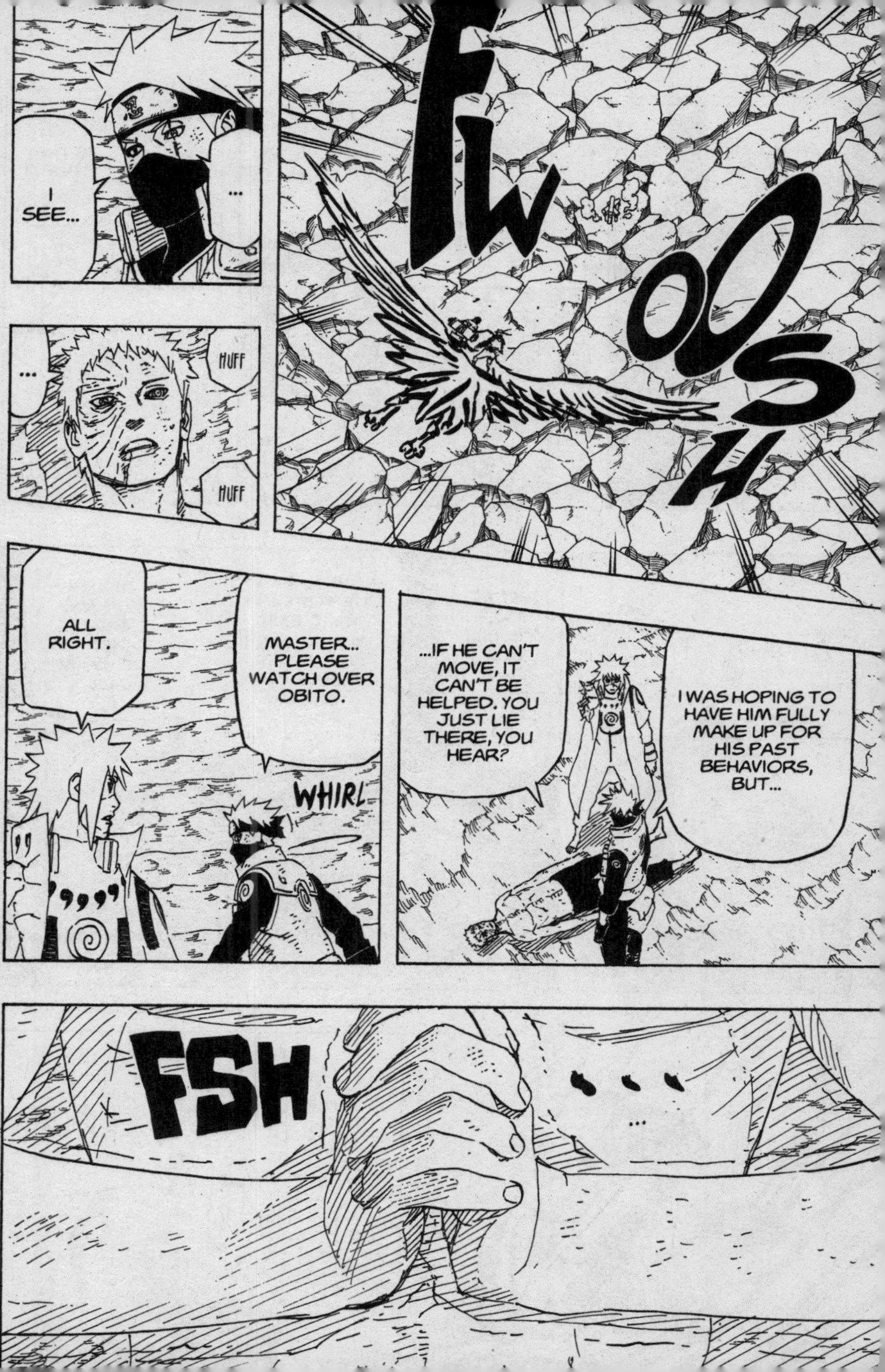
FWOOSH
...
I SEE...
HUFF
...
HUFF
I WAS HOPING TO HAVE HIM FULLY MAKE UP FOR HIS PAST BEHAVIORS, BUT...
...IF HE CAN'T MOVE, IT CAN'T BE HELPED. YOU JUST LIE THERE, YOU HEAR?
MASTER.. PLEASE WATCH OVER OBITO.
ALL RIGHT.
WHIRL
...
...
FSH

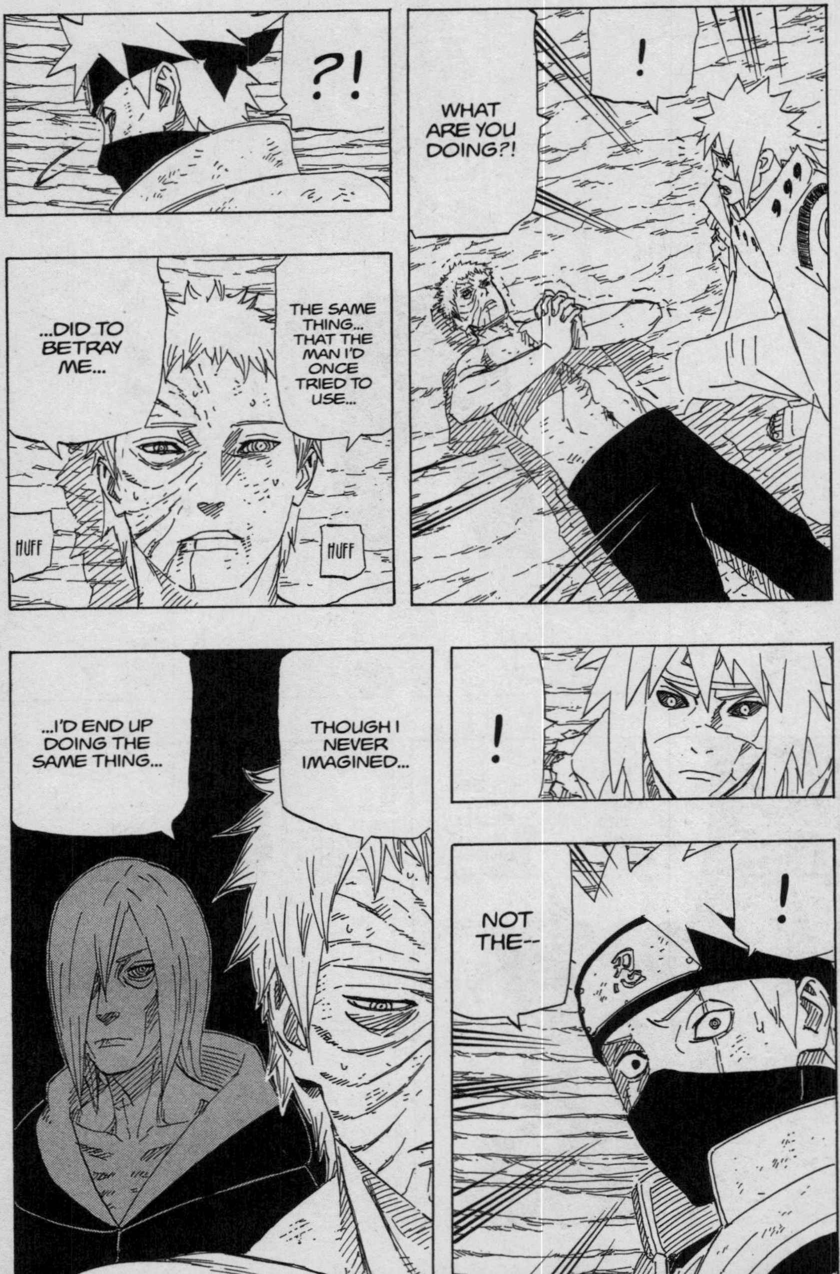
!
WHAT ARE YOU DOING?!
?!
THE SAME THING... THAT THE MAN I'D ONCE TRIED TO USE...
...DID TO BETRAY ME...
HUFF
HUFF
!
!
NOT THE--
THOUGH I NEVER IMAGINED...
...I'D END UP DOING THE SAME THING...

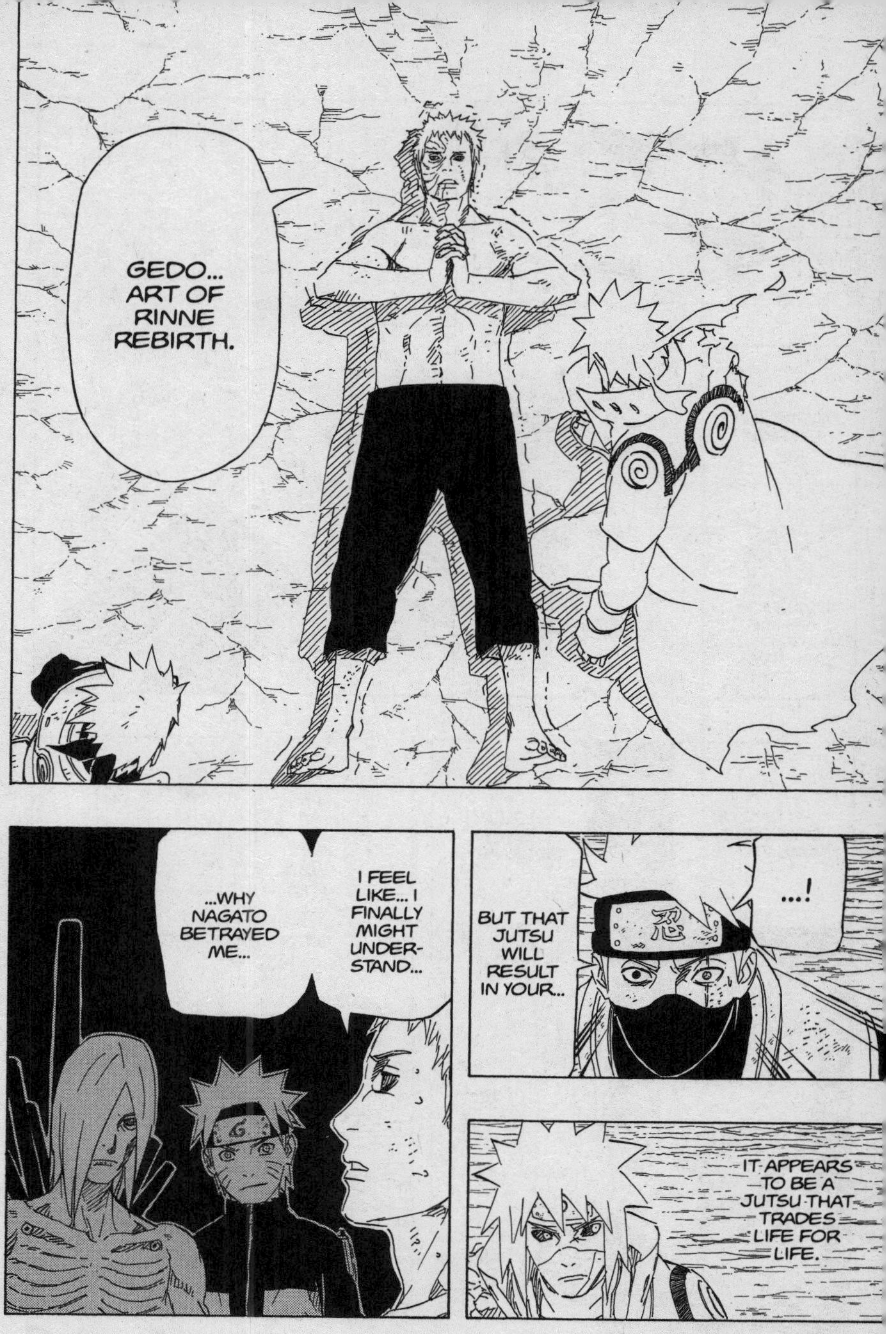
GEDO... ART OF RINNE REBIRTH.
...!
BUT THAT JUTSU WILL RESULT IN YOUR...
IT APPEARS TO BE A JUTSU THAT TRADES LIFE FOR LIFE.
I FEEL LIKE... I FINALLY MIGHT UNDERSTAND...
...WHY NAGATO BETRAYED ME...

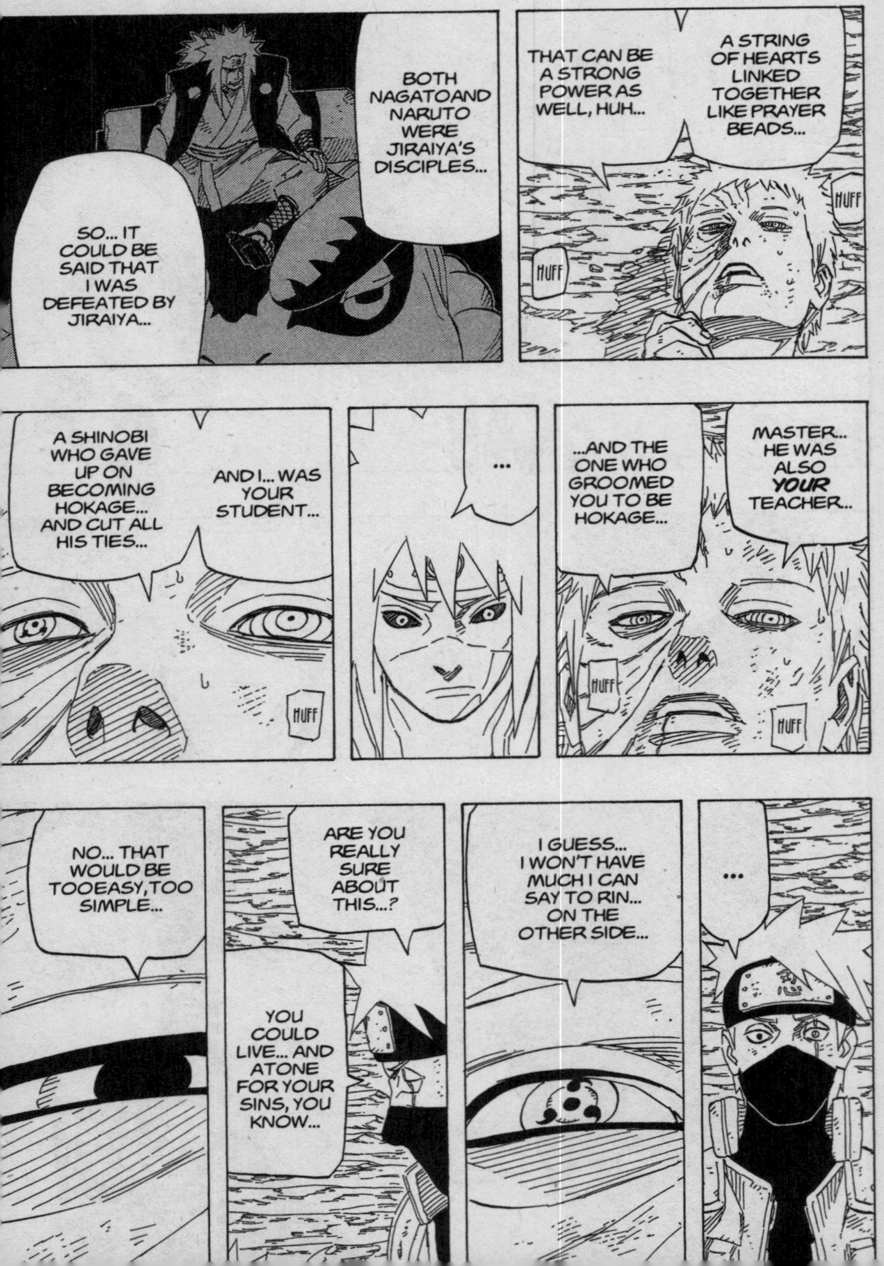
A STRING OF HEARTS LINKED TOGETHER LIKE PRAYER BEADS...
THAT CAN BE A STRONG POWER AS WELL, HUH...
HUFF
HUFF
BOTH NAGATO AND NARUTO WERE JIRAIYA'S DISCIPLES...
SO... IT COULD BE SAID THAT I WAS DEFEATED BY JIRAIYA...
MASTER... HE WAS ALSO *YOUR* TEACHER...
...AND THE ONE WHO GROOMED YOU TO BE HOKAGE...
HUFF
HUFF
...
AND I... WAS YOUR STUDENT...
A SHINOBI WHO GAVE UP ON BECOMING HOKAGE... AND CUT ALL HIS TIES...
HUFF
...
I GUESS... I WON'T HAVE MUCH I CAN SAY TO RIN... ON THE OTHER SIDE...
ARE YOU REALLY SURE ABOUT THIS...?
YOU COULD LIVE... AND ATONE FOR YOUR SINS, YOU KNOW...
NO... THAT WOULD BE TOO EASY, TOO SIMPLE...

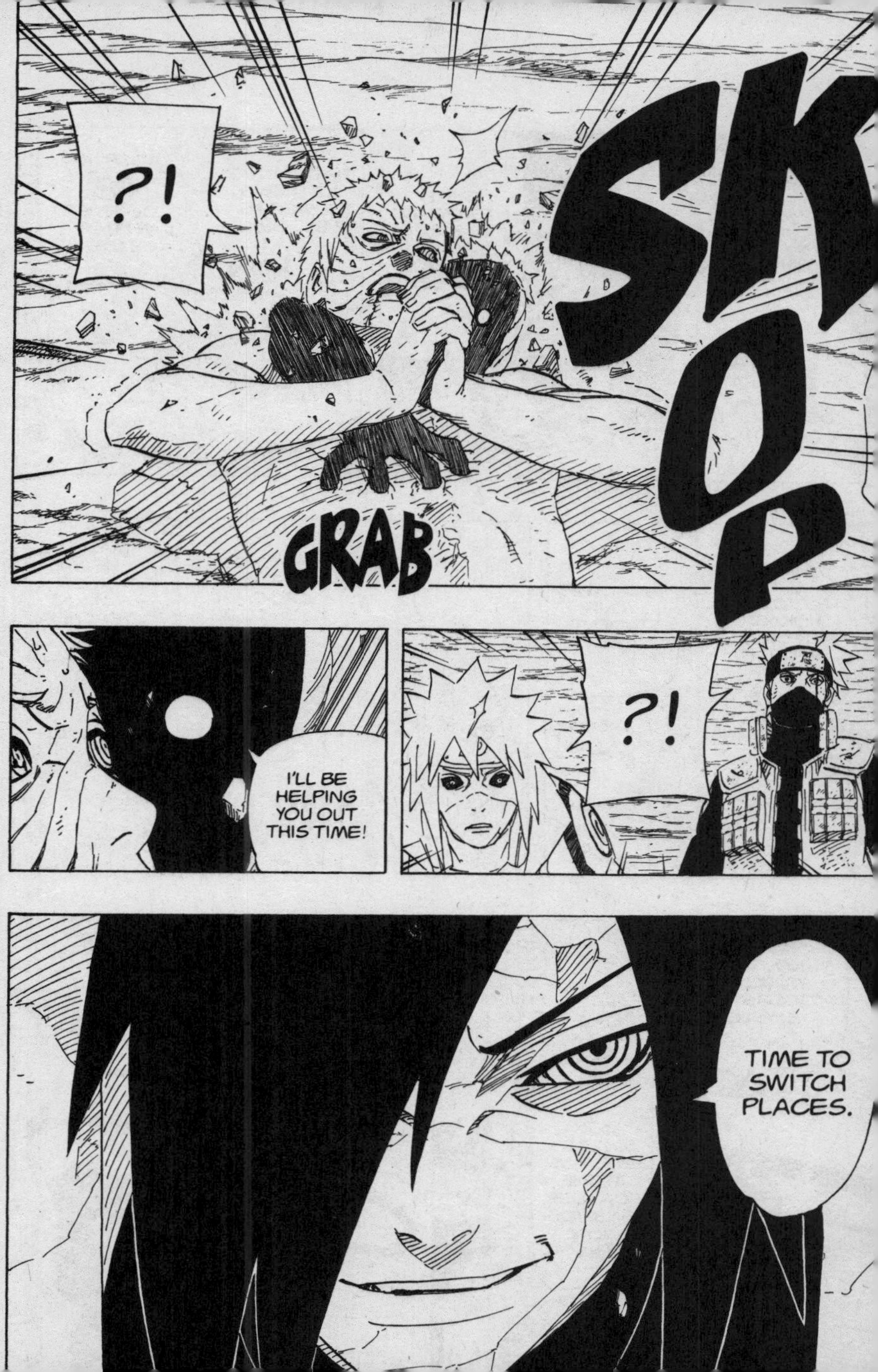
SKOOP
?!
GRAB
?!
I'LL BE HELPING YOU OUT THIS TIME!
TIME TO SWITCH PLACES.

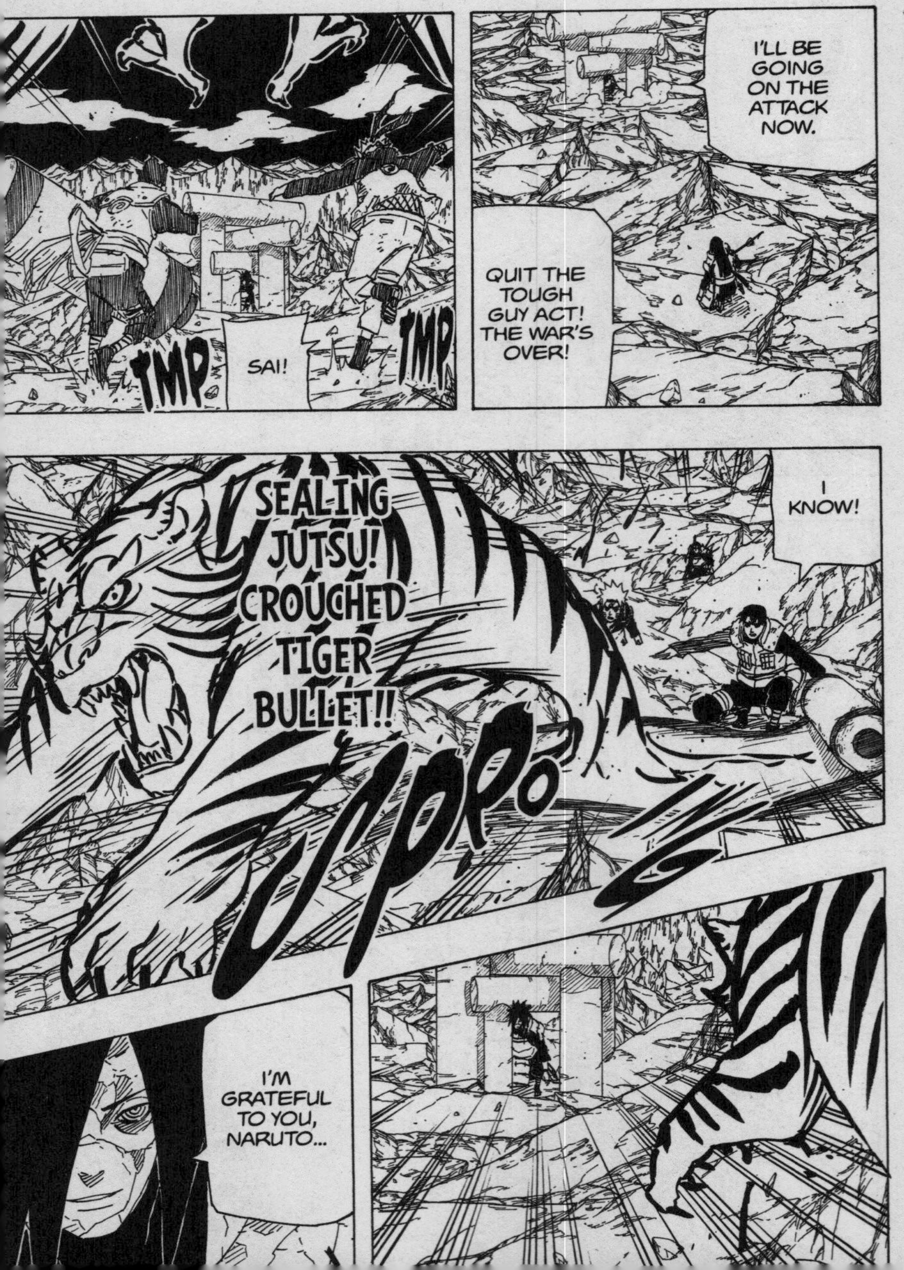
I'LL BE GOING ON THE ATTACK NOW.
QUIT THE TOUGH GUY ACT! THE WAR'S OVER!
SAI!
TMP
TMP
I KNOW!
SEALING JUTSU! CROUCHED TIGER BULLET!!
I'M GRATEFUL TO YOU, NARUTO...

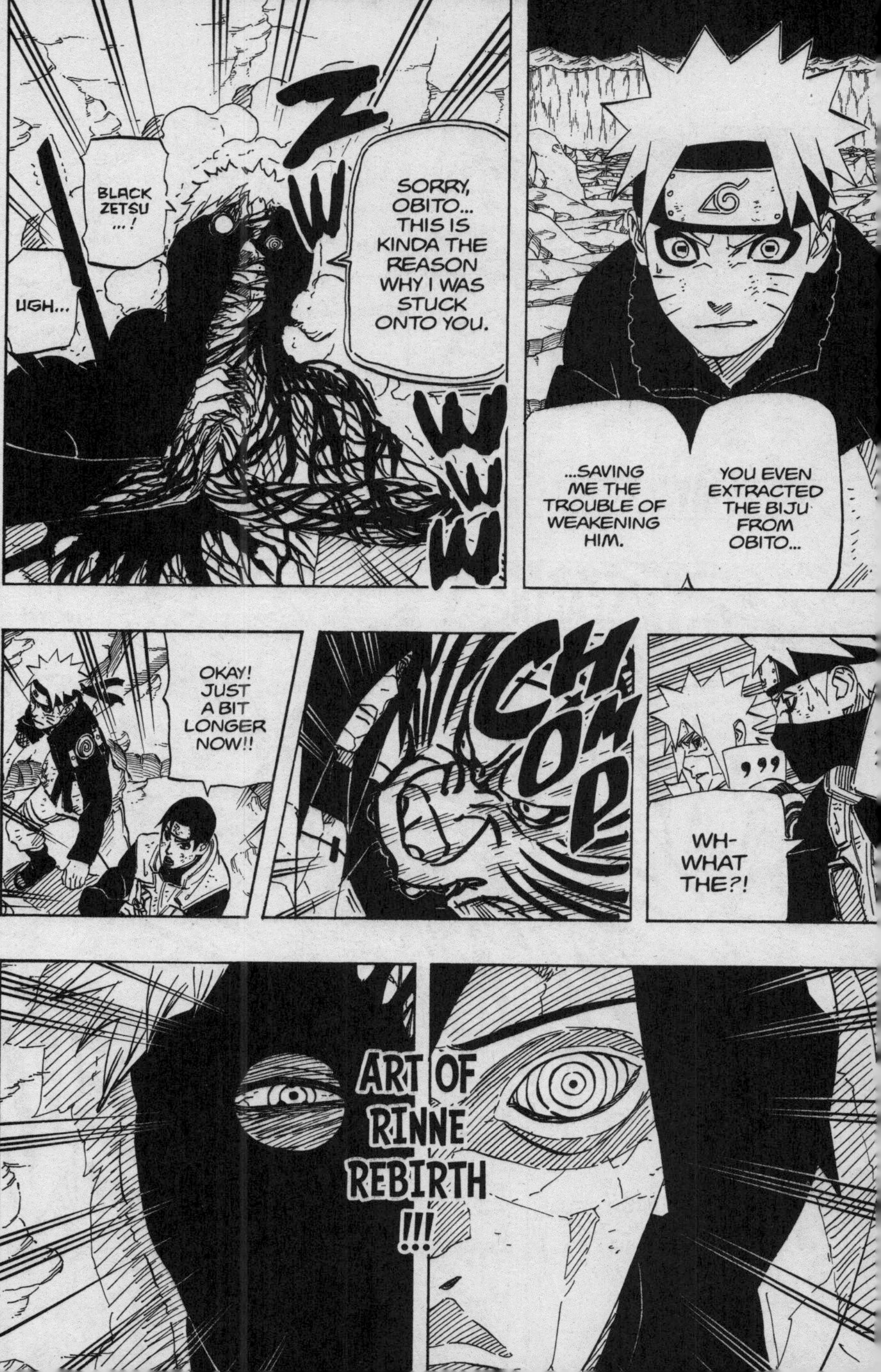
YOU EVEN EXTRACTED THE BIJU FROM OBITO...
...SAVING ME THE TROUBLE OF WEAKENING HIM.
SORRY, OBITO... THIS IS KINDA THE REASON WHY I WAS STUCK ONTO YOU.
ZW
WWWW
BLACK ZETSU ...!
UGH...
"
WH-WHAT THE?!
CHOMP
OKAY! JUST A BIT LONGER NOW!!
ART OF RINNE REBIRTH!!!

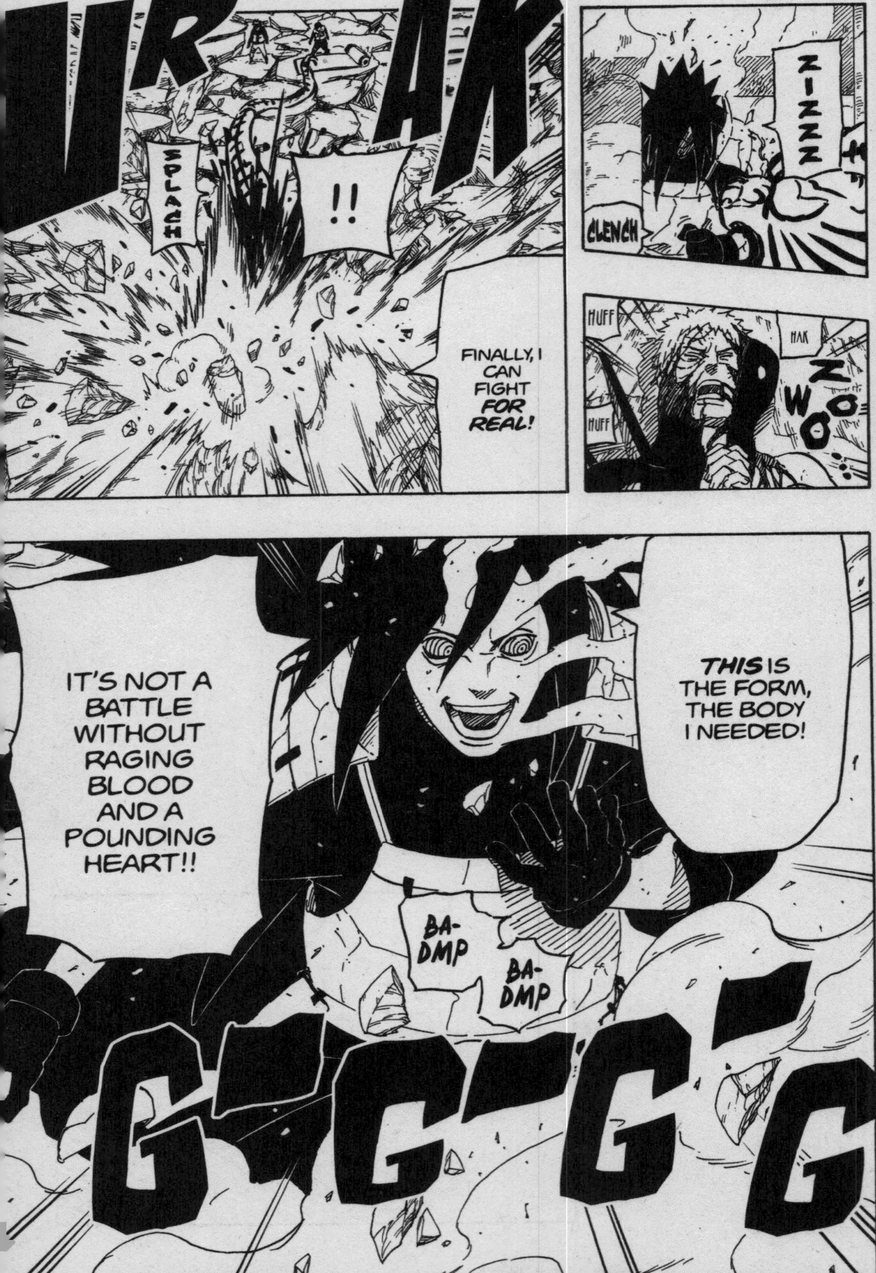
ZIZZZ
CLENCH
HAK
HUFF
HUFF
WOOZ
VRAK
SPLACH
!!
FINALLY, I CAN FIGHT FOR REAL!
THIS IS THE FORM, THE BODY I NEEDED!
IT'S NOT A BATTLE WITHOUT RAGING BLOOD AND A POUNDING HEART!!
BA-DMP
BA-DMP
GGGG

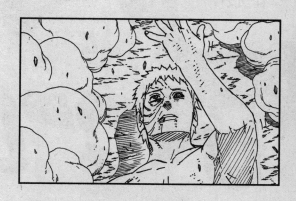

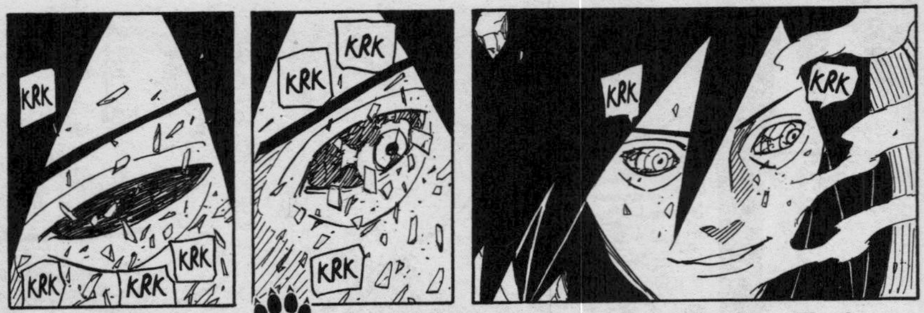
KRK
KRK
KRK
KRK
KRK
KRK
KRK
KRK
KRK

Number 657: Uchiha Madara, in the Flesh

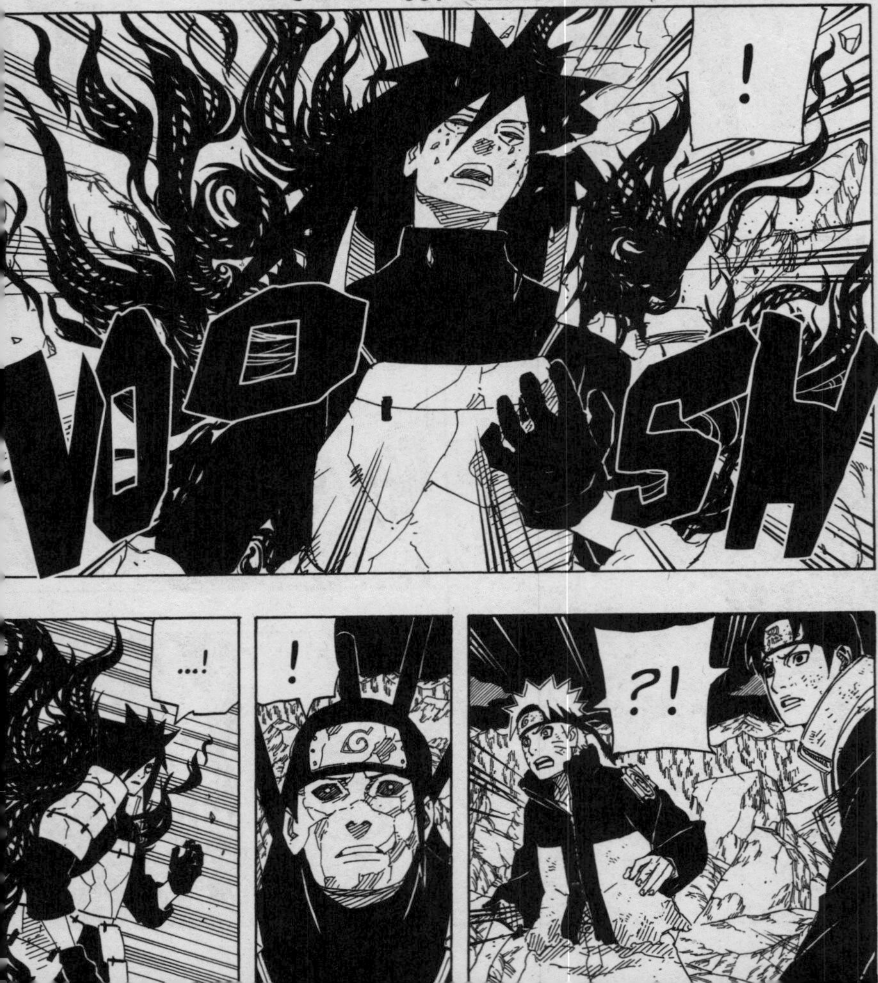
!
VOOSH
?!
!
...!

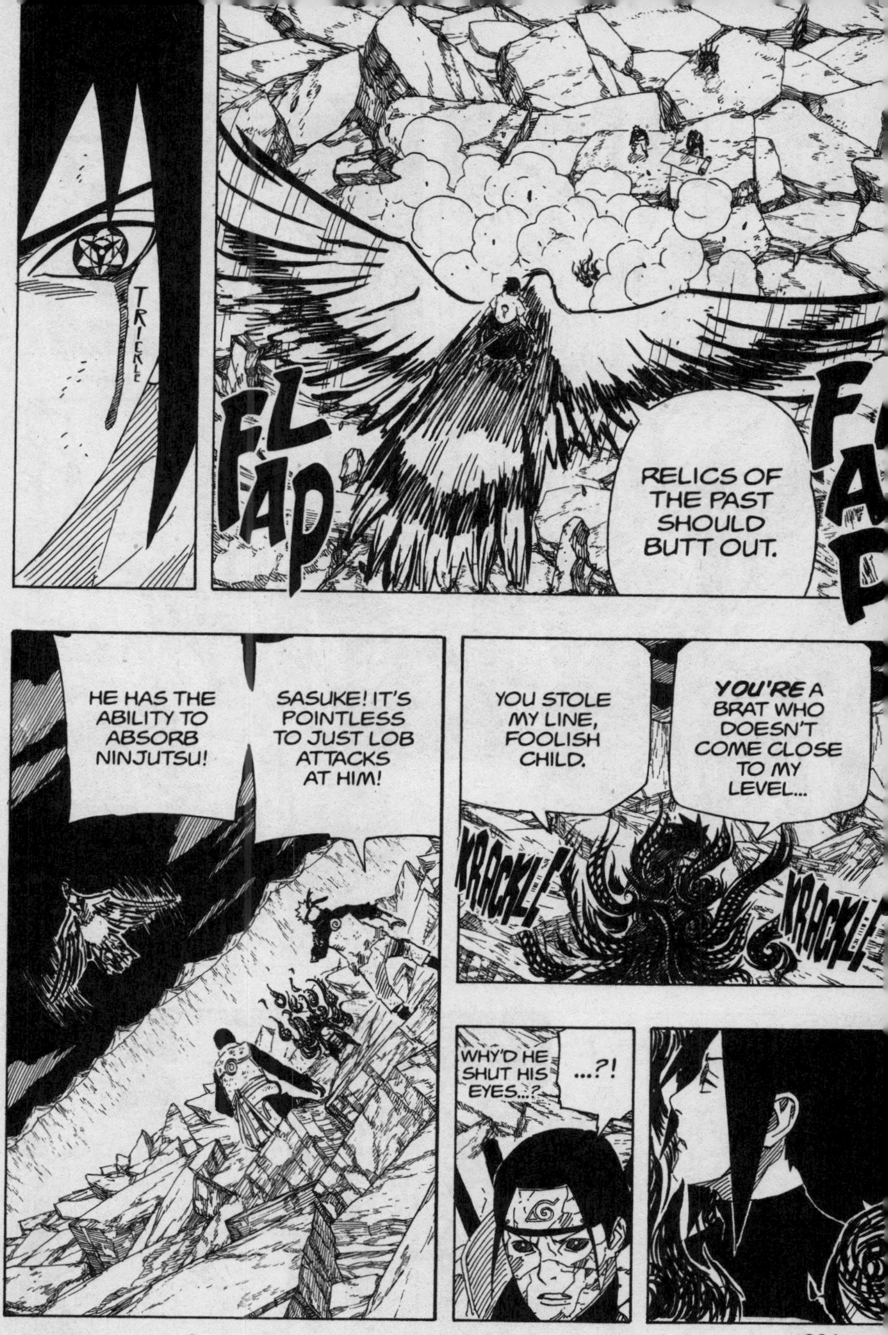

RELICS OF THE PAST SHOULD BUTT OUT.
FLAP
TRICKLE
YOU'RE A BRAT WHO DOESN'T COME CLOSE TO MY LEVEL...
YOU STOLE MY LINE, FOOLISH CHILD.
KRACKLE
KRACKLE
...?!
WHY'D HE SHUT HIS EYES...?
SASUKE! IT'S POINTLESS TO JUST LOB ATTACKS AT HIM!
HE HAS THE ABILITY TO ABSORB NINJUTSU!

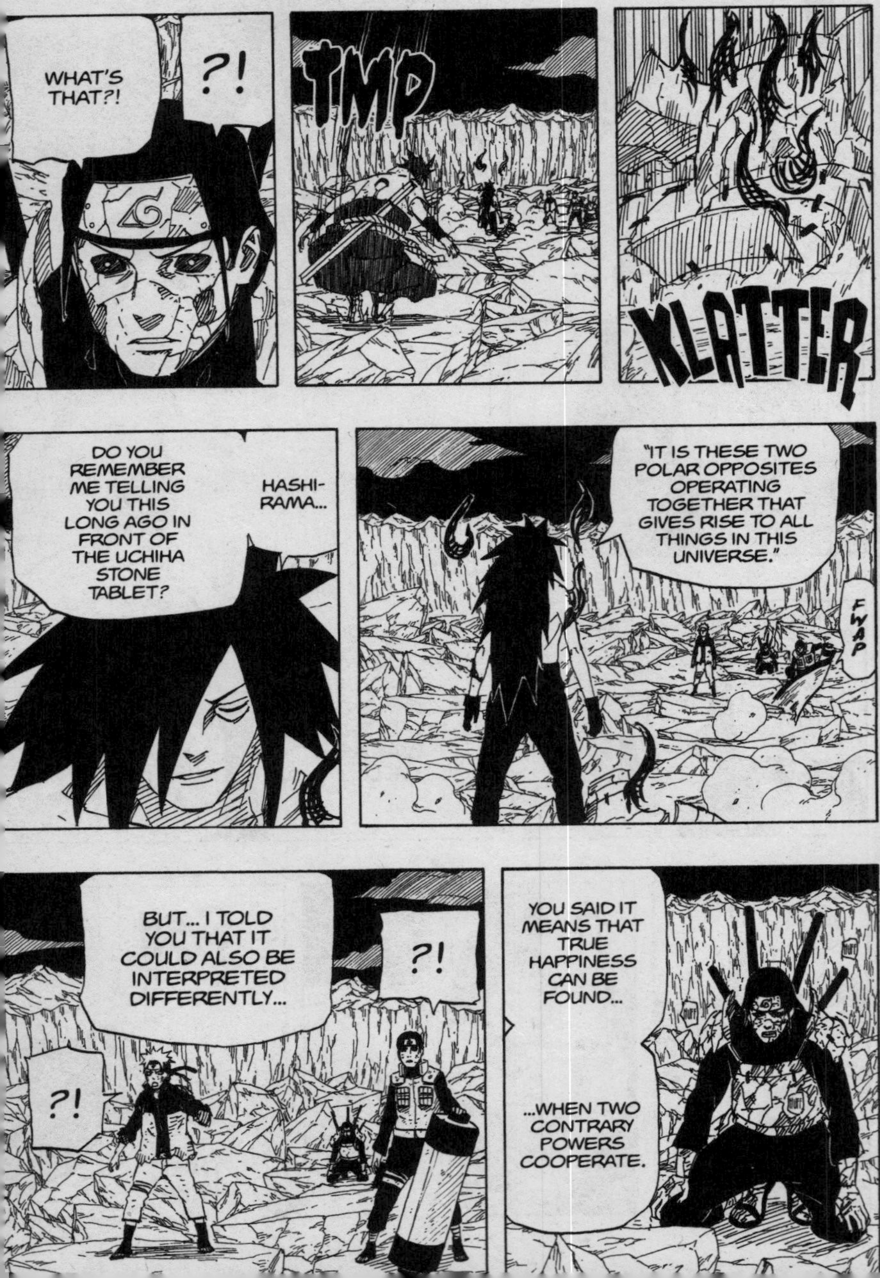
KLATTER
TMP
?!
WHAT'S THAT?!
"IT IS THESE TWO POLAR OPPOSITES OPERATING TOGETHER THAT GIVES RISE TO ALL THINGS IN THIS UNIVERSE."
FWAP
HASHI-RAMA...
DO YOU REMEMBER ME TELLING YOU THIS LONG AGO IN FRONT OF THE UCHIHA STONE TABLET?
YOU SAID IT MEANS THAT TRUE HAPPINESS CAN BE FOUND...
...WHEN TWO CONTRARY POWERS COOPERATE.
?!
BUT... I TOLD YOU THAT IT COULD ALSO BE INTERPRETED DIFFERENTLY...
?!

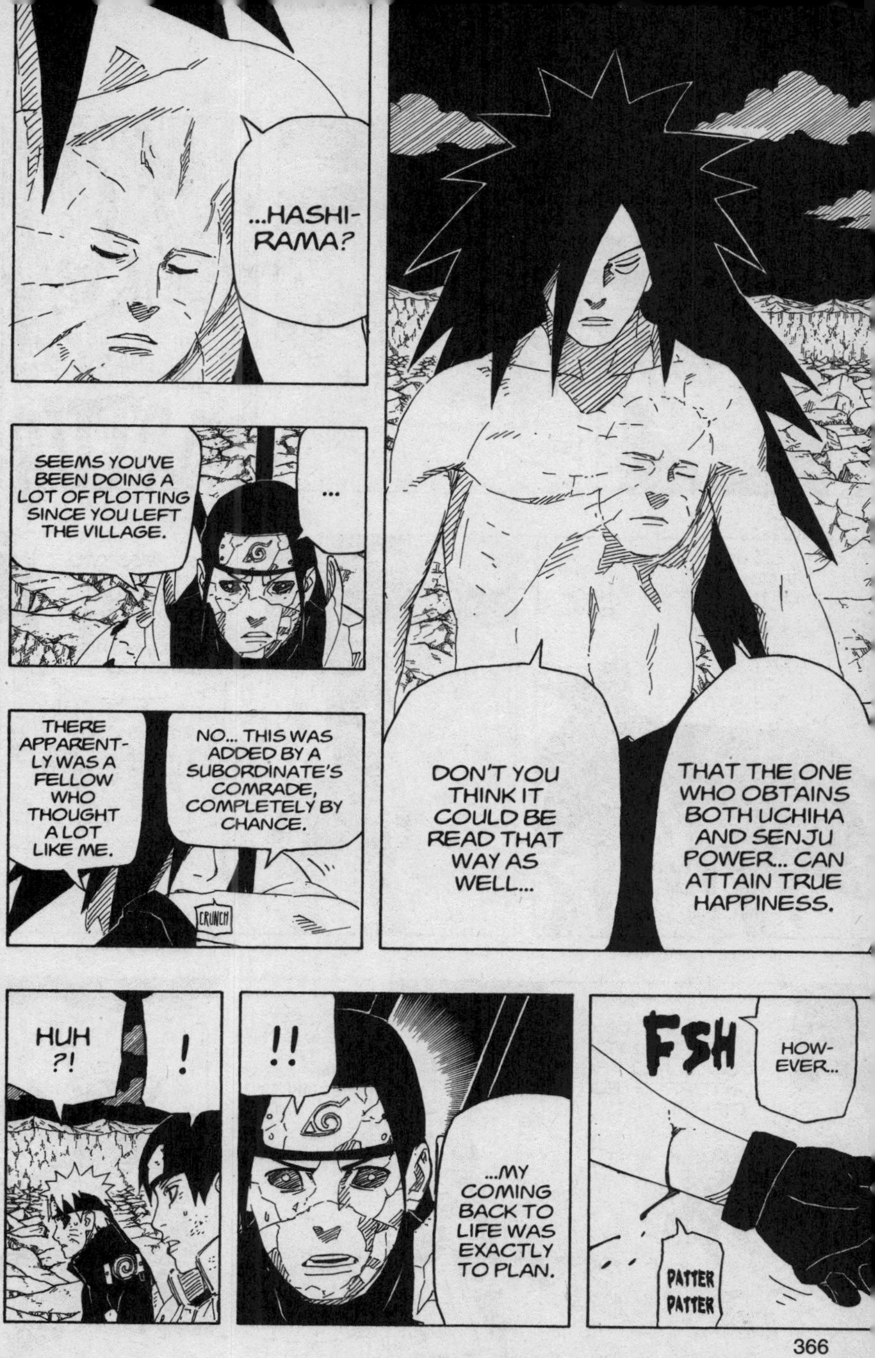

THAT THE ONE WHO OBTAINS BOTH UCHIHA AND SENJU POWER... CAN ATTAIN TRUE HAPPINESS.
DON'T YOU THINK IT COULD BE READ THAT WAY AS WELL...
...HASHI-RAMA?
...
SEEMS YOU'VE BEEN DOING A LOT OF PLOTTING SINCE YOU LEFT THE VILLAGE.
NO... THIS WAS ADDED BY A SUBORDINATE'S COMRADE, COMPLETELY BY CHANCE.
THERE APPARENT-LY WAS A FELLOW WHO THOUGHT A LOT LIKE ME.
CRUNCH
FSH
HOW-EVER...
PATTER PATTER
!!
...MY COMING BACK TO LIFE WAS EXACTLY TO PLAN.
!
HUH ?!

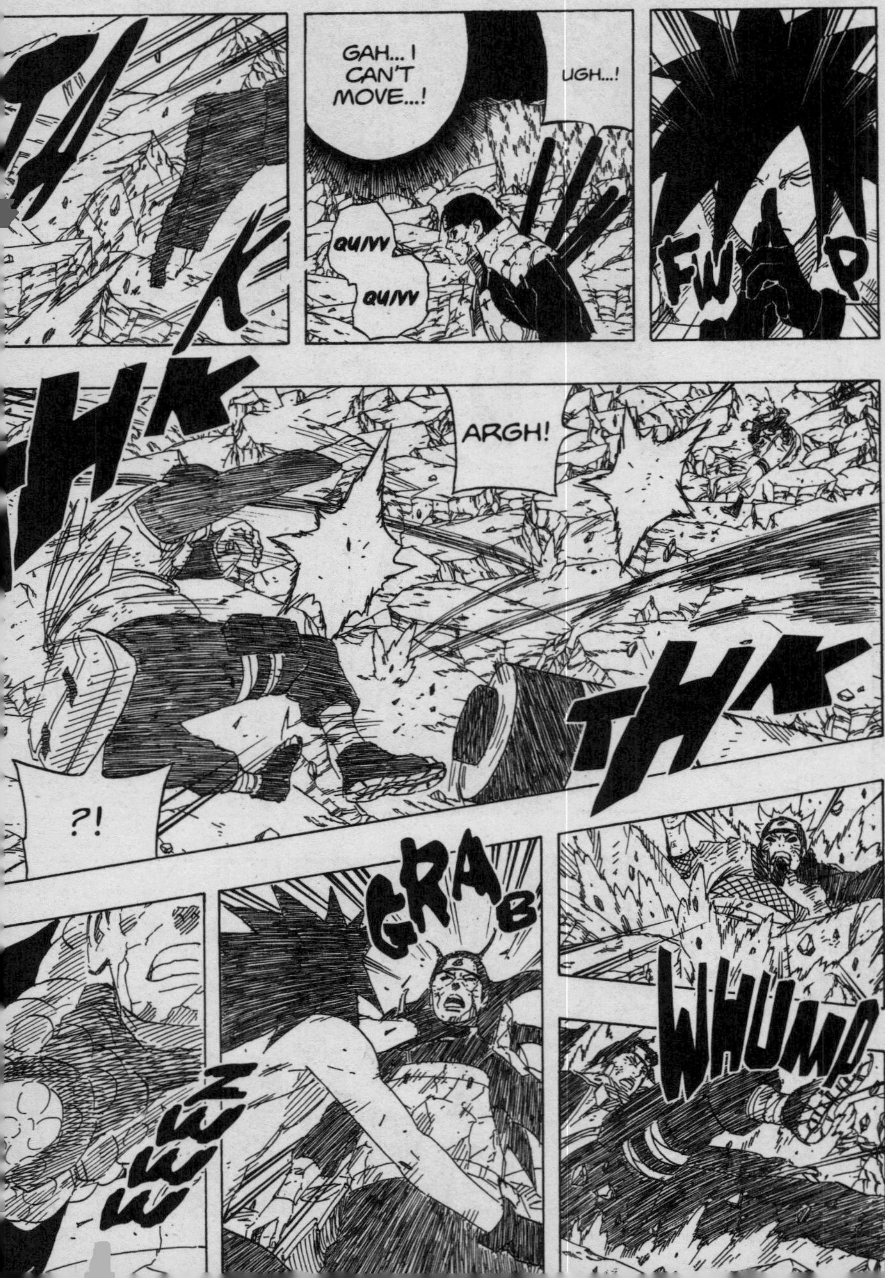
FWAP
UGH...!
GAH... I CAN'T MOVE...!
QUIVV
QUIVV
THWAK
ARGH!
THWAK
THWAK
?!
WHUMP
GRAB

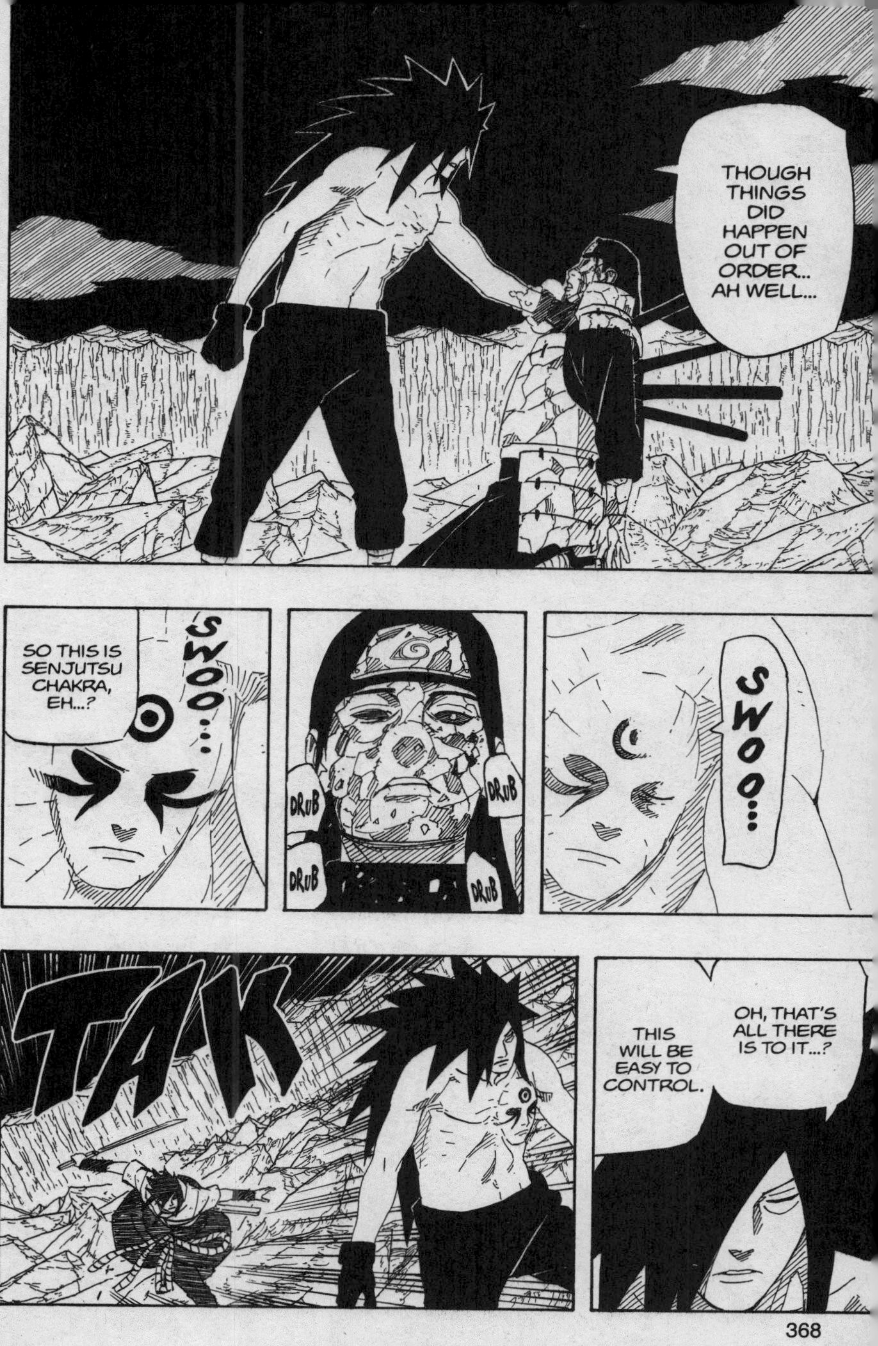
THOUGH THINGS DID HAPPEN OUT OF ORDER... AH WELL...
SWOO...
DRUB
DRUB
DRUB
DRUB
SWOO...
SO THIS IS SENJUTSU CHAKRA, EH...?
OH, THAT'S ALL THERE IS TO IT...?
THIS WILL BE EASY TO CONTROL.
TAK

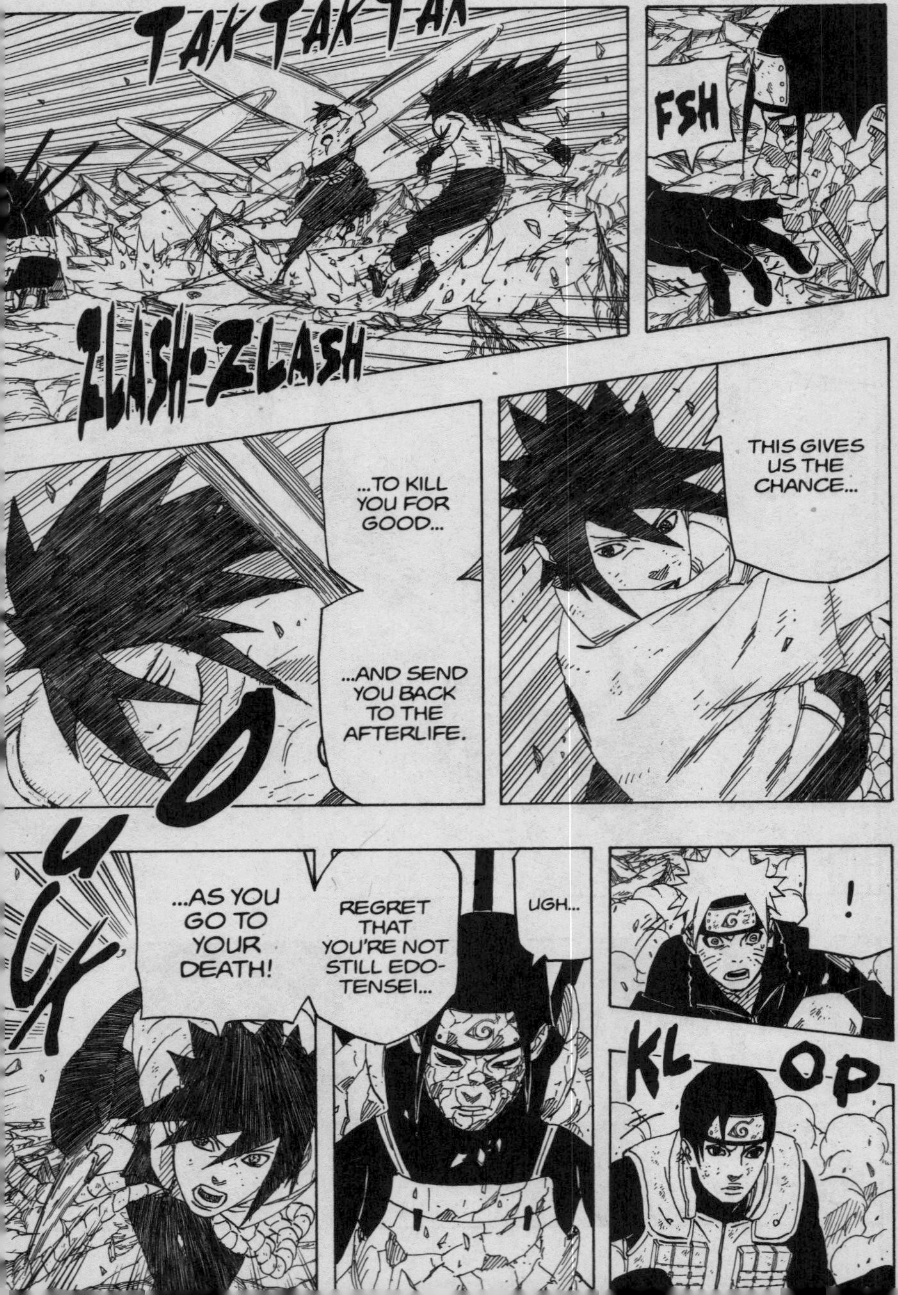
FSH
TAK TAK TAK
ZLASH-ZLASH
THIS GIVES US THE CHANCE...
...TO KILL YOU FOR GOOD...
...AND SEND YOU BACK TO THE AFTERLIFE.
!
KLOP
UGH...
REGRET THAT YOU'RE NOT STILL EDO-TENSEI...
...AS YOU GO TO YOUR DEATH!
UGK

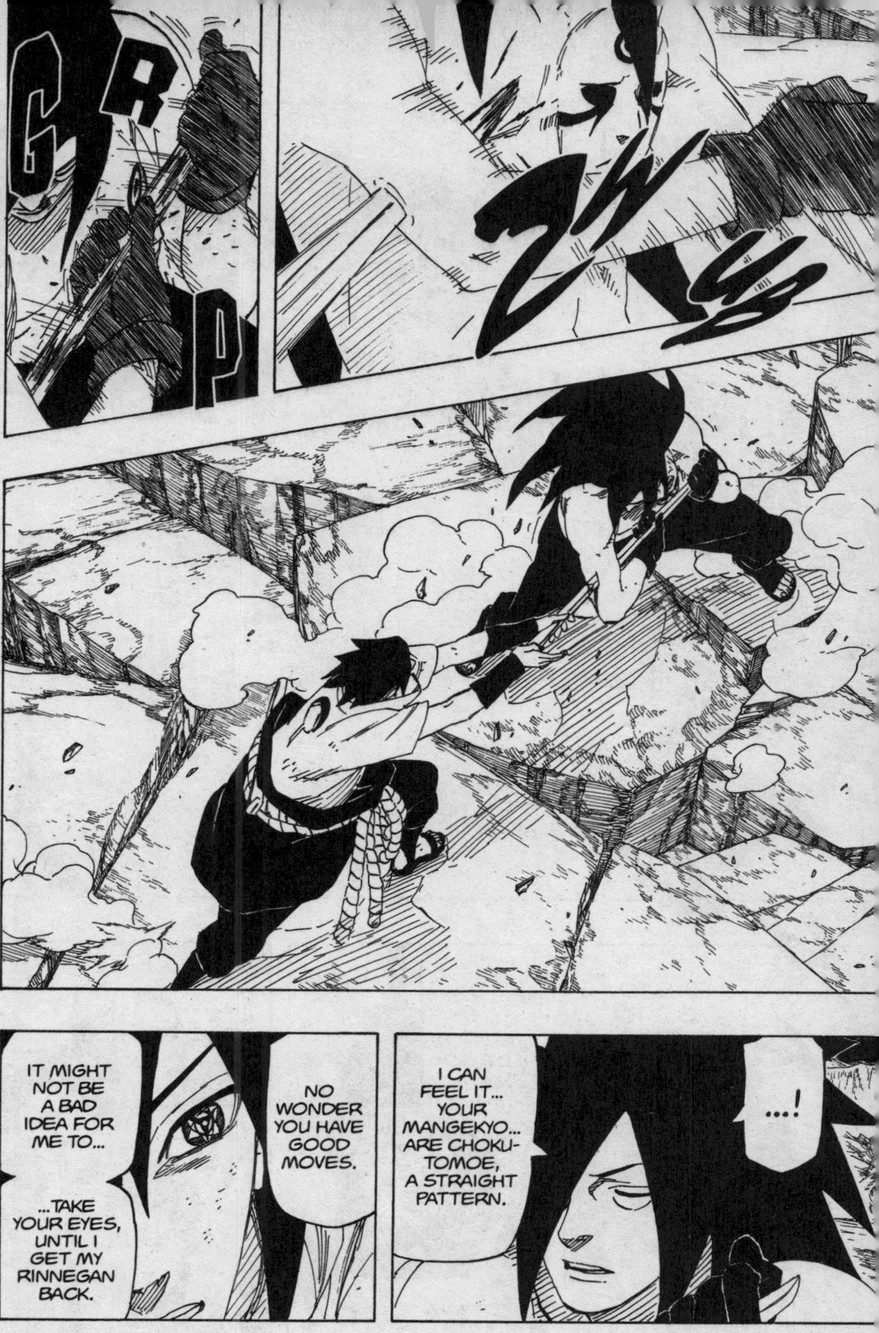
...!
I CAN FEEL IT... YOUR MANGEKYO... ARE CHOKU-TOMOE, A STRAIGHT PATTERN.
NO WONDER YOU HAVE GOOD MOVES.
IT MIGHT NOT BE A BAD IDEA FOR ME TO...
...TAKE YOUR EYES, UNTIL I GET MY RINNEGAN BACK.

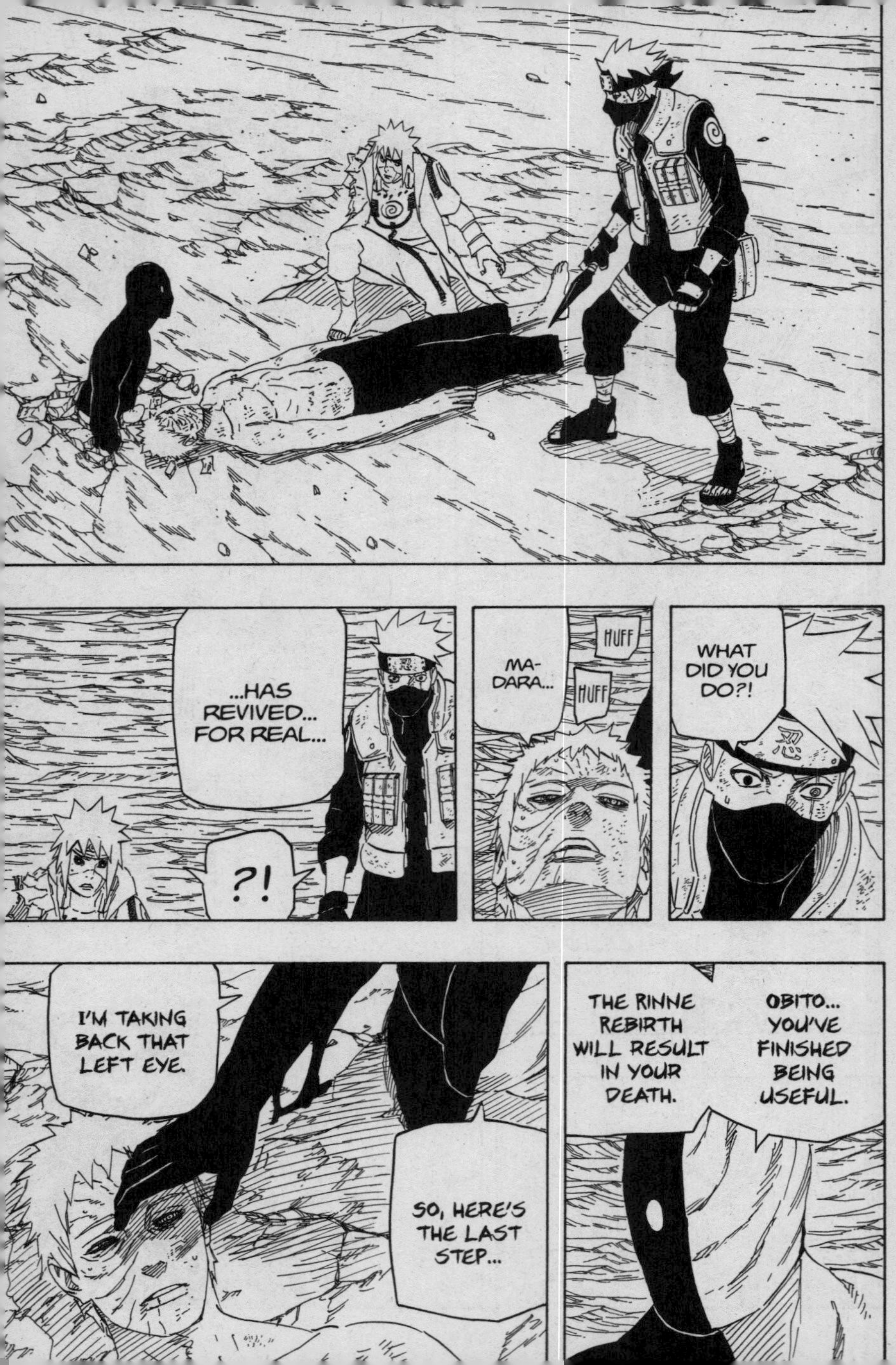
WHAT DID YOU DO?!
HUFF
MA-DARA...
HUFF
...HAS REVIVED... FOR REAL...
?!
OBITO... YOU'VE FINISHED BEING USEFUL.
THE RINNE REBIRTH WILL RESULT IN YOUR DEATH.
I'M TAKING BACK THAT LEFT EYE.
SO, HERE'S THE LAST STEP...

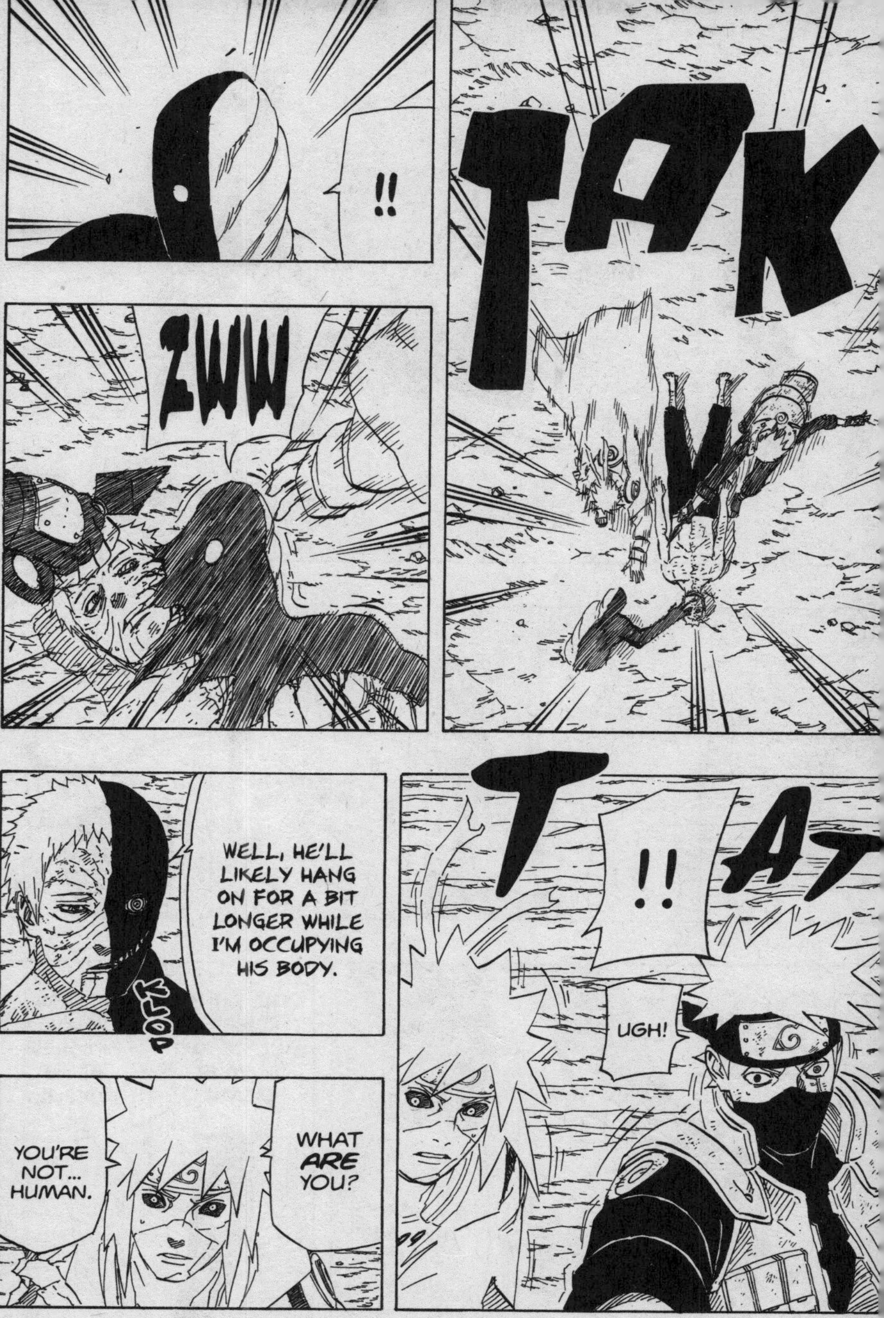
TAK
!!
ZWW
TAT
!!
UGH!
WELL, HE'LL LIKELY HANG ON FOR A BIT LONGER WHILE I'M OCCUPYING HIS BODY.
PLOP
WHAT ARE YOU?
YOU'RE NOT... HUMAN.

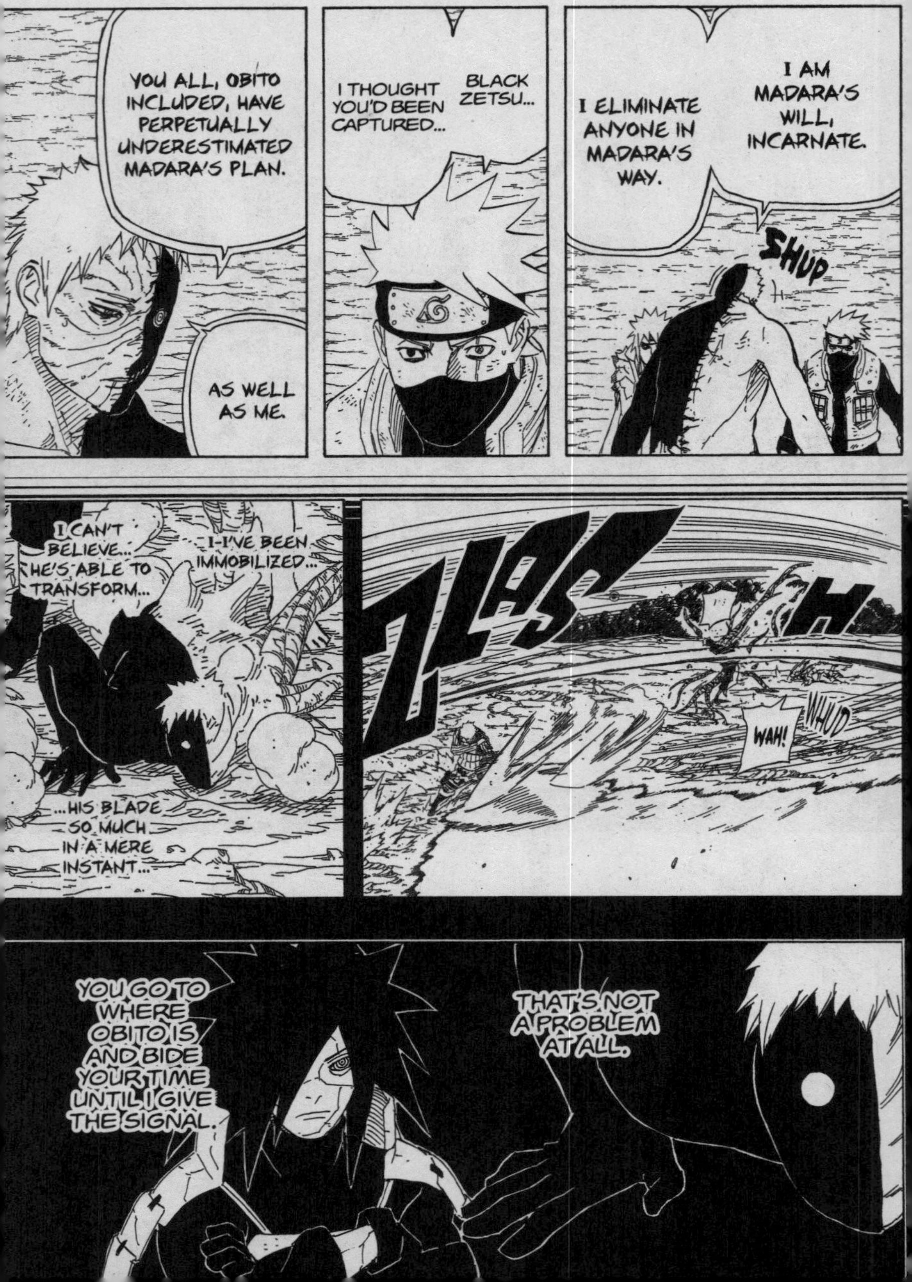

I AM MADARA'S WILL, INCARNATE.
I ELIMINATE ANYONE IN MADARA'S WAY.
SHUP
BLACK ZETSU...
I THOUGHT YOU'D BEEN CAPTURED...
YOU ALL, OBITO INCLUDED, HAVE PERPETUALLY UNDERESTIMATED MADARA'S PLAN.
AS WELL AS ME.
ZLASH
WAH!
WHUD
I-I'VE BEEN IMMOBILIZED...
I CAN'T BELIEVE... HE'S ABLE TO TRANSFORM...
...HIS BLADE SO MUCH IN A MERE INSTANT...
THAT'S NOT A PROBLEM AT ALL.
YOU GO TO WHERE OBITO IS AND BIDE YOUR TIME UNTIL I GIVE THE SIGNAL.

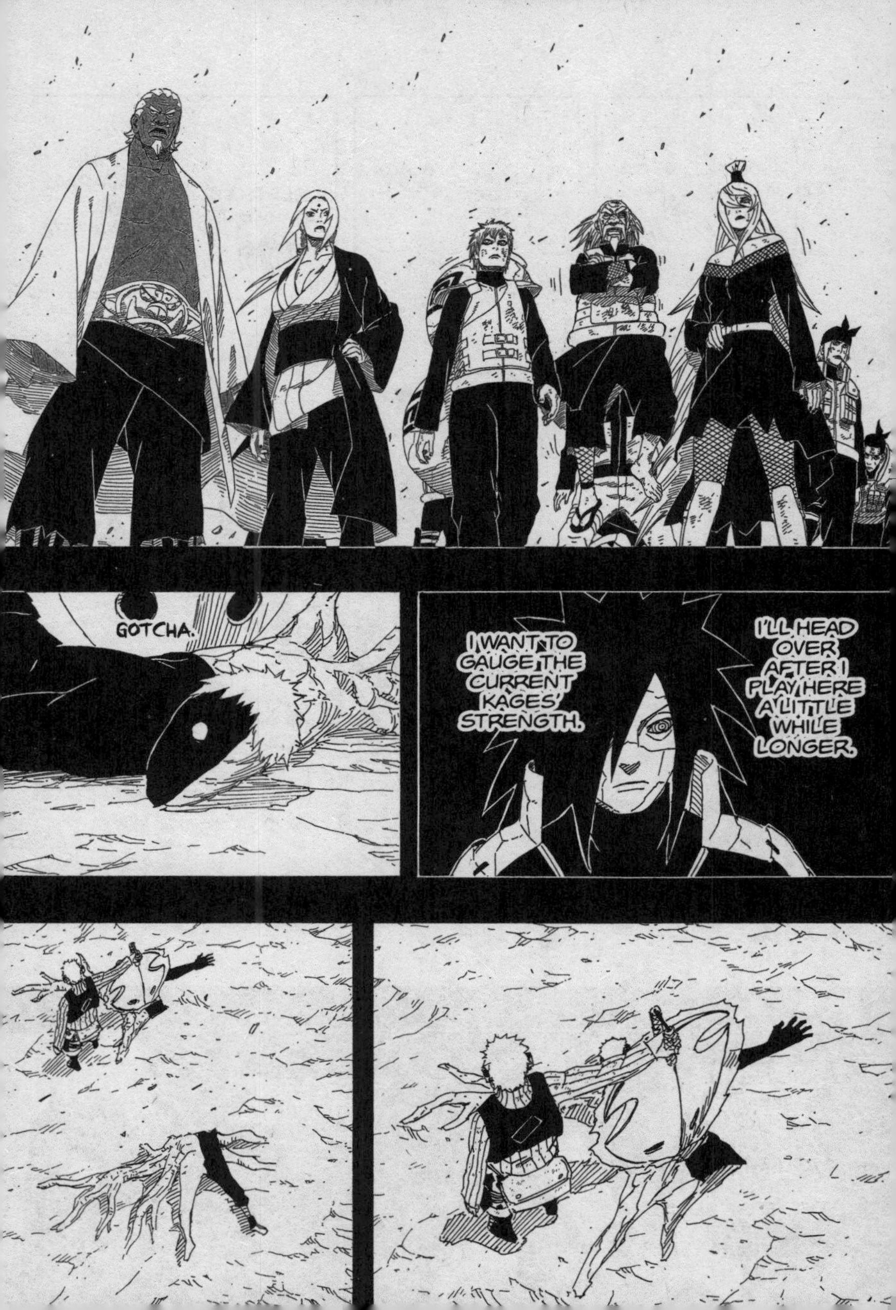
I'LL HEAD OVER AFTER I PLAY HERE A LITTLE WHILE LONGER.
I WANT TO GAUGE THE CURRENT KAGES' STRENGTH.
GOTCHA.

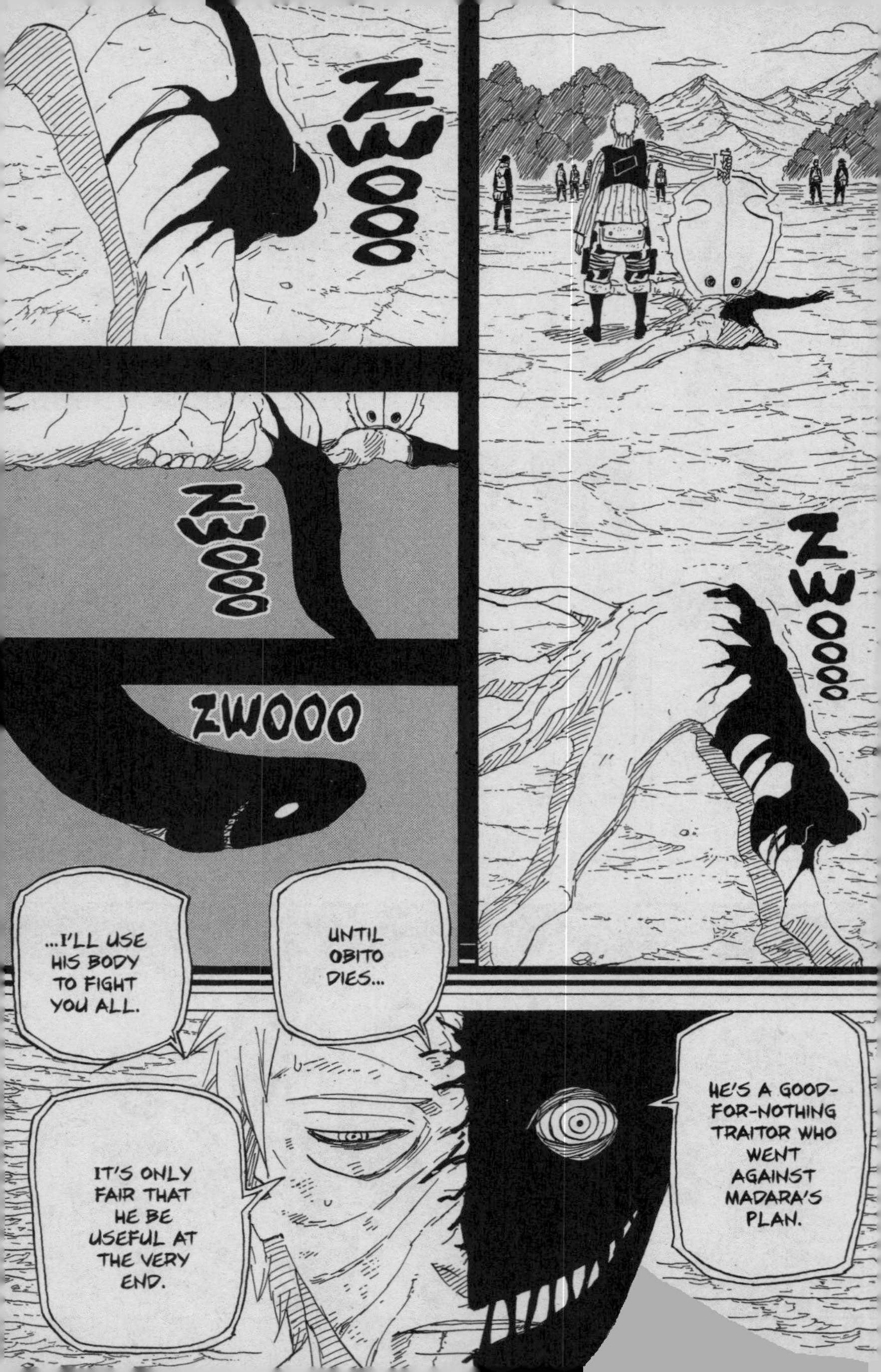
ZWOOOO
ZWOOO
ZWOOO
ZWOOO
HE'S A GOOD-FOR-NOTHING TRAITOR WHO WENT AGAINST MADARA'S PLAN.
UNTIL OBITO DIES...
...I'LL USE HIS BODY TO FIGHT YOU ALL.
IT'S ONLY FAIR THAT HE BE USEFUL AT THE VERY END.

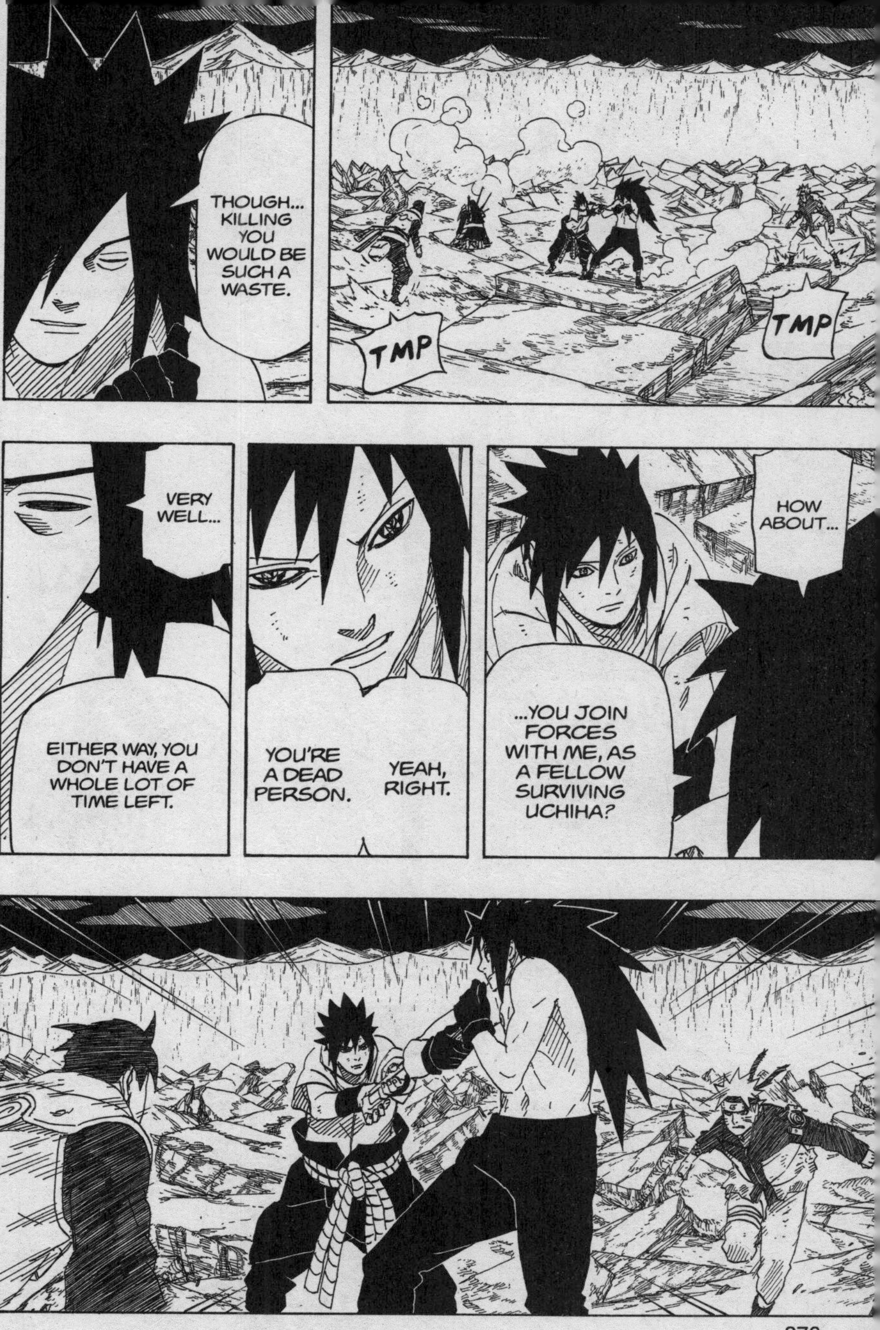
TMP
TMP
THOUGH... KILLING YOU WOULD BE SUCH A WASTE.
HOW ABOUT...
...YOU JOIN FORCES WITH ME, AS A FELLOW SURVIVING UCHIHA?
YEAH, RIGHT.
YOU'RE A DEAD PERSON.
VERY WELL...
EITHER WAY, YOU DON'T HAVE A WHOLE LOT OF TIME LEFT.

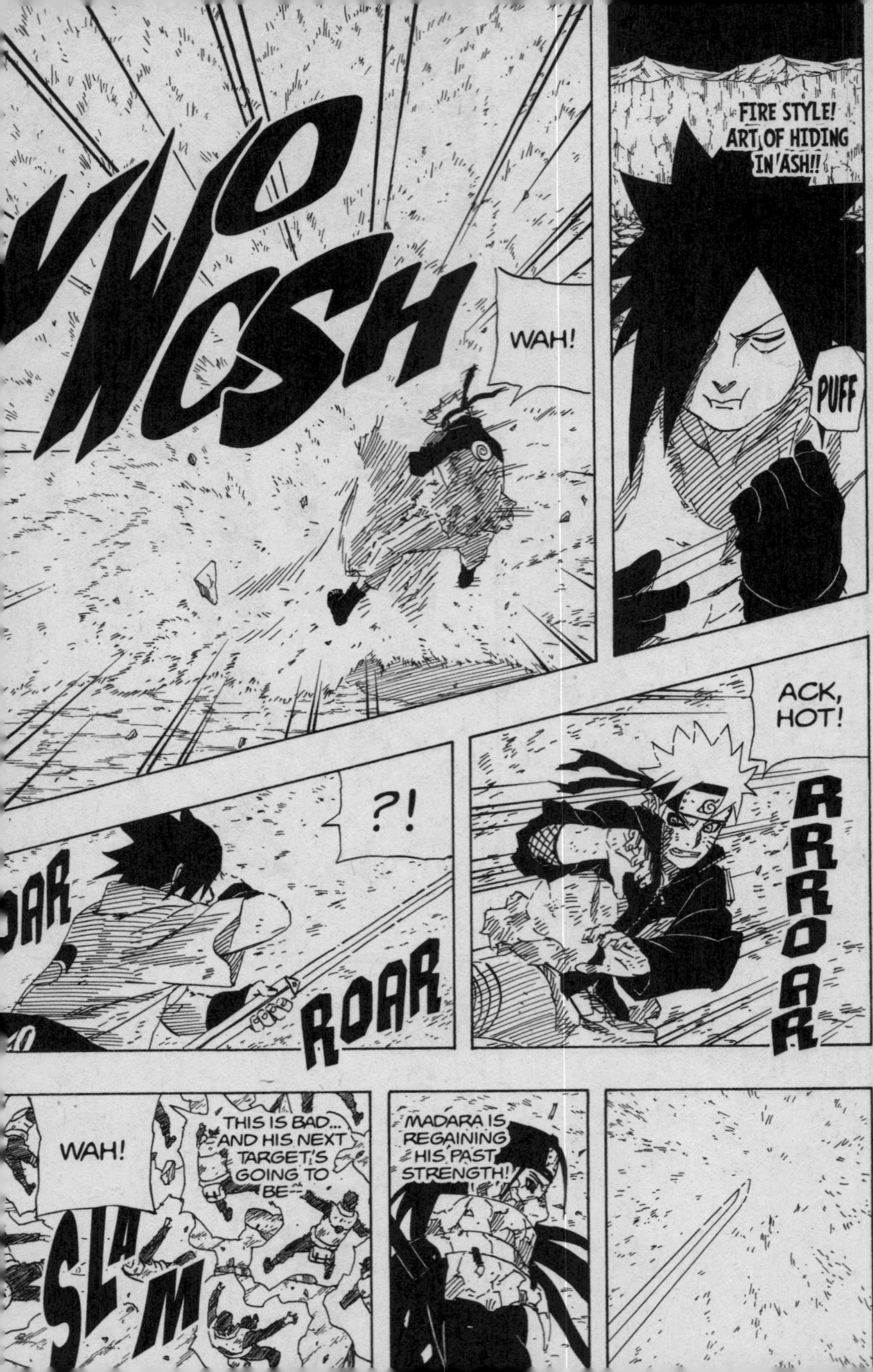
FIRE STYLE! ART OF HIDING IN ASH!!
PUFF
WHOOSH
WAH!
ACK, HOT!
RRRROAR
?!
ROAR
OAR
MADARA IS REGAINING HIS PAST STRENGTH!
THIS IS BAD... AND HIS NEXT TARGET'S GOING TO BE--
WAH!
SLAM

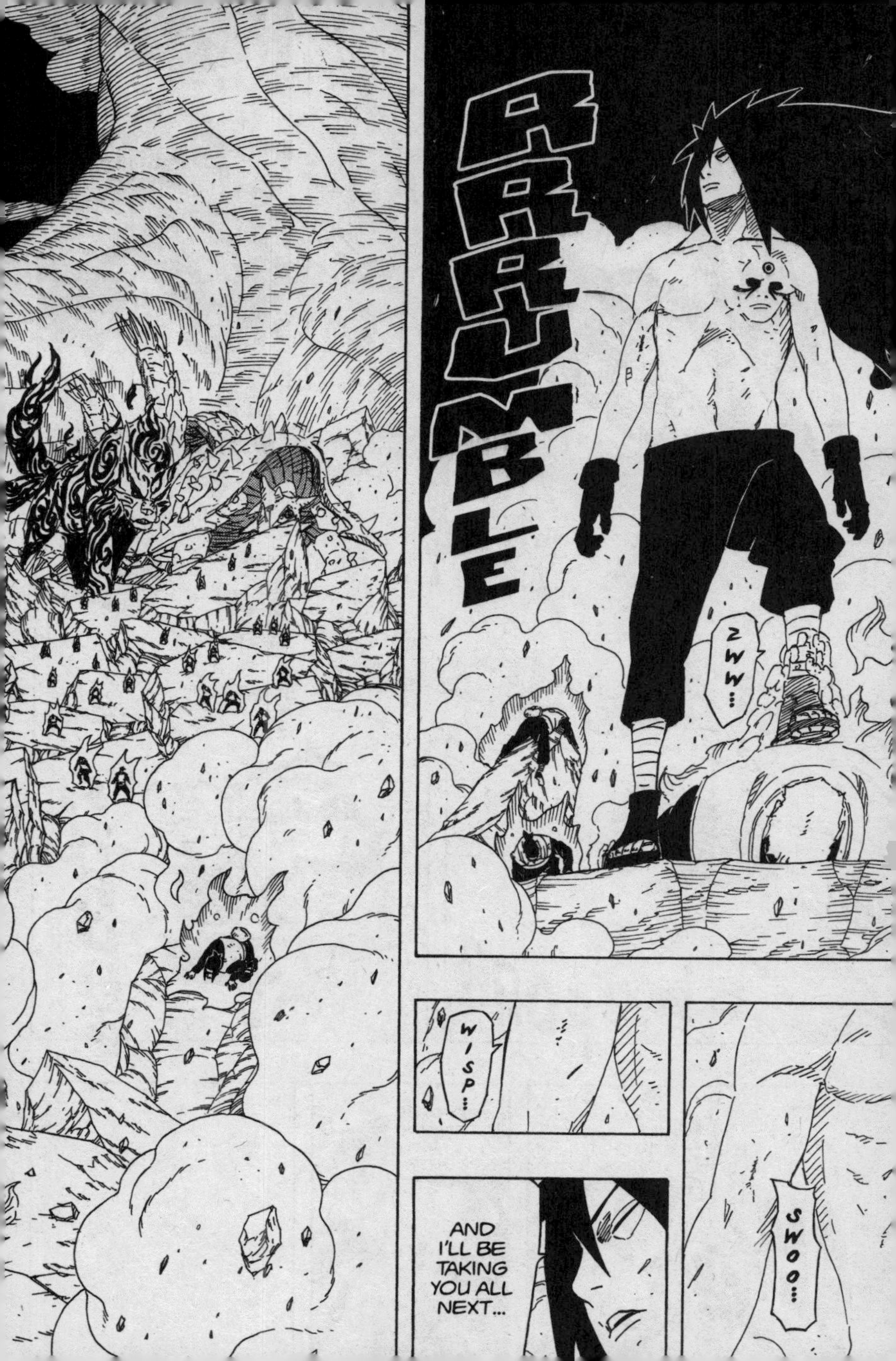
RRRUMBLE
ZWW...
SWOO...
WISP...
AND I'LL BE TAKING YOU ALL NEXT...

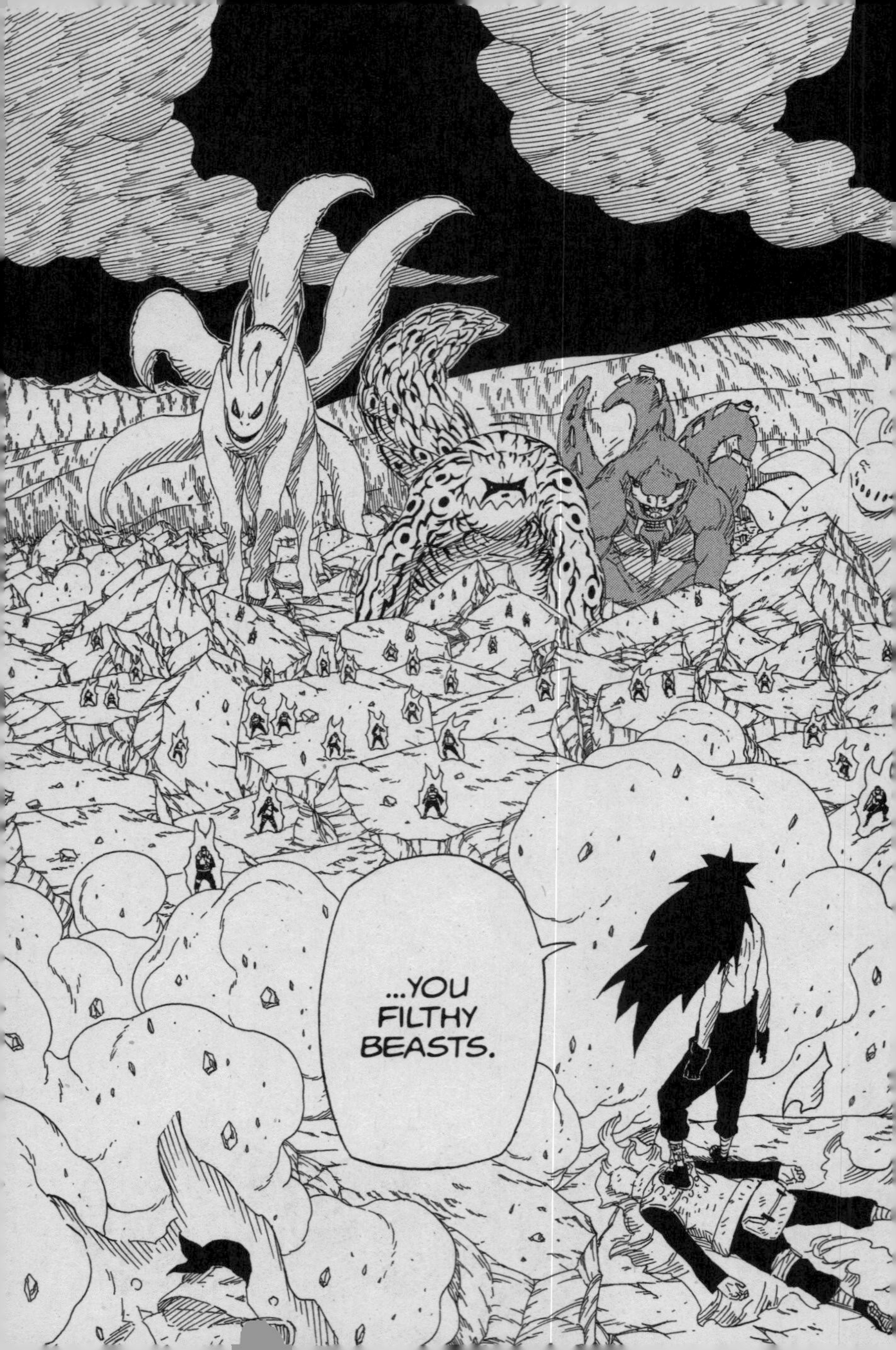
...YOU FILTHY BEASTS.

NARUTO

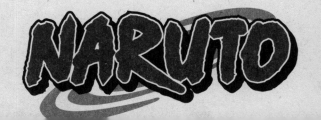

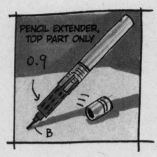

PENCIL EXTENDER,
TOP PART ONLY

0.9

B

岸本斉史

There's something that I discovered only very recently, in regards to how I draw my manga drafts. I found a B lead 0.9 mm mechanical pencil very easy to draw with. And if I stick it in a pencil extender—that socket you put on the end of a pencil stub to keep using it—it's even easier to draw with. It really reduces the time it takes me to complete a draft!

—Masashi Kishimoto, 2014

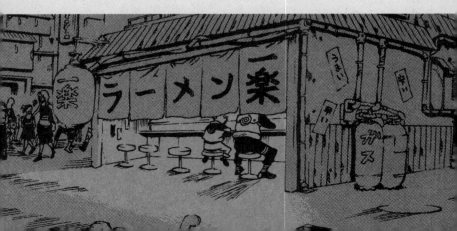

NARUTO

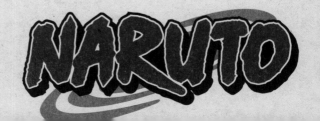

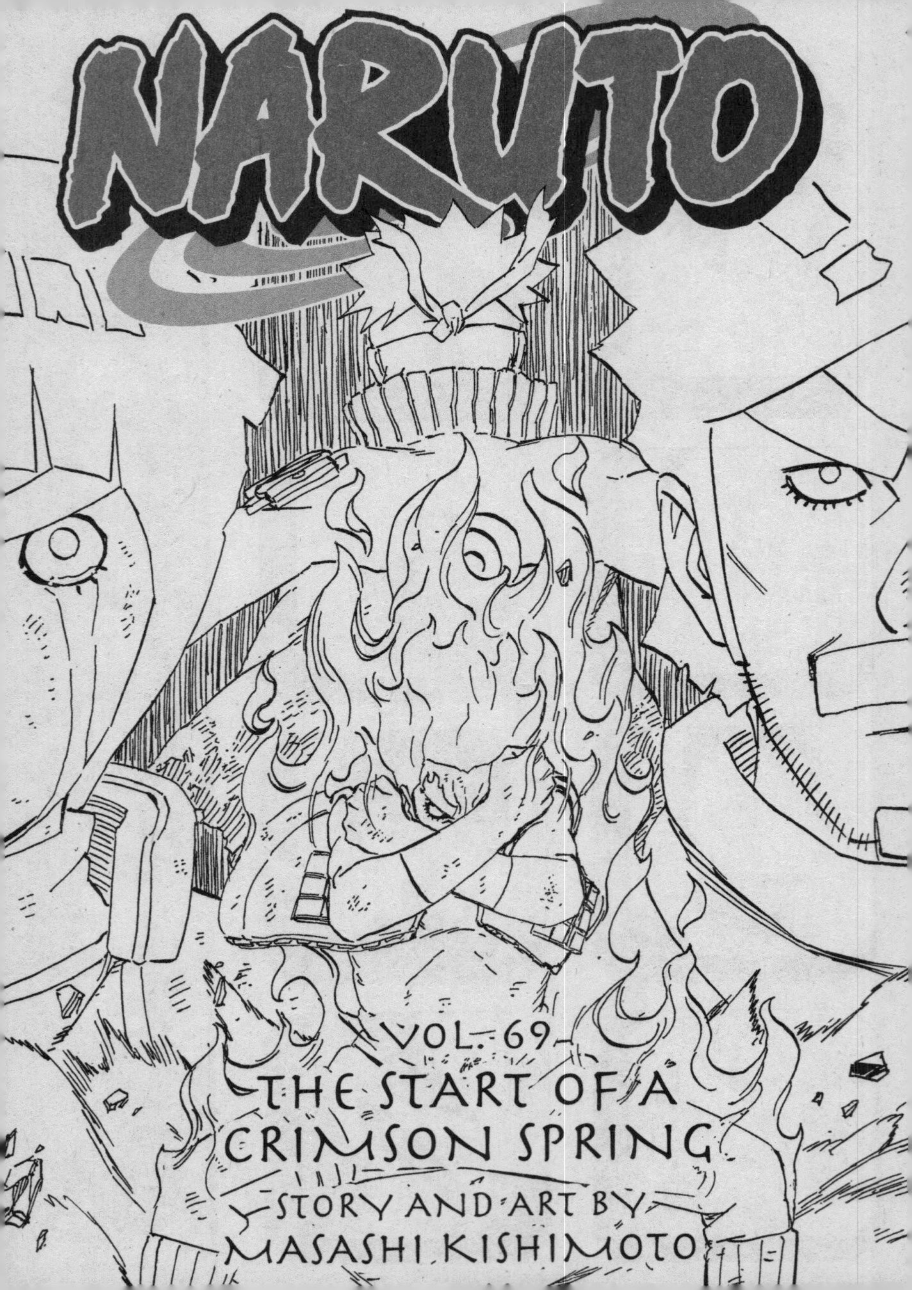
NARUTO
VOL. 69
THE START OF A CRIMSON SPRING
STORY AND ART BY
MASASHI KISHIMOTO

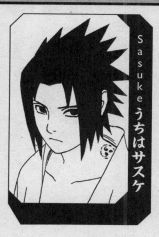

CHARACTERS

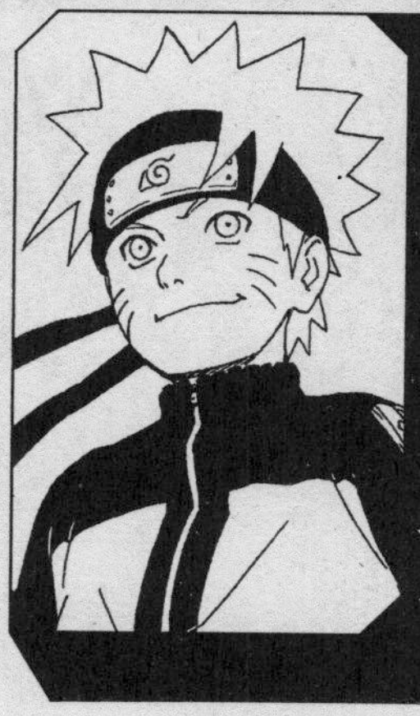

Naruto うずまきナルト

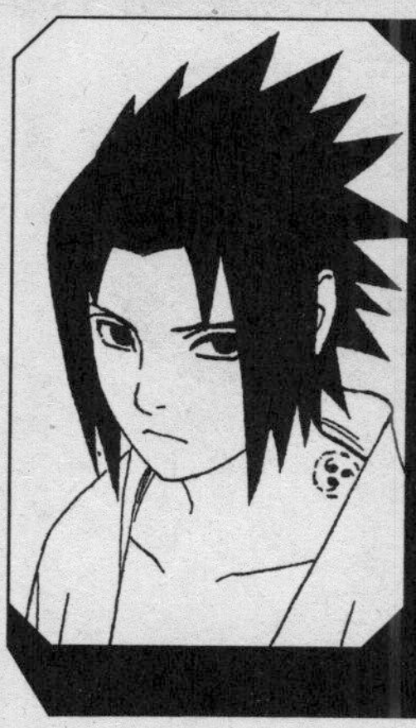

Sasuke うちはサスケ

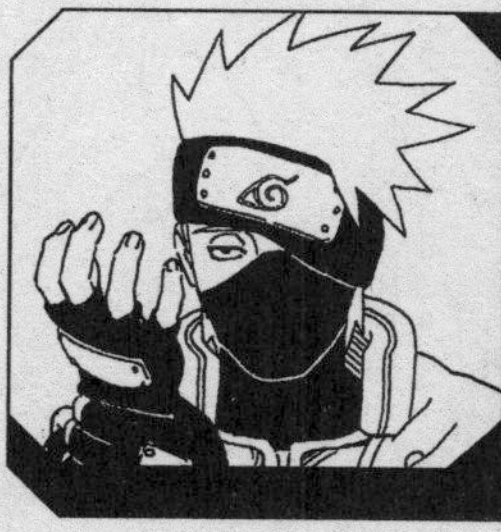

Kakashi はたけカカシ

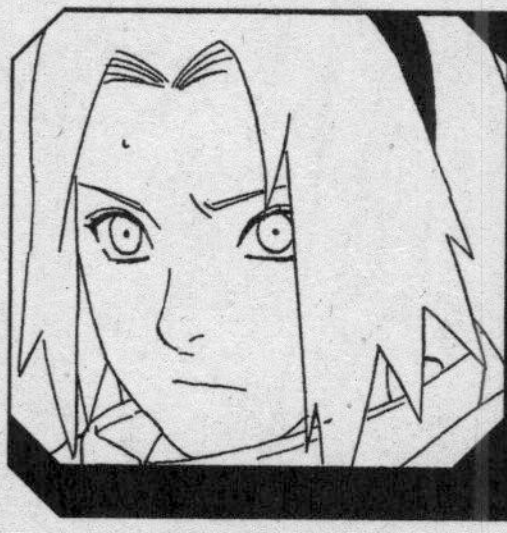

Sakura 春野サクラ

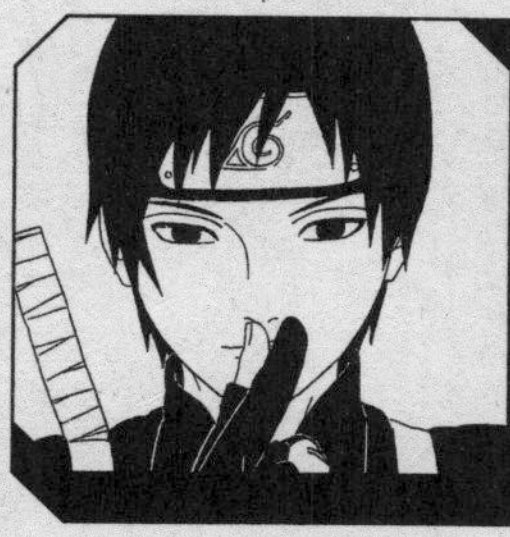

Sai サイ

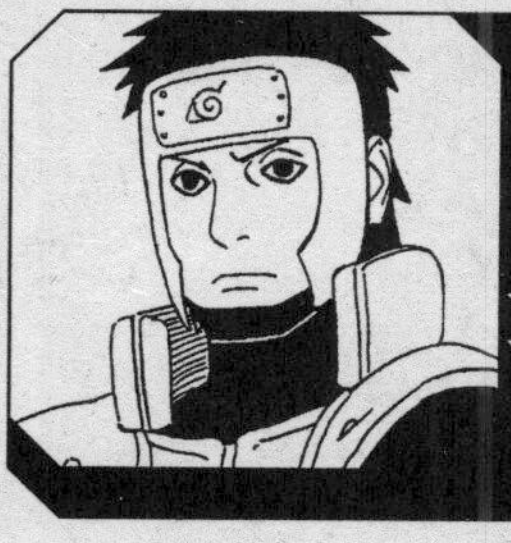

Yamato ヤマト

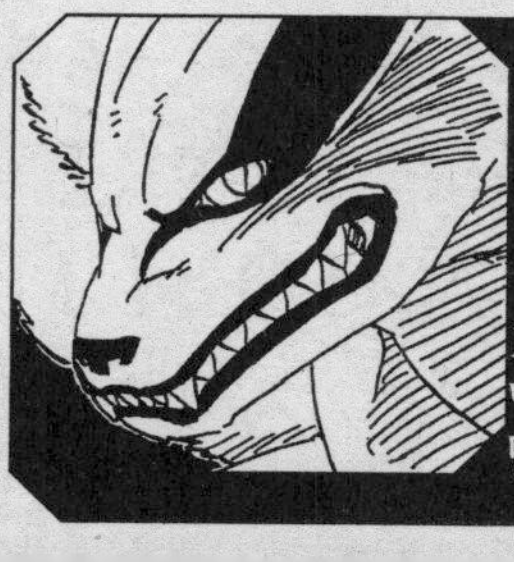

Kurama 九喇嘛

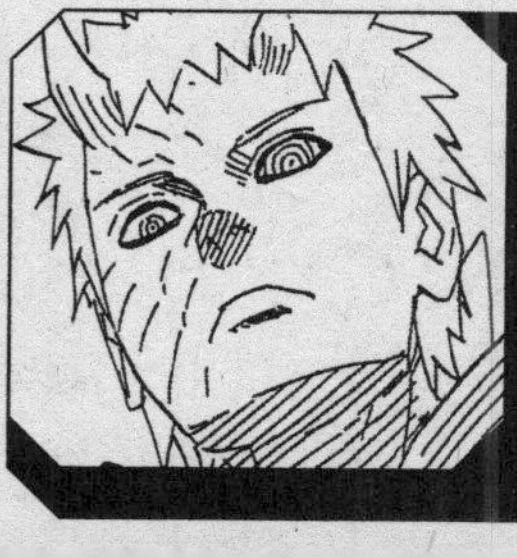

Obito うちはオビト

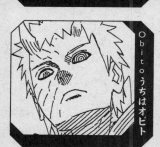

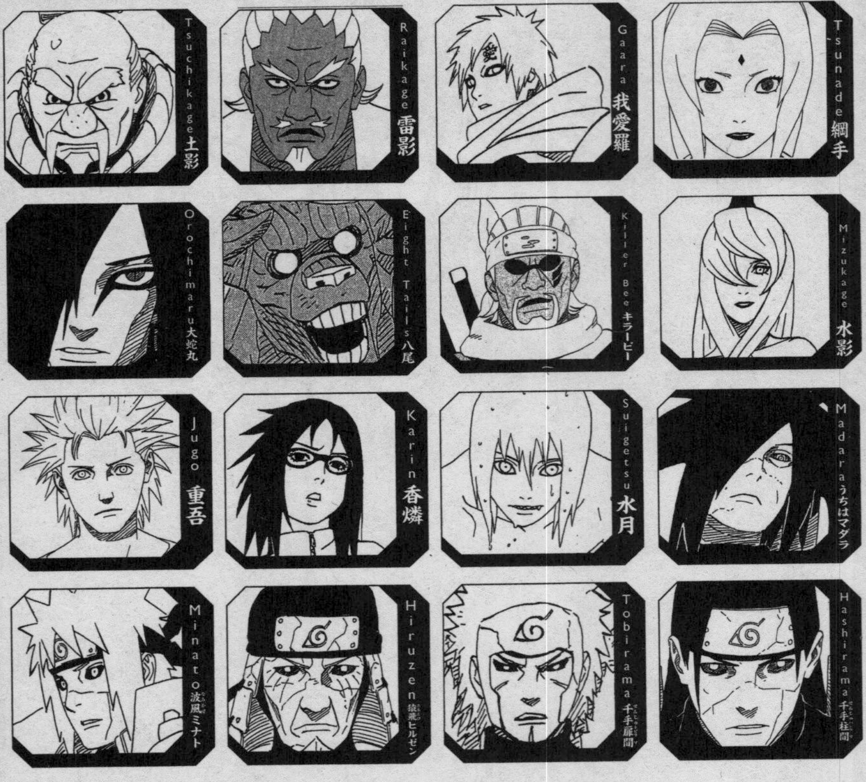
Tsunade 綱手
Gaara 我愛羅
Raikage 雷影
Tsuchikage 土影
Mizukage 水影
Killer Bee キラービー
Eight Tails 八尾
Orochimaru 大蛇丸
Madara うちはマダラ
Suigetsu 水月
Karin 香燐
Jugo 重吾
Hashirama 千手柱間
Tobirama 千手扉間
Hiruzen 猿飛ヒルゼン
Minato 波風ミナト

THE STORY SO FAR...

Naruto, the biggest troublemaker at the Ninja Academy in the Village of Konohagakure, finally becomes a ninja along with his classmates Sasuke and Sakura. They grow and mature through countless trials and battles. However, Sasuke, unable to give up his quest for vengeance, leaves Konohagakure to seek Orochimaru and his power…

Two years pass. Naruto grows up and engages in fierce battles against the Tailed Beast-targeting Akatsuki. And the Fourth Great Ninja War against the Akatsuki finally begins. Obito absorbs the Ten Tails and summons forth the Divine Tree in order to activate the Infinite Tsukuyomi. However, during the battle, Naruto reminds Obito of the days when he wished to be Hokage. Now defeated, Obito tries to make amends for his mistakes, but Madara soon takes control of the situation and the war continues!

NARUTO

VOL. 69
THE START OF A CRIMSON SPRING

CONTENTS

Number 658: Biju vs. Madara...!!

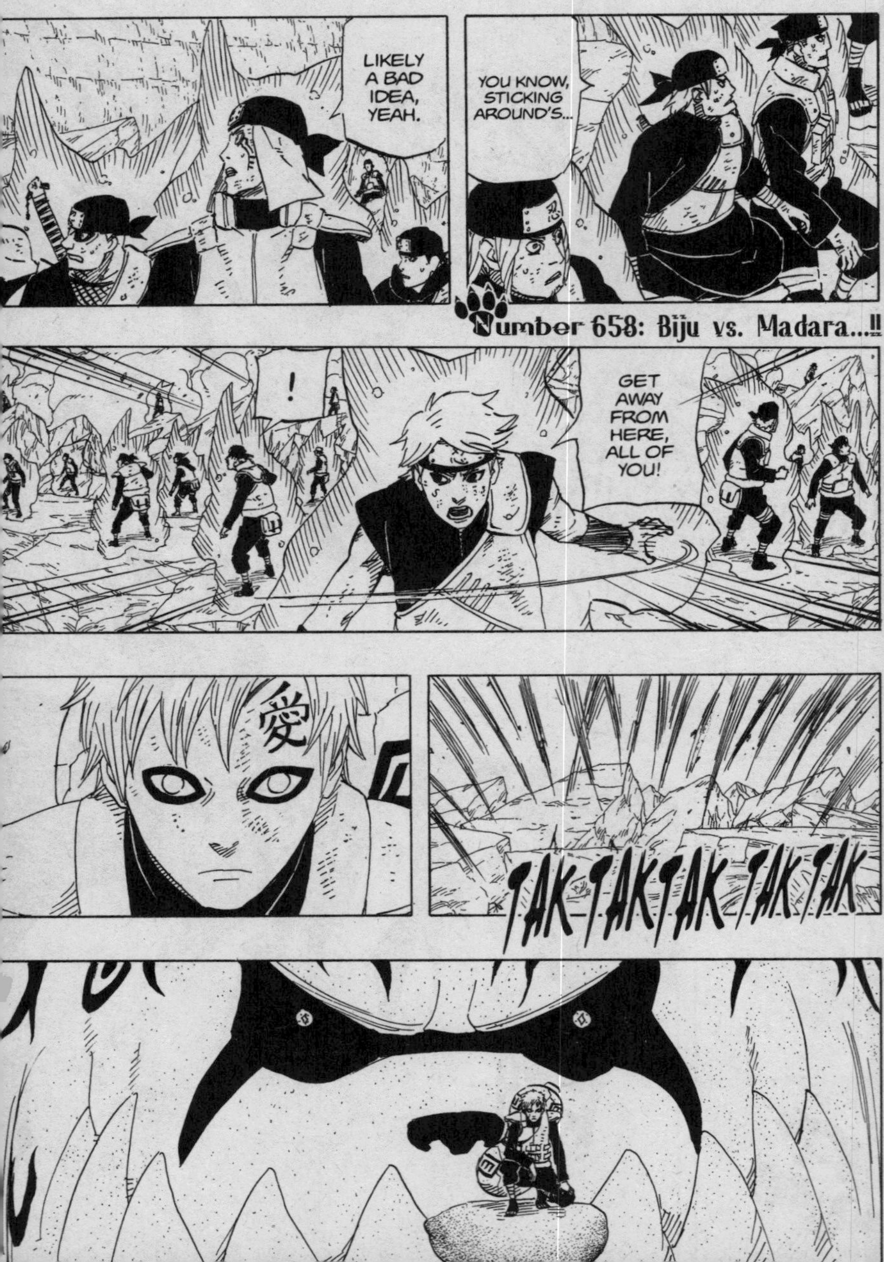
YOU KNOW, STICKING AROUND'S...
LIKELY A BAD IDEA, YEAH.
GET AWAY FROM HERE, ALL OF YOU!
!
TAK TAK TAK TAK TAK

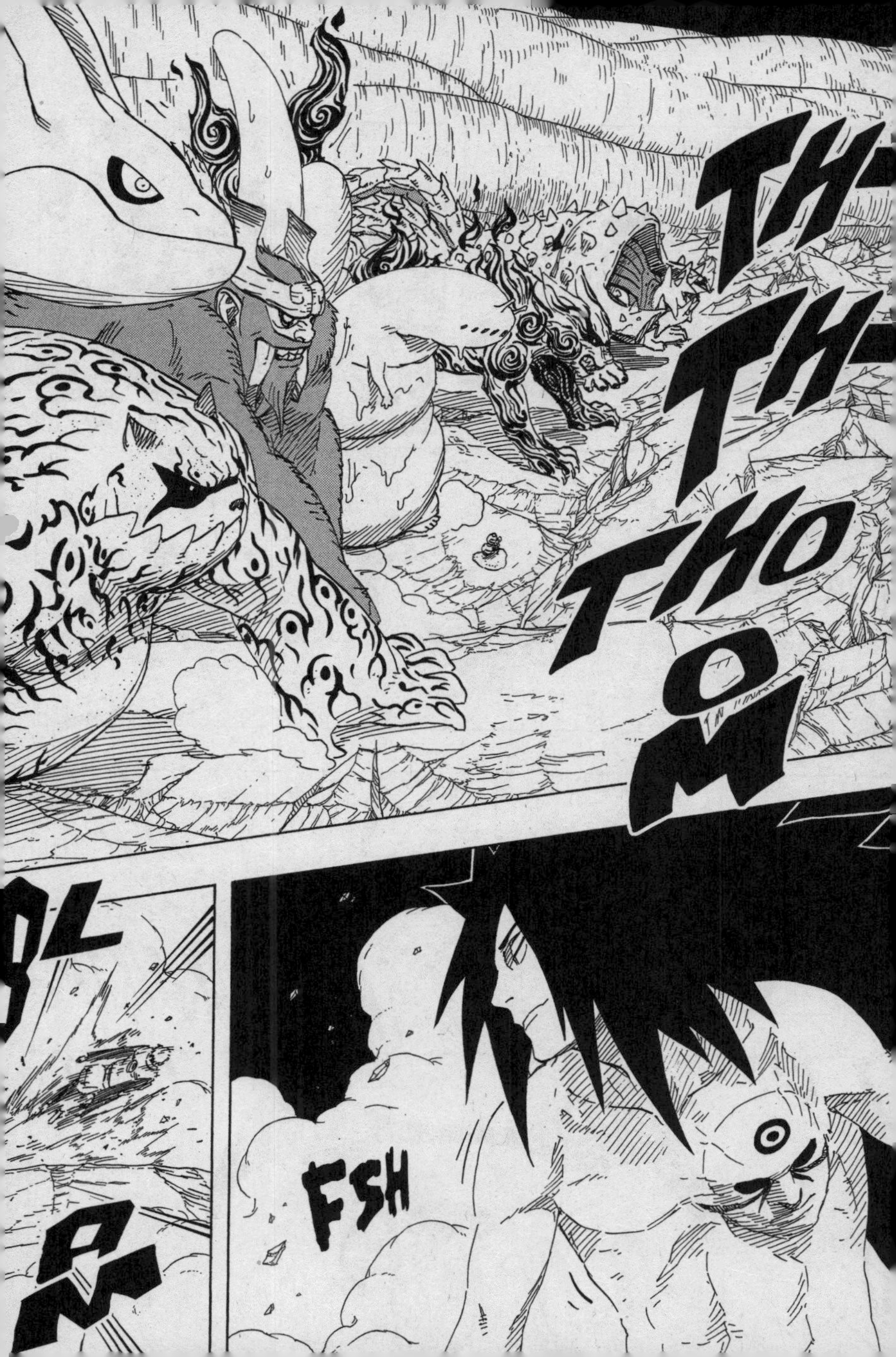
THTHTHOOM
FSH

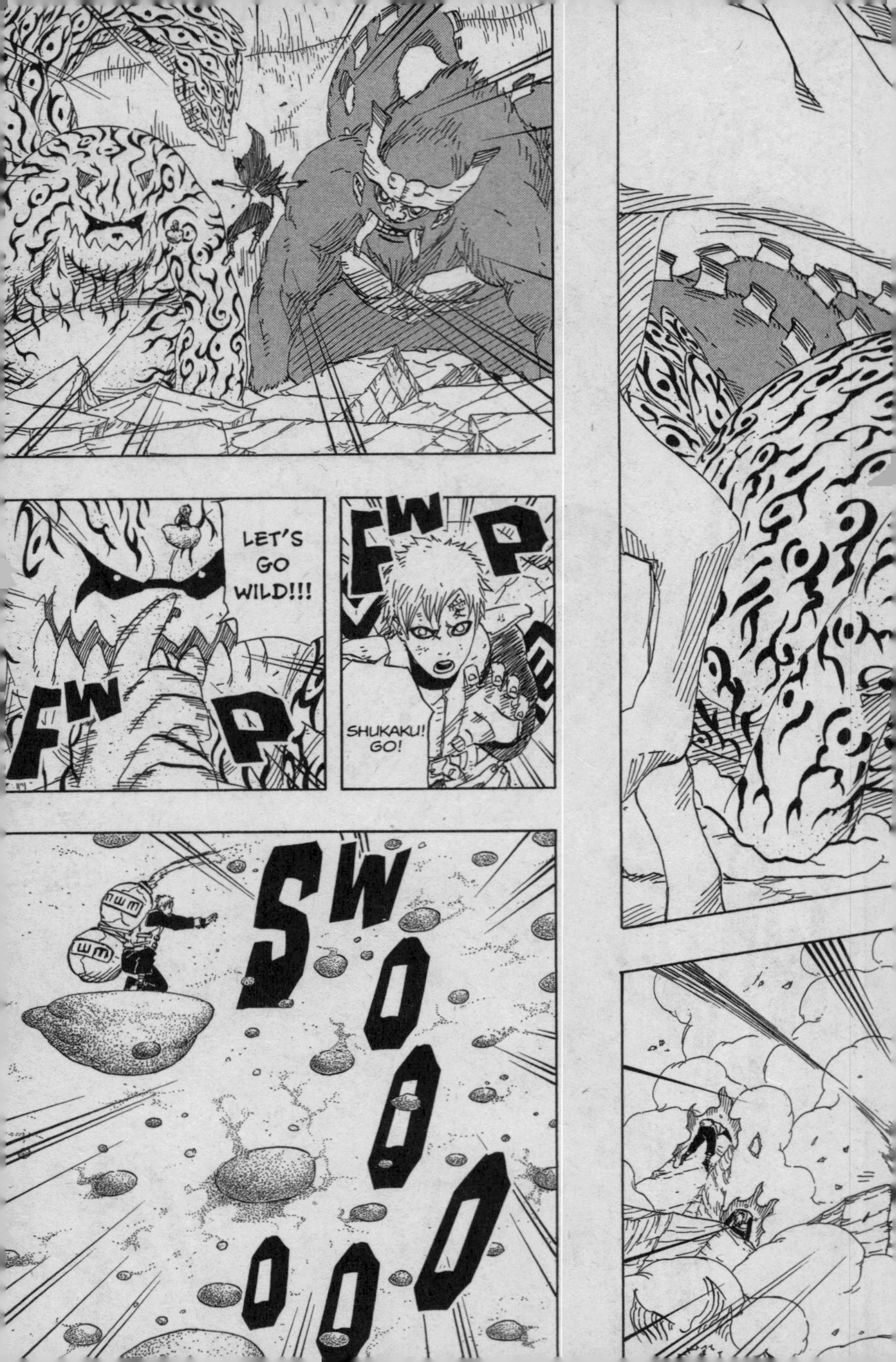
FWP
SHUKAKU! GO!
LET'S GO WILD!!!
FWP
SWOOOOOOOO

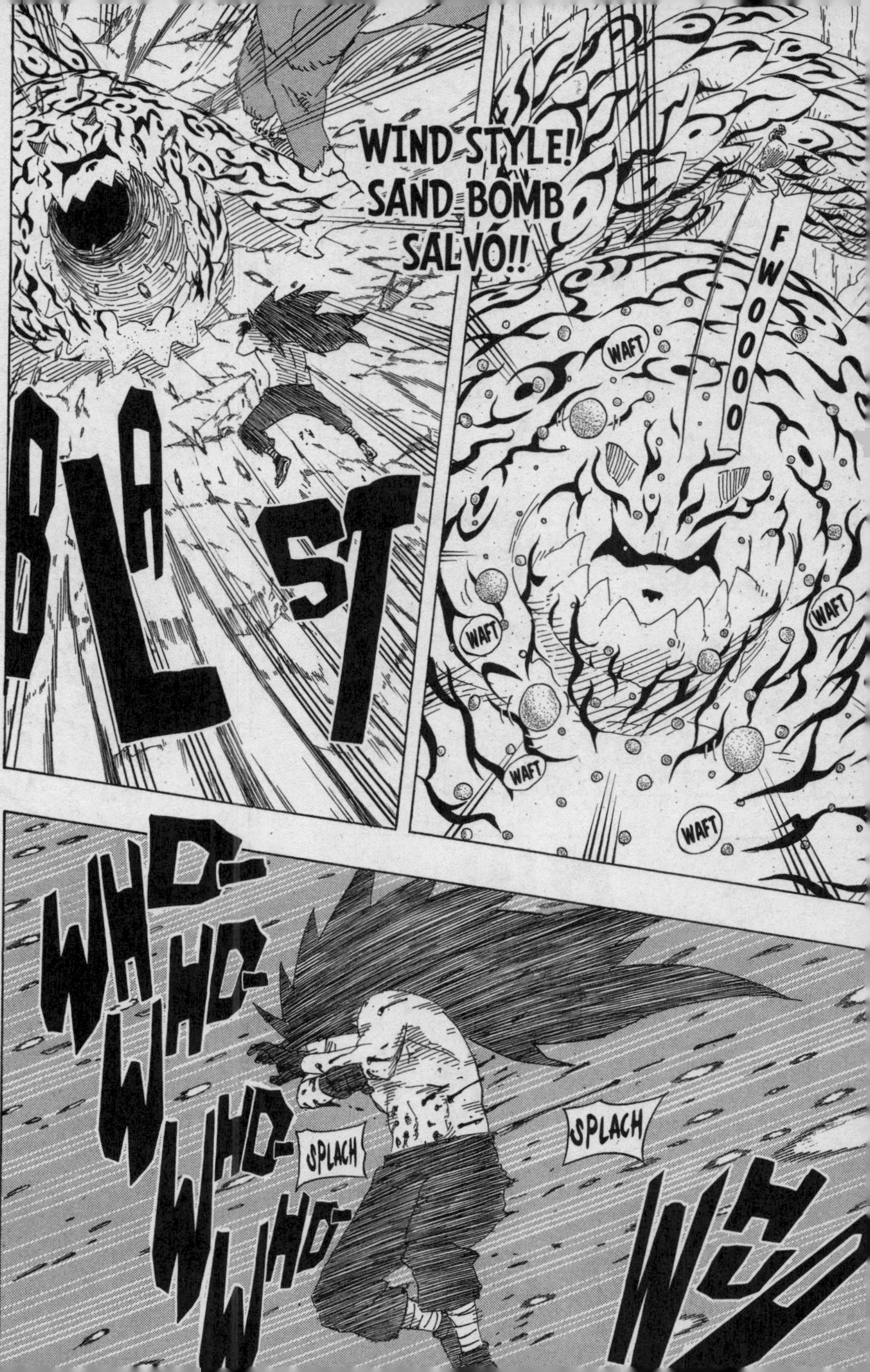
FWOOOOO
WAFT
WAFT
WAFT
WAFT
WAFT
WIND STYLE! SAND BOMB SALVO!!
BLAST
SPLACH
SPLACH
WHO-WHO-WHO-WHO-

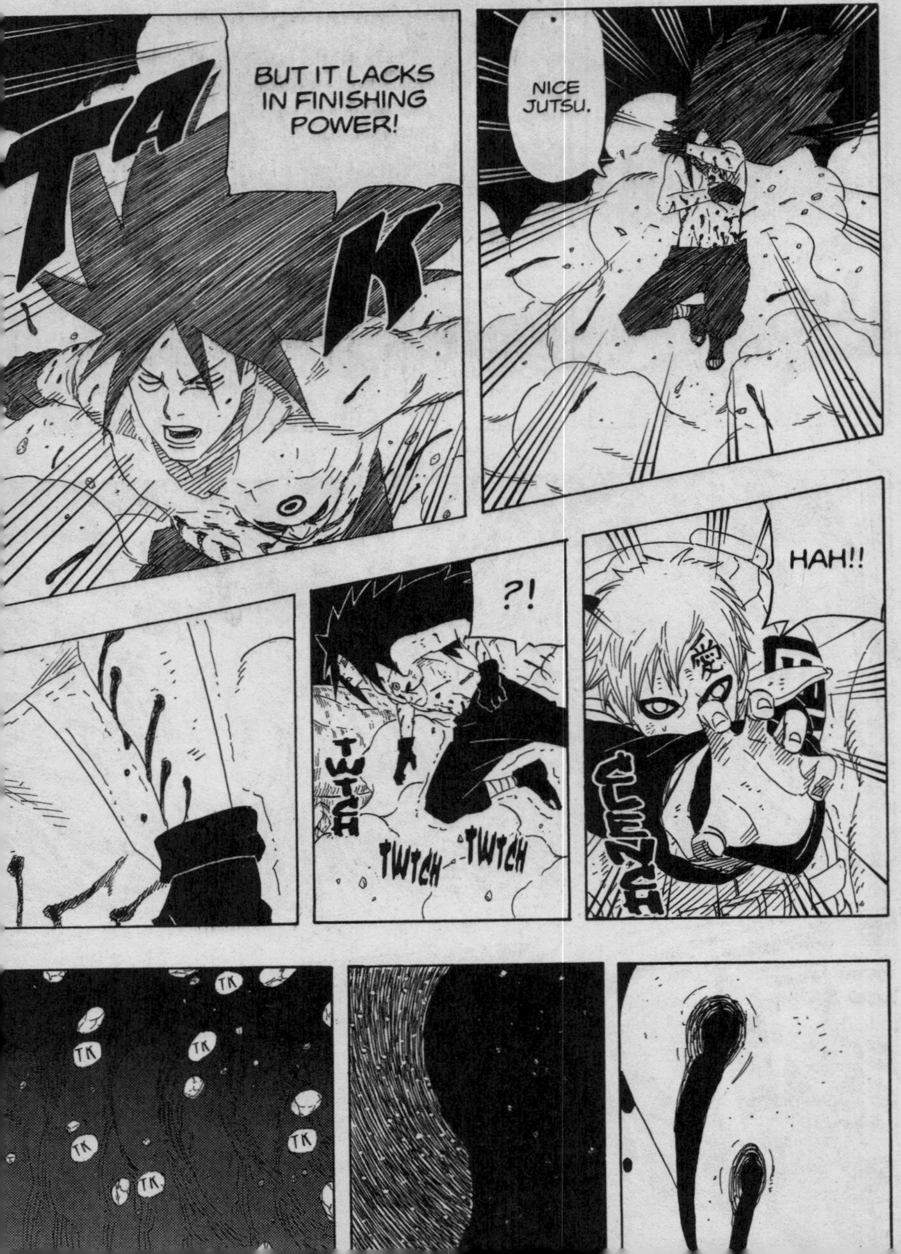
NICE JUTSU.
BUT IT LACKS IN FINISHING POWER!
TAK
HAH!!
CLENCH
?!
TWITCH
TWITCH
TWITCH
TK
TK
TK
TK
TK
TK

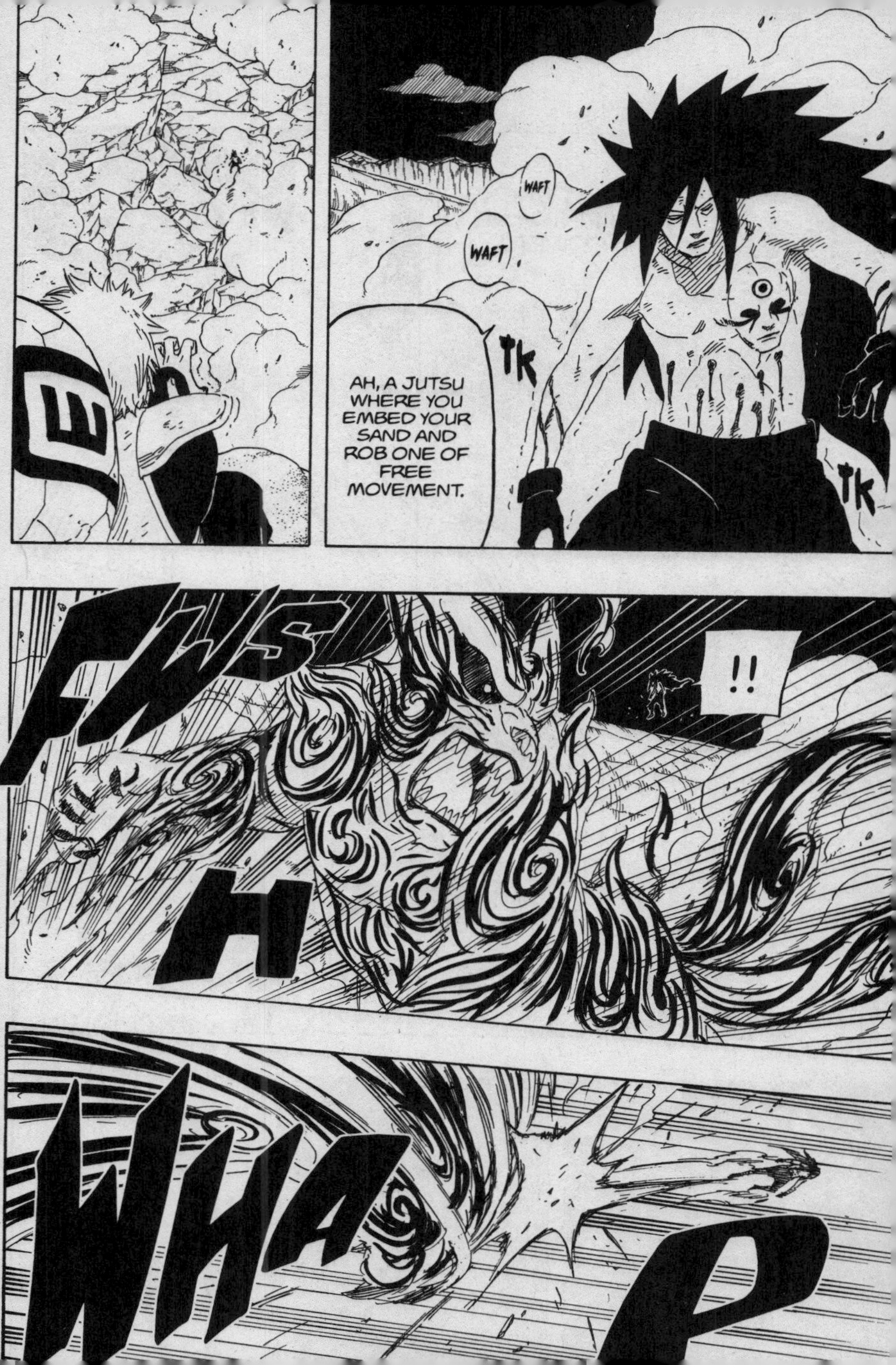
WAFT
WAFT
TK
TK
AH, A JUTSU WHERE YOU EMBED YOUR SAND AND ROB ONE OF FREE MOVEMENT.
!!
FWSH
WHAP

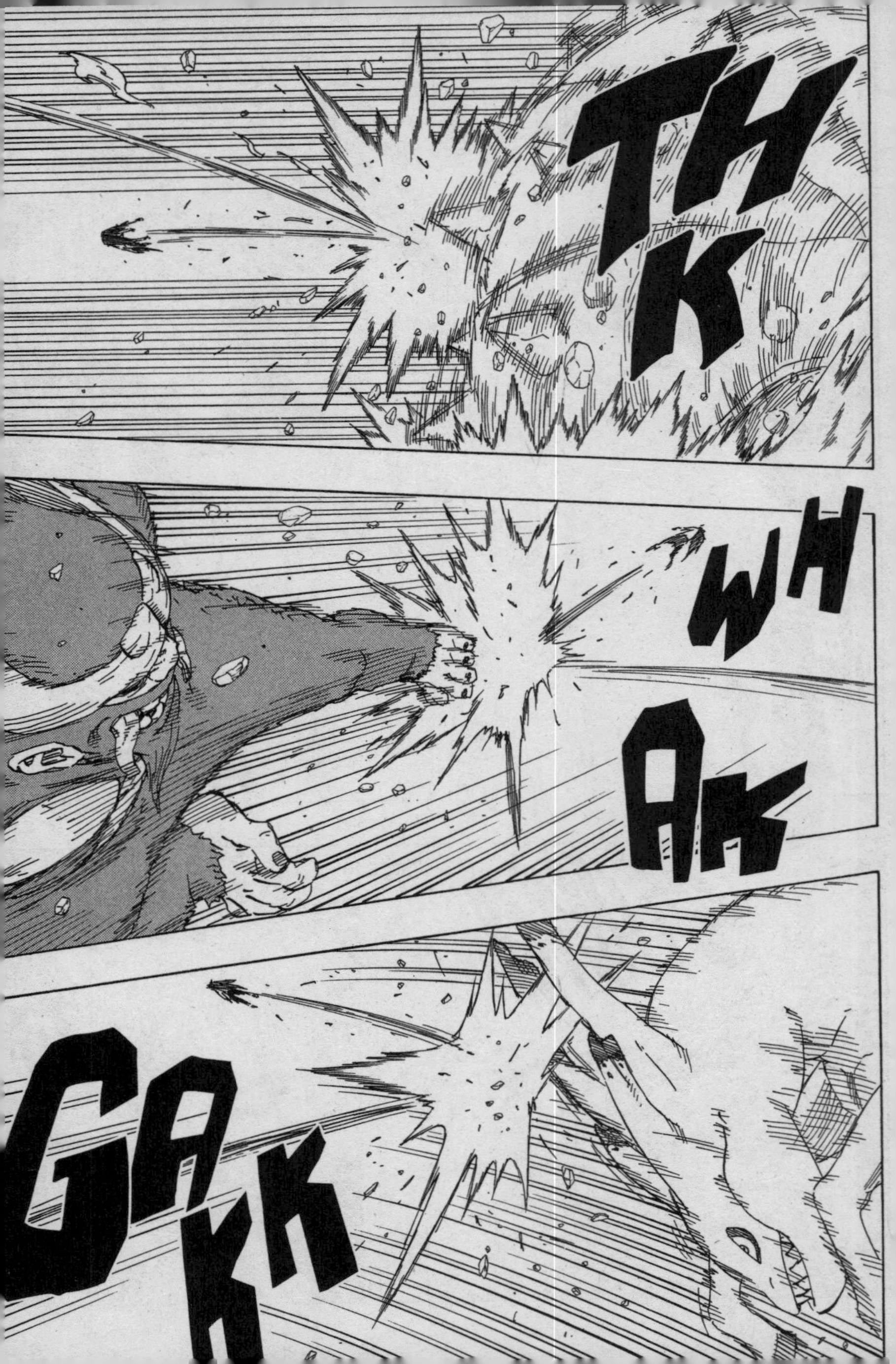
THK
WHAK
GAKK

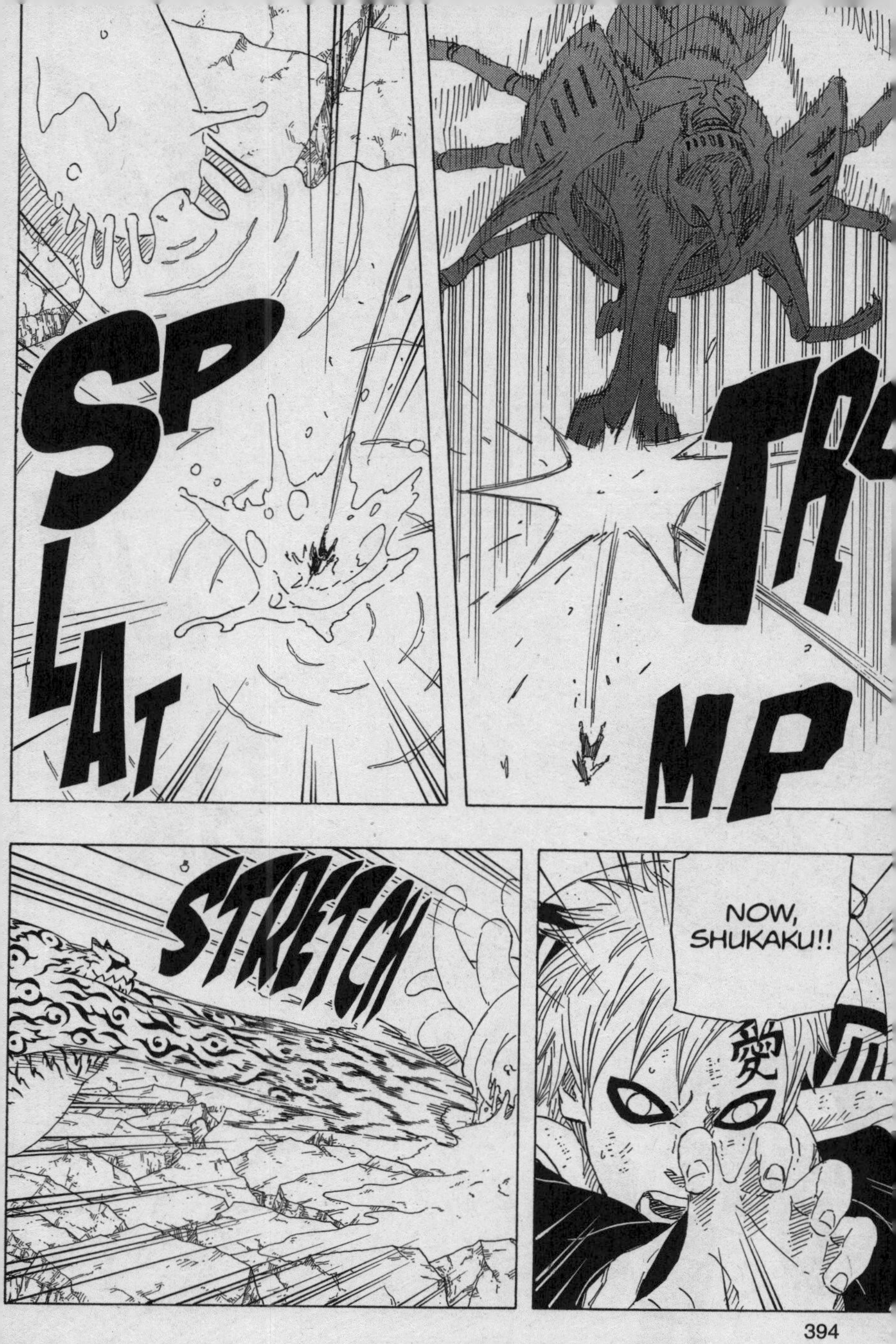
TR
MP
SPLAT
NOW, SHUKAKU!!
STRETCH

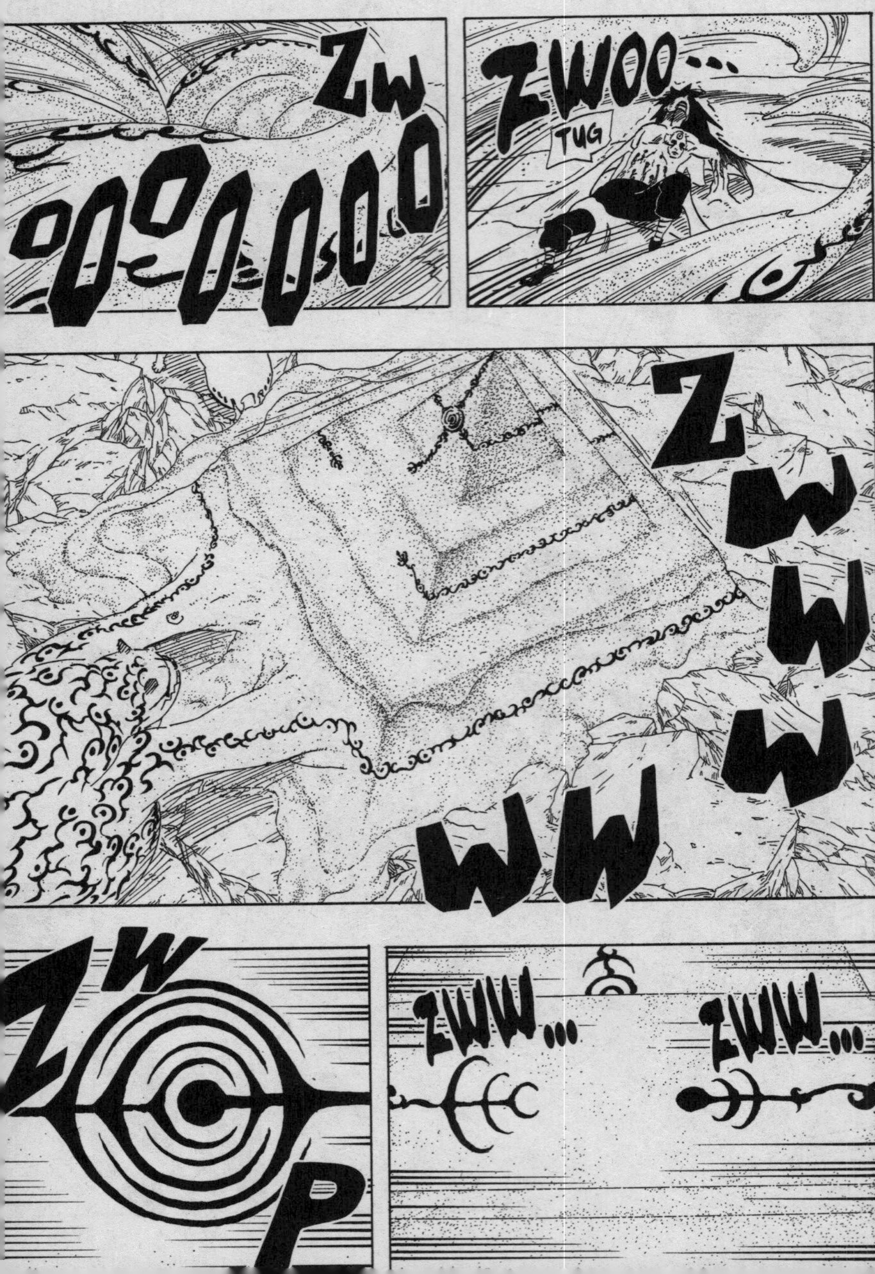
ZWOO...
TUG
ZWOOOOOOOO
ZWWWWWW
ZWW...
ZWW...
ZWOP

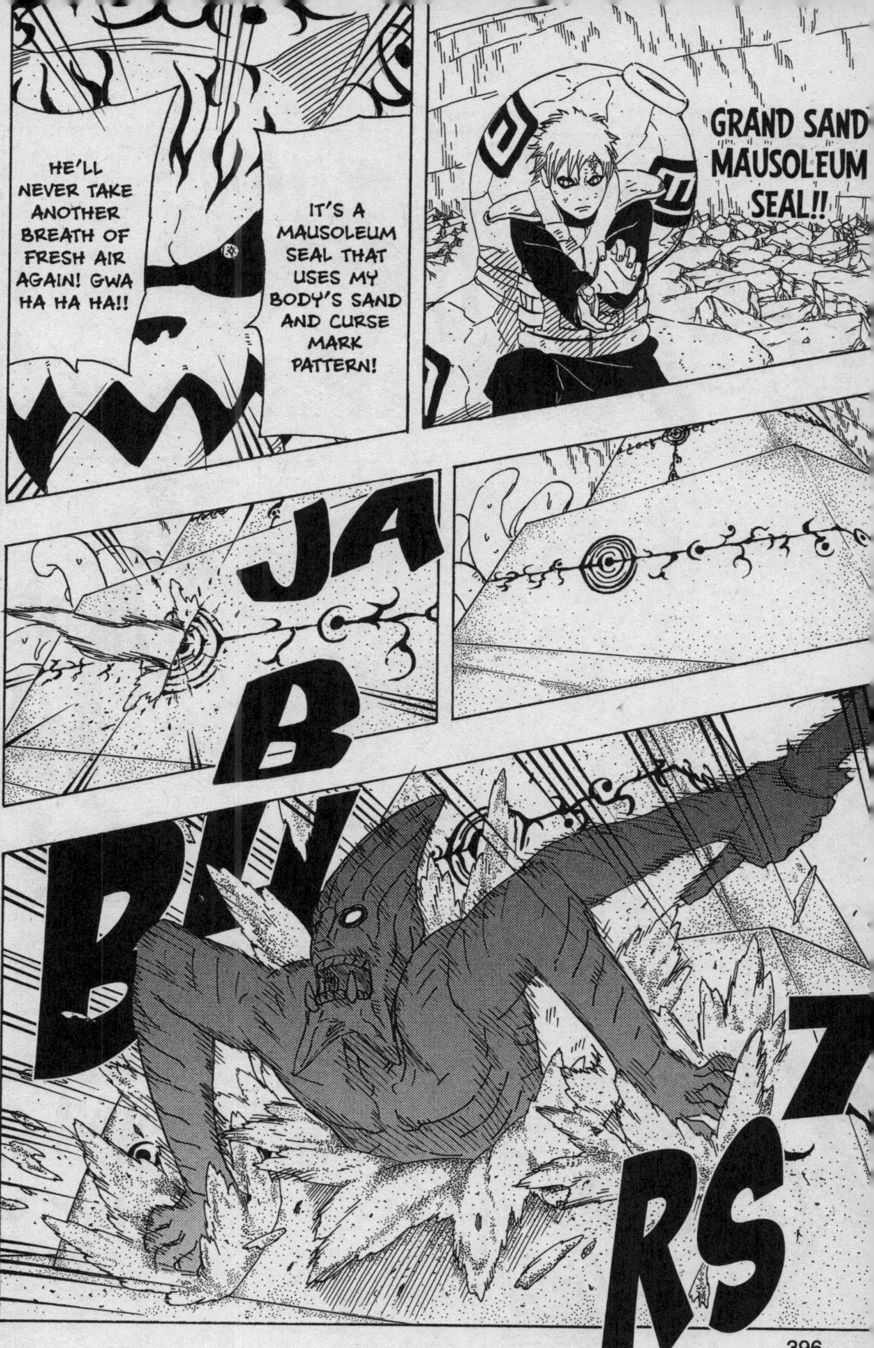
GRAND SAND MAUSOLEUM SEAL!!
IT'S A MAUSOLEUM SEAL THAT USES MY BODY'S SAND AND CURSE MARK PATTERN!
HE'LL NEVER TAKE ANOTHER BREATH OF FRESH AIR AGAIN! GWA HA HA HA!!
JAB

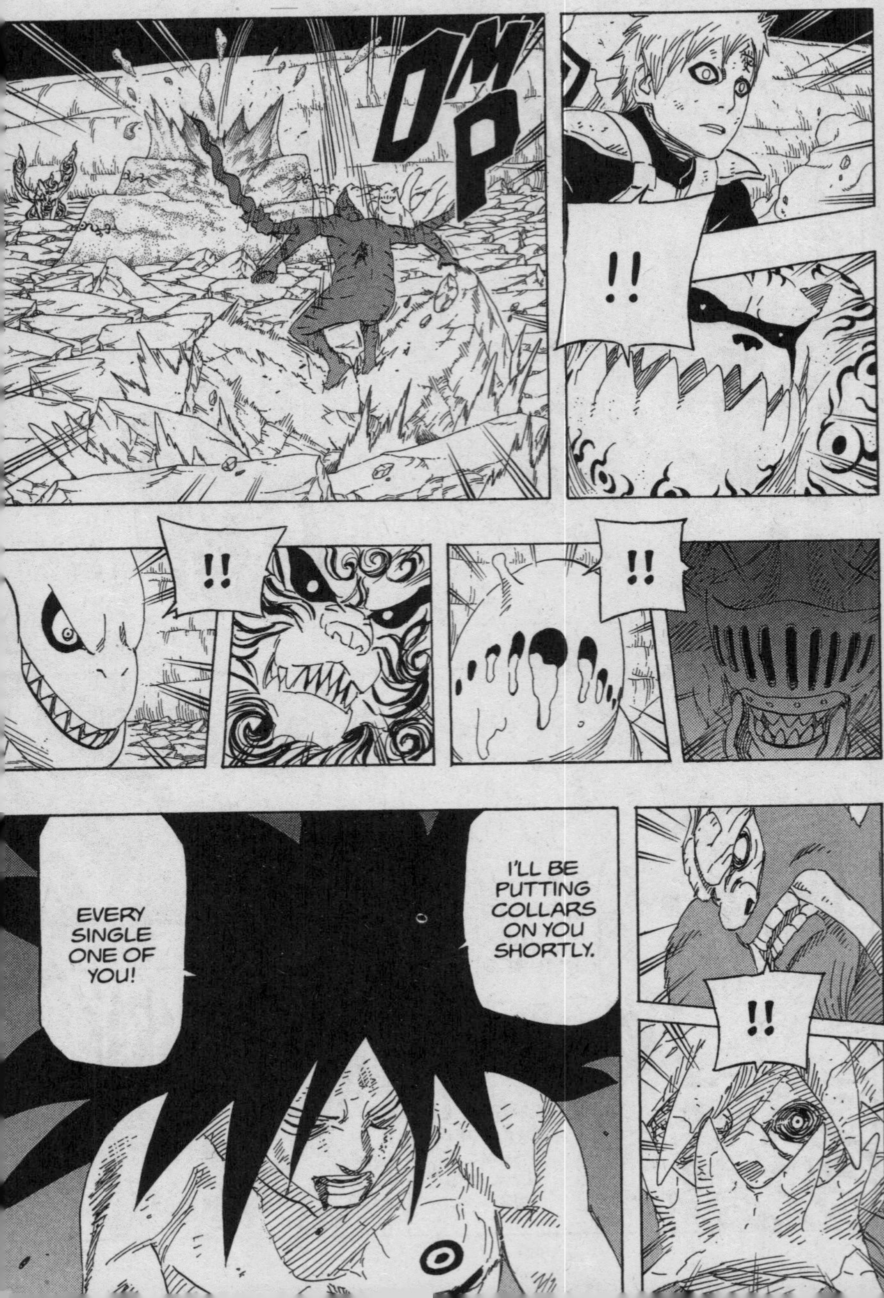
!!
DOMP
!!
!!
!!
I'LL BE PUTTING COLLARS ON YOU SHORTLY.
EVERY SINGLE ONE OF YOU!

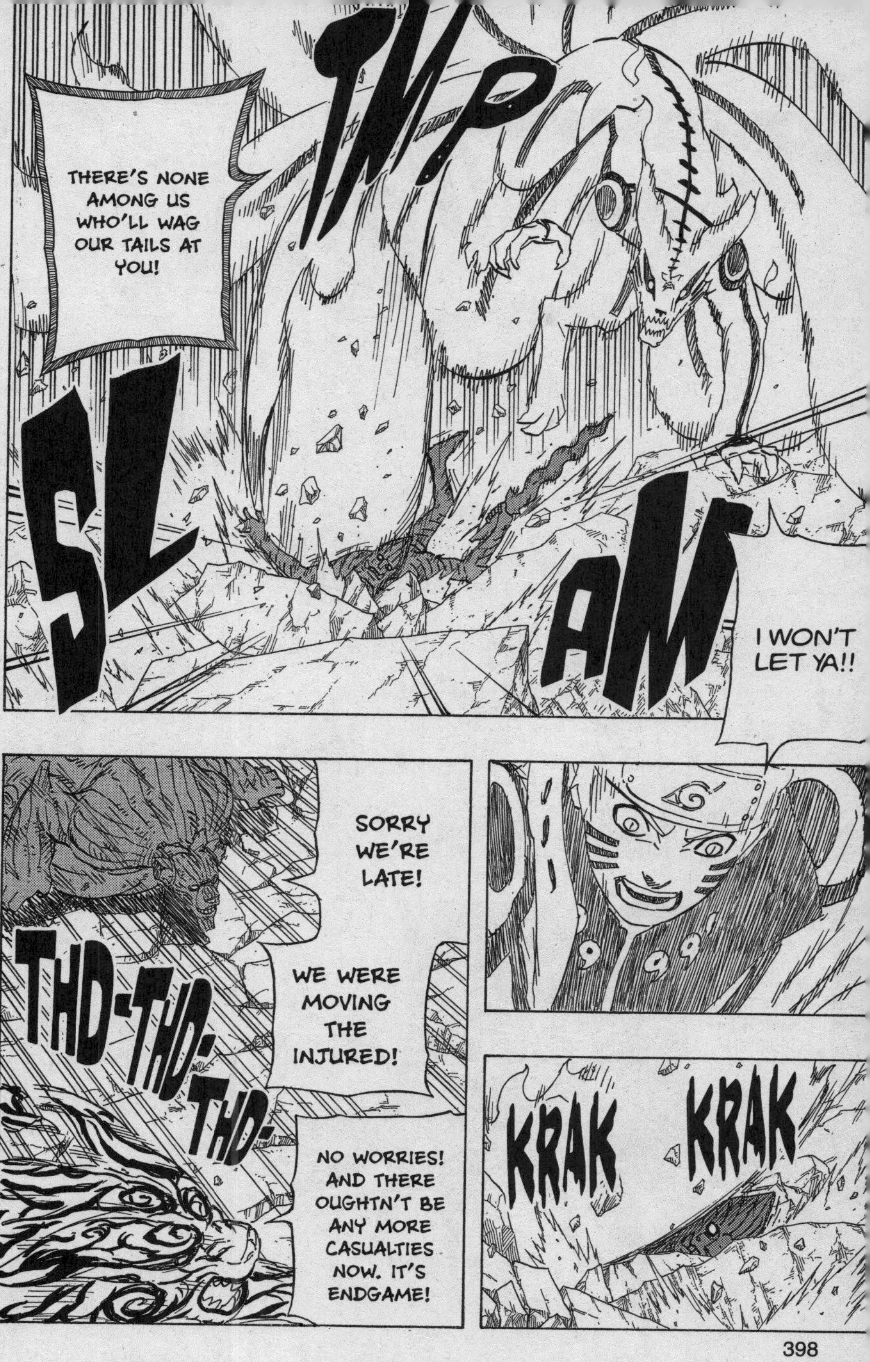
THERE'S NONE AMONG US WHO'LL WAG OUR TAILS AT YOU!
SLAM
I WON'T LET YA!!
KRAK KRAK
SORRY WE'RE LATE!
WE WERE MOVING THE INJURED!
THD-THD-THD-
NO WORRIES! AND THERE OUGHTN'T BE ANY MORE CASUALTIES NOW. IT'S ENDGAME!

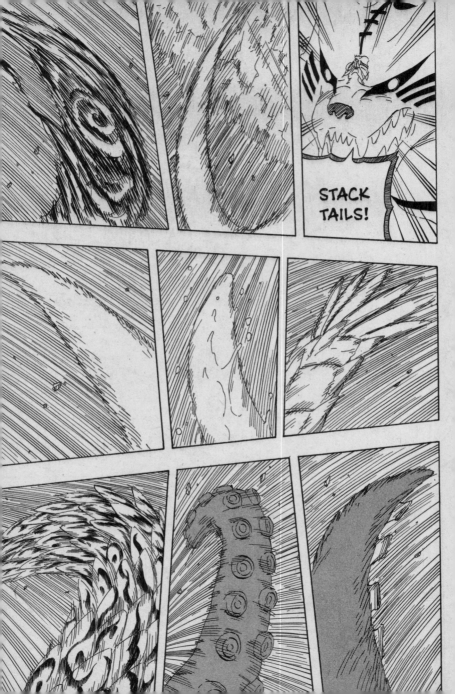

STACK
TAILS!

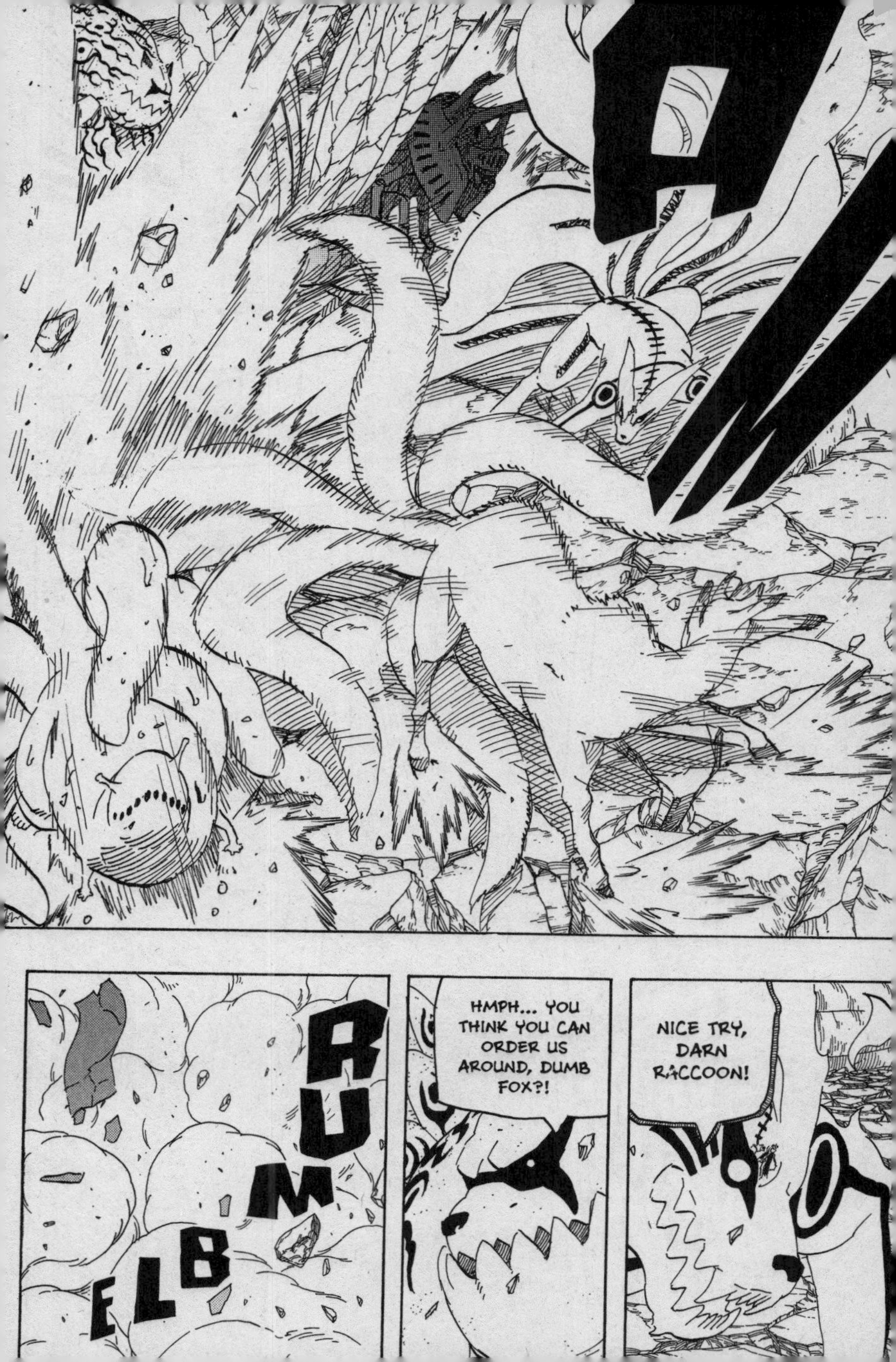
NICE TRY, DARN RACCOON!
HMPH... YOU THINK YOU CAN ORDER US AROUND, DUMB FOX?!
RUMBLE

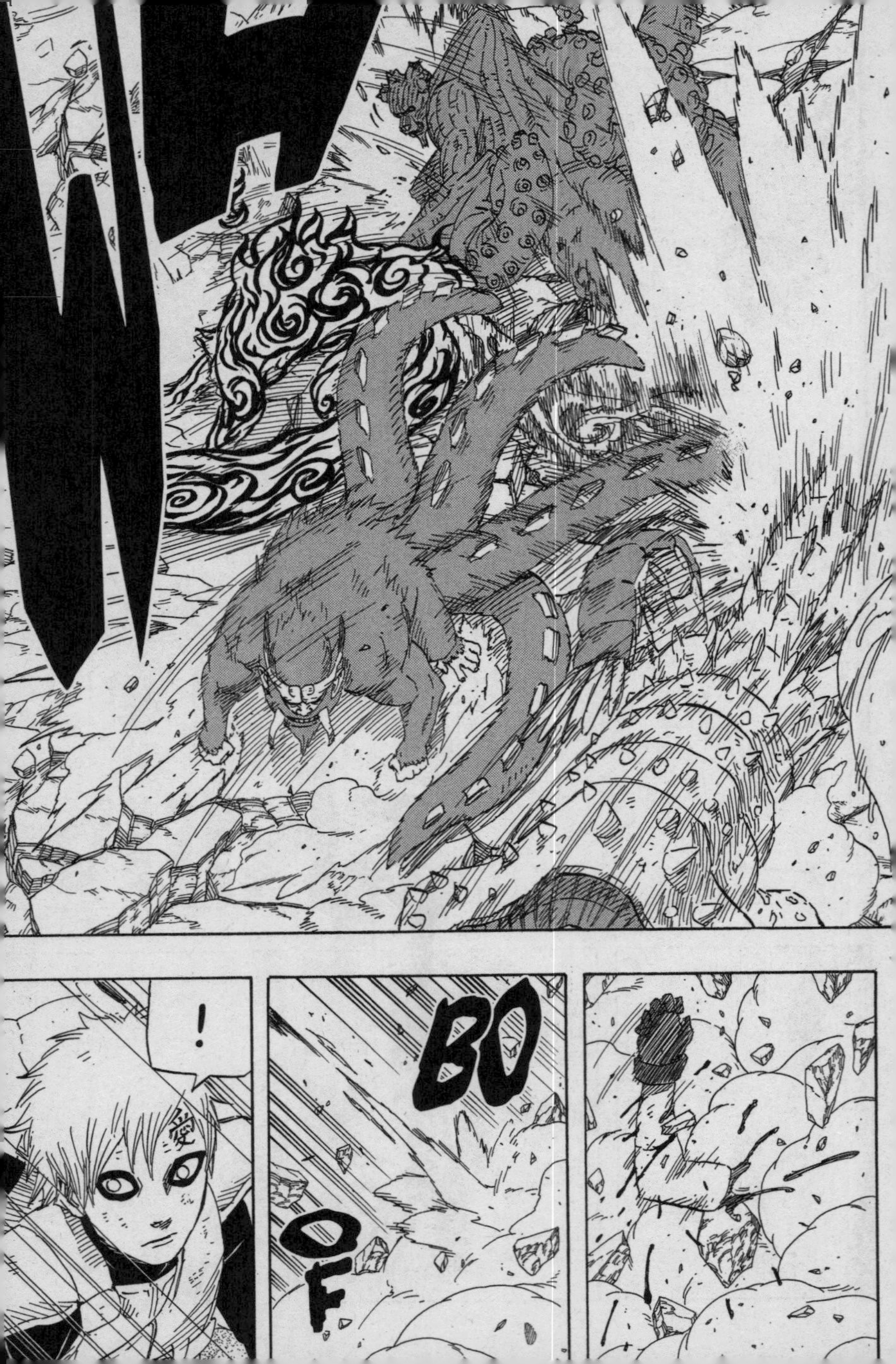
BOOF
!

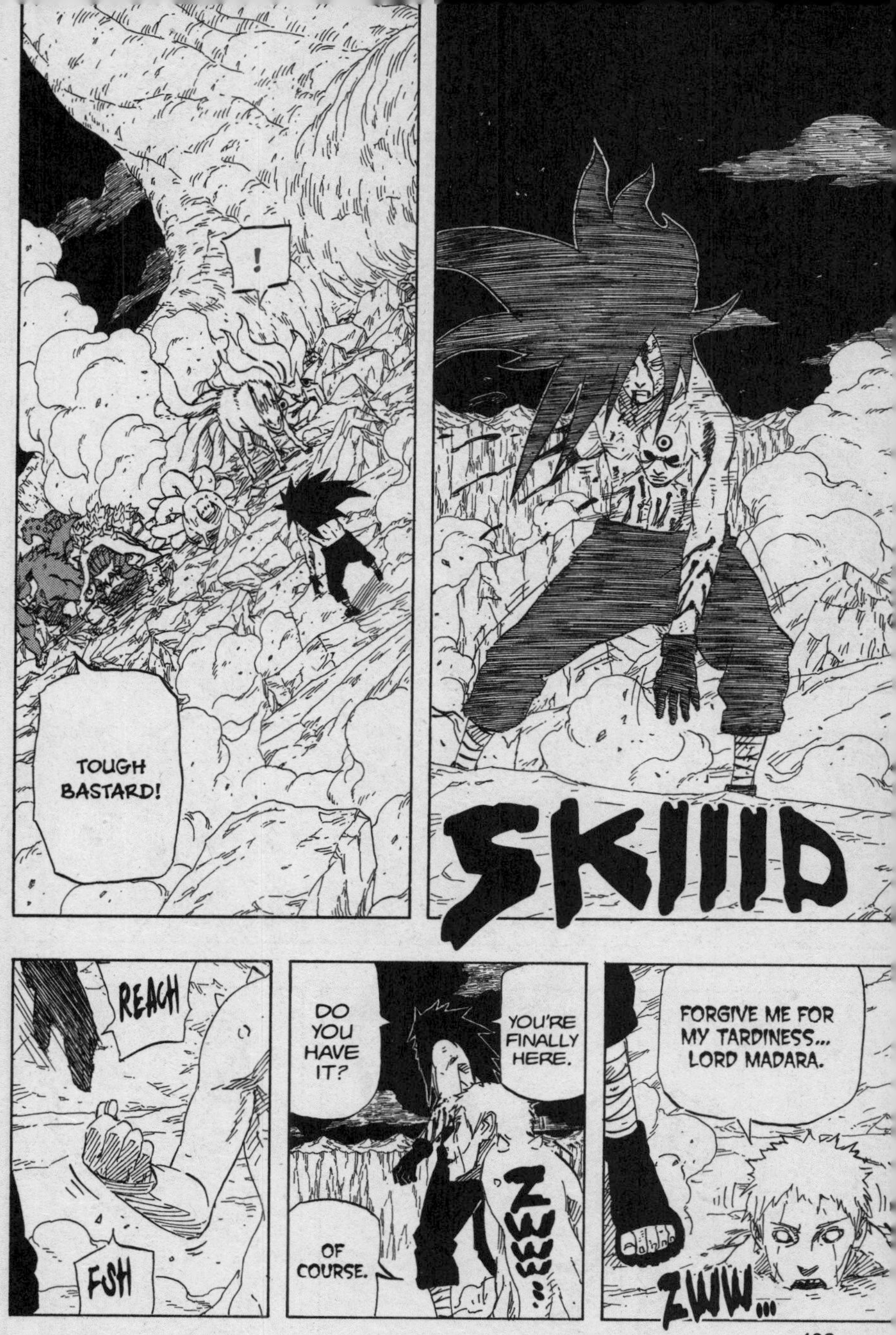
SKIIID
!
TOUGH BASTARD!
FORGIVE ME FOR MY TARDINESS... LORD MADARA.
ZWW...
YOU'RE FINALLY HERE.
DO YOU HAVE IT?
ZWW...
OF COURSE.
REACH
FSH

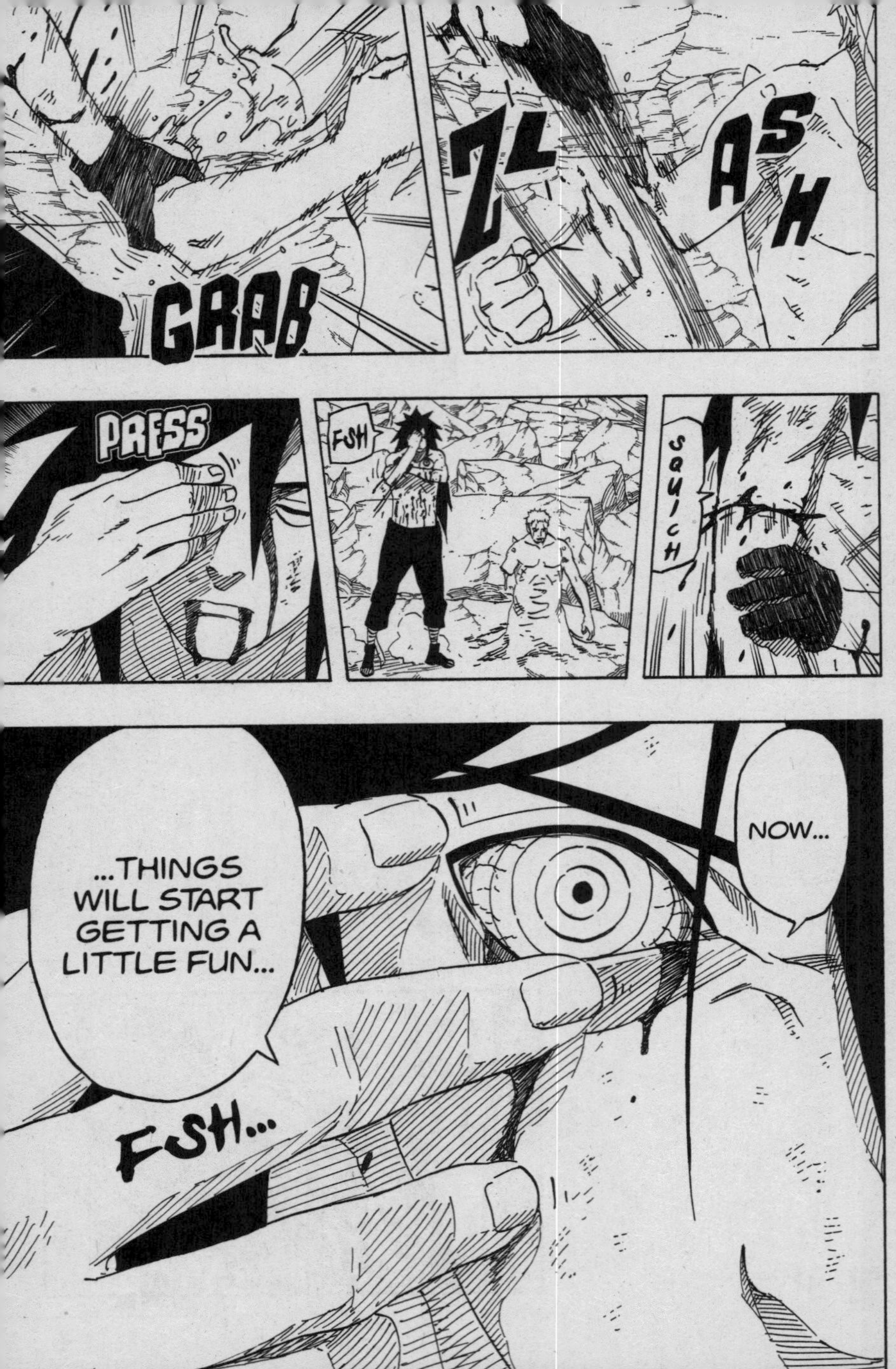
ZLASH
GRAB
SQUICH
FSH
PRESS
NOW...
...THINGS WILL START GETTING A LITTLE FUN...
FSH...

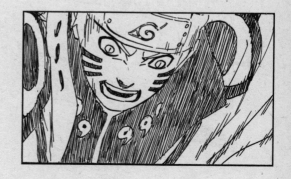

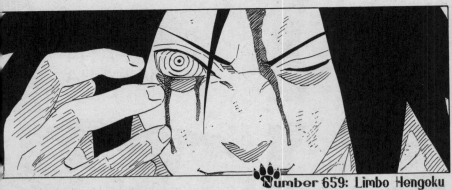

Number 659: Limbo Hengoku

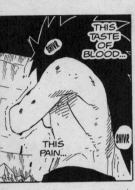

SHIVR

THIS TASTE OF BLOOD...

THIS PAIN...

SHIVR

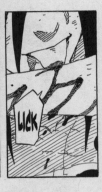

LICK

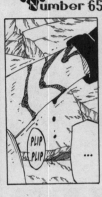

PLIP PLIP

...

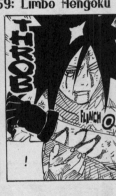

THROB

FLINCH

!

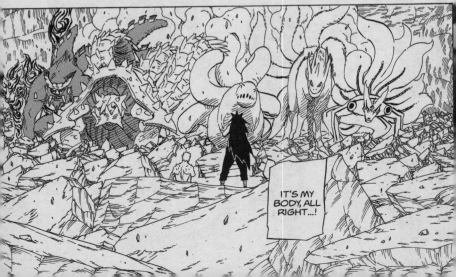

IT'S MY BODY, ALL RIGHT...!

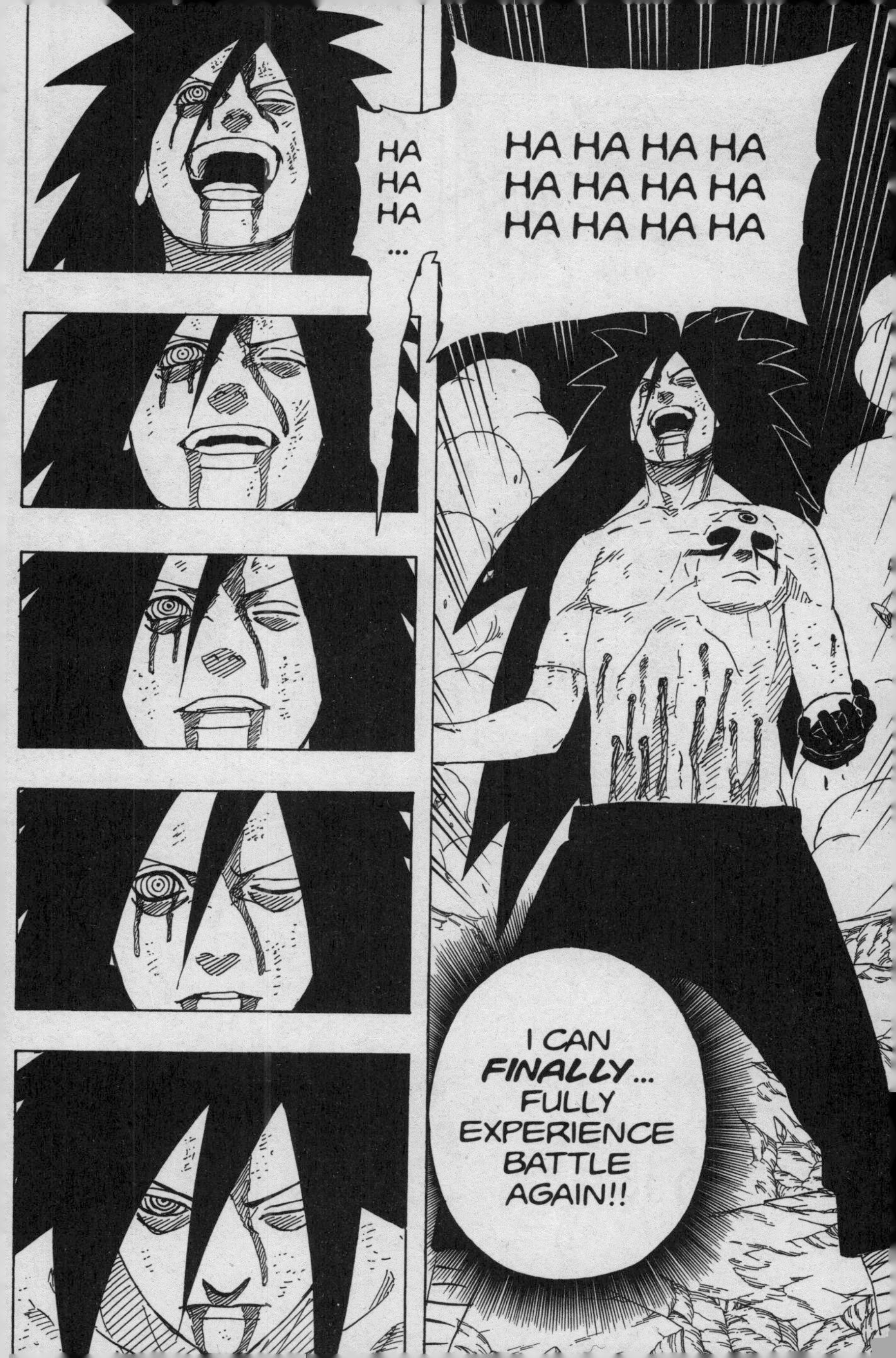
HA HA HA HA
HA HA HA HA
HA HA HA HA
HA
HA
HA
...
I CAN **FINALLY**... FULLY EXPERIENCE BATTLE AGAIN!!

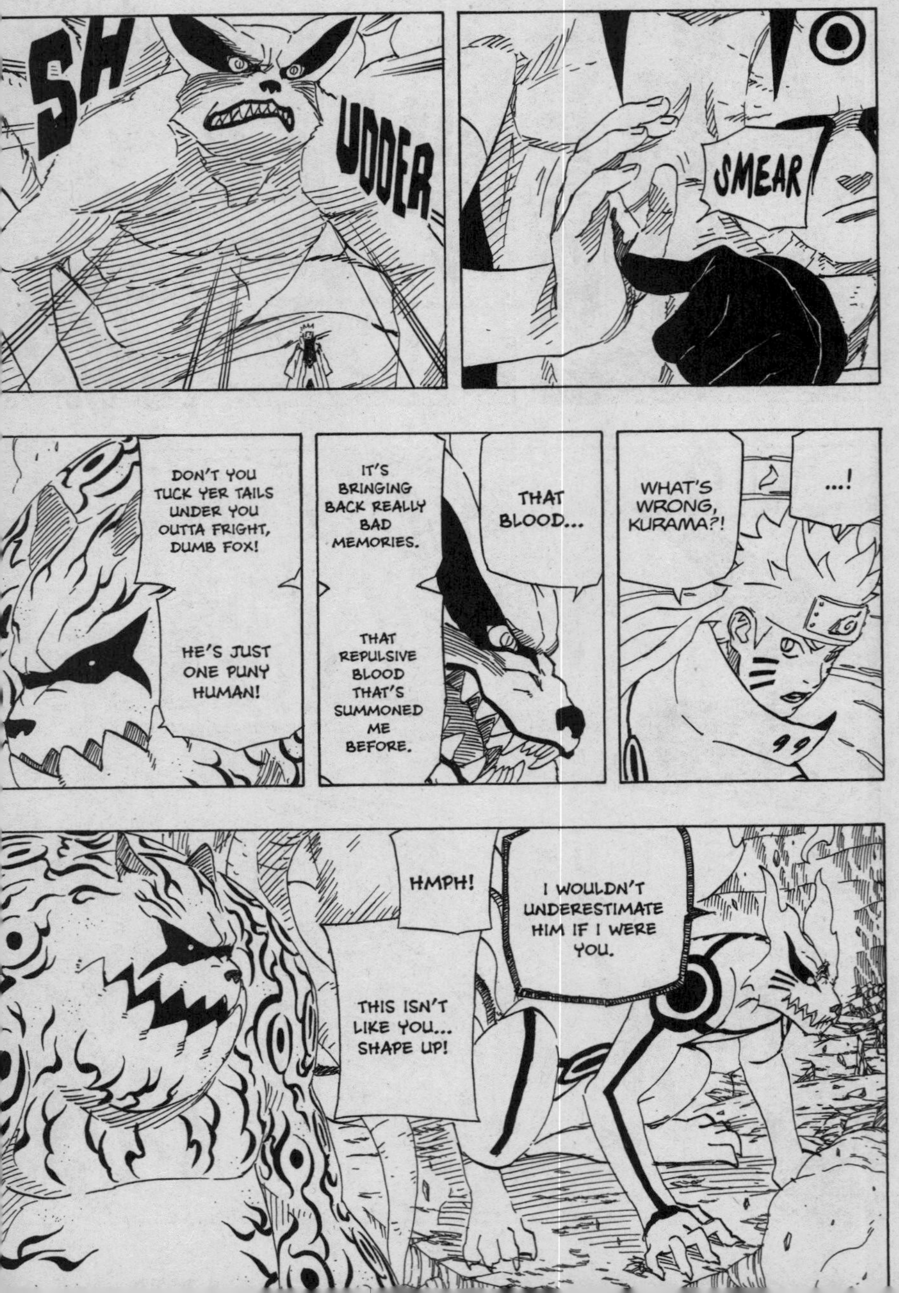
SMEAR
SHUDDER
...!
WHAT'S WRONG, KURAMA?!
THAT BLOOD...
IT'S BRINGING BACK REALLY BAD MEMORIES.
THAT REPULSIVE BLOOD THAT'S SUMMONED ME BEFORE.
DON'T YOU TUCK YER TAILS UNDER YOU OUTTA FRIGHT, DUMB FOX!
HE'S JUST ONE PUNY HUMAN!
I WOULDN'T UNDERESTIMATE HIM IF I WERE YOU.
HMPH!
THIS ISN'T LIKE YOU... SHAPE UP!

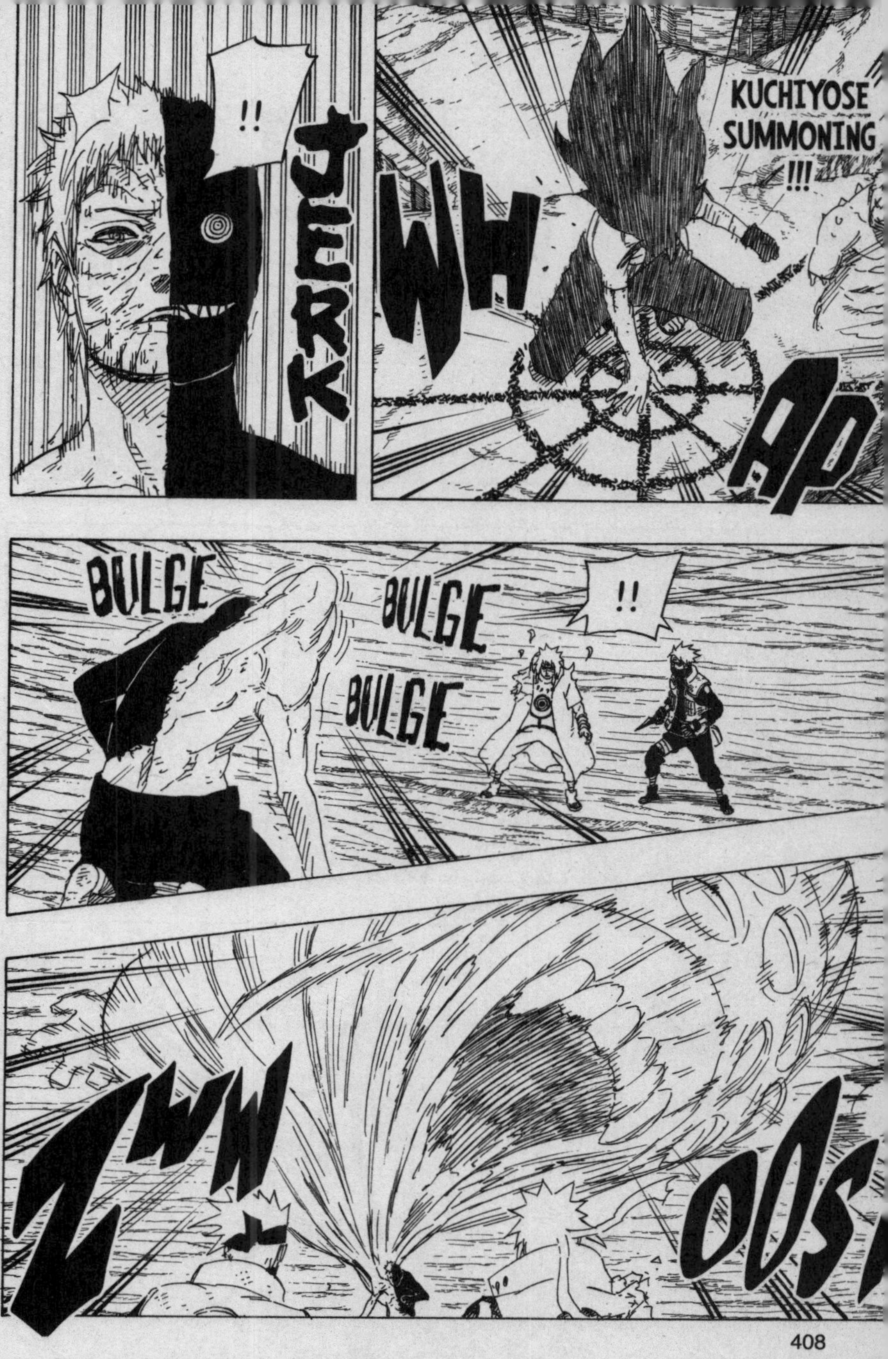
KUCHIYOSE SUMMONING!!!
WH
AP
!!
JERK
!!
BULGE
BULGE
BULGE
ZWW
OOSH

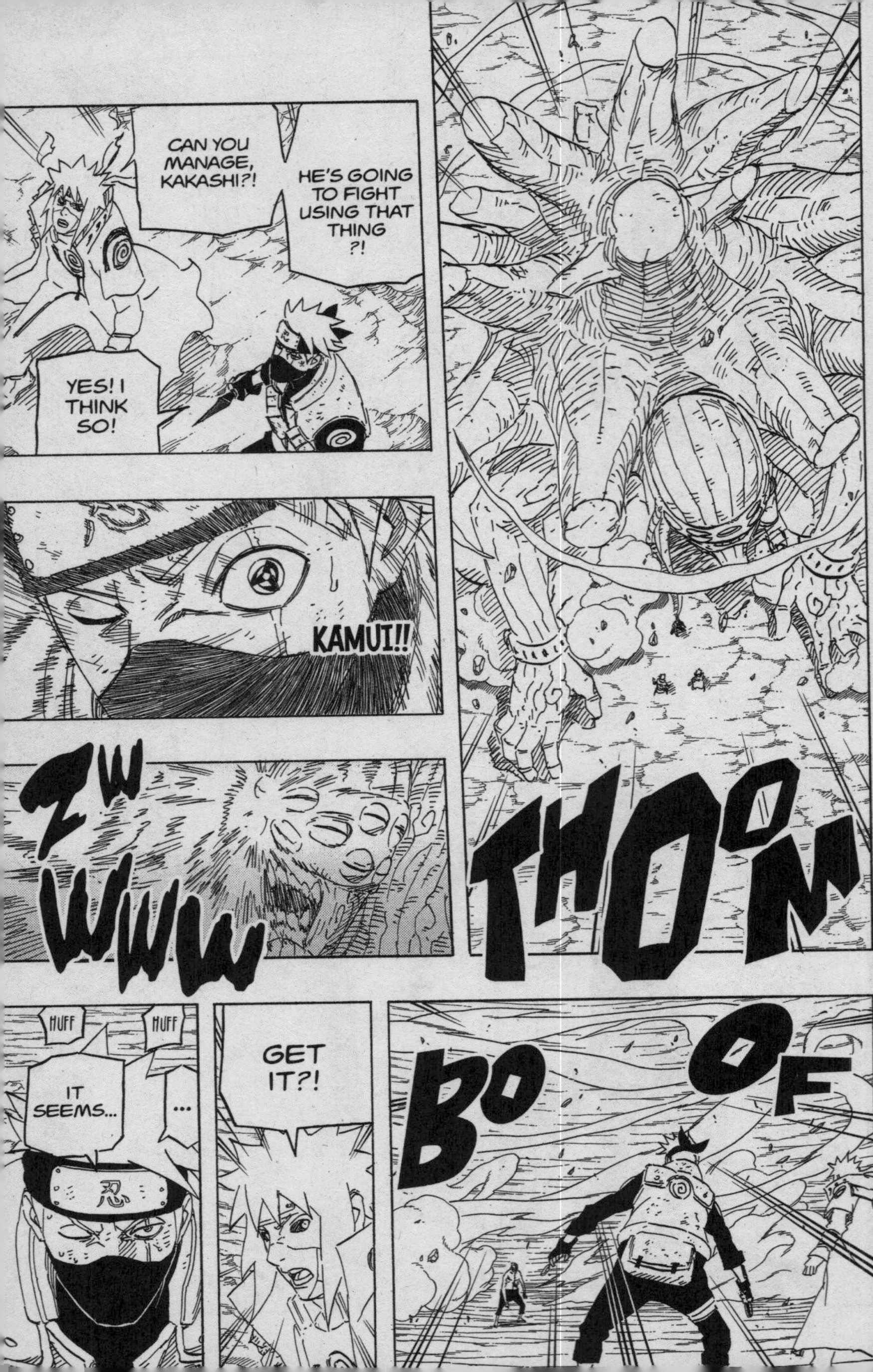
THOOM
HE'S GOING TO FIGHT USING THAT THING ?!
CAN YOU MANAGE, KAKASHI?!
YES! I THINK SO!
KAMUI!!
ZWWWW
BOOF
GET IT?!
HUFF
...
HUFF
IT SEEMS...

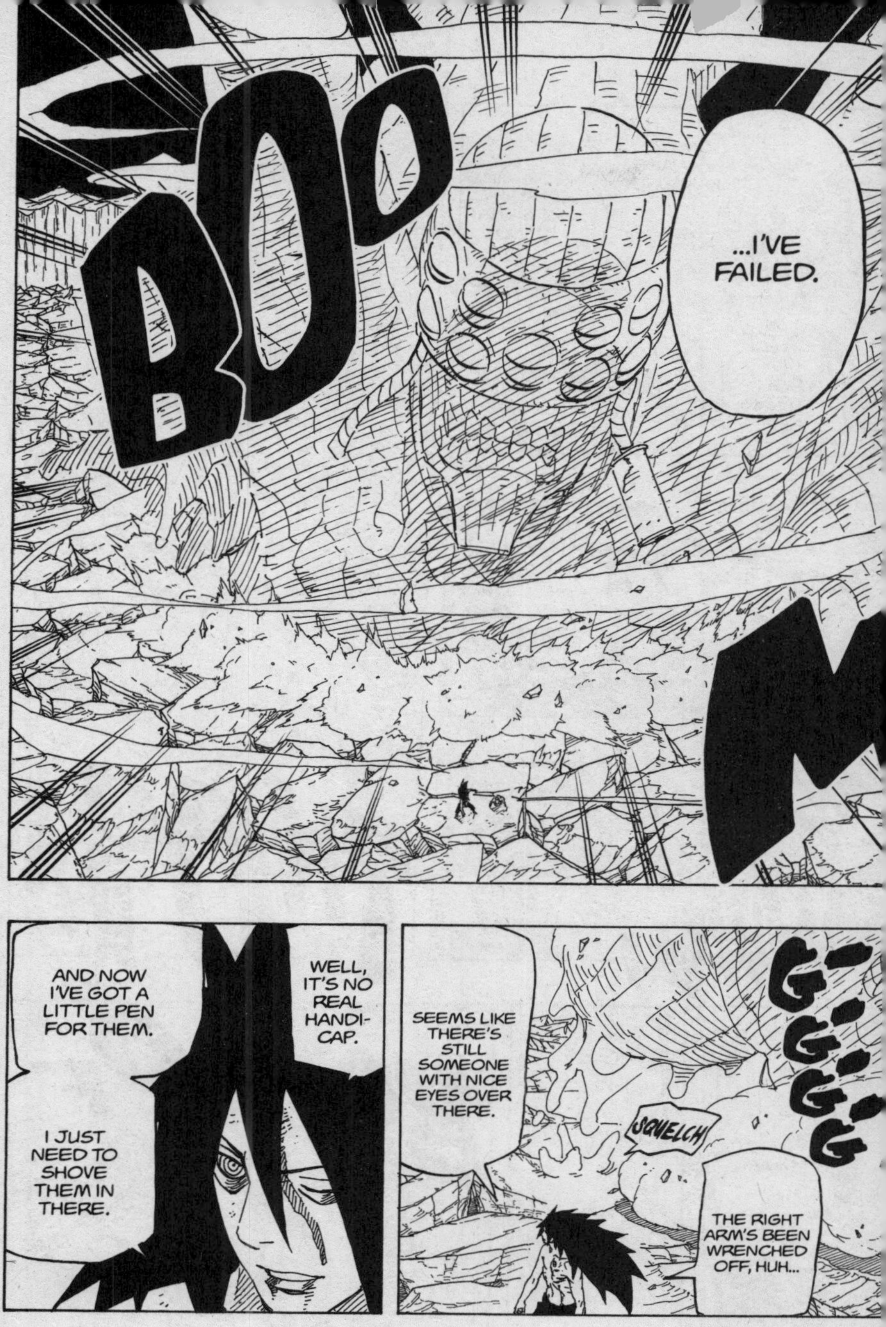
...I'VE FAILED.
BOOM
G-G-G-G-G
SEEMS LIKE THERE'S STILL SOMEONE WITH NICE EYES OVER THERE.
SQUELCH
THE RIGHT ARM'S BEEN WRENCHED OFF, HUH...
WELL, IT'S NO REAL HANDI-CAP.
AND NOW I'VE GOT A LITTLE PEN FOR THEM.
I JUST NEED TO SHOVE THEM IN THERE.

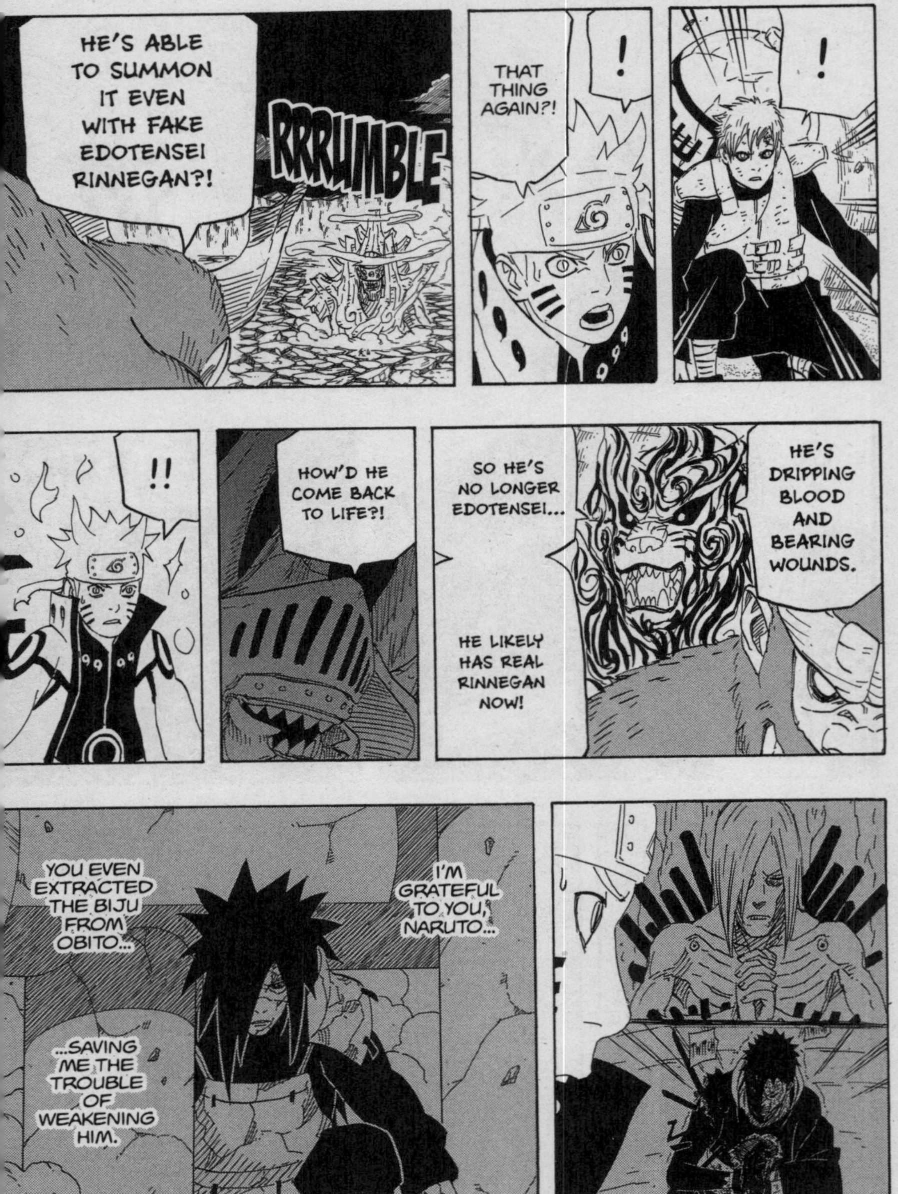
!
!
THAT THING AGAIN?!
HE'S ABLE TO SUMMON IT EVEN WITH FAKE EDOTENSEI RINNEGAN?!
RRRUMBLE
HE'S DRIPPING BLOOD AND BEARING WOUNDS.
SO HE'S NO LONGER EDOTENSEI...
HE LIKELY HAS REAL RINNEGAN NOW!
HOW'D HE COME BACK TO LIFE?!
!!
I'M GRATEFUL TO YOU, NARUTO...
YOU EVEN EXTRACTED THE BIJU FROM OBITO...
...SAVING ME THE TROUBLE OF WEAKENING HIM.

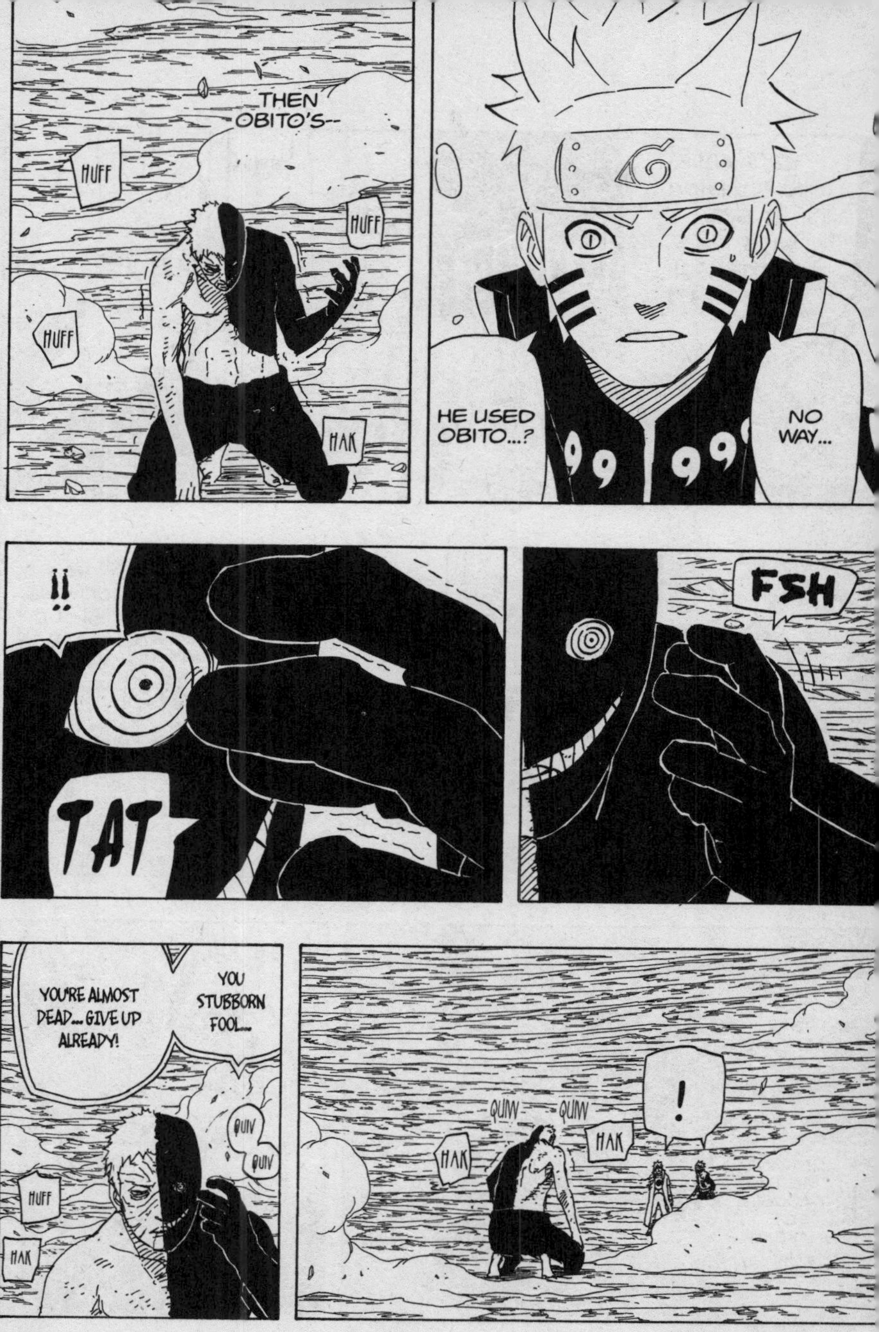
NO WAY...
HE USED OBITO...?
THEN OBITO'S--
HUFF
HUFF
HUFF
HAK
FSH
!!
TAT
!
HAK
QUIVV
QUIVV
HAK
YOU STUBBORN FOOL...
YOU'RE ALMOST DEAD... GIVE UP ALREADY!
QUIV
QUIV
HUFF
HAK

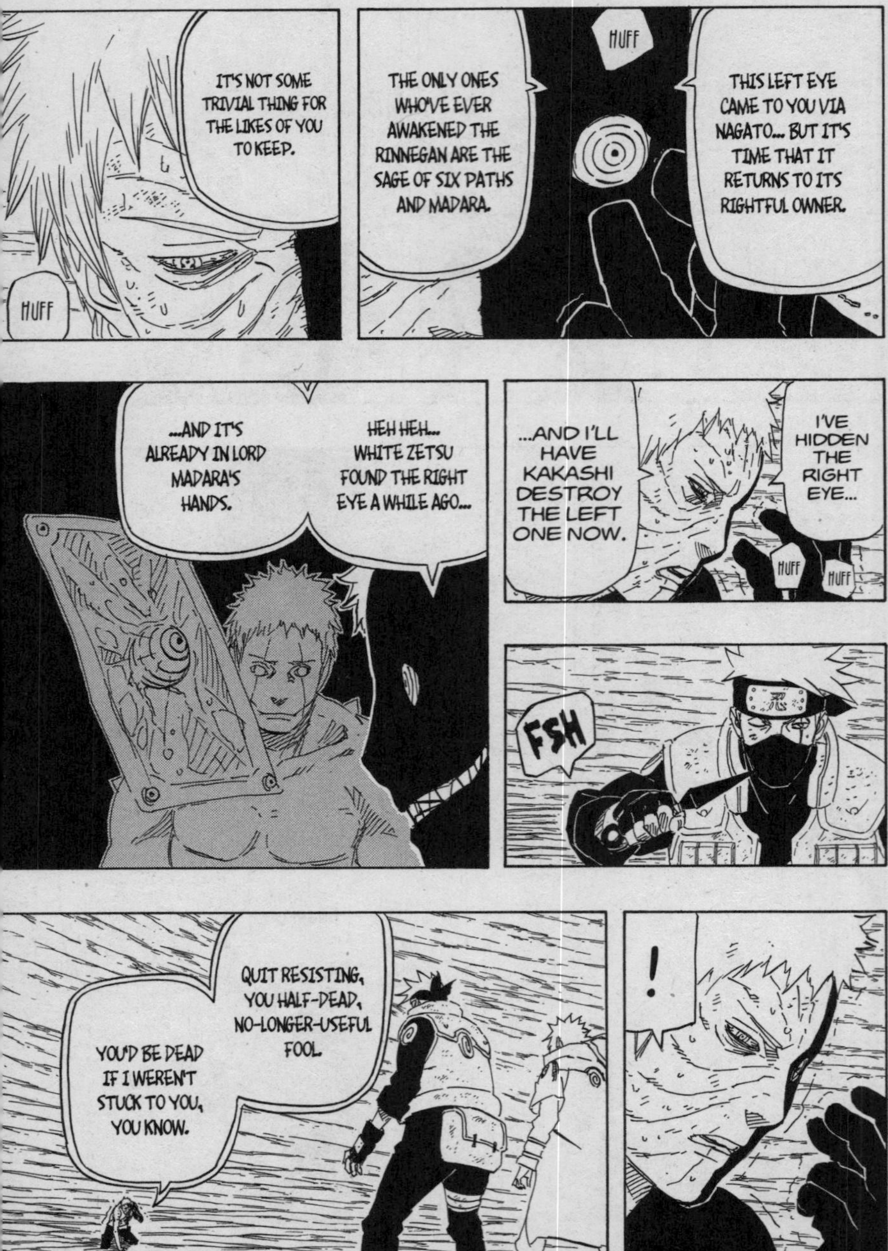
HUFF
THIS LEFT EYE CAME TO YOU VIA NAGATO... BUT IT'S TIME THAT IT RETURNS TO ITS RIGHTFUL OWNER.
THE ONLY ONES WHO'VE EVER AWAKENED THE RINNEGAN ARE THE SAGE OF SIX PATHS AND MADARA.
IT'S NOT SOME TRIVIAL THING FOR THE LIKES OF YOU TO KEEP.
HUFF
I'VE HIDDEN THE RIGHT EYE...
...AND I'LL HAVE KAKASHI DESTROY THE LEFT ONE NOW.
HUFF
HUFF
FSH
HEH HEH... WHITE ZETSU FOUND THE RIGHT EYE A WHILE AGO...
...AND IT'S ALREADY IN LORD MADARA'S HANDS.
!
QUIT RESISTING, YOU HALF-DEAD, NO-LONGER-USEFUL FOOL.
YOU'D BE DEAD IF I WEREN'T STUCK TO YOU, YOU KNOW.

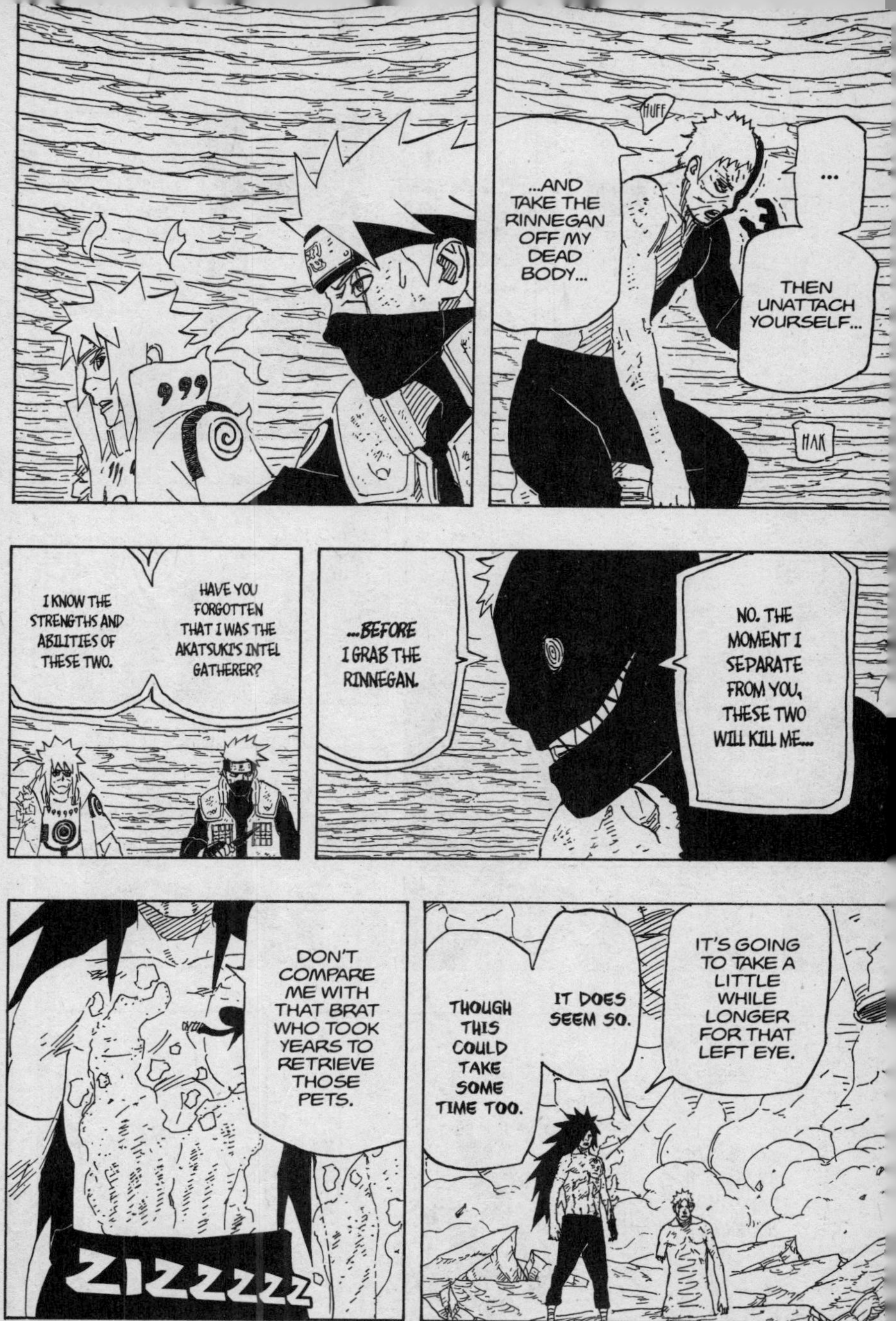
...
THEN UNATTACH YOURSELF...
HUFF
...AND TAKE THE RINNEGAN OFF MY DEAD BODY...
HAK
NO. THE MOMENT I SEPARATE FROM YOU, THESE TWO WILL KILL ME...
...BEFORE I GRAB THE RINNEGAN.
HAVE YOU FORGOTTEN THAT I WAS THE AKATSUKI'S INTEL GATHERER?
I KNOW THE STRENGTHS AND ABILITIES OF THESE TWO.
IT'S GOING TO TAKE A LITTLE WHILE LONGER FOR THAT LEFT EYE.
IT DOES SEEM SO.
THOUGH THIS COULD TAKE SOME TIME TOO.
DON'T COMPARE ME WITH THAT BRAT WHO TOOK YEARS TO RETRIEVE THOSE PETS.
ZIZZZZZ

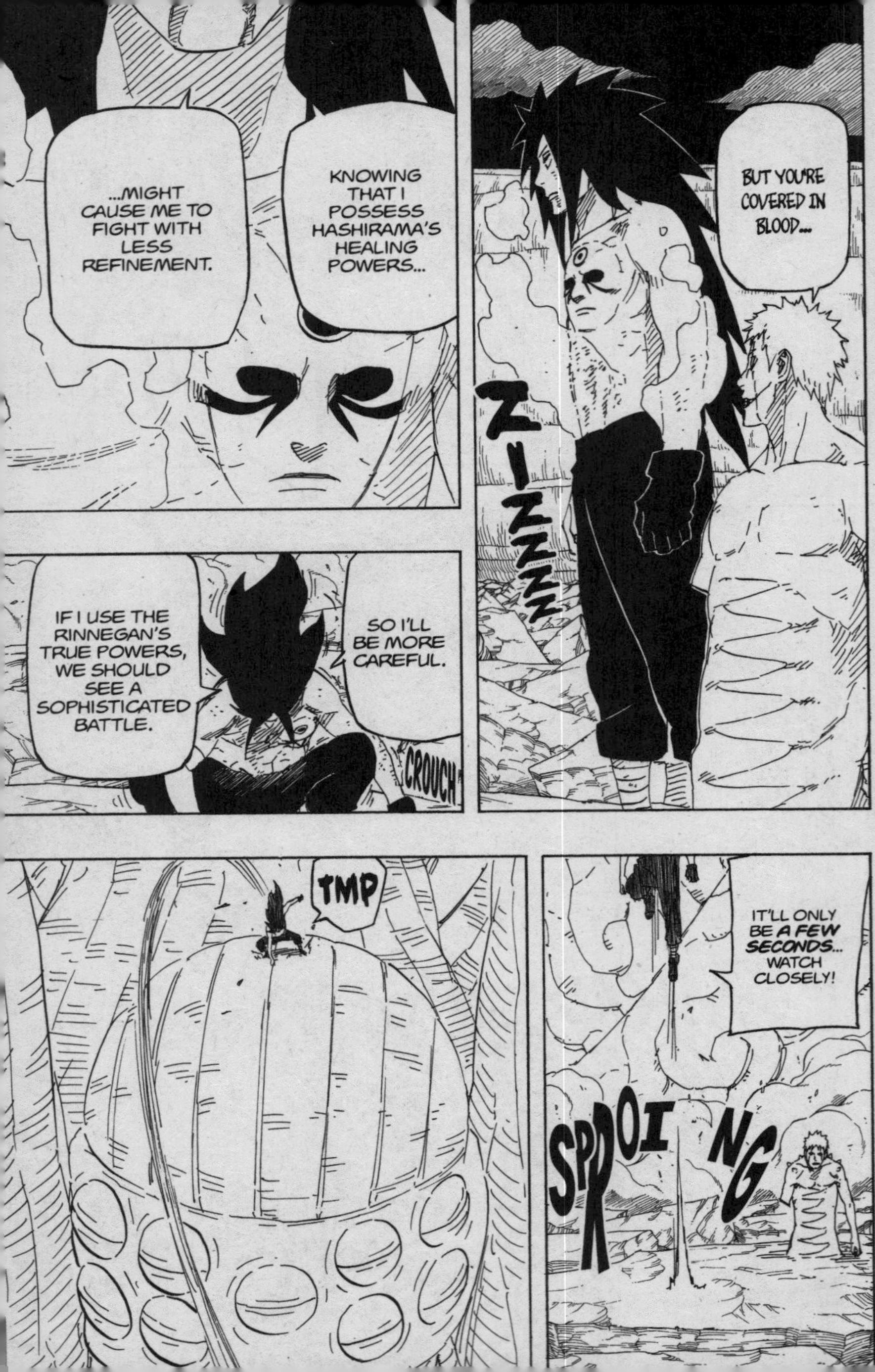
BUT YOU'RE COVERED IN BLOOD...
ZIZZZZ
KNOWING THAT I POSSESS HASHIRAMA'S HEALING POWERS...
...MIGHT CAUSE ME TO FIGHT WITH LESS REFINEMENT.
SO I'LL BE MORE CAREFUL.
IF I USE THE RINNEGAN'S TRUE POWERS, WE SHOULD SEE A SOPHISTICATED BATTLE.
CROUCH
IT'LL ONLY BE ***A FEW SECONDS***... WATCH CLOSELY!
SPROING
TMP

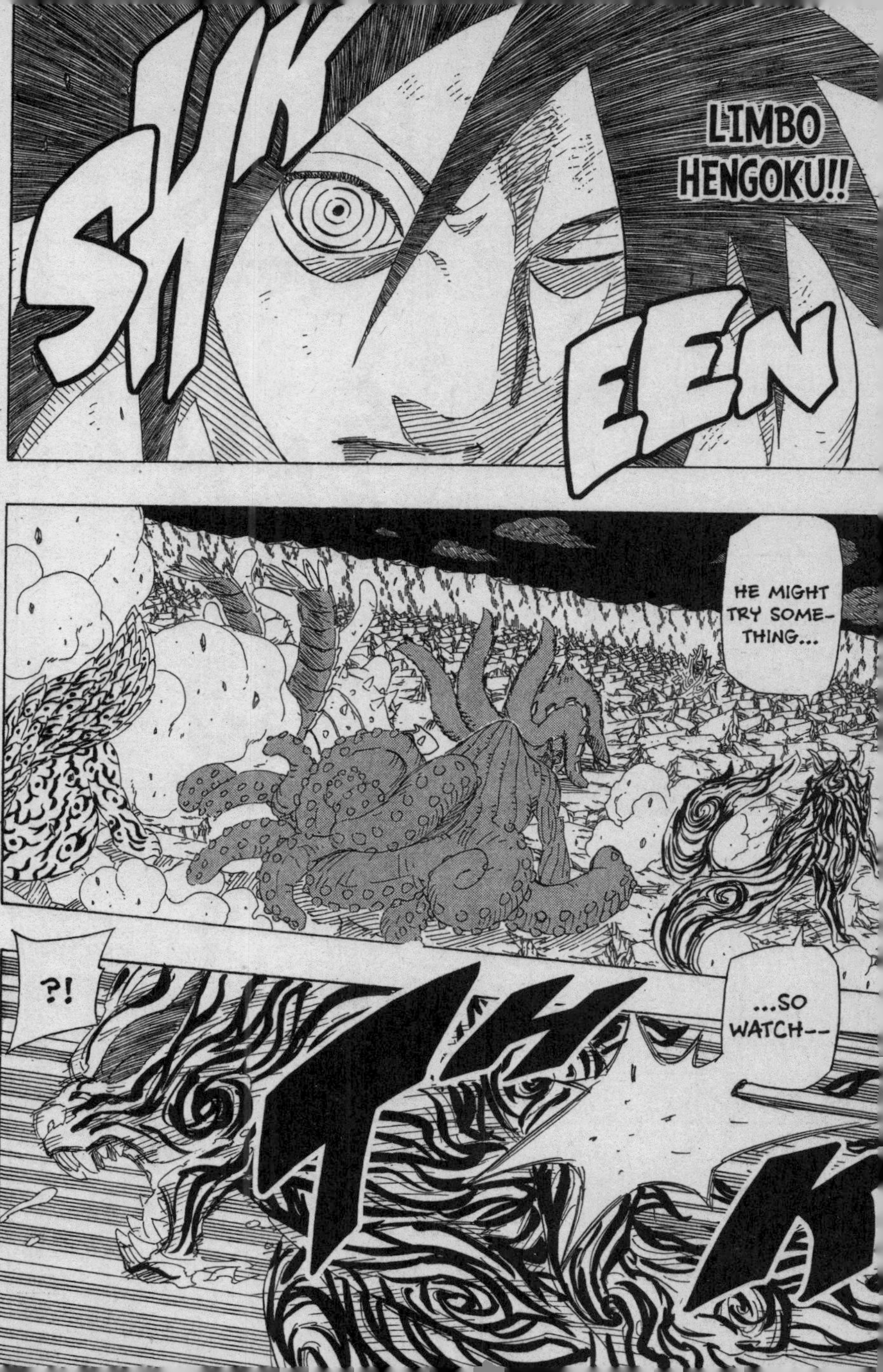
LIMBO HENGOKU!!
SHIN
EEN
HE MIGHT TRY SOME-THING...
...SO WATCH--
?!

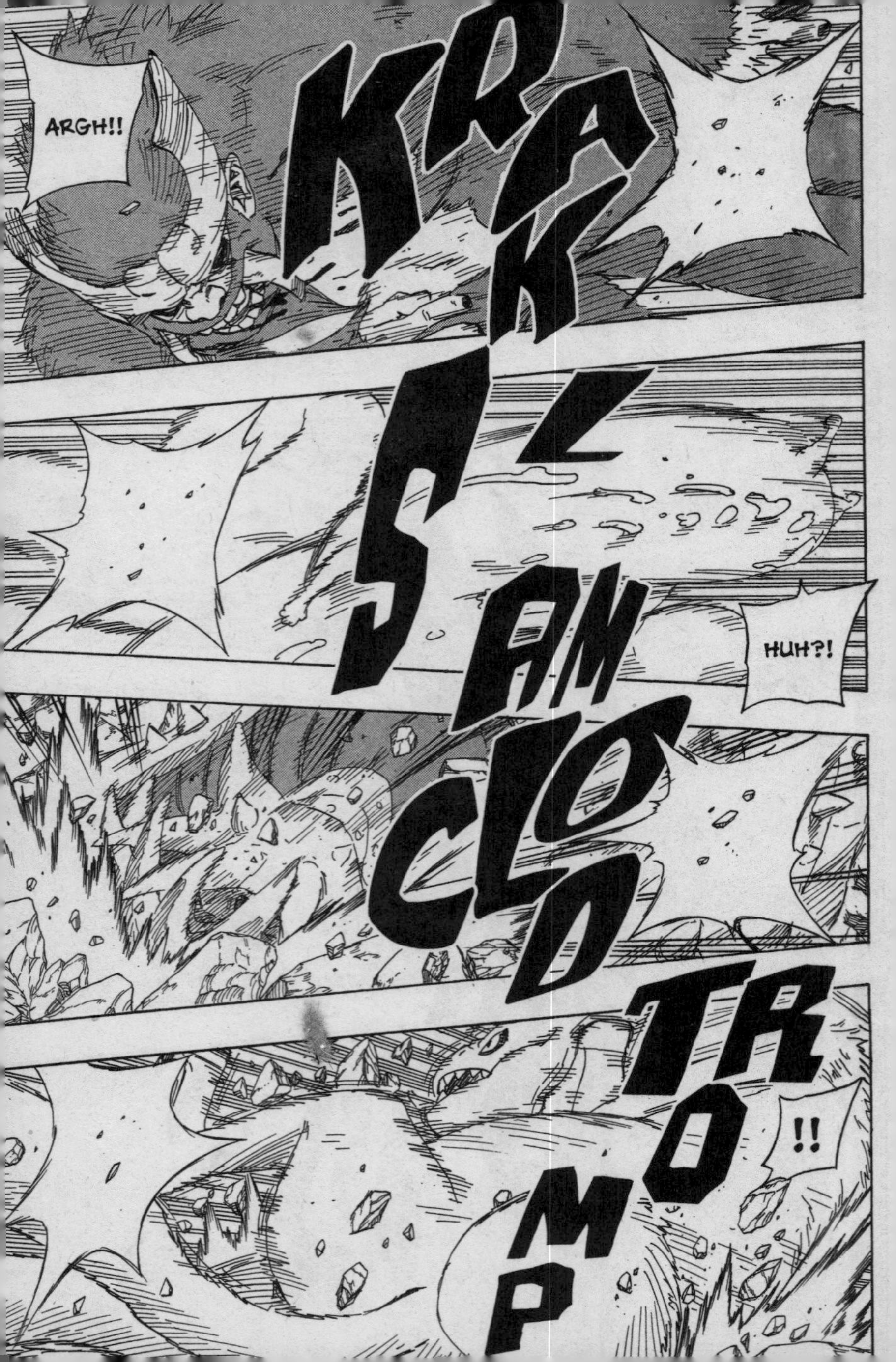
KRAKK
ARGH!!
HUH?!
SLAM
CLOD
!!
TROMP

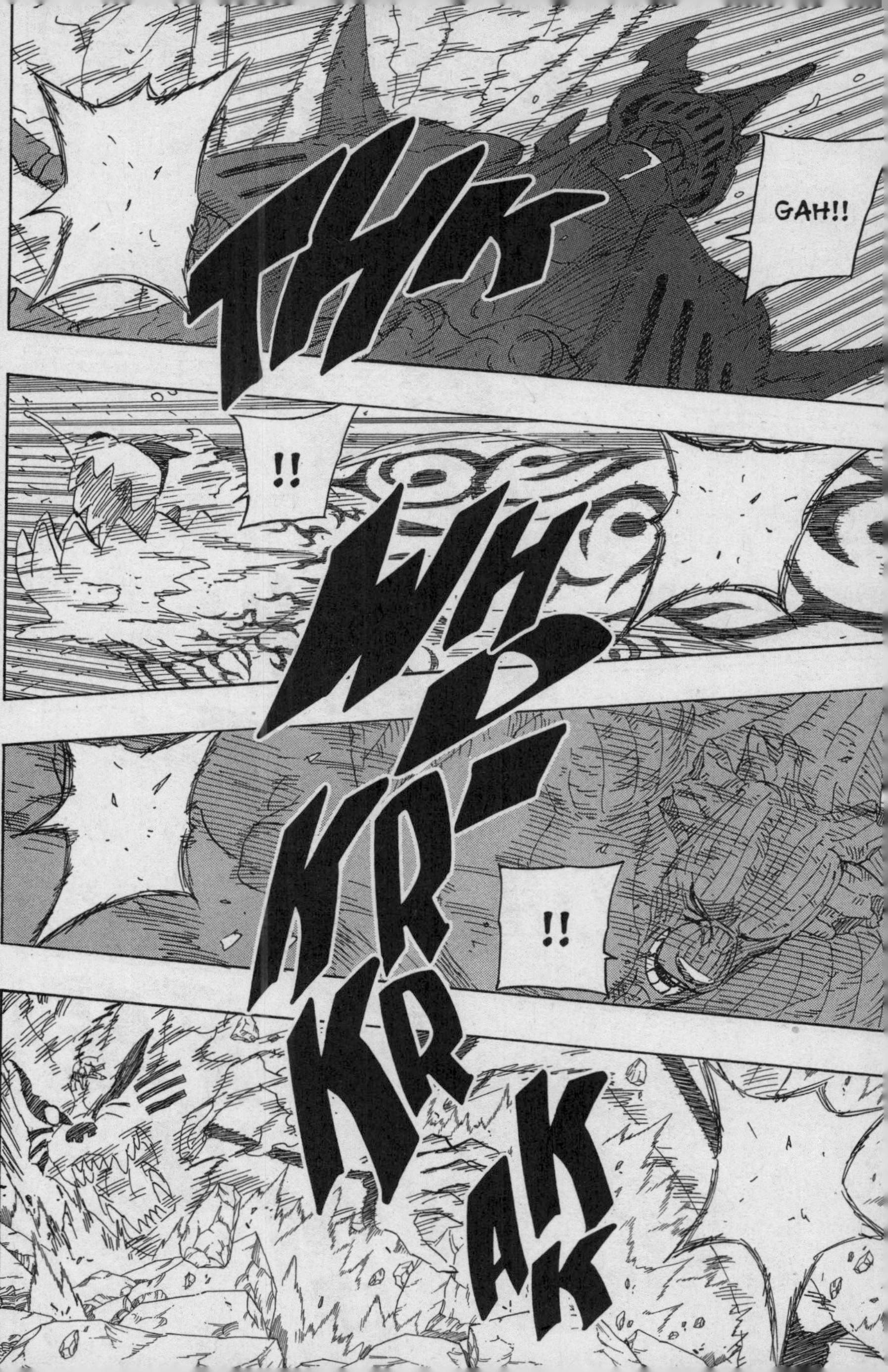
GAH!!
THK
!!
WHD
!!
KR-KRAKAK

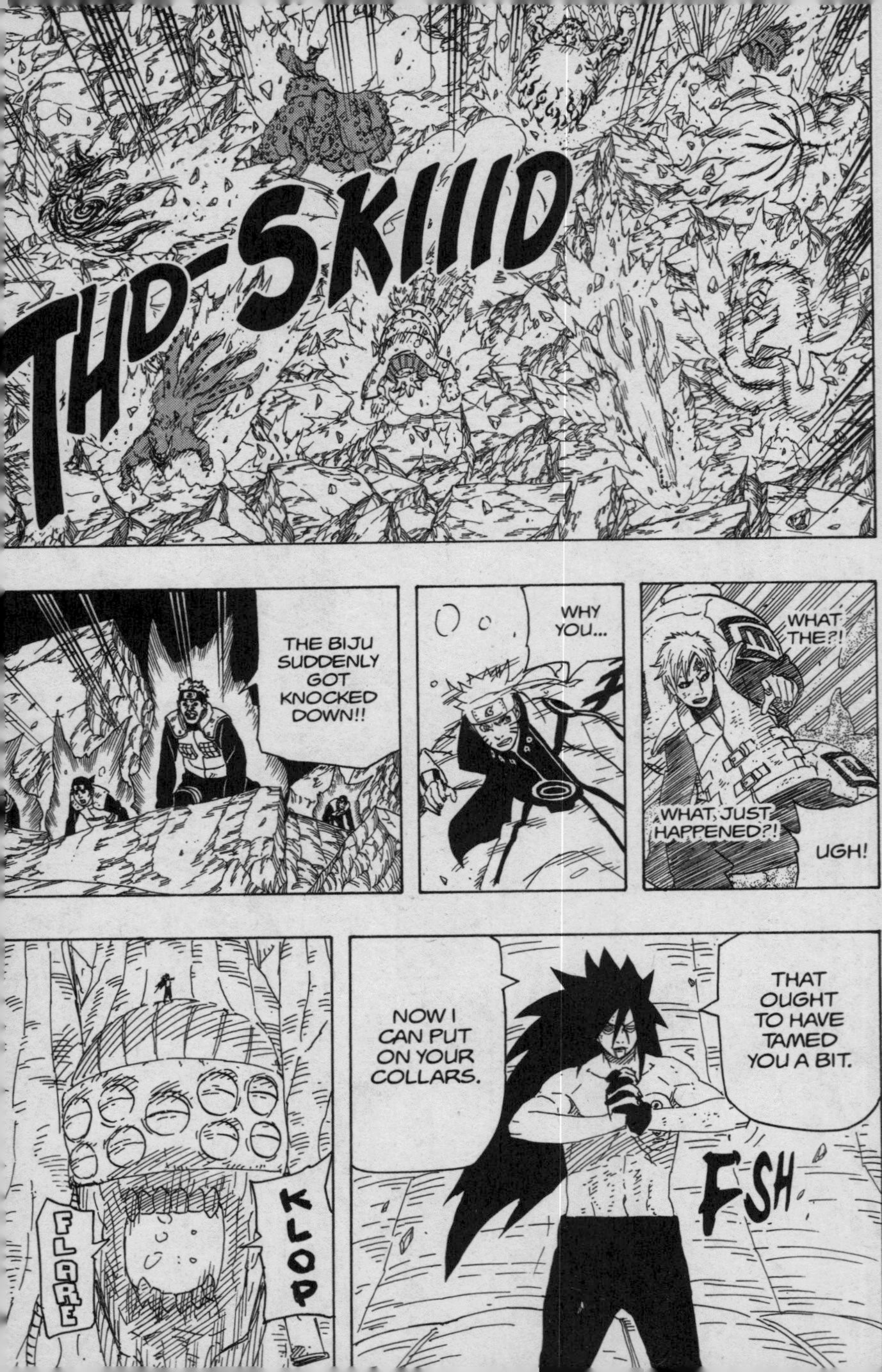
THD-SKIIID
WHAT THE?!
WHAT JUST HAPPENED?!
UGH!
WHY YOU...
THE BIJU SUDDENLY GOT KNOCKED DOWN!!
THAT OUGHT TO HAVE TAMED YOU A BIT.
NOW I CAN PUT ON YOUR COLLARS.
FSH
KLOP
FLARE

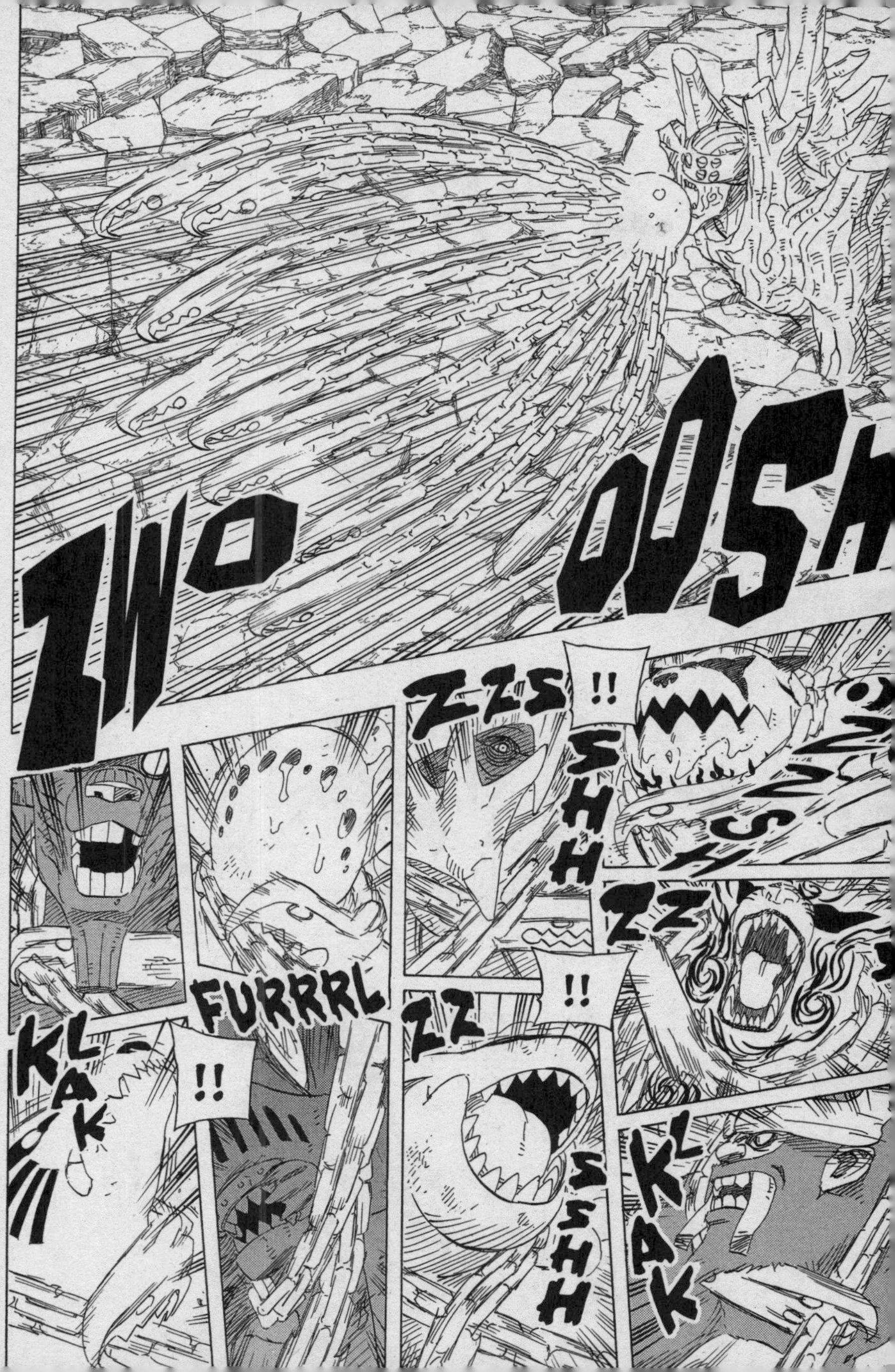

ZWOOOSH
ZZS
!!
SHHH
ZZ
SKLAK
ZZ
!!
SHHH
FURRRL
!!
KLAK

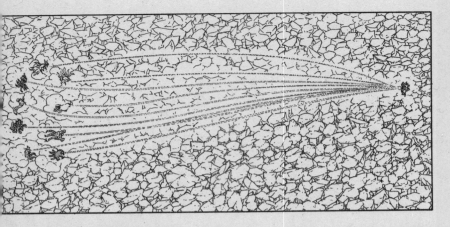

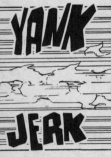

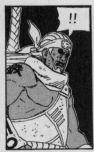

!!

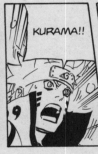

KURAMA!!

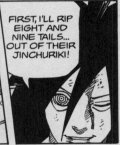

FIRST, I'LL RIP EIGHT AND NINE TAILS... OUT OF THEIR JINCHURIKI!

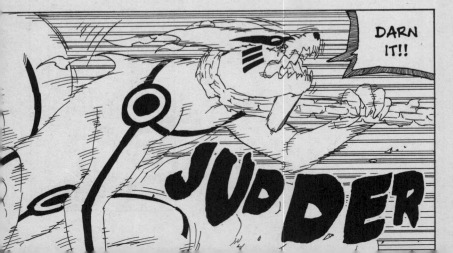

DARN IT!!

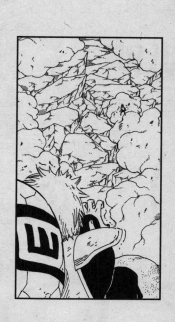

Number 660: One's True Heart

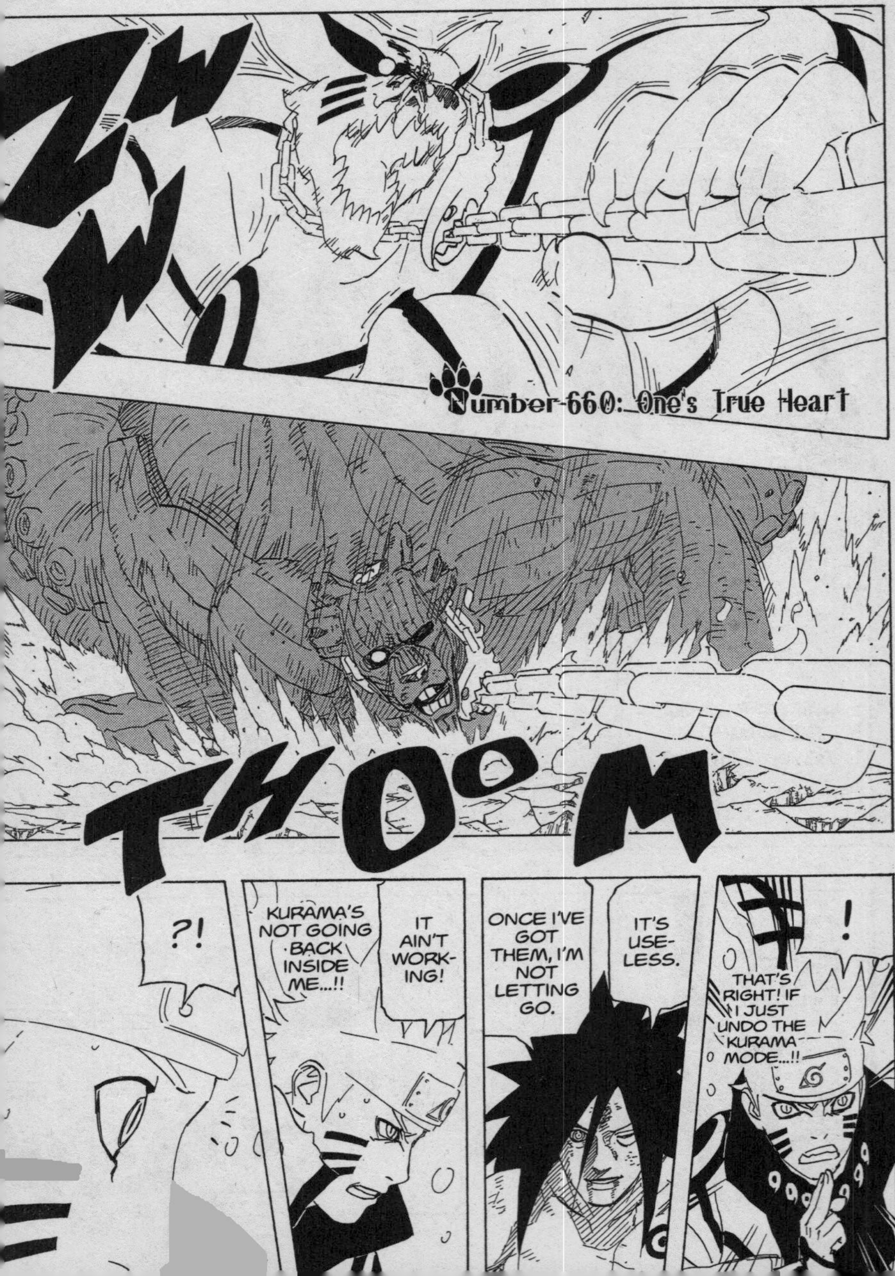
ZWW
THOOM
!
THAT'S RIGHT! IF I JUST UNDO THE KURAMA MODE...!!
IT'S USE-LESS.
ONCE I'VE GOT THEM, I'M NOT LETTING GO.
IT AIN'T WORK-ING!
KURAMA'S NOT GOING BACK INSIDE ME...!!
?!

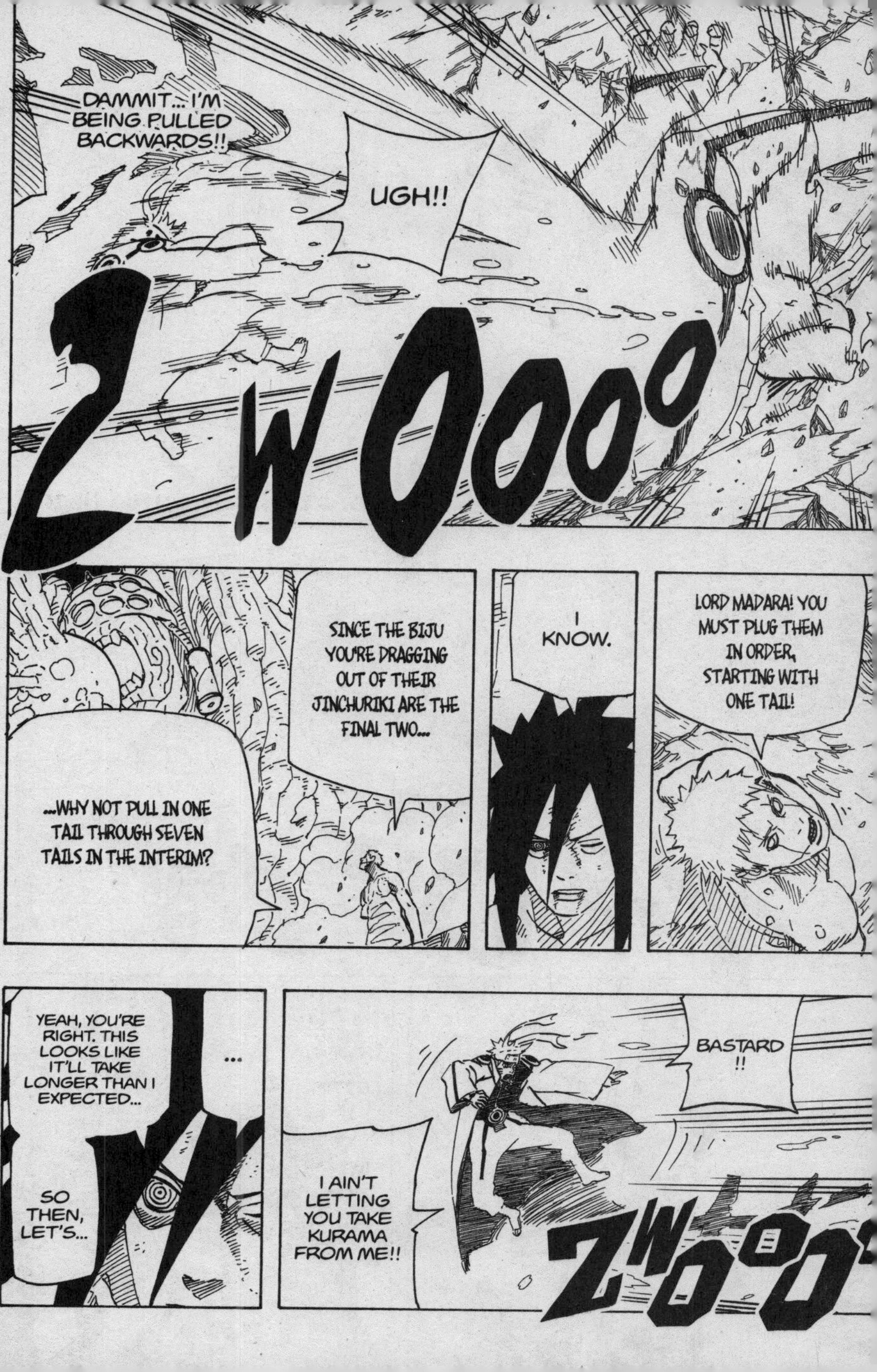
UGH!!
DAMMIT... I'M BEING PULLED BACKWARDS!!
ZWOOOO
LORD MADARA! YOU MUST PLUG THEM IN ORDER, STARTING WITH ONE TAIL!
I KNOW.
SINCE THE BIJU YOU'RE DRAGGING OUT OF THEIR JINCHURIKI ARE THE FINAL TWO...
...WHY NOT PULL IN ONE TAIL THROUGH SEVEN TAILS IN THE INTERIM?
BASTARD !!
I AIN'T LETTING YOU TAKE KURAMA FROM ME!!
ZWOOO
...
YEAH, YOU'RE RIGHT. THIS LOOKS LIKE IT'LL TAKE LONGER THAN I EXPECTED...
SO THEN, LET'S...

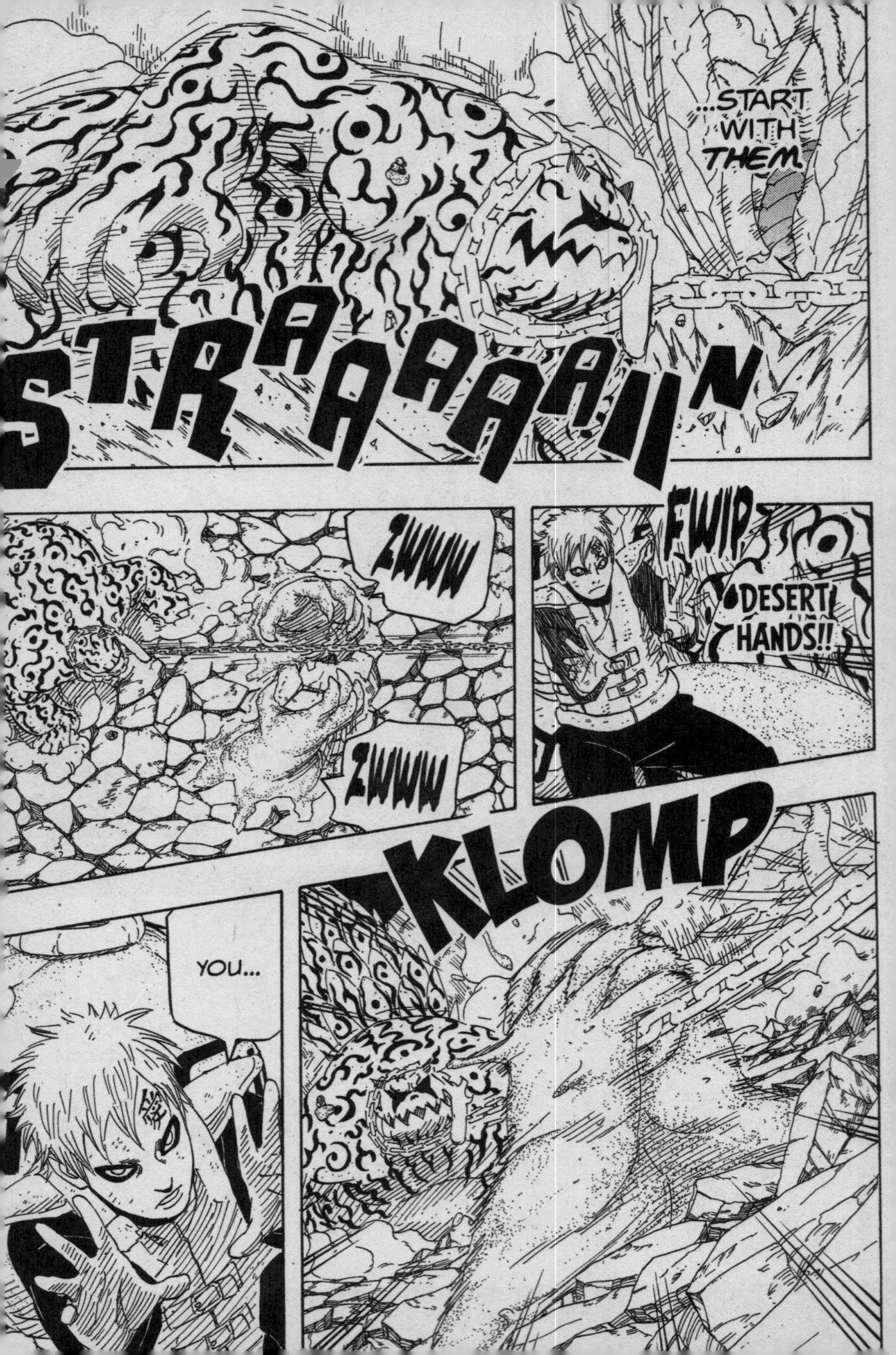
...START WITH THEM.
STRAAAAIN
FWIP
DESERT HANDS!!
ZWWW
ZWWW
KLOMP
YOU...

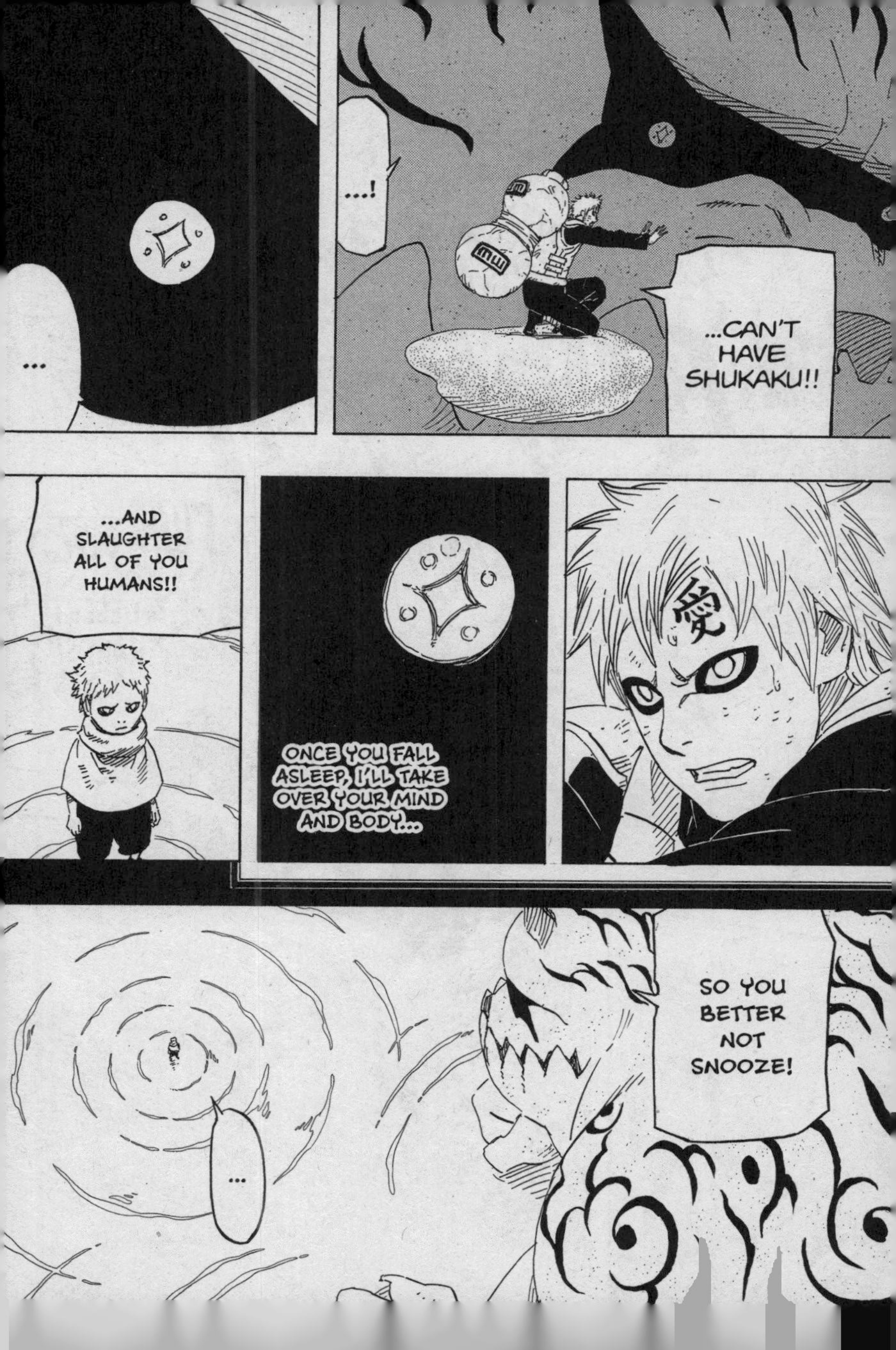

...CAN'T HAVE SHUKAKU!!
...!
...
ONCE YOU FALL ASLEEP, I'LL TAKE OVER YOUR MIND AND BODY...
...AND SLAUGHTER ALL OF YOU HUMANS!!
SO YOU BETTER NOT SNOOZE!
...

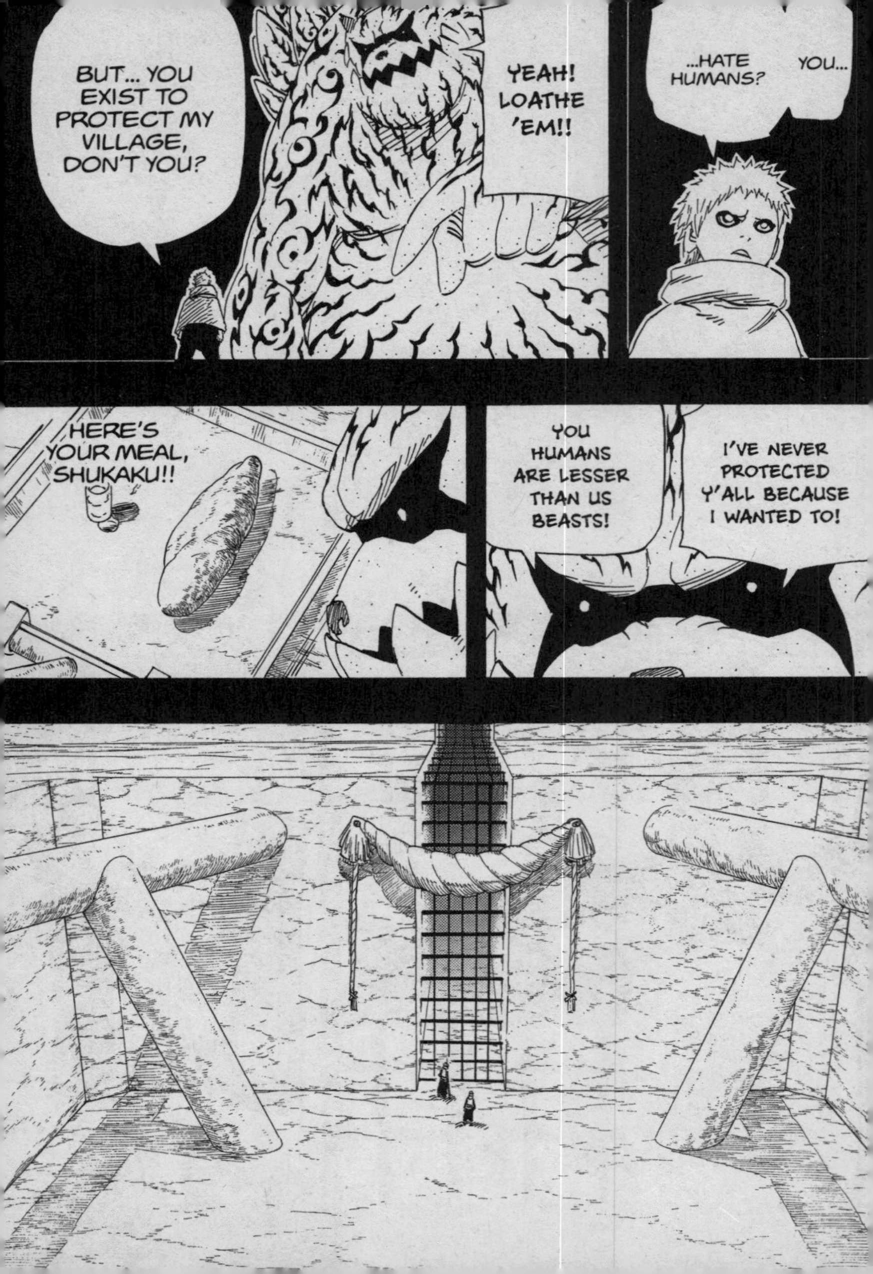
YOU...
...HATE HUMANS?
YEAH! LOATHE 'EM!!
BUT... YOU EXIST TO PROTECT MY VILLAGE, DON'T YOU?
I'VE NEVER PROTECTED Y'ALL BECAUSE I WANTED TO!
YOU HUMANS ARE LESSER THAN US BEASTS!
HERE'S YOUR MEAL, SHUKAKU!!

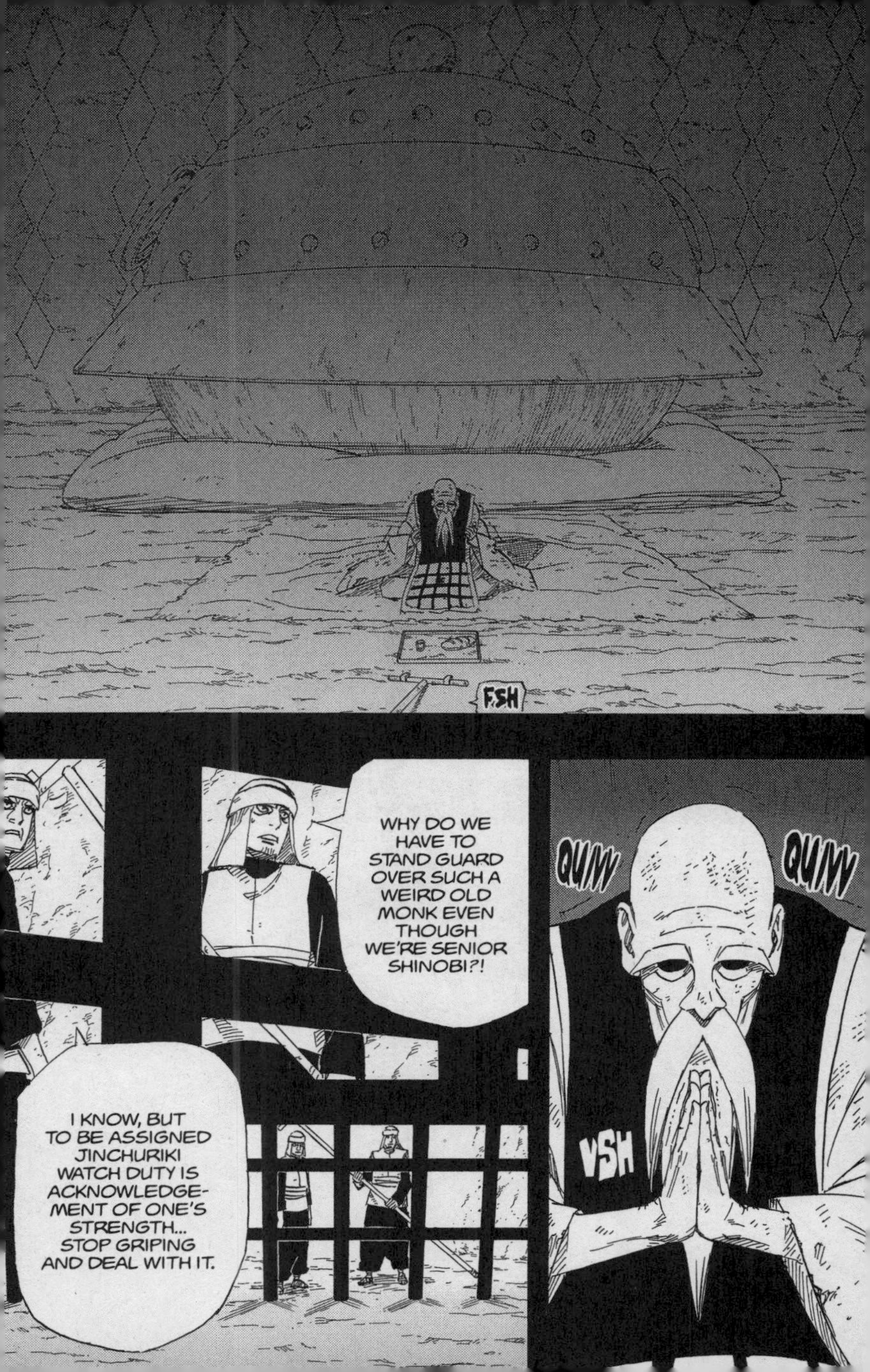
FSH
QUIVV
QUIVV
VSH
WHY DO WE HAVE TO STAND GUARD OVER SUCH A WEIRD OLD MONK EVEN THOUGH WE'RE SENIOR SHINOBI?!
I KNOW, BUT TO BE ASSIGNED JINCHURIKI WATCH DUTY IS ACKNOWLEDGE-MENT OF ONE'S STRENGTH... STOP GRIPING AND DEAL WITH IT.

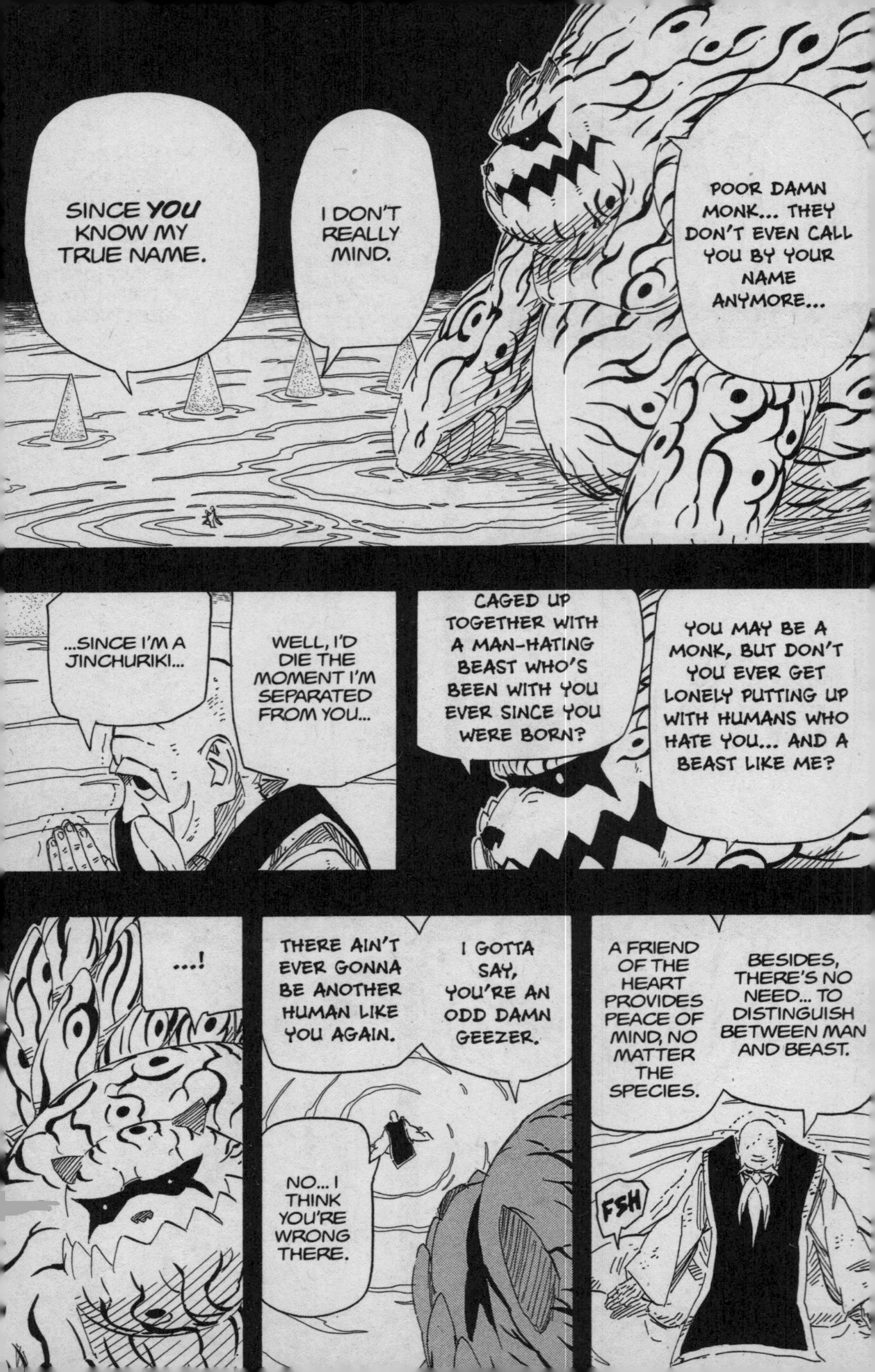
POOR DAMN MONK... THEY DON'T EVEN CALL YOU BY YOUR NAME ANYMORE...
I DON'T REALLY MIND.
SINCE YOU KNOW MY TRUE NAME.
YOU MAY BE A MONK, BUT DON'T YOU EVER GET LONELY PUTTING UP WITH HUMANS WHO HATE YOU... AND A BEAST LIKE ME?
CAGED UP TOGETHER WITH A MAN-HATING BEAST WHO'S BEEN WITH YOU EVER SINCE YOU WERE BORN?
WELL, I'D DIE THE MOMENT I'M SEPARATED FROM YOU...
...SINCE I'M A JINCHURIKI...
BESIDES, THERE'S NO NEED... TO DISTINGUISH BETWEEN MAN AND BEAST.
A FRIEND OF THE HEART PROVIDES PEACE OF MIND, NO MATTER THE SPECIES.
FSH
I GOTTA SAY, YOU'RE AN ODD DAMN GEEZER.
THERE AIN'T EVER GONNA BE ANOTHER HUMAN LIKE YOU AGAIN.
NO... I THINK YOU'RE WRONG THERE.
...!

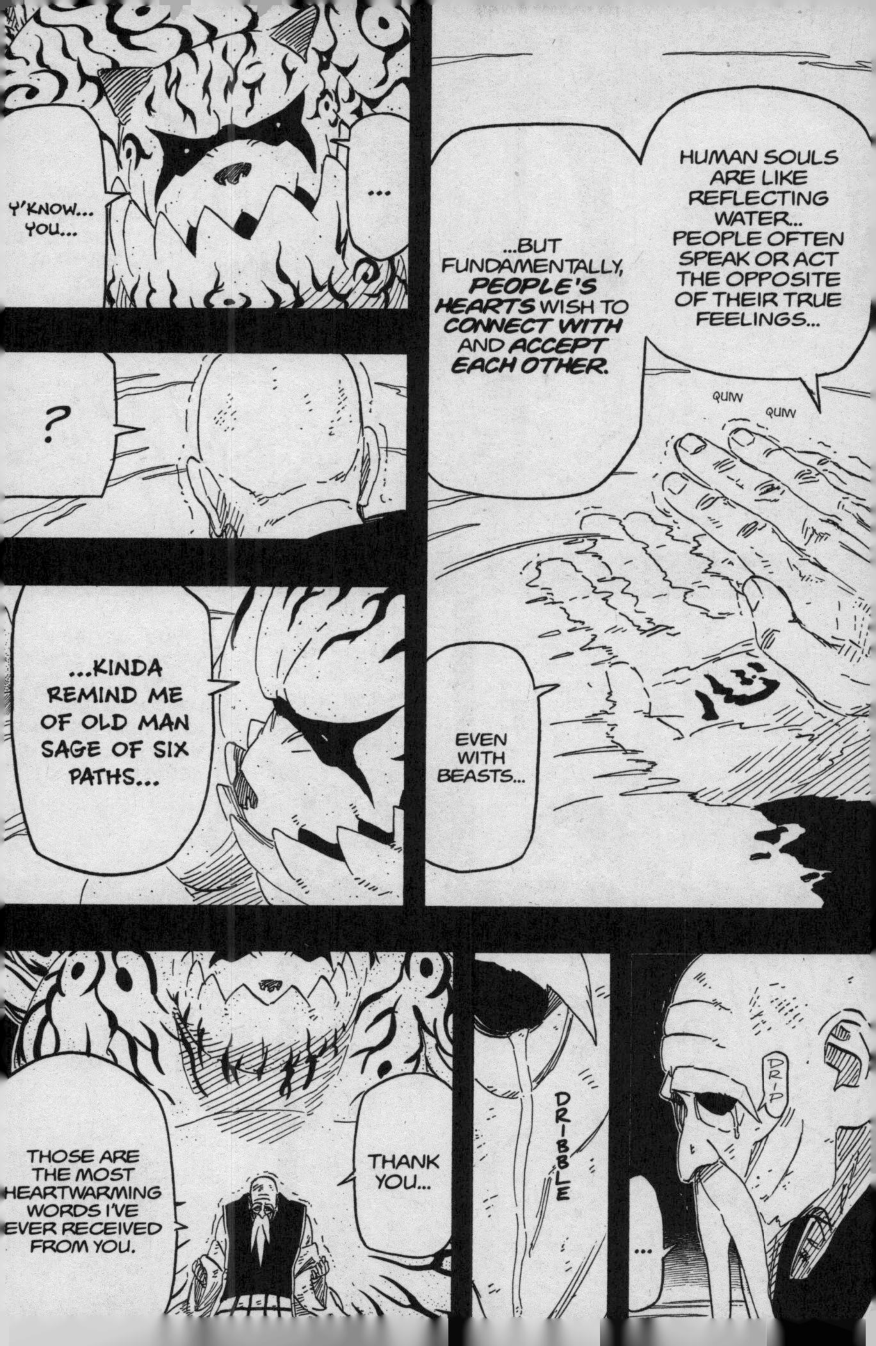
HUMAN SOULS ARE LIKE REFLECTING WATER... PEOPLE OFTEN SPEAK OR ACT THE OPPOSITE OF THEIR TRUE FEELINGS...
...BUT FUNDAMENTALLY, PEOPLE'S HEARTS WISH TO CONNECT WITH AND ACCEPT EACH OTHER.
QUIW
QUIW
EVEN WITH BEASTS...
...
Y'KNOW... YOU...
?
...KINDA REMIND ME OF OLD MAN SAGE OF SIX PATHS...
DRIP
...
DRIBBLE
THANK YOU...
THOSE ARE THE MOST HEARTWARMING WORDS I'VE EVER RECEIVED FROM YOU.

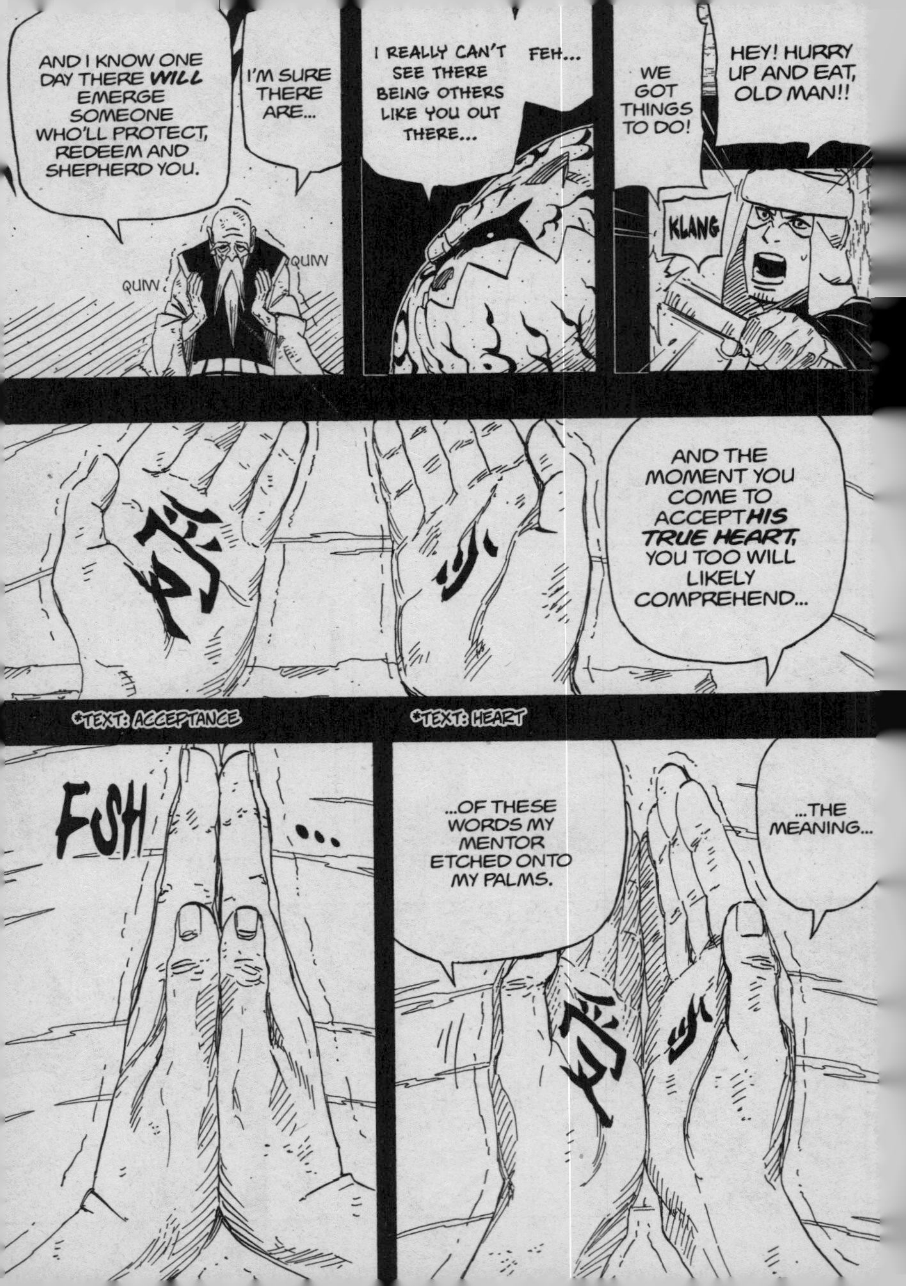
HEY! HURRY UP AND EAT, OLD MAN!!
WE GOT THINGS TO DO!
KLANG
FEH...
I REALLY CAN'T SEE THERE BEING OTHERS LIKE YOU OUT THERE...
I'M SURE THERE ARE...
AND I KNOW ONE DAY THERE **WILL** EMERGE SOMEONE WHO'LL PROTECT, REDEEM AND SHEPHERD YOU.
QUIVV
QUIVV
AND THE MOMENT YOU COME TO ACCEPT **HIS TRUE HEART,** YOU TOO WILL LIKELY COMPREHEND...
*TEXT: HEART
*TEXT: ACCEPTANCE
...THE MEANING...
...OF THESE WORDS MY MENTOR ETCHED ONTO MY PALMS.
...
FSH

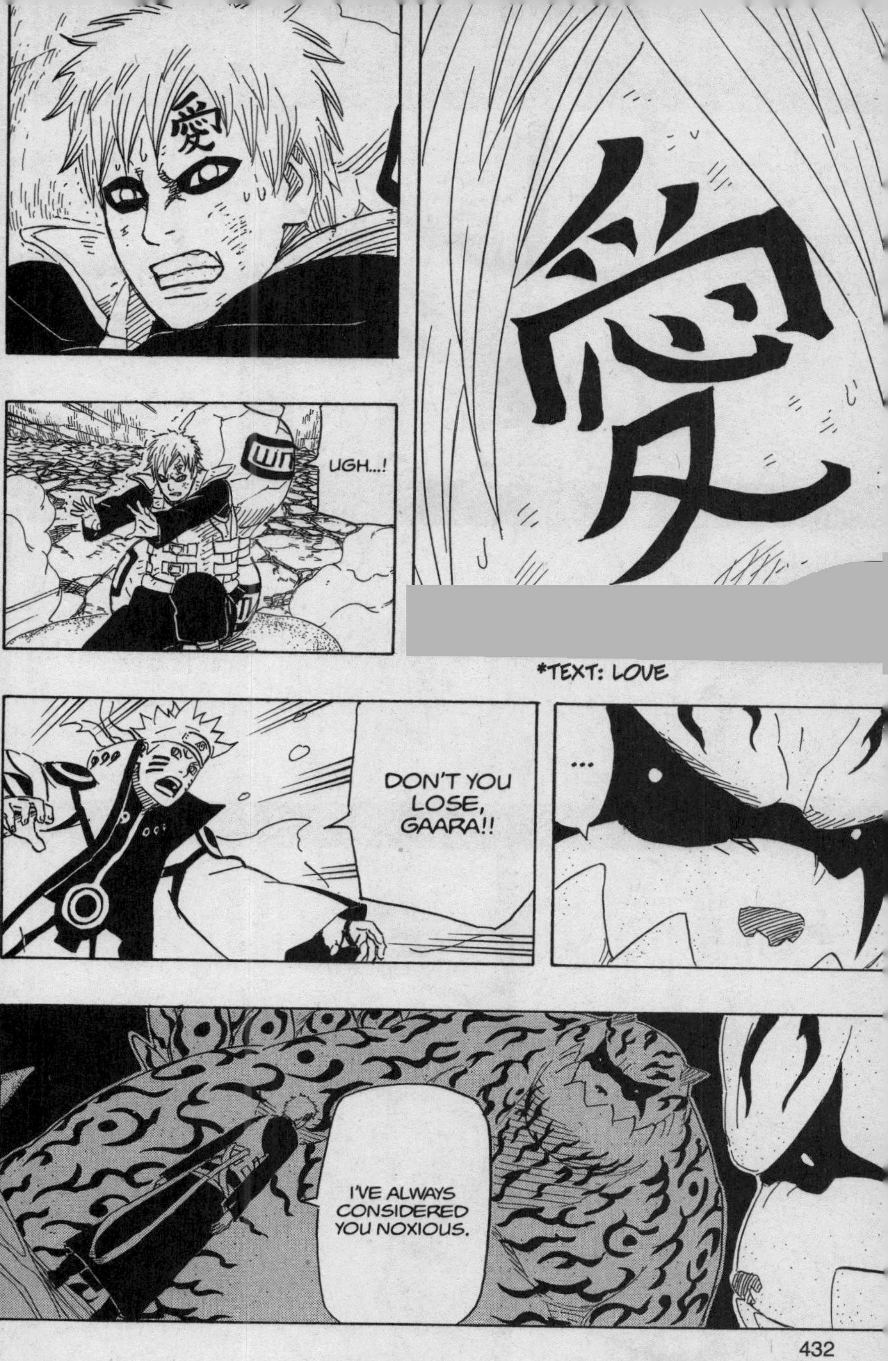
*TEXT: LOVE
UGH...!
...
DON'T YOU LOSE, GAARA!!
I'VE ALWAYS CONSIDERED YOU NOXIOUS.

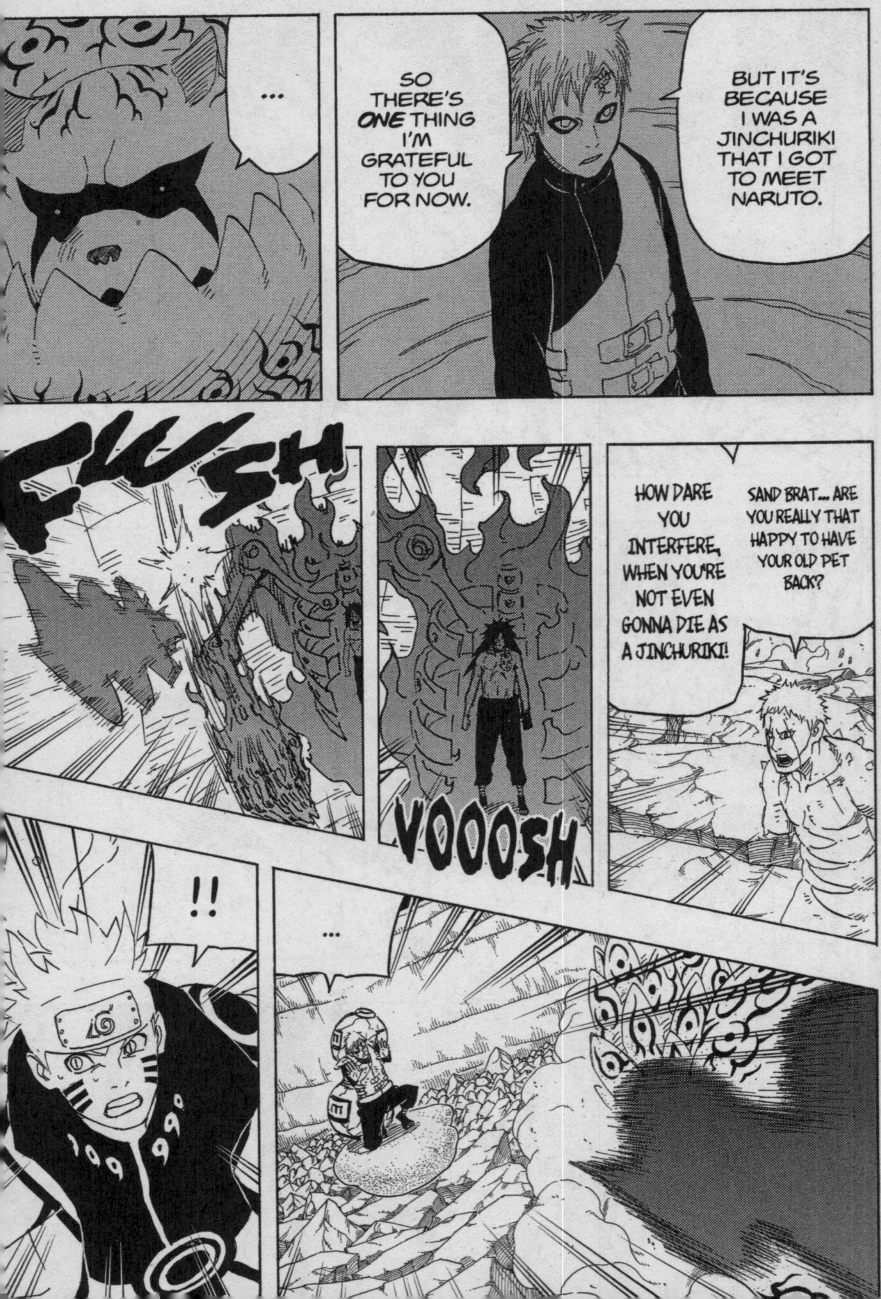
BUT IT'S BECAUSE I WAS A JINCHURIKI THAT I GOT TO MEET NARUTO.
SO THERE'S ONE THING I'M GRATEFUL TO YOU FOR NOW.
...
SAND BRAT... ARE YOU REALLY THAT HAPPY TO HAVE YOUR OLD PET BACK?
HOW DARE YOU INTERFERE, WHEN YOU'RE NOT EVEN GONNA DIE AS A JINCHURIKI!
VOOOSH
FWSH
...
!!

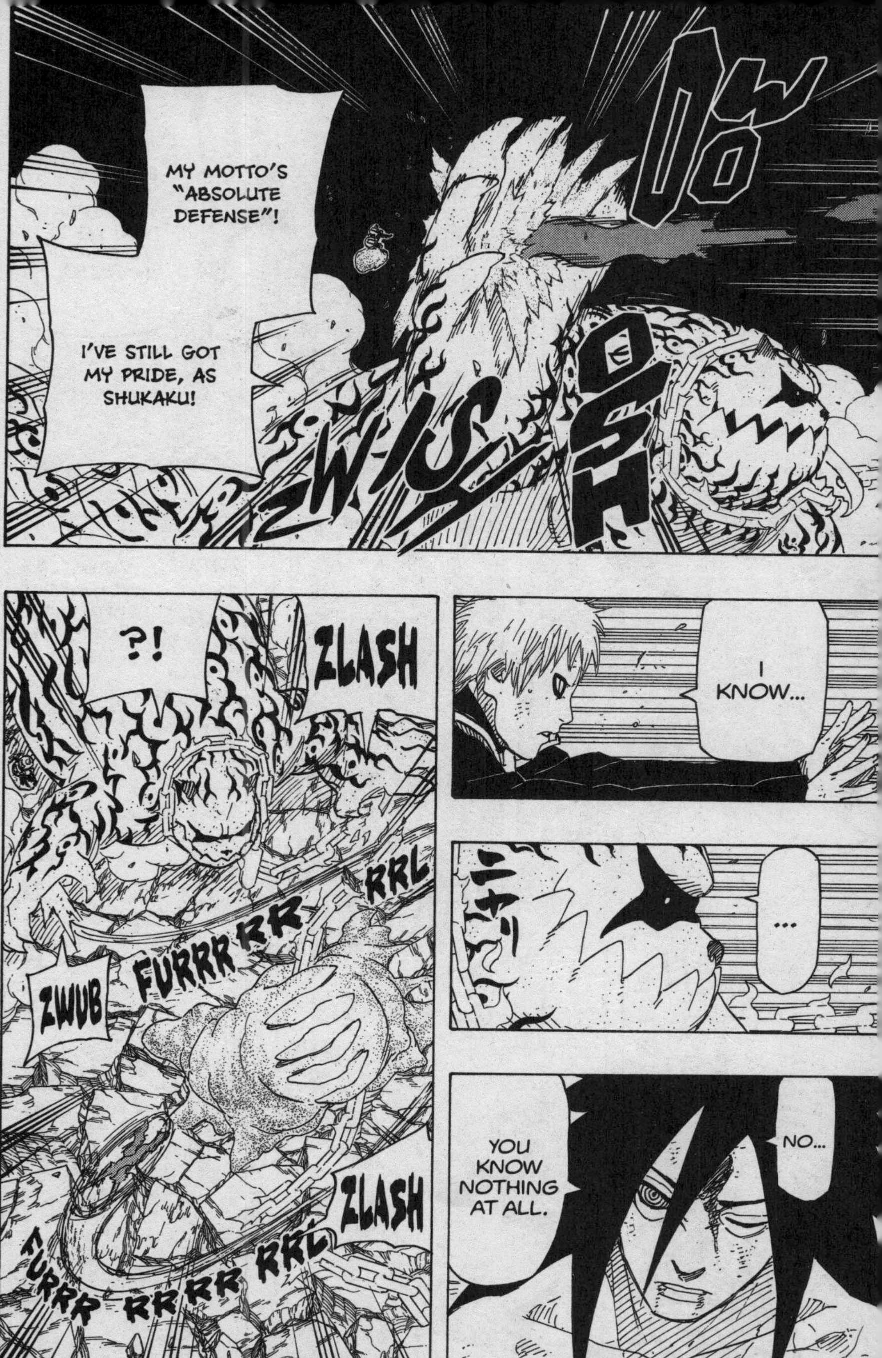
MY MOTTO'S "ABSOLUTE DEFENSE"!
I'VE STILL GOT MY PRIDE, AS SHUKAKU!
I KNOW...
...
NO...
YOU KNOW NOTHING AT ALL.
?!
ZLASH
RRL
FURRRR RR
ZWUB
ZLASH
FURRR RRRR RRL

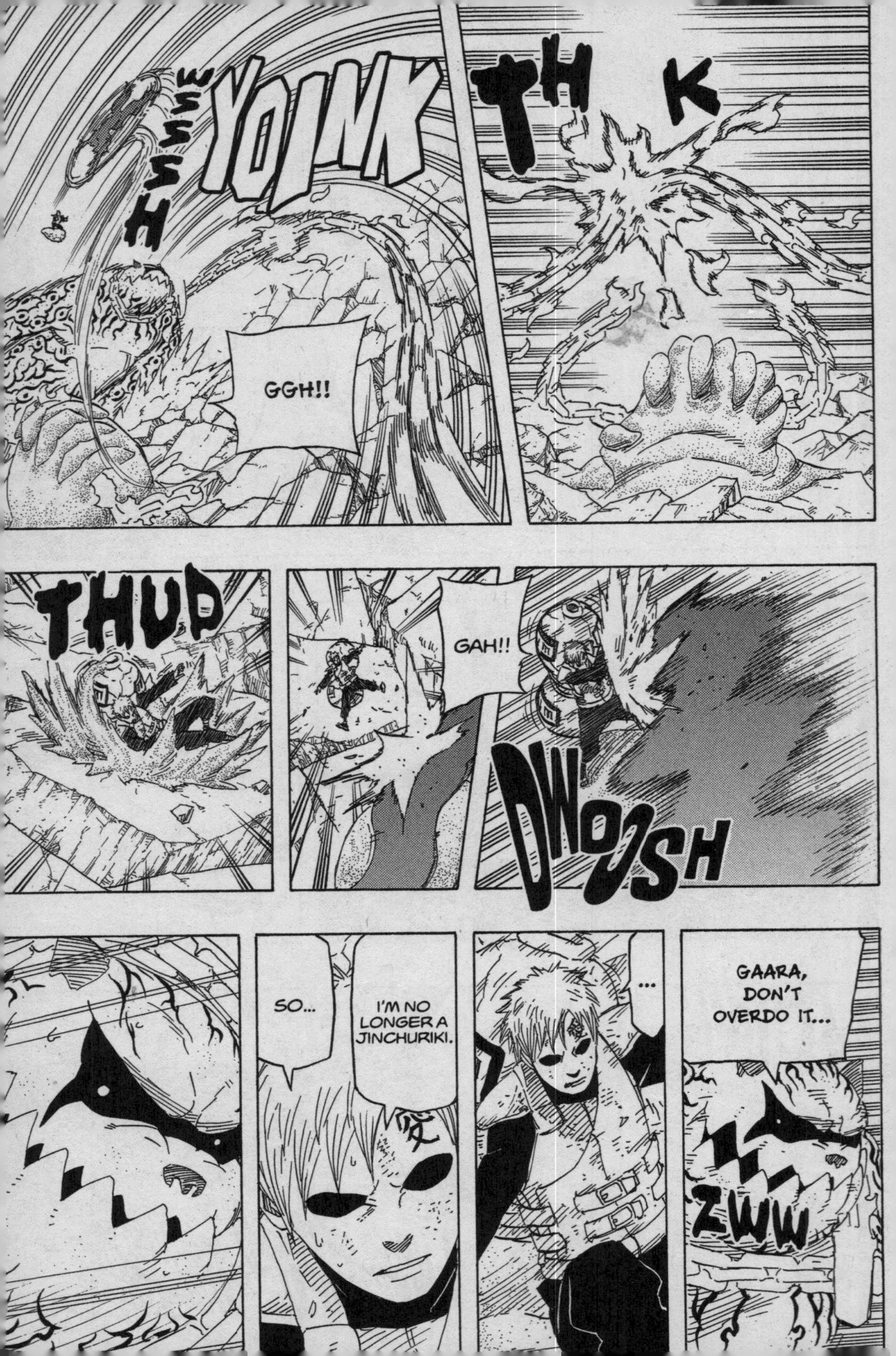
TH K
YOINK
WSSSH
GGH!!
GAH!!
DWOOSH
THUD
GAARA, DON'T OVERDO IT...
ZWW
...
I'M NO LONGER A JINCHURIKI.
SO...

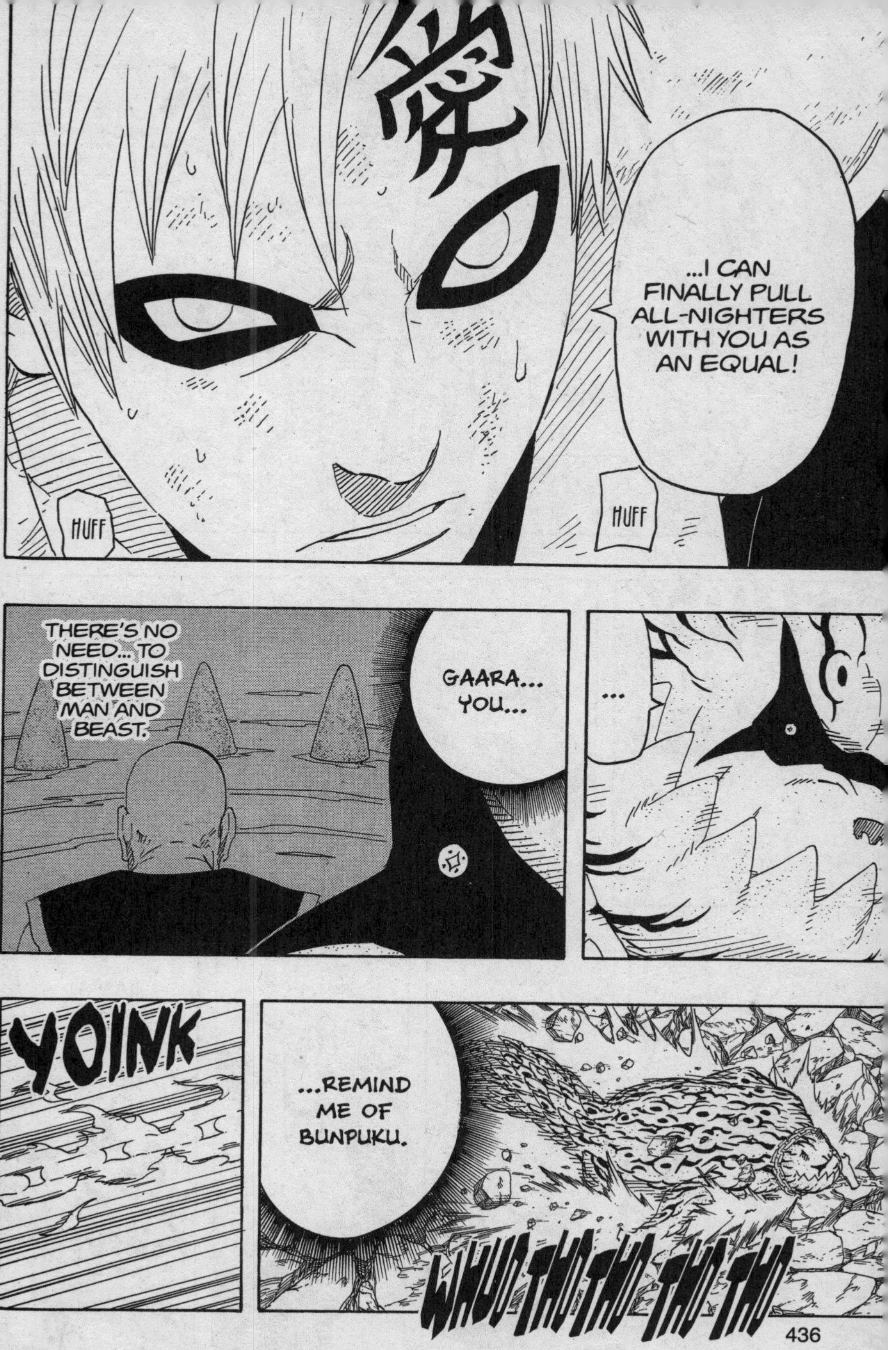
...I CAN FINALLY PULL ALL-NIGHTERS WITH YOU AS AN EQUAL!
HUFF
HUFF
...
GAARA... YOU...
THERE'S NO NEED... TO DISTINGUISH BETWEEN MAN AND BEAST.
...REMIND ME OF BUNPUKU.
WHUD THUD THUD THUD THUD
YOINK

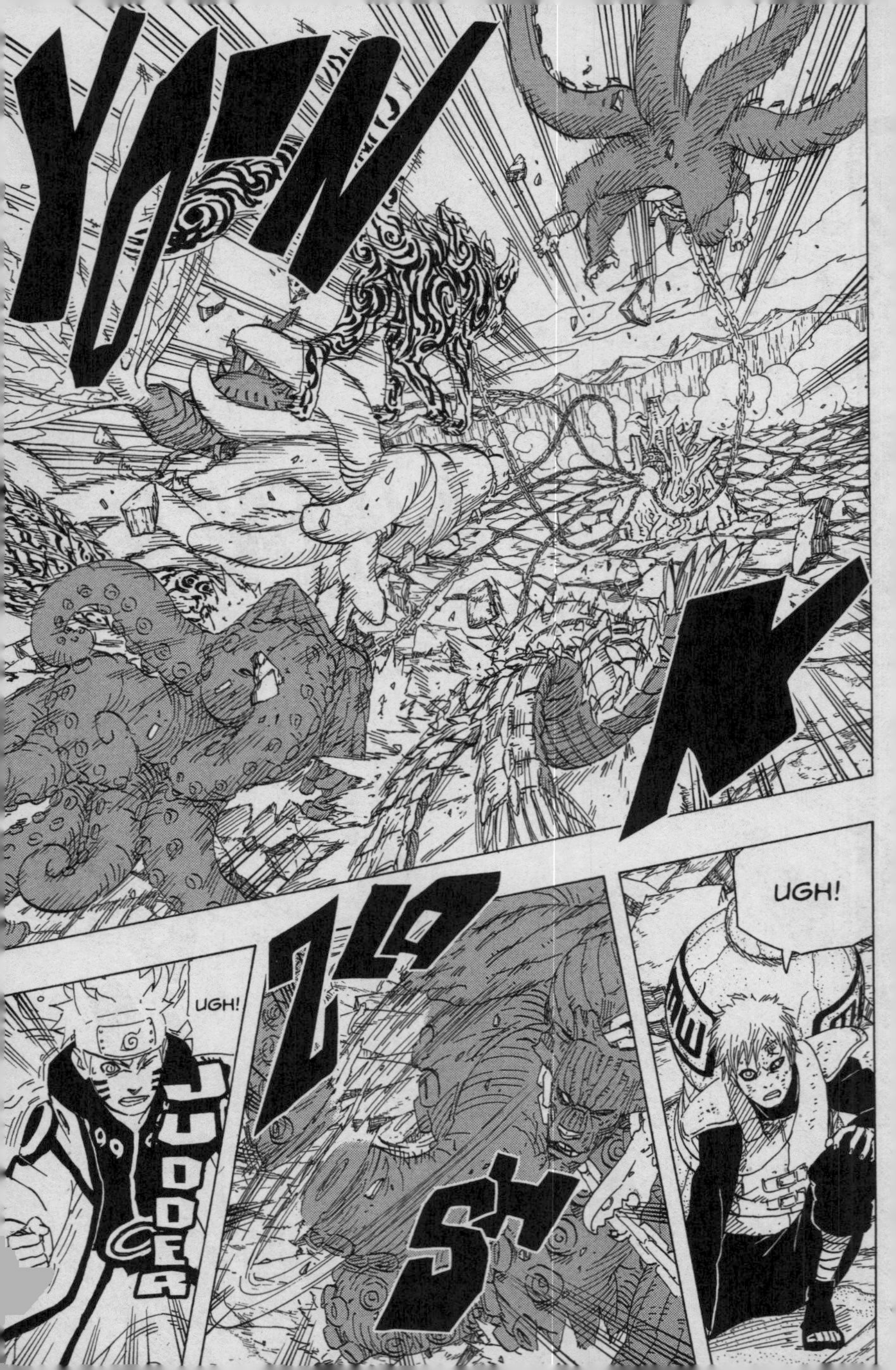
YANK
UGH!
UGH!
JUDDER

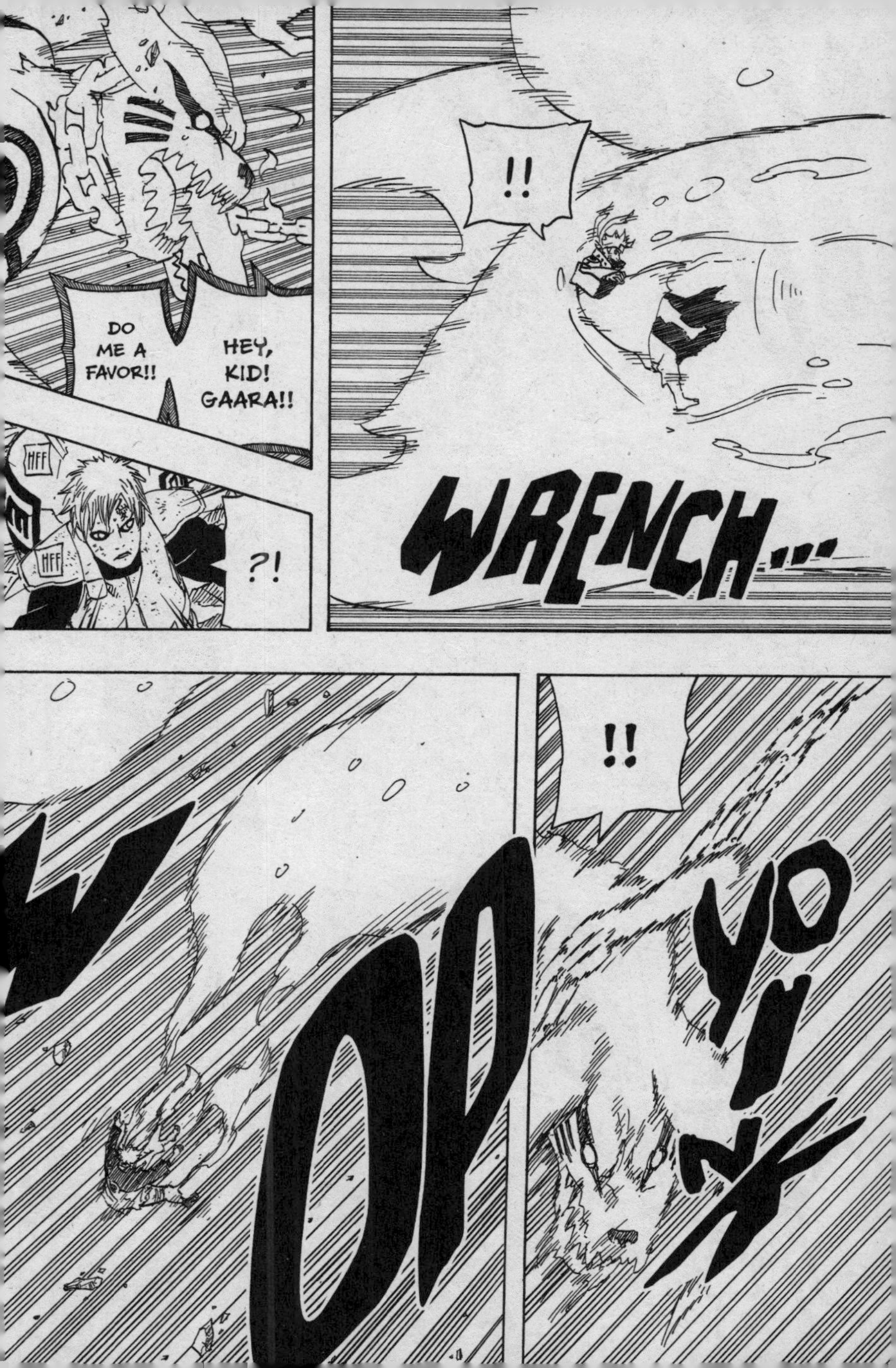
!!
WRENCH...
HEY, KID! GAARA!!
DO ME A FAVOR!!
HFF
HFF
?!
!!

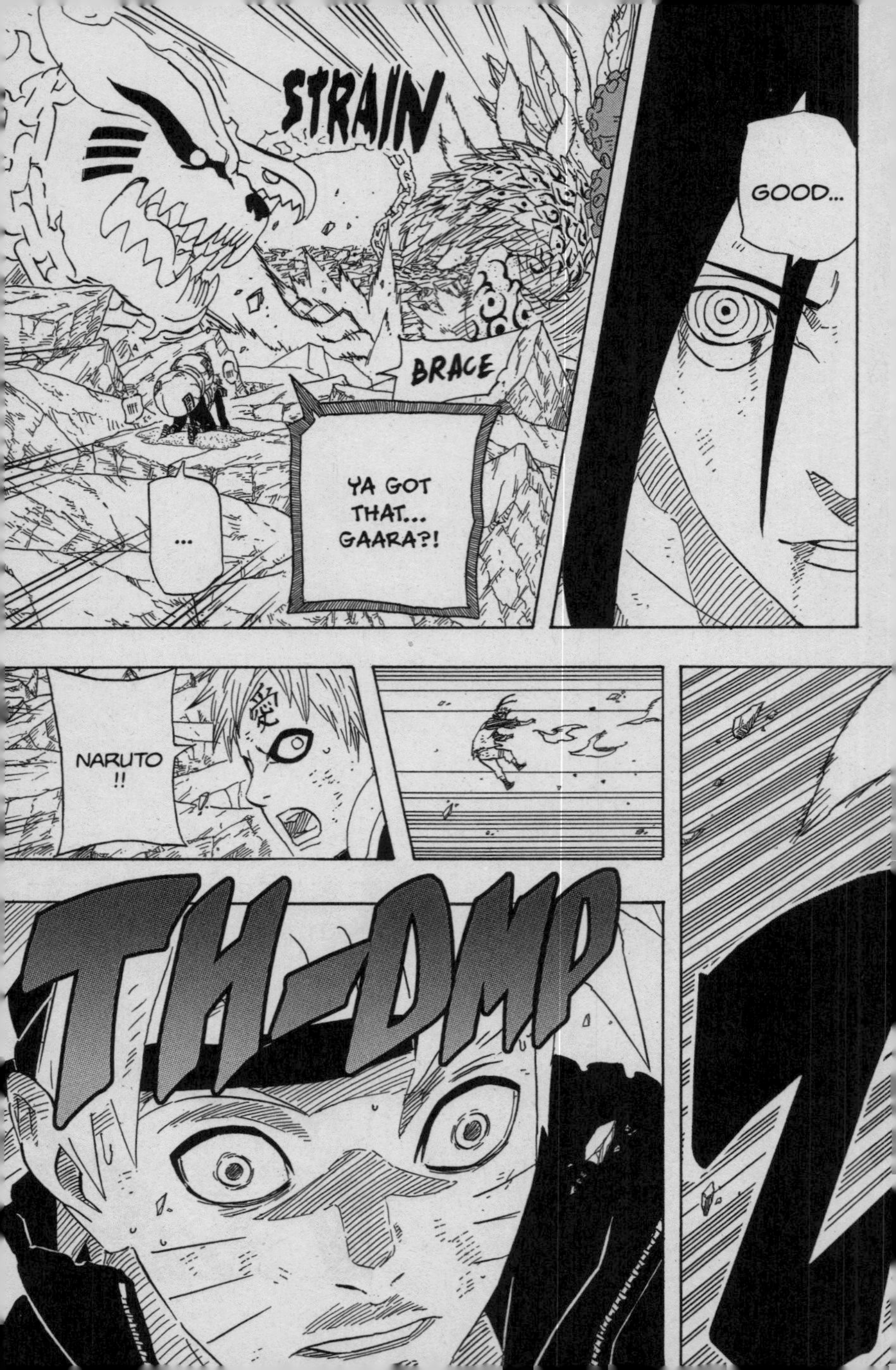
GOOD...
STRAIN
BRACE
YA GOT THAT... GAARA?!
...
NARUTO!!
TH-DMP

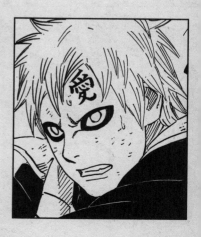

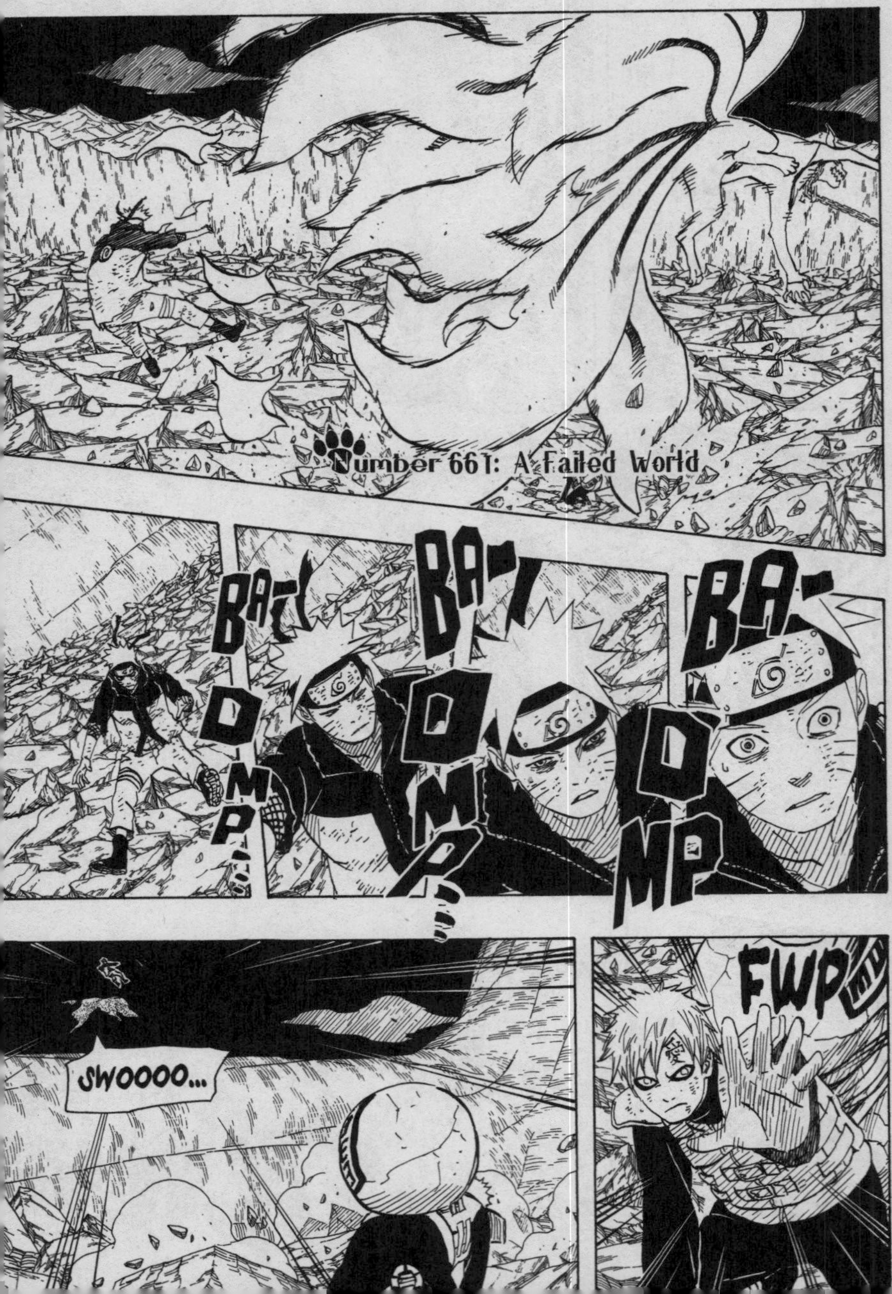
Number 661: A Failed World
BA-DOMP
BA-DOMP
BA-DOMP
FWP
SWOOOO...

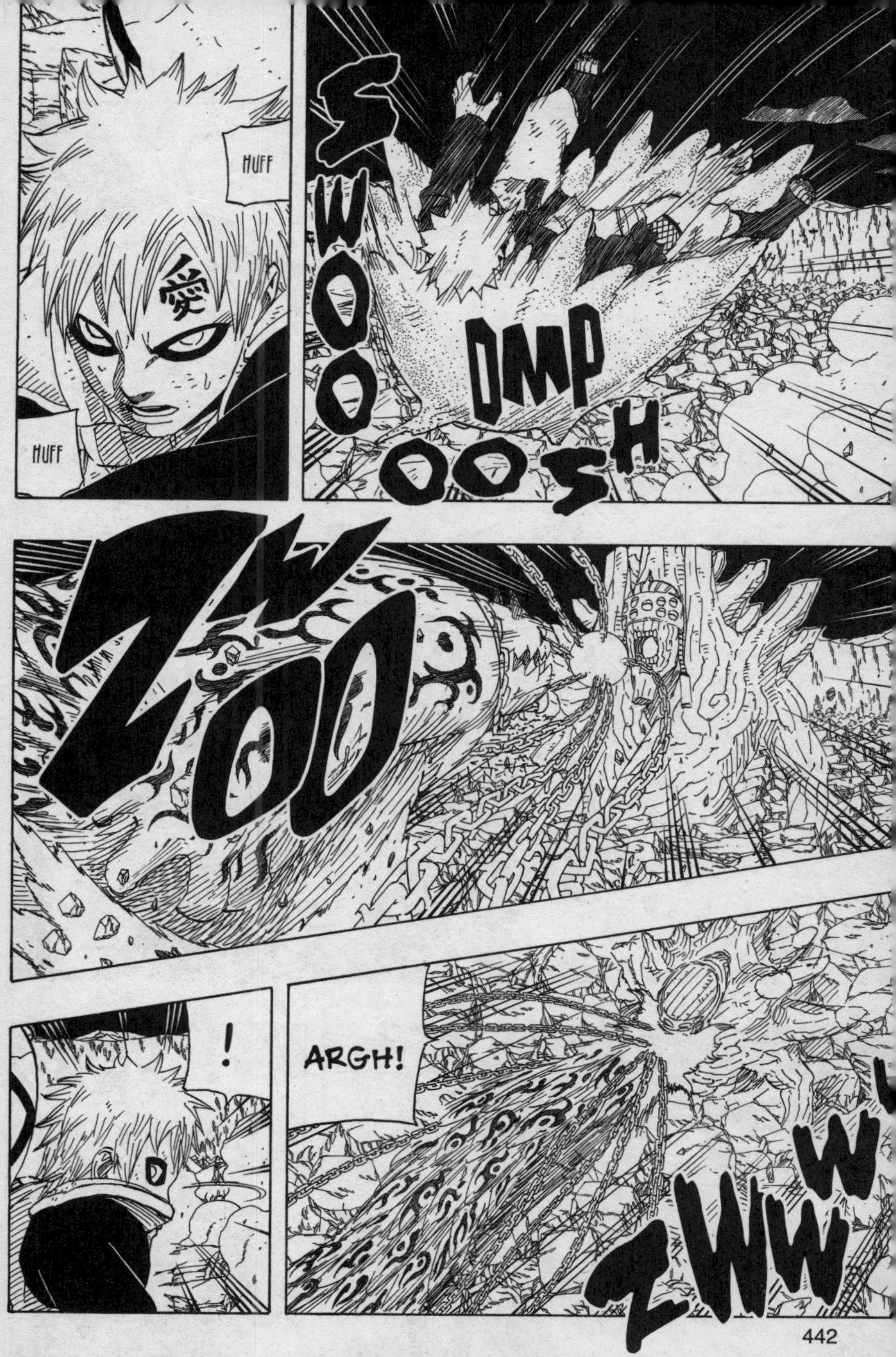

SWOOOOSH
DMP
HUFF
HUFF
ZOOO
ARGH!
ZWWW
!

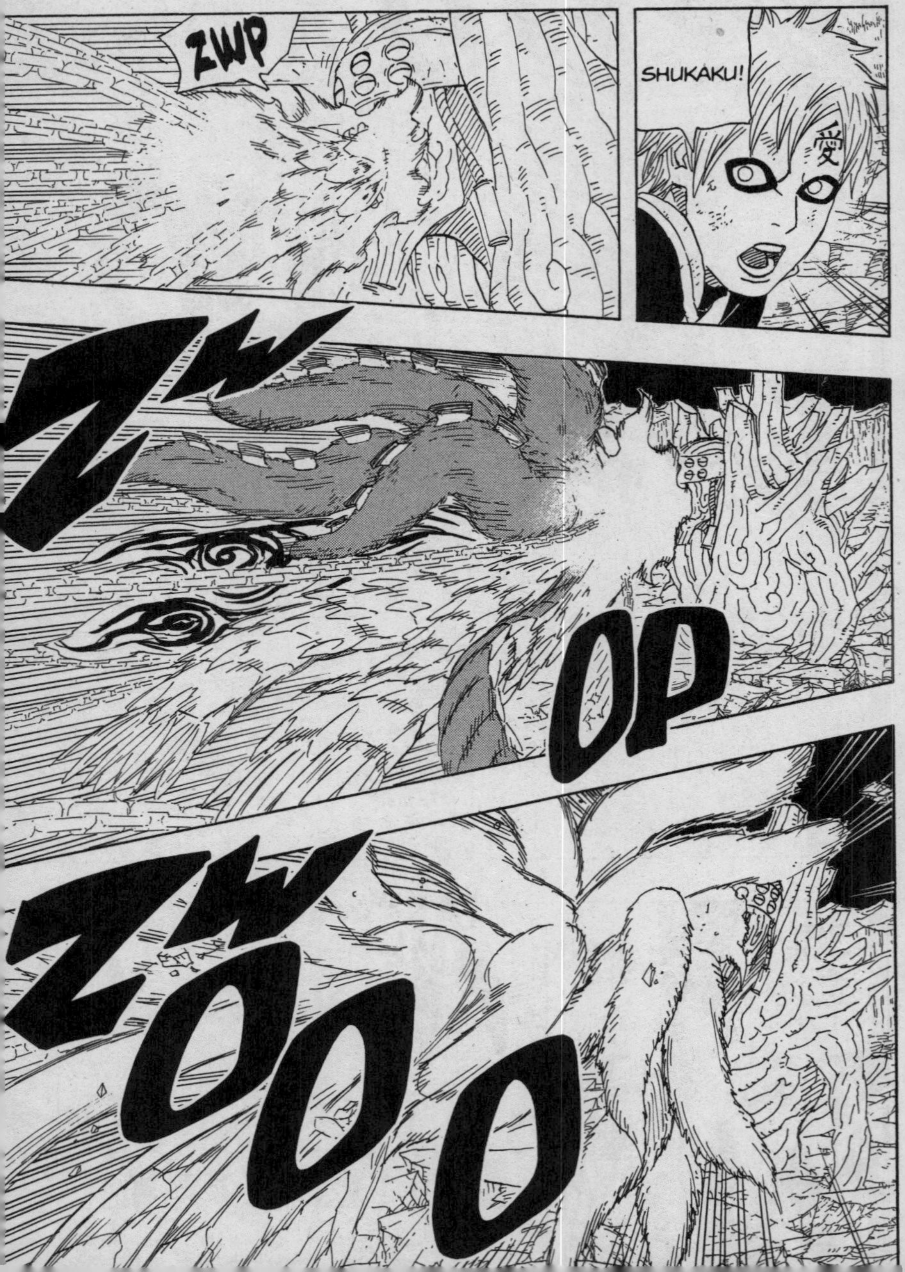
SHUKAKU!
ZWP
ZW
OP
ZW
ZOOOO

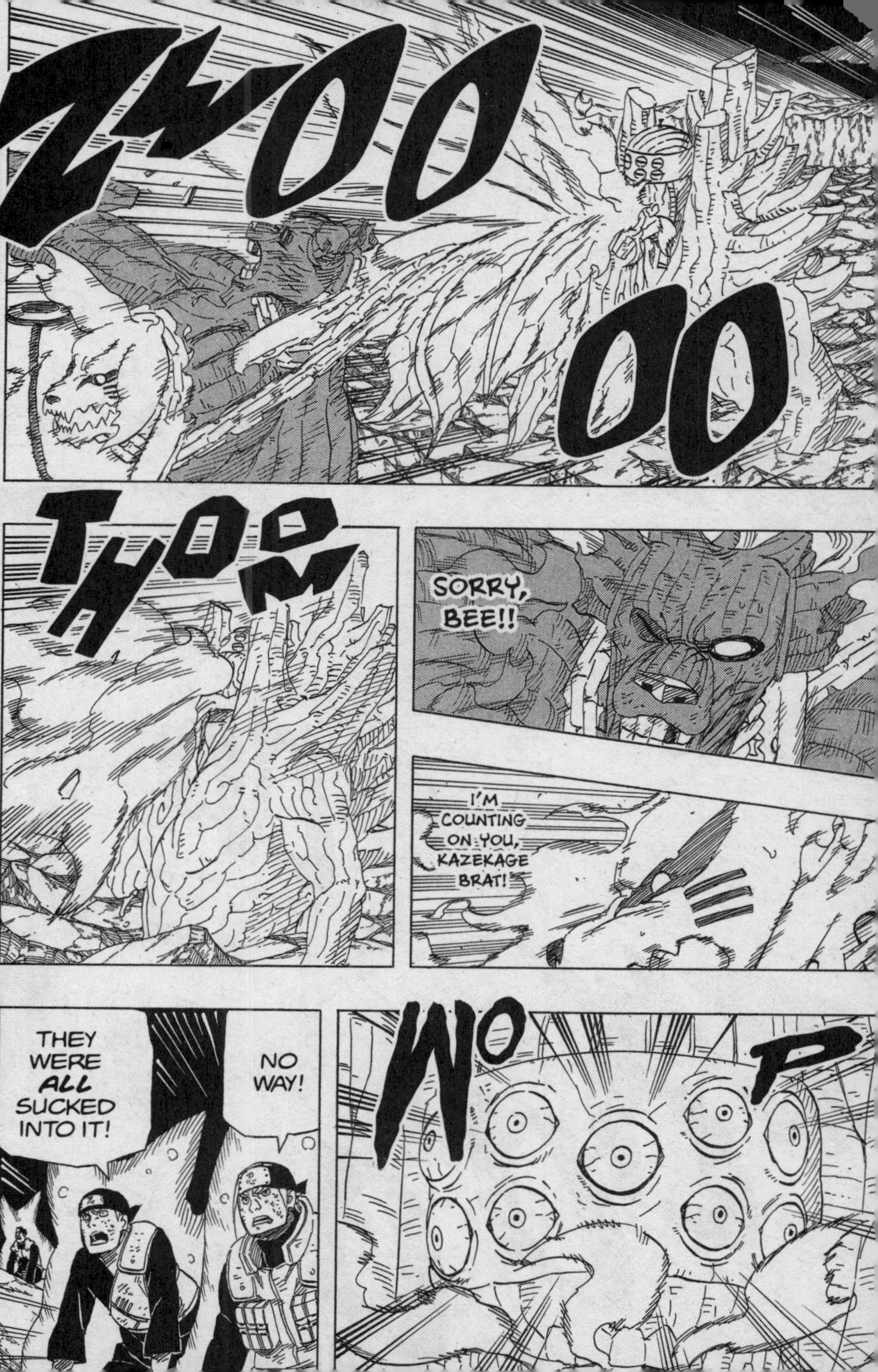
ZWOO
OO
SORRY, BEE!!
I'M COUNTING ON YOU, KAZEKAGE BRAT!
THOOM
WO
P
NO WAY!
THEY WERE **ALL** SUCKED INTO IT!

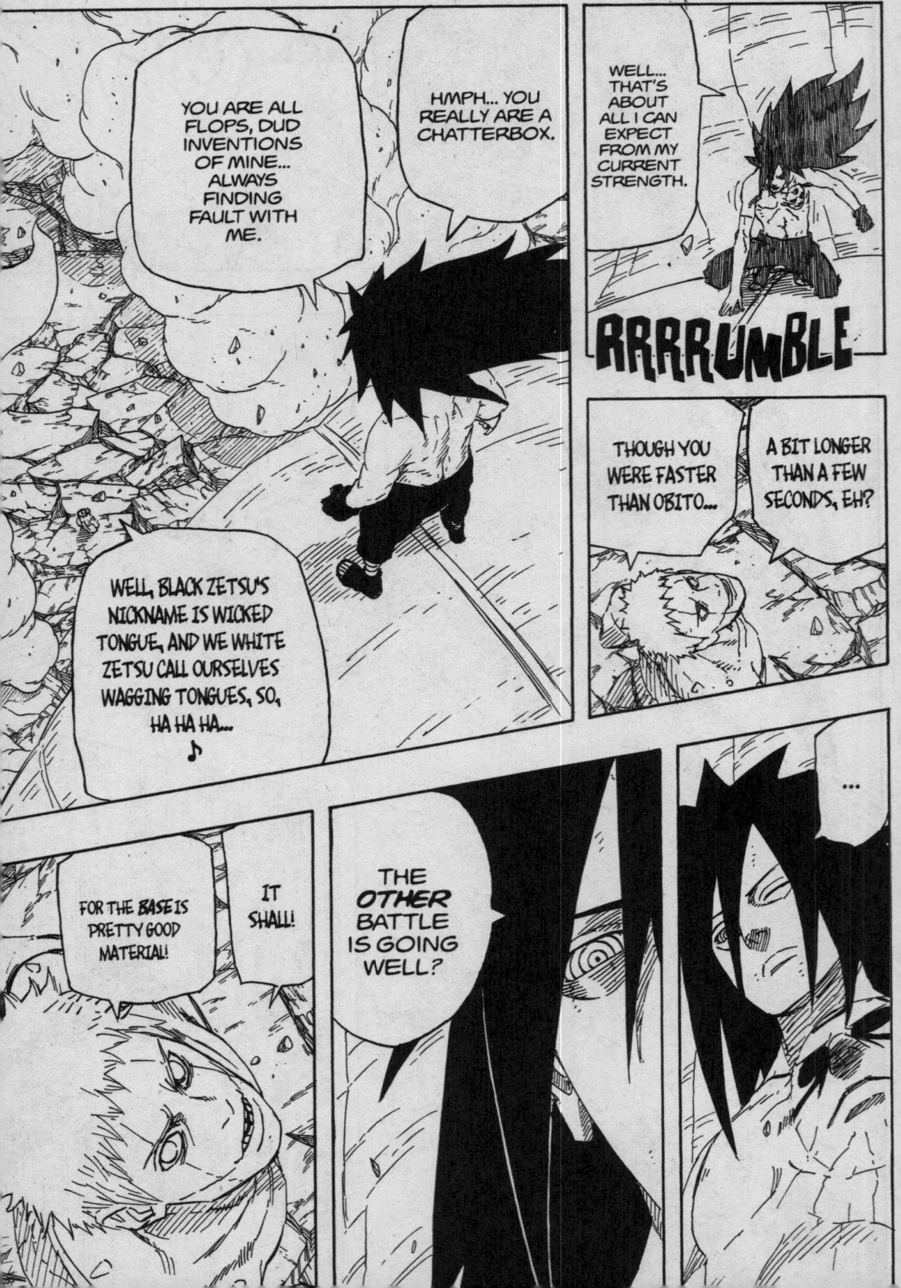
WELL... THAT'S ABOUT ALL I CAN EXPECT FROM MY CURRENT STRENGTH.
RRRRUMBLE
A BIT LONGER THAN A FEW SECONDS, EH?
THOUGH YOU WERE FASTER THAN OBITO...
HMPH... YOU REALLY ARE A CHATTERBOX.
YOU ARE ALL FLOPS, DUD INVENTIONS OF MINE... ALWAYS FINDING FAULT WITH ME.
WELL, BLACK ZETSU'S NICKNAME IS WICKED TONGUE, AND WE WHITE ZETSU CALL OURSELVES WAGGING TONGUES, SO, HA HA HA... ♪
...
THE OTHER BATTLE IS GOING WELL?
IT SHALL!
FOR THE BASE IS PRETTY GOOD MATERIAL!

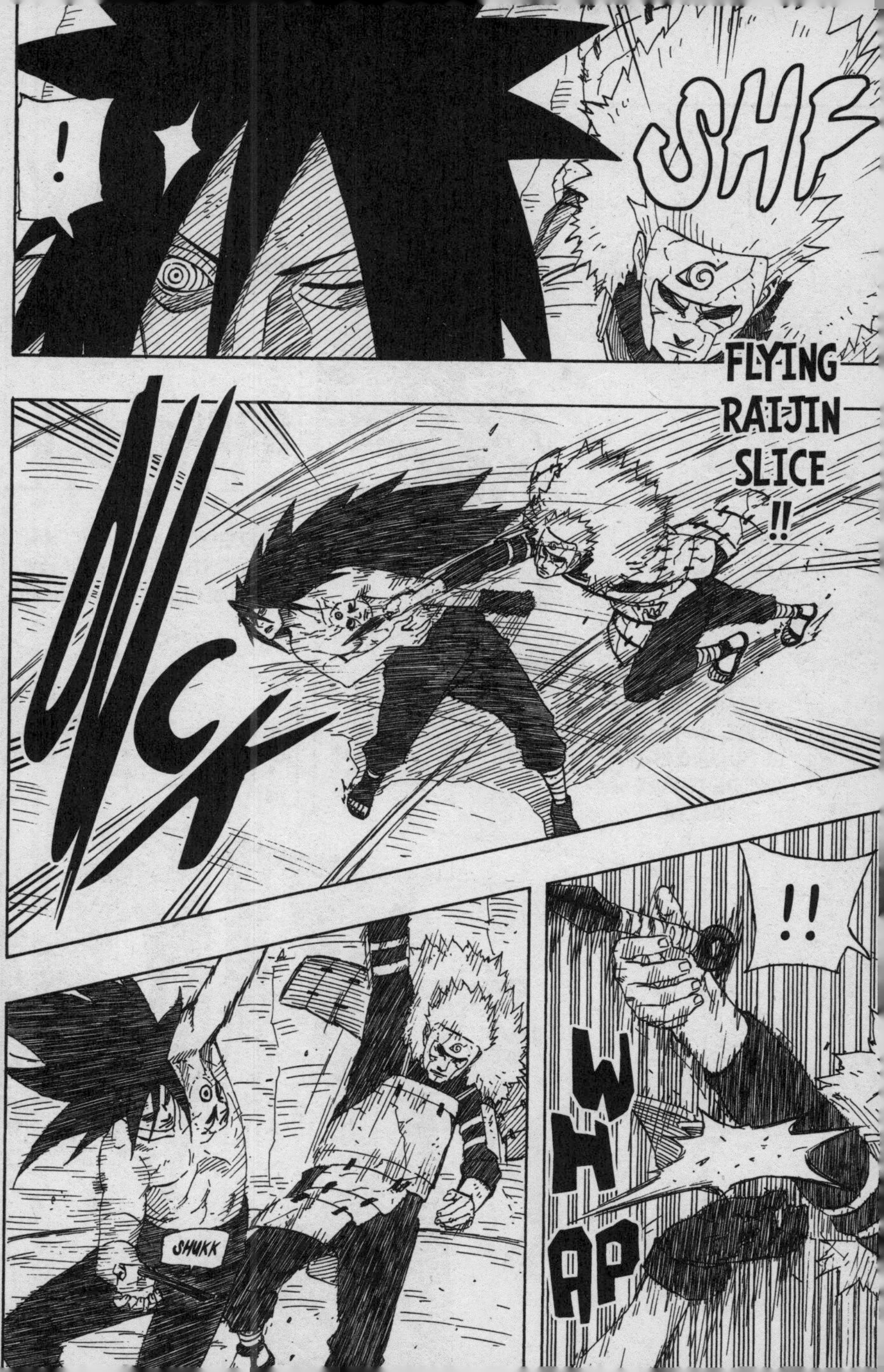
SHF
FLYING RAIJIN SLICE!!
!
!!
WHAP
SHUKK

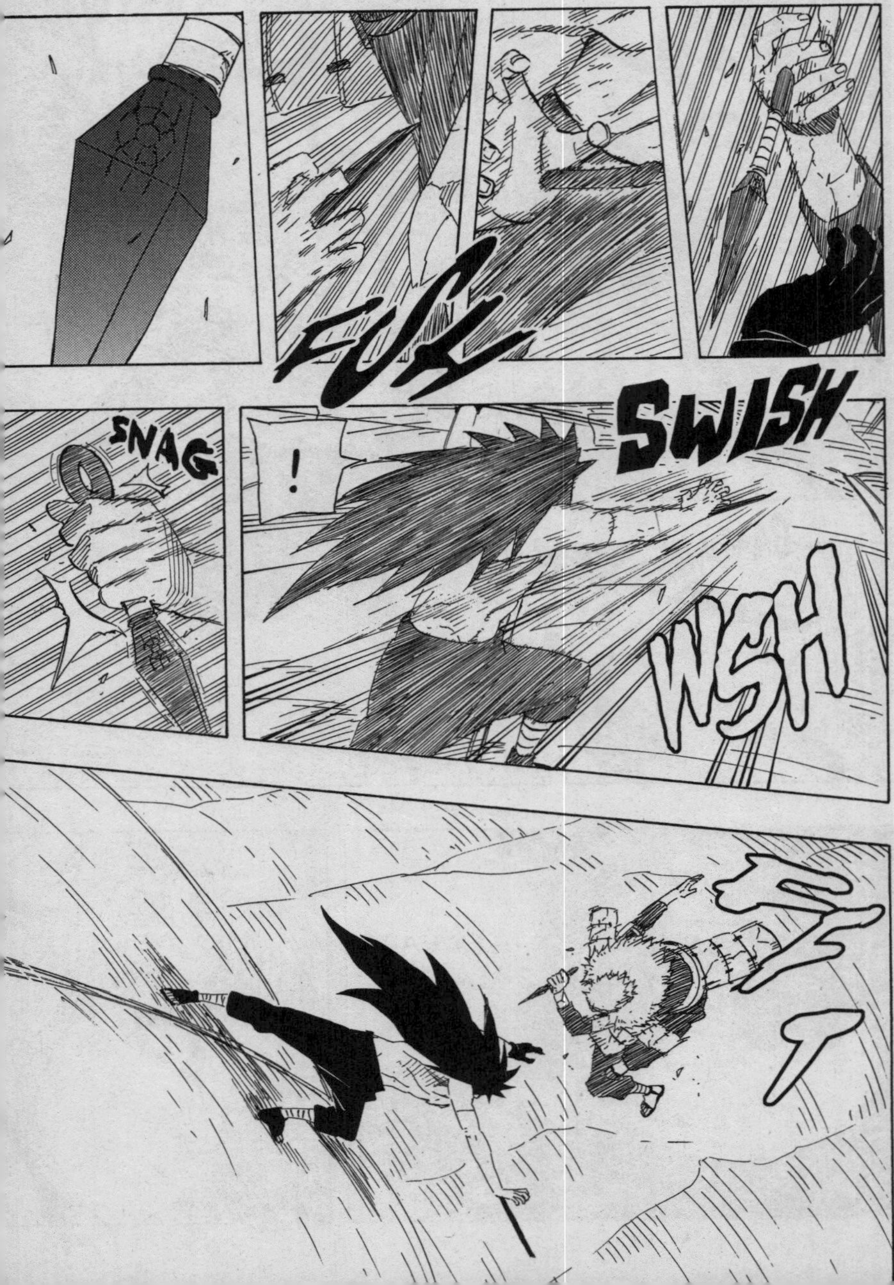
FUA
SWISH
!
WSH
SNAG

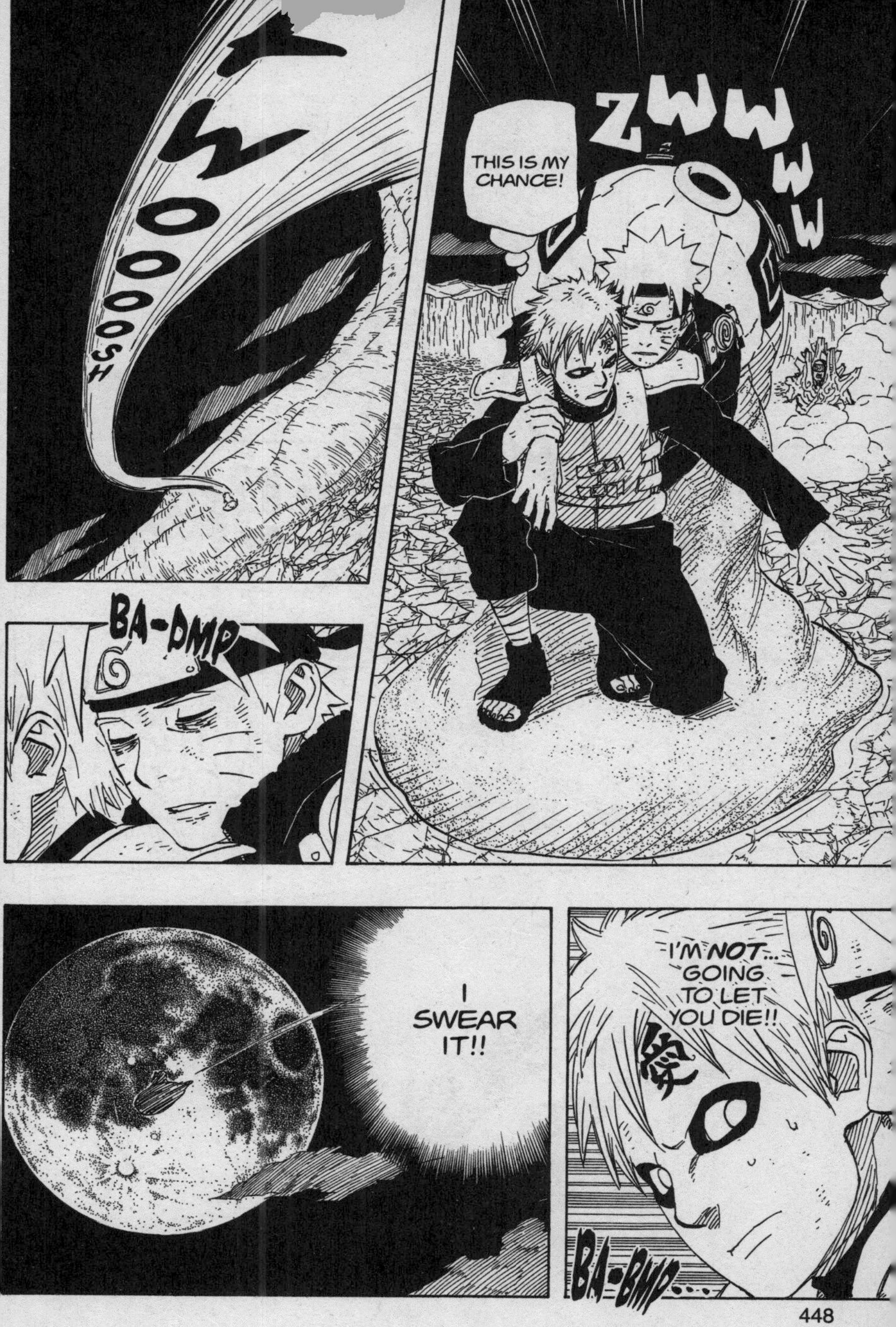
ZWWWWW
THIS IS MY CHANCE!
WOOOOOSH
BA-DMP
I'M NOT... GOING TO LET YOU DIE!!
BA-BMP...
I SWEAR IT!!

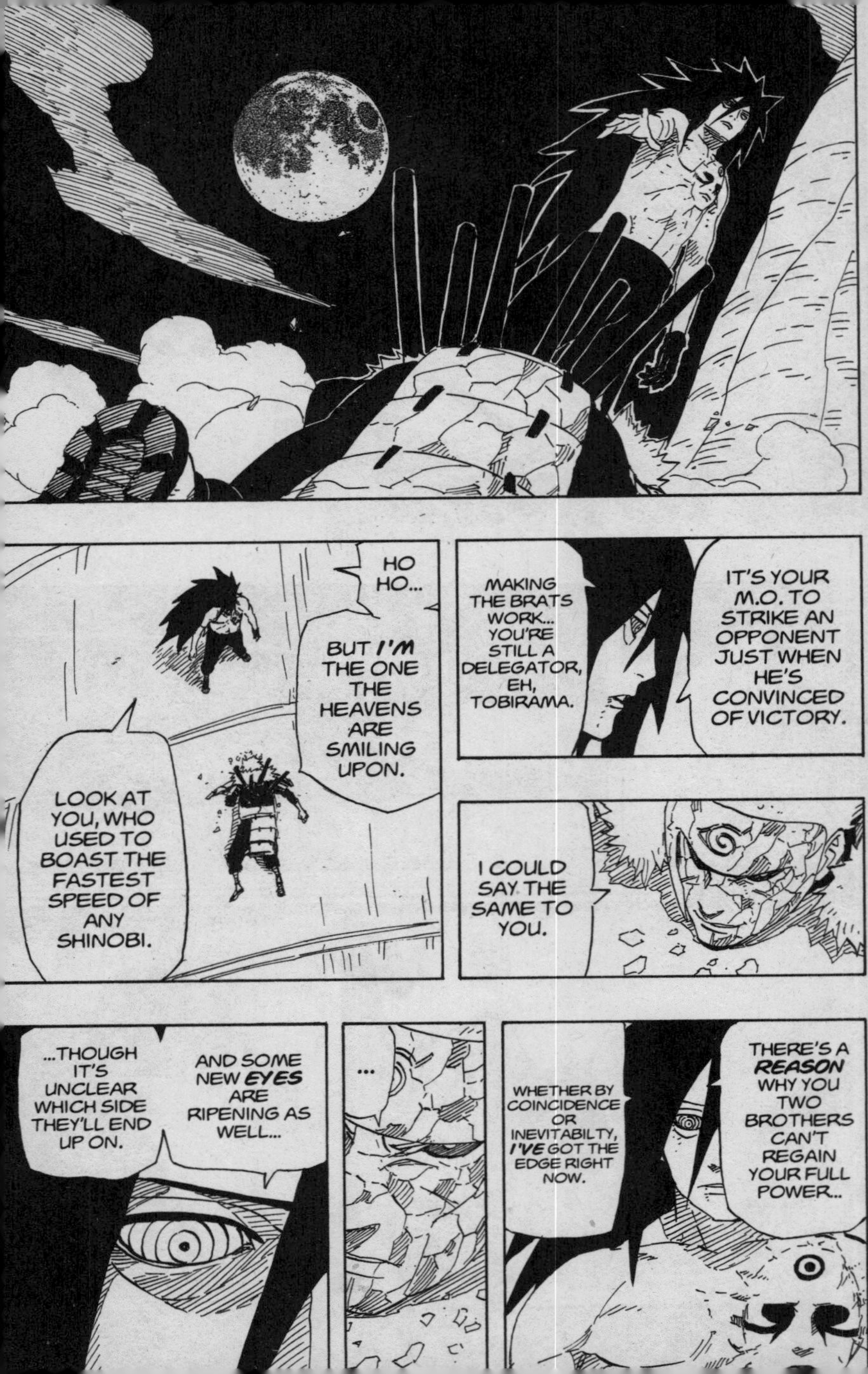
IT'S YOUR M.O. TO STRIKE AN OPPONENT JUST WHEN HE'S CONVINCED OF VICTORY.
MAKING THE BRATS WORK... YOU'RE STILL A DELEGATOR, EH, TOBIRAMA.
I COULD SAY THE SAME TO YOU.
HO HO...
BUT I'M THE ONE THE HEAVENS ARE SMILING UPON.
LOOK AT YOU, WHO USED TO BOAST THE FASTEST SPEED OF ANY SHINOBI.
THERE'S A REASON WHY YOU TWO BROTHERS CAN'T REGAIN YOUR FULL POWER...
WHETHER BY COINCIDENCE OR INEVITABILTY, I'VE GOT THE EDGE RIGHT NOW.
...
AND SOME NEW EYES ARE RIPENING AS WELL...
...THOUGH IT'S UNCLEAR WHICH SIDE THEY'LL END UP ON.

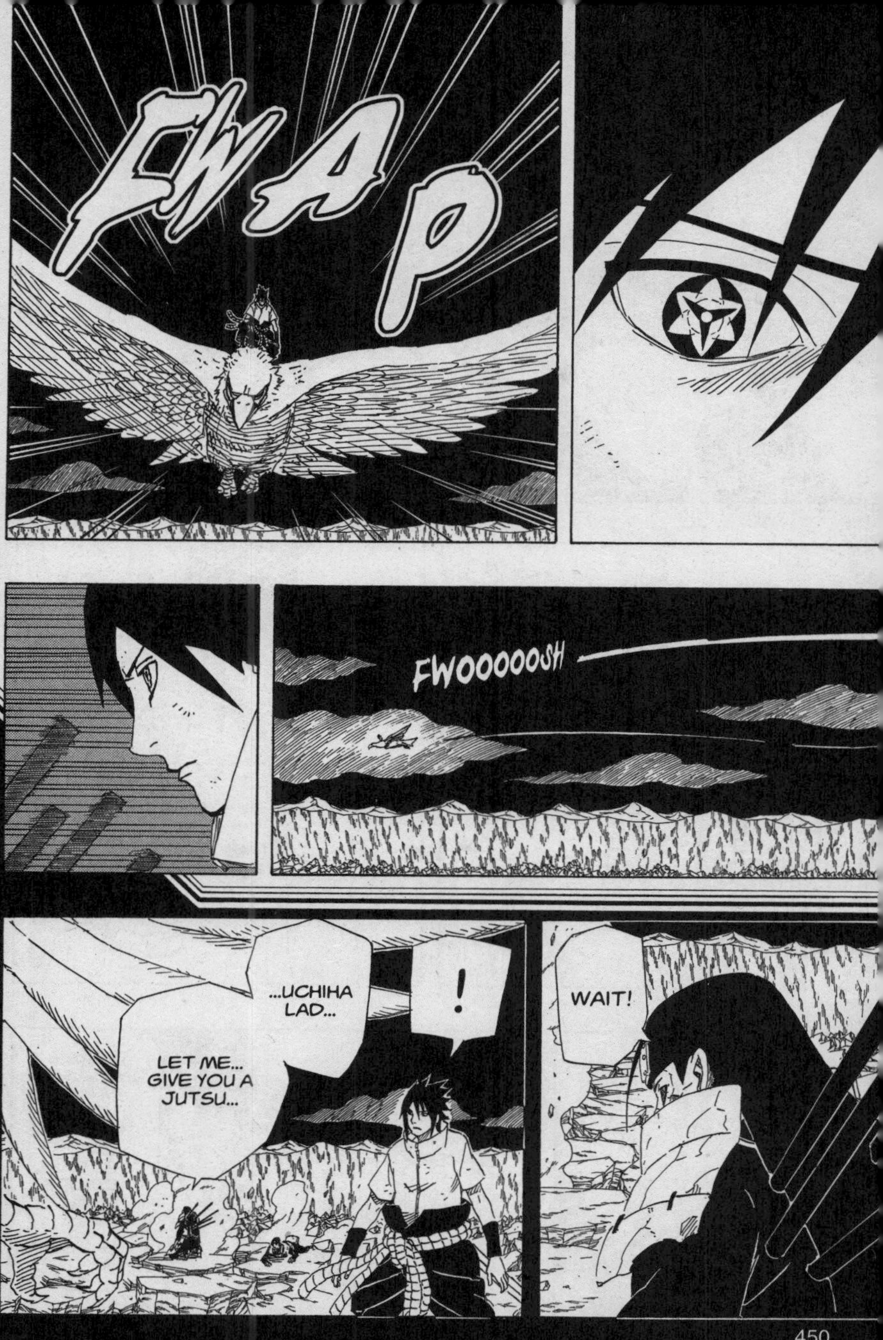
FWAP
FWOOOOOSH
WAIT!
...UCHIHA LAD...
!
LET ME... GIVE YOU A JUTSU...

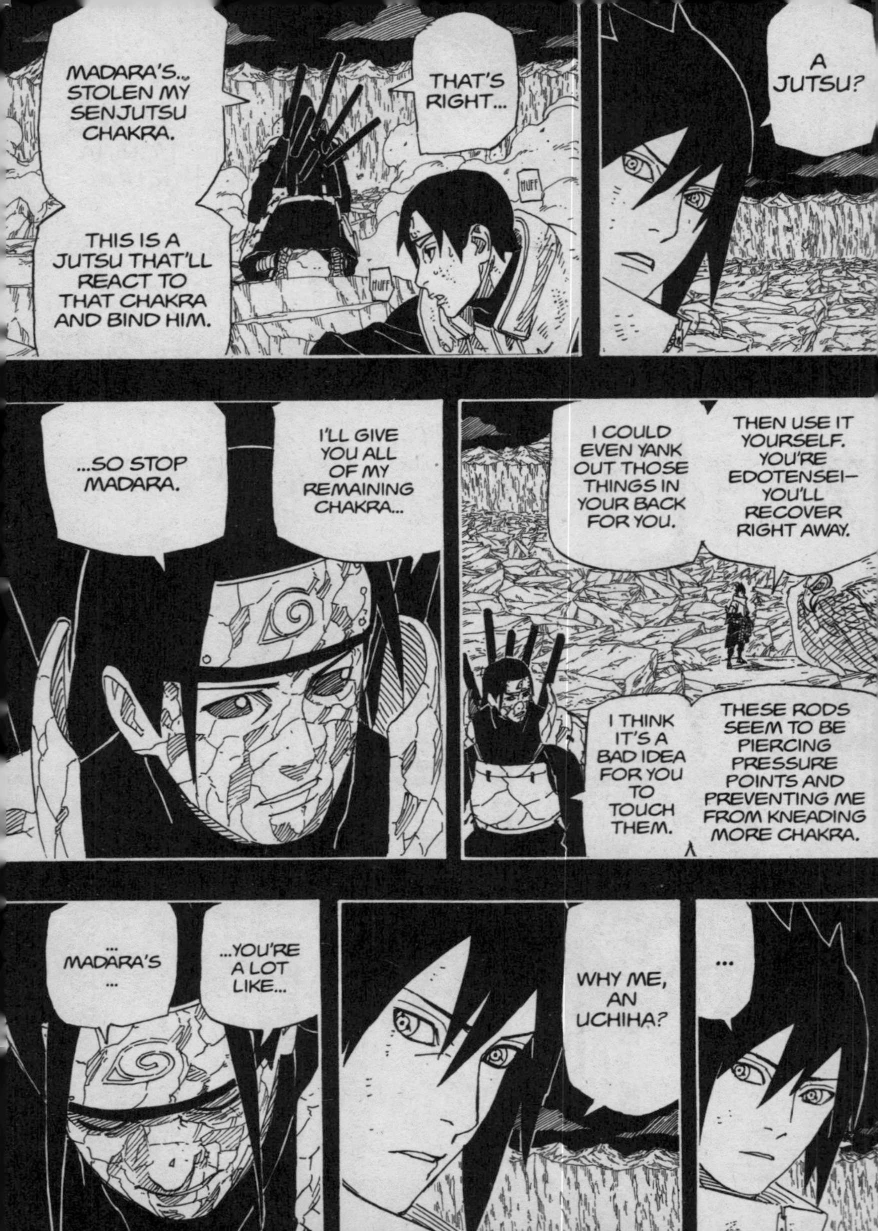
A JUTSU?
THAT'S RIGHT...
HUFF
HUFF
MADARA'S... STOLEN MY SENJUTSU CHAKRA.
THIS IS A JUTSU THAT'LL REACT TO THAT CHAKRA AND BIND HIM.
THEN USE IT YOURSELF. YOU'RE EDOTENSEI— YOU'LL RECOVER RIGHT AWAY.
I COULD EVEN YANK OUT THOSE THINGS IN YOUR BACK FOR YOU.
THESE RODS SEEM TO BE PIERCING PRESSURE POINTS AND PREVENTING ME FROM KNEADING MORE CHAKRA.
I THINK IT'S A BAD IDEA FOR YOU TO TOUCH THEM.
I'LL GIVE YOU ALL OF MY REMAINING CHAKRA...
...SO STOP MADARA.
...
WHY ME, AN UCHIHA?
...YOU'RE A LOT LIKE...
... MADARA'S ...

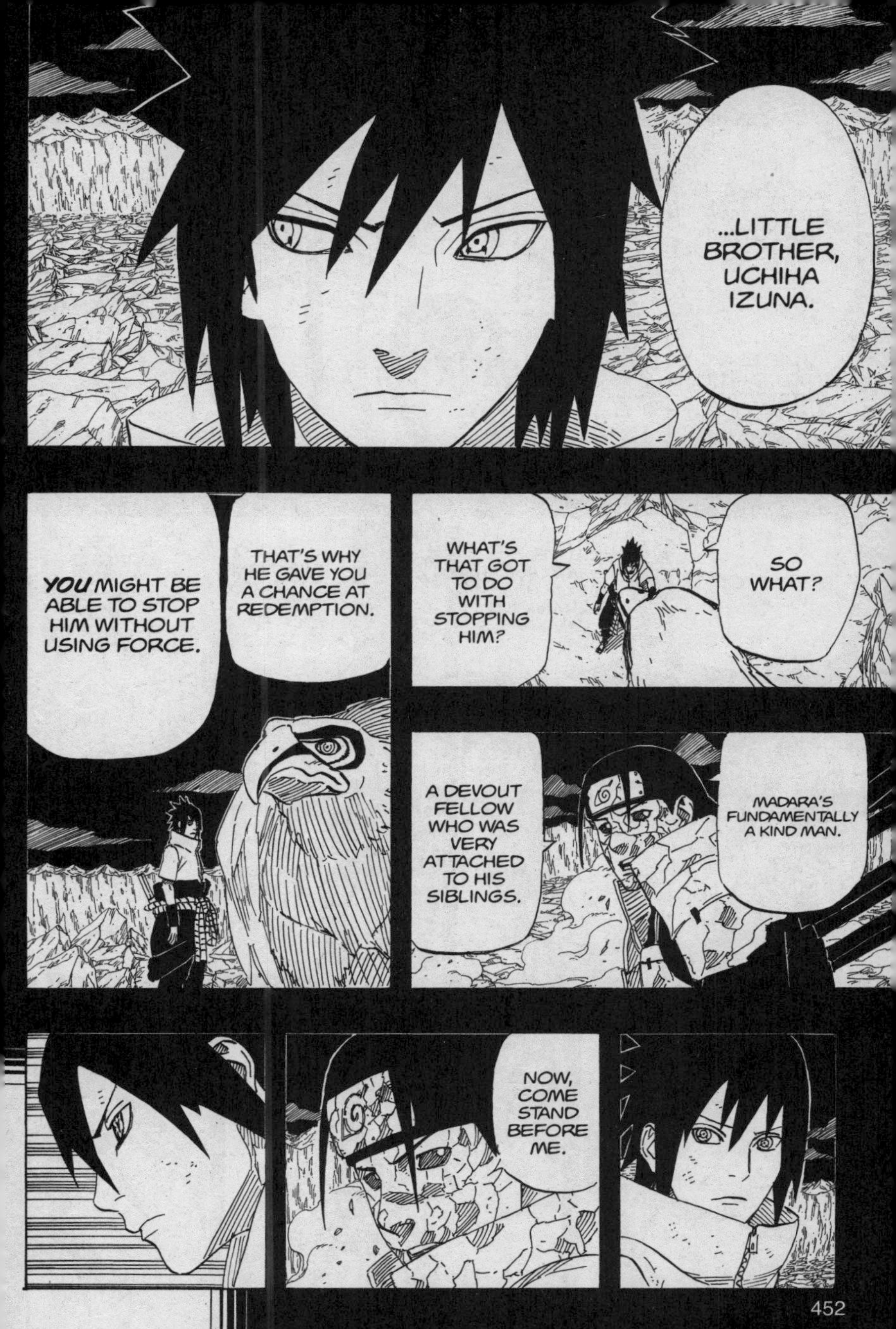
...LITTLE BROTHER, UCHIHA IZUNA.
SO WHAT?
WHAT'S THAT GOT TO DO WITH STOPPING HIM?
MADARA'S FUNDAMENTALLY A KIND MAN.
A DEVOUT FELLOW WHO WAS VERY ATTACHED TO HIS SIBLINGS.
THAT'S WHY HE GAVE YOU A CHANCE AT REDEMPTION.
YOU MIGHT BE ABLE TO STOP HIM WITHOUT USING FORCE.
NOW, COME STAND BEFORE ME.

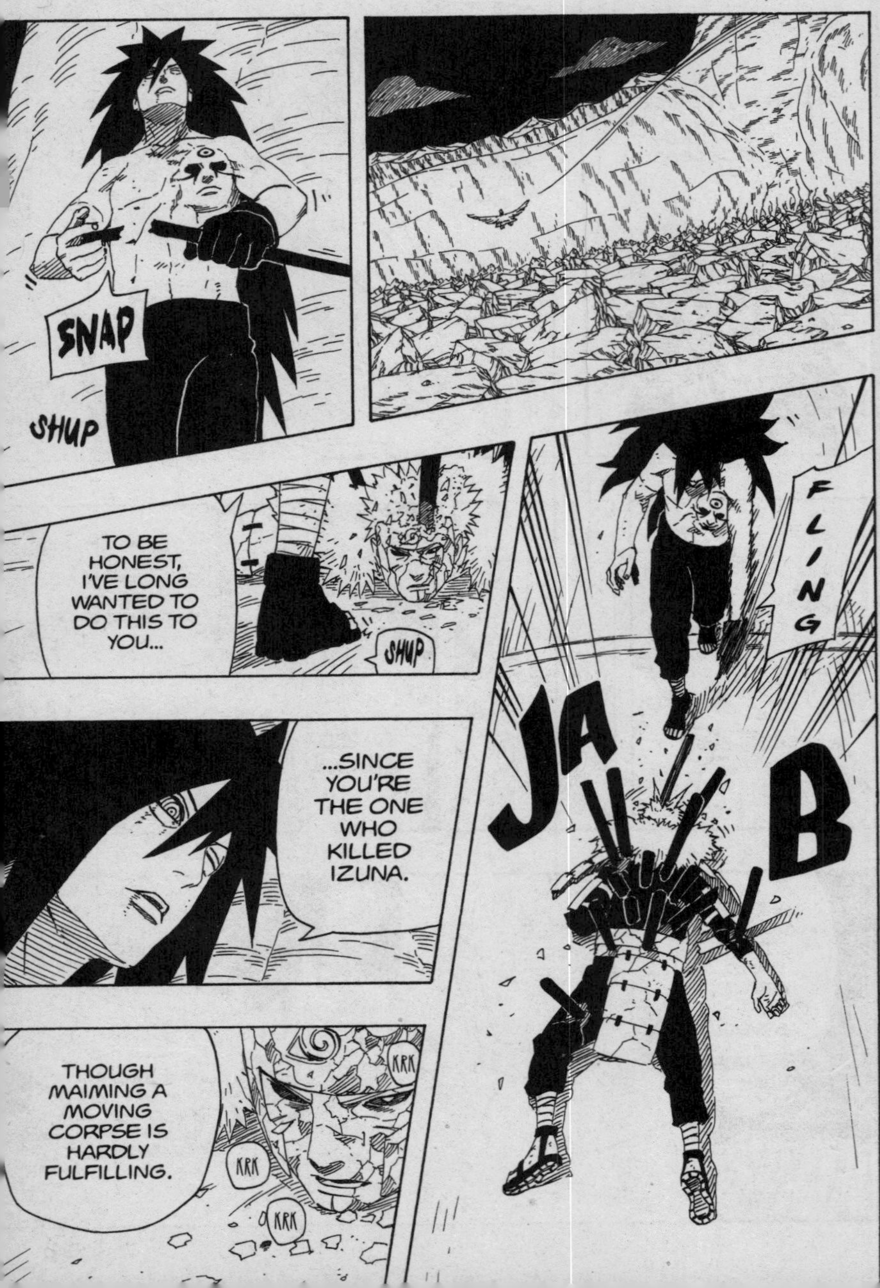
SNAP
SHUP
FLING
JAB
TO BE HONEST, I'VE LONG WANTED TO DO THIS TO YOU...
SHUP
...SINCE YOU'RE THE ONE WHO KILLED IZUNA.
THOUGH MAIMING A MOVING CORPSE IS HARDLY FULFILLING.
KRK
KRK
KRK

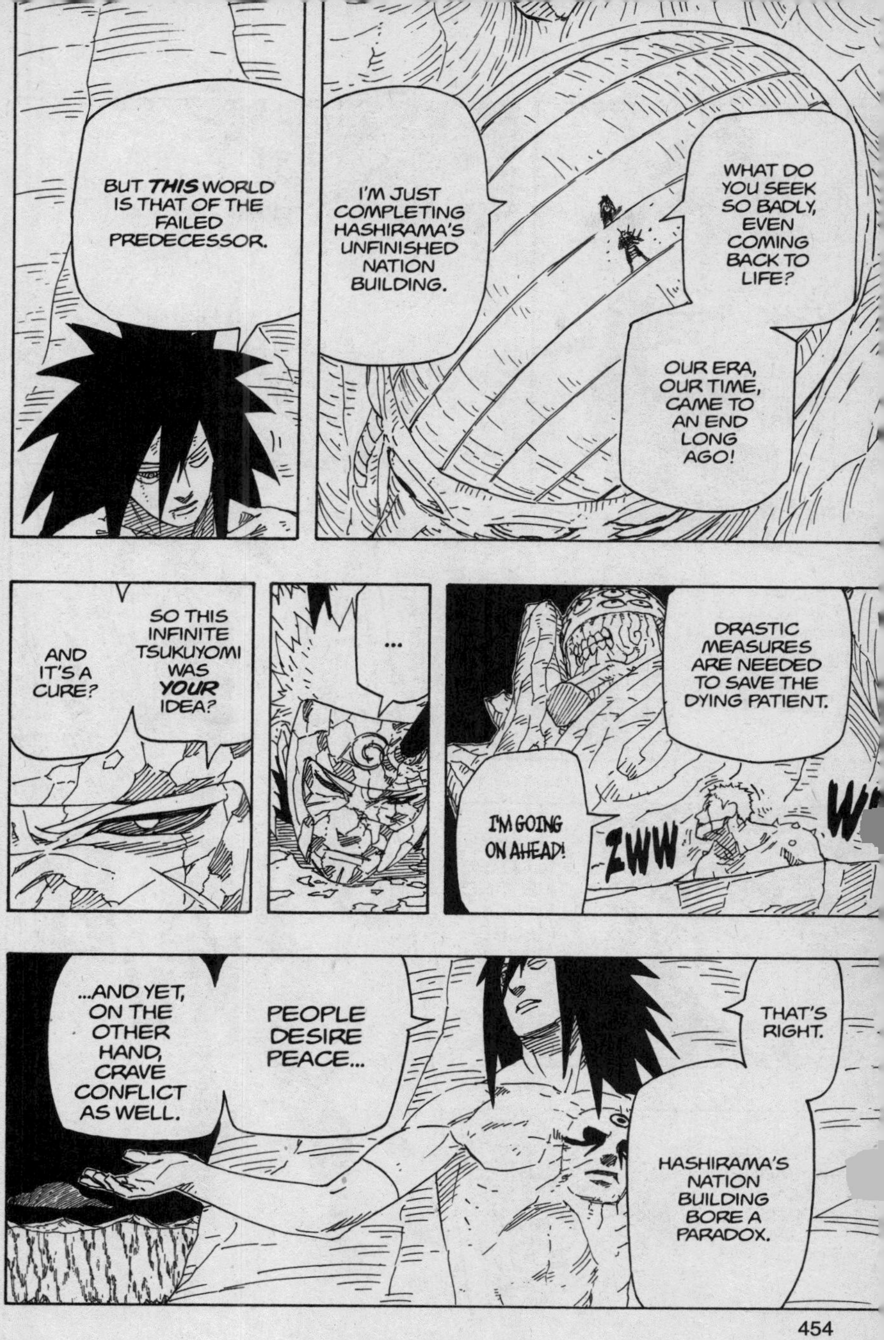
WHAT DO YOU SEEK SO BADLY, EVEN COMING BACK TO LIFE?
OUR ERA, OUR TIME, CAME TO AN END LONG AGO!
I'M JUST COMPLETING HASHIRAMA'S UNFINISHED NATION BUILDING.
BUT **THIS** WORLD IS THAT OF THE FAILED PREDECESSOR.
DRASTIC MEASURES ARE NEEDED TO SAVE THE DYING PATIENT.
I'M GOING ON AHEAD!
ZWW
...
SO THIS INFINITE TSUKUYOMI WAS **YOUR** IDEA?
AND IT'S A CURE?
THAT'S RIGHT.
HASHIRAMA'S NATION BUILDING BORE A PARADOX.
PEOPLE DESIRE PEACE...
...AND YET, ON THE OTHER HAND, CRAVE CONFLICT AS WELL.

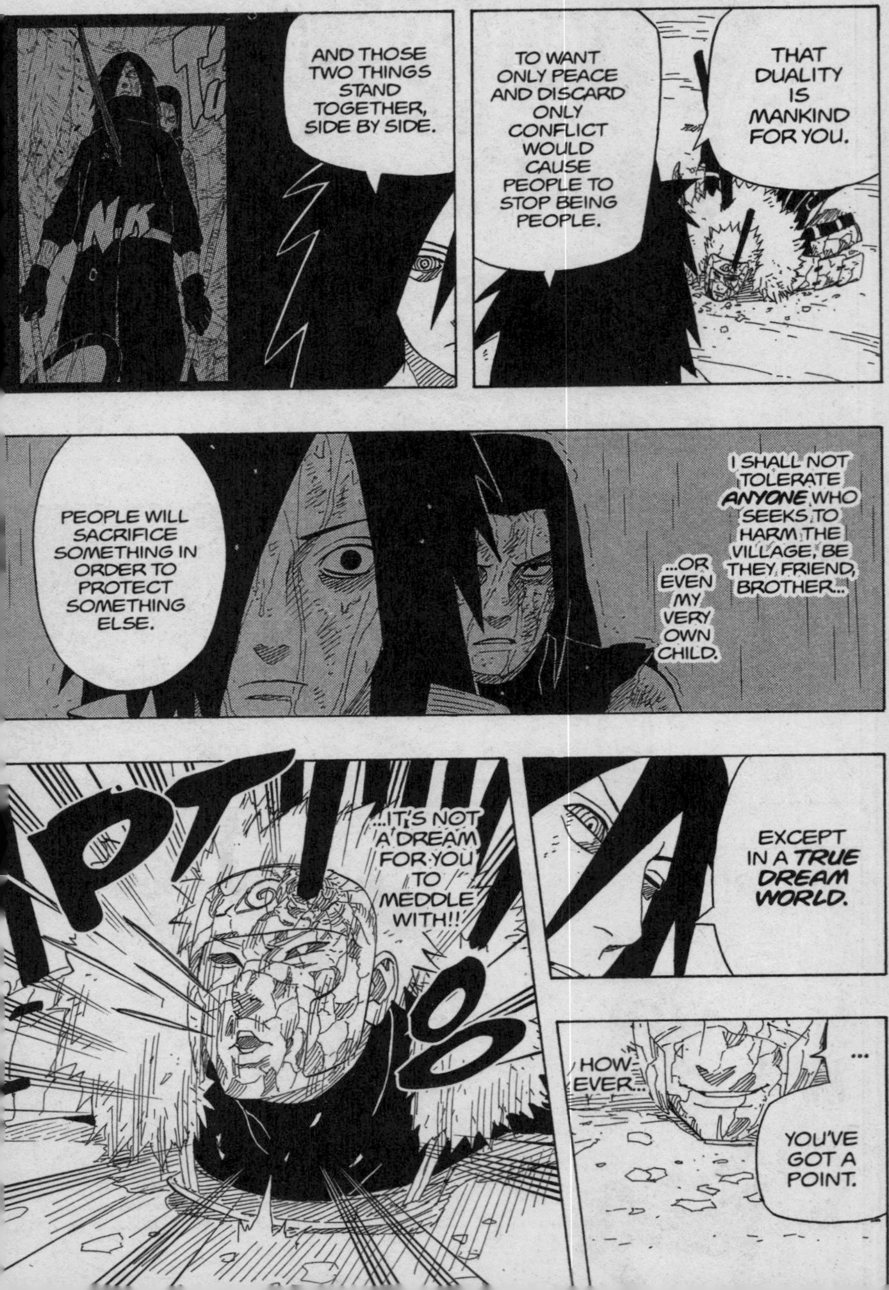
THAT DUALITY IS MANKIND FOR YOU.
TO WANT ONLY PEACE AND DISCARD ONLY CONFLICT WOULD CAUSE PEOPLE TO STOP BEING PEOPLE.
AND THOSE TWO THINGS STAND TOGETHER, SIDE BY SIDE.
I SHALL NOT TOLERATE *ANYONE* WHO SEEKS TO HARM THE VILLAGE, BE THEY FRIEND, BROTHER...
...OR EVEN MY VERY OWN CHILD.
PEOPLE WILL SACRIFICE SOMETHING IN ORDER TO PROTECT SOMETHING ELSE.
EXCEPT IN A *TRUE DREAM WORLD*.
...
YOU'VE GOT A POINT.
HOW-EVER...
...IT'S NOT A DREAM FOR YOU TO MEDDLE WITH!!

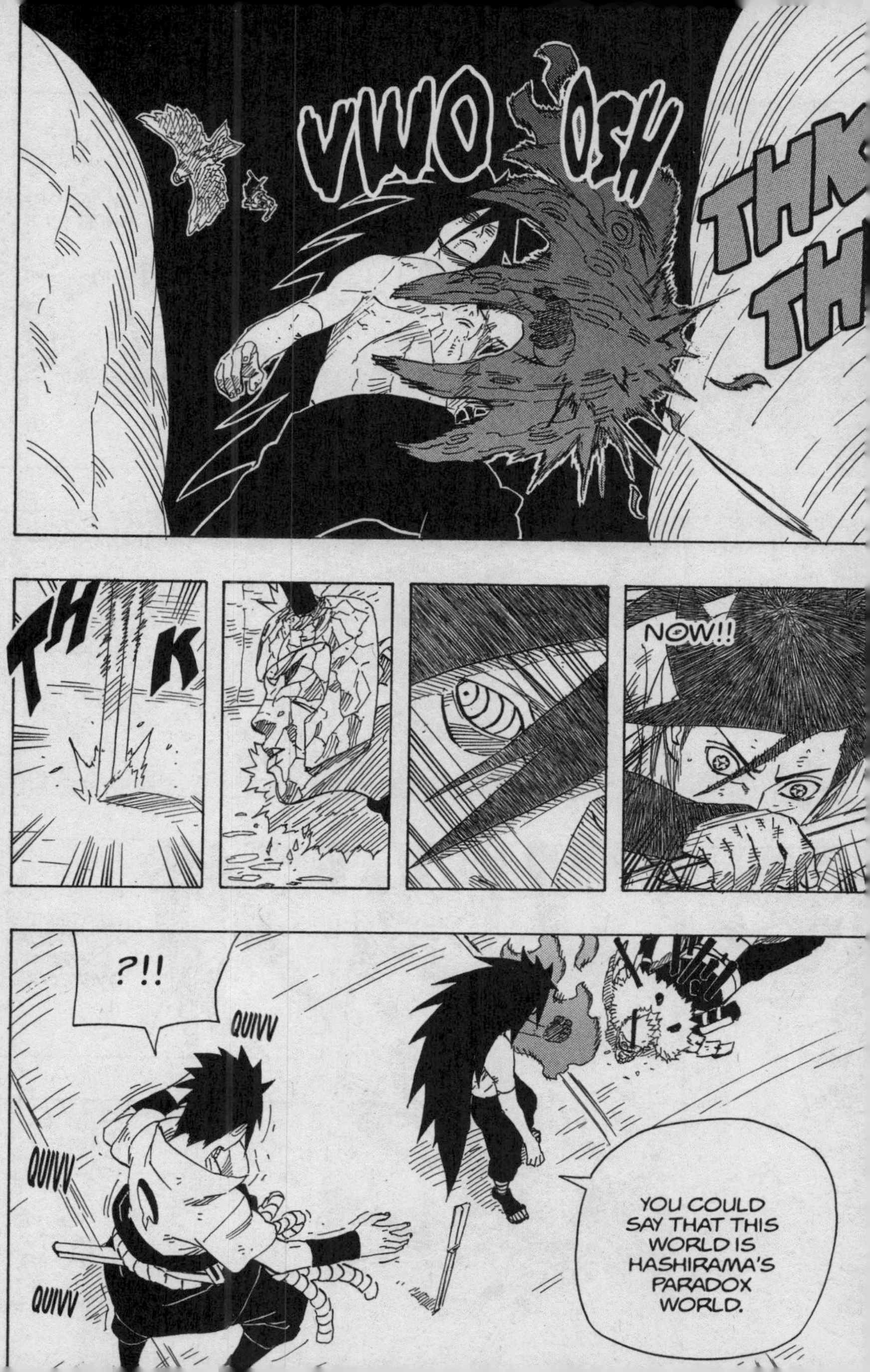
THK
TH
VWO OSH
NOW!!
TH K
YOU COULD SAY THAT THIS WORLD IS HASHIRAMA'S PARADOX WORLD.
?!!
QUIVV
QUIVV
QUIVV

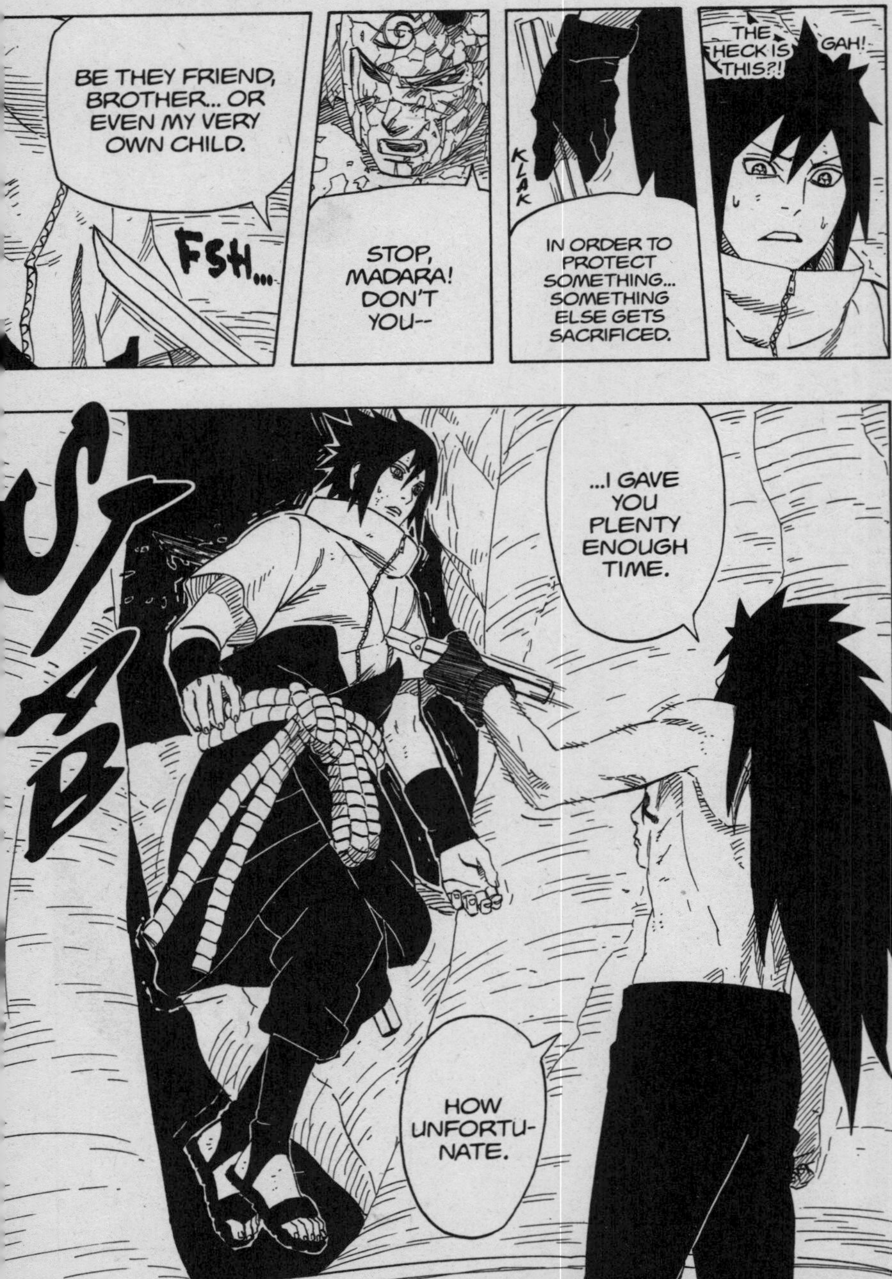
GAH!
THE HECK IS THIS?!
KLAK
IN ORDER TO PROTECT SOMETHING... SOMETHING ELSE GETS SACRIFICED.
STOP, MADARA! DON'T YOU--
BE THEY FRIEND, BROTHER... OR EVEN MY VERY OWN CHILD.
FSH...
...I GAVE YOU PLENTY ENOUGH TIME.
STAB
HOW UNFORTU-NATE.

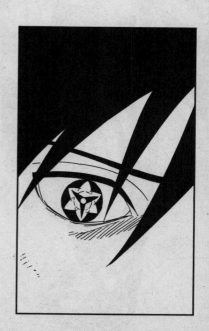

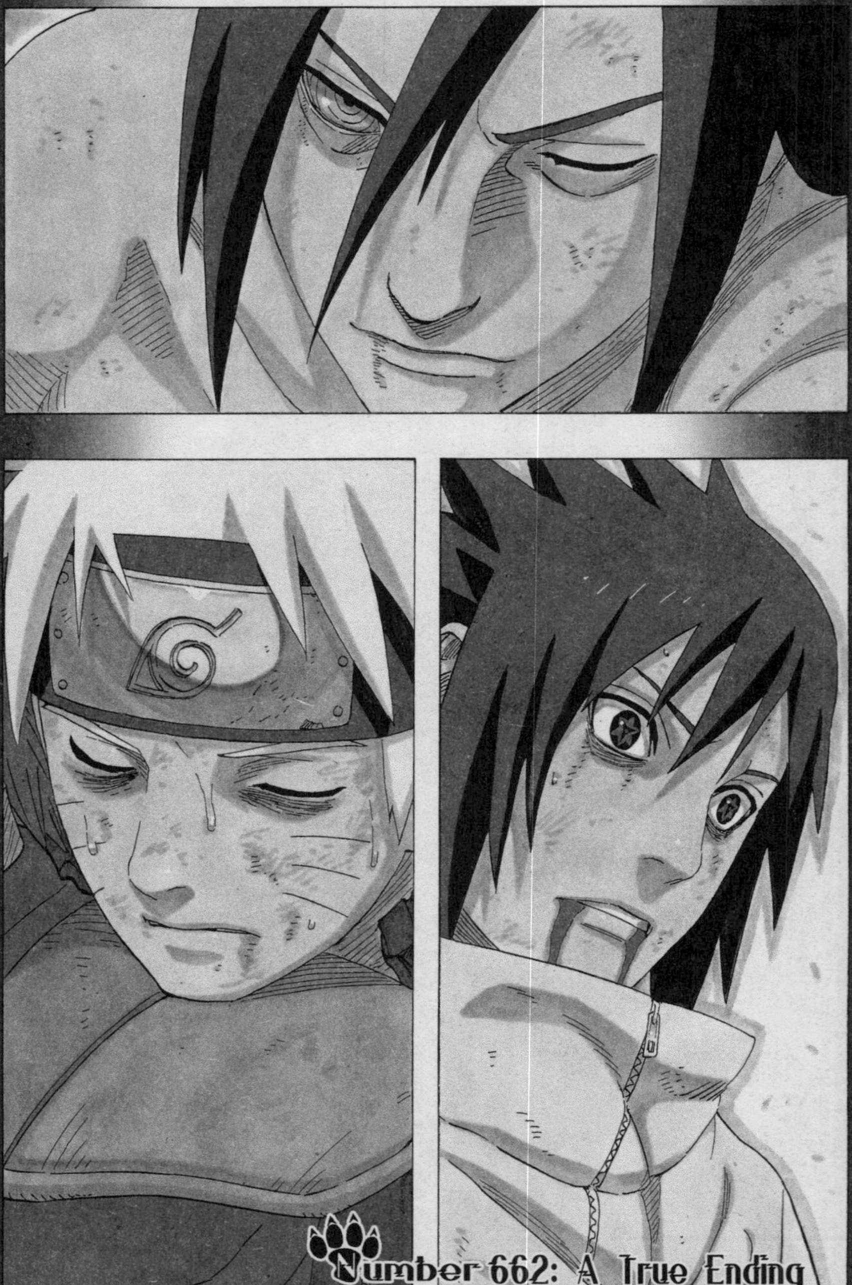
Number 662: A True Ending

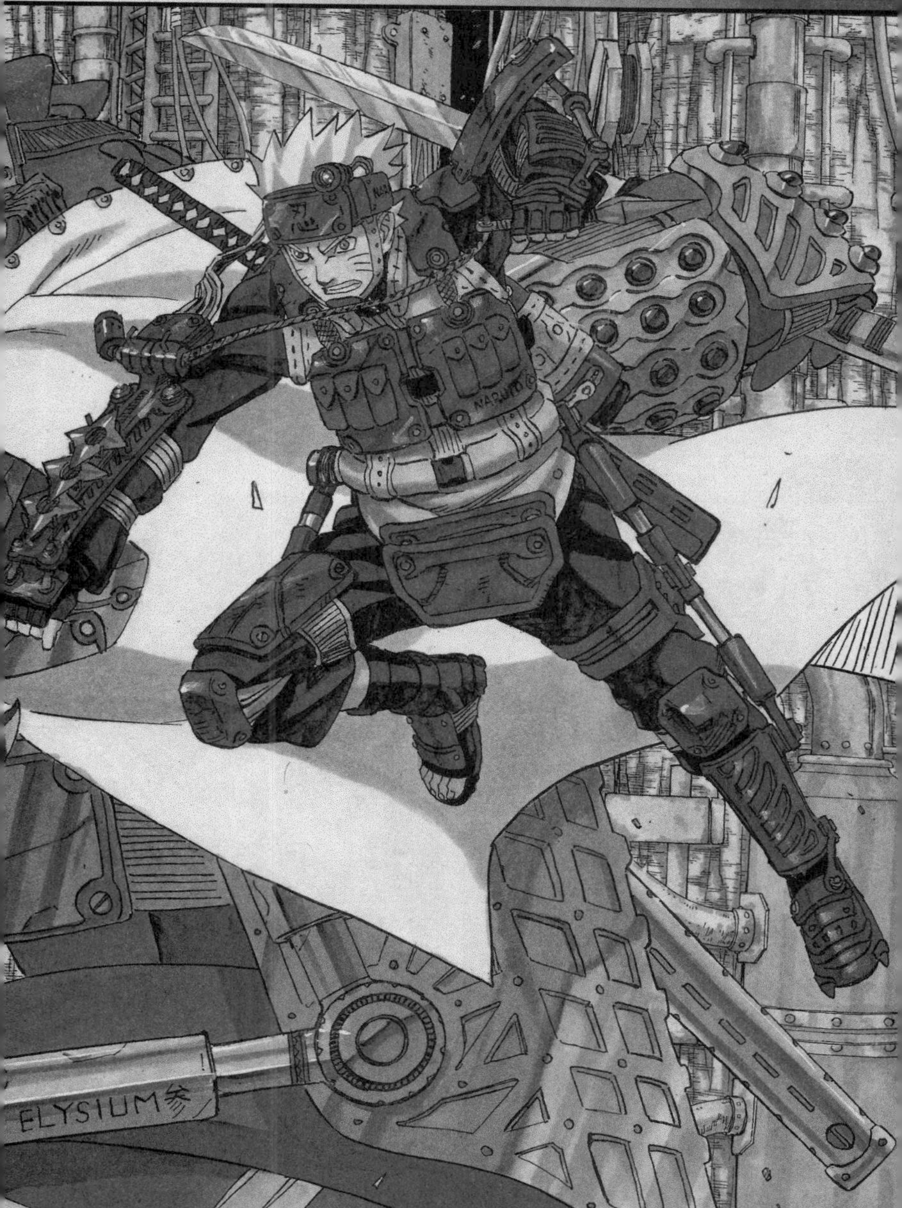
ELYSIUM参

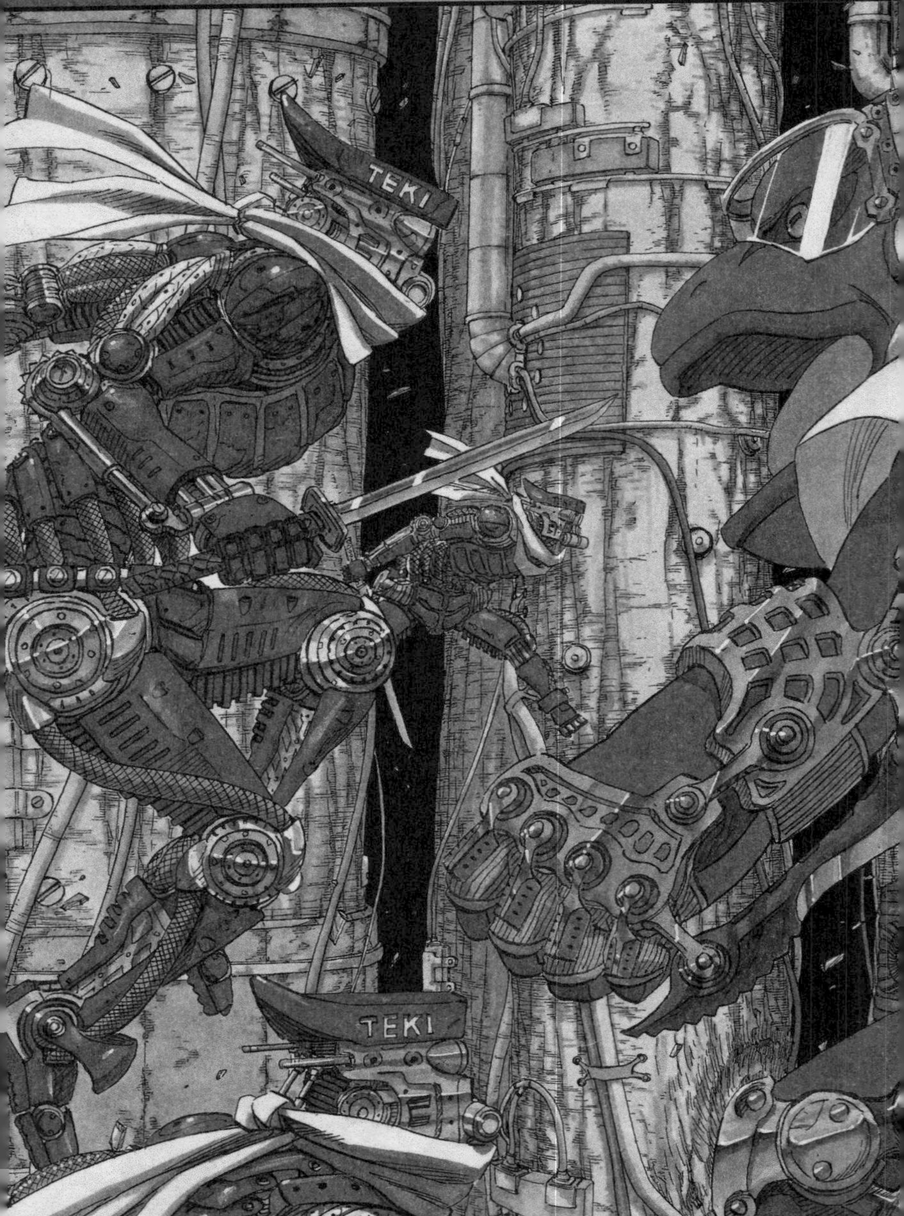
TEKI
TEKI

Number 662: A True Ending

NARUTO

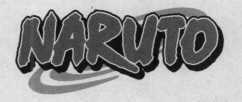

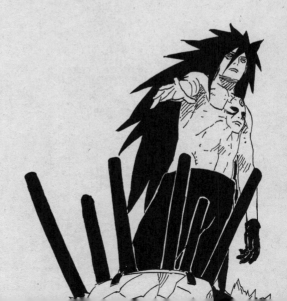

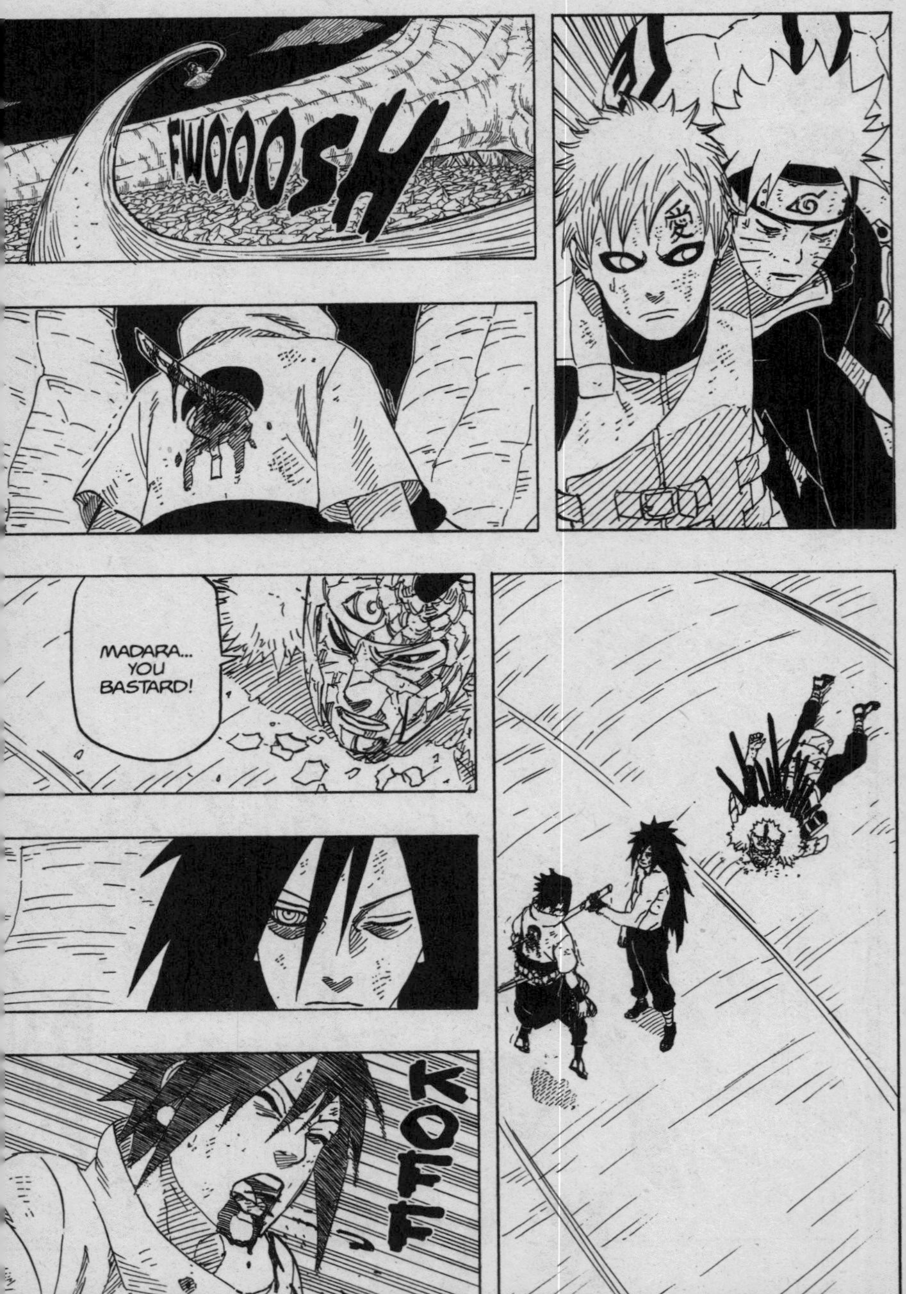
FWOOSH
MADARA... YOU BASTARD!
KOFF

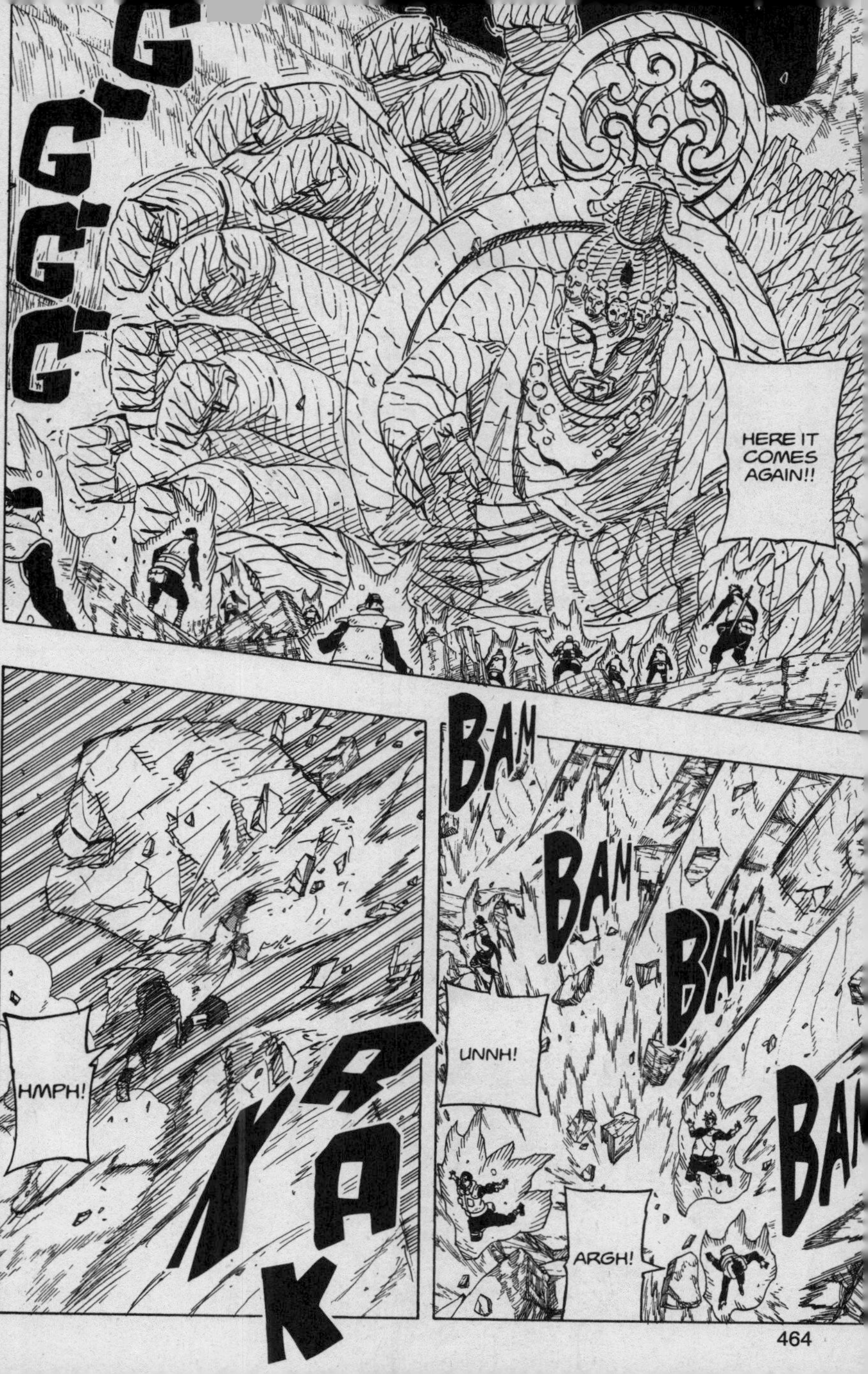
G G G G
HERE IT COMES AGAIN!!
BAM
BAM
BAM
BAM
UNNH!
ARGH!
HMPH!
KRAAK

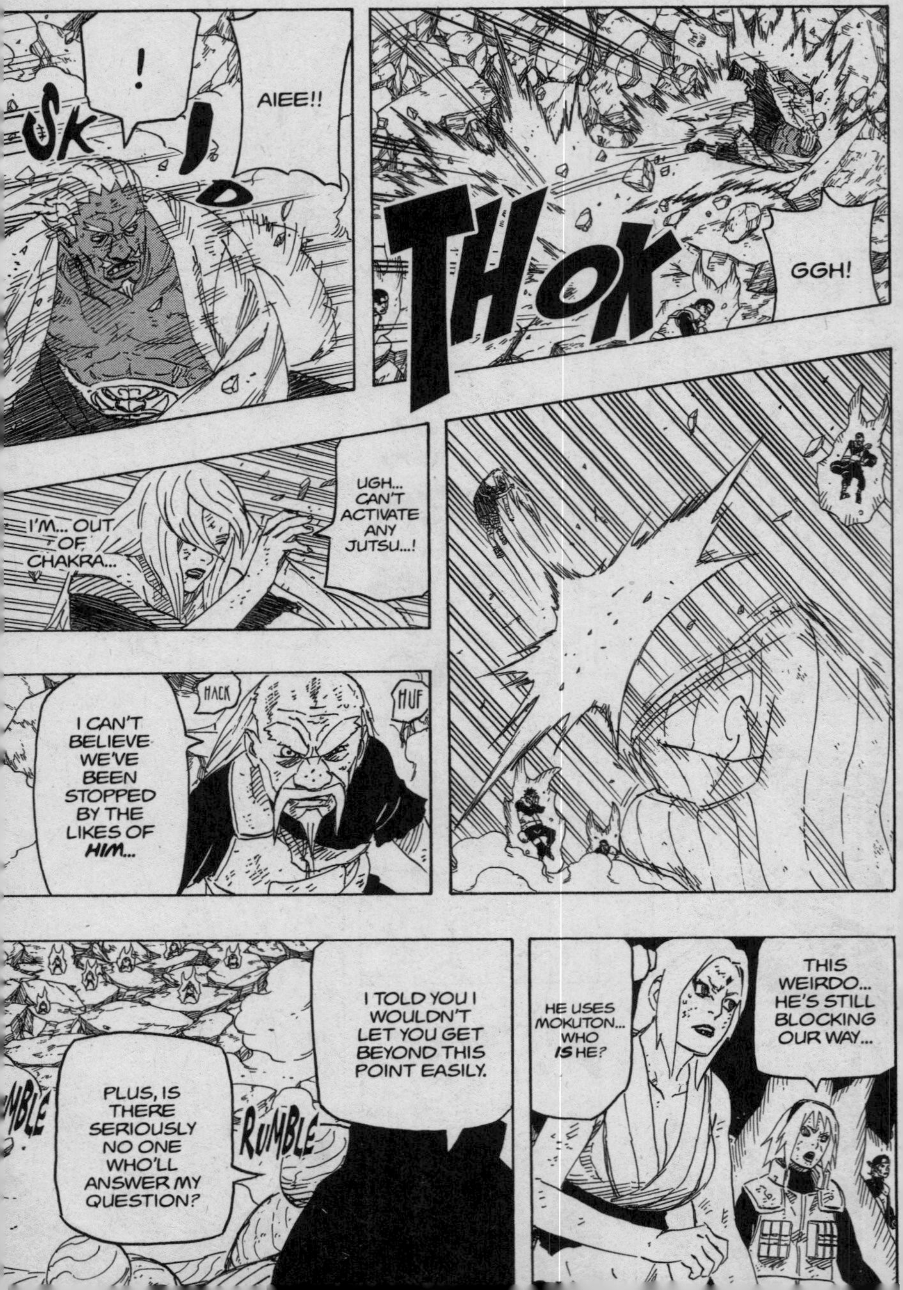
THOK
GGH!
!
AIEE!!
SKID
UGH... CAN'T ACTIVATE ANY JUTSU...!
I'M... OUT OF CHAKRA...
HUF
HACK
I CAN'T BELIEVE WE'VE BEEN STOPPED BY THE LIKES OF *HIM*...
THIS WEIRDO... HE'S STILL BLOCKING OUR WAY...
HE USES MOKUTON... WHO *IS* HE?
I TOLD YOU I WOULDN'T LET YOU GET BEYOND THIS POINT EASILY.
RUMBLE
PLUS, IS THERE SERIOUSLY NO ONE WHO'LL ANSWER MY QUESTION?

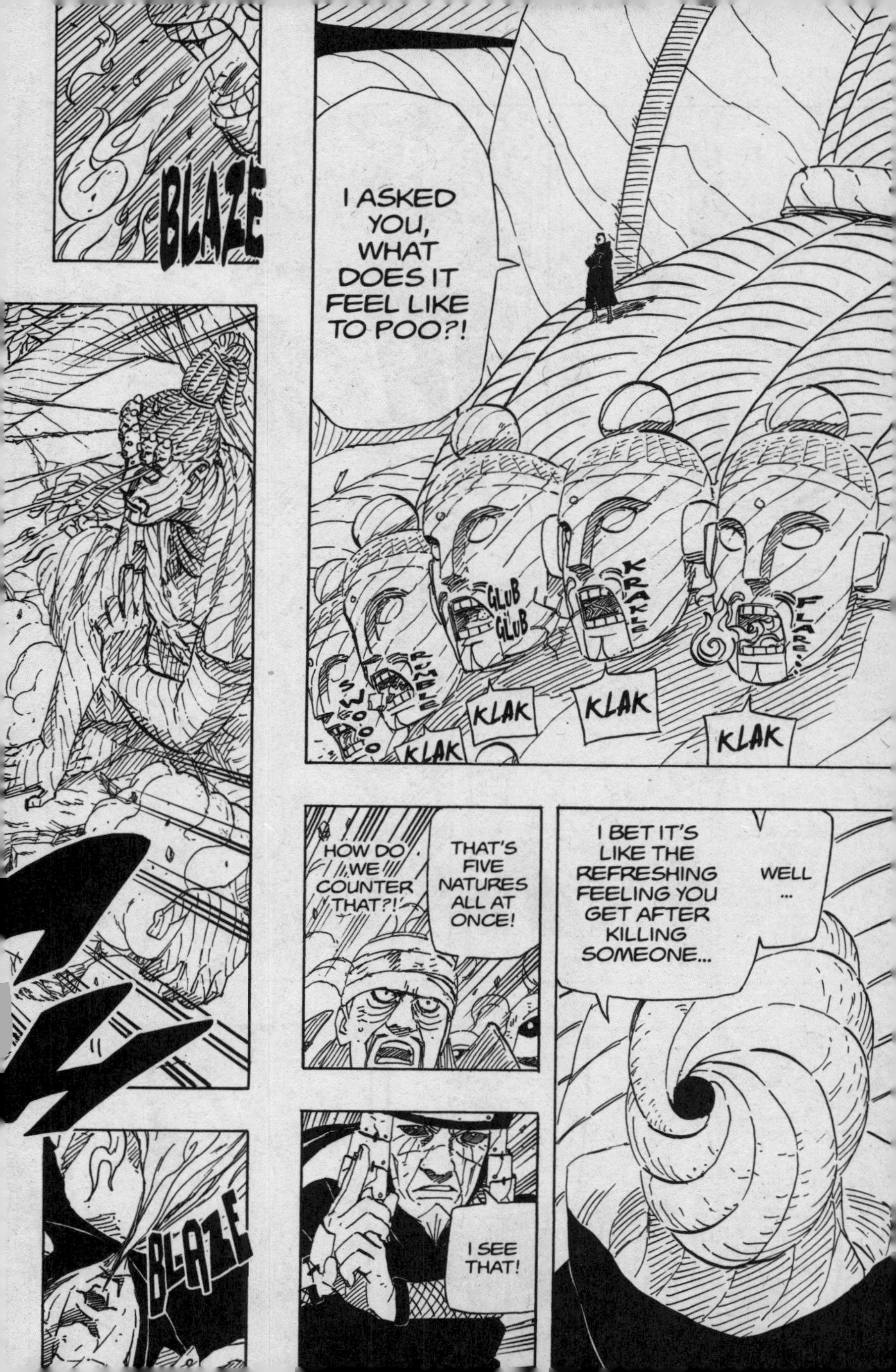
I ASKED YOU, WHAT DOES IT FEEL LIKE TO POO?!
FLARE...
KLAK
KRAKLE
KLAK
GLUB GLUB
KLAK
RUMBLE
SWOOO
KLAK
WELL...
I BET IT'S LIKE THE REFRESHING FEELING YOU GET AFTER KILLING SOMEONE...
THAT'S FIVE NATURES ALL AT ONCE!
HOW DO WE COUNTER THAT?!
I SEE THAT!
BLAZE
BLAZE

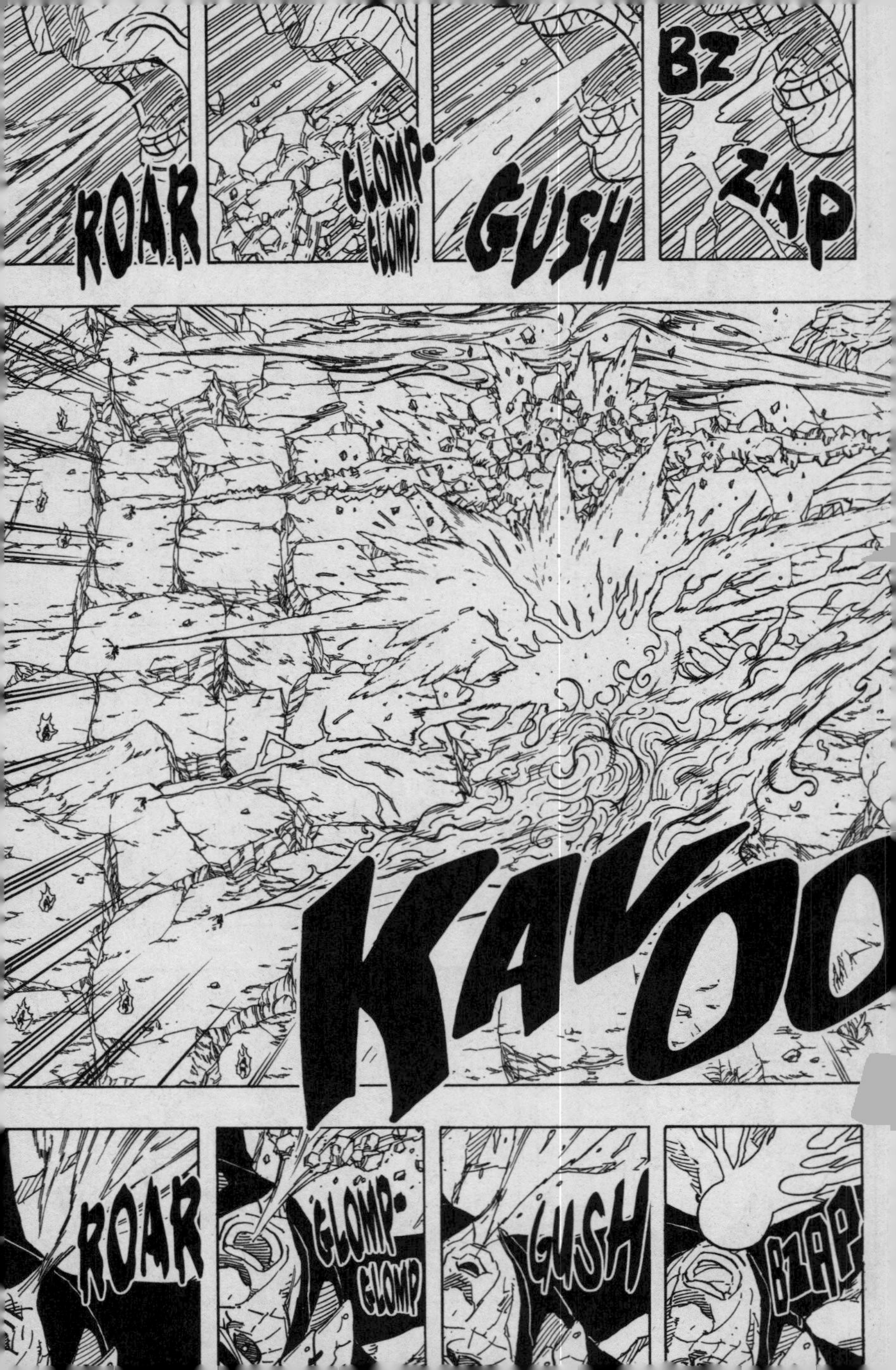
BZ
ZAP
GUSH
GLOMP-GLOMP
ROAR
KAVOO
BZAP
GUSH
GLOMP-GLOMP
ROAR

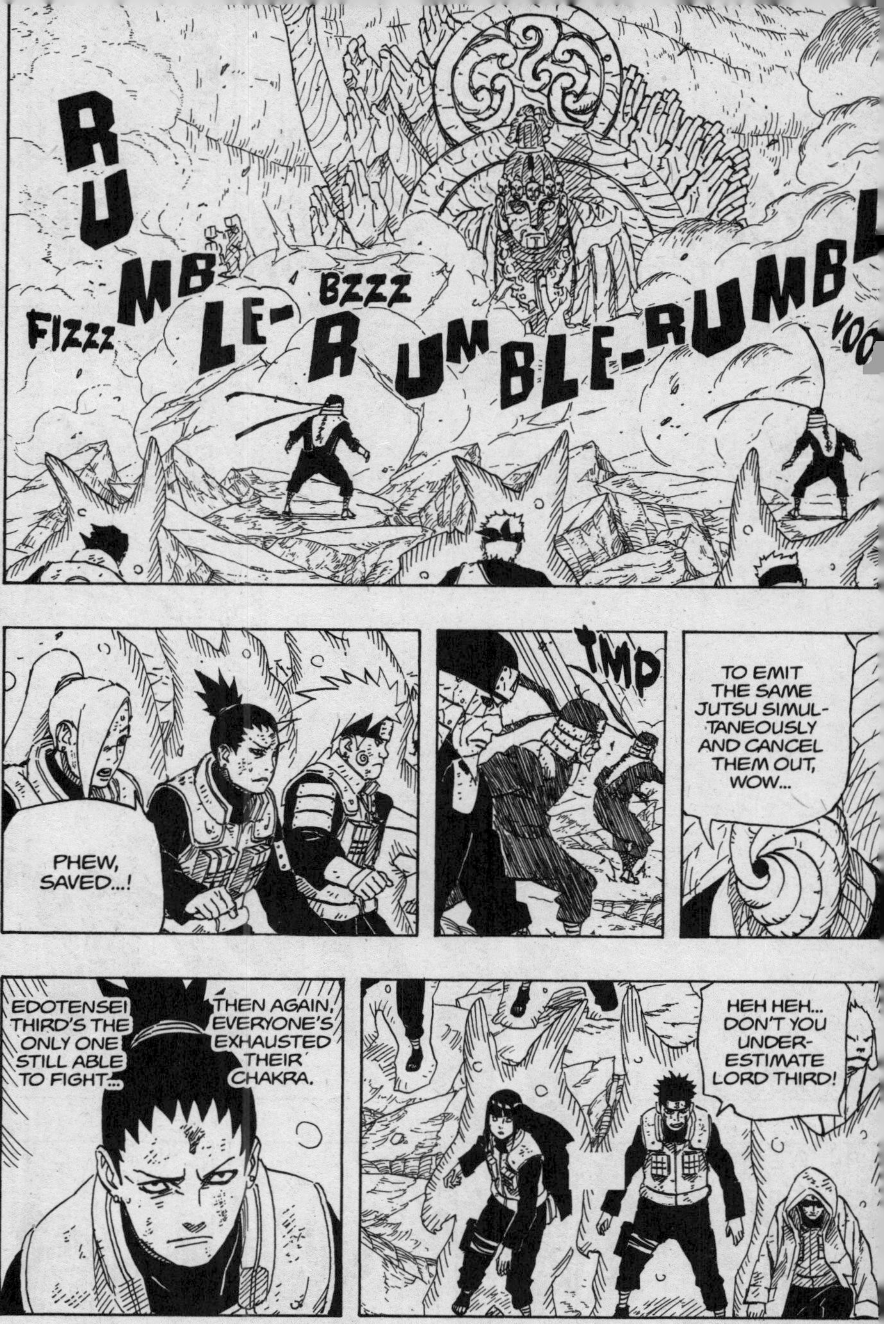
VOO
RUMBLE-RUMBLE-RUMBL
BZZZ
FIZZZ
TO EMIT THE SAME JUTSU SIMULTANEOUSLY AND CANCEL THEM OUT, WOW...
TMP
PHEW, SAVED...!
HEH HEH... DON'T YOU UNDERESTIMATE LORD THIRD!
THEN AGAIN, EVERYONE'S EXHAUSTED THEIR CHAKRA.
EDOTENSEI THIRD'S THE ONLY ONE STILL ABLE TO FIGHT...

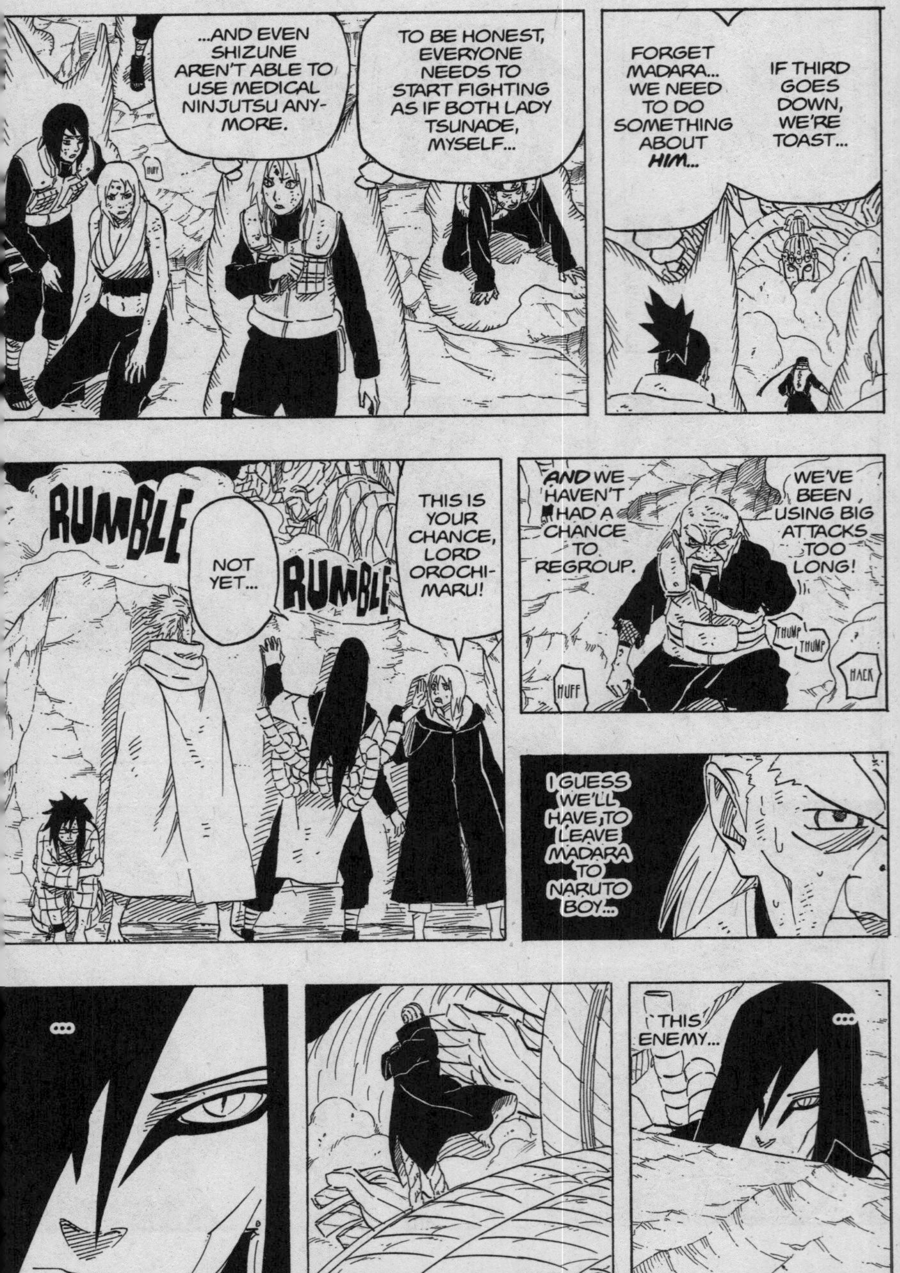
IF THIRD GOES DOWN, WE'RE TOAST...
FORGET MADARA... WE NEED TO DO SOMETHING ABOUT HIM...
TO BE HONEST, EVERYONE NEEDS TO START FIGHTING AS IF BOTH LADY TSUNADE, MYSELF...
...AND EVEN SHIZUNE AREN'T ABLE TO USE MEDICAL NINJUTSU ANYMORE.
HUFF
WE'VE BEEN USING BIG ATTACKS TOO LONG!
AND WE HAVEN'T HAD A CHANCE TO REGROUP.
THUMP
THUMP
HACK
HUFF
I GUESS WE'LL HAVE TO LEAVE MADARA TO NARUTO BOY...
THIS IS YOUR CHANCE, LORD OROCHIMARU!
RUMBLE
RUMBLE
NOT YET...
...
THIS ENEMY...
...

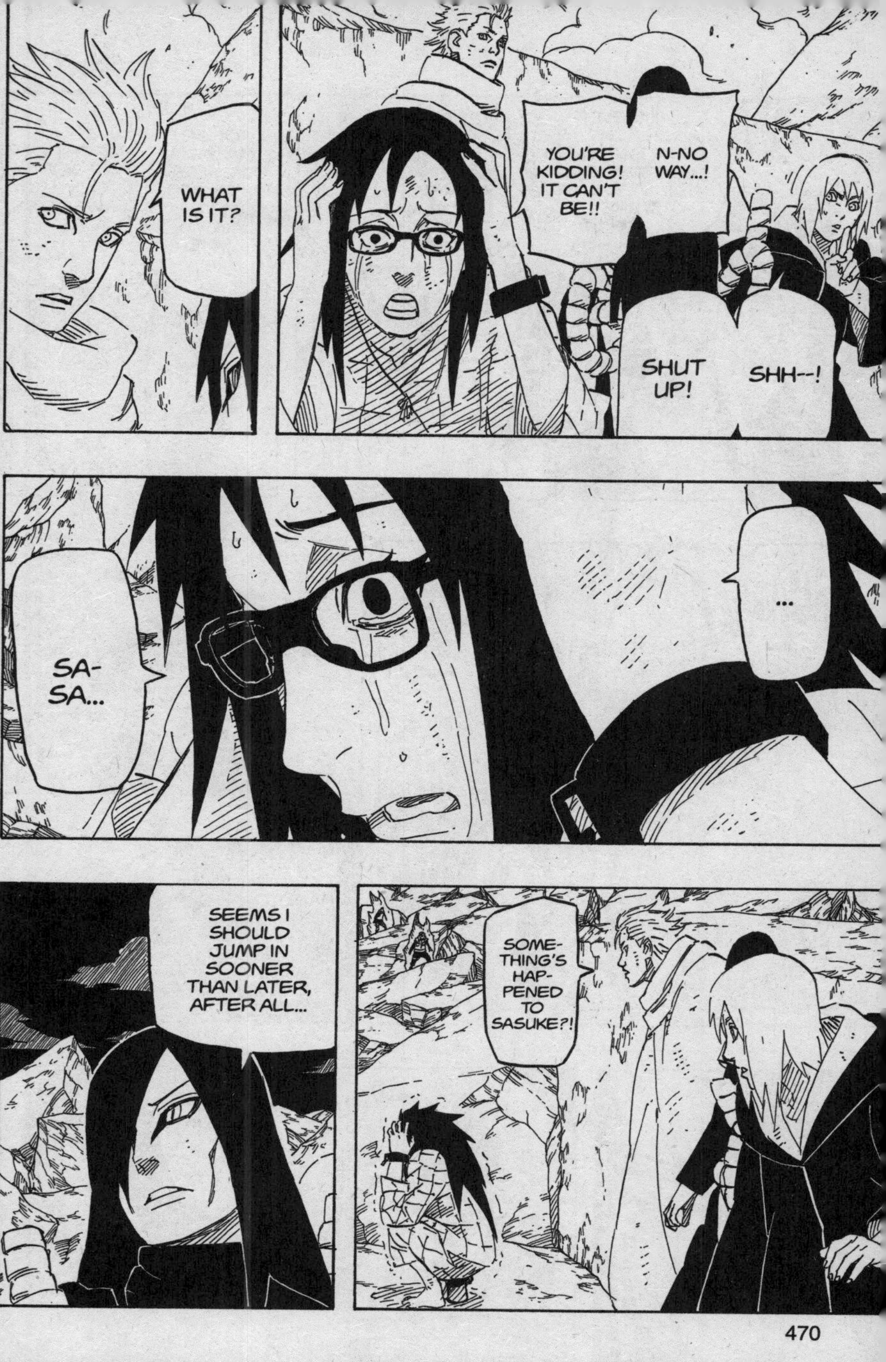
N-NO WAY...!
YOU'RE KIDDING! IT CAN'T BE!!
SHH--!
SHUT UP!
WHAT IS IT?
...
SA-SA...
SOME-THING'S HAP-PENED TO SASUKE?!
SEEMS I SHOULD JUMP IN SOONER THAN LATER, AFTER ALL...

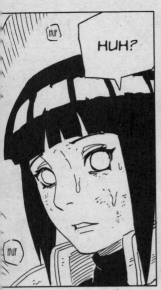

HUF

HUF

HUH?

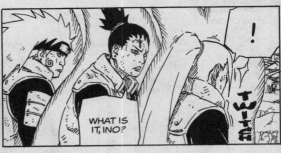

WHAT IS IT, INO?

!

TWITCH

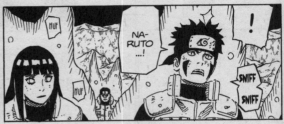

HUF

HUF

NA-
RUTO
...!

!

SNIFF

SNIFF

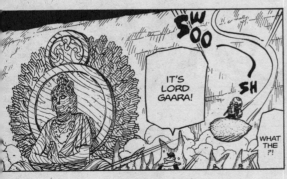

SW
OO

SH

IT'S
LORD
GAARA!

WHAT
THE
?!

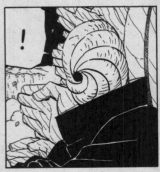

!

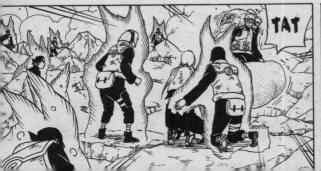

TAT

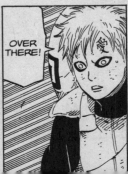

OVER
THERE!

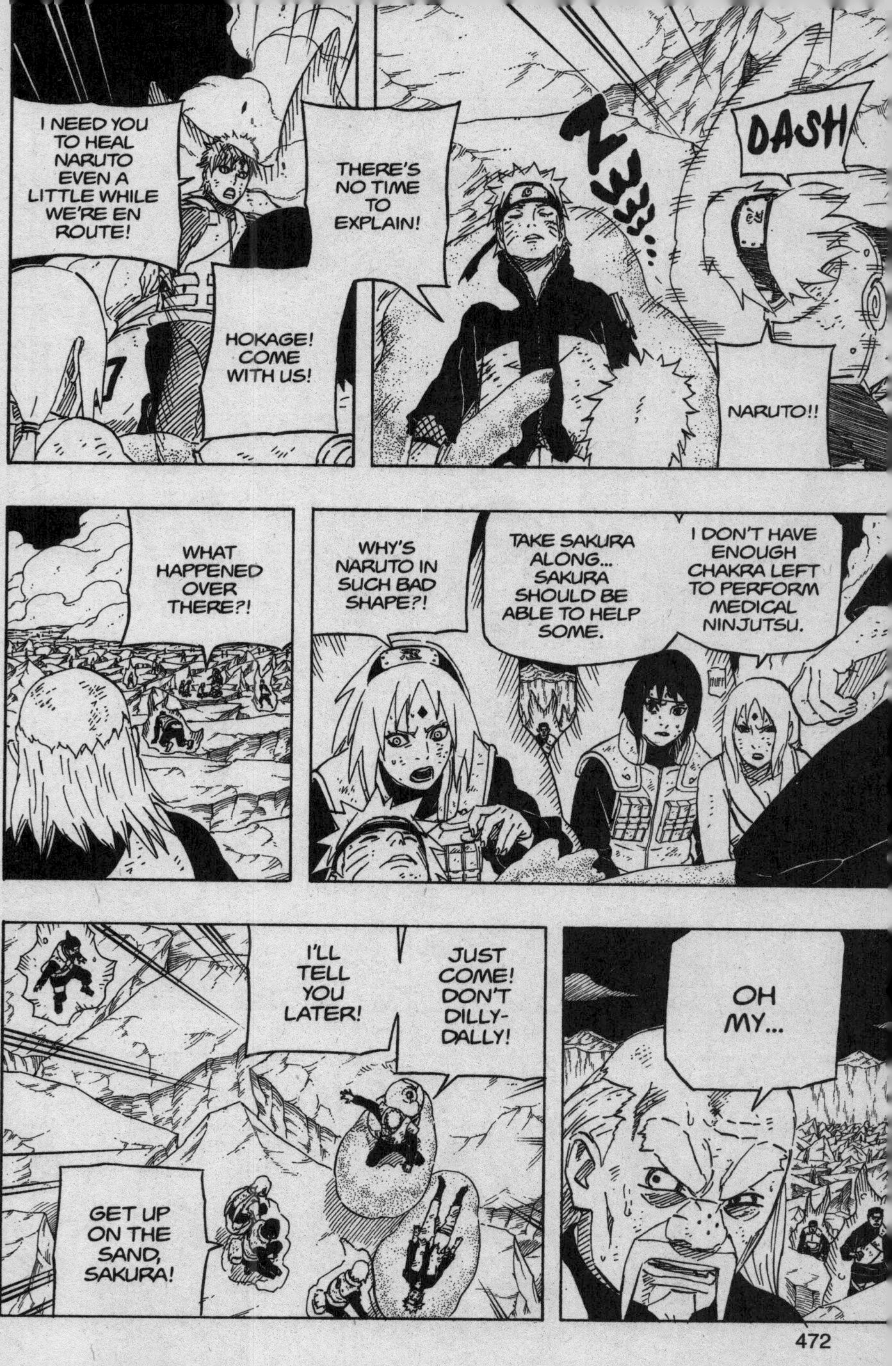
DASH
NARUTO!!
THERE'S NO TIME TO EXPLAIN!
HOKAGE! COME WITH US!
I NEED YOU TO HEAL NARUTO EVEN A LITTLE WHILE WE'RE EN ROUTE!
I DON'T HAVE ENOUGH CHAKRA LEFT TO PERFORM MEDICAL NINJUTSU.
TAKE SAKURA ALONG... SAKURA SHOULD BE ABLE TO HELP SOME.
HUFF
WHY'S NARUTO IN SUCH BAD SHAPE?!
WHAT HAPPENED OVER THERE?!
OH MY...
JUST COME! DON'T DILLY-DALLY!
I'LL TELL YOU LATER!
GET UP ON THE SAND, SAKURA!

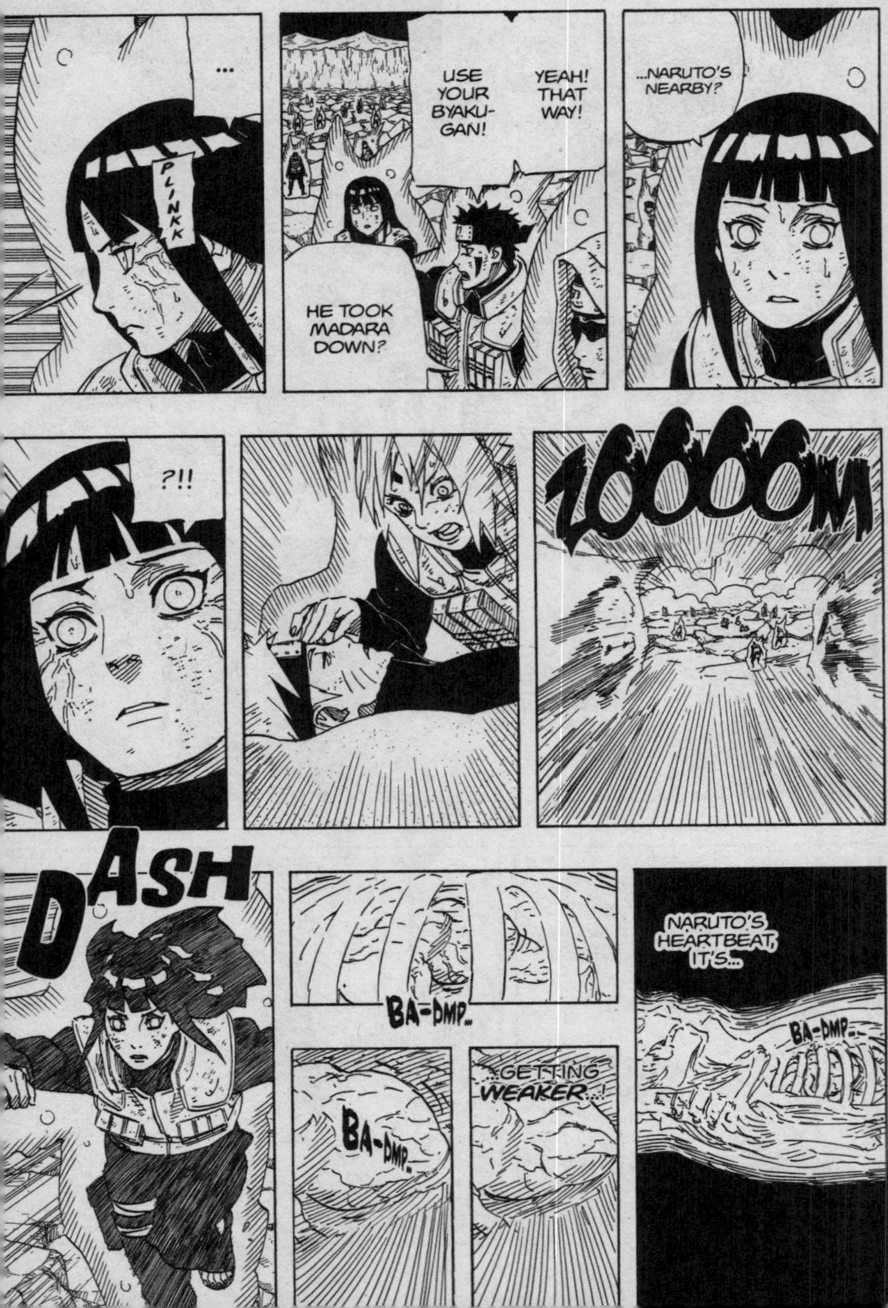
...NARUTO'S NEARBY?
YEAH! THAT WAY!
USE YOUR BYAKU-GAN!
HE TOOK MADARA DOWN?
...
PLINKK
ZOOOOM
?!!
NARUTO'S HEARTBEAT, IT'S...
BA-DMP...
BA-DMP...
...GETTING WEAKER...!
BA-DMP...
DASH

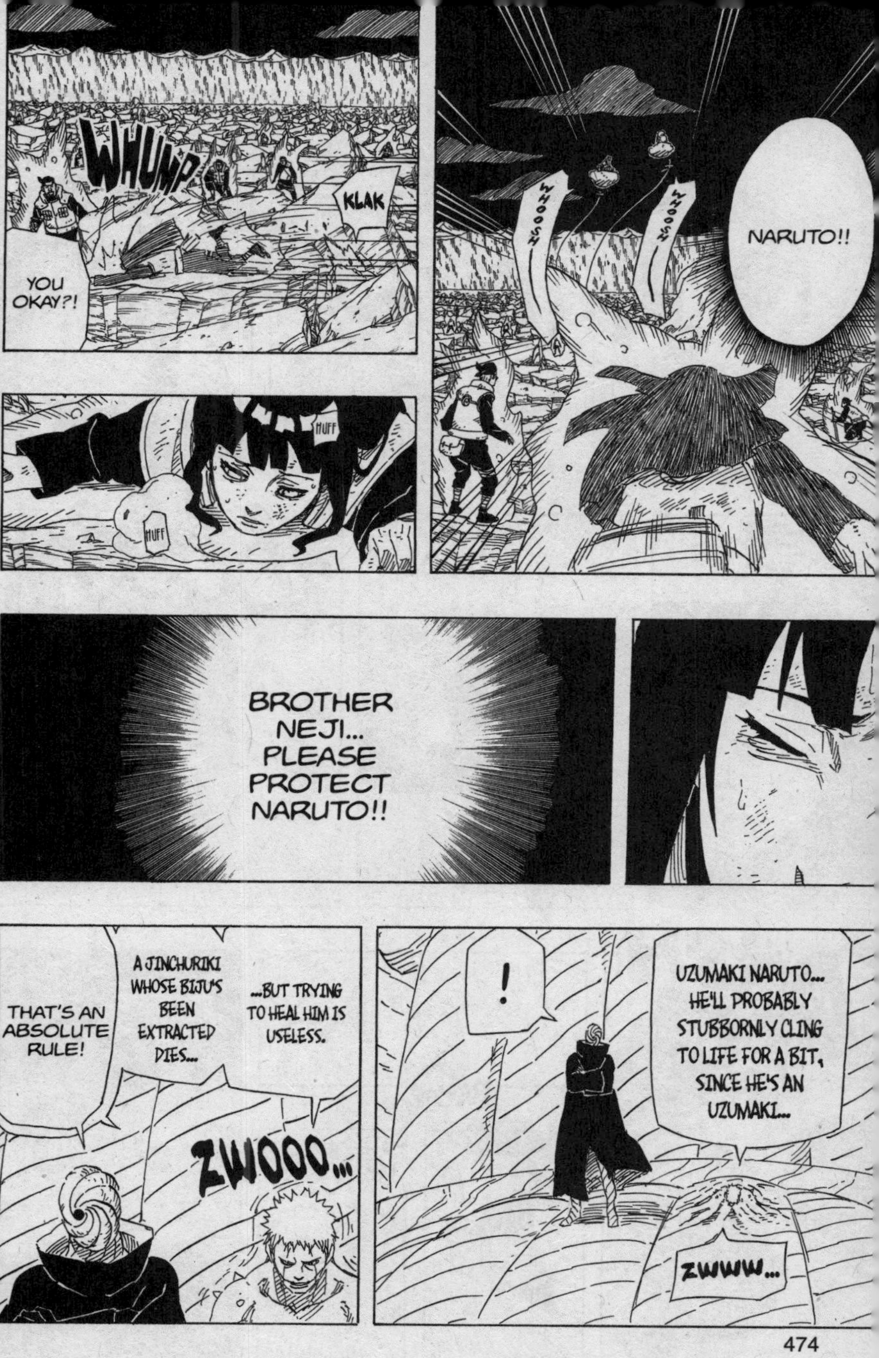
WHOOOSH
WHOOOSH
NARUTO!!
WHUMP
KLAK
YOU OKAY?!
HUFF
HUFF
BROTHER NEJI... PLEASE PROTECT NARUTO!!
!
UZUMAKI NARUTO... HE'LL PROBABLY STUBBORNLY CLING TO LIFE FOR A BIT, SINCE HE'S AN UZUMAKI...
ZWWW...
...BUT TRYING TO HEAL HIM IS USELESS.
A JINCHURIKI WHOSE BIJU'S BEEN EXTRACTED DIES...
THAT'S AN ABSOLUTE RULE!
ZWOOO...

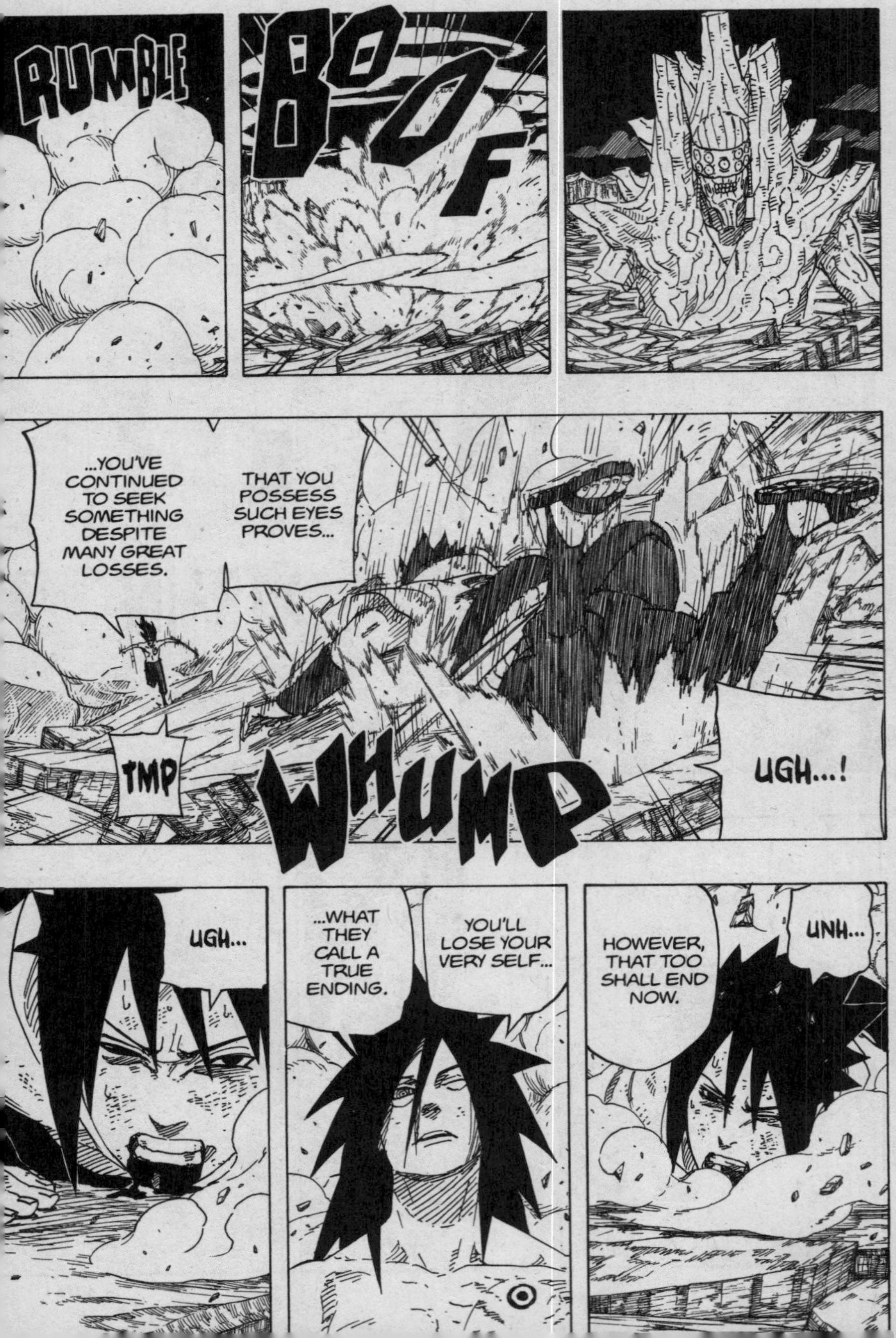
BOOOF
RUMBLE
THAT YOU POSSESS SUCH EYES PROVES...
...YOU'VE CONTINUED TO SEEK SOMETHING DESPITE MANY GREAT LOSSES.
UGH...!
WHUMP
TMP
UNH...
HOWEVER, THAT TOO SHALL END NOW.
YOU'LL LOSE YOUR VERY SELF...
...WHAT THEY CALL A TRUE ENDING.
UGH...

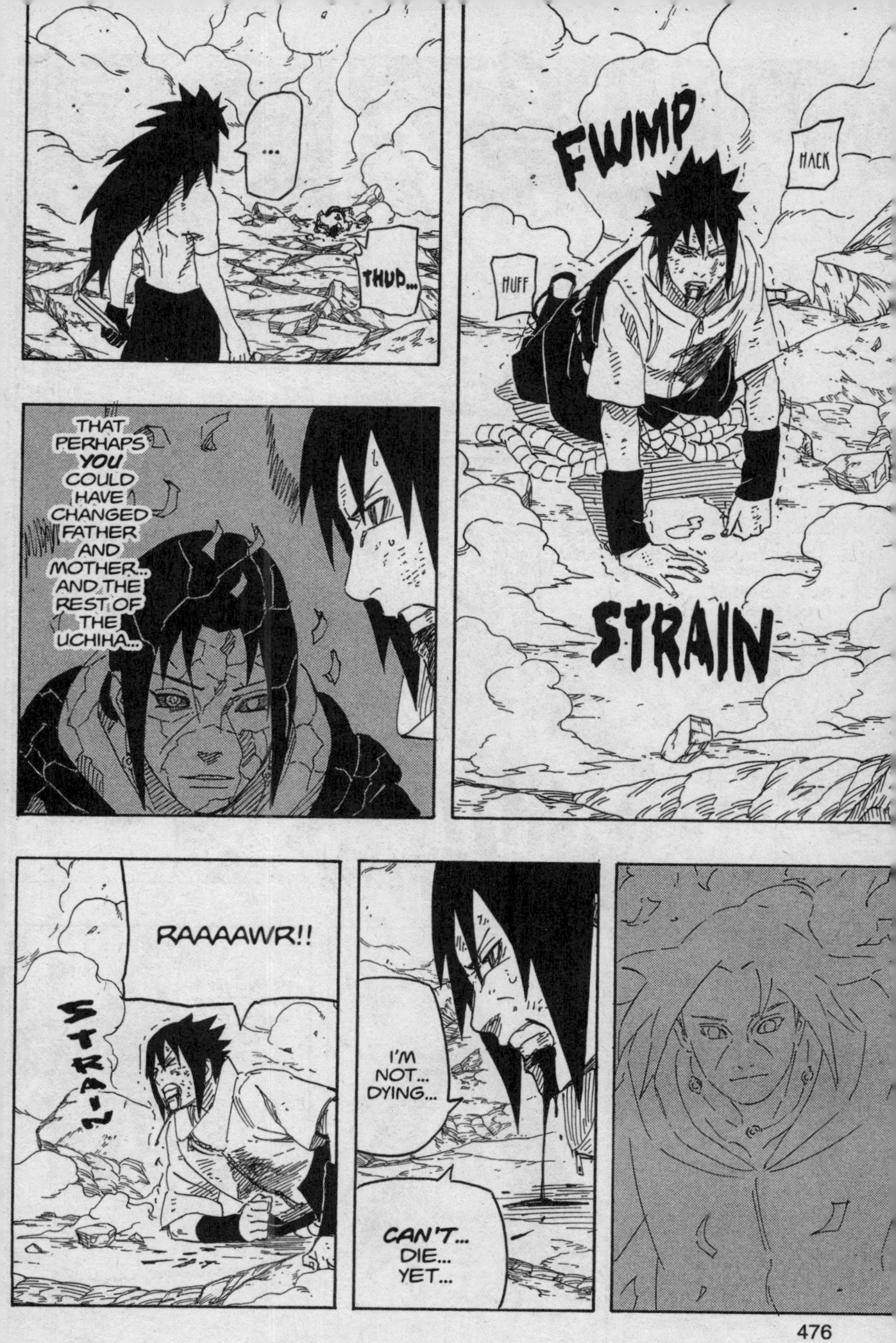
FWUMP
HACK
HUFF
STRAIN
...
THUD...
THAT PERHAPS *YOU* COULD HAVE CHANGED FATHER AND MOTHER... AND THE REST OF THE UCHIHA...
I'M NOT... DYING...
CAN'T... DIE... YET...
RAAAAWR!!
STRAIN

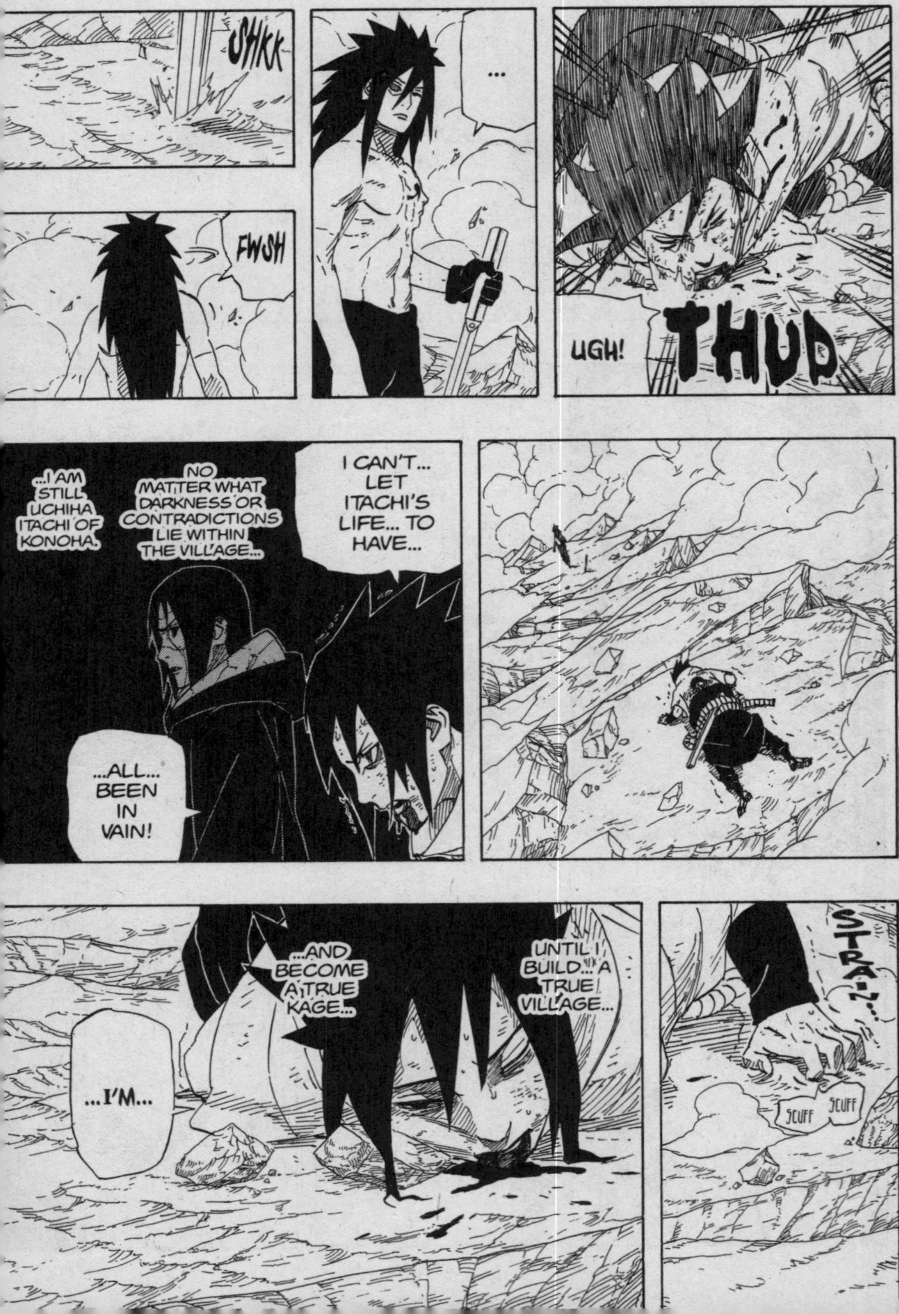
THUD
UGH!
...
SHKK
FWSH
I CAN'T... LET ITACHI'S LIFE... TO HAVE...
NO MATTER WHAT DARKNESS OR CONTRADICTIONS LIE WITHIN THE VILLAGE...
...I AM STILL UCHIHA ITACHI OF KONOHA.
...ALL... BEEN IN VAIN!
STRAIN...
SCUFF
SCUFF
UNTIL I BUILD... A TRUE VILLAGE...
...AND BECOME A TRUE KAGE...
...I'M...

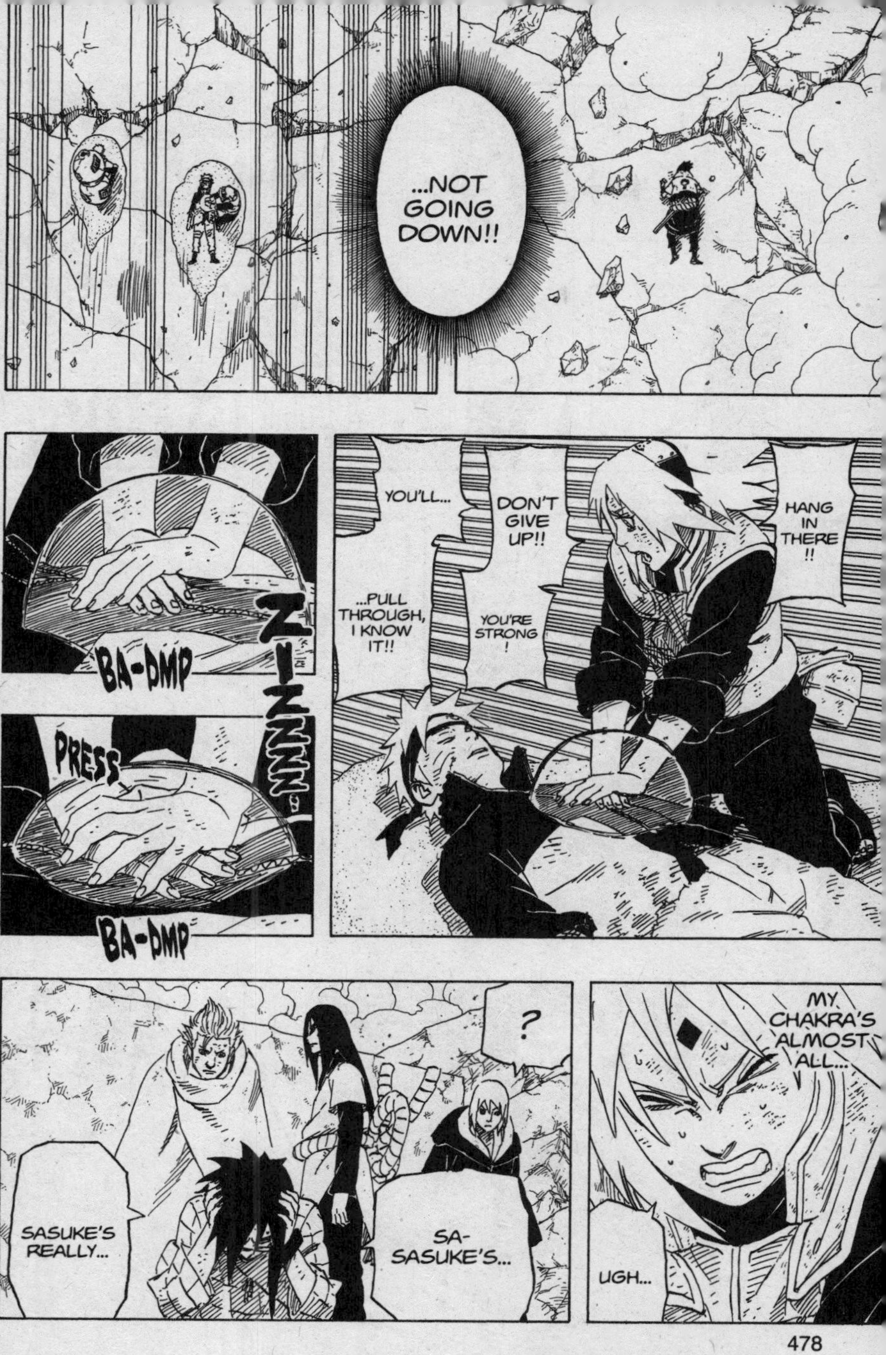
...NOT GOING DOWN!!
HANG IN THERE!!
DON'T GIVE UP!!
YOU'RE STRONG!
YOU'LL...
...PULL THROUGH, I KNOW IT!!
BA-DMP
ZIZNNN..
PRESS
BA-DMP
MY CHAKRA'S ALMOST ALL...
UGH...
?
SA-SASUKE'S...
SASUKE'S REALLY...

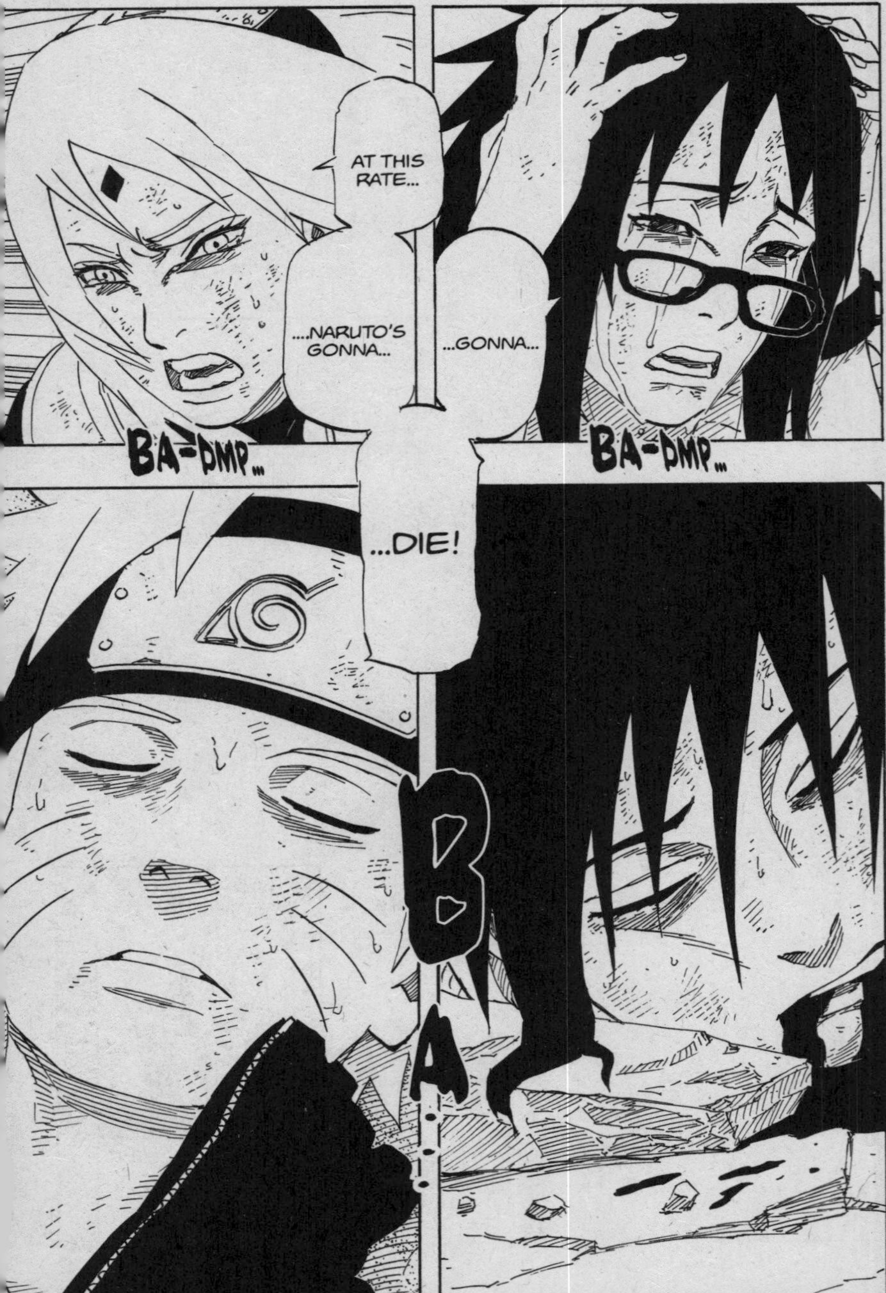
AT THIS RATE...
....NARUTO'S GONNA...
...GONNA...
BA-DMP...
BA-DMP...
...DIE!
BA...

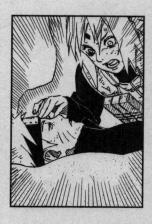

Number 663: No Matter What

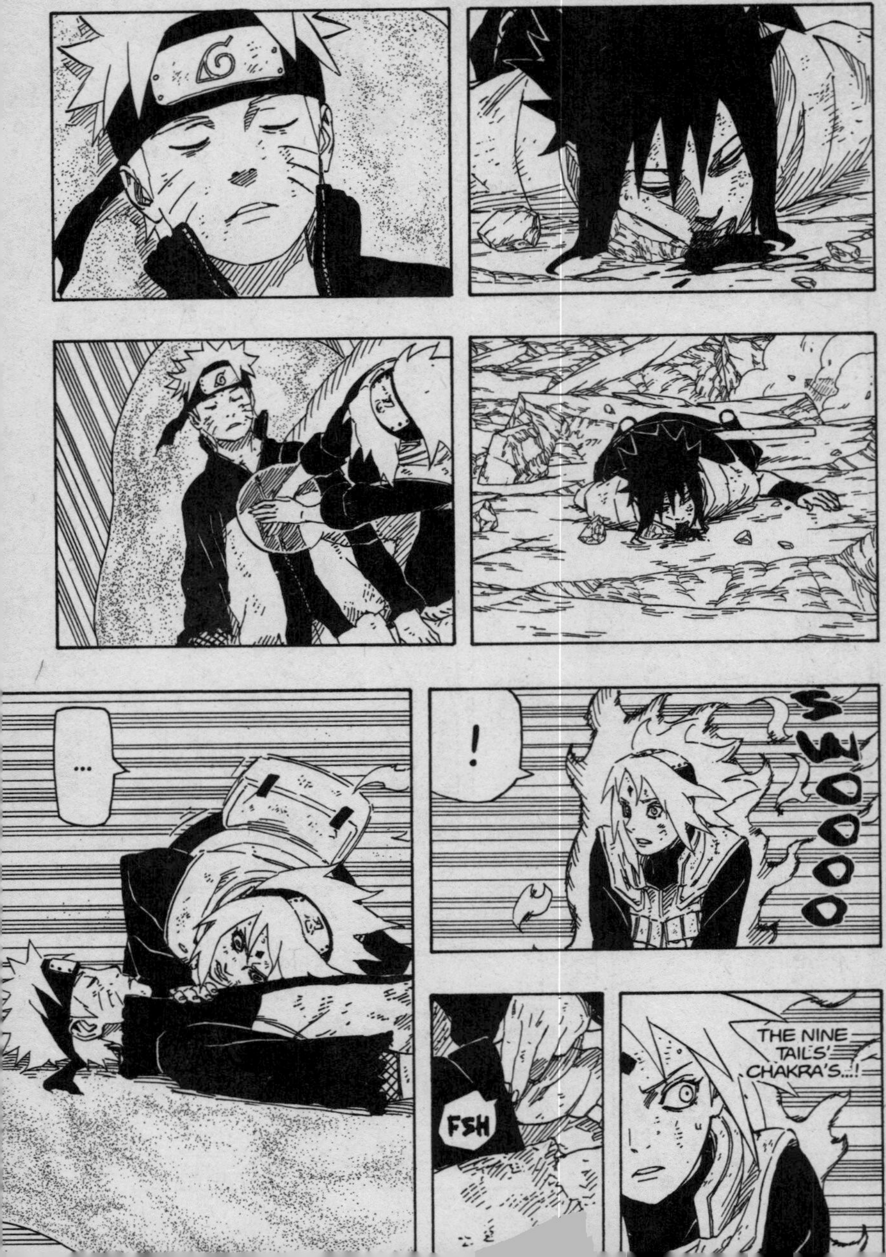
!
SWOOOO
...
THE NINE TAILS' CHAKRA'S...!
FSH

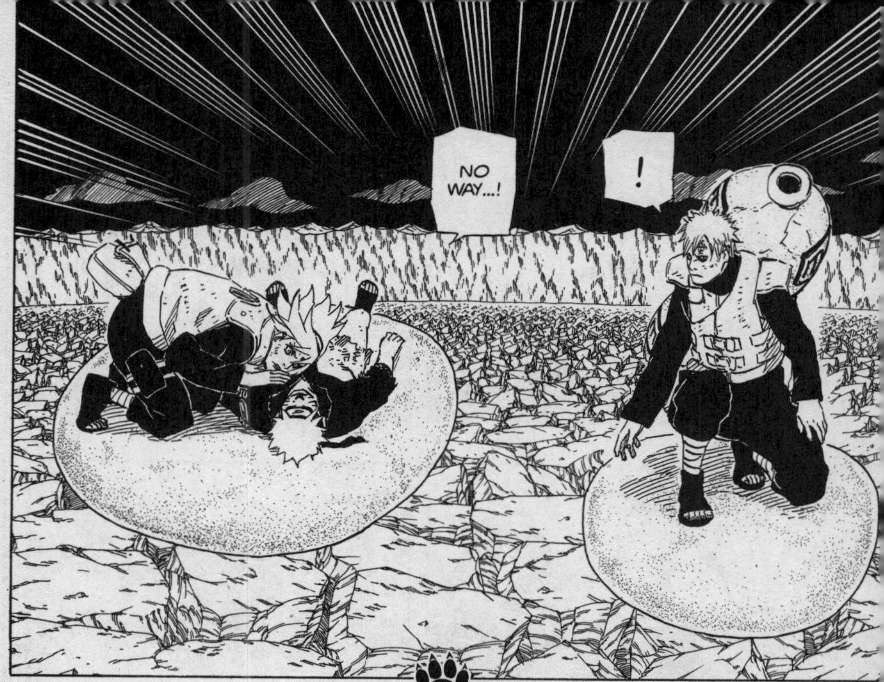
!
NO WAY...!

Number 663: No Matter What

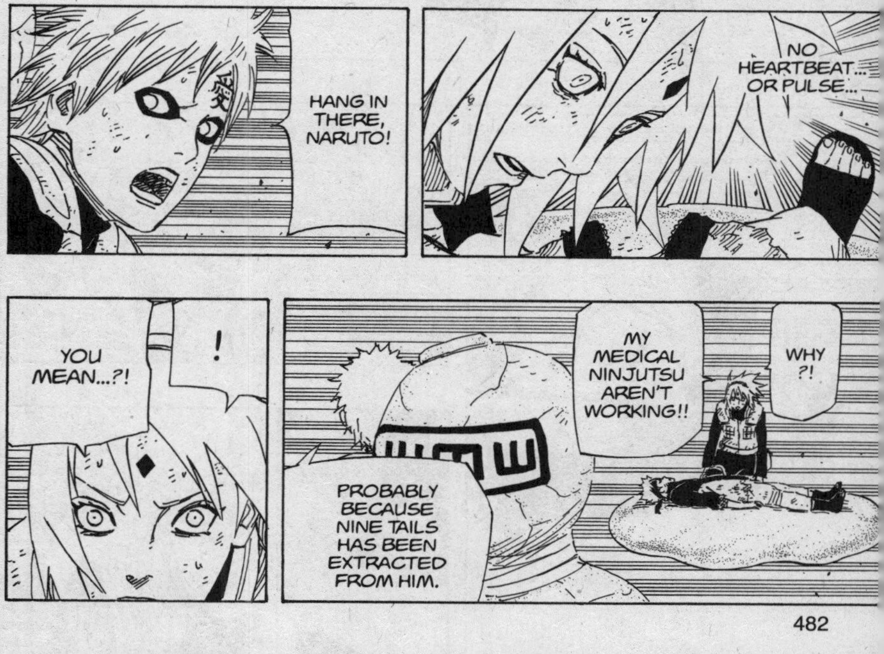
NO HEARTBEAT... OR PULSE...
HANG IN THERE, NARUTO!
WHY ?!
MY MEDICAL NINJUTSU AREN'T WORKING!!
PROBABLY BECAUSE NINE TAILS HAS BEEN EXTRACTED FROM HIM.
!
YOU MEAN...?!

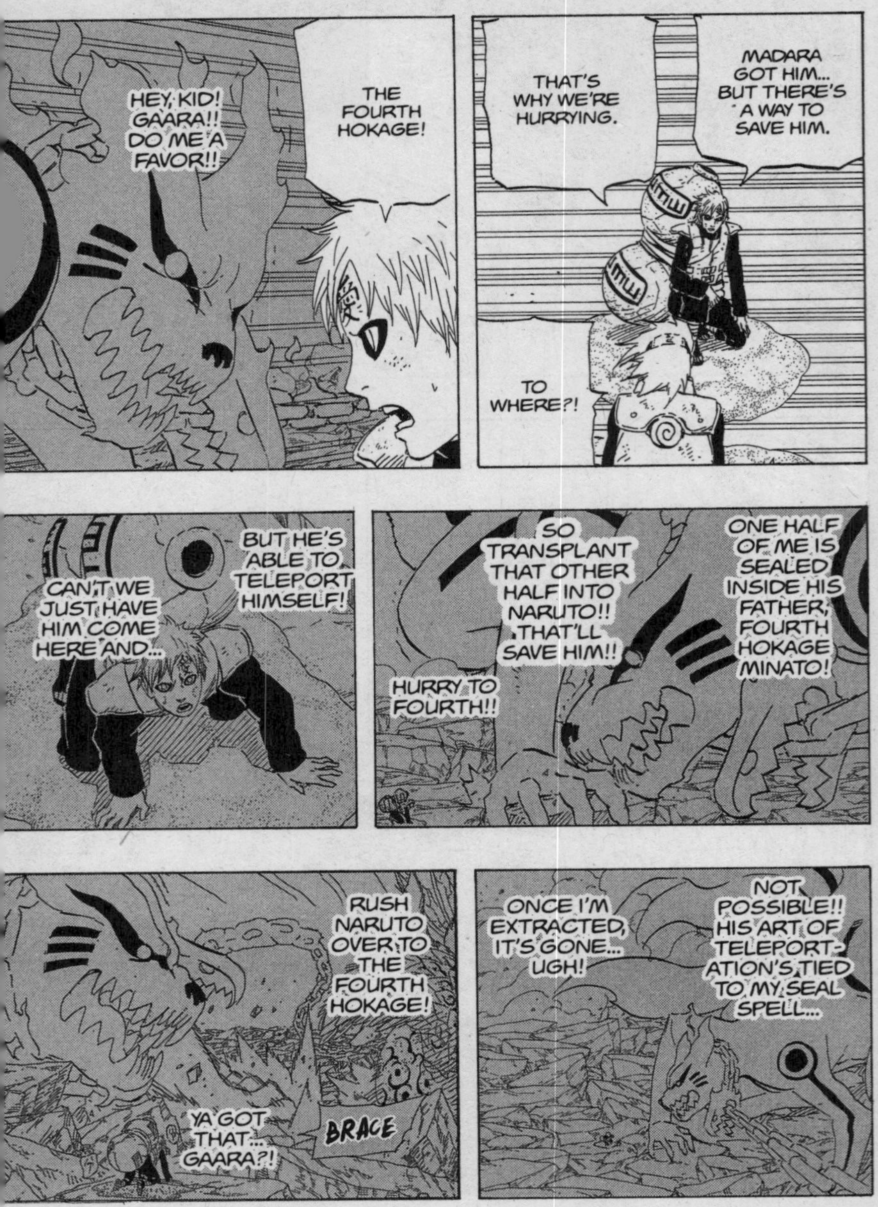
MADARA GOT HIM... BUT THERE'S A WAY TO SAVE HIM.
THAT'S WHY WE'RE HURRYING.
TO WHERE?!
THE FOURTH HOKAGE!
HEY, KID! GAARA!! DO ME A FAVOR!!
ONE HALF OF ME IS SEALED INSIDE HIS FATHER, FOURTH HOKAGE MINATO!
SO TRANSPLANT THAT OTHER HALF INTO NARUTO!! THAT'LL SAVE HIM!!
HURRY TO FOURTH!!
BUT HE'S ABLE TO TELEPORT HIMSELF!
CAN'T WE JUST HAVE HIM COME HERE AND...
NOT POSSIBLE!! HIS ART OF TELEPORT-ATION'S TIED TO MY SEAL SPELL...
ONCE I'M EXTRACTED, IT'S GONE... UGH!
RUSH NARUTO OVER TO THE FOURTH HOKAGE!
BRACE
YA GOT THAT... GAARA?!

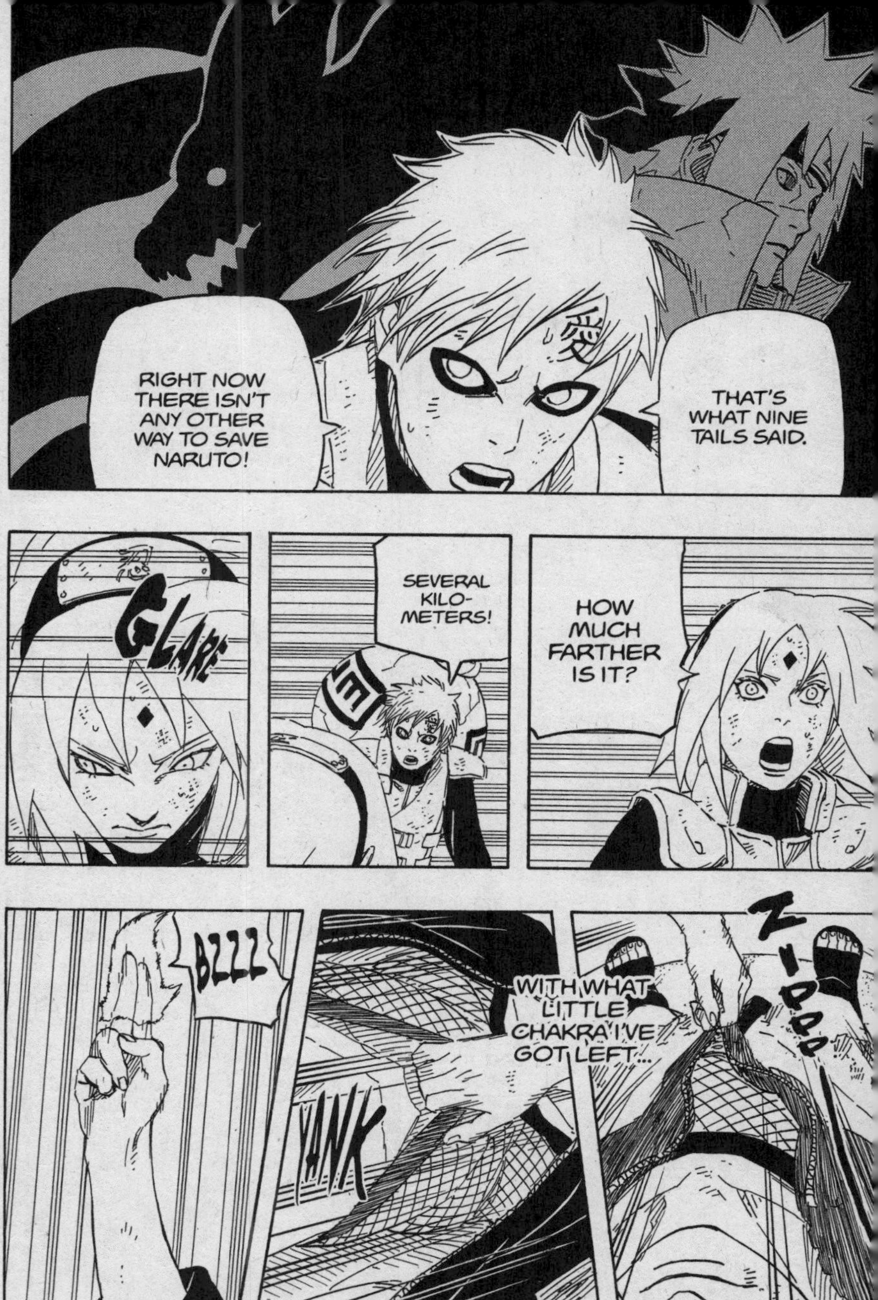
THAT'S WHAT NINE TAILS SAID.
RIGHT NOW THERE ISN'T ANY OTHER WAY TO SAVE NARUTO!
HOW MUCH FARTHER IS IT?
SEVERAL KILO-METERS!
GLARE
ZIPPP
WITH WHAT LITTLE CHAKRA I'VE GOT LEFT...
YANK
BZZZ

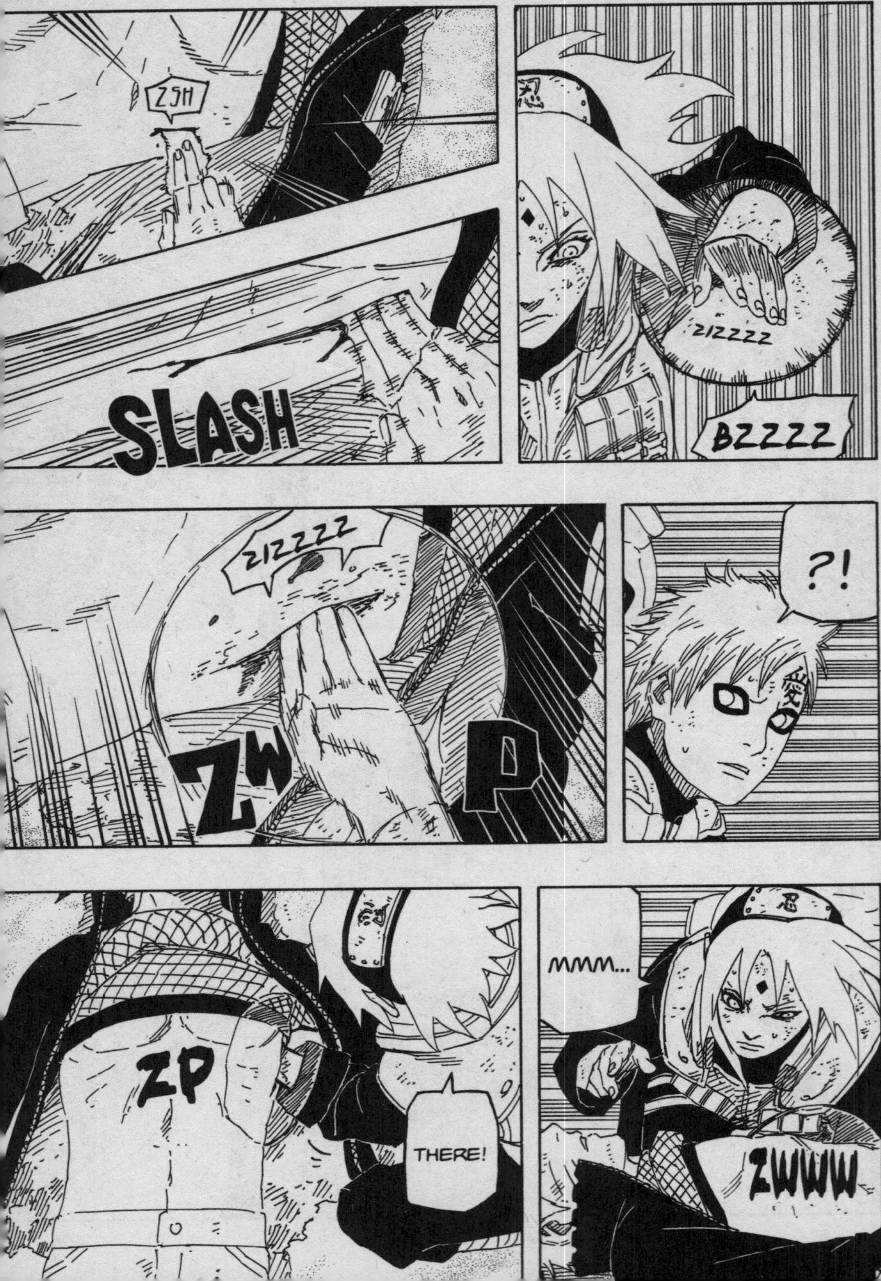
ZIZZZZ
BZZZZ
ZSH
SLASH
?!
ZIZZZZ
ZWP
MMM...
ZWWW
ZP
THERE!

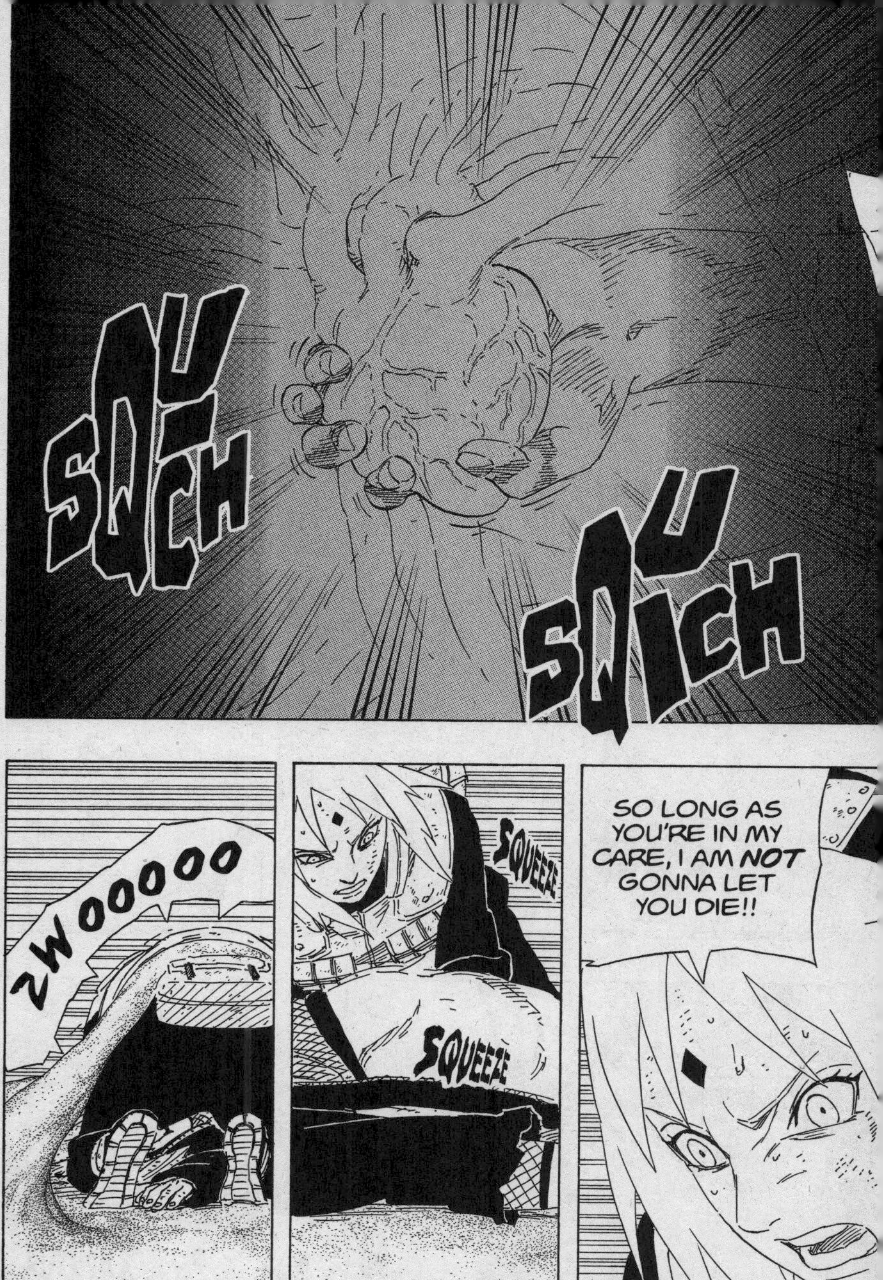
SQUICH
SQUICH
SO LONG AS YOU'RE IN MY CARE, I AM NOT GONNA LET YOU DIE!!
SQUEEZE
SQUEEZE
ZWOOOOO

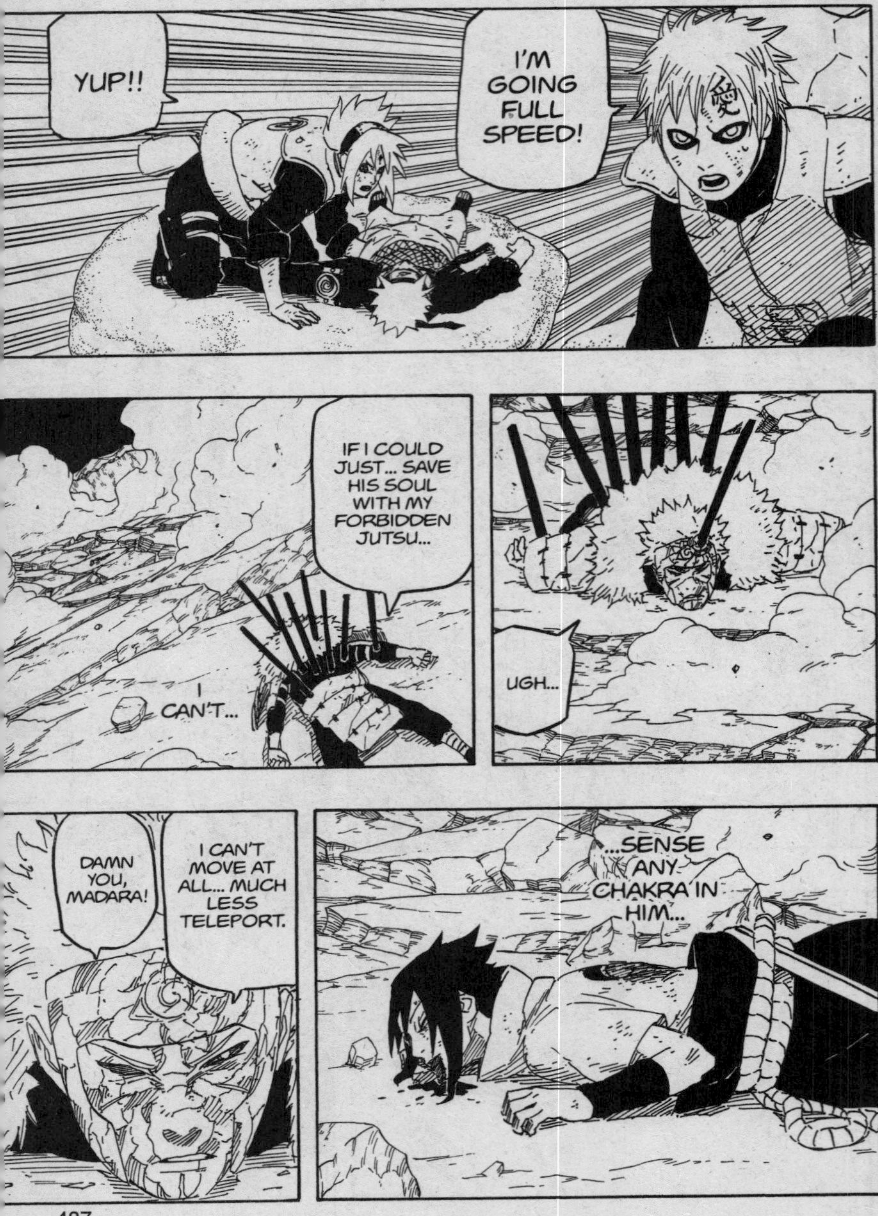
I'M GOING FULL SPEED!
YUP!!
UGH...
IF I COULD JUST... SAVE HIS SOUL WITH MY FORBIDDEN JUTSU...
I CAN'T...
...SENSE ANY CHAKRA IN HIM...
I CAN'T MOVE AT ALL... MUCH LESS TELEPORT.
DAMN YOU, MADARA!

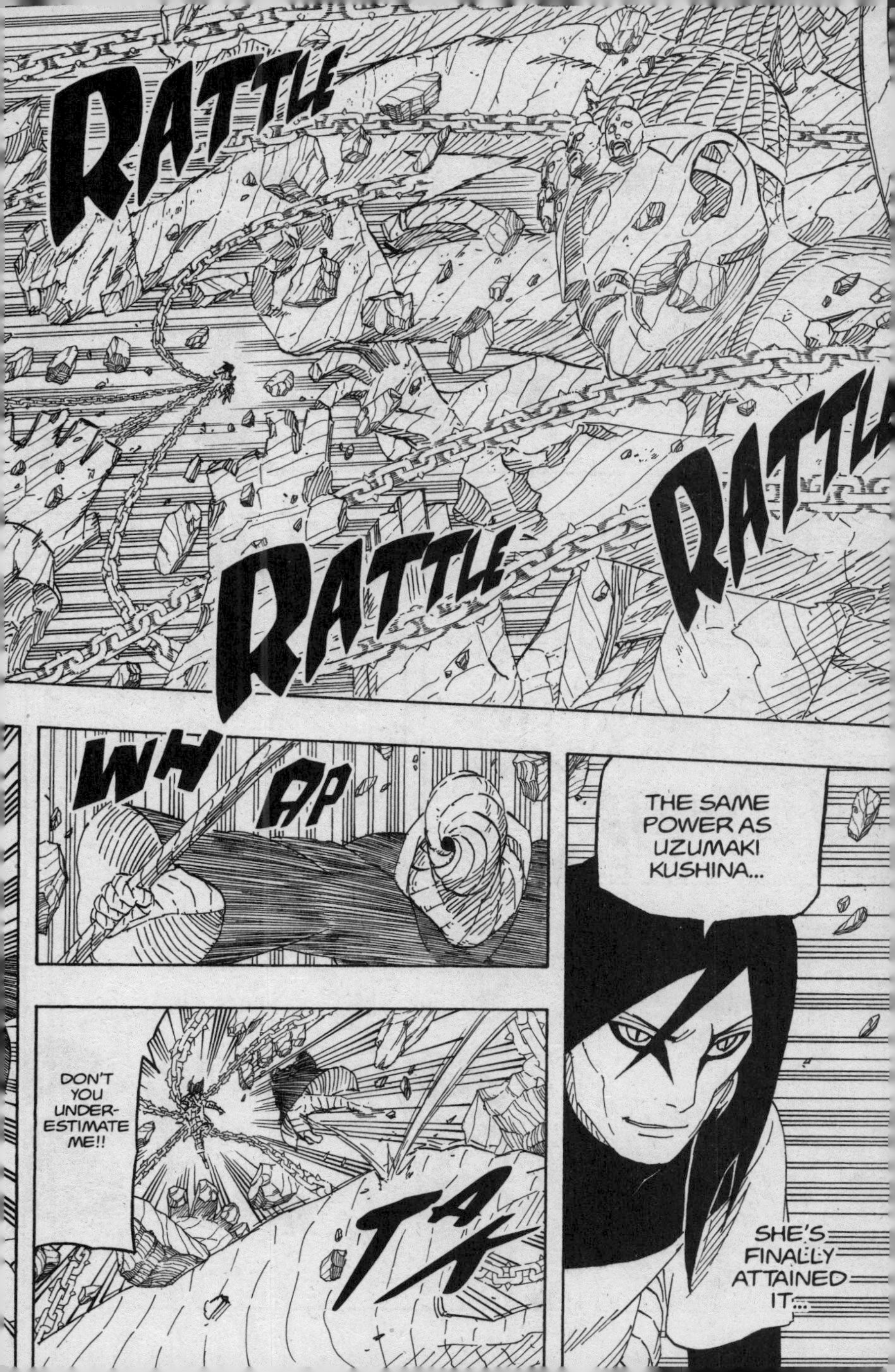
RATTLE
RATTLE
RATTLE
THE SAME POWER AS UZUMAKI KUSHINA...
SHE'S FINALLY ATTAINED IT...
WH AP
DON'T YOU UNDER-ESTIMATE ME!!
TA

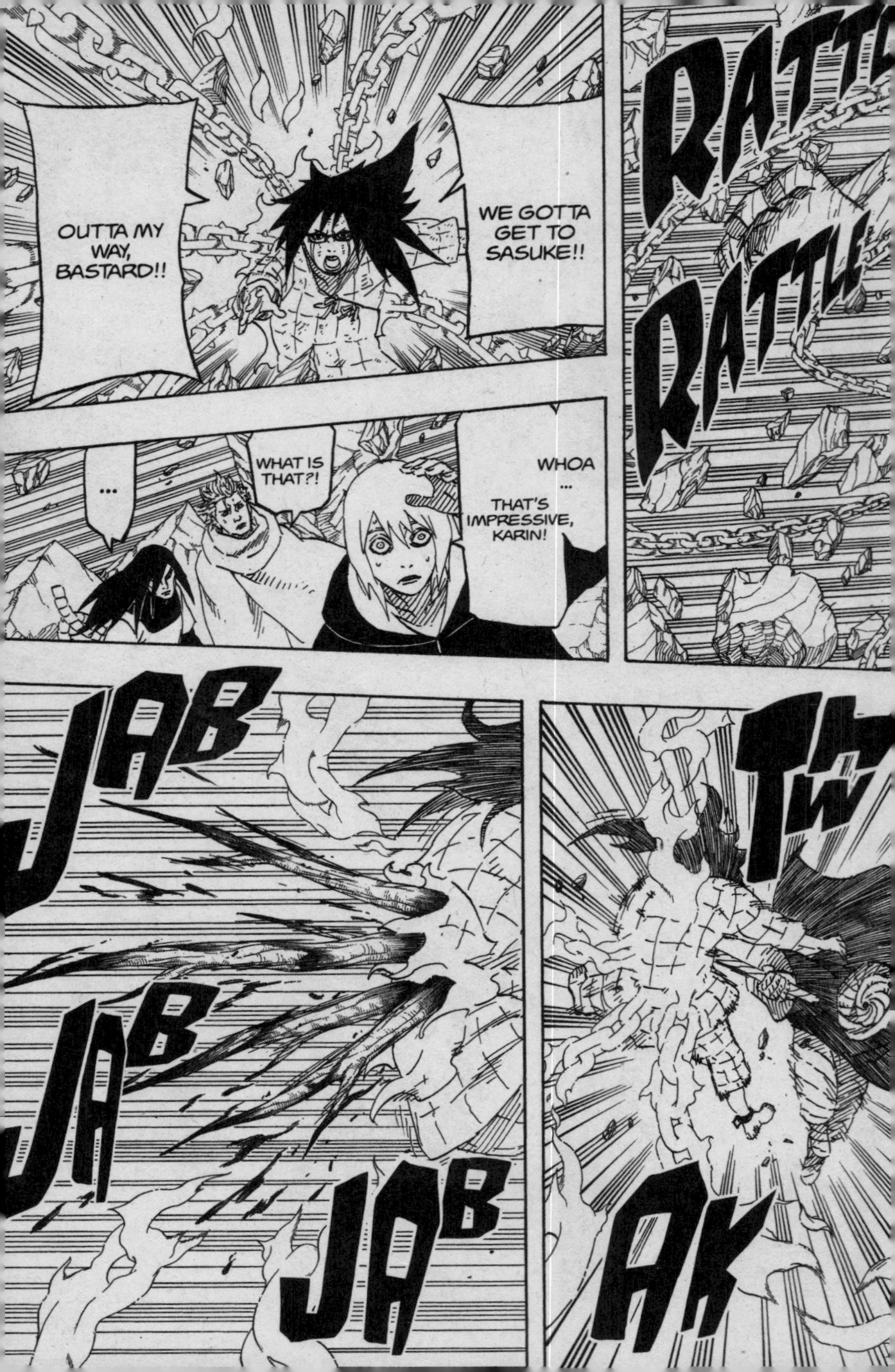
RATTL
RATTLE
WE GOTTA GET TO SASUKE!!
OUTTA MY WAY, BASTARD!!
WHOA ... THAT'S IMPRESSIVE, KARIN!
WHAT IS THAT?!
...
TWAK
JAB
JAB
JAB

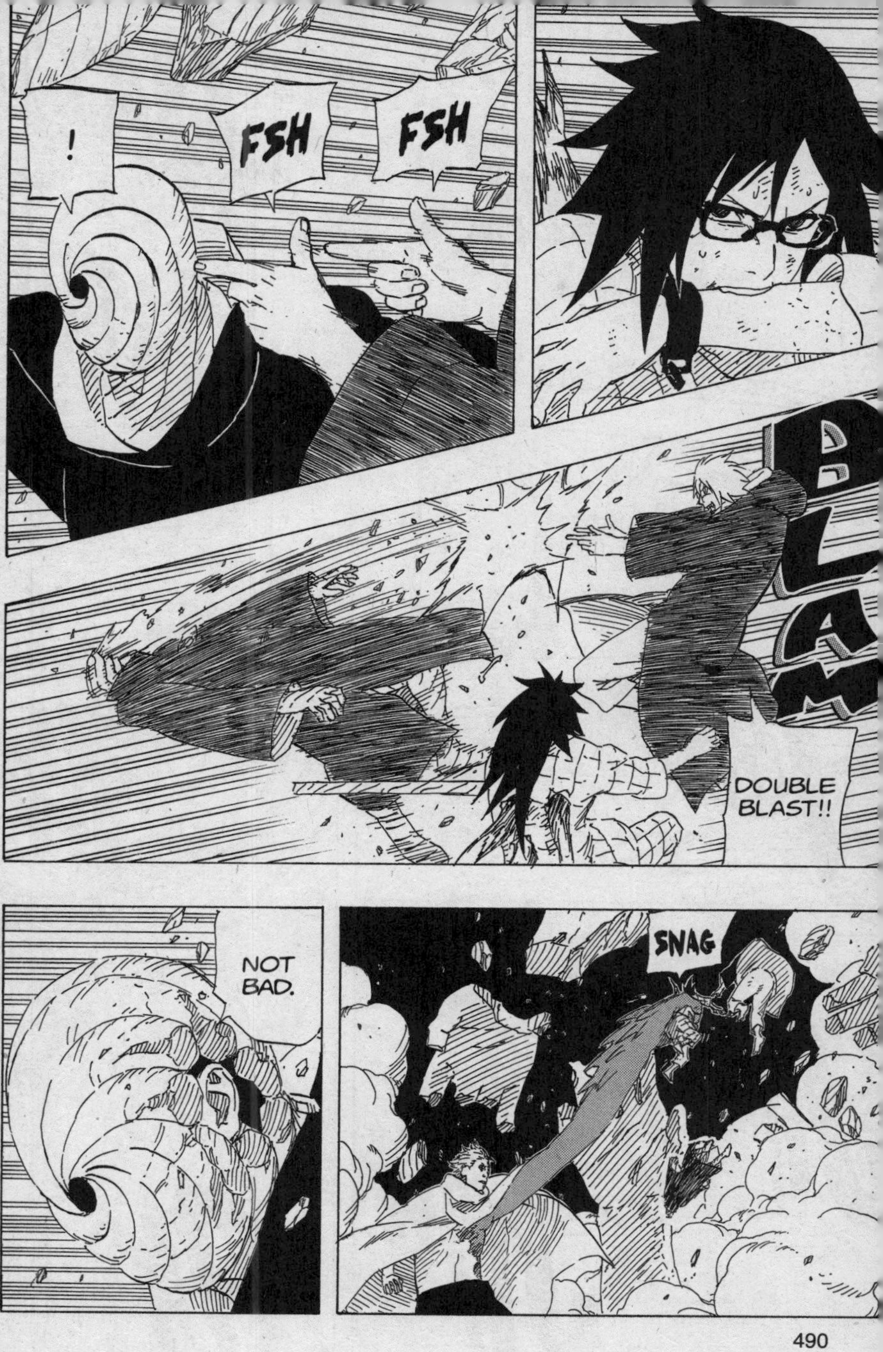
FSH
FSH
!
BLAM
DOUBLE BLAST!!
SNAG
NOT BAD.

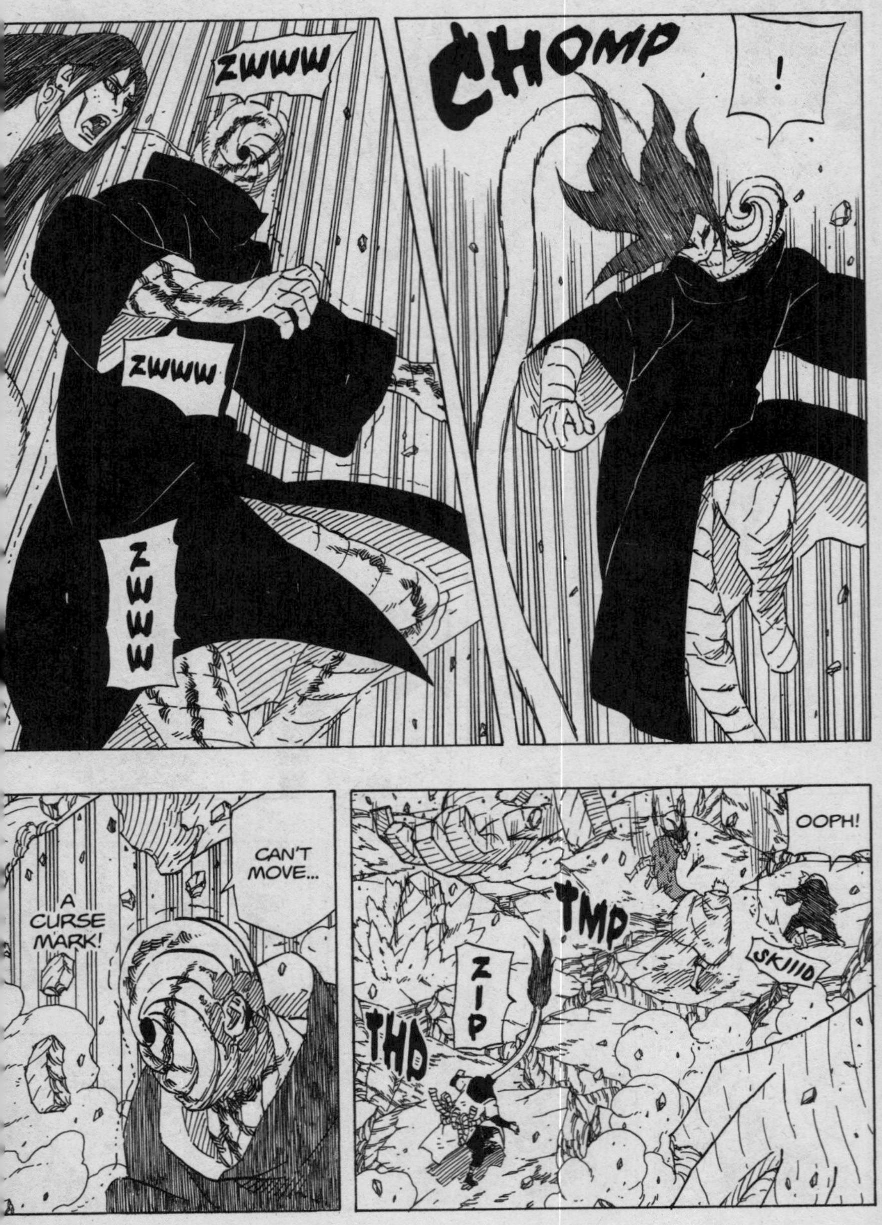
!
CHOMP
ZWWW
ZWWW
ZWWW
OOPH!
SKJIID
TMP
ZIP
THD
CAN'T MOVE...
A CURSE MARK!

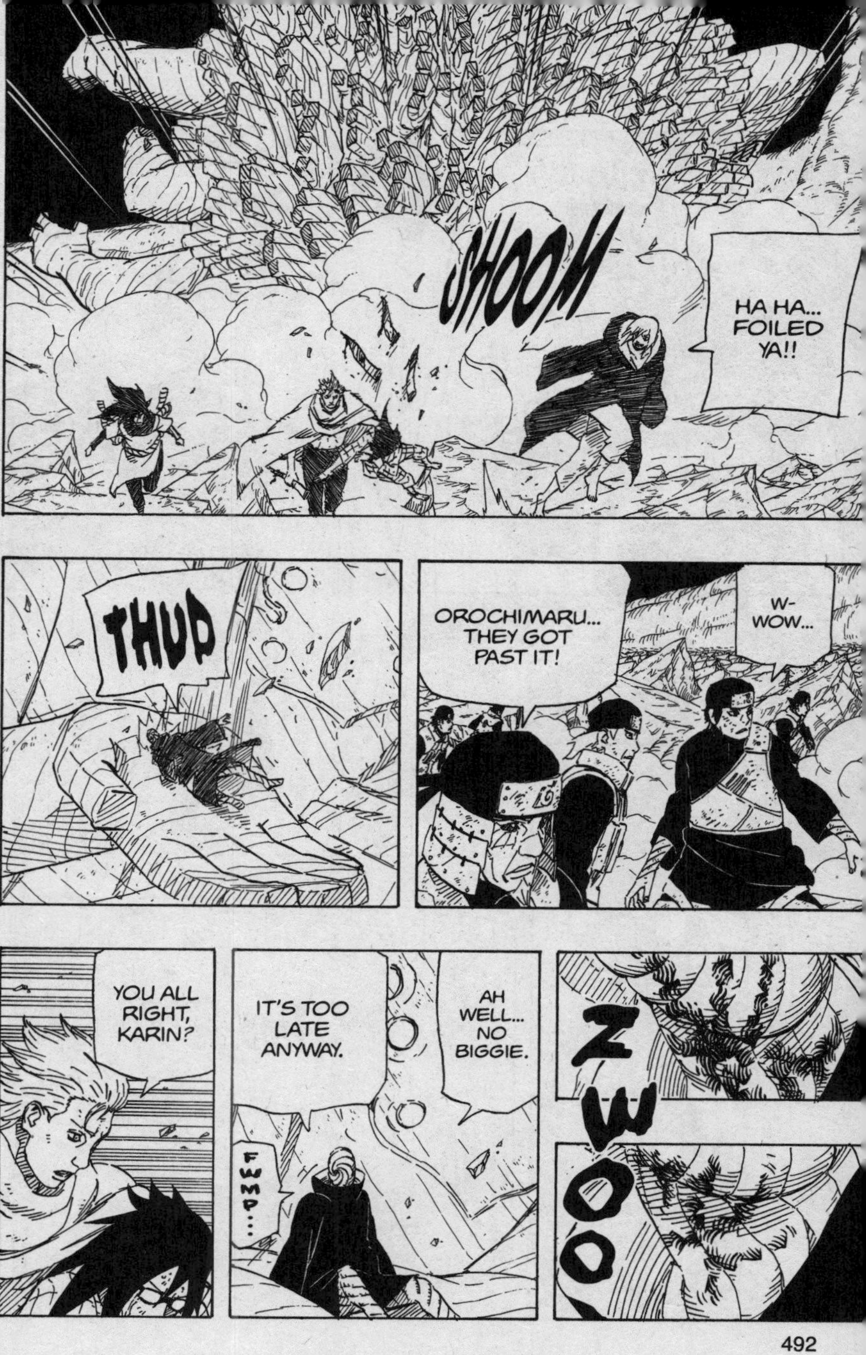
HA HA... FOILED YA!!
SHOOM
W- WOW...
OROCHIMARU... THEY GOT PAST IT!
THUD
ZWOO
AH WELL... NO BIGGIE.
IT'S TOO LATE ANYWAY.
FWMP...
YOU ALL RIGHT, KARIN?

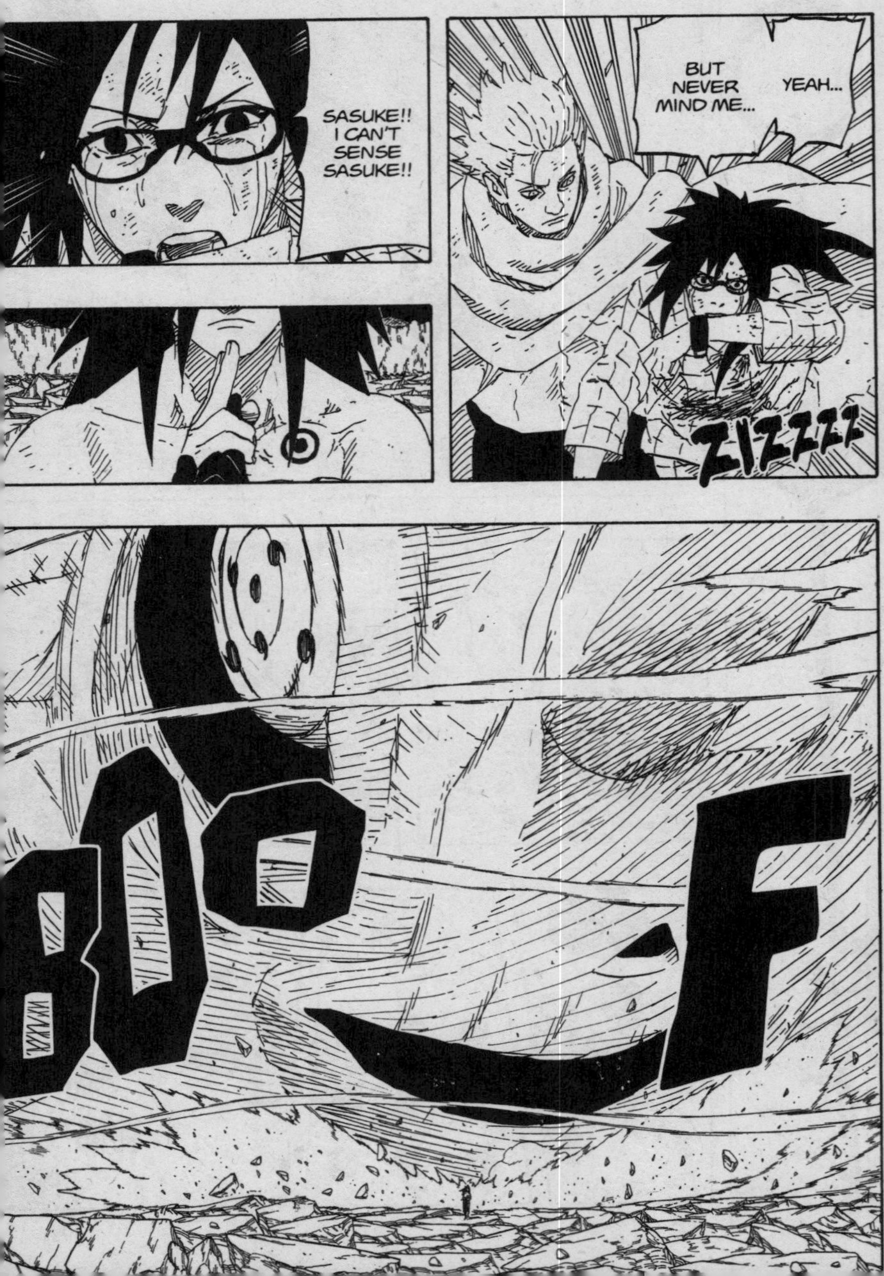
YEAH...
BUT NEVER MIND ME...
ZIZZZZ
SASUKE!! I CAN'T SENSE SASUKE!!
BOOF

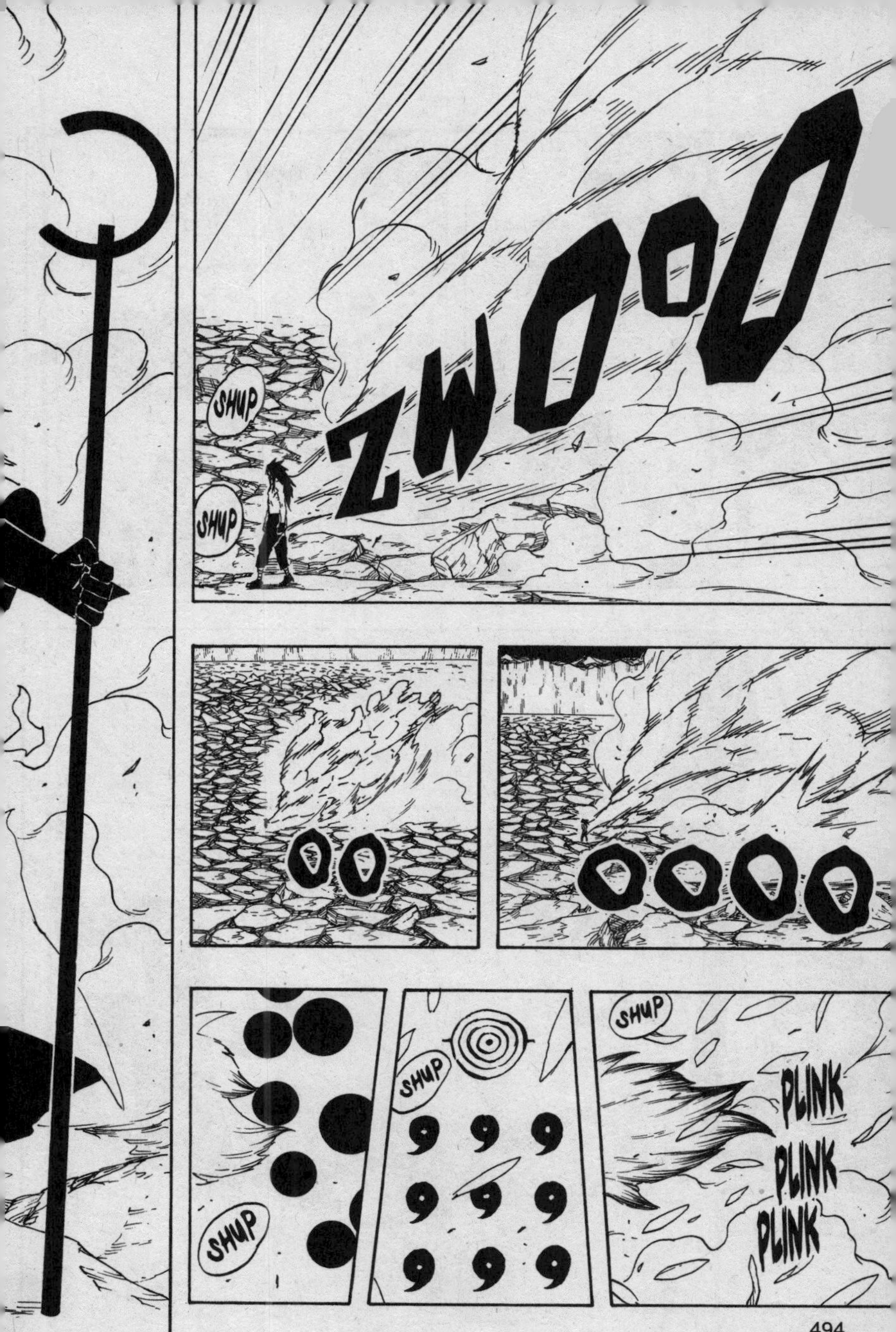
ZWOOOO
SHUP
SHUP
SHUP
PLINK
PLINK
PLINK
SHUP
SHUP

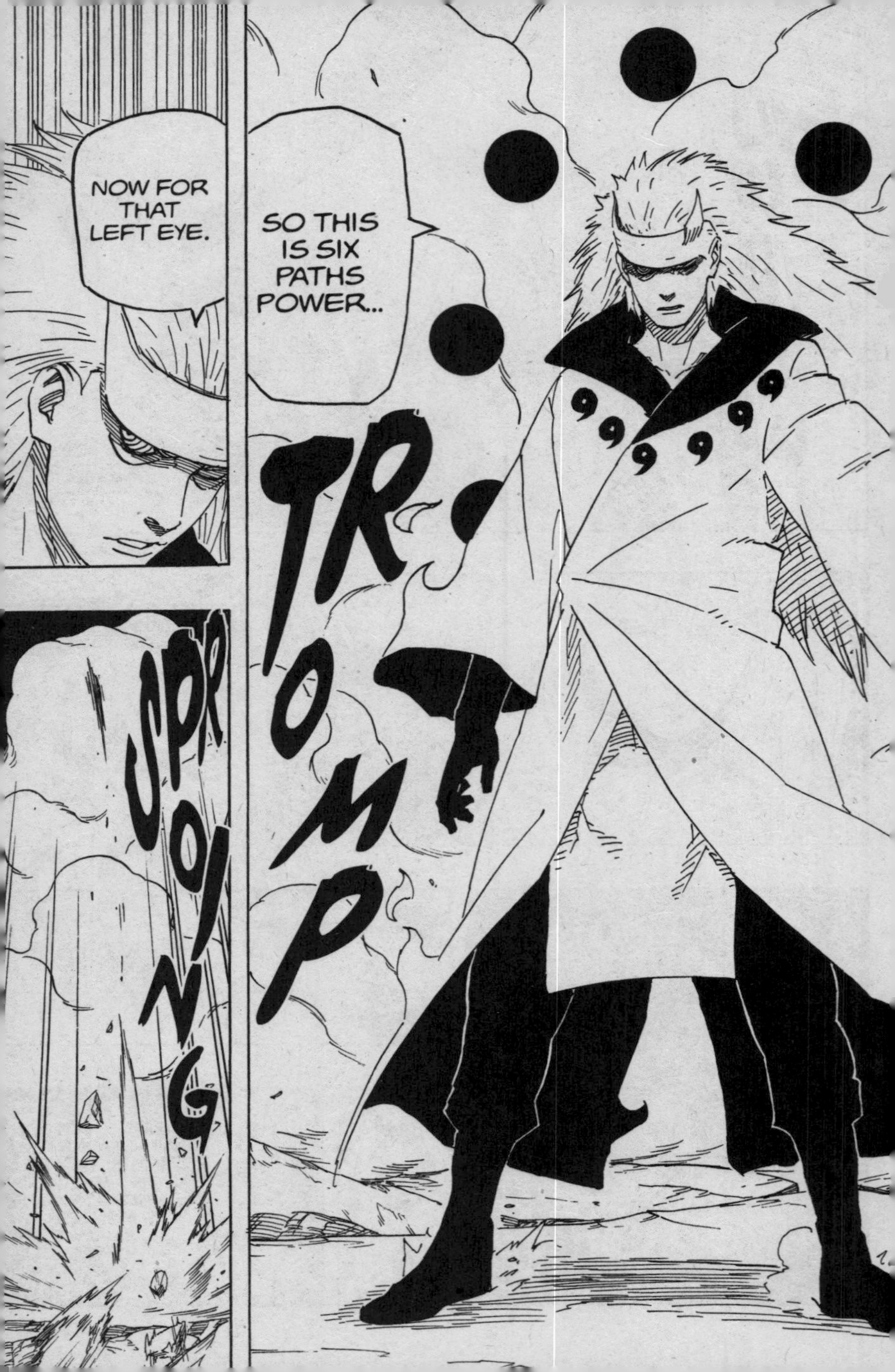
SO THIS IS SIX PATHS POWER...
TROMP
NOW FOR THAT LEFT EYE.
SPROING

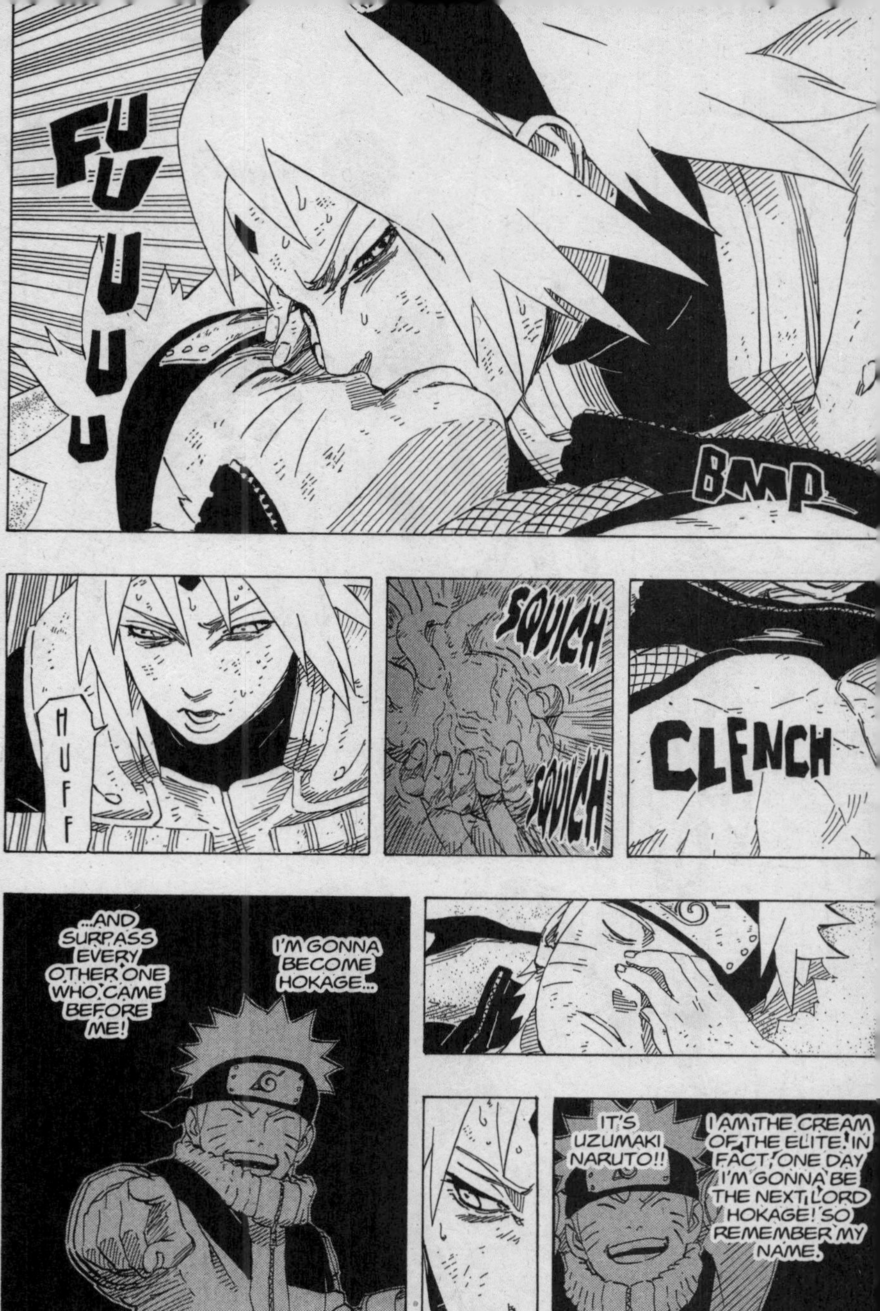
FUUUUU
BMP
CLENCH
SQUICH
SQUICH
HUFF
I AM THE CREAM OF THE ELITE. IN FACT, ONE DAY I'M GONNA BE THE NEXT LORD HOKAGE! SO REMEMBER MY NAME.
IT'S UZUMAKI NARUTO!!
I'M GONNA BECOME HOKAGE...
...AND SURPASS EVERY OTHER ONE WHO CAME BEFORE ME!

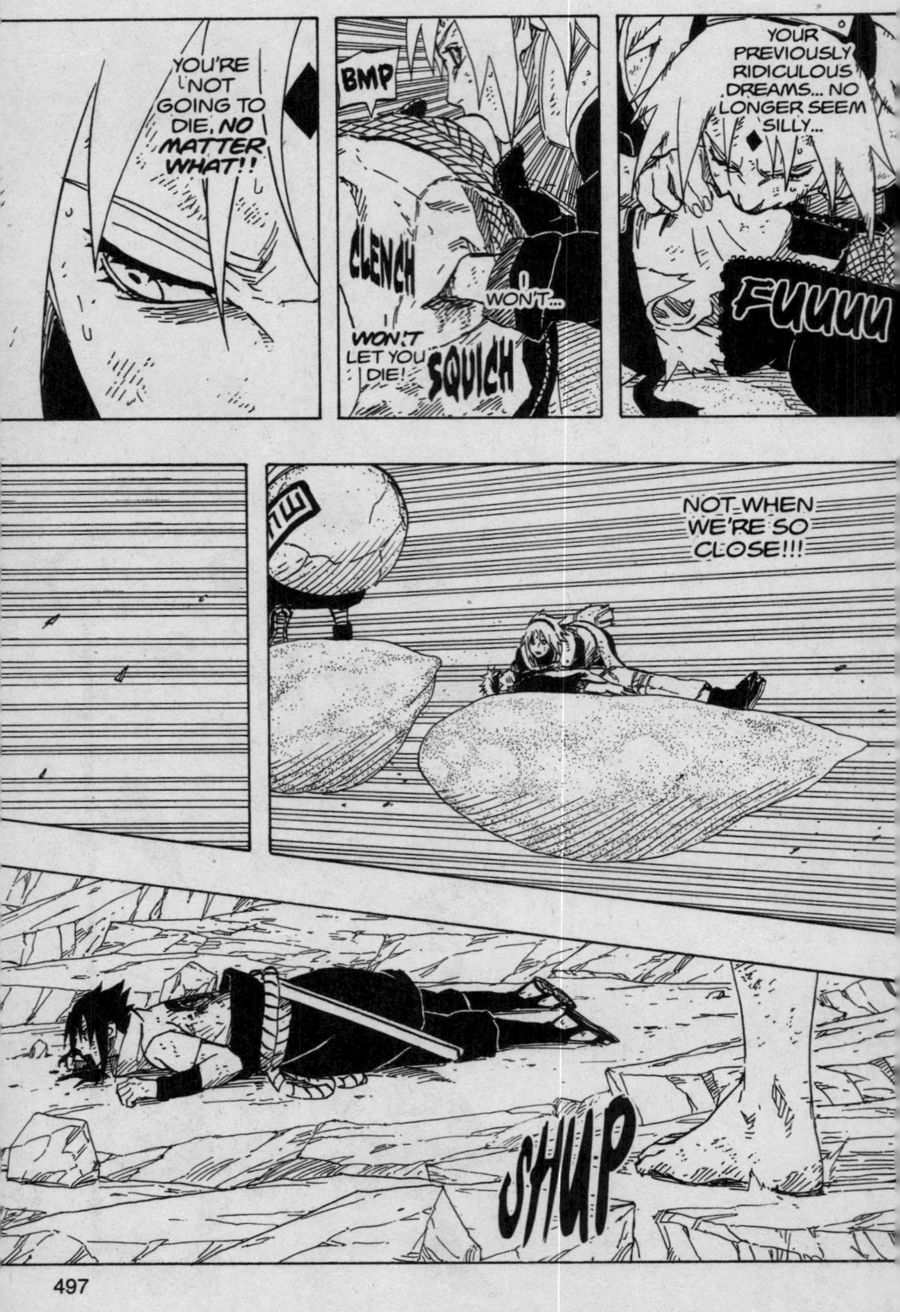
YOUR PREVIOUSLY RIDICULOUS DREAMS... NO LONGER SEEM SILLY...
FUUUU
BMP
CLENCH
I WON'T...
WON'T LET YOU DIE!
SQUICH
YOU'RE NOT GOING TO DIE, NO MATTER WHAT!!
NOT WHEN WE'RE SO CLOSE!!!
SHUP

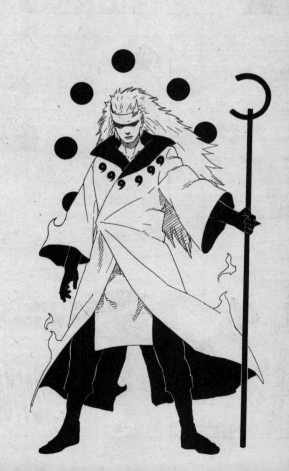

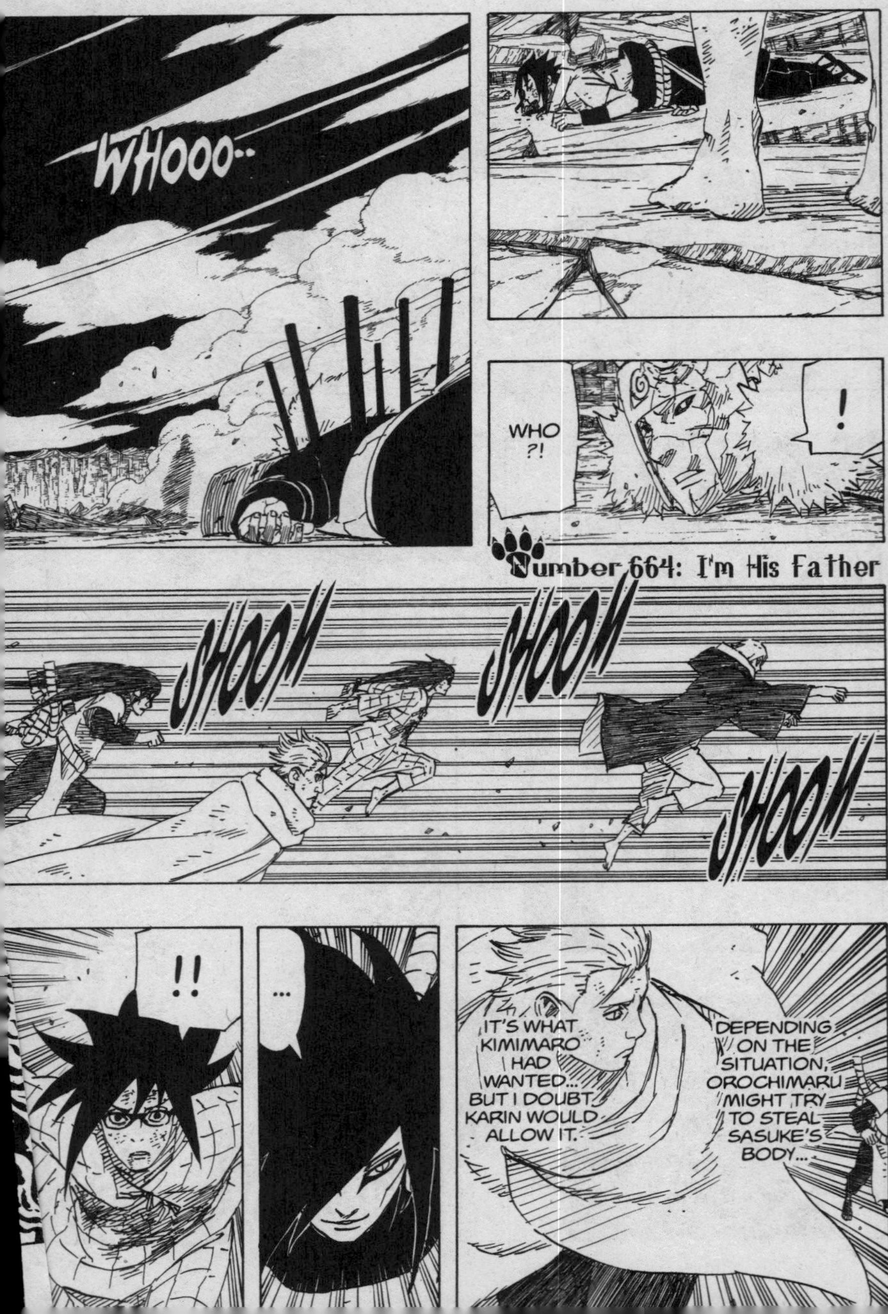
!
WHO ?!
WHOOO..
Number 664: I'm His Father
SHOOM
SHOOM
SHOOM
DEPENDING ON THE SITUATION, OROCHIMARU MIGHT TRY TO STEAL SASUKE'S BODY...
IT'S WHAT KIMIMARO HAD WANTED... BUT I DOUBT KARIN WOULD ALLOW IT.
...
!!

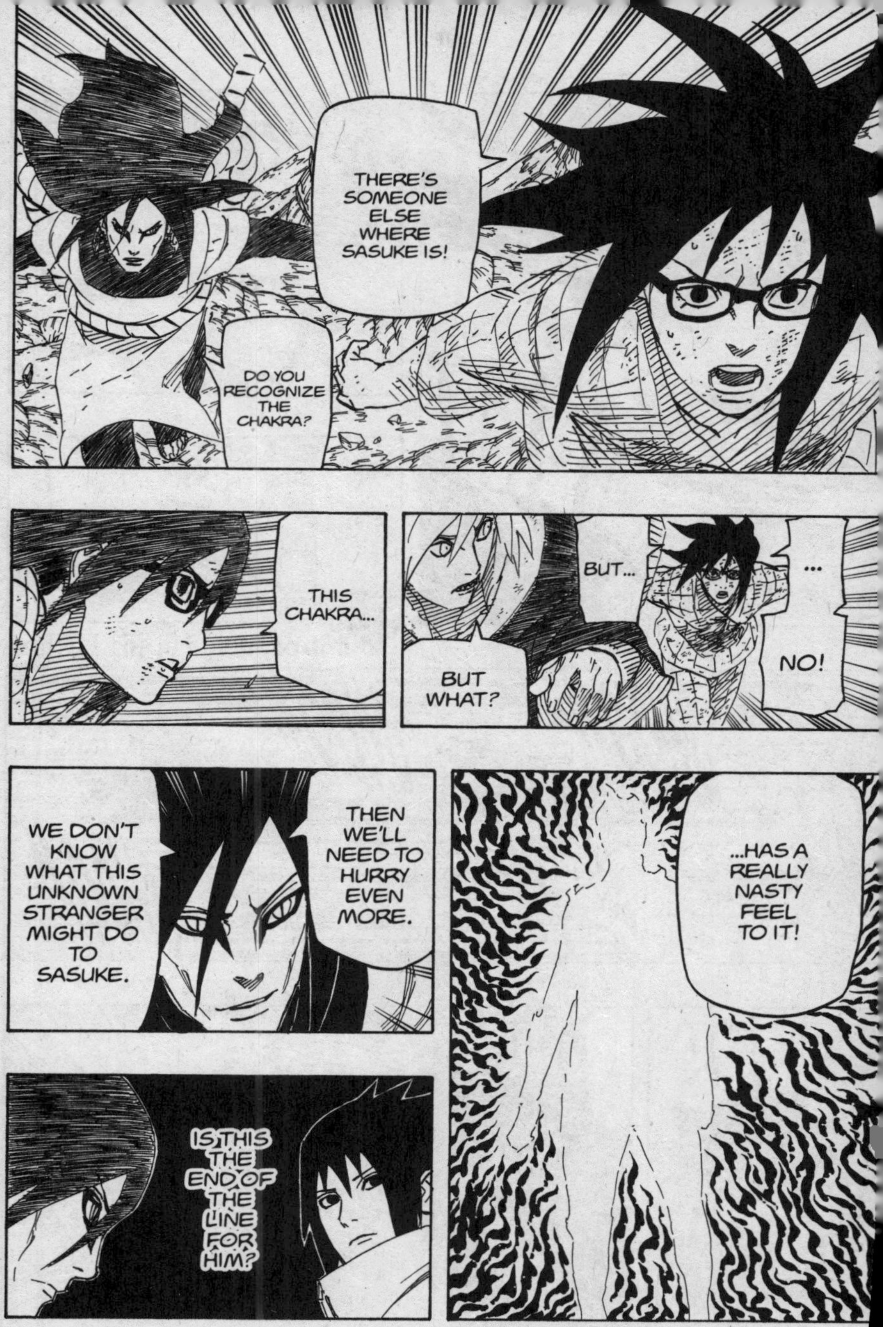
THERE'S SOMEONE ELSE WHERE SASUKE IS!
DO YOU RECOGNIZE THE CHAKRA?
...
BUT...
NO!
BUT WHAT?
THIS CHAKRA...
...HAS A REALLY NASTY FEEL TO IT!
THEN WE'LL NEED TO HURRY EVEN MORE.
WE DON'T KNOW WHAT THIS UNKNOWN STRANGER MIGHT DO TO SASUKE.
IS THIS THE END OF THE LINE FOR HIM?

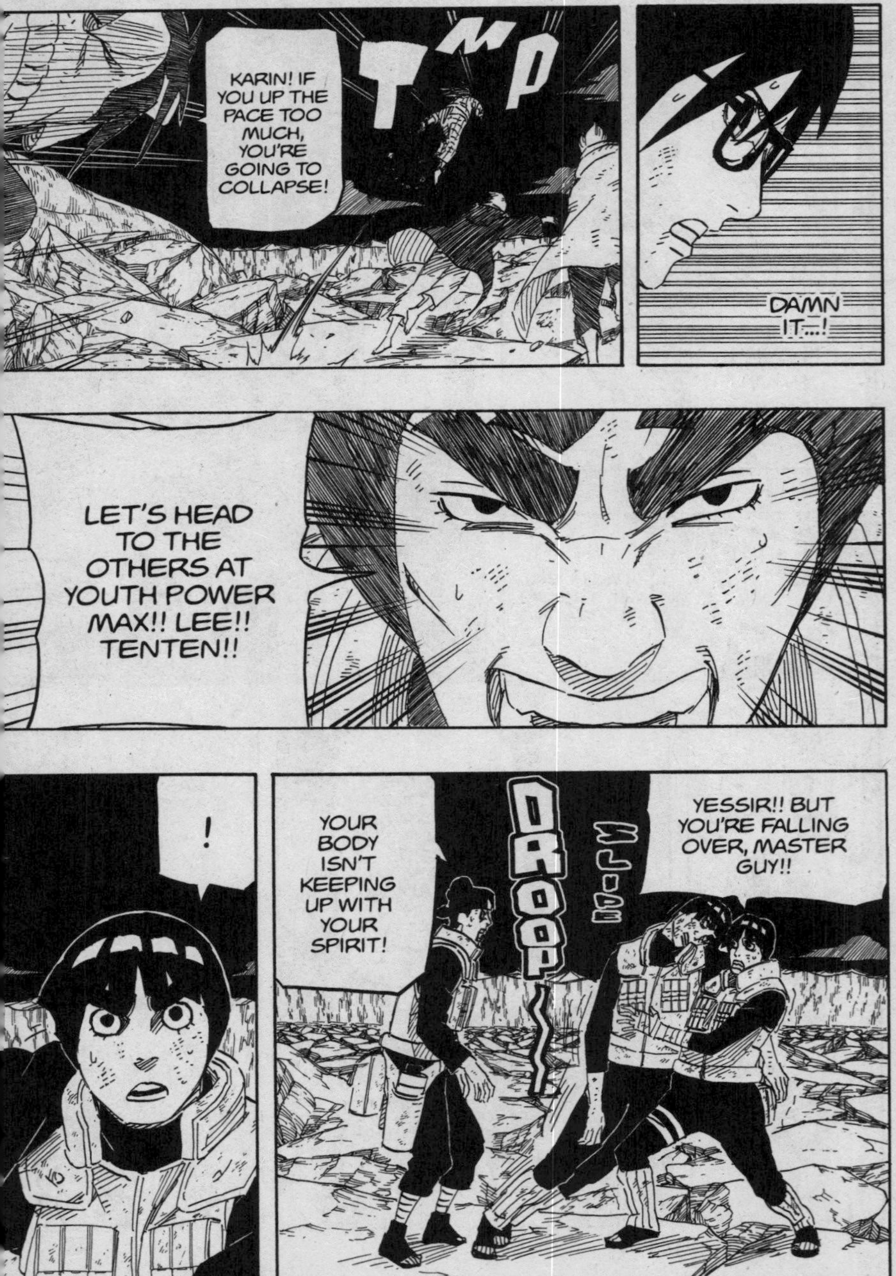
DAMN IT...!
TMP
KARIN! IF YOU UP THE PACE TOO MUCH, YOU'RE GOING TO COLLAPSE!
LET'S HEAD TO THE OTHERS AT YOUTH POWER MAX!! LEE!! TENTEN!!
YESSIR!! BUT YOU'RE FALLING OVER, MASTER GUY!!
SLIDE
DROOP
YOUR BODY ISN'T KEEPING UP WITH YOUR SPIRIT!
!

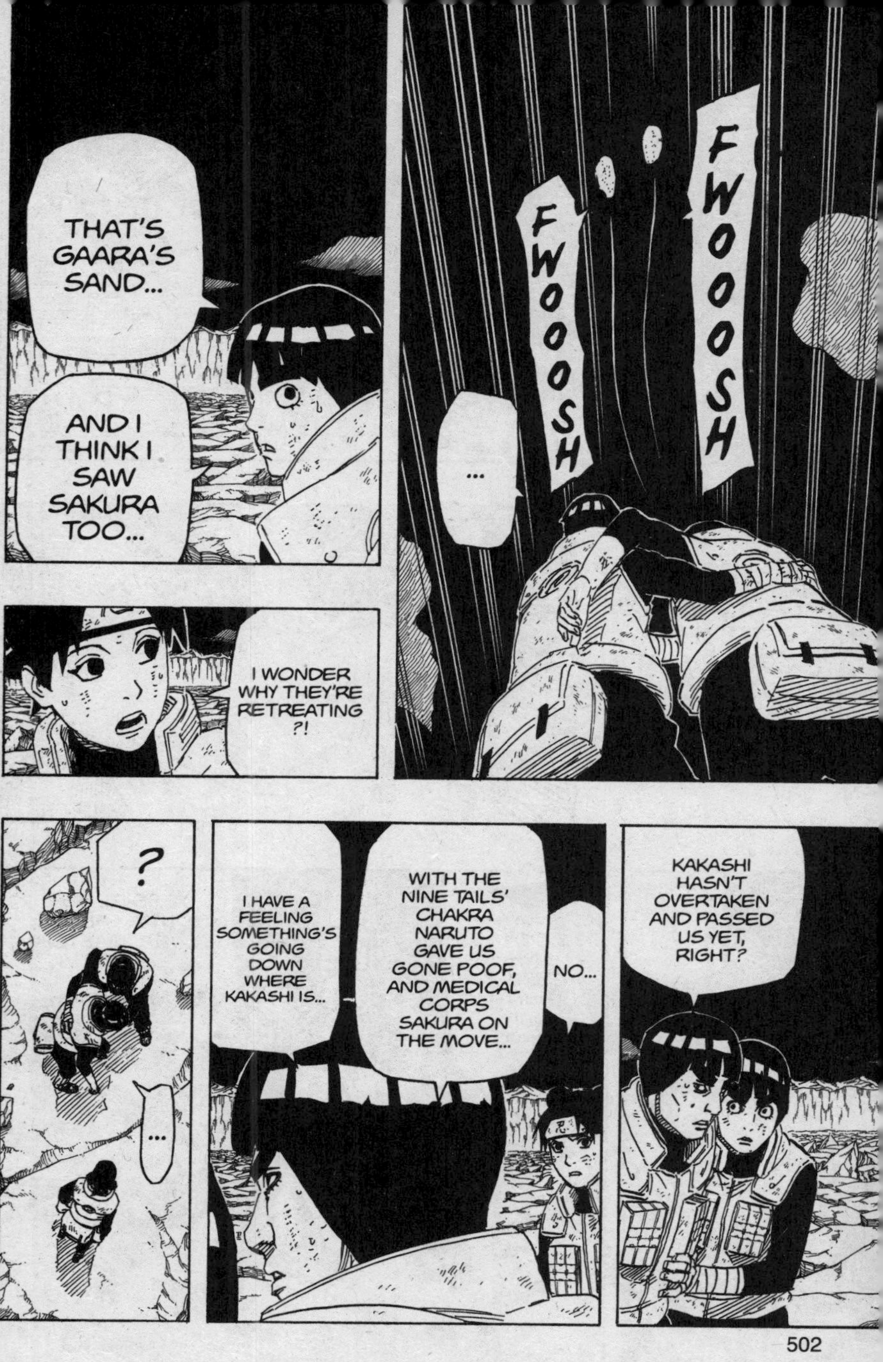
FWOOOSH
FWOOOSH
...
THAT'S GAARA'S SAND...
AND I THINK I SAW SAKURA TOO...
I WONDER WHY THEY'RE RETREATING ?!
KAKASHI HASN'T OVERTAKEN AND PASSED US YET, RIGHT?
NO...
WITH THE NINE TAILS' CHAKRA NARUTO GAVE US GONE POOF, AND MEDICAL CORPS SAKURA ON THE MOVE...
I HAVE A FEELING SOMETHING'S GOING DOWN WHERE KAKASHI IS...
?
...

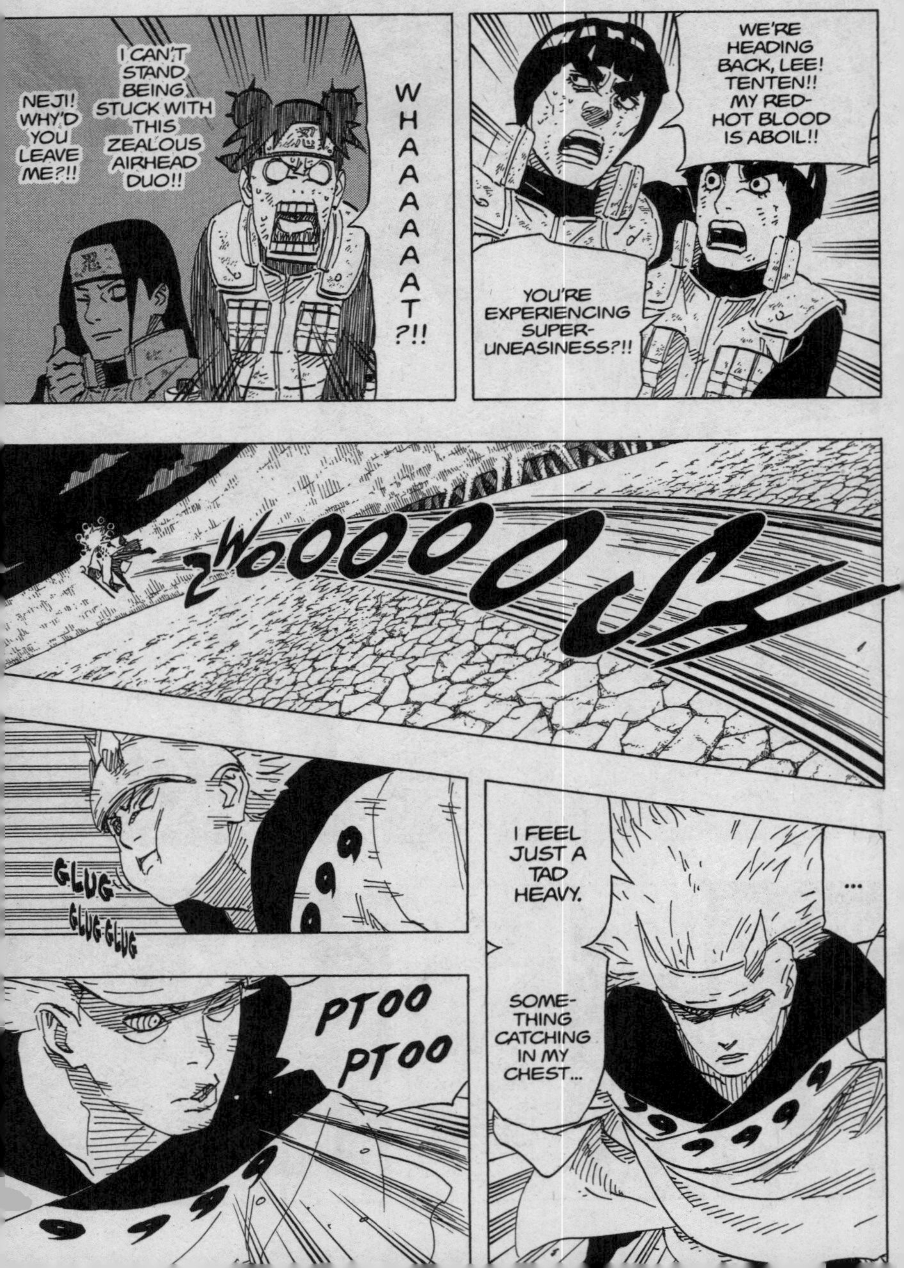
WE'RE HEADING BACK, LEE! TENTEN!! MY RED-HOT BLOOD IS ABOIL!!
YOU'RE EXPERIENCING SUPER-UNEASINESS?!!
WHAAAAAAAT?!!
I CAN'T STAND BEING STUCK WITH THIS ZEALOUS AIRHEAD DUO!!
NEJI! WHY'D YOU LEAVE ME?!!
ZWOOOOOOSH
...
I FEEL JUST A TAD HEAVY.
SOME-THING CATCHING IN MY CHEST...
GLUG
GLUG GLUG
PTOO
PTOO

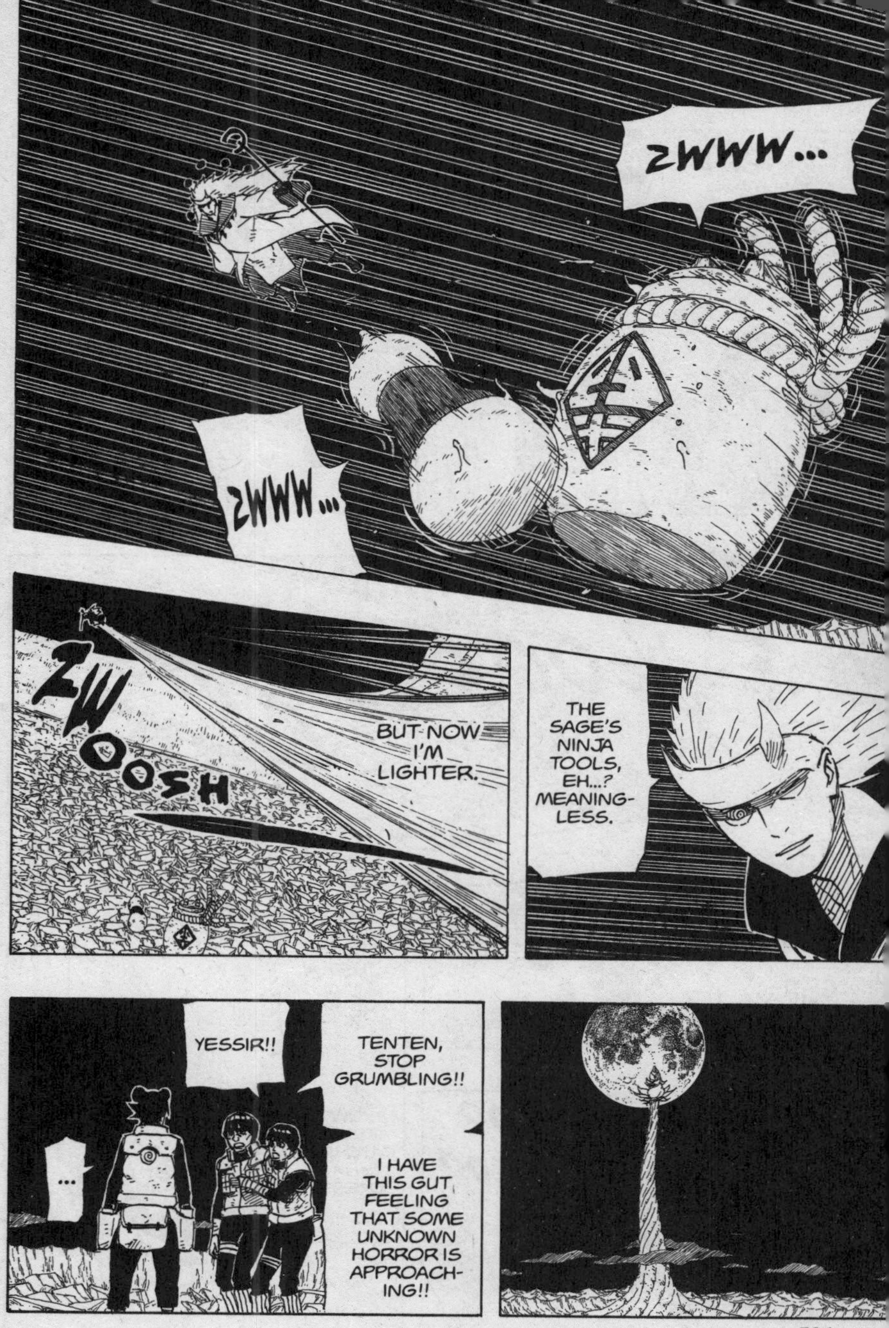
ZWWW...
ZWWW...
THE SAGE'S NINJA TOOLS, EH...? MEANINGLESS.
BUT NOW I'M LIGHTER.
ZWOOSH
TENTEN, STOP GRUMBLING!!
I HAVE THIS GUT FEELING THAT SOME UNKNOWN HORROR IS APPROACHING!!
YESSIR!!
...

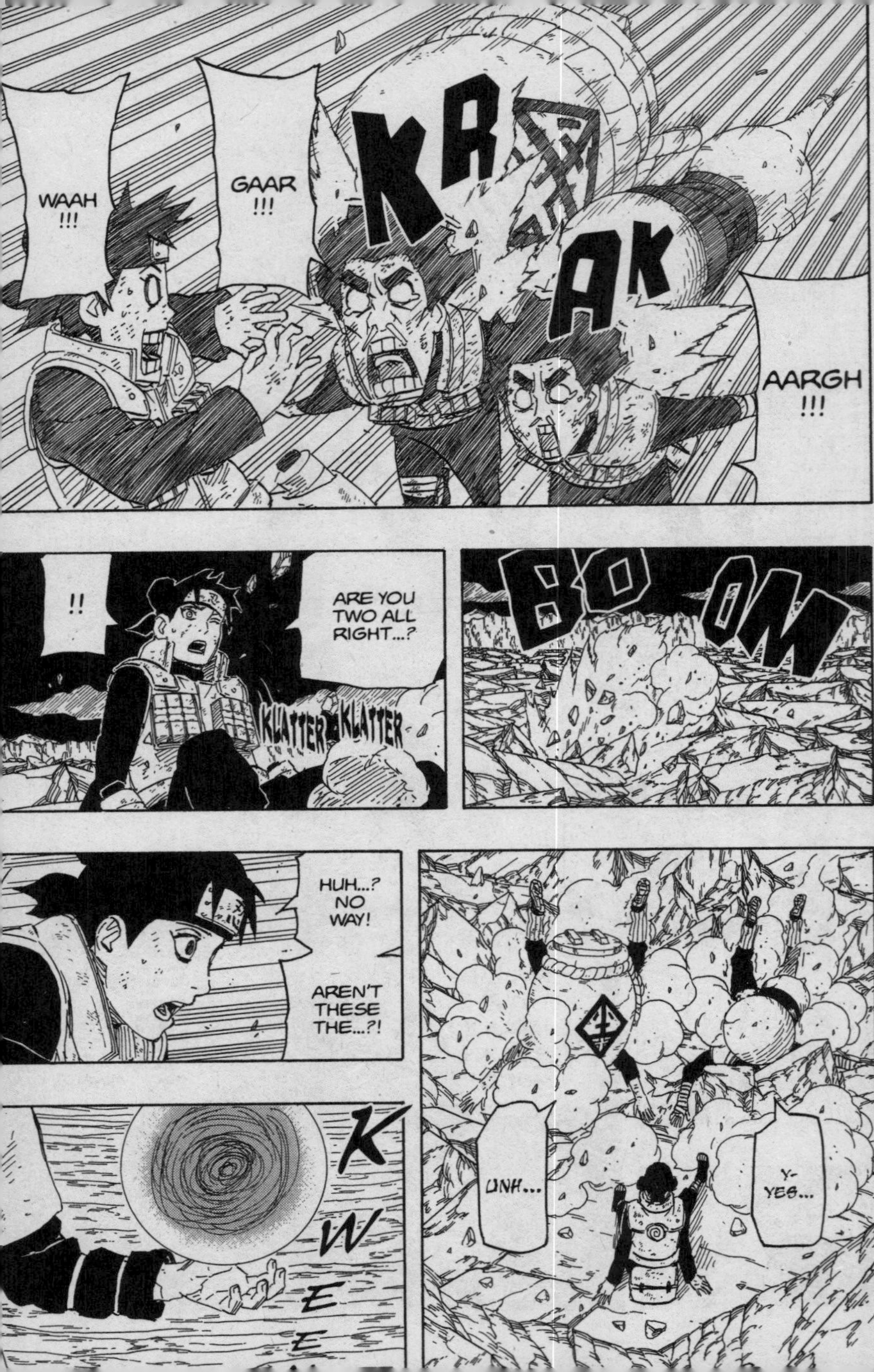
AARGH!!!
KRAKAK
GAAR!!!
WAAH!!!
BOOM
ARE YOU TWO ALL RIGHT...?
!!
KLATTER KLATTER
Y-YES...
UNH...
HUH...? NO WAY!
AREN'T THESE THE...?!
KWEE

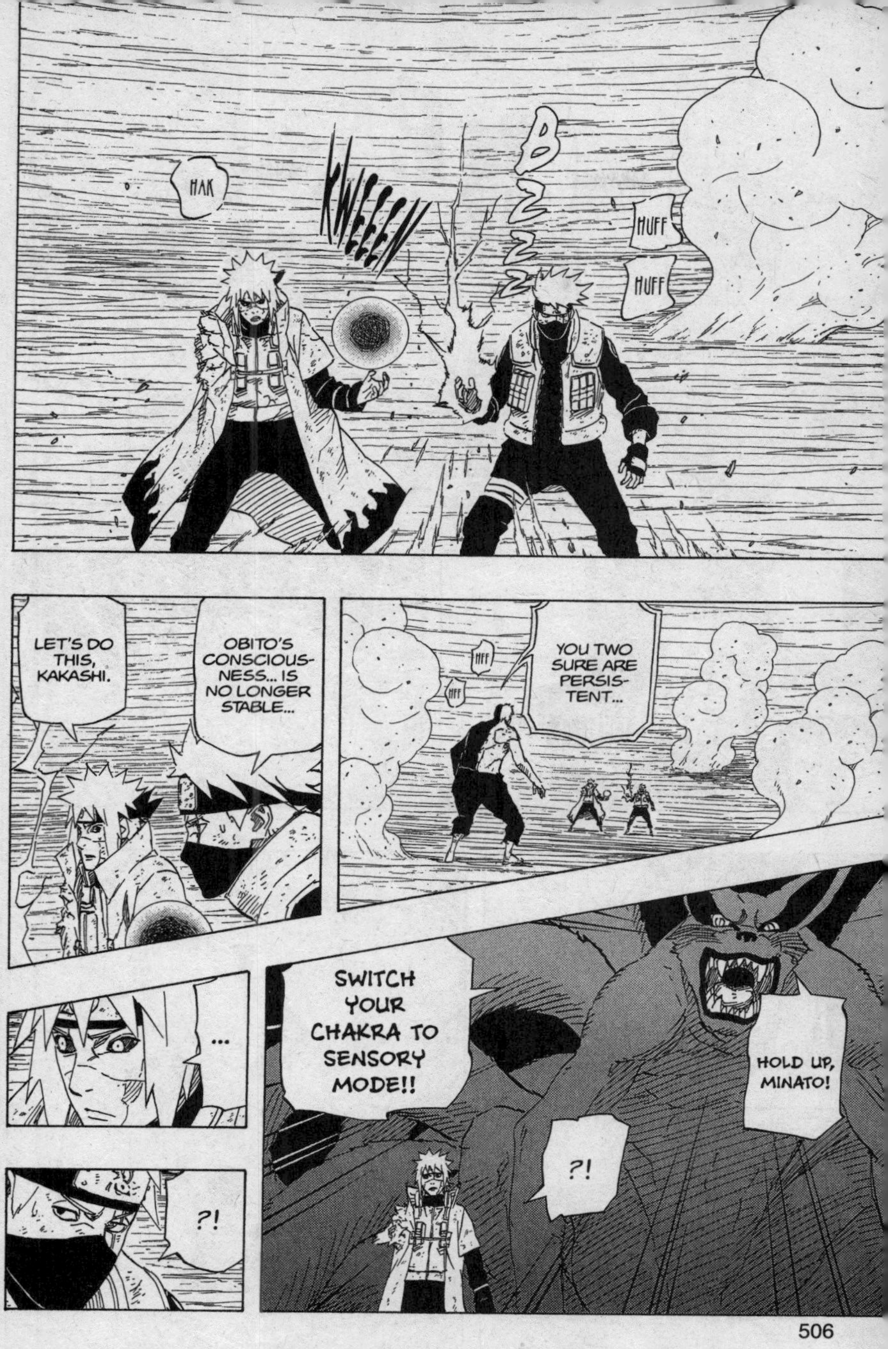
HUFF
HUFF
BZZZZ
KWEEEN
HAK
YOU TWO SURE ARE PERSISTENT...
HFF
HFF
OBITO'S CONSCIOUSNESS... IS NO LONGER STABLE...
LET'S DO THIS, KAKASHI.
HOLD UP, MINATO!
SWITCH YOUR CHAKRA TO SENSORY MODE!!
?!
...
?!

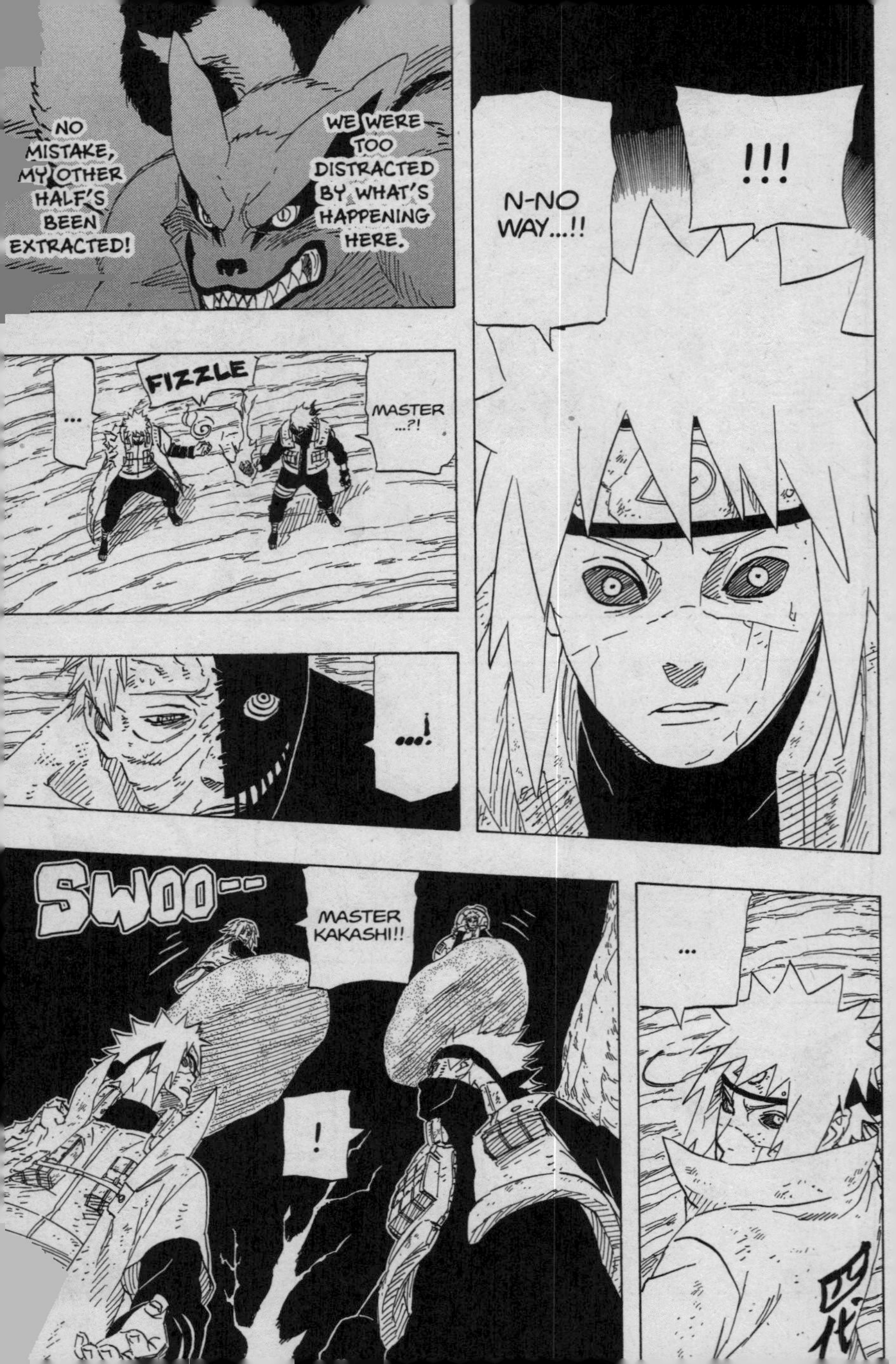

!!!
N-NO WAY...!!
WE WERE TOO DISTRACTED BY WHAT'S HAPPENING HERE.
NO MISTAKE, MY OTHER HALF'S BEEN EXTRACTED!
MASTER ...?!
FIZZLE
...
...!
...
四代
MASTER KAKASHI!!
SWOO--
!

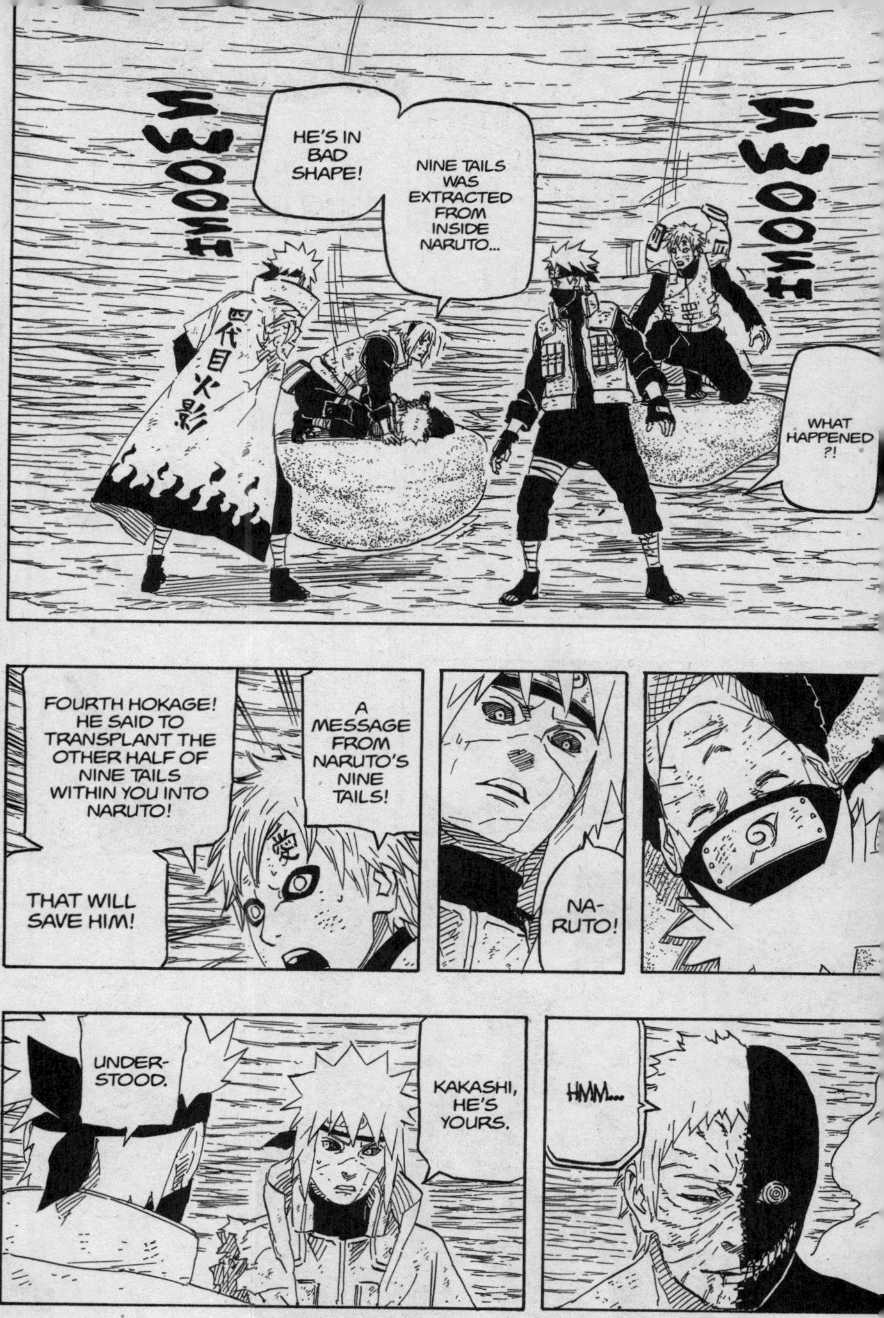
SWOOSH
WHAT HAPPENED?!
HE'S IN BAD SHAPE!
NINE TAILS WAS EXTRACTED FROM INSIDE NARUTO...
SWOOSH
NA-RUTO!
A MESSAGE FROM NARUTO'S NINE TAILS!
FOURTH HOKAGE! HE SAID TO TRANSPLANT THE OTHER HALF OF NINE TAILS WITHIN YOU INTO NARUTO!
THAT WILL SAVE HIM!
HMM...
KAKASHI, HE'S YOURS.
UNDER-STOOD.

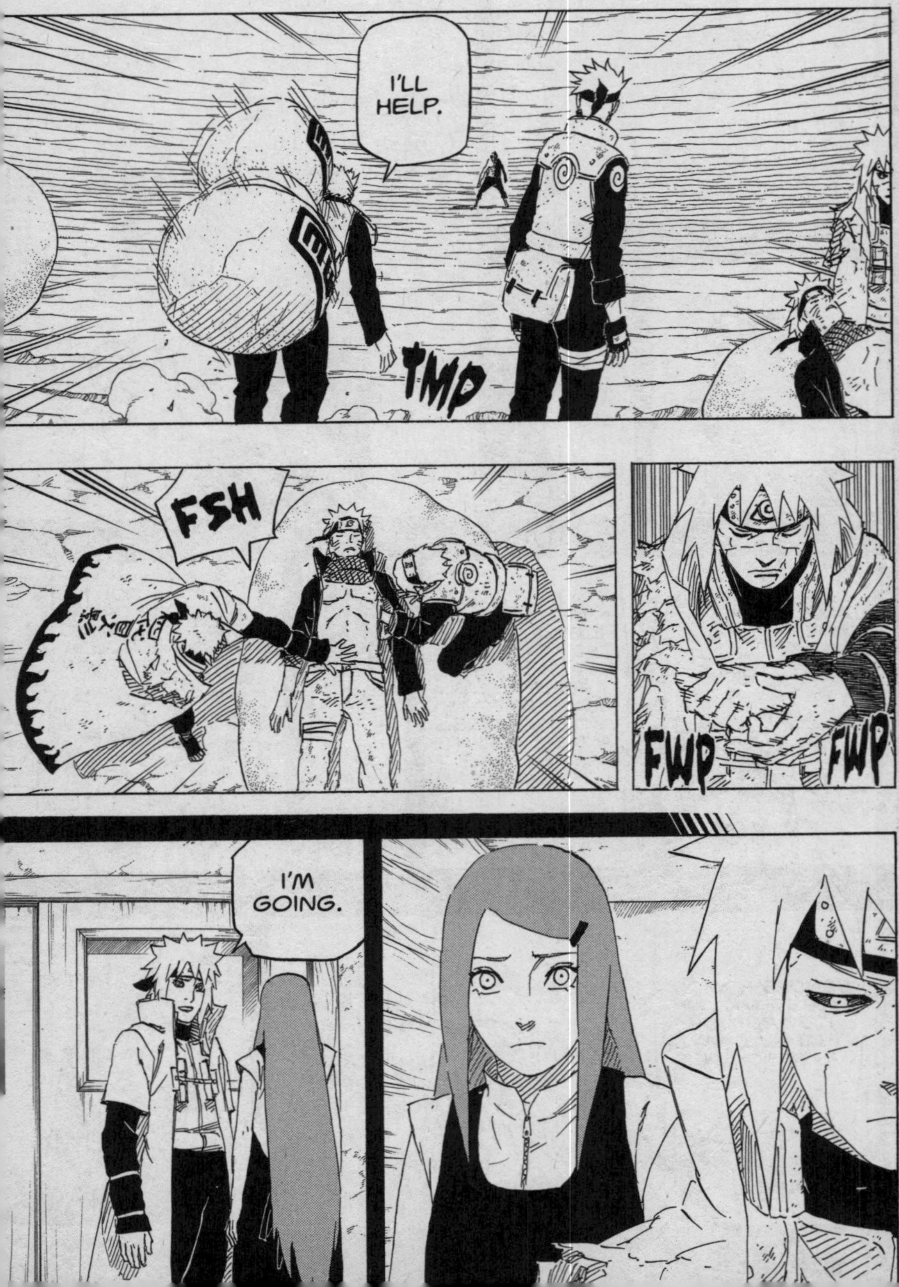
I'LL HELP.
TMP
FWP
FWP
FSH
I'M GOING.

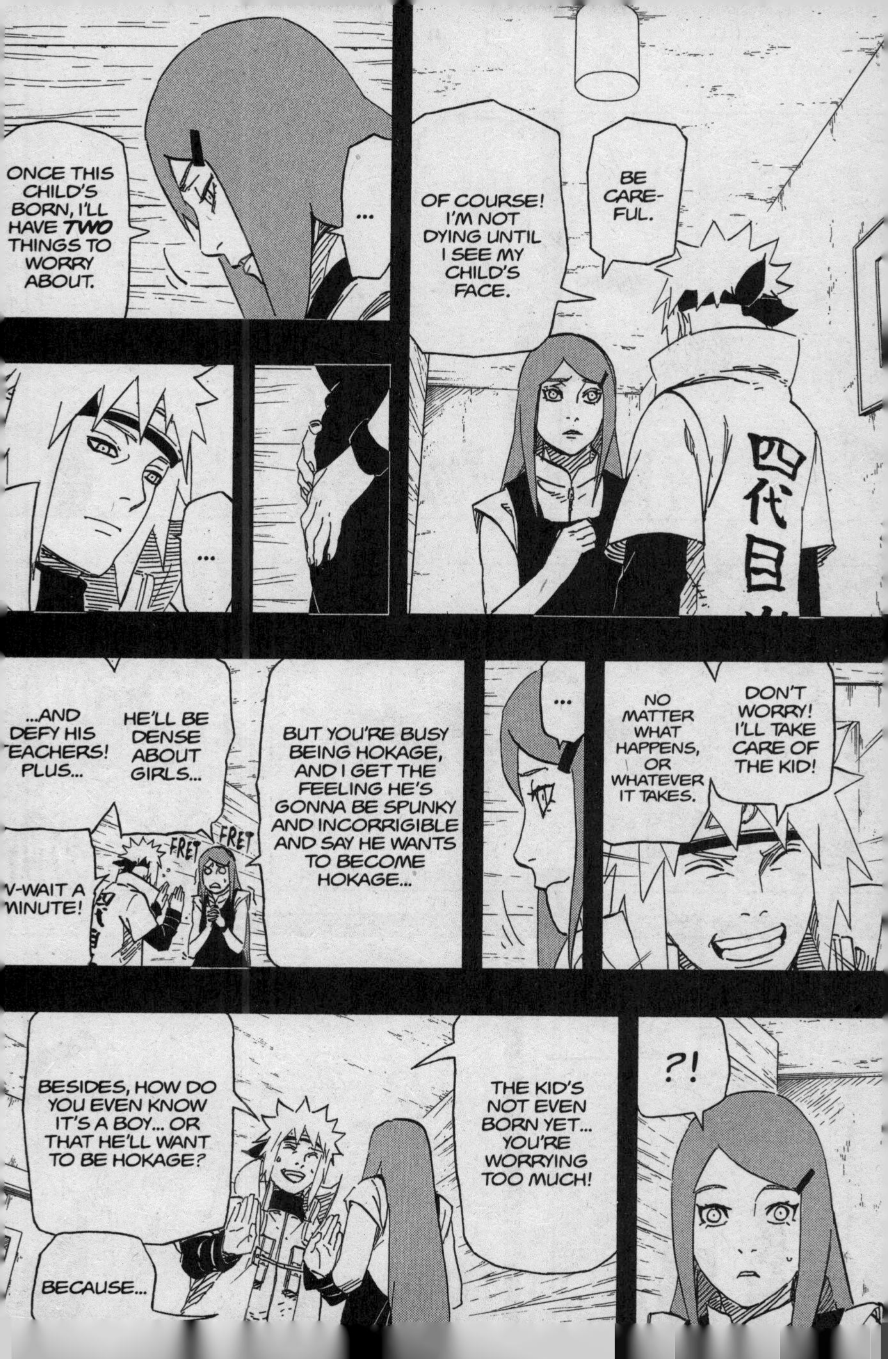
BE CAREFUL.
OF COURSE! I'M NOT DYING UNTIL I SEE MY CHILD'S FACE.
...
ONCE THIS CHILD'S BORN, I'LL HAVE **TWO** THINGS TO WORRY ABOUT.
四代目
...
DON'T WORRY! I'LL TAKE CARE OF THE KID!
NO MATTER WHAT HAPPENS, OR WHATEVER IT TAKES.
...
BUT YOU'RE BUSY BEING HOKAGE, AND I GET THE FEELING HE'S GONNA BE SPUNKY AND INCORRIGIBLE AND SAY HE WANTS TO BECOME HOKAGE...
HE'LL BE DENSE ABOUT GIRLS...
...AND DEFY HIS TEACHERS! PLUS...
FRET FRET
W-WAIT A MINUTE!
?!
THE KID'S NOT EVEN BORN YET... YOU'RE WORRYING TOO MUCH!
BESIDES, HOW DO YOU EVEN KNOW IT'S A BOY... OR THAT HE'LL WANT TO BE HOKAGE?
BECAUSE...

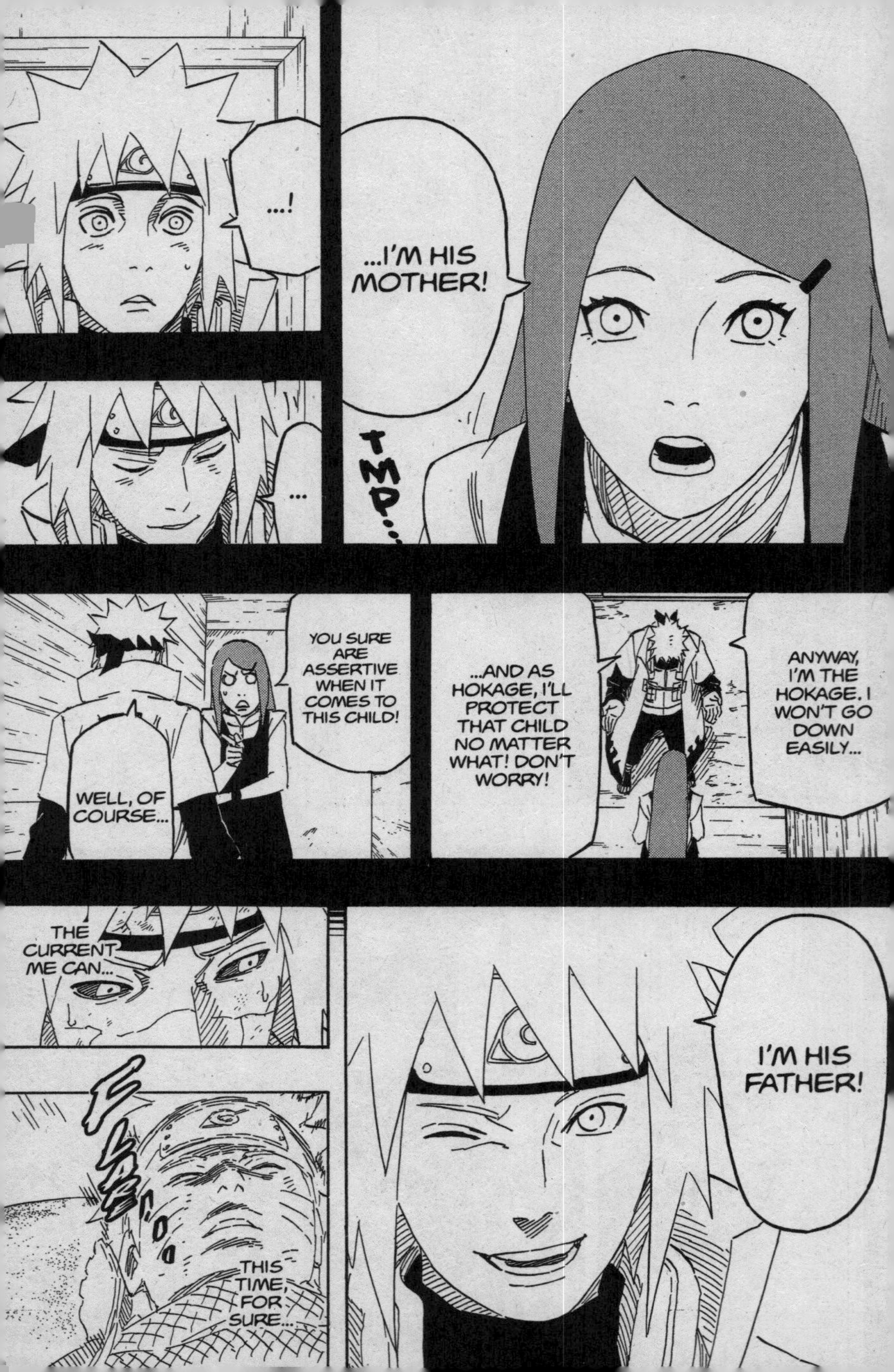

...I'M HIS MOTHER!
TMP...
...!
...
ANYWAY, I'M THE HOKAGE. I WON'T GO DOWN EASILY...
...AND AS HOKAGE, I'LL PROTECT THAT CHILD NO MATTER WHAT! DON'T WORRY!
YOU SURE ARE ASSERTIVE WHEN IT COMES TO THIS CHILD!
WELL, OF COURSE...
I'M HIS FATHER!
THE CURRENT ME CAN...
THIS TIME, FOR SURE...

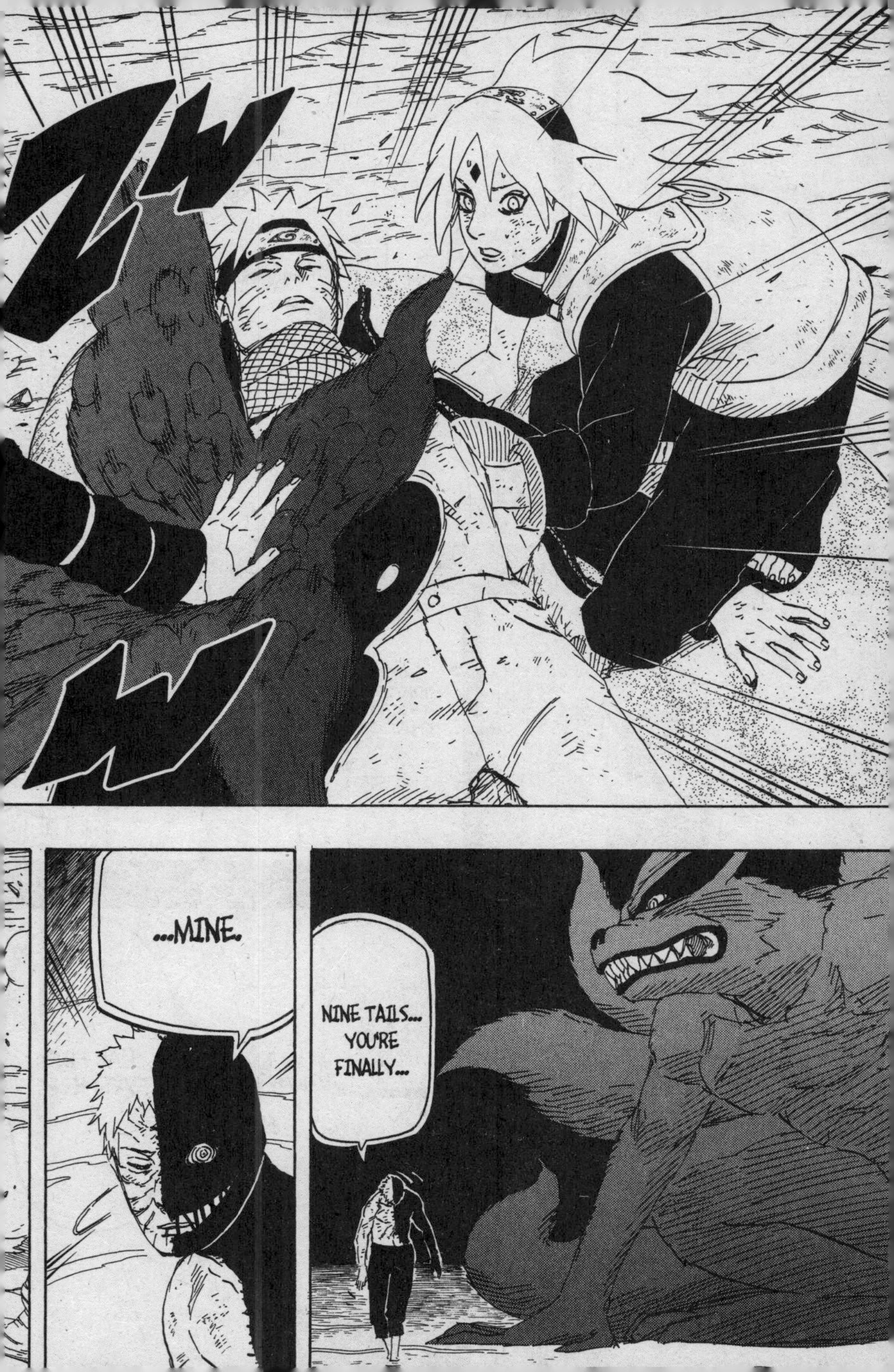
ZWW
NINE TAILS... YOU'RE FINALLY...
...MINE.

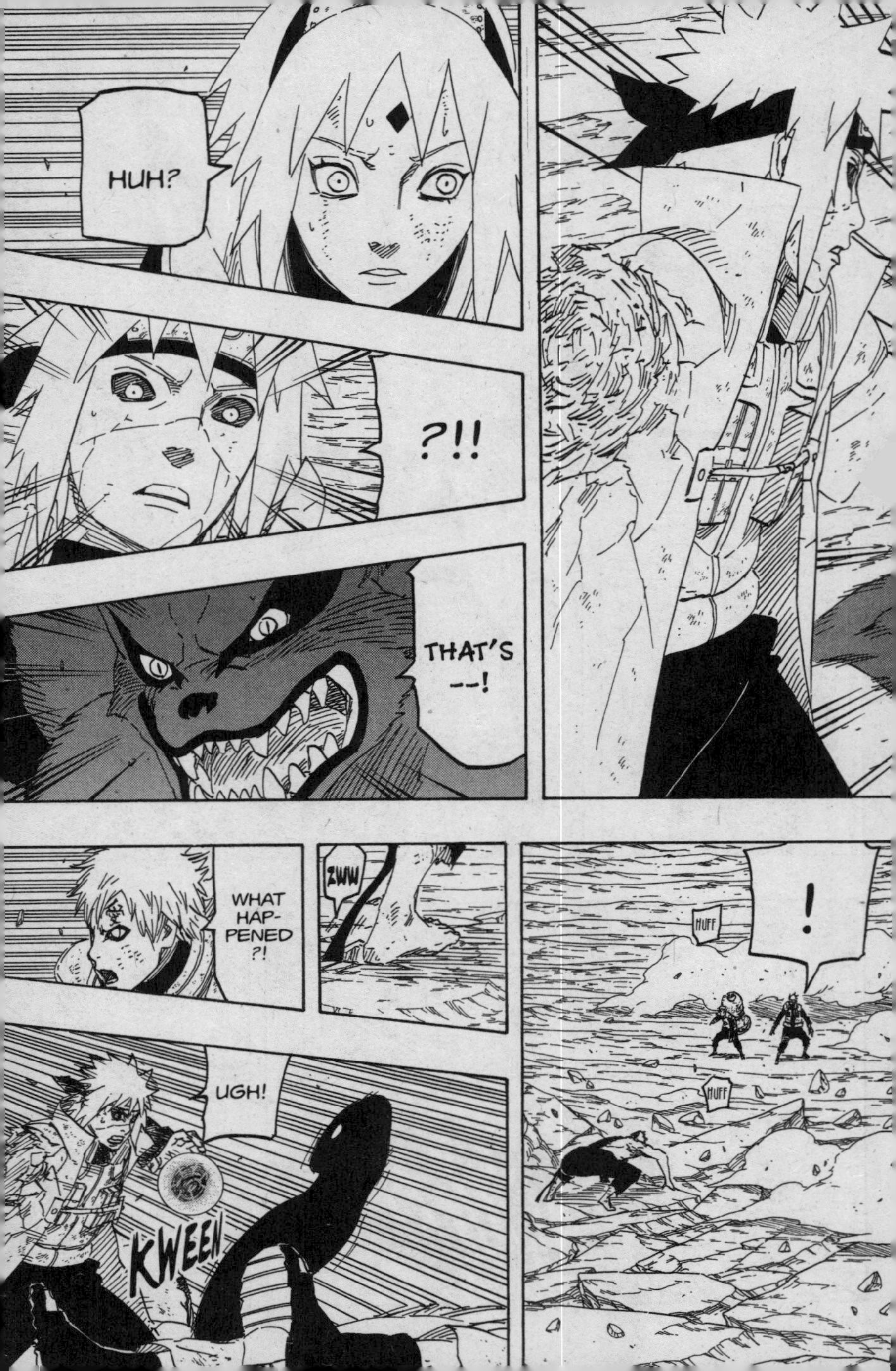
HUH?
?!!
THAT'S --!
!
HUFF
HUFF
ZWW
WHAT HAP-PENED ?!
UGH!
KWEEN

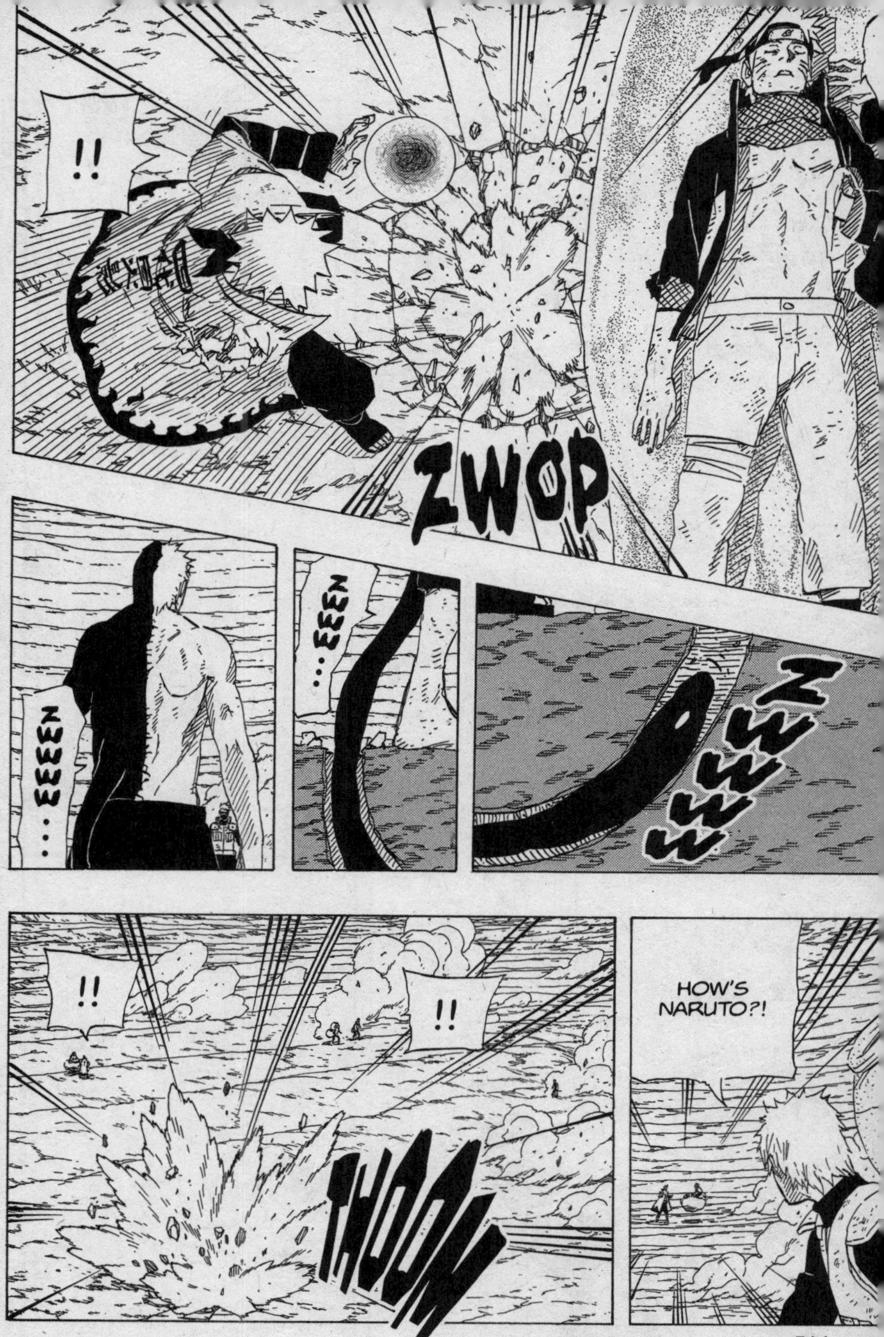
!!
ZWOP
ZWWWWW
ZWWW...
ZWWWWEEEE...
HOW'S NARUTO?!
!!
!!
THOOM

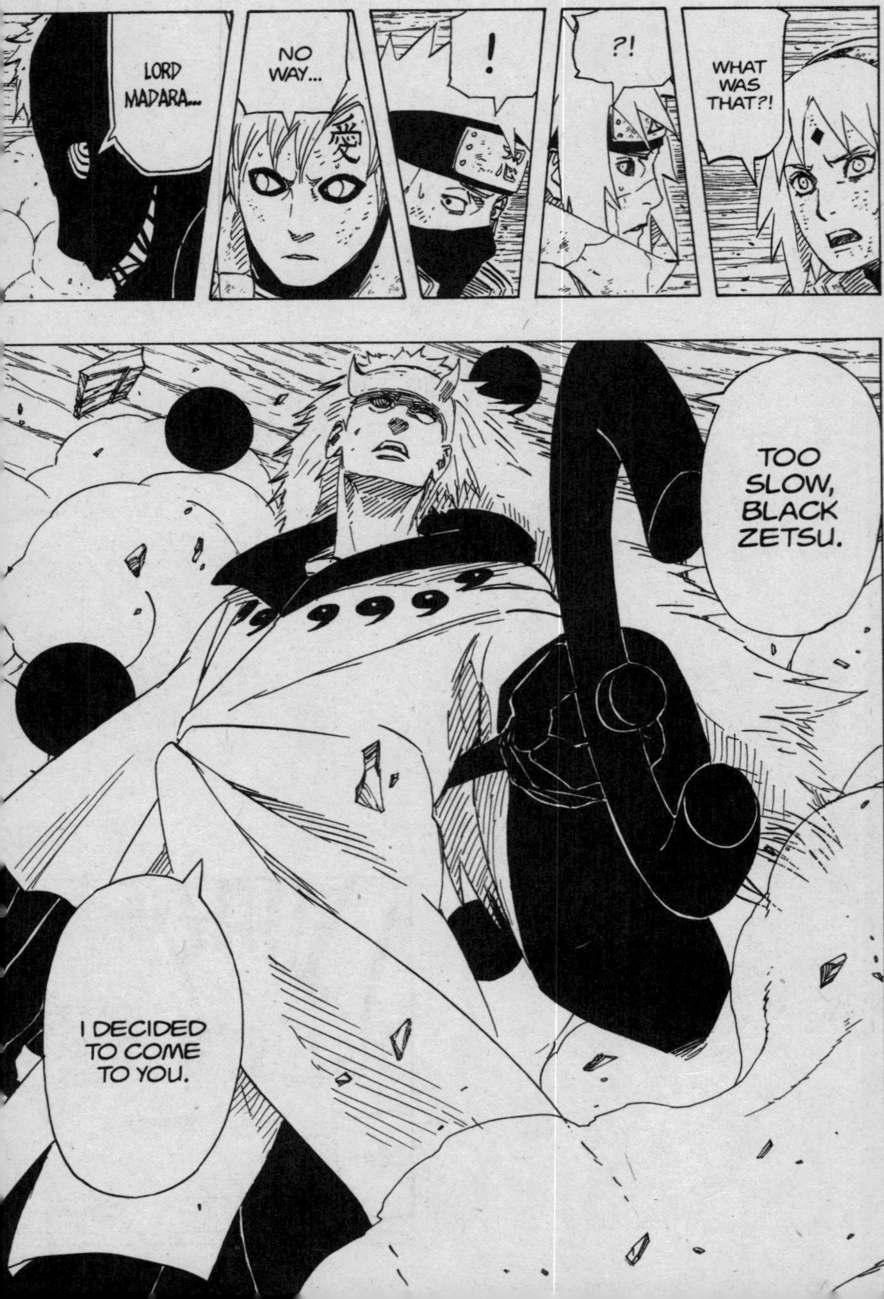
WHAT WAS THAT?!
?!
!
NO WAY...
LORD MADARA...
TOO SLOW, BLACK ZETSU.
I DECIDED TO COME TO YOU.

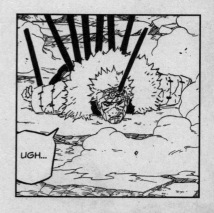

UGH...

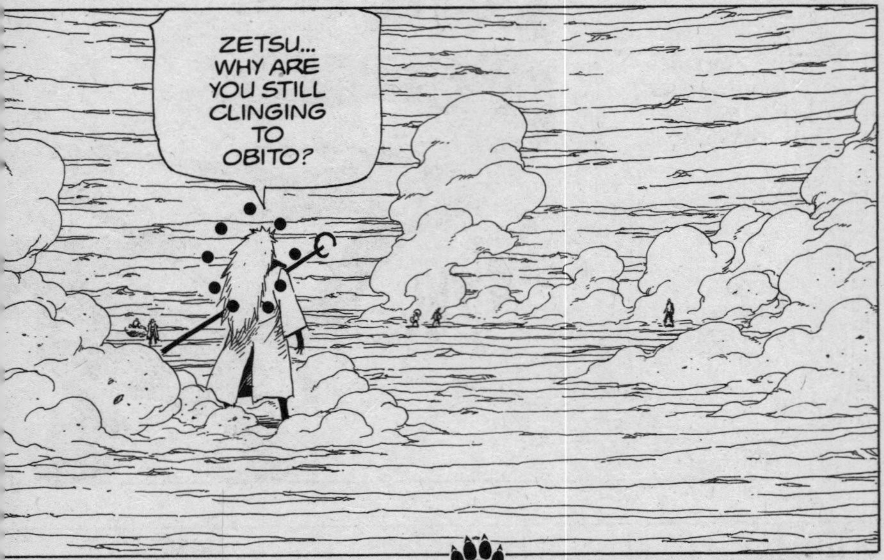
ZETSU... WHY ARE YOU STILL CLINGING TO OBITO?

Number 665: The Current Me

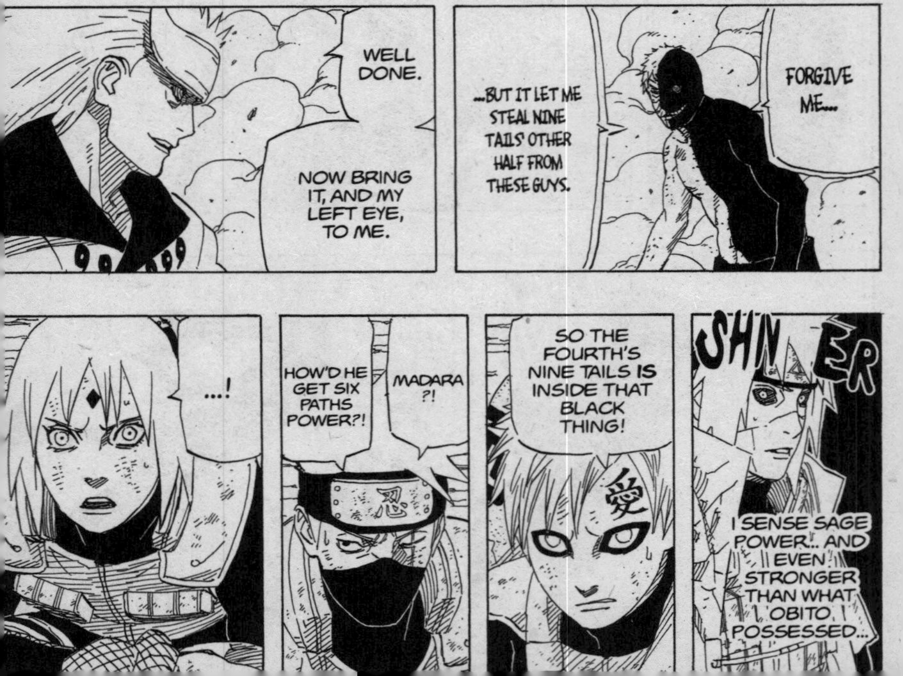
FORGIVE ME...
...BUT IT LET ME STEAL NINE TAILS' OTHER HALF FROM THESE GUYS.
WELL DONE.
NOW BRING IT, AND MY LEFT EYE, TO ME.
SHIN
ER
I SENSE SAGE POWER... AND EVEN STRONGER THAN WHAT OBITO POSSESSED...
SO THE FOURTH'S NINE TAILS IS INSIDE THAT BLACK THING!
MADARA ?!
HOW'D HE GET SIX PATHS POWER?!
...!

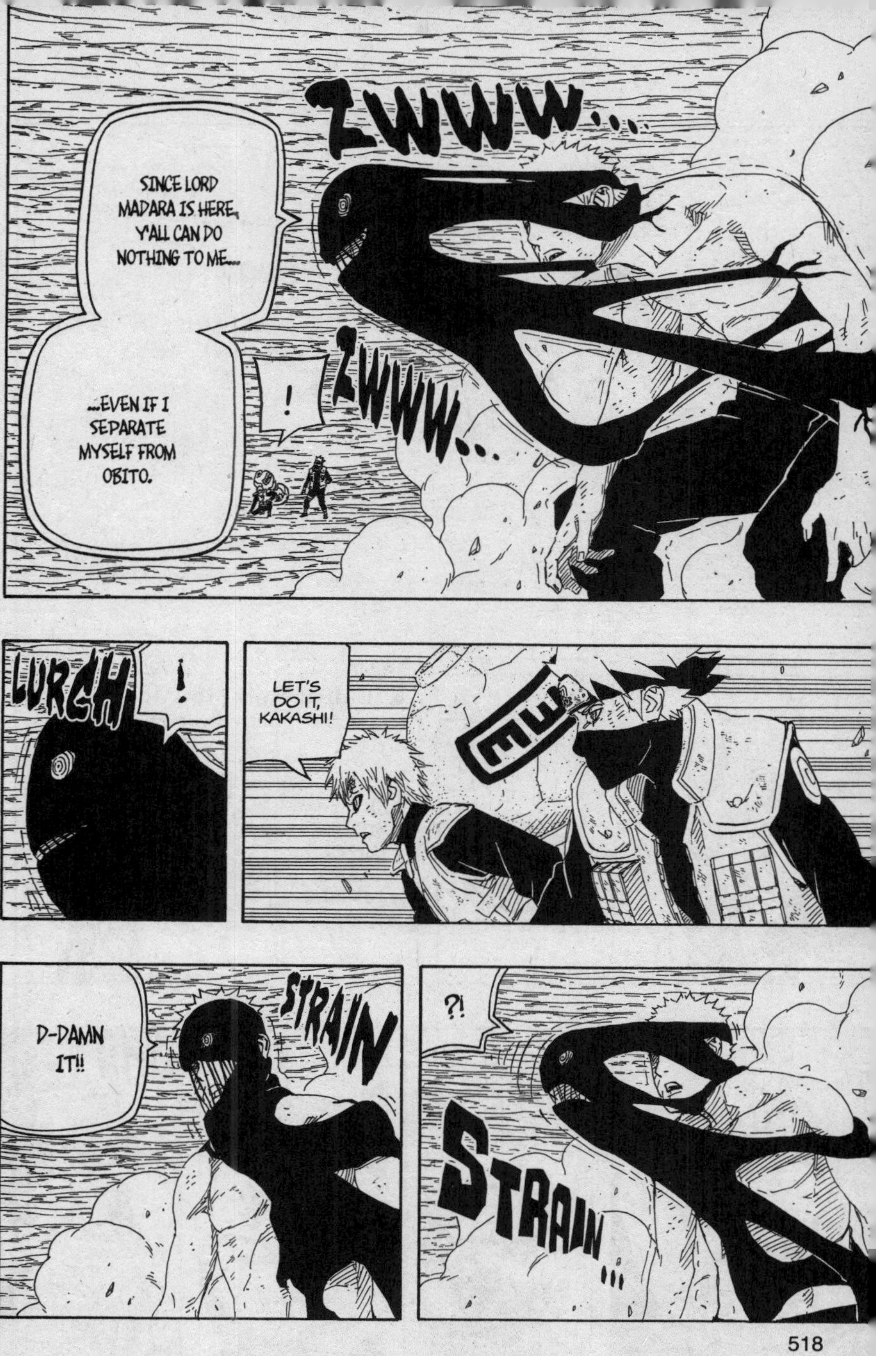
ZWWW...
SINCE LORD MADARA IS HERE, Y'ALL CAN DO NOTHING TO ME...
...EVEN IF I SEPARATE MYSELF FROM OBITO.
ZWWW...
!
LET'S DO IT, KAKASHI!
LURCH
!
?!
STRAIN...
STRAIN
D-DAMN IT!!

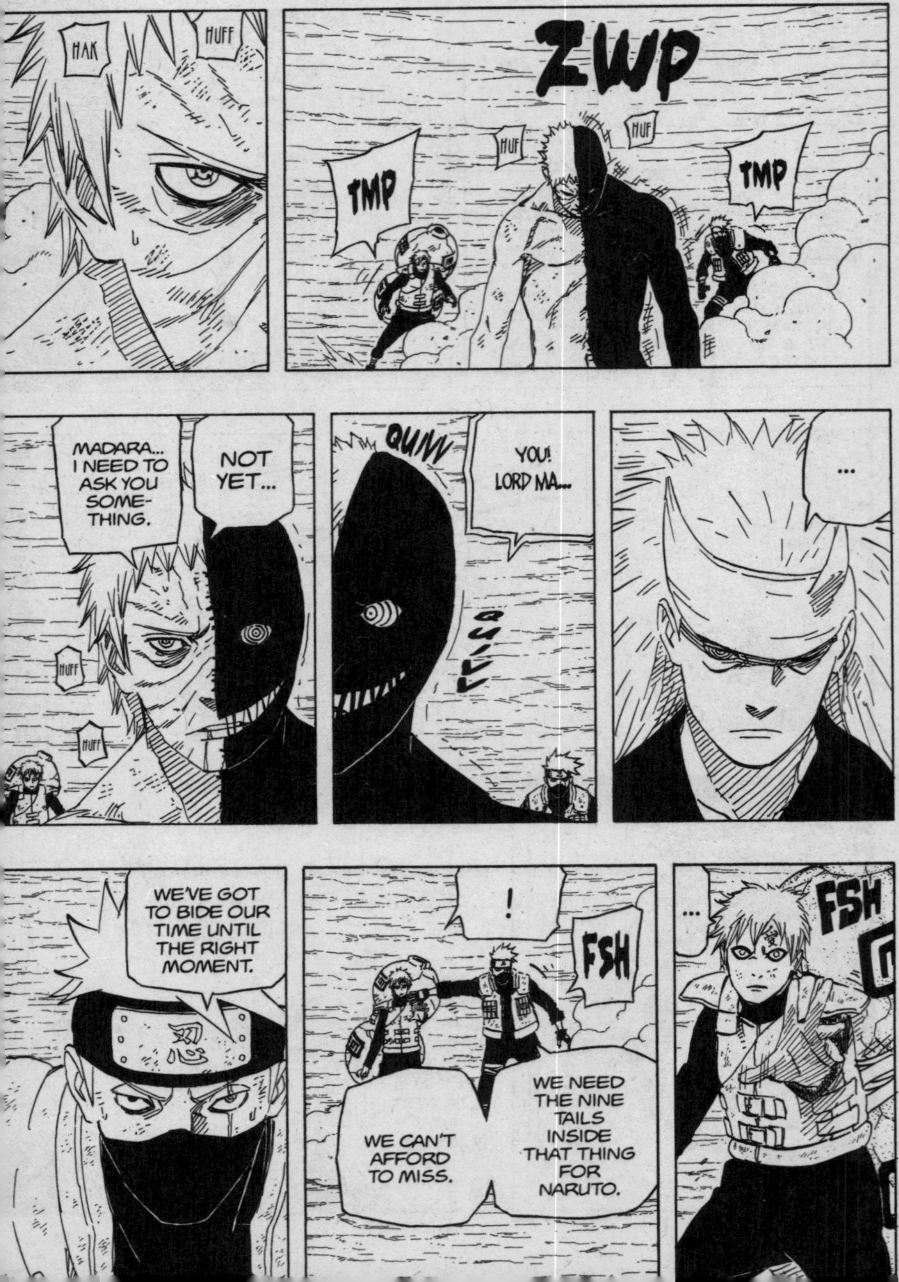
ZWP
HUF
HUF
TMP
TMP
HUFF
HAK
...
QUIVV
YOU! LORD MA...
QUIVV
NOT YET...
MADARA... I NEED TO ASK YOU SOME-THING.
HUFF
HUFF
FSH
...
!
FSH
WE NEED THE NINE TAILS INSIDE THAT THING FOR NARUTO.
WE CAN'T AFFORD TO MISS.
WE'VE GOT TO BIDE OUR TIME UNTIL THE RIGHT MOMENT.

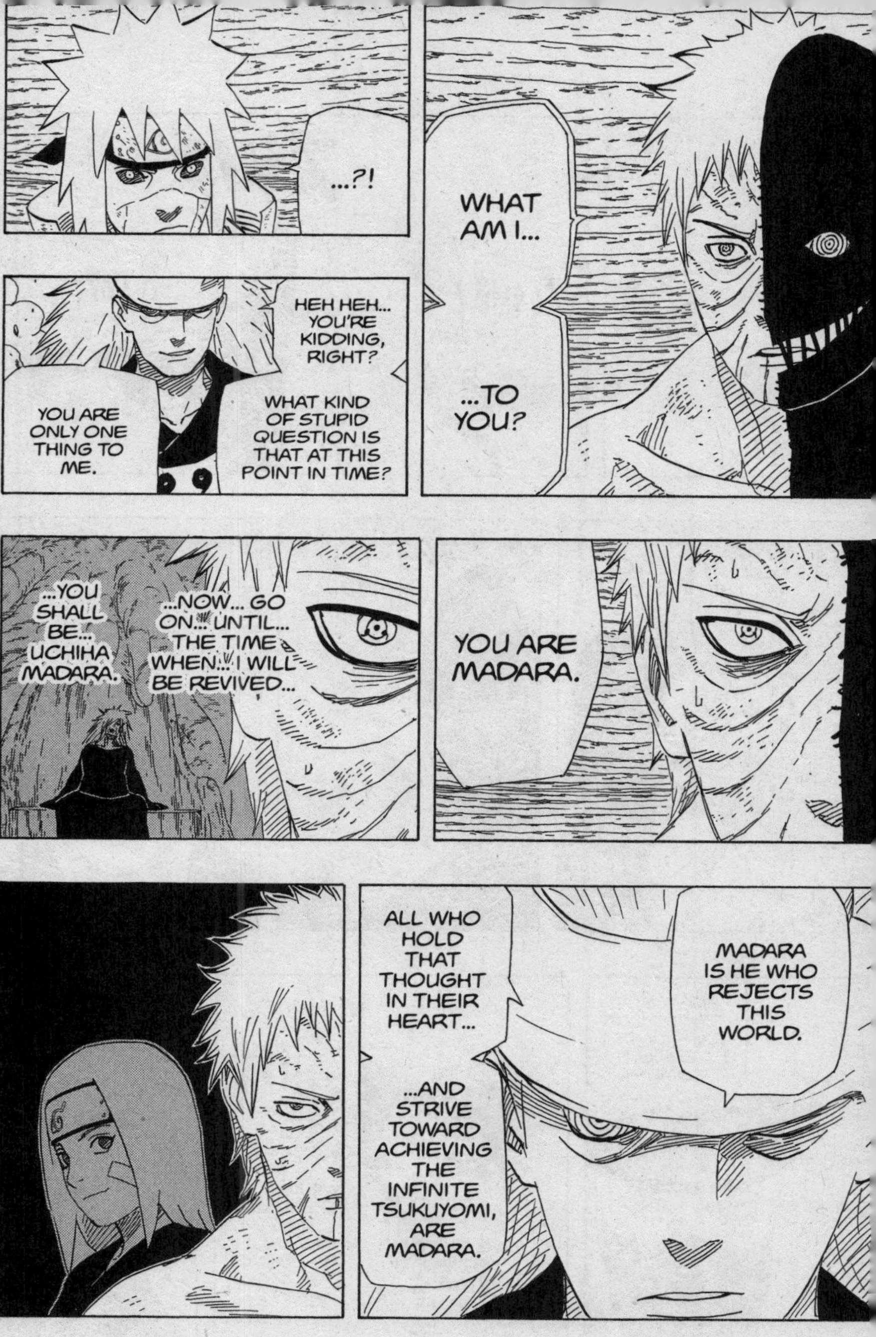
WHAT AM I...
...TO YOU?
...?!
HEH HEH... YOU'RE KIDDING, RIGHT?
WHAT KIND OF STUPID QUESTION IS THAT AT THIS POINT IN TIME?
YOU ARE ONLY ONE THING TO ME.
YOU ARE MADARA.
...NOW... GO ON... UNTIL... THE TIME WHEN... I WILL BE REVIVED...
...YOU SHALL BE... UCHIHA MADARA.
MADARA IS HE WHO REJECTS THIS WORLD.
ALL WHO HOLD THAT THOUGHT IN THEIR HEART...
...AND STRIVE TOWARD ACHIEVING THE INFINITE TSUKUYOMI, ARE MADARA.

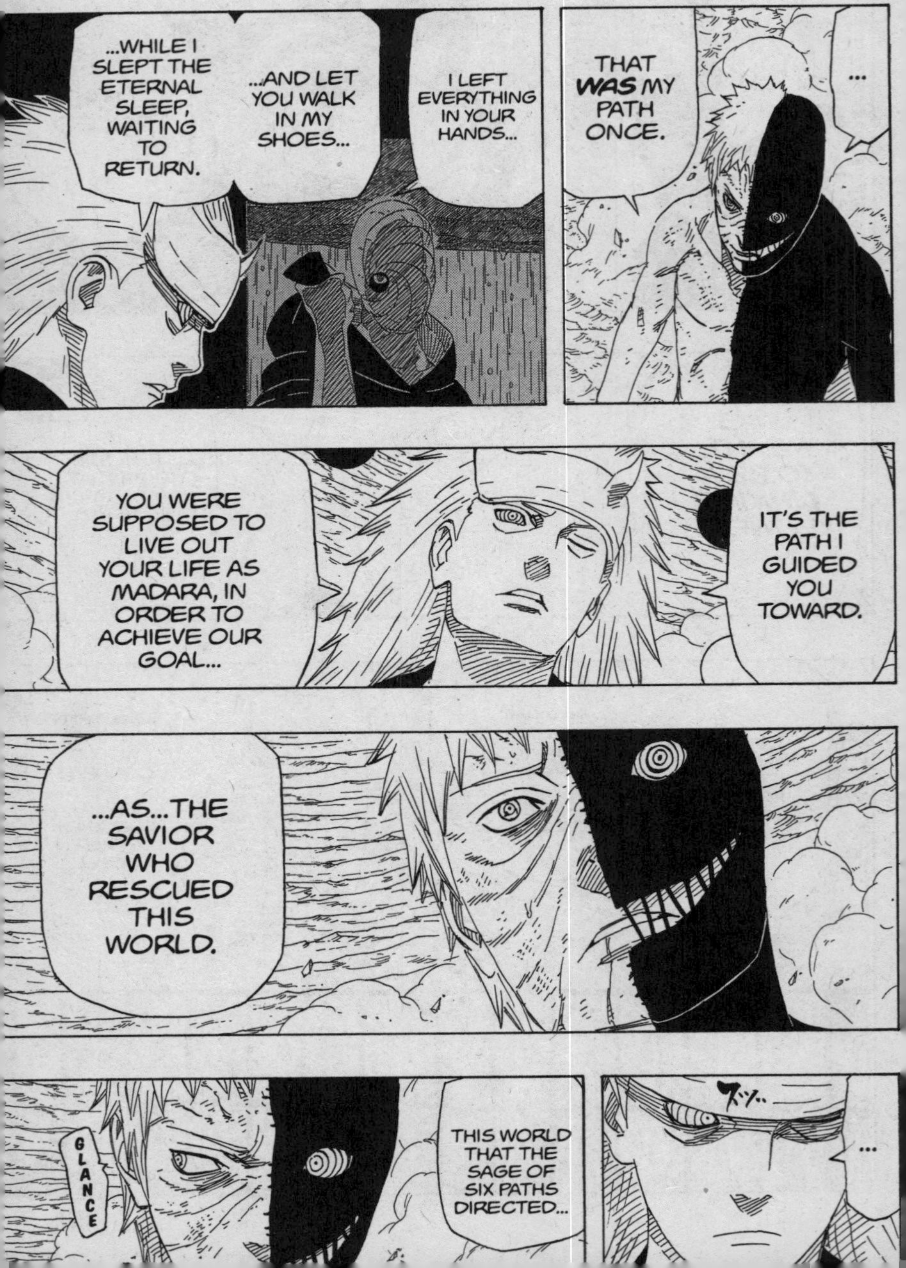
...
THAT WAS MY PATH ONCE.
I LEFT EVERYTHING IN YOUR HANDS...
...AND LET YOU WALK IN MY SHOES...
...WHILE I SLEPT THE ETERNAL SLEEP, WAITING TO RETURN.
IT'S THE PATH I GUIDED YOU TOWARD.
YOU WERE SUPPOSED TO LIVE OUT YOUR LIFE AS MADARA, IN ORDER TO ACHIEVE OUR GOAL...
...AS...THE SAVIOR WHO RESCUED THIS WORLD.
ズッ..
...
THIS WORLD THAT THE SAGE OF SIX PATHS DIRECTED...
GLANCE

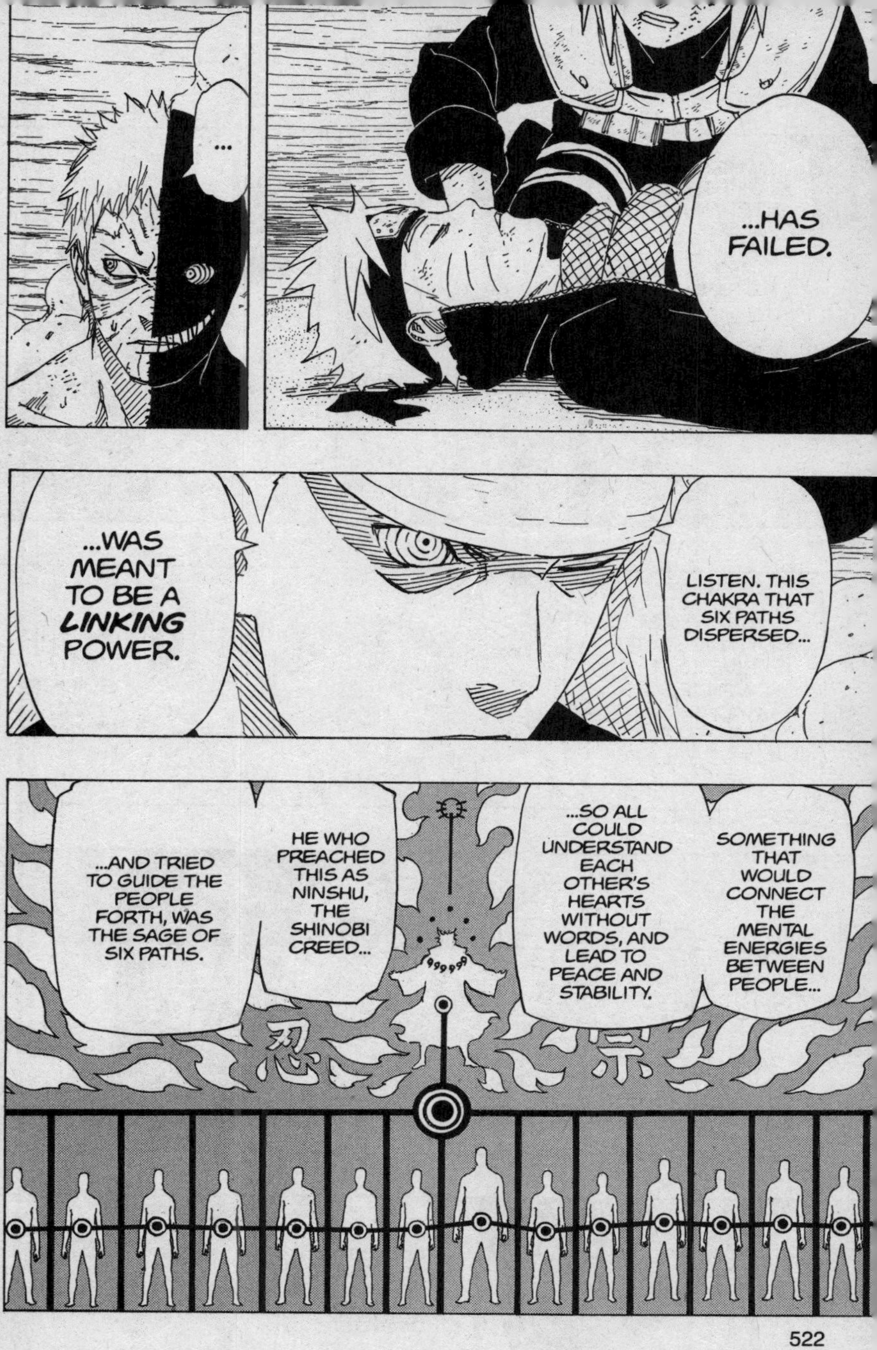
...HAS FAILED.
...
LISTEN. THIS CHAKRA THAT SIX PATHS DISPERSED...
...WAS MEANT TO BE A LINKING POWER.
SOMETHING THAT WOULD CONNECT THE MENTAL ENERGIES BETWEEN PEOPLE...
...SO ALL COULD UNDERSTAND EACH OTHER'S HEARTS WITHOUT WORDS, AND LEAD TO PEACE AND STABILITY.
HE WHO PREACHED THIS AS NINSHU, THE SHINOBI CREED...
...AND TRIED TO GUIDE THE PEOPLE FORTH, WAS THE SAGE OF SIX PATHS.
忍宗

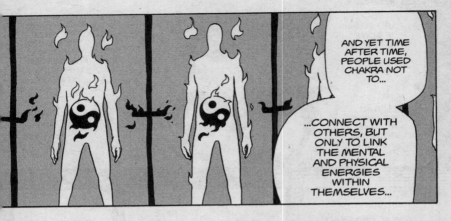

AND YET TIME AFTER TIME, PEOPLE USED CHAKRA NOT TO...
...CONNECT WITH OTHERS, BUT ONLY TO LINK THE MENTAL AND PHYSICAL ENERGIES WITHIN THEMSELVES...
...AS A WAY TO AMPLIFY AND GREATLY INCREASE THE VOLUME OF ONE'S CHAKRA...
...AND CONVERT IT INTO NINJUTSU THAT COULD BE USED AS WEAPONS IN BATTLE.
IRONI-CALLY...
...REVERTING THINGS BACK TO THE WAY SIX PATHS' MOTHER KAGUYA HAD ORIGINALLY EMPLOYED CHAKRA.
WHAT THE HELL IS HE TALKING ABOUT?!
GAARA...
I KNOW...

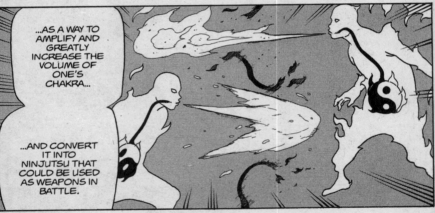

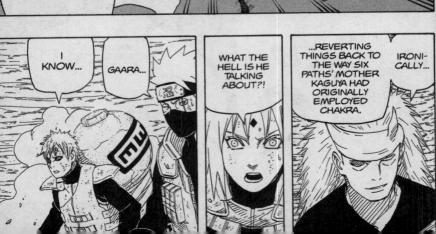

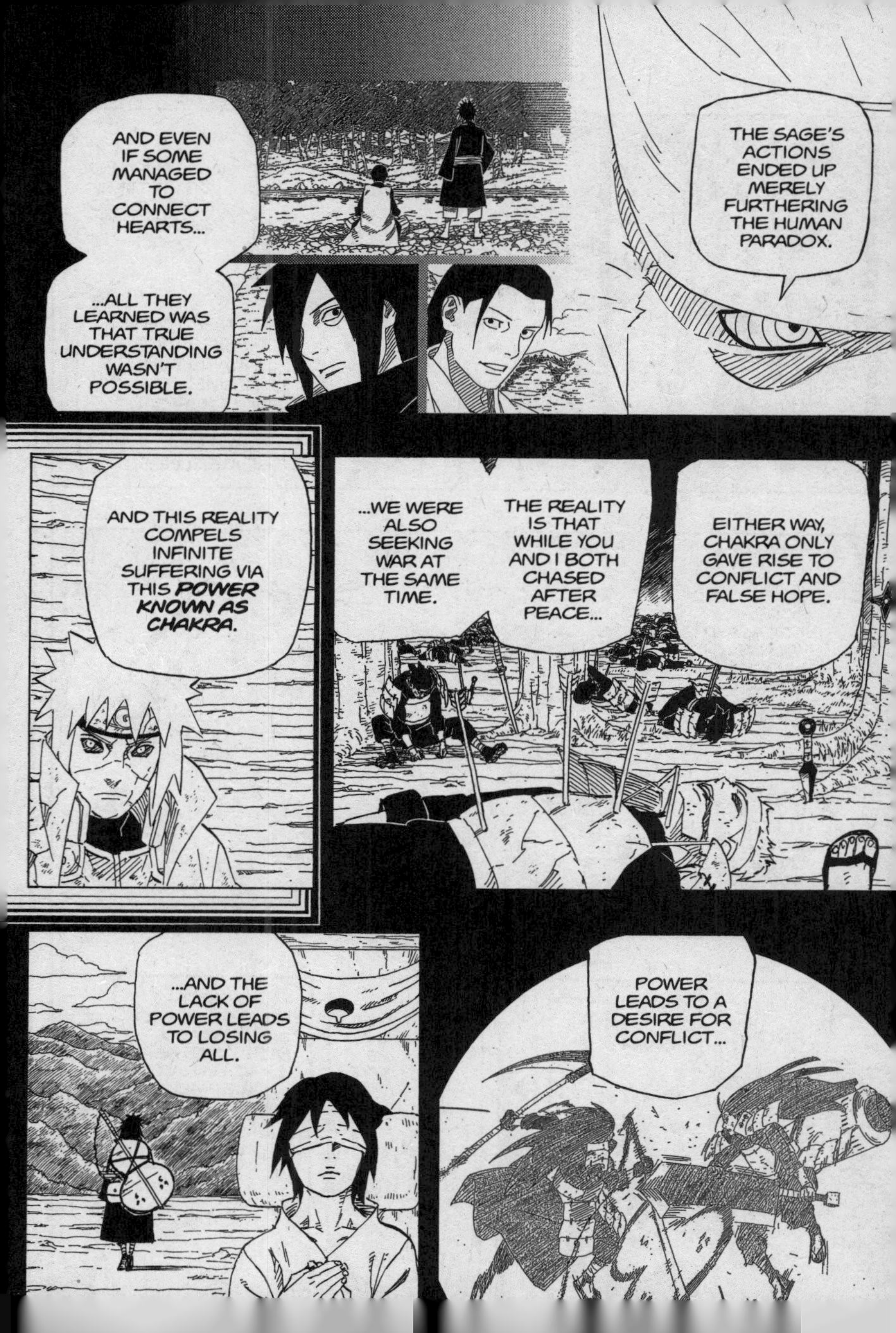
THE SAGE'S ACTIONS ENDED UP MERELY FURTHERING THE HUMAN PARADOX.
AND EVEN IF SOME MANAGED TO CONNECT HEARTS...
...ALL THEY LEARNED WAS THAT TRUE UNDERSTANDING WASN'T POSSIBLE.
EITHER WAY, CHAKRA ONLY GAVE RISE TO CONFLICT AND FALSE HOPE.
THE REALITY IS THAT WHILE YOU AND I BOTH CHASED AFTER PEACE...
...WE WERE ALSO SEEKING WAR AT THE SAME TIME.
AND THIS REALITY COMPELS INFINITE SUFFERING VIA THIS ***POWER KNOWN AS CHAKRA.***
POWER LEADS TO A DESIRE FOR CONFLICT...
...AND THE LACK OF POWER LEADS TO LOSING ALL.

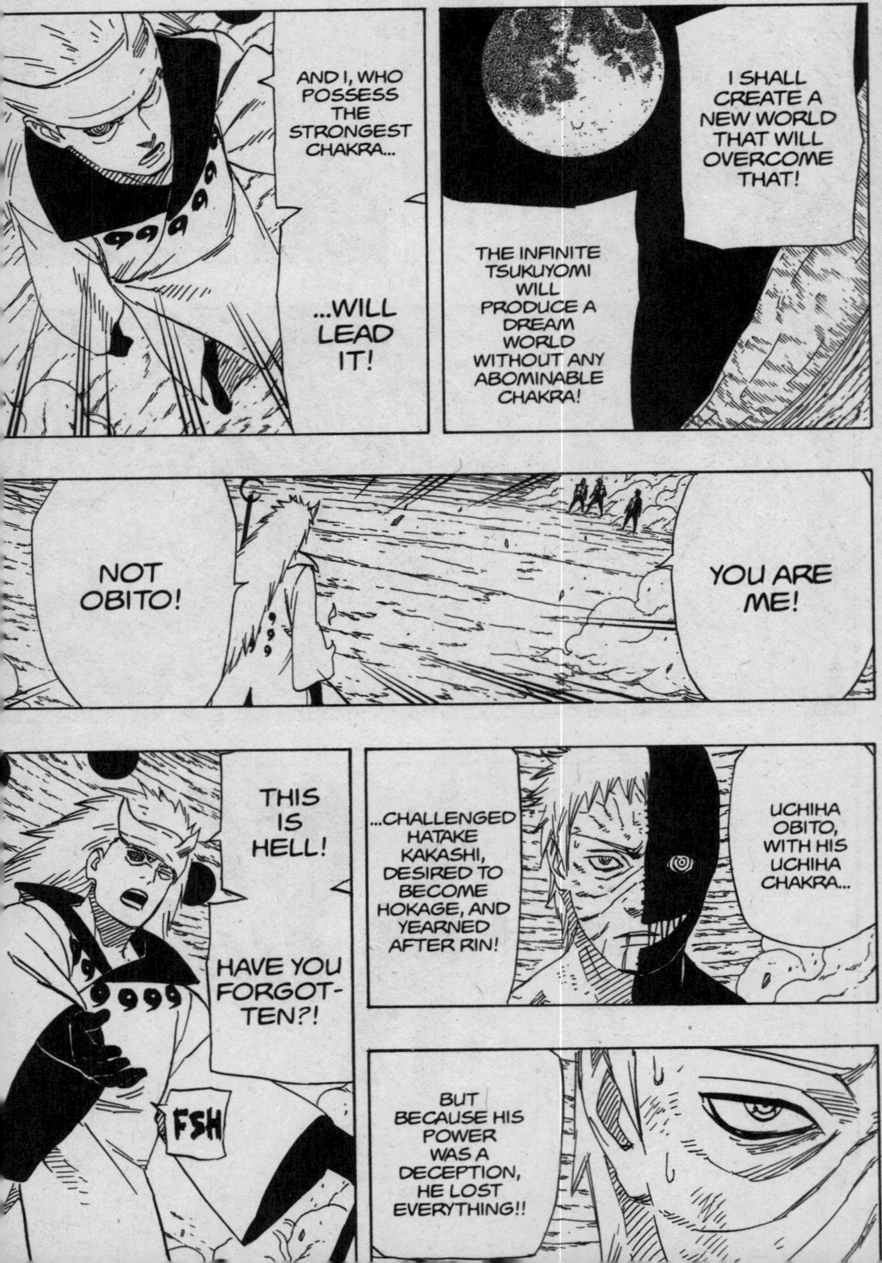
I SHALL CREATE A NEW WORLD THAT WILL OVERCOME THAT!
THE INFINITE TSUKUYOMI WILL PRODUCE A DREAM WORLD WITHOUT ANY ABOMINABLE CHAKRA!
AND I, WHO POSSESS THE STRONGEST CHAKRA...
...WILL LEAD IT!
YOU ARE ME!
NOT OBITO!
UCHIHA OBITO, WITH HIS UCHIHA CHAKRA...
...CHALLENGED HATAKE KAKASHI, DESIRED TO BECOME HOKAGE, AND YEARNED AFTER RIN!
BUT BECAUSE HIS POWER WAS A DECEPTION, HE LOST EVERYTHING!!
THIS IS HELL!
HAVE YOU FORGOT-TEN?!
FSH

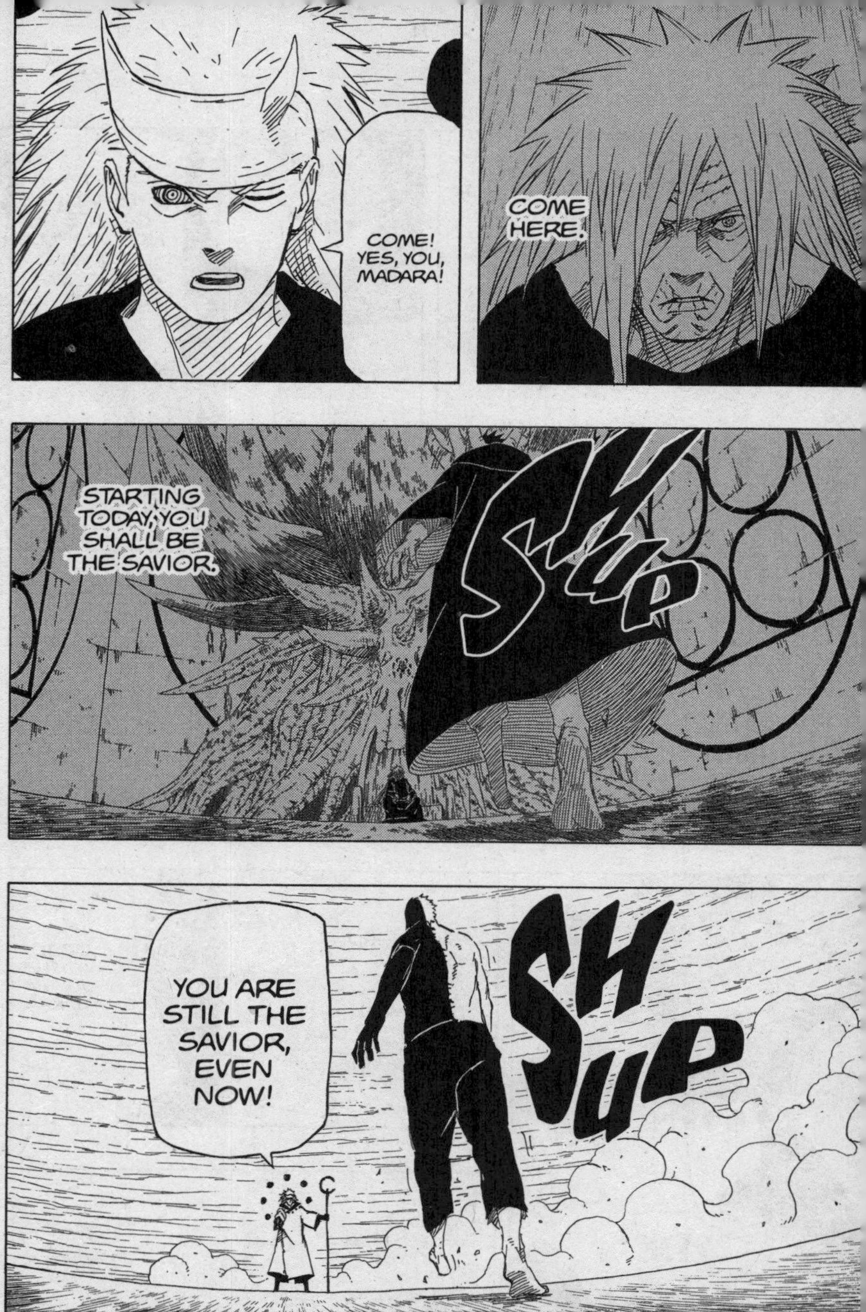
COME HERE.
COME! YES, YOU, MADARA!
STARTING TODAY, YOU SHALL BE THE SAVIOR.
SHUP
YOU ARE STILL THE SAVIOR, EVEN NOW!
SHUP

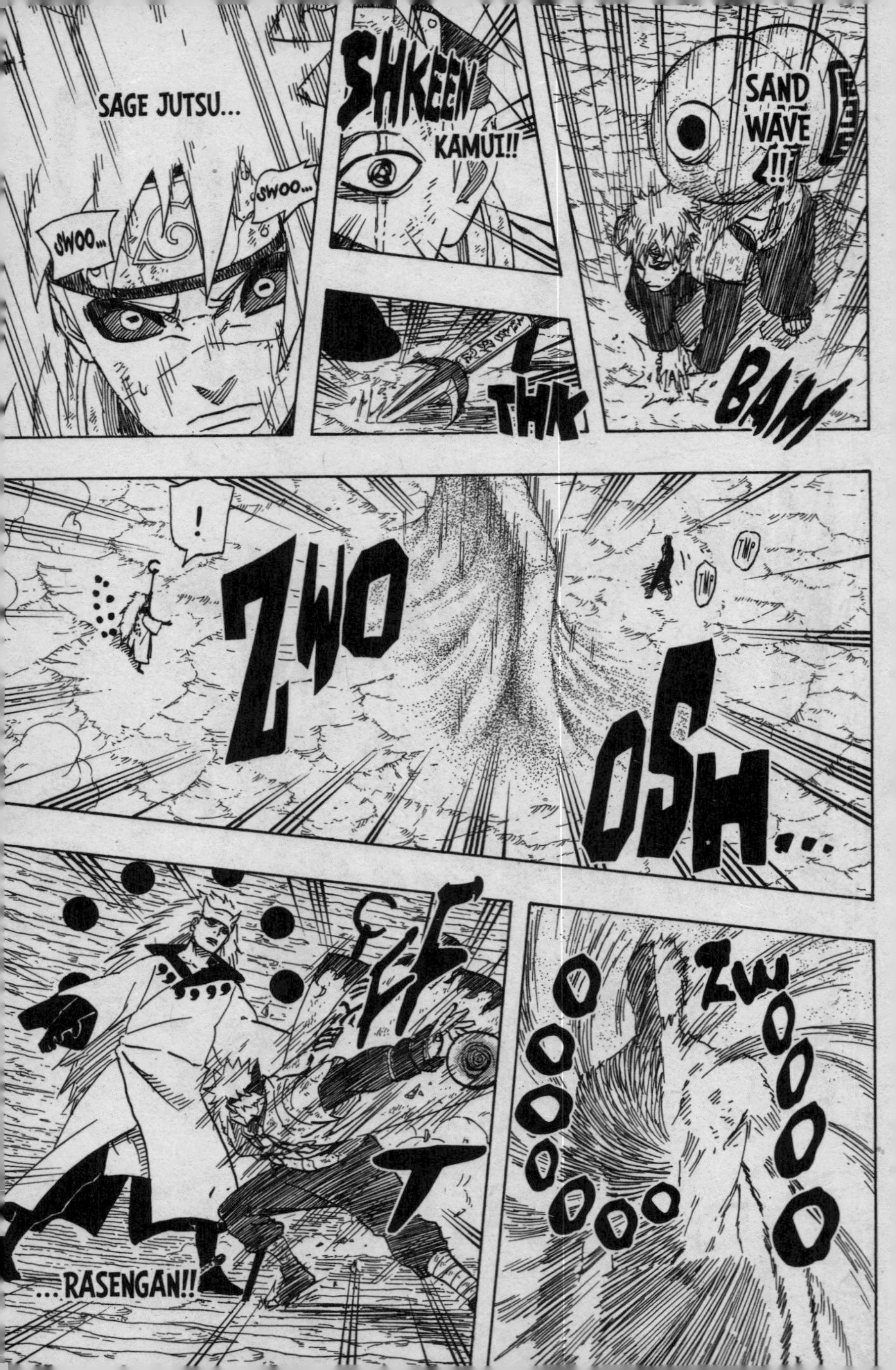

SAND WAVE!!
BAM
SHKEEN
KAMUI!!
THK
SAGE JUTSU...
SWOO...
SWOO...
TMP
TMP
ZWOOSH...
!
ZWOOOOOOOOOOOOOOOO
...RASENGAN!!

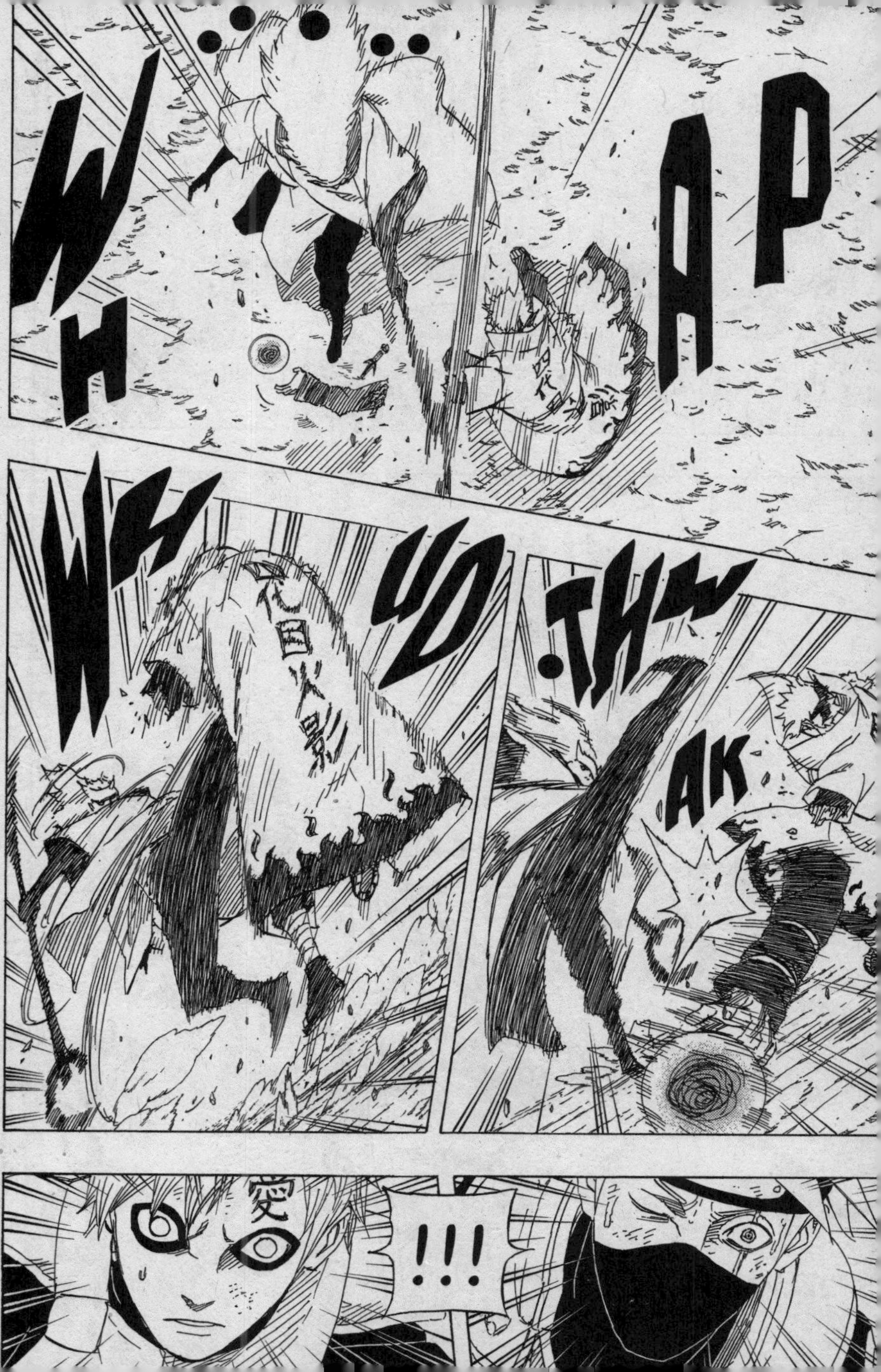
WHAP
THWAK
WHUD
!!!

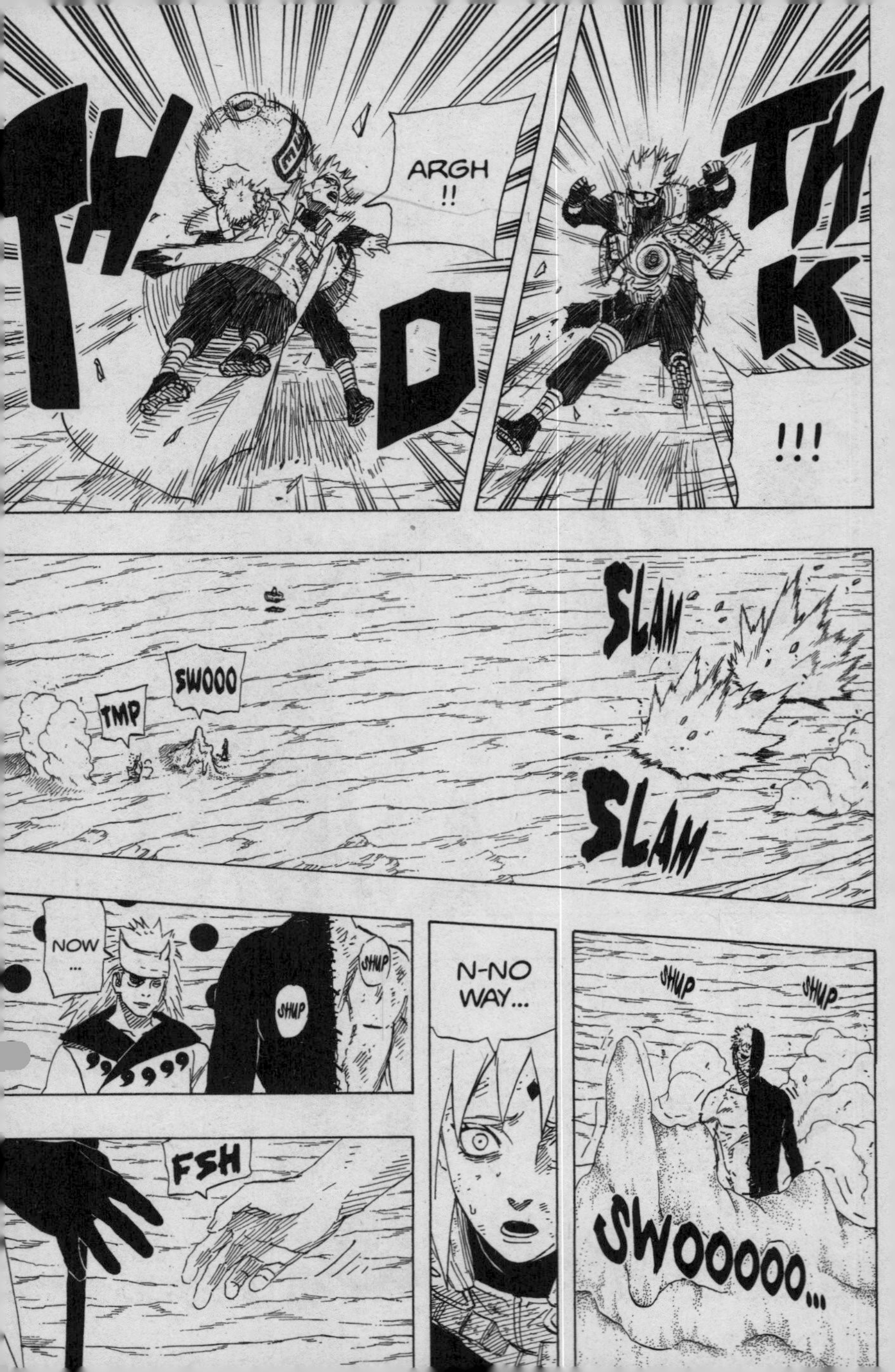
THK
!!!
THD
ARGH !!
SLAM
SLAM
SWOOO
TMP
SHUP
SHUP
SWOOOOO...
N-NO WAY...
NOW...
SHUP
SHUP
FSH

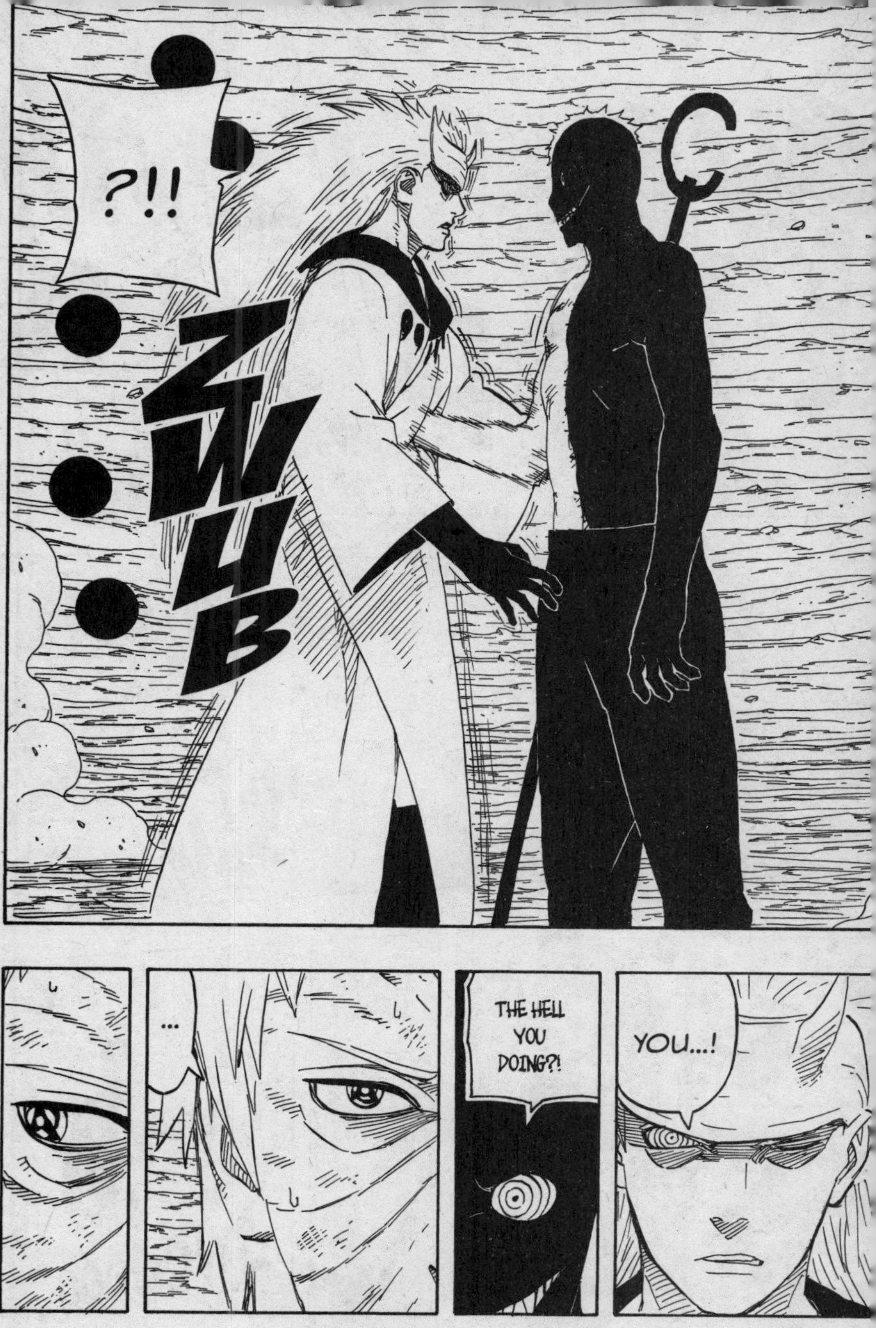
?!!
ZWUB
YOU...!
THE HELL YOU DOING?!
...

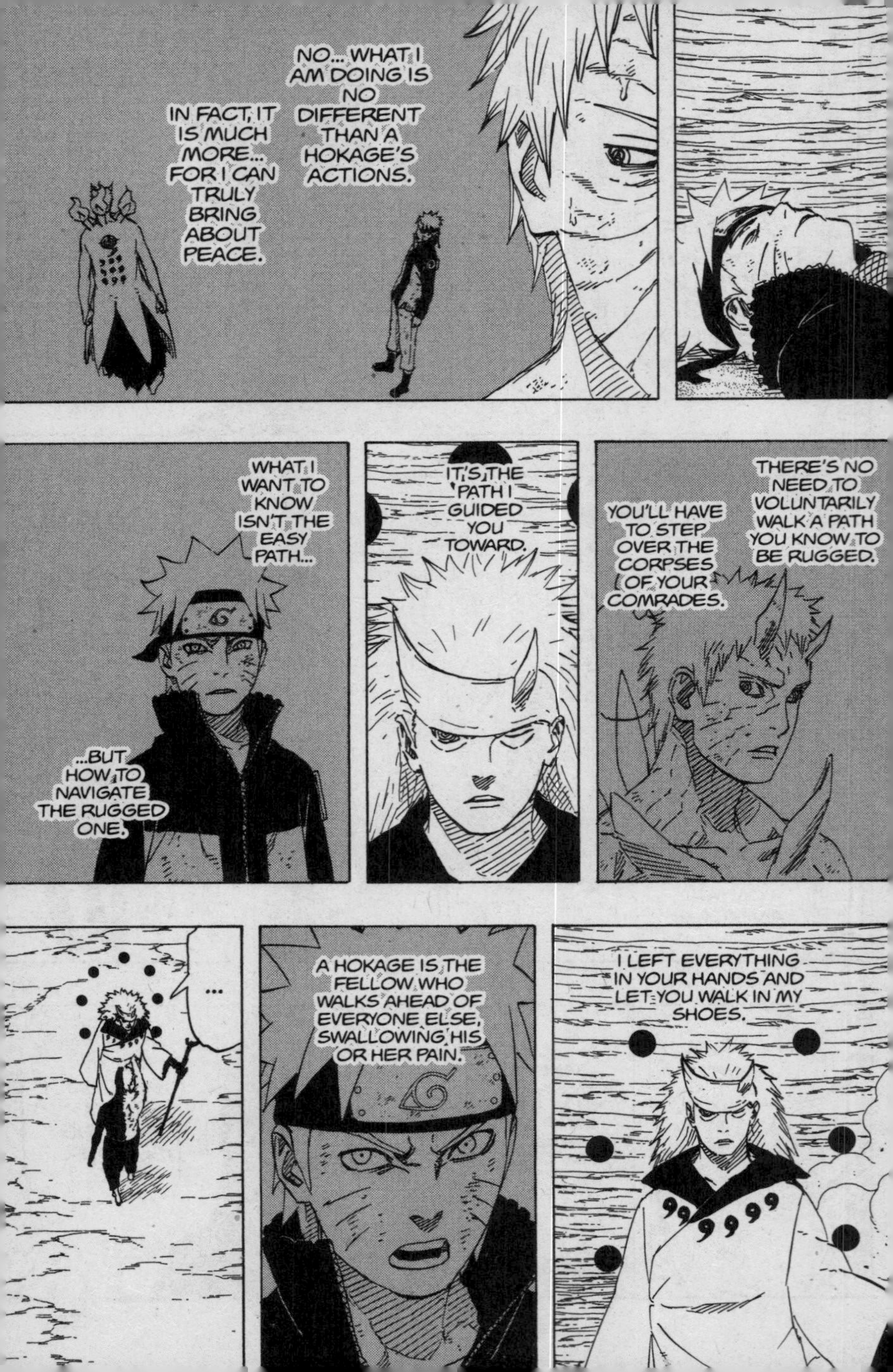
NO... WHAT I AM DOING IS NO DIFFERENT THAN A HOKAGE'S ACTIONS.
IN FACT, IT IS MUCH MORE... FOR I CAN TRULY BRING ABOUT PEACE.
THERE'S NO NEED TO VOLUNTARILY WALK A PATH YOU KNOW TO BE RUGGED.
YOU'LL HAVE TO STEP OVER THE CORPSES OF YOUR COMRADES.
IT'S THE PATH I GUIDED YOU TOWARD.
WHAT I WANT TO KNOW ISN'T THE EASY PATH...
...BUT HOW TO NAVIGATE THE RUGGED ONE.
I LEFT EVERYTHING IN YOUR HANDS AND LET YOU WALK IN MY SHOES.
A HOKAGE IS THE FELLOW WHO WALKS AHEAD OF EVERYONE ELSE, SWALLOWING HIS OR HER PAIN.
...

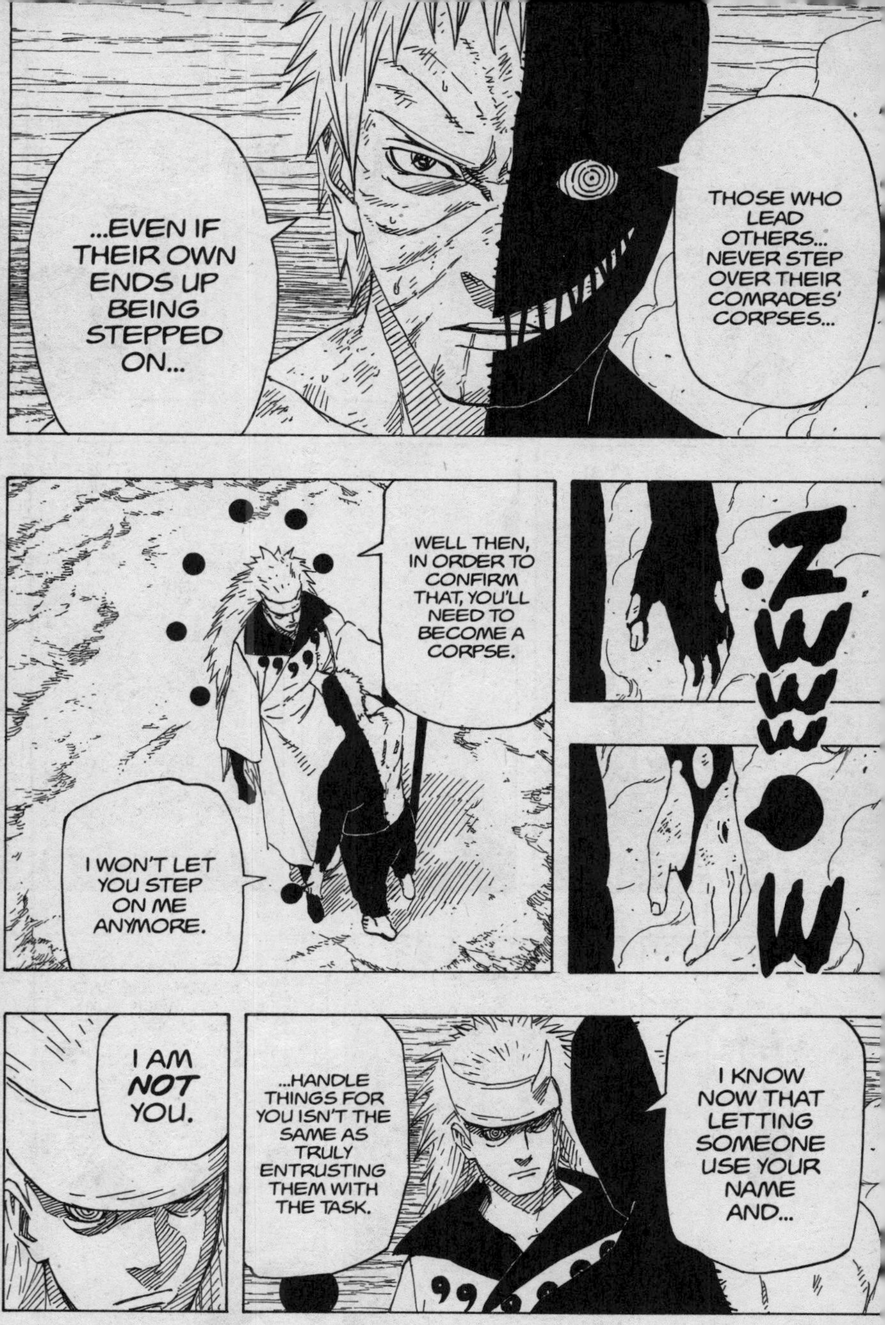
THOSE WHO LEAD OTHERS... NEVER STEP OVER THEIR COMRADES' CORPSES...
...EVEN IF THEIR OWN ENDS UP BEING STEPPED ON...
ZWWWW
WELL THEN, IN ORDER TO CONFIRM THAT, YOU'LL NEED TO BECOME A CORPSE.
I WON'T LET YOU STEP ON ME ANYMORE.
I KNOW NOW THAT LETTING SOMEONE USE YOUR NAME AND...
...HANDLE THINGS FOR YOU ISN'T THE SAME AS TRULY ENTRUSTING THEM WITH THE TASK.
I AM NOT YOU.

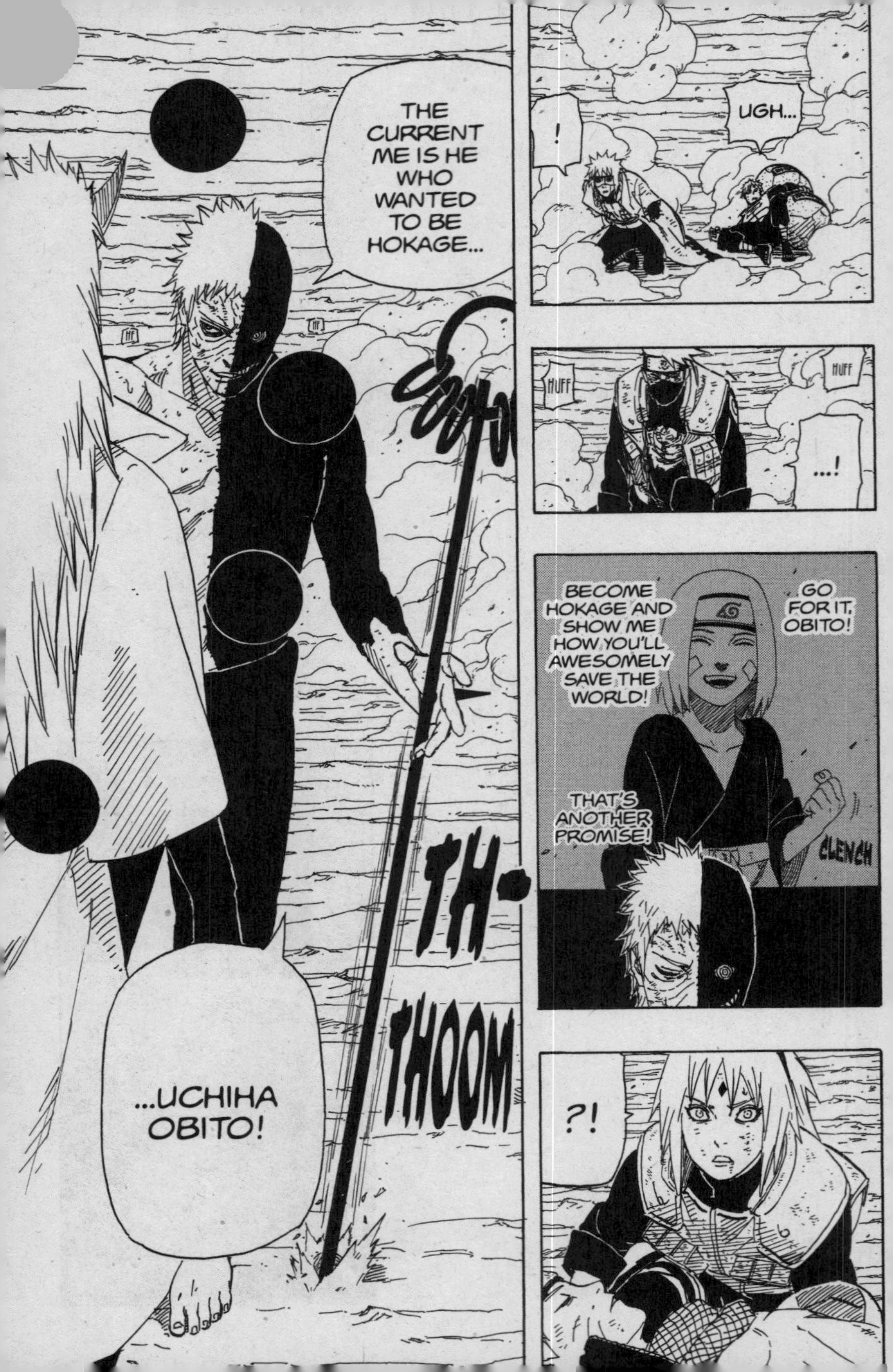
!
UGH...
HUFF
HUFF
...!
GO FOR IT, OBITO!
BECOME HOKAGE AND SHOW ME HOW YOU'LL AWESOMELY SAVE THE WORLD!
THAT'S ANOTHER PROMISE!
CLENCH
?!
THE CURRENT ME IS HE WHO WANTED TO BE HOKAGE...
TH-THOOM
...UCHIHA OBITO!

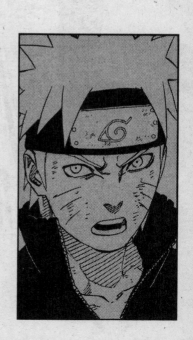

Number 666: The Two Mangekyo

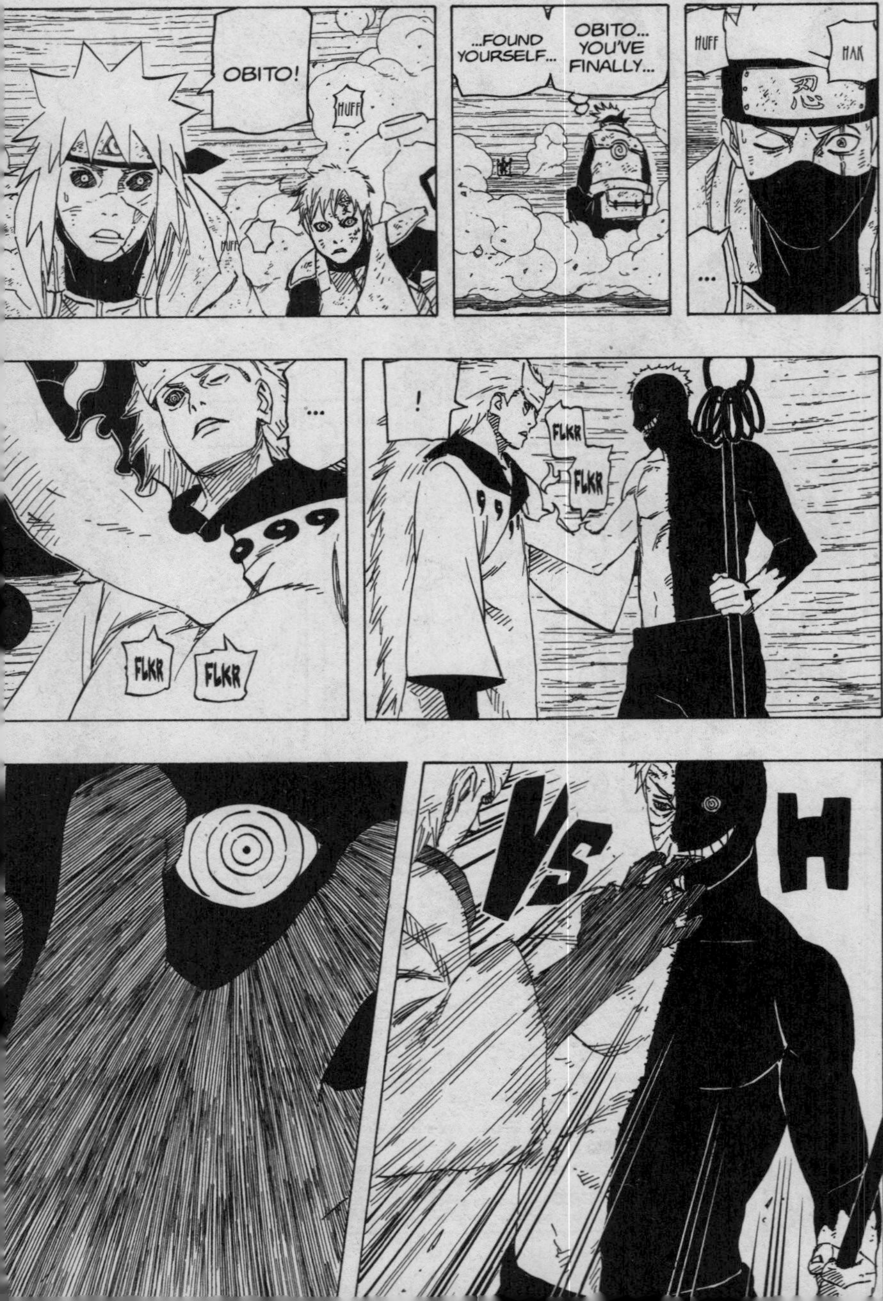
HUFF
HAK
...
OBITO... YOU'VE FINALLY...
...FOUND YOURSELF...
OBITO!
HUFF
HUFF
!
FLKR
FLKR
...
FLKR
FLKR
VSH

Number 666: The Two Mangeky

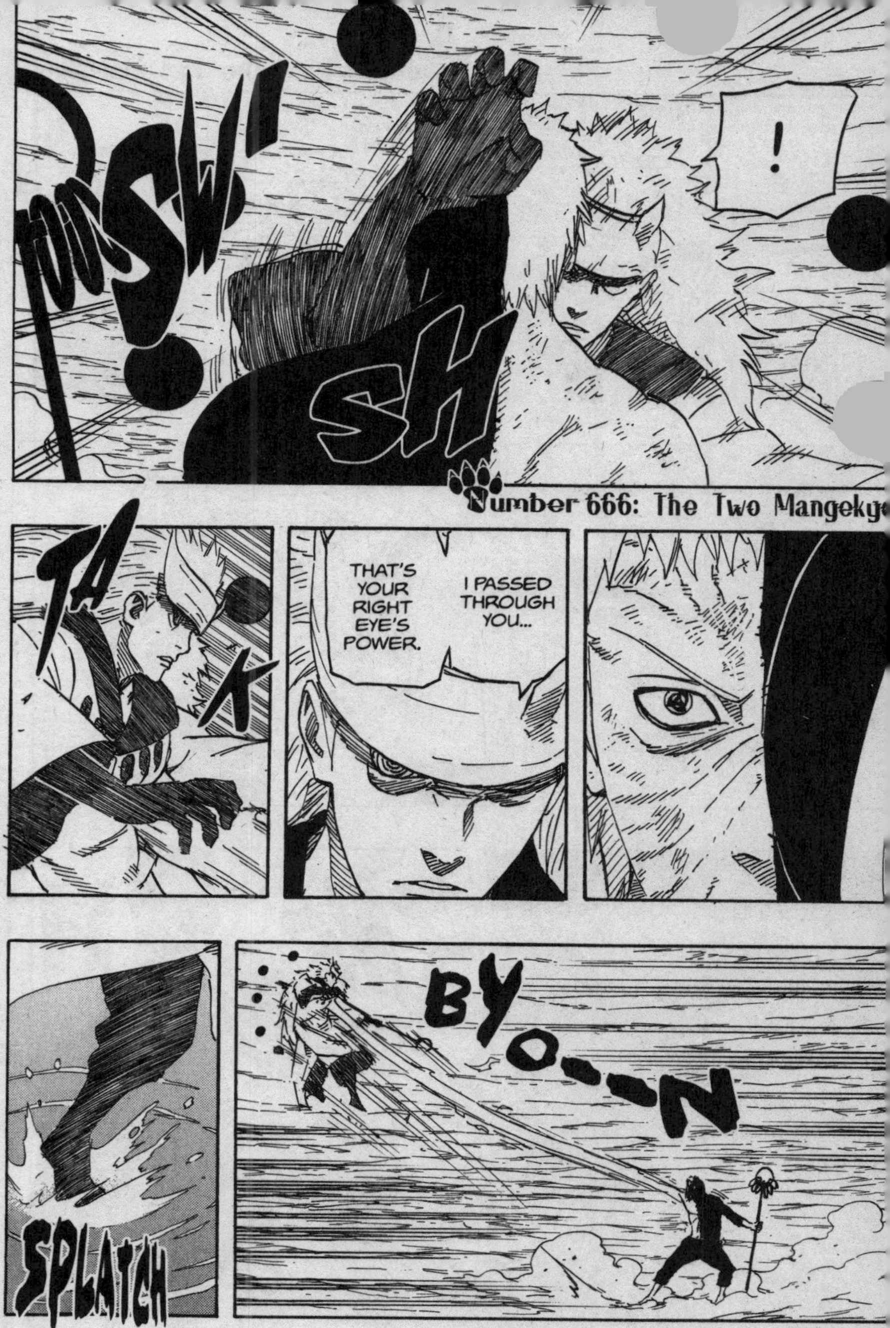
!
SH
I PASSED THROUGH YOU...
THAT'S YOUR RIGHT EYE'S POWER.
TA
K
BYO--N
SPLATCH

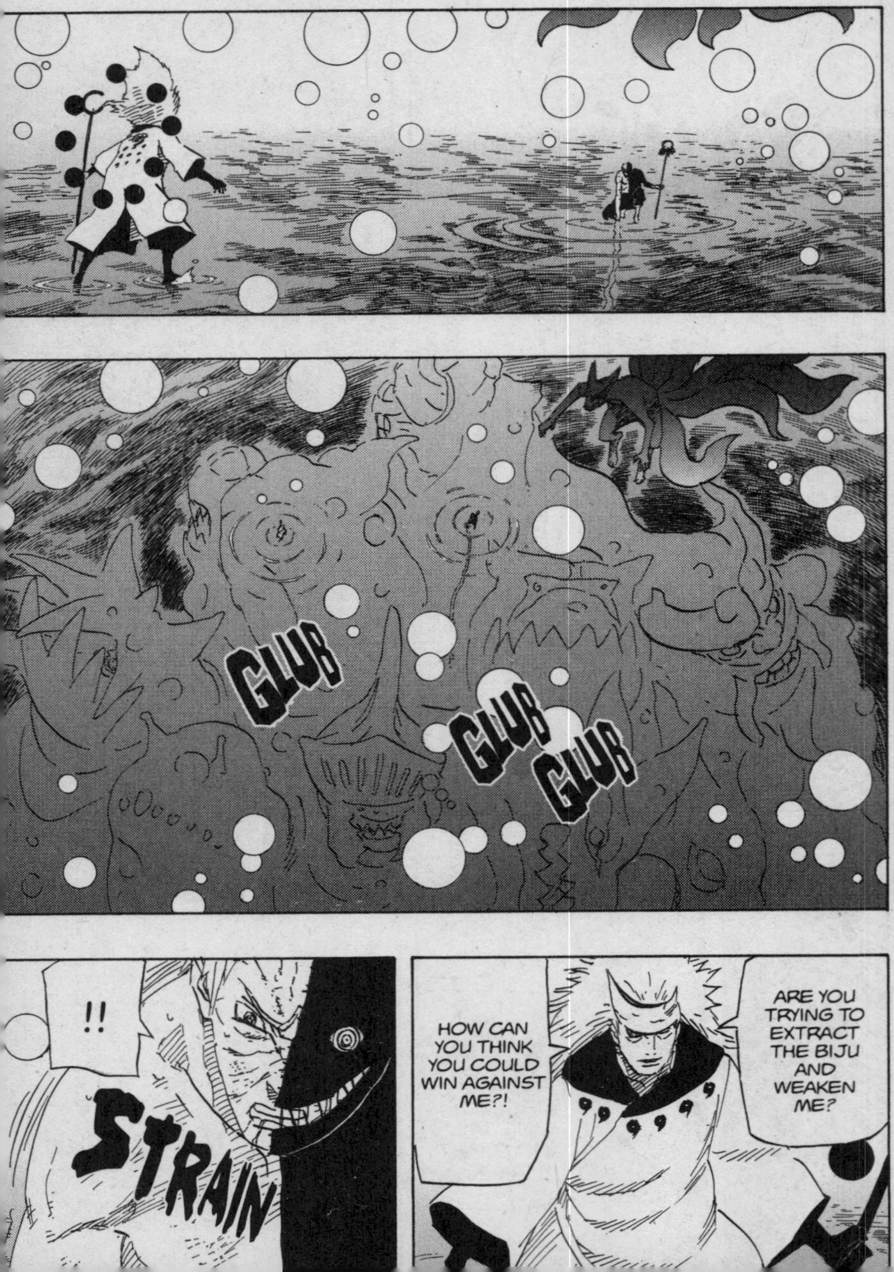
GLUB
GLUB
GLUB
ARE YOU TRYING TO EXTRACT THE BIJU AND WEAKEN ME?
HOW CAN YOU THINK YOU COULD WIN AGAINST ME?!
!!
STRAIN

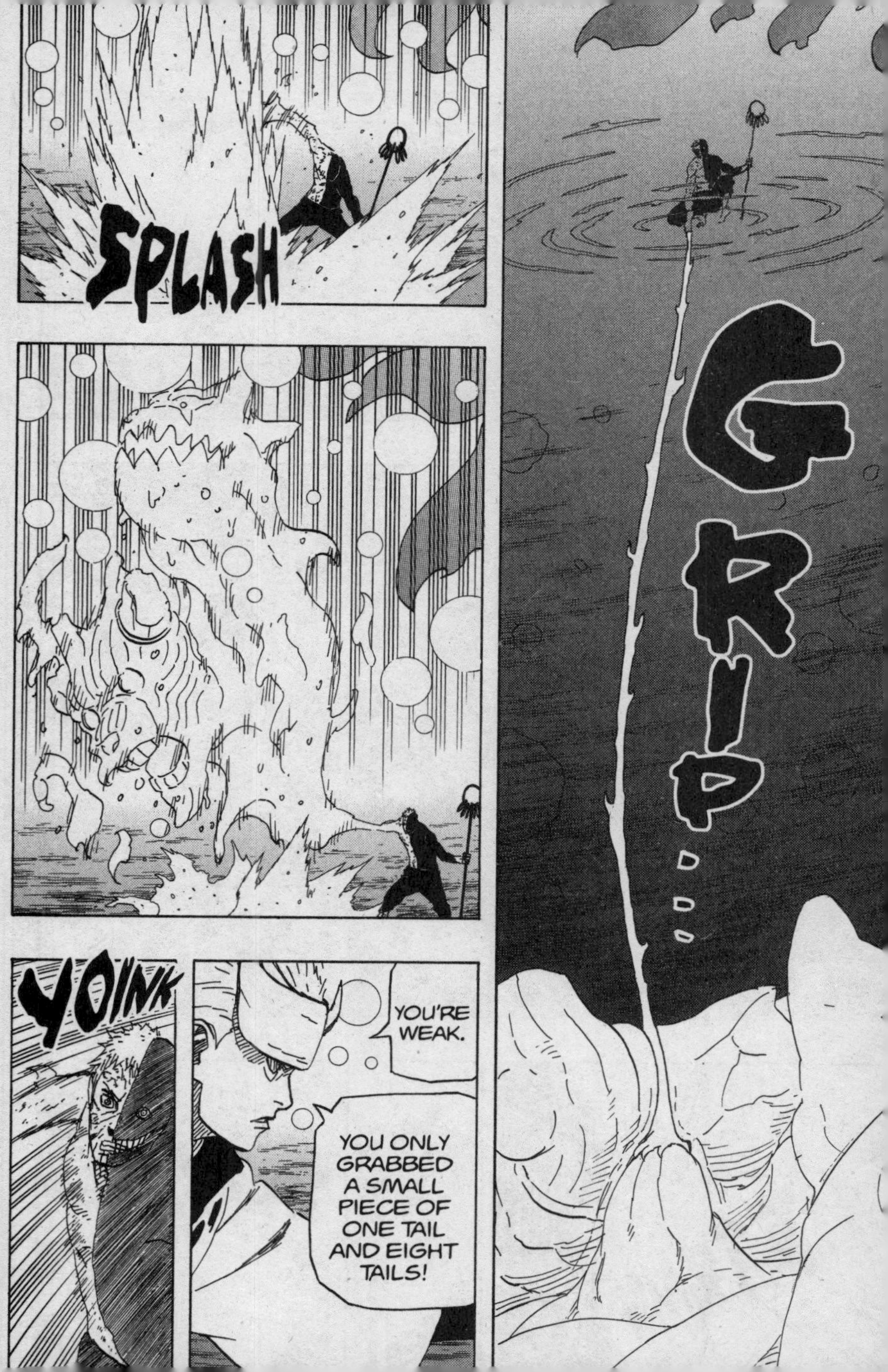
GRIP...
SPLASH
YOU'RE WEAK.
YOU ONLY GRABBED A SMALL PIECE OF ONE TAIL AND EIGHT TAILS!
YOINK

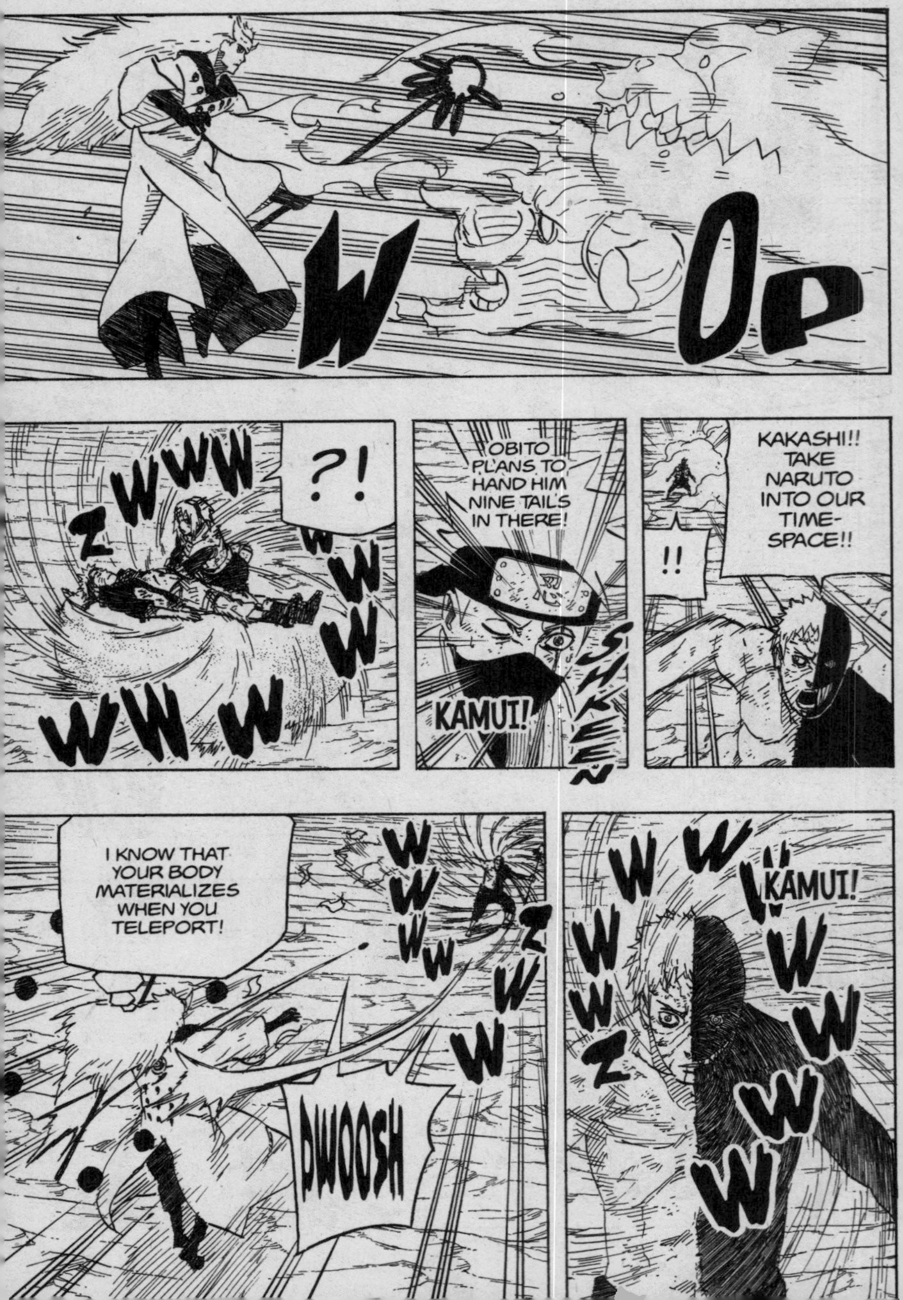
WOOP
KAKASHI!! TAKE NARUTO INTO OUR TIME-SPACE!!
!!
OBITO PLANS TO HAND HIM NINE TAILS IN THERE!
KAMUI!
SHKEEN
?!
ZWWWWWWWWWWW
KAMUI!
ZWWWWWWWWWWWW
I KNOW THAT YOUR BODY MATERIALIZES WHEN YOU TELEPORT!
ZWWWWWWWWW
DWOOSH

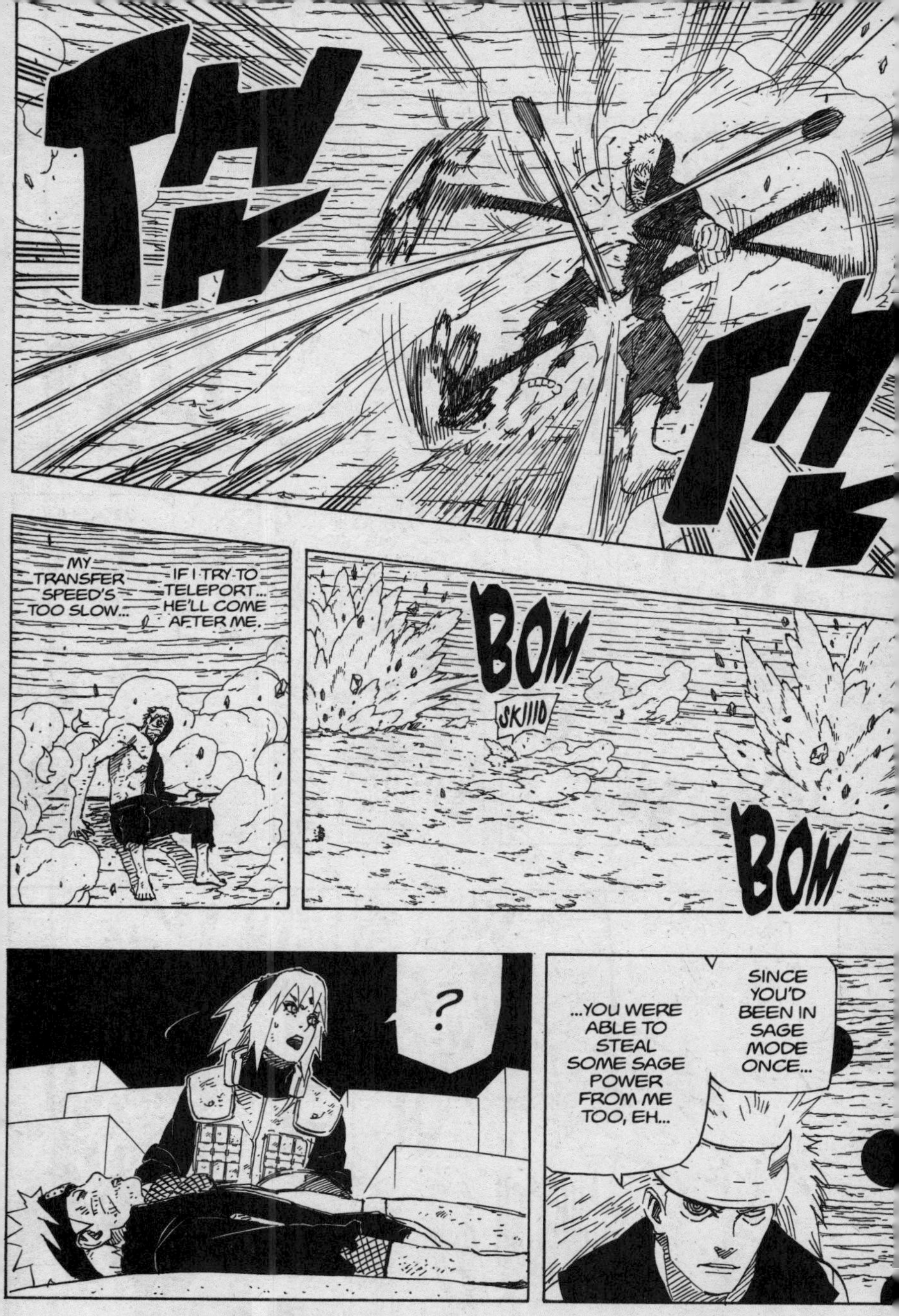
BOM
SKIIID
BOM
IF I TRY TO TELEPORT... HE'LL COME AFTER ME.
MY TRANSFER SPEED'S TOO SLOW...
SINCE YOU'D BEEN IN SAGE MODE ONCE...
...YOU WERE ABLE TO STEAL SOME SAGE POWER FROM ME TOO, EH...
?

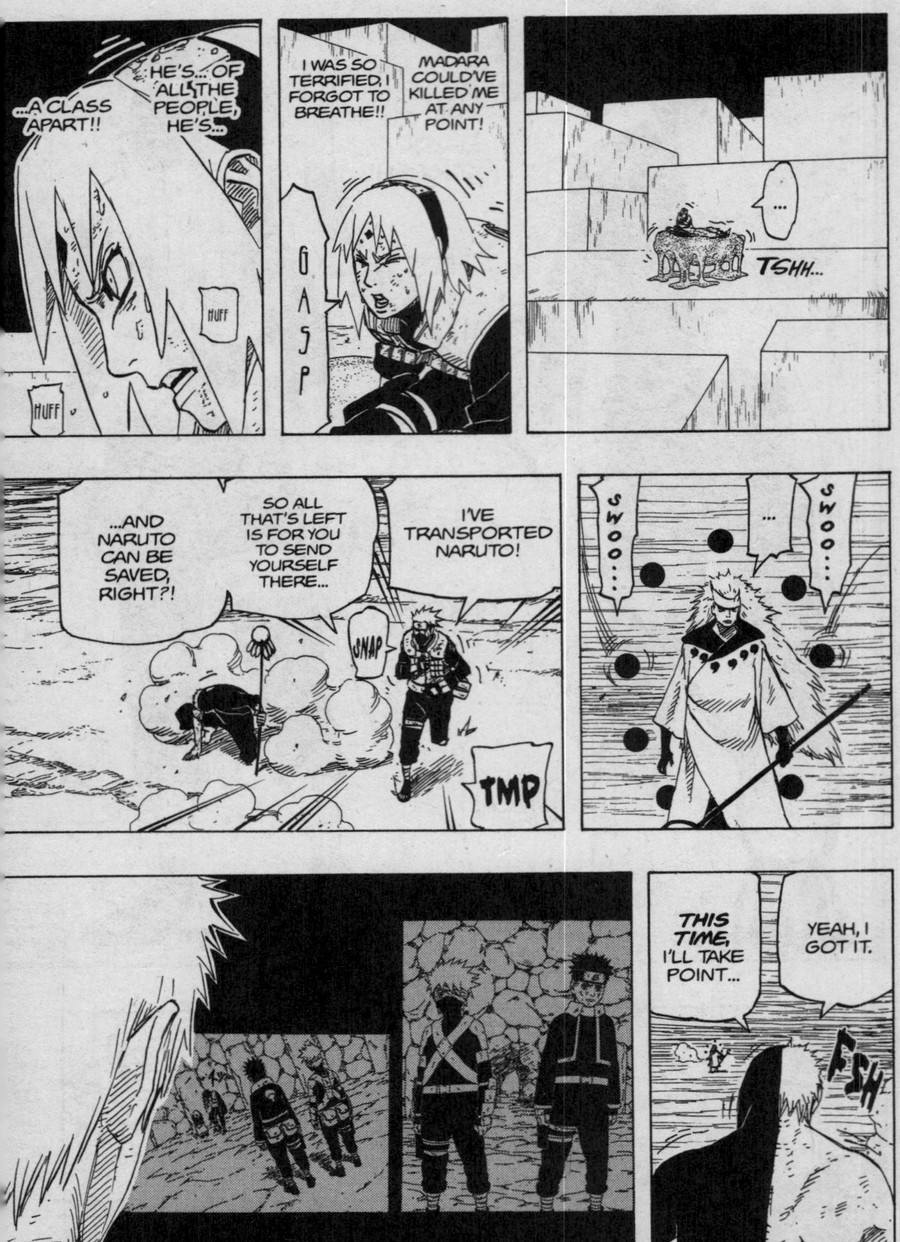
...
TSHH...
MADARA COULD'VE KILLED ME AT ANY POINT!
I WAS SO TERRIFIED, I FORGOT TO BREATHE!!
GASP
HE'S... OF ALL THE PEOPLE, HE'S...
...A CLASS APART!!
HUFF
HUFF
SWOO...
...
SWOO...
I'VE TRANSPORTED NARUTO!
SO ALL THAT'S LEFT IS FOR YOU TO SEND YOURSELF THERE...
...AND NARUTO CAN BE SAVED, RIGHT?!
SNAP
TMP
YEAH, I GOT IT.
THIS TIME, I'LL TAKE POINT...
FSH

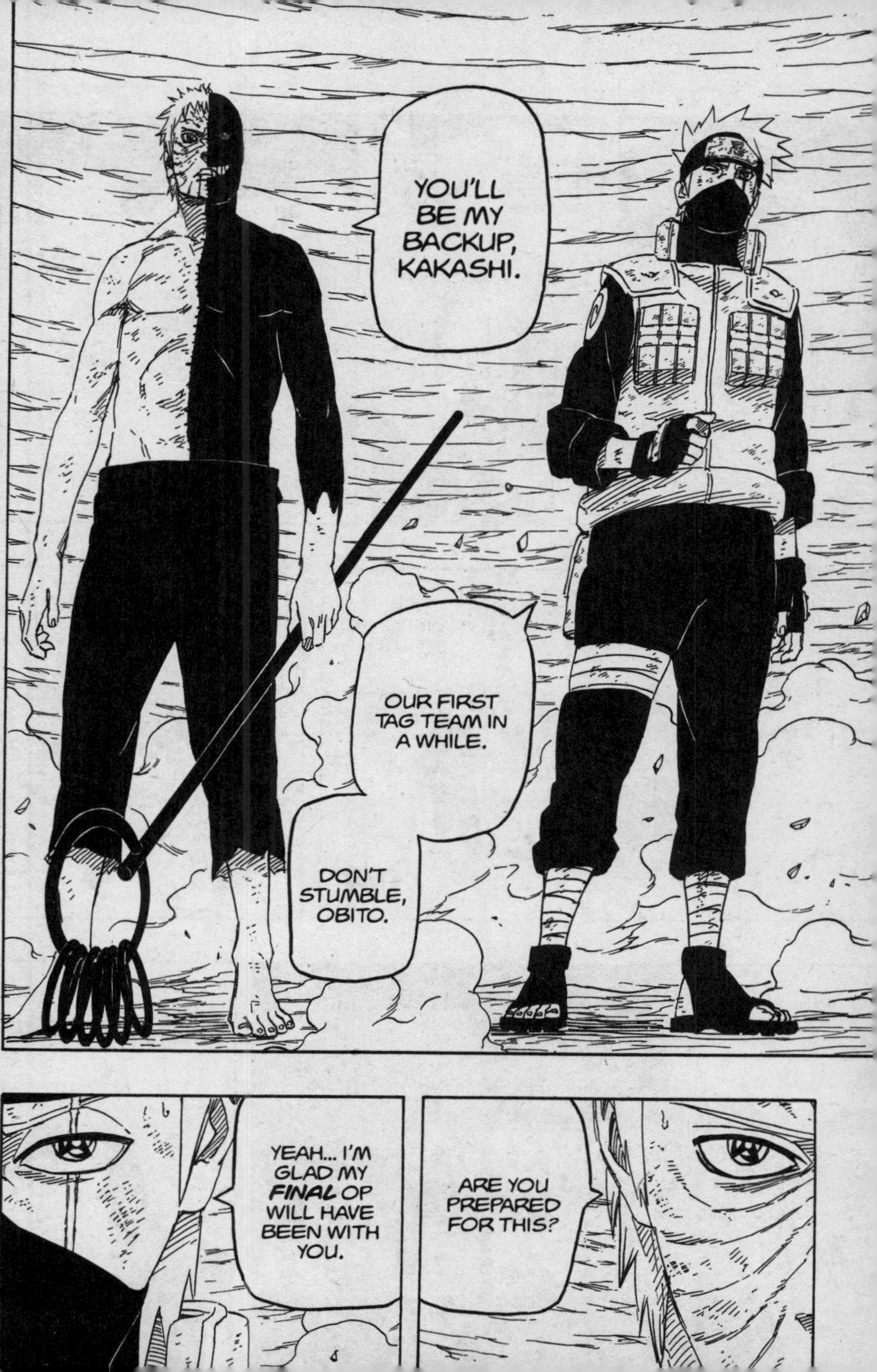
YOU'LL BE MY BACKUP, KAKASHI.
OUR FIRST TAG TEAM IN A WHILE.
DON'T STUMBLE, OBITO.
ARE YOU PREPARED FOR THIS?
YEAH... I'M GLAD MY **FINAL** OP WILL HAVE BEEN WITH YOU.

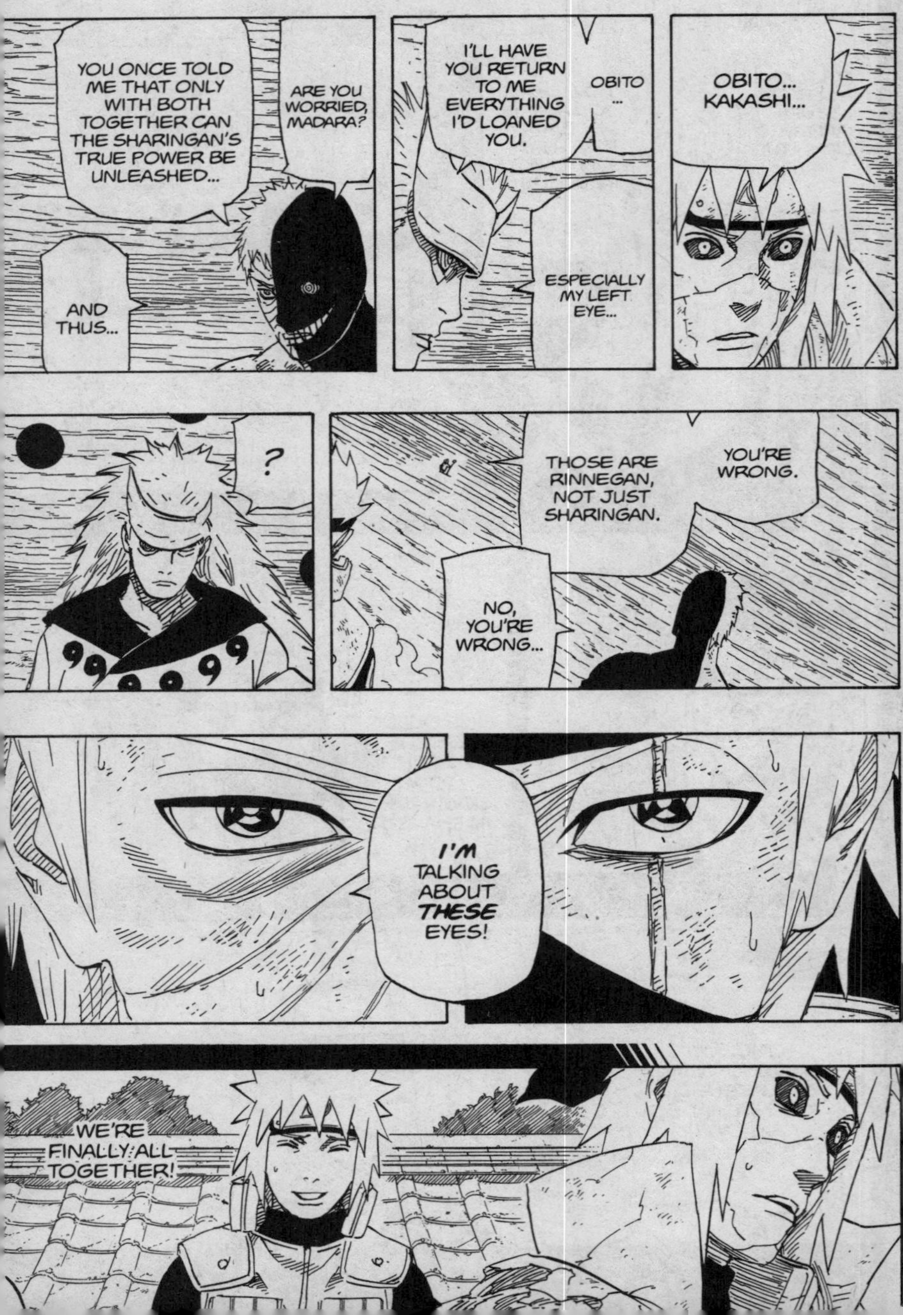
OBITO... KAKASHI...
OBITO ...
I'LL HAVE YOU RETURN TO ME EVERYTHING I'D LOANED YOU.
ESPECIALLY MY LEFT EYE...
ARE YOU WORRIED, MADARA?
YOU ONCE TOLD ME THAT ONLY WITH BOTH TOGETHER CAN THE SHARINGAN'S TRUE POWER BE UNLEASHED...
AND THUS...
YOU'RE WRONG.
THOSE ARE RINNEGAN, NOT JUST SHARINGAN.
NO, YOU'RE WRONG...
?
I'M TALKING ABOUT *THESE* EYES!
WE'RE FINALLY ALL TOGETHER!

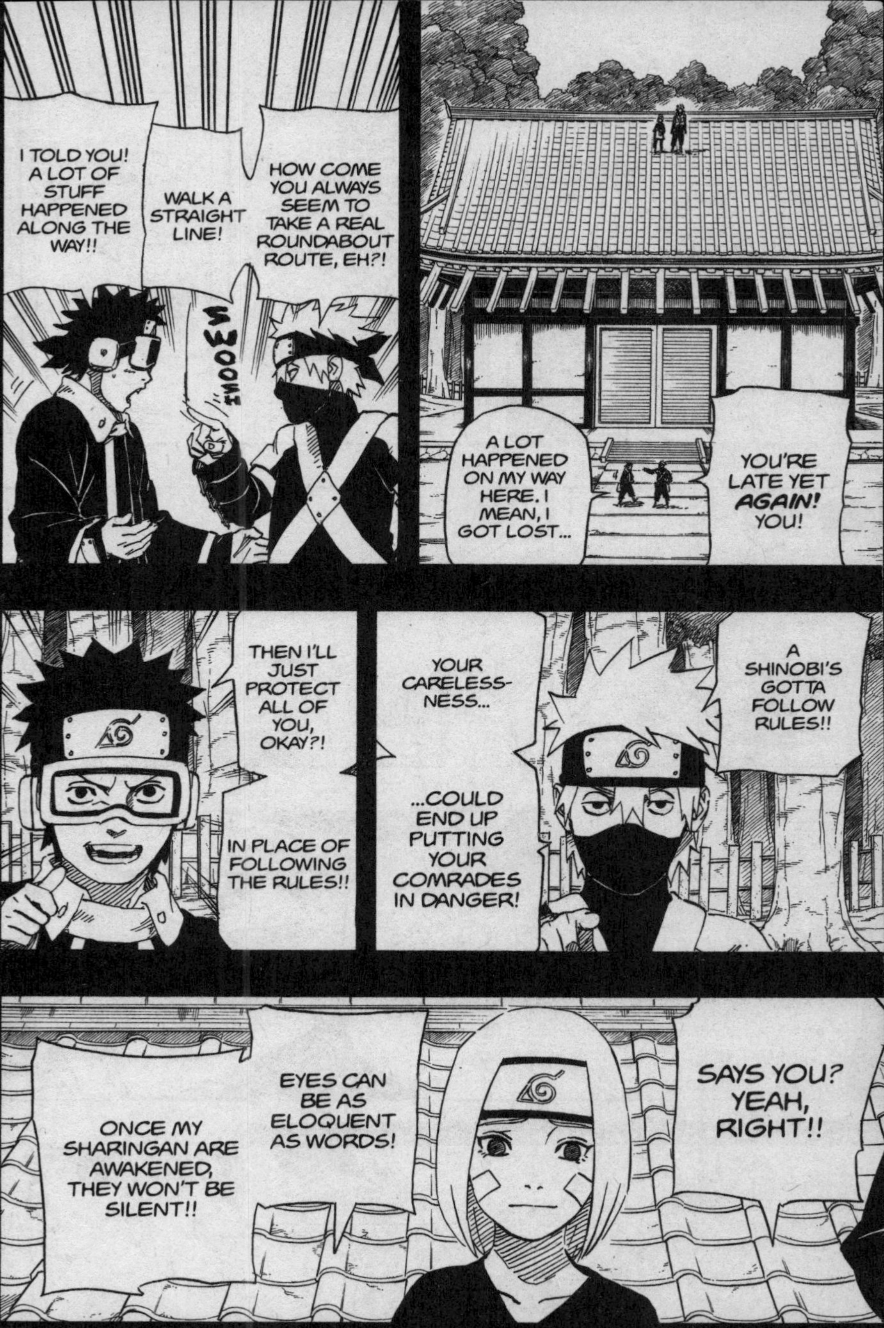
YOU'RE LATE YET AGAIN! YOU!
A LOT HAPPENED ON MY WAY HERE. I MEAN, I GOT LOST...
HOW COME YOU ALWAYS SEEM TO TAKE A REAL ROUNDABOUT ROUTE, EH?!
WALK A STRAIGHT LINE!
I TOLD YOU! A LOT OF STUFF HAPPENED ALONG THE WAY!!
SWOOSH
A SHINOBI'S GOTTA FOLLOW RULES!!
YOUR CARELESS-NESS...
...COULD END UP PUTTING YOUR COMRADES IN DANGER!
THEN I'LL JUST PROTECT ALL OF YOU, OKAY?!
IN PLACE OF FOLLOWING THE RULES!!
SAYS YOU? YEAH, RIGHT!!
EYES CAN BE AS ELOQUENT AS WORDS!
ONCE MY SHARINGAN ARE AWAKENED, THEY WON'T BE SILENT!!

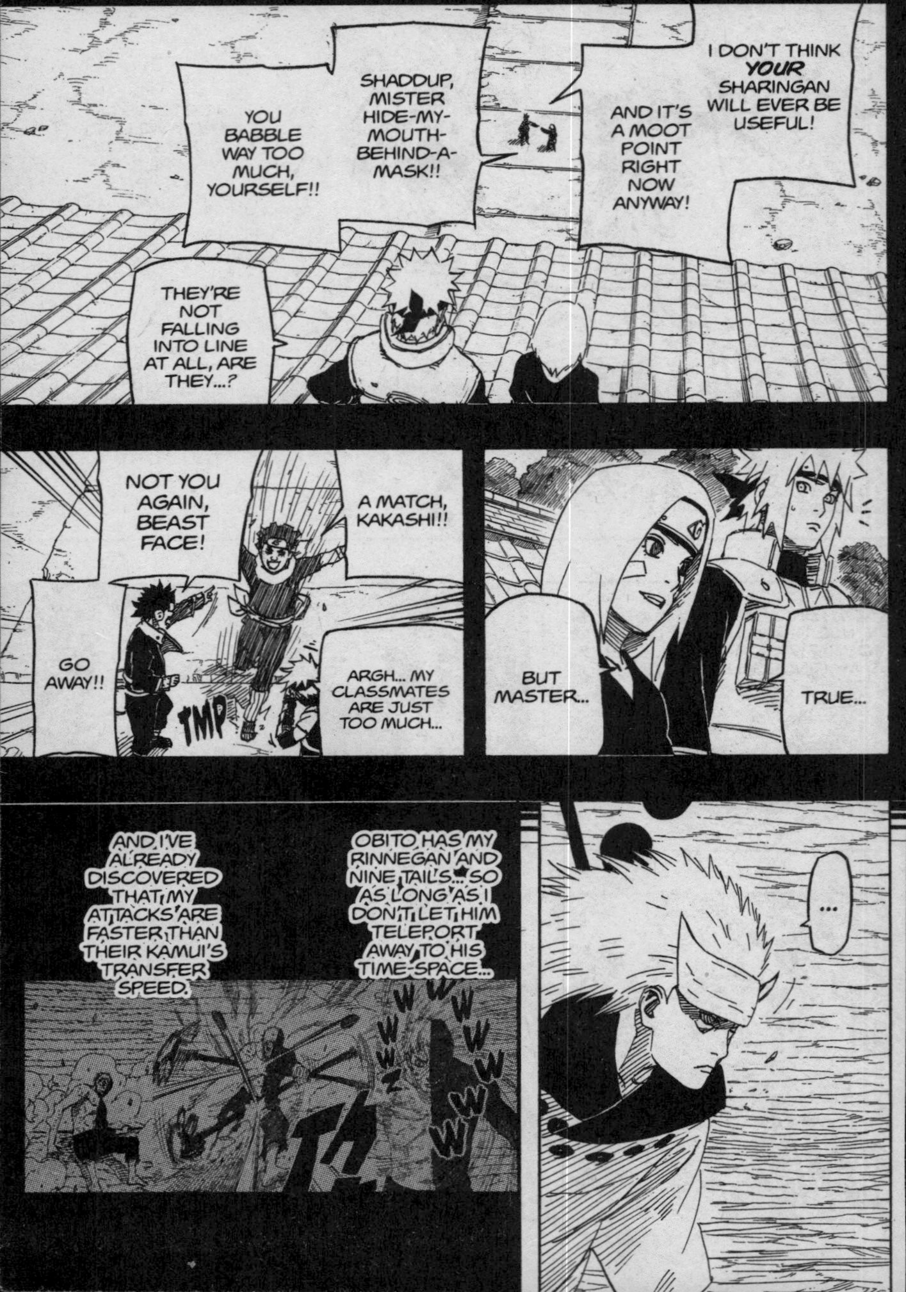
I DON'T THINK **YOUR** SHARINGAN WILL EVER BE USEFUL!
AND IT'S A MOOT POINT RIGHT NOW ANYWAY!
SHADDUP, MISTER HIDE-MY-MOUTH-BEHIND-A-MASK!!
YOU BABBLE WAY TOO MUCH, YOURSELF!!
THEY'RE NOT FALLING INTO LINE AT ALL, ARE THEY...?
TRUE...
BUT MASTER...
A MATCH, KAKASHI!!
NOT YOU AGAIN, BEAST FACE!
GO AWAY!!
TMP
ARGH... MY CLASSMATES ARE JUST TOO MUCH...
...
OBITO HAS MY RINNEGAN AND NINE TAILS... SO AS LONG AS I DON'T LET HIM TELEPORT AWAY TO HIS TIME-SPACE...
AND I'VE ALREADY DISCOVERED THAT MY ATTACKS ARE FASTER THAN THEIR KAMUI'S TRANSFER SPEED.

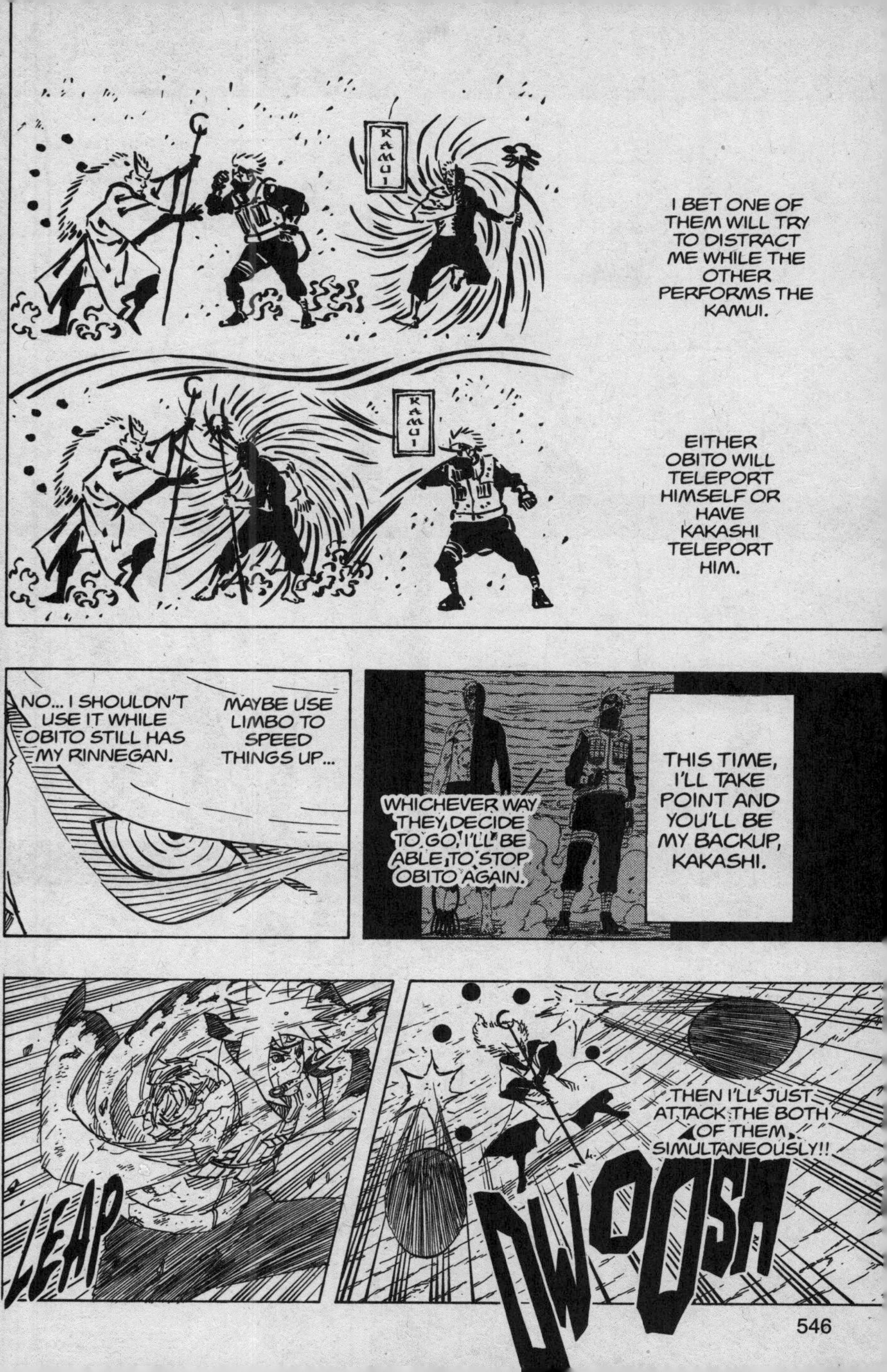
KAMUI
KAMUI
I BET ONE OF THEM WILL TRY TO DISTRACT ME WHILE THE OTHER PERFORMS THE KAMUI.
EITHER OBITO WILL TELEPORT HIMSELF OR HAVE KAKASHI TELEPORT HIM.
THIS TIME, I'LL TAKE POINT AND YOU'LL BE MY BACKUP, KAKASHI.
WHICHEVER WAY THEY DECIDE TO GO, I'LL BE ABLE TO STOP OBITO AGAIN.
MAYBE USE LIMBO TO SPEED THINGS UP...
NO... I SHOULDN'T USE IT WHILE OBITO STILL HAS MY RINNEGAN.
THEN I'LL JUST ATTACK THE BOTH OF THEM SIMULTANEOUSLY!!
DWOOSH
LEAP

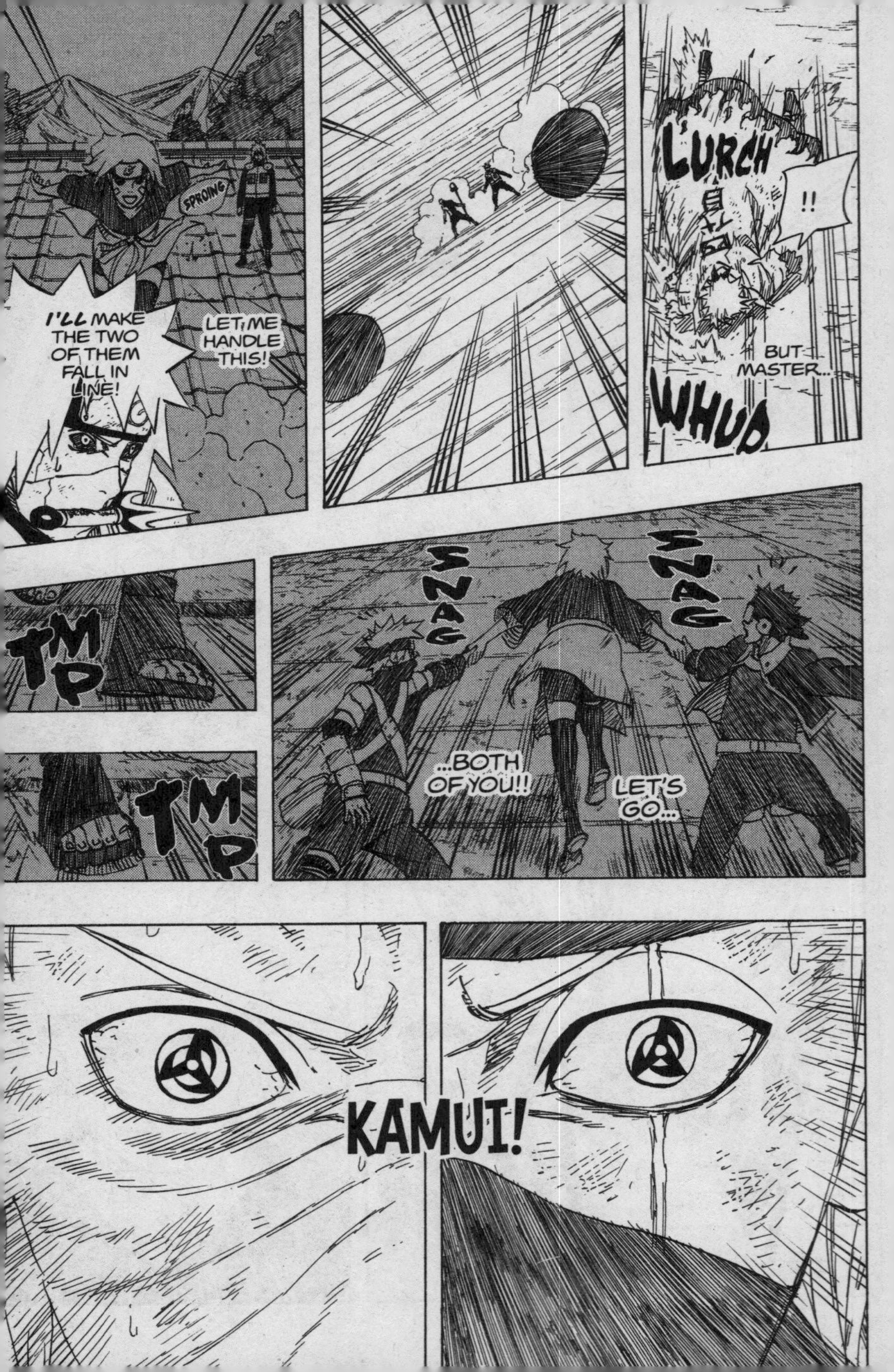
LURCH
!!
BUT MASTER...
WHUD
SPROING
LET ME HANDLE THIS!
I'LL MAKE THE TWO OF THEM FALL IN LINE!
SNAG
SNAG
LET'S GO...
...BOTH OF YOU!!
TMP
TMP
TMP
TMP
KAMUI!

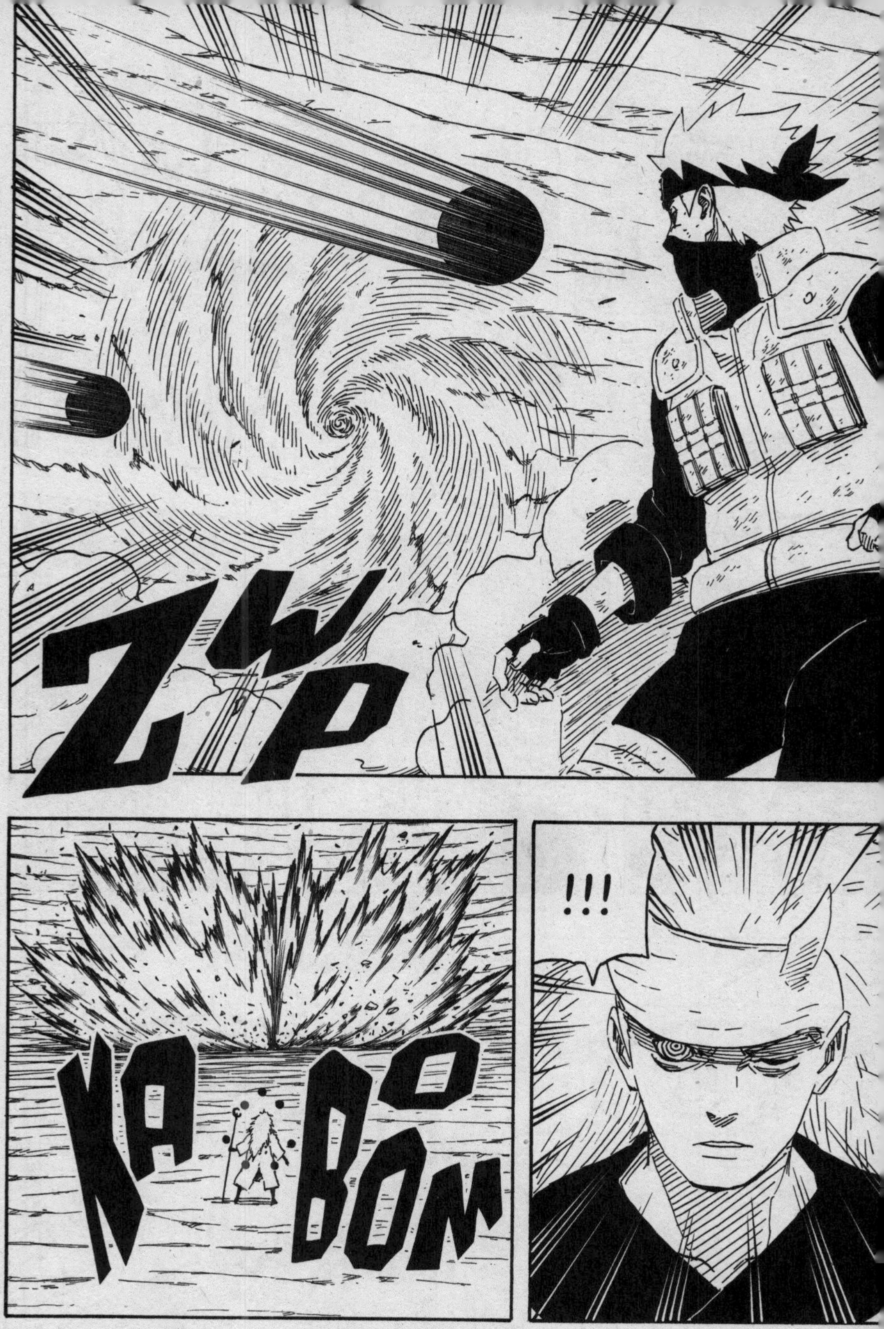
ZWIP
!!!
KA BOOM

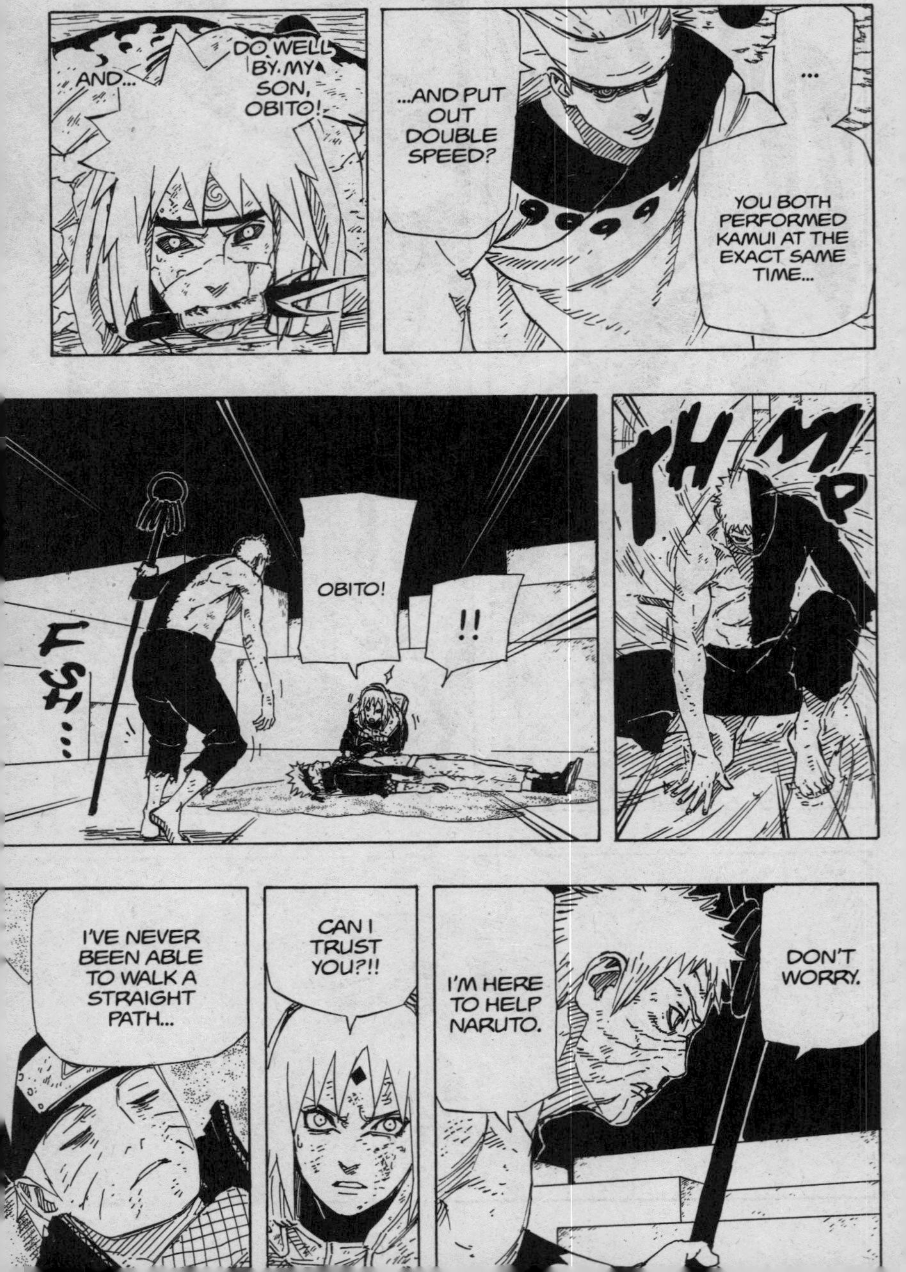
...
YOU BOTH PERFORMED KAMUI AT THE EXACT SAME TIME...
...AND PUT OUT DOUBLE SPEED?
DO WELL BY MY SON, OBITO!
AND...
THMP
!!
OBITO!
FSH...
DON'T WORRY.
I'M HERE TO HELP NARUTO.
CAN I TRUST YOU?!!
I'VE NEVER BEEN ABLE TO WALK A STRAIGHT PATH...

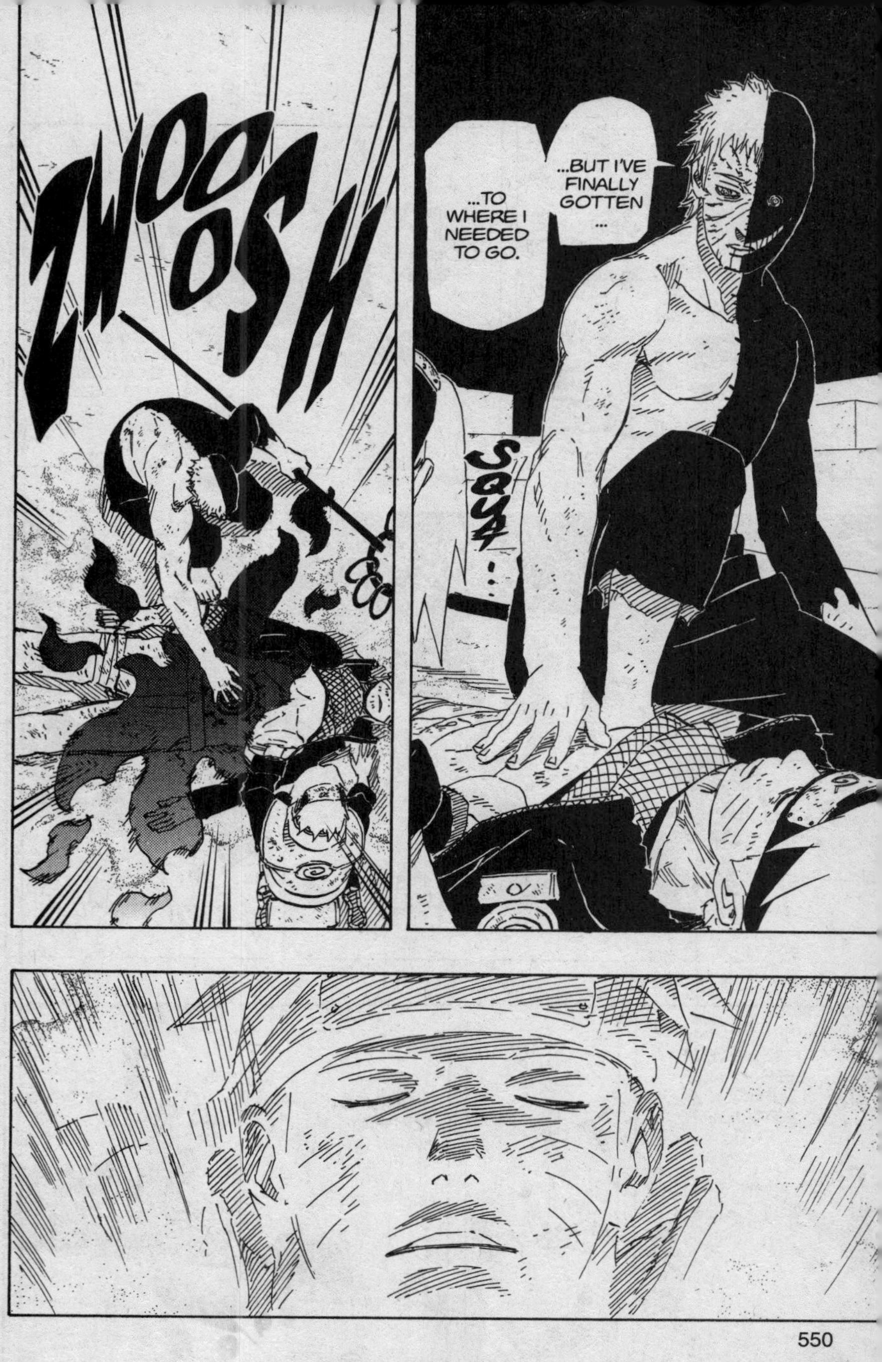
...BUT I'VE FINALLY GOTTEN ...
...TO WHERE I NEEDED TO GO.
SQUA...
ZWOOOSH

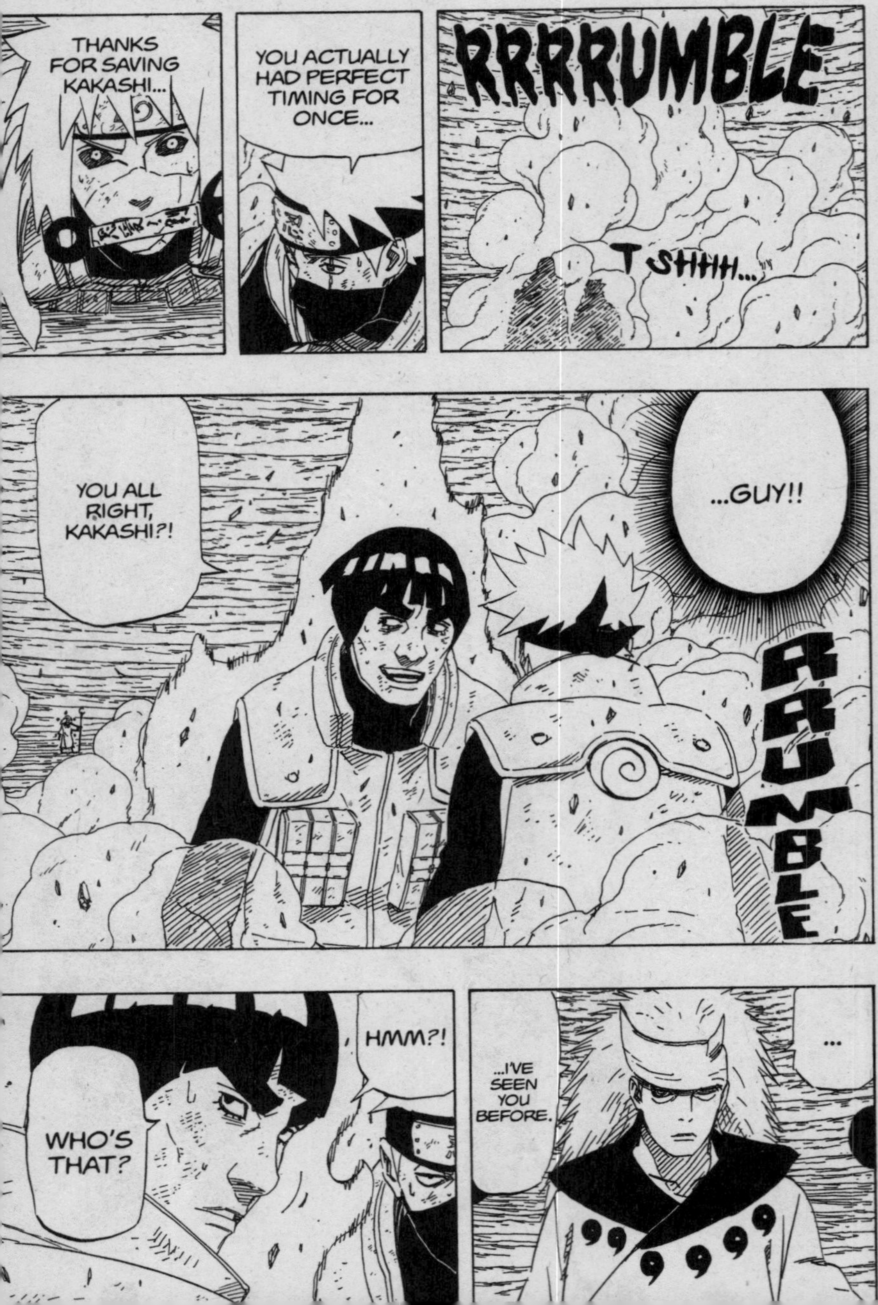
RRRRUMBLE
TSHHH...
YOU ACTUALLY HAD PERFECT TIMING FOR ONCE...
THANKS FOR SAVING KAKASHI...
...GUY!!
RRUMBLE
YOU ALL RIGHT, KAKASHI?!
...
...I'VE SEEN YOU BEFORE.
HMM?!
WHO'S THAT?

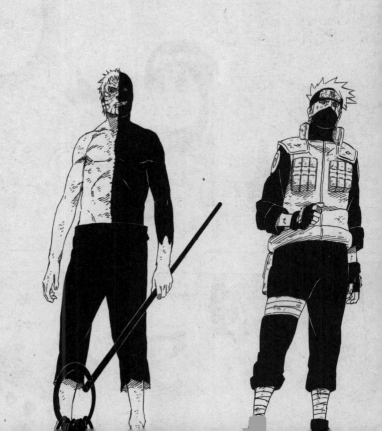

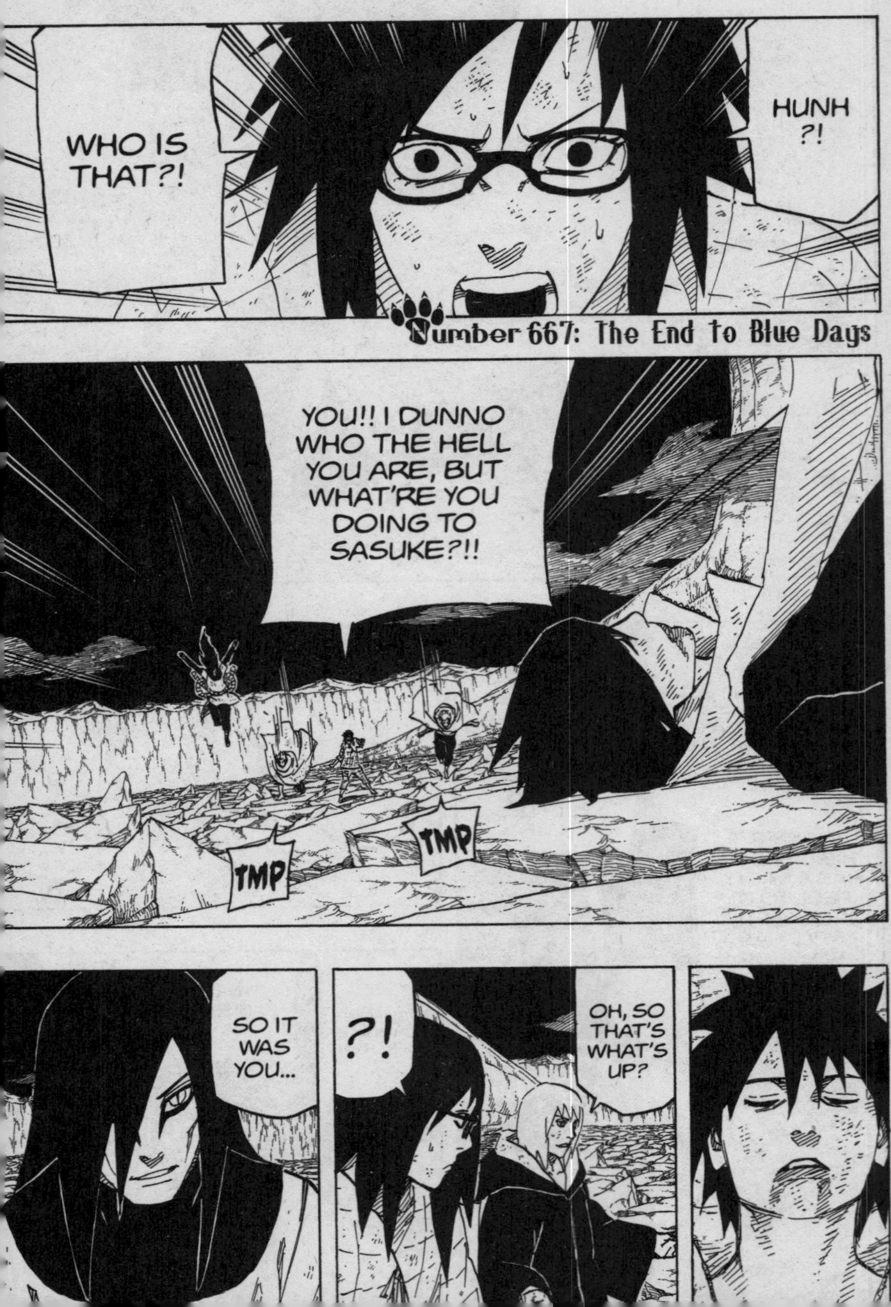
HUNH ?!
WHO IS THAT?!
Number 667: The End to Blue Days
YOU!! I DUNNO WHO THE HELL YOU ARE, BUT WHAT'RE YOU DOING TO SASUKE?!!
TMP
TMP
OH, SO THAT'S WHAT'S UP?
?!
SO IT WAS YOU...

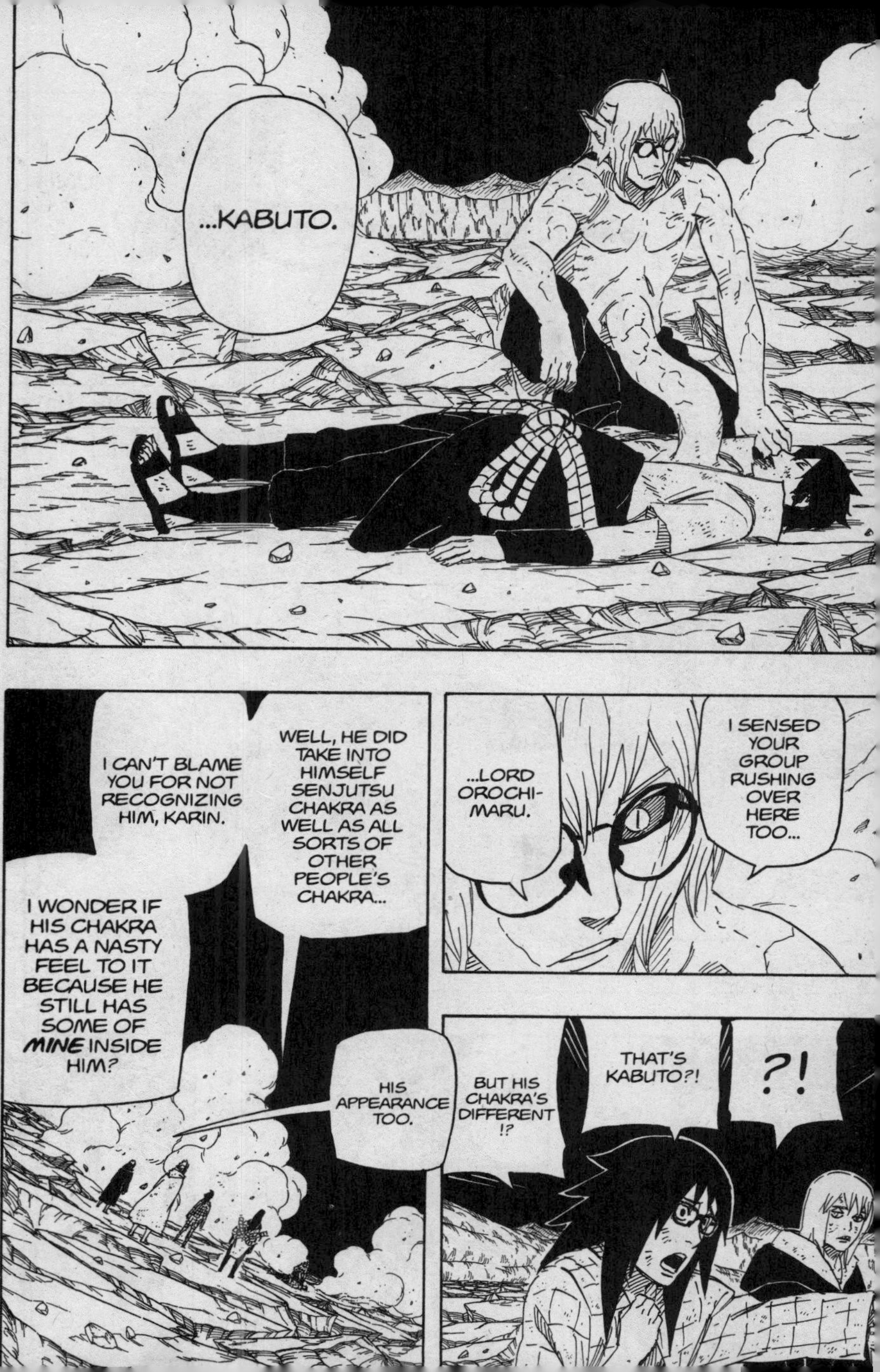

...KABUTO.
I SENSED YOUR GROUP RUSHING OVER HERE TOO...
...LORD OROCHIMARU.
?!
THAT'S KABUTO?!
BUT HIS CHAKRA'S DIFFERENT!?
HIS APPEARANCE TOO.
I CAN'T BLAME YOU FOR NOT RECOGNIZING HIM, KARIN.
WELL, HE DID TAKE INTO HIMSELF SENJUTSU CHAKRA AS WELL AS ALL SORTS OF OTHER PEOPLE'S CHAKRA...
I WONDER IF HIS CHAKRA HAS A NASTY FEEL TO IT BECAUSE HE STILL HAS SOME OF ***MINE*** INSIDE HIM?

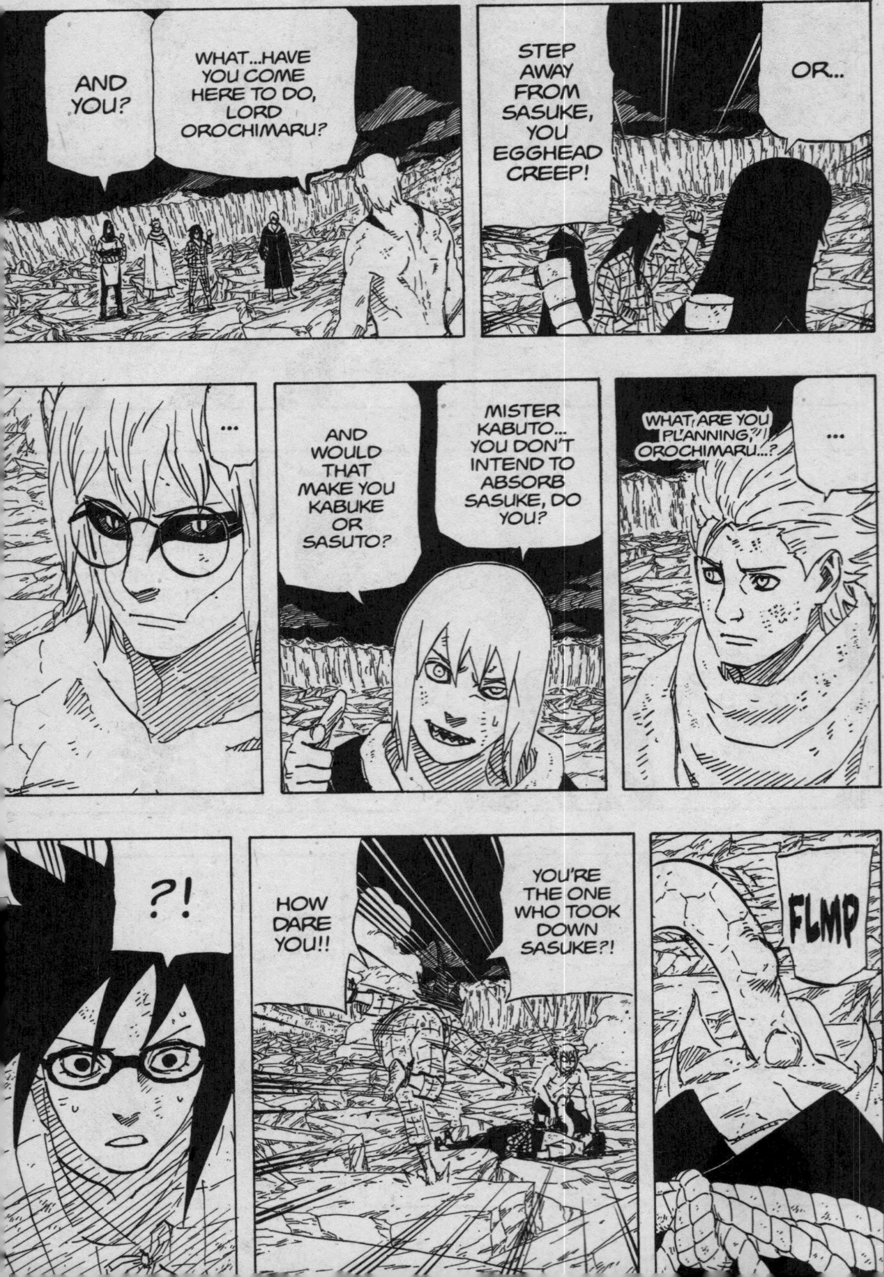
OR...
STEP AWAY FROM SASUKE, YOU EGGHEAD CREEP!
WHAT...HAVE YOU COME HERE TO DO, LORD OROCHIMARU?
AND YOU?
...
WHAT ARE YOU PLANNING, OROCHIMARU...?
MISTER KABUTO... YOU DON'T INTEND TO ABSORB SASUKE, DO YOU?
AND WOULD THAT MAKE YOU KABUKE OR SASUTO?
...
FLMP
YOU'RE THE ONE WHO TOOK DOWN SASUKE?!
HOW DARE YOU!!
?!

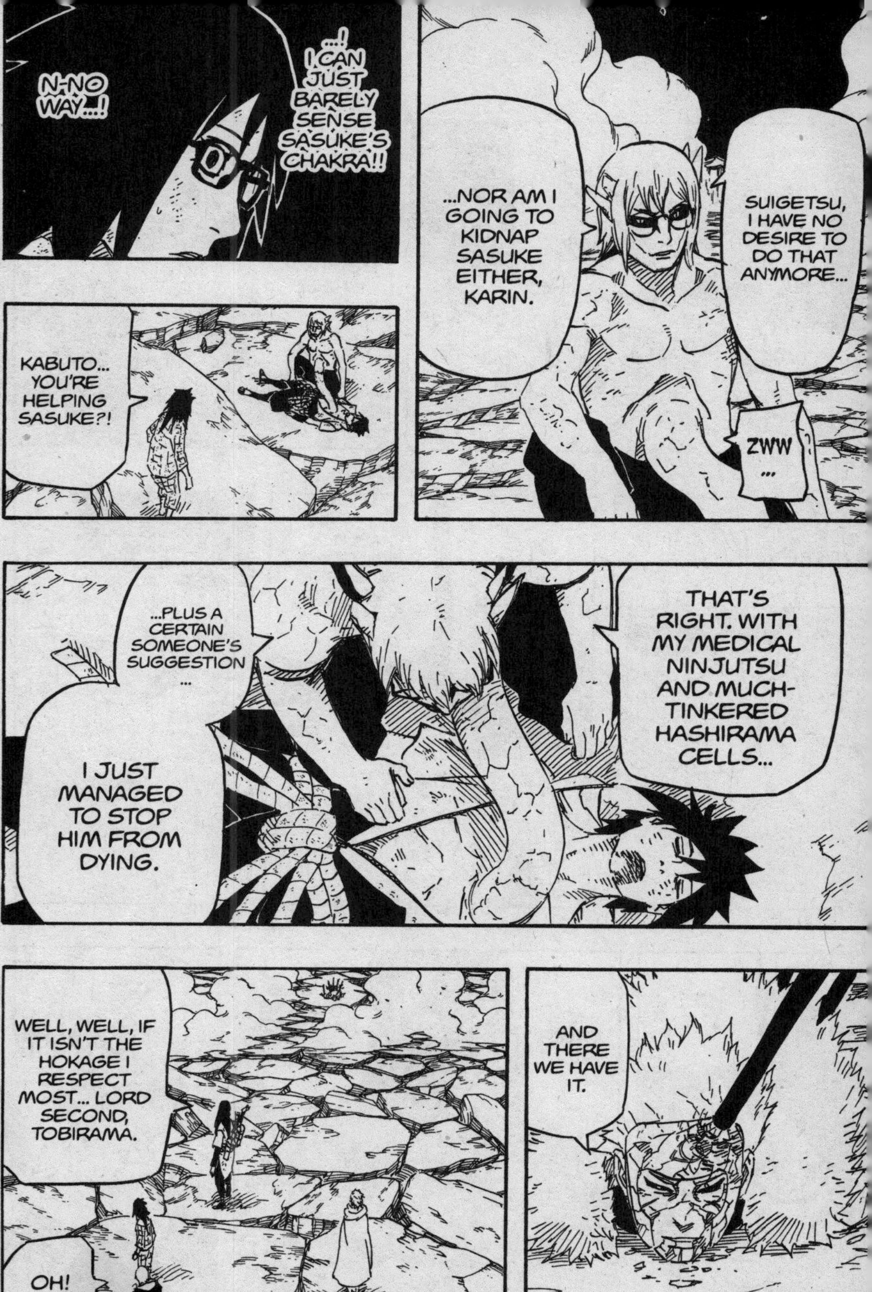
SUIGETSU, I HAVE NO DESIRE TO DO THAT ANYMORE...
...NOR AM I GOING TO KIDNAP SASUKE EITHER, KARIN.
ZWW ...
...! I CAN JUST BARELY SENSE SASUKE'S CHAKRA!!
N-NO WAY...!
KABUTO... YOU'RE HELPING SASUKE?!
THAT'S RIGHT. WITH MY MEDICAL NINJUTSU AND MUCH-TINKERED HASHIRAMA CELLS...
...PLUS A CERTAIN SOMEONE'S SUGGESTION ...
I JUST MANAGED TO STOP HIM FROM DYING.
AND THERE WE HAVE IT.
WELL, WELL, IF IT ISN'T THE HOKAGE I RESPECT MOST... LORD SECOND, TOBIRAMA.
OH!

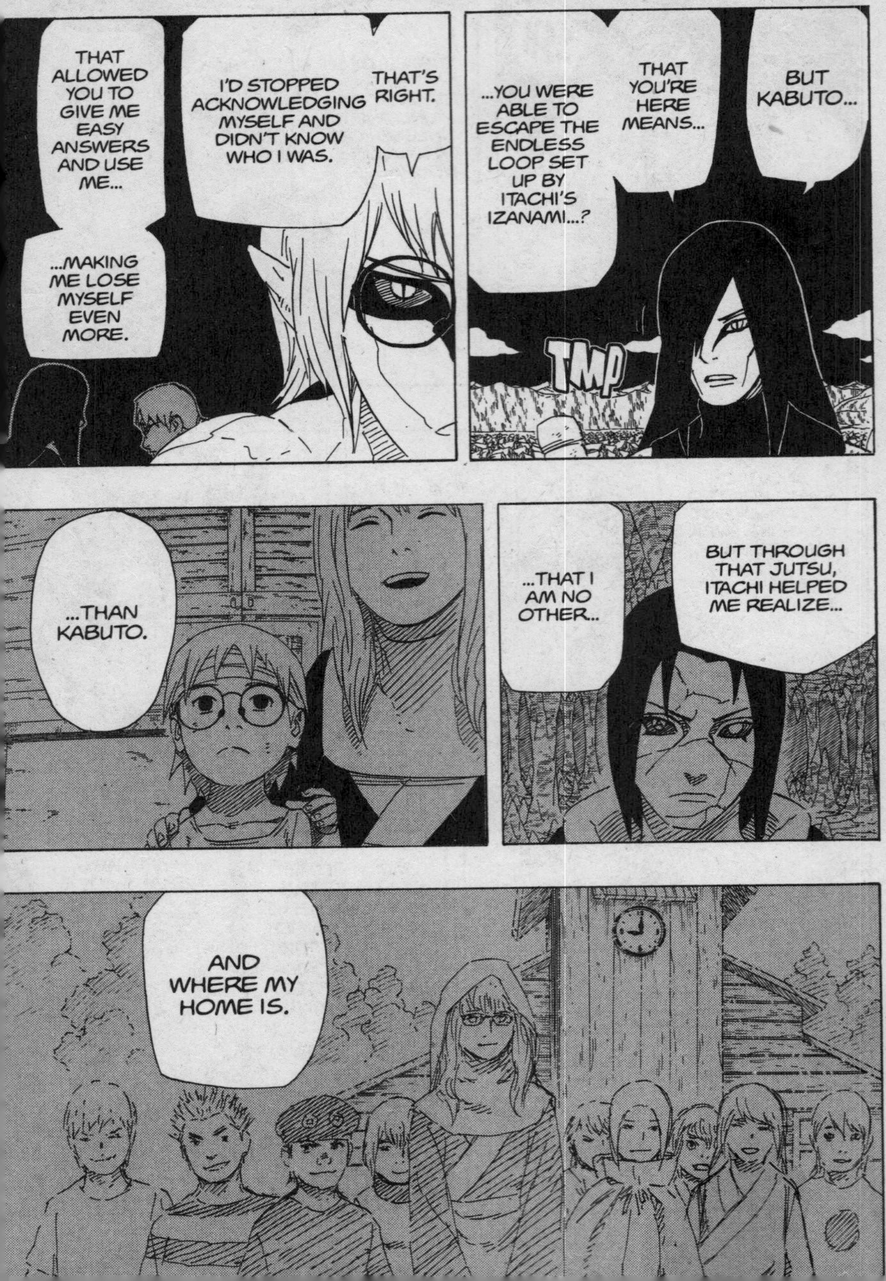
BUT KABUTO...
THAT YOU'RE HERE MEANS...
...YOU WERE ABLE TO ESCAPE THE ENDLESS LOOP SET UP BY ITACHI'S IZANAMI...?
TMP
THAT'S RIGHT.
I'D STOPPED ACKNOWLEDGING MYSELF AND DIDN'T KNOW WHO I WAS.
THAT ALLOWED YOU TO GIVE ME EASY ANSWERS AND USE ME...
...MAKING ME LOSE MYSELF EVEN MORE.
BUT THROUGH THAT JUTSU, ITACHI HELPED ME REALIZE...
...THAT I AM NO OTHER...
...THAN KABUTO.
AND WHERE MY HOME IS.

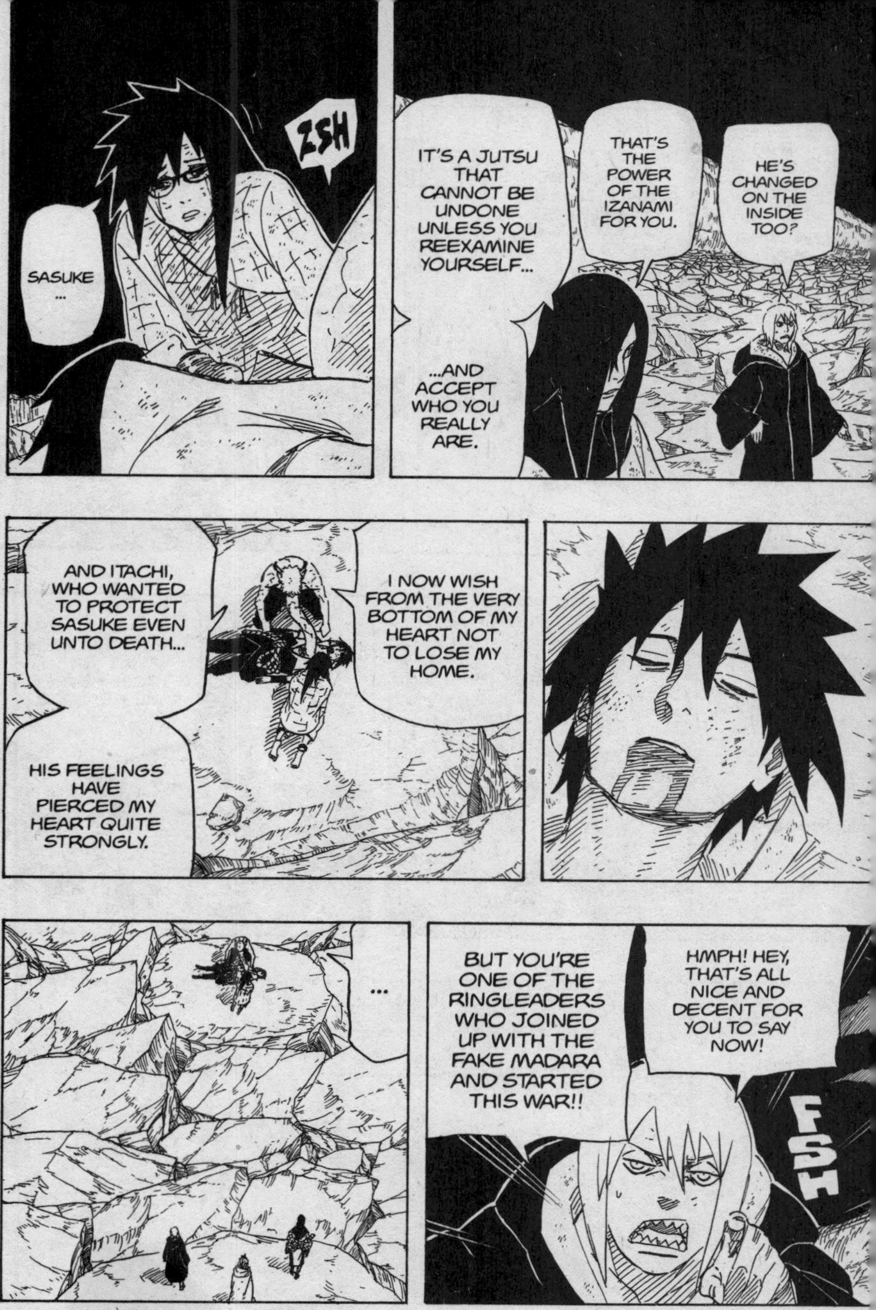

HE'S CHANGED ON THE INSIDE TOO?
THAT'S THE POWER OF THE IZANAMI FOR YOU.
IT'S A JUTSU THAT CANNOT BE UNDONE UNLESS YOU REEXAMINE YOURSELF...
...AND ACCEPT WHO YOU REALLY ARE.
ZSH
SASUKE ...
I NOW WISH FROM THE VERY BOTTOM OF MY HEART NOT TO LOSE MY HOME.
AND ITACHI, WHO WANTED TO PROTECT SASUKE EVEN UNTO DEATH...
HIS FEELINGS HAVE PIERCED MY HEART QUITE STRONGLY.
HMPH! HEY, THAT'S ALL NICE AND DECENT FOR YOU TO SAY NOW!
BUT YOU'RE ONE OF THE RINGLEADERS WHO JOINED UP WITH THE FAKE MADARA AND STARTED THIS WAR!!
FSH
...

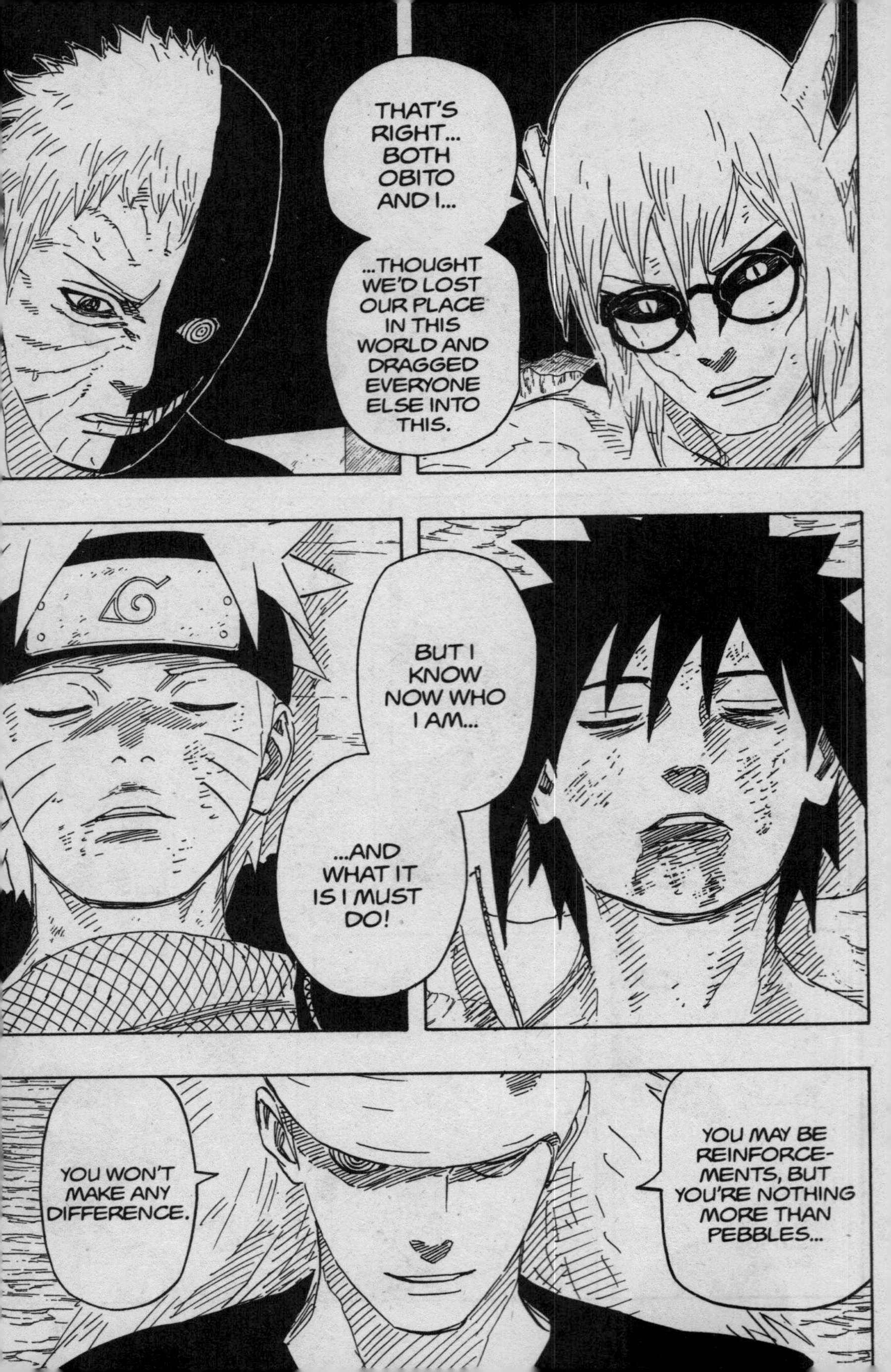
THAT'S RIGHT... BOTH OBITO AND I...
...THOUGHT WE'D LOST OUR PLACE IN THIS WORLD AND DRAGGED EVERYONE ELSE INTO THIS.
BUT I KNOW NOW WHO I AM...
...AND WHAT IT IS I MUST DO!
YOU MAY BE REINFORCE-MENTS, BUT YOU'RE NOTHING MORE THAN PEBBLES...
YOU WON'T MAKE ANY DIFFERENCE.

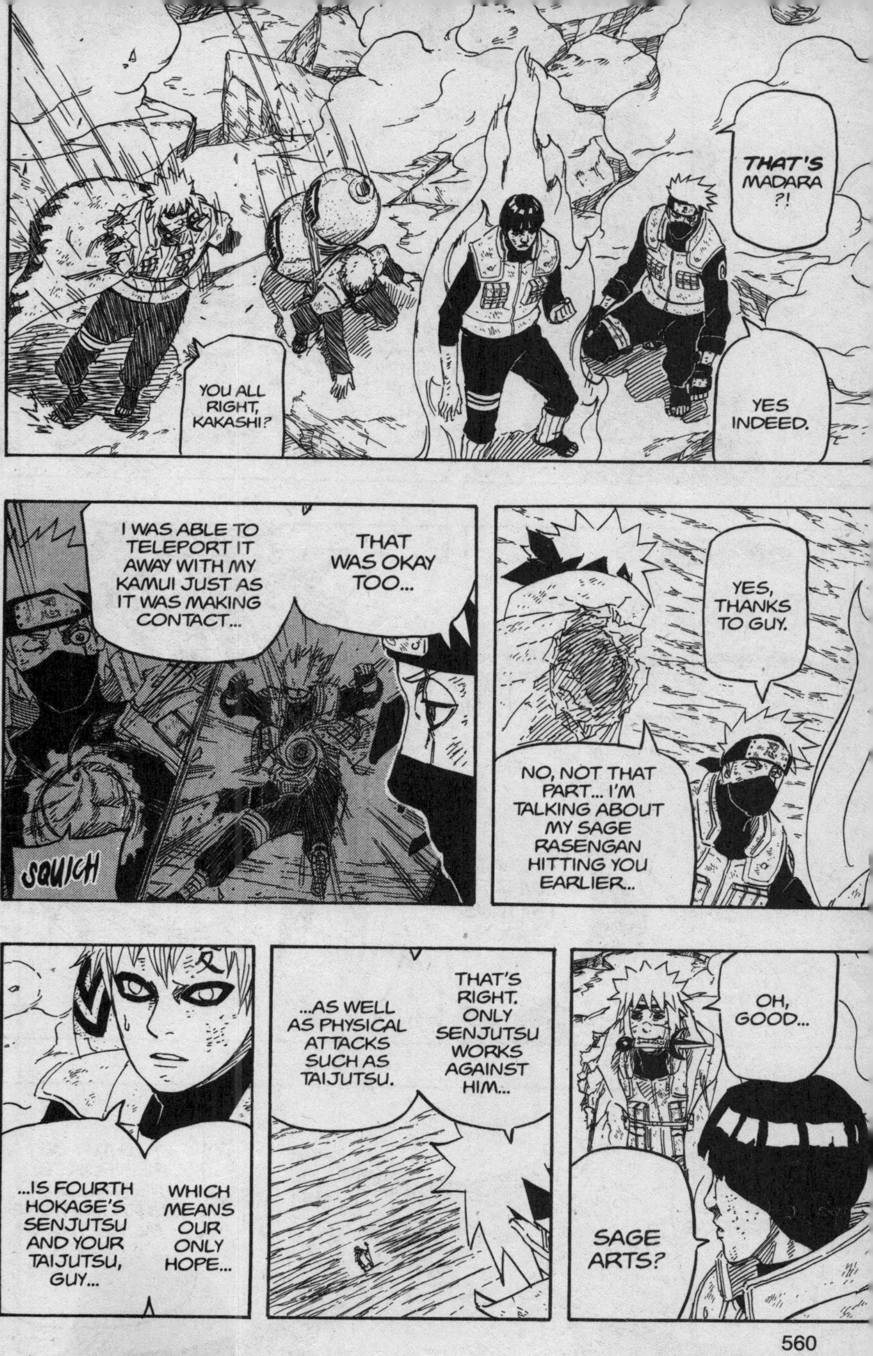
THAT'S MADARA ?!
YES INDEED.
YOU ALL RIGHT, KAKASHI?
YES, THANKS TO GUY.
NO, NOT THAT PART... I'M TALKING ABOUT MY SAGE RASENGAN HITTING YOU EARLIER...
THAT WAS OKAY TOO...
I WAS ABLE TO TELEPORT IT AWAY WITH MY KAMUI JUST AS IT WAS MAKING CONTACT...
SQUICH
OH, GOOD...
SAGE ARTS?
THAT'S RIGHT. ONLY SENJUTSU WORKS AGAINST HIM...
...AS WELL AS PHYSICAL ATTACKS SUCH AS TAIJUTSU.
WHICH MEANS OUR ONLY HOPE...
...IS FOURTH HOKAGE'S SENJUTSU AND YOUR TAIJUTSU, GUY...

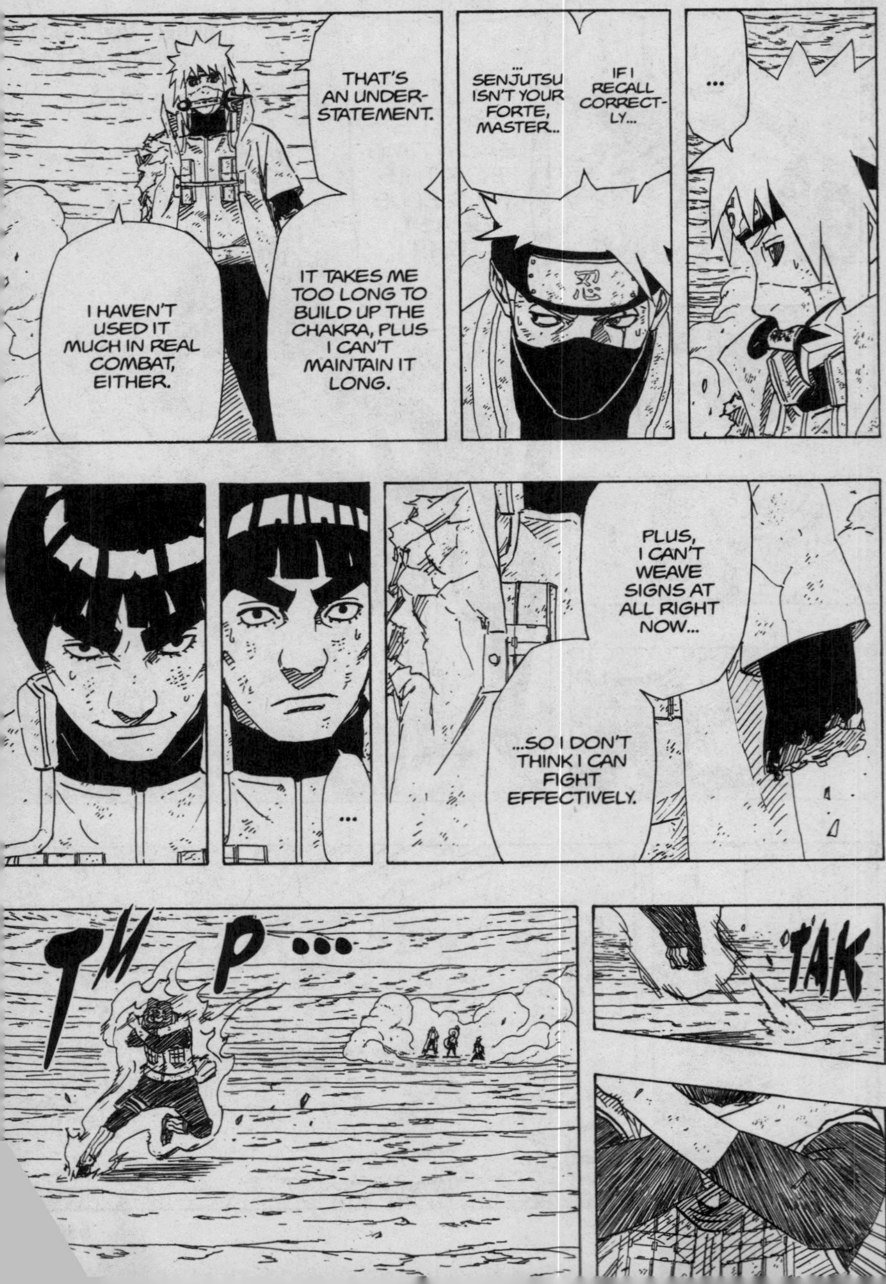
...
IF I RECALL CORRECT-LY...
...SENJUTSU ISN'T YOUR FORTE, MASTER...
THAT'S AN UNDER-STATEMENT.
IT TAKES ME TOO LONG TO BUILD UP THE CHAKRA, PLUS I CAN'T MAINTAIN IT LONG.
I HAVEN'T USED IT MUCH IN REAL COMBAT, EITHER.
PLUS, I CAN'T WEAVE SIGNS AT ALL RIGHT NOW...
...SO I DON'T THINK I CAN FIGHT EFFECTIVELY.
...
TAK
TMP...

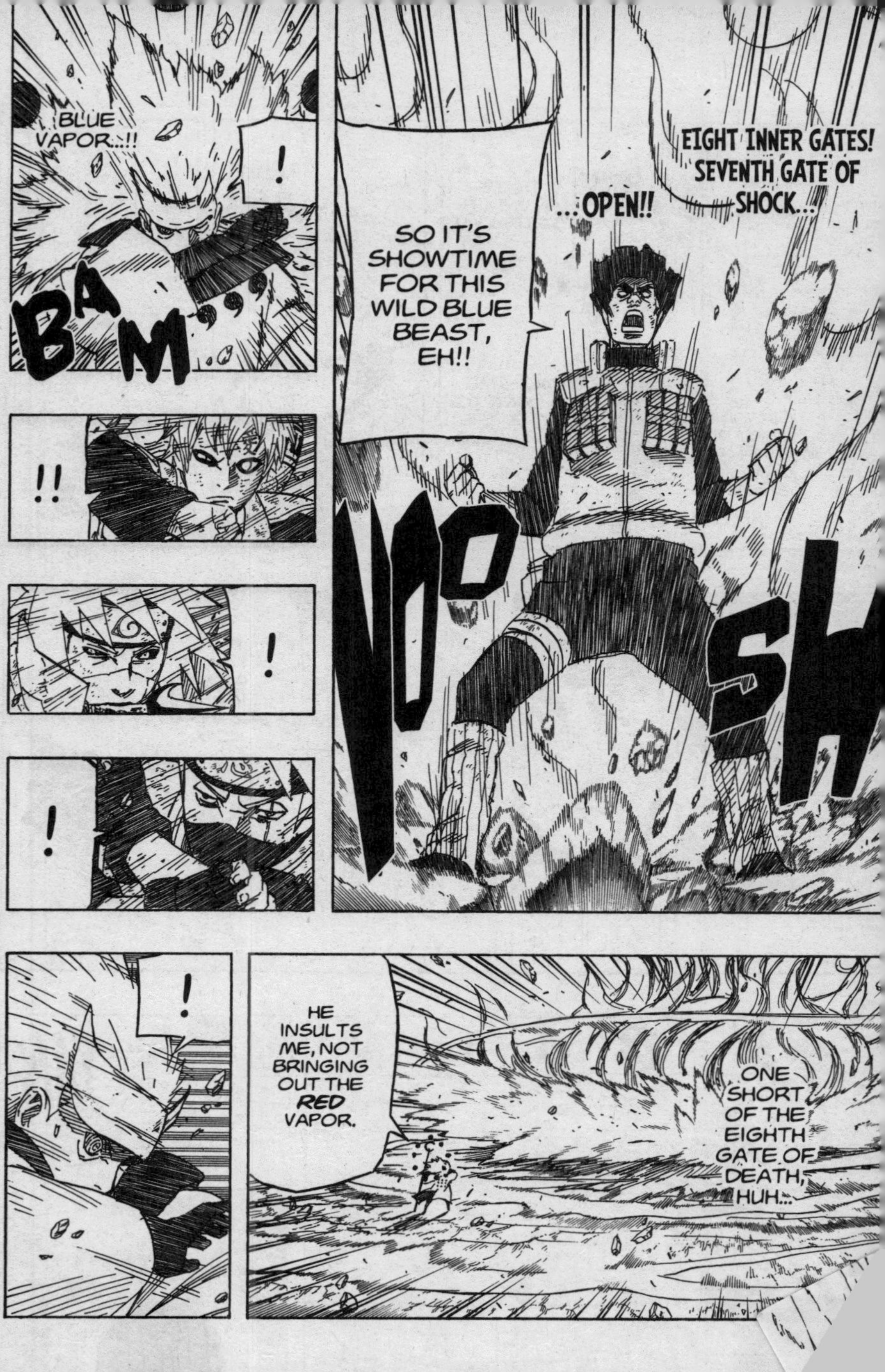
EIGHT INNER GATES! SEVENTH GATE OF SHOCK...
...OPEN!!
SO IT'S SHOWTIME FOR THIS WILD BLUE BEAST, EH!!
VOOSH
!
BLUE VAPOR...!!
BAM
!!
!
!
ONE SHORT OF THE EIGHTH GATE OF DEATH, HUH...
HE INSULTS ME, NOT BRINGING OUT THE *RED* VAPOR.
!

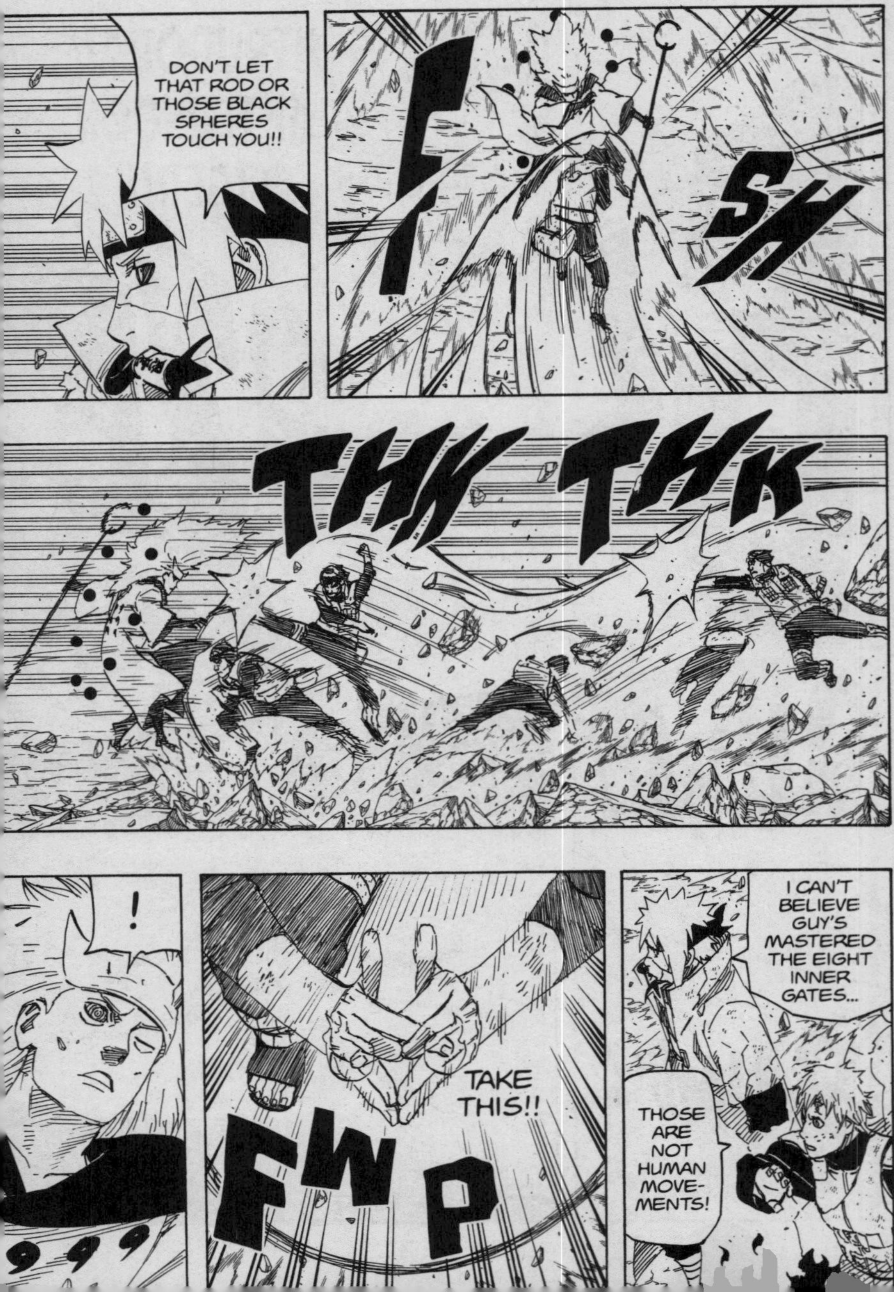
FSH
DON'T LET THAT ROD OR THOSE BLACK SPHERES TOUCH YOU!!
THK THK
I CAN'T BELIEVE GUY'S MASTERED THE EIGHT INNER GATES...
THOSE ARE NOT HUMAN MOVE-MENTS!
TAKE THIS!!
FWP
!

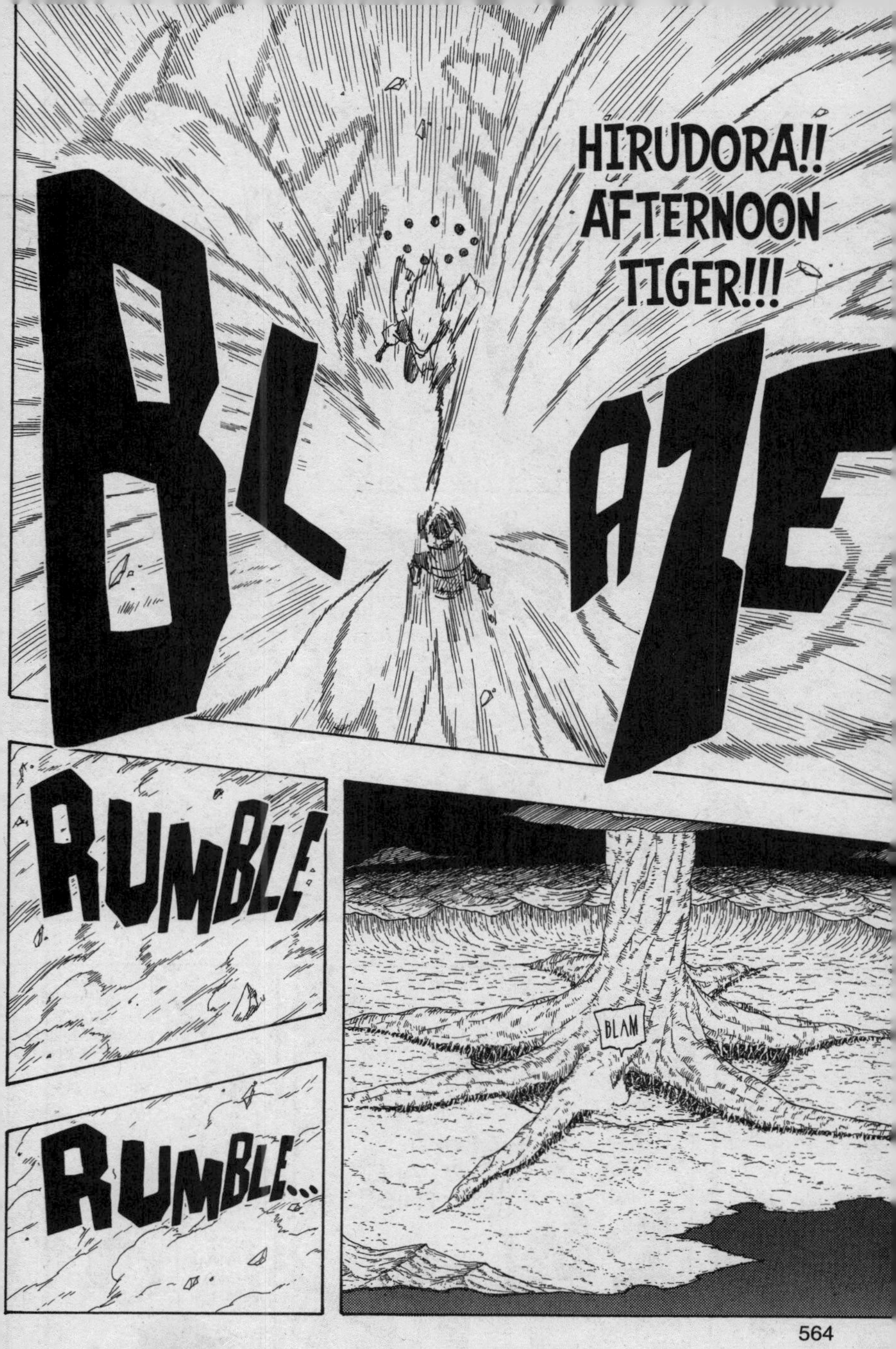
HIRUDORA!! AFTERNOON TIGER!!!
BLAZE
BLAM
RUMBLE
RUMBLE...

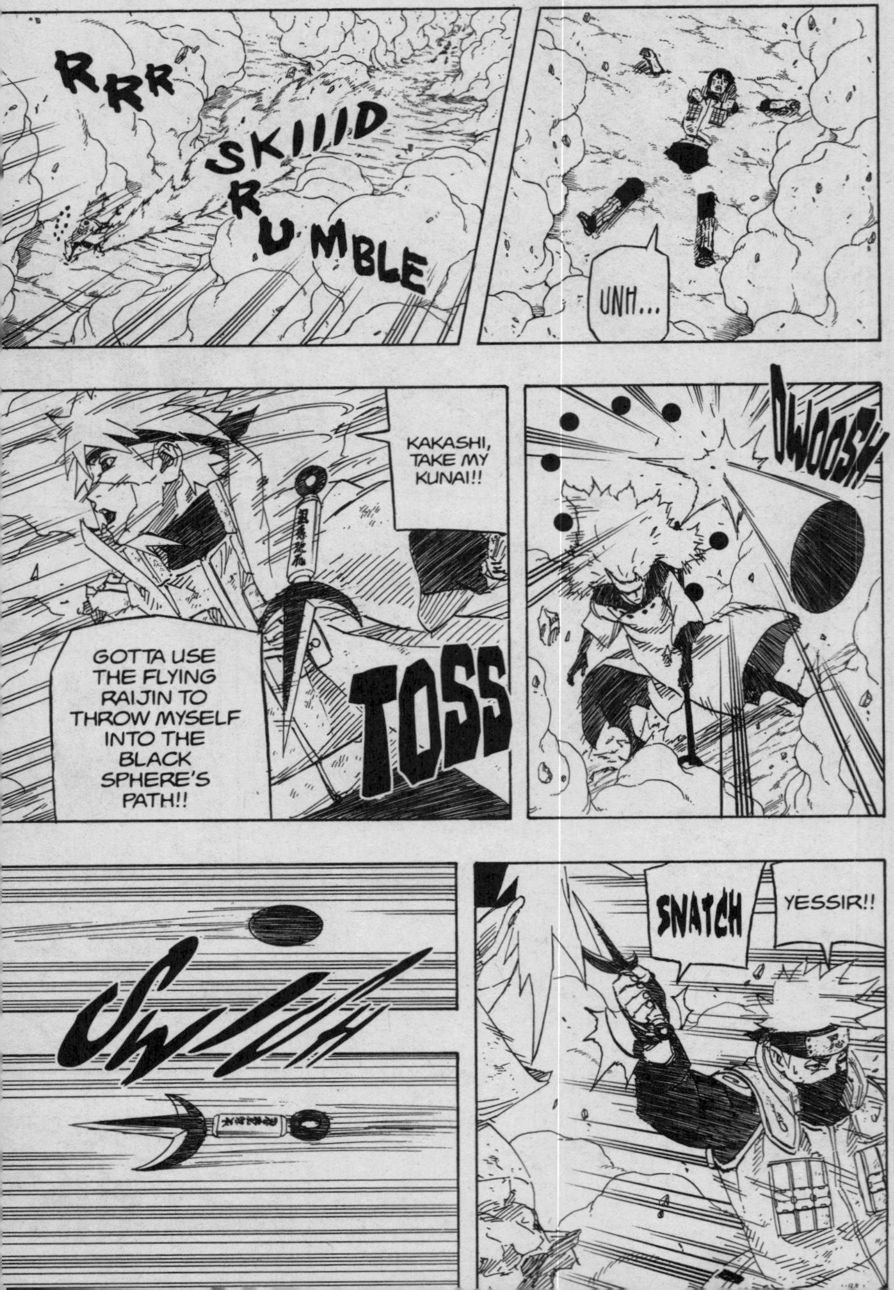

UNH...
RRR
SKIIID
RUMBLE
DWOOSH
KAKASHI, TAKE MY KUNAI!!
GOTTA USE THE FLYING RAIJIN TO THROW MYSELF INTO THE BLACK SPHERE'S PATH!!
TOSS
YESSIR!!
SNATCH
SWISH

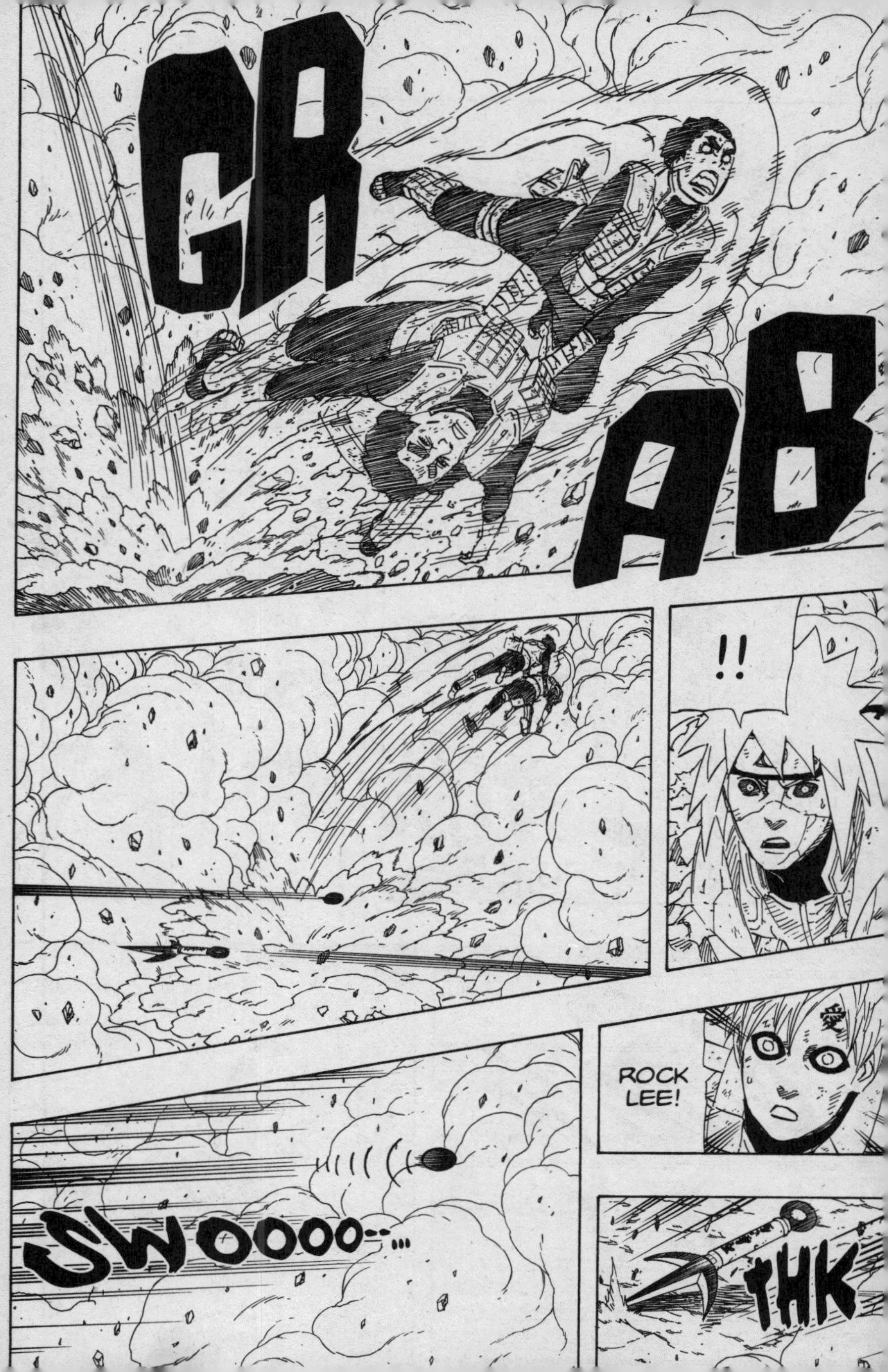
GRAB
!!
ROCK LEE!
THK
SWOOOO...

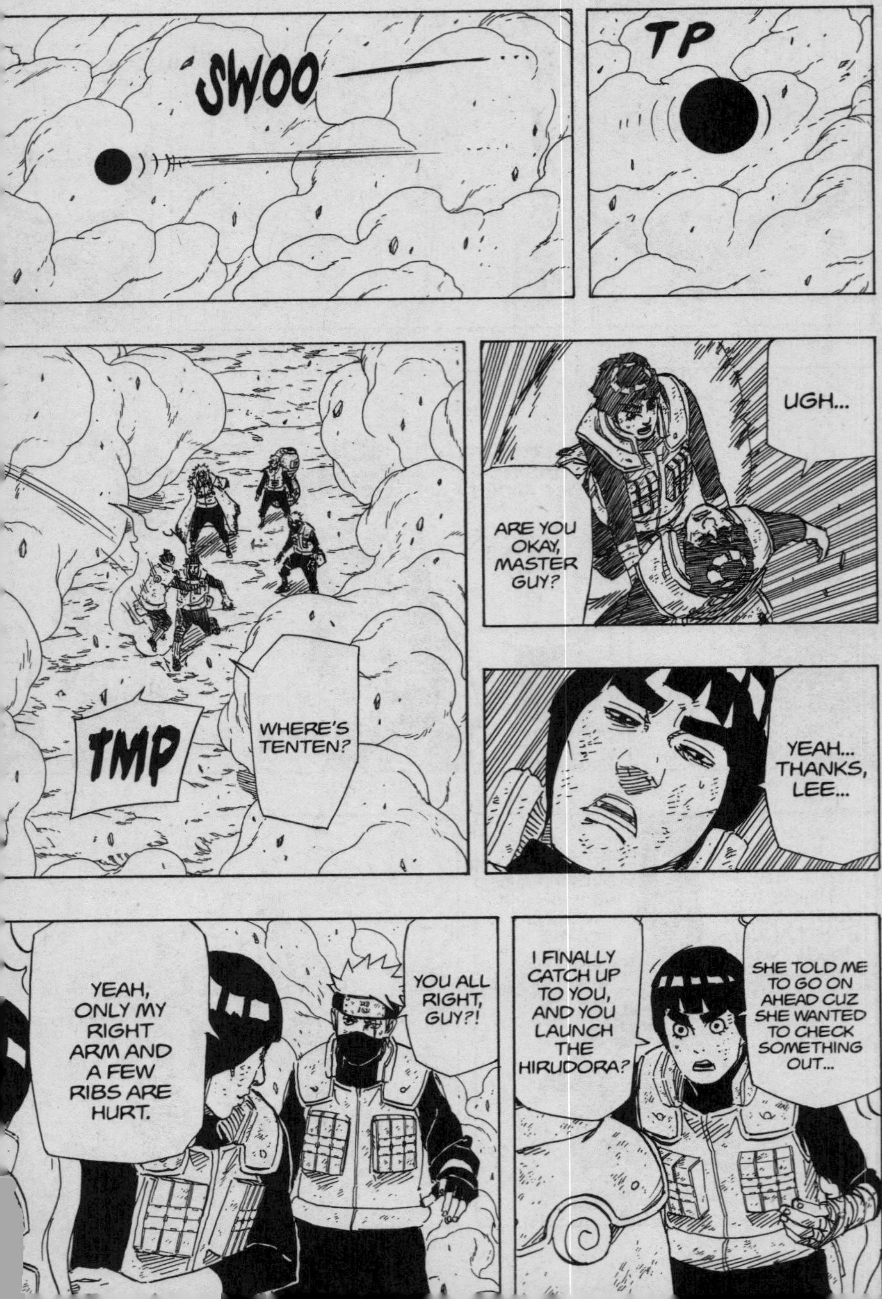
TP
SWOO
UGH...
ARE YOU OKAY, MASTER GUY?
YEAH... THANKS, LEE...
WHERE'S TENTEN?
TMP
SHE TOLD ME TO GO ON AHEAD CUZ SHE WANTED TO CHECK SOMETHING OUT...
I FINALLY CATCH UP TO YOU, AND YOU LAUNCH THE HIRUDORA?
YOU ALL RIGHT, GUY?!
YEAH, ONLY MY RIGHT ARM AND A FEW RIBS ARE HURT.

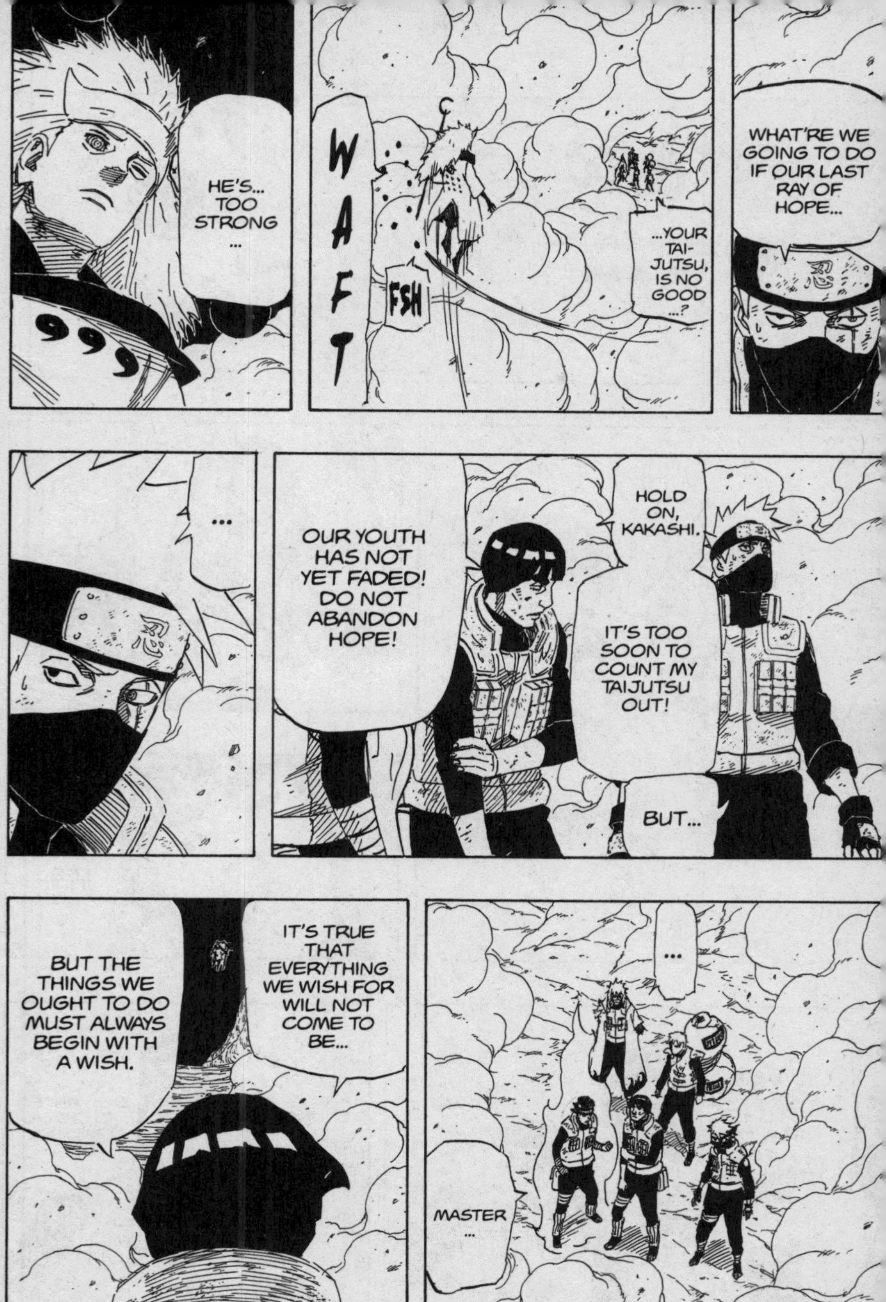
WHAT'RE WE GOING TO DO IF OUR LAST RAY OF HOPE...
...YOUR TAI-JUTSU, IS NO GOOD ...?
WAFT
FSH
HE'S... TOO STRONG ...
HOLD ON, KAKASHI.
IT'S TOO SOON TO COUNT MY TAIJUTSU OUT!
BUT...
OUR YOUTH HAS NOT YET FADED! DO NOT ABANDON HOPE!
...
...
MASTER ...
IT'S TRUE THAT EVERYTHING WE WISH FOR WILL NOT COME TO BE...
BUT THE THINGS WE OUGHT TO DO MUST ALWAYS BEGIN WITH A WISH.

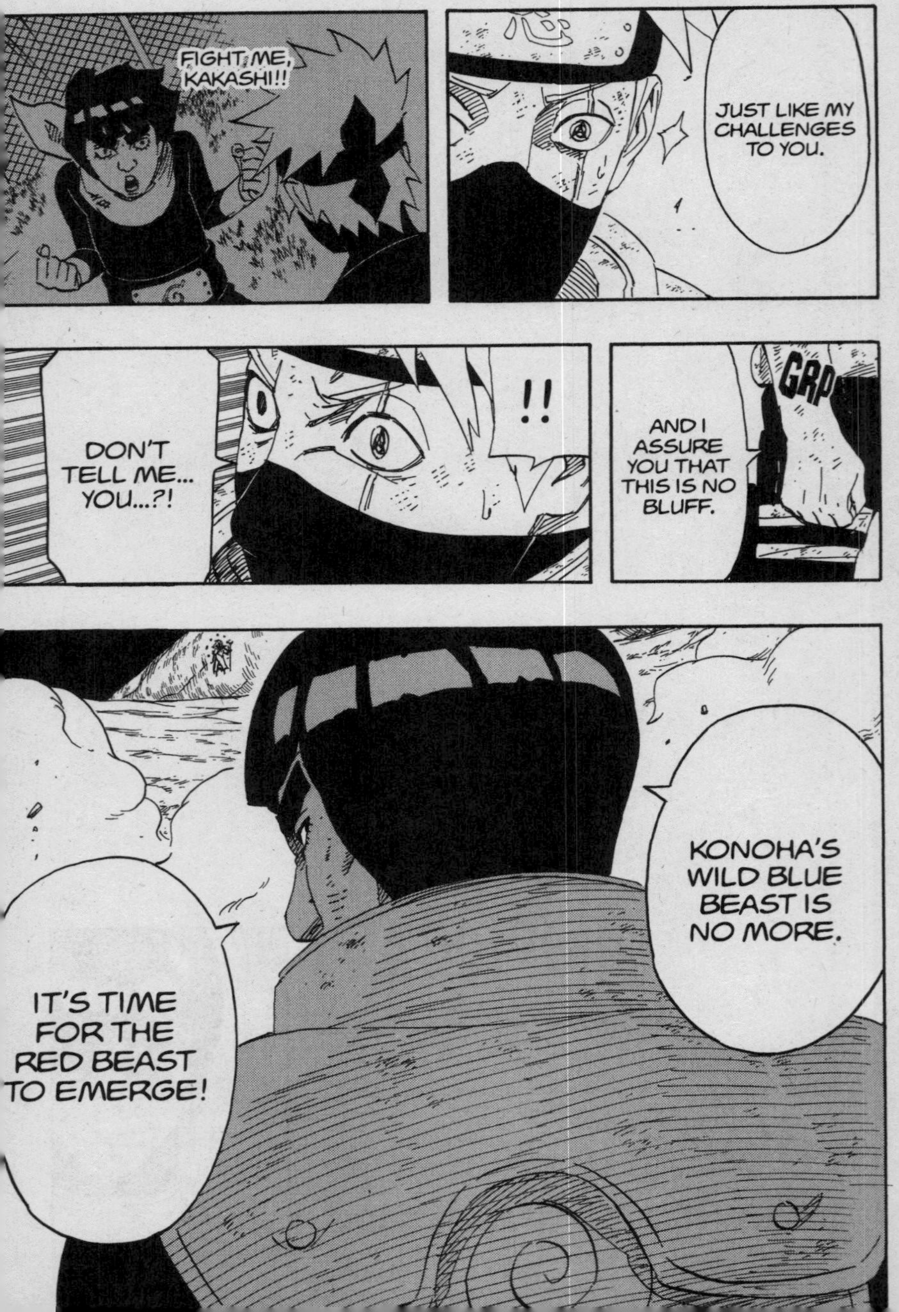
JUST LIKE MY CHALLENGES TO YOU.
FIGHT ME, KAKASHI!!
GRP
AND I ASSURE YOU THAT THIS IS NO BLUFF.
!!
DON'T TELL ME... YOU...?!
KONOHA'S WILD BLUE BEAST IS NO MORE.
IT'S TIME FOR THE RED BEAST TO EMERGE!

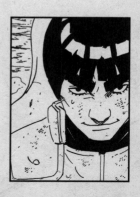

Number 668: The Start of a Crimson Spring

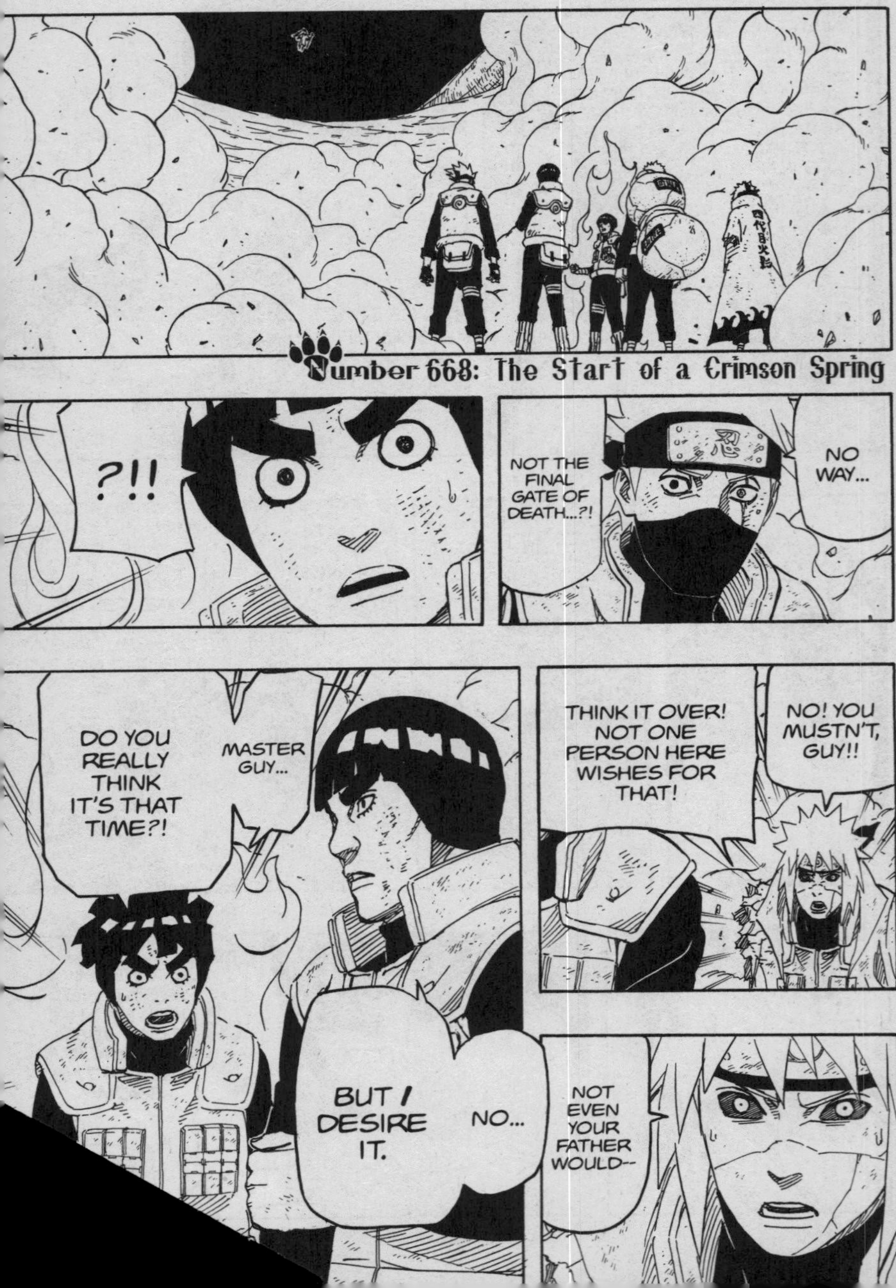
NO WAY...
NOT THE FINAL GATE OF DEATH...?!
?!!
NO! YOU MUSTN'T, GUY!!
THINK IT OVER! NOT ONE PERSON HERE WISHES FOR THAT!
NOT EVEN YOUR FATHER WOULD--
MASTER GUY...
DO YOU REALLY THINK IT'S THAT TIME?!
NO...
BUT I DESIRE IT.

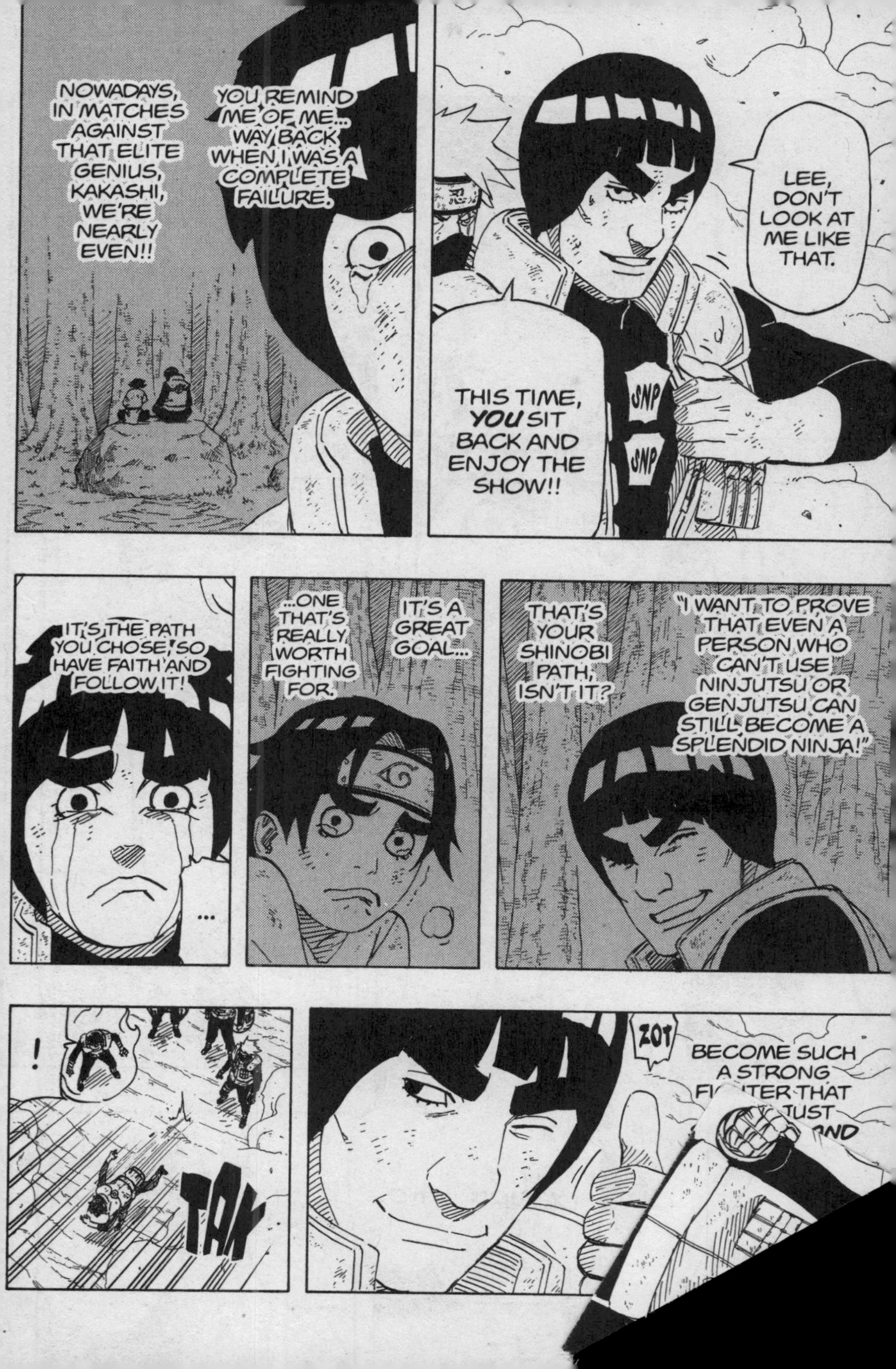
LEE, DON'T LOOK AT ME LIKE THAT.
SNP
SNP
THIS TIME, YOU SIT BACK AND ENJOY THE SHOW!!
YOU REMIND ME OF ME... WAY BACK WHEN I WAS A COMPLETE FAILURE.
NOWADAYS, IN MATCHES AGAINST THAT ELITE GENIUS, KAKASHI, WE'RE NEARLY EVEN!!
"I WANT TO PROVE THAT EVEN A PERSON WHO CAN'T USE NINJUTSU OR GENJUTSU CAN STILL BECOME A SPLENDID NINJA!"
THAT'S YOUR SHINOBI PATH, ISN'T IT?
IT'S A GREAT GOAL...
...ONE THAT'S REALLY WORTH FIGHTING FOR.
IT'S THE PATH YOU CHOSE, SO HAVE FAITH AND FOLLOW IT!
...
ZOT
BECOME SUCH A STRONG
FI TER THAT
JUST
AND
!
TAN

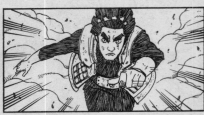

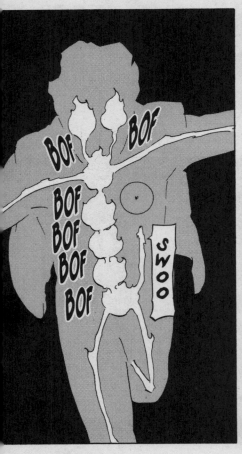

JAB
HIS CHAKRA'S SPREADING TOWARD THE DEATH GATE'S NODE.
BOF BOF
BOF BOF BOF BOF BOF
SWOO
TP
ZWWW
ZWWWW
ZIP

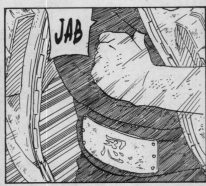

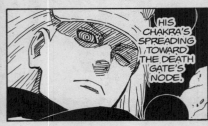

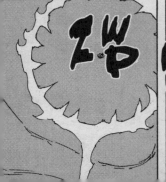

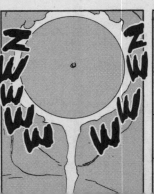

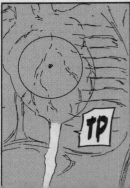

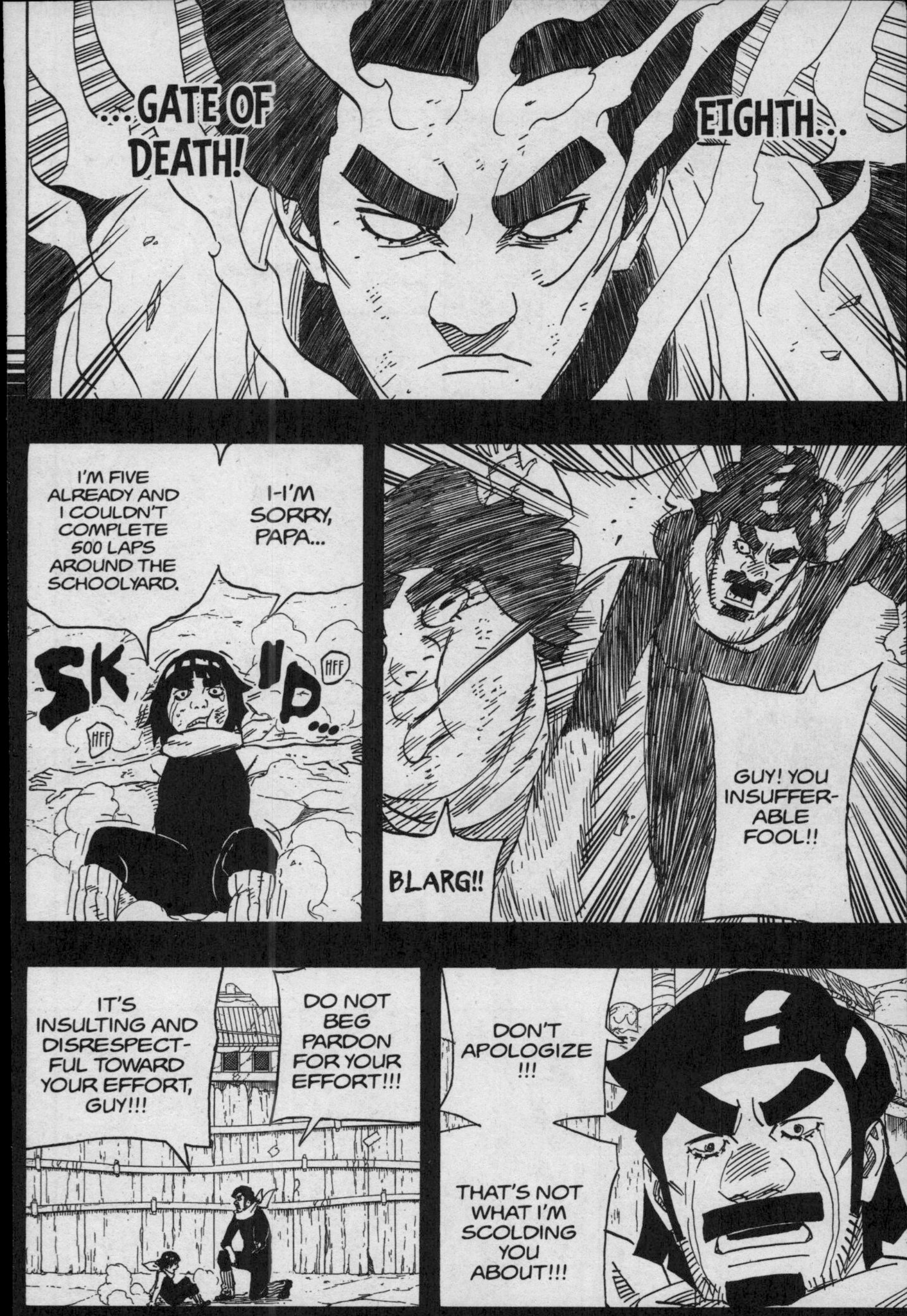
EIGHTH...
...GATE OF DEATH!
GUY! YOU INSUFFER-ABLE FOOL!!
BLARG!!
I-I'M SORRY, PAPA...
I'M FIVE ALREADY AND I COULDN'T COMPLETE 500 LAPS AROUND THE SCHOOLYARD.
SKID...
HFF
HFF
DON'T APOLOGIZE!!!
THAT'S NOT WHAT I'M SCOLDING YOU ABOUT!!!
DO NOT BEG PARDON FOR YOUR EFFORT!!!
IT'S INSULTING AND DISRESPECTFUL TOWARD YOUR EFFORT, GUY!!!

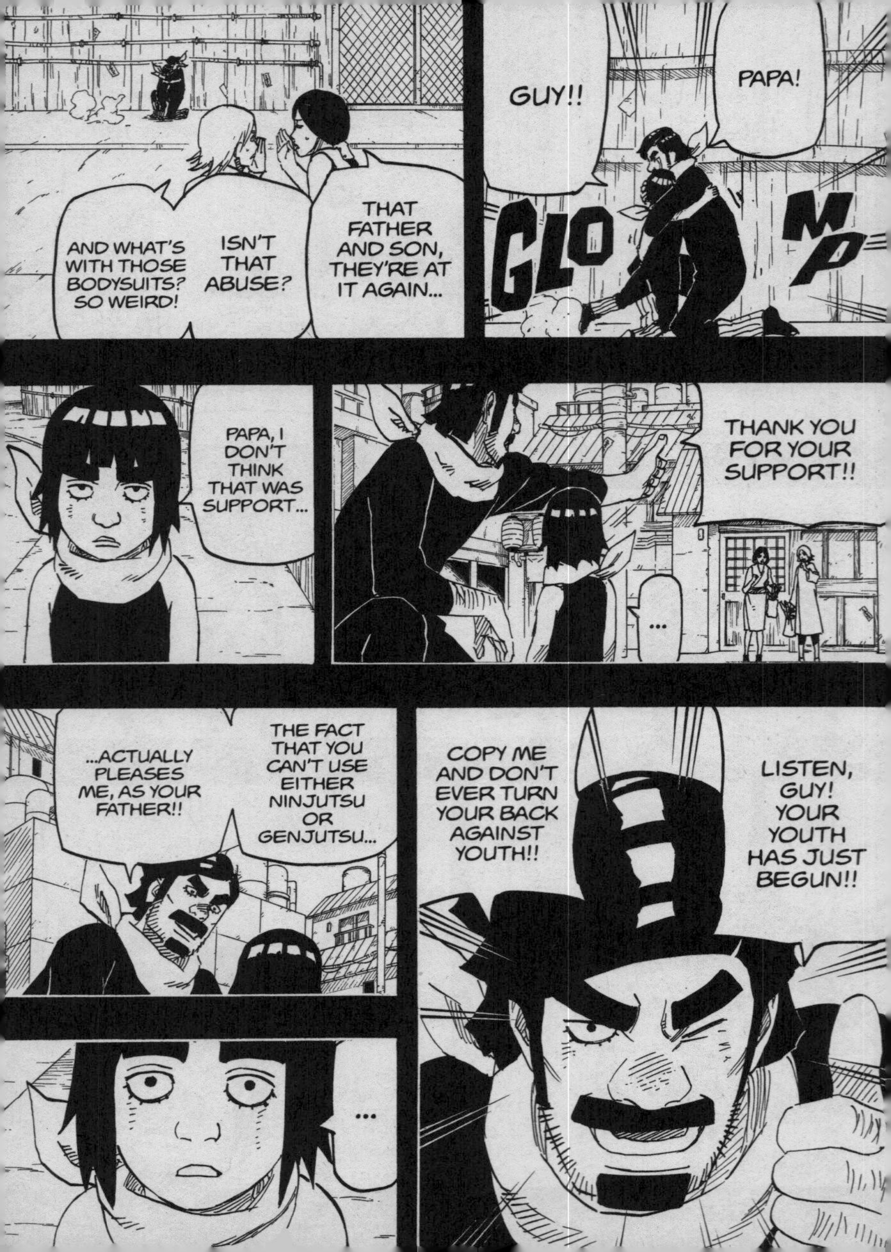
PAPA!
GUY!!
GLOMP
THAT FATHER AND SON, THEY'RE AT IT AGAIN...
ISN'T THAT ABUSE?
AND WHAT'S WITH THOSE BODYSUITS? SO WEIRD!
THANK YOU FOR YOUR SUPPORT!!
...
PAPA, I DON'T THINK THAT WAS SUPPORT...
LISTEN, GUY! YOUR YOUTH HAS JUST BEGUN!!
COPY ME AND DON'T EVER TURN YOUR BACK AGAINST YOUTH!!
THE FACT THAT YOU CAN'T USE EITHER NINJUTSU OR GENJUTSU...
...ACTUALLY PLEASES ME, AS YOUR FATHER!!
...

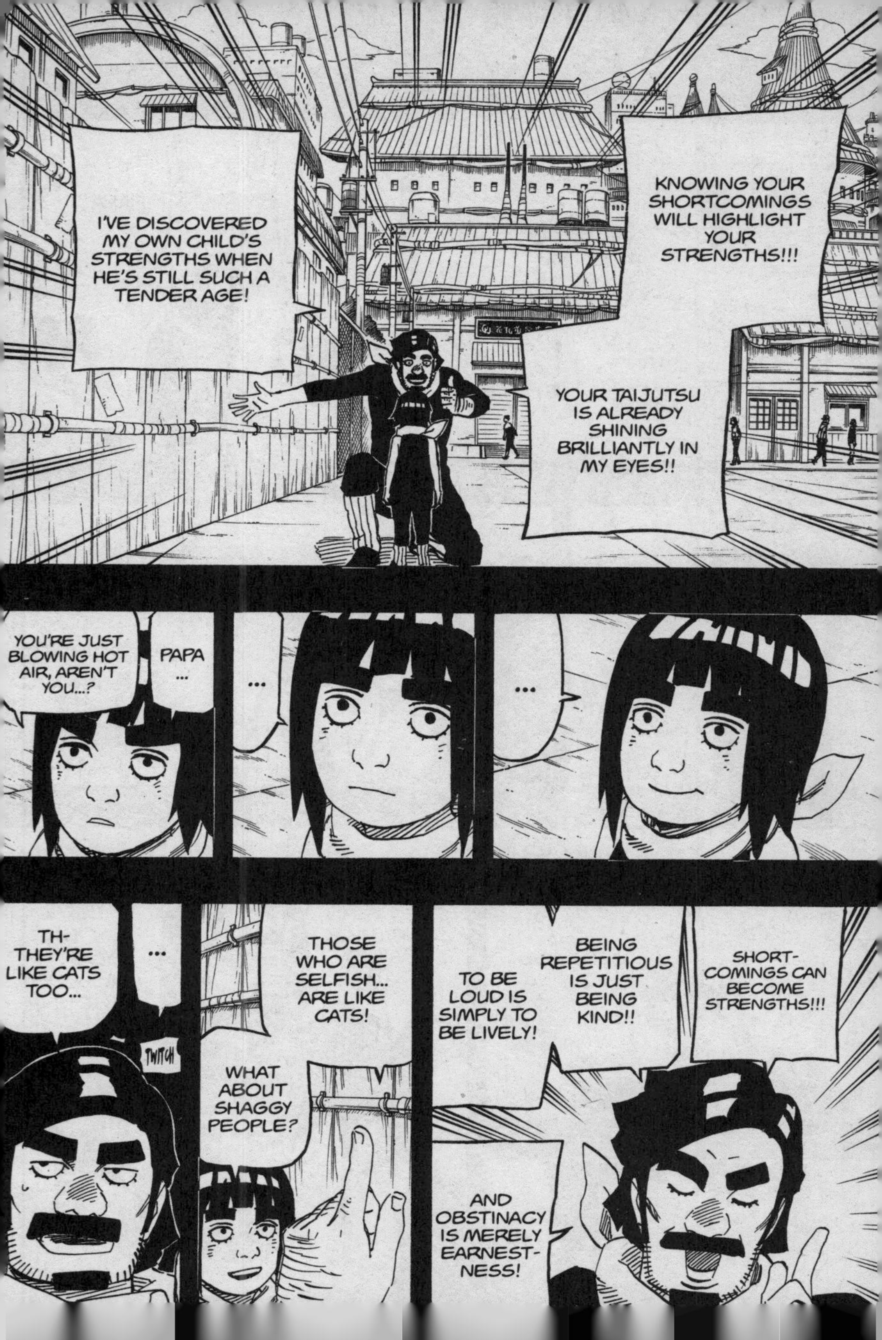
KNOWING YOUR SHORTCOMINGS WILL HIGHLIGHT YOUR STRENGTHS!!!
YOUR TAIJUTSU IS ALREADY SHINING BRILLIANTLY IN MY EYES!!
I'VE DISCOVERED MY OWN CHILD'S STRENGTHS WHEN HE'S STILL SUCH A TENDER AGE!
...
...
PAPA ...
YOU'RE JUST BLOWING HOT AIR, AREN'T YOU...?
SHORT-COMINGS CAN BECOME STRENGTHS!!!
BEING REPETITIOUS IS JUST BEING KIND!!
TO BE LOUD IS SIMPLY TO BE LIVELY!
AND OBSTINACY IS MERELY EARNEST-NESS!
THOSE WHO ARE SELFISH... ARE LIKE CATS!
WHAT ABOUT SHAGGY PEOPLE?
...
TH- THEY'RE LIKE CATS TOO...
TWITCH

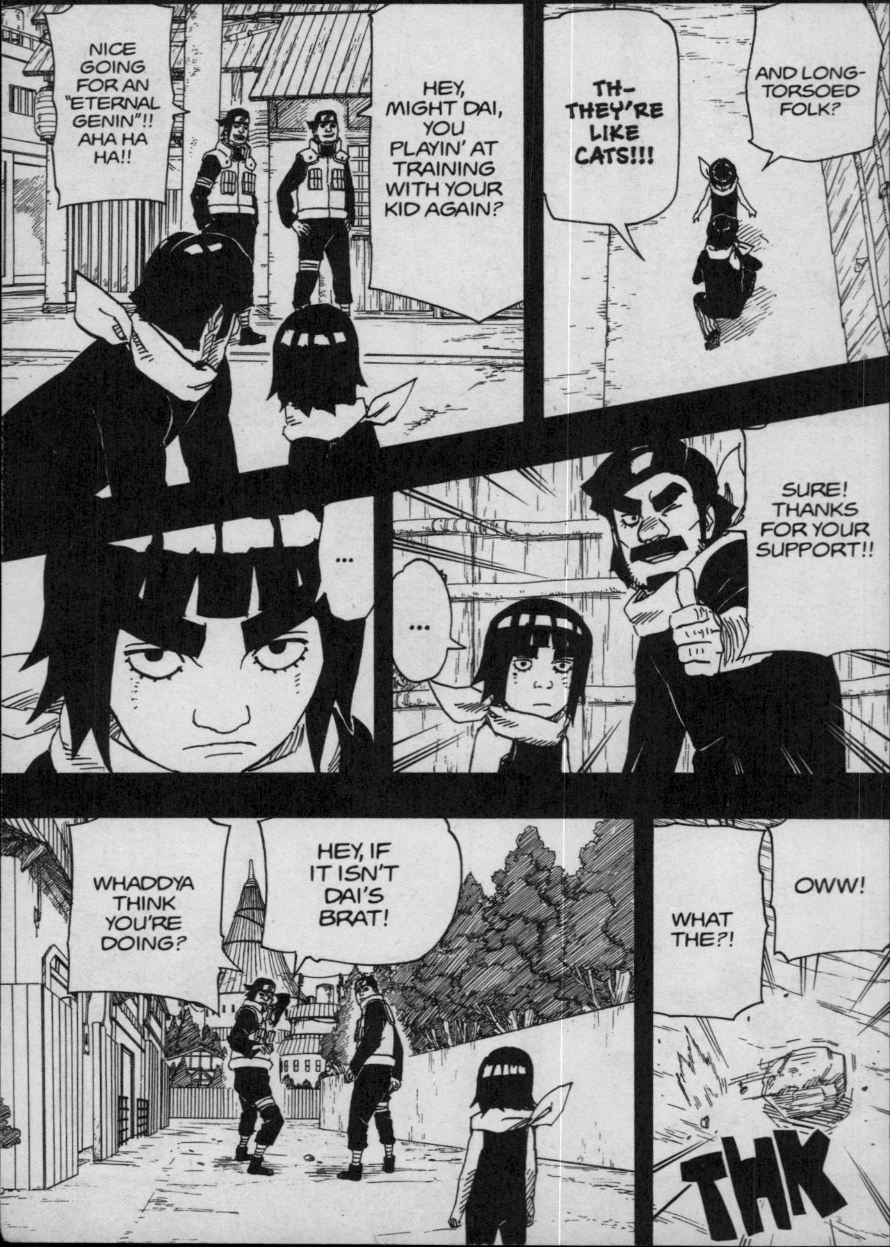
AND LONG-TORSOED FOLK?
TH-THEY'RE LIKE CATS!!!
HEY, MIGHT DAI, YOU PLAYIN' AT TRAINING WITH YOUR KID AGAIN?
NICE GOING FOR AN "ETERNAL GENIN"!! AHA HA HA!!
SURE! THANKS FOR YOUR SUPPORT!!
...
...
OWW!
WHAT THE?!
THK
HEY, IF IT ISN'T DAI'S BRAT!
WHADDYA THINK YOU'RE DOING?

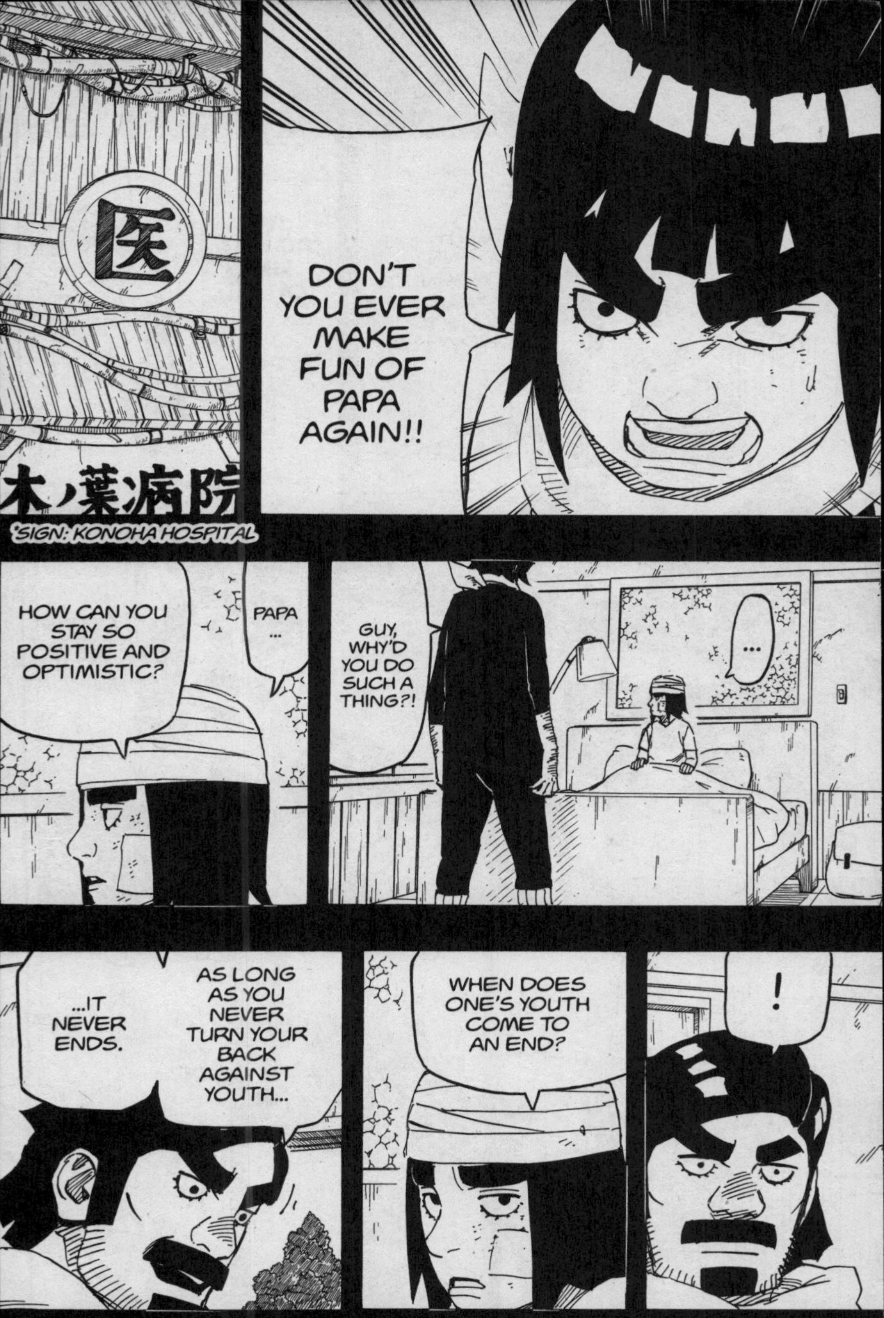
DON'T YOU EVER MAKE FUN OF PAPA AGAIN!!
医
木ノ葉病院
*SIGN: KONOHA HOSPITAL
...
GUY, WHY'D YOU DO SUCH A THING?!
PAPA ...
HOW CAN YOU STAY SO POSITIVE AND OPTIMISTIC?
!
WHEN DOES ONE'S YOUTH COME TO AN END?
AS LONG AS YOU NEVER TURN YOUR BACK AGAINST YOUTH...
...IT NEVER ENDS.

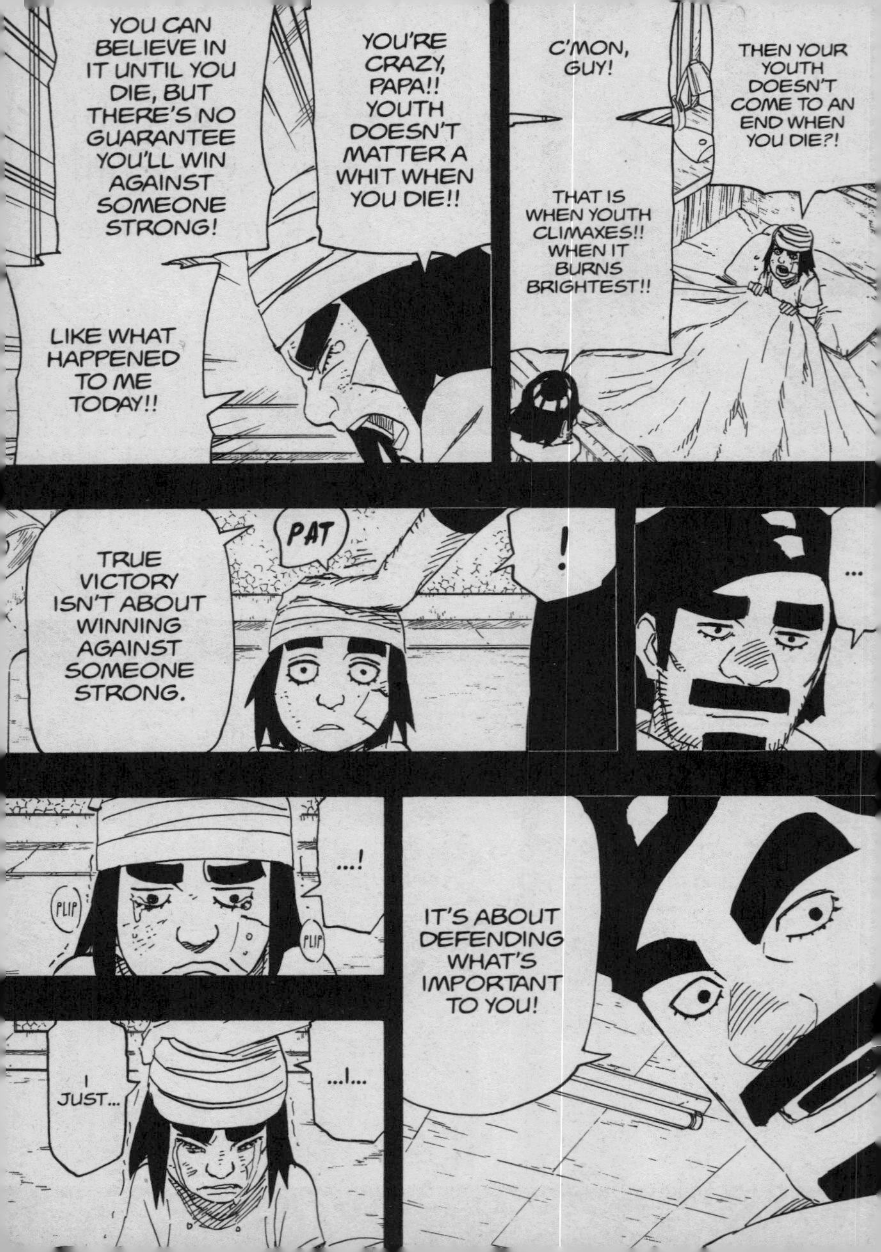
THEN YOUR YOUTH DOESN'T COME TO AN END WHEN YOU DIE?!
C'MON, GUY!
THAT IS WHEN YOUTH CLIMAXES!! WHEN IT BURNS BRIGHTEST!!
YOU'RE CRAZY, PAPA!! YOUTH DOESN'T MATTER A WHIT WHEN YOU DIE!!
YOU CAN BELIEVE IN IT UNTIL YOU DIE, BUT THERE'S NO GUARANTEE YOU'LL WIN AGAINST SOMEONE STRONG!
LIKE WHAT HAPPENED TO ME TODAY!!
...
!
PAT
TRUE VICTORY ISN'T ABOUT WINNING AGAINST SOMEONE STRONG.
IT'S ABOUT DEFENDING WHAT'S IMPORTANT TO YOU!
...!
PLIP
PLIP
...I...
I JUST...

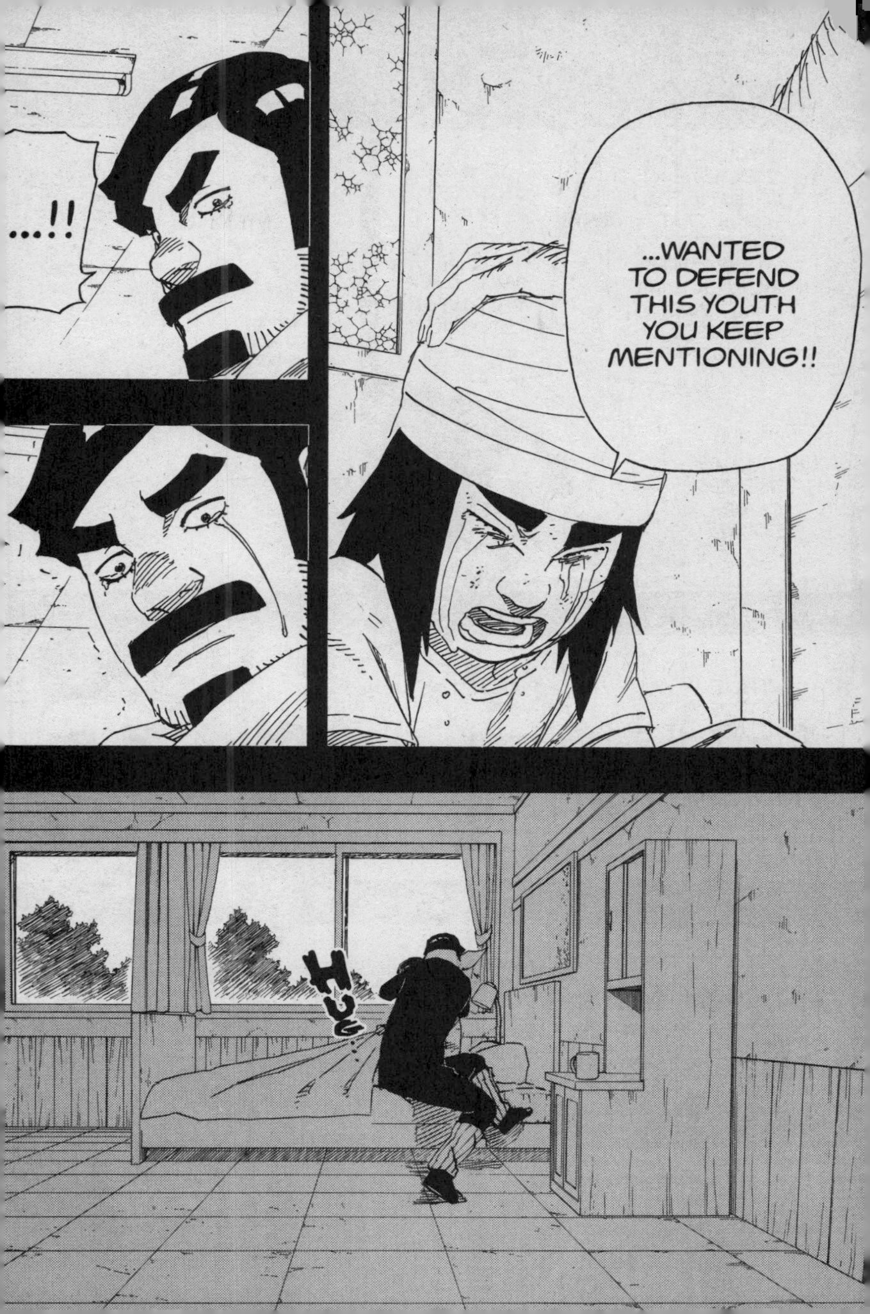
...WANTED TO DEFEND THIS YOUTH YOU KEEP MENTIONING!!
...!!
HUG

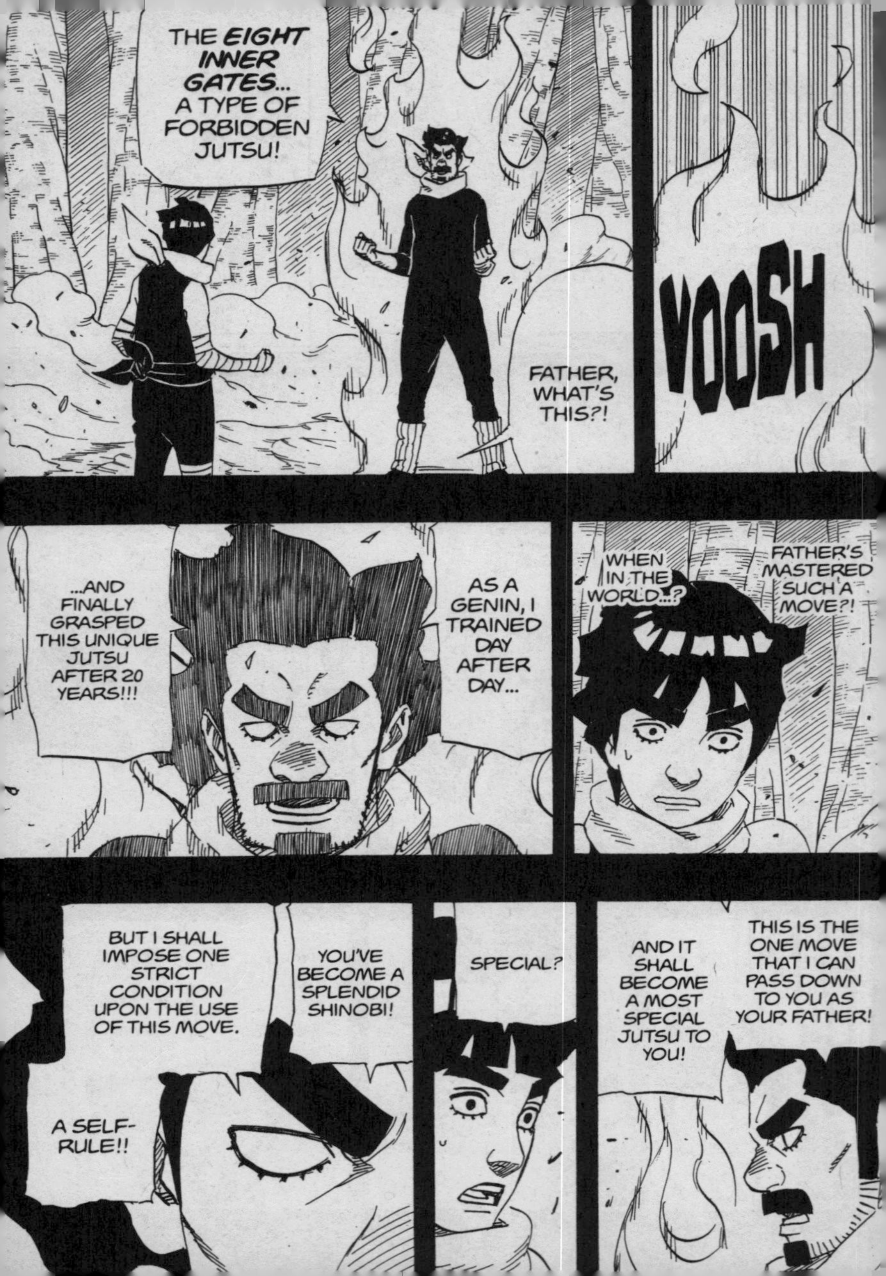
VOOSH
FATHER, WHAT'S THIS?!
THE EIGHT INNER GATES... A TYPE OF FORBIDDEN JUTSU!
FATHER'S MASTERED SUCH A MOVE?!
WHEN IN THE WORLD...?
AS A GENIN, I TRAINED DAY AFTER DAY...
...AND FINALLY GRASPED THIS UNIQUE JUTSU AFTER 20 YEARS!!!
THIS IS THE ONE MOVE THAT I CAN PASS DOWN TO YOU AS YOUR FATHER!
AND IT SHALL BECOME A MOST SPECIAL JUTSU TO YOU!
SPECIAL?
YOU'VE BECOME A SPLENDID SHINOBI!
BUT I SHALL IMPOSE ONE STRICT CONDITION UPON THE USE OF THIS MOVE.
A SELF-RULE!!

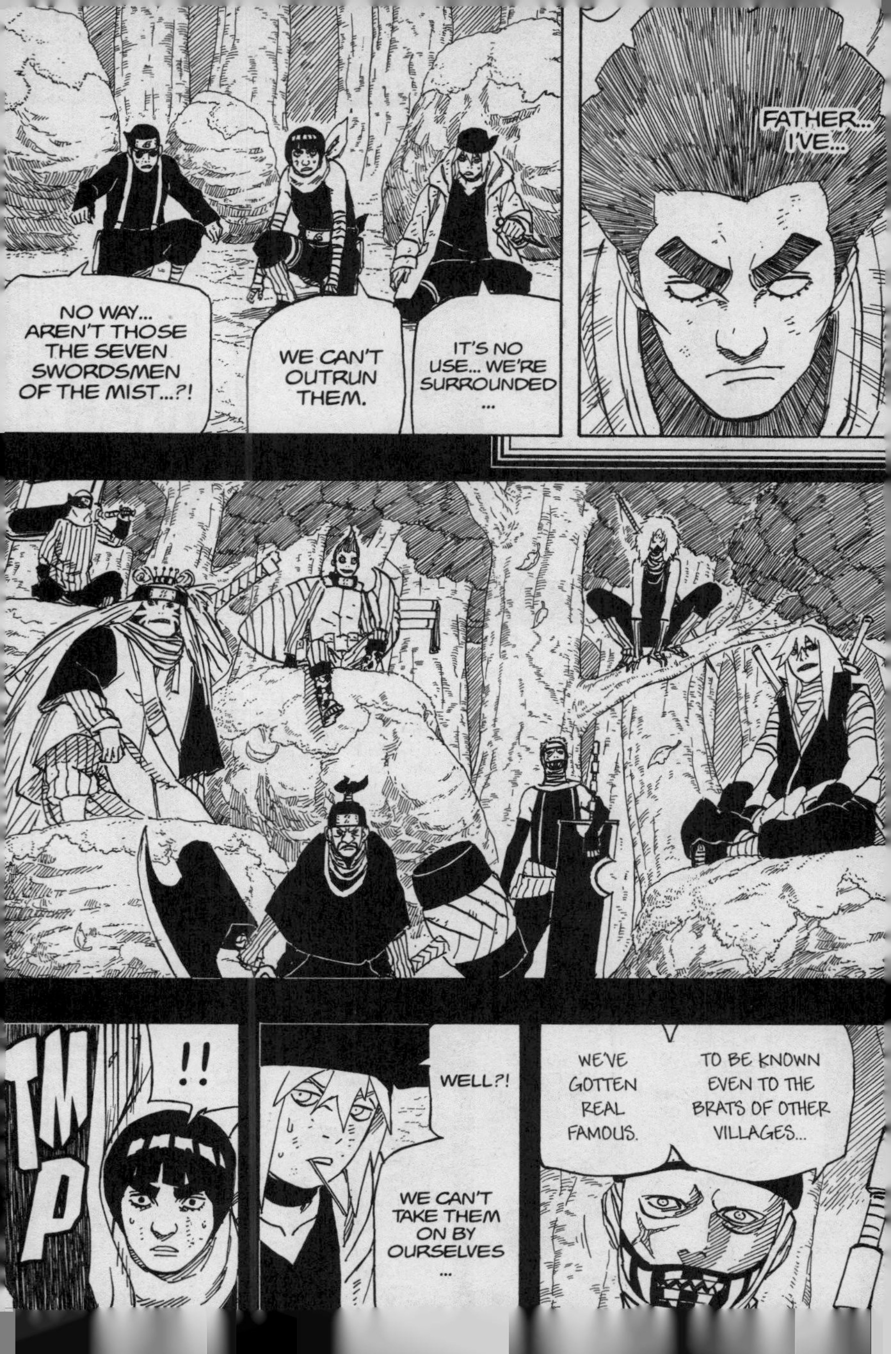
FATHER... I'VE...
IT'S NO USE... WE'RE SURROUNDED ...
WE CAN'T OUTRUN THEM.
NO WAY... AREN'T THOSE THE SEVEN SWORDSMEN OF THE MIST...?!
WE'VE GOTTEN REAL FAMOUS.
TO BE KNOWN EVEN TO THE BRATS OF OTHER VILLAGES...
WELL?!
WE CAN'T TAKE THEM ON BY OURSELVES ...
!!
TMP

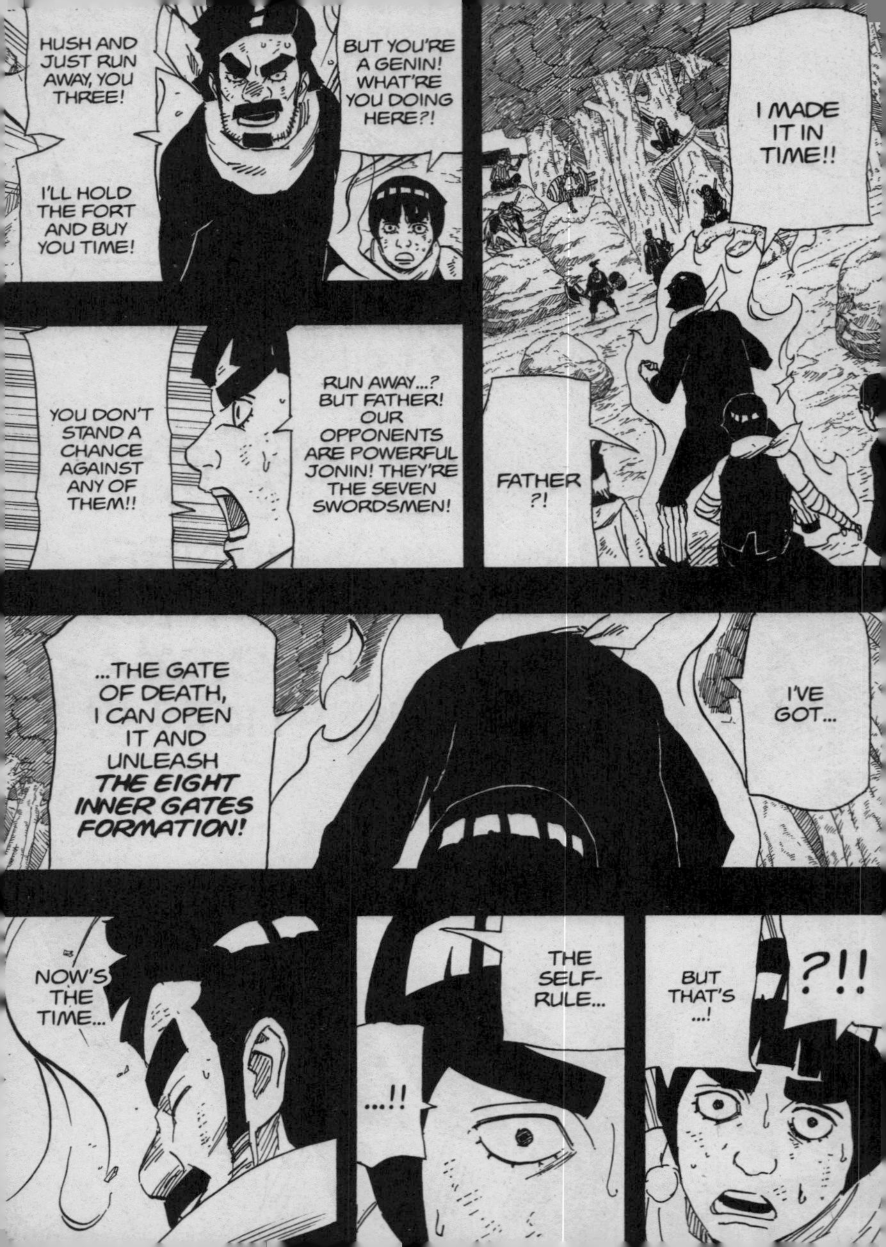
I MADE IT IN TIME!!
FATHER ?!
BUT YOU'RE A GENIN! WHAT'RE YOU DOING HERE?!
HUSH AND JUST RUN AWAY, YOU THREE!
I'LL HOLD THE FORT AND BUY YOU TIME!
RUN AWAY...? BUT FATHER! OUR OPPONENTS ARE POWERFUL JONIN! THEY'RE THE SEVEN SWORDSMEN!
YOU DON'T STAND A CHANCE AGAINST ANY OF THEM!!
I'VE GOT...
...THE GATE OF DEATH, I CAN OPEN IT AND UNLEASH ***THE EIGHT INNER GATES FORMATION!***
?!!
BUT THAT'S ...!
THE SELF-RULE...
...!!
NOW'S THE TIME...

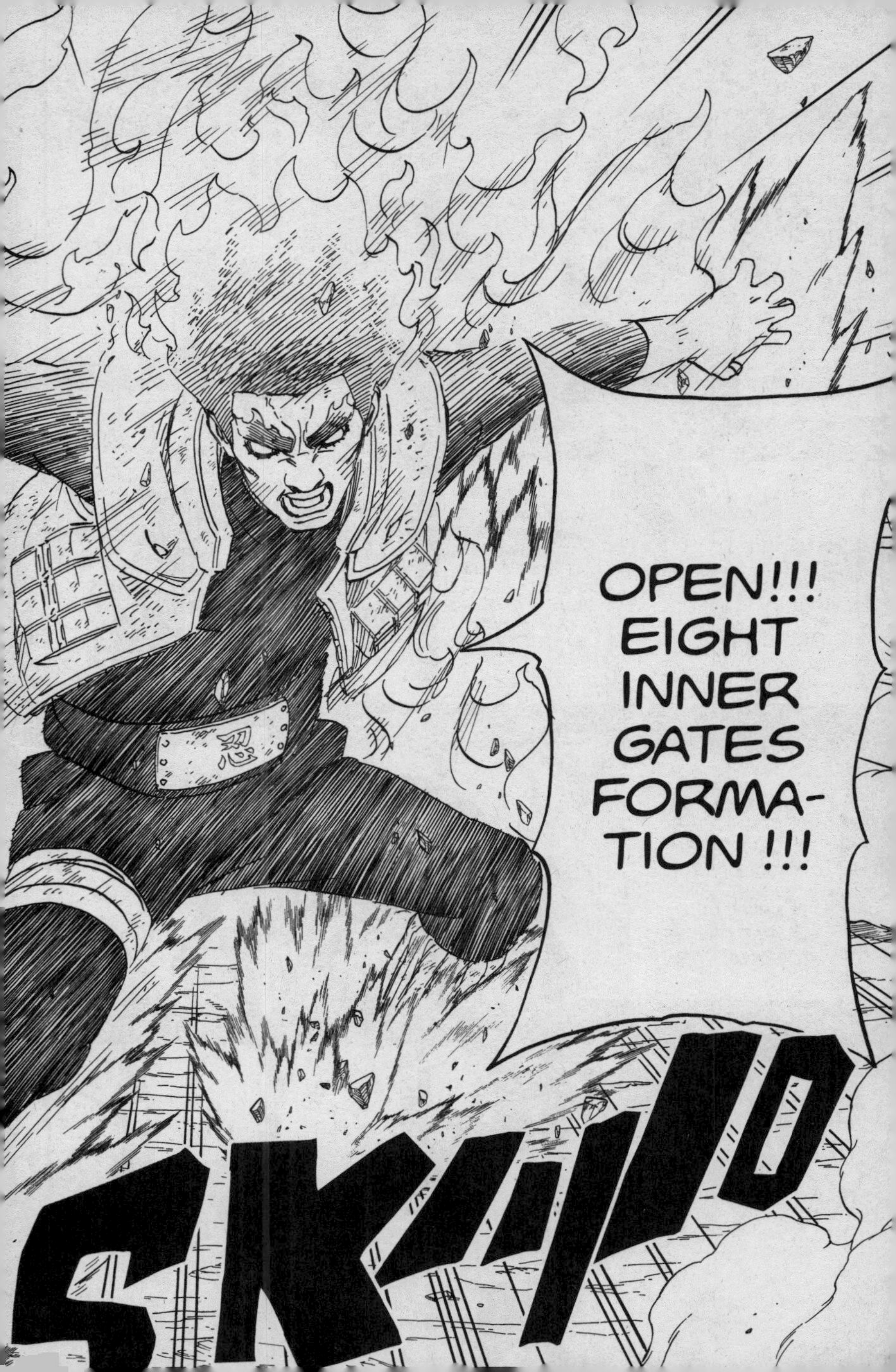
OPEN!!! EIGHT INNER GATES FORMATION!!!

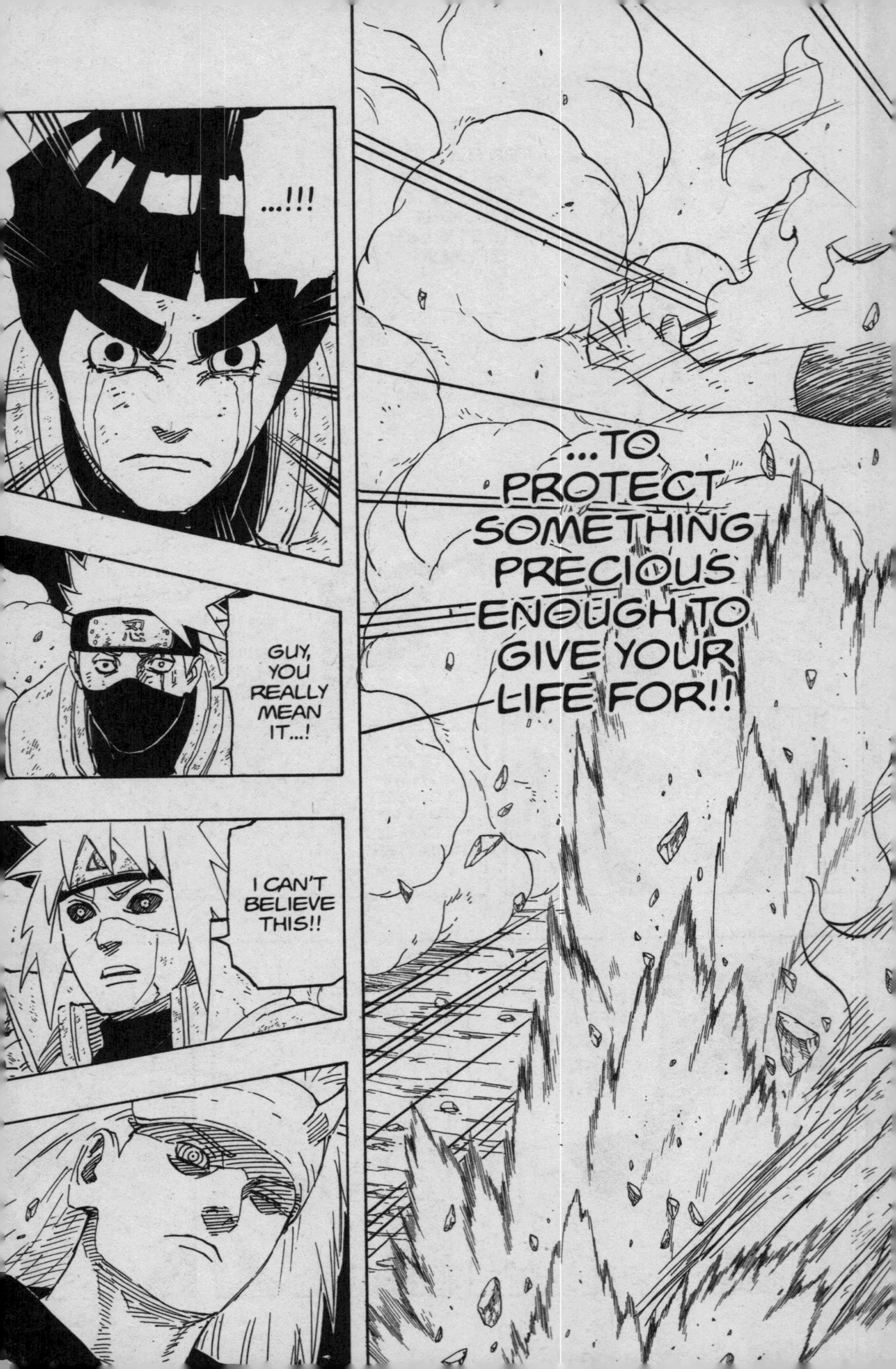
...TO PROTECT SOMETHING PRECIOUS ENOUGH TO GIVE YOUR LIFE FOR!!
...!!!
GUY, YOU REALLY MEAN IT...!
I CAN'T BELIEVE THIS!!

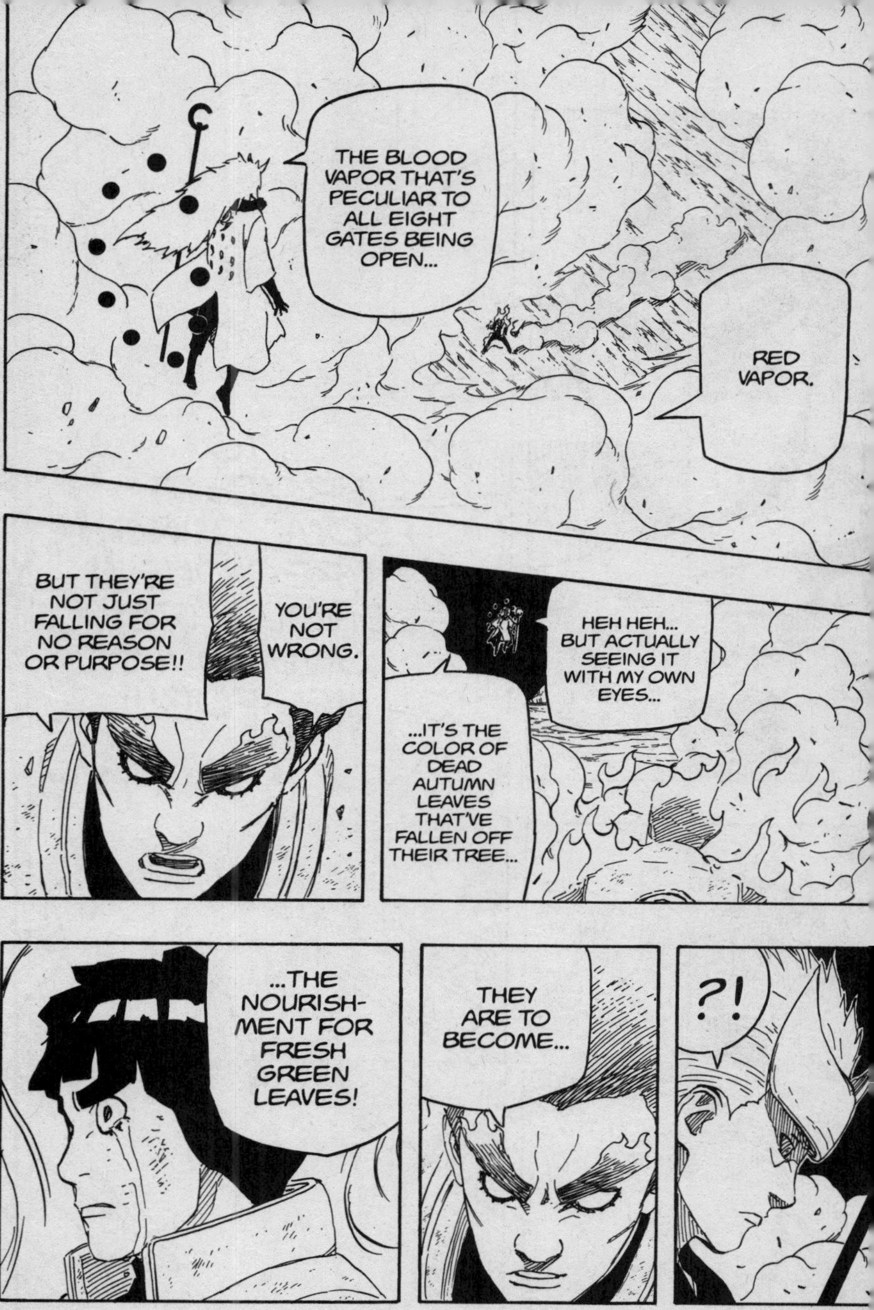
RED VAPOR.
THE BLOOD VAPOR THAT'S PECULIAR TO ALL EIGHT GATES BEING OPEN...
HEH HEH... BUT ACTUALLY SEEING IT WITH MY OWN EYES...
...IT'S THE COLOR OF DEAD AUTUMN LEAVES THAT'VE FALLEN OFF THEIR TREE...
YOU'RE NOT WRONG.
BUT THEY'RE NOT JUST FALLING FOR NO REASON OR PURPOSE!!
?!
THEY ARE TO BECOME...
...THE NOURISH-MENT FOR FRESH GREEN LEAVES!

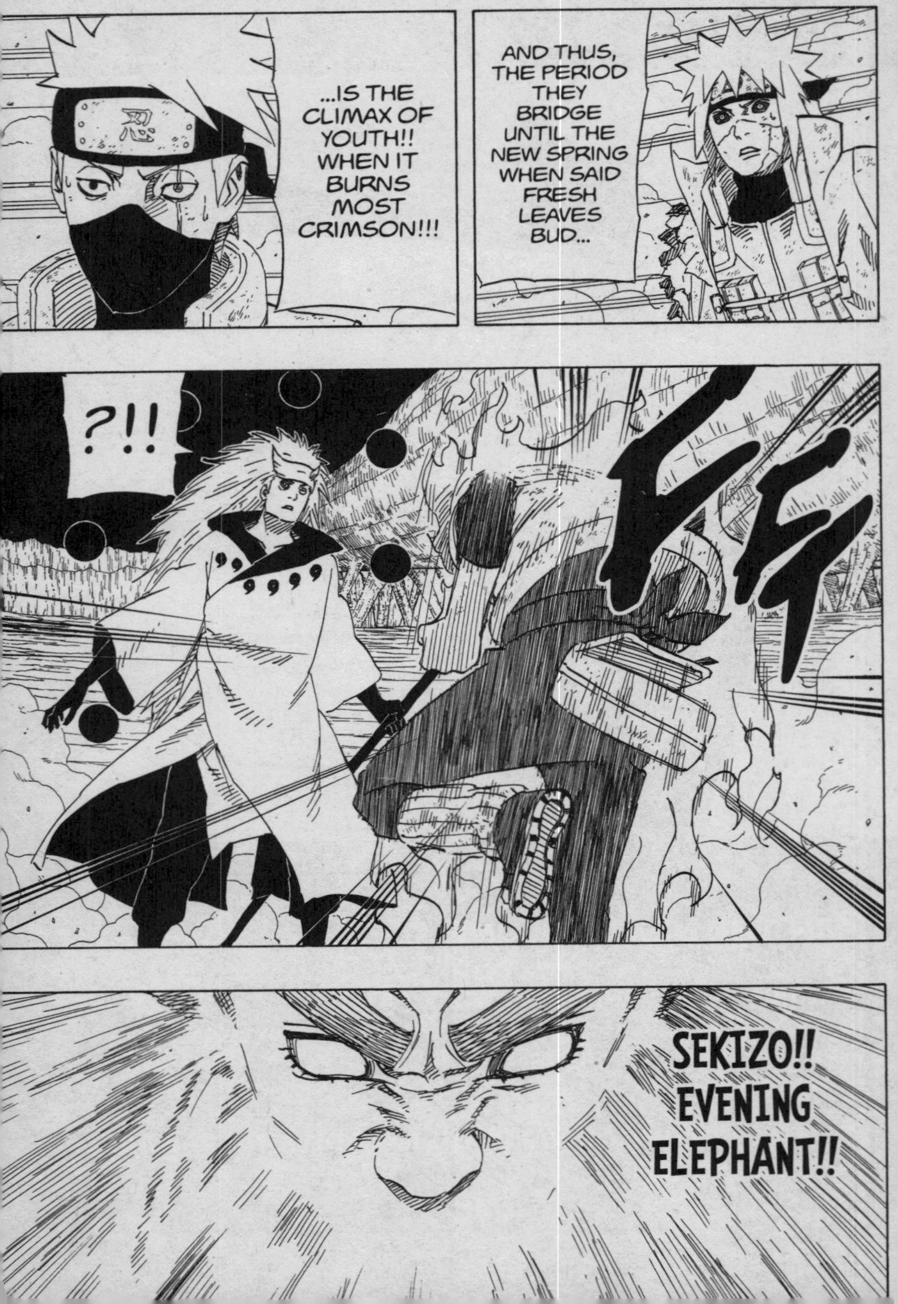
AND THUS, THE PERIOD THEY BRIDGE UNTIL THE NEW SPRING WHEN SAID FRESH LEAVES BUD...
...IS THE CLIMAX OF YOUTH!! WHEN IT BURNS MOST CRIMSON!!!
?!!
SEKIZO!! EVENING ELEPHANT!!

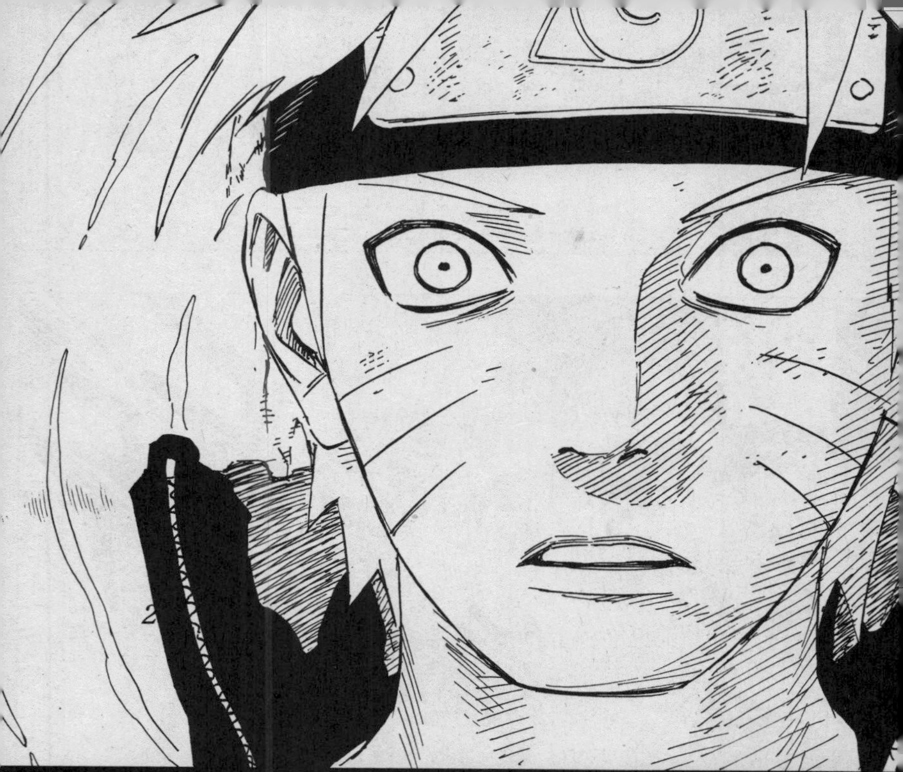

IN THE NEXT VOLUME...

NARUTO AND THE SAGE OF SIX PATHS

Guy risks his life to stop Madara by unleashing his full power. But will it be enough to stop a legendary ninja like Madara? Meanwhile, Naruto and Sasuke are dying. Can they be revived in time to save the ninja world?

FINAL VOLUME OF NARUTO 3-IN-1 EDITION AVAILABLE

Black Clover

STORY & ART BY YŪKI TABATA

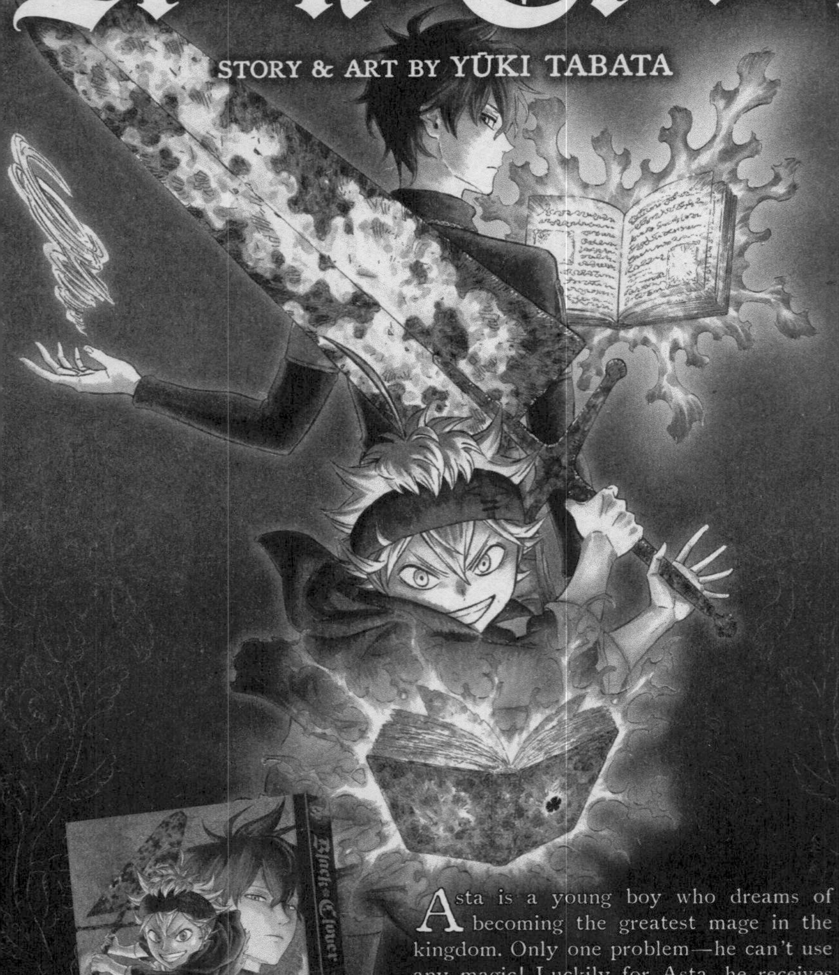

Asta is a young boy who dreams of becoming the greatest mage in the kingdom. Only one problem—he can't use any magic! Luckily for Asta, he receives the incredibly rare five-leaf clover grimoire that gives him the power of anti-magic. Can someone who can't use magic really become the Wizard King? One thing's for sure—Asta will never give up!

SHONEN JUMP

VIZ media
www.viz.com

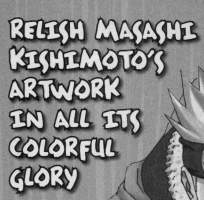
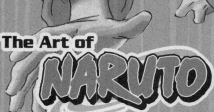
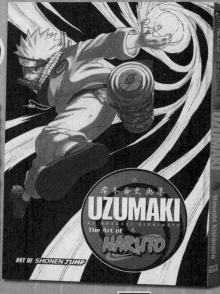

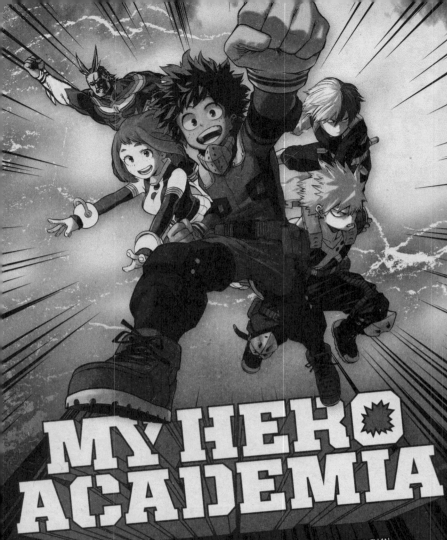

MY HERO ACADEMIA

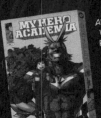

IZUKU MIDORIYA WANTS TO BE A HERO MORE THAN ANYTHING, BUT HE HASN'T GOT AN OUNCE OF POWER IN HIM. WITH NO CHANCE OF GETTING INTO THE U.A. HIGH SCHOOL FOR HEROES, HIS LIFE IS LOOKING LIKE A DEAD END. THEN AN ENCOUNTER WITH ALL MIGHT, THE GREATEST HERO OF ALL, GIVES HIM A CHANCE TO CHANGE HIS DESTINY...

 SHONEN JUMP

viz media
www.viz.com

NARUTO

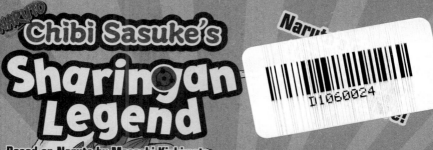

Chibi Sasuke's Sharingan Legend

Based on Naruto by Masashi Kishimoto
Story and Art by Kenji Taira

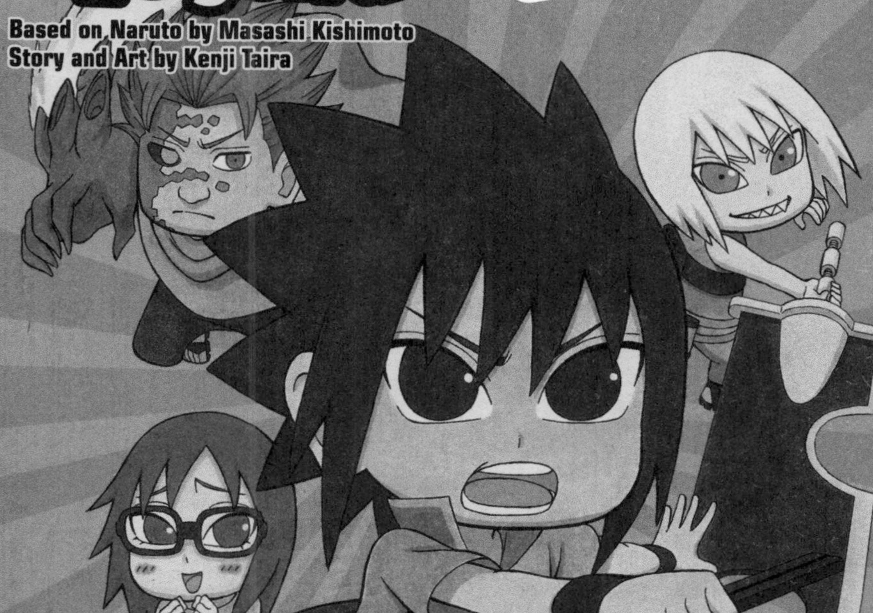

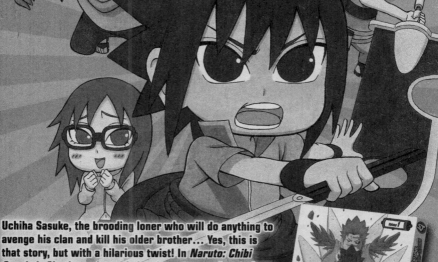

Uchiha Sasuke, the brooding loner who will do anything to avenge his clan and kill his older brother... Yes, this is that story, but with a hilarious twist! In *Naruto: Chibi Sasuke's Sharingan Legend*, the characters and story have been flipped on their heads, all for the sake of comedy! With his Taka teammates Suigetsu, Karin and Jugo, Sasuke travels the land and gets into all kinds of wacky adventures. This is a side of Sasuke you've never seen before. One bit of advice: do not mock the Uchiha!

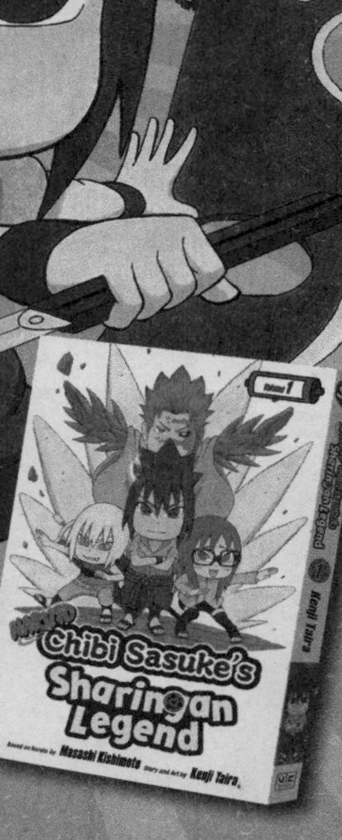
Volume 1
NARUTO
Chibi Sasuke's
Sharingan
Legend
Based on Naruto by Masashi Kishimoto Story and Art by Kenji Taira

VIZ
viz.com

RATED T TEEN